THE GOSPEL ACCORDING TO ST. JOHN

THE AUTHORIZED VERSION
WITH INTRODUCTION AND NOTES

THE GOSPEL ACCORDING TO ST. JOHN

THE AUTHORIZED VERSION
WITH INTRODUCTION AND NOTES

BY B. F. WESTCOTT, D.D., D.C.L.,
LORD BISHOP OF DURHAM

WM. B. EERDMANS PUBLISHING COMPANY
GRAND RAPIDS MICHIGAN

THE present volume is reprinted from *The Speaker's Commentary*. I have corrected a few misprints, defined more exactly a few references, and changed two or three words and phrases which seemed liable to misapprehension. I have not however felt at liberty to make any other alterations or additions.

B. F. W.

CAMBRIDGE,
Dec. 6th, 1881.

ISBN 0-8028-3288-1
Reprinted, October 1975

PHOTOLITHOPRINTED BY CUSHING - MALLOY, INC.
ANN ARBOR, MICHIGAN, UNITED STATES OF AMERICA

CONTENTS

INTRODUCTION.

St. JOHN

INTRODUCTION.

I. The Authorship of the Gospel.

1. *Internal Evidence.*

THE Gospel itself forms the proper starting-point for a satisfactory inquiry into its origin. Doubts may be raised as to the early history of the book owing to the nature of the available evidence, but there can be no question that it is impressed with an individual character, and that it contains indications of the circumstances under which it was composed. These indications, therefore, must first be examined: this character must first be defined so far as it illustrates the relation of the writer to the religious and social circumstances of the first century; and when this is done, we shall be in a position to consider with a fair appreciation the value of the historical testimony in support of the universal tradition of the Early Church which assigned the work to the Apostle St John.

What then is the evidence which the fourth Gospel itself bears to its authorship, first indirectly, and next directly? These are the two questions which we have to answer before we can go further.

i. *The indirect evidence of the Gospel as to its authorship.*

In examining the indirect evidence which the fourth Gospel furnishes as to its authorship, it will be most convenient, as well as most satisfactory, to consider the available materials in relation to successive questions which become more and more definite as we proceed. How far then can we infer from the book itself, with more or less certainty, that the author was, or was not, a Jew, a Jew of Palestine, an eye-witness, an Apostle, and, last of all, St John, the son of Zebedee?

(*a*) *The Author of the Fourth Gospel was a Jew.* A candid examination of the evidence appears to leave no room for reasonable doubt on this point. The whole narrative shews that the author was a Jew. He is familiar with Jewish opinions and customs, his composition is impressed with Jewish characteristics, he is penetrated with the spirit of the Jewish dispensation. His special knowledge, his literary style, his religious faith, all point to the same conclusion. The few arguments which are urged on the other side derive whatever force they have from the isolation of particular phrases which are considered without regard to the general aspect of the life to which they belong.

These statements must be justified in detail.

(α) The familiarity of the author of the fourth Gospel with Jewish opinions is shewn most strikingly by the outline which he gives of the contemporary Messianic expectations. This subject will be brought before us more in detail afterwards (III. § 2). For the present it will be enough to refer to the details which are given or implied in i. 21, iv. 25, vi. 14 f., vii. 40 ff., xii. 34, &c. In all these cases the points are noticed without the least effort as lying within the natural circle of the writer's thoughts. So again he mentions casually the popular estimate of women (iv. 27), the importance attached to the religious schools (vii. 15), the disparagement of "the Dispersion" (vii. 35), the belief in the transmitted punishment of sin (ix. 2), the hostility of Jews and Samaritans (iv. 9), the supercilious contempt of the Pharisees for "the people of the earth" (vii. 49).

The details of Jewish observances are touched upon with equal precision. Now it is the law of the sabbath which is shewn to be overruled by the requirement of circumcision (vii. 22 f.): now the ceremonial pollution which is contracted by entering a Gentile court (xviii. 28). The account of the visit to the Feast of Tabernacles only becomes fully intelligible when we supply the facts at which the writer barely hints, being himself filled with the knowledge of them. The pouring of water from Siloam upon the altar of burnt sacrifice, and the kindling of the lamps in the court of the women, explain the imagery of the "living water" (vii. 38), and of "the light of the world" (viii. 12). And here, again, a Jew only who knew the festival would be likely to describe "the last day of the feast," which was added to the original seven, as "the great day" (vii. 37). The same familiar and decisive knowledge of the people is shewn in glimpses which are opened on domestic life at the marriage feast (ii. 1—10), and at the burial of Lazarus (xi. 17—44). The tumultuary stoning of Stephen (Acts vii. 57 ff.), which could not but be a well-known incident in the early church, would have hindered any one who had not clear information upon the point from recording the answer of the Jews "It is not lawful for us to put any one to death" (xviii. 31); and so in fact these words were afterwards misunderstood by the Greek fathers.

But, on the other hand, it is said that the author of the fourth Gospel was so ignorant of Jewish affairs that he represents the high-priesthood as an annual office when he speaks of Caiaphas as "high-priest in that year" (xi. 49, 51, xviii. 13). It would be sufficient to reply that such ignorance could not be reconciled with the knowledge already indicated; but a consideration of the clause solemnly repeated three times shews that the supposed conclusion cannot be drawn from it. The emphatic reiteration of the statement forces the reader to connect the office of Caiaphas with the part which he actually took in accomplishing the death of Christ. One yearly sacrifice for atonement it was the duty of the high-priest to offer. In that memorable year, when all types were fulfilled in the reality, it fell to Caiaphas to bring about unconsciously the one sacrifice of atonement for sin. He was high-priest before and after, but it was not enough for the Evangelist's purpose to mark this. He was high-priest in that year—"the year of the Lord" (Luke iv. 19),—and so in the way of divine Providence did his appointed part in causing "*one man to die for the people*" (xi. 50).

(β) From the contents of the fourth Gospel we turn now to its form. And it may truly be affirmed that the style of the narrative alone is conclusive as to its Jewish authorship. The vocabulary, the structure of the sentences, the symmetry and numerical symbolism of the composition, the expression and the arrangement of the thoughts, are essentially Hebrew. These points will require to be discussed at greater length when we come to examine the composition of the Gospel (II. § 5). It must suffice now to call attention to such terms as "light," "darkness," "flesh," "spirit," "life," "this world," "the kingdom of God," and the like: to such images as "the shepherd," "the living water," "the woman in travail:" to the simplicity of the connecting particles: to the parallelism and symmetry of the clauses. The source of the imagery of the narrative, to sum up all briefly, is the Old Testament. The words are Greek words, but the spirit by which they live is Hebrew.

(γ) The Old Testament is no less certainly the source of the religious life of the writer. His Jewish opinions and hopes are taken up into and transfigured by his Christian faith; but the Jewish foundation underlies his whole narrative. The land of Judæa was "the home" (τὰ ἴδια; comp. xvi. 32, xix. 27) of the Incarnate Word, and the people of Judæa were "His own people" (i. 11). This was the judgment of the Evangelist when the Messiah had been rejected by those to whom He came; and on the other hand, Christ, when He first entered the Holy City, claimed the Temple as being "the house of His Father" (ii. 16). From first to last Judaism is treated in the Fourth Gospel as the divine starting-point of Christianity. It is true that the author records discourses in which the Lord speaks to the Jews of the Law as being "their Law;" and that he uses the name "the Jews" to mark an anti-Christian body; but even these apparent exceptions really illustrate his main position. The Pharisees as a party strove to keep "the Law" in its widest acceptation, the monument, that is, of the various revelations to Israel (x. 34, xv. 25, notes), for themselves alone, and to bar the progress of the life which it enshrined. In the process it became "their Law." With the same fatal narrowness they reduced the representatives and bearers of the ancient revelation to a national faction; and "the Jews" embodied just that which was provisional and evanescent in the system which they misunderstood (comp. III. § 1). These two characteristic thoughts of the Gospel will become clear when we consider the general development of the history. Meanwhile it must be noticed that the Evangelist vindicates both for the Law and for the people their just historical position in the divine economy. The Law could not but bear witness to the truths which God had once spoken through it. The people could not do away with the promises and privileges which they had inherited. Side by side with the words of Christ which describe the Law as the special possession of its false interpreters (viii. 17, x. 34, xv. 25), other words of his affirm the absolute authority of its contents. It is assumed as an axiom that *The Scripture cannot be broken* (x. 35; see v. 18, note). That which *is written in the prophets* (vi. 45; comp. vi. 31) is taken as the true expression of what shall be. *Moses wrote of Christ* (v. 46. Comp. i. 45). The types of the Old Testament, the brazen serpent (iii. 14), the manna (vi. 32), the water from the rock (vii. 37 f.), perhaps also the pillar of fire (viii. 12), are applied by Christ to Himself as of certain and acknowledged significance. Abraham *saw His day* (viii. 56). It was generally to "the Scriptures" that Christ appealed as *witnessing of Him*. Even the choice of Judas to be an apostle was involved in the portraiture of the divine King (xiii. 18, note, *that the Scripture might be fulfilled;* comp. xvii. 12); and the hatred of the Jews was prefigured in the words *written in their Law, They hated me without a cause* (xv. 25).

Such words of Christ must be considered both in themselves and in the consequences which they necessarily carry with them, if we are to understand the relation of the fourth Gospel to the Old Testament. They shew conclusively that in this Gospel, no less than in the other three, He is represented as offering Himself to Israel as the fulfiller, and not as the destroyer, of "the Law." And it follows also, whatever view is taken of the authorship of the Gospel, that the Evangelist in setting down these sayings of Christ accepts to the full the teaching which they convey.

Nor is this all. Just as the words of the Lord recorded in the fourth Gospel confirm the divine authority of the Old

Testament, so also the Evangelist, when he writes in his own person, emphasizes the same principle. The first public act of Christ reminded the disciples, as he relates, of a phrase in the Psalms (ii. 17). The Resurrection, he says, confirmed their faith *in the Scripture, and the word which Jesus spake*, as if both were of equal weight. In the light of the same event they understood at last what they had done unconsciously in accordance with prophetic utterances (xii. 14 ff.). So again at the close of his record of Christ's public ministry, he points out how the apparent failure of Christ's mission was part of the great scheme of Providence foreshadowed by Isaiah. The experience, and the words of the prophet, made such a result inevitable (xii. 37 ff.). This fulfilment of the wider teaching of prophecy is further confirmed by examples of the fulfilment of its details. Special incidents of the Passion are connected with the language of the Old Testament. The division of the garments, and the casting lots for the seamless robe (xix. 23 f.); the expression of thirst (xix. 28), the limbs left unbroken (xix. 36), the side pierced (xix. 37)—significant parallels with the treatment of the paschal lamb—give occasion to quotations from the Law, the Psalms, and the Prophets; and these fulfilments of the ancient Scriptures are brought forward as solid grounds of faith (xix. 35).

"The Law," in short, is treated by the writer of the fourth Gospel, both in his record of the Lord's teaching, and, more especially, in his own comments, as only a Jew could have treated it. It was misinterpreted by those to whom it was given, but it was divine. So far as it was held, not only apart from, but in opposition to, its true fulfilment, it lost its true character. This character the Evangelist unfolds. The object with which he wrote was to shew that Jesus was not only the *Son of God*, but also *the Christ*, the promised Messiah of the Jews (xx. 31), just as Nathanael, the true representative of Israel (i. 47), had recognised Him at first under this double title.

The portraiture of the people in the fourth Gospel is no less indicative of its Jewish authorship, whatever false deductions may have been popularly drawn from the use of the characteristic title "the Jews" for the adversaries of Christianity. Writing as a Christian the Evangelist still records the central truth, true for all ages, which Christ declared: *We*—as Jews—*worship that which we know, for the salvation*—the salvation promised to the world—*is from the Jews* (iv. 22), rising by a divine law out of the dispensation intrusted to their keeping. Nothing which was said at a later time neutralised these words of the Lord in which He identified Himself with the old people of God, and signalised their inherent prerogatives. The knowledge which the Jews had was the result of their acceptance of the continuous revelation of God from age to age; while the Samaritans who refused to advance beyond the first stage of His manifestation, worshipped the true Object of worship, but ignorantly. They worshipped *that which they knew not* (iv. 22).

This was the rightful position of the Jews towards Christ, which is everywhere presupposed in the Gospel, but they failed to maintain it, and when the Evangelist wrote their national failure was past hope. They received Him not. But the sources and the kinds of their unbelief were manifold, and the narrative reflects the varieties of their character.

For the people are not, as is commonly assumed to be the case, a uniform, colourless mass. On the contrary, distinct bodies reveal themselves on a careful examination of the record, each with its own distinctive marks. Two great divisions are portrayed with marked clearness, "the multitude," and "the Jews." *The multitude* (ὁ ὄχλος) represents the general gathering of the Jewish inhabitants of Palestine, Galilæans for the most part, who are easily swayed to and fro, with no settled policy, and no firm convictions. These, when they saw the signs which Jesus had wrought at Jerusalem, received Him in Galilee (iv. 45), and followed Him, and, at a later time, would have made Him King (vi. 15). When they went up to the feasts they gathered round Him in expectation and doubt, ignorant of the deadly hostility of their rulers to the new prophet (vii. 20), and inclined to believe (vii. 40;

compare the whole chapter). On the eve of the Passion they brought Him in triumph into the city (xii. 12); and, in the last scene in which they are presented in the Gospel, listen in dull perplexity to Christ's final revelation of Himself (xii. 29, 34). In the fourth Gospel they do not appear in the narrative of the Trial and the Crucifixion. They may have been used as instruments, but the guilt of this issue did not belong to them as a body.

In contrast with "the multitude" stand "the Jews[1]." Both titles are general terms, including various elements; both have local centres; both express tendencies of religious feeling. Just as "the multitude" reflect the spirit of Galilee, "the Jews" reflect the spirit of Jerusalem (i. 19), and this term is perhaps used exclusively of those who lived in the limited region of Judæa. "The multitude" have vague, fluent, opinions; "the Jews" hold fast by the popular expectation of a national Messiah, and a national sovereignty. From first to last they appear as the representatives of the narrow finality of Judaism (ii. 18, xix. 38). They begin their opposition by a charge of the violation of the Sabbath (v. 10 ff.; comp. xix. 31). Those of them who are present at Capernaum give expression to "murmurings" at the teaching to which "the multitude" had apparently listened with awed respect (vi. 41, 52; comp. vi. 22—40). They reduce the wavering multitude to silence at Jerusalem (vii. 11—13). If they *believe Christ*, they do not at once *believe on Him*, and while they cling to their own prejudices yield themselves to the perils of fatal error (viii. 31 ff. note). In their zeal for the Law they would at once stone Christ (viii. 59, x. 31); and to them generally the Crucifixion is attributed (xviii. 12, 14, 31, 36, 38, xix. 7, 12, 14). Yet even these are struck with wonder (vii. 15) and doubt (vii. 35, viii. 22); they are divided (x. 19), and ask peremptorily for a clear enunciation of Christ's claim (x. 24); and the defection of many from among them to Him marks the last crisis in the history (xii. 10 f.; comp. xi. 45, 48, ix. 40, xii. 42).

[1] The term occurs rarely in the discourses of the Lord: iv. 22, xiii. 33, xviii. 20, 36. See note on the last passage.

"The Jews" thus presented to a writer who looked back from a Christian point of sight[1] upon the events which he described the aggregate of the people whose opinions were opposed in spirit to the work of Christ. They were not, as they might have been, "true Israelites" (i. 47; comp. *v.* 31). But at the same time he does not fail to notice that there were among them two distinct tendencies, which found their expression in the Pharisees and Sadducees respectively. The latter are not mentioned by name in the fourth Gospel, but the writer describes them more characteristically, and with a more direct knowledge, by their social position at the time. They were "the high-priests," the faction of Annas and Caiaphas (Acts v. 17), the reckless hierarchy, whose policy is sharply distinguished in one or two life-like traits from that of the religious zealots, the Pharisees. Several times indeed the two parties appear as acting together in the great Council (vii. 32, 45, xi. 47, 57, xviii. 3; comp. vii. 26, 48, xii. 42 *the rulers*), yet even in these cases the two are only once so grouped as to form a single body (vii. 45 πρὸς τοὺς ἀρχ. καὶ Φαρ.), and "the chief priests" always stand first as taking the lead in the designs of violence. This is brought out very vividly in the fatal scene in the Sanhedrin after the raising of Lazarus (see xi. 47 note).

In other places when the two parties are mentioned separately the contrast between them familiar to the historian underlies the record. The Pharisees are moved by the symptoms of religious disorder: the high priests (Sadducees) by the prospect of ecclesiastical danger. The Pharisees are the true representatives of "the Jews" (i. 19 || i. 24, ix. 13 || ix. 18, ix. 22 || xii. 42). They send to make inquiries about the mission of John (i. 24); they hear, evidently as of something which deeply concerned them, of baptism among the followers of the Lord (iv. 1); they scornfully reject the opinion of the illiterate multitude (vii. 47); they question the authority of Christ (viii. 13); they condemn His miracles as wrought on the Sabbath (ix.

[1] The phrase "the Passover of the Jews" evidently implies a familiar Christian Passover: ii. 13 note. Comp. ii. 6, v. 1, vii. 2, xix. 42.

13 ff.); they excommunicate His followers (xii. 42; comp. ix. 22); but at last they look with irresolute helplessness upon the apparent failure of their opposition (xii. 19). From this point they appear no more by themselves. "The chief priests" take the direction of the end into their own hands. Five times they are mentioned alone, and on each occasion as bent on carrying out a purpose of death and treason to the faith of Israel. They plotted the murder of Lazarus because *many for his sake believed on Jesus* (xii. 11). Pilate sees in them the true persecutors of Christ: *Thy nation and the chief priests delivered Thee up to me* (xviii. 35). Their voices first raise the cry, *Crucify, Crucify Him* (xix. 6). They make the unbelieving confession, *We have no king but Cæsar* (xix. 15), and utter a vain protest against the title in which their condemnation was written (xix. 21, *the chief priests of the Jews*).

This most significant fact of the decisive action of the Sadducæan hierarchy in compassing the death of the Lord, which is strikingly illustrated by the relative attitude of Pharisees and Sadducees to the early Church as described in the Acts, explains the prominent position assigned to Annas in the fourth Gospel (xviii. 13). Annas was the head of the party. Though he had ceased to be high-priest for many years, he swayed the policy of his successors. St Luke in his Gospel significantly sets him with Caiaphas as "high-priest" (ἐπ' ἀρχιερέως not ἐπ' ἀρχιερέων, iii. 2), as if both were united in one person; and in the Acts he, and not Caiaphas (iv. 6), is alone called "high-priest." The coincidence is just one of those which reveal the actual as distinguished from the official state of things.

One further remark must be made. The general use of the term "the Jews" for the opponents of Christ not only belongs necessarily to the position of an apostle at the close of the first century, but it is even possible to trace in the books of the New Testament the gradual change by which it assumed this specific force. In the Synoptic Gospels it occurs only four times except in the title "king of the Jews;" Matt. xxviii. 15; Mark vii. 3; Luke vii. 3, xxiii. 51; and in the first of these, which is probably the latest in date, the word marks a position of antagonism. In the Acts the title oscillates between the notions of privilege and of opposition, but the course of the history goes far to fix its adverse meaning. The word is comparatively rare in the Epistles of St Paul. It occurs most commonly (twelve times out of twenty-four) in contrast with "Greek," both alike standing in equal contrast with the idea of Christianity; and for St Paul, "a Hebrew of Hebrews," his countrymen, "Jews by nature" (Gal. ii. 15), are already separated from himself. The name of a race has become practically the name of a sect (Rom. iii. 9; 1 Cor. i. 22 ff., ix. 20, x. 32; comp. Gal. ii. 13, i. 13 f.). The word is not found in the Catholic epistles, but in the Apocalypse it is used twice (ii. 9, iii. 9), evidently to describe those who insisted on their literal descent and ceremonial position, and claimed the prerogatives of Israel outside the Church. Such false-styled Jews were the worst enemies of the Gospel; and a Christian writing at the close of the century could not but speak of the people generally by the title which characterized them to his contemporaries.

(*b*) *The Author of the Fourth Gospel was a Jew of Palestine.* The facts which have just been noticed carry us beyond the conclusion which they were alleged to establish. They shew that the writer of the fourth Gospel was not only a Jew, but a Palestinian Jew of the first century. It is inconceivable that a Gentile, living at a distance from the scene of religious and political controversy which he paints, could have realised, as the Evangelist has done, with vivid and unerring accuracy the relations of parties and interests which ceased to exist after the fall of Jerusalem; that he could have marked distinctly the part which the hierarchical class—the unnamed Sadducees—took in the crisis of the Passion; that he could have caught the real points at issue between true and false Judaism, which in their first form had passed away when the Christian society was firmly established: that he could have portrayed the growth and conflict of opinion as to the national hopes of the Messiah side by side with the progress of the Lord's ministry. All these phases of thought and action, which would be ineffaceably impressed upon the memory of one who had lived through the events which the history records, belonged to a state of things foreign to the experience of an Alexandrine, or an Asiatic, in the second century.

For in estimating the value of these conclusions which we have gained, it must be remembered that the old landmarks, material and moral, were destroyed by the Roman war: that the destruction of the Holy City—a true coming of Christ—revealed the essential differences of Judaism and Christianity, and raised a barrier between them: that at the beginning of the second century the influence of Alexandria was substituted for that of the Jewish schools in the growing Church.

(a) And these considerations which apply to the arguments drawn from the religious and political traits of the history, apply also in corresponding degrees to the more special indications that the author of the Fourth Gospel was a Jew of Palestine. Among these, the most convincing perhaps is to be found in his local knowledge. He speaks of places with an unaffected precision, as familiar in every case with the scene which he wishes to recall. There is no effort, no elaborateness of description in his narratives: he moves about in a country which he knows. His mention of sites is not limited to those which are found elsewhere in Scripture, either in the Gospels or in the Old Testament. "Cana of Galilee" (Κανὰ τῆς Γαλιλαίας, ii. 1, 11, iv. 46, xxi. 2), thus exactly distinguished, is not noticed by any earlier writer. "Bethany beyond Jordan" (i. 28), a place already forgotten in the time of Origen, is obviously distinguished from the familiar Bethany "near Jerusalem," the situation of which is precisely fixed as "about fifteen furlongs" from the city (xi. 18). Ephraim, again, situated "near the wilderness" (xi. 54) may be identical with Ophrah (1 Sam. xiii. 17), but it is not otherwise named in Scripture. Once more, Ænon (iii. 23) is not known from other sources, but the form of the name[1] is a sure sign of the genuineness of the reference, and the defining clause, "near to Salim," even if the identification were as difficult now as it has been represented to be, shews that the place was clearly present to the writer[1]. Nothing indeed but direct acquaintance with the localities can account for the description added in each of these cases. A writer for whom these spots were identified with memorable incidents which were for him turning-points of faith, would naturally add the details which recalled them to his own mind: for another the exact definition could have no interest. Other indications of minute knowledge are given in the implied notice of the dimensions of the lake of Tiberias (vi. 19; comp. Mark vi. 47), and of the relative positions of Cana and Capernaum (ii. 12, *went down*).

One name, however, has caused much difficulty. *The city of Samaria named Sychar* (iv. 5) has been commonly identified with Shechem (Sychem, Acts vii. 16), and the changed form has been confidently attributed by sceptical critics to the ignorance of the Evangelist. The importance of Shechem, a city with which no one could have been unacquainted who possessed the knowledge of Palestine which the writer of the fourth Gospel certainly had, might reasonably dispose of such a charge. And more than this: the picture with which the name is connected is evidently drawn from life. The prospect of the corn-fields (*v.* 35), and of the heights of Gerizim (*v.* 20), are details which belong to the knowledge of an eye-witness. The notice of the depth of the well (*v.* 11) bears equally the stamp of authenticity. If then there were no clue to the solution of the problem offered by the strange name, it would be right to acquiesce in the belief that Sychar might be a popular distortion of Shechem, or the name of some unknown

[1] This is true whether the word be taken as an adjectival form "abounding in springs" (comp. Ez. xlvii. 17); or as a corruption of a dual form "the two springs," but it is doubtful whether it can be so rendered. It is said that Ainan and Ainaim, "the two springs," are the names of several places in Arabia. The Syriac versions write the name as two words, "the spring of the dove."

[1] Lieut. Conder in the *Quarterly Statement* of the Palestine Exploration Fund (July, 1874, pp. 191 f.) identifies it with 'Aynún near to Salim, due east of Nablus. The use of the phrase *beyond Jordan* (iii. 26) implies that the country was on the West of the river.

village. But the case does not stand so absolutely without help towards a decision. The earliest ancient authorities (4th cent.) distinguish Shechem and Sychar. Shechem could hardly have been described as *near to the plot of ground which Jacob gave to Joseph* (*v.* 5). There are, moreover, several references to *Sukra*, *Sukar*, *ain-Sukar* (סוכרא, סכר, עין סוכר) in the Talmud; and a village *'Askar* still remains, which answers to the conditions of the narrative. Some difficulty has been felt in identifying 'Askar with Sychar, since it is written at present with an initial *'Ain*, but in a Samaritan Chronicle of the 12th century, the name appears in a transitional form with an initial *Yod* (יסכר), and the Arabic translation of the Chronicle gives 'Askar as the equivalent. The description [of S. John], Lieut. Conder writes, "is most accurately applicable to 'Askar. ... It is merely a modern mud village, with no great indications of antiquity, but there are remains of ancient tombs near the road beneath it." (*Report of the Palestine Exploration Fund*, 1877, pp. 149 f., 1876, p. 197.)

The notices of the topography of Jerusalem contained in the fourth Gospel are still more conclusive as to its authorship than the notices of isolated places in Palestine. The desolation of Jerusalem after its capture was complete. No creative genius can call into being a lost site. And the writer of the fourth Gospel is evidently at home in the city as it was before its fall. He knows much that we learn from independent testimony, and he knows what is not to be found elsewhere. But whether he mentions spots known from other sources, or named only by himself, he speaks simply and certainly. As he recalls a familiar scene he lives again in the past, and forgets the desolation which had fallen upon the place which rises before his eyes. "*There is*," he writes, "*at Jerusalem a pool called Bethesda*" (v. 2), and by the form of the sentence carries us back to the time when the incident first became history. "Bethesda by the sheep-gate," "the pool of Siloam" (ix. 7), "the brook Kidron" (xviii. 1), which are not named by the other evangelists (yet see Luke xiii. 4), stand out naturally in his narrative. What imagination could have invented a Bethesda (or Bethzetha) with its five porches, and exact locality (v. 2)? What except habitual usage would have caused the Kidron to be described as "the winter torrent[1]"? How long must the name Siloam have been pondered over before the perfectly admissible rendering "Sent" was seen to carry with it a typical significance? The *Prætorium* and *Golgotha* are mentioned by the other evangelists; but even here the writer of the fourth Gospel sees the localities, if I may so speak, with the vividness of an actual spectator. The Jews crowd round the Prætorium which they will not enter, and Pilate goes in and out before them (xviii. 28 ff.). Golgotha is "*nigh to the city*," where people pass to and fro, and "*there was a garden there*" (xix. 17, 20, 41). And the fourth Evangelist alone notices the Pavement, the raised platform of judgment, with its Hebrew title, Gabbatha (xix. 13). The places Bethesda and Gabbatha are not, in fact, mentioned anywhere except in the fourth Gospel, and the perfect simplicity with which they are introduced in the narrative, no less than the accuracy of form in the Aramaic titles (whatever be the true reading of Bethesda), marks the work of a Palestinian Jew, who had known Jerusalem before its fall.

The allusions to the Temple shew no less certainly the familiarity of the writer with the localities in which he represents Christ as teaching. The first scene, the cleansing of the Temple, is in several details more lifelike than the similar passages in the Synoptists (ii. 14—16). It is described just as it would appear to an eye-witness in its separate parts, and not as the similar incident is summed up briefly in the other narratives. Each group engaged stands out distinctly, the sellers of oxen and sheep, the money-changers sitting at their work, the sellers of doves; and each group is dealt with individually. Then follows, in the course of the dialogue which ensues, the singularly exact chronological note, "*Forty and six years was this Temple in building*" (ii. 20).

The incidents of the Feast of Taber-

[1] For the discussion of the reading see note on xviii. 1. If the reading "the torrent *of the Cedars*" be adopted, the argument is not affected.

nacles (which are given in chapters vii. and viii.) cannot be understood, as has been already noticed, without an accurate acquaintance with the Temple ritual. The two symbolic ceremonies — commemorating the typical miracles of the wilderness—the outpouring of water on the altar of sacrifice, and the kindling the golden lamps at night, furnish the great topics of discourse. The Evangelist is familiar with the facts, but he does not pause to dwell upon them. Only in one short sentence does he appear to call attention to the significance of the events. "*These things*," he says, "*Jesus spake in the treasury, as he taught in the Temple*" (viii. 20). The mention of the exact spot carried with it to minds familiar with the Herodian Temple a clear revelation of what was in the Apostle's mind. For the treasury was in the court of the women where the great candelabra were placed, looking to which Christ said, "*I am the light*"—not of one people, or of one city, but—"*of the world*." And there is still another thought suggested by the mention of the place. The meeting-hall of the Sanhedrin was in a chamber adjacent to it. We can understand therefore the hasty attempts of the chief priests and Pharisees to seize Christ, and the force of the words which are added, that even there, under the very eyes of the popular leaders, "*no man laid hands on Him*."

The next visit to Jerusalem, at the Feast of Dedication, brings a new place before us. "*It was winter*," we read, "*and Jesus was walking in Solomon's Porch*" (x. 22), a part of the great eastern cloister suiting in every way the scene with which it is connected.

Once again, as I believe, we have a significant allusion to the decoration of the Temple. On the eve of the Passion, at the close of the discourses in the upper chamber, the Lord said, "*Arise, let us go hence*" (xiv. 31). Some time after we read that when He had finished his High-priestly prayer, He went forth with His disciples over the brook Kidron. It seems to be impossible to regard this notice as the fulfilment of the former command. The house, therefore, must have been left before, as is clearly implied in the narrative, and the walk to the Mount of Olives might well include a visit to the Temple; and over the gate of the Temple was spread the great vine of gold, which was reckoned among its noblest ornaments. Is it then a mere fancy to suppose that the image of the vine and its branches was suggested by the sight of this symbolic tracery, lighted by the Paschal moon, and that the High priestly prayer was offered under the shadow of the Temple walls?

However this may be, it is inconceivable that any one, still more a Greek or a Hellenist, writing when the Temple was rased to the ground, could have spoken of it with the unaffected certainty which appears in the fourth Gospel. It is monstrous to transfer to the second century the accuracy of archæological research which is one of the latest acquirements of modern art. The Evangelist, it may be safely said, speaks of what he had seen.

(β) The arguments which have been already drawn from the political, social, religious, and local knowledge of the author of the fourth Gospel, shew beyond all doubt, as it appears, that he was a Palestinian Jew. A presumption in favour of the same conclusion may be derived from the quotations from the Old Testament which are contained in the Gospel. These shew at least so much that the writer was not dependent on the LXX.; and they suggest that he was acquainted with the original Hebrew.

A rapid summary of the facts will enable the student to estimate the weight of this additional evidence.

(1) *Quotations by the Evangelist.*

ii. 17. ...γεγραμμένον ἐστίν Ὁ ζῆλος τοῦ οἴκου σου καταφάγεταί με.

Ps. lxix. (lxviii.) 9. κατέφαγε (Symm. κατηνάλωσε). So Hebr. .... (1)

xii. 14, 15. καθώς ἐστιν γεγραμμένον Μὴ φοβοῦ, θυγάτηρ Σιών· ἰδοὺ ὁ βασιλεύς σου ἔρχεται, καθήμενος ἐπὶ πῶλον ὄνου.

Zach. ix. 9. Χαῖρε σφόδρα, θύγατερ Σιών,...ἰδοὺ ὁ βασιλεὺς σου ἔρχεται...ἐπιβεβηκὼς ἐπὶ...πῶλον νέον. (All the Greek versions have ἐπιβεβηκώς. Theodotion has ἐπὶ ὄνον καὶ πῶλον υἱὸν ὄνου.) Hebr. עַל־חֲמוֹר וְעַל־עַיִר בֶּן־אֲתֹנוֹת. .... (2)

xii. 38. ...ἵνα ὁ λόγος Ἡσαΐου...πληρωθῇ

ὃν εἶπεν Κύριε, τίς ἐπίστευσεν τῇ ἀκοῇ ἡμῶν; καὶ ὁ βραχίων κυρίου τίνι ἀπεκαλύφθη;

Is. liii. 1 (exact). .... (3)

xii. 40. ... ὅτι εἶπεν Ἡσαΐας Τετύφλωκεν αὐτῶν τοὺς ὀφθαλμοὺς καὶ ἐπώρωσεν αὐτῶν τὴν καρδίαν, ἵνα μὴ ἴδωσιν τοῖς ὀφθαλμοῖς καὶ νοήσωσιν τῇ καρδίᾳ καὶ στραφῶσιν, καὶ ἰάσομαι αὐτούς.

Is. vi. 10. ἐπαχύνθη ἡ καρδία τοῦ λαοῦ τούτου...καὶ τοὺς ὀφθαλμοὺς ἐκάμμυσαν, μή ποτε ἴδωσι τοῖς ὀφθαλμοῖς...καὶ τῇ καρδίᾳ συνῶσι καὶ ἐπιστρέψωσι καὶ ἰάσομαι αὐτούς. (The version of Symm. uses the same words generally as LXX.) Comp. Matt. xiii. 13 ff.; Mark iv. 12. .... (4)

xix. 24. ἵνα ἡ γραφὴ πληρωθῇ Διεμερίσαντο τὰ ἱμάτιά μου ἑαυτοῖς καὶ ἐπὶ τὸν ἱματισμόν μου ἔβαλον κλῆρον.

Ps. xxii. (xxi.) 18 (exact). .... (5)

xix. 36. ἵνα ἡ γραφὴ πληρωθῇ Ὀστοῦν οὐ συντριβήσεται αὐτοῦ.

Ex. xii. 46. ὀστοῦν οὐ συντρίψετε ἀπ' αὐτοῦ (al. συντρίψεται). Num. ix. 12. ὀ. οὐ συντρίψουσιν ἀ. αὐ. (al. συντρίψεται). Cf. Ps. xxxiv. (xxxiii.) 20. .... (6)

xix. 37. ἑτέρα γραφὴ λέγει Ὄψονται εἰς ὃν ἐξεκέντησαν. Hebr. דקרו.

Zach. xii. 10. ἐπιβλέψονται πρός με ἀνθ' ὧν κατωρχήσαντο (Theodot. εἰς ὃν ἐξεκέντησαν. Aq. Symm. ἐξεκέντησαν, ἐπεξεκέντησαν).

Comp. Rev. i. 7. .... (7)

(2) *Quotations in the Lord's discourses.*

vi. 45. ἔστιν γεγραμμένον ἐν τοῖς προφήταις Καὶ ἔσονται πάντες διδακτοὶ θεοῦ.

Is. liv. 13. καὶ (θήσω) πάντας τοὺς υἱούς σου διδακτοὺς θεοῦ.

The words are not connected as in LXX. with *v.* 12, but treated as in the Hebrew, independently. .... (8)

vii. 38. καθὼς εἶπεν ἡ γραφὴ ποταμοὶ ἐκ τῆς κοιλίας αὐτοῦ ῥεύσουσιν ὕδατος ζῶντος.

There is no exact parallel. The reference is probably general. .... (9)

x. 34. οὐκ ἔστιν γεγραμμένον...Ἐγὼ εἶπα Θεοί ἐστε;

Ps. lxxxii. (lxxxi.) 6 (exact). ...... (10)

xiii. 18. ἵνα ἡ γραφὴ πληρωθῇ Ὁ τρώγων μου τὸν ἄρτον ἐπῆρεν ἐπ' ἐμὲ τὴν πτέρναν αὐτοῦ.

Ps. xli. (xl.) 9 (10). ...ὁ ἐσθίων ἄρτους μου ἐμεγάλυνεν ἐπ' ἐμὲ πτερνισμόν. (Aq. Symm. Theodot. κατεμεγαλύνθη μου). Hebr. הגדיל עלי עקב. .... (11)

xv. 25. ἵνα πλ. ὁ λόγος...Ἐμίσησάν με δωρεάν.

Ps. xxxiv. (xxxv.) 19. οἱ μισοῦντές με δωρεάν. Ps. lxviii. (lxix.) 5. .... (12)

(3) *Other quotations.*

By John the Baptist.

i. 23. ἐγὼ φωνὴ βοῶντος ἐν τῇ ἐρήμῳ Εὐθύνατε τὴν ὁδὸν Κυρίου.

Is. xl. 3. ἑτοιμάσατε...εὐθείας ποιεῖτε τὰς τρίβους τοῦ θεοῦ ἡμῶν (Aq. Theodot. ἀποσκευάσατε. Symm. εὐτρεπίσατε)....(13)

By Galilæans.

vi. 31. καθώς ἐστιν γεγραμμένον Ἄρτον ἐκ τοῦ οὐρανοῦ ἔδωκεν αὐτοῖς φαγεῖν.

Ps. lxxviii. (lxxvii.) 24... (μάννα φαγεῖν) καὶ ἄρτον οὐρανοῦ ἔδωκεν αὐτοῖς. Ex. xvi. 4, 15. ... ὕω ... ἄρτους ἐκ τοῦ οὐρανοῦ ... οὗτος ὁ ἄρτος ὃν ἔδωκε Κύριος ὑμῖν φαγεῖν. .... (14)

The triumphal cry (xii. 13; Ps. cxvii. 25) can hardly be treated as a quotation. In preserving the Hebrew form *Hosanna* St John agrees with the Synoptic Evangelists and differs from the LXX.

An examination of these fourteen citations (1—7 by the Evangelist; 8—12 by the Lord; 13, 14 by others) shews that they fall into the following groups:

1. Some agree with the Hebrew and LXX., where these both agree;
(3), (5), (10), (12).

2. Others agree with the Hebrew against the LXX.;
(7), (8), (11).

3. Others differ from the Hebrew and LXX. where these both agree;
(1).

4. Others differ from the Hebrew and LXX. where they do not agree;
(2), (4).

5. Free adaptations;
(6), (9), (13), (14).

But there is no case where a quotation agrees with the LXX. against the Hebrew.

(γ) There is yet another argument to be noticed in support of the Palestinian authorship of the fourth Gospel, which appears to be of great weight, though it has commonly been either passed over, or even regarded as a difficulty. The doctrine of the Word, as it is presented in the Prologue, when taken in connexion with the whole Gospel, seems to shew clearly that the writer was of Palestinian and not of Hellenistic training.

In considering St John's teaching on the Logos, "the Word," it is obvious to remark, though the truth is very often neglected in practice, that it is properly a question of doctrine and not of nomenclature. It constantly happens in the history of thought that the same terms and phrases are used by schools which have no direct affinity, in senses which are essentially distinct, while they have a superficial likeness. Such terms (*e. g. idea*) belong to the common dialect of speculation; and it is indeed by the peculiar force which is assigned to them that schools are in many cases most readily distinguished. A new teacher necessarily uses the heritage which he has received from the past in order to make his message readily understood.

It may then be assumed that St John, when he speaks of "the Word," "the Only-begotten," and of His relations to God and to the world, and to man, employs a vocabulary and refers to modes of thought which were already current when he wrote. His teaching would not have been intelligible unless the general scope of the language which he employed, without explanation or preparation, had been familiar to his readers. When he declares with abrupt emphasis that "the Word was in the beginning," and that "the Word became flesh," it is evident that he is speaking of "a Word" already known in some degree by the title, though he lays down new truths as to His being. He does not speak, as in the Apocalypse (xix. 13; comp. Heb. iv. 12) of "the Word of God," but of "the Word" absolutely. Those whom he addressed knew of Whom he was speaking, and were able to understand that which it was his office to make known about Him. In this case, as in every other similar case, the thoughts of men, moving in different directions under the action of those laws of natural growth which are the expression of the divine purpose, prepared the medium and provided the appropriate means for the revelation which was to be conveyed in the fulness of time.

In this respect the manifold forms of speculation, Western and Eastern, fulfilled a function in respect to Christian philosophy similar to that which was fulfilled in other regions of religious experience by the LXX.; and the results which were gained were embodied in Greek modes of speech, which were ready at last for the declaration of the divine message.

It becomes then a question of peculiar and yet of subordinate interest to determine from what source St John derived his language. It is admitted on all hands that his central affirmation, "the Word became flesh," which underlies all he wrote, is absolutely new and unique. A Greek, an Alexandrine, a Jewish doctor, would have equally refused to admit such a statement as a legitimate deduction from his principles, or as reconcileable with them. The message completes and crowns "the hope of Israel," but not as "the Jews" expected. It gives stability to the aspirations of humanity after fellowship with God, but not as philosophers had supposed, by "unclothing" the soul. St John had been enabled to see what Jesus of Nazareth was, "the Christ" and "the Son of God:" it remained for him to bring home his convictions to others (xx. 31). The Truth was clear to himself: how could he so present it as to shew that it gave reality to the thoughts with which his contemporaries were busied? The answer is by using with necessary modifications the current language of the highest religious speculation to interpret a fact, to reveal a Person, to illuminate the fulness of actual life. Accordingly he transferred to the region of history the phrases in which men before him had spoken of "the Logos"—"the Word," "the Reason"—in the region of metaphysics. St Paul had brought home to believers the divine majesty of the glorified Christ: St John laid open the unchanged majesty of "Jesus come in the flesh."

But when this is laid down it still remains to determine in which direction we are to look for the immediate source from which St John borrowed the cardinal term *Logos*, a term which enshrines in itself large treasures of theological speculation.

The scantiness of contemporary religious literature makes the answer more difficult than it might have been if the great Jewish teachers had not shrunk from committing their lessons to writing. And, in one sense, the difficulty is increased by the fact that a striking aspect of Jewish thought has been preserved in the copious writings of PHILO of Alexandria (born c. B.C. 20), who is naturally regarded as the creator of teaching, of which he is in part only the representative. However far this view may be from the truth, the works of Philo furnish at least a starting-point for our inquiry. This typical Alexandrine Jew speaks constantly of "the divine Logos" (ὁ θεῖος λόγος) in language which offers striking, if partial, parallels with the epistle to the Hebrews and St Paul. The divine Logos is "Son of God," "firstborn Son" (πρωτόγονος, I. 414), "image of God" (εἰκὼν θεοῦ, I. 6), "God" (I. 655), "high-priest" (ἀρχιερεύς, I. 653), "man of God," "archetypal man" (ἄνθρωπος θεοῦ, I. 411, ὁ κατ' εἰκόνα ἄνθρωπος, I. 427), "the head of the body" (I. 640; comp. I. 121), "through whom the world was created" (II. 225).

At first sight it might seem that we have here beyond all doubt the source of St John's language. But the ambiguity of the Greek term *Logos*, which means both *Reason* and *Word*, makes it necessary to pause before adopting this conclusion. When Philo speaks of "the divine Logos" his thought is predominantly of the divine Reason and not of the divine Word. This fact is of decisive importance. The conception of a divine Word, that is, of a divine Will sensibly manifested in personal action, is not naturally derived from that of a divine Reason, but is rather complementary to it, and characteristic of a different school of thought. Is it then possible to find any clear traces of a doctrine of a divine Logos elsewhere than at Alexandria?

The Targums furnish an instructive answer to the question. These paraphrases of the Hebrew Scriptures have preserved, as it appears, the simplest and earliest form in which the term "the Word" was employed in connexion with God. They were most probably not committed to writing in the shape in which we now have them, till some time after the Christian æra; but all evidence goes to shew that they embody the interpretations which had been orally current from a much earlier time. In the Targum of Onkelos on the Pentateuch, which is the oldest in date, the action of God is constantly though not consistently referred to "His Word" (*Memra*, מימרא, מימר). Thus it is said that "the Lord protected Noah by His word, when he entered the ark" (Gen. vii. 16): that He "made a covenant between Abraham and His word" (Gen. xvii. 2); that the word of the Lord was with Ishmael in the wilderness (xxi. 20). At Bethel Jacob made a covenant that "the Word of the Lord should be His God" (Gen. xxviii. 21). Moses at Sinai "brought forth the people to meet the Word of God" (Exod. xix. 17). And in Deuteronomy the Word of the Lord appears as a consuming fire talking to His people, and fighting for them against their enemies (Deut. iii. 2, iv. 24).

Such examples might be multiplied indefinitely; and it may be noticed that the term *Debura* (דבורא) occurs in this sense as well as *Memra*. Thus it is said in the Jerusalem Targum on Numb. vii. 89, *the word* (דבורא) *was talking with him;* and again Gen. xxviii. 10, *the word* (ד״) *desired to talk with him.*

In connexion with this usage it must also be observed that "a man's word" is used as a periphrasis for "himself." So we read Ruth iii. 8 ('Targ. Jon.'), "between his word (*i.e.* himself) and Michal" (Buxtorf and Levy, *s. v.*). The "word" is in fact the active expression of the rational character, and so may well stand for the person from whom it issues. As applied to God, the term was free from any rude anthropomorphism, while it preserved the reality of a divine fellowship for man.

One striking difference between the Aramaic and Greek terms will have been remarked. *Logos*, as we have seen, is ambiguous, and may signify either *reason* or *word*, but *Memra* (*Debura*) means *word* only. If now we return to Philo, the importance of this fact becomes obvious. With Philo the Palestinian sense of *word* sinks entirely into the background, if it does not wholly disappear. He has borrowed a term which was already current in the Greek Scriptures, and filled it with a new meaning.

Three currents of thought in fact meet in Philo's doctrine of "the Logos," the Stoic, the Platonic, and the Hebraic. He was nothing less than a creative genius. He felt rightly that the revelation of the Old Testament contained implicitly the harmony of the manifold speculations of men, and he therefore adopted boldly the thoughts of Greek philosophy for the interpretation of its language. He found a "Logos" in the Greek Bible which he accepted as the record of revelation, and he applied to that what Greek writers had said of the "Logos," without thinking it necessary to inquire into the identity of the terms. At one time he borrows from Plato when he speaks of the Logos as "the archetypal idea" ('de spec. leg.' 36, II. p. 333 f.), or as bearing "the idea of ideas" ('de migr. Abr.' 18, I. p. 452 m.). More commonly he uses the Stoic conception of the Logos, as the principle of reason, which quickens and informs matter.

At the same time, while it appears that Philo borrowed both the title of the *Logos* as *Reason*, and the most prominent features of His office, from Hellenic sources, he sought the confirmation of his views in the Old Testament; and in doing this he shews that he was not unacquainted with Jewish speculations on the *Word*. But in spite of the unwavering faith with which he found in the letter of the law the germ and the proof of the teaching which he borrowed from Greece, he abandoned the divine position of the Jew. The whole scope of the writers of the Old Testament is religious. They move in a region of life and history. Their idea of God is that of the Lord who rules the world and His chosen people, not simply as the Author of existence, but as One who stands in a moral relation to men, "speaking" to them. The whole scope of Philo on the other hand is metaphysical. He moves in a region of abstraction and thought. His idea of God is pure being. With him the speculative aspect of the Logos-doctrine overpowers the moral. He does not place the Logos in connexion with the Messiah, nor even specially with Jewish history. It is perhaps of less significance that he speaks of it now as if it were personal, and again as if it were impersonal: now as an attribute, and now as "a second god."

If now we ask with which of these two conceptions of the Logos, current respectively in Palestine and Alexandria, the teaching of St John is organically connected, the answer cannot be uncertain.

Philo occupied himself with the abstract conception of the divine Intelligence, and so laid the foundations of a philosophy. The Palestinian instinct seized upon the concrete idea of "the Word of God," as representing His personal action, and unconsciously prepared the way for a Gospel of the Incarnation. St John started from the conception of "the Word;" and by this means in the end he gave reality to the conception of "the Reason."

The development of the action of the Logos, the Word, in the Prologue to the fourth Gospel places the contrast between Philo and the Evangelist in the broadest light. However wavering and complex Philo's description of the Logos may be, it is impossible not to feel that he has in every case moved far away from the idea of an Incarnation. No one, it is not too much to say, who had accepted his teaching could without a complete revolution of thought accept the statement "the Logos became flesh." The doctrine of the personality of the Logos, even if Philo had consistently maintained it, would not have been in reality a step towards such a fact. On the other hand, in the Prologue the description of the Logos is personal from the first (*ἦν πρὸς τ. θ.*), and His creative energy is at once connected with man. "The Life was the light of men." "The Light was coming into the world (*ἦν.. ἐρχ.*)." And in due time "the Logos became flesh." Thought follows thought naturally, and the last event is seen to crown and complete the history which leads up to it.

Philo and St John, in short, found the same term current, and used it according to their respective apprehensions of the truth. Philo, following closely in the track of Greek philosophy, saw in the Logos the divine Intelligence in relation to the universe: the Evangelist, trusting firmly to the ethical basis of Judaism, sets forth the Logos mainly as the revealer of God to man, through creation, through theophanies, through prophets, through the Incarnation. The Philonean Logos, to express the same thought differently, is a later stage of a divergent interpretation of the term common to Hebrew and Hellenist.

It is however very probable that the teaching of Philo gave a fresh impulse to the study of the complementary conception of the Logos as the divine Reason, which was shadowed forth in the Biblical doctrine of Wisdom (σοφία). Nor is there any difficulty in supposing that the apostolic writers borrowed from him either directly or indirectly forms of language which they adapted to the essentially new announcement of an Incarnate Son of God. So it was that the treasures of Greece were made contributory to the full unfolding of the Gospel. But the essence of their doctrine has no affinity with his. The speculations of Alexandria or Ephesus may have quickened and developed elements which otherwise would have remained latent in Judaism. But the elements were there; and in this respect the evangelic message "the Word became flesh," is the complete fulfilment of three distinct lines of preparatory revelation, which were severally connected with "the Angel of the Presence" (Gen. xxxii. 24 ff.; Exod. xxxiii. 12 ff., xxiii. 20 f.; Hos. xii. 4 f.; Isai. vi. 1 [John xii. 41], lxiii. 9; Mal. iii. 1); with "the Word" (Gen. i. 1; Ps. xxxiii. 6, cxlvii. 15; Isai. lv. 11; comp. Wisd. xviii. 15); and with "Wisdom" (Prov. viii. 22 ff., iii. 19; Ecclus. i. 1—10, xxiv. 9 (14); Bar. iii. 37, iv. 1; comp. Wisd. vii. 7—11).

In short, the teaching of St John is characteristically Hebraic and not Alexandrine. It is intelligible as the final coordination through facts of different modes of thought as to the divine Being and the divine action, which are contained in the Old Testament. And on the other hand it is not intelligible as an application or continuation of the teaching of Philo.

The doctrine of the Logos has been very frequently discussed. An excellent account of the literature up to 1870 is given by Dr Abbot in his appendix to the article on "the Word" in the American edition of the 'Dictionary of the Bible.' Several later works are included in the list given by Soulier, 'La Doctrine du Logos chez Philon d'Alexandrie,' Turin, 1876. The works of Gfroerer, 'Philo u. d. Jud.-Alex. Theosophie,' 1835; Daehne, 'Jud.-Alex. Religions-Philosophie,' 1854; Dorner, 'The Person of Christ' (Eng. Trans.); Jowett, 'St Paul and Philo' ('Epistles of St Paul,' I. 363 ff.); Heinze, 'Die Lehre v. Logos in Griech. Philosophie,' 1872; Siegfried, 'Philo v. Alex.,' 1875, may be specially mentioned. Grossmann has given a complete summary of the word "Logos" in Philo, in his 'Quæstiones Philoneæ,' 1829.

(*c*) *The Author of the fourth Gospel was an eye-witness of what he describes.* The particularity of his knowledge, which has been already noticed summarily, leads at once to the next point in our inquiry. The writer of the Gospel was an eye-witness of the events which he describes. His narrative is marked by minute details of persons, and time, and number, and place and manner, which cannot but have come from a direct experience. And to these must be added various notes of fact, so to speak, which seem to have no special significance where they stand, though they become intelligible when referred to the impression originally made upon the memory of the Evangelist.

(*a*) *Persons.* The portraiture of the chief characters in the Gospel will be noticed afterwards. In this connexion it is sufficient to observe the distinctness with which the different actors in the history rise before the writer. There is no purpose, no symbolism to influence his record. The names evidently belong to the living recollection of the incidents. The first chapter is crowded with figures which live and move: John with his disciples, Andrew, Simon Peter, Philip, Nathanael. Momentous questions are connected with definite persons. *He saith unto Philip, Whence shall we buy bread, that these may eat?...Philip answered him...*(vi. 5, 7; comp. Matt. xiv. 14 ff. and parallels). Certain Greeks said to Philip, *Sir, we would see Jesus. Philip cometh and telleth Andrew: Andrew cometh and Philip and they tell Jesus* (xii. 21 f.). *Thomas saith unto Him, Lord, we know not whither thou goest; how do we know the way?* (xiv. 5). *Philip saith, Lord, shew us the Father, and it sufficeth us* (xiv. 8). *Judas saith, not Iscariot, Lord, how is it that thou wilt manifest thyself to us, and not unto the world?* (xiv. 22). *The disciple whom Jesus loved...falling back upon His breast, saith, Lord, who is it?* (xiii. 25; comp. xxi. 20). Nicodemus (iii. 1 ff., vii. 50, xix. 39), Lazarus (xi. 1 ff., xii. 1 ff.), Simon the father of Judas Iscariot[1] (vi. 71, xii. 4, xiii. 2, 26), and Malchus (xviii. 10), are mentioned only in the fourth Gospel. The writer of this Gospel alone mentions the relationship of Annas to Caiaphas (xviii. 13), and identifies one of those who pointed to Peter as the kinsman of him whose ear Peter cut off (xviii. 26).

(β) *Time.* The details of time belong perhaps more obviously to the plan of the narrative than the details of persons. The greater seasons, even though they are not noted in the Synoptists, may be supposed to have been preserved in tradition, as the first Passover (ii. 13, 23), the Feast of the New Year (v. 1), the Second Passover (vi. 4), the Feast of Tabernacles (vii. 2), the Feast of Dedication (x. 22); but other specifications of date can only be referred to the knowledge of actual experience. Such are the indications of the two marked weeks at the beginning and end of Christ's ministry (i. 29, 35, 43, ii. 1, xii. 1, 12 (xiii. 1), xix. 31, xx. 1), of the week after the Resurrection (xx. 26), the enumeration of the days before the raising of Lazarus (xi. 6, 17, 39), the note of the duration of Christ's stay in Samaria (iv. 40, 43; compare also vi. 22, vii. 14, 37). Still more remarkable is the mention of the hour or of the time of day which occurs under circumstances likely to have impressed it upon the mind of the writer, as *the tenth hour* (i. 40), *the sixth hour* (iv. 6), *the seventh hour* (iv. 52), *about the sixth hour* (xix. 14), *it was night* (xiii. 30), *in the early morning* (xviii. 28, xx. 1, xxi. 4), *the evening* (vi. 16, xx. 19), *by night* (iii. 2).

(γ) *Number.* The details of number, though fewer, are hardly less significant. It is unnatural to refer to anything except experience such definite and, as it appears, immaterial statements as those in which the writer of the fourth Gospel mentions the *two* disciples of the Baptist (i. 35), the *six* waterpots (ii. 6), the *five* loaves and *two* small fishes (vi. 9), the *five-and-twenty* furlongs (vi. 19), the *four* soldiers (xix. 23. Cp. Acts xii. 4), the *two hundred* cubits (xxi. 8), the *hundred and fifty and three* fishes (xxi. 11).

The number of the loaves and fishes is preserved in the Synoptic narrative, but this single parallel does not in any way lessen the value of the whole group of examples as a sign of immediate observation in the Evangelist. Other records of number shew the clearness if not the directness of the writer's information, as the *five* husbands (iv. 18), the *thirty and eight* years sickness (v. 5), the estimate of *three hundred* pence (xii. 5; comp. Mark xiv. 5), the weight of a *hundred* pounds (xix. 39).

(δ) *Place.* Many of the local details characteristic of the fourth Gospel have been already noticed. Here it is only necessary to observe that the manner in which the scenes of special acts and utterances are introduced shews that they belong to the immediate knowledge of the writer. We cannot naturally account for the particularity except on the supposition that the place was an integral part of the recollection of the incidents. Thus the scenes of John's baptism are given at *Bethany* and *Ænon* (i. 28, iii. 23; comp. x. 40). The son of the nobleman was sick *at Capernaum* while Jesus was at *Cana* (iv. 46 f.). Jesus found the paralytic whom He had healed *in the Temple* (v. 14). He gained many adherents when He went towards the close of His ministry *beyond Jordan to the place where John was at first baptizing* (x. 40 ff.). When Mary came to Him He had not yet come to the village, but *was in the place where Martha met Him* (xi. 30). He spent the interval between the raising of Lazarus and His return to Bethany on the eve of the Passion *in the country near the wilderness, in a city called Ephraim* (xi. 54). The people as

[1] In this connexion it is interesting to notice that the writer of the fourth Gospel knew that the title Iscariot was a local or family name. He applies it both to Judas and to his father Simon: vi. 71, xiii. 2, 26, xii. 4, xiv. 22.

they *stood in the Temple* speculated on His reappearance (xi. 56).

So again Christ spoke certain memorable words *in a solemn gathering* (ἐν συναγωγῇ) *at Capernaum* (vi. 59, note), in *the treasury* (viii. 20), in *Solomon's porch* (x. 23), before crossing the Cedron (xviii. 1).

(ε) *Manner.* More impressive still are the countless small traits in the descriptions which evince either the skill of a consummate artist or the recollection of an observer. The former alternative is excluded alike by the literary spirit of the first and second centuries and by the whole character of the Gospel. The writer evidently reflects what he had seen. This will appear most clearly to any one who takes the record of a special scene and marks the several points which seem to reveal the impressions of an eye-witness, as (for example) the calling of the first disciples (i. 35—51), or the foot-washing (xiii. 1—20), or the scene in the high-priest's court (xviii. 15—27), or the draught of fishes (xxi. 1—14). In each one of these narratives, and they are simply samples of the nature of the whole narrative, it is almost impossible to overlook the vivid touches which correspond with the actual experience of one who had looked upon what he describes. Thus, to take a single illustration from the first (i. 35—51), we cannot but feel the life (so to speak) of the opening picture. John is shewn standing, in patient expectation of the issue, as the tense implies (εἱστήκει, comp. vii. 37, xviii. 5, 16, 18, xix. 25, xx. 11), with two of his disciples. As Christ moves away, now separate from him, he fixes his eyes upon Him (ἐμβλέψας, comp. *v.* 43), so as to give the full meaning to the phrase which he repeats, in order that his disciples may now, if they will, take the lesson to themselves. Each word tells; each person occupies exactly the position which corresponds to the crisis. And the description becomes more significant when contrasted with the notice of the corresponding incident on the former day (i. 29 ff.).

Not to dwell at length on these scenes, one or two detached phrases may be quoted which will serve to shew the kind of particularity on which stress is laid. The loaves used at the feeding of the five thousand are *barley* loaves which a boy has (vi. 9; comp. *v.* 13); when Mary came to Jesus she *fell at His feet* (xi. 32; contrast *vv.* 20 f.); after the ointment was poured out *the house was filled from its fragrance* (xii. 3); the branches strewn in the way of Jesus were taken from *the palm-trees* which were by the road-side (xii. 13); *it was night* when Judas went forth (xiii. 30); Judas brings a band of Roman soldiers as well as officers of the priests to apprehend Jesus (xviii. 3); Christ's tunic was *without seam, woven from the top throughout* (xix. 23); the napkin which had been about His head was *wrapped together in a place by itself* (xx. 7); Peter *was grieved* because Jesus said to him the third time, Lovest thou me? (xxi. 17).

Compare also xiii. 24, xviii. 6, xix. 5, xxi. 20. Each phrase is a reflection of a definite external impression. They bring the scenes as vividly before the reader as they must have presented themselves to the writer.

If it be said that we can conceive that these traits might have been realised by the imagination of a Defoe or a Shakespeare, it may be enough to reply that the narrative is wholly removed from this modern realism; but besides this, there are other fragmentary notes to which no such explanation can apply. Sometimes we find historical details given bearing the stamp of authenticity, which represent minute facts likely to cling to the memory of one directly concerned (i. 40), though it is in fact difficult for us now to grasp the object of the writer in preserving them. It is equally impossible to suppose that such details were preserved in common tradition or supplied by the imagination of the writer. Examples are found in the exact account of Andrew finding *first his own brother* Simon (i. 41), of the passing visit to Capernaum (ii. 12), of John's baptism (iii. 23), of the boats from Tiberias (vi. 22 f.), of the retirement to Ephraim (xi. 54).

Sometimes the detail even appears to be in conflict with the context or with the current (Synoptic) accounts, though the discrepancy vanishes on a fuller realisation of the facts, as when the words *Arise, let us go hence* (xiv. 31) mark the separation betw~en the discourses in the upper chamber and those on the way to the garden (compare i. 21 with Matt. xi. 14; iii. 24 with Matt. iv. 12).

Elsewhere a mysterious saying is left wholly unexplained. In some cases the obscurity lies in a reference to a previous but unrecorded conversation, as when the Baptist says to the disciples who had followed him, *Behold the Lamb of God* (i. 29; comp. vi. 36, xii. 34), or, perhaps, to unknown local circumstances (i. 46). In others it lies in a personal but unexpressed revelation, as in the words which carried sudden conviction to Nathanael, *Before Philip called thee, when thou wast under the fig-tree, I saw thee* (i. 48). Apparent contradictions are left without any comment, as v. 31 compared with viii. 14; xiii. 36 compared with xvi. 5; xiv. 19 compared with xvi. 19; and, on the other hand, an explanation is given which, though it might appear superfluous at a later time, becomes at once natural in one who in the process of narration is carried back to the scene itself with all its doubts and perplexities, as when it is said in interpretation of the words, *ye are clean, but not all;* "for He knew him that betrayed (was betraying) Him; for this reason He said, Ye are not all clean" (xiii. 11).

(*d*) *The Author of the fourth Gospel was an Apostle.* Such touches as those which have been now enumerated, and every page of the Gospel will supply examples, shew that the writer was an eye-witness of many at least of the scenes which he describes. The age of minute historical romance had not yet come when the fourth Gospel was written, even if such a record could possibly be brought within the category. A further examination of the narrative shews that the eye-witness was also an apostle. This follows almost necessarily from the character of the scenes which he describes, evidently as has been shewn from his own knowledge, the call of the first disciples (i. 19—34), the journey through Samaria (iv.), the feeding of the five thousand (vi.), the successive visits to Jerusalem (vii. ix. xi.), the Passion, the appearances after the Resurrection. But the fact is further indicated by the intimate acquaintance which he exhibits with the feelings of "the disciples." He knows their thoughts at critical moments (ii. 11, 17, 22, iv. 27, vi. 19, 60 f., xii. 16, xiii. 22, 28, xxi. 12; comp. Luke xxiv. 8; Matt. xxvi. 75). He recalls their words spoken among themselves (iv. 33, xvi. 17, xx. 25, xxi. 3, 5) as to their Lord (iv. 31, ix. 2, xi. 8, 12, xvi. 29).

He is familiar with their places of resort (xi. 54, xviii. 2, xx. 19).

He is acquainted with imperfect or erroneous impressions received by them at one time, and afterwards corrected (ii. 21 f., xi. 13, xii. 16, xiii. 28, xx. 9, xxi. 4).

And yet more than this, the writer of the fourth Gospel evidently stood very near to the Lord. He was conscious of His emotions (xi. 33, xiii. 21). He was in a position to be well acquainted with the grounds of His action (ii. 24 f., iv. 1, v. 6, vi. 15, vii. 1, xvi. 19). Nor is this all; he speaks as one to whom the mind of the Lord was laid open. Before the feeding of the five thousand he writes, *This He* (Jesus) *said trying him, for He Himself knew what He was about to do* (vi. 6). *Jesus knew in Himself* the murmurings of the disciples (vi. 61); *He knew from the beginning who they were that believed not, and who it was that would betray Him* (vi. 64); *He knew the hour of His Passion* (xiii. 1, 3), and who should betray Him (xiii. 11); *He knew* indeed *all the things that were coming upon Him* (xviii. 4); He *knew* when *all things were accomplished* (xix. 28).

(*e*) *The Author of the fourth Gospel was the Apostle John.* Such statements when they are taken in connexion with the absolute simplicity of the narrative necessarily leave the impression that the Evangelist was conscious of having had the opportunity of entering, more deeply even than others, into the conditions of the Lord's life. And this reflection brings us to the last point. If the writer of the fourth Gospel was an apostle, does the narrative indicate any special apostle as the writer? In the Epilogue (xxi. 24) the authorship of the book is assigned, as we shall see afterwards, to *the disciple whom Jesus loved* (ὃν ἠγάπα ὁ Ἰησοῦς). This disciple appears under the same title twice in the narrative of the Passion (xiii. 23, xix. 26), as well as twice afterwards (xxi. 7, 20), and once in connexion with St Peter under a title closely resembling it (xx. 2, ὃν ἐφίλει ὁ Ἰησοῦς).

He is known to the high-priest (xviii. 15), and stands in very close relationship with St Peter (xiii. 24, xx. 2, xxi. 7; comp. xviii. 15; Acts iii.). Though his name is not mentioned, there is nothing mysterious or ideal about him. He moves about among the other apostles quite naturally, and from the enumeration (xxi. 2; comp. i. 35 ff.) of those present at the scene described in the last chapter, it follows that he must have been either one of *the sons of Zebedee*, or one of the *two other disciples* not described more particularly.

If now we turn to the Synoptic narrative we find three disciples standing in a special sense near to Jesus, Peter and the sons of Zebedee, James and John. There is then a strong presumption that the Evangelist was one of these. St Peter is out of the question. Of the two sons of Zebedee, James was martyred very early (Acts xii. 2), so that he could not have been the author of the Gospel. John therefore alone remains; and he completely satisfies the conditions which are required to be satisfied by the writer, that he should be in close connexion with St Peter, and also one admitted to peculiar intimacy with the Lord.

Does then this definite supposition that St John was the anonymous disciple who wrote the fourth Gospel find any subsidiary support from the contents of the history? The answer cannot be doubtful. St John is nowhere mentioned by name in the Gospel; and while it appears incredible that an apostle who stands in the Synoptists, in the Acts (iii. 1, iv. 13, &c.), and in St Paul (Gal. ii. 9), as a central figure among the twelve, should find no place in the narrative, the nameless disciple fulfils the part which would naturally be assigned to St John. Yet further, in the first call of the disciples one of the two followers of the Baptist is expressly named as Andrew (i. 40); the other is left unnamed. Andrew, it is said, found *first his own brother Simon* (i. 41). The natural interpretation of the words suggests that the brother of some other person, and if so, of the second disciple, was also found. A reference to the last scene at the sea of Galilee (xxi. 2) leads to the certain inference that these two brothers were the sons of Zebedee, and so that the second disciple was St John. Another peculiarity of the Gospel confirms the inference.

The Evangelist is for the most part singularly exact in defining the names in his Gospel. He never mentions Simon after his call (i. 42 f.) by the simple name, as is done in the other Gospels, but always by the full name Simon Peter, or by the new name Peter. Thomas is three times out of four further marked by the correlative Greek name Didymus (xi. 16, xx. 24, xxi. 2), which is not found in the Synoptists. Judas Iscariot is described as the son of a Simon not elsewhere noticed (vi. 71, xii. 4, xiii. 2, 26). The second Judas is expressly distinguished from Iscariot even when the latter had left the eleven (xiv. 22). Nicodemus is identified as *he that came to Jesus by night* (xix. 39 [vii. 50]). Caiaphas on each of the two separate occasions where he is introduced is qualified by the title of his office as *the high-priest of that year* (xi. 49, xviii. 13).

But in spite of this habitual particularity the Evangelist never speaks of the Baptist, like the three other Evangelists, as "John the Baptist," but always simply as "John." It is no doubt to be noticed that in most places the addition of the title would have been awkward or impossible; but elsewhere such an identification might have been expected (i. 15 and v. 33, 36; comp. Matt. iii. 1, xi. 11 ff.). If however the writer of the Gospel were himself the other John of the Gospel history, it is perfectly natural that he should think of the Baptist, apart from himself, as John only[1].

But it is said that if it is admitted that the Apostle John is to be identified with the nameless disciple of the fourth Gospel, the second of the two disciples of the Baptist, the companion of St Peter, the disciple whom Jesus loved; it is still impossible, in spite of the attestation of the Epilogue, that he could have written the Gospel. The Gospel, such is the contention, must have been written by some one else, for it is argued that the author could not have spoken

[1] It is also to be observed that the writer of the fourth Gospel does not give the name of Salome, the wife of Zebedee (xix. 25. Comp. Matt. xxvii. 56), or of James (xxi. 2), or of the Mother of the Lord.

of himself as *the disciple whom Jesus loved*, claiming in this way for himself, and not as he might reasonably have done for another whom he took as his hero, a pre-eminence over his fellow-apostles; and (it is further urged in particular) that St John would not have "studiously elevated himself in every way above the Apostle Peter" as this writer does.

The last objection may be disposed of first. The notion that the author of the fourth Gospel wishes to present St John as the victorious rival of St Peter, is based mainly upon the incident at the Last Supper, where St Peter beckoned to St John to ask a question which he did not put himself (xiii. 24 ff.); and it is asserted that the same idea is supported by the scenes in the court of the High Priest, and by the Cross. It would be sufficient to reply that all these incidents belong to details of personal relationship, and not to official position, and St John was (as it appears) the son of the sister of the Mother of the Lord. But if we go into details an examination of the narrative as a whole shews that it lends no support whatever to the theory of any thought of rivalry or comparison between St Peter and St John existing in the writer's mind. St John stands, just as he stands in the Acts, silent by the side of the Apostle to whom the office of founding the Church was assigned (cf. xxi. 21; Acts iii. 1). And as for the incident at the Last Supper, the person who occupied the third and not the second place would be in a position to act the part assigned to St John (John xiii. 23, note). Here then St Peter takes the precedence; and elsewhere he occupies exactly the same place with regard to the Christian Society in the fourth Gospel as in the other three. He receives the promise of his significant surname (i. 42); he gives utterance to the critical confession of Christ's majesty (vi. 68); he is placed first (as it seems) at the foot-washing during the Last Supper (xiii. 6); he is conspicuous at the betrayal in defence of his Lord (xviii. 10); he stands patiently without the high priest's door till he is able to obtain admission (xviii. 16); the message of the Resurrection is brought to him and to "the other disciple" only as second to him (xx. 2); he first sees the certain signs that Christ had risen (xx. 7); he directs the action of the group of apostles during their time of suspense (xxi. 3); he is the first to join the Lord upon the seashore, and the chief in carrying out His command (xxi. 7, 11); he receives at last the Great Commission (xxi. 15 ff.).

The representative official precedence of St Peter thus really underlies the whole narrative of the fourth Gospel. The nearness of St John to the Lord is a relation of sympathy, so to speak, different in kind.

But this ascription of a special relation of the unnamed disciple to the Lord as *the disciple whom Jesus loved*, with a feeling at once general (ἠγάπα) and personal (ἐφίλει, xx. 2), requires in itself careful consideration. And if it were true, as is frequently assumed, that St John sought to conceal himself by the use of the various periphrases under which his name is veiled, there might be some difficulty in reconciling the use of this exact title with the modest wish to be unnoticed. But in point of fact the writer of the fourth Gospel evidently insists on the peculiarity of his narrative as being that of a personal witness. He speaks with an authority which has a right to be recognised. It is taken for granted that those whom he addresses will know who he is, and acknowledge that he ought to be heard. In this respect the fourth Gospel differs essentially from the other three. They are completely impersonal, with the exception of the short preface of St Luke. We can then imagine that St John as an eye-witness might either have written his narrative in the first person throughout, or he might have composed an impersonal record, adding some introductory sentences to explain the nature of the book, or he might have indicated his own presence obliquely at some one or other of the scenes which he describes. There is no question of self-concealment in the choice between these alternatives; and there can be also no question as to the method which would be most natural to an apostle living again, as it were, in the divine history of his youth. The direct personal narrative and the still more formal personal preface to an impersonal narrative seem to be alien from the circumstances of the composition. On the other hand, the oblique allusion corresponds with the devout contemplation from a distance of events seen only after a long interval in their full significance. The facts and the actors alike are all separated from the Evangelist as he recalls them once more in the centre of a Christian Society[1].

But if it be admitted that the oblique form of reference to the fact that the writer of the fourth Gospel was an eye-witness of what he describes was generally the most natural, does it appear that this particular form of oblique reference, to which objection is made, was itself natural? The answer must be looked for in the circumstances under which it is used. After the distinct but passing claim to be an eye-witness (i. 14), the Evangelist does not appear personally in the Gospel till the scenes of the Passion. He may be discovered in the call of the disciples (i. 41), but only by a method of exhaustion. So far there was nothing to require his explicit attestation. But in the review of the issue of Christ's work it might well be asked whether the treachery of Judas was indeed foreseen by Christ. St John shews how deeply he felt the importance of the question (vi. 70, 71, xiii. 11; comp. xiii. 18 f.). It was then essential to his plan that he should place on record the direct statement of the Lord's foreknowledge on the authority of him to whom it was made. That communication was a special sign of affection. Can we then be surprised that, in recalling the memorable fact that it was made to himself, he should speak of himself as *the disciple whom Jesus loved* (ἠγάπα)? The words express the grateful and devout acknowledgment of something received, and contain no assumption of a distinction above others. Christ loved all (xiii. 1, 34, xv. 9); St John felt, and confesses, that Christ loved him, and shewed His love in this signal manner. The same thought underlies the second passage where the phrase occurs (xix. 26). The charge to receive the Mother of the Lord almost necessarily calls out the same confession. In the last chapter (xxi. 7, 20) the title seems to be repeated with a distinct reference to the former passages, and no difficulty can be felt at the repetition.

The remaining passage (xx. 2) is different, and ought not to have been confounded with those already noticed. There can be no doubt that if the words *she cometh to Simon Peter and the other disciple whom Jesus loved*, had stood alone, the reader would have included St Peter under the description; the word "other" has no meaning except on this interpretation (contrast xxi. 7). But it has been assumed that the entirely different phrase used here (ὃν ἐφίλει) must be identical with that used elsewhere of St John alone (ὃν ἠγάπα), and the passage has been accordingly misunderstood. Yet the contrast between the two words equally translated "love," gives the clue to the right meaning. St Peter and St John shared alike in that peculiar nearness of personal friendship to Christ (if we may so speak) which is expressed by the former word (φιλεῖν, see xi. 3, 36), while St John acknowledges for himself the gift of love which is implied in the latter; the first word describes that of which others could judge outwardly; the second that of which the individual soul alone is conscious. The general conclusion is obvious. If that phrase (ὃν ἐφίλει ὁ Ἰησοῦς) had been used characteristically of St John which is in fact used in relation to St Peter and St John, there might have been some ground for the charge of an apparent assumption of pre-eminence on the part of the Evangelist; as it is, the phrase which is used is no affectation of honour; it is a personal thanksgiving for a blessing which the Evangelist had experienced, which was yet in no way peculiar to himself.

As far therefore as indirect internal evidence is concerned, the conclusion

[1] In illustration of this view, reference may be made to Mr Browning's noble realisation of the situation in his 'Death in the Desert.'

> "...much that at the first, in deed and word,
> Lay simply and sufficiently exposed,
> Had grown (or else my soul was grown to match,
> Fed through such years, familiar with such light,
> Guarded and guided still to see and speak)
> Of new significance and fresh result;
> What first were guessed as points I now knew stars."

towards which all the lines of inquiry converge remains unshaken, that the fourth Gospel was written by a Palestinian Jew, by an eye-witness, by *the disciple whom Jesus loved*, by John the son of Zebedee. We have now to consider the direct evidence which the Gospel offers upon the question.

ii. *The direct evidence of the Gospel as to its authorship.*

Three passages of the Gospel appear to point directly to the position and person of the author: i. 14, xix. 35, xxi. 24. Each passage includes some difficulties and uncertainties of interpretation which must be noticed somewhat at length.

(*a*) Ch. i. 14. *The Word became flesh and dwelt* (*tabernacled*) *among us, and we beheld His glory*...(ὁ λόγος σὰρξ ἐγένετο, καὶ ἐσκήνωσεν ἐν ἡμῖν, καὶ ἐθεασάμεθα τὴν δόξαν αὐτοῦ...). The main question here is as to the sense in which the words *we beheld* are to be taken. Are we to understand this "beholding" of the historical sight of Christ, so that the writer claims to have been an eye-witness of that which he records? or can it be referred to a spiritual vision, common to all believers at all times?

Our reply cannot but be affected by the consideration of the parallel passage in the beginning of the first Epistle of St John, which was written, it may certainly be assumed, by the same author as the Gospel: *That which was from the beginning, which we have heard, which we have seen with our eyes, which we beheld, and our hands handled, concerning the Word of life*...(1 John i. 1, ὃ ἦν ἀπ' ἀρχῆς, ὃ ἀκηκόαμεν, ὃ ἑωράκαμεν τοῖς ὀφθαλμοῖς, ὃ ἐθεασάμεθα καὶ αἱ χεῖρες ἡμῶν ἐψηλάφησαν, περὶ τοῦ λόγου τῆς ζωῆς...). Now there cannot be any doubt that the "beholding" here, from the connexion in which it stands (*we have seen with our eyes, our hands handled*), must be understood literally. Language cannot be plainer. The change of tense moreover emphasizes the specific historical reference (*we beheld*, and not as of that which ideally abides, *we have beheld* [1 John iv. 14; John i. 32, n.]). This being so, the same word in the same tense and in the same general connexion cannot reasonably be understood otherwise in the Gospel. It may also be added further, that the original word (θεᾶσθαι) is never used in the New Testament of mental vision (as θεωρεῖν)[1]. The writer then (such must be our conclusion) claims to have *beheld* that *glory* which his record unfolds.

But it is said that the phrase *among us* cannot be confined to the apostles or immediate disciples of Christ exclusively, and that it must be taken to include *all* Christians (Luke i. 1), or even all men. If however this interpretation of *among us* admits the wider interpretation of the pronoun, it does not exclude the apostles, who are in this connexion the representatives of the Church and of humanity, and it does not therefore touch the meaning of the following clause, in which the sense of *beheld* is fixed independently. The whole point of the passage is that the Incarnation was historical, and that the sight of the Incarnate Word was historical. The words cannot without violence be made to give any other testimony. The objection is thus, on a view of the context, wholly invalid; and the natural interpretation of the phrase in question, which has been already given, remains unshaken. The writer professes to have been an eye-witness of Christ's ministry[2].

(*b*) Ch. xix. 35. This second passage, which, like the former one, comes into the narrative parenthetically, is in some respects more remarkable. After speaking of the piercing of the Lord's side, the writer adds, *And forthwith came there out blood and water. And he that hath seen hath borne witness, and his witness is true: and he knoweth that he saith true, that ye also may believe. For these things came to pass that*... (καὶ ὁ ἑωρακὼς μεμαρτύρηκεν καὶ ἀληθινὴ αὐτοῦ ἐστὶν ἡ μαρτυρία, καὶ ἐκεῖνος οἶδεν ὅτι ἀληθῆ λέγει ἵνα καὶ ὑμεῖς πιστεύητε. ἐγένετο γὰρ... John xix. 35 ff.). One point in this passage, the contrast between the two words rendered *true*, cannot be given adequately in an English version. The wit-

[1] The word occurs in John i. 32, 38, iv. 35, vi. 5, xi. 45; 1 John i. 1, iv. 12, 14.

[2] The significant variation of language in *v.* 16 supports the view which has been given. The Apostolic *we* is distinguished from the Christian *we all*. The use of the direct form in these two cases (*we* beheld, *we* received) is remarkable. Contrast xx. 30 (ἐνώπ. τῶν μαθ.).

ness is described as "fulfilling the true conception of witness" (ἀληθινός), and not simply as being correct (ἀληθής); it is true to the idea of what witness should be, and not only true to the fact in this special instance (comp. viii. 16, note) so far as the statement is true. There is therefore no repetition in the original in the two clauses, as there appears to be in the English version. This detail is not without significance for the right understanding of the whole comment. It brings out clearly the two conditions which testimony ought to satisfy, the first that he who gives it should be competent to speak with authority, and the second that the account of his experience should be exact. But the main question to be decided is whether the form of the sentence either suggests or admits the belief that the eye-witness to whose testimony appeal is made is to be identified with the writer of the Gospel.

The answer to this question has been commonly made to turn upon a false issue. It has been argued, with a profusion of learning, that the use in the second clause of the pronoun which expresses a remote, or rather an isolated personality (ἐκεῖνος), is unfavourable to the identification of the Evangelist and the eye-witness, or, at least, lends no support to the identification. It has also been asserted, as might have been expected, by less cautious scholars, that the use of this pronoun is fatal to the identification. On the other hand, it has been shewn by examples from classical authors and also from St John's Gospel (ix. 37) that a speaker can use this pronoun of himself[1]. But in reality the problem contained in the passage must be solved at an earlier stage. If the author of the Gospel could use the first clause (*he that hath seen*, &c.) of himself, there can be no reasonable doubt that he could also use of himself the particular pronoun which occurs in the second clause; and to go even further, there can be no reasonable doubt that according to the common usage of St John he would use this particular pronoun to resume and emphasize the reference (i. 18, v. 39, 37). No one, in other words, with any knowledge of St John's style can seriously dispute the fact that the "he" of the second clause is the same as the "witness" of the first clause.

This being so, only two interpretations of the passage are possible. The Evangelist either makes an appeal to an eye-witness separate from himself, but not more definitely described, who is said to be conscious of the truth of his own testimony; or he makes an appeal to his own actual experience, now solemnly recorded for the instruction of his readers.

We are thus brought to the right issue. Is it the fact that the second alternative is, as has been confidently affirmed, excluded by the nature of the case? Is it the fact that we cannot suppose that St John, if he were the writer, would have referred to his own experience obliquely? On the contrary, if we realise the conditions under which the narrative was drawn up, it will be seen that the introduction of the first person in this single place would have been more strange. The Evangelist has been already presented as a historical figure in the scene (*vv.* 26, 27); and it is quite intelligible that an Apostle who had pondered again and again, as it may well have been, what he had gradually shaped, should pause at this critical point, and, dwelling upon that which he felt to be a crucial incident, should separate himself as the witness from his immediate position as a writer. In this mental attitude he looks from without upon himself (ἐκεῖνος) as affected at that memorable moment by the fact which he records, in order that it may create in others the present faith (πιστεύητε) which it had created in his own soul. The comment from this point is therefore perfectly compatible with the identification of the witness and the author.

We may however go further. The comment is not only compatible with the identification; it favours the identification, not indeed by the use of the particular pronoun, which tells neither one way nor the other, but by the whole construction of the passage. The witness is spoken of as something which abides after it has been given; *he hath borne*

[1] The most complete discussion of this part of the problem is to be found in a set of papers in the 'Studien u. Kritiken,' 1859, 1860, by Steitz on the one side, and by Ph. Buttmann on the other.

witness; and, more than this, the witness is given still; *he knoweth that he saith true;* and, yet again, the giver of the witness sets himself in contrast with his readers; *he hath given his witness...that ye may believe.* It is not possible then to doubt that the words taken in their context assert that the eye-witness was still living when the record was written[1]; and if so, it is most natural to suppose that his present utterance, to which appeal is made, is that contained in the Gospel itself. It is difficult to appreciate the evidential force of an appeal to the consciousness of an undefined witness.

In this connexion another point must be observed. If the author were appealing to the testimony of a third person he would almost necessarily have used an aorist and not a perfect, *he that saw bore witness*, and not *he that hath seen hath borne witness.* For the mere narrator the testimony centres in the moment at which it was rendered; for the witness himself it is a continuous part of his own life.

The conclusion to which these remarks converge will appear still more certain if the comment be reduced to its simplest elements. If it had stood, *He that hath seen hath borne witness, that ye also may believe*, no ordinary reader would have doubted that the writer was appealing to his own experience, recorded in the history, since no other testimony is quoted. But the intercalated clauses do not in any way interfere with this interpretation. They simply point out, as has been already noticed, the relation in which this special statement stands to its attestation. They shew that this testimony satisfies the two conditions, which must be ratified for the establishment of its authority, that it is adequate in relation to its source, and that it is correct in its actual details. For a witness may give true evidence and yet miss the essential features of that of which he speaks. Hence the writer affirms the competency of the witness, while he affirms also that the testimony itself was exact.

On the whole therefore the statement which we have considered is not only compatible with the identity of the eye-witness and the writer of the Gospel, but it also suggests, even if it does not necessarily involve, the identification of the two. On the other hand, the only other possible interpretation of the passage is wholly pointless. It supposes that an appeal is made with singular emphasis to an unknown witness, who is said to be conscious of the truthfulness of his own testimony. Such a comment could find no place in the connexion in which the words stand.

(*c*) Ch. xxi. 24. The third passage which occurs in the appendix to the Gospel (ch. xxi.) is different in character from the other two. After the narrative of the Lord's saying with regard to "the disciple whom he loved," the record continues: *this is the disciple who witnesseth concerning these things, and who wrote these things: and we know that his witness is true* (οὗτός ἐστιν ὁ μαθητὴς ὁ μαρτυρῶν περὶ τούτων καὶ ὁ γράψας ταῦτα, καὶ οἴδαμεν ὅτι ἀληθὴς αὐτοῦ ἡ μαρτυρία ἐστίν). There can be no doubt as to the meaning of the words. The writing of the Gospel is distinctly assigned by them to "the beloved disciple" (*v.* 21). But it is not at once obvious to whom the words are to be assigned. Is the author of the Gospel himself the speaker? or must the note be referred to others who published his Gospel, as, for example, to the Ephesian elders? Before we attempt to answer this question it must be observed that whichever view be taken, the sentence contains a declaration as to the authorship of the Gospel contemporaneous with its publication, for there is not the least evidence that the Gospel was ever circulated in the Church without the epilogue (ch. xxi.). And yet further, the declaration extends both to the substantial authorship (*he that witnesseth concerning these things*) and also to the literal authorship of the record (*he that wrote these things*). So much is clear; but perhaps it is impossible to press the present tense (*he that witnesseth*) as a certain proof that the author was still alive when the work was sent forth. The form as it stands here by itself may simply indicate the vital continuity of his testimony. However this may be, the note at least emphasizes what was felt to be a real presence of the writer in the society to which he belonged.

If we now proceed to fix the author-

[1] This conclusion holds good to whomsoever the comment be referred.

ship of the note, it will at once appear that the passage (xix. 35) which has been already considered practically decides the question. The contrast between the two notes is complete. In that the note is given in the singular and in the third person; in this it is given in the plural and in the first person. In that the witness is regarded as isolated and remote (*he that...and he...*); in this the witness is regarded as present (*this is...*). If we believe that the former is, as has been shewn, a personal affirmation of the writer himself, it seems almost impossible to believe that this is a personal affirmation also. No sufficient reason can be given for the complete change of position which he assumes towards his own work. The plural (*we know*) by itself would be capable of explanation, but the transition from the historical singular (*this is...*) to the direct plural (*we know...*) is so harsh and sudden as to be all but inadmissible; and the difficulty is aggravated by the occurrence of the first person singular (*I suppose*) in the next sentence. On the other hand, if we bear in mind that the Gospel as originally composed ended with xx. 31, to which xxi. 25 may have been attached, and that the narratives in xxi. 1—23 were drawn up by the same author at a later time under circumstances which called for some authoritative interpretation of a mistaken tradition, we can readily understand how the note was added to the record by those who had sought for this additional explanation of the Lord's words, and preserved when the completed Gospel was issued to the Church. At the same time, if *v.* 25 formed the last clause of the original Gospel, it would naturally be transferred to the end of the enlarged record.

The general result of the examination of these passages is thus tolerably distinct. The fourth Gospel claims to be written by an eye-witness, and this claim is attested by those who put the work in circulation.

2. *External evidence as to the authorship.*

In considering the external evidence[1] for the authorship of the Fourth Gospel, it is necessary to bear in mind the conditions under which it must be sought. It is agreed on all hands that the Gospel was written at a late date, towards the close of the first century, when the Evangelic tradition, preserved in complementary forms in the Synoptic Gospels, had gained general currency, and from its wide spread had practically determined the popular view of the life and teaching of the Lord. And further, the substance of the record deals with problems which belong to the life of the Church and to a more fully developed faith. On both grounds references to the contents of this Gospel would naturally be rarer in ordinary literature than references to the contents of the other Gospels. Express citations are made from all about the same time.

Christian theological literature practically begins for us with Irenæus, Clement of Alexandria, and Tertullian, and these writers use the four Gospels as fully and decisively as any modern writer. The few letters and apostolic treatises and fragments which represent the earlier literature of the second century give very little scope for the direct use of the New Testament. But it is most significant that Eusebius, who had access to many works which are now lost, speaks without reserve of the Fourth Gospel as the unquestioned work of St John, no less than those three great representative Fathers who sum up the teaching of the century. If he had known of any doubts as to its authorship among ecclesiastical writers, he would without question have mentioned these, as he has quoted the criticism of Dionysius of Alexandria on the Apocalypse.

We start then with the undeniable fact that about the last quarter of the second century, when from the nature of the case clear evidence can first be obtained, the Gospel was accepted as authoritative by heretical writers like Ptolemæus and

[1] The character of the present Introduction necessarily excludes detailed criticism of the authorities which are quoted. But it may be said, once for all, that the passages which are set down are used after a careful examination of all that has been urged against their validity. The original texts have been discussed in detail by Dr Sanday ('The Gospels in the Second Century,' 1876) and by Dr Lightfoot in the 'Contemporary Review,' 1875, f., who have noticed at length the most recent literature on the subject.

Heracleon, and used by the opponents of Christ like Celsus, and assigned to St John by Fathers in Gaul, Alexandria, and North Africa, who claimed to reproduce the ancient tradition of their churches, and this with perfect naturalness, there being evidently no trace within their knowledge of a contrary opinion. It is true that the Gospel was not received by Marcion, but there is no evidence to shew that he was influenced by anything but subjective considerations in the formation of his collection of Scriptures. Irenæus also mentions an earlier sect, of doubtful affinity, which, claiming for itself the possession of prophetic gifts, rejected the Gospel of St John and its characteristic promises of the Paraclete (Iren. 'c. Hær.' III. 11. 9, "Alii ut donum Spiritus frustrentur quod in novissimis temporibus secundum placitum Patris effusum est in humanum genus, illam speciem non admittunt quæ est secundum Joannis evangelium, in qua Paracletum se missurum Dominus promisit; sed simul et evangelium et propheticum repellunt Spiritum"). But the language of Irenæus lends no support to the supposition that this sect questioned the authority of the Gospel on critical grounds. At the same time it must be noticed that Epiphanius ('Hær.' LI. 3) and Philastrius ('Hær.' 60) assert that a body of men whom they call *Alogi* assigned the authorship of the Gospel and of the Apocalypse to Cerinthus. The statement as it stands is scarcely intelligible; and it seems to have arisen from the mistaken extension to the authorship of the Gospel, by way of explaining its rejection, of a late conjecture as to the authorship of the Apocalypse.

Such an exception can have no weight against the uniform ecclesiastical tradition with which it is contrasted. This tradition can be carried still further back than Irenæus, who is its fullest exponent. The first quotation of the Gospel by name is made by THEOPHILUS of Antioch (c. 181 A.D.): "...The holy Scriptures teach us, and all the inspired men (οἱ πνευματοφόροι), one of whom John saith: *In the beginning was the Word, and the Word was God*...Afterwards he saith: *and the Word was God: all things were made through Him, and without Him was not even one thing made* ('ad Autol.' II. 22). ATHENAGORAS (c. 176 A.D.) paraphrases and combines the language of the Gospel in such a way as to shew that it was both familiar and authoritative, and had been carefully weighed by him: "The Son of God is *the Word* of the Father in idea and actually (ἐν ἰδέᾳ καὶ ἐνεργείᾳ). For *all things were made* in dependence on Him and *through Him* (πρὸς αὐτοῦ [Acts xxvii. 34] καὶ δι' αὐτοῦ), *the Father and the Son being One.* But since *the Son is in the Father and the Father in the Son*, by unity and power of the Spirit (ἑνότητι καὶ δυνάμει πνεύματος), the Son of God is the Mind and Word of the Father" ('Leg.' 10; comp. John i. 3, x. 30, xvii. 21). About the same time CLAUDIUS APOLLINARIS, bishop of Hierapolis, speaking of the different opinions as to the day of the Last Supper, evidently treats "the disagreement of the Gospels" (*i.e.* the Synoptists and St John) as something really out of the question (Routh, 'Rell.' I. 167 ff.; comp. 'Hist. of N. T. Canon,' p. 224); and he gives an explanation of John xix. 34 (see note), which shews that the incident had become a subject of deep speculation. Still earlier TATIAN, the scholar of Justin (c. 160 A.D.), quotes words of the Gospel as well known: "This is in fact," he says, "that which hath been said: *The darkness apprehendeth not the light*" ('Orat.' 13, τοῦτο ἔστιν ἄρα τὸ εἰρημένον [Acts ii. 16] ἡ σκοτία τὸ φῶς οὐ καταλαμβάνει, John i. 5; comp. John i. 3 with 'Orat.' 19); and the latest criticism confirms the old belief that his 'Diatessaron' was constructed from the texts of the four Canonical Gospels (Lightfoot, 'Contemporary Review,' May, 1877).

So far the line of testimony appears to be absolutely beyond doubt. The traces of the use of the fourth Gospel in the interval between 100—160 A.D. are necessarily less clear; but as far as they can be observed they are not only in perfect harmony with the belief in its apostolic origin, but materially strengthen this belief.

The EPISTLE OF CLEMENT to the Corinthians was probably written before the Gospel of St John, but already this writing shews traces of the forms of thought which are characteristic of the book (cc. VII. XXXVI. 'Hist. of Canon of

N. T.' pp. 25 f.). The EPISTLE OF BARNABAS again offers some correspondences and more contrasts with the teaching of St John in the common region of "mystical" religious thought. In the LETTERS OF IGNATIUS, which even if they are not authentic certainly fall within the first half of the century, the influence of the teaching, if not demonstrably of the writings, of St John is more direct. The true meat of the Christian, for example, is said to be the "bread of God, *the bread of heaven, the bread of life*, which is *the flesh of Jesus Christ*," and his drink is "*Christ's blood*, which is love incorruptible" ('ad Rom.' VII.; comp. John vi. 32, 51, 53). And again: "The Spirit is not led astray, as being from God. For it *knoweth whence it cometh and whither it goeth*, and *testeth* (ἐλέγχει) that which is hidden" ('ad Philad.' VII.; comp. John iii. 8, xvi. 8).

It is however with POLYCARP and PAPIAS[1] that the decisive testimony to the authenticity of St John's writings really begins. Recent investigations, independent of all theological interests, have fixed the martyrdom of Polycarp in 155—6 A.D. (See Lightfoot, 'Contemporary Review,' 1875, p. 838.) At the time of his death he had been a Christian for eighty-six years ('Mart. Polyc.' c. IX.). He must then have been alive during the greater part of St John's residence in Asia, and there is no reason for questioning the truth of the statements that he "associated with the Apostles in Asia (*e.g.* John, Andrew, Philip; comp. Lightfoot's 'Colossians,' pp. 45 f.), and was entrusted with the oversight of the Church in Smyrna by those who were eye-witnesses and ministers of the Lord" (Euseb. 'H. E.' III. 36; comp. Iren. 'c. Hær.' III. 3. 4). Thus, like St John himself, he lived to unite two ages. When already old he used to speak to his scholars of "his intercourse with John and the rest of those who had seen the Lord" (Iren. 'Ep. ad Flor.' § 2); and Irenæus, in his later years, vividly recalled the teaching which he had heard from him as a boy (Iren. *l. c.*; comp. 'c. Hær.' III. 3. 4). There is no room in this brief succession for the introduction of new writings under the name of St John. Irenæus cannot with any reason be supposed to have assigned to the fourth Gospel the place which he gives to it unless he had received it with the sanction of Polycarp. The person of Polycarp, the living sign of the unity of the faith of the first and second centuries, is in itself a sure proof of the apostolicity of the Gospel. Is it conceivable that in his lifetime such a revolution was accomplished that his disciple Irenæus was not only deceived as to the authorship of the book, but was absolutely unaware that the continuity of the tradition in which he boasted had been completely broken? One short letter of Polycarp, with which Irenæus was acquainted (Iren. *l. c.*), has been preserved. In this there is a striking coincidence with the language of 1 John: "Every one," he writes, "who doth not confess that Jesus Christ hath come in the flesh, is antichrist" ('ad Phil.' VII.; comp. 1 John iv. 2, 3). The sentence is not a mere quotation, but a reproduction of St John's thought in compressed language which is all borrowed from him (πᾶς, ὃς ἄν, ὁμολογεῖν 'I. X. ἐν σαρκὶ ἐληλυθέναι, ἀντίχριστος). The words of St John have, so to speak, been shaped into a popular formula. And if it be said that the reference to the Epistle shews nothing as to the Gospel, the reply is that the authorship of the two cannot reasonably be separated. A testimony to one is necessarily by inference a testimony to the other.

The testimony of PAPIAS to the Gospel of St John, is, like that of Polycarp, secondary and inferential. Papias, according to Eusebius, "used testimonies from the former epistle of John" (Euseb. 'H. E.' III. 39). The mention of this fact, as the epistle was universally received, is remarkable; but the Catholic Epistles formed an exceptional group of writings, and it is perhaps on this account that Eusebius goes beyond his prescribed rule in noticing the use which was made even of those among them which were "acknowledged." At any rate the use of the Epistle by Papias points to his acquaintance with the Gospel. Several minute details in the fragment of the

[1] For a complete discussion of the historical position of these two Fathers in regard to early Christian teaching and literature, see the articles of Dr Lightfoot in the 'Contemporary Review' for May, August and October, 1875.

preface to his "Exposition of Oracles of the Lord" tend in the same direction. And there is a remarkable tradition found in a preface to a Latin MS. of the Gospel which assigns to Papias an account of the composition of the Gospel similar to that given in the Muratorian fragment (see 'Canon of N. T.' p. 76, n.).

But it is said that if Papias had used the Gospel Eusebius would not have neglected to notice the fact. The statement rests on a complete misunderstanding of what Eusebius professed to do. He did not undertake to collect references to "the acknowledged books," among which he placed the four Gospels, so that however often Papias might have quoted St John's Gospel, Eusebius would not according to his plan have noticed the fact, unless something of special interest had been added to the reference (comp. 'Hist. of N. T. Canon,' pp. 229 f.; Lightfoot, 'Contemporary Review,' 1875, pp. 169 ff.).

The object of Papias was, as has been shewn elsewhere, to illustrate the evangelic records by such information as he could gain from the earliest disciples; and it is by no means unlikely that the "history of the woman taken in adultery," which has found a place in the Gospel of St John, was recorded by him in illustration of John viii. 15 (see note *ad loc.*).

In close connexion with Papias stand "the elders" quoted by Irenæus, among whose words is one clear reference to St John (Iren. v. 36. 2): "for this reason [they taught] the Lord said, *there are many mansions in my Father's home* (ἐν τοῖς τοῦ πατρός μου μονὰς εἶναι πολλάς. John xiv. 2. Comp. Luke ii. 49). The quotation is anonymous, but it is taken from a writing and not from tradition; and the context makes it at least highly probable that the passage was quoted from Papias' 'Exposition.'

Whatever may be thought of the passing references of Polycarp and Papias to the writings of St John, the main value of their testimony lies in the fact that they represent what can justly be called a school of St John. Papias like Polycarp may himself have heard the Apostle (Iren. v. 33. 4). At least he studied with Polycarp (Iren. *l. c.*). And he had still another point of connexion with the apostolic body. He conversed at Hierapolis with two daughters of the Apostle Philip (Euseb. 'H. E.' III. 39; Lightfoot, 'Colossians,' 45 ff.). Nor were these two men alone. There were many about them, like the elders quoted by Irenæus, who shared in the same life. The succession was afterwards continued at Sardis through Melito, at Ephesus through Polycrates (comp. Euseb. 'H. E.' v. 22), at Hierapolis through Claudius Apollinaris, at Lyons through Pothinus and Irenæus (compare also the 'Epistle of the Churches of Vienne and Lyons,' c. 4, 177 A.D.); and the concordant testimony of the latest witnesses in these different Churches is a sure proof that they preserved the belief which had been held from the first by the school to which they belonged (comp. Lightfoot, 'Contemporary Review,' August, 1876).

The testimony to the Gospel of St John is, as might have been expected on the assumption of its authenticity, most clear among the writers who stood in the closest connexion with his teaching. But it is not confined to them. Justin Martyr certainly appears to have been acquainted with the book. His evidence is somewhat obscure. All his references to the Gospels are anonymous; but at the same time his description of "the Memoirs" as written "by the *Apostles* and those who followed them" ('Dial.' 103), exactly answers to our present collection of four. And though the coincidences of language between Justin and St John are not such as to establish beyond question Justin's dependence on the Evangelist, this at least is the most natural explanation of the similarity ('Hist. of N. T. Canon,' p. 166, n.). And more than this, his acquaintance with the Valentinians ('Dial.' 35; comp. Iren. III. 11. 7, "qui a Valentino sunt eo [Evangelio] quod est secundum Iohannem plenissime utentes...") shews that the fourth Gospel could not have been unknown to him.

Justin's teaching on the Word is perhaps a still more important indication of the influence of St John. This teaching presupposes the teaching of St John, and in many details goes beyond it. Thoughts which are characteristically Alexandrine, as distinguished from Hebraic, find a place in Justin; and he shews not only how little power there was in the second century to fashion such a doctrine as that of the fourth Gospel, but also how little Christian speculation was able to keep within the limits laid down by the Apostles.

The SHEPHERD OF HERMAS offers an instructive example of the precariousness of the argument from silence. The book contains no definite quotations from the Old or New Testament. The allusions which have been found in it to the characteristic teaching of St John are I believe real, but they are not unquestionable. Yet it is certain from an independent testimony, that the Gospel was accepted as one of the four Gospels almost at the same date when the book was written, and probably in the same place. The Muratorian Fragment notices that the Shepherd was written "very lately (c. 170 A.D.) in our times, in the city of Rome," and at the same time speaks of the Gospel according to St John as "the fourth" Gospel in such a way as to mark its general recognition ('Hist. of N. T. Canon,' pp. 211 ff.; see below, II. § 2). To the same date also must be referred the two great translations of the East and West, the Syriac and Latin, in which the four Gospels stand without rivals.

Outside the Church the testimony to the general use of St John's Gospel is both early and decisive. In the quotations from early heretical writers the references to it are comparatively frequent. In many cases its teaching formed the starting-point of their partial and erroneous conclusions. The first Commentary on the Gospel was written by Heracleon (c. 175 A.D.); and his copy of the book had already been defaced by false readings. At an earlier date the Gospel was used by the author of the Clementine Homilies, by Valentinus and his school, by the Ophites, and by Basilides ('Hist. of N. T. Canon,' 282 ff., Sanday, 'The Gospels in the Second Century,' pp. 292 ff.).

The testimony of Basilides is of singular interest. 'The Refutation of Heresies,' attributed to Hippolytus, which was first published in 1851, contains numerous quotations from his writings and from the writings of his school. In one passage at least where there can be no reasonable doubt that the author of the 'Refutation' is quoting Basilides himself (c. 130 A.D.), a phrase from the Gospel of St John is used as the authoritative basis for a mystical explanation ('Ref. Hær.,' VII. 22).

In reviewing these traces of the use of the Gospel in the first three-quarters of a century after it was written, we readily admit that they are less distinct and numerous than those might have expected who are unacquainted with the character of the literary remains of the period. But it will be observed that all the evidence points in one direction. There is not, with one questionable exception, any positive indication that doubt was anywhere thrown upon the authenticity of the book. It is possible to explain away in detail this piece of evidence and that, but the acceptance of the book as the work of the Apostle adequately explains all the phenomena without any violence; and hitherto all the new evidence which has come to light has supported this universal belief of the Christian Society, while it has seriously modified the rival theories which have been set up against it.

II. THE COMPOSITION OF THE GOSPEL.

1. *The Author.*

The facts bearing upon the life of St John which are recorded in the New Testament are soon told. He was the son, apparently the younger son, of Zebedee and Salome (Mark xv. 40, xvi. 1, compared with Matt. xxvii. 56). Salome, as it appears from John xix. 25 (see note), was the sister of "the Mother of the Lord," so that St John was the cousin of the Lord "according to the flesh." He was probably younger than the Lord and than the other apostles. It is therefore easily intelligible that his near connexion by birth, combined with the natural enthusiasm of youth, offered the outward occasion for the peculiar closeness in which he stood to Christ.

Of his father Zebedee, a fisherman probably of Bethsaida or the neighbour hood (John i. 41 ff.), nothing is known except that he was sufficiently prosperous to have hired servants (Mark i. 20). At a later time Salome appears as one of the women who followed the Lord and "ministered to Him of their substance" (Mark xv. 40 f., compared with Luke viii. 3). And it is clear from John xix. 27 that the apostle had some means.

Like the other apostles, with the single exception of Judas Iscariot, St John was a Galilæan. The fact has a moral value. When the rest of the Jewish nation was drawn partly to political intrigues, partly to speculations of the schools, the people of Galilee retained much of the simple faith and stern heroism of earlier times. It was made a reproach to them that they were unskilled in the traditions, and kept to the letter of the Law (comp. vii. 52, note). The rising of Judas "in the days of the taxing" (Acts v. 37) may have been a hopeless outburst of fanaticism, but at least it shewed that there were many in Galilee who were ready to die for the confession that they had "no lord or master but God." The same spirit appears in the multitude who would have "taken Jesus by force" at the lake of Tiberias and made Him king (vi. 14 f.). They were ready to do and to suffer something for their eager if mistaken Messianic hope. It was amidst the memories of such conflicts, and in an atmosphere of passionate longing, that St John grew up. And in some measure he shared the aspirations of his countrymen if he avoided their errors. When the Baptist proclaimed the advent of Christ, St John was at once ranged among his disciples. And more than this: though "simple and unlettered" (Acts iv. 13), he appears to have grasped with exceptional power the spiritual import of the Baptist's message, who directed him immediately to Christ as "the Lamb of God." St John obeyed the sign, and followed without delay the Master who was mysteriously pointed out to him. Thus from the first the idea of sovereignty was mingled with that of redemption, the issue of victory with the way of suffering, in the conception of the work of the Messiah whom he welcomed.

The ardour of the Galilæan temper remained in the apostle. St John with his brother St James received from the Lord (Mark iii. 17) the remarkable surname, Boanerges, "sons of thunder." Thunder in the Hebrew idiom is "the voice of God;" and the sons of Zebedee appear to have given swift, startling, vehement utterance to the divine truth which they felt within them. Theirs was not characteristically the decisive action, but the sudden moving word which witnessed to the inner fire. It may have been some stern voice which marked St James as the first martyr among the apostles. Certainly the sayings of St John which are recorded by St Luke correspond with the prophetic energy which the title indicates (Luke ix. 49 || Mark ix. 38; comp. Num. xi. 28; Luke ix. 54). His zeal was undisciplined, but it was loyal and true. He knew that to be with Christ was life, to reject Christ was death; and he did not shrink from expressing the thought in the spirit of the old dispensation. He learnt from the Lord, as time went on, a more faithful patience, but he did not unlearn the burning devotion which consumed him. To the last, words of awful warning, like the thunderings about the throne, reveal the presence of that secret fire. Every page of the Apocalypse is inspired with the cry of the souls beneath the altar, "How long" (Rev. vi. 10); and nowhere is error as to the Person of Christ denounced more sternly than in his Epistles (2 John 10; 1 John iv. 1 ff.).

The well-known incident which occurred on the last journey to Jerusalem reveals the weakness and the strength of St John's character. His mother, interpreting the desire of her sons, begged of Christ that they might sit, the one on His right hand and the other on His left, in His Kingdom (Matt. xx. 20 ff., comp. Mark x. 35 ff.). So far they misunderstood the nature of that especial closeness to their Lord which they sought. But the reply shewed that they were ready to welcome what would be only a prerogative of suffering. To be near Christ, even if it was "to be near the fire" and "near the sword," was a priceless blessing. And we can feel that the prayer was already granted when Salome and St John waited by the Cross (John xix. 25 ff.).

This last scene reveals St John nearest of all the apostles to Christ, as "the disciple whom Jesus loved" (ch. xiii. 23, note). Together with his brother St James and St Peter, he was one of the three admitted to a closer relationship with Christ than the other apostles (Luke viii.

51, ix. 28; Mark xiv. 33); and of the three his connexion was the closest. He followed Christ to judgment and to death (John xviii. 15, xix. 26), and received from Him the charge of His Mother as her own son (xix. 27, note).

After the Ascension St John remained at Jerusalem with the other apostles. He was with St Peter at the working of his first miracle; and afterwards he went with him to Samaria (Acts i. 13, iii. 1 ff., viii. 14). At the time of St Paul's first visit to Jerusalem he seems to have been absent from the city (Gal. i. 18); but on a later occasion St Paul describes him as one of those accounted to be "the pillars of the Church" (Gal. ii. 9). At what time and under what circumstances he left Jerusalem is wholly unknown. At the opening of the Apocalypse (i. 9) he speaks of himself as "in the island called Patmos, for the word and the testimony of Jesus." Beyond this there is no further notice of him in the New Testament[1].

When we pass beyond the limits of Scripture, St John is still presented to us under the same character, as the Son of Thunder, the prophetic interpreter of the Old Covenant. Now it is related that he refused to remain under the same roof with Cerinthus (or according to another account "Ebion"), who denied the reality of the Incarnation: "Let us fly," he said, "lest the bath fall on us, since Cerinthus is within, the enemy of the truth" (Iren. III. 3. 4; comp. Epiph. 'Hær.' xxx. 24). Now he is described as a "priest wearing the plate (or diadem)" prescribed by the law (Ex. xxxix. 30 f.) for the high-priest (Polycrates ap. Euseb. 'H. E.' III. 31, v. 24; comp. ch. xviii. 15, note). Now he is shewn, in one of the most beautiful of early histories, seeking out the lost and enforcing the obligation of ministerial duty (Euseb. 'H. E.' III. 23, on the authority of Clement of Alexandria). Once again we read that "when he tarried at Ephesus to extreme old age, and could only with difficulty be carried to the church in the arms of his disciples, and was unable to give utterance to many words, he used to say no more at their several meetings than this, 'Little children, love one another.' At length," Jerome continues, "the disciples and fathers who were there, wearied with hearing always the same words, said, 'Master, why dost thou always say this?' 'It is the Lord's command,' was his worthy reply, 'and if this alone be done, it is enough.'" (Hieron. 'Comm. in Ep. ad Gal.' vi. 10)[1].

These traditions are in all probability substantially true, but it is impossible to set them in a clear historical framework. Nothing is better attested in early Church history than the residence and work of St John at Ephesus. But the dates of its commencement and of its close are alike unknown. It began after the final departure of St Paul, and it lasted till about the close of the first century (Iren. II. 22. 5, μέχρι τῶν Τραιάνου χρόνων, A.D. 98—117). This may be affirmed with confidence; but the account of his sufferings at Rome (Tert. 'de Præscr. Hær.' 36..."in oleum demersus nihil passus est;" comp. Hieron. 'ad Matt.' xx. 23), and of the details of his death at Ephesus, are quite untrustworthy. One legend, which is handed down in various forms, is too remarkable to be wholly omitted. It was widely believed that St John was not dead, but sleeping in his grave; and that he would so remain till Christ came. Meanwhile, it was said, "he shewed that he was alive by the movement of the dust above, which was stirred by the breath of the saint." "I think it needless," Augustine adds, "to contest the opinion. Those who know the place must see whether the soil is so affected as it is said; since I have heard the story from men not unworthy of credence" ("revera non e levibus hominibus id audivimus." Aug. 'In Joh. Tract.' CXXIV. 2).

These words of Augustine are part of his commentary on the mysterious saying of the Lord which, as is seen from the Gospel (xxi. 21 ff), was perceived to mark in some way the future work of the apostle: "If I will that he tarry till I come, what is that to thee?" St John

[1] This is not the place to discuss the authorship of the Apocalypse. Its doctrinal relation to the Gospel of St John, which will be discussed afterwards, appears to be decisive in support of the early date of the banishment.

[1] These traditions are collected in a very agreeable form in Dean Stanley's 'Sermons and Essays on the Apostolic Age.' The later legends are given by Mrs Jameson, in her 'Sacred and Legendary Art,' I

did most truly "tarry till the Lord came." It is impossible for us to realise fully what was involved in the destruction of the Holy City for those who had been trained in Judaism. It was nothing else than the close of a divine drama, an end of the world. The old sanctuary, "the joy of the whole earth," was abandoned. Henceforth the Christian Church was the sole appointed seat of the presence of God. When Jerusalem fell Christ came, and with His coming came also the work of St John. During the period of conflict and fear and shaking of nations which preceded that last catastrophe, St John had waited patiently; and we may believe that he had fulfilled his filial office to the Mother of the Lord in his own home in Galilee to the last, gaining by that a fuller knowledge of the revelation of the Son of God, and bringing into a completer harmony the works which he had seen, and the words which he had heard.

In these scattered traits we can gain a consistent if imperfect conception of St John. The central characteristic of his nature is intensity, intensity of thought, word, insight, life. He regards everything on its divine side. For him the eternal is already: all is complete from the beginning, though wrought out step by step upon the stage of human action. All is absolute in itself, though marred by the weakness of believers. He sees the past and the future gathered up in the manifestation of the Son of God. This was the one fact in which the hope of the world lay. Of this he had himself been assured by evidence of sense and thought. This he was constrained to proclaim: "We have seen and do testify." He had no laboured process to go through: he saw. He had no constructive proof to develope: he bore witness. His source of knowledge was direct, and his mode of bringing conviction was to affirm.

2. *The Occasion and Date.*

An early and consistent tradition represents the Gospel of St John as written at the request of those who were intimate with the Apostle, and had, as we must suppose, already heard from his lips that teaching which they desired to see recorded for the perpetual guidance of the Church. CLEMENT OF ALEXANDRIA has preserved the tradition in its simplest form. He states on the authority "of the elders of an earlier generation" (παράδοσις τῶν ἀνέκαθεν πρεσβυτέρων) that "St John, last [of the Evangelists], when he saw that the outward (bodily) facts had been set forth in the [existing] Gospels, impelled by his friends, [and] divinely moved by the Spirit, made a spiritual Gospel" (Clem. Alex. ap. Euseb. 'H. E.' VI. 14.) This general statement is given with additional details in the MURATORIAN FRAGMENT on the Canon. "The fourth Gospel [was written by] John, one of the disciples (*i.e.* Apostles). When his fellow-disciples and bishops urgently pressed (*cohortantibus*) him, he said, 'Fast with me [from] to-day, for three days, and let us tell one another any revelation which may be made to us, either for or against [the plan of writing] (*quid cuique fuerit revelatum alterutrum*)'. On the same night it was revealed to Andrew, one of the Apostles, that John should relate all in his own name, and that all should review [his writing]" (see 'Hist. of N. T. Canon,' p. 527). There can be no doubt that JEROME had before him either this fragment, or, as appears more probable, the original narrative on which it was based, when he says that "ecclesiastical history records that John, when he was constrained by his brothers to write, replied that he would do so, if a fast were appointed and all joined in prayer to God; and that after this [fast] was ended, filled to the full with revelation (*revelatione saturatus*), he indited the heaven-sent preface: *In the beginning was the Word...*" ('Comm. in Matt.' Prol.) Eusebius, to whom we are indebted for the testimony of Clement, adds in another place, as a current opinion, that St John wrote after the other Evangelists, to the truth of whose narrative he bore witness, in order to supply an account of the early period of the Lord's ministry which they omitted; and at the same time he implies, what is otherwise most likely, that the Apostle committed to writing what he had long delivered in unwritten preaching (Euseb. 'H. E.' III. 24).

Other writers attempt to define more exactly the circumstances under which

St John was induced to compose his Gospel. Thus in the Scholia on the Apocalypse attributed to VICTORINUS of Pettau († c. 304), it is said that "he wrote the Gospel after the Apocalypse. For, when Valentinus and Cerinthus and Ebion and the others of the school of Satan were spread throughout the world, all the bishops from the neighbouring provinces came together to him, and constrained him to commit his own testimony to writing" (Migne, 'Patrol.' v. p. 333). This statement appears to be an amplification of the Asiatic tradition preserved by Irenæus, which has been already noticed; and is only so far interesting as it shews the current belief that the fourth Gospel was written as an answer to the questionings of a comparatively advanced age of the Church. So much indeed seems to be historically certain; for, though it is impossible to insist upon the specific details with which the truth was gradually embellished, there can be no reason to question the general accuracy of a tradition which was widely spread in the last quarter of the second century. The evidence of Clement of Alexandria is independent of that of the Muratorian Canon, while both appear to point back to some common authority, which cannot have been far removed from the time of the Apostle. The fourth Gospel, we may thus conclude from the earliest direct evidence, was written after the other three, in Asia, at the request of the Christian churches there, as a summary of the oral teaching of St John upon the life of Christ, to meet a want which had grown up in the Church at the close of the Apostolic age (comp. Epiph. 'Hær.' XLI. 12).

The contents of the Gospel go far to support this view of its relatively late date. It assumes a knowledge of the substance of the Synoptic narratives. It deals with later aspects of Christian life and opinion than these. It corresponds with the circumstances of a new world.

(*a*) The first of these statements will come under examination at a later time, and will not be contested in its general shape. The two others can be justified by a few references to the Gospel, which will repay careful study.

(*b*) No one can read the fourth Gospel carefully without feeling that the writer occupies a position remote from the events which he describes. However clear it is that he was an eye-witness of the Life of the Lord, it is no less clear that he looks back upon it from a distance[1]. One plain proof of this is found in the manner in which he records words which point to the spread of the Gospel beyond the limits of Judaism. This characteristic view is distinctly brought out in the interpretation which he gives of the judgment of Caiaphas: *Now this he said not of himself, but being high-priest in that year, he prophesied that Jesus should die for the nation* (τοῦ ἔθνους, see note), *and not for the nation only, but in order that he might gather together in one the children of God that were scattered abroad* (xi. 51 f.). It is beyond question that when the Evangelist wrote these words, he was reading the fulfilment of the unconscious prophecy of Caiaphas in the condition of the Christian Church about him.

The same actual experience of the spread of the Gospel explains the prominent position which St John assigns to those sayings of Christ in which He declared the universality of His mission: *other sheep I have which are not of this fold: them also must I lead...and they shall become one flock, one shepherd* (x. 16). *I, if I be lifted up from the earth, will draw all men unto myself* (xii. 32). The Son has *authority over all flesh* (xvii. 2). *All that which the Father giveth me*, He said, *shall come to me; and him that cometh to me I will in no wise cast out* (vi. 37). The knowledge of God and of Jesus Christ *is eternal life* (xvii. 3); and this knowledge, the knowledge of the truth, conveys the freedom, of which the freedom of the children of Abraham was only a type (viii. 31 ff.). The final form of worship is the worship of "the Father," in which all local and temporal worships, typified by Gerizim and Jerusalem, should pass away (iv. 21 ff.).

This teaching receives its final seal in the answer to Pilate: *Thou sayest that I*

[1] This is the impression which is conveyed by the notes which he adds from time to time in interpretation of words or facts: vii. 39, xii. 33, xviii. 9, 32, xix. 36, xxi. 19. These notes offer a remarkable contrast to those in which attention is called in the first Gospel to the present and immediate fulfilment of prophecy, Matt. i. 22, xxi. 4, &c. (γέγονεν ἵνα πληρωθῇ).

am a king. To this end have I been born, and to this end am I come into the world, that I should bear witness unto the truth. Every one that is of the truth heareth my voice (xviii. 37). The relation of the believer to Christ is thus shewn to rest on a foundation which is of all most absolute. Christ, while He fulfilled "the Law," which was the heritage of the Jews, revealed and satisfied the Truth, which is the heritage of humanity.

There are indeed traces of the announcement of this universalism of the Gospel in the Synoptic narratives, and especially in that of St Luke. It is taught there that Christ came as *the salvation prepared before the face of all the peoples, a light for revelation to Gentiles, and a glory to God's people Israel* (ii. 31, 32). *Repentance unto remission of sins* was to be preached *in His name unto all the nations beginning from Jerusalem* (xxiv. 47). It may be possible also to see in the fate of the Prodigal Son an image of the restoration of the heathen to their Father's home. But in these cases the truth is not traced back to its deepest foundations; nor does it occupy the same relative position as in St John. The experience of an organized Christian society lies between the two records.

This is plainly intimated by the language of the Evangelist himself. He speaks in his own person of the great crisis of the choice of Israel as over. *He came to His own home and His own people received Him not* (i. 11); and so in some sense, the choice of the world was also decided, *the light hath come into the world, and men loved the darkness rather than the light* (iii. 19). The message of the Gospel had already been proclaimed in such a way to Jew and Gentile that a judgment could be pronounced upon the general character of its acceptance.

This typical example serves to shew how St John brings into their true place in the completed Christian edifice the facts of Christ's teaching which were slowly realised in the course of the apostolic age. And while he does so, he recalls the words in which Christ dwelt upon that gradual apprehension of the meaning of His Life and work, which characterized in fact the growth of the Catholic Church. Throughout the last discourses of the Lord, the great charge to the apostolate, we seem to hear the warning addressed to St Peter at the outset: *What I do thou knowest not now, but thou shalt come to know* (γνώσῃ) *afterwards* (xiii. 7). It is implied in the recital that the words of patient waiting had found their accomplishment by the mission of the new Advocate. *I have yet many things to say unto you, but ye cannot bear them now. Howbeit when He is come, even the Spirit of truth, He shall guide you into all the truth* (xvi. 12; comp. xv. 26). Even if Christ had already *made known all things* (xv. 15), there was need of the long teaching of time, that His disciples might master the lessons which they had implicitly received.

The record of these appeals to a future growth of knowledge can admit of only one interpretation. In dwelling on such aspects of Christ's teaching, it is clear that the Evangelist is measuring the interval between the first imperfect views of the Apostles as to the kingdom of God, and that just ideal, which he had been allowed to shape, under the teaching of the Paraclete, through disappointments and disasters. Now at length, on the threshold of a new world, he can feel the divine force of much that was before hard and mysterious. He had waited till his Lord came; and he was enabled to recognise His Presence, as once before by the lake of Galilee, in the unexpected victories of faith.

(*c*) In the last quarter of the first century, the world relatively to the Christian Church was a new world; and St John presents in his view of the work and Person of Christ the answers which he had found to be given in Him to the problems which were offered by the changed order. The overthrow of Jerusalem, carrying with it the destruction of the ancient service and the ancient people of God, the establishment of the Gentile congregations on the basis of St Paul's interpretation of the Gospel, the rise of a Christian philosophy (γνῶσις) from the contact of the historic creed with Eastern and Western speculation, could not but lead one who had lived with Christ to go back once more to those days of a divine discipleship, that he might find in them, according to the promise, the anticipated replies to the questionings of a later age. This St John has done; and it is impossible not to feel how in each of these cardinal directions he points his readers to words and facts which are still unexhausted in their applications.

(α) We have already touched upon the treatment of the Jewish people in the fourth Gospel. They appear as the heirs of divine blessings who have Esau-like despised their birthright. The prerogatives of the people and their misuse of them are alike noted. But in this respect there is one most striking difference between the fourth Gospel and the other three. The Synoptic Gospels are full of warnings of judgment. Pictures of speedy desolation are crowded into the record of the last days of the Lord's ministry (Matt. xxiv., Mark xiii., Luke xxi.). His coming to judgment is a central topic. In St John all is changed. There are no prophecies of the siege of the Holy City; there is no reiterated promise of a Return; the judgment had been wrought. Christ had come. There was no longer any need to dwell upon the outward aspects of teaching which had in this respect found its accomplishment. The task of the Evangelist was to unfold the essential causes of the catastrophe, which were significant for all time, and to shew that even through apparent ruin and failure the will of God found fulfilment. Inexorable facts had revealed the rejection of the Jews. It remained to shew that this rejection was not only foreseen, but was also morally inevitable, and that it involved no fatal loss. This is the work of St John. He traces step by step the progress of unbelief in the representatives of the people, and at the same time the correlative gathering of the children of God by Christ to Himself. There was a divine law of inward affinity to good or evil in the obedience and disobedience of those who heard. *I am the good shepherd; and I know mine own, and mine own know me, even as the Father knoweth me and I know the Father* (x. 14, 15). *Ye believe not, because ye are not of my sheep. My sheep hear my voice, and I know them, and they follow me* (x. 26, 27). *This is the judgment, that the light is come into the world, and men loved the darkness rather than the light, for their works were evil* (iii. 19).

The fourth Gospel reveals in these and similar passages the innermost cause of the rejection of the Jewish people. The fact underlies the record, and the Evangelist lays open the spiritual necessity of it. He reveals also the constitution of the Spiritual Church. The true people of God survived the ruin of the Jews: the ordinances of a new society replaced in a nobler shape the typical and transitory worship of Israel. When this Gospel was written, the Christian congregations, as we see from St Paul's Epistles, were already organized, but the question could not but arise, how far their organization was fitted to realise the ideal of the kingdom which Christ preached. The Evangelist meets the inquiry. He shews from the Lord's words what are the laws of His service, and how they are fulfilled by the institutions in which they were embodied. The absolute worship was to be in *spirit and truth* (iv. 23), as distinguished from letter and shadow; and the discourses with Nicodemus and at Capernaum set forth by anticipation how the sacraments satisfy this condition for each individual. On the other hand, the general ministerial commission, which is contained only in the fourth Gospel (xx.), gives the foundation of the whole. In that lies the unfailing assurance of the permanence of the new society.

(β) So far the fourth Gospel met difficulties which had not been and could not be realised till after the fall of Jerusalem. In like manner it met difficulties which had not been and could not be felt till the preaching of St Paul had moulded the Christian Society in accordance with the law of freedom. Then first the great problems as to the nature of the object of personal faith, as to the revelation of the Deity, as to the universality of the Gospel, were apprehended in their true vastness; and the Evangelist shews that these thoughts of a later age were not unregarded by Christ Himself. The experience of the life of the Church—which is nothing less than the historic teaching of the Holy Spirit—made clear in due time what was necessarily veiled at first. Sayings became luminous which were riddles before their solution was given. Christ, in relation to humanity, was not characteristically the Prophet or the King, but the Saviour of the world, the Son of Man, the Son of God. In this connexion the fact of the Incarnation obtained its full significance. By the Incarnation alone the words which were partially interpreted through the crowning miracle of the Lord's ministry were brought home to all men; *I am the Resurrection and the Life* (xi. 25).

Thus by the record of the more mysterious teaching of the Lord, in connexion with typical works, St John has given a historical basis for the preaching of St Paul. His narrative is at once the most spiritual and the most concrete. He shews how Faith can find a personal object. The words *He that hath seen me hath seen the Father* (xiv. 9) mark an epoch in the development of religious thought. By them the idea of God receives an abiding embodiment, and the Father is thereby brought for ever within the reach of intelligent devotion. The revelation itself is complete (xvii. 6, 26), and yet the interpretation of the revelation is set forth as the work of the Holy Spirit through all ages (xiv. 26). God in Christ is placed in a living union with all creation (v. 17; comp. i. 3, note). The world, humanity and God are presented in the words and in the Person of Christ under new aspects of fellowship and unity.

It will be evident how this teaching is connected with that of St Paul. Two special points only may be noticed: the doctrine of the sovereignty of the divine will, and the doctrine of the union of the believer with Christ. The foundations of these two cardinal doctrines, which rise supreme in the Pauline Epistles, lie deep in the fourth Gospel.

The first, the doctrine of Providence, Predestination, however it be called, not only finds reiterated affirmation in the discourses of the Lord contained in the fourth Gospel, but it is also implied as the rule of the progress of the Lord's life. His "hour" determines the occurrence of events from man's point of view; and the Evangelist refers to it in connexion with each crisis of the Gospel history, and especially with the Passion in which all crises were consummated (ii. 4, vii. 30, viii. 20, xii. 23, 27, xiii. 1, xvi. 4, xvii. 1; comp. vii. 6—8, ὁ καιρός). So also the will or "the gift" of the Father is the spring of the believer's power (iii. 27, vi. 37, 44, 65, xvii. 12); and Christ fulfils and applies that will to each one who comes to Him (xv. 16, 5, v. 21).

Faith again assumes a new aspect in the narrative of St John. It is not merely the mediative energy in material deliverances, and the measure (so to speak) of material power; it is an energy of the whole nature, an active transference of the whole being into another life. Faith in a Person—in One revealed under a new "name"—is the ground of sonship (i. 12), of life (xi. 25), of power (xiv. 12), of illumination (xii. 36, 46). The keywords of two complementary views of truth are finally combined: *this is the work of God, that ye believe*—believe with a continuous ever-present faith (πιστεύητε not πιστεύσητε)—*on Him whom He sent* (vi. 29; comp. viii. 30, note).

(γ) Once again; when the fourth Gospel was written Christianity occupied a new intellectual position. In addition to social and doctrinal developments, there were also those still vaster questions which underlie all organization and all special dogma, as to the function and stability of knowledge, as to the interpretation and significance of life, as to the connexion of the seen and unseen. The new faith had made these questions more urgent than before, and the teaching of the Lord furnished such answers to them as man can apprehend. Knowledge was placed in its final position by the declaration *I am the Truth ... The Truth shall make you free* (xiv. 6, viii. 31 ff.). Everything real is thus made tributary to religious service. Again, the eternal is revealed as present, and life is laid open in all its possible nobility. The separation which men are inclined to make arbitrarily between "here" and "there" in spiritual things is done away. *This is life eternal...* (xvii. 3); *He that heareth my word hath life eternal...* (v. 24). Once more, the essential unity and the actual divisions of the world are alike recognised. *All things were made* (ἐγένετο) *through Him* [in the Word] (i. 3);...*and the Light shineth in the darkness* (i. 5); and *the Word became* (ἐγένετο) *flesh*. Thus in Christ there is offered the historic reconciliation of the finite and the infinite, by which the oppositions of thought and experience are made capable of being reduced to harmony.

These internal indications of date completely accord with the historical tradition, and lead to the conclusion that the composition of the Gospel must be placed late in the generation which followed the destruction of Jerusalem. The shock of that momentous revolution was over, and Christians had been enabled to interpret it. There is no evidence to determine the date exactly. St John, according to the Asiatic tradition recorded by Irenæus (II. 22. 5; III. 3. 4) lived "till the times of Trajan" (A.D. 98—117), and the writing of the Gospel must be placed at the close of his life. It is probable therefore that it may be referred to the last decennium of the first century, and even to the close of it.

Tradition is uniform in fixing St John's residence at Ephesus (Iren. III. 3. 4; Polycr. ap. Euseb. 'H. E.' III. 31; Clem. Alex. 'Quis div. salv.' c. 42; Orig. ap. Euseb. 'H. E.' III. 1, &c.), and naming that city as the place where he wrote his Gospel (Iren. III. 1. 1, &c.); and no valid objection has been brought against the belief which was preserved on the spot by a continuous succession of Church teachers[1].

3. *The Object.*

From what has been already said it will be clear that the circumstances under which the fourth Gospel was written served to define its object. This is clearly expressed by St John himself: *Many other signs did Jesus in the presence of His disciples which have not been written in this book; but these have been written that ye may believe* (πιστεύητε, cf. vi. 29) *that Jesus is the Christ, the Son of God, and that believing ye may have life in His name* (xx. 30 f.). The record is therefore a selection from abundant materials at the command of the writer, made by him with a specific purpose, first to create a particular conviction in his readers, and then in virtue of that conviction to bring life to them. The conviction itself which the Evangelist aims at producing is twofold, as corresponding with the twofold relation of Christianity to the chosen people and to mankind. He makes it his purpose to shew that Jesus, who is declared by that human name to be truly and historically man, is at once *the Christ*, in whom all types and prophecies were fulfilled[1], and also *the Son of God*, who is, in virtue of that divine being, equally near to all *the children of God*—His Father and their Father (xx. 17)—*scattered throughout the world* (xi. 52; comp. i. 49). The whole narrative must therefore be interpreted with a continuous reference to these two ruling truths, made clear by the experience of the first stage in the life of the Church; and also to the consequence which flows from them, that life is to be found in vital union with Him who is made known in this character (ἐν τῷ ὀνόματι αὐτοῦ). Each element in the fundamental conviction is set forth as of equal moment. The one (*Jesus is the Christ*) bears witness to the special preparation which God had made; the other (*Jesus is the Son of God*) bears witness to the inherent universality of Christ's mission. The one establishes the organic union of Christianity with Judaism; the other

[1] The denial of the Asiatic residence of St John does not call for serious discussion. To suppose that the belief grew out of Irenæus' confusion of "John the presbyter" with "John the apostle," involves the further assumption that Polycarp himself led him into the error (Iren. 'Ep. ad Flor.'). Comp. Steitz, 'Stud. u. Krit.' 1868; Hilgenfeld, 'Einl.' 394 ff.

[1] It is not without instruction to notice that writers of very different schools have unconsciously omitted the words "the Christ" in quoting this verse, and thereby obscured the full design of the Apostle. Among others I may quote as representatives:

Reuss, 'Hist. de la Théologie Chrétienne' ed. 2, II. 426, "Ceci, dit-il dans ses dernières lignes, ceci est écrit, afin que vous croyiez que Jésus est le Fils de Dieu, et afin que vous ayez la vie par cette croyance."

Weisz, 'Lehrbuch d. Bibl. Theol.' Ausg. 2, s. 636, "Der Glaube, welcher die Bedingung des Heilsaneignung bildet...ist die zuversichtliche Ueberzeugung davon, dasz Jesus der Sohn Gottes ist."

Lias, 'The Doctrinal System of St John,' p. 2. [The purpose for which the Gospel was written] "is stated in express language by the author: 'These things have been written that ye might believe that Jesus is the Son of God, and that, believing, ye might have life through His name' (John xx. 31)."

liberates Christianity from Jewish limitations[1].

It will at once appear that this pregnant description of the object of the Gospel coincides completely with the view which has been given as to the date and occasion of its composition. To establish that *Jesus is the Christ* is to prove that Christianity is the true spiritual heir of Judaism, through which a divine society and a divine service have been established for all time. To establish that *Jesus is the Son of God* is to place the doctrine of St Paul upon a firm basis, inasmuch as the Saviour is revealed in His essential relation of Creator to all the world. To establish that *life is* to be had *in His name*, is to raise all being, all thought, into a new region, where rests the hope (at least) of the reconciliation of the conflicts and contradictions of our present order.

So far then the fourth Gospel is distinguished from the other three in that it is shaped with a conscious design to illustrate and establish an assumed conclusion. If we compare the avowed purpose of St John with that of St Luke (i. 1—4), it may be said with partial truth that the inspiring impulse was in the one case doctrinal, and in the other case historical. But care must be taken not to exaggerate or misinterpret this contrast. Christian doctrine is history, and this is above all things the lesson of the fourth Gospel. The Synoptic narratives are implicit dogmas, no less truly than St John's dogmas are concrete facts. The real difference is that the earliest Gospel contained the fundamental facts and words which experience afterwards interpreted, while the latest Gospel reviews the facts in the light of their interpretation. But in both cases the exactness of historical truth is paramount. The discovery of the law of phenomena does not make the record of the phenomena less correct than before in the hands of him who has ascertained it. On the contrary, such knowledge keeps the observer from many possibilities of error, while it enables him to regard facts in new relations, and to present them in such a way that they may suggest to others the general truth which he has gained. The historic interest of St John in the substance of his narrative is, in other words, purified and made more intense by the dogmatic significance with which he feels that each incident is charged.

If the scope of the fourth Gospel is thus distinctly apprehended in all its fulness according to the Evangelist's own description, it becomes unnecessary to discuss at any length the different special purposes which have been assigned as the motive of his work. The narrative is not in express design polemical, or supplementary, or didactic, or harmonizing; and yet it is all this, because it is the mature expression of apostolic experience perfected by the teaching of the Holy Spirit in the writer's own life and in the life of the Church.

i. The Gospel is not specifically polemical (Iren. 'Adv. Hær.' III. 11, Hieron. 'Comm. in Matt.' Prol.; comp. 'De Virr. Ill.' 9). It is quite true that many passages in the Gospel of St John are conclusive against particular points of Ebionitic and Docetic error (comp. 1 John ii. 22, iv. 2), and against false claims of the disciples of the Baptist (comp. Acts xix. 3 f.); but it does not follow that it was the particular object of St John to refute these false opinions. The full exhibition of the Truth was necessarily their refutation; and in this respect their existence may have called attention to points which had been overlooked or misunderstood before. But the first Epistle shews with what directness the Apostle would have dealt with adversaries if controversy had been the purpose immediately present to his mind.

ii. The same remark applies to the "supplemental" theory (Eusebius, 'H. E.' III. 24; comp. Hieron. 'De Virr. Ill.' 9). As a matter of fact the fourth Gospel does supplement the other three, which it presupposes. It supplements them in the general chronology of the Lord's life, as well as in detailed incidents. But this is because the Gospel is the vital analysis of faith and unbelief. It traces in order the gradual development of the popular views of Christ among those to whom He came. As a natural consequence it records the successive crises in the

[1] This definition of the object of the Gospel must be compared with the parallel definition of the object of the First Epistle, 1 John i. 1—4.

divine revelation which happened in Jerusalem, the centre of the religious activity of the Jewish theocracy. The scope of the Gospel is from the nature of the case supplementary to that of the other three; and this being so, the history is also supplementary.

iii. But though the scope of the fourth Gospel is supplementary to that of the other three, it cannot rightly be said that the aim of the Evangelist was essentially didactic (comp. Clem. Alex. ap. Euseb. 'H. E.' VI. 14) in such a sense that he has furnished an interpretation of the Gospel rather than a historical record. The substance of the narrative is distinctly affirmed to be facts (*these signs are written*); and the end contemplated is practical (*that ye may have life*), and speculative only so far as right opinion leads to right action.

iv. Once again: The conciliatory—irenical—effect of the Gospel cannot be questioned, but this effect is due to the teaching on Christ's Person which it discloses, and not to any conscious aim of the writer. Just as it rises above controversy while it condemns error, it preserves the characteristic truths which heresy isolated and misused. The fourth Gospel is the most complete answer to the manifold forms of Gnosticism, and yet it was the writing most used by Gnostics. It contains no formal narrative of the institution of sacraments, and yet it presents most fully the idea of sacraments. It sets forth with the strongest emphasis the failure of the ancient people, and yet it points out most clearly the significance of the dispensation which was committed to them. It brings together the many oppositions—antitheses—of life and thought, and leaves them in the light of the one supreme fact which reconciles all, *the Word became Flesh;* and we feel from first to last that this light is shining over the record of sorrow and triumph, of defeat and hope.

4. *The Plan.*

The view which has been given of the object of the Gospel enables us to form a general conception of what we must call its plan. This is, to express it as briefly as possible, the parallel development of faith and unbelief through the historical Presence of Christ. The Evangelist is guided in the selection, and in the arrangement, and in the treatment of his materials by his desire to fulfil this purpose. He takes a few out of the vast mass of facts at his disposal (xxi. 25, xx. 30), which are in his judgment suited to produce a particular effect. Every part of his narrative is referred to one final truth made clear by experience, that "Jesus is the Christ, the Son of God." He makes no promise to compose a life of Christ, or to give a general view of His teaching, or to preserve a lively picture of the general effect which He produced on average observers, or to compose a chapter on the general history of his own times, or to add his personal recollections to memoirs of the Lord already current; nor have we any right to judge his narrative by the standard which would be applicable to any one of such writings. He works out his own design, and it is our first business to consider how he works it out. When this is done we shall be in a position to consider fairly the historical characteristics of the Gospel.

The development and details of St John's plan are considered at length elsewhere. Here it will be sufficient to indicate in a tabular form the outlines of the history.

THE PROLOGUE, i. 1—18.

The Word in His absolute, eternal Being; and in relation to Creation.

THE NARRATIVE, i. 19—xxi. 23.

The Self-revelation of Christ to the world and to the Disciples.

I.—THE SELF-REVELATION OF CHRIST TO THE WORLD (i. 19—xii. 50).

1. *The Proclamation* (i. 19—iv. 54).

i. The testimony to Christ (i. 19—ii. 11)
of *the Baptist*, i. 19—34,
disciples, i. 35—51,
signs (water turned to wine), ii. 1—11.

ii. The work of Christ (ii. 13—iv. 54)
in Judæa (Nicodemus), ii. 13—iii. 36,
Samaria (the woman of Samaria), iv. 1—42,
Galilee (the nobleman's son healed), iv. 43—54.
Unbelief as yet passive.

2. *The Conflict* (v. 1—xii. 50).

i. The Prelude (v., vi.),
(*a*) *In Jerusalem* (the impotent man healed on the Sabbath), v.
The Son and the Father.
(*b*) *In Galilee* (the five thousand fed), vi.
Christ and men.

ii. The great Controversy (vii.—xii.).
(*a*) *The Revelation of faith and unbelief*, vii.—x.
The Feast of Tabernacles, vii., viii.
The Feast of Dedication (the blind man healed on the Sabbath), ix., x.
(*b*) *The decisive Judgment*, xi., xii.
The final sign and its issues (the raising of Lazarus), xi.
The close of Christ's public ministry, xii.

II.—The Self-revelation of Christ to the Disciples (xiii.—xxi.).

1. *The last ministry of love* (xiii.—xvii.).

i. The last acts of love (xiii. 1—30).
ii. The last discourses (xiii. 31—xvi. 33),
In the chamber, xiii. 31—xiv.,
On the way, xv., xvi.
iii. The prayer of consecration, xvii.

2. *The Victory through death* (xviii.—xx.).

i. The Betrayal (xviii. 1—11).
ii. The double Trial (xviii. 12—xix. 16).
iii. The end (xix. 17—42).
iv. The new life (xx.).

3. *The Epilogue*, xxi.

i. The Lord and the body of disciples (the miraculous draught of fishes), xxi. 1—14.
ii. The Lord and individual disciples (xxi. 15—23).
Concluding notes, xxi. 24, 25[1].

[1] The data for fixing the chronology are very meagre. The following appears to be the best arrangement of the main events.

Early spring: the calling of the first disciples, i. 19—ii. 11.
First Passover (April), ii. 13—iii. 21;
iii. 22—iv. 54.
The Feast of the New Year (September), v. See Additional Note.
Second Passover (April), vi.
The Feast of Tabernacles (October), vii., viii.
The Feast of Dedication (December), ix., x.;
xi., xii.
Third Passover (April), xiii.—xx.

Such in a rough outline appears to be the distribution of the parts of the Gospel. It will be felt at once how fragmentary the record is, and yet how complete. The incidents all contribute to the orderly development of the truths which it is the object of the Evangelist to commend to his readers. In developing the plan thus broadly defined he dwells on three pairs of ideas, witness and truth, glory and light, judgment and life. There is the manifold attestation of the divine mission: there is the progressive manifestation of the inherent majesty of the Son: there is the continuous and necessary effect which this manifestation produces on those to whom it is made; and the narrative may be fairly described as the simultaneous unfolding of these three themes, into which the great theme of faith and unbelief is divided. A rapid survey of their treatment will bring out many instructive features in the composition.

(*a*) *The Truth and the Witness.* It is characteristic of Christianity that it claims to be "the Truth." Christ spoke of Himself as "the Truth" (xiv. 6). God is revealed in Christ as "the only true (ἀληθινός) God" (xvii. 3). The message of the Gospel is "the Truth." This title of the Gospel is not found in the Synoptists, the Acts or the Apocalypse; but it occurs in the Catholic Epistles (James v. 19; 1 Pet. i. 22; 2 Pet. ii. 2), and in the Epistles of St Paul (2 Thess. ii. 12; 2 Cor. xiii. 8; Eph. i. 13, &c.). It is specially characteristic of the Gospel and Epistles of St John.

According to the teaching of St John, the fundamental fact of Christianity includes all that "is" in each sphere. Christ the Incarnate Word is the perfect revelation of the Father: as God, He reveals God (i. 18). He is the perfect pattern of life, expressing in act and word the absolute law of love (xiii. 34). He unites the finite and the infinite (i. 14, xvi. 28). And the whole history of the Christian Society is the progressive embodiment of this revelation.

In the presence of Pilate, the representative of earthly power, Christ revealed the object of His coming, as a permanent fact, to be that He might "bear witness to the truth" (γεγέννημαι, ἐλήλυθα, not ἦλθον, ἵνα μαρτυρήσω τῇ ἀληθείᾳ, xviii. 37). This "Truth," it is implied, was already, in some sense, among men even if it was unrecognised. There were some who "were of the Truth," drawing, as it were, their power of life from it (comp. 1 John ii. 21, iii. 19). Over these Christ claimed the supremacy of a King.

Among the chosen people this testimony of conscience was supplemented by the voice of the representative of the prophets. The Baptist bore, and still bears, witness to the Truth (v. 33, μεμαρτύρηκε).

But Christ came not only to maintain a Truth which was present among men, but to make known a new fulness of Truth. The "Truth came (ἐγένετο "was realised as the right issue of things") through Him" (i. 17; comp. *v.* 14 πλήρης ...ἀληθείας). His teaching was "the Truth" (viii. 40; comp. xvii. 17, ὁ λόγος ὁ σός). He is Himself the Truth (xiv. 6).

And this work is carried out step by step by the Spirit (xvi. 13 ff.) who is sent in Christ's name by the Father (xiv. 26), as He also is sent by Christ Himself (xvi. 7). Under this aspect the Spirit, like Christ, is the Truth which He makes known (1 John v. 6).

And again, the whole sum of the knowledge of Christ and of the Spirit is "the Truth" (1 John ii. 21; 2 John 1), which can be recognised by man (John viii. 32, γνώσεσθε τὴν ἀλήθειαν), and become the object of fixed knowledge (1 John ii. 21, οἴδατε τὴν ἀλ.); though on the other hand men can withstand and reject its claims (viii. 44 f.; comp. Rom. i. 18).

So far the Truth is regarded as a whole without us (objectively), working and witnessing (3 John 8, 12). But at the same time the Spirit, as the Spirit of Truth, or rather of "the Truth," brings the Truth into direct communication with man's spirit (xiv. 17, xv. 26, xvi. 13; 1 John iv. 6, opposed to τὸ πν. τῆς πλάνης); and "the Truth" becomes an inward power in the believer (1 John i. 8, ii. 4; 2 John 2).

Truth therefore reaches to action. *We do* or *do not the Truth* (iii. 21; 1 John i. 6)[1]. It follows that the reception of the Truth

[1] This aspect of the Truth is brought out specially by St Paul, who contrasts "unrighteousness" with "truth": Rom. i. 18, ii. 8; 1 Cor. xiii. 6; 2 Thess. ii. 12. Comp. Eph. iv. 24, v. 9.

brings freedom (viii. 32), because the Truth corresponds with the law of our being. By the Truth we are sanctified (xvii. 17).

No one therefore can fail to see how inconsistent it is with the apostolic conception of Christianity to represent the Faith as antagonistic to any form of Truth. It is interpreted by every fragment of Truth. All experience is a commentary on it. And we must be careful to keep ourselves open to every influence of light.

The message which St John has to convey in his Gospel is "the Truth," and this is commended to men by various forms of witness (μαρτυρία). There is nothing in the Synoptic Gospels to prepare for the remarkable development which he gives of this idea. It evidently belongs to a time when men had begun to reason about the faith, and to analyse the grounds on which it rested. The end of the witness is the confirmation of the truth (xviii. 37); and the Evangelist, looking back upon his own experience, is able to distinguish the several forms which the witness assumed and still essentially retains.

The witness to Christ which he records is therefore manifold, and extends over the whole range of possible attestation of divine things. In due succession there is, (1) the witness of the Father; (2) the witness of Christ Himself; (3) the witness of works; (4) the witness of Scripture; (5) the witness of the Forerunner; (6) the witness of disciples; and that which illuminates and quickens all, (7) the witness of the Spirit.

(1) The witness of the Father is that to which Christ appeals as the proper witness of Himself: *I* (ἐγώ) *receive not my witness from a man...the Father which sent me, He* (ἐκεῖνος) *hath borne witness concerning me* (v. 34, 37). *If I* (ἐγώ) *bear witness concerning myself, my witness is not true. There is another that beareth witness of me, and I know that the witness which He beareth concerning me is true* (v. 31 f.; contrast viii. 14). *I am he that beareth witness concerning myself, and the Father that sent me beareth witness concerning me* (viii. 18). This witness then is distinguished from the witness of a prophet (*e.g.* John the Baptist), and from the witness of Christ standing (if we can so conceive) in the isolation of His Personality. It lies in the absolute coincidence between the will and words and works of Christ and the will of the Father, realised by Christ in His divine-human Person (*I know*, v. 32). Such witness carries conviction to men so far as they have themselves been brought into unity with God. Man can feel what is truly divine while he reaches after it and fails to attain to it. The sense of his own aspirations and of his own shortcomings enables him to appreciate the perfection of Christ. Thus the witness of the Father is (what we speak of as) the "character" of Christ. The witness is continuous, present and abiding (μαρτυρεῖ, μεμαρτύρηκε), and it reposes upon the general conception of God as Father (*the Father* not *my Father*), standing in this paternal relation to all men. As soon as the thought of "the Fatherhood of God" is gained, it is felt that "the Son" expresses it absolutely. The witness of this perfect coincidence therefore finds its cogency in the response which it calls out from the soul of man. Man recognises the voice as naturally and supremely authoritative (1 John v. 9).

(2) The witness of the Father finds a special expression in the witness of the Son concerning Himself. This witness is valid because it reposes on a conscious fellowship with God (comp. x. 30), in which no element of selfishness can find any place, and on a direct and absolute knowledge of divine things (iii. 11, 32 f.), and of a divine mission seen in its totality (viii. 14; comp. *v.* 55). In this sense Christ said, *Even if I bear witness concerning myself my witness is true, because I know whence I came and whither I go* (viii. 14). Such witness necessarily derives power from what can be seen of the witness of the Father in Christ's character. And more than this, Christ's claim to universal sovereignty lay in the fact that He came *into the world in order to bear witness to the truth* (xviii. 37). *Every one* therefore, He adds, *that is of the truth heareth my voice* (id.). Thus it is seen that the final power of the witness of Christ to Himself is derived from man's affinity to truth which is found perfectly in Him. *His sheep*, according to the fa-

miliar image, *know His voice* (x. 4 f.). And He has a special message for each: *He calleth* (φωνεῖ) *His own sheep by name* (x. 3). The end of this is that *he that believeth on Him hath the witness in himself* (1 John v. 10).

(3) This divine witness, the internal witness which is addressed to man's moral constitution, takes a special and limited form in the witness of works. Thus Christ said, *The witness which I have is greater than that of John; for the works which the Father hath given me to accomplish, the very works that I do bear witness concerning me that the Father hath sent me* (v. 36, note). Within a narrow range and in a concrete and sensible manner, His works revealed His perfect communion with the Father (v. 17 ff.). Men could see in them, if not otherwise, tokens of His real nature and authority. *The works which I do in my Father's name*, claiming a special connexion with Him, making Him known as *my Father*, *these bear witness concerning me* (x. 25; comp. xiv. 11, xv. 24). And this kind of witness which was given in one form by Christ Himself during His historical presence is still continued. His disciples are enabled to perform *greater works* than those to which He appealed (xiv. 12 ff.). The Christian Society has still the living witness of "signs."

For in the record of the "works" of Christ St John draws no line between those which we call natural and supernatural. The separate "works" are fragments of the one "work" (iv. 34, xvii. 4). Whether they are predominantly works of power or of love, wrought on the body or on the spirit, they have the same office and end (comp. v. 20 f., 36, ix. 3 f., xiv. 10). They are "shewn:" they require that is a sympathetic interpretation (x. 32; comp. v. 20). The earliest emotion which they produce may be simply "wonder" (v. 20), but wonder is the first step to knowledge. This follows both in its decisive apprehension and in its progressive extension (x. 38, ἵνα γνῶτε καὶ γινώσκητε).

Works therefore according to St John are signs (vi. 26); and their witness, from their want of directness and from their outwardness of form, is secondary to that of "words" (xiv. 11, xv. 22 ff.). The internal witness, according to our mode of speaking, is placed above the external. The former is an appeal to the spiritual consciousness, the latter to the intellect.

(4) So far we have seen that the witness to Christ is found in Himself, in what He is, and in what He did and does through His disciples. But He stood also in a definite relation to the past. Witness was borne to Him both by the records of the ancient dispensation and by the last of the prophets. *Ye search the Scriptures*, Christ said to the Jews, *because ye think that in them ye have eternal life*—that they are in themselves the end, and not the preparation for the end—*and they are they which witness concerning me; and ye will not come to me that ye may have life* (v. 39, 40). Without Christ the Old Testament is an unsolved riddle. By the writings of Moses and the prophets (v. 46, i. 45) He was seen to be the goal and fulfilment of immemorial hopes which became a testimony to Him in whom they were satisfied. The Old Testament was to the first age and is to all ages, if regarded in its broad and indisputable outlines, a witness to Christ.

(5) The witness of the Old Testament found a final expression in the latest of the prophets. John the Baptist occupied a position which was wholly peculiar. *He came for witness, to bear witness concerning the Light, that all men might believe through him* (i. 7). His own light was borrowed and kindled (v. 35, i. 8); yet it was such as to attract and arrest (v. 35), and served to prepare men for that which should follow. In this sense Christ appealed to it. *Ye have sent to John, and he hath borne witness to the truth. But I receive not my witness from a man, but these things I say that ye may be saved* (v. 33 f.). The witness was, so to speak, an accommodation to the moral condition of those for whom it was given. It was the attestation of a personal conviction based upon a specific proof. The Baptist realised his own character and office (i. 19 ff.); and he recognised Christ by the sign which had been made known to him (i. 32 ff.). He realised the sternest form of Judaism, and at the same time perceived the universality of that in

which Judaism should be crowned. In a signal example he offered the witness of the leader of men who sways the thoughts of the multitude.

(6) The witness of the Baptist was to one decisive event. By this was revealed to him the relation of Christ to the old covenant of which he was himself the last representative. His was the individual witness of an exceptional man. To this was added the witness, so to speak, of common life. The witness of the disciples was in various degrees a witness to what they had experienced in their intercourse with Christ, a witness to facts. *Ye also*, Christ said to the eleven, *bear witness, because ye are with me from the beginning* (xv. 27). *He that hath seen hath borne witness* (xix. 35). *This is the disciple that witnesseth concerning these things and wrote these things* (xxi. 24; comp. 1 John i. 2, iv. 14).

(7) But in all these cases there was need of an interpreter. Neither the mission nor the Person of Christ could be understood at once. It was necessary that He should be withdrawn in order that the disciples might be able to receive the full revelation of His Nature. This was their consolation in the prospect of persecution and hatred. *When the Paraclete is come whom I will send from the Father, even the Spirit of Truth, which proceedeth from the Father, He shall bear witness concerning me* (xv. 26). In this witness lies the continual unfolding of the infinite significance of the Incarnation. The Spirit takes of that which is Christ's, and declares it (xvi. 14). It is the Spirit, as St John himself says elsewhere, *that beareth witness, because the Spirit is the truth* (1 John v. 6).

If now we look back over these seven types of witness to which St John appeals in the Gospel, it will be seen that they cover the whole range of the possible proof of religious truth, internal and external. The witness of the Father and of Christ Himself is internal, and rests on the correspondence of the Gospel with that absolute idea of the divine which is in man. The witness of works and of Scripture is external and historical, and draws its force from the signs which the Gospel gives of fulfilling a divine purpose. The witness of the prophet and of the disciples is personal and experiential, and lies in the open declaration of what men have found the Gospel to be. Lastly, the witness of the Spirit is for the believer the crown of assurance and the pledge of the progress of the Truth.

(*b*) *Light and Glory*. The second pair of words, Light and Glory, which characterize St John's narrative correspond to a certain extent with the Witness and the Truth. The Witness becomes effective through Light. The Truth is revealed in Glory.

The description of God as Light (1 John i. 5) expresses in its final form that idea of self-communication which is realised in many ways. The works of God are a revelation of Him (i. 4 f., note); and among these man's own constitution, though this is not specially brought out by St John (comp. Matt. vi. 23; Luke xi. 35). The Word as Light visited men (ix. 5, ὅταν) before the Incarnation (i. 9 f.; comp. v. 38; Rom. ii. 15 f.), at the Incarnation (viii. 12, xii. 46, iii. 19—21; comp. xi. 9 f.), and He still comes (xiv. 21); even as the Spirit who still interprets His "name" (xiv. 26, xvi. 13; comp. 1 John ii. 20 ff., 27).

St John draws no distinction in essence between these three different forms of revelation, in nature, in conscience, in history: all alike are natural or supernatural, parts of the same harmonious plan. But man has not independently light in himself. The understanding of the outward revelation depends upon the abiding of the divine word within (v. 37 f.). Love is the condition of illumination (xiv. 22 ff.). And the end of Christ's coming was that those who believe in Him may move in a new region of life (xii. 46), and themselves *become sons of light* (xii. 35 f.), and so, as the last issue of faith, have *the light of life* (viii. 12).

Under the action of the Light the Truth is seen in Christ as Glory. Christ, "the Light of the world," is seen by the believer to be the manifested glory of God.

(1) Step by step the Gospel of St John lays open the progress of this manifestation. The summary of its whole course is given by the Apostle at the outset: *The Word became flesh and tabernacled*

among us, and we beheld His glory, glory as of an only son from a father (i. 14), absolutely representing, that is, Him from whom He came. The beginning of Christ's signs was a manifestation of His glory (ii. 11), and that it might be so, it was shewn only when *the hour was come* (ii. 4). For the glory of the Son was not of His own seeking (viii. 50), but was wholly the expression of His Father's will through Him (viii. 54). And conversely the Son by His perfect conformity to the Father's will *glorified the Father upon earth* in the fulfilment of His appointed work (xvii. 4), wherein He was also glorified Himself (xvii. 10).

(2) The glory of Christ was therefore in a true sense the glory of God. *This sickness*, the Lord said in regard to Lazarus, *is not unto death*, as its real issue, *but for the glory of God, that the Son of God may be glorified through it* (xi. 4). And so the restoration of Lazarus to life was a vision of *the glory of God* (xi. 40), as producing faith in Him whom He sent (xi. 42). The glorification of "the name" of the Father was the historic work of the Son (xii. 28). When the crisis was past, *Jesus saith, Now was the Son of man glorified* (ἐδοξάσθη), *and God was glorified in Him* (xiii. 31). At the end the correlation is not between the Son and the Father, but between the Son of man and God. In Him, little by little, under the conditions of human existence, the absolute idea of manhood was fulfilled.

(3) It follows that the thought of Christ's glory is extended beyond the Incarnation. The glory which was consummated through the Incarnation *he had with the Father before the world was* (xvii. 5); and when the prophet was allowed to look upon *the Lord, sitting upon a throne, high and lifted up* (Is. vi. 1 ff.), what he saw was *the glory of Christ* (xii. 41).

(4) And on the other hand, as the glory of the Son is extended backward, so also the glory of *Jesus, the Son of man*, consummated on the divine side even in God (xiii. 32) at the Ascension (vii. 39, xii. 16), to which the way was opened by the Passion (xii. 23, xiii. 31), is to be realised by men little by little in the course of ages. The petitions of believers are granted *that the Father may be glorified in the Son* (xiv. 13): their fruitfulness, already regarded as attained, is a source of this glory (xv. 8). And one chief office of the Spirit is *to glorify Christ* by making Him more fully known (xvi. 14).

(*c*) *Judgment and Life.* The glory of Christ and of God in Christ, which is thus presented as the substance of revelation, belongs to a spiritual sphere. It can therefore only be perceived by those who have true spiritual vision. As an inevitable consequence, the revelation of the divine glory carries with it a judgment, a separation.

The fundamental notion of this Judgment lies in the authoritative and final declaration of the state of man as he is in relation to God and standing apart from God. It follows as a necessary consequence that Judgment in this sense is contrasted with "salvation," "life." *He that believeth* [on the Son] *is not judged* (iii. 18). He *hath passed out of death into life* (v. 24; comp. v. 29). For Christ has life (i. 4, v. 26), and His words are life (vi. 53; comp. vi. 68, xii. 50). He came to offer life to men (x. 28, xvii. 2), that they too may have it (iii. 15 f., v. 40, vi. 40, x. 10). He is indeed Himself "the Life" (xi. 25, xiv. 6) and the support of life (vi. 33, 35, 48, 51; comp. iv. 14). To know the Father and Him is eternal life (xvii. 3); and he that "believeth in Him," he that is united with Him by faith, hath the life as a present possession (iii. 36, v. 24, vi. 47, 54; comp. viii. 12), which otherwise he cannot have (vi. 53). The relation of the believer to Christ is made parallel with the relation of the Son to the Father (vi. 57). *Because I live*, Christ said to the eleven, *ye shall live also* (xiv. 19). Thus the believer, in virtue of the vital connexion which he has realised with God in His Son, is no longer considered apart from Him. Judgment therefore in his case is impossible.

This conception of judgment explains the apparent contradiction in the views which are given of the part of Christ in regard to it. On the one side judgment is realised as self-fulfilled in the actual circumstances of life. *This is the judgment, that the light is come into the world and men loved the darkness rather than the light, for their works were evil* (iii. 19);

and by this contrast the unbeliever is convicted from within: *he hath one that judgeth him: the word that I spake*, Christ said, *shall judge him at the last day* (xii. 48). Hence it is said: *God sent not the Son into the world to judge the world, but that the world may be saved through Him* (iii. 17). *I came not to judge the world, but to save the world* (xii. 47).

And yet on the other side judgment belongs to Christ, and satisfies the utmost ideal of judgment because it reposes upon adequate knowledge. Thus we read: *the Father hath given all judgment unto the Son* (v. 22; comp. v. 27); and *for judgment* (κρίμα) *came I into this world*...(ix. 39; comp. viii. 26). *I judge no man; yea, and if I* (ἐγώ) *judge, my judgment is true* (ἀληθινή, viii. 15 f.). *As I hear I judge, and my judgment is just* (v. 30).

Striking as the contrast between these passages appears to be, it is only necessary to consider what the judgment is in order to feel their harmony. Spiritual judgment is a consequence involved in the rejection of the revelation which Christ made. His will was to unite men to Himself, so that they might have life and not be judged. So far then as they rejected Him and stood away from Him, His Presence shewed them as they truly were. He judged them; and judgment was equivalent to condemnation. Thus the exhibition of the contrast of the true and the false became one of the means for developing belief and unbelief according to the character of Christ's hearers (viii. 26). Whatever might be the result, His message must be delivered.

In one sense therefore judgment, like the gift of life, is immediate. It lies in the existence of an actual relation (iii. 18) which carries with it its final consequences. In another sense it is still future, so far as it will be realised in a spiritual order of being *in the last day* (xii. 48). There is *a resurrection of life* and *a resurrection of judgment* (v. 29), in which the issues of both begun here will be completely fulfilled. Meanwhile the process is going on upon earth. The manifestation of perfect holiness presented to the world in perfect self-sacrifice (v. 30) has set up a standard which cannot be put out of sight. Under this aspect Christ's coming was a sentence of judgment (κρίμα, ix. 39). The judgment of the sovereign power of the world in the Passion (xii. 31) has left men no excuse (see xvi. 11, note). In that they can see the mind of God, and according as they surrender themselves to it or resist it, they find life or judgment.

So far the judgment is self-fulfilled. It cannot but be carried out. The word of Christ sooner or later must justify itself (xii. 48). There is no need that He should seek to assert and vindicate its supremacy. *There is one that seeketh and judgeth* (viii. 50), the eternal power of righteousness symbolized in the Law (v. 45), and expressed in the Gospel (xii. 48 ff.).

But though this is so, the idea of divine action is never lost in the Bible in an abstraction, however emphatic. And while the eternal necessity of judgment is thus set forth, the historical execution of judgment, both present and final, is recognised as a work of the Son; and though it was not the purpose of His mission, yet it was committed to Him in virtue of His mission. *The Father doth not judge any man, but hath given all judgment to the Son* (v. 22). Even as the Father gave Him *to have life in Himself*, and so to be a spring of life to all who are united with Him, so also He *gave Him authority to execute judgment because He is a Son of man*—not *the* Son of man—(v. 27), because He is truly man, and not only the representative of humanity. His judgment therefore (comp. Hebr. iv. 14 ff.) is essentially united with His complete sympathy with man's nature, and extends to the fulness of human life. It finds place always and everywhere.

These contrasts bring out into full relief the conflict between faith and unbelief, which, as has been said, is the main subject of St John's Gospel. In the Synoptic Gospels faith occupies a different position. It is in these almost exclusively relative to a particular object (Matt. viii. 10, ix. 2, 22, 29, &c.; Mark ix. 23, &c.). Only once does the full expression for faith in the Person of Christ occur (πιστεύειν εἰς, Matt. xviii. 6, || Mark ix. 42). In St John, on the other hand, this is the characteristic form under which faith is presented. The simple noun is not found in his Gospel. Faith is the attitude of the whole believing man. Such faith in Christ is the condition of eternal life (i. 12, vi. 40). To produce it was the object of the Evangelist (xx. 31). And the history marks in typical crises the progress of its development.

The first sign is followed by an access of faith in the disciples (ii. 11). The first entrance into Jerusalem was followed by faith disturbed by preconceived ideas (ii. 23, iii. 12 ff.). The preaching in Samaria called out a complete confession of faith (iv. 39 ff.), which stands in contrast with the faith resting on signs which followed in Galilee (iv. 48 ff.).

From this point active unbelief appears side by side with faith. By claiming authority over the Sabbath, and "making Himself equal with God" (v. 17 f.), the Lord offered a test of devotion to those who followed Him: He fulfilled that to which Moses pointed (v. 39, 45 ff.). The decisive trial in Galilee caused a fresh division between those who had hitherto been disciples. It was now revealed that life was to be gained by the personal appropriation of the virtue of Christ's Life and Death (vi. 53 ff.). Some turned aside, and St Peter confessed the Apostolic faith even in the mysterious prospect of the Passion (vi. 66 ff.). At the Feast of Tabernacles the antagonism of the hierarchy was more decided (vii. 32, 47 ff.), and the Lord traced it to its source in an analysis of the spirit of those who believed Him with a view to the execution of their own designs (viii. 31, note). At the same time He revealed His preexistence (viii. 31 ff., 58). The separation between the old Church and the new, which was implicitly included in these discourses, was openly shewn in the scenes which followed. Christ offered Himself openly as the object of faith as "the Son of man" (ix. 35 ff.), and declared the universality of His work (x. 16). The raising of Lazarus, which carried with it the condemnation of the Lord, shewed Him to be the conqueror of death and through death (xi. 25 f., 50, xii. 23 ff.). So the public revelation was completed, and with it faith and unbelief were brought to their last issue (xii. 37 ff.).

The last discourses and the last prayer point to the future victories of faith; and the narrative closes with the beatitude of the Risen Christ: *Blessed are they that have not seen, and yet have believed* (xx. 29), which crowned the loftiest confession of faith triumphant over doubt: *My Lord and my God* (xx. 28).

Even from this rapid summary it will be seen that the self-revelation of Christ became stage by stage the occasion of fuller personal trust and more open personal antagonism. In Him *thoughts from many hearts were revealed* (Luke ii. 35). And St John lays open the course of the original conflict which is the pattern of all conflicts to the end of time.

5. *The Style.*

The characteristic repetition and development of the three pairs of ideas, Witness and Truth, Glory and Light, Judgment and Life, in the structure of St John's Gospel, serve to indicate the peculiarities of the style of the book. There is both in the vocabulary and in the form of the sentences a surprising simplicity, which becomes majestic by its solemn directness.

(*a*) It is not necessary to dwell upon the vocabulary. Any one who will trace out the use of the six words already discussed will feel how the apparent monotony contains a marvellous depth and fulness. An examination of other words, as *sign* (σημεῖον), and *works* (ἔργα), and *name* (ἐν τῷ ὀνόματι, εἰς τὸ ὄνομα), *the Father* (ὁ πατήρ), and *my Father* (ὁ πατήρ μου), the *world* (κόσμος, not ὁ αἰὼν οὗτος and the like), to *love*, to *know* (εἰδέναι and γινώσκειν), will lead to the same conclusion (compare Additional Notes on i. 10, iv. 21). The apparent sameness of phraseology produces throughout an impressive emphasis.

(*b*) This emphatic monotony is still more observable in the form and in the combination of the sentences. The constructions are habitually reduced to the simplest elements. To speak of St John's Gospel as "written in very pure Greek" is altogether misleading. It is free from solecisms, because it avoids all idiomatic expressions. The grammar is that which is common to almost all language. Directness, circumstantiality, repetition, and personality, are the characteristic marks of the separate sentences. And the sentences and thoughts are grouped together in a corresponding manner. They are co-ordinated and not subordinated. The sequence of the reasoning is not wrought out, but left for sympathetic interpretation.

The narrative is uniformly direct. Even the words and opinions of others are given directly and not obliquely. Any one of the detailed incidents in St John's narrative will illustrate this characteristic of his style. Thus we read in the opening scene: *This is the witness of John when the Jews sent...to ask him, Who art thou? and he confessed...I am not the Christ. And they asked him, What then? Art thou Elijah? And he saith, I am not*...(i. 19 ff.). And again, *Certain of the multitude therefore, when they heard these words, said, This is of a truth the Prophet. Others said, This is the Christ. But some said, What, doth the Christ come out of Galilee?* (vii. 40 f.; comp. ii. 3 ff., iv. 27 ff., v. 10 ff., vi. 14, viii. 22, ix. 2 ff., &c.)[1].

It is a part of the same method that illustrative details are added parenthetically or as distinct statements, and not wrought into the texture of the narrative (vi. 10, iv. 6, x. 22, xiii. 30, xviii. 40).

The circumstantiality of St John's style is a necessary result of this directness. Each element in the action is distinguished, as a general rule, and set out clearly. Thus while the other Evangelists write habitually according to the common Greek idiom [*Jesus*] *answering said* (ἀποκριθεὶς εἶπε), St John never uses this form, but writes instead [*Jesus*] *answered and said* (ἀπεκρίθη καὶ εἶπεν). He places the two parts of the act in equal prominence; and though it might appear at first sight that the phrases are exactly equivalent, yet the co-ordination of details brings a certain definiteness to the picture which fixes the thought of the reader. The same tendency is shewn in St John's analysis of other actions, *Jesus cried aloud and said* (xii. 44). *Jesus cried aloud in the temple, teaching and saying* (vii. 28). *John beareth witness of Him and hath cried, saying*...(i. 15). *They questioned him, and said* (i. 25). In these and similar cases it will be found that the separation of the whole into its parts adds to the impressiveness, and to the meaning of the description.

One remarkable illustration of this particularity is found in the combination of the positive and negative expression of the same truth. *All things were made through Him, and without Him was not any thing made* (i. 3). *He confessed, and denied not* (i. 20). *Jesus did not trust Himself unto them, for that He knew all men, and because He needed not that any one should bear witness concerning man* (ii. 24 f.). *God...gave His only Son that whosoever believeth on Him may not perish, but have eternal life* (iii. 16). Comp. x. 5, xviii. 20; 1 John i. 6, ii. 4, 27.

The circumstantiality of St John's style leads to frequent repetition of the subject or of the significant word in a sentence (i. 1, *Word*; i. 7, *witness*; i. 10, *world*; iv. 22, *worship*; v. 31 f., *witness*; vi. 27, *meat*; xi. 33, *weeping*).

Such repetitions are singularly marked in the record of dialogues, in which the persons are constantly brought into prominence. Sentence after sentence begins with words, "Jesus said," "the Jews said," and the like, so that the characters in the great conflict are kept clearly present to the mind of the reader in sharp contrast (ii. 18 ff., iv. 7 ff., viii. 48 ff., x. 23 ff.).

This usage leads to what has been called above the personality of St John's narrative. This is shewn by the special frequency with which he introduces a demonstrative pronoun to call back the subject, when a clause has intervened between the subject and the verb. This he does in two ways. Sometimes he employs the pronoun of present reference: *He that abideth in me and I in him, this man* (οὗτος) *beareth much fruit* (xv. 5; comp. vii. 18, &c.); and sometimes, which is the more characteristic usage, the pronoun of remote, isolated reference: *He that entereth not by the*

[1] This directness of construction is so universal in the Gospel that the only example (so far as I have observed) of an oblique sentence is in iv. 51, where the true reading appears to be *met him, saying that his son liveth*, in place of *met him and told him, saying, Thy son liveth*; for, on the other hand, the common oblique reading in xiii. 24 is incorrect; and the vivid phrase, *and saith to him, Say, who is it?* must be substituted for *that he should ask who it should be of whom he spake*.

This is in fact a characteristic of the New Testament style generally; see Winer, § LX. 9; but in St John it is most marked.

door...that man (ἐκεῖνος) *is a thief and a robber* (x. 1; comp. i. 18, 33, v. 11, 37, 38, xii. 48, xiv. 21, 26, xv. 26).

Another feature of the same kind is the frequency of St John's use of the personal pronouns, and especially of the pronoun of the first person. In this respect much of the teaching of the Lord's discourses depends upon the careful recognition of the emphatic reference to His undivided Personality. *Yea, and if I* (ἐγώ) *judge*—I, who am truly God, and truly man—*my judgment is true; for I am not alone, but I and the Father that sent me* (viii. 16). In this case, as in most cases, the pronoun calls attention to the nature of the Lord: elsewhere it marks the isolation (so to speak) of His personality; so that we read two sentences which, being in appearance directly contradictory, are harmonized by giving due emphasis to the exact force of the pronoun (v. 31, viii. 14 note).

(*c*) The method of combining sentences in St John corresponds completely to the method of their separate construction. The simplicity, directness, circumstantiality, repetition, which mark the constituent sentences, mark also whole sections of his work. Words, sentences, paragraphs follow one another in what must appear to an unreflecting reader needless iteration, though in fact it is by this means that the central thought is placed in varied lights, so that its fulness can at last be grasped. The multiplication of simple elements in this instance, as elsewhere, produces in the end an effect of commanding grandeur, and so the student learns to pause in order that he may carefully consider the parts which separately contribute to it. (See, for example, ch. xvii.)

The most obvious illustration of this feature lies in St John's constant habit of framing his record of events and discourses without connecting particles. When the feeling is most intense clause follows clause by simple addition. No conjunction binds the parts together. The details are given severally, and the reader is left to seize them in their unity (iv. 7, 10 ff., xi. 34, 35, xiv. 15 ff., xv. 1—20).

At the same time St John does in fact insist more than the other Evangelists upon the connexion of facts, even if he commonly leaves them in simple juxtaposition. His most characteristic particle in narrative (it is rare in the discourses) is *therefore* (οὖν), and this serves in very many cases to call attention to a sequence which is real, if not obvious. *There arose* therefore *a question on the part of John's disciples with a Jew about purifying* (iii. 25). *When* therefore *He heard that he was sick, He abode for the time two days in the place where He was* (xi. 6). Comp. iii. 29, iv. 46, vii. 28.

In like manner the unusual frequency of the phrase *in order that* (ἵνα), which marks a direct object, is a sign of the habitual tendency of St John to regard things in their moral and providential relations. Even where the usage departs most widely from the classical standard, it is possible to see how the irregular construction springs out of a characteristic mode of thought (*e.g.* iv. 34, v. 36, vi. 29, viii. 56, xii. 23, xiii. 34, xvii. 3); and frequently the particle suggests a profound interpretation of the divine counsel (v. 20, x. 17, xii. 38, xv. 8, xvi. 2).

The simple coordination of clauses is frequently assisted by the repetition of a marked word or phrase, such as occurs in separate sentences. In this way a connexion is established between two statements, while the idea is carried forward in a new direction. Sometimes the subject is repeated: *I am the good Shepherd. The good Shepherd layeth down his life for the sheep* (x. 11). Sometimes a word is taken up from a former clause and repeated with significant emphasis: *Greater love hath no man than this, that a man lay down his life for his friends. Ye are my friends...No longer do I call you servants...but I have called you friends*...(xv. 13 ff.). Sometimes a clause is repeated which gives (so to speak) the theme of the passage: *I am the door of the sheep...I am the door: by me if any man enter in, he shall be saved...* (x. 7 ff.). *I am the good Shepherd: the good shepherd layeth down his life for the sheep...I am the good Shepherd...and I lay down my life for my sheep* (x. 11, 14). *I am the true vine...I am the vine: ye are the branches* (xv. 1, 5). Sometimes a clause is repeated which gives a closing cadence: *The world hated them because they are not of the world, even as I am not of the world...They are not of the world, even as I am not of the world... Sanctify them in the truth...that they themselves may be sanctified in truth* (xvii. 14 ff.). Three times in the sixth chapter the clause recurs: *I will* (*may*) *raise him up at the last day* (39, 40, 44). And even in the simple narrative of St Peter's denial the scene is impressed upon the reader by the solemn repetition of the words: *Peter was standing and warming himself* (xviii. 18, 25)[1].

(*d*) This repetition in some cases leads to a perfect poetic parallelism: (xiv. 26, 27).

And in fact the spirit of parallelism, the instinctive perception of symmetry in thought and expression, which is the essential and informing spirit of Hebrew poetry, runs through the whole record, both in its general structure and in the structure of its parts. From first to last the Truth is presented, so to speak, in ever-widening circles. Each incident, each discourse, presupposes what has gone before, and adds something to the result.

6. *Historical Exactness.*

Our inquiry up to this point has established beyond doubt that the structure of the fourth Gospel corresponds with the fulfilment of a profound purpose. It is composed both generally and in detail with singular symmetry. There is a growing purpose wrought out from stage to stage in the great divisions of the record; and there are subtle and minute traits in each separate narrative which reveal to careful examination the presence of an informing idea throughout it. The correspondences of part with part may indeed be due as much to the one fundamental conception of the whole work as to special and conscious adaptation of details; but none the less we must feel that the historical elements are means to an end; that the narrative expresses distinctly (as it professes to do) the writer's interpretation of the events with which he deals. We must feel that it is not an exhaustive exposition (so far as the Evangelist's knowledge went) of the incidents of the Lord's life; that it does not preserve some features of His work which were unquestionably prominent; that we could not put together from it a complete picture of *Jesus of Nazareth* as He *went about doing good, and healing all that were oppressed of the devil* (Acts x. 38). We allow, or rather we press, the fact that the fourth Gospel, so far as it is regarded as a biography, or as a biographical sketch, is confined to certain limited aspects of the Person and Life and Work with which it deals. But while we make the fullest acknowledgment of these truths, we affirm also that the literal accuracy of the contents of the Gospel is not in any way prejudiced by the existence of this particular purpose. The historical illustrations of the writer's theme—if we even so regard the incidents which he relates—are no less historical because they are illustrations: the Evangelist's conception of the real significance of Christ's Presence is not to be set aside because it is his conception: the special traits which are given are in no degree open to suspicion, because they are special traits emphasized with a definite object. Neither the apostolical authorship nor the historical trustworthiness of the narrative is affected by the admission that the writer fulfils his work, according to his own words, with an express purpose in view.

The first point is not before us now; but there is one argument directly bearing upon it, which underlies very much of the popular criticism of the Gospel though it is not very often put into a distinct shape, which may be most conveniently noticed here. It is sometimes plainly said, and more often silently assumed, that an Apostle could not have spoken of One with whom he had lived familiarly, as the writer of the fourth Gospel speaks of the Lord. In reply to this argument one sentence only is necessary. In order to have any force the argument takes for granted all that is finally at issue, and implies that it is *not* true that "the Word became flesh." If, on the other hand, this revelation is true, as we believe, then the fourth Gospel helps us to understand how the overwhelming mystery was gradually made known: how the divine Nature of Christ was revealed little by little to those with whom He had conversed as man. Un-

[1] So also words are repeated through considerable sections of the Gospel: *love, to love* (xiii.—xvii.); *life* (v., vi.); *light* (viii.—xii.).

less our faith be false, we may say that we cannot conceive any way in which it could have been historically realised except that which is traced out in the experience reflected in the writings of St John. The Incarnation is confessedly a great mystery, in every sense of the word, but no fresh difficulty is occasioned by the fact that in due time it was laid open to those among whom the Son of God had moved.

Moreover, it may be added, the difficulty of admitting that an Apostle came to recognise the true divinity of One with whom he had lived as man with man is not done away by denying the apostolic authorship of the Gospel. The most conspicuous critics who refuse to assign the Gospel to St John agree in assigning the Apocalypse to him; and it is no easier for us to understand how (not to quote xxii. 13) an Apostle could speak of the Master whom he had followed to the Cross as being the Holy and the True, who has the key of David, "who openeth, and no man shutteth; and shutteth, and no man openeth" (iii. 7), as joined with "Him that sitteth on the throne," in being "worthy to receive blessing, and honour, and glory, and might, for ever and ever" (v. 13), than to understand how he could look back upon His *life* as the life of the Incarnate Word. The Christology of the Gospel and the Christology of the Apocalypse are alike, we may venture to say, historically inexplicable unless we take as the key to their interpretation the assertion of the fact, "the Word became flesh," apprehended under the action of the Spirit, in the consciousness of those who had known Christ "from the Baptism of John to the Resurrection."

These considerations however carry us away from our immediate subject; for we are not concerned at present with the apostolic authorship of the Gospel. We have to inquire how far its trustworthiness is affected by the existence of a specific didactic design in the writing. But before discussing this question one other topic must be referred to, only to be set aside, which will be examined in detail afterwards. The arguments against the trustworthiness of the Gospel drawn from the fact that its contents do not for the most part coincide with the contents of the Synoptic Gospels may be dismissed, or, at least, held in suspense. For this end it will be enough to insist on the obvious fact that a general difference in the contents of two narratives relating to a complex history, which are both avowedly incomplete, cannot be used to prejudice the accuracy of either. And the most cursory consideration of the fragmentariness of the records of Christ's life will make it evident that the mere addition of the facts related by St John to those preserved in the other Gospels cannot create any difficulty. They do not differ in kind from incidents related by the Synoptists; and we have no external means for determining the principles by which the choice of incidents embodied in the Synoptic narratives was determined. There is certainly no reason for supposing that these narratives would have included the incidents peculiar to St John, if they had been familiarly known at the time when the records were drawn up. The Synoptists indicate summarily cycles of events which they do not relate; and St John refers definitely to "many other signs" with which he was personally acquainted.

Thus we are brought back to the proper subject of our inquiry. Does the author of the fourth Gospel forfeit his claim to observe accuracy of fact because the facts are selected with a view to a definite purpose? He professes to write, as we have seen, in the hope of creating in others the faith which he holds himself (xix. 35, xx. 31). Now that faith is in reality a special interpretation of all history drawn from a special interpretation of One Life. We may therefore modify our question and ask, Does the Evangelist forfeit his claim to be a truthful historian, because he turns his eye steadily to the signs of the central laws of being? The answer to the question must be sought finally in the conditions of the historian's work. These conditions include in every case choice, compression, combination of materials. And he fulfils his work rightly who chooses, compresses, combines his materials according to a certain vital proportion. In other words, the historian, like the poet, cannot but interpret the facts which he records. The truth of history is simply the truth of the interpretation of an infinitude of details contemplated together. The simplest statement of a result presents a broad generalization of particulars. The generalization may be true or false; it may be ruled by an outward or by an inward principle; but in any case it only represents a total impression of the particulars seen in one way. It does not represent either all the particulars or all the impressions which they are capable of producing. What is called pure "objective" history is a mere phantom. No one could specify, and no one would be willing to specify, all the separate details which man's most imperfect observation can distinguish as elements in any one "fact;" and the least reflection shews that there are other elements not less numerous or less important than those open to our observation, which cannot be observed by us, and which yet go towards the fulness of the "fact." The subjectivity of history is consequently a mere question of degree. A writer who looks at the outside of things, and reproduces the impression which this would convey to average men, is as far from the whole truth as the writer who brings his whole power to bear upon an individual realisation of it. Thus every record of a "fact" is necessarily limited to the record of representative details concerning it. The truthfulness of the historian as a narrator lies therefore in his power of selecting these details so as to convey to others the true idea of the fact which he has himself formed. In this respect the literal accuracy of any number of details is no guarantee for the accuracy of the impression conveyed by the sum of them regarded as a whole; and it is no paradox to say that a "true" detail which disturbs the proportion of the picture becomes in the connexion false.

What has been said of separate "facts" is obviously true of the sequence of facts. It is impossible not to feel that a true conception of the character of a life or (if such a phrase may be used) of the spirit of a social movement would illuminate the connexion and meaning of the external details in which they are manifested, and that many details regarded externally would be liable to the gravest misapprehension if the conception were either false or wanting. And further, it is no less clear that the necessity for this interpretative power becomes more urgent as the subject becomes more complex.

There is undoubtedly at present a strong feeling in favour of realistic, external, history; but it may reasonably be questioned whether this fashion of opinion will be permanent, and it is obviously beset by many perils. Realistic history often treats only of the dress and not of the living frame, and it can never go beyond the outward circumstances of an organization which is inspired by one vital power. The photographer is wholly unable to supply the function of the artist; and realism must be subordinated to the interpretation of the life, if history is to take its true place as a science. This is the thought which underlies the Hebrew type of historic record. In the Old Testament the prophet is the historian. The facts which he records are significant, if fragmentary, expressions of an inner divine law wrought out among men. His interest is centred in the life which is manifested in action, but not exhausted by it. His aim is to reveal this life to others through the phenomena which the life alone makes truly intelligible to him.

We are not now concerned to inquire whether the prophetic interpretation of the life of men and nations and humanity be true or false. All that needs to be insisted upon is that the historian must have some view of the life whereby the events which he chronicles are held together. This view will influence him both in the choice of incidents and in the choice of details. And he will be the best historian who grasps the conception of the life most firmly, and who shews the absolute and eternal in the ordinary current of events. For him each event will be a sign.

Now whatever debates may arise on other points it cannot be doubted that the writer of the fourth Gospel has a distinct conception of a spiritual law of the life of humanity which found its final realisation in the Incarnation. This conception is therefore his clue in the choice and arrangement of facts. He takes just so many events and so much of each as will illustrate the central truth which he finds in a particular view of the Person of Christ. If his view of Christ be right, it cannot be seriously questioned that the traits on which he chiefly dwells are intrinsically natural; and no other view appears to be able to explain the phenomena of the belief attested by the earliest Christian literature, the letters of St Paul and the Apocalypse, and by the existence of the Christian Church. Thus the Gospel of St John adds that express teaching on the relation of Christ to God—of the Son to the Father—which underlies the claims to exclusive and final authority made by Him in the Synoptists. And the definiteness of the Evangelist's aim does not diminish but rather increases his interest in the exact conditions and circumstances under which Christ acted and spoke; for our historic interest must always vary directly with our sense of the importance of the history.

Some of these points will come before us again in greater detail, but so much at least is clear, that the "subjectivity" of the fourth Evangelist affords in itself no presumption against his historical accuracy. Every historian is necessarily subjective. And it must be shewn that the Evangelist's view of the Person of Christ, which is established independently of his Gospel, is false, before any argument against his trustworthiness can be drawn from a representation of Christ's works and words which corresponds with that view.

It is then no disparagement of the strict historical character of the fourth Gospel that the writer has fulfilled the design which he set before himself, of recording such "signs" out of the whole number of Christ's works as he considered likely to produce a specific effect. But even if it is admitted that historical exactness is generally reconcileable in theory with the execution of a particular design in the selection and exhibition and combination of facts, and further that this particular design may be the interpretation of the innermost meaning of the life, while it includes only a small fraction of the outward events, yet it will be urged that this method of explanation does not apply to all the phenomena of St John's Gospel: that the discourses of the Lord, in especial as given there, cannot be regarded otherwise than as free compositions of the Evangelist; that their contents are monotonous and without progress from first to last; that they are of the same character under different circumstances; that they have no individuality of style; that, on the contrary, they are almost undistinguishable in form and substance from the first epistle in which the writer speaks in his own person, and from the speeches which he places in the mouth of other characters, as the Baptist. These objections, it will be seen, are quite independent of any supposed incompatibility of the accounts of St John and of the Synoptists, and require a separate examination. They arise out of the study of the book itself, and must be considered first. The apparent contrasts between the records of the teaching of the Lord given in the first three Gospels and in the fourth will be noticed afterwards.

1. What has been already said as to the conditions which determine the selection of representative details and of representative incidents in a narrative of events applies with necessary limitations to the historical record of teaching. It is obvious that if a record of a debate of several hours length is to be compressed into a few sentences, the value of the record will depend not upon the literal reproduction of the exact words used here and there or in a brief episode of the discussion, but upon the power of the historian to enter into the spirit of the debate and to sketch its outline in right proportion. The thoughts of the speakers are more important than the style of the speakers. And it is quite conceivable that the meaning and effect of a long discourse, when reduced to a brief abstract, may be conveyed most truly by the use of a different style, and even, to a certain extent, of different language from that actually employed.

Again: the style of a speaker enters in very various degrees into his teaching, according to his subject and his circumstances. At one time it is of the essence: at another time, it is wholly subordinate to the general drift of the exposition. The keen, pregnant saying, the vivid illustration must be preserved exactly, or their character is lost. The subtle argument may be best touched suggest ively, so that the sympathetic reader can supply the links which cannot be given in full. A many-sided speaker will thus furnish materials for very different studies. But it would be wholly wrong to conclude that the sketch which preserves most literally those fragments of his words, which are capable of being so preserved, is more true than the sketch which gives a view of the ultimate principles of his doctrine. The former may give the manner and even the outward characteristics: the latter may reveal the soul.

Now to apply these principles to the discourses contained in the fourth Gospel, it is undeniable that the discourses of the Lord which are peculiar to St John's Gospel are, for the most part, very brief summaries of elaborate discussions and expositions in relation to central topics of faith. It is wholly out of the question that they can be literally complete reports of what was said. From the necessities of the case the Evangelist has condensed his narrative. He has not given, and he could not have given, consistently with the nature of this work, all the words which were actually spoken; and this being so, it follows that he cannot have given the exact words or only the words which were spoken. Compression involves adaptation of phraseology. And when once we realise the inevitable conditions of condensation, we find ourselves constrained to trust (in this case as in others) to the insight and power of him who selects, arranges, emphasizes words which are in his judgment best suited to convey the proportionate impression of discourses which he apprehends in their totality.

One or two illustrations will shew how a conversation is compressed in St John's narrative. A simple example is found in xii. 34. The question of the Jews turns upon the title "Son of man," which has not been recorded in the context. But it is easy to see how the previous references to the sufferings of Christ in connexion with the universality of His mission gave a natural opportunity for the use of it. The Evangelist however has noticed only the fundamental facts. The reader himself supplies what is wanting for the explanation of the abrupt use of names. The idea of "elevation" is the key to the thought, and that word St John has preserved in his record of what had gone before (*v.* 32): the title "Son of man" was already familiar, and he passes over the particular phrase in which it occurred.

In viii. 34 ff. there is a more complicated and still more instructive example of the compression of an argument. The recorded words do no more than give the extreme forms: the course which the spoken words must have followed can only be determined by careful thought, though it can be determined certainly. Men are sinners, and if sinners then slaves of sin. What, therefore, is the essential conception of slavery? It is an arbitrary, an unnatural, relation: the opposite of sonship, which expresses a permanent, an absolute connexion answering to the very constitution of things. The communication of sonship to the slave is consequently the establishment of his freedom. And in spiritual things He alone can communicate the gift to whom the dispensation of it has been committed. If, therefore, "the Son"—the one absolute Son—give freedom, they who receive it are free indeed. The imagery of a whole parable lies implicitly in the brief sentence.

In other cases "answers" of the Lord evidently point to detailed expressions of feeling or opinion with which the Evangelist was familiar, and which yet he has not detailed *e.g.* xii. 23, 35. At the close of his account of the public ministry of Christ he gives, without any connexion of place or time, a general summary of the Lord's judgment on His hearers (xii. 44—50). The passage is apparently a compendious record and not a literal transcription of a single speech.

And so elsewhere it is probable that where no historical connexion is given, words spoken at different times, but all converging on the illumination of one truth, may be brought together: *e.g.* x. (λόγοι, *v.* 19).

The force of these considerations is increased if, as seems to be surely established, most of the discourses recorded by St John were spoken in Aramaic. Whatever may have been the case in some other parts of Palestine, a large and miscellaneous crowd gathered at Jerusalem was able to understand what was spoken to them "in the Hebrew tongue" (Acts xxi. 40), and the favour of the multitude was conciliated by the use of it. The divine voice which St Paul heard was articulate to him in Hebrew words (Acts xxvi. 14). St Peter evidently spoke in an Aramaic dialect in the court of the high-priest, and the bystanders not only understood him but noticed his provincialism (Matt. xxvi. 73; Mark xiv. 70). Aramaic, it is said, in the Acts (i. 19), was the proper language of "the dwellers in Jerusalem" (τῇ διαλέκτῳ αὐτῶν). And again, the title with which Mary addressed the risen Lord was "Hebrew" (Ῥαββουνεί, John xx. 16). The phrase which the Lord quoted from the Psalms upon the cross was "Hebrew" (Mark xv. 34). These indications, though they are not absolutely conclusive, are yet convergent, and lead to the conclusion that at the Holy City and in intercourse with the inner circle of the disciples Christ used the vernacular Aramaic dialect. As claiming to be the fulfiller of the Law, He could hardly have done otherwise without offering violence to the religious instincts of the nation. If then He spoke in Aramaic on those occasions with which St John chiefly deals, the record of the Evangelist contains not only a compressed summary of what was said, but that also a summary in a translation[1].

It may be remarked yet further that the providential office of St John was to preserve the most universal aspect of Christ's teaching. His experience fitted him to recall and to present in due proportions thoughts which were not understood at first. In this way it is probable that his unique style was slowly fashioned as he pondered the Lord's words through long years, and delivered them to his disciples at Ephesus. And there is nothing arbitrary in the supposition that the Evangelist's style may have been deeply influenced by the mode in which Christ set forth the mysteries of His own Person. Style changes with subject, according to the capacity of the speaker; and St John's affinity with his Lord, which enabled him to reproduce the higher teaching, may reasonably be supposed to have enabled him also to preserve, as far as could be done, the characteristic form in which it was conveyed.

However this may have been, such a view of St John's record of the Lord's discourses as has been given derogates in no respect from their complete authority and truthfulness. A complete reproduction of the words spoken would have been as impossible as a complete reproduction of the details of a complicated scene. Even if it had been possible it would not have conveyed to us the right impression. An inspired record of words, like an inspired record of the outward circumstances of a life, must be an interpretation. The power of the prophet to enter into the divine thoughts is the measure of the veracity of his account.

Thus the question finally is not whether St John has used his own style and language in summarising the Lord's teaching, but whether he was capable of so entering into it as to choose the best possible method of reproducing its substance. It may or may not be the case that the particular words, in this sentence or that, are his own. We are only concerned to know whether, under the circumstances, these were the words fitted to gather into a brief space and to convey to us the meaning of the Lord. We may admit then that St John has recorded the Lord's discourses with "freedom." But freedom is exactly the reverse of arbitrariness, and the phrase in this connexion can only mean that the Evangelist, standing in absolute sympathy with the thoughts, has brought them within the compass of his record in the form which was truest to the idea[1].

These considerations seem to be amply sufficient to meet the objections which are urged against the general form

[1] It may be sufficient to add, without entering further into the subject, that the testimony of Josephus 'Antt.' XX. 11 2 is explicit as to the feeling with which Jews regarded Greek as a foreign language, and to the fact that the Jews of Jerusalem habitually spoke Aramaic ('c. Apion.' I. 9, μόνος αὐτὸς συνίην).

[1] In this connexion the notes which are given by the Evangelist in ii. 21, vii. 39, xii. 33, are of the greatest importance. If he had not kept strictly to the essence of what Christ said, he might easily have brought out in the saying itself the sense which he discovered in it at a later time.

of the discourses in St John. A more particular examination will shew now far the more special objections which are based upon their alleged monotony are valid.

2. St John, as we have seen, writes with the purpose of revealing to his readers the Person of the Lord, and shews Him to be "the Christ," and "the Son of God." As a natural consequence he chooses for his record those discourses which bear most directly upon his theme, and dwells on that side of those discourses which is most akin to it. It will be seen later that the Synoptists have preserved clear traces of this teaching, but it was not their object to follow it out or to dwell upon it predominantly. With St John it was otherwise. He wished to lead others to recognise Christ as what he had himself found Him to be. There is therefore in the teaching which he preserves an inevitable monotony up to a certain point. The fundamental truths of the Gospel as an object of faith are essentially simple. They do not, like questions of practice and morals, admit of varied illustration from life. Christ is Himself the sum of all, and St John brings together just those words in which on exceptional occasions (as it appears) He revealed Himself to adversaries and doubters and friends. For there is an indication that the discourses recorded by St John are not (so to speak) average examples of the Lord's popular teaching, but words called out by peculiar circumstances. Nothing in the fourth Gospel corresponds with the circumstances under which the Sermon on the Mount, or the great group of parables were spoken. On the other hand, the private discussions with Nicodemus and the woman of Samaria find no parallels in the other Gospels, and yet they evidently answer to conditions which must have arisen. The other discourses, with the exception of those in ch. vi., which offer some peculiar features, were all held at Jerusalem, the centre of the true and false theocratic life. And more than this: they were distinctively festival discourses, addressed to men whose religious feelings and opinions were moved by the circumstances of their meeting. On such occasions we may naturally look for special revelations. The festivals commemorated the crises of Jewish history; and a closer examination of the discourses shews that they had an intimate connexion with the ideas which the festivals represented. As long as the Jewish system remained, this teaching would be for the most part unnoticed or unintelligible. When the old was swept away, then it was possible, as the result of new conditions of religious growth, to apprehend the full significance of what had been said.

Yet further: while there is so far a "monotony" in the discourses of St John that the Lord, after the beginning of His public ministry, turns the thoughts of His hearers in each case to Himself, as the one centre of hope, yet the form in which this is done presents a large variety of details corresponding with the external circumstances under which the several discourses were held, and there is also a distinct progress in the revelation. The first point will be touched upon in the next section: the second becomes evident at once, if account be taken of the order of the successive utterances of the Lord, and of the limits of possible change in the variable element which they contain.

It is undoubtedly true that as we read St John's Gospel in the light of the Prologue we transfer the full teaching which that contains into all the later parts of the narrative, and that they derive their complete meaning from it. But if the discourses are examined strictly by themselves, it will be seen that they offer in succession fresh aspects of the Lord's Person and work: that the appearances of repetition are superficial: that each discourse, or rather each group of discourses, deals completely with a special topic. Thus in ch. v. the Son and the Jews are contrasted in their relation to God, and from this is traced the origin of unbelief. In ch. vi. the Son is shewn to be the Giver and the Support of life. In cc. vii., viii. He is the Teacher and the Deliverer: in cc. ix., x., the Founder of the new Society. The discourses of the eve of the Passion have, as will be seen afterwards, a character of their own.

3. There is, then, a clear advance and historical development in the self-revelation of Christ as presented by St John. There is also an intimate correspondence between the several dis-

courses and their external conditions. For the most part the discourses grew (so to speak) out of the circumstances by which they were occasioned. The festival discourses, for example, are coloured by the peculiar thoughts of the season. The idea of the Passover is conspicuous in ch. vi., that of the Feast of Tabernacles in cc. vii., viii., that of the Dedication in ch. x. The traits of connexion are often subtle and unemphasized, but they are unmistakable. There is a psychological harmony between the words and the hearers for the time being. Nothing less than a complete and careful analysis of the Gospel can bring home the force of this argument, but two illustrations will indicate the kind of details on which it rests. The scene by the well at Sychar illustrates one type of teaching (iv. 4—42): the discourse after the healing at Bethesda another (v. 19—47).

There can be no question as to the individuality of the discourse with the woman of Samaria. The scene, the style, the form of opinion are all characteristic. The well, the mountain (*v.* 20), the fertile corn-fields (*v.* 35), form a picture which every traveller recognises. The style of the conversation is equally life-like. The woman, with ready intelligence, enters into the enigmatic form of the Lord's sentences. She gives question for question, and, like Nicodemus, uses His imagery to suggest her own difficulties. At the same time, her confession keeps within the limits of her traditional faith. For her the Christ is a prophet. And it is easy to see how the fuller testimony of her countrymen unparalleled in the Gospels was based upon later teaching (*v.* 42), which their position enabled them to receive as the Jews could not have done.

The discourse in ch. v. is characteristic in other ways. It is the recorded beginning of Christ's prophetic teaching. He unfolds the nature of His work and of His Person in answer to the first accusations of the Jews before some authoritative body (see v. 19, note). It is not a popular discourse, but the outline of a systematic defence. It springs naturally out of the preceding act, and it appears to refer to the circumstances of the Feast. It is not so much an argument as a personal revelation. At the same time it offers an analysis of the religious crisis of the time. It discloses the relation in which Jesus stood to the Baptist (33—35), to Moses (46), to revelation generally (37 f.), to Judaism (39 f.). It deals, in other words, with just those topics which belong to the beginnings of the great controversy at Jerusalem[1].

One other illustration may be given to shew the inner harmony which underlies the progress of the self-revelation of the Lord as recorded by St John. Without reckoning the exceptional personal revelations to the woman of Samaria (iv. 26), and to the man born blind (ix. 37), the Lord reveals Himself seven times with the formula "I am," five times in His public ministry, and twice in the last discourses. It must be enough here to enumerate the titles. Their general connexion will be obvious.

(1)	vi. 35 ff.	*I am the Bread of life.*
	viii. 12.	*I am the Light of the world.*
	x. 7.	*I am the Door of the sheep.*
	x. 11.	*I am the good Shepherd.*
	xi. 25.	*I am the Resurrection and the Life.*
(2)	xiv. 6.	*I am the Way, and the Truth, and the Life.*
	xv. 1 ff.	*I am the true Vine.*

4. But it is said that the language attributed to the Baptist and that of the Evangelist himself are undistinguishable from that of the discourses of the Lord. What has been said already shews to what extent this must be true. St John

[1] It may be added also that the occasion and contents of the discourse are in complete agreement with the Synoptic narrative. In these no less than in St John the open hostility of the Jews starts from the alleged violation of the Sabbath (Matt. xii. 2; Mark ii. 27 f.); and they offer the following correspondences of thought with St John's record:

v. 14, Matt. xii. 45 (Luke xvii. 19).
vv. 19 f., Matt. xi. 27; Luke x. 22.
v. 20, Matt. iii. 17.
v. 22, Matt. xxviii. 18.
v. 23, Luke x. 16 (Matt. x. 40).
vv. 22, 27, Matt. xvi. 27.
v. 29, Matt. xxv. 32, 46.
v. 30, Matt. xxvi. 39.
v. 39, Luke xxiv. 27 (Matt. xxvi. 54).
v. 43, Matt. xxiv. 5.
v. 44, Matt. xiii. 14 ff., xviii. 1 ff.
v. 46, Luke xvi. 31.

deals with one aspect of the truth, and uses the same general forms of speech to present the different elements which contribute to its fulness. But beneath this superficial resemblance there are still preserved the characteristic traits of the teaching of each speaker. There is, as has been pointed out, a clear progress in the Lord's revelation of Himself. The words of the Baptist, coming at the commencement of Christ's work, keep strictly within the limits suggested by the Old Testament. What he says spontaneously of Christ is summed up in the two figures of the "Lamb" and "the Bridegroom," which together give a comprehensive view of the suffering and joy, the redemptive and the completive work of Messiah under the prophetic imagery. Both figures appear again in the Apocalypse; but it is very significant that they do not occur in the Lord's teaching in the fourth Gospel or in St John's epistles. His specific testimony, again, *this is the Son of God* (i. 34), is no more than the assertion in his own person of that which the Synoptists relate as a divine message accompanying the Baptism (Matt. iii. 17, and parallels). And it is worthy of notice, that that which he was before prepared to recognise in Christ (i. 33) was the fulness of a prophetic office which the other Evangelists record him to have proclaimed as ready to be accomplished (Matt. iii. 11)[1].

Even in style too, it may be added, the language assigned to the Baptist has its peculiarities. The short answers, *I am not; No; I am not the Christ* (i. 20 f.), are unlike anything else in St John, no less than the answer in the words of prophecy (i. 23). Comp. iii. 29, note.

The correspondences of expression between the language attributed to the Lord in the Gospel and the Epistles of St John are more extensive and more important. They are given in the following table:

John iii. 11. *We speak that we do know, and testify that we have seen.*	1 John i. 1—3. *That which was from the beginning ... which we have seen with our eyes ... for the life was manifested, and we have seen it, and bear witness (testify) ... that which we have seen and heard declare we unto you.*
v. 32 ff. *There is another that beareth witness of me; and I know that the witness which he witnesseth of me is true ... I receive not witness from man ...*	v. 9 ff. *If we receive the witness of men, the witness of God is greater: for this is the witness of God which he hath testified of his Son...*
v. 24. *He that heareth my word ... is passed from death unto life.*	iii. 14. *We know that we have passed from death unto life, because we love the brethren.*
v. 38. *... ye have not his word abiding in you.*	ii. 14. *... the word of God abideth in you.*
vi. 56. *He that eateth my flesh and drinketh my blood, dwelleth in me, and I in him.* Comp. xiv. 17.	iv. 15. *Whosoever shall confess that Jesus is the Son of God, God dwelleth in him, and he in God.* Comp. *v.* 16; iii. 24.
viii. 29. *I do always those things that please him.*	iii. 22. *...because we...do those things that are pleasing in his sight.*
viii. 44. *He (the devil) was a murderer from the beginning.*	iii. 8. *... the devil sinneth from the beginning.* Comp. iii. 12, 15.
viii. 46. *Which of you convinceth me of sin?*	iii. 5. *... in him is no sin.*
viii. 47. *He that is of God heareth God's words: ye therefore hear them not, because ye are not of God.*	iv. 6. *We are of God: he that knoweth God heareth us; he that is not of God heareth not us.*
x. 15. *I lay down my life for the sheep.*	iii. 16. *... he laid down his life for us.*

[1] The passage, iii. 31—36, is to be attributed to the Evangelist and not to the Baptist. See note.

John xii. 35. *He that walketh in darkness knoweth not whither he goeth.*	1 John ii. 11. *...he that hateth his brother ... walketh in darkness, and knoweth not whither he goeth ...*
xiii. 34. *A new commandment I give unto you, That ye love one another; as I have loved you, that ye also love one another.*	iii. 23. *This is his commandment, That we should believe in the name of his Son Jesus Christ, and love one another, as he gave us commandment.* iv. 11. *Beloved, if God so loved us, we ought also to love one another.* Comp. ii. 7 ff., iii. 11, 16.
xv. 10. *If ye keep my commandments, ye shall abide in my love.*	iv. 16. *God is love, and he that dwelleth in love dwelleth in God, and God in him.*
xv. 18. *If the world hate you ...*	iii. 13. *Marvel not, my brethren, if the world hate you.*
xvi. 24. *Ask and ye shall receive, that your joy may be fulfilled.*	i. 4. *These things write we unto you, that your joy may be fulfilled.* Comp. 2 John 12.
xvi. 33. *I have overcome the world.*	v. 4 f. *This is the victory that overcometh* (ἡ νικήσασα) *the world, even our faith.*

Compare also the following passages:

iv. 22 f.	v. 20.
vi. 69 (πεπιστ. κ. ἐγνώκ.).	iv. 16.
viii. 35.	ii. 17.

In addition to these phrases there are single terms, more or less characteristic, which are common to the Lord's discourses and the Epistle: "true" (ἀληθινός), "murderer," "to ask" (ἐρωτᾷν), "to receive witness," "the Son;" and the frequent use of the final particle (ἵνα) is found in both (xv. 12, xvii. 3; compared with iii. 23).

An examination of the parallels can leave little doubt that the passages in the Gospel are the originals on which the others are moulded. The phrases in the Gospel have a definite historic connexion: they belong to circumstances which explain them. The phrases in the Epistle are in part generalisations, and in part interpretations of the earlier language in view of Christ's completed work and of the experience of the Christian Church. This is true of the whole doctrinal relation of the two books, as will be seen later on. The Epistle presupposes the Gospel, and if St John had already through many years communicated his account of the Lord's teaching orally to his circle of disciples, it is easy to see how the allusions would be intelligible to the readers of the Epistle if it preceded the publication of the Gospel. If the Epistle was written after the Gospel was published, the use of the Lord's words in what is practically a commentary upon them can cause no difficulty.

The Prologue to the Gospel offers the real parallel to this Epistle. In this there is the same application of the teaching of the Gospel from the point of view of the advanced Christian society. The exposition of the truth assumes the facts and words which follow in the narrative, while it deals with them freely and in the Apostle's own phraseology.

This will appear from the following table:

v. 1. *In the beginning was the Word.*	i. 1. *That which was from the beginning ... concerning the word of life ...*
... the Word was with God (ἦν πρός). Contrast xvii. 5.	i. 2. *... the eternal life, which was with the Father* (ἦν πρός).
... the Word was God.	v. 20.

v. 9. *The true light ... was coming into the world.*	ii. 8. *The darkness is past, and the true light now shineth.*
v. 5. *The light shineth in the darkness.* Comp. xii. 35.	
v. 12. *As many as received him, to them gave he right to become children of God ...*	iii. 1. *Behold, what manner of love the Father hath given unto us, that we should be called children of God, and such we are* (καὶ ἐσμέν).
— *... to them that believe on his name.*	v. 13. *... you that believe on the name of the Son of God.*
v. 13. *Which were born ... of God* (ἐγενν. ἐκ).	v. i. *Whosoever believeth that Jesus is the Christ is born of God* (γεγένν. ἐκ).
v. 14. *The Word became flesh.*	iv. 2. *Every spirit that confesseth that Jesus Christ is come in the flesh is of God.*
— *... we beheld his glory.*	i. 1. *That which we beheld.*
v. 18. *No man hath seen* (ἑώρακεν) *God at any time.* Comp. vi. 46.	iv. 12. *No man hath beheld* (τεθέαται) *God at any time.* Comp. v. 20.

These parallels, which are found in eighteen verses only, offer, as it will be felt, a close affinity to the Epistle not in language only, but in formulated thought. And further, the Prologue and the Epistle stand in the same relation of dependence to the discourses. In this respect it is interesting to compare what is said in the Prologue on "the Life," and "the Light," and "the Truth," with the passages in the Lord's words from which the Evangelist draws his teaching.

(1) The Life. Comp. v. 26, xi. 25, xiv. 6.

(2) The Light. Comp. viii. 12, ix. 5, xii. 46.

(3) The Truth. Comp. viii. 32, xiv. 6.

It will be remembered that the cardinal phrases "the Word," "born (begotten) of God," are not found in the discourses of the Lord[1].

Elsewhere in the Gospel there are in the narrative natural echoes, so to speak, of words of the Lord (ii. 4 compared with vii. 30, *his hour was not yet come*); and correspondences which belong to the repetition of corresponding circumstances (iv. 12 || viii. 53; iii. 2 || ix. 33), or to the stress laid upon some central truth (vii. 28 || ix. 29 f. || xix. 9). Still the conclusion remains unshaken that the discourses of the Lord have a marked character of their own, that they are the source of St John's own teaching, that they perfectly fit in with the conditions under which they are said to have been delivered.

7. *The Last Discourses.*

But it may be said that the last discourses, in which there may have been some compression yet not such as to alter their general form, offer peculiar difficulties: that they are disconnected, indefinite, and full of repetitions: that it is most improbable that thoughts so loosely bound together could have been accurately preserved in the memory for half a century: that we must therefore suppose that the Evangelist here at least has allowed his own reflections to be mingled freely with his distant recollections of what the Lord said.

It may be at once admitted that these discourses offer a unique problem. They belong to an occasion to which there could be no parallel, and it may be expected that at such a crisis the Lord would speak much which "the disciples understood not at the time," over which still some of them would untiringly reflect. Our modes of thought again follow a logical sequence; Hebrew modes of thought follow a moral sequence. With us, who trust to the instruction of books, the power of memory is almost untrained: a Jewish disciple was disciplined to retain the spoken words of his master.

Thus we have to inquire primarily

[1] The remarks made upon the Prologue generally, including the brief comment on the Baptist's testimony (i. 16—18), apply also to the two comments of the Evangelist upon the conversation with "the teacher of Israel" (iii. 16—21), and on the Baptist's last testimony (iii. 31—36). See notes.

whether the teaching really suits the occasion? whether there is a discernible coherence and progress in the discourses? If these questions are answered in the affirmative, it will be easy to understand how a sympathetic hearer, trained as a Jew would be trained, should bear them about with him till his experience of the life of the Church illuminated their meaning, when the promised Paraclete "taught him all things and brought all things to his remembrance which Christ had spoken."

If the discourses are taken as a whole it will be found that their main contents offer several peculiarities. Three topics are specially conspicuous: the mission of the Paraclete, the departure and the coming of Christ, the Church and the world. And generally a marked stress is laid throughout upon the moral aspects of the Faith.

It is scarcely necessary to point out the fitness of such topics for instruction at such a time. If the Lord was what the Apostles announced Him to be it is scarcely conceivable that He should not have prepared them by teaching of this kind before His departure, in order that they might be fitted to stand against the antagonism of the Jewish Church, and to mould the spiritual revolution which they would have to face. The book of the Acts—"the Gospel of the Holy Spirit"—is in part a commentary upon these last words.

At the same time it is most important to observe that the ideas are not made definite by exact limitations. The teaching gains its full meaning from the later history, but the facts of the later history have not modified it. The promises and warnings remain in their typical forms. At first they could not have been intelligible in their full bearing. The fall of Jerusalem at length placed them in their proper light, and then they were recorded.

The moral impress of the last discourses is clear throughout. They are a sermon in the chamber to the Apostles, completing the Sermon on the Mount to the multitudes. In this section only Christ speaks of His "commandments" (ἐντολαί, ἐντολή, xiv. 15, 21, xv. 10, xiii. 34, xv. 12; comp. xv. 14, 17), and by the use of the word claims for them a divine authority. The commandments are summed up in one, "to love one another." The love of Christian for Christian is at once the pattern and the foundation of the true relation of man to man. And as the doctrine of love springs out of Christ's self-sacrifice (xv. 13, xiii. 34), so is it peculiar to these discourses in the Gospel. The time had come when it could be grasped under the influence of the events which were to follow.

The successive forms under which the principle of love is inculcated illustrate the kind of progress which is found throughout the chapters (*e.g.* xiii. 34, xv. 12). The three following passages will indicate what is meant:

xiv. 15. *If ye love me, ye will keep* (τηρήσετε) *my commandments.*

xiv. 21. *He that hath my commandments, and keepeth them, he it is that loveth me: and he that loveth me shall be loved of my Father, and I will love him, and will manifest myself to him.*

xv. 10. *If ye keep my commandments, ye shall abide in my love; even as I have kept my Father's commandments, and abide in his love.*

At a first reading it might be easy to miss the advance from obedience resting on love to progressive knowledge, and then to a divine certainty of life. When the relation of the three connected texts is seen, it is difficult not to feel that what appears to be repetition is a vital movement.

A similar progress is noticeable in the four chief passages which describe the work of the Paraclete:

xiv. 16, 17.

I will ask the Father, and
he shall give you another Paraclete,
that he may be with you for ever;
even the Spirit of truth,
whom the world cannot receive...

xiv. 26.

The Paraclete, even the Holy Spirit,
whom the Father will send in my name,
he shall teach you all things, and
bring to your remembrance all things that I said unto you.

xv. 26.

When the Paraclete is come
whom I will send unto you from the Father

even the Spirit of truth,
which proceedeth from the Father,
he shall bear witness of me.

xvi. 7 ff.

If I go not away, the Paraclete will not come to you;
but if I go, I will send him unto you.
And he, when he is come, will convict the world...
...when he is come, even the Spirit of truth,
he will guide you into all the truth...

Step by step the relation of the Paraclete to Christ is made clear: (1) *I will ask, another Paraclete;* (2) *the Father will send in my name;* (3) *I will send;* (4) *if I go I will send him.* And again His work is defined more and more exactly: (1) *be with you for ever;* (2) *teach all things...that I said unto you;* (3) *bear witness of me;* (4) *convict the world, guide into all the truth.* Such subtle correspondences are equally far from design and accident: they belong to the fulness of life.

The teaching on the relation of the Church to the world, which is peculiar to this section, moves forward no less plainly. In xiv. 17, 22 ff., it is shewn that the world is destitute of that sympathy with the divine Spirit which is the necessary condition of the reception of revelation. Afterwards the hatred of the world is foretold as natural (xv. 18 ff.); and then this hatred is followed out to its consequences (xvi. 1 ff.). Yet, on the other hand, it is promised that the Spirit shall convict the world; and at last Christ declares that He Himself has already conquered the world (xvi. 33).

The same general law of progress applies to the notices of Christ's departure and return in cc. xiv., xvi. In the first passage the central thought is "I come;" attention is concentrated on what Christ will do (xiv. 3, 18, 23). In the second the thought is rather of the relation of the disciples to Him (xvi. 16, 22).

These examples indicate at least the existence of a real coherence and development of thought in the discourses. It is unquestionably difficult to follow out the development of thought in detail. In the notes an endeavour has been made to do this. Here it must be sufficient to give a brief outline of the general course which the addresses take. These form two groups, the discourses in the chamber (xiii. 31—xiv.) and on the way (xv., xvi.). The predominant thoughts in the first are those of separation from Christ as He had been hitherto known, and of sorrow in separation: in the second, of realised union with Christ in some new fashion, and of victory after conflict.

I. The Discourses in the Chamber (xiii. 31—xiv.).

1. *Separation, its necessity and issue* (xiii. 31—38).

(α) Victory, departure, the new Society (31—35).

(β) The discipline of separation (St Peter) (36—38).

2. *Christ and the Father* (xiv. 1—11).

(α) The goal and purpose of departure (1—4).

(β) The way to the divine (St Thomas) (5—7).

(γ) The knowledge of the Father (St Philip) (8—11).

3. *Christ and the disciples* (xiv. 12—21).

(α) The disciples continue Christ's work (12—14).

(β) He still works for them (15—17).

(γ) He comes to them Himself (18—21).

4. *The law and the progress of revelation* (22—31).

(α) The conditions of revelation (St Jude) (22—24).

(β) The mode of revelation (25—27).

(γ) Christ's work perfected by His return (28—31).

The teaching springs from the facts of the actual position, and then deals with successive difficulties which it occasions.

II. The Discourses on the Way (xv., xvi.).

1. *The living union* (xv. 1—10).

(α) The fact of union (1, 2).

(β) The conditions of union (3—6).

(γ) The blessings of union (7—10).

2. *The issues of union: the disciple and Christ* (11—16).

(α) Christ's joy comes from sacrifice (12, 13).

(β) The disciple's connexion with Christ is by love (14, 15).

(γ) It is stable as resting on His choice (*v.* 16).

3. *The issues of union: the disciples and the world* (17—27).

(α) Love of Christ calls out hatred of the world (17—21).

(β) With this inexcusable hatred the disciples must contend (22—27).

4. *The world and the Paraclete* (xvi. 1—11).

(α) The last issues of hatred (1—4).

(β) The necessity of separation (4—7).

(γ) The conviction of the world (8—11).

5. *The Paraclete and the disciples* (12—15).

(α) He completes Christ's work (12, 13),

(β) and glorifies Christ (14, 15).

6. *Sorrow turned to joy* (16—24).

(α) A new relation (16, 17).

(β) Sorrow the condition of joy (19—22).

(γ) Joy fulfilled (23, 24).

7. *Victory at last* (25—33).

(α) A summary (25—28).

(β) A confession of faith (29, 30).

(γ) Warning and assurance (31—33).

The form of the discourse is changed. The Lord reveals uninterruptedly the new truths, till the close, when the disciples again speak no longer separately, but, as it were, with a general voice. The awe of the midnight walk has fallen upon them.

It is not of course affirmed that this view of the development of the discourses is exhaustive or final; but at least it is sufficient to shew that they are bound together naturally, and that the dependence of the parts is such as could be easily apprehended and retained by those who listened. There is novelty under apparent sameness: there is variety under apparent repetition: there is a spiritual connexion underneath the apparently fragmentary sentences. This is all that it is necessary to shew. As far as we can venture to judge the words befit the occasion: they form a whole harmonious in its separate parts: they are not coloured by later experiences: they might easily have been preserved by the disciple who was in closest sympathy with the Lord.

III. Characteristics of the Gospel.

1. *Relation to the Old Testament.*

St John recognises in his narrative the divine preparation for the advent of Christ which was made among the nations. Such a discipline is involved in the view which he gives of the general action of the Word before His Incarnation (i. 5), and particularly in his affirmation of His universal working (i. 9). Nor was this discipline wholly without immediate effect. At the time of the advent Christ had *other sheep*, which were not of the Jewish *fold* (x. 16). There were *children of God scattered abroad* (xi. 52): some who had yielded themselves to the guidance of the divine light which had been given to them, and who were eager to welcome its fuller manifestation (iii. 20 ff.): citizens of a kingdom of truth waiting for their king (xviii. 37).

But while these broader aspects of the divine counsel find a place in the fourth Gospel, St John brings out with especial force that the discipline of Israel was the true preparation for the Messiah, though Judaism had been perverted into a system antagonistic to Christianity, and Christ had been rejected by His own people. If he affirms more distinctly than the other apostolic writers, from the circumstances of his position, that the Jews had proved to be ignorant of the contents and scope of the revelation which had been committed to them (v. 37 ff.), and of the nature of the Lord whom they professed to worship with jealous reverence (xvi. 3, vii. 28, viii. 19, 54 f., xv. 21); if he affirms that their proud confidence in the literal interpretation of the facts of their providential history was mistaken and delusive (v. 37; contrast Gen. xxxii. 30; Exod. xx. 18 ff., xxiv. 10; Deut. iv. 12, 36, v. 4, 22:—vi.

32, cf. Ps. lxxviii. 24); he affirms no less distinctly that the old Scriptures did point to Christ, and that the history was instinct with a divine purpose. This appears by (*a*) his general recognition of the peculiar privileges of the Jews; (*b*) his interpretation of types; (*c*) his application of prophecies; and particularly by his treatment of the Messianic expectations of the people.

(*a*) The words of the Prologue, *He came to His own home* (τὰ ἴδια), *and His own people* (οἱ ἴδιοι) *received Him not* (i. 11, note), place beyond question the position which the Evangelist assigned to his countrymen in the divine order. They were in a peculiar sense the subjects of the Christ. In this sense Christ claimed their allegiance, and sovereign authority in the centre of their religious life. His greeting to Nathanael was: *Behold an Israelite indeed* (i. 47): His command in the temple at His first visit: *Make not my Father's house a house of merchandise* (ii. 16). In answer to the questionings of the Samaritan woman, who placed the tradition of her fathers side by side with that of the Jews, He asserted the exceptional knowledge and the unique office of His people: *we worship that which we know* (iv. 22), and *salvation*—the promised salvation (ἡ σωτηρία)—*is from* (ἐκ) *the Jews* (iv. 22), two phrases which mark at once the progressive unfolding of the divine truth (Heb. i. 1), and the office of the old dispensation to furnish the medium out of which the new should spring. In the beginning of His conflict with official Judaism, Christ assigns to the Scriptures their proper function towards Himself (v. 39, 46 f.). From this point "the Jews" take up a position of antagonism, and their privileges perish in their hands (comp. pp. lxxxv., lxxxvi.).

(*b*) It is a significant fact that three and three only of the old saints, Abraham, Moses, and Isaiah, are mentioned by the Lord or by the Evangelist in connexion with Messiah. These three cover and represent the three successive periods of the training of the people: so subtle and so complete are the harmonies which underlie the surface of the text. Christ claimed for Himself testimonies from the patriarchal, the theocratic, and the monarchical stages of the life of Israel.

viii. 56. *Your father Abraham rejoiced to see*—in the effort to see (ἵνα ἴδῃ)—*my day: and he saw it, and was glad.*

The point of the reference lies in the view which it gives of the first typical example of faith as reaching forward to a distant fulfilment. It was not stationary, but progressive. In that onward strain lies the secret of the Old Testament.

The second reference to the patriarchal history in the Gospel of St John is the complement of this effort after the remote. Abraham looked onwards to that which was not yet revealed: Jacob rested in his present covenant with God. This aspect of faith also is recognised by the Lord.

i. 51. *Verily, verily, I say unto you, ye shall see heaven opened, and the angels of God ascending and descending upon the Son of man.*

The desire of Abraham was fulfilled in the universal sovereignty of Christ: the vision of Jacob was fulfilled in the abiding presence of Christ. A greater than Abraham brought freedom for all through the Truth: a greater than Jacob opened a well whose waters sprang up within the believer unto eternal life.

The references to Moses are not less pregnant. It is shewn that just as Christ was the object to whom the patriarch looked in the future and in the present, so He was the object in regard of whom all the discipline of the law was shaped. Jesus said to the leaders of the Jews: *Had ye believed* (*Did ye believe*) *Moses, ye would have believed* (*would believe*) *me, for he wrote of me* (v. 46).

This thought is brought out by references both to details of the Law and also to the circumstances which accompanied the promulgation of the Law.

Twice the Lord defended Himself from the charge of violating the Sabbath. On each occasion He laid open a principle which was involved in this institution.

v. 17. *My Father worketh even until now, and I work.*

The cessation from common earthly work was not an end, but a condition for something higher: it was not a rest *from* work, but *for* work (see note *ad loc.*).

vii. 22. *For this cause*—by which I have been moved in my healing—*hath Moses given you circumcision* (*not that it is of Moses, but of the fathers), and on the sabbath ye circumcise a man.*

The Sabbath, therefore, was subordinate to the restoration of the fulness of the divine covenant. It was made to give way to acts by which men were "made whole."

The one reference to the idea of the Passover is equally significant. *These things*, the Evangelist writes in his record of the crucifixion, *were done that the Scripture should be fulfilled, A bone of him shall not be broken* (xix. 36, note). The words come like an after-thought. They are left without definite application, and yet in that single phrase, by which the Lord is identified as the true Paschal Lamb, the meaning of the old sacrifices is made clear. "The Lamb of God" is revealed as the one offering to whom all offerings pointed.

The two interpretations of facts in the history of the Exodus which St John has given are even more remarkable than these lights thrown upon the Mosaic discipline and the Mosaic ritual. The first is the interpretation of the brazen serpent: the second the interpretation of the manna.

Jesus said to Nicodemus: *As Moses lifted up the serpent in the wilderness, even so must the Son of man be lifted up* (iii. 14). The Jews said: *Our fathers did eat the manna in the wilderness; as it is written, He gave them bread from heaven to eat. Jesus therefore said unto them, Verily, verily, I say unto you, Moses gave you not that bread from heaven; but my Father giveth you the true bread from heaven ... I am the bread of life* ... (vi. 31 ff.). Thus the most significant deliverance from the effects of sin, and the most striking gift of divine Providence recorded in the Pentateuch, are both placed in direct connexion with Christ. In each case that which was temporal is treated as a figure of that which is eternal. Great depths of thought are opened. The life-long wanderings of the Jews are shewn to be an image of all life[1].

(*c*) St John's dealing with the later teaching of the prophets, the interpreters of the kingdom, is of the same character. He does not deal so much with external details as with the inner life of prophecy. He presents Christ as being at once the Temple (ii. 19), and the King (xii. 13). He makes it clear that the new dispensation towards which the prophets worked was one essentially of spiritual blessing. The sense of complete devotion to God, of the union of man with God in Christ, of the gift of the Spirit through Him, were the thoughts in which he found the stamp of their inspiration. Thus it is that he has preserved the words in which the Lord gives us the prophetic description of the Messianic times: *They shall all be taught of God* (vi. 45); and those again in which He gathers up the whole doctrine of Scripture on this head: *If any man thirst, let him come unto me and drink. He that believeth on me, as the scripture hath said, out of his belly shall flow rivers of living water* (vii. 37 f., note); and those in which He shewed that the conception of the union of God and man was not foreign to the Old Testament, when it was said even of unjust judges, *Ye are gods*, because the Word of God, in which was a divine energy, came to them (x. 34 f., note).

On the other hand St John has recorded how the Lord recognised in the hostile unbelief of the Jews the spirit of their fathers, *who hated* the Lord's Anointed *without a cause* (xv. 25), and pointed out how the treachery of Judas had its counterpart in that of Ahitophel, of whom it was written, *He that eateth bread with me hath lifted up his heel against me* (xiii. 18).

There is the same mysterious depth, the same recognition of a spiritual undercurrent in common life, in the references which the Evangelist himself makes to the later books of Scripture. Once at the beginning of the Gospel he tells how the disciples were enabled to see fulfilled in the Lord the words of the suffering prophet, *The zeal of thine house shall consume me* (ii. 17); and at the close of the account of the public ministry he points out how the unbelief of the Jews, the most tragic of all mysteries, had been foreshadowed of old. *These things*, he writes, *said Isaiah, because—because*, not *when* (ὅτι not ὅτε, see note)—*he saw* Christ's *glory, and spake of Him* in the most terrible description of the unbelief and blindness of Israel (xii. 37 ff.[1]).

[1] Compare also the notes on vii. 37, viii. 12, and above, p. vii.

[1] The following table of the prophecies quoted

It seems to be impossible to study such passages without feeling that the writer of the fourth Gospel is penetrated throughout—more penetrated perhaps than any other writer of the New Testament—with the spirit of the Old. The interpretations which he gives and records, naturally and without explanation or enforcement, witness to a method of dealing with the old Scriptures which is of wide application. He brings them all into connexion with Christ. He guides his readers to their abiding meaning, *which cannot be broken;* he warns the student against trusting to the letter, while he assures him that no fragment of the teaching of *the Word of God* is without its use. And in doing this he shews also how the scope of revelation grows with the growth of men. Without the basis of the Old Testament, without the fullest acceptance of the unchanging divinity of the Old Testament, the Gospel of St John is an insoluble riddle.

2. *The unfolding of the Messianic idea.*

The history of the Gospel of St John is, as has been seen, the history of the development of faith and unbelief, of faith and unbelief in Christ's Person. It is therefore under another aspect the history of the gradual unfolding of the true Messianic idea in conflict with popular expectations. On the one side are the hopes and the preoccupations of the Jews: on the other side are the progressive revelations of the Lord. And there is nothing which more convincingly marks the narrative as a transcript from life than the clearness with which this struggle is displayed. A summary outline of the Gospel from this point of view will probably place the facts in a distinct light.

The opening scene reveals the contrasted elements of expectation as they had been called into activity by the preaching of the Baptist (i. 19 ff.). The Baptist's words and testimonies (i. 29, 33, 36) were fitted to check the popular zeal, and at the same time to quicken the faith of those who were ready to receive and to follow that greater One who should come after according to the divine promise (i. 29 f., 36). So it came to pass that some of his disciples found in Jesus, to whom he mysteriously pointed, the fulfilment of the old promises and of their present aspirations (i. 35—42). Others at once attached themselves to the new Teacher (*Rabbi*, i. 38); and He was acknowledged as *Messiah* (i. 41); *the Son of God, and King of Israel* (i. 49). The "sign" which followed confirmed the personal faith of these first followers (ii. 11); but so far there was nothing to shew how the titles which had been at least silently accepted were to be realised.

The cleansing of the temple was in this respect decisive. Messiah offered Himself in His Father's house to His own people, and they failed to understand, or rather they misunderstood, the signs which He gave them. As a consequence, He *did not commit himself unto them, because He knew all men; and... what was in man* (ii. 23 ff.). The origin of this misunderstanding is shewn in the imperfect confession of Nicodemus (iii. 2 ff.), and in the complaint of the disciples of the Baptist (iii. 26). On the other hand, the testimony of Christ and the testimony of the Baptist set the real issue before men, as the Evangelist shews in his comments on the words. The Messiah of those whom the Evangelist characterizes as "the Jews" had no place in the work of Jesus; and His work as Messiah had no place in their hearts.

Such was the situation at Jerusalem. It was otherwise in Samaria. There Jesus

in the Gospel will suggest further illustrations:

Prophecies,

(1) Design marked (ἵνα πληρ. Comp. xviii. 9).
- (α) By the Evangelist.
  - xii. 38.
  - [xii. 40, ὅτι εἶπεν Ἡσ.]
  - xix. 24.
  - — 36.
  - [xix. 37, ἑτέρα γρ. λέγει.]
- (β) By Christ.
  - xiii. 18.
  - xv. 25.
  - [xvii. 12.]

(2) Coincidence marked (καθώς ἐστι γεγρ.)
- (α) By the Evangelist.
  - ii. 17.
  - xii. 14 f.
- (β) By Christ.
  - vi. 45.
  - (Comp. vii. 38.)
  - x. 34.

Compare also above, pp. xiii. f.

could openly announce Himself to be the Christ, inasmuch as the claim was rightly though imperfectly understood (iv. 25 f.); and the confession of the Samaritans who had sought His fuller teaching shewed how far they were from resting in any exclusive or temporal hopes (iv. 42, *the Saviour of the world*, according to the true reading).

The next visit to Jerusalem (ch. v.) gave occasion for a fundamental exposition of the nature and work of the Lord, and of the manifold witness to Him, side by side with an analysis of the causes of Jewish unbelief. The later history is the practical working out of the principles embodied in this discourse.

The first decisive division between the followers of Christ was in Galilee. There superficial faith was more prevalent and more eager. The "multitude" wished to precipitate the issue according to their own ideas (vi. 14 f.). In answer to this attempt Christ turned the minds of those who came to Him by most startling imagery from things outward, and foreshadowed His own violent death as the condition of that personal union of the believer with Himself, to bring about which was the end of His work. So He drove many from Him (vi. 60), while He called out a completer confession of faith from the twelve (vi. 69). Words which had been used before (ch. i.), have now a wholly different meaning. To believe in Christ now was to accept with utter faith the necessity of complete self-surrender to Him who had finally rejected the homage of force.

The issue at Jerusalem was brought about more slowly. The interval between ch. v. and ch. vii. was evidently filled with many questionings (vii. 3 f., 11 f.); and when Jesus appeared at Jerusalem He created divisions among the multitude (vii. 30 f., 43). Some thought that He must be the Christ from His works (vii. 31), and from His teaching (vii. 26, 37 ff., 46 ff.). They even questioned whether possibly their leaders had reached the same conclusion (vii. 26, ἔγνωσαν). But they did not see that He satisfied the prophetic tests which they applied to Messiah (vii. 27, 42, 52).

In the midst of this uncertainty the rulers openly declared themselves (vii. 32, 48); and under their influence the mass of the people fell away when Christ set aside their peculiar claims and purposes (viii. 33, 58 f.). He still however continued to lay open more truths as to Himself, and revealed Himself to the outcast of the synagogue as "the Son of man" (ix. 35, note). Divisions spread further (ix. 16, x. 19); and at last the request was plainly put: *If thou art the Christ, tell us plainly* (x. 24). Again, the result of the answer was a more bitter hostility (x. 39), and wider faith (x. 42).

The end came with the raising of Lazarus. This was preceded by the confession of Martha (xi. 27), and followed by the counsel of Caiaphas (xi. 47 ff.). There was no longer any reason why Christ should shrink from receiving the homage of His followers. He accepted openly the title of King when He entered the Holy City to die there (xii. 13 ff.); and the public ministry closed with the questioning of the people as to "the Son of man," who seemed to have usurped the place of Him who should reign for ever (xii. 34).

Such a history of the embodiment of an idea, an office, carries with it its own verification. The conflict and complexity of opinion, the growth of character, the decisive touches of personal and social traits, which it reflects, stamp it not only as a transcript from life, but also as an interpretation of life by one who had felt what he records. The whole history moves along with a continuous progress. Scene follows scene without repetition and without anticipation. The revelation of doctrine is intimately connected with a natural sequence of events, and is not given in an abstract form. Thoughts are revealed, met, defined from point to point. We not only see individualised characters, but we see the characters change under intelligible influences as the narrative goes forward. And this is all done in the narrowest limits and in a writing of transparent simplicity. Art can shew no parallel. No one, it may be confidently affirmed, who had not lived through the vicissitudes of feeling, which are indicated often in the lightest manner, could have realised by imagination transient and complicated modes of thought which had no existence in the second century.

It did not fall within the scope of the Synoptists to trace out the unfolding of the Messianic idea in the same way; but the teaching upon the subject which they record is perfectly harmonious with that of St John.

The Synoptists and St John agree in describing (α) the universal expectation at the time of the Advent (Matt. iii. 5, and parallels; John i. 41, 19, 20, iii. 26, iv. 25); (β) the signs by which the Christ should be heralded (Matt. xvi. 1; John vi. 30 f.); the preparation by Elijah (Matt. xi. 14, xvii. 10; John i. 21), and (none the less) the suddenness of His appearance (Matt. xxiv. 26 f.; John vii. 27); (γ) the readiness of some to welcome Him even as He came (Luke ii. 25 ff., Symeon; 36, Anna; John i. 45, Philip; 49, Nathanael).

They agree likewise in recording that the Lord pointed to His death under figures from an early time (Matt. ix. 15, and parallels; John iii. 14); and that open hostility to Him began in consequence of His claims to deal authoritatively with the traditional law of the Sabbath (Matt. xii. 13 ff.; John v. 16); and of His assumption of divine attributes (Mark ii. 6; John v. 18).

There is, however, one difference in this far-reaching agreement. All the Evangelists alike recognise the prophetic, royal, and redemptive aspects of Christ's work; but St John passes over the special reference to the Davidic type, summed up in each of the two Synoptists by the title "Son of David" (yet see vii. 42; Rev. v. 5, xxii. 16)[1]. The explanation is obvious. The national aspect of Messiah's work passed away when "the Jews" rejected Him. It had no longer in itself any permanent significance. The Kingdom of Truth (xviii. 37) was the eternal antitype of Israel. The Gospel was a message for the world. The fall of Jerusalem proclaimed the fact; and that catastrophe which interpreted the earlier experience of the Apostle made the recurrence of like experience impossible.

Thus the fall of Jerusalem determined the work of St John with regard to the conception of the Lord's office. The apprehension of the absolute office of Messiah corresponds with the apprehension of Christianity as essentially universal. These truths St John established from Christ's own teaching; and so by his record the title of "the Son of God" gained its full interpretation (xx. 31; 1 John iv. 15, v. 13, 20).

St John shews in a word how Christ and the Gospel of Christ satisfied the hopes and destinies of Israel, though both were fatally at variance with the dominant Judaism. And in doing this he fulfilled a part which answered to his characteristic position. The Judaism in which the Lord lived and the early Apostles worked, and the Judaism which was consolidated after the fall of Jerusalem, represented two distinct principles, though the latter was, in some sense, the natural issue of the former. The one was the last stage in the providential preparation for Christianity: the other was the most formidable rival to Christianity.

3. *The Characters.*

The gradual self-revelation of Christ which is recorded in St John's Gospel carries with it of necessity the revelation of the characters of the men among whom He moved. This Gospel is therefore far richer in distinct personal types of unbelief and faith than the others.

Attention has been called already (pp. viii. ff.) to the characteristic traits by which the classes of people who appear in the history are distinguished—"the multitude," "the Jews," "the Pharisees," "the high-priests." In them the broad outlines of the nature of unbelief are drawn. In the events of the Passion three chief actors offer in individual types the blindness, and the weakness, and the selfishness, which are the springs of hostility to Christ. Blindness—the blindness which will not see—is consummated in the high-priest: weakness in the irresolute governor: selfishness in the traitor apostle. The Jew, the heathen, the disciple become apostate, form a representative group of enemies of the Lord.

These men form a fertile study. All that St John records of Caiaphas is contained in a single sentence; and yet in that one short speech the whole soul of

[1] The title occurs twice only in the Epistles, but in important passages: Rom. i. 3; 2 Tim. ii. 8.

the man is laid open. The Council in timid irresolution expressed their fear lest "the Romans might come and take away both their place and nation if Christ were let alone." They had petrified their dispensation into a place and a nation, and they were alarmed when their idol was endangered. But Caiaphas saw his occasion in their terror. For him Jesus was a victim by whom they could appease the suspicion of their conquerors: *Ye know nothing at all, nor consider that it is expedient for you that one man should die for the people, and that the whole nation perish not* (xi. 49 f.). The victim was innocent, but the life of one could not be weighed against the safety of a society. Nay rather it was, as his words imply, a happy chance that they could seem to vindicate their loyalty while they gratified their hatred. To this the divine hierarchy had come at last. Abraham offered his son to God in obedience to the Father whom he trusted: Caiaphas gave the Christ to Cæsar in obedience to the policy which had substituted the seen for the unseen.

Caiaphas had lost the power of seeing the Truth: Pilate had lost the power of holding it. There is a sharp contrast between the clear, resolute purpose of the priest, and the doubtful, wavering answers of the governor. The judge shews his contempt for the accusers, but the accusers are stronger than he. It is in vain that he tries one expedient after another to satisfy the unjust passion of his suitors. He examines the charge of evil-doing and pronounces it groundless; but he lacks courage to pronounce an unpopular acquittal. He seeks to move compassion by exhibiting Jesus scourged and mocked and yet guiltless; and the chief-priests defeat him by the cry, *Crucify, Crucify* (xix. 6). He hears His claim to be a "King not of this world" and "the Son of God," and is "the more afraid;" but his hesitation is removed by an argument of which he feels the present power: *If thou let this man go, thou art not Cæsar's friend* (xix. 12). The fear of disgrace prevailed over the conviction of justice, over the impression of awe, over the pride of the Roman. The Jews completed their apostacy when they cried: *We have no king but Cæsar* (xix. 15); and Pilate, unconvinced, baffled, overborne, delivered to them their true King to be crucified, firm only in this, that he would not change the title which he had written in scorn, and yet as an unconscious prophet.

Caiaphas misinterpreted the divine covenant which he represented: Pilate was faithless to the spirit of the authority with which he was lawfully invested: Judas perverted the very teaching of Christ Himself. If once we regard Judas as one who looked to Christ for selfish ends, even his thoughts become intelligible. He was bound to his Master not for what He was, but for what he thought that he would obtain through Him. Others, like the sons of Zebedee, spoke out of the fulness of their hearts, and their mistaken ambition was purified; but Judas would not expose his fancies to reproof: St Peter was called Satan—an adversary—but Judas was a devil, a perverter of that which is holy and true. He set up self as his standard, and by an easy delusion he came to forget that there could be any other. Even at the last he seems to have fancied that he could force the manifestation of Christ's power by placing Him in the hands of His enemies (vi. 70, xviii. 6, notes). He obeys the command to "do quickly what he did," as if he were ministering to his Master's service. He stands by in the garden when the soldiers went back and fell to the ground, waiting, as it were, for the revelation of Messiah in His Majesty. Then came the end. He knew the sovereignty of Christ, and he saw Him go to death. St John says nothing of what followed; but there can be no situation more overwhelmingly tragic than that in which he shews the traitor for the last time standing (εἱστήκει) with those who came to take Jesus.

The types of faith in the fourth Gospel are no less distinct and representative. It is indeed to St John that we owe almost all that we know of the individual character of the disciples. St Peter, it is true, stands out with the same bold features in all the Evangelists. St Matthew and St Mark have preserved one striking anecdote of the sons of Zebedee. St Luke gives some traits of those who were near the Lord in His Infancy, of Zacchæus, of Martha and Mary. But we learn only from St John to trace the workings of faith in Nathanael, and Nicodemus, and Andrew, and Philip, and Thomas, and "the disciple whom Jesus loved;" in the woman of Samaria, and in Mary Magdalene. As in the case of Caiaphas, Pilate and Judas, a few words and acts lay open the souls of all these in the light of Christ's presence.

Of St John it is not necessary to speak again. His whole nature, his mode of thought, his style of speech, pass by a continuous reflection into the nature, the thought, the style, of the Master for whom he waited. In the others there is a personality more marked because more limited. To regard them only from one point of view, in Nicodemus and the woman of Samaria we can trace the beginnings of faith struggling through the prejudice of learning and the prejudice of ignorance. In St Philip and St Thomas we can see the growth of faith overcoming the hindrances of hesitation and despondency. In St Peter and St Mary Magdalene we can see the activity of faith chastened and elevated.

The contrast between Nicodemus and the woman of Samaria, the two to whom Christ, according to the narrative of St John, first unfolds the mysteries of His kingdom, cannot fail to be noticed. A rabbi stands side by side with a woman who was not even qualified in popular opinion to be a scholar: a Jew with a Samaritan: a dignified member of the Council with a fickle, impulsive, villager. The circumstances of the discourses are not less different. The one is held in Jerusalem, the other almost under the shadow of the schismatical temple in Gerizim: the one in the house by night, the other in the daylight by the well-side. Christ is sought in the one case; in the other He asks first that so He may give afterwards. The discourses themselves open out distinct views of the kingdom. To Nicodemus Christ speaks of a new birth, of spiritual influence witnessed by spiritual life, of the elevation of the Son of man in whom earth and heaven were united: to the Samaritan He speaks of the water of life which should satisfy a thirst assumed to be real, of a worship in spirit and truth, of Himself as the Christ who should teach all things.

But with all this difference there was one thing common to the Jewish ruler and to the Samaritan woman. In both there was the true germ of faith. It was quickened in the one by the miracles which Jesus did (iii. 2); in the other by His presence. But both were drawn to Him and rested in Him. Both expressed their difficulties, half seizing, half missing His figurative language. Both found that which they needed to bring them into a living union with God. The pretensions of superior knowledge and discernment were cast down. The suspicions of rude jealousy were dispelled. The revelation of a suffering Redeemer scattered the proud fancies of the master of Israel: the revelation of a heavenly Father raised the conscience-stricken woman to new hope. Even after the Crucifixion Nicodemus, "who came by night at first," openly testified his love for Christ; and the Samaritan at once, forgetful of all else, hastened to bring her countrymen to Him whom she had found.

Here we see the beginning of faith: in St Philip and in St Thomas we see something of the growth of faith. It is an old tradition (Clem. Alex. 'Strom.' III. 4, § 25) that St Philip was the disciple who asked the Lord that he might first go and bury his father, and received the stern reply, "Follow thou me, and let the dead bury their dead." Whether this be true or not, it falls in with what St John tells us of him. He appears to hang back, to calculate, to rest on others. "Jesus," we read, "findeth Philip" (i. 43). He had not himself come to Jesus, though the words imply that he was ready to welcome, or even waiting for, the call which was first spoken to him. So again, when the Lord saw the multitude in the wilderness, it was to Philip He addressed the question, to "prove him," "Whence shall we buy bread, that these may eat?" (vi. 5 ff.). And even then he could only estimate the extent of the want. He had no suggestion as to how it must be met. But if his was a slow and cautious and hesitating faith, it was diffusive. He had no sooner been strengthened by the words of Christ than he in turn found Nathanael. "We have found," he saith, "Him of whom Moses in the Law and the prophets wrote" (i. 45). He appealed, as we must believe, to the witness of their common search in the Scriptures in times gone by, and his only answer to his friend's doubt—the truest answer to doubt at all times—was simply "Come and see." Yet his own eyes were holden too in part. Even at the last he could say, "Lord, shew us the Father, and it sufficeth us" (xiv. 8). But he said this in such a spirit that he received the answer which for him and for us gives faith an object on which it can rest for ever: "Jesus saith unto him, Have I been so long time with you, and yet hast thou not known me, Philip? he that hath seen me hath seen the Father" (xiv. 9 f.).

Philip believed without confidence. Thomas believed without hope. The whole character of Thomas is written in the first sentence which we hear him speak: "Let us also go, that we may die with him" (xi. 16). He could love Christ even to the last, though he saw nothing but suffering in following Him. He knew not whither He went; how could he know the way? (xiv. 5). But even so, he could keep close to Him: one step was enough, though that was towards the dark. No voice of others could move him to believe that which of all he wished most. The ten might tell him that the Lord was risen, but he could not lightly accept a joy beyond all that for which he had looked. "Except I shall see in His hands the print of the nails, and put my finger into the print of the nails, and thrust my hand into His side, I will not believe" (xx. 24 ff.). But when the very test which he had laid down was offered, the thought of proof was lost in the presence of Christ. He saw at once what had not yet been seen. The most complete devotion found the most fervent expression in those last words of faith, "My Lord, and my God" (xx. 27 f.).

In this way disciples were led on little by little to know the Master in whom they trusted. Often they failed through want of enthusiasm or want of insight. Some there were also who failed by excess of zeal. Mary Magdalene, when the blindness of sorrow was removed, would have clung to the Lord whom she had again found, lest again He should be taken from her. She would have kept Him as she had known Him. She would have set aside the lesson that it was good that He should go away. Then came those words which at once satisfied and exalted her affection, "Go unto my brethren, and say to them, I ascend unto my Father and your Father, and my God and your God" (xx. 15 ff.). She, the tender, loving woman, is made the messenger of this new Gospel: she is first charged to declare the truth in which her own passionate desire was transfigured: she who would have chained down heaven to earth is commissioned to proclaim that earth is raised to heaven.

Something of the same kind may be noticed in the history of St Peter. Unlike Philip he is confident, because he knows the strength of his love: unlike Thomas he is hopeful, because he knows whom he loves. But his confidence suggests the mode of his action: his hope fashions the form of its fulfilment. Peter saith unto Jesus, "Thou shalt never wash my feet," and then with a swift reaction, "Lord, not my feet only, but also my hands and my head" (xiii. 6 ff.). If he hears of a necessary separation, he asks, "Lord, why cannot I follow thee now? I will lay down my life for thy sake" (xiii. 36 ff.). He draws his sword in the garden (xviii. 10 f.).: he presses into the courtyard of the high-priest (xviii. 16 ff.). He dares all and doubts nothing. But when the trial came he was vanquished by a woman. He had chosen his own part, and the bitterness of utter defeat placed him for ever at the feet of the Saviour whom he had denied. He knew, though it was with grief, the meaning of the last triple charge: he knew, though it was through falls, the meaning of the answer to his last question: *If I will that he tarry till I come, what is that to thee? Follow thou me* (xxi. 22).

There is one other character common to all four Evangelists which cannot be altogether passed by. St John's notices of the Baptist have little externally in common with the Synoptic narratives, but they reveal a character which answers to the stern figure of the preacher of repentance. His last testimony to Christ (iii. 27—30) completely corresponds with the position of one who is looking forward to a future dimly seen. The herald must fulfil his herald's work to the end.

His glory is to accept the necessity of decline (iii. 30).

It is needless to add any comments to this rapid enumeration of the characters who people the brief narrative of St John. The vividness, the vigour, the life, of their portraitures cannot be mistaken or gainsaid. The different persons shew themselves. They come forward and then pass out of sight as living men, and not like characters in a legendary history. They have an office not only separately but in combination. They witness, in other words, not only to the exactness but also to the spiritual completeness of the record.

This fulness of characteristic life in the fourth Gospel is practically decisive as to its apostolic authorship. Those who are familiar with the Christian literature of the second century will know how inconceivable it is that any Christian teacher could have imagined or presented as the author of the fourth Gospel has done the generation in which the Lord moved. The hopes, the passions, the rivalries, the opinions, by which His contemporaries were swayed had passed away, or become embodied in new shapes. A great dramatist could scarcely have called them back in such narrow limits as the record allows. Direct knowledge illuminated by experience and insight, which are the human conditions of the historian's inspiration, offers the only adequate explanation of the dramatic power of the Gospel.

4. *Symbolism.*

It will be evident from the illustrations which have been already given that there is a subtle and yet unmistakable harmony within the different parts of St John's Gospel; that each narrative which it contains is to be considered not only in itself, but also in relation to the others with which it is connected: that fact is interpreted by thought and thought by fact: that the historical unity of the book is completed by a moral and spiritual unity. Under one aspect the lessons of the Old Testament are illuminated by Christ's presence. Under another aspect the characters which move about the Lord offer typical representations of faith and unbelief in their trials and issues. And in all this there is not the least violence done to the outward history, but there is simply a practical recognition of the necessary fulness which there was in the Life, in the Words, and in the Works of the Son of man.

St John himself is careful to explain that all which he saw when he wrote his Gospel was not clear to the disciples at once. The words of the Lord to St Peter had a wider application than to any one detail: *What I do thou knowest not now, but thou shalt come to know* (γνώσῃ) *hereafter* (xiii. 7). The Resurrection was the first great help to this advance in knowledge (ii. 22, xii. 16); and the meaning of the Resurrection itself was extended when Christ raised a new Temple in place of the old after the fall of Jerusalem, and His Church was finally established (ii. 19, note).

There can then be no cause for surprise if St John, looking back over the whole range of his experience, selects just those parts of Christ's ministry for his record which fit together with the most complete mutual correspondences. Such a selection would not be so much the result of a conscious design as of a spiritual intuition. His Gospel was in the truest sense of the word a "prophecy," a revelation of the eternal under the forms of time.

In this respect the miracles of the Lord which he has related form an instructive illustration of his method. Taken together they are a revelation of Christ, of "His glory." A very brief examination of them will be sufficient to establish by this one example that principle of a spiritual meaning in the plan and details of the Gospel which I have called the symbolism of St John.

The two characteristic names which miracles bear in St John's Gospel mark distinctly the place which he assigns to them in relation to the general course of the divine government. They are *signs* (ii. 11, note) and they are *works* (v. 20, note). They are "signs" so far as they lead men to look beneath the surface for some deeper revelations of the method and will of God, to watch for the action of that spiritual ministry—"the angels ascending and descending upon the Son of man"—which belongs to the new dispensation. They are "works" so far as they take their place among the ordinary phenomena of life (v. 17), differing from them not because they involve any more real manifestation of divine energy but simply because they are suited to arrest attention. They are "signs" in short, for they make men feel the mysteries which underlie the visible order. They are "works," for they make them feel that this spiritual value is the attribute of all life.

St John has recorded in detail seven miracles of Christ's ministry and one of the risen Christ. Their general connexion with the structure of his Gospel (see p. xlii.) will appear from the following table:

1. *The water turned to wine*, ii. 1—11.
   The nobleman's son healed, iv. 46—54.
2. *The paralytic at Bethesda*, v. 1—15.
   The feeding of the five thousand, vi. 1—15.
   The walking on the sea, vi. 16—21.
   The restoration of the man born blind, ix. 1—12.
   The raising of Lazarus, xi. 17—44.
3. *The miraculous draught of fishes*, xxi. 1—12.

Of these the first two give the fundamental character of the Gospel, its nature and its condition: the next five are signs of the manifold working of Christ, as the restoration, the support, the guidance, the light and the life of men: the last is the figure of all Christian labour to the end of time.

The first two miracles, which the Evangelist significantly connects together as wrought at Cana, seem at first sight to have nothing in common. They are given without any comment except the record of their effects (ii. 11, iv. 53). But these two brief notes give the clue to the interpretation of the signs. They shew from the beginning that Christianity is the ennobling of all life, and that its blessings are appropriated only by faith.

The change of the water into wine has always been rightly felt to be a true symbol of Christ's whole work. The point of the second miracle at Cana lies in the discipline of faith. The request to Christ (iv. 47) was itself a confession of faith, yet that faith was not accepted as it was. It was necessary at once to raise faith to the unseen. Whatever outward signs may be granted they do but point to something beyond. At the commencement of His ministry Christ declared in act what He repeated afterwards at its close: *Blessed are they that see not, and yet believe.*

The four chief miracles which are connected with Christ's conflict form the basis on each occasion of discourses in which their lessons are enforced. Here there can be no doubt of the symbolism: it is declared unmistakably that the works are "signs," charged with a divine purpose. In the case of the paralytic suffering is definitely connected with sin (v. 14). Christ removes the malady spontaneously and on a Sabbath. Such action is revealed to be after the pattern of God's action: *My Father worketh even until now, and I work* (v. 17). God seeks without ceasing to repair by tenderness and chastisement the ravages which sin has made in His creation, and to lead it onward to its consummation.

In the feeding of the five thousand the teaching is carried a step further. Man needs not restoration only but support. He has wants as well as defects: he has to struggle against material difficulties. Christ reveals Himself as sufficient to supply every craving of man, and as sovereign over the forces of nature: *I am the bread of life. He that cometh to me shall never hunger; and he that believeth on me shall never thirst*... (vi. 35). *What then if ye should behold the Son of man ascending where He was before? It is the spirit that quickeneth* (vi. 62 f.). So the works are invested with a permanent prophetic power.

Man needs support and he needs enlightenment also; for we must go forward, and in one sense we are "blind from our birth." This is the next lesson of the miracles which St John records. Before the blind regained his sight at Siloam Christ said: *When* (ὅταν) *I am in the world, I am the light of the world* (ix. 5). Sight was given to the obedient disciple. The Pharisees refused to read the sign which conflicted with their prejudices. And He then added: *For judgment I came into this world, that they which see not may see; and that they which see may be made blind* (ix. 39).

But even if failings be remedied, if wants be satisfied, if light be given, there yet remains one more terrible enemy: death, physical death, comes at last. Here also Christ gave a sign of His power. In the very agony of apparent loss He said: *He that believeth in me, even though he die, shall live; and whosoever liveth and believeth in me shall never die* (xi. 25 f.). And so far as any single fact offered to the senses can confirm the truth, the raising of Lazarus shewed that there is a Life sovereign over physical life, a Life victorious over death.

The sequence of these "signs," these living parables of Christ's action, these embodiments of truth in deed, can hardly be mistaken. Nor is the meaning of the one miracle of the risen Lord less obvious. The narrative is the figure of the history of the Church. The long night passes in what seems to be vain effort. Christ stands in the dawn upon the shore, and at first His disciples know Him not. Even so in due time He is revealed in blessing; and men are charged afresh to use the new gifts which He has enabled them to gather.

It would be easy to follow out these correspondences and connexions of the different parts of St John's Gospel in other directions and in fuller detail; but enough has been said to direct attention to the subject. If the principle be acknowledged the application will follow.

IV. Relation of the Gospel to the other Apostolic Writings.

1. *The Relation of the Fourth Gospel to the Synoptists.*

It is impossible for any one to turn directly from the first three Gospels to the Fourth without feeling that he has been brought in the later record to a new aspect of the Person and Work of Christ, to a new phase of Christian thought, to a new era in the history of the Christian Church. In this there is a halo of divine glory always about the Saviour even in scenes of outward humiliation: the truths of the Gospel are presented in their relations to the broadest speculations of men: the society of believers, of "the brethren" (xx. 17, xxi. 23), stands out with a clear supremacy above the world. As we compare the pictures more carefully, and in this view they are two and not four, we find that the general difference between the Gospels which is thus obvious reaches throughout their whole composition. The Synoptists and St John differ in the general impression which they convey as to the duration, the scene, the form, the substance of the Lord's teaching. They differ also in regard to the circumstances under which they were composed. The latter difference furnishes the final explanation of the former. And here it may be well to make one remark on the total effect which these differences produce upon the student of the New Testament. At first they are not realised in their true weight and value. The conception of the Lord which is brought to the study of any Gospel includes elements which are derived from all. Contrasts are already reconciled. So it was with the early Church. No teacher found the Fourth Gospel at variance with the other three, though they recognised its complementary character. Then follows in many cases an exaggerated estimate of the importance of the differences which are apprehended upon a careful comparison of the books. Fresh results impress us more in proportion as they are unexpected, and at variance with our preconceived opinions. Still later perhaps that comprehensive conception of the subject of the Gospel is regained by labour and thought, from which, as a tradition, the study began; and it is felt that a true and intelligible unity underlies external differences, which are now viewed in their proper position with regard to the records and to the subject.

Before considering the differences or the correspondences of the Synoptists and St John, it is necessary to apprehend distinctly the fragmentary character of the documents which we have to compare. The narrative of St John, and the narratives of the Synoptists, are alike partial, and alike recognise a large area of facts with which they do not deal.

1. *Limited range of St John's Gospel.* The Gospel of St John forms, as we have seen, a complete whole in relation to "its purpose;" but as an external history

it is obviously most incomplete. It is a Gospel and not a Biography, an account of facts and words which have a permanent and decisive bearing upon the salvation of the world, and not a representation of a life simply from a human point of sight. The other Gospels, as based upon the popular teaching of the Apostles, include more details of directly human interest, but these also are Gospels and not Biographies. All the Gospels are alike in this: they contain in different shapes what was necessary to convey the message of redemption to the first age and to all ages in the unchangeable record of facts. Their completeness is moral and spiritual and not historical. The striking Jewish legend as to the Manna was fulfilled in Christ. He was to each true believer, from the absolute completeness of His Person, that which each desired; and the Evangelists have preserved for the society typical records of apostolic experience.

The fragmentariness of St John's record is shewn conclusively by his notice of periods of teaching of undefined length of which he relates no more than their occurrence:

iii. 22. *Jesus and his disciples came into the land of Judæa; and there he tarried* (διέτριβεν) *with them and baptized* ... (iv. 1—3) *making and baptizing more disciples than John.* Comp. iv. 54.

vii. 1. *After these things Jesus walked* (περιεπάτει) *in Galilee; for he would not walk in Judæa, because the Jews sought to kill him.*

x. 40—42. *And he went away again beyond Jordan, into the place where John was at first baptizing; and there he abode* (the reading is uncertain, ἔμεινεν or ἔμενεν) ... *and many believed on him there.*

xi. 54. *Jesus therefore walked no more openly among the Jews, but departed thence into the country near to the wilderness, into a city called Ephraim; and there he abode* (ἔμεινεν) *with the disciples.*

The last passage seems to describe a period of retirement, but the others imply action and continuous labour in Judæa, Galilee and Peræa, of which St John has preserved no details. He passed these over (such is the obvious explanation) because they did not contribute materials necessary for the fulfilment of his special purpose. And so again the two days teaching in Samaria, at which he was present, is represented only by the confession which it called out (iv. 42).

The same conclusion follows from the frequent general notices of "signs" and "works" which find no special recital:

ii. 23. *Many believed on his name beholding his signs which he did* (ἐποίει). Comp. iv. 45, *The Galilæans received him, having seen all the things that he did* (ὅσα ἐποίησεν) *in Jerusalem at the feast;* and iii. 2, *No man can do these signs that thou doest, except God be with him.*

vi. 2. *And a great multitude followed him, because they beheld the signs which he did* (ἐποίει) *on them that were sick.*

vii. 3. *His brethren therefore said unto him, Depart hence and go into Judæa, that thy disciples also may behold thy works which thou doest.*

vii. 31. *But of the multitude many believed on him; and they said, When the Christ shall come, will he do more signs than those which this man hath done* (ἐποίησεν)*?*

x. 32. *Jesus answered them, Many good works have I shewed you from the Father; for which of those works do ye stone me?*

xi. 47. *The chief priests ... said, What do we? for this man doeth many signs.*

xii. 37. *Though he had done so many signs before them, yet they believed not on him.*

xx. 30. *Many other signs therefore did Jesus in the presence of the disciples which are not written in this book ...*

xxi. 25. *And there are also many other things which Jesus did, the which, if they should be written every one, I suppose that even the world itself would not contain the books that should be written.*

A consideration of what the Lord's Life was, as it has been made known to us, shews that this last summary statement is only a natural expression of the sense of that which we must feel to be its infinite fulness. And the other passages open glimpses of a variety and energy of action of which St John's narrative itself gives no completer view. Of "all that the Lord did" at Jerusalem, which moved the faith alike of "the teacher of Israel," and of "the Galilæans," he has noticed only the cleansing of the temple. Of the healings of the sick in Galilee, he has recorded only one. He tells us nothing of "the disciples in Judæa" (vii. 3), who might desire to see works such as Christ wrought in other places. Of the "many good works" shewn at Jerusalem (x. 32), two only are given at length. A fair appreciation of these facts will leave no doubt that St John omitted far more events than he related out of those which he knew. The Gospel of the Church, which it was his office to write, might be expected to take shape in special festival discourses at the centre of the Old Faith. He deals with aspects of Christ's Life and teaching which were not clear at first, but became clear afterwards. And in doing this he leaves ample room for other accounts widely differing in character from his own.

One other point deserves notice in this connexion. The abrupt breaks in St John's narrative shew that he was guided by something different from a purely historic aim in his work. The simple phrase *after these things* (iii. 22, v. 1, vi. 1) is used to mark a decided interval in time and place; and if the interpretation of x. 22 which has been adopted be correct, the transition in ix. 1 is not less sharp[1].

2. *Limited range of the Synoptists.* The Synoptic Gospels, no less than St John, imply much more than they record. The commencement of the Galilæan ministry in their narratives not only leaves room for, but points to, earlier work.

Matt. iv. 12. *Now when he heard that John was delivered up, he withdrew* (ἀνεχώρησεν) *into Galilee.*

Mark i. 14. *Now after that John was delivered up, Jesus came into Galilee preaching the Gospel of God.*

The words have no force unless it be supposed that the Evangelists referred to an earlier ministry in Judæa which is deliberately passed over (comp. John ii., iii.). Nor is there anything in Luke iv. 14 f. opposed to this view. The summary which is there given may include any period of time, and specifies a wide area of place (comp. *v.* 23).

Again, the Sermon on the Mount involves some previous teaching in Judæa in which the character of the Scribes and Pharisees had been revealed. It is most unlikely that their "righteousness" would have been denounced (Matt. v. 20) unless the Lord had met them in the seat of their power and proved them.

Still more instructive is the great episode in St Luke (Luke ix. 51—xviii. 14, see note), which shews how much material there was at hand of which no use was made in the oral Gospel of the Apostles. At the same time it is of interest to observe that this peculiar section has in one incident (x. 38 ff.) a point of connexion with St John, and the notices of the Samaritans which it contains (x. 33, xvii. 16, [ix. 52]) offer in some respects a parallel to the fourth chapter of his Gospel.

3. *The differences of the Synoptists and St John.* Taking account of these characteristics of the Gospels we can form a juster estimate of their differences. The Synoptists and St John differ at first sight (as has been already said) as to the time, the scene, the form, and the substance of the Lord's teaching.

If we had the Synoptic Gospels alone it might be supposed that the Lord's ministry was completed in a single year: that it was confined to Galilee till the visit to Jerusalem at the Passover by which it was terminated: that it was directed in the main to the simple peasantry, and found expression in parables, and proverbs, and clear, short discourses, which reach the heart of a multitude: that it was a lofty and yet practical exposition of the Law, by One who spake as man to men. But if we look at St John all is changed. In that we see that the public ministry of Christ opened as well as closed with a Paschal journey: that between these journeys there intervened another Passover and several visits to Jerusalem: that He frequently used modes of speech which were dark and mysterious, not from the imagery in which they were wrapped, but from the thoughts to which they were applied: that at the outset He claimed in the Holy City the highest prerogatives of Messiah, and at later

[1] It may be added that St John nowhere notices *scribes* (viii. 3 is an interpolation), *taxgatherers* ("publicans"), *lepers*, or *demoniacs*.

times constantly provoked the anger of His opponents by the assumption of what they felt to be divine authority. And beyond all these differences of arrangement and manner, the first three Gospels and the Fourth have very few facts in common. They meet only once (at the Feeding of the five thousand), before the last scenes of the Passion and Resurrection. And in this common section they are distinguished by signal differences. To mention only two of the most conspicuous: the Synoptists do not notice the raising of Lazarus, which marks a crisis in the narrative of St John; and on the other hand, St John does not mention the Institution of the Holy Eucharist, which is given in detail by each of the Synoptists (see notes on cc. xi., xiii.).

A student of the Gospels can have no wish to underrate the significance of phenomena like these, which must powerfully affect his view of the full meaning both of the documents and of their subject. But he will interrogate them, and not at once assume that they have only to witness to discrepancies. From such questioning one result is gained at once. It is seen (to omit the question of time for the present) that differences of form and substance correspond to differences of persons and place. On the one side there is the discourse at Nazareth, the Sermon on the Mount, the groups of parables, words first spoken to the Galilæan multitudes with the authority of the Great Teacher, and then continued afterwards when they came up to the Feast full of strange expectations, which were stimulated by the Triumphal Entry. On the other side there are the personal communings with individual souls, with "the Master of Israel" and the woman of Samaria, unveilings of the thoughts of faithless cavillers, who had been trained in the subtleties of the Law, and rested on the glories of their worship: glimpses of a spiritual order opened at last to loving disciples, in which they were prepared to find, even through sorrow, the accomplishment of their early hopes. On the one side there is the Gospel of "the common people who heard gladly:" on the other side the Gospel of such as felt the deeper necessities and difficulties of faith. The lessons which appealed to broad sympathies are supplemented by those which deal with varieties of personal trial and growth. The cycle of missionary teaching is completed by the cycle of internal teaching: the first experience of the whole band of Apostles by the mature experience of their latest survivor.

These general remarks are supported by numerous minute details which indicate that the Synoptists do in fact recognise an early Judæan ministry and teaching similar to that of St John, and that St John recognises important work in Galilee and teaching similar to that of the Synoptists.

(α) *The scene of the Lord's teaching.* The general description of the Lord's following as including multitudes "*from Judæa and Jerusalem*" (Matt. iv. 25; comp. Mark iii. 7 f.) cannot be pressed as proving that He had Himself worked there. Similar language is used in connexion with the Baptist (Matt. iii. 5). But the reading of St Luke iv. 44, *he was preaching in the synagogues of Judæa* (for *Galilee*), which is supported by very strong MSS. authority (ℵBCLQR *Memph.*), taken in connexion with Luke v. 17, may fairly be urged in favour of such a view. Indeed the feeling of the people of Jerusalem on the Lord's last visit is scarcely intelligible unless they had grown familiar with Him on former visits. So again the well-known words of the lamentation over Jerusalem, *How often would I have gathered thy children...and thou wouldest not* (Matt. xxiii. 37 ff.), scarcely admit any other sense than that Christ had personally on many occasions sought to attach the inhabitants to Himself, as now when the issue was practically decided. The visit to Martha and Mary (Luke x. 38 ff.) suggests previous acquaintance with them, and so probably previous residences in the neighbourhood of Jerusalem (John xi. 1 ff.). The circumstances connected with the preparation for the last visit (Matt. xxi. 2 f., xxvi. 17 ff., and parallels), point to the same conclusion. Compare Acts x. 37, 39. On the other hand St John when he notices a brief sojourn of the Lord and His first disciples at Capernaum (ii. 12), seems to imply a longer abode there at another time; and in a later passage he records words which shew that Galilee was the ordinary scene of Christ's ministry (vii. 3). It might indeed have been plausibly argued from these words that when they were spoken He had not wrought any conspicuous works in Judæa.

(β) *The manner of the Lord's teaching.* It has been already shewn that the form of the Lord's teaching could not but depend upon the occasion on which it was delivered; and there is no scene in St John which answers to those under which the Sermon on the Mount, or the chief groups of parables were delivered; and conversely there are no scenes in the Synoptists like those with Nicodemus and the woman of Samaria. The discourses at Jerusalem recorded by the Synoptists were spoken after Christ had openly accepted the position of Messiah by His triumphal entry: those recorded by St John belong to earlier times, when He was gradually leading His hearers to grasp the truth of faith in Him. As the circumstances become more like in character there is a growing resemblance in style. In John x., xii., we have the implicit parables of the Sheepfold, the Good Shepherd, the Grain of Corn. In Matt. xi. 25 ff.; Luke x. 21 ff., there is a thanksgiving spoken in regard to the disciples' work which in character is not unlike the last discourses.

(γ) *The duration of the Lord's teaching.* The data for determining the length of the Lord's ministry are singularly few. The time of its commencement is approximately fixed by the different elements given by St Luke (iii. 1), as marking the Call of the Baptist. But there is nothing in the Gospels to connect its close with any particular year of Pilate's procuratorship. Pilate was recalled in A.D. 36, and Herod was banished in A.D. 39. They may therefore have met at Jerusalem in any year during Pilate's term of office. Caiaphas retained his office till the end of Pilate's procuratorship. The date of the death of Annas is not known, but he lived to old age. So far there is a wide margin of uncertainty; and this can only be removed by the assumption that the Gospels supply a complete chronology of the Ministry, for the earliest tradition is both late and conflicting. Here however we are left to probability. The Synoptists appear to include the events of their narrative in a single year; but it is very difficult to bring the development of faith and unbelief to which they witness, the missions of the Twelve and of the Seventy, and the different circuits of the Lord, within so brief a space[1]. St John, on the other hand, notices three Passovers, but he gives no clear intimation that he notices every Passover which occurred in the course of the Lord's work. In such a case the fragmentariness of the records is a conclusive answer to the supposed discrepancy.

4. *The coincidences of the Synoptists and St John.* So far we have dwelt upon the differences between the Synoptists and St John. Their correspondences are less obvious and impressive, but they are scarcely less important.

The common incidents with which they deal are the following:

1. *The Baptism of John* (St John adds the mention of *the Levites*, i. 19: the questions, i. 20 ff.: the place, *Bethany*, i. 28: the *abiding* of the Spirit on Christ, i. 32 f.: the after testimony to Christ, i. 26 ff.).

2. *The Feeding of the five thousand* (St John notices the time, *the Passover was near*, vi. 4: the persons, *Philip* and *Andrew*, vi. 5, 8: the command to collect the fragments, *v.* 12: the issue of the miracle and the retirement of Jesus, *v.* 14 f.).

3. *The Walking on the Sea* (St John mentions the distance, vi. 19: the feeling of the disciples, *v.* 21: the result, *ib.*).

4. *The Anointing at Bethany* (St John mentions the time, xii. 1, *six days before the Passover:* the persons, *Mary*, *v.* 3 (comp. Matt. xxvi. 7; Mark xiv. 3), and *Judas*, *vv.* 4, 6: the full details of the action, *v.* 3).

5. *The Triumphal Entry* (St John mentions the time, *on the next day*, xii. 12: the reference to Lazarus, *v.* 18: the judgment of the Pharisees, *v.* 19).

6. *The Last Supper* (St John records the feet-washing, xiii. 2 ff.: the question of St John, *v.* 23: the ignorance of the Apostles, *v.* 28: the discourses in the chamber and on the way[2]).

[1] The reading and interpretation of Luke vi. 1 (δευτεροπρώτῳ) is too uncertain to be pressed. Yet see note on Mark ii. 23.

[2] On the apparent difference between the

7. *The Betrayal.* See notes on c. xviii.

8. *The Trial.* Ib.

9. *The Crucifixion.* Ib.

10. *The Burial* (St John notices the action of Nicodemus, xix. 39: the garden, *v.* 41).

11. *The Resurrection.* See note on c. xx.

Not to enter in detail upon an examination of the parallels, it may be said that in each case St John adds details which appear to mark his actual experience; and also that the facts in all their completeness form a natural part of both narratives. They do not appear either in the Synoptists or in St John as if they were borrowed from an alien source.

The passages in which St John implies an acquaintance with incidents recorded by the Synoptists are more numerous.

i. 19 ff.	The general effect of John's preaching (Matt. iii. 5, &c.).
— 32 ff.	The circumstances of the Lord's Baptism (Matt. iii. 16 f.).
— 40.	Simon Peter is well known.
— 46.	Nazareth the early home of Christ (Matt. ii. 23, &c.).
ii. 12.	Capernaum the later residence of Christ.
—	The family of Christ. Comp. vi. 42, vii. 3, xix. 25 f.
— 19.	The false accusation; Matt. xxvi. 61.
iii. 24.	The date of John's imprisonment (Matt. iv. 12; comp. John iv. 43).
vi. 3.	Retirement to "the mountain."
— 62.	The Ascension.
— 67.	"The twelve." Comp. *vv.* 13, 70, xx. 24 (not in cc. i.—iv.).
xi. 1, 2.	Mary and Martha are well known.
xviii. 33.	The title "the King of the Jews."
xviii. 40.	Barabbas suddenly introduced.
xix. 25.	The ministering women (Matt. xxvii. 55, &c.).

Synoptists and St John as to the day of the Last Supper, see note on Matt. xxvi. This question is of importance in regard to the Synoptists and not in regard to St John. The narrative of St John is perfectly definite and consistent: it bears every mark of exact accuracy, and is in harmony with what seems to be the natural course of the events.

There are also several coincidences in the use of imagery between St John and the Synoptists, and not a few sayings of which the substance is common to them.

Common imagery.

iii. 29.	The Bride and the Bridegroom. Matt. ix. 15, and parallels.
iv. 35 ff.	The harvest. Matt. ix. 37 f.
xiii. 4 ff.	Serving. Matt. x. 24; Luke xii. 37, xxii. 27.
xv. 1 ff.	The vine. Matt. xxi. 33.
— 2.	The unfruitful tree. Matt. vii. 19.

Common sayings.

iv. 44.	Comp. Matt. xiii. 57; Mark vi. 4; Luke iv. 24 (used in different connexions).
vi. 42.	Comp. *ll. cc.*
— 69.	Comp. Matt. xvi. 16, and parallels (corresponding confessions).
xii. 25.	Comp. Matt. x. 39, xvi. 25; Luke xvii. 33 (used in different connexions).
xiii. 16.	Comp. Luke vi. 40; Matt. x. 24 (used in different connexions).
(xiii.) 20.	Comp. Matt. x. 40, (xxv. 40); Luke x. 16 (used in different connexions).
xvi. 2 f.	Comp. Matt. xxiv. 10 f.

In other parallels there are not a few verbal coincidences:

i. 23.	I am *the voice of one crying in the wilderness*, Make straight *the way of the Lord.*
— 26 f.	*I baptize in water...He that cometh after me, the latchet of whose shoe I am not worthy to unloose.*
— 32.	*...descending as a dove...*
— 43.	*Follow me.* Matt. viii. 22, &c.
iii. 5.	*to enter into the kingdom of God.*
v. 8.	*Arise, take up thy bed and walk.* Mark ii. 9.
vi. 20.	*It is I: be not afraid.*
viii. 52.	*taste of death.* Mark ix. 1.

xii. 5.	*to be sold for three hundred pence and given to the poor.* Mark xiv. 5.
— 13.	*Hosanna, blessed is he that cometh in the name of the Lord.*
xiii. 21.	*One of you shall betray me.*
— 38.	*The cock shall not crow till thou shalt deny me thrice.*
xix. 3.	*Hail, King of the Jews.*
xx. 19.	*He saith unto them, Peace be unto you.*

Coincidences more or less striking are found in the following passages.

i. 18.	Matt. xi. 27.
—33.	— iii. 11.
iii. 18.	Mark xvi. 16.
iv. 44.	— vi. 4.
v. 22.	Matt. vii. 22 f.
vi. 7, 10.	Mark vi. 37—39.
— 35.	Matt. v. 6.
— 37.	— xi. 28.
— 39.	— xviii. 14.
— 46.	— xi. 27.
— 70.	Luke vi. 13.
vii. 45 f.	Matt. vii. 28.
ix. 16.	— xii. 2.
x. 15.	— xi. 27.
xi. 25.	— x. 39.
xii. 8.	— xxvi. 11.
—13.	Mark xi. 9.
—44.	Luke ix. 48.
xiii. 1.	Mark xiv. 41.
— 3.	Matt. xi. 27.
—16.	— x. 24.
—20.	— x. 40.
—21.	Mark xiv. 18—21.
xiv. 18.	Matt. xxviii. 20.
— 28.	Mark xiii. 32.
xv. 8.	Matt. v. 16.
—14.	— xii. 49 f.
—20.	— x. 25.
—21.	— x. 22.
xvi. 1 f.	— x. 17 ff.; xiii. 21.
xvii. 2.	— xxviii. 18.
xviii. 11.	— xxvi. 42, 52.
— 15, 18, 22.	Mark xiv. 64 f.
— 20.	Matt. xxvi. 55.
— 39.	Mark xv. 6.
xix. 1—3, 17.	— — 16, 19, 22.
— 6.	Luke xxiii. 21.
[— 19.	— — 38, an interpolation in St Luke.]
xx. 14.	Mark xvi. 9.
23.	Matt. xvi. 19.

The connexion between St John and St Luke is of especial interest. From the relation of St Luke to St Paul it is natural to expect that the peculiarities of his Gospel would furnish indications of transition to the form of the Gospel which St John has preserved. Instances of this relation have been already given in the notices of Samaritans, and of Martha and Mary (p. lxxix.). The following coincidences in thought or language may be added:

i. 19 ff.	Luke iii. 15 f.
vi. 42.	— iv. 22.
x. 27 ff.	— xii. 32.
xiii. 1, xiv. 30.	— ix. 51 (ἀναλήψεως); xxii. 53.
— 4 ff.	— xxii. 27.
— 17.	— xi. 28.
— 22.	— xxii. 23.
— 27.	— — 3.
— 37.	— — 33.
xiv. 30.	— iv. 13 (ἄχρι καιροῦ).
xvi. 7.	— xxiv. 49 (ἐγὼ ἐξαποστέλλω).
xviii. 36 f.	— xvii. 20 f.
— 38.	— xxiii. 4.
xx. 3, 6.	— xxiv. 12 (the reading is doubtful).
— 19 ff.	— — 36 ff.

Such correspondences prove nothing as to the direct literary connexion of the two Gospels, nor do the few significant words which are common to St Luke and St John (*e.g.* τὸ ἔθνος of Jews, μονογενής), but they do shew the currency of a form of the apostolic Gospel with characteristic features approximating to characteristic features in St John.

5. *The relation of the Synoptists to St John in regard of the Lord's Person.* But it may be said that even if the considerations which have been urged establish the possibility of reconciling the apparent differences of the Synoptists and St John as to the place, the manner and the duration of the Lord's Teaching: if they shew that there is theoretically room for the events and the discourses of both narratives: if they supply in both cases indications of a wider field and a more varied method than is habitually recorded in the two histories

respectively; yet the fundamental difference between the first three Gospels and the Fourth as to the general view of the Lord's Person practically excludes such a reconciliation.

This difficulty unquestionably underlies the other difficulties and gives force to them. It is not possible to do more here than to point out the main arguments by which it can fairly be met.

The Person of the Lord is as truly the centre of the teaching of the Synoptists as of the teaching of St John. It is not His doctrine but Himself which is to redeem the world (Matt. xx. 28).

The narratives of the Nativity, though they did not form part of the apostolic oral Gospel, are completely harmonious with it. There is no contrast (for example) in passing from the history of the Nativity to that of the Baptism.

The claims of the Lord which are recorded by the Synoptists, if followed to their legitimate consequences, involve the claims recorded by St John.

Matt. vii. 22.	*in my name.*
— ix. 2 ff.	*Thy sins be forgiven thee.*
— x. 1.	(Gives power to work signs.)
— — 39.	*he that loseth his life for my sake...*
— xi. 27.	*All things are delivered unto me...*
— xiii. 41.	*The Son of man will send forth his angels.* Comp. xvi. 27, xxv. 31.
— xviii. 20.	*Where two or three are gathered together in my name, there am I* ...(as said of Shekinah).
— xx. 28.	*his life a ransom for many.*
— xxi. 37 ff.	*They will reverence my son.*
— xxii. 45.	*If David call him Lord.*
— xxv. 31.	*When the Son of man shall come in his glory.* Comp. xxvi. 64.
— xxvi. 28.	*My blood of the covenant.*
— xxviii. 20.	*I am with you alway.*
Luke xxi. 15.	*I will give you a mouth and wisdom.*
— xxiv. 49.	*I send the promise of my Father upon you.*

A careful estimate of these passages will make it clear that the Synoptists recognise in the Lord the power of judgment, of redemption, and of fellowship, which are the main topics of the teaching in St John. In one respect only St John adds a new truth to the doctrine of the Lord's Person which has no direct anticipation in the Synoptists. These do not anywhere declare His pre-existence. (Yet compare Luke xi. 49 with Matt. xxiii. 34 and John x. 35.)

The general conclusion however stands firm. The Synoptists offer not only historical but also spiritual points of connexion between the teaching which they record and the teaching in the Fourth Gospel; and St John himself in the Apocalypse completes the passage from the one to the other.

2. *The Apocalypse and the Fourth Gospel.*

The Apocalypse is doctrinally the uniting link between the Synoptists and the Fourth Gospel. It offers the characteristic thoughts of the Fourth Gospel in that form of development which belongs to the earliest apostolic age. It belongs to different historical circumstances, to a different phase of intellectual progress, to a different theological stage, from that of St John's Gospel; and yet it is not only harmonious with it in teaching, but in the order of thought it is the necessary germ out of which the Gospel proceeded by a process of life.

1. *Affinities of the Apocalypse with the Gospel.* The points of connexion between the Apocalypse and the Gospel of St John are far more numerous than are suggested by a first general comparison of the two books. The main idea of both is the same. Both present a view of a supreme conflict between the powers of good and evil. In the Gospel this is drawn mainly in moral conceptions; in the Apocalypse mainly in images and visions. In the Gospel the opposing forces are regarded under abstract and absolute forms, as light and darkness, love and hatred; in

the Apocalypse under concrete and definite forms, God, Christ, and the Church warring with the devil, the false prophet and the beast.

But in both books alike Christ is the central figure. His victory is the end to which history and vision lead as their consummation (see xvi. 33, note). His Person and Work are the ground of triumph, and of triumph through apparent failure (Rev. i. 5, vi. 16, vii. 14, xii. 11).

It follows that in both books the appearance of Christ is shewn to issue in a judgment, a separation, of elements partially confused before. The "hatred" of evil gains a new intensity (Rev. ii. 6; 2 John 10). The Apocalypse gives, so to speak, in an ideal history the analysis of the course of unbelief which is laid open in John viii.

On man's part the conflict with evil is necessarily a conflict in action. The Apocalypse and the Gospel therefore lay stress on obedience and works. To "keep the commandments" is now the fulfilment of Christian duties (John xiv. 23, note; 1 John ii. 3 f.; v. 2 f.; 2 John 6; Rev. xii. 17, xiv. 12 [xxii. 14, a false reading]).

The universality of the Gospel is an immediate consequence of the proclamation of its moral character. And there is not the least trace in the Apocalypse of the doctrine of the permanent or general obligation of the Law or of circumcision. The particular injunctions which are enforced in ii. 14, 20 are combined in the Acts (xv. 28 f., xxi. 25) with the removal of such an obligation from the Gentiles. External ceremonies fall wholly into the background, as symbols only of that which is universal and spiritual (Rev. v. 8 ff., xiv. 6 f.; comp. 1 John ii. 2).

At the same time the Apocalypse no less than the Gospel recognises the preparatory office of Judaism. In both it is assumed that "Salvation is of the Jews" (John iv. 22, 38). The Seer shews that the sovereignty which the prophets foretold was established in Jesus, "the Christ" (xii. 5, 10, xi. 15); and the imagery of the old Scriptures is used from first to last to foreshadow the conflict, the victory and the judgment of the divine King (*e.g.* Zech. xii. 10; John xix. 37; Rev. i. 7).

In correspondence with the universality of the Gospel is the office of personal "witness" on which the firmest stress is laid in all the writings of St John. The experience of the believer finds expression in a testimony which is strong in the face of death. In the Apocalypse the characteristic form in which this "witness" appears is as "the testimony of Jesus" (i. 2, 9, xii. 17, xix. 10, xx. 4). The true humanity of the Saviour is that revelation on which faith reposes.

This testimony to the Incarnation leads to a final correspondence between the Apocalypse and the Fourth Gospel which is of the highest importance. Both present the abiding of God with man as the issue of Christ's work. *If any man love me, he will keep my word, and my Father will love him, and we will come to him and make our abode with him* (John xiv. 23). *Behold I stand at the door and knock: If any man hear my voice and open the door, I will come in to him, and will sup with him and he with me* (Rev. iii. 20). *Behold the tabernacle of God is with men, and He will dwell* (σκηνώσει) *with them* (Rev. xxi. 3).

2. *Contrasts of the Apocalypse with the Gospel.* Side by side with these coincidences of thought, which reach to the ruling conceptions of the books, there are also important contrasts in their subject-matter and their modes of dealing with common topics.

The most striking contrast lies in the treatment of the doctrine of Christ's Coming in the two books. This is the main subject of the Apocalypse, while it falls into the background in the Gospel and in the Epistles of St John. In the Apocalypse the thought is of an outward coming for the open judgment of men: in the Gospel of a judgment which is spiritual and self-executing. In the Apocalypse the scene of the consummation is a renovated world: in the Gospel "the Father's house." In the former the victory and the transformation are from without, by might, and the "future" is painted under historic imagery: in the latter, the victory and the transformation are from within, by a spiritual influence, and the "future" is present and eternal.

It is part of this same contrast that the progress of the conflict between good and evil is presented very differently in the Apocalypse and in the Gospel. In the Apocalypse it is portrayed under several distinct forms as a conflict of Christ with false Judaism, with idolatry, with the Roman empire allied with false prophecy: in the Gospel it is conceived in its essence as a continuous conflict between light and darkness. On the one side are outward persecutors; on the other the spirit of falsehood: on the one side, the working of the revelation of Christ; on the other the revelation of Christ itself. Or, to put the facts under another aspect, the Apocalypse gives a view of the action of God in regard to men, in a life full of sorrow, and partial defeats and cries for vengeance: the Gospel gives a view of the action of God with regard to Christ who establishes in the heart of the believer a Presence of completed joy.

In regard to Judaism this contrast assumes a special form. In the Apocalypse the triumph of Christianity is described under the imagery of Judaism. The Church is the embodied fulfilment of Old Testament prophecy. The outlines are drawn of the universal, ideal, Israel (vii. 4), the ideal Jerusalem (iii. 12, xxi. 2, 10), and the ideal worship (xx. 6, xxii. 3; comp. viii. 3, v. 8), yet so that there is no longer any temple (xxi. 22). In the Gospel Christianity is proclaimed as the absolute truth. Outward Judaism is shewn in its opposition to Christ's word, not as fulfilled by it, standing without, isolated and petrified; and not taken up with it, quickened and glorified (compare Rev. ii. 9, iii. 9, with John viii. 39 ff.).

The conception of God in the two books shews corresponding differences. The conception of God in the Apocalypse follows the lines of the Old Testament. He is "the Lord God, the Almighty" (i. 8, iv. 8, &c.), "which was and is" (xi. 17, xvi. 5. Comp. i. 4, 8, iv. 8), who executes righteous judgment on the world (xi. 18, xiv. 10, xvi. 19, xix. 15). Nothing is said of His love in sending His Son; nor of the Paraclete. In the Gospel God is revealed characteristically by Christ as "the Father" and not only as "my Father" (see iv. 21, note); and specially in connexion with the work of redemption. In the one case it may be said that His action is revealed in relation to the sinful history of the world: and in the other His being in relation to the purpose of the world[1].

Besides these differences of substance there are also differences of language both in vocabulary and style. The difference in the scope of the books accounts in part for these. The irregularities of style in the Apocalypse appear to be due not so much to ignorance of the language as to a free treatment of it, by one who used it as a foreign dialect. Nor is it difficult to see that in any case intercourse with a Greek-speaking people would in a short time naturally reduce the style of the author of the Apocalypse to that of the author of the Gospel. It is however very difficult to suppose that the language of the writer of the Gospel could pass at a later time in a Greek-speaking country into the language of the Apocalypse.

Such very briefly are the coincidences and differences between the Apocalypse and the Fourth Gospel. Several conclusions appear to follow from them.

The differences answer to differences in situation; and are not inconsistent with identity of authorship.

Of the two books the Apocalypse is the earlier. It is less developed both in thought and style. The material imagery in which it is composed includes the idea of progress in interpretation. The symbols are living. On the other hand, to go back from the teaching of the Gospel to that of the Apocalypse, to clothe clear thought in figures, to reduce the full expression of truth to its rudimentary beginnings, seems to involve a moral miracle, which would introduce confusion into life.

The Apocalypse is after the close of St Paul's work. It shews in its mode of dealing with Old Testament figures a close connexion with the Epistle to the Hebrews (2 Peter, Jude). And on the

[1] The difference between the two books as to subordinate spiritual powers, angels and evil spirits, follows from the difference in their structure. Comp. i. 51, note.

other hand it is before the destruction of Jerusalem.

The crisis of the Fall of Jerusalem explains the relation of the Apocalypse to the Gospel. In the Apocalypse that "coming" of Christ was expected, and painted in figures: in the Gospel the "coming" is interpreted.

Under this aspect the Gospel is the spiritual interpretation of the Apocalypse. The materials of the Gospel were treasured up, pondered, illuminated as time went on. Meanwhile the active and manifold religious thought of Ephesus furnished the intellectual assistance which was needed to exhibit Christianity as the absolute and historical religion in contrast with Judaism and Heathenism. The final desolation of the centre of the old Theocracy was the decisive sign of the form which the new Faith must take. Then first, according to the divine law of order, the Spirit would guide the Apostle into all the Truth.

This is not the place to work out in detail the likeness and difference of the Apocalypse and the Fourth Gospel on special points of doctrine; but the Christology of the two books illustrates very remarkably the position which has been assigned to the Apocalypse as connecting the Synoptists and St John. It is necessary then to indicate shortly the teaching of the Apocalypse on Christ's work and being.

The work of Christ is presented summarily as the victory through death of One who was truly man. Christ was the representative of David (v. 5, xxii. 16), pierced (i. 7), crucified (xi. 8), and again quickened (i. 5; comp. Col. i. 18). So He "bought" the redeemed (v. 9, xiv. 3 f.); and His blood brings to them release (i. 5, λύσαντι ἀπὸ τ. ἁ), cleansing (vii. 14), and victory (xii. 11). And in this He fulfilled the divine will for men (i. 1 [ἔδωκεν], ii. 26, 5, 10, 16, iii. 10, 5, 21, v. 5, xxi. 23).

The exaltation of Christ followed on the completion of His earthly work. The "Lamb slain" was raised to glory (v. 9, 12). The "seven spirits of God" are His (v. 6, iii. 1; comp. i. 4; John xv. 26). In the heavenly sanctuary He is revealed as the divine High Priest (i. 12—17; comp. ii. 9, x. 5 f.) "like a son of man" (i. 13, xiv. 14); truly man, and yet more than man, "the living One" (i. 17; comp. John v. 26). He possesses divine knowledge (ii. 2, 9, 13, 19, &c., ii. 23; comp. Jer. xi. 20, &c.); and divine power (xi. 15, xii. 10, xvii. 14, xix. 16). He receives divine honour (v. 8 ff., xx. 6); and is joined with God (iii. 2, v. 13, vi. 16 f., vii. 10, xiv. 4, xxi. 22, xxii. 1, 3; comp. John v. 20, 23), so that with God He is spoken of as one (xi. 15, βασιλεύσει, xx. 6, μετ' αὐτοῦ, xxii. 3, οἱ δοῦλοι αὐτοῦ λατρεύσουσιν αὐτῷ); He shares also in part the divine titles (i. 7, iii. 7, xix. 11; comp. vi. 10, iii. 14; comp. Isai. lxv. 16, but not xxii. 13).

The full importance of these passages is brought out by the stern denunciations against every form of idolatry with which the book abounds (comp. 1 John v. 21). Christ therefore is wholly separated from creatures. And further, the passages shew that the imagery which is used in the Old Testament to describe the revelation of God is transferred by the writer to Christ (comp. John xii. 41, note).

One other point remains to be noticed. In the Synoptists there is no direct statement of the pre-existence of Christ. The truth is recognised in the Apocalypse, but relatively rather than absolutely. Christ is spoken of as *the first and the last* (i. 17, ii. 8); *the beginning of the creation of God* (iii. 14; comp. Prov. viii. 22; Col. i. 15); and *the Word of God* (xix. 13). In these phrases we find the earliest form of the "Logos doctrine," which is still kept within the lines of the Old Testament ideas. But the later unfolding of the truth is included in this earliest confession. If an Apostle was enabled to see in the Master whom he had followed the Being to whom all creation pays homage in the spiritual world, there is no difficulty in apprehending how he could rise, without doing violence to the laws of human thought, to the enunciation of the fact on which the Fourth Gospel is a commentary, *the Word became flesh and dwelt among us, and we beheld His glory.*

In a word, the study of the Synoptists, of the Apocalypse and of the Gospel of St John in succession enables us to see under what human conditions the full majesty of Christ was perceived and declared, not all at once, but step by step, and by the help of the old prophetic teaching.

3. *The Gospel and the Epistles of St John.*

The relation of the Gospel of St John to his Epistles is that of a history to its accompanying comment or application. The first Epistle presupposes the Gospel either as a writing or as oral instruction. But while there are numerous and striking resemblances both in form and thought between the Epistle and the Evangelist's record of the Lord's discourses and his own narrative, there are still characteristic differences between them. In the Epistle the doctrine of the Lord's true and perfect humanity (σάρξ) is predominant: in the Gospel that of His divine glory (δόξα). The burden of the Epistle is "the Christ is Jesus:" the writer presses his argument from the divine to the human, from the spiritual and ideal to the historical. The burden of the Gospel is "Jesus is the Christ:" the writer presses his argument from the human to the divine, from the historical to the spiritual and ideal. The former is the natural position of the preacher, and the latter of the historian.

The difference between the Epistle and the Gospel in their eschatological teaching follows from this fundamental difference. In the Gospel the doctrine of the "coming" of the Lord (xxi. 22, xiv. 3), and of "the last day" (vi. 40, 44), and of "the judgment" (v. 28 f.), are touched upon generally. In the Epistle "the manifestation" of Christ (ii. 28) and His "presence" stand out as clear facts in the history of the world. He comes, even as He came, "in flesh" (2 John 7); and "antichrists" precede His coming (1 John ii. 18 ff.).

Again, in the Epistle the doctrine of propitiation is more distinct and fully expressed than in the Gospel (ἱλασμός, 1 John ii. 2, iv. 10; comp. Heb. ii. 17; καθαρίζειν, 1 John i. 7, 9); and in connexion with this the duty of the confession of sins (1 John i. 9), and the office of the Lord as Paraclete (Advocate) (1 John ii. 1; comp. John xiv. 16, note). But it is most worthy of notice that no use is made in the Epistle of the language of the discourses in John iii. and vi. On the other hand, the conception of the "unction" of Christians (1 John ii. 20, 27; comp. Rev. i. 6) is a later interpretation of the gift of the Spirit which Christ promised.

Generally too it will be found on a comparison of the closest parallels, that the Apostle's own words are more formal in expression than the words of the Lord which he records. The Lord's words have been moulded by the disciple into aphorisms in the Epistle: their historic connexion has been broken. At the same time the language of the Epistle is in the main direct, abstract, and unfigurative. The Apostle's teaching, so to speak, is "plain" (παρρησίᾳ), while that of the Lord was "in proverbs" (ἐν παροιμίαις, John xvi. 25).

One or two examples will illustrate the contrast which has been indicated:

John viii. 12. *I am the Light of the world: he that followeth me shall not walk in darkness, but shall have the light of life.*

1 John i. 5, 7. *This then is the message we have heard of him, and declare unto you, that God is light, and in him is no darkness at all... If we walk in the light as he is in the light, we have fellowship one with another...*

John xv. 23. *He that hateth me hateth my Father also.*

1 John ii. 23. *Whosoever denieth the Son, the same hath not the Father; but he that acknowledgeth the Son hath the Father also.*

Compare also pp. lxi. ff.

Generally it will be felt that there is a decisive difference (so to speak) in the atmosphere of the two books. In the Epistle St John deals freely with the truths of the Gospel in direct conflict with the characteristic perils of his own time: in the Gospel he lives again in the presence of Christ and of the immediate enemies of Christ, while he brings out the universal significance of events and teaching not fully understood at the time.

V. The History of the Gospel.

1. *The Text.*

The materials for determining the text of the Gospel of St John are, as in the case of the other Gospels, and of the books of the New Testament generally, ample and varied. It will be sufficient to notice the most important authorities in which the Gospel of St John is preserved.

I. GREEK MANUSCRIPTS.

Cod. Sinaiticus (ℵ). The entire Gospel.

Cod. Alexandrinus (A). Wants vi. 50—viii. 52.

Cod. Vaticanus (B). The entire Gospel.

Cod. Ephraemi (C). Eight considerable fragments. (1) i. 1—41. (2) iii. 33—v. 16. (3) vi. 38—vii. 3. (4) viii. 34—ix. 11. (5) xi. 8—46. (6) xiii. 8—xiv. 7. (7) xvi. 21—xviii. 36. (8) xx. 26—end.

Cod. Bezæ (D). Wants i. 16—iii. 26; and xviii. 13—xx. 13 has been supplied by a later hand, perhaps from the original leaves.

Cod. Paris. (L). Wants xxi. 15—end.

There are besides eight other uncial MSS. containing the Gospel complete or nearly complete; and thirteen which contain more or less considerable fragments.

The cursive mss., which are almost of every degree of excellence, are more than 600.

II. ANCIENT VERSIONS.

(1) *The Old* (Curetonian) *Syriac* (*Syr. vt.*). Four fragments: (1) i. 1—42. (2) iii. 5—vii. 37. (3) vii. 37—viii. 53, omitting vii. 53—viii. 11. (4) xiv. 11—29.

The Vulgate Syriac (Peshito, *Syr. psh.*). The entire Gospel.

The Harclean Syriac (*Syr. hcl.*). The entire Gospel.

(2) *The Old Latin* (*Lat. vt.*). The entire Gospel in several distinct types.

The Vulgate Latin (*Vulg.*). The entire Gospel.

The Memphitic (Coptic, in the dialect of Lower Egypt). The entire Gospel.

The Thebaic (Sahidic, in the dialect of Upper Egypt). Very considerable fragments have been published in the Appendix to Woide's 'Cod. Al. N. T.' of which a collation is given in Schwartze's edition of the Memphitic Gospels.

III. FATHERS.

In addition to isolated quotations there remain, from early times: the Commentaries of CYRIL of ALEXANDRIA (nearly complete); the Explanatory Homilies of AUGUSTINE and CHRYSOSTOM; and large fragments of the Commentaries of ORIGEN and THEODORE of MOPSUESTIA.

This is not the place to enter in detail upon the methods of textual criticism. It must suffice to say that the problem is in the first stage essentially historical. The primary object of the critic is to discover in the case of variations the most ancient reading. When this has been done it remains to take account of any arguments which may be urged against the authenticity of the earliest text. Unless these are of great weight the prerogative of age must prevail. But this first process cannot be accomplished by simply taking the reading of the most ancient copies, or giving a fixed value, so to speak, to each copy according to its antiquity. The most ancient copy is *ceteris paribus* likely to give the most ancient text on the whole, and with a less degree of probability in each particular case. But the ancient authorities often disagree. Hence it is a necessary condition for the determination of the most ancient text to study the chief authorities *as wholes* (1) separately, and (2) in their mutual relations. In this way it can be ascertained beyond doubt what MSS. (for example) preserve a distinctly ante-Nicene text. When this is done the mass of evidence can be reduced to manageable dimensions. If it cannot be shewn that a reading has any ante-Nicene authority, it may in almost all cases be confidently set aside.

No one of the existing MSS. of the New Testament is older than the fourth century; but the earliest, which have been already enumerated, represent very different types of text, and are, as far as can be ascertained, of very different origin. To speak of them all as "Alexandrine" is in every way misleading.

(1) A most careful examination of B leaves it in possession of the title to supreme excellence. Its readings have no specific colouring. It is not unlikely that it represents the text preserved in the original Greek Church of Rome.

(2) The texts of ℵ and D, which have much in common, are of very high antiquity, dating from the end of the second century. Their common element is closely akin to an element in the Old Syriac and Old Latin versions, and shews much license in paraphrase and in the introduction of synonymous phrases and words. The characteristics of these MSS. are probably of Palestinian origin.

(3) The characteristic readings of C and L indicate the work of a careful grammatical revision. They seem to be due to Alexandria.

(4) In the Gospels A gives a revised (Antiochene) text which formed the basis of the later Byzantine texts. These texts were almost exclusively reproduced from the sixth century onwards.

The characteristic readings of B, of ℵD, and of C, L, have all more or less support in the ante-Nicene age. The characteristic readings of A, on the other hand, cannot be traced back beyond the fourth century, though it has also a valuable ancient element in common with BCL rather than with ℵD.

It follows therefore (speaking generally) that a reading which is found in B and in a primary representative of one of the other groups has very high claims to be considered the original reading. On the other hand a reading which is found only in the representatives of one of the three last groups is likely to be a correction; and the same may be said of a reading which is given only in representatives of the third and fourth groups. Very few readings in the Gospels will be found to stand the test of a comprehensive examination which are not supported by ℵ or B or D.

These conclusions necessarily depend upon an exhaustive induction of particulars. No process can be more precarious than the attempt to settle each case of variation as it arises. A reading, which taken alone may appear to be plausible or even true, is often seen to be an ingenious correction from a consideration of the characteristics of the authorities by which it is supported taken as a group. No authority has an unvarying value. No authority is ever homogeneous. It is only by taking a wide view of the grouping of the authorities that a solid conclusion can be gained. And in this respect the evidence which is available for determining the text of the New Testament is so copious and varied that little final doubt can be left.

Very little has been said in detail on various readings in the notes, except on a few passages of unusual interest. It will therefore be useful to give a brief summary of the authorities for a selection of variations which have a critical interest. This may serve as basis for further study to those who wish to pursue the subject; and at the same time it will illustrate the comparative value of the different authorities in their different combinations[1].

1. *Interpretative or Supplementary Glosses.*

i. 24. *and they were sent from the Pharisees* (καὶ ἀπεσταλμένοι), ℵ*A*BC*L *Memph.* See note.
and they that were sent were of the Pharisees (καὶ οἱ ἀπεσταλμένοι), ℵ^{cb}A^{2}C^{3}X (MSS. mss.) *Latt. Syrr.*

—27. *coming after me*, ℵ*B(C*LT^b), *Syr. vt. Memph. He it is who coming after me is preferred before me*, AC^{3}X (MSS. mss.) *Latt.* Comp. *v.* 15.

iii. 15. *may have eternal life.*
may not perish but have eternal life. See note.

— 25. *a Jew* ℵ^{c}ABL (MSS. mss.) *Syr. psh.*
Jews ℵ* (MSS. mss.) *Latt. Syr. vt. Memph.*

— 34. *he giveth not*, ℵBCLT^b 1 33 (*Lat. vt.*).
God giveth not, AC^{2}D (MSS. mss.) Verss.

iv. 42. *the Saviour of the world*, ℵB C*T^b *Latt. Syr. vt. Memph.*
the Christ the Saviour of the world, ADL (MSS. mss.).

v. 4. See note.

[1] No attempt is made to give a complete summary of the evidence. "MSS." signifies many (or the remainder of) uncial and "mss." many (or the remainder of) cursive manuscripts. *Latt.* and *Syrr.* the Latin and Syrian versions in agreement; and verss. versions generally. If the title of an authority is enclosed in ( ), this indicates that the evidence is modified by some circumstance or other.

v. 16. *did ... persecute*, ℵBCDL 1 33 (*Latt.*) *Syr. vt.*
did...persecute and sought to slay him, A (MSS. mss.). Comp. v. 18.

vi. 9. *a boy.*
a single boy. See note.

— 22. *except one*, ℵ^c ABL 1 (*Latt.*).
except that one (or *one*), *into which his disciples* (or *the disciples of Jesus*) *entered*, ℵ*D (MSS. mss.) *Syrr.*

— 51. *my flesh for the life of the world*, BCDLT 33 *Latt. Syrr. vt. Theb.* (and ℵ in a changed order).
my flesh which I will give for the life of the world, MSS. mss. (A is defective) (*Syrr.*) *Memph.* See note.

— 59. *teaching...on a sabbath*, D (*Lat. vt.*).

vii. 46. *never man so spake*, ℵ^c BLT *Memph.*
never man so spake as this man (speaketh), ℵ*(D)X MSS. mss.

viii. 59. *out of the temple*, ℵ*BD *Latt. Theb.*
out of the temple, and going through the midst of them went on his way (ἐπορεύετο) *and so passed by*, ℵ^ca CLX 33 *Memph.*
out of the temple, going through the midst of them and so passed by, A (MSS. mss.) *Syrr.*

x. 13, 26. See notes.

xi. 41. *the stone*, ℵBC*DLX 33 *Latt. Theb.* (*Syrr.*).
the stone where he was, A 1.
the stone where he that was dead was laid, C^3 (MSS. mss.).

xii. 7. *suffer her...to keep it* (ἵνα...τηρήσῃ), ℵBDLQX 33 (*Latt.*) *Memph. Theb.*
leave her alone; she hath kept it (τετήρηκεν), A (MSS. mss.).

xiii. 14. *ye ought also.*
by how much more ought ye also, D (*Lat. vt.*).

— 32. *And God shall glorify*, ℵ*BC* DLX *Lat. vt.*
If God was glorified in him, God shall also glorify, ℵ^c A (MSS. mss.) *Vg. Memph.*

xiv. 4. *and whither I go ye know the way*, ℵBC*LQX *Memph.*
and whither I go ye know, and the way ye know, ADN (MSS. mss.) *Latt. Syrr.*

— 5. *how know we the way*, BC*D (*Lat. vt.*).
how can we know the way, (ℵ)ALNQX *Vg. Syrr.*

xvi. 16. *shall see me*, ℵBDL (*Lat. vt.*).
shall see me, because I go to the Father, A MSS. mss. (*Memph.*) *Syrr.* Comp. *vv.* 5, 10.

xvii. 21. *that they may be in us*, BC*D (*Lat. vt.*) *Theb.*
that they may be one in us, ℵAC^3 LX MSS. mss. *Vg. Memph. Syrr.*

See also iii. 13, note.

In connexion with these explanatory additions, a few passages may be noticed in which an easy word has been substituted for a more difficult one.

i. 16. Note.
vi. 63. Note.
viii. 16. *true* as satisfying the idea (ἀληθινή), BDLTX 33.
true to facts (ἀληθής), ℵ MSS. mss.
x. 38. *that ye may know and may understand* (γινώσκητε), BLX 1 33 *Theb. Memph.*
that ye may know and believe, ℵA (MSS. mss.) *Latt.*

2. *Paraphrases.*

The group ℵ D *Syr. vt.* and *Lat. vt.* are specially marked by paraphrastic variations.

i. 4. *in him is life*, ℵD *Syr. vt. Lat. vt.* See note.
— 34. *the chosen one of God*, ℵ *Syr. vt.* See note.
ii. 3. *they had not wine for the wine of the marriage was consumed*, ℵ* (*Lat. vt.*).
iii. 5. *kingdom of heaven*, ℵ*.
— 6. *is spirit because God is spirit, and he is born of God*, *Syr. vt.* (*Lat. vt.*).
— 8. *from water and the spirit*, ℵ *Lat. vt. Syr. vt.*
v. 13. *he that was sick*, D (*Lat. vt.*).

v. 19. *the Father doeth*, *Syrr. Memph.*
vi. 15. *and declare* (ἀναδεικνύναι) *him king*, ℵ*.
— — *he fleeth again*, ℵ* (*Latt.*) *Syr. vt.* See note.
— 17. *darkness overtook* (κατέλαβεν) *them*, ℵD.
— 51. *from my bread*, ℵ (*Lat. vt.*).
x. 38. *if ye are not willing to believe me*, D *Latt.*
xi. 9. *how many hours hath the day?* D.
— 33. *was troubled in spirit, as moved with indignation* (ὡς ἐμβριμώμενος), D 1 *Theb.*
xii 32. *all things*, ℵ*D *Latt.*
xiv. 7. *ye will know my Father also*, ℵD (*Lat. vt.*).
xvii. 3. *didst send into this world*, D.
— 10. *thou didst glorify me*, D.
xviii. 37. *concerning the truth*, ℵ*.

Other examples of readings characteristic of this group will be found in the following passages:

i. 14 (πλήρη), 48.
ii. 15.
iv. 24, 42, 46, 51.
v. 9, 13, 25, 32, 42.
vi. 3, 23, 25, 27, 37, 46, 56 (note), 64, 66.
vii. 1, 6, 12, 26, 37, 47, 48, 50, 52.
viii. 16, 21, 27.
ix. 35.
x. 11, 15, 25, 34, 39.
xi. 14.
xiv. 11.
xv. 20.
xvi. 13, 19.
xvii. 2, 7, 10, 23 (ἠγάπησα), 26.
xviii. 1 (note), 35.
xix. 4, 13, 33, 38.
xx. 1, 11, 15, 24 f.
xxi. 17, 18.

It is not probable that any one of these readings will commend itself to the student; but it must be added that in the case of omission it appears that the authority of this group is sometimes of greater weight. The omissions in St John's Gospel which they support in the following passages are by no means unlikely to be correct:

iii. 25, 32, note.
iv. 9, *for...Samaritans.*

On the other hand their omissions in vi. 23, x. 8 (*before me*), xxi. 23, are not to be admitted.

The readings of ℵ when they are unsupported are often quite arbitrary: *e. g.* iii. 36, vi. 10, 23, viii. 57, xi. 31, xiv. 16, xix. 13.

3. Passages in which the sense is considerably affected by the variation are not very numerous:

i. 16. Note.
—18. Note.
—28. Note.
—39 (40). *and ye shall see*, BC*LT[b] 1 33 (mss.) *Syrr.*
and see, ℵAX MSS. (mss.) *Latt. Memph.* Comp. *v.* 47.
—51. Note.
ii. 17. *will eat me up*, ℵABLPT[b] (MSS. mss.).
hath eaten me up, a few mss.
iii. 15. Note.
v. 1. Note.
—3 f. Note.
vi. 69. Note.
vii. 8. *I go not up yet*, BLTX (MSS. mss.) *Theb. Syrr.*
I go not up, ℵD (some MSS. mss.) *Lat. vt. Syr. vt. Memph.* In such a case it is right to follow that combination of ancient authority which is elsewhere most trustworthy. For the combination in favour of "*not*" see note on vi. 15.
vii. 39. Note.
— 53—viii. 11. Note.
viii. 38. *do ye* (or *ye do*) *that which ye heard from the father* (τοῦ πατρός) or *your father*, ℵ[c]BCLX 1 33 *Memph.*
ye do that which ye have seen with your father, ℵ*D(T) (MSS. mss.) *Latt.*
— 44. Note.
ix. 35. Note.
x. 14. *mine know me*, ℵBDL *Latt. Memph. Theb.*
I am known of mine, AX MSS. mss. (*Syrr.*).
—22. Note.
xii. 17. *when he called*, ℵABX (MSS. mss.) *Vg.*
that he called, DL *Lat. vt. Theb. Memph.*

xii. 41. *because he saw*, ℵABLX 1 33 *Memph. Theb.*
when he saw, D (MSS. mss.) *Latt. Syrr.*

— 47. *and keep them not*, ℵABDLX 1 33 *Latt. Syrr. Theb. Memph.*
and believe not, (MSS. mss.).

xiii. 2. *during a supper* (γινομένου), ℵ*BLX.
a supper having been made (γενομένου), ℵ^c AD (MSS. mss.).

— 24. *and saith to him, Tell us who it is of whom he speaketh*, (ℵ)BCLX 33 *Latt.*
that he should ask who it was of whom he spake, AD MSS. mss. *Syrr.*

— 25. *leaning back as he was* (ἀναπεσὼν οὕτως), (ℵ^c) BCLX.
falling upon (ἐπιπεσών), ℵ*AD (MSS. mss.).

xiv. 10. *doeth his works*, ℵBD.
himself doeth the works, AQ (LX) (MSS. mss.).

— 15. *ye will keep*, ℵBL *Memph.*
keep, ADQX MSS. mss. *Latt. Syrr.*

xvii. 11. *keep them in thy name which* (ᾧ) *thou hast given me*, ℵABCL (MSS. mss.), *Syrr. Theb.* (ὃ D*X mss.).
keep in thy name those whom thou hast given me, a few mss. *Vg. Memph.*

— 12. *thy name that thou*, BC*L 33 (ℵ^c *Theb. Memph.*).
thy name: those that thou, ADX (MSS. mss.) *Latt. Syrr.*

xviii. 15. Note.
— 24. Note.

xix. 3. *and they came unto him and said*, ℵBLX 33 (MSS. mss.) *Latt. Theb. Memph.*
and said, A (MSS. mss.).

A careful examination of these passages will shew how rarely A gives a certain ante-Nicene reading when authorities are divided. The relative lateness of its text compared with the texts of ℵBD and C, will be further apparent from the following passages: i. 26 (δέ), 39 (ἴδετε), 49; iv. 21 (πίστευσον), 46 (ὁ Ἰησοῦς); v. 3 (πολύ), 15 (καί); vi. 40 (τοῦ πέμψαντός με), 45 (οὖν); ix. 11, 41 (οὖν); x. 4 (τὰ ἴδια πρόβατα), 14; xi. 31 (λέγοντες).

In the case of proper names A seems to have adopted the later corrections, as in writing *Capernaum* for *Capharnaum* (ℵBCD, &c.); and *Jonas* for *John*, as the name of the father of St Peter (i. 42). This remark is not without weight in regard to the readings of A in v. 2; xviii. 1 (see notes).

On the other hand it will be no less evident that in the examples given the readings of B are almost beyond question correct; and further inquiry will tend to prove that no reading of B which is supported by independent authority, and certainly no reading of B which is supported by a primary uncial (*e.g.* ℵ, C. D, A), can be altogether set aside.

The following examples will repay study. Combination of Bℵ:

iv. 15.	διέρχωμαι.
v. 17.	*om.* Ἰησοῦς.
ix. 20.	ἀπεκρ. οὖν.
— 23.	ἐπερωτήσατε.
— 28.	καὶ ἐλοιδ.
xii. 4.	λέγει δέ.
xiv. 17.	*om.* αυτό sec.
xvii. 11.	αὐτοί.
xix. 24.	*om.* ἡ λέγουσα.
— 35.	πιστεύητε.
— 39.	ἕλιγμα.

Such considerations carefully checked and followed out lead to conclusions which can be confidently accepted even where the most ancient evidence is unusually divided, *e.g.* i. 21, iii. 15, vii. 39, viii. 39, x. 29.

In most cases of slight variation the reading of the text from which A.V. was taken has been silently corrected, and a translation of that which seems to be the true text substituted for A.V.

It will be convenient to add a list of these passages in addition to those variations which have been already noticed.

i. 29. *he* (John); 42, Omit *and*, 43.
ii. 4. Add *And;* 10, Omit *then.*
—11, 17,
22. Omit *unto them.*
iii. 2. *him* (*Jesus*); 18, Omit *but.*
iv. 30, 35,
43. Omit *departed thence and;* 50,

Omit *and* (1); 52, *therefore* (*and*).
v. 10. Add *and;* 11, Add *But;* 12, Omit *Then;* 27, 30, 37, Omit *himself;* add *he.*
vi. 2. *the* (*his*); 7, 10, 11, *therefore* (*and*); 14, 17, 24, Omit *also;* 35, 38, 39, 42, *now* (*then*); 43, Omit *therefore;* 47, 55, 58, *the* (*your*); Omit *manna;* 63, 65, *the F.* (*my F.*), 68, 71.
vii. 9. Add *And;* 10, Transpose *to the feast;* 15, *therefore* (*and*); 16, Add *therefore;* 20, 26, Omit *very;* 29, 32, 33, Omit *unto them;* 40, *certain* (*many*), 46, 50.
viii. 14. *or* (*and*); 20, 21, 25, 28, Omit *unto them;* 29, 41, 46, Omit *and;* 48, 52
ix. 4, 6, 8, 9, Add *No, but;* 10, 12, 14, 17, Add *therefore;* 20, 21, 25, 26, 28, 30, 31, 36, 37, Omit *And;* 40.
x. 12, 19, 31, 32, 33, 39.
xi. 12. Add *to him;* 29, 41, 44, 45, *that...he* (*the things...Jesus*); 49, *you* (*us*); 53, Omit *together;* 37.
xii. 1, 4, 6, 7, 13, 22, 23, 25, 34, 35, *among* (*with*).
xiii. 2, 3, 6, 22, 23, Omit *Now,* 26.
xiv. 2. Add *for;* 7, 9, 12, 14, 16, 17, *is* (*shall be*); 28.
xv. 7, 10, 11, 14, 26.
xvi. 3, 4, *their* (*the*); 10, 15, 19, 20, 23, 25, 27, 29, 32, 33.
xvii. 1, 4, 17, *the* (*thy*); 20, 21, 23, 24.
xviii. 4, 13, 18, Add *also,* 28, 30, 31, 40, Omit *all.*
xix. 7, 11, Add *him;* 13, 14, Omit *and;* 15, 16, 17, 20, 24, 29, 35, Add *also;* 38, 39.
xx. 6, 14, 16, 17, 18, 19, 20, 21, 28, 29.
xxi. 3, 4, 11, 12, 13, 15, 21.

Two general conclusions will follow from a careful study of the different lists of variations which include, I believe, all the passages where the text of St John is in any way doubtful, (1) that the utmost extent of variation is comparatively unimportant; and (2) that the most ancient text adds in almost every case some minute touch which increases the vigour or clearness of the language. The criterion of apparent fitness which is most ambiguous when applied to separate readings becomes trustworthy when it is applied to a considerable group of readings.

2. *The interpretation of the Gospel.*

The first commentary on the Gospel of St John of which any distinct record has been preserved was written by HERACLEON, "the most esteemed (δοκιμώτατος) representative of the School of Valentinus" (Clem. Al. 'Strom.' IV. 9. 73), whose friend he is said to have been. The work must therefore probably be assigned to the first half of the second century. The quotations preserved by Origen shew that Heracleon dealt with long continuous passages of the Gospel (*e.g.* c. iv.), but it is not certain that he commented on the whole. The text which he followed had one important various reading (iv. 18, ἕξ, *six*, for πέντε, *five*); and the manner in which he treats the book shews that he regarded it as of divine authority in the minutest details, though he frequently distorts its meaning by strange mystical interpretations [1].

The Commentary of ORIGEN was written at the injunction of his friend Ambrosius ('in Joh. Tom.' I. §§ 3, 6). The work was begun and the first five books were written at Alexandria (*c.* A.D. 225, Euseb. 'H.E.' VI. 24), before his ordination at Cæsarea (A.D. 228). The troubles which followed this event interrupted the task and it seems not to have been completed, if indeed it ever was completed, till more than ten years after its commencement (comp. Tom. VI. § 1). Eusebius mentions that of the whole work "only twenty-two books" (τόμοι) had come down to his time. He does not say how many there were originally. Jerome, according to the common texts, speaks of "thirty-four" or "thirty-nine" books ('Præf. Hom. in Luc.'), but these readings

[1] Part of the fragments of Heracleon are printed after Grabe and Massuet in Stieren's Irenæus, I. 938 ff. Jerome mentions a Commentary on the four Gospels attributed to Theophilus of Antioch, but questions its authenticity ('De Virr. Ill.' 25; 'Præf. ad Matt.' Ep. CXXI. 6).

are commonly altered to "thirty-two" on the authority of Rufinus (Huet, Orig. III. 2. 7). At present there remain Books I. II. (John i. 1—7 *a*), VI. (John i. 19—29), X. (John ii. 12—25), XIII. (John iv. 13—44), XIX. (part John viii. 19—24), XX. (John viii. 37—52), XXVIII. (John xi. 39—57), XXXII. (John xiii. 2—33), with fragments of IV. V. At the beginning of the thirty-third book, which deals with c. xiii., Origen speaks with doubt as to the completion of the whole Commentary, nor does he at the end of the book give, as he sometimes does, a promise of the immediate continuation of the work. It is possible therefore that his labours may have ended at this point. Certainly the whole Commentary would have occupied at least fifty books.

The work has Origen's faults and excellencies in full measure. It is lengthy, discursive, fanciful, speculative; but it abounds with noble thoughts and intuitions of the truth. As a commentator Origen created a new form of theological literature.

Little remains of the works of the earlier Greek Commentators of the fourth century, THEODORUS of Heraclea (Perinthus), (Theodor. 'H. E.' II. 3, Hieron. 'De Virr. Ill.' 90), and DIDYMUS of Alexandria (Hieron. 'De Virr. Ill.' 105). The 'Homilies' of CHRYSOSTOM, composed while he was still at Antioch (before A.D. 398), form the foundation of a historical interpretation of the Gospel. His explanations and applications of the text are clear, vigorous and eloquent. The reader will probably miss the signs of a spontaneous sympathy with the more mysterious aspects of the Gospel.

AUGUSTINE in his 'Lectures on St John' (*Tractatus in Joh.* CXXIV.) is strongest where Chrysostom is weakest. His ignorance of Greek constantly betrays him into the adoption of a false sense of the words, but his genius no less frequently enables him to enter with the fullest insight into the thought of a passage which may escape the verbal interpreter. I have ventured not unfrequently to quote his terse and pregnant comments in their original form. No translation can do them justice.

The Commentaries of THEODORE of Mopsuestia were popularly considered the best of the Antiochene school. Considerable fragments of his Commentary on St John remain.

At the opposite extreme to Theodore is CYRIL of Alexandria, whose Commentary on St John remains nearly complete. In this dogmatic interests overpower all other considerations. It was natural that Cyril should read the Gospel in the light of the controversies in which he was absorbed; but under his treatment the divine history seems to be dissolved into a docetic drama. At the same time his speculations, like those of the other Alexandrines, abound in isolated thoughts of great subtlety and beauty.

The two distinct 'Catenæ' of Corderius and Cramer contain extracts from other Greek Commentaries, Ammonius of Alexandria, Apollinaris of Laodicea, Severus of Antioch, Theodore of Heraclea, &c., but Cyril closes the series of the great patristic interpreters of St John. The Greek Commentaries of THEOPHYLACT († 1107), and EUTHYMIUS († *c.* 1118), are mainly epitomes of Chrysostom, but both are clear and sensible. The Latin Commentaries of Beda and Walafrid Strabo (*Glossa ordinaria*) depend largely on Augustine.

RUPERT of Deutz ('Comm. in Joh.' Libb. XIV.) in this subject as in others shewed original power. His Commentaries on St John are marked by great fertility in subtle speculation, though he claims to deal more with humble details than Augustine. The fragments of the Commentary of JOHANNES SCOTUS ERIGENA are not less interesting, and he explains the text carefully.

More comprehensive however and serviceable than these commentaries is the 'Golden Chain' (*Catena aurea*) of THOMAS AQUINAS, which brings together a large selection of comments from Greek and Latin writers. It must however be used with great caution, for a considerable proportion of the quotations adduced from early writers are taken from spurious books.

Of the Commentaries of the sixteenth century it must be sufficient to mention a few which will serve as representatives. Those of Ferus (*i. e.* Wild, of Mainz, 1536), Corn. a Lapide (*i. e.* Van der Steen, Louvain and Rome, † 1637), and Maldonatus (Maldonato, of Salamanca and Paris, 1596; St John is unfinished), among Roman Catholic scholars; of Brentius (*i.e.* Brenz, 'Homilies,' of Stuttgart, 1528), and J. Gerhard (of Jena, 1617), among Lutherans; of Musculus (*i.e.* Meusslin of Berne, 1548), and R. Gualther ('Homilies,' of Berne, 1565), among the "Reformed," are all conspicuous for thought, research and vigour. Lampe (of Utrecht, 1724) has given a very complete list of the Commentaries down to his own time; and his own work is a mine of learning, which it is, however, painful to work from the form in which he has arranged his materials.

The spread of idealism in Germany in the first quarter of the present century gave a fresh impulse to the study of St John. Fichte (1806, 'Anw. z. sel. Leben,' VI.) and Schelling (1841, 'Werke,' II. 4, pp. 302 f.), in different ways and with a partial conception of the scope of the Gospel, insisted upon its primary importance for the apprehension of Christian truth in relation to the present age. When Neander began his public work (1813), he lectured on the Gospel of St John, and on his deathbed (1850) he announced as the subject of his next course "The Gospel of St John considered in its true historical position." Meanwhile great light had been thrown upon the composition and contents of the Gospel. The commentaries of Lücke (1st ed. 1820—24), of Tholuck (1st ed. 1827), of Klee (1829), of Olshausen (1st ed. 1832), of Meyer (1st ed. 1834), and of De Wette (1st ed. 1837), contributed in various degrees to illustrate its meaning.

It does not fall within my scope to criticise these or later books[1].

For obvious reasons I have thought it best to refrain from using modern English Commentaries, with one partial exception. Otherwise I have endeavoured to take account as far as possible of the writings of every school which seemed likely to contribute to the understanding of St John. My one aim has been to express what seems to me the sense and teaching of his words. With this view I have, except in a few cases, simply given the conclusion at which I have arrived without reviewing rival opinions, or citing the authorities by which it is supported or opposed. I have not however consciously passed over or extenuated any difficulty which I have been able to feel: nor again, have I called particular attention to details which happen to have come into undue prominence in modern controversy.

It would be an idle task to enumerate all the names of those from whose writings I have sought and gained help; and I should be unable to measure the debts which I owe to scholars who often teach much when they do not command assent. Yet there are some names which cannot be passed over in silence. When I began to work seriously at the Gospel of St John more than twenty-five years ago I felt that I owed most to Origen, Neander, Olshausen, Luthardt, and, from a very different point of view, to F. C. Baur. In arranging my thoughts during the last eight years I feel that I owe most to Godet, whose Commentary, except on questions of textual criticism, seems to me to be unsurpassed. And on the other hand Keim has continually offered criticisms and suggestions which have opened fresh sources of illustration for the text. But throughout this space of Cambridge work, the living voice of friends has been far more helpful to me than books. The fulness of sympathy in common labour brings light and fresh power of vision, and not only materials for thought.

Throughout the notes I have quoted the renderings of the Latin Vulgate in the hope of directing more attention to the study of it. It seems to me that we have lost much in every way from our neglect of a Version which has influenced the Theology of the West more profoundly than we know.

One department of illustration, it must be added, still calls for systematic study. The didactic method and not only the language of St John is essentially Hebraic; and very much has still to be learnt especially from the *Midrashim* before the full force of his record

[1] An admirable summary of the literature dealing with the authenticity of St John's Gospel has been added by Dr C. R. Gregory to the English translation of Luthardt's 'St John the Author of the Fourth Gospel,' Edinburgh, 1875.

can be apprehended. The collections which Wetstein has made from Lightfoot and other early Rabbinic scholars, Delitzsch's 'Horæ Hebraicæ' (in the 'Ztschr. f. Luth. Theol.'); the recent work of Wünsche ('Neue Beiträge zur Erläuterung der Evangelien aus Talmud u. Midrash,' Göttingen, 1878), which is very useful, but by no means always exact; Siegfried's 'Philon von Alexandria' (indirectly), and Mr Taylor's excellent edition of the 'Sayings of the Jewish Fathers' (*Pirke Aboth*), rather point to the rich mine than exhaust it[1].

There is a remarkable legend ('Shemoth R.' c. v.), that when the LORD gave the Law from Sinai He wrought great marvels with His voice (Job xxxvii. 5). "The voice sounded from the South; and as the people hastened to the South, lo! it sounded from the North. They turned to the North, and it came from the East. They turned to the East, and it came from the West. They turned thither, and it came from heaven. They lifted up their eyes to heaven, and it came from the depths of the earth. And they said one to another, Where shall wisdom be found? (Job xxviii. 12).

"And the Voice went forth throughout the world, and was divided into seventy voices, according to the seventy tongues of men, and each nation heard the Voice in its own tongue, and their souls failed them; but Israel heard and suffered not.

"And each one in Israel heard it according to his capacity; old men, and youths, and boys, and sucklings and women: the voice was to each one as each one had the power to receive it."

The student of St John will find the parable fulfilled as he ponders the Apostle's words with growing experience, and unchanged patience. He himself limits the meaning which he finds in them.

"Omnes carnalium sordes affectuum ab oculis cordis abstergendæ sunt iis qui in scholâ Christi venerabilibus student litteris; ut hanc aliquatenus valeant Aquilam prosequi, quam cordis munditia juvit ut claritatem solis æterni, plus ceteris divinæ visionis animalibus, irreverberata posset mentis acie contemplari" (RUPERTUS OF DEUTZ).

[1] The 'Kôl Kôré' of R. Soloweyczyk translated into French under the title 'La Bible, le Talmud et l'Evangile,' Paris, 1875, St Matthew and St Mark, is of little value in this respect.

THE GOSPEL ACCORDING TO

St. JOHN

CHAPTER I.

1 *The divinity, humanity, and office of Jesus Christ.* 15 *The testimony of John.* 39 *The calling of Andrew, Peter, &c.*

IN the beginning was the Word, and the Word was with God, and the Word was God.

THE GOSPEL ACCORDING TO ST JOHN] The title of the Gospel, which is found in very different forms in ancient authorities, is no part of the book itself. The earliest authorities, and those which represent the earliest text, give the simplest form: *According to John* (κατὰ Ἰωάννην [-άνην] ℵBD; *secundum Iohannem* (as the running heading) Lat. vt.; and so Syr. vt.: *of John*). The word *Gospel* which is implied in this title is supplied by the mass of MSS. (εὐαγγέλιον κατὰ Ἰ. [without the article] ACLX, &c.; and so, as the initial heading, Lat. vt., Syr. vt.). Very many of the later MSS. add the definite article (τὸ κατὰ Ἰ. εὐαγγ.), and very many also add an epithet: *The holy Gospel according to John* (τὸ κατὰ Ἰ. ἅγιον εὐαγγ.). A few MSS. give the remarkable title: *Of the* [*holy*] *Gospel according to John* (ἐκ τοῦ κατὰ Ἰ. [ἁγίου] εὐαγγ.). The printed texts of the Peshito give: *The holy Gospel of the preaching of John the preacher.* There is a similar variety in the titles given in the English Versions: *Đæt Godspell aefter Iohannes gerecednesse* [narration] (Anglo-Saxon). *The Gospel (Euuangelie) of Joon* [or *Joon* simply] (Wycliffe). *The Gospel of Saint John* (Tyndale 1526, 1534, 1535, Coverdale, Matthew, Great Bible). *The Gospel after S. John* (Taverner 1539, with the running heading *The Gospel of S. John*). *The Gospel by Saint Iohn* (Bishops' Bible 1568, 1572). *The Holy Gospel of Jesus Christ according to John* (Geneva 1560, Rheims 1582 with the running heading *The Gospel according to S. John*, Tomson 1583). *The Gospel according to S. John* (A. V. 1611).

THE PROLOGUE (i. i.—18).

Though the narrative of St John's Gospel is not marked off by any very distinct line from the introductory verses, it has been generally acknowledged that i. 1—18 forms an introduction to the whole work. This conclusion appears to be completely established by a careful analysis of the contents of the section, which present in a summary form the main truths that are illustrated by the records of the history. The first verse appears to stand by itself: the remaining verses give an outline of the relations of the Word to Creation. The connexion of the different parts, and the order of progress, will be best seen in a tabular form:

I. THE WORD IN HIS ABSOLUTE, ETERNAL BEING (*v.* 1).

1. His *Existence:* Beyond time.
2. His *Personal Existence:* In active Communion with God.
3. His *Nature:* God in Essence.

II. THE WORD IN RELATION TO CREATION (*vv.* 2—18).

1. *The essential facts* (*vv.* 2—5).
   - i. The source of creation. In the divine counsel (*v.* 2).
   - ii. The act of creation (*v.* 3).
     - The Word the Agent (*through Him*).
     - The Word the Quickening Presence (*not apart from Him*).
   - iii. The being of things created (*vv.* 4, 5).
     - *a.* In the divine Idea (*v.* 4).
       - As to the World.
       - As to Man.
     - *b.* In human history (*v.* 5).
       - The continuous conflict of Light and Darkness following on a critical assault of Darkness.
2. *The historic manifestation of the Word generally* (*vv.* 6—13).
   - i. The testimony of prophecy represented by John (*vv.* 6—8).
     - *a.* John's personality (*v.* 6).
     - *b.* The end of his mission (*v.* 7).
     - *c.* His nature (*v.* 8).
   - ii. The manifestations of the Word (as Light) before the Incarnation (*vv.* 9, 10).
     - *a.* By special revelations (*v.* 9).
     - *b.* By His immanent Presence (*v.* 10).
   - iii. The Coming of the Word to the

Chosen People consummated at the Incarnation (*vv.* 11—13).
a. National unbelief (*v.* 11).
b. Individual faith (*vv.* 12, 13).

3. *The Incarnation as apprehended by personal experience* (*vv.* 14—18).
i. The personal witness (*v.* 14).
a. The fact.
b. The observation of the fact.
c. The moral nature of the fact.
ii. The witness of prophecy (John) (*v.* 15).
a. The promised Christ.
b. His essential dignity.
iii. The nature of the revelation (*vv.* 16—18).
a. In the experience of believers.
b. In relation to the Law.
c. In its final source.

Other arrangements of the Prologue have been proposed which bring out different aspects. It has been divided into two parts: 1—5 (the essential nature of the Word), 6—18 (the historical manifestation of the Word); and again into three parts: 1—5, 6—13, 14—18, which have been supposed to present the progressive revelation of the Word, either in fuller detail from section to section, or in historical order, as He is essentially, as He was made known under the Old Covenant, as He was made known under the New; and yet again into three parts: 1—4 (the activity of the Word before the Incarnation generally), 5—11 (the revelation of unbelief), 12—18 (the revelation of faith).

The detailed examination of the text will shew how far these arrangements correspond with the structure of the whole passage.

I. THE WORD IN HIS ABSOLUTE, ETERNAL BEING (*v.* 1).

CHAP. I. 1. The first sentence of the Gospel offers a perfect example of the stately symmetry by which the whole narrative is marked. The three clauses of which it consists are set side by side (...*and*...*and*...); the Subject (*the Word*) is three times repeated; and the substantive verb three times occupies the same relative position. The symmetry of form corresponds with the exhaustiveness of the thought. The three clauses contain all that it is possible for man to realise as to the essential nature of the Word in relation to time, and mode of being, and character: He was (1) *in the beginning:* He was (2) *with God:* He was (3) *God.* At the same time these three clauses answer to the three great moments of the Incarnation of the Word declared in *v.* 14. He who "was God," *became flesh:* He who "was with God," *tabernacled among us* (comp. 1 John i. 2): He who "was in the beginning," *became* (in time).

This revelation is the foundation of the whole Gospel of St John. It sets aside the false notion that the Word became "personal" first at the time of Creation or at the Incarnation. The absolute, eternal, immanent relations of the Persons of the Godhead furnish the basis for revelation. Because the Word was personally distinct from "God" and yet essentially "God," He could make Him known. Compare an interesting passage of Irenæus: II. 30. 9.

In the beginning] The phrase carries back the thoughts of the reader to Gen. i. 1, which necessarily fixes the sense of the *beginning*. Here, as there, "the beginning" is the initial moment of time and creation; but there is this difference, that Moses dwells on that which starts from the point, and traces the record of divine action *from* the beginning (comp. 1 John i. 1, ii. 13), while St John lifts our thoughts *beyond* the beginning and dwells on that which "was" when time, and with time finite being, began its course. Comp. Prov. viii. 23. Already when "God created the heaven and the earth," "the Word *was*." The "being" of the Word is thus necessarily carried beyond the limits of time, though the pre-existence of the Word is not definitely stated. The simple affirmation of existence in this connexion suggests a loftier conception than that of pre-existence; which is embarrassed by the idea of time. Pre-existence however is affirmed in a different connexion: ch. xvii. 5.

This force of *in the beginning* is brought out by a comparison with the corresponding phrase in 1 John i. 1, *from the beginning*. The latter marks the activity of the Word in time from the initial point: the former emphasizes the existence of the Word at the initial point, and so before time.

was] The verb *was* does not express a completed past, but rather a continuous state. The imperfect tense of the original suggests in this relation, as far as human language can do so, the notion of absolute, supra-temporal, existence.

the Word] This translation of the original (λόγος, Vulg. *verbum*, though some early Latin authorities give *sermo*) ought undoubtedly to be kept. It is probable that there is a reference to the language of Gen. i. 3 ff. "God said." For the history and meaning of the term Logos see Introduction p. xv. Here it will be sufficient to observe:

1. The personal title *Logos* is used absolutely only in *vv.* 1, 14 (Rev. xix. 13; Heb. iv. 12—*the Word of God*). In 1 John i. 1 the phrase *the Word of life* is not personal, but equivalent to "the revelation of the life."

2. The term λόγος never has the sense of *reason* in the New Testament.

3. St John introduces the term without any explanation. He assumes that his readers are familiar with it.

4. The theological use of the term appears

1. 1. 2 [a]The same was in the beginning
with God.
1. 16. 3 [b]All things were made by him;
and without him was not any thing
made that was made.

---

to be derived directly from the Palestinian *Memra*, and not from the Alexandrine *Logos*.

5. Though the term is not used in the apostolic writings in the sense of *Reason*, yet the first verse deals with the divine relations independently of the actual revelation to men. The "Word" (λόγος) of *v.* 1 includes the conception of the immanent word (λόγος ἐνδιάθετος) of Greek philosophy in thought though not in language. But the idea is approached from the side of historical revelation. He who has been made known to us as "the Word" *was* in the beginning. Thus the economic Trinity, the Trinity of revelation, is shewn to answer to an essential Trinity. The Word as personal (ἐνυπόστατος) satisfies every partial conception of the *Logos*.

6. The personal titles "the Word" and "the Word of God" must be kept in close connexion with the same terms as applied to the sum of the Gospel in the New Testament, and with the phrase "the word of the Lord" in the prophecies of the Old Testament. The Word, before the Incarnation, was the one source of the many divine words; and Christ, the Word Incarnate, is Himself the Gospel.

7. The evangelist uses the title *Word* and not *Son* here, because he wishes to carry his readers to the most absolute conceptions.

was with God] The phrase (ἦν πρός, Vulg. *erat apud*) is remarkable. It is found also Matt. xiii. 56; Mark vi. 3; Mark ix. 19; Mark xiv. 49; Luke ix. 41; 1 John i. 2. The idea conveyed by it is not that of simple coexistence, as of two persons contemplated separately in company (εἶναι μετά, iii. 26, &c.), or united under a common conception (εἶναι σύν, Luke xxii. 56), or (so to speak) in local relation (εἶναι παρά, ch. xvii. 5), but of being (in some sense) directed towards and regulated by that with which the relation is fixed (v. 19). The personal being of the Word was realised in active intercourse with and in perfect communion with God. Compare Gen. i. 26, where the same truth is expressed under distinct human imagery. The Word "was with God" before He revealed God. The main thought is included in the statement that *God is love* (1 John iv. 16; comp. ch. xvii. 24); and it finds expression in another form in the description of "the life, the life eternal, which was manifested to men." This life "was with the Father" (ἦν πρὸς τὸν πατέρα, not πρὸς τὸν θεόν, 1 John i. 2): it was realised in the intercommunion of the divine Persons when time was not.

the Word was God] The predicate (*God*) stands emphatically first, as in iv. 24. It is necessarily without the article (θεός not ὁ θεός) inasmuch as it describes the nature of the Word and does not identify His Person. It would be pure Sabellianism to say "the Word was ὁ θεός." No idea of inferiority of nature is suggested by the form of expression, which simply affirms the true deity of the Word. Compare for the converse statement of the true humanity of Christ v. 27 (ὅτι υἱὸς ἀνθρώπου ἐστίν note).

On the other hand it will be noticed that "the Word" is placed in personal relation to "God" (ὁ θεός) spoken of absolutely in the second clause; while in the third clause "the Word" is declared to be "God," and so included in the unity of the Godhead. Thus we are led to conceive that the divine nature is essentially in the Son, and at the same time that the Son can be regarded, according to that which is His peculiar characteristic, in relation to God as God. He is the "image of God" (εἰκὼν τοῦ θεοῦ) and not simply of the Father.

II. THE WORD IN RELATION TO CREATION (*vv.* 2—18).

This main section of the Prologue falls into three parts:

1. *The essential facts* (*vv.* 2—5).
2. *The historic manifestation of the Word generally* (*vv.* 6—13).
3. *The Incarnation as apprehended by personal experience* (*vv.* 14—18).

The Evangelist having given in the first verse such an idea as man can receive of the Word in Himself, next traces out step by step the mode in which the Word has entered into relation with Creation.

1. *The essential facts* (*vv.* 2—5).

This sub-section lays open the source of creation in the divine counsel (*v.* 2), the act of creation through the Word and by His Presence (*v.* 3), the being of things created in the divine idea (*v.* 4), and as manifested in history (*v.* 5).

2. In passing from the thought of the Personal Being of the Word in Himself to the revelation of the Word, the Evangelist brings the revelation into the closest connexion with the essential Nature of the Word by the repetition in combination of the three clauses of the 1st verse: *The same was in the beginning with God*. At the moment of creation that relation, which *was* eternally, was actually effective. Creation itself was (in some sense) the result of the eternal fellowship expressed in the relation of the Word to God.

The same] Literally, *This* [Word]; He who has just been declared to be God. The pronoun implies and emphasizes the whole previous definition. Comp. vi. 46, vii. 18, &c.

4 In him was life; and the life was the light of men.

5 And the light shineth in darkness; and the darkness comprehended it not.

3. *All things*] The exact form (πάντα) expresses all things taken severally, and not all things regarded as a defined whole (τὰ πάντα, Col. i. 16). The thought to be brought out is that of the vast multiplicity of created things (spirits, matter, &c.). Of all these no one came into being without the Word. For this reason the term "the world" (ὁ κόσμος, *vv.* 9, 10) is purposely avoided.

were made] Literally, *became* (ἐγένετο). Creation itself is represented as a "becoming" in contrast with the "being" emphasized before. The same contrast recurs in *vv.* 6, 9.

Three distinct words are used in the New Testament to convey the conception of creation, (1) to *create* (κτίζειν), and (2) to *make* (ποιεῖν), in reference to the Creator; and (3) to *become* (γίγνεσθαι), in reference to that which is created. The first word (Rev. iv. 11, x. 6; Col. i. 16, &c.) suggests the idea of design, plan, purpose; the second (Rev. xiv. 7; Mark x. 6, &c.), of an actual result or object produced (comp. Eph. ii. 10); the third, of the law fulfilled in the production of the object. The use of "become" in *vv.* 14, 17, brings out its force as expressive of the unfolding of a divine order.

by him] **through Him.** The Word is described as the mediate Agent of Creation (διά, *through*, not ὑπό, *by*). Comp. Col. i. 16; Heb. i. 2. The Father is the one spring, source (πηγή), and end of all finite being, as He is of the Godhead. *All things are of Him ...through Jesus Christ*...(1 Cor. viii. 6). Thus in different relations creation can be attributed to the Father and to the Son. Comp. v. 17.

without him] Literally, *apart from Him* (comp. xv. 5). Creation is set forth under a twofold aspect, as depending on the divine Agency and on the divine Presence. It is first called into being by the Word, and then sustained in being by Him (Heb. i. 3). Compare the use of *in Him*, Col. i. 16, 17; Acts xvii. 28.

was not any thing made] The true form of the text gives **not even one thing** (οὐδὲ ἕν), for "not anything" (οὐδέν). St John emphasizes the universality of the action of the Word. The same thought is expressed in detail by St Paul: Col. i. 16.

For the combination of a positive and negative expression to express the fulness of truth, see ch. iii. 16, vi. 50; 1 John i. 5, ii. 4, 27, v. 12.

was made] **hath been made.** The change of tense (from ἐγένετο to γέγονεν) distinguishes the act of creation (*aor.*) from the continuance of things created (*perf.*). Compare Col. i. 16 (ἐκτίσθη, ἔκτισται).

3, 4. ...*that was made* (**hath been made**). *In him was life*...] The original words admit two very distinct divisions. The last clause of *v.* 3 may be taken either (1) with the words which precede, as A.V., or (2) with the words which follow. It would be difficult to find a more complete consent of ancient authorities in favour of any reading, than that which supports the second punctuation: *Without Him was not anything made. That which hath been made in Him was life.* See Note at the end of the Chapter.

4. *the life was the light of men*] The works of the Word supplied for a time, from within and from without, that which He supplied more completely by His personal manifestations (ix. 5, note), and afterwards by His historical Presence (viii. 12, xii. 46), and yet more completely by His Presence through the Spirit in the Church. He is Himself, however revealed, the Light of men and of the world (viii. 12, ix. 5).

the light] the one light. It must be observed that the Word is not here spoken of directly as "the Light of men." He is "the Light" through the medium of "Life." In part and according to the divine constitution of things He is made known, and makes Himself known, in and through the vital processes of creation.

of men] of men as a class (τῶν ἀνθρώπων) and not of individuals only. Comp. iii. 19, xvii. 6. Man as made in the image of God stood in a special relation to the Word. "He saith not the Light of the Jews only but of all men; for all of us, in so far as we have received intellect and reason from that Word which created us, are said to be illuminated by Him" (Theophylact, quoted by Thomas Aqu.).

5. In *v.* 4 the divine essence and the divine purpose of creation are declared from the side of God; in *v.* 5 the Evangelist describes the actual state of things from the side of man. The description holds good generally. It embraces the experience of Judaism and Heathendom, of pre-Christian and post-Christian times. The truth which found its most signal fulfilment in the historical Presence of Christ, was established in various ways both before and after it. The conflict of Light and Darkness which represents one aspect of the history of the Gospel, represents also one aspect of all human history.

the light] It is probable that the word must be taken in a somewhat wider sense in this clause than in the last, so as to include not only the manifestations of the Word (as "Life") through "Nature" in the widest sense of the term, but also the Personal manifestations of the Word. It is impossible for us to judge how far the two series of manifestations may be in fact united. Comp. Ps. xxxvi. 9.

Matt. 3. 6 ¶ [c]There was a man sent from God, whose name *was* John.

7 The same came for a witness, to bear witness of the Light,

---

shineth] Comp. 1 John ii. 8. The light does not "appear" only; it "lightens," Gen. i. 17; Ps. lxxvii. 18, xcvii. 4 (LXX.). It is of the essence of light to invade the realm of darkness. The word (φαίνειν) describes that which is the action of light in itself, as distinguished from its effects as "illuminating" men (φωτίζειν, *v.* 9). This action of the Light is not to be limited to any one point. It is continuous from the creation to the consummation of things, though there have been times when it has flashed forth with peculiar splendour.

in darkness] *in* **the darkness.** Side by side with the light the darkness appears suddenly and without preparation. An acquaintance with the history of the Fall is evidently presupposed. The perfect fellowship of man and God has been broken. Man in his self-will has separated, isolated himself. He has made for himself, so to speak, an atmosphere of darkness, by seeking to sever his life from the Source of life. For all that is without God, apart from Him, is darkness. Comp. 1 John i. 5.

comprehended (**overcame**) *it not*] The verb in the original (κατέλαβεν) has received two very different renderings—*overcame* and *apprehended.* It is found again in a parallel passage, xii. 35, *that darkness overtake you not;* and also in an old reading of vi. 17, *the darkness overtook them.* In these cases the sense cannot be doubtful. The darkness comes down upon, enwraps men. As applied to light this sense includes the further notion of overwhelming, eclipsing. The relation of darkness to light is one of essential antagonism. If the darkness is represented as pursuing the light it can only be to overshadow and not to appropriate it. And this appears to be the meaning here. The existence of the darkness is affirmed, and at the same time the unbroken energy of the light. But the victory of the light is set forth as the result of a past struggle; and the abrupt alteration of tense brings into prominence the change which has passed over the world. It could not but happen that the darkness when it came should seek to cover all; and in this attempt it failed: *the light is shining in the darkness, and the darkness overcame it not.*

This general interpretation of the word, which is completely established by the usage of St John (comp. 1 Thess. v. 4), is supported by the Greek Fathers; but the Latin version gives the rendering *comprehenderunt*, "took hold of," "embraced." This sense, however, and that of "understood" (expressed in the New Testament by the middle voice of the verb: Acts iv. 13, x. 34, xxv. 25; Eph. iii. 18) seem to be inconsistent with the image and foreign to the context. The darkness, as such, could not "seize," "appropriate," the light. In doing this it would cease to exist. And yet further, the notion of the historical development of revelation is not at present pursued. The great elements of the moral position of the world are stated: their combinations and issues are outlined afterwards. In this respect *v.* 5 is parallel with 9—13, indicating the existence and continuance of a conflict which is there regarded in its contrasted issues. The whole phrase is indeed a startling paradox. The light does not banish the darkness: the darkness does not overpower the light. Light and darkness coexist in the world side by side.

2. *The historic manifestation of the Word generally* (*vv.* 6—13).

In the former section the great facts which issue in the spiritual conflict of life have been set forth. The Evangelist now traces in outline the course of the conflict which is apprehended in its essential character in the final manifestation of the Light. This manifestation was heralded by prophecy, of which John the Baptist was the last representative (*vv.* 6—8). It had been prepared also by continuous revelations of the Word, as light, at once through special communications (*v.* 9), and by His immanent Presence (*v.* 10). But when He came to His own in the fulness of time, He found, as the Incarnate Saviour, national unbelief (*v.* 11) relieved only by individual faith (*vv.* 12, 13). The conflict shadowed out before (*v.* 5) still continued.

6—8. The office of prophecy is shewn through the work of the Baptist; of whom the Evangelist speaks in regard to his personality (*v.* 6), the end of his mission (*v.* 7), his nature (*v.* 8). The abrupt introduction of John is explained by the fact that the review of the revelation, preparatory to the Incarnation, starts from the last, that is the most intelligible, stage in it. The Baptist—a priest and a Nazarite—was the completed type of the Prophet (Matt. xi. 9 f. and parallels); and it was by the Baptist, an interpreter of the Old Dispensation and herald of the New, that St John himself was guided to Christ (*vv.* 35 ff.).

6. *There was...*] More exactly, *There arose, became* (ἐγένετο)...Each of the three words in the original which describe the advent of John is expressive. His "becoming" is contrasted with the "being" of the Word (*v.* 9). He is spoken of as "a man" with a significant reference to the mystery realised in *v.* 14. And at the same time he was charged with a divine mission.

that all *men* through him might believe.
8 He was not that Light, but *was sent* to bear witness of that Light.
9 *That* was the true Light, which

---

sent from God] *from* (παρά) and not simply *by* God (comp. xv. 26). On the word used here for *send* (ἀποστέλλω), see xx. 21 note. Comp. Mal. iii. 1, ch. iii. 28. The two words (*was, sent*) are not a mere periphrasis for "was sent:" they fix attention separately on the person and on the mission of the Baptist.

whose name...] Rather (in accordance with St John's sharp brief style; so iii. 1), **his** *name was*.... Possibly an allusion to the meaning of the name (Theodore, Gotthold, God's gracious gift) underlies the clause. Compare Luke i. 63.

John] On the use of the simple name without any title in the fourth Gospel, see Introd.

7. *The same*] He who was of such a nature, so commissioned, so named. Comp. *v.* 2, and contrast the pronoun in *v.* 8.

came for a witness, to bear...that...] *came* **for witness, that he might** *bear... that all men*...John's mission is first set forth under its generic aspect: he came **for witness** (εἰς μαρτυρίαν), not *for a witness;* and then its specific object (ἵνα μαρτ. περὶ τ. φ.) and its final object (ἵνα π. πιστ.) are defined coordinately (*that...that*...). This combination of successive and related ends under one form of construction, is characteristic of St John's style: comp. xx. 31, xv. 16, xvii. 21, 23 f. For the phrase "for witness" compare the kindred phrase Matt. viii. 4, x. 18, xxiv. 14 (εἰς μαρτύριον); Mark vi. 11. The coming of the Baptist (ἦλθε) in the fulfilment of his office is contrasted with his personal coming (ἐγένετο *v.* 6).

for witness] On the idea of "witness" see Introd. The office of the prophet in the fullest sense is to make known Another. This office had been fulfilled "in many parts and in many fashions" by all God's messengers in earlier times, and at last eminently by the Baptist (comp. iii. 30). He came, as his predecessors, but with a clearer charge, *to bear witness concerning the Light*, to interpret to men the signs of a divine will and guidance without them and within them, and then to point to Him who was Himself the Life and the Light. In this way provision was made for leading men in human ways to recognise the divine.

all men] The prophets had prepared the way for the extension of the divine call beyond Israel (comp. Isai. xlix. 6). The Baptist at last delivered a message which in its essence was universal. As the last prophet, the last interpreter of the Law, he carried the preparatory discipline to its final application. He spoke to men as men; outward descent, national privileges, disappeared from their place in the divine order from the time of his preaching. The basis of his preaching was repentance—inner self-renunciation—the end was faith. In this connexion it is to be noticed that the conception of faith is sharpened by being left in an absolute form: *that all men might believe* (contrast *v.* 12) *through him* (John). There can be but one adequate object of faith, even God made known in the Son. *Believe* is used similarly *v.* 51, v. 44, xi. 15, xiv. 29, &c., iv. 41 f., 53, xix. 35, xx. 29, 31.

The character of the Baptist's preaching is implied in its scope. The phrase "all men" is unintelligible except on the supposition that the universal gospel was preceded by a call to repentance. But it is worthy of remark that St John does not notice explicitly his call to repentance, nor do the terms "repent," "repentance" find a place in his Gospel or Epistles ("Repent" occurs frequently in the Apocalypse). Thus the correspondence between St John and the Synoptists as to the character of the Baptist's work is complete without a correspondence of letter.

through him] that is the Baptist, not the Light. The message of the Baptist has an absolute and enduring power. He still in spirit goes before Christ.

8. *He was not that* (**the**) *Light*] From this passage and other similar passages (*v.* 20, iii. 26 ff.) it has been plausibly argued that the Evangelist was familiar with some who unduly exalted the Baptist. Comp. Acts xix. 3 f. John was "the lamp" (v. 35) and not the light. The pronoun of reference which is used (ἐκεῖνος) isolates and so fixes attention upon the person referred to. Comp. i. 18, note, ii. 21, note.

but was sent to...] Literally, *but that*... The ellipse is best filled up from *v.* 7: *but* **came that he might**... Comp. ix. 3, xv. 25, note.

9, 10. The preparation of prophecy, represented by John, was one part of the education of the world. The Word Himself as light (*v.* 5) visited the world which He had made (*v.* 9), and was in it still (*v.* 10).

9. *That was* (**There** *was*) *the true Light ...that cometh* (**coming**) *into the world*] The original text is ambiguous. The participle *coming* (ἐρχόμενον) may agree either (1) with *man*, or (2) with *light*. Thus there are two distinct series of interpretations. (1) If *coming* be taken with *man*, the sense will be either (*a*) simply "every man" according to a common Hebrew idiom, or (*b*) "every man at the moment of his birth." But it is scarcely possible that the words "coming into the

lighteth every man that cometh into
the world.

or. 11. 10 He was in the world, and [d]the
world was made by him, and the
world knew him not.

11 He came unto his own, and his
own received him not.

12 But as many as received him,
to them gave he ‖power to become ‖ Or, *the*
the sons of God, *even* to them that *right*, or, *privilege.*
believe on his name:

13 Which were born, not of blood,
nor of the will of the flesh, nor of the
will of man, but of God.

---

world" can be without distinct meaning; and, in spite of Wordsworth's greatest ode, it is hardly true to say that the illumination of the Light, which comes through Life, is most complete at man's entrance into the world.

(2) If, on the other hand, *coming* be taken to agree with *light*, it may be directly connected either (*a*) with "lighteth," or (*b*) with "was." In the first case (*a*) the sense will be "lighteth every man by coming;" but the context does not call for any statement as to the mode of the action of the Light; and the Light illuminates by "being" as well as by "coming." If then (*b*) "was...coming" be taken together, there is still some ambiguity remaining. The phrase has been interpreted to mean (α) "was destined to come," and (β) "was on the point of coming," and (γ) "was in the very act of coming."

But it seems best to take it more literally and yet more generally as describing a coming which was progressive, slowly accomplished, combined with a permanent being, so that both the verb (*was*) and the participle (*coming*) have their full force, and do not form a periphrasis for an imperfect. The mission of John was one and definite; but all along up to his time "the Light" of which he came to witness continued to shine, being revealed in many parts and in many ways. **There was the Light, the true Light,** *which lighteth every man;* that Light was, and yet more, that Light was **coming into the world.** The same idea of a constant, continuous coming of the Word to men is found in vi. 33, 50, where "that cometh" (ὁ καταβαίνων) stands in marked contrast with "that came" (ὁ καταβάς, *vv.* 51, 58). Taken in relation to the context, the words declare that men were not left alone to interpret the manifestations of the Light in the Life around them and in them. The Light from whom that Life flows made Himself known more directly. From the first He was (so to speak) on His way to the world, advancing towards the Incarnation by preparatory revelations. He came in type and prophecy and judgment.

The identification of "the Word" with "the Light" is natural and prepared by *v.* 5. But, at the same time, the titles are not coextensive. "The Light" (as the other special titles, the Bread of Life, &c.) describes "the Word" only in a special relation towards creation and particularly towards men.

In this relation the Light is characterized as (1) *the true* (ἀληθινός) Light, and (2) that *which lighteth every man.* The former expression (1) marks the essential nature of the Light as that of which all other lights are only partial rays or reflections, as the archetypal Light (see iv. 23, vi. 32, xv. 1). The "true light" in this sense is not opposed to a "false light," but to an imperfect, incomplete, transitory light.

The latter (2) describes the universal extent of its action. The words must be taken simply as they stand. No man is wholly destitute of the illumination of "the Light." In nature, and life, and conscience it makes itself felt in various degrees to all. The Word is the spiritual Sun: viii. 12 (xi. 9). This truth, it may be added, is recognised here by St John, but he does not (like Philo) dwell upon it. Before the fact of the Incarnation it falls into the background. For the Jewish idea of "the light of Creation" (Is. xxx. 26), see Taylor's 'Sayings of the Jewish Fathers,' p. 72.

lighteth] Comp. Luke xi. 35, 36. The Light is contrasted in each particular with the Witness to the Light. He "arose" (ἐγένετο); the Light "was" (ἦν). He guided his disciples away from himself; the Light illuminated in virtue of its own nature. He came once for all; the Light was ever coming through the ages.

every man] The idea is distinct from that of "all men" (*v.* 7). The relation is not collective, corporate, as it is here presented, but personal, and universal while personal. The reality of this relation furnished the basis for the crowning fact of the Incarnation. The world was made for this re-gathering.

coming *into the world*] Comp. iii. 19, xii. 46.

10, 11. Verse 9, according to the interpretation which has been given, presents a comprehensive view of the action of the Light. This action is now divided into two parts. The first part (*v.* 10) gathers up the facts and issues of the manifestation of the Light as immanent. The second part (*v.* 11) contains an account of the special personal manifestation of the Light to a chosen race. The two parts are contrasted throughout as to the mode (*was, came*), the scene (*the world, His own home*), the recipients (*the world, His own people*), the end (*not know, not receive*), of the manifestation. The world failed to recognise Him who was doubly shewn as its Creator and as its Preserver. The people of God failed to welcome Him whom they had been prepared to receive.

10. *He was in the world*] Comp. *v.* 5, note. It is impossible to refer these words simply to the historical Presence of the Word in Jesus as witnessed to by the Baptist. The whole scope and connexion of the passage requires a wider sense. The Word acts by His Presence as well as by His special Advent. The continuance and progress of things, no less than their original constitution, are fitted to make Him known.

the world] the sum of created being, which belongs to the sphere of human life as an ordered whole considered apart from God, and in its moral aspect represented by humanity. See Note at the end of the Chapter.

knew] "recognised." Comp. ii. 25, note.

him] The personal character which has been already implied now finds expression (αὐτόν, contrasted with the neuter in *v.* 5, αὐτό). The previous pronoun is ambiguous in the original (δι' αὐτοῦ), but it is most natural to suppose that this also is masculine (as in A.V.).

The form of the sentence is peculiarly characteristic. The clauses are placed simply side by side (...*and the world...and the world*...). In this way the statement of the issue (*and the world knew Him not*) gains in pathos. For a similar use of *and* see viii. 20, note.

11. The Evangelist now passes from the universal action of the Word as the Light to His special action. Creation and mankind were His, and not unvisited by Him; but in "the world" and in humanity one spot and one people were in a peculiar sense devoted to Him. The land of Israel was "His own home," and the children of Israel were "His own people." The Word came to the holy land and to the holy nation, and they "received Him not."

came] The word forms a climax when combined with those which precede: *was, was in the world, came to His own;* and in this connexion it appears to contain an allusion to the technical sense of "he that cometh." Comp. ix. 39. The tense (ἦλθε, comp. *v.* 7) seems necessarily to mark a definite advent, the Incarnation, which consummated the former revelations of the Word to Israel. It does not seem possible that the manifestations before the Incarnation and separate from it could be so spoken of. Nor is there anything in this interpretation which detracts from the force of *v.* 14. The Incarnation is regarded in the two places under different aspects. Here it is regarded in relation to the whole scheme of Redemption, as the crowning revelation to the ancient people of God; in *v.* 14, it is regarded in its distinctive character as affecting humanity. Here it is seen from the side of national failure, there of individual faith.

He came...received him not] **He came unto his own home and his own people received him not.** The Vulgate rightly preserves the significant variation of the original: *in propria (sua) venit, et sui eum non receperunt.*

unto his own (neut.)] *i.e.* "to His own home" (εἰς τὰ ἴδια). Compare xvi. 32, xix. 27; Acts xxi. 6 (Esther v. 10, vi. 12, LXX.). There can be no reasonable doubt that this phrase, and the corresponding masculine which follows, "his own" (οἱ ἴδιοι) *i.e.* "his own people," describe the land and the people of Israel as being, in a sense in which no other land and people were, the home and the family of GOD, of Jehovah. "The holy land" (Zech. ii. 12. Comp. 2 Macc. i. 7) was "the LORD's land" (Hos. ix. 3; Jer. ii. 7, xvi. 18. Comp. Lev. xxv. 23); and Israel was His portion (Ex. xix. 5; Deut. vii. 6, xiv. 2, xxvi. 18, xxxii. 9; Ps. cxxxiv. (cxxxv.) 4. Comp. Ecclus. xxiv. 8 ff.). The development of the thought of the apostle is certainly destroyed by supposing that here the earth is spoken of as the Lord's home, and man as His people.

It must be noticed that by this appropriation of the Old Testament language that which was before applied to Jehovah is now applied to Christ. Comp. xii. 41 note.

received] The word used here (παρέλαβον) as distinguished from that used in the next verse (ἔλαβον) suggests in this connexion the notion of "receiving that which has been handed down by another" (as opposed to παρέδωκα, comp. 1 Cor. xv. 1, 3, xi. 23), as distinct from that of "taking." The divine teachers of Israel, through John their representative, "offered" Christ to the people as Him whom the Lord had promised; and the leaders of the people refused to acknowledge Him as their King.

12. The Jews as a nation did not receive Christ as Him for whose advent they had been disciplined; but this national rejection was qualified by the personal belief of some. These however believed as *men*, so to say, and not as *Jews*. They became on an equality with those who believed from among the heathen. The Christian Church was not, as it might have been, the corporate transfiguration of the old Church, but was built up of individuals. To these, whether Jews or Gentiles by ancestry, *as many as received Him* [Christ] *gave* **right** *to become* **children** *of God*. The privilege of Israel (Ex. iv. 22) was extended to all the faithful.

The irregular construction of the original (ὅσοι δὲ ἔλαβον...ἔδωκεν αὐτοῖς...) gives prominence to the act of personal faith which distinguishes the first-fruits of the new Israel. Thought is first fixed on the character of those who believed, and then by a change of subject on the Word, and what He did.

received] The word indicates the action of him who "takes" that which is within reach as anxious to make it his own. Comp. v. 43, xiii. 20, xix. 6.

power (**right**)] The word (ἐξουσία) does not describe mere ability, but legitimate, rightful authority, derived from a competent source which includes the idea of power. Comp. v. 27, x. 18, xvii. 2, xix. 10, 11; Rev. ii. 26, &c. This right is not inherent in man, but "given" by God to him. A shadow of it existed in the relation of Israel to God. But that which was in that case outward and independent of the individual will was replaced in the Christian Church by a vital relationship.

As far as we can conceive of "this right to become children," it lies in the potential union with the Son, whereby those who receive Him are enabled to realise their divine fellowship. They are adopted—placed, if we may so speak, in the position of sons—that so they may become children actually. Comp. 2 Pet. i. 3, 4; Gal. iv. 6. The fruit is not given at once, but the seed. It is of God to give, but man must use His gift, which faith appropriates. It is thus important to observe how throughout the passage the divine and human sides of the realisation of Sonship are harmoniously united. The initial act is at once a "begetting" (ἐγεννήθησαν) and a "reception" (ἔλαβον). The growth follows from the use of a gift. The issue is complete on the part of God, but man must bring it to pass by continuous exertion (γενέσθαι τέκνα, τοῖς πιστεύουσιν).

to become] Comp. Matt. v. 45.

the sons] **children** (τέκνα). Comp. xi. 52; 1 John iii. 1, 2, 10, v. 2; Rom. viii. 16, 17, 21, ix. 8; Phil. ii. 15. The idea of "child," as distinguished from "son," which does not occur in this connexion in St John except Rev. xxi. 7, is that of a community of nature (*v.* 13) as distinguished from that of a dignity of heirship. It is an illustration of this limitation of the idea of spiritual "childship," that in the divine relation τέκνον is not found (as υἱός is) in the singular (yet see Tit. i. 4; 1 Tim. i. 2; Philem. 10). It may be added that the divine Sonship with which the New Testament deals is always regarded in connexion with Christ. Yet comp. Acts xvii. 28 f.

even *to them that*...] The words are in apposition with the preceding *them*. The effective reception of Christ is explained to be the continuous energy of faith which relies upon Him as being for the believer that which He has made Himself known to be. The faith is regarded as present and lasting (τοῖς πιστεύουσιν), and not simply as triumphant in the crisis of trial (τοῖς πιστεύσασιν, Heb. iv. 3); and its object is the revealed Person of the Incarnate Word. Comp. 1 John v. 13 (τοῖς πιστεύουσιν).

believe on his name] ii. 23; 1 John v. 13. Contrast *believe the name* (1 John iii. 23, πιστ. τῷ ὀν.). See v. 24, note, viii. 30 f., note.

his name] The revealed name gathers up and expresses for man just so much as he can apprehend of the divine nature. Compare iii. 18, xx. 31. From these passages it is clear that the "name" to the believer is that which describes the Incarnate Word as "the Christ, the Son of God." For the use of "the name" as applied to the Father in St John, see v. 43, x. 25, xii. 13, 28, xvii. 6, 11, 12, 26; Rev. iii. 12, xi. 18, xiii. 6, xiv. 1, xv. 4, 9, xxii. 4; as applied to the Son, ii. 23, iii. 18, xiv. 13, 14, 26, xv. 16, xvi. 23, 24, 26, xx. 31; 1 John ii. 12, iii. 23, v. 13; Rev. ii. 3, 13, iii. 12, xiv. 1. Comp. 3 John 7 (the name). Comp. ii. 23 note.

13. The spring of the new life to which the believer has "right" lies solely in God. The beginning of it cannot be found in the combination of the material elements, by which physical life is represented, nor in the natural instinct, in obedience to which beings are reproduced, nor in the will of the rational man. This appears to be the meaning of the threefold negation. The progress is from that which is lowest in our estimate of the origin of life to that which is highest. At the same time the three clauses naturally admit a moral interpretation. The new birth is not brought about by descent, by desire or by human power.

blood] Lit. *bloods*. The use of the plural (ἐξ αἱμάτων, Vulg. *ex sanguinibus*) appears to emphasize the idea of the element out of which in various measures the body is framed.

flesh...man...] These two clauses differ from the former by referring the beginning of life to purpose; and they differ from one another in that the first marks the purpose which comes from the animal nature, and the second that which comes from the higher human nature (ἀνήρ).

were born] Literally, *were begotten*, as 1 John ii. 29, iii. 9, iv. 7, v. 1, 4, 18. The thought is of the first origin of the new life, and not of the introduction of the living being into a new region. The phrase appears to be parallel with *as many as received*. The act of reception coincided with the infusion of the divine principle, by which the later growth became possible.

It is important to notice generally that St John dwells characteristically upon the communication of a new life, while St Paul dwells upon the gift of a new dignity and relation (υἱοθεσία, Rom. viii. 15; Gal. iv. 5; Eph. i. 5). When St Paul brings out the newness of the Christian's being he speaks of him as a new "creation" (κτίσις, Gal. vi. 15; 2 Cor. v. 17). The language of St James (i. 18) and of St Peter (1 Pet. i. 3, 23) corresponds with that of St John.

[e] Matt. i. 16.

14 [e]And the Word was made flesh, and dwelt among us, (and we beheld his glory, the glory as of the only begotten of the Father,) full of grace and truth.

The statement as to the fact of the new birth is made quite generally, but it is natural to see in it the contrast between the spiritual birth which makes "a child of GOD," and the fleshly descent in which the Jews trusted, and which had been recognised under the old dispensation. Comp. Matt. iii. 9.

3. *The Incarnation as apprehended by personal experience* (14—18).

This section, like the former, falls into three parts. St John gives first the substance of the apostolic witness (*v.* 14); and then the witness of prophecy, represented by the Baptist (*v.* 15); and thirdly, a general account of the nature of the revelation (*vv.* 16—18).

14. The construction of the verse is somewhat irregular. It consists of a main clause, which describes the fact and the character of the Incarnation (*The Word became flesh and tabernacled among us, full of grace and truth*), broken by a parenthesis (*and we beheld His glory ...from the Father*), which records the observation of the fact, so that it presents in succession the Incarnation, the witness to the Incarnation, the character of the Incarnate Word.

The Incarnation, which has been touched upon in *v.* 11 in its relation to the whole course of revelation, is now presented in its essential character. In the former place the Advent was considered in reference to particular promises (*He came*) and to a chosen people: now it is revealed in its connexion with humanity. Thus there is no retrogression or repetition, but a distinct progress in the development of thought. The special aspect of Messiah's coming, followed by the national failure to recognise His coming, prepares the way for the universal aspect of it.

The general scope of the whole verse may be briefly summed up under four heads:

1. The nature of the Incarnation. *The Word became flesh.*

2. The historical life of the Incarnate Word. *He tabernacled among us.*

3. The personal apostolic witness to the character of that human-divine Life. *We beheld His glory.*

4. The character of the Incarnate Word as the Revealer of God. *Full of grace and truth.*

It may be added that the fact of the miraculous Conception, though not stated, is necessarily implied by the Evangelist. The coming of the Word into flesh is presented as a Creative act in the same way as the coming of all things into being was.

And the Word...] The conjunction carries the reader back to *v.* 1, with which this verse is closely connected by this repetition of the title, *the Word*, which is now at length resumed. All that has intervened is in one sense parenthetical. The Incarnation presupposes and interprets the Creation and the later history of man, and of man's relation to God. Thus the thoughts run on in perfect sequence: *In the beginning was the Word;...and the Word was God. And the Word became flesh.* This connexion is far more natural than that which has been supposed to exist between *v.* 14 and *v.* 9 or *v.* 11.

The announcement of the mystery of the Incarnation, embracing and completing all the mysteries of revelation, corresponds (as has been already noticed) to the declaration of the absolute Being of the Word in *v.* 1. "He was God;" and "He became flesh:" eternity and time, the divine and the human, are reconciled in Him. "He was with God;" and "He tabernacled among us:" the divine existence is brought into a vital and historical connexion with human life. "He was in the beginning;" and "we beheld His glory:" He who "was" beyond time was revealed for a space to the observation of men.

was made (**became**) *flesh*] (σὰρξ ἐγένετο, Vulg. *Verbum caro factum est*, Tert. *Sermo caro factus est*). Owing to the inherent imperfection of human language as applied to the mystery of the Incarnation, both these words are liable to misinterpretation. The word *became* must not be so understood as to support the belief that the Word ceased to be what He was before; and the word *flesh* must not be taken to exclude the rational soul of man. The clear apprehension of the meaning of the phrase, so far as we can apprehend it, lies in the recognition of the unity of the Lord's Person, before and after the Incarnation. His Personality is divine. But at the same time we must affirm that His humanity is real and complete. He, remaining the same Person as before, did not simply assume humanity as something which could be laid aside: *He became flesh.* He did not simply become "a man:" He became "man." The mode of the Lord's existence on earth was truly human, and subject to all the conditions of human existence; but He never ceased to be God. And the nature which He so assumed He retains in its perfection (1 John iv. 2 ἐν σαρκὶ ἐληλυθότα. 2 John 7 ἐρχομενον ἐν σαρκί). As compared with the corresponding phrase *to come in the flesh* (1 John l.c.), the phrase *became flesh* brings out especially one aspect of the Incarnation. The former marks the unchanged continuity of the Lord's Personality, and the latter the complete reality of His Manhood.

How this "becoming" was accomplished we cannot clearly grasp. St Paul describes it as an "emptying of Himself" by the Son of God (Phil. ii. 6 f.), a laying aside of the mode of divine existence (τὸ εἶναι ἴσα θεῷ); and this declaration carries us as far as we can go in defining the mystery.

Thus briefly the following main truths must be held as expressed in the words when they are fairly interpreted:

1. The Lord's humanity was complete, as against various forms of Apollinarianism, according to which the divine Logos supplied the place of part of that which belongs to the perfection of Manhood. (The Word became *flesh*, and not *a body* or the like.)

2. The Lord's humanity was real and permanent, as against various forms of Gnosticism, according to which He only assumed in appearance, or for a time, that which was and remained foreign to Himself. (The Word *became* flesh, and did not *clothe Himself in* flesh.)

3. The Lord's human and divine natures remained without change, each fulfilling its part according to its proper laws, as against various forms of Eutychianism, according to which the result of the Incarnation is a third nature, if the humanity has any real existence. (The *Word* became *flesh*, both terms being preserved side by side.)

4. The Lord's humanity was universal and not individual, as including all that belongs to the essence of man, without regard to sex or race or time. (The Word became *flesh* and not *a man*.)

5. The Lord's human and divine natures were united in one Person, as against various forms of Nestorianism, according to which He has a human personality and a divine personality, to which the acts &c. belonging to the respective natures must be referred. (*The Word became flesh and dwelt*, &c., without any change of the subject to the verb.)

6. The Word did not acquire personality by the Incarnation. He is spoken of throughout, not as a principle or an energy, but, whatever may be the inherent imperfection of such language, as a Person.

So far, perhaps, we can see generally a little of the Truth, but the attempt to express the Truth with precision is beset with difficulty and even with peril. Thus in using the words "personality" and "impersonal" in relation to Christ, it is obviously necessary to maintain the greatest reserve. For us "personality" implies limitation or determination, *i.e.* finiteness in some direction. As applied to the divine nature therefore the word is not more than a necessary accommodation required to give such distinctness to our ideas as may be attainable. The word "impersonal" again, as applied to the Lord's human nature, is not to be so understood as to exclude in any way the right application of the word "man" (ἄνθρωπος) to Him, as it is used both by Himself (viii. 40) and by St Paul (1 Tim. ii. 5).

The phrase *the Word became flesh* is absolutely unique. The phrases which point towards it in St John (1 John iv. 2), in the Epistle to the Hebrews (ii. 14), and in St Paul (Rom. viii. 3; Phil. ii. 7; 1 Tim. iii. 16) fall short of the majestic fulness of this brief sentence, which affirms once for all the reconciliation of the opposite elements of the final antithesis of life and thought, the finite and the infinite.

became] This term (ἐγένετο) forms a link between this verse and verse 3. As "all things *became* through the Word," so He Himself "*became flesh*." The first creation and the second creation alike centre in Him. By His own will He "became" that which first "became" through and in Him.

flesh] Humanity from the side of its weakness and dependence and mortality is naturally described as "flesh." In this respect "flesh" expresses here human nature as a whole regarded under the aspect of its present corporeal embodiment, including of necessity the "soul" (xii. 27), and the "spirit" (xi. 33, xiii. 21, xix. 30), as belonging to the totality of man (comp. Heb. ii. 14). At the same time the word marks the points of connexion between man and the material world, so that it has a further significance as presenting in a familiar contrast the spiritual and the material (*the Word, flesh*). Thus several ante-Nicene Fathers speak of the Word, or the Son, as Spirit with reference to this passage (Tertull. 'de Carne Christi' 18; Hippol. 'c. Noet.' 4; Hermas, 'Sim.' V. 6, IX. 1; Theoph. 'ad Autol.' II. 10; Clem. 'II. ad Cor.' IX. with Lightfoot's note).

dwelt (**tabernacled**)] The original word (ἐσκήνωσεν, Vulg. *habitauit* [*inhabitauit*]) describes properly the occupation of a temporary habitation. The tent or tabernacle was easily fixed and easily removed, and hence it furnished a natural term for man's bodily frame. Yet apparently the original idea of "tent" (σκηνή) was lost in the form σκῆνος which expresses the idea of "frame" apart from any further figurative meaning: Wisd. ix. 15; 2 Cor. v. 1, 4; 2 Pet. I. 13 f. (σκήνωμα). And so also the verb itself (σκηνόω) is used without any reference to the notion of transitoriness: Rev. vii. 15, xii. 12, xiii. 6, xxi. 3.

Whether however the thought of the temporariness of Christ's sojourn upon earth is indicated by the term or not, there can be no doubt that it serves to contrast the Incarnation with the earlier "Christophanies," which were partial, visionary, evanescent, and at the same time to connect the Personal Presence of the Lord with His earlier Presence in the Tabernacle wh ch foreshadowed it, Ex. xxv. 8; Lev. xxvi 11. The Lord in old times *walked in a tent and in a tabernacle* (2 S. vii. 6; cf. Ps. lxxviii. 67 ff.), as now. He dwelt among men according to the promises expressed after that type (Joel III. 21; Ezek. xxxvii.). The parallelism becomes more striking if we accept the current view that the Tabernacle was a symbol of the world.

Many also have found in the word itself a distinct reference to the *Shekinah;* but before any stress can be laid upon the coincidence of form, it is necessary that the history of the term *Shekinah* should be examined far more carefully than it has been examined at present, with a view to determining: 1. The earliest use of the term. 2. The comparative use of the word in the different Targums. 3. The exact senses in which it is used in relation to (α) the Word, and (β) the Glory.

among us] in our midst (ἐν ἡμῖν). Among those who, like the Evangelist, were eye-witnesses of His life. Compare Gen. xxiv. 3 (LXX.).

The supposition that the plural marks the dwelling of the Word as being realised in the nature or in the race, as distinguished from the individual, is quite inconsistent with the historical purport of the whole phrase. Moreover this truth has been already stated by the use of the term "flesh."

and we beheld...Father] The breaking of the construction by this parenthetical clause, marks the pause which the Evangelist makes to contemplate the mystery which he has declared. He looks, as it were, from without upon the record and comments upon it. The same phenomenon in different forms recurs *v.* 16, iii. 16, 31, xix. 35; 1 John i. 2.

we beheld] 1 John i. 1. The abode of the Word among men was only for a brief space, but yet such that those near Him could contemplate His glory at leisure and calmly. His historical Presence was real if transitory. And while the appearance of the Lord was in humility, yet even under the limitations of His human form, those who looked patiently could see the tokens of the divine revelation made through Him. Comp. Luke ix. 32; 2 Pet. i. 16 ff.; 1 John iv. 14 (τεθεάμεθα).

his glory] The word "glory" (δόξα) carries on the parallel between the divine Presence in the Tabernacle and the divine Presence by the Word Incarnate among men. From time to time the Lord manifested His glory in the wilderness (Exod. xvi. 10, xxiv. 16, xl. 34, &c.); in the Temple of Solomon (1 K. viii. 11); and to the prophets (Isai. vi. 3. Comp. ch. xii. 41; Ezek. i. 28, &c.; Acts vii. 55); and even so Christ's glory flashed forth at crises of His history. It is not possible for us to define exactly in what way this majesty was shewn, by signs, by words, by events. Comp. Luke ix. 31 f. It is enough that the Evangelist records his own experience. The Son of Man had a glory which corresponded with His filial relation to the Father, even when He had laid aside His divine glory (xvii. 5).

For the general idea of "glory" in St John, see Introd.

the glory as of] Rather, **glory** *as of*... This glory of the Incarnate Word is described as being "glory as of an only son from his father," a glory, that is, of one who represents another, being derived from him, and of the same essence with him. The particle of comparison and the absence of articles in the original shew that the thought centres in the abstract relation of father and son; and yet in the actual connexion this abstract relation passes necessarily into the relation of "the Son" to "the Father."

as of] Comp. Rev. v. 6, xiii. 3.

only begotten] Comp. iii. 16; 1 John iv. 9. This rendering somewhat obscures the exact sense of the original word (μονογενής), which is rather "only-born." That is, the thought in the original is centred in the personal Being of the Son and not in His generation. Christ is the One only Son, the One to whom the title belongs in a sense completely unique and singular, as distinguished from that in which there are many children of God (*vv.* 12 f.). The use of the word elsewhere in the New Testament to describe an only child (Luke vii. 12, viii. 42, ix. 38; Heb. xi. 17) brings out this sense completely. The ideas of the Son as "begotten" of the Father, and as "the only Son," are expressed separately in the ancient Creeds (*e.g.* 'Ep. Syn. Ant.' Routh, 'Rell.' III. 290, γεννητόν, μονογενῆ υἱόν. 'Symb. Nic.' γεννηθ. ἐκ τ. π. μονογενῆ, &c.).

In the LXX. the word occurs seven times: Tobit iii. 15 (vi. 11), viii. 17 (of only children); Wisd. vii. 22; and (as a translation of יחיד) Ps. xxii. (xxi.) 21, xxxv. (xxxiv.) 17 (of the soul, the one single, irreparable life of man), xxv. (xxiv.) 16 (of the sufferer left alone and solitary). The Hebrew word thus translated is in seven other places represented by ἀγαπητός, which carries with it also the notion of an only child (Gen. xxii. 2, 12, 16; Judges xi. 34; Jer. vi. 26; Amos viii. 10; Zech. xii. 10).

Christian writers from early times have called attention to the connexion of the two words applied in the New Testament to Christ "the only Son" (μονογενής) and "the first-born" (πρωτότοκος, Col. i. 15), which present the idea of His Sonship under complementary aspects. The first marks His relation to God as absolutely without parallel, the other His relation to creation as preexistent and sovereign. Comp. Lightfoot on Coloss. i. 15.

of (**from**) *the Father*] Or, *from a father.* The idea conveyed is not that of sonship only, but of mission also. Christ was a Son, and a Son sent to execute a special work (comp. *v.* 6, ἀπεστ. παρὰ θεοῦ, vi. 46, vii. 29, xvi. 27, xvii. 8). The converse thought is expressed in *v.* 18 (ὁ ὢν εἰς τ. κ. τ. π.).

full of grace and truth] The phrase is

15 ¶ John bare witness of him, and cried, saying, This was he of whom I spake, He that cometh after me is preferred before me: for he was before me.

16 And of his *f* fulness have all we received, and grace for grace. *f* Col. 1. 19.

17 For the law was given by Moses, *but* grace and truth came by Jesus Christ.

---

connected with the main subject of the sentence, *the Word...dwelt among us...full of grace.* For a moment the Evangelist had rested upon the glorious memories of that which he had seen (comp. 1 John i. 1, 2). Now he goes on to characterize Christ's Presence by its inward marks. Each of the two elements is laid open in *vv.* 16, 17. The combination recalls the description of Jehovah, Exod. xxxiv. 6 (Ps. xxv. 10); and is not unfrequent in the O.T.: Gen. xxiv. 27, 49, xxxii. 10; Ps. xl. 10, 11, lxi. 7 (חסד ואמת). As applied to the Lord, the phrase marks Him as the Author of perfect Redemption and perfect Revelation. Grace corresponds with the idea of the revelation of God as love (1 John iv. 8, 16) by Him who is Life; and Truth with that of the revelation of God as light (1 John i. 5) by Him who is Himself Light.

15. The testimony of John is introduced in the same manner as before, as representing the final testimony of prophecy. John gave not only a general witness to "the Light," but also pointed out the true position which Christ occupied towards himself in virtue of His Nature.

bare witness...and cried...] **beareth** *witness...and* **crieth (hath cried)**] The witness of John is treated as present and complete; present because his mission was divine, complete because it was directed to a special end which was reached (μαρτυρεῖ, κέκραγεν). Comp. *v.* 34.

The words of John are given here in a form different from that in which they appear in *v.* 30, and with a different scope. *This was He of whom I spake* (ὃν εἶπον, Vulg. *quem dixi*), to whom my teaching pointed generally; and not "in behalf of whom (ὑπὲρ οὗ, all. περὶ οὗ, Vulg. *de quo*) I made a special statement." The words which follow are therefore most probably to be taken as an independent statement: "This is the Christ of whom I spake; and He has now entered on His office. He that cometh after me is come to be (become) before me..."

crieth (κέκραγεν)] vii. 28, 37, xii. 44. The voice of the Baptist was more than that of a witness. It was the loud, clear voice of the herald who boldly proclaimed his message so that all might hear it.

was he] The Baptist throws himself backward in thought to the time when he looked forward to the Christ who had not yet appeared, and proclaimed His coming.

He that cometh after me is preferred before me] **is come to be before me** (ἔμπροσθέν μου, Vulg. *ante me*). The words express the Baptist's witness to Christ from the moment when His Messiahship was signified. As soon as He was manifested He took up a position in advance of His Forerunner, though the Forerunner had already been long labouring. The witness of the Baptist before Christ's Baptism was simply in general terms, "He that cometh after me is mightier than I" (Matt. iii. 11; Luke iii. 16); but St John gives his recognition of the actual present majesty of his successor. "After" and "before" are both used in a metaphorical sense from the image of progression in a line. He who comes later in time comes "after;" and he who advances in front shews by that his superior power. The supposed reference to the pre-existence of the Word, as if the Baptist said, "He that cometh after me in respect of my present mission hath already been active among men before I was born," seems to be inconsistent with the argument which points to a present consequence (*is now come to be*) of an eternal truth (*He was before me*).

for **(because)** *he was before me*] The precedence in dignity (iii. 33) which Christ at once assumed when He was manifested, was due to His essential priority. He *was* in His essence (viii. 58) before John, and therefore at His revelation He took the place which corresponded with His nature.

before me] The original phrase in the second clause (πρῶτός μου, Vulg. *prior me*) is very remarkable. It expresses not only relative, but (so to speak) absolute priority. He was first altogether in regard to me, and not merely former as compared with me. Comp. xv. 18.

16. *And of his fulness...*] According to the true reading, **Because** *of his fulness...* The words depend on *v.* 14, *full of grace and truth*, so that the sense is, We have knowledge of His character as "full of grace and truth" because... The intercalated witness of the Baptist, pointing to the true nature of Christ, marks the source of this spiritual wealth.

These words and those which follow are certainly words of the Evangelist and not of the Baptist. This is shewn not only by their general character, but by the phrase *we all.*

of his fulness] *out of it* (ἐκ), as a copious source of blessing.

fulness (πλήρωμα, Vulg. *plenitudo*)] the plenitude, the full measure of all the divine powers and graces which were concentrated absolutely in Christ, the Incarnate Word. The term occurs here only in St John's writings; but it is found five times in the two Epistles of St Paul to the Colossians and Ephesians, which form the connecting link

g 1 Tim. 6. 16. 1 John 4. 12.

18 g No man hath seen God at any time; the only begotten Son, which is in the bosom of the Father, he hath declared *him*.

---

between the writings of St Paul and St John (Col. i. 19, ii. 9; Eph. i. 23, iii. 19, iv. 13). Of these passages the two in the Epistle to the Colossians illustrate most clearly the meaning of St John. St Paul says that "all the fulness dwelt" in Christ (i. 19), and more definitely, that "all the fulness of the Godhead dwells in Him," "and ye," he continues, addressing the Christians to whom he is writing, "are in Him, fulfilled (πεπληρωμένοι)..." (ii. 9 f.). Here St Paul's thought is evidently that the whole sum of the divine attributes exists together in Christ, and that each Christian in virtue of his fellowship with Him draws from that "fulness" whatever he needs for the accomplishment of his own part in the great life of the Church. And so, from another point of sight, the Church itself, made up of the many parts, thus severally perfected, is "the body of Christ," His "fulness" realising in actual fact that which answers to the whole divine power in its Head (Eph. i. 23). St John's idea in the present passage is the same: Christians receive from Christ, as from a spring of divine life, whatever they severally require according to their position and work. All is in Him, and all in Him is available for the believer. Comp. v. 20, xv. 15, xvii. 22. For a complete discussion of the word see Lightfoot, 'Colossians,' pp. 323 ff.

all we] The addition of *all* here (as compared with *v.* 14) appears to place us in a new company. The circle of the eye-witnesses passes into the larger fellowship of the Christian Church. Speaking from the centre of the new Society the Apostle can say "*We all*—whether we saw Christ's glory or not—can attest the reality of His gifts. **We all received** (ἡ. π. ἐλάβομεν, not *have all we received*) *of His fulness*, when we were admitted into His fold, and at each succeeding crisis of our spiritual life." The essential universality of the blessing excludes the special claims of every select body. Comp. iii. 34.

received] The verb is without any direct object, since *of his fulness* is not partitive. The conception of "the fulness" however at once suggests one: "*we all received* that which answered to our wants."

and grace for grace] Each blessing appropriated became the foundation of a greater blessing. To have realised and used one measure of grace was to have gained a larger measure (as it were) in exchange for it (χάριν ἀντὶ χ.). Thus this clause is not an explanation of that which has preceded, but a distinct addition to it. The phrase is illustrated by a saying in 'Aboth' IV. 5, "the reward of a precept is a precept."

17. *For* (**Because**) *the law*...] The clause is parallel with *v.* 16, and not the ground of it.

the law was given by (**through**)...*grace and truth came by* (**through**)...] The Law is represented as an addition to the essential scheme of redemption. Comp. Gal. iii. 19; Rom. v. 20. It was "given" for a special purpose. On the other hand, the Gospel "came" (ἐγένετο), as if, according to the orderly and due course of the divine plan, this was the natural issue of all that had gone before. Judaism was designed to meet special circumstances; Christianity satisfies man's essential nature.

grace and truth] Grace and Truth are now presented under the aspect of their complete embodiment (ἡ χ. καὶ ἡ ἀλ.: comp. *v.* 14, χ. καὶ ἀλ.). The Gospel is spoken of as "grace," so far as it is the revelation of God's free love, and as "truth," so far as it presents the reality and not the mere images or shadows of divine things. Comp. iv. 23. In both respects it was contrasted with the Law. The Law had a reward for obedience (Gal. iii. 12), and consequently brought a knowledge of sin (Rom. iii. 20; comp. vi. 14); and on the other hand, it had only the shadow of the good things to come (Heb. x. 1; Col. ii. 17). This exact and subtle correspondence of St John's teaching with that of the other apostolic writings is to be noticed. The word "grace" does not occur elsewhere in his writings except in salutations, 2 John 3; Rev. i. 4, xxii. 21.

For the idea of Truth see Introd.

by (**through**) *Jesus Christ*] The Person who has been present to the Evangelist throughout is now at last fully named. Comp. xvii. 3, xx. 31. The "name" thus given includes the declaration of the true humanity of the Saviour (*Jesus*), and of His relation to the earlier dispensation (*Christ*). His divine nature is set forth in the next verse. Compare 1 John i. 3.

18. This last verse justifies the claim of the Gospel to be the Truth, while it lays down the inherent limitations of human knowledge. It is impossible, so far as our experience yet goes, for man to have direct knowledge of God as God. He can come to know Him only through One who shares both the human and divine natures, and who is in vital fellowship both with God and with man. In Christ this condition is satisfied. He who as the Word has been declared to be God, who as the Son is one in essence with the Father, even He set forth that which we need to know. It is tacitly assumed throughout,

as it will be observed, that "the Truth" and "the knowledge of God" are identical terms.

No man hath seen God at any time (**ever yet seen**)] Comp. 1 John iv. 12. In both places the original of "God" is without the article (θεόν, not τὸν θεόν). By this manner of expression thought is turned to the divine Nature rather than to the divine Person: "God as God" (comp. i. 1, n.). The Theophanies under the Old Dispensation did not fall under this category. Comp. Exod. xxxiii. 12 ff. (xxxii. 30). Even Christ Himself was not "seen" as God. The perception of His true divine Nature was not immediate, but gained by slow processes (xiv. 9). The words set aside the false views of Judaism and Heathenism (v. 37, 1 John v. 20 f.). They do not deny the possibility of a true knowledge of God, but of a natural knowledge of God, such as can be described by "sight." The sight of God is the final transfiguration of man (1 John iii. 2). The simple act of vision is marked here (ἑώρακεν, *seen*), while in the Epistle it is the calm sight of beholding (τεθέαται). Comp. xiv. 9, xii. 45.

By the use of the words **ever yet** (πώποτε) the Evangelist perhaps points forward to that open vision of the Divine which shall be granted hereafter, 1 John iii. 2; Matt. v. 8.

the only begotten Son] The remarkable variation of reading in this place, "one who is God only-begotten" (θεὸς μονογενής) for "the only-begotten Son" (ὁ μονογενὴς υἱός) (see Additional Note), makes no difference in the sense of the passage; and, however strange the statement may appear, does not seriously affect the form in which it is conveyed to us. "One who is God only-begotten," or "God the only Son" (μονογενὴς θεός), One of whom it can be predicated that He is unique in His Being, and God, is none other than "the only-begotten Son" (ὁ μονογενὴς υἱός). The word Son—"the only-begotten Son"—carries with it the idea of identity of essence. The article in the one case defines as completely as the predicate in the other. But the best-attested reading (μονογενὴς θεός) has the advantage of combining the two great predicates of the Word, which have been previously indicated (*v.* 1 θεός, *v.* 14 μονογενής).

which is in the bosom] The image is used of the closest and tenderest of human relationships, of mother and child (Num. xi. 12), and of husband and wife (Deut. xiii. 6), and also of friends reclining side by side at a feast (comp. xiii. 23), and so describes the ultimate fellowship of love. The exact form of the original words is remarkable. The phrase is not strictly "in the bosom," but "into the bosom" (ὁ ὢν εἰς τ. κ.). Thus there is the combination (as it were) of rest and motion, of a continuous relation, with a realisation of it (comp. i. 1, ἦν πρός). The "bosom of the Father" (like heaven) is a state and not a place.

The words, as used by the Evangelist, may point to the exaltation of the ascended Christ; but in connexion with "God the only Son" (μονογ. θεός) it is more natural to take them as an absolute description of the nature of the Son, so that the participle will be timeless. In fact the Ascension of Christ is essentially connected with the divine glory which He had "before the foundation of the world" (xvii. 5).

of the Father] The choice of this title in place of God (τοῦ θεοῦ) serves to mark the limits of the revelation made through Christ. Even this was directed to one aspect (so to speak) of the Godhead. The Son made God known not primarily as God, but as the Father. At the same time this title lays the foundation of revelation in the essential relation of the Persons of the Godhead. Comp. 1 John i. 2.

In this connexion the description of the relation of the Word to God (*v.* 1, ὁ λόγος ἦν πρὸς τὸν θεόν) is seen to be complementary to that of the relation of the Son to the Father. The one marks an absolute relation in the Godhead. The other a relation apprehended with regard to creation. Hence in the latter the form of expression is borrowed from human affection.

he] The pronoun (ἐκεῖνος) emphasizes the attributes of the person already given, and isolates Him for the distinct contemplation of the reader. Comp. *v.* 33. This usage finds an interesting illustration in the fact that in 1 John this pronoun is used distinctively for the Lord: 1 John ii. 6, iii. 3, 5, 7, 16, iv. 17.

hath declared him] More exactly **he declared** Him, once and for ever. The word which occurs here (ἐξηγήσατο, Vulg. *enarravit* [*disseruit, exposuit*]) is constantly used in classical writers of the interpretation of divine mysteries. Cf. Gen. xli. 8, 24; Lev. xiv. 57. The absence of the object in the original is remarkable. Thus the literal rendering is simply, *he made declaration* (Vulg. *ipse enarravit*). Comp. Acts xv. 14.

The position of the object of the former clause (God) at the beginning of the sentence, leads naturally to the supplying of it in thought here; or rather suggests that which corresponds with it in connexion with the new verb, "the truth concerning Him, revealed as a Father, as man could bear the revelation." The knowledge of God, which Christ had as God, He set forth to men as man. Comp. Matt. xi. 27. Men *hear* from Him that which He *saw*. Comp. vi. 45 f. note.

Several important reflections follow from the consideration of the Prologue.

1. The writer occupies a distinct historical position. He speaks as one (i) who was originally a Jew, (ii) who had been an eye-witness, (iii) who is surrounded by a Christian society.

(i) His Jewish descent appears to be marked by the use of "his own home" (τὰ ἴδια), and "his own people" (οἱ ἴδιοι, *v.* 11); by the mode in which creation is spoken of (ἐν ἀρχῇ); by the implied reference to the Fall (*v.* 5).

(ii) It is impossible to interpret *v.* 14 (ἐθεασάμεθα) without violence otherwise than as containing a direct statement of the writer's experience, and that too given in a form which is strikingly natural.

(iii) The phrase "we all" (*v.* 16) can only be an appeal to the experience of the Christian body in which the writer was living.

2. There is no effort on the part of the writer to establish, or to enforce, or to explain. He sets forth what is matter of experience to him with complete conviction and knowledge. Nothing can be farther from the appearance of introducing any new teaching. The Evangelist takes for granted that his readers understand perfectly what he means by "the Word," "the Father." He does not expressly affirm but assumes the identification of the Word with Jesus Christ (*v.* 17).

3. There is no trace of any purely speculative interest in the propositions which are laid down. The writer at once passes to life and history from the contemplation of the divine in itself (*v.* 1). After the first verse everything is set down with a view to the revelation of God through the Word to men; and this revelation is treated historically in its different elements, and from the side of man. Moreover the Person of the Revealer is one from first to last, though He is regarded successively as the Word, the Life, the Light, the Word made flesh, even Jesus Christ And the last term under which God is spoken of is "the Father," in which the abstract idea is lost in the personal.

4. Though the purely speculative is absent from the Prologue, as it is from the Gospel generally, the treatment of the subject is such that the Evangelist supplies the clues for the prosecution of the highest problems so fai as man can pursue them. This he does (1) By opening a momentary vision of the Godhead itself in which can be seen the Immanent Trinity, (2) By shewing the relation of Creation to the Creator as Preserver, (3) By the declaration of the fact of the Incarnation, in which the Unity of the Finite and the Infinite is realised. And the more the Prologue is studied under these aspects, the more conspicuous become its originality and exhaustiveness.

5. The Prologue does in fact define the scope of the Gospel and interpret it. In this respect it corresponds with the close, xx. 31, which expresses in other terms *vv.* 14, 18.

And while the phraseology is peculiar, this section contains nothing which is not either directly affirmed in the Lord's discourses, or directly deducible from them.

1. The Preexistence of Christ, vi. 62, viii. 58, xvii. 5, 24.
2. His Creative energy, v. 17.
3. The Universality of His work, viii. 12, x. 16.

The main subject of the Gospel which has been prepared by the Prologue is THE SELF-REVELATION OF CHRIST TO THE WORLD AND TO THE DISCIPLES. Under this aspect the Gospel falls into two great divisions, THE SELF-REVELATION OF CHRIST TO THE WORLD (i. 19—xii. 50); and THE SELF-REVELATION OF CHRIST TO THE DISCIPLES (xiii. 1—xxi. 23).

The first of these two great divisions falls also into two parts, THE PROCLAMATION (i. 19—iv. 54), and THE CONFLICT (v. 1—xii. 50).

THE PROCLAMATION (i. 19—iv. 54).

The record of the beginning of the Gospel contained in the first four chapters presents in act and word the main elements of the Message which Christ claimed to bring and to be, and typical examples of the classes of men to whom it was offered. So far He meets with misunderstanding, but with no active hostility. Principles and tendencies are laid open, but they await their development.

The Proclamation consists of two parts, which are marked distinctly in the construction of the narrative (ii. 11, iv. 54). The first part deals with (i) THE TESTIMONY TO CHRIST (i. 19—ii. 11), and the second with (ii) THE WORK OF CHRIST (ii. 13—iv. 54).

i. THE TESTIMONY TO CHRIST (i. 19—ii. 11).

This section consists of three divisions, which deal with three forms of witness, three typical relations of Christ, three modes of revelation. The first gives the witness of the prophet, the relation of Christ to the preparatory dispensation, the revelation by direct divine communication (i. 19—34). The second gives the witness of disciples, the relation of Christ to individual men, the revelation through spiritual insight (i. 35—51). The third gives the witness of acts, the relation of Christ to nature, the revelation through signs (ii. 1—11). In each case there is an activity of faith in recognising the divine message, half-veiled, half-open; and the section closes characteristically with the joyful confirmation of believers (ii. 11).

The period covered by the incidents is marked as a week (i. 29, 35, 43, ii. 1), which corresponds with the week at the close of the Lord's ministry.

The incidents are peculiar to St John, and he writes as an eye-witness throughout: i. 35, 41, ii. 2.

19 ¶ And this is the record of John, when the Jews sent priests and Levites from Jerusalem to ask him, Who art thou?

---

1. THE TESTIMONY OF THE BAPTIST (i. 19—34).

The narrative of St John starts from the same point as the original Apostolic Gospel (compare Acts i. 22, x. 37, xiii. 24; Mark i. 1); but, as belonging to a later period in the growth of the Church, it distinguishes more exactly than that did the relation of the Baptist both to the old Covenant and to Christ.

The first part of the Baptist's testimony is concerned with the popular expectations to which his preaching had given fresh life, and contains the announcement of the Christ (19—28). The second part gives his personal recognition of the Christ who had now entered on His work (29—34). The verses which follow (35—37) form a transition, but belong most properly to the next section.

The circumstances of the Baptism of Christ are evidently presupposed as known; and the Baptism itself had already taken place before the mission from Jerusalem. This follows both from the record of time (*vv.* 29, 35, &c.), and from the fact that the Baptist already "knew" Jesus as the Christ (*v.* 26, "whom *ye* know not." Comp. *v.* 33). *See note at the end of the Section.*

St John says nothing of the Baptist's preaching of repentance, though it is implied in the words by which the Baptist described his office (*v.* 23). This did not fall within the scope of the Evangelist, which was confined to the direct relations of the Herald and the Christ. How fully these relations are defined will appear from the following analysis of the Baptist's testimony as given by the Evangelist:

The Testimony of John.
- *a.* In answer to the mission of the Jews. *The Christ announced* (i. 19—28).
  - α. His own position (*vv.* 19—23).
    - (1) Negatively (*vv.* 19—21).
      - Not the Christ (*v.* 20).
      - Not the promised Forerunner of the day of the Lord (*v.* 21).
      - Not the prophet, of undefined mission (*v.* 21).
    - (2) Positively (*vv.* 22, 23).
      - "A voice."
  - β. His office (*vv.* 24—28).
    - To baptize (*v.* 25)
      - with a preparatory baptism of water (*v.* 26),
      - before the coming of a mightier One (*v.* 27).
- *b.* Spontaneously in the presence of Christ. *The Christ revealed* (*vv.* 29—34).
  - α. The fulfilment of prophecy (*vv.* 29—31).
    - The Person (*v.* 29).
    - The work (*v.* 30).
    - The relation to the precursor (*v.* 31).
  - β. The sign of the fulfilment (*vv.* 32—34).
    - The sign itself (*v.* 32).
    - The sign in relation to the promise (*v.* 33).
    - The sign interpreted (*v.* 34).

The Christ announced in answer to the official inquiries of the Jews (19—28).

This mission from Jerusalem, which is not mentioned by the Synoptists, took place, as has been seen, after the Baptism, and was probably caused by some rumours which arose from that event. It may be regarded as being, in some sense, a Temptation of John corresponding to the (simultaneous) Temptation of Christ. John refused the titles in which the hierarchical party expressed their false views, even as Christ refused to satisfy their expectations by the assumption of external power. The position which John occupies relatively to the Jewish teachers on the one side, and to Christ on the other, offers a remarkable picture of the religious circumstances of the time. Both negatively and positively the scene is a living picture of a crisis of transition. The answer of the Baptist to the people (Luke iii. 15 ff.; Matt. iii. 11) is distinct from, and yet perfectly harmonious with, St John's record.

19. *And*] The conjunction takes up the references already made to John's testimony: *vv.* 15, 6, 7. Thus the history is bound up with the dogmatic Prologue, the transition lying in *v.* 17 (*Jesus Christ*); and so the loftiest thoughts pass at once and naturally into simple facts. It may be noticed also that the narrative evidently begins with the immediate, personal knowledge of the writer; and perhaps from the fact to which he referred the beginning of his own faith.

the record (**witness**)] Comp. i. 7, iii. 11, v. 31, and notes.

John] Comp. *v.* 6, note.

the Jews] Specifically *the Pharisees* as the representative class (*v.* 24). On the use of the term generally see Introd. p. ix. *a.* In this case the envoys were probably despatched by the Sanhedrin. Compare ch. v. 33.

sent priests...from Jerusalem] **sent unto him from Jerusalem priests...** Those who were sent came directly from the religious centre of the people.

priests and Levites] The two classes representing the ecclesiastical side of the nation. The compound phrase is nowhere else used in

20 And he confessed, and denied not; but confessed, I am not the Christ.

21 And they asked him, What then? Art thou Elias? And he saith, I am not. Art thou ‖that prophet? And he answered, No.

‖ Or, *a prophet*.

22 Then said they unto him, Who art thou? that we may give an answer to them that sent us. What sayest thou of thyself?

23 [h] He said, I *am* the voice of one crying in the wilderness, Make straight the way of the Lord, as said the prophet Esaias.

h M 3.

24 And they which were sent were of the Pharisees.

25 And they asked him, and said

---

the New Testament; and "Levite" occurs only in Luke x. 32 (with "priest" in significant connexion), and Acts iv. 36. The exact description of those sent marks the special knowledge of the Evangelist. It may be added that he nowhere uses the titles *scribes and elders* found in the other Gospels (viii. 3 is unauthentic). On the popular expectation of the Messiah see vii. 41, note.

Who art thou?] The pronoun is emphatic, "As for thyself, who art thou?"

20. *he confessed, and denied not*] For the combination compare *v.* 3, note. The first term (*confessed*) marks the readiness of the testimony; the second (*denied not*) the completeness of it. Both terms are used absolutely. A similar phrase is quoted from Josephus ('Antt.' VI. 7. 4), "Saul confessed that he was guilty, and denied not the sin."

but confessed] **and he confessed.** The substance of the confession is added to the statement of the fact of the confession.

I am not] The position of the pronoun, according to the true reading, is emphatic. "*I* am not the Christ for whom you take me, but the Christ is indeed among you." Thus the answer is addressed rather to the spirit than to the form of the question. The emphatic insertion of the pronoun (ἐγώ) throughout the section is remarkable: *I* am the voice (*v.* 23); *I* baptize (*v.* 26); *I* am not worthy (*v.* 27); of whom *I* said (*v.* 30); *I* knew him not (*vv.* 31, 33); *I* came (*v.* 31); *I* have seen (*v.* 34). The relation of the Baptist to Christ is suggested everywhere.

the Christ] As some then supposed, Acts xiii. 25; Luke iii. 15, note.

21. *What then? Art thou Elias?*] The construction of the original words adopted in A. V. is not found elsewhere in St John, though it occurs in St Paul (Rom. vi. 15, xi. 7). The words can also be rendered, *What then* (not *Who*) *art thou?* What is the function which thou hast to discharge? *Art thou Elias?*

Elias] Mal. iv. 5, the forerunner of the day of the Lord. Matt. xi. 14, xvii. 10—13. In a spiritual sense John was Elias (comp. Luke i. 17), yet not so as the Jews literally understood the promise. Thus the denial of the Baptist is directed to the Jewish expectation of the bodily return of Elijah, of which Lightfoot has collected interesting notices on Matt. xvii. 10. And at the same time the mission of the Baptist did not exhaust the promise of the coming of Elijah; beyond that coming there was yet another: Matt. *l. c.* (ἔρχεται καὶ ἀποκαταστήσει. See Chrysostom on the passage). Comp. Luke ix. 30.

that prophet] **the** *prophet*. The abruptness of the form of the question in the original is remarkable (The prophet art thou?). The reference is probably to Deut. xviii. 15, interpreted not of the Christ (Acts iii. 22, vii. 37), but in some lower sense. Comp. vii. 40, vi. 14. The general expectation often took a special shape, Matt. xvi. 14.

he answered, No] The replies grow shorter from time to time: "I am not the Christ," "I am not," "No."

22. *Then said they...*] **They said therefore...** This consequential (not temporal) *then* (οὖν) is very common in St John; and it is necessary in most cases to give it the full rendering *therefore* in order to mark the connexion (often subtle) which the Evangelist indicates. The fresh question was a consequence of the former answer.

Who art thou? that...] The same natural ellipsis occurs ix. 36.

23. *the voice*] Or, **a** *voice*. The Baptist was simply "a voice of one crying," not invested with a distinct personality ("thou art to me No bird, but an invisible thing, A voice, a mystery"). Moreover, the answer comes wholly from Isai. xl. 3, where the words herald the revelation of the glory of the Lord. In the Synoptists the quotation is applied to the Baptist: Matt. iii. 3; Mark i. 3; Luke iii. 4.

in the wilderness] as once before in the triumphal march from Egypt. Comp. Ps. lxviii. 7. In the original (Hebrew) these words are joined with the verb which follows, and it may be so here, *make straight in the wilderness...* In either case the moral application of the words is obvious.

24. *they which were sent were of...*] According to the oldest reading (καὶ ἀπεσταλμένοι ...not καὶ οἱ ἀπεσταλμένοι) the translation is, **they had been sent from...**

the Pharisees] and therefore men whose

unto him, Why baptizest thou then,
if thou be not that Christ, nor Elias,
neither that prophet?
26 John answered them, saying, I
baptize with water: but there standeth one among you, whom ye know
att. 3. not;
s 19. 4. 27 [i]He it is, who coming after
me is preferred before me, whose
shoe's latchet I am not worthy to
unloose.
28 These things were done in
Bethabara beyond Jordan, where
John was baptizing.
29 ¶ The next day John seeth
Jesus coming unto him, and saith,

---

attention would be fixed on the solemn and startling rite with which the new movement was inaugurated.

25. *Why...then*] They wished to condemn him from his own admission.

baptizest] The obvious symbolism of the rite—already adopted, as it seems, at the reception of proselytes—as marking spiritual defilement in the chosen people, would make it distasteful to legalists. It was however connected with the work of Messiah, Ezek. xxxvi. 25; Isai. lii. 15; Zech. xiii. 1. Comp. Heb. x. 22.

if thou be not that Christ...that prophet...] *if thou* **art** *not* **the** *Christ*...**the** *prophet*...

26. *I baptize with* (**in**) *water*] The answer is in two parts, and suggestive rather than explicit. "I baptize, because the form of this baptism shews that, however striking outwardly, it does not belong to the work of the Christ; and still it is designed to prepare for the recognition of the Christ actually present in the midst of you. My work is the work of a servant, and the work of a herald. There is nothing to condemn in my conduct, if you consider what my baptism is, and what the Christ's baptism is, and know that He is among you, so that the preparatory rite has a just place." The order of the words in the Greek (comp. 31) shews that the first thought is of the baptism as such, and next of its special character. Comp. Acts i. 5.

but there standeth one among you...] **in the midst of you** *standeth one*...The absence of the conjunction, according to the true text, and the position of the adjective (μέσος) at the beginning of the sentence, bring out sharply the opposition between the Baptist (*I* baptize) and his Successor.

standeth] The word (στήκει), as distinguished from "is," marks the dignity and firmness of the position which Christ was shewn to hold. (Mark xi. 25; 1 Thess. iii. 8, &c.)

ye know not] The *ye* is emphatic. St John had at this time recognised Jesus; he knew Him, but his questioners did not.

27. *He it is...before me*] The most probable text gives simply *coming after me*, which is to be taken closely with the words which precede.

shoe's latchet] To loose this, or to "carry the shoes" (Matt. iii. 11), was the business of a slave. Compare Mark i. 7, note.

The Pharisees hear words which might well move them to deeper questionings; but for this they had no heart. It is enough to have discharged their specific duty.

28. *Bethabara*] This name (Judg. vii. 24?) is a mere correction, made as early as the end of the second century (*Syr. vt.*), for *Bethany*, which was probably an obscure village in Peræa, and not to be confounded with the Bethany (xi. 18) on the Mount of Olives. According to a possible derivation Bethany may mean "the house of the boat" as Bethabara "the house of the passage," both equally marking the site of a ferry or ford across the Jordan.

The mention of the locality adds to the force of the preceding recital; and incidentally shews that the date of the mission falls after the first stage of the ministry of the Baptist, when he had left "the wilderness of Judæa" (Matt. iii. 1) and retired "beyond Jordan." Compare x. 40, iii. 23.

John was baptizing] The form of expression in the original, where the imperfect of the verb is represented by the imperfect of the substantive verb and the participle, is characteristic of the New Testament writers, and serves to emphasize the idea of continued action. Comp. viii. 18, v. 39, xi. 1.

The Christ revealed as the fulfilment of the Forerunner's work (29—34).

The inquiries made from Jerusalem would naturally create fresh expectation among John's disciples. At this crisis (*the next day*) the Lord, who had retired for a time after His Baptism (Luke iv. 1), returned, and John solemnly marked Him out, not by name but by implication, as the promised Saviour.

29. *John* (**he**) *seeth...coming unto him*] Compare *v.* 36. Christ was probably coming directly from the Temptation. It was fitting that His active ministry should begin with the solemn recognition by His herald. The omission of the Temptation by St John can cause no difficulty except on the irrational supposition that he was bound to relate all he knew, and not that only which belonged to his design.

saith] No one is directly addressed. The

Behold the Lamb of God, which ‖taketh away the sin of the world.

‖Or, *beareth.*

30 This is he of whom I said, After me cometh a man which is

words (as in *v.* 36) are spoken for those who "had ears to hear them."

Behold] "Lo, here is before you (ἴδε)..." Compare *v.* 47, xix. 5, 14; and contrast Luke xxiv. 39.

the Lamb of God] It seems likely from the abrupt definiteness of the form in which the phrase is introduced that it refers to some conversation of the Baptist with his disciples, springing out of the public testimony given on the day before. The reference which he had made to Isaiah might naturally lead to further inquiries as to the general scope of the prophet; and there can be no doubt that the image is derived from Isaiah liii. (comp. Acts viii. 32). But the idea of vicarious suffering endured with perfect gentleness and meekness, which is conveyed by the prophetic language (compare Jer. xi. 19), does not exhaust the meaning of the image. The lamb was the victim offered at the morning and evening sacrifice (Exod. xxix. 38 ff.), and thus was the familiar type of an offering to God. And yet more, as the Passover was not far off (ii. 12, 13), it is impossible to exclude the thought of the Paschal Lamb, with which the Lord was afterwards identified (xix. 36. Cp. 1 Pet. i. 19). The deliverance from Egypt was the most conspicuous symbol of the Messianic deliverance (Rev. xv. 3; Heb. iii. 3 ff.; Ezek. xx. 33 ff.); and "the lamb" called up all its memories and its promises. And it has been plausibly conjectured that this thought may have been brought home by the sight of the flocks of lambs passing by to Jerusalem as offerings at the coming Feast. However this may have been, the title as applied to Christ, under the circumstances of its utterance, conveys the ideas of vicarious suffering, of patient submission, of sacrifice, of redemption, not separately or clearly defined, but significant according to the spiritual preparation and character of those before whom the words were spoken. A corresponding glimpse of Christ's sufferings is given by Symeon in Luke ii. 25 ff.; and there can be no difficulty in believing that at this crisis the Forerunner had a prophetic insight into a truth which was afterwards hidden from the disciples (Matt. xvi. 21 ff.).

It must be further noticed that the Lamb which the Baptist recognises was not one of man's providing. Christ is *the Lamb of God*, that is, the Lamb which God Himself furnishes for sacrifice (Gen. xxii. 8), while the accessory notions of "fitness for," "belonging to," are also necessarily included in the genitive.

The explanation which has been given of the definite article appears to be the most simple; but it is possible that the article may represent some earlier and well-known use of the phrase, as in "the prophet" (*v.* 21), "the root of David" (Rev. v. 5). Nor can any stress be laid upon the fact that the application of the title to Christ is strange and unprepared. The title *the Lion of the tribe of Judah* (Rev. v. 5; comp. Gen. xlix. 9) is not less singular; and, according to many (but see Note on *v.* 51), the title "the Son of man" rests upon the single passage of Daniel (vii. 13) in the Old Testament. The figure is found again in Rev. v. 6 ff. (ἀρνίον) and in 1 Pet. i. 19 f.

which taketh away] It seems to be most in accordance with St John's usage to take this phrase as defining the character of "the Lamb of God," and not as presenting Christ under a new aspect, "even He that taketh away the sin of the world." The majority of the Old and Vulgate Latin copies, the Old Syriac and other early authorities, however, adopt the latter rendering by repeating "Behold" (Vulg. *Ecce agnus Dei, Ecce qui tollit...*). The word (αἴρει) may mean either (1) *taketh upon him*, or (2) *taketh away*. But the usage of the LXX. and the parallel passage 1 John iii. 5, are decisive in favour of the second rendering (Vulg. *qui tollit*, all. *qui aufert*); and the Evangelist seems to emphasize this meaning by substituting another word for the unambiguous word of the LXX. (φέρει, *beareth*). It was however by "taking upon Himself our infirmities" that Christ took them away (Matt. viii. 17); and this idea is distinctly presented in the passage of Isaiah (liii. 11). The present tense marks the future result as assured in the beginning of the work and also as continuous (comp. 1 John i. 7).

the sin of the world] The singular (as contrasted with the plural, 1 John iii. 5) is important, so far as it declares the victory of Christ over *sin* regarded in its unity; as the common corruption of humanity, which is personally realised in the *sins* of separate men. The parallel passage in the Epistle (*l.c.*) shews that the redemptive efficacy of Christ's Work is to be found in His whole Life (*He was manifested*) crowned by His Death. Of the two aspects of the Atonement, as (1) The removal of the punishment of sin, and (2) The removal of sin, St John dwells habitually on the latter. Yet see iii. 36; 1 John ii. 2.

The plural (*sins*), which has been transferred into our own Prayer-Book from the early Western Service-Books (*O Lamb of God that takest away the sins of the world*), occurs in Latin quotations from the time of Cyprian (*qui tollis peccata*), but it is not found in any of the best MSS. of the Old Latin or of the Vulgate. It occurs also in the Morning Hymn of the Alexandrian Church (*Gloria in*

preferred before me: for he was before me.

31 And I knew him not: but that he should be made manifest to Israel, therefore am I come baptizing with water.

32 [k]And John bare record, saying, I saw the Spirit descending from heaven like a dove, and it abode upon him. [k Matt. 3. 16.]

33 And I knew him not: but he that sent me to baptize with water,

---

excelsis), though not in immediate connexion with "the Lamb of God," and this is probably the source of the liturgical use which slightly influenced the Latin texts.

the world] Creation summed up in humanity considered apart from (viii. 12, ix. 5, 1 John iv. 9), and so at last hostile to God (xiv. 17, xv. 18). Yet potentially the work of Christ extends to the whole world (vi. 33; 1 John ii. 2). Compare Additional Note on *v.* 10.

The Synoptists have preserved a trace of this extension of the work of Messiah from the Jews to mankind in the teaching of the Baptist (Matt. iii. 9). His call to confession and repentance included the idea of the universality of his message. He addressed men as men. Comp. *v.* 7 note.

30. *of whom*] Literally, according to the true text, *in behalf of whom* (ὑπὲρ οὗ), *i.e.* vindicating whose glorious office as compared with my own.

I (ἐγώ) *said*] The pronoun is purposely expressed: *I*, the prophetic messenger of His advent, declared His superior majesty.

After me...which is **come to be** *before me*] See *v.* 15, note.

a man] The word chosen (ἀνήρ, Vulg. *vir*) is emphatic, and here serves to give dignity to the person described (contrast ἄνθρωπος, *v.* 6). Elsewhere, except in the sense of "husband," it occurs in St John only in vi. 10, where the two terms (ἀνήρ, ἄνθρωπος) are contrasted.

31. *I knew him not*] I (emphatic), his precursor, trained for my work in the deserts (Luke i. 80) till the day for my mission came, knew Him not as Messiah (*v.* 26). From the narrative in St Luke it appears to be doubtful whether the Baptist had any personal knowledge of Jesus.

but that he should be made manifest] but apart from such special knowledge I had a distinct charge; and I knew that my mission was to lead up to the present manifestation of the Christ to the chosen people.

Israel] The term is always used with the idea of the spiritual privileges attaching to the race, i. (50) 49, iii. 10, xii. 13.

The popular belief that Messiah would be unknown till He was anointed by Elijah, is given in a very remarkable passage of Justin's 'Dialogue,' c. 8.

am I come baptizing with **(in)** *water*] Rather, **came I**, fulfilling my initiatory work. The order of the words differs from that in *vv.* 26, 33, so that the subordinate character of his baptism is here the predominant idea.

32. *bare record*] bare **witness**. It is important to preserve the identity of language throughout: *vv.* 7, 8, 15, 19, 34.

I saw] Rather, **I have beheld** (τεθέαμαι), "gazed on," with calm, steady, thoughtful gaze, as fully measuring what was presented to my eyes (1 John i. 1). The perfect is found only 1 John iv. 12, 14. The aorist occurs frequently, i. 14, 38, &c. The verb in *v.* 34 is different (ἑώρακα).

the Spirit descending] This communication of the Spirit to Christ belongs to the fulfilment under human conditions of His whole work. Hitherto that work had been accomplished in the perfection of individual Life. Messiah now enters on His public office, and for that receives, as true Man, the appropriate gifts. The Spirit by whom men are subjectively united to God descends upon the Word made Flesh, by whom objectively God is revealed to men.

from **(out of)** *heaven like* **(as)** *a dove*] This definite revelation may be compared with that of the "tongues of fire," Acts ii. 3. The word used of the Spirit "moving on the face of the waters" in Gen. i. 2, describes the action of a bird hovering over its brood, and the phrase is explained in the Talmud, "The Spirit of God was borne over the water as a dove which broods over her young" ('Chag.' 15 a). To those who had not "eyes to see" the outward phenomenon may not have appeared anything extraordinary, just as the articulate voice of God was said by such to be thunder (xii. 29). But Christ Himself, who "saw" this visible manifestation in its divine fulness (Matt. iii. 16; Mark i. 10), heard also the divine words as a definite message. The dove, as a symbol here, suggests the notion of (1) Tenderness, (2) Innocence, Matt. x. 16, (3) Gentle and tranquil movement.

and it abode upon him] The transition to the finite verb gives emphasis to this fact. The phrase occurs Isai. xi. 2. The Spirit came to the prophets only from time to time (comp. 2 K. iii. 15), but with Christ it remained unchangeably.

33. *And I knew him not*] The phrase is solemnly repeated from *v.* 31. The mission and the sign of the fulfilment of the mission are treated in the same way.

the same said unto me, Upon whom thou shalt see the Spirit descending, and remaining on him, the same is he which baptizeth with the Holy Ghost.

34 And I saw, and bare record that this is the Son of God.

he that sent me...the same (**he**) *said*] This detail is peculiar to St John. In what form this revelation was conveyed to the Baptist we cannot tell. He was conscious of a direct personal charge. This is brought out prominently by the repetition of the pronoun "*he* (ἐκεῖνος) said." Comp. *v.* 18.

Upon whom] Rather, **Upon whomsoever**, so that the dependence of the Baptist's knowledge on the divine sign is placed in a stronger light.

remaining] **abiding**, as *v.* 32. Both elements (the descent and the resting) in this sign are obviously significant. The Spirit "descended" for the fulfilment of a ministry on earth; He "abode" on Christ so that from henceforth that which was immanent in the "Word"—His "glory"—was continuously manifested to believers. The Son became the Giver of the Spirit who revealed Him, even as the Spirit enabled Him to reveal the Father. He Himself received the Spirit, as it was His office to baptize with the Spirit.

The "abiding" no less than the "descent" of the Spirit was an object of "sight" to the herald of Christ. He was enabled to discern in the Lord after His return from the Temptation the permanence of His divine endowment.

baptizeth with (**in**) *the Holy Ghost*] the atmosphere, the element of the new life. Comp. iii. 5; Matt. iii. 11, "with the Holy Ghost *and fire*." The inward and outward purification are thus combined. The transference of the image of baptism to the impartment of the Holy Spirit was prepared by such passages as Joel ii. 28 (Acts ii. 17).

The "descent" and "abiding" of the Spirit upon Him "who was in the beginning with God" illustrates the perfect order with which the divine counsel is accomplished. As "the Son of Man" (comp. *v.* 51), Christ was thus "consecrated" to His public Work. Such a consecration is spoken of as wrought by the Father before the Incarnation (x. 36), and by the Son before the Passion (xvii. 19).

34. *I saw, and bare record*] Rather, **I** (emphatic) **have seen** as a fact, without the accessory notion of attentive observation (*v.* 32), **and have given my witness** *that...* So far my experience and my work are now completed. The sign for which I waited has been given; the Messiah whom I was sent to herald has been revealed.

the Son of God] Dan. iii. 25. The phrase is to be interpreted according to the context in which it occurs of those who are in each case regarded as the direct representatives of God, as sometimes of kings, &c. (Ps. lxxxii. 6): and so here it is used in the highest sense (comp. Ps. ii. 7). Some very early authorities (א, *Syr. vt.*, &c.) read *the chosen one of God.*

In comparing this section with the corresponding passage in the Synoptists, we notice:

1. The Baptism and Temptation must precede *v.* 19. John knew Jesus as Messiah (*v.* 26), of which he was first assured at His Baptism (*v.* 33). And the succession of time (29, 35) leaves no interval for the Temptation, of which the Baptist would naturally have no knowledge. It is probable that *v.* 29 marks the return of the Lord from the Temptation.

2. The testimony of John given in the Synoptists belongs to the time before the Baptism, and is addressed to a popular audience: that in St John, to special messengers (as it seems) from the Sanhedrin, and to the immediate disciples of the Baptist. The substance of the testimonies corresponds to these differences of circumstances. The former is general, and combined with the idea of judgment; the latter is carefully defined with regard to current belief, and stimulative to faith. Moreover, the testimony recorded by St John distinctly refers to the earlier testimony (*v.* 30).

3. The particularity and exactness of St John's narrative, preserving the exact marks of time, and place, and look, and position, mark the work of an eye-witness.

4. The testimony of John, which was the first recognition and the first manifestation of Christ, is the natural beginning of St John's Gospel, whose design is to give the historic development of faith and unbelief. Comp. xx. 31. In this incident faith in Christ was first shewn and first tried. The testimony of John was a word of inspiration answering to the faith which regarded outward facts in a divine light.

5. The descent of the Holy Spirit upon Christ at His Baptism is presented by St John simply as an objective sign to the Baptist. He does not speak of any communication of the Holy Spirit to Christ. The "abiding" is part of the sign, the completion of the "descent." By a comparison of the other Gospels we see that the manifestation was a sign to Christ also as well as to the Baptist; just as the words which contained the divine revelation (*My beloved Son*) were heard in their twofold application, as addressed to others, *This is my beloved Son* (Matt.), and as addressed to the Lord, *Thou art my beloved Son* (Mark, Luke). To the Baptist the sign shewed that his work was consummated by the open advent of Him whose way he was himself sent to prepare: to Christ, that the hour of His public ministry was come, a ministry com-

35 ¶ Again the next day after John stood, and two of his disciples;

36 And looking upon Jesus as he walked, he saith, Behold the Lamb of God!

---

menced by an act of self-humiliation. At the same time we cannot but believe (so far as we realise the perfect humanity of Christ) that Christ at this crisis first became conscious as man of a power of the Spirit within Him corresponding to the new form of His work. See *v.* 33, note.

For the rest it will be seen that the narratives of this event lend no support to the Ebionitic view that the Holy Spirit was first imparted to Christ at His Baptism; or to the Gnostic view that the Logos was then united to the man Jesus. And at the same time this event enables us to apprehend the different spheres of the Word and of the Spirit. By the Word God is revealed objectively to man: by the Spirit man is subjectively brought into fellowship with God. We could not, without destroying the essential idea of the Christian Faith, suppose either that the Spirit was made flesh or that the Word descended upon Christ.

2. THE TESTIMONY OF DISCIPLES (i. 35—51).

The work of the Baptist passed naturally into the work of Christ. His testimony found a true interpretation from some of his disciples, and they first attached themselves to the Lord. Christ who had been announced and revealed was welcomed and followed.

The whole section consists of a series of examples of spiritual insight. Christ reveals His power by shewing His knowledge of men's thoughts (*vv.* 42, 48); and the disciples recognise their Master by their experience of what He is (*vv.* 39, 41, 49). The incidents are a commentary on the words "Come and see" (*vv.* 46, 39), and the promise with which the section closes opens the prospect of a more perfect divine vision (*v.* 51).

The very mixture of Hebrew (Simon, Nathanael) and Greek (Andrew, Philip) names seems to indicate the representative character of this first group of disciples; and there is a progress in the confessions which they make: "*We have found the Messiah*" (*v.* 41): "*We have found him of whom Moses in the Law, and the Prophets, did write...*" (*v.* 45): "*Rabbi, thou art the Son of God, thou art the King of Israel*" (*v.* 49).

The history falls into two parts, and deals with two groups of disciples. First, John's work is crowned (35—42); and then Christ's work is begun (43—51). This will be seen in the subjoined table.

The Testimony of Disciples.

a. The first group. John's teaching crowned (*vv.* 35—42).
  - *α.* John's word understood and obeyed (35—39).
    - (1) John's disciples and John (35—37).
    - (2) John's disciples and Christ (38, 39).
  - *β.* The new message proclaimed (40—42).
    - (1) The mission (40, 41).
    - (2) The blessing (42).

b. The second group. Christ's teaching begun (*vv.* 43—51).
  - *α.* Christ's call and its issue (outward power) (43—46).
  - *β.* Christ's knowledge of the heart (inward power) (47—51).

The work of the first day of Christ's Ministry. John's teaching crowned (35—42).

On this first day of His teaching Christ is recognised by those who have been already prepared to receive Him. The disciples of John are shewn in their true position towards him and his Successor. Christ is not said to have called any one to Himself. Two pairs of brothers, as it appears, form the first group of disciples, of whom the first pair are named, Andrew and Simon; and the second pair, John and James, are only faintly indicated. The first disciples become the first preachers.

The date is shortly before the Passover (ii. 1, 12); and in accordance with this an early tradition fixed the beginning of Christ's Ministry at the vernal equinox ('Clem. Hom.' I. 16).

35. *Again the next day after John stood*] Again **the next day John was standing.** The picture is one of silent waiting. The hearts of all were full with thoughts of some great change. **Was standing:** compare vii. 37, xviii. 5, 16, 18, xix. 25, xx. 11.

two of his disciples] Comp. viii. 17. One of them is identified (*v.* 40) as Andrew; and the other was evidently the Evangelist. This appears from the absence of all further designation, and from the fact that the narrative bears the marks of having been written by an eye-witness for whom each least detail had a living memory.

36. *looking upon*] **having looked on.** The word (ἐμβλέψας) describes one penetrating glance, as again in *v.* 42, the only other place where it is found in St John. Comp. Mark x. 21, 27; Luke xx. 17, xxii. 61.

as he walked] no longer "coming unto him" (*v.* 29), but evidently (37, 38) going away. So for the last time the Baptist and the Christ were together; and the Baptist

37 And the two disciples heard
him speak, and they followed Jesus.
38 Then Jesus turned, and saw
them following, and saith unto them,
What seek ye? They said unto him,
Rabbi, (which is to say, being interpreted, Master,) where ‖dwellest
thou?

‖ Or, *abidest.*

39 He saith unto them, Come and
see. They came and saw where he
dwelt, and abode with him that day:
for it was ‖about the tenth hour.
40 One of the two which heard
John *speak*, and followed him, was
Andrew, Simon Peter's brother.
41 He first findeth his own brother

‖ Th two befo nig

gave by anticipation a commentary on his own sublime words (iii. 30) when he pointed his scholars to their true Lord.

Behold the Lamb of God!] The words are not at this time a new revelation (as *v.* 29) and therefore the explanatory clause is omitted. They are a suggestion by the Baptist to those who had hitherto faithfully followed him, that now they were called away to a greater Master. The first disciples of Christ naturally came from among the Baptist's disciples. So the divine order was fulfilled, and the preparatory work had fruit. The new Church grew out of the old Church, as its proper consummation. The revelation of Christ as He was (*v.* 29) shewed to those whose souls were rightly disciplined that He would complete what the Baptist had begun. At the same time the disciples of the Baptist could leave their teacher only in obedience to his own guidance as he interpreted their thoughts. And the direction came not as a command, but in a form which tested their faith. The words spoken answered to their inmost thoughts, and so they could understand and obey them. But without this spiritual correspondence the decisive sentence could have no power of constraint, for it does not appear that St John even addressed them, but rather he spoke indefinitely (*v.* 29), and the message came home to them: *He saith...and the two disciples heard him speak* (*as he spoke*, ἤκουσαν λαλοῦντος), *and followed Jesus.*

37. *followed*] The word expresses the single act as their choice was made once for all. The circumstance has a significance for all time. Christ's first disciples were made by the practical interpretation of a phrase which might have been disregarded.

38. *Then* (**But**) *Jesus turned*] as He was going away. This action hindered the two disciples from following Him silently and unperceived as they might have done (*they ... followed* ... **but** *Jesus* ...).

saw them] **beheld** *them.* Comp. vi. 5.

What seek ye?] Not *whom?* It is of interest to compare the first words of Christ recorded in the several Gospels. *Suffer* it to be so *now; for thus it becometh us to fulfil all righteousness* (Matt. iii. 15). *The time is fulfilled, and the kingdom of heaven is at hand: repent ye and believe the gospel* (Mark i. 15). *How is it that ye sought me? wist ye not that I must be about my Father's business?* (Luke ii. 49). The first words in the text followed by *Come and* **ye shall see**, the searching question and the personal invitation, are a parable of the message of faith.

They said (**And** *they said*)...*Rabbi*] The fresh recollection of the incident seems to bring back the original terms which had almost grown to be foreign words (*vv.* 41, 42). The English *Master* is to be taken in the sense of "Teacher." Comp. iii. 2, note.

dwellest] Rather **abidest**, as *v.* 39 (*dwelt*, **abode**).

The answer implies that if they could be with Christ, that, and nothing less than that, would satisfy their want. For a thing (*what? v.* 38) these first disciples substituted a Person. They were in need of Christ first and not of any special gift of Christ.

39. *Come and see*] According to the most probable reading, *Come and* **ye shall see**. The present imperative (ἔρχεσθε, compare *v.* 47, vii. 37, xi. 34, and on the other hand iv. 16, ἐλθέ) describes an immediate act contemplated as already begun. The act of faith goes first: knowledge is placed definitely after. The double repetition, *So they came and saw*, must be noticed.

They came...day...for it was...] *They came* **therefore** (**So** *they came*)...*day...it was...*

that day] that memorable day, from which the Christian society took its rise. Compare xx. 19 note.

the tenth hour] *i.e.* 10 a.m. Comp. iv. 6, note, and Additional Note on ch. xix. An early hour seems to suit best the fulness of the day's events. The mention of the time is one of the small traits which mark St John. He is here looking back upon the date of his own spiritual birth.

40. *One of the two...*] The other being St John; *v.* 35, note.

heard John speak] Literally, *heard from John*, heard the great tidings from him, *i.e.* that Jesus was the Lamb of God. For the construction see vi. 45.

Andrew] Compare vi. 8, xii. 22; Mark xiii. 3, where the same four disciples appear together as here. See note.

Simon Peter's brother] Thus Peter is treated as the better known.

Simon, and saith unto him, We have
found the Messias, which is, being
interpreted, ‖ the Christ. ‖ the ...ated
42 And he brought him to Jesus.
And when Jesus beheld him, he said,
Thou art Simon the son of Jona:
thou shalt be called Cephas, which is
by interpretation, ‖ A stone. ‖ Or, Peter.

---

41. *first findeth his own brother*] **findeth first** *his own brother*. The words imply that someone else was afterwards found; and from the form of the sentence we may conclude that this was the brother of the second disciple, that is James the brother of John. All this evidently took place on the same day (*vv.* 35, 43).

findeth] The use of the word in this chapter is most remarkable. It occurs again in this verse and in 43 (44), and twice in *v.* 45 (46). The search and the blessing go together.

We have found] This was the result of their intercourse with Christ. The verb stands first, thus giving prominence to the search (*v.* 38) now joyously ended. It is otherwise in *v.* 45. The plural shews the sympathy but not the presence of St John.

Messias ... interpreted the (omit) *Christ*] The Hebrew name is found only here and iv. 25. Compare *v.* 38 (*Rabbi*), note, *v.* 42 (*Cephas*); and contrast *vv.* 20, 25. On the form (Μεσσίας or Μεσίας) as representing the Aramaic (מְשִׁיחָא) see Delitzsch, 'Ztschr. f. Luth. Theol.' 1876, s. 603.

The announcement was an interpretation of the disciples' own experience. It does not appear that the title was used by the Baptist. The prerogatives of the Christ, the works of the Christ, were laid open, and it was the office of faith to recognise Him in whom they were found.

The title "the Christ" is found in the narrative of St John's Gospel, just as in the Synoptists. It is not unfrequently used by the people doubting and questioning (vii. 26 f., 31, 41 f., x. 24, xii. 34. Comp. ix. 22); and by the Baptist in answer to them (i. 20, 25, iii. 28); but very rarely in a confession of faith, as here and xi. 27. Comp. iv. 25, 29. The word is introduced wrongly in iv. 42, vi. 69. For the usage of St John himself see xx. 31; 1 John ii. 22, v. 1; 2 John 9; Rev. xi. 15, xii. 10, xx. 4. Comp. i. 17 note. Perhaps the Hebrew form is definitely preserved in order to connect the Lord with the Jewish hope and to exclude Gnostic speculations on the Æon Christ.

41, 42. *findeth ... saith ... brought*] The change of tense gives vividness to the narrative.

42. *And he brought...And when Jesus beheld him he said*] **He brought...Jesus looked on him and said.**

beheld him] Comp. *v.* 36 note.

Thou art] This is not necessarily a prophetic declaration by divine knowledge. It rather means simply "this is your natural name." Some take the phrase interrogatively: *Art thou...?* placing the old and the new in sharper contrast.

son of Jona] Here and in ch. xxi. the best text gives *son of* **John**.

thou shalt be called Cephas] Hereafter thou shalt win the name of Cephas. This promise received its fulfilment, Matt. xvi. 18 (*Thou art Peter*), where the earlier naming is implied. The title appears to mark not so much the natural character of the Apostle as the spiritual office to which he was called.

Cephas] The Aramaic name (כיפא) is found in the New Testament elsewhere only in 1 Cor. i. 12, iii. 22, ix. 5, xv. 5; Gal. i. 18, ii. 9, 11, 14.

by interpretation, A stone] The sense would perhaps be given better by keeping the equivalent proper name: *by interpretation Peter, that is a stone*, or rather *a mass of rock* detached from the living rock (Vulg. *Cephas quod interpretatur Petrus*).

As to the *relation* of this meeting with St Peter to the call recorded in Matt. iv. 18—22; Mark i. 16—20; Luke v. 1—11, it may be observed that

1. All the features are different.
   (*a*) Place—Judæa: Galilee.
   (*b*) Time—Close on the Baptism: Some time after.
   (*c*) Persons—Philip and Nathanael are not named by Synoptists.
   (*d*) Circumstances—A simple meeting: A miracle.
2. The narrative in the Synoptists implies some previous connexion.
3. This was the establishment of a personal relationship: that was a call to an official work. The former more naturally belongs to St John's scope, as giving the history of the growth of faith. The latter falls in with the record of the organization of the Church.
4. The teaching in Galilee to which the call recorded in the Synoptists belongs was really the beginning of a new work, distinct from the Lord's first work at Jerusalem.
5. The occupation of the disciples with their ordinary work after the first call finds a complete parallel in John xxi.

The work of the second day of Christ's ministry. Christ's own work begun (43—51).

The record of the fulfilment of John's work in the attachment of his disciples to Christ is followed by the record of the beginning of Christ's work. Jesus now "seeks" and commands (*v.* 43), and reveals both His authority and His insight.

43 ¶ The day following Jesus would go forth into Galilee, and findeth Philip, and saith unto him, Follow me.

44 Now Philip was of Bethsaida, the city of Andrew and Peter.

45 Philip findeth Nathanael, and saith unto him, We have found him, of whom *l* Moses in the law, and the *m* prophets, did write, Jesus of Nazareth, the son of Joseph.

46 And Nathanael said unto him,

l Gen... 10. ... 18. 1... *m* Isa...

---

43. *The day following Jesus would go forth ...and findeth...and saith...*] **The next day** (*vv.* 29, 35) **he was minded to** *go forth... and* **he** *findeth*...**and Jesus** *saith*... The transposition of the subject by the best authorities creates no real ambiguity. Compare xix. 5. The purpose is evidently spoken of as in accomplishment.

The coordination of the two clauses (*he was minded, and he saith*), which would commonly be placed in dependence, is characteristic of St John's style. Comp. ii. 13 ff.

go forth into Galilee] "His hour was not yet come" for a public manifestation at Jerusalem, and therefore He returned for a time to His usual place of abode.

findeth] How and where "Jesus found Philip" must remain unknown; but the word implies that the meeting was not accidental. Compare *vv.* 43, 45 (46): v. 14. The Lord "found" those who were "given" to Him: xvii. 6 ff., vi. 37. Comp. iv. 23.

Philip] See vi. 5, 7, xii. 21 ff., xiv. 8, 9. These passages throw light on the character of the disciple whom Christ sought. The name Philip is pure Greek. Comp. xii. 20 f.

Follow me] As a disciple bound to my service. The words are here first pronounced by Christ. Comp. Matt. viii. 22, ix. 9, xix. 21, and parallels; ch. xxi. 19, 22. The phrase in Matt. iv. 19 is different.

44. *was of Bethsaida, the city...*] More exactly, *was* **from** (ἀπό) *Bethsaida*, **of** (ἐκ) *the city*... The Synoptists mention that Simon and Andrew had a house at Capernaum (Mark i. 21, 29; comp. Matt. viii. 5, 14; Luke iv. 31, 38).

Bethsaida] Defined as *Bethsaida of Galilee*, xii. 21; and identified by Dr Thomson with *Abu Zany* on the west of the entrance of the Jordan into the lake, and by Major Wilson with *Khan Minyeh* (Wilson, 'Sea of Galilee,' in Warren's 'Recovery of Jerusalem,' pp. 342, 387). Comp. Matt. xiv. 22 note; Mark viii. 22 note.

The notice of the home of Philip explains how he was prepared to welcome Christ. He knew and was in sympathy with Andrew and Peter; and probably he too with them had followed the Baptist.

45. *Philip findeth*] Probably on the journey. Nathanael was "of Cana in Galilee" (xxi. 2). The first disciple who "found Christ," and the first disciple whom Christ "found," became alike evangelists at once.

Nathanael] = Theodore. He is probably to be identified with Bartholomew, for the following reasons:

(1) The mention of him in this place and in xxi. 2 shews that he occupied a prominent position among the disciples. Those with whom he is classed in each place are Apostles.

(2) No mention is made of Nathanael in the Synoptists, or of Bartholomew in St John; while the name Bartholomew is a patronymic (Son of Tolmai) like Barjona (Matt. xvi. 17), and Barjesus (Acts xiii. 6).

(3) In the list of Apostles Bartholomew is coupled with Philip by St Matthew (x. 3), St Luke (vi. 14), St Mark (iii. 18), so that the six first are the six first called. In xxi. 2 Thomas is added, as in Acts i. 13.

We have found] Here, in the original, the verb stands last. "Him of whom Moses wrote and the prophets, we have found." This form of the sentence (contrast *v.* 41) seems to imply that Philip and Nathanael had often dwelt on the Old Testament portraiture of Messiah. By the use of the plural, Philip unites himself to the little group of disciples, and his words shew that he had been before in communication with them.

Moses in the law] By types (ch. iii. 14 f.) and by more distinct words (Deut. xviii. 15. Comp. Acts iii. 22, vii. 37). Comp. v. 46.

Jesus of Nazareth, the son of Joseph] *i.e.* in Jesus of Nazareth. Philip describes the Lord by the name under which He would be commonly known. Comp. Matt. xxi. 11; and ch. vi. 42 (vii. 42).

46. *Can there any good thing come out of Nazareth?*] Literally, *From Nazareth can any good thing be? i.e.* can any blessing, much less such a blessing as the promised Messiah, arise out of a poor village like Nazareth, of which not even the name can be found in the Old Testament? Contrast Isai. ii. 3 (*Zion*). There is no evidence, unless the conduct of the Nazarenes to the Lord be such (Luke iv. 16 ff.), that Nazareth had a reputation worse than other places in Galilee (Matt. xiii. 58; Mark vi. 6). It was proverbial, however, that "out of Galilee ariseth no prophet" (vii. 52); and the candour of Nathanael would not hide a misgiving even when it was to the dishonour of his own country. The phrase *be out of* (εἶναι ἐκ) denotes more than the simple home. It expresses the ideas of

Can there any good thing come out
of Nazareth? Philip saith unto him,
Come and see.
47 Jesus saw Nathanael coming
to him, and saith of him, Behold an
Israelite indeed, in whom is no guile!
48 Nathanael saith unto him,
Whence knowest thou me? Jesus
answered and said unto him, Before
that Philip called thee, when thou
wast under the fig tree, I saw thee.
49 Nathanael answered and saith
unto him, Rabbi, thou art the Son of
God; thou art the King of Israel.

---

derivation and dependence, and so of moral correspondence. Comp. iii. 31 note, iv. 22.

Come and see] Compare *v.* 39. The words contain the essence of the true solution of religious doubts. The phrase is common in Rabbinic writers (בוא וראה). See Wetstein on *v.* 40.

47. *coming*] Nathanael at once accepted the challenge.

of him] not *to him*, but to the bystanders, as reading the soul of the man approaching Him.

It will be noticed how the Lord interprets the thoughts of all whom He meets in these opening chapters of St John: St Peter (*v.* 42), St Philip (*v.* 43), Nathanael (*v.* 47), the Blessed Virgin (ii. 4), Nicodemus (iii.), the Woman of Samaria (iv.). Compare ii. 25.

an Israelite indeed] one, that is, who answers in character to the name which marks the spiritual privileges of the chosen nation—"soldiers of God." There is already here a reference to Jacob's victories of faith (*v.* 51), which is made yet clearer by the second clause.

indeed] Literally, *in truth* (ἀληθῶς). The adverb is characteristic of St John: iv. 42, vi. 14, vii. 40, viii. 31; 1 John ii. 5.

in whom is no guile] who is frank, simple, with no selfish aims to hide, no doubts to suppress. In whom the spirit of Jacob—the supplanter—has been wholly transformed to the type of Israel. The future growth of St Peter had formed the main topic of Christ's welcome to him (*v.* 42), as here the present character of Nathanael.

48. *Whence knowest thou me?*] Nathanael must have overheard the words spoken about him, and found in them some clear discernment of his thoughts (comp. ii. 25), which roused him to this question of surprise uttered without reserve.

Before that...] The love of Christ had anticipated the love of the friend in finding Nathanael.

when thou wast under the fig tree, I saw thee] This sentence, like the former one, points to some secret thought or prayer, by knowing which the Lord shewed His divine insight into the heart of man. He *saw* not that which is outward only, but that which was most deeply hidden. Compare iv. 19. There is nothing to shew whether Nathanael was still in meditation when Philip found him or not.

the fig tree] which would be in leaf about this time (Matt. xxi. 10 ff., ch. ii. 13). The definite article (*the* fig-tree) calls up the exact scene. Compare Mic. iv. 4; Zech. iii. 10, &c. The form of the phrase (ὑπὸ τὴν συκῆν, contrasted with ὑποκάτω τῆς συκῆς, *v.* 50, **underneath**) implies that Nathanael had *withdrawn* under the fig-tree, for thought or prayer. This meditation turned (as we must suppose) upon the ideas recognised in the Lord's words. Augustine's narrative of the crisis of his own conversion is a singular commentary on the scene. He too had retired beneath a fig-tree for solitary thought when the voice "Tolle, lege" decided his choice. 'Confessiones,' VIII. 12. 28. A passage is also quoted from the Jerusalem Talmud ('Berachoth,' II. 8), in which R. Akiva is described as studying the law under a fig-tree.

49. *answered and saith unto him*] **answered him**, according to the best text.

Rabbi] All prejudice and doubt is laid aside, and the title is given by instinct which before (*v.* 48) he had withheld.

thou art the Son of God; thou art the King (**art King**) *of Israel*] Thus Messiah was described in relation to (1) His divine origin (2) His human sovereignty. Both attributes are implied in the conception of a kingdom of God. "The 'true Israelite,'" as it has been well said, "acknowledges his king." Compare Peter's confession in Matt. xvi. 16, and in ch. vi. 68, 69, and that of Thomas in xx. 28.

the Son of God] The words are an echo of the testimony of the Baptist (*v.* 34). Nothing can be more natural than to suppose that the language of John had created strange questionings in the hearts of some whom it had reached, and that it was with such thoughts Nathanael was busied when the Lord "saw" him. If this were so, the confession of Nathanael may be, as it were, an answer to his own doubts.

King of Israel] As here at the beginning, so once again this title is given to Christ at the close of His ministry, xii. 13. Compare Matt. xxvii. 42; Mark xv. 32, where the mockery is made more bitter by the use of this theocratic phrase in place of the civil title, "King of the Jews." See xviii. 33 note.

50 Jesus answered and said unto him, Because I said unto thee, I saw thee under the fig tree, believest thou? thou shalt see greater things than these.

51 And he saith unto him, Verily, verily, I say unto you, Hereafter ye shall see heaven open, and the angels of God ascending and descending upon the Son of man.

---

50. *believest thou?*] The words can also be taken affirmatively; but the same sense is given more forcibly by the question (comp. xvi. 31, xx. 29), which conveys something of surprise that the belief was accorded so readily, and something of warning that even this expression of belief did not exhaust the power of faith.

see greater things than these] actually experience greater proofs of my divine mission than are shewn in these revelations of thy thoughts. The plural (*these things*) marks the class and not the special incident. Comp. 3 John 4.

51. *he saith unto him...I say unto you...ye*] The word is for Nathanael, but the blessing is for all believers.

Verily, verily] *i.e. Amen, Amen.* The phrase is found in the New Testament only in the Gospel of St John (who never gives the simple *Amen*), and (like the simple *Amen* in the Synoptists) it is used only by Christ. The word *Amen* is represented by *in truth* or *truly* in Luke iv. 25, ix. 27. In the LXX. the original word is retained only in responsive phrases (Neh. v. 13, viii. 6). Elsewhere it is translated, "be it so" (γένοιτο), Ps. xli. 13, lxxii. 19, lxxxix. 52. The word is properly a verbal adjective, "firm," "sure." Comp. Isai. lxv. 16 (*God of the Amen.* LXX. ὁ θεὸς ὁ ἀληθινός); Rev. iii. 14 (*the Amen*). See Delitzsch, 'Ztschr. f. Luth. Theol.' 1856, II. 422 ff.

Hereafter (**From henceforth**)] This word must be omitted according to decisive authority. If it were genuine it would describe the communion between earth and heaven as established from the time when the Lord entered on His public ministry.

heaven open] Rather, **opened.** The phrase is the symbol of free intercourse between God and man. Comp. Isai. lxiv. 1.

angels ... ascending and descending] The order is remarkable. The divine messengers are already on the earth though we see them not; and they first bear the prayer to God before they bring down the answer from Him. So it was in the vision of Jacob (Gen. xxviii. 12), which furnishes the image here; and by the Incarnation that vision was made an abiding reality. That which was a dream to the representative of Israel was a fact for the Son of Man. Thus the reference is to the continuing presence of Christ (Matt. xxviii. 20), in whom believers realise the established fellowship of the seen and the unseen, and not to the special acts of angelic ministration to Christ alone during His earthly life. There is an interesting discussion of Jacob's vision in Philo, 'De Somn.' §§ 22 ff. pp. 640 ff.

The locality of the conversation may have been near Bethel or the ford Jabbok, so that the references to Jacob's history were forcibly suggested by the places made famous through the patriarch.

angels] ch. xx. 12 (comp. xii. 29). There are no other references (v. 4 is a gloss) to the being and ministry of angels in the Gospel or Epistles of St John.

the Son of man] By the use of this title the Lord completes the revelation of His Person, which has been unfolded step by step in the narrative of this chapter, in which He has been acknowledged as the greater Successor of the Baptist (*vv.* 26 f.), the Lamb of God (*vv.* 29, 36), the Son of God (*vv.* 34, 49), the Messiah (*vv.* 41, 45), the King of Israel (*v.* 49). These titles had been given by others. He chooses for Himself that one which definitely presents His work in relation to humanity in itself, and not primarily in relation to God or to the chosen people, or even to humanity as fallen. If, as appears probable, the title was now first adopted, it is to be noticed that it was revealed in answer to a signal confession of faith (Matt. xiii. 12). See Additional Note.

ADDITIONAL NOTES on Chap. I.

3, 4. The last words of *v.* 3 (ὃ γέγονεν [*that*]*which hath been made*) can be taken either (1) with the words which follow, or (2) with the words which go before. In the former case the text will run...χωρὶς αὐτοῦ ἐγένετο οὐδὲ ἕν. ὃ γέγονεν ἐν αὐτῷ ζωὴ ἦν...*without Him was not anything made: that which hath been made was life in Him* (*in Him was life*); in the latter case...χωρὶς αὐτοῦ ἐγένετο οὐδὲ ἓν ὃ γέγονεν. ἐν αὐτῷ ζωὴ ἦν...*without Him was not anything made that hath been made. In Him was life...*

The former (to speak generally) was the punctuation of the ante-Nicene age: the latter is that of the common texts, and of most modern versions and popular commentaries.

The evidence in greater detail is as follows:

(1)...χωρὶς αὐτοῦ ἐγένετο οὐδὲ ἕν. ὃ γέγονεν

ἐν αὐτῷ ζωὴ ἦν...This punctuation is supported by overwhelming ancient authority of MSS., versions, and Fathers.

(*a*) *Manuscripts.* AC (firsthand) D place a distinct point before ὃ γέγονεν, and no point after it[1]. The remaining two (ℵB) of the five most ancient MSS. make no punctuation. Other important but later MSS. give the same stopping, as *e.g.* L.

(*β*) *Versions.* One of the most important of the *Old Latin* copies (*b*) inserts *autem*, so that the connexion is unquestionable: *Quod autem factum est, in eo vita est.* Others (*a*, *e*, *f*, *ff*² &c.) give the same connexion by punctuation. But in themselves the words are ambiguous; and therefore it is not surprising that in *c* and in MSS. of the Vulgate generally (as in the editions) the *quod factum est* is connected with the words which go before.

The *Old Syriac* (Curetonian), like *b*, introduces a conjunction, so as to leave no doubt as to the punctuation which it follows: *But that which was*... The Thebaic and Æthiopic versions support the same connexion.

(*γ*) *Fathers.* The same connexion is supported by Clem. Alex., Orig., (Euseb.), Cyr. Alex., Hil., Aug., and by the earliest heretical writers quoted by Irenæus, Hippolytus, Clem. Alex.

Ambrose gives both readings, but he adopts the reading *quod factum est in ipso vita est*, and evidently implies that this was known to be the oldest reading, though it was felt to be ambiguous in sense. Jerome's quotations appear to recognise both punctuations.

(2) χωρὶς αὐτοῦ ἐγένετο οὐδὲ ἓν ὃ γέγονεν. ἐν αὐτῷ ζωὴ ἦν. This punctuation is supported by

(*a*) *Manuscripts.* The mass of secondary uncials and later manuscripts.

(*β*) *Versions.* The Memphitic and the printed Latin texts. But the clause "which hath been made" is omitted in one MS. of the Memphitic.

(*γ*) *Fathers.* The modern stopping was due to the influence of the Antiochene School, who avowedly adopted it to make it clear that the former words applied only to "things created" and not, as had been alleged, to the Holy Spirit.

So Chrysostom (*in loc.*) "Without Him was made not even one thing which hath been made," "that is of things made (τῶν γενητῶν) both visible and mental (νοητῶν) none has been brought to being without the power of Christ. For we shall not put the full point at 'not even one thing,' as the heretics do (κατὰ τοὺς αἱρετικούς); for they say thus 'that which hath become in Him was life,' wishing to speak of the Holy Spirit as a creation (κτίσμα)." At the same time he takes the next clause ἐν αὐτῷ ζωὴ ἦν as meaning "that in Him all things live and are in Him providentially ordered (προνοεῖται), so that that which has been said of the Father might properly be said also of Him, that in Him we live and move and have our being."

The punctuation thus recommended was supported also by Theodoret and Theodore of Mopsuestia, and prevailed in later times.

Epiphanius in his 'Ancoratus' (c. LXXV.) written in 374 A. D., after quoting the passage according to the old punctuation (c. LXXIV.), goes on to say that the words have been used by some to derogate from the honour of the Holy Spirit. The true way of reading the passage is, he continues, *All things were made through Him, and without Him was nothing made that hath been made in Him.* Nothing can be said for this division of the words, and it may be fairly concluded that Epiphanius is simply hazarding a hasty judgment. In 'Hær.' LXIX. § 56 (p. 779), he treats the words ὃ γέγονεν as the subject of ζωὴ ἦν, while he connects them with the words which go before (ἐπειδὴ ἦν καὶ ἦν καὶ ἦν (*v.* 1) καὶ τὰ ἐν αὐτῷ ζωὴ ἦν).

The interpretation of the passage is undoubtedly most difficult, but it does not seem that the difficulty is increased by the ancient punctuation. The difficulty in either case centres in the use of the imperfect ("*was* life..." "*was* the light..."), for which several ancient authorities read *is* in the first place, a substitution which can only be regarded as an arbitrary correction. It is indeed by no means clear in what sense it can be said: *Life was in the Word, and the Life* [thus spoken of as in the Word] *was the Light of men*; or again: *That which hath been made was Life in the Word, and the Life* [thus enjoyed by creation in the Word] *was the Light of men.* Yet the second conception will be seen upon consideration to fall in with the scope of St John's view of the nature and action of the Word.

The Apostle deals with the two main aspects of finite being, origin and continuance. As to the first, he says exhaustively that *all things became through the Word* as Agent; and *Nothing, no not one thing, became without—apart from—Him.* At this point, then, the view of the act of creation is completed. But the continuance of created things has yet to be noticed. That which "became" still lasts. And as Creation (on one side) was "in the Word," so too continuance is in Him. The

[1] A careful and repeated examination of D satisfies me completely that this MS. has no stop after γέγονεν. There is a slight flaw in the vellum which extends towards γέγονεν from the top of the following ε, of which the upper boundary is above the level of the writing, but this is certainly not the vestige of a stop. The stops are below the level of the writing. And again, there is no increased space between γέγονεν and ἐν such as is found where a stop occurs, as between οὐδέν and ὅ. On holding the leaf to the light, the point of a C falls within the flaw and gives the semblance of a stop.

endurance of the universe is due to its essential relation to the Creator. Creation has not "life in itself" (v. 26), but it had and has life in the Word.

It will however be objected that the phrase of the Apostle is "was life in Him," and not "has life in Him." At first sight the objection appears to be strong. The latter phrase would no doubt be far simpler than that which is actually used, and it would express part of the truth more clearly; but at the same time it would fall short of the fulness of what is written. As it is, the thought of the reader is carried away from the present, and raised (so to speak) to the contemplation of the essence of things. For a moment we are taken from phenomena—"that which hath become"—to being, to the divine "idea" of things. From this point of sight the Life of the world was included in the Word, and with the Life also the destination of the Life. Even in that which is fleeting there is that which "was," something beyond time, of which particular issues are shewn in time. In regard to God things "were" in their absolute, eternal, perfection; in regard to men "they have become." The thought occurs once again in the writings of St John. There is the same contrast between the "idea" and the temporal realisation of the idea, in the Hymn of the Elders in the Apocalypse (iv. 11): *Thou art worthy, our Lord and our God, to receive glory and honour and power, for thou didst create all things, and for thy pleasure* (θέλημα) *they were* (ἦσαν, according to the true reading), *and were created.*

Human language is necessarily inadequate to express distinctly such a conception as has been faintly indicated; but at least it will be seen that the early punctuation of the passage suggests a view of the relation of the Creation to the Creator which claims to be reverently studied. That which was created and still continues, represents to us what was beyond time (if we dare so speak) in the Divine Mind. In its essence it was not only living, but *life* in the Word, in virtue, that is, of its connexion with Him (comp. ch. v. 17, note). And through it—through the finite—the Word made Himself known; so that Creation was essentially a manifestation of the Word to men who were able to observe and to interpret in part the phenomena of life.

According to this view the word *life* is used both times in the same sense to express the divine element in creation, that in virtue of which things "are," each according to the fulness of its being. It is the sum of all that *is* physically, intellectually, morally, spiritually in the world and in man. This "life" is for rational beings a manifestation of God through the Word; and it was the Divine Will that it should be so: *the life was the light of men.* Comp. Rom. i. 19, 20, ii. 14, 15; Acts xiv. 17, xvii. 23 ff.

It will be seen that in this explanation the words *in Him* are connected with *was life*, and not with *that which hath been made*. The unusual but emphatic order finds a parallel in the true reading of iii. 15. The other combination however has very early authority (comp. Iren. I. 8. 5). Thus Clement of Alexandria applies the words to the Christian reborn in Christ. "He that hath been baptized (ὁ πεφωτισμένος) is awake unto God and such a one lives: For that which hath been made in Him is life" ('Pæd.' II. 9 § 79; comp. 'Pæd.' I. 6 § 27).

Cyril of Alexandria, who grasps with singular vigour the double relation of Creation to the Word as Creator and Preserver of all things, which is conveyed in the passage, appears to invert the description of the continuous vital connexion of the Word and the world. "As for that which hath come into being"—so he paraphrases—"the Life, the Word that is the Beginning and Bond (σύστασις) of all things, was in it"..."The Word, as Life by nature, was in the things which have become, mingling Himself by participation in the things that are" ('Comm.' *ad loc.*). This construction seems to be quite impossible; and the meaning suffers, inasmuch as things are not referred to their one centre of living unity, but on the contrary this one life is regarded as dispersed.

Augustine ('Comm.' *in loc.*) has illustrated the meaning well. "*Quod factum est;* hic subdistingue [he has just set aside the punctuation *quod factum est in illo, vita est*] et deinde infer, *in illo vita est.* Quid est hoc?...Quomodo possum dicam....Faber facit arcam. Primo in arte habet arcam: si enim in arte arcam non haberet, unde illam fabricando proferret?...In arte invisibiliter est, in opere visibiliter erit....Arca in opere non est vita, arca in arte vita est; quia vivit anima artificis, ubi sunt ista omnia antequam proferantur: Sic ergo, fratres carissimi, quia Sapientia Dei, per quam facta sunt omnia, secundum artem continet omnia antequam fabricat omnia, hinc quæ fiunt per ipsam artem non continuo vita sunt, sed *quidquid factum est, vita in illo est.* Terram vides...caelum vides...foris corpora sunt, in arte vita sunt."

Thus the ancient division of the clauses gives a consistent if mysterious sense to every phrase. If however the other punctuation, that of A.V., be adopted, the addition of the words "that hath been made" adds nothing to the sense, and the harmony of the rhythm of the original is spoiled, especially if the true reading (οὐδὲ ἕν for οὐδέν) be taken. Then further there is a certain abruptness in the beginning, *In Him was life*, unlike the repetition of the subject in the adjacent clauses (*vv.* 1, 2...*the Word...the same was, vv.* 4, 5, *the light...the light shineth...*). It is a still further objection to this arrangement of the passage, that nothing is said of the means by which the Life became the Light of men. The 3rd verse naturally prepares the way for the announcement of the revelation of the Word through and in His works.

But still, even in this arrangement of the clauses, the sense, though less clearly expressed, will remain substantially the same. The mention of "life" in the Word must be made in reference to finite being and not in reference to Himself. He was the centre and support of all things according to their several natures; and the life thus derived from Him was the light of men. According to this view the verb *was* describes what was the historical relation of things at the moment after creation, and not what was the archetypal idea of things. Still even so that which "was" when God pronounced all things "very good," represents the essential law of being.

4. *In him* was (ἦν) *life*] An important and well-marked group of ancient authorities, which represent a text of the second century, ℵD, MSS. of Orig., *Lat. vt.*, *Syr vt.*, read *in him* is (ἐστίν) *life*. The variant is without doubt a very early gloss; and it may be observed, once for all, that these authorities, both separately and collectively, are characterized by a tendency to introduce interpretative readings. In such cases where they stand alone against the other authorities, their reading, though of great antiquity and once widely current, is very rarely to be received.

10. *The world*, ὁ κόσμος.

1. The conception of the "world" (κόσμος) is eminently characteristic of the writings of St John. He nowhere uses αἰών (ὁ νῦν αἰών, ὁ αἰὼν οὗτος, &c.) for the moral order; and conversely κόσμος is very rarely used with a moral sense, as the sphere of revelation, by the Synoptists (comp. Matt. v. 14, xiii. 38, xviii. 7, xxvi. 13; [Mk. xvi. 15]), though it occurs more frequently in St Paul (Rom. iii. 19; 1 Cor. i. 21, &c.).

2. The fundamental idea of κόσμος in St John is that of the sum of created being which belongs to the sphere of human life as an ordered whole, considered apart from God (xvii. 5, 24). The world is relative to man as well as to God. So far as it includes the material creation, this is regarded as the appointed medium and scene of man's work (comp. Wisd. ix. 2 f., x. 1). Spiritual existences (angels, &c.) are not included in this conception of the world: they are "of the things above" as contrasted with "the things below" (viii. 23).

In this widest sense "the world was made through (διά)" the Word (i. 10). Comp. Rev. xiii. 8, xvii. 8.

3. More specially the world is that system which answers to the circumstances of man's present life. At birth he "comes into the world" (vi. 14, xvi. 21), and "is in the world" till death (xiii. 1, xvii. 11), comp. xvii. 15. The Lord during His earthly Life, or when He submits to its conditions, is "in the world" (ix. 5, xvii. 11, 13) in a more definite manner than that in which He is "in the world" from creation (i. 10), "coming into the world" (i. 9, xi. 27, xii. 46, xvi. 28, xviii. 37), and being "sent into the world" by the Father (x. 36, xvii. 18; 1 John iv. 9), and again "leaving the world" (xvi. 28). Comp. Rev. xi. 15.

4. So far "the world" represents that which is transitory and seen as opposed to the eternal (1 John ii. 15 ff., iii. 17). And these particular ideas of the transitoriness, the externality, the corruption of "the world" are emphasized in the phrase "this world" (ὁ κόσμος οὗτος, viii. 23, xi. 9, xii. 25, 31, xiii. 1, xviii. 36, xvi. 11; 1 John iv. 17. Comp. xiv. 30). So far as it is regarded under this aspect the "world" has no direct connexion with God (comp. 1 John v. 19).

5. It is easy to see how the thought of an ordered whole relative to man and considered *apart* from God passes into that of the ordered whole *separated* from God. Man fallen impresses his character upon the order which is the sphere of his activity. And thus the "world" comes to represent humanity in its present state, alienated from its Maker, and so far determining the character of the whole order to which man belongs. The world instead of remaining the true expression of God's will under the conditions of its creation, becomes His rival (1 John ii. 15—17). St John says little as to cause or process of this alienation. It is referred however to the action of a being without, who is the source and suggestor of evil (viii. 44, xiii. 2; 1 John iii. 8).

6. Through this interruption in its normal development, the world which was made by the Word, recognised Him not (i. 10; comp. xvii. 25; 1 John iii. 1). It became exposed to destruction (ἀπώλεια, iii. 16, viii. 24; 1 John v. 19 ff., ii. 2). Still it was the object of God's love (iii. 16 f.), and Christ took on Him its sin (i. 29). He was "the light" (viii. 12, ix. 5, xii. 46); "the Saviour of the world" (iv. 42, xii. 47; 1 John iv. 14), giving life to it (vi. 33, 51). He spoke not to a sect or to a nation, but to the world (xviii. 20, viii. 26). He is a propitiation "for the whole world" (1 John ii. 2).

7. The coming of Christ into the world was necessarily a judgment (ix. 39). Out of the whole, regarded as a system containing within itself the spring of a corresponding life (xv. 19, xvii. 14, 16; 1 John iv. 5, ii. 16), some were chosen by (xv. 19) or "given" to Him (xvii. 6). Thus the whole has become divided. Part attaches itself to God in answer to His call: part still stands aloof from Him. In contrast with the former the latter is called the world. In this sense the "world" de-

scribes the mass of men (comp. xii. 19) distinguished from the people of God, characterized by their peculiar feelings (vii. 7, xiv. 27, xv. 18 f., xvi. 20, xvii. 14; 1 John iii. 13, iv. 5) and powers (xiv. 17; 1 John iii. 1), hostile to believers, and incapable of receiving the divine spirit. The disciples and "the world" stand over against one another (xiv. 19, 22). On the one side are the marks of "light" and "love" and "life;" on the other, "darkness" and "hatred" and "death." The world has its champions (1 John iv. 1 ff.), its inspiring power (1 John iv. 4, v. 19), its prince (xiv. 30, xvi. 11). In the world the disciples have tribulation, though Christ has conquered it (xvi. 33); and His victory is repeated by them through the faith (1 John v. 4 f.).

8. But even this "world" is not uncared for, though for a time it was left (xvii. 9). The disciples are sent into it (xvii. 18). The Paraclete's Mission is to convict it (xvi. 8), the self-surrender of Christ (xiv. 31), the unity (xvii. 21) and the glory of the disciples (xvii. 23), are to the end that the world may come to knowledge and faith.

9. From this analysis of St John's usage of the term it will be seen how naturally the original conception of an order apart from God passes into that of an order opposed to God: how a system which is limited and transitory becomes hostile to the divine: how the "world" as the whole scene of human activity is lost in humanity: how humanity ceases to be "of the world" by its union with God in Christ.

13. In some of the early Latin copies (*b*, Tertullian and perhaps the translator of Irenæus) a very remarkable variation was introduced into this verse, by which it was referred to the Word as subject, *Who ... was born.* The variation arose from the ambiguity of the relative in Latin, which was taken with the nearest antecedent (*ejus, qui ... natus est*).

15. *of whom I spake*] The variations in a few of the most ancient authorities here suggest the possibility of some very early corruption of the text. The original hand of ℵ gives, *This was he that cometh after me* who *is become before me* (οὗτος ἦν ὁ ὀπ. μ. ἐρχ. ὃς ἔμ. μ. γ.). This insertion of the relative (ὅς) finds some support in one old Latin copy. The first hands of B and C and a very early corrector of ℵ read *who spake* (ὁ εἰπών for ὃν εἶπον); and this reading gives an intelligible sense by emphasizing the reference to the Baptist's testimony: "this John and no other was he who spake the memorable words."

16. *And of ...*] This reading, which is supported by A, the secondary uncials, almost all the cursives, three Syriac versions and the Vulgate, is a good example of a change introduced, probably by the unconscious instinct of the scribe, for the sake of smoothness and (as it was supposed) of clearness. At a very early time (second century) verse 16 was regarded as a continuation of the words of the Baptist, so that the true reference of the second *because* (ὅτι) was lost, and the repetition of the conjunction in two consecutive clauses was felt to be very harsh. The true reading, *because of ...* (ὅτι ἐκ ...) is supported by an overwhelming concurrence of the representatives of the most ancient texts (B, ℵD, CLX, 33, *Lat. vt.*, *Memph.*) though it practically disappeared from later copies.

18. *the only begotten Son*] Two readings of equal antiquity, as far as our present authorities go, though unequally supported, are found in this passage. Of these the first, followed by A.V., *the only begotten Son* (ὁ μονογενὴς υἱός), is found in AX, the secondary uncials, all known cursives except 33, the *Lt. vt.*, *Syr. vt.*, *Syr. Hcl. and Hier.*, the *Vulgate*, *Arm.*

The second, *one who is God, only begotten* (μονογενὴς θεός), is found in ℵ*BC*L, *Peshito*, *Syr. Hcl.*, *mg.* [D is defective.]

A third reading, *the only begotten God* (ὁ μονογενὴς θεός), which is found in ℵ^c, 33 (the reading of the Memphitic version is ambiguous: it *may* express *the only-begotten of God*, but it is more probable that it expresses *the only-begotten God* (ὁ μονογενὴς θεός): Schwartze rejects the former rendering, which is that of Wilkins, too peremptorily), probably arose from a combination of the two readings, and may be dismissed at once. The strangely inaccurate statement of many commentators that ὁ μον. θεός is the reading of "ℵBCL, &c.," shews a complete misapprehension not only of the facts but of the significance of the readings. The tempting reading of one Latin copy, *the only begotten*, has still less real claim to be taken into account in the face of the facts of the case. In considering this evidence it will appear that

1. The most ancient authorities for the reading, *the only-begotten Son*, the *Old Latin* and *Old Syriac* versions, are those which are inclined to introduce interpretative glosses (see note on *v.* 4), and on this occasion their weight is diminished by the opposition of ℵ.

2. The reading, *God, only-begotten*, in the Peshito, can hardly have been a correction of the original text, because this reading is not found in the type of text (*e.g.* AX) by the help of which the version appears to have been revised.

3. There is no ancient Greek authority for the reading, *the only-begotten Son*, while the Greek authorities for *God, only-begotten*, represent three great types, B, ℵ, CL.

4. The universal agreement of the later copies in the reading, *the only-begotten Son*, shews that there was no tendency in scribes to change it, while the correction of ℵ (*the only-begotten God*) shews us the reading, *God, only-*

begotten, modified under the influence of the common reading.

5. The substitution, intentional or accidental, of *God* (θ̅ς) for *Son* (υ̅ς) does not explain the omission of the article in the reading, *God, only-begotten;* while, on the contrary, the substitution of *Son* for *God* would naturally carry with it the addition of the article (ch. iii. 16, 18).

6. The occurrence of the word "Father" in the context would suggest the use of the word "Son," while the word God would appear at first sight out of place in the relation described.

Thus the testimony of the direct documentary evidence for the text very decidedly preponderates in favour of the reading, *God, only-begotten.*

The patristic testimony is complicated, and it is impossible to discuss it at length. It must be enough to say that

1. The phrase *God only begotten* (μονογενὴς θεός) is found from very early times in Greek writers of every school. By Clement, Irenæus and Origen it is connected with this passage. [The Latin writers, almost without exception, have *unicus* or *unigenitus filius.*]

2. It is very unlikely that a phrase in itself most remarkable should have obtained universal and unquestioned currency among Greek writers if it were not derived from apostolic usage.

It may further be added that the Valentinian writers, the earliest writers by whom the text is quoted, could have had no reason for introducing the reading, *God, only-begotten*, which they give. While on the other hand the substitution of *the only-begotten Son* for *God only-begotten* is not unlike the style of "Western" paraphrase (*e.g. vv.* 4, 34; Mark i. 20, vi. 36, 56, &c.; Luke xxiii. 35).

On the whole, therefore, the reading *God only-begotten* must be accepted, because (1) It is the best attested by ancient authority; (2) It is the more intrinsically probable from its uniqueness; (3) It makes the origin of the alternative reading more intelligible.

An examination of the whole structure of the Prologue leads to the same conclusion. The phrase, which has grown foreign to our ears though it was familiar to early Christian writers, gathers up the two thoughts of sonship and deity, which have been separately affirmed of the Word (*vv.* 14, 1).

The reading has been discussed in detail by Dr E. Abbot ('Bibliotheca Sacra,' Oct. 1861; 'Unitarian Review,' June, 1875); and by Dr Hort ('Two Dissertations...,' Camb. 1875). The conclusion of Dr Hort in favour of μονογενὴς θεός, after a full examination of Prof. Abbot's arguments for ὁ μονογενὴς υἱός, is pronounced by Prof. Harnack in an elaborate review of his essay in 'Theol. Lit. Zeit.' 1876, pp. 541 ff., to have been "established beyond contradiction."

24. All the most ancient MSS. (א*A*BC*, D is defective), with Origen (and *Memph.*) read ἀπεσταλμένοι ἦσαν in place of οἱ ἀπεστ. ἦσαν. This reading can be rendered either: *they had been sent from...*, or, *certain had been sent from among...* Origen expressly distinguishes two missions, the first in *v.* 19, and the second here.

28. *Bethabara*] The great preponderance of authorities is in favour of the reading *Bethany.* Origen implies that a diversity of reading existed here in his time. "Almost all the copies," he says, "have *Bethany*, but I am convinced that we ought to read *Bethabara*," which probably was the reading of the minority. His reasons are simply geographical; and it is a striking fact that even his authority thus boldly exerted was unable to induce scribes to alter the reading which they found in their archetypes, so that *Bethabara* still remains the reading only of a small minority. The oldest authority which gives *Bethabara* is *Syr. vt.*, but this very early translation frequently admits glosses (see next note).

34. For the words *the Son of God* a group of authorities characteristically "Western" (see *v.* 4, note), א, *e*, *Syr. vt.*, Ambr., read *the chosen of God.* The two readings are combined curiously in several early Latin authorities (*electus Dei filius*).

42. There is no doubt that Ἰωάνου (אBL, *Lat. vt.*, *Memph.*) should be read for Ἰωνᾶ. Comp. xxi. 15, 16, 17. Both words are used as Greek representatives of יְהוֹחָנָן *Johanan.* Comp. 2 K. xxv. 23 (LXX.).

51. The words ἀπ' ἄρτι (*from henceforth*) must be omitted on the authority of the witnesses which preserve the purest ancient text (אBL, *Latt.*, *Memph.*, Orig.). They were probably added from Matt. xxvi. 64, where the words are undisturbed.

THE SON OF MAN.

1. The title "the Son of man" stands in significant contrast with the other titles which are assigned to the Lord, and particularly with that title which in some respects is most akin to it, "the Son of David." It was essentially a new title; it was used, so far as we know, with one exception only, by the Lord and of Himself; it expresses a relationship not to a family or to a nation, but to all humanity.

2. The title was a new one. It is common to regard it as directly derived from the book of Daniel. But in reality the passage (vii. 13) in which the title is supposed to be found has only a secondary relation to it. The vision of Daniel brings before him not "the Son of man," but one "like a son of man." The phrase is general (Ezek. ii. 1), and is in-

troduced by a particle of comparison. The Greek represents the original exactly: ὡς υἱὸς ἀνθρώπου ἐρχόμενος ἦν, and the true parallel is found in Rev. i. 13, xiv. 14. The thought on which the seer dwells is simply that of the human appearance of the being presented to him (comp. Dan. x. 16; Ezek. i. 26). The force of this comparison comes out more plainly if the context be taken into account. The divine kingdom is being contrasted with the kingdoms of the world. These are presented under the images of beasts. The brute forces symbolized them, just as man, to whom originally dominion was given, symbolized the rightful sovereignty which was to be established. "I saw," the seer writes, "in my vision by night...and four great beasts came up from the sea. The first was like a lion,...and...a second...like a bear,...and lo another like a leopard....I saw in the night visions, and behold one like a son of man came with the clouds of heaven..." (vii. 2 ff.). The dominion which had been exercised by tyrants was henceforward to be entrusted to "the saints of the Most High" (vii. 17 f., 27). The former rulers had come forth from the sea—the symbol of all confusion and instability—the divine ruler came from heaven.

3. It is true that the image of Daniel found fulfilment in the sovereignty of Christ, and so the words of the seer, with the substitution of "the Son of man" for "one like a son of man" were applied by the Lord to Himself (Matt. xvi. 27, xxiv. 30, xxvi. 64). But He was not only "like a son of man," He was "the Son of man." The less is of necessity included in the greater; but in itself the language of Daniel furnishes no parallel to the language of the Gospels.

4. The same may be said of all the other passages in which the phrases "the sons of men" or "Son of man" occur in the Old Testament. They describe man as dependent, limited, transitory. The singular, except in Ezekiel as addressed to the prophet, is of rare occurrence; and (as I believe) it is never found with the article (*e.g.* Ps. viii. 5, lxxx. 17).

5. But there can be no doubt that the image in Daniel exercised some influence upon later apocalyptic writings. The remarkable use of the title "Son of man" in reference to the Messiah in the Book of Henoch is directly based upon it. The sense of the title however remains equally limited as before. The Messiah is "a Son of man," and not properly "the Son of man" (c. 46, §§ 1, 2, 3, 4; c. 48, § 2). In these places the chosen messenger of the Most High is described simply as a man, and not as one who stands in any special relation to the human race.

6. There is very little in the Gospels to shew how far the fuller applications of the title found in the apocalypse of Henoch obtained currency, or how the people commonly understood the title. There is at least nothing to shew that the title was understood to be a title of Messiah. On the contrary, "the Son of man" and "the Messiah" are, as it were, set one against the other, Matt. xvi. 13, 16 (the parallels, Mark viii. 27; Luke ix. 18, give simply *me*); John xii. 34. And it is inconceivable that the Lord should have adopted a title which was popularly held to be synonymous with that of Messiah, while He carefully avoided the title of Messiah itself.

7. The title, then, as we find it in the Gospels, *the Son of man* absolutely, was a new one. It is out of the question to suppose that the definite article simply expressed "the prophetic Son of man." The manner in which the title is first used excludes such an interpretation. The title is new, and the limits within which its usage is confined serve to fix attention on its peculiarity. In the Gospels it is used only by the Lord in speaking of Himself; and beyond the range of His discourses it is found only in Acts vii. 56.

8. In the Lord's discourses the title is distributed generally. It is found both in the earlier and in the later discourses in about equal proportions. It is not however found in the discourses after the Resurrection. The title occurs many times in St John's Gospel, but less frequently than in the other three; and in the last discourses which St John gives at length it occurs only once, in the opening sentence, xiii. 31. [In St Matthew 30 times; in St Mark 13; in St Luke 25; in St John 12.]

9. The passages in which the title is found in the Synoptic Gospels may be grouped into two great classes: (1) those which refer to the earthly work of the Lord in the time of His humility; and (2) those which refer to His future coming in glory. The usage in St John is strictly parallel, but the occurrence of the title in his Gospel will be considered more in detail on ix. 35.

(1) The earthly presence of the Lord as the Incarnate Son presented a series of startling contrasts. (α) He was to outward eyes despised, and yet possessing supreme authority; (β) He lived as men live, and yet He was at all times busy with His Father's work; (γ) His true nature was veiled, and yet not wholly hidden; (δ) His mission was a mission of love, and yet it imposed on those to whom He came heavy responsibility; (ε) to misinterpret Him was to incur judgment, and yet the offence was not past forgiveness; (ζ) He foresaw the end from the beginning, with its sorrows and glory.

The following passages in which the title occurs illustrate these different thoughts:

(α) Matt. viii. 20 ‖ Luke ix. 58. Matt. ix. 6 ‖ Mark ii. 10 ‖ Luke v. 24.

(β) Matt. xi. 19 ‖ Luke vii. 34. Matt. xiii. 37. Matt. xii. 8 ‖ Mark ii. 28 ‖ Luke vi. 5.

(γ) Matt. xvi. 13.

(δ) Luke xix. 10, xvii. 22.

(ε) Mark viii. 38 ‖ Luke ix. 26. Comp. Luke xii. 8. Matt. xii. 32 ‖ Luke xii. 10. (Mark iii. 28, τοῖς υἱ. τῶν ἀνθρ.).

(ζ) Mark viii. 31 ‖ Luke ix. 22. Comp. xxiv. 7. Matt. xvii. 12 ‖ Mark ix. 12. Matt. xvii. 22 ‖ Mark ix. 31 ‖ Luke ix. 44. Matt. xx. 18 ‖ Mark x. 33 ‖ Luke xviii. 31. Matt. xxvi. 2. Matt. xxvi. 24 ‖ Mark xiv. 21 ‖ Luke xxii. 22. Matt. xxvi. 45 ‖ Mark xiv. 41. Matt. xii. 40 ‖ Luke xi. 30. Matt. xvii. 9 ‖ Mark ix. 9. Matt. xx. 28 ‖ Mark x. 45. Luke xxii. 69 (ἀπὸ τοῦ νῦν). Matt. xxvi. 64 (ἀπ' ἄρτι) ‖ Mark xiv. 62. Luke xxii. 48.

(2) Side by side with these traits of the human life of the Son of man, visions are opened of another life of glory, sovereignty, judgment. (α) Though He had come, yet He still spoke of His coming as future. (β) Meanwhile men are left on their trial, to which an end is appointed in a swift and unexpected catastrophe. This "presence" of the Son of man at "the consummation of the age" is to be followed by a (γ) judgment of men and nations, and (δ) by the gathering of the elect into a divine kingdom.

These thoughts are illustrated by the following passages in which the title occurs:

(α) Matt. x. 23, xvi. 27 f., xxiv. 44. Comp. Luke xii. 40.

(β) Luke vi. 22, xvii. 30, xviii. 8, xxi. 36; Matt. xxiv. 27, 37 (comp. Luke xvii. 24, 26), 39.

(γ) Matt. xiii. 40 f., xix. 28, xxv. 31 ff., Matt. xxiv. 30 ‖ Mark xiii. 26 ‖ Luke xxi. 27.

10. A consideration of these passages will enable us to seize the outlines of the teaching which is summed up in the title. The idea of the true humanity of Christ lies at the foundation of it. He was not only "like a son of man," but He was "a Son of man:" His manhood was real and not apparent. But He was not as one man among many (yet the title ἄνθρωπος occurs John viii. 40; 1 Tim. ii. 5). He was the representative of the whole race; "*the* Son of man" in whom all the potential powers of humanity were gathered.

11. Thus the expression which describes the self-humiliation of Christ raises Him at the same time immeasurably above all those whose nature He had assumed. Of no one, simply man, could it be said that he was "the man," or "the Son of man," in whom the complete conception of manhood was absolutely attained.

12. The teaching of St Paul supplies a striking commentary upon the title when he speaks of Christ as the "second Adam" (1 Cor. xv. 45. Comp. Rom. v. 14), who gathers up into Himself all humanity, and becomes the source of a higher life to the race.

13. As a necessary conclusion from this view of Christ's humanity which is given in the title "the Son of man," it follows that He is in perfect sympathy with every man of every age and of every nation. All that truly belongs to humanity, all therefore that truly belongs to every individual in the whole race, belongs also to Him. (Compare a noble passage in Goldwin Smith's 'Lectures on History,' pp. 134 ff.)

14. The thought is carried yet further. We are allowed to see, and it can only be as it were "by a mirror in a riddle" (1 Cor. xiii. 12), that the relation which exists in the present order of things between every man and Christ, is continued in another order. As "the Son of man" He is revealed to the eyes of His first martyr, that Christians may learn that that which is begun in weakness shall be completed in eternal majesty (Acts vii. 56).

15. It may well be admitted that the early disciples did not at first apprehend all that the later history of the race enables us to see in the title. Perhaps it may have been from some sense of the mysterious meaning of the term, which had not yet been illuminated by the light of a Catholic Church, that they shrank themselves from using it. But we cannot be bound to measure the interpretation of Scripture by that which is at once intelligible. The words of the Lord are addressed to all time. They stand written for our study, and it is our duty to bring to their interpretation whatever fulness of knowledge a later age may have placed within our reach.

CHAPTER II.

1 *Christ turneth water into wine,* 12 *departeth into Capernaum, and to Jerusalem,* 14 *where he purgeth the temple of buyers and sellers.* 19 *He foretelleth his death and resurrection.* 23 *Many believed because of his miracles, but he would not trust himself with them.*

AND the third day there was a marriage in Cana of Galilee; and the mother of Jesus was there:

---

3. THE TESTIMONY OF SIGNS (ii. 1—11). The manifestation of the glory of Christ (ii. 11) follows naturally upon the recognition of His claims in virtue of testimony and experience. He shews by a significant sign, spontaneously offered in the presence of an acknowledged want and significant only to disciples (*v.* 11), the nature of the new order which He has already described (i. 51). He has been announced, and followed; He is now believed in. The scene still lies in the circle of the family, and not among "the people" or in "the world."

The narrative proceeds in a simple and

2 And both Jesus was called, and
his disciples, to the marriage.
3 And when they wanted wine,
the mother of Jesus saith unto him,
They have no wine.
4 Jesus saith unto her, Woman,

---

exact sequence. The Evangelist describes the time and scene (*vv.* 1, 2), the occasion (*vv.* 3—5), the manner (*vv.* 6—8), the result (*vv.* 9, 10), and the effect (*v.* 11) of Christ's first sign.

CHAP. II. 1, 2. The details of time, place, and persons contribute to the meaning of "the beginning of signs." It was shewn in close connexion with the faith of the first disciples (*the third day*), at the village where one at least of them dwelt (xxi. 2), at a festival of the highest natural joy.

1. *the third day*] *i.e.* from the last day mentioned, i. 43. The distance from the place where John was baptizing to Nazareth was about sixty miles, three days journey.

a marriage] or *a marriage feast*, which was frequently celebrated for several (seven) days, Gen. xxix. 22 ff.; Judges xiv. 12. It is wholly unknown in whose honour the feast was held.

Cana of Galilee] So called each time when it is mentioned in the Gospel, to distinguish it from a Cana in Cœlo-Syria (Jos. 'Antt.' xv. 5. 1, &c.). This village is mentioned in the N. T. (comp. Jos. 'Vita,' § 16) only by St John here and iv. 46, xxi. 2. It has been traditionally identified (from the 8th century) with *Kefr Kenna*, about 4½ miles north-west of Nazareth. Recently the site has been sought at a village about nine miles north of Nazareth, *Khurbet-Cana*, which is said (though this is doubtful) to have retained the name *Kana-el-Jelil.* The Syriac versions agree in inserting a *-t-* in the name (*Katna*). This may point to local knowledge; and it has been conjectured that *Kana* may be identified with *Katana*, a place about four miles from Nazareth.

the mother of Jesus] In St John alone the name of "the mother of Jesus" is not mentioned, even when Joseph is named (vi. 42). Comp. xix. 25 ff., note.

was there] From *v.* 5 it is evident that the Virgin Mary was closely connected with the family; and so she was already at the house when Jesus arrived at Cana with His disciples. The absence of all mention of Joseph here and elsewhere (see xix. 27) has been reasonably supposed to imply that he was already dead. See Mark vi. 3, note.

2. *And both Jesus...and*] Rather, *And Jesus* **also**...*and* (iii. 23, xviii. 2, 5, xix. 39).

was called] *i.e.* on his return from the Baptist, and not *had been called.*

his disciples] This is the first distinct mention of the relation in which the little group gathered from "the disciples of John" (i. 35, 37) now stood to the greater Teacher ("Rabbi," 49).

3—5. The depth, obscurity, and (at the same time) naturalness of this conversation witness to the substantial truth of the record. The words only become intelligible when the exact relation between the mother of Jesus and her divine Son is apprehended. As soon as this is grasped the implied request, the apparent denial, the persistence of trust, the triumph of faith, are seen to hang harmoniously together.

3. *when they wanted wine*] Rather, **when the wine failed**, as it might be expected to do from the unexpected addition of seven guests to the party already gathered. The fact that the arrival of Jesus had brought the difficulty, made it more natural to apply to Him for the removal of it. There is a Jewish saying, "Without wine there is no joy" ('Pesach.' 109 a, Wünsche), and the failure of the wine at a marriage feast would be most keenly felt. The reading of some early authorities ($\aleph$* and copies of *Lat. vt.*) is a remarkable example of the paraphrases which are characteristic of the "Western" text: *they had no wine, for the wine of the marriage was consumed* (συνετελέσθη).

They have no wine] It is enough to state the want. To describe the circumstance is in such a case to express a silent prayer. Compare xi. 3, and contrast that passage with iv. 47.

The Mother of the Lord having heard of the testimony of the Baptist, and seeing the disciples gathered round her Son, the circumstances of whose miraculous birth she treasured in her heart (Luke ii. 19, 51), must have looked now at length for the manifestation of His power, and thought that an occasion only was wanting. Yet even so she leaves all to His will. Contrast Luke ii. 48.

4. *Jesus saith*] **And** *Jesus saith.* These two clauses are joined together closely, just as *vv.* 7, 8, while *vv.* 5 and 7 are not connected with what immediately precedes.

The order here is, *What have I to do with thee, woman?* It is otherwise in xix. 26. Here the contrast comes first; there the personality.

Woman] In the original there is not the least tinge of reproof or severity in the term. The address is that of courteous respect, even of tenderness. See xix. 26. Comp. iv. 21, xx. 13, 15. At the same time it emphasizes the special relation which it expresses; as here the contrast between the divine Son and the human Mother.

what have I to do with thee?] Or, *what hast thou to do with me?* Literally, *what is*

what have I to do with thee? mine hour is not yet come.
5 His mother saith unto the servants, Whatsoever he saith unto you, do *it*.
6 And there were set there six waterpots of stone, after the manner of the purifying of the Jews, containing two or three firkins apiece.
7 Jesus saith unto them, Fill the waterpots with water. And they filled them up to the brim.
8 And he saith unto them, Draw

---

there to me and thee? (τί ἐμοὶ καὶ σοί, γύναι; Vulg. *quid mihi et tibi est, mulier?*) "Leave me to myself; let me follow out my own course." The phrase occurs not unfrequently in the Old Testament, 2 S. xvi. 10; 1 K. xvii. 18; 2 Chro. xxxv. 21 (Judg. xi. 12). It is found also in the New Testament: Matt. viii. 29, and parallels. Comp. Matt. xxvii. 19. Everywhere it marks some divergence between the thoughts and ways of the persons so brought together. In this passage it serves to shew that the actions of the Son of God, now that He has entered on His divine work, are no longer dependent in any way on the suggestion of a woman, even though that woman be His Mother. Henceforth all He does springs from within, and will be wrought at its proper season. The time of silent discipline and obedience (Luke ii. 51) was over. Comp. Matt. xii. 46 ff.

mine hour is not yet come] the due time for the fulfilment of my work. The words are here used of that part of Christ's work which was shewn in the first revelation of His glory; but more commonly they refer to the consummation of it in the Passion. See viii. 20, note, xvii. 1, note. Mary may have believed that the first manifestation of Christ would lead at once to full triumph; and to that fancy the words are a pregnant answer.

There is no inconsistency between this declaration of Christ that "His hour was not yet come," and the fulfilment of the prayer which followed immediately. A change of moral and spiritual conditions is not measured by length of time. Comp. xiii. 1, note.

5. The Lord's reply left the faith which rests absolutely in Him unshaken. Nowhere else perhaps is such trust shewn. Whether divine help was given through Him or not, so much at least could be provided, that if the right moment came—and it is impossible to use a temporal measure for moral changes—all should be ready for His action. *Whatsoever he saith unto you, do it;* the command is wholly unlimited: all is left to Christ.

6—8. The manner of working the miracle is described with singular minuteness and yet with singular reserve. The wine is found to be present; the water shews the contents of the source from which it was drawn.

6. *And there...set there...of stone*] More exactly: **Now** *there...there...of stone* **set...** *there*] in the court of the house as it seems (*v.* 8) and not in the guest-chamber.

six waterpots] The large number would be required in consequence of the many guests assembled at the feast. They were *of stone*—as our canon directs fonts to be—since that material is less liable to impurity. Vessels of stone or earthenware were prescribed by Jewish tradition for the washings before and after meals ('Sota,' 4, Wünsche). The "purifying" extended not only to the "washing of hands," but also to "the washing of cups and brasen vessels and couches" (Mark vii. 3, 4). For the washing of vessels, which were immersed and not only sprinkled, later tradition prescribed a receptacle holding "forty Sata," about five times as large as one of these.

Dr E. D. Clarke gives a remarkable illustration of the passage: "...walking among these ruins [at Cana] we saw large, massy stone water-pots...not preserved nor exhibited as reliques, but lying about, disregarded by the present inhabitants... From their appearance and the number of them, it was quite evident that a practice of keeping water in large stone pots, each holding from eighteen to twenty-seven gallons, was once common in the country." ('Travels,' II. p. 445, referred to by Van Lennep, 'Bible Customs,' p. 45, note.)

the purifying of the Jews] See *v.* 13. The words seem to contain an allusion to a Christian purification. Comp. iii. 25; Heb. i. 3; 2 Pet. i. 9.

two or three firkins apiece] The measure here (*metretes*) probably corresponds with the Bath, which was equivalent to three Sata (*measures*, Matt. xiii. 33), about 8¾ gallons. It is reasonable to suppose that the vessels provided for this extraordinary gathering were of different sizes, but all large.

7. *unto them*] The sixth verse is substantially parenthetical, and in thought *v.* 7 follows *v.* 5 directly.

they filled them up to the brim] This preliminary work was done completely, so that the contents of the vessels were obvious to all.

8. *Draw out*] Rather, **Draw**. There is considerable obscurity as to the meaning of these words. According to the current interpretation the water in the vessels of purification was changed into wine, and the servants are bidden to draw from these. There is

out now, and bear unto the governor of the feast. And they bare *it*.

9 When the ruler of the feast had tasted the water that was made wine, and knew not whence it was: (but the servants which drew the water knew;) the governor of the feast called the bridegroom,

10 And saith unto him, Every man at the beginning doth set forth good wine; and when men have well drunk, then that which is worse: *but* thou hast kept the good wine until now.

11 This beginning of miracles did Jesus in Cana of Galilee, and mani-

---

nothing in the text which definitely points to such an interpretation; and the original word is applied most naturally to drawing water from the well (iv. 7, 15), and not from a vessel like the waterpot. Moreover the emphatic addition of *now* seems to mark the continuance of the same action of drawing as before, but with a different end. Hitherto they had drawn to fill the vessels of purification: they were charged *now* to "draw and bear to the governor of the feast." It seems most unlikely that water taken from vessels of purification could have been employed for the purpose of the miracle. On the other hand, the significance of the miracle comes out with infinitely greater force if the change is wrought through the destination of the element. That which remained water when kept for a ceremonial use became wine when borne in faith to minister to the needs, even to the superfluous requirements, of life. This view, that the change in the water was determined by its destination for use at the feast, can be held equally if the water so used and limited to that which was used were "drawn" from the vessels, and not from the well.

If, however, the traditional view of the miracle be retained no real difficulty can be felt in the magnitude of the marriage gift with which Christ endowed the house of a friend.

the governor (**ruler**, as *v.* 9) *of the feast*] Some have supposed this "ruler" to be the chief servant, "steward," to whose care all the arrangements of the feast were entrusted, and not one of the guests. This is the classical usage of the term employed, and hence Juvencus speaks of *summus minister*. But on the other hand, in Ecclus. xxxv. 1, 2, one of the guests is described as "ruler" (ἡγούμενος), and there is no certain evidence that the Jews had any such an officer among their servants, who certainly would not in any case be likely to be found in such a household as this.

9, 10. The independent witness to the two parts of the miracle establishes its reality. The ruler of the feast declares what the element *is*, the servants knew what it *was*.

9. *When the ruler...the governor...called*] **And** *when the ruler...the* **ruler...calleth** (φωνεῖ, Vulg. *vocat*). See xviii. 33.

that was made] Literally, *when it had become*, *after it had become*. The clause is predicative and not simply descriptive.

and knew not...knew] This clause is most probably to be taken as a parenthesis: *When the ruler tasted...(and he knew not...but...knew) he calleth*...Comp. i. 14, note. His ignorance of the source from which the wine came did not lead to his inquiry, but rather gave weight to his spontaneous testimony to its excellence.

which drew] *which* **had drawn**. Vulg. *qui haurierant*.

10. The words are half playful and fall in with the character of the scene. The form of the first part of the sentence is proverbial, and there is nothing to offend in the strong term, *have well drunk* (comp. Gen. xliii. 34, LXX.), "drunk freely," which has no immediate application to the guests present. The last clause seems to be one of those unconscious prophecies in which words spoken in recognition of a present act reveal the far deeper truth of which it is a sign.

at the beginning doth set] **first setteth on.**

good wine] Rather, **the** *good wine* from his store. The definite article is made pointed by the end of the verse.

worse] **poorer**. Literally, *smaller*. Omit *then*.

kept] The idea of the verb (τηρεῖν) is that of watchful care rather than of safe custody (φυλάσσειν). Comp. ch. xii. 7.

11. *This beginning ...*] Rather, according to the true reading, *This as a beginning of his signs ...*

miracles] **signs** (σημεῖα, Vulg. *signa*). The value of the work was rather in what it indicated than in what it was. Miracles, in this aspect which is commonest in the New Testament, are revelations of truth through the symbolism of the outward acts.

The translation *signs* is always preserved in the Synoptists except Luke xxiii. 8 (see Matt. xvi. 3); but in St John we frequently find the rendering *miracles*, even where the point of the teaching is lost by this translation, *e.g.* John vi. 26, *not because ye saw* **signs** *but*..., where the motive was not the prospect of something yet nobler to be revealed, but acquiescence in the gross satisfaction of earthly wants. Whenever the word is used of Christ's works it is always with distinct reference to a higher character which

fested forth his glory; and his disciples believed on him.

12 ¶ After this he went down to Capernaum, he, and his mother, and his brethren, and his disciples: and they continued there not many days.

---

they indicate. Those who call them "signs" attach to Him divine attributes in faith, ii. 23, iii. 2, &c., or fear, xi. 47; and each sign gave occasion to a growth of faith or unbelief according to the spirit of those who witnessed it. The word was adopted into the Aramaic dialect (סימן) in the general sense of "sign."

It may be added that the word *power* (δύναμις) for *miracle* never occurs in St John, while he very commonly includes miracles under the term *works*, xiv. 11, &c.

In this passage the twofold effect of the sign is described by St John, first as a manifestation of Christ's glory, and next as a ground of faith in those who were already disciples. The office of miracles towards those who do not believe is wholly left out of sight.

manifested forth] **manifested.** The word (φανεροῦν) is frequent in St John, ch. i. 31, vii. 4, xxi. 1, &c.

his glory] The glory (comp. i. 14, note) is truly, inherently, Christ's glory. A prophet would manifest the glory of God. The manifestation of His glory in this "sign" must not be sought simply in what we call its "miraculous" element, but in this taken in connexion with the circumstances, as a revelation of the insight, the sympathy, the sovereignty of the Son of Man, who was the Word Incarnate. See Additional Note.

his disciples believed on him] Testimony (i. 36) directs those who were ready to welcome Christ to Him. Personal intercourse converts followers into disciples (ii. 2). A manifestation of power, as a sign of diviner grace, converts discipleship into personal faith.

believed on him] The original phrase (ἐπίστευσαν εἰς αὐτόν, Vulg. *crediderunt in eum*) is peculiarly characteristic of St John. It is found in one place only in the Synoptic Gospels (Matt. xviii. 6 || Mark ix. 42), and but rarely in St Paul's Epistles (Rom. x. 14; Gal. ii. 16; Phil. i. 29). The idea which it conveys is that of the absolute transference of trust from oneself to another.

As the beginning of Christ's signs this miracle cannot but have a representative value. We may observe

1. Its essential character. A sign of sovereign power wrought on inorganic matter, not on a living body.

2. Its circumstantial character. The change of the simpler to the richer element. In this respect it may be contrasted with the first public miracle of Moses, with whose history the record of miracles in the Old Testament commences.

3. Its moral character The answer of love to faith, ministering to the fulness of human joy in one of its simplest and most natural forms. Contrast this feature with the action of the Baptist, Matt. xi. 18, 19.

In each respect the character of the sign answers to the general character of Christ as a new creation, a transfiguration of the ceremonial Law into a spiritual Gospel, the ennobling of the whole life. It may be added also that the scene of the "sign"—a marriage feast—is that under which the accomplishment of Christ's work is most characteristically prefigured, ch. iii. 29; Matt. xxii. 2 ff., xxv. 1 ff.; Rev. xix. 7, xxi. 2.

This miracle alone of those recorded by St John has no parallel in the Synoptists; and we cannot but conclude from the minuteness of the details of the history that the Mother of the Lord made known some of them to the Apostle to whose care she was entrusted. Moreover in this miracle only does she occupy a prominent place.

12. This verse forms a transition. As yet the family life was not broken. Till "His hour was come" in a new sense the Lord still waited as He had hitherto lived.

Capernaum] Caphar-nahum, according to the most ancient authorities (Καφαρναούμ, כפר נחום. Josephus gives both Κεφαρναούμ and Κεφαρνώμη). This town was on the shores of the lake, so that Christ *went down* thither from Nazareth or Cana, which were on the table-land above. Caphar (a *hamlet*, cf. Luke ix. 12. *Syr.*) is found in late names of places not unfrequently, answering to the Arabic *Kefr*. The site of Capernaum has now been identified beyond all reasonable doubt with *Tell-Hûm* (Wilson, 'Sea of Galilee,' in Warren's 'Recovery of Jerusalem,' pp. 342 ff.; Tristram, 'Land of Israel,' pp. 428 ff. ed. 3). Compare Matt. iv. 13, note.

From the mention of "his brethren," who are not noticed *vv.* 1, 2, it appears likely that the Lord had returned to Nazareth from Cana. The passing reference to a sojourn at Capernaum falls in with what is said in the Synoptists (Matt. iv. 13) of the Lord's subsequent removal thither from Nazareth at the commencement of His Galilæan ministry, though this fact is not expressly mentioned by St John. Comp. vi. 24 ff.

his brethren] Most probably the sons of Joseph by a former marriage. See an exhaustive essay by Dr Lightfoot, 'Galatians,' Essay II.

not many days] This is perhaps mentioned to shew that at present Capernaum was not made the permanent residence of the Lord, as it became afterwards.

13 ¶ And the Jews' passover was at hand, and Jesus went up to Jerusalem,

14 And found in the temple those that sold oxen and sheep and doves, and the changers of money sitting:

---

ii. THE WORK OF CHRIST (ii. 13—iv. 54).

The formation of a small group of disciples inspired by true faith (*v.* 11) was followed by the commencement of the Lord's public work. This is presented in three forms as undertaken in three distinct scenes, Judæa, Samaria, Galilee.

Hitherto the Revelation of Christ has been given mainly through the confession of disciples (i. 51, note). The Evangelist now, as he traces the sequence of events, crowns the record of the testimony rendered to Christ by the record of His first self-revelation. He shews how He satisfied anticipations and wants; how He was misunderstood and welcomed. Unbelief is as yet passive, though it is seen by Christ (ii. 25).

The narrative deals still for the most part with representative individuals, and not with the masses of the people.

The general contents of the section are thus distributed:

1. The work in Judæa (ii. 13—iii. 36).
   - *a.* At Jerusalem in the temple (ii. 13—22).
     - i. The symbolic act (13—16).
       Effect on the disciples (*v.* 17).
     - ii. The promised sign (18—21).
       Effect on the disciples (*v.* 22).
   - *b.* At Jerusalem with Jews (ii. 23—iii. 21).
     - i. Generally (23—25).
     - ii. Specially (iii. 1—21).
   - *c.* In Judæa generally (iii. 22—36).
2. The work in Samaria (iv. 1—42).
   iv. 1—3, transitional.
   - *a.* Specially (4—38).
   - *b.* Generally (39—42).
3 The work in Galilee (iv. 43—54).
   - *a.* Generally (43—45).
   - *b.* A special sign (46—54).

1. THE WORK IN JUDÆA (ii. 13—iii. 36).

It was fitting that the Lord's public work should commence in Judæa and in the Holy City. The events recorded in this section really determined the character of His after ministry. He offered Himself by a significant act intelligible to faith as the Messiah: His coming was either not understood or misunderstood; and, after a more distinct revelation of His Person in Samaria, He began his work afresh as a prophet in Galilee. Henceforward He appeared no more openly as Messiah at Jerusalem till His final entry.

Christ's work at Jerusalem in the temple (ii. 13—22).

It is impossible not to feel the change which at this point comes over the narrative. There is a change of place, of occasion, of manner of action. Jerusalem and Cana, the passover and the marriage feast, the stern Reformer and the sympathizing Guest. So too the spiritual lessons which the two signs convey are also complementary. The first represents the ennobling of common life, the second the purifying of divine worship. Or, to put the truth in another light, the one is a revelation of the Son of man, and the other a revelation of the Christ, the Fulfiller of the hope and purpose of Israel.

The history falls into two parts, the symbolic act (13—17), the promised sign (18—22). The contents of the section are peculiar to St John, who was an eye-witness, ii. 17.

13—17. The record is a commentary on Mal. iii. 1 ff. Comp. Zech. xiv. 20 f. The first step in Messiah's work was the abolition of the corruptions which the selfishness of a dominant and faithless hierarchy had introduced into the divine service. Origen ('in Joh.' t. x. § 16) justly points out the spiritual application of this first act of Christ's ministry to His continual coming both to the Church and to individual souls.

13. *the Jews' passover*] ch. xi. 55. Comp. vi. 4. The exact rendering, **the passover of the Jews**, brings out the sense more clearly. The phrase appears to imply distinctly the existence of a recognised "Christian Passover" at the time when the Gospel was written. Compare *v.* 6. Origen ('in Joh.' t. x. § 14) thinks that the words mark how that which was "the Lord's Passover" had been degraded into a merely human ceremonial.

For the general sense in which the term *the Jews* is used in St John, see Introd. pp. ix, x.

went up] ch. v. 1, vii. 8, 10, xi. 55, xii 20. Comp. Luke ii. 41 f.

14. *And found*] **And He found.** There is a pause at the end of *v.* 13 which must be marked by the commencement of a new sentence. The visit to the Holy City is recorded first, and then the visit to the temple. It was natural that the Lord's work should begin not only at Jerusalem but also at the centre of divine worship, the sanctuary of the theocracy. He now comes in due time to try the people in His Father's house, and to judge abuses which He must have seen often on earlier visits. The event is to be placed before the

15 And when he had made a scourge of small cords, he drove them all out of the temple, and the sheep, and the oxen; and poured out the changers' money, and overthrew the tables;
16 And said unto them that sold doves, Take these things hence; make not my Father's house an house of merchandise.
17 And his disciples remembered that it was written, [a]The zeal of thine house hath eaten me up. [a] Psal. 69. 9.
18 ¶ Then answered the Jews

---

passover (*v.* 23), and probably on the eve of the feast, when leaven was cleared away, Exod. xii. 15; 1 Cor. v. 7.

in the temple] *i.e.* in the outer court, the court of the Gentiles, where there was a regular market, belonging to the house of Hanan (Annas). See note on Mark xi. 15.

The two words translated "temple" in A.V. require to be distinguished carefully, (1) *Hieron*, the whole sacred enclosure, with the courts and porticoes, which is never used metaphorically; and (2) *Naos*, the actual sacred building, used below of the body of the Lord (*v.* 21), and of Christians who form His spiritual body (1 Cor. iii. 16, 17, vi. 19; 2 Cor. vi. 16). The distinction is often very interesting. Contrast Matt. iv. 5, xii. 6, xxiv. 1; Luke ii. 37, 46; John x. 23; Acts iii. 10, xxi. 28 (*Hieron*, the temple-courts), with Matt. xxiii. 17, 35, xxvii. 5, note, 51; Luke i. 21; John ii. 20 (*Naos*, the sanctuary).

those that sold] Not simply men engaged in the traffic, but those who were habitually engaged in it.

oxen...sheep...doves] Comp. Matt. xxi. 12, note. Caspari, 'Einl. in d. L. J.' s. 102.

changers of money] The word used here (κερματιστής) is different from that in *v.* 15 (κολλυβιστής). The present word indicates properly the changer of large into smaller coins; the second word is derived from the fee paid for the exchange (κόλλυβος), which appears in the vernacular Aramaic (Buxtorf, 'Lex.' s.v. קלבום). Obviously no coins bearing the image of the Emperor or any heathen symbol could be paid into the temple treasury, and all offerings of money would require to be made in Jewish coins. The yearly payment of the half-shekel, which could be made in the country (Matt. xvii. 24), was also received at the temple, and the exchange required for this gave abundant business to the exchangers. Lightfoot has collected an interesting series of illustrations on Matt. xxi. 12.

15. *a scourge of small cords*] as a symbol of authority and not as a weapon of offence. The "cords" (σχοινία, properly of twisted rushes) would be at hand. No corresponding detail is mentioned in the parallel narratives. Jewish tradition ('Sanh.' 98 b, Wünsche) figured Messiah as coming with a scourge for the chastisement of evil-doers. On this occasion only, when He came to claim authority by act, did the Lord use the form of force. For the effect compare xviii. 6.

them all] apparently the sellers as well as the animals, though the next clause must be translated, **both** *the sheep and the oxen* (τά τε πρόβατα καί...).

and poured...and said...] *and* **he** *poured... and* **he** *said...* Each stage in the action is to be distinguished.

changers'] See *v.* 14.

16. *Take these things hence*] Since these could not be driven. There is no reason to think that those who sold the offerings of the poor were as such dealt with more gently than other traffickers.

my Father's house] Compare Luke ii. 49 ("in that which belongs to my Father"). The speciality of the title (*my* Father's house, not *our* Father's house) must be noticed. When Christ finally left the temple (Matt. xxiv. 1) He spoke of it to the Jews as *your house* (Matt. xxiii. 38); the people had claimed and made their own what truly belonged to God. It must be observed also that the Lord puts forth His relation to God as the fact from which His Messiahship might be inferred. This formed the trial of faith.

house of merchandise] Contrast Matt. xxi. 13 (*a den of robbers*). Here the tumult and confusion of worldly business is set over against the still devotion which should belong to the place of worship.

merchandise] Vulg. *negotiationis*. The word (ἐμπόριον) means the place of traffic, the mart, and not the subject or the art of trafficking (ἐμπορία). Comp. Ezek. xxvii. 3 (LXX.). Thus the "house" is here regarded as having become a market-house, no longer deriving its character from Him to whom it was dedicated, but from the business carried on in its courts.

17. *And* (omit) *his disciples*] We notice here on the occasion of the first public act of Christ, as throughout St John, the double effect of the act on those who already believed, and on those who were resolutely unbelieving. The disciples *remembered* at the time (contrast *v.* 22) that this trait was characteristic of the true prophet of God, who gave himself for his people. The Jews found in it an occasion for fresh demands of proof.

it was written] Or more exactly, *it is written*, *i.e.* stands recorded in Scripture (γεγραμ-

and said unto him, What sign shewest thou unto us, seeing that thou doest these things?

19 Jesus answered and said unto them, [b]Destroy this temple, and in three days I will raise it up. [b] Ma 61

μένον ἐστίν). Compare vi. 31, 45, x. 34, xii. 14. St John prefers this resolved form to the simple verb (γέγραπται) which prevails almost exclusively in the other books. Comp. iii. 21.

The words occur in Ps. lxix. 9. The remainder of the verse is applied to the Lord by St Paul, Rom. xv. 3. Other passages from it are quoted as Messianic, John xv. 25 (*v.* 4), xix. 28 and parallels (*v.* 21); Rom. xi. 9, 10 (*v.* 22); Acts i. 20 (*v.* 25).

For a general view of the quotations from the Old Testament in St John see Introd.

The zeal of thine house] the burning jealousy for the holiness of the house of God, and so for the holiness of the people who were bound by service to it, as well as for the honour of God Himself. Comp. Rom. x. 2; 2 Cor. xi. 2.

hath eaten me] According to the true text, **will eat** (devour) *me*. The reference is not to the future Passion of the Lord, but to the overpowering energy and fearlessness of His present action. It is not natural to suppose that the disciples had at the time any clear apprehension of what the issue would be. They only felt the presence of a spirit which could not but work.

18 ff. The act in which the Lord offered a revelation of Himself called out no faith in the representatives of the nation. Thereupon in answer to their demand He takes the temple, which He had vainly cleansed, as a sign, having regard to the destruction which they would bring upon it. The end was now visible though far off. Comp. Matt. ix. 15.

The words are an illustration of Luke xvi. 31. To those who disregarded the spirit of Moses, the Resurrection became powerless.

18. *Then answered the Jews*] *The Jews* **therefore** *answered* (and so in *v.* 20). See i. 22, note. The connexion is with *v.* 16 directly.

answered] The term is not unfrequently used when the word spoken is a reply to or a criticism upon something done, or obviously present to the mind of another: *e.g.* v. 17, xix. 7; Matt. xi. 25, xvii. 4, xxviii. 5; Mark x. 51, xii. 35; Luke i. 60, xiii. 14; Acts iii. 12, v. 8; Rev. vii. 13. And once even in reference to the significant state of the barren fig-tree; Mark xi. 14.

What sign shewest thou...] By what clear and convincing token (comp. 1 Cor. i. 22) can we be made to see that thou hast the right to exercise high prophetic functions, *seeing that* (ὅτι, comp. ix. 17) *thou doest these things* which belong to a great prophet's work? Comp. Matt. xxi. 23.

The same demand for fresh evidence in the presence of that which ought to be decisive is found ch. vi. 30; Matt. xii. 38 f., xvi. 1 ff.

doest] The work was not past only, but evidently charged with present consequences.

19. *Destroy this temple...*] The phrase here placed in its true context appears twice as the basis of an accusation, (1) Matt. xxvi. 61, note; Mark xiv. 57, 8, and (2) Acts vi. 14. In both cases the point of the words is altered by assigning to Christ the work of destruction which he leaves to the Jews. (*I am able to* (*I will*) destroy as contrasted with *Destroy*.)

In the interpretation of the words two distinct ideas have to be brought into harmony, (1) the reference to the actual temple which is absolutely required by the context, and (2) the interpretation of the Evangelist (*v.* 21). At the same time the "three days" marks the fulfilment as historical and definite. The point of connexion lies in the conception of the temple as the seat of God's presence among His people. So far the temple was a figure of the Body of Christ. The rejection and death of Christ, in whom dwelt the fulness of God, brought with it necessarily the destruction of the temple, first spiritually, when the veil was rent (Matt. xxvii. 51), and then materially (observe ἀπ' ἄρτι Matt. xxvi. 64). On the other hand the Resurrection of Christ was the raising again of the Temple, the complete restoration of the tabernacle of God's presence to men, perpetuated in the Church, which is Christ's body.

In this connexion account must be taken of the comparison of the temple with Christ, Matt. xii. 6. Compare ch. i. 14 (ἐσκήνωσεν).

The Resurrection of Christ was indeed the transfiguration of worship while it was the transfiguration of life.

In the Synoptic Gospels Christ connects the destruction of the temple with the faithlessness of the people: Matt. xxiv. 2 ff., xxiii. 38.

It may be noticed that on a similar occasion the Lord referred to the "sign of the prophet Jonah," as that alone which should be given (Matt. xii. 39, xvi. 4). Life through death; construction through dissolution; the rise of the new from the fall of the old; these are the main thoughts.

The imperative *destroy* is used as in Matt. xxiii. 32, *fill ye up*. Comp. xiii. 28. Thus in the first clear antagonism Christ sees its last issue. The word itself (λύσατε) is a very remarkable one. It indicates a destruction which comes from dissolution, from the breaking of that which binds the parts into a whole,

20 Then said the Jews, Forty and six years was this temple in building, and wilt thou rear it up in three days?

21 But he spake of the temple of his body.

22 When therefore he was risen from the dead, his disciples remembered that he had said this unto them; and they believed the scripture, and the word which Jesus had said.

---

or one thing to another. Comp. 2 Pet. iii. 10 ff.; Acts xxvii. 41; Eph. ii. 14; and also v. 18 note; 1 John iii. 8.

I will...] The Resurrection is here assigned to the action of the Lord, as elsewhere to the Father (Gal. i. 1; see *v.* 22, note).

20. *Forty and six ... building*] Rather, *In forty and six...was this temple built* as we now see it. The work is regarded as complete in its present state, though the reparation of the whole structure was not completed till 36 years afterwards. Herod the Great began to restore the temple in B.C. 20 (Jos. 'B. J.' I. 21 (16). 1: comp. 'Antt.' XV. 11 (14. 1), and the design was completed by Herod Agrippa A.D. 64. The tense of the verb (ᾠκοδομήθη) marks a definite point reached; that point probably coincided with the date of the Lord's visit; but the form of expression makes it precarious to insist on the phrase as itself defining this coincidence.

rear it up] **raise it up**: the same word is used as before. That which Christ raises (x. 18) is that which was (raise *it* up) and not another. The old Church is transfigured and not destroyed. The continuity of revelation is never broken.

in three days] Comp. Hos. vi. 2.

21. *But he* (ἐκεῖνος) ...] The pronoun (i. 18, note) is emphatic and marks a definite contrast, not only between the Lord and the Jews, but also between the Lord and the apostles. St John seems to look back again upon the far distant scene as interpreted by his later knowledge, and to realise how the Master foresaw that which was wholly hidden from the disciples.

of (περί) ...] *i.e. concerning...* This was the general topic of which He was speaking, not the direct object which He indicated, as in vi. 71 (ἔλεγεν τὸν Ἰ.), from which usage it must be carefully distinguished. Compare Eph. v. 32 (λέγω εἰς), where the ultimate application is marked.

the temple of his body] *i.e.* the temple defined to be His body, as in the phrase "the cities of Sodom and Gomorrah" (2 Pet. ii. 6). Compare Acts iv. 22; 2 Cor. v. 1; Rom. iv. 11 (v. l.). For the usage see 1 Cor. vi. 19; Rom. viii. 11.

St John notices on other occasions the real meaning of words of the Lord not understood at first: vii. 39, xii. 33, xxi. 19; and in each case he speaks with complete authority. This trait of progressive knowledge is inexplicable except as a memorial of personal experience.

22. *was risen*] Rather, *was* **raised**: so also xxi. 14. The full phrase would be, "was raised by God from the dead," as in the corresponding expression, "whom God raised from the dead" (Acts iii. 15, iv. 10, v. 30, x. 40, xiii. 30, 37; Rom. iv. 24, viii. 11, x. 9; 1 Cor. xv. 15, &c.). In all these cases the resurrection is regarded as an awakening effected by the power of the Father. Much less frequently it is presented simply as a rising again, consequent on the awakening, in reference to the manifestation of the power of the Son, Mark viii. 31, ix. 9; Luke xxiv. 7. Comp. John xi. 23, 24; and *v.* 19, note.

remembered] *v.* 17. The repetition of the word seems to mark the facts of Christ's life as a new record of revelation, on which the disciples pondered even before the facts were committed to writing. Compare xii. 16.

had said] Rather, **spake** (omit *unto them*). The original tense (ἔλεγεν) implies either a repetition of or a dwelling upon the words. Comp. v. 18, vi. 6, 65, 71, viii. 27, 31, xii. 33, iv. 33, 42, &c.

believed] A different construction is used here (ἐπίστευσαν τῇ γραφῇ) from that in *v.* 11: they trusted the Scripture as absolutely true. Comp. iv. 50, v. 46, 47, xx, 9.

the scripture] The phrase "the Scripture" occurs elsewhere ten times in St John, vii. 38, 42, x. 35, xiii. 18 (xvii. 12), xix. 24, 28, 36, 37 (xx. 9), and in every case except xvii. 12 and xx. 9 the reference is to a definite passage of Scripture given in the context, according to the usage elsewhere, Mark xii. 10 [xv. 28]; Luke iv. 21; Acts i. 16, viii. 35, &c. (though St Paul appears also to personify Scripture), while the plural is used for Scripture generally, v. 39; Luke xxiv. 32; 1 Cor. xv. 3, 4, &c. In xvii. 12 the reference appears to be to the words already quoted, xiii. 18, so that the present and the similar passage, xx. 9, alone remain without a determinate reference. According to the apostle's usage, then, we must suppose that here also a definite passage is present to his mind, and this, from a comparison of Acts ii. 27, 31, xiii. 35, can hardly be any other than Ps. xvi. 10.

the word ... had said (εἶπεν)] the revelation which St John has just recorded, not as an isolated utterance (ῥῆμα), but as a comprehensive message (τῷ λόγῳ).

The Synoptists narrate a cleansing of the

23 ¶ Now when he was in Jerusalem at the passover, in the feast *day*, many believed in his name, when they saw the miracles which he did.

---

temple as having taken place on the day of the triumphal entry into Jerusalem before the last passover (Matt. xxi. 12 ff.; Mark xi. 15 ff.; Luke xix. 45 ff.). Of such an incident there is no trace in St John (xii. 12 ff.), and conversely the Synoptists have no trace of an earlier cleansing. It has been supposed that the event has been transposed in the Synoptic narratives owing to the fact that they give no account of the Lord's ministry at Jerusalem before the last journey; but a comparison of the two narratives is against the identification.

1. The exact connexion of the event in each case is given in detail.

2. There is a significant difference in the words used to justify the act, Mark xi. 17; John ii. 16.

3. The character of the two acts is distinct. The history of St John presents an independent assumption of authority: the history of the Synoptists is a sequel to the popular homage which the Lord had accepted.

4. The cleansing in St John appears as a single act. The cleansing in the Synoptists seems to be part of a continued policy (Mark xi. 16).

5. In the record of the later incident there is no reference to the remarkable words (ii. 19) which give its colour to the narrative of St John, though the Synoptists shew that they were not unacquainted with the words (Matt. xxvi. 61; Mark xiv. 58).

Nor on the other hand, is there any improbability in the repetition of such an incident. In each case the cleansing was effected in immediate connexion with the revelation of Jesus as the Messiah. This revelation was twofold: first when He claimed His royal power at the entrance on His work, and then when He claimed it again at the close of His work. In the interval between these two manifestations He fulfilled the office of a simple prophet. In the first case, so to speak, the issue was as yet doubtful; in the second, it was already decided; and from this difference flows the difference in the details of the incidents themselves. For example, there is a force in the addition "a house of prayer *for all nations*," in the immediate prospect of the Passion and of the consequent rejection of the Jews, which finds no place at the beginning of the Lord's ministry, when He enters as a Son into "His Father's house." And again, the neutral phrase, "a house of merchandise," is in the second case represented by its last issue "a den of robbers."

Assuming that the two cleansings are distinct, it is easy to see why St John records that which occurred at the beginning, because it was the first crisis in the separation of faith and unbelief; while the Synoptists necessarily, from the construction of their narratives, recorded the later one. This, on the other hand, was virtually included in the first, and there was no need that St John should notice it.

Christ's work at Jerusalem with the people (ii. 23—iii. 21).

The record of the great Messianic work (ii. 14—16), which was the critical trial of the representatives of the theocracy, is followed by a summary notice of the thoughts which it excited among the people generally, and also in one who was fitted to express the feelings of students and teachers. The people imagined that they had found the Messiah of their own hopes: the teacher acknowledged the presence of a prophet who should continue, and probably reform, what already existed. In both respects the meaning of Christ's work was missed: the conclusions which were drawn from His "signs" (ii. 23, iii. 2) were false or inadequate.

The section falls into two parts: Christ's dealing with the people (ii. 23—25), and with "the teacher of Israel" (iii. 1—21).

The contents are peculiar to St John. It is probable that he writes from his own immediate knowledge throughout (comp. iii. 11).

23—25. *Christ's dealing with the people generally.* In this brief passage the false faith of the people is contrasted with the perfect insight of Christ. The people were willing to accept Him, but He knew that it would be on their own terms. Comp. vi. 14 f. (*Galilee*).

The explanation which St John gives of the reserve of Christ shews a characteristic knowledge of the Lord's mind. It reads like a commentary gained from later experience on what was at the time a surprise and a mystery.

23. *in Jerusalem*] if not in the temple, yet still in the Holy City. It may be noticed that of the two Greek forms of the name, that which is alone found (in a symbolic sense) in the Apocalypse (iii. 12, xxi. 2, 10, Ἱερουσαλήμ) is not found in the Gospel, in which (as in St Mark) the other form (Ἱεροσόλυμα) is used exclusively (twelve times).

The triple definition of place (*in Jerusalem*), time (*at the passover*), circumstance (*during the feast*) is remarkable. The place was the city which God had chosen: the time was the anniversary of the birth of the nation: the circumstances marked universal joy.

in the feast day] Rather, **at the feast**, *i.e.* of unleavened bread, kept on the seven

24 But Jesus did not commit himself unto them, because he knew all *men*,

25 And needed not that any should testify of man: for he knew what was in man.

---

days which followed the actual passover (Lev. xxiii. 5, 6). It has been conjectured, not unreasonably, that the purifying of the temple took place on the eve of the passover, when the houses were cleansed of leaven.

many] Among these there may have been some Galilæans, who had come to the feast, as "the Jews" (*v.* 20) are not distinctly mentioned. Comp. viii. 30 f., iv. 45.

believed in (**on**) *his name*] Comp. i. 12 and viii. 30, note. In this place the phrase seems to imply the recognition of Jesus as the Messiah, but such a Messiah as Him for whom they looked, without any deeper trust (for the most part) in His Person (*v.* 24). They believed not *on Him* (iii. 18), but *on His name*, as Christ (comp. Matt. vii. 22. Orig. 'in Joh.' t. x. § 28). The phrase occurs again in connexion with the title "Son of God," 1 John v. 13, where there is no limitation of the fulness of the meaning. For the use of "believe on" (πιστεύειν εἰς) with other than a personal object, see 1 John v. 10.

when they saw] *when they* **beheld** (θεωροῦντες) with the secondary notion of a regard of attention, wonder, reflection. The word (θεωρεῖν) is so used in vii. 3, xii. 45, xiv. 19, xvi. 16 ff., &c. In this place it connects the imperfect faith of the people with the immediate effect of that which arrested their attention. Contrast iv. 45 (ἑωρακότες).

the miracles (**his signs**) *which he did*] time after time (ἃ ἐποίει). Here the Evangelist dwells on the works as still going on (*which He was doing*): in iv. 45 he regards the same works in their historical completeness (*all that He did*, ὅσα ἐποίησεν). The conviction was wrought not at once, nor on a survey of all the works, but now by one, now by another. The same idea is given by the present participle (*when they beheld*, θεωροῦντες) in combination with the aorist (*believed*). The incidental notice of these "signs" (comp. vii. 31, xi. 47, xx. 30) is an unquestionable proof that St John does not aim at giving an exhaustive record of all he knew. Similar references to cycles of unrecorded works are found in the Synoptists: Mark iii. 10, vi. 56.

24. *But Jesus*] The contrast is emphasized in the original by the preceding pronoun, *But on His part Jesus* (αὐτὸς δὲ Ἰ.).

commit] The same word (ἐπίστευεν) is used here as that rendered *believe* (*v.* 23). Compare Luke xvi. 11. The kind of repetition would be in some degree, though inadequately, expressed in English by "many trusted on His name ... but Jesus did not trust Himself to them." There is at the same time a contrast of tenses. The first verb marks a definite, completed, act: the second a habitual course of action. A partial commentary on this reserve of Christ is found in vi. 14 f., where He refuses to accept the homage of the people which is offered with false beliefs and hopes. Comp. Matt. vii. 21 ff.

24, 25. *because he knew ... And needed not ...*] The original is more exact and expressive: **owing to the fact that—for that**—*He knew* (διὰ τὸ γινώσκειν) *all men, and* **because He** *needed not...* (Vulg. *eo quod ...quia...*). The ultimate reason lay in His knowledge of all men: the immediate reason in the fact that He needed no testimony to the character of any man.

24. *he knew*] The pronoun is emphatic. Christ knew "by Himself," "in virtue of His Own power."

knew] It is of great importance to distinguish in the narrative of St John the knowledge (1) of discernment and recognition from that (2) of intuition and conviction. The one word (γινώσκειν), used here, implies movement, progress: the other (εἰδέναι) satisfaction, rest. For the contrast between the words compare (1) i. 49, iii. 10, vi. 69, xiii. 12 (γινώσκειν): (2) i. 26, 31, iii. 2, 11, ix. 29 (εἰδέναι). See Additional Note.

25. *testify of man*] **bear witness concerning** *man* generically (περὶ τοῦ ἀνθρώπου). The original (τοῦ ἀνθρώπου) may mean also "the man with whom from time to time he had to deal," as it appears to do in the second case. Compare vii. 51 (τὸν ἄνθρωπον); Matt. xii. 43, xv. 11.

he knew] as in *v.* 24, "*He* **Himself** *knew*, by His Own power on each occasion ...." The pronoun is repeated a third time (αὐτός—αὐτόν—αὐτός).

what was in man] This knowledge is elsewhere attributed to Jehovah (Jer. xvii. 10, xx. 12). It was immediate (*of Himself*), universal (*all men*), complete (*what was in man, i.e.* the thoughts and feelings as yet unexpressed).

ADDITIONAL NOTES on CHAP. II. 11, 24.

11. This passage brings forward very vividly one feature of St John's Gospel which has been overlooked by one school of critics and exaggerated by another. It represents the whole human life of Christ, under its actual conditions of external want and suffering and of internal conflict and sorrow, as a continuous and conscious manifestation of divine glory. He shews from first to last how "the eternal life was manifested which was with the Father" (1 John i. 2) in the works, and in the words of Christ, in what He did and in what He suffered. (Compare Introd.) Such a view, it has been argued, is inconsistent with the portraiture of the Saviour in the other Gospels, and with the teaching of St Paul upon the "exinanition" of Christ (Phil. ii. 5—11).

This objection appears to rest upon a totally inadequate conception of human life. If life is potentially the expression of a divine purpose, it is evident that all the circumstances which it includes are capable of ministering to the divine end. A want or a sorrow cannot be regarded in itself. It has a relation to a whole, and is interpretative at once and preparatory. A perfect human life, a life lived, that is, in absolute harmony with the divine, will therefore in every point reveal to those who have the eyes to see, something of God, of His "glory." And further, a human consciousness, which has complete insight into the true order of things, or so far as it has insight, will be able to realise at any moment the actual significance of each detail of experience. This being so, it is clear that all the acts and sufferings of "the Son of Man" were essentially revelations of glory, and become so to us so far as we are enabled to apprehend their meaning. They are at the same time to be regarded externally, but that external realisation is only a condition for their spiritual understanding. From the nature of the case each fact in the life of Christ was the vehicle for conveying some eternal truth. It could not be otherwise. St John lays open in some representative instances what this truth was, and while he does so he shews how the knowledge of it was present to the mind of Christ. Humiliation, shame, death are thus not regarded outwardly, as they may rightly be in suitable connexions, but as the appointed, and so the best, means for the attainment of the highest end, and recognised as such. In this light they become "glories" (1 Pet. i. 11).

These remarks hold true in regard to each event in the Lord's life; but St John, from his point of sight, regards the whole work of Christ as one, as the complete fulfilment of the divine counsel. All is present at each moment, "one act at once," while we "as parts can see but part, now this, now that." The Passion *is* the Victory; and this not only in relation to divine knowledge but also in relation to perfect human knowledge, which from point to point is in accordance with the divine.

St John therefore, while from time to time he dwells on Christ's glory and on Christ's assertion of His glory, is not recording, as has been said, that which can be understood only of the Eternal Word, but that which properly belongs to the Son of Man, who at each stage, in each fragment of His life, recognised the perfect fulfilment through Himself of the purpose of the Father towards the world. Compare i. 51, viii. 28, xi. 40 ff., xiii. 31, xvii. 4.

24. All the Evangelists agree in representing the Lord as moving among men with a complete and certain knowledge of their characters and needs. Only on very rare occasions does He ask anything, as if all were not absolutely clear before His eyes (*e.g.* Mark viii. 5; comp. Mark xi. 13; John xi. 34). But St John exhibits this attribute of complete human knowledge most fully, and dwells upon it as explaining Christ's action at critical times. He describes the knowledge both as relative, acquired (γινώσκειν), and absolute, possessed (εἰδέναι). In some cases the "perception" (γνούς, ἔγνω, γινώσκει) is that which might be gained "naturally" by the interpretation of some intelligible sign (v. 6, vi. 15, xvi. 19, iv. 1). At other times it appears to be the result of an insight which came from a perfect spiritual sympathy, found in some degree among men (i. 42, 47, ii. 24 f., v. 42, x. 14 f., 27: comp. xxi. 17), which reaches from the knowledge of the heart even to the knowledge of God (xvii. 25). The absolute knowledge (εἰδώς, εἰδέναι) is shewn in connexion with divine things (iii. 11, v. 32, vii. 29, viii. 55, xi. 42, xii. 50), and with the facts of the Lord's being (vi. 6, viii. 14, xiii. 1, 3, xix. 28), and also in relation to that which was external (vi. 61, 64, xiii. 11, 18, xviii. 4). A careful study of these passages seems to shew beyond doubt that the knowledge of Christ, so far as it was the discernment of the innermost meaning of that which was from time to time presented to Him, and so far as it was an understanding of the nature of things as they are, has its analogues in human powers. His knowledge appears to be truly the knowledge of the Son of Man, and not merely the knowledge of the divine Word, though at each moment and in each connexion it was, in virtue of His perfect humanity, relatively complete. Scripture is wholly free from that Docetism—that teaching of an illusory Manhood of Christ—which, both within the Church and without it, tends to destroy the historic character of the Gospel.

CHAPTER III.

1 *Christ teacheth Nicodemus the necessity of regeneration.* 14 *Of faith in his death.* 16 *The great love of God towards the world.* 18 *Condemnation for unbelief.* 23 *The baptism, witness, and doctrine of John concerning Christ.*

1 THERE was a man of the Pharisees, named Nicodemus, a ruler of the Jews:

Christ's dealing with the representative teacher (iii. 1—21).

This first conversation is, together with the Evangelist's comment, the personal application of the general call to repentance, with which the other Gospels open. It is, like the public message of the Baptist or of Christ, a proclamation of the kingdom of heaven, but given under new circumstances.

Under another aspect the history is complementary to the passage which precedes. Christ was unwilling to commit Himself—His Person—to those who had false views; and in the same spirit He laid open the truth to one who sought it. By refusal and by compliance alike He shewed His knowledge of men.

The record consists of two parts. The first part (1—15) contains a summary of the actual conversation: the second gives the commentary of St John (16—21).

It is interesting to notice that according to the Sarum Use, following the old Roman Use, the section *vv.* 1—15 is read as the Gospel for Trinity Sunday. This Gospel is retained in our Prayer Book, while the modern Roman Use gives Matt. xxviii. 18 ff. The fitness of the selection is obvious. The narrative shews how the Lord deals with the difficulties of the thoughtful man, reproving presumption and elevating faith.

CHAP. III. **1—15.** The general outline of the discourse can be marked with fair distinctness, and places the relation in which the new order—the kingdom of God, established through Christ—stands to the old in a clear light.

Nicodemus comes as the representative of the well-instructed and thoughtful Jew who looked for the consummation of national hope to follow in the line along which he had himself gone, as being a continuation and not a new beginning (*v.* 2).

The Lord at once checks this anticipation. The kingdom of God cannot, He says, be seen—outwardly apprehended—without a new birth. The right conception of it depends upon the possession of corresponding and therefore fresh powers (*v.* 3).

But the obvious answer is, Such a change in man is impossible. He is physically, morally, spiritually, one: the result of all the past (*v.* 4).

This objection would be valid if the change belonged to the same order as that to which we naturally belong. But the Lord replies that the birth which He reveals is an entrance to a new order, and wrought by a new power. It has an external element, because it belongs to men now in life: it has an internal element, because it carries men into a new world (*v.* 5).

No change of man in himself, so far as the life of sense is concerned, would be adequate (*v.* 6).

But none the less the change, though wrought by a mysterious and unseen Power, coming we know not whence, going we know not whither, in the interspace of earthly life, is manifested by its results (7 f.).

Such ideas were strange to Nicodemus, and to the traditional Judaism of the time (*v.* 9).

Yet even already there were some with the Lord who had known and seen the reality of the teaching and facts by which these ideas were established (10 f.).

And, beyond these "earthly things" of which sensible experience was possible, the new kingdom included in its principles "heavenly things," still farther removed from current beliefs (*v.* 12).

Such was the doctrine of the Person of the Lord; and flowing from it the doctrine of the Redemption through His Cross (13 ff.).

The circle of thought is thus complete. Christianity—in consideration of the completed work of Christ, which is presupposed—stands contrasted with Judaism both as an organization and as a divine economy. The entrance to the Church is through a sacrament not outward only but spiritual also. The facts on which it rests and which it proclaims belong essentially to heaven, not to earth. Viewed in these relations the discourse expands and explains the truth stated generally in its outward form in the Sermon on the Mount: *Except your righteousness shall exceed the righteousness of the Scribes and Pharisees, ye shall in no case enter into the kingdom of heaven* (Matt. v. 20).

1. *There was a man...*] **Now** *there was a man....* The word *man* is repeated to emphasize the connexion with ii. 25. Nicodemus offered at once an example of the Lord's inward knowledge of men, and an exception to this general rule which He observed in not trusting Himself to them.

Pharisees] i. 24 note.

Nicodemus] Comp. vii. 50, xix. 39. The name was not uncommon among the Jews. Nicodemus ben Gorion (Bunai) who lived to the siege of Jerusalem, has been identified (falsely, *v.* 4 *old*) with this one. The traditions as to Bunai, which are very vague and untrust-

2 The same came to Jesus by night, and said unto him, Rabbi, we know that thou art a teacher come from God: for no man can do these miracles that thou doest, except God be with him.

3 Jesus answered and said unto him, Verily, verily, I say unto thee, Except a man be born [1]again, he cannot see the kingdom of God.

[1] Or, above

4 Nicodemus saith unto him, How can a man be born when he is old?

---

worthy, have been collected by Lightfoot on this place, and by Delitzsch, Zeitschr. f. Luth. Theol.' 1854.

a ruler] *i.e.* a member of the Sanhedrin (ἄρχων, Vulg. *princeps*): vii. 50. Comp. vii. 26, xii. 42; Luke xxiii. 13, 35, xxiv. 20; Acts iv. 8. The word however is used in Rabbinic literature (ארכון) generally for a "great man" or "prince." See Buxtorf, *s. v.*; Matt. ix. 18; Luke xii. 58, xiv. 1, xviii. 18.

2. *to Jesus*] *unto* **him**.

by night] This detail is noticed again in xix. 39 (but not according to the true reading in vii. 50). On each occasion where Nicodemus is mentioned we may see other traces of the timidity to which it was due. He defended Jesus without expressing any personal interest in Him: he brought his offering only after Joseph of Arimathæa had obtained the Body from Pilate.

Rabbi] Such a style of address in the mouth of Nicodemus (*v.* 10) is significant (comp. i. 38). The title was one of late date, not having come into use till the time of Herod the Great, with the Schools of Shammai and Hillel. It is formed like "Master" from a root meaning *great*, and was used in three forms, Rab, Rabbi, Rabban (Rabbun, John xx. 16). According to the Jewish saying, "Rabbi was higher than Rab, Rabban than Rabbi, but greater than all was he who [like the prophets] was not called by any such title."

we know] The pronoun is not emphatic. There is however a symptom of latent presumption in the word. Nicodemus claims for himself and for others like him the peculiar privilege of having read certainly the nature of the Lord's office in the signs which He wrought. So much at least he and they could do, if the common people were at fault. Comp. ix. 24. It is natural to connect such a recognition of the divine mission of Jesus with the report of the envoys sent to John: i. 19. Contrast Matt. xii. 24; c. ix. 29.

from God] The words stand first emphatically: "it is from God, not from man, thy title to teach is derived." Jesus had not studied in the schools, but possessed the right of a Rabbi from a higher source. Comp. vii. 15, 16.

a teacher] not different in kind from other teachers. In this conception lay the essence of the error of Nicodemus. The word used here (διδάσκαλος) is commonly rendered *master*, after the Vulgate (*magister*), a rendering which is apt to suggest false associations (i. 38, viii. 4, xi. 28, xiii. 13 f., xx. 16).

miracles] **signs**. Comp. ii. 11 note. The address of Nicodemus is incomplete, but he evidently wishes to invite the Lord to give a fuller view of His teaching, and that, it may reasonably be supposed, with regard to the kingdom of God of which John had spoken.

except...him] Comp. Acts x. 38; 1 S. xviii. 14; c. ix. 31 f.

3. *answered*] not the words, but the thoughts. The Lord's answers to questions will be found generally to reveal the true thought of the questioner, and to be fitted to guide him to the truth which he is seeking. Nicodemus implied that he and those like him were prepared to understand and welcome the Lord's teaching. This appeared to him to be of the same order as that with which he was already familiar. He does not address the Lord as if he were ready to welcome Him as "the Christ" or "the prophet." On the other hand, the Lord's reply sets forth distinctly that His work was not simply to carry on what was already begun, but to recreate. The new kingdom of which He was the founder could not be comprehended till after a new birth.

Verily, verily] i. 51, note. The words by their emphasis generally presuppose some difficulty or misunderstanding to be overcome; and at the same time they mark the introduction of a new thought carrying the divine teaching further forward, *vv.* 5, 11. Comp. v. 19, vi. 47, 53.

unto thee] The address was general: the reply is personal.

born again] See Additional Note.

he cannot see the kingdom of God] Without this new birth—this introduction into a vital connexion with a new order of being, with a corresponding endowment of faculties — no man can see—can outwardly apprehend—the kingdom of God. Our natural powers cannot realise that which is essentially spiritual. A new vision is required for the objects of a new order. Elsewhere there are references to the change required (Matt. xviii. 3; 1 Cor. ii. 14) in order that we may observe that which though about us is unregarded (Luke xvii. 20, 21).

cannot] The impossibility lies in the moral characteristics of the man, and not in any external power. Comp. vi. 44, note.

The sense which is commonly given to "see" in this passage, as if it were equivalent

can he enter the second time into his mother's womb, and be born?

5 Jesus answered, Verily, verily, I say unto thee, Except a man be born of water and *of* the Spirit, he cannot enter into the kingdom of God.

---

to "enjoy," "have experience of" (Luke ii. 26, *see death*; Acts ii. 27, *see corruption*; 1 Pet. iii. 10, *see good days*), entirely sacrifices the marked contrast between "seeing" and "entering into" the kingdom. Part of the same thought is found in Luke xvii. 20.

the kingdom of God] The phrase occurs only here and in *v.* 5 in St John's Gospel (yet compare xviii. 36, 37; Rev. xii. 10), while it is frequent in the Synoptists. St Matthew alone uses, in addition, the phrase "the kingdom of heaven," which is found as an early variant in *v.* 5 (in א, &c.). The phrase "the kingdom of God" is found in the Acts, and in each group of St Paul's epistles; but it does not occur in the Epistle to the Hebrews or in the Catholic Epistles (comp. 2 Pet. i. 11). The words have always a twofold application, external and internal; and the immediate application in each case leads on to a more complete fulfilment in the same direction. Thus under the old dispensation the visible Israel was the kingdom of God as typical of the visible catholic church, the spiritual Israel as typical of the true spiritual church. And now again the visible church is the type of the future universal reign of Christ, as the spiritual church is of the consummation of Christ's reign in heaven.

4. *Nicodemus saith*] It is commonly supposed that Nicodemus either misunderstood the general scope of the Lord's answer, or half-mockingly set it aside. But in fact he employs the image chosen by the Lord in sober earnest to bring out the overwhelming difficulties with which the idea suggested by it was encompassed. It is one indication of the point of his argument that he substitutes for the indefinite phrase used by the Lord (*except one* (τίς) *be born*...) the definite title (*how can a man* (ἄνθρωπος) *be born*...).

How can a man be born...] How is it possible for a man whose whole nature at any moment is the sum of all the past, to start afresh? How can he undo, or do away with, the result which years have brought and which goes to form himself? His "I" includes the whole development through which he has passed; and how then can it survive a new birth? Can the accumulation of long ages be removed and the true "self" remain?

when he is old] Nicodemus evidently applies the Lord's words to his own case. The trait is full of life.

can he enter the (a) *second time into his mother's womb, and be born?*] Nicodemus takes one part of a man's complex personality only. Is it possible to conceive physical birth repeated? And if not, Nicodemus seems to say to Christ, how then can there be any such moral new birth as you claim? For all life from its first beginning has contributed to the moral character which belongs to each person. The result of all life is one and indivisible.

This thought is one which cannot but occur to every one. It goes to the very root of faith. The great mystery of religion is not the punishment, but the forgiveness, of sin: not the natural permanence of character, but spiritual regeneration. And it is one aspect of this mystery which Nicodemus puts forth clearly.

5. *Jesus answered*] Christ meets the difficulty by an enlarged repetition of the former statement. As before He had insisted on the fact of the new birth, He now reveals the nature of the birth. This involves an outward and an inward element, which are placed side by side.

Except a man be born of water and of the Spirit (or, *and spirit*)] The preposition used (ἐξ) recalls the phrase "baptize—plunge—*in* water, *in* spirit" (Matt. iii. 11), so that the image suggested is that of rising, reborn, out of the water and out of that spiritual element, so to speak, to which the water outwardly corresponds.

The combination of the words *water and spirit* suggests a remote parallel and a marked contrast. They carry back the thoughts of hearer and reader to the narrative of creation (Gen. i. 2), and to the characteristics of natural birth, to which St John has already emphatically referred (i. 13). The water and the spirit suggest the original shaping of the great Order out of Chaos, when the Spirit of God brooded on the face of the waters; and at the same time this new birth is distinctly separated from the corruptible element (blood) which symbolizes that which is perishable and transitory in human life.

These distant references serve in some degree to point to the true sense of the passage. If further we regard the specific Biblical ideas of *water* and *spirit*, when they are separated, it will be seen that *water* symbolizes purification (comp. i. 25, note) and *spirit* quickening: the one implies a definite external rite, the other indicates an energetic internal operation. The two are co-ordinate, correlative, complementary. Hence all interpretations which treat the term *water* here as simply figurative and descriptive of the cleansing power of the Spirit are essentially defective, as they are also opposed to all ancient tradition.

This being so, we must take account of the application of these ideas of cleansing and quickening to the circumstances under which

6 That which is born of the flesh
is flesh; and that which is born of
the Spirit is spirit.
7 Marvel not that I said unto
thee, Ye must be born ‖again.
8 The wind bloweth where it

‖ Or abo

the words were first spoken, and of their application to the fulness of the Christian economy. The words had an immediate, if incomplete, sense, as they were addressed to Nicodemus: they have also a final and complete sense for us. And yet more, the inceptive sense must be in complete harmony with the fuller sense, and help to illustrate it.

It can, then, scarcely be questioned that as Nicodemus heard the words, *water* carried with it a reference to John's baptism, which was a divinely appointed rite (i. 33), gathering up into itself and investing with a new importance all the lustral baptisms of the Jews: the *spirit*, on the other hand, marked that inward power which John placed in contrast with his own baptism. Thus the words, taken in their immediate meaning as intelligible to Nicodemus, set forth, as required before entrance into the kingdom of God, the acceptance of the preliminary rite divinely sanctioned, which was the seal of repentance and so of forgiveness, and following on this the communication of a new life, resulting from the direct action of the Holy Spirit through Christ. The Pharisees rejected the rite, and by so doing cut themselves off from the grace which was attached to it. They would not become as little children, and so they could not enter into the kingdom of heaven.

But the sense of the words cannot be limited to this first meaning. Like the corresponding words in ch. vi., they look forward to the fulness of the Christian dispensation, when after the Resurrection the baptism of water was no longer separated from, but united with, the baptism of the spirit in the "laver of regeneration" (Titus iii. 5. Comp. Eph. v. 26), even as the outward and the inward are united generally in a religion which is sacramental and not only typical. Christian baptism, the outward act of faith welcoming the promise of God, is incorporation into the Body of Christ, and so the birth of the Spirit is potentially united with the birth of water. The general inseparability of these two is indicated by the form of the expression, *born of water and spirit* (ἐξ ὕδ. καὶ πν.), as distinguished from the double phrase, *born of water and of spirit*.

According to this view the words have a distinct historical meaning, and yet they have also a meaning far beyond that which was at first capable of being apprehended. They are in the highest sense prophetic, even as the following words, in which the Lord speaks of His Passion; and at the same time they contemplate the fulness of the organized life of the Christian society (*enter into the kingdom of heaven—not see life*, *v.* 36).

enter into] become a citizen of the kingdom, as distinguished from the mere intelligent spectator (see *v.* 3) of its constitution and character. The image suggested by the words *enter into* is that of entering into the promised land—the type of the kingdom of heaven—as in Ps. xcv. 11.

A new birth is necessary to gain a true conception of the divine kingdom: a new birth, distinctly specified as having an outward fulfilment as well as an inward, is necessary for admission into the kingdom, which is itself at once outward and spiritual. This conclusion follows from a very simple consideration. No principle can produce results superior to itself. If man is to enjoy a spiritual life, that by which he enters it—his birth—must be of a corresponding character. The flesh (i. 13, see note) can only generate flesh. Spiritual life cannot come forth from it.

The fact which the Lord affirms is at once more marvellous and more natural than that by which Nicodemus typified it. A mere repetition of the natural birth would not bring that which man requires.

6. *That which is born* ...] The original tense (τὸ γεγεννημένον) conveys an idea which can only be reproduced by a paraphrase: "that which hath been born, and at present comes before us in this light." There is an important difference observed in the narrative between the *fact* of the birth (*aorist*, *vv.* 3, 4, 5, 7) and the *state* which follows as the abiding result of the birth (*perfect*, *vv.* 6, 8). In 1 John v. 18 the true interpretation depends upon the contrast between the one historic Son of God (ὁ γεννηθείς, opposed to *the evil one*) and the sons of God, who live in virtue of their new birth (ὁ γεγεννημένος). Compare also Gal. iv. 23, 29 for a fainter representation of a corresponding difference of tenses.

The neuter (*that which is born* ...) states the principle in its most abstract form. In *v.* 8 a transition is made to the man (*every one that is born*). There is a similar contrast in 1 John v. 4 (neuter) and 1 John v. 1, 18 (masc.).

flesh ... spirit] The words describe the characteristic principles of two orders. They are not related to one another as evil and good; but as the two spheres of being with which man is connected. By the "spirit" our complex nature is united to heaven, by the "flesh," to earth. Comp. vi. 63, note.

listeth, and thou hearest the sound thereof, but canst not tell whence it cometh, and whither it goeth: so is every one that is born of the Spirit.

---

flesh] This term probably includes all that belongs to the life of sensation, all that by which we are open to the physical influences of pleasure and pain, which naturally sway our actions. Thus, though it does not of itself include the idea of sinfulness (i. 14; 1 John iv. 2), it describes human personality on the side which tends to sin, and on which actually we have sinned.

It must also be noticed that that which is born of flesh and spirit is described not as "fleshly" and "spiritual," but as "flesh" and "spirit." In other words, the child, so to speak, is of the same nature with the parent, and does not only partake in his qualities. The child also occupies in turn the position of a parent, from which a progeny springs like to himself. Compare the corresponding usage, 1 John i. 5 (light), iv. 8 (love).

of the Spirit] Or, *of spirit*. While the term is essentially abstract and expresses spirit as spirit, the quickening power is the Spirit. The idea of nature passes into that of Person. The *water* is not repeated, because the outward rite draws its virtue from the action of the Spirit.

Many early authorities (*Lat. vt., Syr. vt.*) add the gloss, *quia Deus spiritus est et de (ex) Deo natus est*. Ambrose ('De spir.' III. § 59) accuses the Arians of having removed the words *quia Deus spiritus est* from their MSS. The charge is an admirable illustration of the groundlessness of such accusations of wilful corruption of Scripture. The words in question have no Greek authority at all, and are obviously a comment.

7. *Marvel not...*] If then this is a necessary law—such is the force of the Lord's words—that the offspring must have the essential nature of the parent, and if the kingdom of God is spiritual and its citizens therefore spiritual, while the nature of man, as all experience it to be, is fleshly, swayed by powers which belong to earth, *Marvel not that I said unto thee, Ye must be born again*, even *ye* who think that you have penetrated to the true conception of Messiah's work and prepared yourselves adequately for judging it and entering into it.

There appears also to be in the emphatic *ye* an implied contrast between the Lord, who needed no re-birth, and all other men. He does not say, as a human teacher, '*We* must be born again.'

The passage from the singular (*I said unto thee*) to the plural (*ye must*) ought not to be overlooked, comp. i. 51; and especially Luke xxii. 31, 32.

8. *The wind...the Spirit*] In Hebrew, Syriac, Latin, the words are identical (as properly *Geist* and *Ghost*) and Wiclif and the Rhemish Version keep "spirit" in both cases, after the Latin. But at present the retention of one word in both places could only create confusion, since the separation between the material emblem and the power which it was used to describe is complete. The use of the correlative verb (πνεῖ, ch. vi. 18; Rev. vii. 1; Matt. vii. 25, 27; Luke xii. 55; Acts xxvii. 40), and of the word *sound* (voice), is quite decisive for the literal sense of the noun (πνεῦμα); and still at the same time the whole of the phraseology is inspired by the higher meaning. Perhaps also the unusual word (πνεῦμα, 1 K. xviii. 45, xix. 11; 2 K. iii. 17) is employed to suggest this. The comparison lies between the obvious physical properties of the wind and the mysterious action of that spiritual influence to which the name "spirit," "wind," was instinctively applied. The laws of both are practically unknown; both are unseen; the presence of both is revealed in their effects.

where it listeth] The phrase is not to be pressed physically. The wind obeys its own proper laws, which depend on a complication of phenomena which we cannot calculate, and consequently for us it is a natural image of freedom. For a similar phrase applied to the Spirit, see 1 Cor. xii. 11.

the sound] Rather, **the voice**. The word commonly implies an articulate, intelligible voice, as even in a passage like 1 Cor. xiv. 7 ff.; yet in the Apocalypse the word is used more widely, *e.g.* ix. 9, xiv. 2, &c.

canst not tell] More simply, **knowest not**. Comp. Eccles. xi. 5.

so is every one...] The form of the comparison is irregular. The action of the spirit on the believer is like the action of the wind in the material world. As the tree (for example) by waving branches and rustling leaves witnesses to the power which affects it; *so is every one that hath been born of the Spirit*. The believer shews by deed and word that an invisible influence has moved and inspired him. He is himself a continual sign of the action of the Spirit, which is freely determined, and incomprehensible by man as to source and end, though seen in its present results.

It is not unreasonable to suppose that this image of the wind was suggested by the sound of some sudden gust sweeping through the narrow street without. Thus the form of the Lord's teaching corresponds with the teaching by parables in the Synoptists (Matt. xiii. 4, note).

born of the Spirit] *v.* 6. An important group of ancient authorities (א, *Lat. vt., Syr. vt.*) read *born of water and the spirit*. The gloss is a good example of a natural corruption by assimilation.

9 Nicodemus answered and said
unto him, How can these things be?
10 Jesus answered and said unto
him, Art thou a master of Israel, and
knowest not these things?
11 Verily, verily, I say unto thee,
We speak that we do know, and testify that we have seen; and ye receive not our witness.
12 If I have told you earthly
things, and ye believe not, how shall
ye believe, if I tell you *of* heavenly
things?
13 And no man hath ascended up

---

9. *How can these things be?*] *How can these things* **come to pass** (γενέσθαι, Vulg. *fieri*)? How can this new birth, issuing in a new life, be realised? The idea is of change, transition, not of essence, repose. The emphasis lies on *can* (πῶς δύναται, *v.* 4).

10. *Art thou a master* (**the teacher**) *of Israel*] the authorized teacher of the chosen people of God. The definite article (ὁ διδάσκαλος) marks the official relation of Nicodemus to the people generally.

knowest not] perceivest (γινώσκεις) not, by the knowledge of progress, recognition. Comp. ii. 24 note. Though Nicodemus had previously been ignorant of that which the Lord declared, he ought to have recognised the teaching as true when he heard it.

these things] the reality and character of the spiritual influence shewn in the actions of man, which yet is not of man, but comes from another region.

11. *We speak*] The plural contrasted with the singular *vv.* 3, 5, 7, 12 (all are unemphatic) is remarkable. It has been explained as a simple rhetorical plural, or as containing an allusion to John the Baptist, to the Prophets, to the Holy Spirit, to the Father (viii. 16, 18), but all these explanations appear to fail when taken in connexion with the *you* and *ye*. The Lord and those with Him, of whom some, including the Evangelist, may have been present at the interview, appear to stand in contrast to the group represented by Nicodemus. Comp. iv. 22. There were already gathered round Christ those who had had personal (*we have seen*) and immediate (*we know*) knowledge of the divine wonders which He announced. Their witness is indeed distinguished from His afterwards (*v.* 13), but so far it reached as to meet the difficulties, and fill up the shortcomings of the faith which Nicodemus had attained to. The plural, it will be noticed, is used in connexion with "the things on earth," but the singular only (εἴπω) of "the things in heaven."

we do know—absolutely and immediately (οἴδαμεν)—*and testify* (**bear witness of**)...] The words answered to actual knowledge, the witness declared actual experience. The object in each stands first: "That which we know, we speak; and that which we have seen, we witness."

and ye receive not] The pronoun is unemphatic, as the *we* before. The stress lies on *our witness*. "What we have seen we witness, and our witness ye receive not." Comp. *v.* 27 n. For the use of the simple *and* in this connexion of sad contrast see i. 10, v. 32, vii. 28, 30, xiv. 24, xvi. 32.

12. *If I have told*] *If* **I told**. As, for example, in what He had just said to Nicodemus of the spiritual birth, though this was but as a sample of the teaching which He had already addressed to men (*you*, not *thee*) such as Nicodemus. Comp. Wisd. ix. 16.

earthly things] The word "earthly" is ambiguous, and may mean that which is "of the nature *of earth*" (cf. *v.* 31) or which "has its sphere and place *on earth*." The original word expresses the second notion distinctly (ἐπίγειος, Vulg. *terrenus*); and it must be so interpreted in the other places where it occurs: 1 Cor. xv. 40 (bodies fitted for life on earth). Comp. Col. iii. 2; 2 Cor. v. 1; Phil. ii. 10. iii. 19 (whose thoughts rest on earth); James iii. 15 (wisdom which finds its consummation on earth, and reaches no higher). Thus the strictly local meaning (1 Cor. xv. 40; Phil. ii. 10) passes insensibly into a meaning predominantly moral (Phil. iii. 19; James iii. 15).

Here the phrase "earthly things" will mark those facts and phenomena of the higher life as a class (τὰ ἐπίγεια) which have their seat and manifestation on earth: which belong in their realisation to our present existence: which are seen in their consequences, like the issues of birth: which are sensible in their effects, like the action of the wind: which are a beginning and a prophecy, and not a fulfilment.

how shall ye believe] The words are spoken with a view to the future already realised. The question is not abstract (*How can ye?*), but framed in regard of actual circumstances.

of (omit) *heavenly things*] those truths which belong to a higher order, which *are* in heaven (τὰ ἐπουράνια), and are brought down thence to earth as they can *become* to men. Such was the full revelation of the Son, involving the redemption of the world and the reunion of man with God, which is indicated in the three following verses. The reality of these truths finds no outward confirmation as the new birth in its fruits. The difference thus indicated between the "earthly" and the "heavenly" elements of the Lord's teaching serves to shew the ground of the contrast between St John and the earlier Evangelists. The teaching of the Lord was on one side,

to heaven, but he that came down from heaven, *even* the Son of man which is in heaven.

14 ¶ [a]And as Moses lifted up the serpent in the wilderness, even so must the Son of man be lifted up:

15 That whosoever believeth in him should not perish, but have eternal life.

---

like the teaching of the Baptist, a preparation for the Kingdom of Heaven (Mark i. 15); and on the other a revelation of the kingdom both in its embodiment and in its life.

13. *And no man...*] The transition by "and" is completely according to the Hebrew idiom, which adds new thoughts without defining the exact relation in which they stand to what has gone before. That must be determined by the thoughts regarded in juxtaposition. Men might be unprepared to receive the teaching of heavenly things, yet side by side with this fact were two others: that Christ alone could teach them, and that His mission was but for a time. While also these facts included the two great mysteries of the spiritual life: the truths as to the Person and as to the Work of the Son of Man.

hath ascended up (**gone up**) *to heaven*] Comp. Deut. xxx. 12; Prov. xxx. 4. No man hath risen into the region of absolute and eternal truth, so as to look upon it face to face, and in the possession of that knowledge declare it to men; but the Son of Man, He in whom humanity is summed up, has the knowledge which comes from immediate vision. And His elevation is yet more glorious than a mere ascent. He did not mount up to heaven, as if earth were His home, but came down thence **out of** *heaven*, as truly dwelling there; and therefore He has inherently the fulness of heavenly knowledge. Comp. Plato's myth in the 'Phædrus.'

but...the Son of man] The particle *but* (εἰ μή) does not imply that Christ had ascended to heaven, as though He were one of a class and contrasted with all the others (*except*), but simply that He in fact enjoyed that directness of knowledge by nature which another could only attain to by such an ascension. The exception is to the whole statement in the preceding clause, and not to any part of it. Comp. Luke iv. 26 f.; Matt. xii. 4; Gal. i. 7.

came down from (**out of**) *heaven*] That is, at the Incarnation. Comp. vi. 32, 33 ff., 42, &c. The phrase is used of the manifestation of God in the Old Testament; Ex. xix. 11 ff.; Num. xi. 17, 25, xii. 5.

The exact form of expression is very remarkable. It preserves the continuity of the Lord's personality, and yet does not confound His natures: "He that came down from heaven, even He who being Incarnate is the Son of man, without ceasing to be what He was before." Comp. i. 14, vi. 38.

which is in heaven] These words are omitted by many very ancient authorities, and appear to be an early gloss bringing out the right contrast between the ascent of a man to heaven and the abiding of the Son of Man in heaven. See Additional Note at the end of the Chapter.

14. *as Moses...*] The character of the revelation through the Son of Man has been set forth in the former verse, and in this the issue of that revelation in the Passion is further indicated. This mystery is shadowed forth under the image of an Old Testament symbol (Num. xxi. 7 ff.), just as the Resurrection had been half veiled, half declared, under the figure of a restored temple (ii. 19). In the last miracle of Moses, on the borders of the promised land, the serpent had been "lifted up," and made a conspicuous object to all the stricken people; and so too was Christ to be "lifted up," and with the same life-giving issue. How this "lifting up" should be accomplished is not yet made clear. See Additional Note. The point of connexion between *v.* 13 and *v.* 14 lies in the repetition of the title "the Son of Man." The Incarnation, under the actual circumstances of humanity, carried with it the necessity of the Passion.

so must the Son of man be lifted up] The same phrase (*lifted up*, ὑψωθῆναι, Vulg. *exaltari*) occurs viii. 28, xii. 32, note, 34, in reference to the Passion; and elsewhere (Acts ii. 33, v. 31; [Phil. ii. 9]) in reference to the Ascension consequent upon it. Thus the words imply an exaltation in appearance far different from that of the triumphant king, and yet in its true issue leading to a divine glory. This passage through the elevation on the cross to the elevation on the right hand of God was a necessity (*so must*, δεῖ) arising out of the laws of the divine nature. Comp. xx. 9 note, *v.* 30 note.

It is important to notice that similar figurative references to the issue of the Lord's work in His Death are found in the Synoptic record: Matt. ix. 14 ff., x. 38; Mark viii. 34; Luke xiv. 27.

15. *believeth in him*] Or, according to another reading, *every one* **that believeth may have in Him** *eternal life*, according to the familiar formula of St Paul, *in Christ*. To "believe" is used absolutely *v.* 12, i. 50, iv. 42, 53, vi. 36, xi. 15, xx. 29; and the exceptional order of the words (ἐν αὐτῷ ἔχῃ) finds a justification in v. 39, xvi. 33.

should (rather, **may**) *not perish, but have eternal life*] The words *not perish but* in this

[b] 1 John 4. 9.

16 ¶ [b] For God so loved the world, that he gave his only begotten Son, that whosoever believeth in him should not perish, but have everlasting life.

---

verse are to be omitted on decisive authority. See Additional Note.

eternal life] As the wounded who looked on the brazen serpent were restored to temporal health, so in this case *eternal life* follows from the faith of the believer on the crucified and exalted Lord.

The exact phrase, *have eternal life*, as distinguished from *live for ever*, is characteristic of St John. It occurs *vv.* 16, 36, v. 24, vi. 40, 47, 54; 1 John iii. 15, v. 12 f. (x. 10, xx. 31, *hath life*). Comp. Matt. xix. 16. The use of the auxiliary verb marks the distinct realisation of the life as a personal blessing (*have* life), as being more than the act of living. Comp. xvi. 22, *have sorrow*.

The record of the conversation comes to an end without any formal close. There is nothing surprising in this. The history is not that of an outward incident, but of a spiritual situation. This is fully analysed; and the issue is found in the later notices of Nicodemus, so far as it has an immediate personal value.

Several observations are suggested by the narrative, which will be illustrated by later passages of the Gospel.

1. The account of the conversation is evidently compressed. The Evangelist does little more than indicate the great moments of the discussion. The full meaning and connexion of the parts can only be gained by supplying what he merely indicates.

2. In spite of the compression there is a distinct progress and completeness in the record. The order of thought is real and natural.

3. The thoughts are not obvious, but when they are understood they deal with critical difficulties; and with difficulties which belong to the first stage of the preaching of the Gospel.

4. The form and substance of the discussion keep completely within the line of Jewish ideas. All that is said belongs to a time before the full declaration of the nature of Christ's work, while the language is fitted to move a hearer to deeper questionings, and is in perfect harmony with later and plainer revelations.

5. The occurrence of the phrase "Kingdom of God" here only in St John's Gospel belongs to the exact circumstances of the incident.

6. If the narrative were a free composition of a late date, it is inconceivable that the obscure allusions should not have been made clearer; and if it were composed for a purpose, it is inconceivable that the local colouring of opinion and method should have been what it is.

7. The recorded external circumstances, the meeting with Christ at the time of His first public appearance, of one in whom pride of descent and pride of knowledge were united, explains the subject and manner of the discourse. And the essential principles involved in it explain why this Evangelist was guided to report it. The narrative belongs to one definite point in the history of religious development, and also to all time

16—21. This section is a commentary on the nature of the mission of the Son, which has been indicated in Christ's words (*vv.* 13, 14), and unfolds its design (16, 17), its historic completion (18, 19), the cause of its apparent failure (20, 21). It adds no new thoughts, but brings out the force of the revelation already given in outline (1—15) by the light of Christian experience. It is therefore likely from its secondary character, apart from all other considerations, that it contains the reflections of the Evangelist, and is not a continuation of the words of the Lord. This conclusion appears to be firmly established from details of expression.

1. The tenses in *v.* 19 (*loved, were*) evidently mark a crisis accomplished, and belong to the position which St John occupied but not to that in which the Lord stood, when the revelation of His Person and Work had not been openly presented to the world.

2. The phrase *only begotten Son* (*vv.* 16, 18) is used of Christ elsewhere only in i. 14, 18; 1 John iv. 9; and in each case by the Evangelist.

3. The phrase *believe in the name of* (*v.* 18) is not found in the recorded words of Christ, while it occurs in St John's narrative, i. 12, ii. 23; 1 John v. 13.

4. *To do truth* occurs elsewhere in the New Testament only in 1 John i. 6.

The addition of such a comment finds a parallel in i. 16—18.

There is also an obvious fitness in the apostolic exposition of the Lord's words at this crisis, as in that of the Baptist's words which follows (*vv.* 31—36). The questionings of Nicodemus and the testimony of John give, so to speak, the last utterances of Judaism, the last thoughts of the student, and the last message of the prophet. They shew the difference and the connexion of the Old and New Dispensations. This difference and this connexion appeared under a changed aspect after Jerusalem had fallen, and it was of importance for the Evangelist to shew that from the first the crisis was foreseen.

The succession of thoughts appears to be the following:—

1. The divine purpose in the Incarnation (16, 17)

12. 17 [c] For God sent not his Son into the world to condemn the world; but that the world through him might be saved.

This is set forth negatively and positively in relation to
(*a*) Man himself (personal), that he may not perish, but have everlasting life.
(*β*) The Son (general) not to judge the world, but that the world through Him may be saved.
2. The actual result (18, 19).
A judgment.
(*a*) The application of the judgment.
Those whom it reaches not,
Those whom it has reached.
(*β*) The nature of the judgment.
Light offered,
Darkness chosen.
3. The cause of the result in man (20, 21).
A twofold moral condition.
(*a*) Those who do ill shrink from the light in fear of testing.
(*β*) Those who do the Truth come to the light that their deeds may be made manifest.

16 ff. The pregnant declaration of the character and issue of the Lord's work given by Him to Nicodemus, as the representative of the old wisdom, leads the Evangelist to unfold its meaning more fully in relation to the actual circumstances in which he was himself placed. The issue of the proclamation of the Gospel had not in appearance corresponded with its promise and its power. But this issue did not modify its essential character.

16, 17. The divine purpose in the Incarnation was a purpose of universal love, even though it was imperfectly realised by man: a purpose of life to the believer, of salvation to the world.

16. *For God...*] Short explanatory remarks are frequently added in the same way (γάρ), ii. 25, iv. 44, vi. 6, 64, vii. 39, xiii. 11, xx. 9.

loved the world] loved all humanity considered as apart from Himself. See i. 29, note. The love of God shewn in the surrender and gift of His Son for men, is thus set forth as the spring of Redemption. The Father gave the Son even as the Son gave Himself.

so ..that] The supreme act serves as a measure of the love. Comp. 1 John iv. 11.

gave his only begotten Son] The word *gave*, not *sent*, as in *v.* 17, brings out the idea of sacrifice and of love shewn by a most precious offering. The title "only begotten" is added to enhance this conception, and the exact form in which the title is introduced (τὸν υἱὸν τὸν μονογενῆ), which is different from that in *v.* 18 (τοῦ μονογενοῦς υἱοῦ) further emphasizes it; "His Son, His only Son." Comp. 1 John iv. 9; and Matt. iii. 17, &c. (ὁ υἱὸς ὁ ἀγαπητός). There is an obvious reference to Gen. xxii. 2.

should (**may**) *not perish* (ἀπόληται) once for all, *but have* (ἔχῃ) with an abiding present enjoyment **eternal** (as in *v.* 15) *life*] In this verse and in the next the negative and positive aspects of the truth as regards individuals and the race (*every one, the world*) are definitely opposed; and there is striking parallelism in the related clauses: *perish, judge; have eternal life, be saved*. The addition of the clause, *may not perish, but*, in this verse, as distinguished from *v.* 15, is explained naturally by the actual state of things which St John saw in the church and the world about him.

the world...whosoever believeth] The love of God is without limit on His part (*v.* 17, note), but to appropriate the blessing of love, man must fulfil the necessary condition of faith.

17. *For God sent not his* (**the**) *Son...*] A transition is here made from the notion of sacrifice, love, gift (*v.* 16), to that of work and authority. (Yet see 1 John iv. 9, ἀπέσταλκεν, not ἀπέστειλεν.) There are two words equally translated "send," which have different shades of meaning. The one used here (ἀποστέλλω), which contains the root of "apostle," suggests the thought of a definite mission and a representative character in the envoy; the other (πέμπω) marks the simple relation between the sender and the sent. See xx. 21, note. It will be observed also that the title *Son* (**the** *Son*, not *his Son*), which is that of dignity, takes the place of *only begotten Son*, which is the title of affection.

condemn] Rather, **judge** (κρίνῃ, and so in verses 18, 19), as in the exact parallel, xii. 47. It is worthy of notice that St John does not use the compound verb (κατακρίνω), commonly translated *condemn*, nor its derivatives, though they occur in the history of the woman taken in adultery (viii. 10, 11).

In the later Jewish Messianic anticipations the judgment of the nations by Messiah is the most constant and the most prominent feature.

that the world...might (**may**) *be saved*] The divine purpose is, like the divine love, without any limitation. The true title of the Son is "the Saviour of the world" (ch. iv. 42; 1 John iv. 14. Comp. ch. i. 29; 1 John ii. 2). The sad realities of present experience cannot change the truth thus made known, however little we may be able to understand in what way it will be accomplished. The thought is made more impressive by the threefold repetition of "the world." Comp. i. 10, xv. 19. The general result is given here (*be saved*) in

18 ¶ He that believeth on him is not condemned: but he that believeth not is condemned already, because he hath not believed in the name of the only begotten Son of God.

19 And this is the condemnation, [d]that light is come into the world, and men loved darkness rather than light, because their deeds were evil.

20 For every one that doeth evil

[d] ch. 4.

---

1 John iv. 9 the individual appropriation of the blessing (*may live*).

18, 19. But though judgment was not the object of Christ's mission, judgment is in fact the necessary result of it. This judgment is self-executed, and follows inevitably from the revealed presence of Christ. (Comp. Luke ii. 34, 35.)

18. *is not condemned* (**judged**); *but* (omit)...*is condemned* (**hath been judged**) *already*] The change of tense is most significant. In the case of the believer there is no judgment. His whole life is *in* Christ. In the case of the unbeliever, the judgment is completed; he is separated from Christ, because he hath not believed on the revelation made in the person of Him who alone can save. The epithet *only begotten*, applied here again to the Son, brings out in relation to God (as has been seen) the idea of the Father's love (*v.* 16); in relation to man the singleness of our hope.

hath not believed in the name of...] hath not acknowledged Christ as being the only Son of God, such as He is revealed to be. Comp. ii. 23, note, i. 12, note. The belief in Christ under this one cardinal aspect leads to the full faith in His Person. Comp. 1 John v. 10, 13. The tense (*hath not believed*) is emphatic and corresponds with *hath been judged:* he is not in the state of one who believed when it was open to him to do so.

19. *And this*...] The reality—the necessity—of the judgment of the unbelieving is involved in the recognition of the character of Christ's coming. Judgment is not an arbitrary sentence, but the working out of an absolute law.

The exact form of expression (*αὕτη ἐστίν... ὅτι*) is characteristic of St John. Comp. 1 John i. 5, v. 11, 14.

condemnation] **judgment.** But more exactly the process (*κρίσις*), and not the result (*κρίμα*): the *judging* rather than the *judgment*. The manifestation of Christ was in fact both a process of judgment and also a sentence of judgment upon man. Comp. ix. 39, note. For the idea of "judgment," see Introd.

that...is come...and...] The two facts are placed simply side by side (comp. i. 10, 11, &c.), each in its independent completeness.

light is come...] **the light**, not simply *light*. Comp. i. 4. And so again, *men loved* **the darkness** *rather than* **the light**. The alternatives were offered to men in their most absolute form; the contrast of "the light" and "the darkness" was complete; and so men made their choice.

and men...] This was the immediate and general issue on which the apostle looked. Men as a class (*οἱ ἄνθρωποι*, ch. xvii. 6) passed sentence on themselves in action. Comp. xii. 48.

loved...were] The past tenses are used in the retrospect of the actual reception of the revelation of Christ made to men. Men *loved* (*ἠγάπησαν*) the darkness at the time when the choice was offered, because their works were habitually (*ἦν*) evil.

the *darkness*] Comp. i. 5. There are two words thus translated. The one, which occurs here (*σκότος*), and 1 John i. 6, only in St John's writings, expresses darkness absolutely as opposed to light; the other (*σκοτία*) which is found i. 5, viii. 12, xii. 35, 46; 1 John i. 5, ii. 8, 9, 11, darkness realised as a state.

rather than...] *i.e.* choosing it in preference to. The decision was final. Comp. xii. 43.

because (**for**) *their deeds* (**works**) *were evil*] The order of the original is very remarkable. Its force might be suggested in English by the inversion, "for evil were their works." It is best to keep the usual rendering of the original (*ἔργα*) "works" not "deeds" here and in the following verses (*vv.* 20, 21).

20, 21. The tragic issue of Christ's coming, the judgment which followed it, was due to the action of a moral law. All that has affinity with the light comes to it, all that is alien from it shrinks from it. Men's works were evil, and therefore they sought to avoid conviction under the darkness.

20. *doeth evil* (**ill**)] The word rendered *evil* here (*φαῦλος*) is different from the common word (*πονηρός*) used in *v.* 19. It occurs v. 29; Rom. ix. 11; 2 Cor. v. 10 (in each case contrasted with *good*); Tit. ii. 8; James iii. 16; and corresponds to the English *bad*, as expressing that which is poor, mean, worthless, of its kind, and so unfit for careful scrutiny.

doeth] The words translated *doeth* here and in *v.* 21 are different. That used here (*πράσσων*) expresses the scope and general character of a man's activity: that used in *v.* 21 (*ποιῶν*) the actual result outwardly shewn. There is a similar contrast in Rom. i. 32, ii 3, vii. 15, 19, 20. Bad actions have a moral weight, but no real and permanent being like the Truth.

hateth the light, neither cometh to
the light, lest his deeds should be
‖reproved.
21 But he that doeth truth cometh
to the light, that his deeds may be
made manifest, that they are wrought
in God.
22 ¶ After these things came Je-

---

hateth the light...] He both hates the light in itself and shrinks from it in consideration of its effects.

lest his deeds should...] Rather, **in order that his works may not**... The particle is the same as in the following verse, and marks the direct object of the evil-doer.

be reproved] Properly "sifted, tried, tested," and then, if need be, "convicted," "shewn faulty and reproved," as by one having authority and aptitude to judge. Comp. xvi. 8, note; Rev. iii. 19, and especially Eph. v. 13.

21. *But he that*...] In addition to the contrast of the verbs already noticed (*v.* 20), there is a further contrast in the forms of the two expressions "doing ill" and "doing the truth." In the one case action is represented by the many separate bad works (φαῦλα πράσσων), in the other by the realisation of the one Truth (ποιῶν τὴν ἀλήθειαν), which includes in a supreme unity all right deeds.

doeth truth] *doeth* **the truth**. The phrase is a remarkable one. Right action is true thought realised. Every fragment of right done is so much truth made visible. The same words occur 1 John i. 6. Comp. Neh. ix. 33; Gen. xxiv. 49, xlvii. 29. The phrase is not unfrequent in Rabbinic writings. St Paul gives emphasis to the same thought by contrasting "the truth" with "unrighteousness:" 2 Thess. ii. 12; 1 Cor. xiii. 6; Rom. i. 18, ii. 8. Comp. Eph. iv. 24, v. 9.

cometh to...] It is not said even of him that "he loveth the light." This perhaps could not be said absolutely of man. Action is for him the test of feeling. It must be noticed that the words recognise in man a striving towards the light. Comp. vii. 37 (*thirst*), xi. 52, xviii. 37.

be made manifest, that...] Whatever may be the imperfection of the deeds of the Christian in themselves, he knows that they were wrought in virtue of his fellowship with God. He is not therefore proudly anxious that they may be tested, and that so the doer may have praise since they abide the test; but looks simply to this that their spring may be shewn.

Hence it follows that A. V. is right in the rendering *that*. The other rendering *because* introduces a thought foreign to the argument. For the construction, see 1 John ii. 19.

be made manifest] for they have a character which bears the light. Comp. Eph. v. 13.

are wrought (**have been wrought**) *in God*] in union with Him, and therefore by His power. The original order lays the emphasis on *God:* "that it is in God, and not by the man's own strength, they have been wrought." The perfect participle (ἐστὶν εἰργασμένα) has its full force. The works of the believer are wrought in God, and as they have been once wrought they still abide. St John elsewhere adopts the same resolved form. Comp. ii. 17 note (γεγραμμένον ἐστίν).

Christ's teaching in Judæa generally (*vv.* 22—36).

This section forms the natural sequel to the visit of Christ to Jerusalem. He had offered Himself there with a significant sign as Messiah. The sign was generally not interpreted or misinterpreted; and leaving the Holy City, He began His work (so to speak) again as a prophet, following in part the method of the Baptist. Thus slowly by act and word He prepared a body of disciples to recognise Him, and to believe in Him, and to accept the true conception of Messiah's nature and work.

The section falls into three parts. There is a summary notice of Christ's work (22—24). This is followed by John's testimony (25—30); which is drawn out at greater length by the Evangelist (31—36).

The contents of the section are peculiar to St John, who writes as a companion of the Lord.

22—24. For a time Christ and the Baptist worked side by side, preaching "repentance" (Mark i. 15), and baptizing. The Messiah took up the position of a prophet in Judæa, as afterwards in Galilee. (See *v.* 24.)

22. *After these things*] The phrase does not indicate immediate connexion. Comp. v. 1, note. The first preaching of Christ was in the temple. When He found no welcome there He spoke in the Holy City: then in Judæa: afterwards in Galilee, which thenceforth became the centre of His teaching.

Jesus and his disciples] Comp. ii. 2, 12. The phrase occurs also in Matt. ix. 10 (Mark ii. 15), 19; Mark viii. 27. In each case there is a special force in the vivid representation of the great Teacher and of the accompanying disciples as two distinct elements in the picture.

the land of Judæa] as distinguished from Jerusalem itself. The exact phrase occurs here only in the New Testament. Compare Mark i. 5; Acts xxvi. 20, where "the country of Judæa" is similarly contrasted with the capital.

tarried] The stay was probably prolonged for some time. See Additional Note on v. 1.

and baptized] This baptism, actually ad-

sus and his disciples into the land of Judæa; and there he tarried with them, [e] and baptized.

[e] chap. 4. 2.

23 ¶ And John also was baptizing in Ænon near to Salim, because there was much water there: and they came, and were baptized.

24 For John was not yet cast into prison.

25 ¶ Then there arose a question between *some* of John's disciples and the Jews about purifying.

26 And they came unto John, and said unto him, Rabbi, he that was

---

ministered by the disciples, iv. 2, would belong to the preparation for the kingdom, like John's baptism. It was not and indeed could not be an anticipation of the Christian Sacrament which it foreshadowed. Comp. Matt. iv. 17; Mark i. 14, 15. At this point then the work of Christ and of His Forerunner met. Christ had not been acknowledged as king in the chief seat of the theocracy: therefore He began His work afresh on a new field and in a new character.

23. *And John also...*] The Baptist continued to fulfil his appointed work though he had acknowledged Christ.

in Ænon near to Salim] The word Ænon is probably an adjectival form from the familiar *ain* (eye, spring), meaning simply "abounding in springs" (fountains). The situation of Salim is disputed. In the time of Eusebius Salim was identified with a place on the confines of Galilee and Samaria on the west of Jordan, six or eight miles south of Scythopolis (*Bethshan*). A place bearing the name of *'Aynûn* has been found not far from a valley abounding in springs to the north of the *Salim* which lies not far to the east of *Nablous* ('Palestine Exploration Report,' 1874, pp. 141 f., comp. 1876, p. 99). Comp. Introd.

much water] The form of the phrase (πολλὰ ὕδατα) probably indicates many fountains or streams or pools of water. Mark ix. 22; Matt. xvii. 15. Elsewhere the plural is used of the gathered or troubled waters; Matt. viii. 32, xiv. 28, 29; Rev. i. 15, &c.

they came] There is no antecedent: "Men continued to come to him (the Baptist) and ...." Comp. xv. 6, xx. 2; Mark x. 13; Acts iii. 2.

24. *For John...*] More exactly, *For John* **had not yet been** *cast...* This note of time must be taken in connexion with Matt. iv. 12, 13, 17; Mark i. 14. The public ministry of the Lord in Galilee did not begin till after this time, after John was cast into prison as the Synoptists record. The events in Galilee, which the evangelist has already related (ii. 1—12), were preparatory to the manifestation at Jerusalem which was the real commencement of Christ's Messianic work. St John records the course and issue of this manifestation: the other Evangelists start with the record of the Galilæan ministry which dates from the imprisonment of the Baptist. Comp. Mark i. 14, note.

25—30. The outward similarity of the work of Christ and of the Baptist gave an occasion (25, 26) for the last testimony of the Baptist to Christ. In the eyes of some Christ appeared as his rival. To these the Baptist himself shewed what his own work was, and then he left his hearers to recognise Christ.

25. *Then there arose*] The particle (οὖν) is one not of time but of consequence: *There arose* **therefore...** as a consequence of this double work of baptizing

a question between some of...] Rather, "**a questioning** (a discussion, disputation) **on the part of** (ἐκ, Vulg. *ex*) *John's* disciples **with...**" For the word "questioning" (ζήτησις) see Acts xv. 2; 1 Tim. vi. 4; 2 Tim. ii. 23; Tit. iii. 9.

the Jews] According to the most probable reading, **a Jew**, which gives a definiteness to the incident otherwise wanting.

about purifying] that is, as we may suppose, about the religious value of baptism, such as John's. We cannot but believe that Christ, when He administered a baptism through His disciples, explained to those who offered themselves the new birth which John's baptism and this preparatory baptism typified. At the same time He may have indicated, as to Nicodemus, the future establishment of Christian Baptism, the sacrament of the new birth. In this way nothing would be more natural than that some Jew, a direct disciple, should be led to disparage the work of John, contrasting it with that of which Christ spoke; and that thereupon John's disciples, jealous for their master's honour, should come to him complaining of the position which Christ had taken.

26. *Rabbi...*] The title of reverence is emphatic. The speakers first contrast the new Teacher with their own, and then describe his present action. *Rabbi, he that was with thee*, in thy company as one of thy disciples, *beyond Jordan*, in the most conspicuous and successful scene of thy ministry, *to whom thou* (σύ) **hast borne** *witness*, as the authoritative judge, *behold he is baptizing...*

to whom] *i.e.* in whose favour, to support whose claims. Comp. v. 33, xviii. 37; 3 John 12; Luke iv. 22; Acts x. 43 (xiii. 22), xiv. 3, xv. 8; Rom. x. 2; Gal. iv. 15; Col. iv. 13. Elsewhere from the context *against*, Matt. xxiii. 31. Cf. James v. 3.

thou barest witness] The original expresses

1. 7, with thee beyond Jordan, *f* to whom
thou barest witness, behold, the same
baptizeth, and all *men* come to him.
r. 5. 27 John answered and said, *g* A
ake man can ‖ receive nothing, except it
im- be given him from heaven.

28 Ye yourselves bear me witness,
that I said, *h* I am not the Christ, but *h* chap. 1. 20.
that I am sent before him.
29 He that hath the bride is the
bridegroom: but the friend of the
bridegroom, which standeth and hear-

---

not only the fact, "barest witness," but by the perfect, "*thou* **hast borne witness**," marks the testimony as being yet effective: ch. i. 34.

behold] The form here used (ἴδε) is characteristic of St John. Comp. i. 29; xix. 5, 14; &c.

baptizeth] This appeared to be an invasion of John's work.

all men] The natural exaggeration (*v.* 23) of angry zeal. Contrast *v.* 32.

27—30. The words of the Baptist meet the jealous zeal of his disciples. He (1) lays down the principle of revelation (*v.* 27); and then (2) applies it to his own work, both as to (*a*) The past witness (*v.* 28), and as to (β) The present fulfilment (*v.* 29); and then (3) draws the main conclusion (*v.* 30).

27. Every contrast of teacher with teacher is harmonized by the truth that each has only that which God has given him.

answered] The answer lies in the simple explanation of the essential relation between the Forerunner and the Christ, drawn from the universal truth. When this is once apprehended all possibility of rivalry is gone. The message which was brought to John by his disciples as a complaint, in his eyes crowns his proper joy.

A man...heaven] The principle is general, and must not be interpreted either of Christ, or of the Baptist, alone. It has an application to both. The Baptist says in fact: "I cannot claim any new authority which has not been directly assigned to me; He, of whom you speak, cannot effectually exercise His power unless it be of divine origin."

A man...] The word has force (comp. *v.* 4). It is the law of human existence as dependent upon God, to which even Messiah is subject.

receive] The original word (λαμβάνειν) includes the conceptions of "receiving" and "taking." Comp. *v.* 32, note. The thought here is that there is but one source of spiritual power, and that opened by God's love, and not by man's own will.

be given] More exactly, **have been given**. The divine gift, already complete in itself, makes the human appropriation possible.

from (ἐκ, out of) *heaven*] The phrase is not the same as "from God:" out of the treasury, so to speak, of all true and abiding blessings. Comp. xix. 11.

28, 29. The principle stated in *v.* 27 is applied directly by the Baptist to himself, according to his earlier definition of his work, and, under a figure, to Christ.

28. *Ye yourselves*] You need no teacher to meet your difficulty. The zeal which you display is shewn to be mistaken if you only recall what I said. When I announced my mission I declared it to be provisional. No word of mine can have given occasion to the error whereby you claim for me the highest place.

The exact emphatic phrase (αὐτοὶ ὑμεῖς) occurs 1 Thess. iv. 9 (Mark vi. 31 is different). Comp. Acts xxiv. 15.

before him] The Baptist now distinctly identifies Him of whom he had spoken before in general terms (i. 26, 30) as "the Christ." The manifestation to Israel had taken place. The difference of language is very significant.

29. The Baptist spoke plainly of himself, but he speaks of Christ's office and position in mysterious language, answering exactly to the situation. That position must be recognised in order that He may be known, as the Baptist knew Him.

the bride...the bridegroom] The image is commonly used in the prophetical books of the Old Testament from first to last to describe the relation between Jehovah and His people, Hos. ii. 19; Ezek. xvi.; Mal. ii. 11. In the New Testament it is applied to Christ and the church as here, Rev. xix. 7, xxi. 2, 9, xxii. 17 (comp. Eph. v. 32 ff.); and also to the connexion of Christ with any particular body of Christians, 2 Cor. xi. 2.

Similar imagery is used in the Synoptic Gospels; Matt. xxii. 1 ff. (the marriage feast), xxv. 1 ff. (the ten virgins). Comp. Matt. ix. 15.

the friend of the bridegroom] To whom it fell to demand the hand of the bride, and to prepare everything for the due reception of the bride and bridegroom. Comp. Buxtorf, 'Lex. Rabb.,' or Levy, 'Chald. Wörterb.' s. v. שושבינא. The Baptist had fulfilled his office in preparing and bringing the representatives of the spiritual Israel—the new divine Bride—to Christ—the Bridegroom.

standeth] in the attitude of expectation and ready service, *and heareth him* not only as cognisant of his presence, but as waiting to fulfil his commands. Comp. xii. 29 (Mark ix. 1, τῶν ἑστηκότων).

rejoiceth greatly] Literally, *with joy rejoiceth*. In this rejoicing there is no alloy. Comp. Luke xxii. 15 (so A. V.); Acts iv. 17, v. 28,

eth him, rejoiceth greatly because of the bridegroom's voice: this my joy therefore is fulfilled.

30 He must increase, but I *must* decrease.

31 He that cometh from above is above all: he that is of the earth is earthly, and speaketh of the earth: he that cometh from heaven is above all.

---

xxiii. 14; James v. 17. The idiom is common in the LXX. as the representative of the Hebrew construction with the inf. abs., but it is found also in classical writers. It is significant that it is found here only in St John's writings.

because of the bridegroom's voice] when he has entered his new home, bringing his bride with him, and there first spoken with her at the marriage feast. The full, clear voice of the bridegroom's love is contrasted with all the words of those who have prepared for His coming.

this my joy] The form of the original is emphatic: *this joy*, the joy of seeing a work happily consummated, *which is mine.* Comp. xv. 9, note.

is fulfilled] Literally, **hath been fulfilled** already, when, as you announce, the Christ is gathering round Him the disciples who are the beginnings of His church. Comp. i. 34.

30. *He must...*]. That lies in the divine law of things. Comp. *vv.* 7, 14, ix. 4, x. 16, xx. 9, note; Rev. i. 1, iv. 1, xx. 3, &c.

decrease] in imprisonment, suspense, martyrdom. These last words of St John are the fulness of Christian sacrifice, and fitly close his work, and with it the old dispensation. At the same time, they have an ever-germinant fulfilment. The progress from the Law to the Gospel, from the fulness of self to the fulness of Christ, is the law of Christian life. For the later mission from the Baptist to Christ in relation to this testimony, see Matt. xi. 3, note.

31—36. This section contains reflections of the Evangelist on the general relation of the Son to the Forerunner, and to the teachers of the earlier dispensation generally. The Baptist had spoken figuratively in the language of the Old Testament of what Christ was, and so directed his disciples to acknowledge Him. The Evangelist looking over the long interval of years reaffirms in clearer words the witness of the Herald, and shews how it has been fulfilled.

The passage is distinguished from the answer of the Baptist by

(1) A marked contrast of style. The verses 27—30 are in form clear and sharp, with echoes of the abrupt prophetic speech. These (31—36) have a subtle undertone of thought, which binds them together closely, and carries them forward to the climax in *v.* 36.

(2) Parts of it contain clear references to words of the Lord, *e.g. vv.* 31, 32, refer to *vv.* 11 ff., *v.* 35 to x. 28, 29.

(3) The use of the title "Son" absolutely (*vv.* 35, 36) appears to be alien from the position of the Baptist.

(4) The historical position marked in *v.* 32 (*no man*) is strikingly different from that marked in *v.* 29.

(5) The aorists in *v.* 33 describe the later experience of Christian life. Comp. i. 16.

On the other hand, the use of the present tense, *v.* 32 (*testifieth*, *receiveth*), *vv.* 31. 34 (*speaketh*), is not inconsistent with the position of the Evangelist.

The section falls into the following divisions:

1. The contrast of the earthly and the heavenly teacher (*vv.* 31, 32).
2. The experience and the endowment of the church (33—35).
   (*a*) The experience of faith (*v.* 33).
   (β) Christ the perfect and abiding Teacher (*v.* 34).
   (γ) The Son the supreme King (*v.* 35).
3. The issues (36).
   (*a*) Of Faith—Life.
   (β) Of Disobedience—wrath.

31, 32. The earthly teacher, and such were all who came before Christ, is contrasted with the One Teacher from heaven, (1) in origin (*of the earth*, *from above*, *of heaven*), (2) in being (*of the earth*, *above all*), (3) in teaching (*of the earth*, *what he hath seen and heard* in the kingdom of truth). Comp. Matt. xi. 11.

31. *He that cometh from above*] not *He that came*. The work of Christ is regarded not as past nor as future, but as ever-present (vi. 33).

from above] from a higher region. The same word occurs in the original (ἄνωθεν) as that used in *v.* 3 (*again*, *anew*); see note. It seems to be chosen from its connexion with the *above* (ἐπάνω) which follows.

above all] that is, *sovereign over all things* (*v.* 35), and not *over all men* only (as Vulg., *supra omnes*), though this is the prominent idea here, where the Son is compared with former teachers.

of the earth...earthly (**of the earth**)...*of the earth*] The same phrase (ἐκ τῆς γῆς) is thrice repeated. The rendering "earthly" in the second case obscures the thought and introduces confusion with the "earthly," *i.e.* realised on the earth, and not springing out of the earth, in *v.* 12 (ἐπίγειος, see note). The

32 And what he hath seen and heard, that he testifieth; and no man receiveth his testimony.

33 He that hath received his testimony [i] hath set to his seal that God [i] Rom. 3. 4.
is true.

"earth," as distinguished from the "world," expresses the idea of the particular limitations of our being, without any accessory moral contrast with God. Its opposite is heaven. Contrast 1 John iv. 5 (ἐκ τοῦ κόσμου). The term does not occur elsewhere in St John's writings in this sense. Comp. 1 Cor. xv. 47.

he that is of the earth] He who draws his origin from the earth, a child of earth, a man of men (comp. Matt. xi. 11), *is of the earth*, draws likewise the form and manner of his life from the earth, *and speaketh of the earth*. His birth, his existence, his teaching, are all of the same kind. The phrase *to be of* (εἶναι ἐκ), expressing a moral connexion, is characteristic of St John. It includes the ideas of derivation and dependence, and therefore of a moral correspondence between the offspring (issue) and the source. Thus according to the essential affinity of their character men are said to be *of the truth*, xviii. 37; 1 John ii. 21, iii. 19; or *of the world*, xv. 19, xvii. 14, 16, xviii. 36; 1 John ii. 16, iv. 5; and again with a personal relation *of God*, vii. 17, viii. 47; 1 John iii. 10, iv. 1—7, v. 19; 3 John 11, and *of the Father*, 1 John ii. 16; or, on the other side, *of the devil*, 1 John iii. 8 (comp. John viii. 44), and *of the evil one*, 1 John iii. 12. So Christ describes Himself as being *from above* (ἐκ τῶν ἄνω), and "the Jews" as being *from below* (ἐκ τῶν κάτω), viii. 23. The phrase is comparatively rare in the other writings of the New Testament, but when it occurs it is deserving of notice, Matt. i. 20, xxi. 25 f., and parallels; Luke ii. 4; Acts v. 38 f.; Rom. ix. 5; 1 Cor. i. 30, xi. 12 (2 Cor. v. 18); 2 Cor. iv. 7; Gal. iii. 10, 20; Col. iv. 11.

The phrase *to be begotten* (*born*) *of* (γεγεννῆσθαι ἐκ) has a kindred meaning. *To be of* expresses the essential, permanent, relation; *to be begotten of* refers to the initial moment of the relation, i. 13, iii. 5, 6, 8, viii. 41; 1 John ii. 29, iii. 9, iv. 7, v. 1, 4, 18. It is not said of any that "they are born of the evil one." Compare iv. 22, note.

speaketh of the earth] The earth is the source from which he draws his words. Even divine things come to him through earth. He has not looked on truth absolute in the heavenly sphere. But this "speaking of the earth" is not of necessity a "speaking of the world" (1 John iv. 5). On the contrary *he that cometh from heaven* is not only supreme over all creation, and therefore unlimited by the earth, but *v.* 32, **witnesseth**—testifieth with solemn authority, in this connexion perhaps in contrast with *speaketh*—*what he hath seen and heard* in heaven.

that cometh] as on a conspicuous mission. In this case the thought is not of the source of being (*he that is of the earth*), but of the source of authority.

from heaven] This phrase, as contrasted with *from above*, gives the exact correlative to *from the earth*.

31, 32. It is not improbable that the words *is above all* and *and* should be omitted, so that the words should run on: *he that cometh from heaven testifieth what he hath seen and heard*. See Additional Note.

32. *hath seen and heard*] The change of tense appears to mark a contrast between that which belonged to the existence (*hath seen*, ἑώρακεν), and to the mission (*heard*, ἤκουσεν, not *hath heard*) of the Son. Comp. viii. 26, 40, xv. 15 (vi. 45), and viii. 38 with *varr. lectt.*

testifieth] **witnesseth.** Even after the historical manifestation of Christ on earth has ended, He still speaks through His church. The present here is co-ordinate with the plural in *v.* 11. In that passage the Lord connects the testimony of the disciples with His own; and so here St John regards the testimony of the disciples as being truly the testimony of Christ.

and no man...] The issue, as elsewhere (*v.* 11, vii. 30, viii. 20), is simply added to the description of the revelation. For the time the testimony of Christ through His church found no acceptance. The close of the apostolic age was a period of singular darkness and hopelessness. Comp. 1 John v. 19 (2 Tim. i. 15). It was possible then for St John to say *no man receiveth* (literally, *is receiving*) *his testimony* (**witness**). This sad judgment stands in sharp contrast with *v.* 29, and *v.* 26.

receiveth his testimony (**witness**, and so in *v.* 33)] Two words are translated *receive*, one used here (λαβεῖν) marking that something is taken, the other (δέξασθαι, ch. iv. 45 only in St John), adding the notion of welcoming or receiving from another (Luke xvi. 6, 7). The former word includes also the idea of retaining that which is taken, while the latter presents only the act of reception. Hence St John uses the former of "receiving the Word" (i. 12; comp. v. 43, xiii. 20). The phrase "receive the witness" is peculiar to St John: *vv.* 11, 33, v. 34, 1 John v. 9. (Comp. xii. 48, xvii. 8.) The witness is not welcomed only but kept. It becomes an endowment, a possession.

33—35. But even so, though the current of faith was checked, the church was in existence. There were disciples who had received the testimony at an earlier time, and found that in so doing they had been solemnly

34 For he whom God hath sent speaketh the words of God: for God giveth not the Spirit by measure *unto him.*

35 [k]The Father loveth the Son, and hath given all things into his hand.

36 [l]He that believeth on the Son

[k] Ma[tt.] 27.
[l] Hab[.] 1 Joh[n] 10.

---

united with God; and this experience of faith is still assured by the fact of Christ's absolute knowledge and absolute power.

33. *He that hath received* (*that* **received**, ὁ λαβών)] The reference appears to be directly historic, going back to the time when the disciples were first gathered round the Lord.

hath set to his seal] hath confirmed in the most solemn manner the statement which follows, *that God is true*. The term *seal* is used here only in this sense. Elsewhere the word is used of marking as reserved for a special destination: vi. 27; Rev. vii. 3. Comp. Eph. i. 13, iv. 30. There is a noble Jewish saying, quoted by Lightfoot ('Hor. Hebr.' John vi. 27), that "the seal of God is Truth." See xviii. 37, note.

that God is true] This affirmation admits of two senses. (1) It may mean that in accepting the teaching of Christ the believer accepts the teaching of God, for the words of Christ are in truth the words of God. The believer therefore by receiving these really attests what is a direct message of God; and in so doing he feels that he enters into a certain fellowship with Him, than which man can have no higher glory. The rejection of the testimony of Christ is, according to this interpretation, spoken of as "making God a liar" (1 John i. 10, v. 10). (2) The statement may also be taken in a wider sense. The believer finds in Christ the complete fulfilment of every promise of God. By his experience of what Christ is and what Christ says to him he gladly confesses that "God is true," that He has left nothing unsatisfied of the hope which He has given to man. Comp. viii. 26.

The first explanation appears at first sight to fall in best with *v.* 34, but the second in fact embraces the first in a larger thought.

34. The proof of God's truth is found in the absolute fulness of Christ's spiritual endowment.

he whom God hath sent] the one heavenly messenger as contrasted with all the earthly.

the words...] Not "words" only (vi. 68), but the complete, manifold expression (τὰ ῥήματα) of the divine message.

for God giveth not...by measure unto him] **for he giveth not...by measure.** The words *God* and *unto him* have no place in the original text. If these are omitted it is doubtful whether the subject of the sentence is "God," or "Messiah." The object in any case must be general.

If, as in the common interpretation, God be taken as the subject, the sense appears to be: "Christ speaks the words of God, for God giveth not the Spirit by measure, only in a definite degree, to all, but He gives it completely."

If, on the other hand, Messiah is the subject (as Cyril takes it), the sense will be: "Christ speaks the words of God, for His words are attested by His works, in that He giveth the Spirit to His disciples as dispensing in its fulness that which is His own."

This second interpretation, which appears to have been neglected in late times owing to the false text, has much to recommend it (xv. 26).

35. The ground of what has been said lies in the actual relation of God to Messiah, as the Father to the Son.

hath given] Contrast *giveth* (*v.* 34).

all things] *v.* 31. The term is not to be limited in any way.

36. The absolute supremacy of the Christian revelation as compared with all that went before is seen in its final issues of life, and incapacity for life.

that believeth] with a faith which is continuous, not momentary (ὁ πιστεύων).

hath everlasting (**eternal**) *life*] *To believe and confess that Jesus is the Son of God* (1 John iv. 15) is the pledge of new and abiding life By that belief our whole relation to the world, to man and to God, is changed; and changed already: *This is life eternal*...(xvii. 3, note).

believeth not] **disobeyeth** (ὁ ἀπειθῶν). Disbelief is regarded in its activity. The same word occurs 1 Peter iv. 17; Rom. ii. 8, xi. 30, 31, &c. Nothing is said of those who have no opportunity of coming to the true knowledge of Christ. Comp. Mark xvi. 16 (πιστεύσας, ἀπιστήσας).

shall not see life] shall be unable to form any true conception of life, much less enjoy it. Comp. *v.* 3. The future is contrasted with the present (*hath...shall not...*): the simple idea of *life* with the full conception *eternal life*. Comp. v. 24, 39 f.

the wrath of God] The phrase is commonly used of a distinct manifestation of the righteous judgment of God (Rom. i. 18, iii. 5, ix. 22, xii. 19), and especially of "the coming wrath" (ἡ μέλλουσα ὀργή, Matt. iii. 7; Luke iii. 7; ἡ ὀργὴ ἡ ἐρχομένη, 1 Thess. i. 10; comp. Luke xxi. 23, ὀργὴ τῷ λαῷ τούτῳ; 1 Thess. ii. 16; Rom. ii. 5 (v. 9); Eph. v. 6; Col. iii. 6).

In this sense it is not unfrequent in the Apocalypse (xi. 18, xiv. 10, xvi. 19, xix. 15),

hath everlasting life: and he that believeth not the Son shall not see life; but the wrath of God abideth on him.

---

where "the wrath of God" is set side by side with "the wrath of the Lamb" (vi. 16 f.).

The phrase is very common in the Old Testament. (Comp. Hebr. iii. 11.)

Here "the wrath of God" describes the general relation in which man as a sinner stands towards the justice of God. Comp. Eph. ii. 3. St John goes back from the revelation of God as Father to the original idea of God as God.

abideth on him] The natural law is inexorable. Only faith in the revelation through Christ can remove the consequences of sin which must otherwise bring God's wrath upon the sinner. Comp. 1 John iii. 14.

ADDITIONAL NOTES on CHAP. III.

3. The word translated *again* (ἄνωθεν) properly means "from the top," "from the beginning," "from above." Thus it is used literally of the rending of the vail of the temple "from the top" (Matt. xxvii. 51; Mark xv. 38; compare John xix. 23), and temporally of knowledge possessed from an early date (Acts xxvi. 5), or traced from the source (Luke i. 3), and locally, with a spiritual application, of the wisdom which cometh "from above" (James iii. 15, 17; comp. James i. 17). The word occurs in a sense similar to this last in John iii. 31, xix. 11. In Gal. iv. 9 it is combined with the simple term for "again" (πάλιν ἄνωθεν), as implying the complete repetition of an entire process, starting, as it were, afresh, so as to obliterate every trace of an intermediate change.

Two interpretations of the word, derived from distinct applications of the fundamental idea, have found favour in the present place from early times: (1) "from the beginning," "over again," "anew," and (2) "from above," "from heaven." The Syriac (Peshito), Memphitic, Æthiopic, and Latin versions give the rendering "anew" (Vulgate, "renatus (natus) denuo"); the Greek writers (from Origen) generally adopt the sense, "from heaven;" the Harclean Syriac, Armenian, and Gothic versions translate "from above." The English versions have vacillated strangely. Tyndale and Coverdale, agreeing with Vulgate, Luther ("von neuen"), and Erasmus, Ed. 1., gave "anew;" but Coverdale, in the Great Bible, with the Zurich version ("von oben herab"), and Erasmus, in his later editions ("e supernis"), gave "from above." The Bishops' Bible of 1568 reads "born again," but this is changed back again in 1572 to "born from above."

It has been urged in favour of the second rendering that St John constantly speaks of "being born of God" (γενν. ἐκ τοῦ θεοῦ), i. 13; 1 John iii. 9, iv. 7, v. 1, 4, 18, while he does not speak (as St Paul) of a "new creation." But it may be questioned whether the phrase used here (γενν. ἄνωθεν) could be used to convey this idea of being "born of God," and it would be most strange under any circumstances that the usual mode of expressing it should be abandoned. It is further of great importance to notice that in the traditional form of the saying (*e.g.* Just. M. 'Ap.' I. 61) a word is used (ἀναγεννᾶσθαι) as equivalent to the ambiguous phrase of St John (γεννηθῆναι ἄνωθεν), which unquestionably can only mean "to be reborn" (comp. 1 Pet. i. 3, 23). And, once again, the idea of "a birth from God" (i. 13) does not suit the context. The reality of the new birth has to be laid down first, and then its character (*v.* 5). The emphasis lies on "to be born." This too was evidently the sense in which Nicodemus understood the sentence (*a second time*). If he had found a reference to the divine action in the Lord's words he could not have left it unnoticed. There seems then to be no reason to doubt that the sense given by the Vulgate and A. V. is right, though the notion is not that of mere repetition (*again*), but of an analogous process (*anew*).

14. The narrative of the setting up of the brazen serpent (Num. xxi. 4 ff.) presents at first sight several difficulties. The use of an image in spite of the general prohibition, and that image the image of a serpent, is mysterious. Justin Martyr presses his Jewish opponent with this apparent violation of the divine law, and asks for an explanation. "We cannot give one," is the answer: "I have often asked my teachers about this, and no one could account for it" ('Dial.' § 94, p. 322 B).

The earliest reference to the incident is in the Book of Wisdom. "[The murmuring people] were troubled for a little while, for warning, having a symbol (σύμβολον not σύμβουλον) of salvation, to remind them of Thy commandments; for he that turned to it was saved, not by reason of that which he beheld (διὰ τὸ θεωρούμενον), but by reason of the Saviour of all" (Wisd. xvi. 6 f.). This explanation of the efficacy of the symbol is commonly given by Jewish writers. So the Targum of Jonathan: "it shall come to pass that if [one bitten] look upon it, he shall live, if his heart be directed to the Name of the Word (*Memra*) of the Lord."

Philo interprets the serpent as the antithesis of the serpent of the Temptation, an idea which is found also in Rabbinic writings. "The serpent of Eve," he says, "was pleasure: the serpent of Moses was temperance (σωφροσύνη) or endurance (καρτερία). It is only by this spirit of self-denial that the allurements of vice are overcome" ('de Leg. alleg.' II. T. i. pp. 80 ff.; 'de Agric.' T. i. p. 315 f.).

This interpretation found some currency among the Christian Fathers. Ambrose, evidently following some earlier authority, speaks of "my serpent, the good serpent (comp. Matt. x. 16), who sheds not poison but its antidotes from his mouth...The serpent which after the winter is past puts off his fleshly dress (*exuit se corporis amictu*), that he may appear in fair beauty" (In Ps. cxliii. 'Serm.' VI. § 15).

The belief that the serpent was the emblem of healing and life (Knobel on Num. xxi.) according to the heathen conception, which was developed among the Ophite sects (comp. Tertull. 'de Præscr. Hær.' 47), carries out this conception to a more extravagant form.

There can however be little doubt that the serpent in Scripture is the symbol of the personal power of evil (Rev. xii. 9 ff.; 2 Cor. xi. 3; Gen. iii. 1 ff.); and that the central thought in the Mosaic narrative is that of the evil by which the people suffered being shewn openly as overcome (comp. Col. ii. 15). He who looking upon the symbol recognised in it the sign of God's conquering power, found in himself the effects of faith. The evil was represented as overcome in a typical form (*a brazen serpent*) and not in an individual form (*a natural serpent*), and therefore the application of the image was universal.

If now we consider the immediate application of the symbol, it is at once clear that by transferring the image of the elevation of the serpent to Himself Christ foreshewed that He was to be presented in some way conspicuously to men, and that being so presented He was to be the source of life to those who looked to Him with faith. So much Nicodemus would be able to gather. Can we now after the event follow out the parallel yet further?

The elevation of the serpent on the pole, and the serpent itself, have been supposed to be directly significant of the circumstances of the death of Christ upon the cross. As to the first point, it seems to be reasonable to say that the mode in which the brazen serpent was shewn to the eye of faith aptly prefigured the mode in which Christ was presented to men with redemptive power (comp. xii. 32). The second point presents greater difficulty, but it is frequently pressed by early writers. Thus the author of the Epistle of Barnabas supposes Moses to address the people in these words: "Whenever any one of you is bitten, let him come to the serpent which is placed upon the tree (ἐπὶ τοῦ ξύλου), and let him hope in faith, that he [the symbolic serpent] being dead can make alive, and immediately he shall be saved" (Barn. 'Ep.' XII.). In this aspect the harmlessness of the typical serpent was naturally dwelt upon. So Origen writes: "A brazen serpent was a type of the Saviour," for He was not a serpent truly; but "represented (*imitabatur*) a serpent..." ('Hom. XI. in Ezech.' § 3). Others follow out this idea more in detail. For example, Gregory of Nyssa, explaining the history at some length, says: "The law shews us that which is seen upon the tree (τὸ ἐπὶ ξύλου φαινόμενον), and this is the likeness of a serpent and not a serpent, as also the divine Paul saith, 'in likeness of flesh of sin' (Rom. viii. 3). The true serpent is sin; and he that deserts to sin puts on the nature of the serpent. Man therefore is freed from sin by Him who assumed (ὑπελθόντος) the form (εἶδος) of sin, and was made after our fashion (γενομένου καθ' ἡμᾶς), who were changed to the form of the serpent" ('De vit. Mos.' I. pp. 414 f. Migne. Comp. Chrys. and Theoph. *ad loc.*).

Epiphanius, adopting the same view, that the serpent represented Christ, explains the connexion quite differently. "The Jews," he writes, "treating Christ as a serpent, were wounded by the wiles of the serpent, that is the devil, and then healing came to those who were bitten, as by the lifting up of the serpent" ('Hær.' XXXVII. § 7, pp. 273 f.).

Tertullian, on the other hand, saw in the serpent the image of the devil slain, though he implies that the figure was variously interpreted in his time ('de Idol.' V. Comp. 'adv. Jud.' X.).

Justin Martyr dwells only upon the figure of the cross (σημεῖον LXX.), on which the serpent was raised, and not on the serpent itself, as the emblem of the Lord's saving Passion ('Apol.' I. 60, 'Dial.' 94).

In the face of these and other differences of interpretation in detail, it seems to be far best to compare the two acts together as wholes, the elevation of the serpent, and the elevation of Christ on the cross, without attempting to follow out the comparison of the parts separately. The lifting up of the serpent, as Augustine says, is the death of Christ, the cause being signified by the effect (Aug. 'De pecc. mer. et remiss.' I. 32). In Christ sin was slain, and he who had the power of sin (Rom. vi. 6; Col. ii. 14). Christ lifted up upon the cross "draws all men unto Him for eternal salvation" Ign. (interpol. 'ad Smyrn.' 2). Looking to Him the believer finds life. (Comp. Bas. 'de Sp. s.' XIV.)

In the type and the antitype the same great ideas are conspicuous. There is in both the open manifestation of a source of healing to those smitten, effectual by faith, and that under the form of a triumph over the cause of suffering when it has been allowed to do its worst.

The Jewish writers are singularly silent as to the incident of the Brazen Serpent. "The thing was done by God's command, and it is not for us to inquire into the why and wherefore of the serpent form" (Aben Ezra, quoted by Taylor, 'The Gospel in the Law,' pp. 119 ff.). They discuss however the manner in which the symbol was efficacious, and commonly agree in supposing that it was by directing men to lift up their eyes to their Father in heaven, and to see in Him the conqueror of their enemy. The chief passages bearing upon the question are collected by the younger Buxtorf in his treatise 'De serpente æneo' ('Exercitationes,' pp. 458 ff. Basileæ, 1659). The general interpretation of the history has been frequently discussed at length. Two essays may be mentioned: Menken, 'Ueber die eherne Schlange,' 1812 ('Schriften' VI. 351 ff. 1858), and Erskine, 'The Brazen Serpent, or Life coming through Death,' 1831.

NOTE ON READINGS IN CHAP. III.

There are three readings of considerable interest in ch. iii. which require to be noticed in some detail, as they involve important principles of textual criticism. They are the omission of the words

(1) *v.* 15, *may not perish but* (μὴ ἀπόληται ἀλλ').

(2) *v.* 13, *which is in heaven* (ὁ ὢν ἐν τῷ οὐρανῷ).

(3) *vv.* 31, 32, *is above all things, and* (ἐπάνω πάντων ἐστί, καί).

(1) Of these *v.* 15 is the simplest case, and may be taken first.

The words in question are omitted by

(α) MSS.: ℵBLT[b]1,33 and a few mss.
(β) *Versions:* (*Old Lat.*, some), *Old Syr.*, *Jerus. Syr.*, *Memph.*, (*Æth.*), (*Arm.*).
(γ) *Fathers:* Cyr. Al., Cypr., Lcfr.

They are found in

(α) MSS.: A 69 and nearly all other MSS. and mss. (CD are defective).
(β) *Versions:* (*Old Lat.*, some), *Vulg.*, *Syr. P.* and *Hcl.*, (*Arm.*), (*Æth.*).
(γ) Chr., Theodt., Victorin.

The same words occur in *v.* 16, where they are omitted by no early authority except *Old Syr.*

The consideration of this evidence shews that

1. The only ancient (ante-Nicene) evidence for the words is that of some old Latin texts (represented among the Greek MSS. by 69).

2. The words were adopted by the Antiochene school in the fourth century, and thence passed into the current Greek text.

3. The origin of the insertion is obvious; while there was no cause for omission.

The words therefore must be omitted without doubt.

In connexion with this omission, it must be observed that the primary authorities are greatly divided as to the preposition and pronoun which precede. We find εἰς αὐτόν ℵ and mass of MSS., (*Vulg.*), &c., ἐπ' αὐτῷ L, ἐπ' αὐτόν A, ἐν αὐτῷ BT, some Latin copies. In *v.* 16 L reads ἐπ' αὐτῷ.

The common phrase πιστ. εἰς αὐτόν evidently could not have given rise to these variations, and it can only be regarded as an early correction. Of the other readings ἐν αὐτῷ is at once the best attested, and by its difficulty explains the tendency to change.

(2) The problem in *v.* 13 is more difficult. The words are omitted by

(α) MSS.: ℵBLT[b]33.
(β) *Versions:* (*Memph.*), (*Æth.*).
(γ) *Fathers:* Eus., Cyr. Al. (constantly: 12 times. See Pusey, Cyril VII. 1, Pref. p. xx.), Orig. *int.*

They are found in

(α) MSS.: (A) and apparently in all other MSS. and mss. (CD are defective).

In A the words ων εν τω ουνω have been written over an erasure, and it is supposed that the original reading was ο εν τω ουνω. The ο by the first hand is unaltered.

(β) *Versions:* *Old Lat.*, *Old Syr.*, *Vulg.*, *Syr. Pesh. and Hcl.*, *Arm.*, (*Memph.*), (*Æth.*).
(γ) *Fathers:* Hippol., Dion. Alex., Did., (Orig. *int.*), Novat., Hil., Lcfr.

Here it will be seen that the ancient MSS are on the side of omission, and the ancient versions on the side of retention. But it is obvious that an interpretative gloss in a version is easier of explanation than an omission in a copy of the original text. Such glosses are found not unfrequently in the old Latin and old Syriac copies (*e.g.* iii. 6, 8), though they are commonly corrected in the revised Latin and Syriac texts of the 4th (5th) cent. (*Vulg.*, *Pesh.*). In this case however the words are contained in the Syrian Greek text (A), and so, even if they were a gloss, they would be left undisturbed (comp. *v.* 25). And the omission of the words by ℵ, which is the Greek correlative of the *old Lat.* and *old Syr.*, greatly detracts from their weight here. In regard to the Patristic evidence, the constant usage of Cyril balances the quotations of Dionysius and Didymus. On the whole, therefore, there seems to be no reason for deserting the Greek authorities, which have been found unquestionably right in (1); the words being thus regarded as a very early (2nd cent.) insertion. There was no motive for omission; and the thought which they convey is given in i. 18.

(3) The third case, *vv.* 31, 32, is of a different kind. Of the words in question καί is omitted by overwhelming authority, and may be set aside at once.

The words ἐπάνω πάντων ἐστί are omitted by

(α) MSS.: ℵ[1]D 1 and a few mss.
(β) *Versions:* (*Old Lat.*), *Old Syr.*, *Arm.*
(γ) *Fathers:* Orig., Eus., (Tert.), Hil.

They are found in

(α) MSS.: ℵ^{c}ABLT^b and all others (C is defective).

(β) *Versions:* (*Old Lat.*, some), *Vulg.*, *Memph.*, *Syr. P.* and *Hcl.*, *Æth.*

(γ) *Fathers:* (Orig.), Chrys., (Tert.), (Orig. *int.*).

The authorities for omission represent the most ancient element (*Old Lat.*. *Old Syr.*, with ℵ and D) of the authorities for the insertion of the disputed words in (2). It appears, however, from an examination of all the cases of omission by this group (*e.g.* iv. 9), that its weight is far greater for omission than for the addition or the substitution of words. In this case the motive (1) for the repetition of *ἐπάνω πάντων ἐστίν*, and then (2) for the addition of *καί*, is sufficiently clear. The words therefore cannot but be regarded with great suspicion; and the sense certainly does not lose by their absence. On the contrary, the opposition of *ὁ ὢν ἐκ τῆς γῆς ἐκ τῆς γῆς λαλεῖ* to *ὁ ἐκ τοῦ οὐρανοῦ ἐρχόμενος ὃ ἑώρακεν καὶ ἤκουσεν τοῦτο μαρτυρεῖ* becomes far more impressive if the words in question are omitted.

CHAPTER IV.

1 *Christ talketh with a woman of Samaria, and revealeth himself unto her.* 27 *His disciples marvel.* 31 *He declareth to them his zeal to God's glory.* 39 *Many Samaritans believe on him.* 43 *He departeth into Galilee, and healeth the ruler's son that lay sick at Capernaum.*

WHEN therefore the Lord knew
how the Pharisees had heard
that Jesus made and baptized more
disciples than John,
2 (Though Jesus himself baptized
not, but his disciples,)
3 He left Judæa, and departed
again into Galilee.
4 And he must needs go through
Samaria.
5 Then cometh he to a city of Sa-

---

2. THE WORK IN SAMARIA (iv. 1—42).

This section consists of three parts. The opening verses (1—3) form the historical transition from the notice of the teaching in Judæa (iii. 22 ff.). This is followed by the detailed account of the Lord's conversation with the Samaritan woman (4—38), and by a summary of His intercourse with the people (39—42).

The whole section is peculiar to St John, and bears evident traces of being the record of an eye-witness. Other notices of the Lord's dealing with Samaritans are found Luke ix. 52 ff., xvii. 16. Comp. Luke x. 33.

CHAP. IV. **1—3.** The Lord changes the scene of His ministry that He may avoid a premature collision with the Pharisaic party. Comp. vii. 1, x. 39 f.

These verses serve as a transition passage. The Lord left Judæa, as He had left Jerusalem, and went again to Galilee, there to carry on His prophet's work.

1. *When therefore the Lord knew...*] The word *therefore* carries back the reader to the narrative, iii. 22 ff. The action which roused controversy was necessarily notorious. Nothing implies that the knowledge of the Lord was supernatural (see ii. 24, note). It could not but be that as Christ's work spread, He should become acquainted with the thoughts which it revealed outside the circle of His disciples.

the Lord] The absolute title occurs in the narrative of St John, vi. 23, xi. 2, xx. 20. Comp. xx. 2, 13, 18, 25, xxi. 7. It is found also not unfrequently in the narrative of St Luke, x. 1, xvii. 5 f., xxii. 61, &c.

the Pharisees] If they heard of the success of Christ's teaching, and the word perhaps implies that they continued to observe the new Prophet who had appeared at Jerusalem, there could be no doubt how they would regard Him. It is worthy of notice that St John never notices (by name) the Sadducees or the Herodians. The Pharisees were the true representatives of the unbelieving nation.

The direct form of the sentence reproduces the message which was brought to them: *Jesus* [whose name they knew] **is making and baptizing** *more disciples than John.*

than John] had done, as by this time he was probably thrown into prison. Though John had more points of contact with the Pharisees than Christ, coming as he did *in the way of righteousness*, even he had excited their apprehensions. Cf. Matt. xxi. 32.

2. *Though* (**And yet,** *καίτοιγε*) *Jesus...*] The words are a correction of the report which has been just quoted. Comp. iii. 26. Christ did not personally baptize (comp. iii. 22) because this Judaic baptism was simply a symbolic act, the work of the servant and not of the Lord. The sacrament of baptism presupposes the Death and Resurrection of Christ. This is very well set forth by Tertullian, 'de Bapt.' 11.

3. *He left*] The original word (*ἀφίημι*) is a very remarkable one (*καταλείπω* might have been expected, Matt. iv. 13, Heb. xi. 27); and there is no exact parallel in the New Test. to this usage (yet compare ch. xvi. 28). The general idea which it conveys seems to be that of leaving anything to itself, to its own

maria, which is called Sychar, near to
33. the parcel of ground [a] that Jacob gave
18.
h. to his son Joseph.
6 Now Jacob's well was there.
Jesus therefore, being wearied with
his journey, sat thus on the well:
and it was about the sixth hour.
7 There cometh a woman of Sa-

---

wishes, ways, fate; of withdrawing whatever controlling power was exercised before. Christ had claimed Jerusalem as the seat of His royal power, and Judæa as His kingdom. That claim He now in one sense gave up.

again] The reference is to i. 43. There was a danger of confusing these two visits to Galilee in the Synoptic accounts. St John therefore sharply distinguishes them.

into Galilee] Where His preaching would excite less hostility on the part of the religious heads of the people, while they would also have less power there.

The Conversation with the Woman of Samaria (4—38).

The record of the conversation consists of two main parts, (1) the account of the conversation itself (4—26), and (2) the account of its issues (27—38), both immediately (27—30), and in its spiritual lessons (31—38).

The whole passage forms a striking contrast and complement to iii. 1—21. The woman, the Samaritan, the sinner, is placed over against the Rabbi, the ruler of the Jews, the Pharisee. The nature of worship takes the place of the necessity of the new birth; yet so that either truth leads up to the other. The new birth is the condition for entrance into the Kingdom: true worship flows from Christ's gift.

There is at the same time a remarkable similarity of method in Christ's teaching in the two cases. Immediate circumstances, the wind and the water, furnished present parables, through which deeper thoughts were suggested, fitted to call out the powers and feelings of a sympathetic listener.

The mode in which the Lord dealt with the woman finds a parallel in the Synoptic Gospels, Luke vii. 37 ff. Comp. Matt. xxvi. 6 ff. The other scattered notices of the Lord's intercourse with women form a fruitful subject for study, ch. xi., xx. 14 ff.; Matt. ix. 20 and parallels, xv. 22 ff. and parallels, xxvii. 55 and parallels, xxviii. 9 f.; Luke viii. 2 f., x. 38 ff., xi. 27 f., xiii. 11 ff.

4—26. The order of thought in the conversation is perfectly natural. A simple request raises the question of the difference of Jew and Samaritan (4—9). The thought of this difference gives occasion to the suggestion of a unity springing from a gift of love greater than that of "a cup of cold water" (*v.* 10). How can such a gift be conceived of? how can a poor wayfarer provide it (*v.* 11 f.)? The answer lies in the description of its working (*vv.* 13 f.). Then follows the personal petition (*v.* 15), followed by the personal conviction (*vv.* 16 ff.), and confession (*v.* 19). This leads to the expression of a central religious difficulty (*v.* 20), which Christ resolves (21—24). Hereupon the word of faith (*v.* 25) is crowned by the self-revelation of Christ (*v.* 26).

4. *must needs*] *i.e.* this was the natural route from Jerusalem to Galilee. Josephus ('Antiq.' xx. 5. 1) speaks of it as that usually adopted by Galilæan pilgrims; and in one place uses the same phrase as St John: "Those who wish to go away quickly [from Galilee to Jerusalem] must needs (ἔδει) go through Samaria, for in this way it is possible to reach Jerusalem from Galilee in three days" ('Vita,' § 52). Sometimes travellers went on the other side of Jordan. Comp. Luke ix. 52 f. This "passing through" gave occasion for a prophetic revelation of the future extension of the Gospel (comp. Acts i. 8), and stands in no opposition to the special charge to the Apostles, Matt. x. 5.

5. *Then cometh he...*] **So** (οὖν) **he cometh...**

a city...which is called Sychar...] **a city called** *Sychar*, as xi. 54; Matt. ii. 23. The term "city" is used widely, as in the passages quoted, and does not imply any considerable size, but rather one of the "little walled villages with which every eminence is crowned."

Sychar] This name has been commonly regarded as an intentional corruption of *Sichem* (Acts vii. 16, *Shechem*, *Neapolis*, *Nablous*) as signifying either "drunken-town" (Isai. xxviii, 1, שֵׁכָר) or "lying-town" (Hab. ii. 18, שֶׁקֶר). But the earlier writers (*e.g.* Euseb. 'Onom.' s. v.) distinguish Shechem and Sychar; and the latter is said to lie "in front of Neapolis." Moreover a place Sychar (עין סוכר, סוכרא, סוכר) is mentioned several times in the Talmud; and it is scarcely possible that so famous a place as Shechem would be referred to as Sychar is referred to here. There is at present a village, *'Askar*, which corresponds admirably with the required site. The name appears in a transitional form in a Samaritan Chronicle of the 12th cent. as *Iskar* (Conder, in 'Palestine Exploration Report,' 1877, p. 150). Compare Delitzsch 'Ztschr. f. Luth. Theol.' 1856, pp. 240 ff., who has collected the Talmudic passages.

the parcel of ground (χωρίον, Vulg. *prædium*, comp. Matt. xxvi. 36)...*Joseph*] Comp. Gen. xxxiii. 19, xlviii. 22 (xxxiv. 25); Josh. xxiv. 32. The blessing of Jacob treated the purchase which he had made, and the warlike act of his sons in the district, as a pledge of the future conquests of the sons of **Joseph, to**

maria to draw water: Jesus saith unto her, Give me to drink.
8 (For his disciples were gone away unto the city to buy meat.)
9 Then saith the woman of Samaria unto him, How is it that thou, being a Jew, askest drink of me, which am a woman of Samaria? for

---

whom he gives the region as a portion (שְׁכֶם). The LXX. play upon the word and introduce *Shechem* (Σίκιμα) as the substantial (not literal) rendering. In recognition of the promise the bones of Joseph were deposited at Shechem on the occupation of Palestine (Josh. xxiv. 32; Acts vii. 15, 16).

6. *Jacob's well*] *Jacob's* **spring**. The word "spring" (πηγή, עַיִן, Vulg. *fons*) is used here (twice) and in *v.* 14. Comp. James iii. 11 (βρύει); Rev. vii. 17, xxi. 6, and *well* (φρέαρ, בְּאֵר, *puteus*) in *vv.* 11, 12. Comp. Rev. ix. 1, 2. Both names are still given to the well, *Ain Yakûb* and *Bîr-el-Yakûb*. The labour of constructing the well in the neighbourhood of abundant natural springs, shews that it was the work of a "stranger in the land." Comp. Gen. xxvi. 19. Lieut. Anderson, who descended to the bottom in May, 1866, found it then seventy-five feet deep and quite dry. "It is," he says, "lined throughout with rough masonry, as it is dug in alluvial soil" (Warren's 'Recovery of Jerusalem,' pp. 464 f.). The well is now being carefully examined and restored under the direction of the Palestine Exploration Society ('Report,' 1877, p. 72).

wearied] It is important to notice in St John the clearest traces of the Lord's perfect manhood. He alone preserves the word "I thirst" in the account of the Passion, xix. 28.

thus] The word may mean (1) either "thus wearied as He was," or (2) simply, just as He was, without preparation or further thought. In the former sense it would have been natural that the adverb should precede the verb (οὕτως ἐκαθέζετο) as in Acts vii. 8, xx. 11, xxvii. 17.

on the well] **by the spring** (ἐπί, ch. v. 2).

and it was...the sixth hour] The clause stands by itself: **It** *was*... The time indicated is probably six in the evening. The night would not close so rapidly as to make the subsequent description (*v.* 35) impossible. Compare Additional Note on ch. xix.

7. *a woman of Samaria*] A *woman*, and as such lightly regarded by the popular doctors (comp. *v.* 27): a *Samaritan*, and as such despised by the Jews. Thus prejudices of sex and nation were broken down by this first teaching of the Lord beyond the limit of the chosen people. Yet more, the woman was not only an alien, but also poor; for *to draw water* was no longer, as in patriarchal times (Gen. xxiv. 15, xxix. 9 ff.; Exod. ii. 16 f.; comp. Tristram, 'Land of Israel,' pp. 25 f.), the work of women of station.

The later legends give the woman the significant name *Photina*.

Give me to drink] The request must be taken in its literal and obvious meaning (*v.* 6); but at the same time to ask was in this case to give. The Teacher first met His hearer on the common ground of simple humanity, and conceded to her the privilege of conferring a favour.

8. *For his disciples*] If they had been present they could have supplied the want. "Something to draw with" (*v.* 11), a "bucket" of skin, often found by the well sides, would form naturally part of the equipment of the little travelling party. This seems to be a better explanation of the reason than to suppose that the absence of the disciples gave the opportunity for the conversation.

were gone away] Perhaps St John remained with Christ. The narrative is more like that of an eye-witness than a secondary account derived from the woman, or even from the Lord Himself. Yet it may be urged that *v.* 33 naturally suggests that the Lord had been left alone.

meat] *i.e. food*, as commonly (Matt. iii. 4, vi. 25, &c.), but here only in the New Testament in the plural. Eggs, fruit, and the like might be purchased from Samaritans, as they could not contract defilement. Compare Lightfoot on *v.* 4. The later rules however were stricter. "To eat the bread of a Samaritan" it was said "was as eating the flesh of swine."

9. *Then saith the woman of Samaria...*] **The Samaritan woman therefore saith** ... The form in this verse (ἡ γ. ἡ Σαμαρεῖτις) is different from that in *v.* 7 (γ. ἐκ τῆς Σ.). The stress is laid on character as implied in national descent and not on mere local connexion.

The strangeness of the request startles the woman; "What further," she seems to ask, "lies behind this request?" The original is perfectly symmetrical (*thou which art a Jew ...of me which am a Samaritan woman...*). There is force also in the distinct addition of the word *woman* (γυναικός). That the request was made not only of a Samaritan but of a woman completed the wonder of the questioner.

thou, being a Jew] Some peculiarity of dress or dialect or accent would shew this (comp. Mark xiv. 70).

for the Jews have no dealings with the Samaritans] **for Jews...with Samaritans.** These words, which are omitted by an important group of ancient authorities, are, if genuine,

the Jews have no dealings with the Samaritans.

10 Jesus answered and said unto her, If thou knewest the gift of God, and who it is that saith to thee, Give me to drink; thou wouldest have asked of him, and he would have given thee living water.

11 The woman saith unto him, Sir, thou hast nothing to draw with, and the well is deep: from whence then hast thou that living water?

---

an explanatory note of the Evangelist. In this relation the present form (*have no dealings*) is remarkable. The origin of the hostility of the two peoples, which lasts to the present day, may be traced to the Assyrian colonisation of the land of Israel (2 K. xvii. 24). From this followed the antagonism of the Samaritans to the Jews at the Return (Ezra iv., Neh. vi., which led to the erection of a rival temple on Mount Gerizim. Comp. Ecclus. l. 25, 26. 'Dict. of Bible,' III. p. 1117.

have...dealings] The original word (συγχρῶνται, Vulg. *coutuntur*) suggests the relations of familiar intercourse and not of business. Offices of kindness were not expected between Jews and Samaritans. The spirit of religious bitterness still lingers on the spot. "On asking drink from a woman [near Nablous] who was filling her pitcher, we were angrily and churlishly refused:—'The Christian dogs might get it for themselves'" (Tristram, 'Land of Israel,' p. 134, ed. 3).

10. *If thou knewest* (**hadst known**) *the gift of God...*] The words are, as commonly in St John's Gospel, an answer to the essential idea of the foregoing question. The woman had sought an explanation of the marvel that a Jew should ask a favour of a Samaritan woman. This however, as she dimly guessed, was only a part of the new mystery. The frank appeal to a human charity deeper than religious antagonism did indeed indicate a possibility of union greater than hope. Had she known what God had now done for men, and who that Jewish Teacher was whom she saw, she would herself have boldly asked of Him a favour far greater than He had asked of her, and would have received it at once: she would have become the petitioner, and not have wondered at the petition: her present difficulty would have been solved by her apprehension of the new revelation which had been made not to Jew or Samaritan but to man. Had she known *the gift of God*, the gift of His Son (iii. 16) in which was included all that man could want, she would have felt that needs of which she was partly conscious (*v.* 25) could at length be satisfied. Had she known *who it was that said to her*, *Give me to drink*. she would have laid open her prayer to Him without reserve or doubt, assured of His sympathy and help.

the gift] The word here used (δωρεά) occurs only in this place in the Gospels. It carries with it something of the idea of bounty, honour, privilege; and is used of the gift of the Spirit (Acts ii. 38, viii. 20, x. 45, xi. 17), and of the gift of redemption in Christ (Rom. v. 15; 2 Cor. ix. 15), manifested in various ways (Eph. iii. 7, iv. 7; Hebr. vi. 4). This usage shews that there is here a general reference to the blessings given to men in the revelation of the Son, and not a simple description of what was given to the woman in the fact of her interview with Christ. "The gift of God" is all that is freely offered in the Son.

thou wouldest have asked] The pronoun is emphatic (σὺ ἂν ᾔτ.).

living water] that is perennial, springing from an unfailing source (Gen. xxvi. 19), ever flowing fresh (Lev. xiv. 5). The request which Christ had made furnished the idea of a parable; the bodily want whereby He suffered suggested an image of the spiritual blessing which He was ready to bestow.

The Jews were already familiar with the application of the phrase (*living water*) to the quickening energies which proceed from God (Zech. xiv. 8; Jer. ii. 13, xvii. 13. Comp. *v.* 14, note), though it may be doubtful how far the prophetic language would be known to Samaritans. Here the words indicate that which on the divine side answers to the spiritual thirst, the aspirations of men for fellowship with God. This under various aspects may be regarded as the Revelation of the Truth, or the gift of the Holy Spirit, individually or socially, or whatever, according to varying circumstances, leads to that eternal life (*v.* 14) which consists in the knowledge of God and His Son Jesus Christ (xvii. 3).

11, 12. The woman's answer is in spirit exactly like the first. Her thoughts reach forward to some truth which she feels to be as yet far from her. How can she conceive of the gift? The well of Jacob is, in one sense, a well of "living water," yet it cannot be that which supplies the Speaker with His gift, for "the well is deep," and He has "nothing to draw with." He offers in word that for which He asks. How again can she conceive of Him who speaks to her? He is wearied and thirsty, and yet professes to command resources which were sealed to the patriarchs.

11. *the well is deep*] The well is at present partially choked up with rubbish. See *v.* 6, note. In Maundrell's time (March,

12 Art thou greater than our father Jacob, which gave us the well, and drank thereof himself, and his children, and his cattle?

13 Jesus answered and said unto her, Whosoever drinketh of this water shall thirst again:

14 But whosoever drinketh of the water that I shall give him shall never thirst; but the water that I shall give him shall be in him a well of water springing up into everlasting life.

15 The woman saith unto him,

1697), it was 105 feet deep and had fifteen feet of water in it. Dr Tristram found in it only "wet mud" in December ('Land of Israel,' p. 143, ed. 3), but towards the end of February it was "full of water" (*id.* p. 401).

that living water] Simply **the** *living water*, whereof thou speakest.

12. *Art thou*] The pronoun is emphatic: "Art thou, a poor, wearied traveller, of more commanding power than the patriarch who gained by labour what he gave us?"

our father Jacob] The Samaritans claimed descent from Joseph as representing the ancient tribes of Ephraim and Manasseh. (Joseph. 'Ant.' XI. 8. 6.)

gave us] left, that is, to his descendants as a precious heritage. The tradition is independent of the Old Testament.

children] **sons**, the special representatives of his house.

cattle] The original word (θρέμματα, Vulg. *pecora*) may mean slaves, but the sense given in A. V. is more natural. The well was sufficient for large wants. The word occurs here only in the New Testament, and is not found in LXX.

13, 14. The words of Christ carry on the parable of the tenth verse, and in doing so still answer the thought and not the words of the woman. They imply that she had felt rightly that it was some other water than that for which Christ asked which He was waiting to give: that one greater than Jacob was there. The water which the patriarch had drunk and given satisfied a want for the moment: the living water satisfied a want for ever, and in such a way that a fresh and spontaneous source supplied each recurrent need of refreshment.

The mode in which the new thought is developed corresponds exactly with vi. 49 f.

13. *Whosoever*] More exactly, **Every one that...** The form of expression is contrasted with the hypothetical *whosoever* in *v.* 14. With this change of form follows also a change of tense (ὁ πίνων = habitual; ὃς ἂν πίῃ = once for all).

of this water] pointing to the well.

14. *that I shall give*] The pronoun in the first case is emphatic and carries the answer to the contrast which the woman had drawn between Jacob and Christ. The gift, consequent in its realisation upon the fulfilment of Christ's work, is still future (ἐγὼ δώσω).

shall never...] The phrase (οὐ μὴ...εἰς τὸν αἰῶνα) is a very remarkable one, and recurs viii. 51, 52, x. 28, xi. 26, xiii. 8. Elsewhere it is found in the New Testament in 1 Cor. viii. 13, where the translation "I will eat no flesh while the world standeth" expresses the literal force of the words.

thirst] in the sense of feeling the pain of an unsatisfied want, Rev. vii. 16. But the divine life and the divine wisdom bring no satiety, Ecclus. xxiv. 21.

shall be...a well of water...everlasting life] *shall* **become**...*a* **spring** *of water...* **eternal** *life*. It shall not serve for the moment only, but shall also preserve power to satisfy all future wants if it be appropriated by the receiver. The communication of the divine energy, as a gift of life, necessarily manifests itself in life. The blessing welcomed proves a spring of blessing, which rises towards and issues in *eternal life;* for this is as the infinite ocean in which all divine gifts find their end and consummation. The life comes from the Source of life and ascends to Him again.

The image is developed in three stages. Christ's gift is as a spring of water, of water leaping up in rich abundance, and that not perishing or lost but going forth to the noblest fulfilment.

springing up into] The original word (ἁλλομένου εἰς) describes the "leaping" of a thing of life, and not the mere "gushing up" of a fountain.

There is a Jewish saying that "when the Prophets speak of water they mean the Law" (Wünsche, *ad loc.*). The Incarnate Word was what the Scribes wished to make the Scriptures. Compare also 'Aboth,' I. 4; 12.

15. The relation of the persons is now changed. A greater want supersedes the less. The woman is no longer able to follow the thoughts which lie before her in their mysterious depth; but at least she can ask for the gift which has already been assured to her (*v.* 10). She seeks a favour in turn before she has granted that which was sought of her. *Sir, give me this water, that I thirst not, neither come hither to draw.* The gift appeared to her to have two virtues, corresponding to the twofold description just given of it. It would satisfy her own personal wants: and it would also, as being a source of blessing no less than

Sir, give me this water, that I thirst not, neither come hither to draw.

16 Jesus saith unto her, Go, call thy husband, and come hither.

17 The woman answered and said, I have no husband. Jesus said unto her, Thou hast well said, I have no husband:

18 For thou hast had five husbands; and he whom thou now hast is not thy husband: in that saidst thou truly.

19 The woman saith unto him, Sir, I perceive that thou art a prophet.

20 Our fathers worshipped in this mountain; and ye say, that in [b] Jerusalem is the place where men ought to worship.

[b] Deut. 12. 5.

---

a blessing, enable her to satisfy the wants of those to whom she had to minister.

come hither] The original word according to the best authorities (διέρχωμαι) gives the idea of "come all the way hither" across the intervening plain.

16. *Jesus* (**He**) *saith...* The apparently abrupt transition seems to be suggested by the last words of *v.* 15. In those the speaker passed beyond herself. She confessed by implication that even the greatest gift was not complete unless it was shared by those to whom she was bound. If they thirsted, though she might not thirst, her toilsome labour must be fulfilled still. According to this interpretation Christ again reads her thought; and bids her summon him to whom it was her duty to minister. The gift was for him also; and the command was at the same time a test of the woman's awakening faith.

17. *I have no husband*] The words are half sad, half apologetic, as of one who shrinks from the trial conscious of weakness, and who seeks further assurance of power before rendering complete obedience. The command might disprove the knowledge and claims of the mysterious Teacher. The exact form of the Lord's answer suggests that a pause for a brief space followed. *Jesus said* (**saith**) *to her, Thou saidst well, I have no husband...in that thou hast said truly.* The plea had been left, as it were, to be solemnly pondered (**Thou saidst**, not *Thou hast said*), and the transposition of the words in the repetition of it, by which the emphasis is thrown in the original on *husband* which lay before on *I have not*, at once reveals how the thoughts of the woman were laid bare.

well said] It is possible that there is something of a sad irony in the words, as there is in Matt. vii. 9; 2 Cor. xi. 4.

18. *five husbands*] Though the facilities for divorce are said to have been fewer among the Samaritans than among the Jews, there is no reason to suppose that the woman's former marriages were illegally dissolved. That which was true in her statement pointed the rebuke. Her present position, though dishonourable, was not expressly forbidden by the Mosaic Law.

The singular details which are given of the woman's life have led many commentators to regard her as offering in her personal history a figure of the religious history of her people, which had been united to and separated from "five gods" (Jos. 'Antt.' IX. 14. 3; 2 K. xvii. 29 ff.), and was at last irregularly serving the true God.

in that saidst thou truly] **this thou hast said** *truly.* The form is different (εἴρηκας) from that used in *v.* 17 (εἶπας).

19. *I perceive*] The word (θεωρῶ) marks contemplation, continued progressive vision, not immediate perception. See ii. 23. We cannot tell in what way the Lord's words were more significant to the woman than to us (see i. 48, 49), but they evidently bore with them to her a complete conviction that her whole life was open to the eyes of the speaker (*v.* 29).

a prophet] The emphasis lies on the title and not on the pronoun (ὅτι προφήτης εἶ σύ). The first thought in the Samaritan's mind is that the connexion of man with God has been authoritatively restored; and if so, then, she argues, it may be that discrepancies as to local worship will be solved.

20. *Our fathers ... and ye say ...*] To the student of the law the exclusive establishment of worship at Jerusalem must have been a great difficulty. To a Samaritan no question could appear more worthy of a prophet's decision than the settlement of the religious centre of the world. Thus the difficulty which is proposed is not a diversion, but the natural thought of one brought face to face with an interpreter of the divine will.

Our fathers] that is, either simply our ancestors from the time of the erection of the Samaritan Temple after the Return, or, more probably, the patriarchs. See below. The Samaritan Temple was destroyed by John Hyrcanus c. B.C. 129 (Jos. 'Antt.' XIII. 9. 1).

worshipped] For this absolute use of the verb (προσκυνεῖν) see xii. 20; Rev. v. 14 (true reading); Acts viii. 27, xxiv. 11.

in this mountain] pointing to Mount Gerizim, at the foot of which the well lies. According to the Samaritan tradition it was on this mountain that Abraham prepared the

21 Jesus saith unto her, Woman, believe me, the hour cometh, when ye shall neither in this mountain, nor yet at Jerusalem, worship the Father.

22 Ye worship ye know not what: we know what we worship: for salvation is of the Jews.

23 But the hour cometh, and now

---

sacrifice of Isaac, and here also that he met Melchisedek. In Deut. xxvii. 12 f. Gerizim is mentioned as the site on which the six tribes stood who were to pronounce the blessings for the observance of the law. And in the Samaritan Pentateuch, Gerizim and not Ebal is the mountain on which the altar was erected, Deut. xxvii. 4.

The natural reference to the unnamed mountain is an unmistakable trait from the life.

A striking passage is quoted from 'Bereshith R.' § 32, by Lightfoot and Wünsche: "R. Jochanan, going to Jerusalem to pray, passed by [Gerizim]. A certain Samaritan seeing him asked him, Whither goest thou? I am, saith he, going to Jerusalem to pray. To whom the Samaritan, Were it not better for thee to pray in this holy mountain than in that cursed house?" Compare 'Bereshith R.' § 81.

and ye say ...] *ye* (ὑμεῖς), on your side... The whole problem is stated in its simplest form. The two facts are placed side by side (*and*, not *but*), traditional practice, Jewish teaching.

the place] that is, the one temple.

ought to worship] **must** *worship* (*v.* 24), according to a divine obligation (δεῖ). Comp. iii. 30, note.

21. The rival claims of Gerizim and Jerusalem are not determined by the Lord, for they vanish in the revelation of a universal religion.

Woman, believe me] The true form of the original (πίστευέ μοι) marks the present beginning of faith, which is to grow to something riper. Compare x. 38, xii. 36, xiv. 1, 11. On the other hand, the single act of faith is marked (πίστευσον) in Acts xvi. 31. In the two parallel narratives, Mark v. 36, Luke viii. 50 (πίστευσον), the two forms are used: that which is general and continuous in the first passage is concentrated into a special act in the second by the addition of, "and she shall be saved." In the present connexion the unique phrase (*believe me*) corresponds to the familiar "Verily, verily," as introducing a great truth. Comp. Mal. i. 11.

the (rather *an*) *hour cometh*] This consummation was still future. The temple still claimed the reverent homage of believers (ii. 16). Contrast *v.* 23.

the hour] There is a divine order in accordance with which each part of the whole scheme of salvation is duly fulfilled. Comp. v. 25, 28, xvi. 2, 4, 25, 32. So Christ had "His hour," ii. 4, note.

neither ... nor yet (**nor**) *at Jerusalem*] The two centres of worship are spoken of in the same terms (οὔτε ... οὔτε) in the prospect of the future.

worship the Father] The word *worship* was used indefinitely in *v.* 20: here it finds its true complement. The object of worship determines its conditions. He who is known as the Father finds His home where His children are. This absolute use of the title, "the Father," is characteristic of St John, and almost peculiar to him. Other examples are found, Matt. xi. 27 and parallels; Acts i. 4, 7; Rom. vi. 4; Eph. ii. 18. See Additional Note. The revelation of God as the Father sums up the new tidings of the Gospel. In this place the title stands in a significant relation to the boast of a special descent (*our fathers*, *v.* 20).

22. *Ye* (emphatic) *worship ye know not what* (**that which ye know not**) (Vulg. *adoratis quod nescitis*)] Your worship, that is, is directed to One with whose character, as He has revealed Himself through the prophets and in the history of His people, you are really unacquainted. You know whom to worship, but you do not know Him. By confining your faith to the law you condemn yourselves to ignorance of the God of Israel. *We* Jews, on the other hand (the pronoun again is emphatic), *worship* **that which we know**; *for* the promised *salvation is of the Jews*. The power of Judaism lay in the fact that it was not simple deism, but the gradual preparation for the Incarnation. The Jew therefore *knew that which he worshipped*, so far as the will, and in that the nature, of God was gradually unfolded before him. Contrast viii. 54.

ye ... we ...] The sharp contrast between Samaritans and Jews which runs through the narrative (*vv.* 9, 20, *ye say*), and the pointed reference to "the Jews" which follows, fix beyond all reasonable doubt the interpretation of the pronouns.

what ...] not *Him whom* ... The abstract form suggests the notion of God, so far as His attributes and purposes were made known, rather than of God as a Person, revealed to men at last in the Son: xiv. 9. Compare Acts xvii. 23 (ὃ οὖν).

salvation] Rather, *the* promised and expected *salvation* (ἡ σωτηρία) to be realised in the mission of Messiah. So Acts iv. 12. Compare Acts xiii. 26. See also Rev. vii. 10, xii. 10, xix. 1.

is of ...] that is, "proceeds from" (ἐστὶν ἐκ), not "belongs to." Comp. i. 46, note,

is, when the true worshippers shall worship the Father in spirit and in truth: for the Father seeketh such to worship him.

24 [c]God *is* a Spirit: and they that worship him must worship *him* in spirit and in truth.

[c] 2 Cor. 3. 17.

25 The woman saith unto him, I

---

vii. 22, 52, (x. 16). The thought is expressed in a symbol in Rev. xii. 5.

23. *But...*] The old differences of more and less perfect knowledge were to be done away.

the (rather *an*) *hour cometh, and now is*] The presence of Christ among men brought with it this result at once, though local worship (*v.* 21) was not yet abolished. Compare v. 25 as contrasted with v. 28. In each case the subtle contrast between the immediate and ultimate issues which are pointed to is most significant and characteristic of the exact circumstances to which the words belong. See also xvi. 25, 32.

the true worshippers] The original term "true" (ἀληθινός) describes that which is not only truly but also completely what it professes to be. Thus it is used in connexion with those material objects under which Christ represents Himself. See i. 9, vi. 32, vii. 28, viii. 16, xv. 1, note, xvii. 3, xix. 35. The popular sense of the word "ideal"—fulfilling the complete conception—comes near to this usage.

in spirit and (om. *in*) *truth*] The words describe the characteristics of worship in one complex phrase (ἐν πνεύματι καὶ ἀληθείᾳ) and not in two co-ordinate phrases. Worship involves an expression of feeling and a conception of the object towards whom the feeling is entertained. The expression is here described as made *in spirit:* the conception as formed *in truth.* Judaism (speaking generally) was a worship of the letter and not of spirit (to take examples from the time): Samaritanism was a worship of falsehood and not of truth. By the Incarnation men are enabled to have immediate communion with God, and thus a worship in spirit has become possible: at the same time the Son is a complete manifestation of God for men, and thus a worship in truth has been placed within their reach. These two characteristics answer to the higher sense of the second and third commandments, the former of which tends to a spiritual service, and the latter to a devout regard for the "name" of God, that is, for every revelation of His Person or attributes or action.

spirit] In biblical language, that part of man's nature which holds, or is capable of holding, intercourse with the eternal order is the spirit (1 Thess. v. 23). The spirit in man responds to the Spirit of God. Comp. vi. 63. The sphere of worship was therefore now to be that highest region where the divine and human meet, and not, as in an earlier period of discipline, material or fleshly. Comp. Rom. i. 9.

truth] Worship is necessarily limited by the idea of the being worshipped. A true idea of God is essential to a right service of Him. Comp. Hebr. viii. 5, x. 1.

for] The phrase in the original (καὶ γάρ, Vulg. *nam et*) is remarkable. It alleges a reason which is assumed to be conclusive from the nature of the case: *for the Father also on His part*, which is expressed fairly by *for in fact*, *for indeed.* Comp. Matt. viii. 9 and parallel, xxvi. 73 and parallels; Mark x. 45; Luke vi. 32 ff., xi. 4, xxii. 37; Acts xix. 40; Rom. xi. 1, and not unfrequently in St Paul.

seeketh] There is a real correspondence between the true worshipper and God. Comp. i. 43 (*findeth*), note. The true (ἀληθινός) worshipper answers to the true (ἀληθινός) God (xvii. 3).

such to worship him] *such* **for His worshippers.**

24. *God is a Spirit*] *God is* **Spirit**, absolutely free from all limitations of space and time. The nature and not the personality of God is described, just as in the phrases, *God is light* (1 John i. 5), or *God is love* (1 John iv. 8). This premiss is drawn from a true interpretation of the old revelation (Isai. xxxi. 3), but the conclusion which follows belongs to the new. The declaration in its majestic simplicity is unique; though St John implies in the two other revelations of God's being which he has given (*ll. cc.*) the truth which is declared by it.

worship him in spirit and in truth] More exactly, **worship in spirit and truth** (*v.* 23).

25. The woman's answer to the declaration made to her helps us to understand why it was made. She had acknowledged the Lord as a prophet, but she felt that such truths could be affirmed only by one who was more than a prophet, and for such a one she looked. In her hope Messiah was the perfect lawgiver and not the conqueror. Truth and not dominion was the blessing she connected with His mission. The confession, like the revelation by which it was followed, is unique in the gospels.

I know] Compare iii. 2, *we know.* The object and the ground of knowledge are characteristically different.

which is called Christ] The words may be part of the speech of the woman, in which case they imply that the Greek title was that which was popularly current (cf. *v.* 29). At

know that Messias cometh, which is called Christ: when he is come, he will tell us all things.

26 Jesus saith unto her, I that speak unto thee am *he*.

27 ¶ And upon this came his disciples, and marvelled that he talked with the woman: yet no man said, What seekest thou? or, Why talkest thou with her?

28 The woman then left her waterpot, and went her way into the city, and saith to the men,

29 Come, see a man, which told me all things that ever I did: is not this the Christ?

30 Then they went out of the city, and came unto him.

31 ¶ In the mean while his disciples prayed him, saying, Master, eat.

---

least, the different form in which the interpretation is given in i. 41 must be noticed. This exact form (ὁ λεγόμενος χριστός) is used as part of a title elsewhere, xi. 16, xx. 24, xxi. 2 (cf. Luke xxii. 1).

For the Samaritan conceptions of Messiah see 'Introd. to Study of the Gospels,' pp. 159 f.

when he is come] *when He* **comes.** The pronoun (ἐκεῖνος) is emphatic, and fixes the attention on Messiah as contrasted with, and standing apart from, all other teachers.

he will tell us all things] More exactly, *He will announce all things unto us.* The word (ἀναγγελεῖ, Vulg. *adnunciabit*) is used of the fresh and authoritative message of the Advocate, xvi. 13 ff. The teaching so given would be absolute and complete.

26. The woman was prepared to welcome Messiah in His prophetic dignity, and in this He makes Himself known to her. Compare ix. 35 ff. In each case the revelation answers to the faith of the recipient. With these acknowledgments prompted by grace contrast the acknowledgment yielded to legal authority, Matt. xxvi. 63, 64.

I that speak] Or rather, *I that talk* (ὁ λαλῶν): the word suggests the notion of free, familiar conversation, which is brought out in the next verse. It was by this intercourse of loving and searching sympathy, that Christ revealed Himself as the hope of men. Comp. ix. 37, note.

27—30. The conversation being ended, its immediate effects are noticed. The disciples reverently wonder. The woman is filled with a hope beyond hope. Her countrymen are moved by her enthusiasm. The whole picture is full of life.

27. *And...came and marvelled...*] *And... came; and* **they** *marvelled.* The change of tense, which marks the pause of wonder, requires the insertion of the pronoun.

talked with the woman] **was talking with a woman**, against the custom of the doctors by whom it was said that "a man should not salute a woman in a public place, not even his own wife," and that it was "better that the words of the law should be burnt than delivered to women." Compare 'Aboth' I. 5 (Taylor); and Buxtorf, 'Lex. Rabb.' p. 1146; and contrast Gal. iii. 28. One of the thanksgivings in the daily service of the Synagogue is: "Blessed art Thou, O Lord... Who hast not made me a woman."

A double question arose in the minds of the disciples. Could their master require a service from a woman? or could He wish to commune with her as a teacher? Yet they were content to wait. In due time He would remove their doubts. Even thus early they had learnt to abide His time.

28. *The woman then left...went her way...*] **So** *the woman left...went* **away...** This time the woman's answer is in action. The Lord had set aside His own want: she set aside her own purpose. But she shewed that her absence was to be but for a brief space by "leaving her water-pot." And meanwhile the message which she bore to the city was for all, for *the men*, the inhabitants generally, and not for her "husband" only.

29. The Samaritan woman, like the first disciples (i. 41, 45), at once tells what she has found, and with the same appeal *Come, see* (i. 46).

all things that ever I did (*that I did*)] The words here and *v.* 39 are more definite in their reference than A. V.; and the truth of the exaggerated phrase lies in the effect which Christ's words had upon the woman's conscience (18 ff.). She was convinced that He knew all, and in the revelation which He had made, she seemed to feel that He had told her all, because He had by that called up all before her eyes.

is not this the Christ?] The original words cannot be so rendered. The form of the woman's question (μήτι οὗτός...; Vulg. *numquid*...?), suggests the great conclusion as something even beyond hope: **Can this be the Christ?** Is it possible to believe that the highest blessing has suddenly been given to us? The form of the sentence grammatically suggests a negative answer (*v.* 33), but hope bursts through it. Compare Matt. xii. 23. The same phrase occurs Matt. xxvi. 22, 25; John viii. 22, xviii. 35; James iii. 11, &c.

30. Omit *Then.* The result of the woman's

32 But he said unto them, I have meat to eat that ye know not of.
33 Therefore said the disciples one to another, Hath any man brought him *ought* to eat?
34 Jesus saith unto them, My meat is to do the will of him that sent me, and to finish his work.
35 Say not ye, There are yet four months, and *then* cometh harvest?

---

message is given abruptly. The trust of the hearers is the measure of her zeal.

came unto] The tense of the original (ἤρχοντο, comp. c. xx. 3) is vividly descriptive. The villagers started on their journey, and are seen, as it were, pursuing it. Comp. *v.* 35. *They went out of the city and* **came on their way towards** *him* (Vulg. *exierunt et veniebant*).

31—38. The deeper lessons of the incident are unfolded when the Lord was left alone with His disciples. Their natural and loving request leads Him to point to wants more truly imperious than those of the body, thus carrying on the teaching of the act and word just given to and by the woman (31—34). The actual, unexpected, condition of the Samaritans, is used to illustrate the urgency and the fruitfulness of the work to which the apostles were called.

31. *his disciples*] **the** *disciples.* The love of the disciples overpowered their wonder. They strive to satisfy the wants of their Master and not their own curiosity (*v.* 27).

prayed] begged, asked (ἠρώτων, Vulg. *rogabant*): *vv.* 40, 47, xii. 21, &c.

Master] The original preserves the Hebrew form **Rabbi** (comp. i. 38) which has been translated here and in ix. 2, xi. 8. Elsewhere *Rabbi* has been rightly kept in this Gospel.

32. *meat to eat that ye* (emphatic) *know not of*] *that ye* **know not**; that is meat of which ye know not the virtue and power. Comp. *v.* 22. For the image, see vi. 27.

33. *one to another*] not venturing to ask more from their Lord. Comp. xvi. 17.

34. *to do...and to finish...*] The exact form of the expression (ἵνα π.) emphasizes the *end* and not the *process*, not *the doing...and finishing* but *that I may do...and finish.* Comp. vi. 29, xv. 8, xvii. 3; 1 John iii. 11, v. 3. The distinction in tenses between the two verbs (ποιῶ, τελειώσω) which is found in the common texts is not supported by the best authorities.

that sent me] Comp. v. 36 f.

finish] **accomplish.** The original word (τελειώσω) is remarkable. It expresses not merely "finishing," "bringing to an end," but "bringing to the true end," "perfecting." It is characteristic of St John, and the Epistle to the Hebrews: ch. v. 36, xvii. 4, 23, xix. 28; 1 John ii. 5, iv. 12, 17 f.; Hebr. ii. 10, v. 9, vii. 28, &c.

his work] Comp. v. 19, note.

34 ff. The train of thought in these verses appears to be this. "My true food lies in working for the fulfilment of my Father's will, and the partial accomplishment of this end is even now before my eyes. You, as you traverse these corn plains, anticipate without doubt the coming harvest. And the labour of the sower is a parable of all spiritual labour. The issue of that labour is not less certain than the issue of this. Nay, further: the spiritual harvest of which that natural harvest is a figure is even now ready for the sickle. In this sense, the reaper already has his reward and the sower through him. For the work of these two is essentially separate. In spiritual labour the homely proverb is fulfilled: He who reaps sows not what he reaps, he who sows reaps not what he sows. Still the joy of the reaper crowns the toil of the sower; and these first-fruits of Samaria, the first-fruits of a spiritual harvest, crown my joy." Comp. Matt. ix. 37, 38.

Say not ye (ὑμεῖς)...*harvest*] These words have been understood in two ways, either (1) as a proverbial saying, marking roughly the interval between some familiar date (seedtime) and harvest; or (2) as a description of the actual state of things at the time, so that when the words were spoken there were four months to the harvest. The emphatic "ye" (*say not ye*), which appears to indicate men's clear calculation of natural events, favours the first interpretation; but the form of the sentence (*there are yet*...) and the period named, which is less than the interval between seedtime and harvest, favour the second. If this latter view be adopted we have an approximate date for the narrative. The harvest began about the middle of April, and lasted to the end of May (Tristram, 'The Land of Israel,' pp. 583 f.). The conversation therefore might be placed about the end of January (or early in February). By this time the fields would be already green. Dr Tristram found the wheat and barley near Jerusalem, sown just after Christmas, four inches high on February 20th (*l. c.* p. 399). But on this supposition it would follow from this passage, compared with ii. 13 and iv. 3, that the Lord must have continued about ten months in Judæa, a supposition which seems to be inconsistent with iv. 45. See Additional Note on v. 1.

Lift up your eyes] Comp. Isai. xlix. 18. This prophetic passage offers a striking parallel in thought and language.

behold, I say unto you, Lift up your
[d] Matt. 9. 37 eyes, and look on the fields; [d]for they
are white already to harvest.
36 And he that reapeth receiveth
wages, and gathereth fruit unto life
eternal: that both he that soweth
and he that reapeth may rejoice together.
37 And herein is that saying true,
One soweth, and another reapeth.
38 I sent you to reap that whereon
ye bestowed no labour: other men laboured, and ye are entered into their
labours.
39 ¶ And many of the Samaritans
of that city believed on him for the
saying of the woman, which testified,
He told me all that ever I did.
40 So when the Samaritans were
come unto him, they besought him
that he would tarry with them: and
he abode there two days.
41 And many more believed because of his own word;

---

the fields] At the present time the plain at the foot of Gerizim is fertile corn-land (Stanley, 'S. and P.' 233 ff.). The detail has the truth of life in it. The disciples saw the promise of rich crops: but Christ saw the spiritual harvest of which the fields were the image (Matt. xiii. 3 ff., &c.), even now come in its first-fruits, as the people from the city approached.

for] Rather, **that**. *Look on* (i. 38) *the fields*, and observe *that* ... The woman, we may suppose, with the Samaritans (*v.* 30), was seen returning to the well.

35, 36. The punctuation and reading at the end of verse 35 are uncertain, but it seems best to omit *already* at the close of it, and to substitute it for *and* at the beginning of *v.* 36: **Already he that** *reapeth* ... The harvest was strangely anticipated in this first welcome of the word beyond the limits of Judaism.

36. *receiveth wages ... that both* (omit) *he*...] There is even now work for him to do, which has an immediate reward, and he *gathereth fruit* which shall not perish or be consumed, but endure *unto life eternal*. Comp. *v.* 14, vi. 27, xii. 25. There in that higher order the sower shall "see of his travail" and be glad: the forerunner who has long passed away shall meet him who has received the harvest of his earlier work and share his joy. The application seems to be to lawgiver and priest and prophet, and all who "went before" Christ's coming in old times and even now go before Him. Christ Himself stands as the Lord of the Harvest (*v.* 38) and not here as the Sower.

37. *And herein is that saying* ...] **For** *herein is* **the** *saying* ... "I say this," so the words imply, "to prepare you by the lesson of your immediate success for future disappointment, for in this spiritual sowing and harvesting the common proverb finds its complete, ideal, fulfilment (ἀληθινός): *one soweth and another reapeth*."

herein] *i.e.* in the fact that you are reaping already (*v.* 36) what others sowed. And the principle was to find application in their labours also.

38. *I sent you ... ye bestowed no labour* (**ye have not laboured**) ...] The words probably point to the successful labours of the Apostles in Judæa (*v.* 2). At the same time their whole mission was included in their call.

other men laboured (**have laboured**) ... *into their labours* (**labour**)] The reference, as in the case of the sower, is to all who had in any manner prepared the way for Christ. He was, as has been said, like Joshua, who brought His Own people to "a land for which they did not labour" (Josh. xxiv. 13); and it is possible that the words may contain a reference to that passage of the Old Testament. The "you" is emphatic throughout. The word "laboured" is the same as that used for "wearied" in *v.* 6 (κοπιᾶν). The result is identified with the effort (*labour, that which you have not wrought by your labour*, ὃ οὐ κεκοπ., Vulg. *quod non laborastis*). Comp. Ecclus. xiv. 15.

The work in Sychar (39—42).

39—42. The ready faith of the woman was found also among her countrymen. As she had looked for a religious teacher in the Christ, they acknowledged in Him "the Saviour of the world."

39. *believed ... for the saying*] Rather, **because of the word** (*v.* 41), the narrative (διὰ τὸν λόγον), and not the simple statement only, *of the woman* **as** (or **while**) **she** (earnestly, constantly, and not once for all) *testified* (τῆς γυναικὸς μαρτυρούσης) ...

40. *So when ... were come* (**came**) ...] Their belief went thus far, that they wished to hear more of His teaching.

that he would tarry] Rather, **to abide** (i. 38, 39), as in the second clause.

41. *many more*] The phrase is comparative, *far more* (in reference to *v.* 39), and not positive (πολλῷ πλείους). This isolated notice is an instructive illustration of our frag-

42 And said unto the woman, Now we believe, not because of thy saying: for we have heard *him* ourselves, and know that this is indeed the Christ, the Saviour of the world.

43 ¶ Now after two days he departed thence, and went into Galilee.

44 For [e] Jesus himself testified, that a prophet hath no honour in his own country. [e] Matt. 13. 57.

---

mentary knowledge of the Lord's whole work.

because of his (omit *own*) *word*] Comp. *v.* 39.

42. *Now we believe ... heard him ourselves*] More exactly, **No longer is it because of thy speech that we believe,** *for we have* **heard for ourselves.** The order is remarkable. The word *speech* (*talking*, λαλιά) corresponds with *talk* in *vv.* 26, 27. It occurs elsewhere in New Testament only ch. viii. 43; Matt. xxvi. 73 (Mark xiv. 70). It does not appear that the Samaritans asked for signs like the Jews (comp. *v.* 48), or that any outward miracles were wrought among them.

the Christ, the Saviour of the world] The words *the Christ* must be omitted, in accordance with an overwhelming concurrence of ancient authorities. The simple title, *the Saviour of the world* (Vulg. *Salvator mundi*), is found once again in 1 John iv. 14; and it is a significant fact that this magnificent conception of the work of Christ was first expressed by a Samaritan, for whom the hope of a Deliverer had not been shaped to suit national ambition. So at last faith rose to the level of the promise, *v.* 21. The "salvation" (*v.* 22) sprang from the Jews, and was recognised by Samaritans.

3. THE WORK IN GALILEE (43—54).

This notice of Christ's Galilæan work consists of a general account of the welcome which He found (*vv.* 43—45), followed by the narrative of a second "sign" (*vv.* 46—54).

It seems probable that the earlier part of the Synoptic narratives (Mark i. 14—ii. 14 and parallels) must be placed in the interval which extended from iv. 43—v. 1. So far there are no signs of the special hostility which seems to have been called out by the healing on the Sabbath wrought on the next visit to Jerusalem.

The contents of the section are peculiar to St John. It has indeed been questioned whether "the healing of the nobleman's son" is not identical with "the healing of the centurion's servant," recorded by St Matthew (viii. 5 ff.) and St Luke (vii. 2 ff.). Both miracles were wrought at Capernaum, and wrought in the same manner, at a distance. But in all other respects the incidents are characteristically unlike, as to

(1) *Place.* The request was made here at Cana, there at Capernaum.

(2) *Time.* Here immediately after the return to Galilee, there after some time had elapsed.

(3) *Persons.* Here the subject was a son, there a slave: here the petitioner was probably a Jew, there a heathen soldier.

(4) *Character.* Here the faith of the father, as interpreted by the Lord, is weak; there the faith of the centurion is exceptionally strong.

(5) *Manner.* Here the request is granted in a way opposed to the prayer, there in accordance with it: here the Lord refuses to go, there He offers to go to the sufferer.

The two miracles are in fact complementary. In the one, weak faith is disciplined and confirmed: in the other, strong faith is rewarded and glorified. The fame of the former miracle may easily have encouraged the centurion to appeal to the Lord in his distress.

In one other case the Lord is recorded to have exercised His power at a distance, Matt. xv. 22 and parallels.

43. *Now after two days he departed thence, and went ...*] *After* **the** *two days* (mentioned in *v.* 40) *he* **went forth** (ἐξῆλθεν) **thence** *into Galilee.*

44. *Jesus himself*] The testimony of Christ was the same as the testimony of the Apostles after the fall of Jerusalem.

testified ... country] The general meaning of this clause depends upon the sense given to *his own country.* This has been understood to be (1) Galilee generally, (2) Nazareth, (3) Lower Galilee, in which Nazareth was situated, as distinguished from Upper Galilee, in which was Capernaum, (4) Judæa. Against the first three lies the fatal objection, that it seems impossible that St John should speak of Galilee in this connexion as Christ's "own country" (ἡ ἰδία πατρίς. Compare vii. 41, 42). Both by fact and by the current interpretation of prophecy, Judæa alone could receive that title (comp. Orig. 'Tom.' XIII. 54). Moreover, Judæa is naturally suggested by the circumstances. The Lord had not been received with due honour at Jerusalem. His Messianic claim had not been welcomed. He did not trust Himself to the Jews there. He was forced to retire. If many followed Him, they were not the representatives of the people, and their faith reposed on miracles. No apostle was a Jew in this narrower sense. Nothing then can be more appropriate than to mark this outward failure of the appeal to Judæa by an application of the common proverb (comp. Matt. xxiii. 37; Luke xiii. 34),

45 Then when he was come into Galilee, the Galilæans received him, having seen all the things that he did at Jerusalem at the feast: for they also went unto the feast.

46 So Jesus came again into Cana of Galilee, *f* where he made the water wine. And there was a certain ‖ nobleman, whose son was sick at Capernaum.

f chap. 2. 1.

‖ Or, *courtier*, or, *ruler*.

47 When he heard that Jesus was come out of Judæa into Galilee, he went unto him, and besought him that he would come down, and heal his son: for he was at the point of death.

48 Then said Jesus unto him, Except ye see signs and wonders, ye will not believe.

49 The nobleman saith unto him, Sir, come down ere my child die.

---

followed by the notice of the ready welcome given to Christ by Galilæans (*v.* 45).

If this interpretation of "his own country" be accepted, it will be enough simply to notice the other interpretations which have found favour. Thus the words have been supposed to mean, (1) Jesus departed into Upper Galilee (or Capernaum), for He testified that a prophet hath no honour in his own country (Lower Galilee or Nazareth). (2) Jesus departed into Galilee, ennobled by the fame which He had gained in Jerusalem, and which He could not have gained in Galilee, for He testified that a prophet hath no honour in his own country, and therefore must win it in some strange place. (3) Jesus departed into Galilee to meet what He knew would be a hopeless conflict; or to seek there rest from labour.

It may be noticed that the emphatic epithet *own* distinguishes the phrase used here from that found in Matt. xiii. 54, 57 (where "own" is inserted by some copies) and in Luke iv. 23, 24. The addition indicates the special force which the Evangelist attached to the words.

45. *Then when he was come...*] **So when He came...** The issue justified the proverb. In Galilee, which was not Messiah's country, not even in popular estimation a prophet's home (vii. 52), Jesus found a ready reception. His works at Jerusalem, which had produced no permanent effect upon the spot, impressed the Galilæans more deeply; and it is not unlikely that Galilæan pilgrims formed the greater part of "the many" who "believed on His name" at the Passover (ii. 23).

received] "welcomed" (ἐδέξαντο, Vulg. *exceperunt*). See iii. 27, note.

they also went...] and therefore if in one sense they were strangers yet they were not religious aliens.

46. *So Jesus came again...*] **He came therefore** *again...* In consequence of the welcome which He received He went on to Cana, where He had first "manifested forth His glory" (ii. 11).

nobleman] Rather, *officer in the service of the king*, *i.e.* Herod Antipas, tetrarch of Galilee, who was popularly known as "king:" Matt. xiv. 9. The word (βασιλικός) is used by Josephus (*e.g.* 'B. J.' I. 13 (11). 1) for any person employed at court. The Vulgate, following an early but false reading (βασιλίσκος), gives *regulus*, "a petty king," "a chieftain." Some have conjectured that this officer was Chuza, "Herod's steward" (Luke viii. 3), or Manaen, his foster-brother (Acts xiii. 1).

Capernaum] ii. 12, note.

47. *went*] Literally, *went away* (ἀπῆλθεν, Vulg. *abiit*). The word emphasizes the thought that the father left his son for the time.

come down] Comp. ii. 12.

he was at the point of death] The Vulgate rendering is worthy of notice: *incipiebat mori*. Comp. Acts xxvii. 33. Contrast xii. 33, *esset moriturus*.

48. *Then said Jesus...*] *Jesus* **therefore** *said...* The Lord read the character of the petitioner even through a petition which might seem to shew faith.

see] Comp. xx. 29. His faith required the support of sight.

signs and wonders] The two words (σημεῖα καὶ τέρατα) are combined Matt. xxiv. 24; Mark xiii. 22; Acts (ii. 19), ii. 22, 43, iv. 30, v. 12, vi. 8, vii. 36, viii. 13, xiv. 3, xv. 12; Rom. xv. 19; 2 Cor. xii. 12; (2 Thess. ii. 9); Hebr. ii. 4. They severally mark the two chief aspects of miracles: the spiritual aspect, whereby they suggest some deeper truth than meets the eye, of which they are in some sense symbols and pledges; and the external aspect, whereby their strangeness arrests attention. "Sign" and "work" (see v. 20) are the characteristic words for miracles in St John. The word here translated "wonders" is never used by itself in the New Testament.

ye will not believe] *ye will* **in no wise** *believe*. The plural (*ye*) marks the nobleman as the representative of a class, to whom miracles were the necessary support of a faith which was not reluctant but feeble. The negative phrase (οὐ μὴ πιστεύσητε) does not express the simple fact, but in some degree connects it with the state of things of which it is the result: "There is no likelihood—no possibility—that ye should believe." Perhaps however the phrase is better taken as an interrogation: *Will ye in no wise believe?* Comp. ch. xviii. 11; (Rev. xv. 4). Luke xviii. 7 (οὐ μὴ ποιήσῃ).

50 Jesus saith unto him, Go thy way; thy son liveth. And the man believed the word that Jesus had spoken unto him, and he went his way.

51 And as he was now going down, his servants met him, and told *him*, saying, Thy son liveth.

52 Then inquired he of them the hour when he began to amend. And they said unto him, Yesterday at the seventh hour the fever left him.

53 So the father knew that *it was* at the same hour, in the which Jesus said unto him, Thy son liveth: and himself believed, and his whole house.

54 This *is* again the second miracle *that* Jesus did, when he was come out of Judæa into Galilee.

The temper of the Galilæans is placed in sharp contrast with that of the Samaritans.

49. *Sir, come down...*] The faith, however imperfect, which springs out of fatherly love is unshaken. It clings to what it can grasp. Compare Mark ix. 24, which offers a complete spiritual parallel.

child] The diminutive (τὸ παιδίον) is used significantly here; not "son" (*v.* 47) or "boy" (*v.* 51). Compare Mark v. 23, 35.

50. *Go thy way; thy son liveth*] The assurance thus given is the final test, and it is sustained. So far the father endured without seeing. The crisis of life and death was present; hence it is enough to say "liveth" (*v.* 51) and not "is healed." Comp. Mark v. 23.

And the man...Jesus had spoken...] *The man...Jesus* **spake**...

51. *met him, and told him, saying, Thy son liveth*] *met him, saying* **that his boy** (παῖς) **liveth.** Here only (according to the true reading) St John uses the oblique form ("that his boy liveth"), and not as in A. V., the direct ("Thy son liveth").

52. *Then inquired he...And they said...*] *He inquired* **therefore**...**So** *they said* (εἶπαν οὖν)...

he began to amend] The original phrase is remarkable (κομψότερον ἔσχεν, Vulg. *melius habuerit*), and appears to have been used in familiar conversation, as we might say "he begins to do nicely," or "bravely." The closest parallel is in Arrian: "When the doctor comes in you must not be afraid as to what he will say; nor if he says 'You are doing bravely' (κόμψως ἔχεις), must you give way to excessive joy" ('Dissert. Epict.' III. 10. 13; comp. Dissert. II. 18. 14).

Yesterday at the seventh hour...] *i.e.* 7 *p.m.* See note on ch. xix. Such a phrase could scarcely be used of one o'clock in the afternoon in the evening of the same natural day.

at the seventh hour] The original expresses duration of time (ὥραν ἑβδόμην, "in the seventh hour") and not a point of time.

53. *believed*] that Jesus was the Christ Comp. iii. 15 note. The belief in *v.* 50 is simply belief in the specific promise.

54. *This is again the second miracle...when he was come...*] More closely: *This did Jesus again as a second sign having come* (*after He came*)... The point lies in the relation of the two miracles as marking two visits to Cana, separated by a visit to Jerusalem. The form of the phrase corresponds with that in ii. 11.

In looking back over this section (ii. 13—iv. 54), the signs of harmonious progress in the development of the Lord's work are obvious. At first He stands before men with words and deeds of power, and they interpret and misinterpret His character, yet so that He cannot enter upon His kingdom by the way of a universal welcome from the ancient theocracy (ii. 13—25). Then follows the beginning of the direct revelation of a divine presence, which is shewn at once to have a larger significance than for Israel. Christ sets Himself forth in two representative scenes as satisfying the hope of men, yet otherwise than they had expected (iii., iv.). He acknowledges that He is the Messiah in the sense of the woman of Samaria; but the higher teaching which He addressed to Nicodemus is veiled in riddles. At the same time a new confession is added to those of the first chapter (i. 51, note). The Samaritans acknowledge Christ to be "the Saviour of the world" (iv. 42, note).

ADDITIONAL NOTE on CHAP. IV. 21.

On the titles "the Father," "my Father," in St John.

Very much of the exact force of St John's record of the Lord's words appears to depend upon the different conceptions of the two forms under which the Fatherhood of God is described. God is spoken of as "the Father" and as "my Father." Generally it may be said that the former title expresses the original relation of God to being and specially to humanity, in virtue of man's creation in the divine image, and the latter more particularly the relation of the Father to the Son Incarnate, and so indirectly to man in virtue of the Incarnation. The former suggests those thoughts, which spring from the consideration of the absolute moral connexion of man with God: the latter, those which spring from what is made known to us through revelation of the connexion of the Incarnate Son with God and with man. "The Father" corresponds, under this aspect, with the group of ideas gathered up in the Lord's titles, "the Son," "the Son of man:" and "my Father" with those which are gathered up in the title "the Son of God," "the Christ."

The two forms are not unfrequently used in close succession. Thus for example, we read:

v. 43. I have come in the name of *my Father*.

v. 45. Do not think that I will accuse you to *the Father*.

The coming of Christ was a new revelation: the accusation of the unbelieving lies already in the primal constitution of things.

vi. 27. Which the Son of man will give you, for him *the Father* sealed, even God.

vi. 32. *My Father* giveth you the true bread from heaven.

In the one place the Lord appears as satisfying the wants of humanity: in the other, the new dispensation is contrasted with the old.

x. 17. Therefore doth *the Father* love me, because I lay down my life.

x. 18. This commandment received I from *my Father*.

The one statement rests on the conception of true self-sacrifice: the other deals with the mission of Christ.

Other instructive examples will be found: viii. 18 f., x. 29 ff., 36 ff., xiv. 6—10, xv. 8—10, 15 f., 23—26. In many cases it will be seen that the absolute conception of Fatherhood is that on which the main teaching of a passage really depends: iv. 21 ff., vi. 45 f., xvi. 23 ff., and to such pregnant sentences as x. 30, xx. 21, the title "*the Father*" gives a singular depth of meaning. Of the two phrases *the Father* is by far the more common, and yet in many places *my Father* has been substituted for it in the later texts, to express a more obvious sense: vi. 65, viii. 28, 38, x. 29, 32, xv. 10, xvi. 10.

The form *my Father* is the true reading in the following passages: ii. 16, v. 17, 43, vi. 32, 40, viii. 19, 49, 54, x. 18, 25, 29, 37, xiv. 2, 7, 20, 21, 23, xv. 1, 8, 15, 23 f., xx. 17.

It may be added that St John never uses the phrase "our Father," which is not unfrequent in St Paul, nor yet the phrase "your Father," except xx. 17. Nor does he use πατήρ without the article by itself (comp. 2 John 3) of God, except (of course) in the vocative case; xi. 41, xii. 27 f., xvii. 1, 5, (11), 21, 24, (25). Comp. i. 14, note.

CHAPTER V.

1 Jesus on the sabbath day cureth him that was diseased eight and thirty years. 10 The Jews therefore cavil, and persecute him for it. 17 He answereth for himself, and reproveth them, shewing by the testimony of his Father, 32 of John, 36 of his works, 39 and of the scriptures, who he is.

THE CONFLICT (v. 1—xii. 50).

Up to the present time the Lord has offered Himself to typical representatives of the whole Jewish race at Jerusalem, in Judæa, in Samaria, and in Galilee, in such a way as to satisfy the elements of true faith. Now the conflict begins which issues in the Passion. Step by step faith and unbelief are called out in a parallel development. The works and words of Christ become a power for the revelation of men's thoughts. The main scene of this saddest of all conceivable tragedies is Jerusalem. The crises of its development are the national Festivals. And the whole controversy is gathered round three miracles.

(1) *The healing of the impotent man at Bethesda* (v.).

(2) *The healing of the man born blind* (ix.)

(3) *The raising of Lazarus* (xi.).

The sixth chapter is a Galilæan episode, marking the crisis of faith and unbelief outside Judæa proper.

The unity of the record is marked by the symptoms of the earlier conflict which appear at the later stages, *e.g.* vii. 19 ff. compared with v. 18 ff.; x. 27 ff. compared with x. 1 ff.; xi. 47 ff.

With the exception of parts of ch. vi. the contents of this division of the Gospel are peculiar to St John.

The narrative falls into two parts: THE PRELUDE (v., vi.), and THE GREAT CONTROVERSY (vii.—xii.).

I. THE PRELUDE (v., vi.).

The Prelude consists of two decisive incidents with their immediate consequences; one at Jerusalem (ch. v.), the other in Galilee (ch. vi.). In the first we have Christ's revelation of Himself in answer to false views of His relation to God (v. 18); in the other, His revelation of Himself in answer to false views of His work for men (vi. 15, 26). In the first case the revelation is indirect ("the Son;" compare *vv.* 24, 30, 31 ff.); in the second case the revelation is predominantly direct ("I am," yet see *vv.* 40, 53).

The section closes with the first division

23. AFTER [a]this there was a feast of
16. 1. the Jews; and Jesus went up to
Jerusalem.
2 Now there is at Jerusalem by
the sheep ‖*market* a pool, which is ‖ Or, gate.
called in the Hebrew tongue Bethesda, having five porches.
3 In these lay a great multitude of

---

in the circle of the disciples (vi. 66), and the foreshadowing of the end (vi. 70 f.).

i. THE SON AND THE FATHER (ch. v.).

The record of the healing (*vv.* 2—9*a*), and of the immediate sequel to it (*vv.* 9*b*—18), is followed by a long discourse addressed by "the Lord" to "the Jews," in answer to their charge that "He spake of God as His own Father, as His Father in a sense wholly unique (πατὴρ ἴδιος)." This discourse consists of two main divisions.

(*a*) *The nature and prerogatives of the Son* (*vv.* 19—29).

(β) *The witness to the Son, and the ground of unbelief* (*vv.* 31—47).

v. 30 serves as a connecting link between the two parts.

The contents of these two sections form the foundation of all the later teaching in the Gospel.

The discourse appears to have been addressed to a small (official) gathering: perhaps to the Sanhedrin, and certainly not to the multitude (comp. *vv.* 33, 39). Perhaps there is a reference to it in vii. 26 (ἔγνωσαν).

The sign (*vv.* 2—9 *a*).

The healing of the impotent man was a work wrought by the Lord spontaneously. He chose both the object of it and the occasion. The malady of the sufferer was not urgent in such a sense that the cure could not have been delayed. The cure therefore was not wrought on a Sabbath although it was a Sabbath, but because it was Sabbath, with the view of bringing out a deeper truth (comp. vii. 21 ff.).

For other healings on Sabbaths see Matt. xii. 9 ff. and parallels; Luke xiii. 10 ff., xiv. 1 ff.

CHAP. V. 1. *After this*...(**these things**...)] There is a slight difference between *after this* (μετὰ τοῦτο, ii. 12, xi. 7, 11, xix. 28 [Hebr. ix. 27]), and *after these things* (μετὰ ταῦτα, *v.* 14, iii. 22, vi. 1, xiii. 7, xix. 38, xxi. 1, &c.). The former implies a connexion of some kind (of time or dependence) between the preceding and subsequent events, which is not suggested by the latter.

a feast] The evidence for the identification of this unnamed feast is very slight. The tradition of the early Greek Church identified it with Pentecost. Most modern commentators suppose it to be the Feast of Purim (March), from a comparison of iv. 35 and vi. 4. But see Additional Note.

went up to Jerusalem] If the feast were that of Purim, this journey was not of obligation; but compare x. 22 (the Feast of Dedication).

2. *there is at Jerusalem...*] The use of the present tense does not prove that the narrative was written before the destruction of Jerusalem. It is quite natural that St John in recalling the event should speak of the place as he knew it. It has indeed been conjectured that a building used for a benevolent purpose might have been spared in the general ruin, but this explanation of the phrase is improbable.

by the sheep market] by the sheep **gate** (ἐπὶ τῇ προβατικῇ, *super probatica* Am.), which lay near the temple on the east of the city (Neh. iii. 1, 32, xii. 39), though it cannot now be certainly fixed ('Dict. of Bible,' *s. v.*). The ellipsis, which is most naturally supplied by *gate*, is (apparently) without parallel.

a pool] This has been identified by some with an intermittent spring known as the *Fountain of the Virgin*, in the Valley of Kidron. The traditional site is the *Birket Israil* by the modern gate of St Stephen, on the north-east of the city. But neither spot fully answers to the conditions of the pool.

in the Hebrew] that is, in the language "of those beyond the river" brought from Babylon, and not in the classical language of the Old Testament. Compare Lightfoot *ad loc.*

Bethesda] The original reading and the meaning of the name are both very uncertain. The common interpretation of the form Bethesda is *House of mercy* (בית חסדא); but this is open to objection on the ground of the usage of חסדא, and it has been supposed to represent the *House of the portico* (בית אסטיו, οἶκος στοῆς). See Delitzsch, 'Ztschr. f. Luth. Theol.' 1856, 622 f. The true reading appears to contain the element *-zatha* (*-saida*), which suggests בית זיתא, the *House of the olive.* The pool is not mentioned by any Jewish writer.

five porches] Cloisters, or covered spaces round the pool, such as are commonly found by tanks in India.

3, 4. The words from *waiting for...he had* are not part of the original text of St John, but form a very early note added to explain *v.* 7, while the Jewish tradition with regard to the pool was still fresh. Some authorities add the last clause of *v.* 3 only; others *v.* 4 only; others add both, but with considerable verbal variations. See Additional Note.

3. *In these lay a great multitude of impotent folk*] *In these* **were lying a multitude** *of* impotent folk, of blind, halt, withered, waiting for the moving of the water.

4 For an angel went down at a certain season into the pool, and troubled the water: whosoever then first after the troubling of the water stepped in was made whole of whatsoever disease he had.

5 And a certain man was there, which had an infirmity thirty and eight years.

6 When Jesus saw him lie, and knew that he had been now a long time *in that case*, he saith unto him, Wilt thou be made whole?

7 The impotent man answered him, Sir, I have no man, when the water is troubled, to put me into the pool: but while I am coming, another steppeth down before me.

8 Jesus saith unto him, Rise, take up thy bed, and walk.

9 And immediately the man was made whole, and took up his bed, and walked: and on the same day was the sabbath.

10 ¶ The Jews therefore said unto him that was cured, It is the sabbath day: [b]it is not lawful for thee to carry *thy* bed. [b] Jer. 22.

---

sick *folk...* The healing properties of the pool may have been due to its mineral elements. Eusebius ('De situ et nom.' *s. v.*) describes the waters of the pool identified with it in his time as "marvellously red," *i.e.* probably from deposits of iron on the stones. A chalybeate spring would be efficacious generally in cases of weakness.

A similar scene is still presented by the hot sulphureous springs near Tiberias (*Hammath*, Josh. xix. 35): Tristram, 'Land of Israel,' 416.

4. *an angel...*] Comp. Rev. xvi. 5.

5. *thirty and eight years*] This period of time, corresponding with the period of the punishment of the Israelites in the wilderness, has led many, from a very early date, to regard the man as a type of the Jewish people paralysed by faithlessness at the time of Christ's coming. The detail may however be added simply to mark the inveteracy of the disease (ix. 1, *blind from his birth*).

6. *saw him lie* (**lying**) *and knew* (γνούς)] by the information of bystanders, or (more probably) by His divine intuition (see p. 46). The life of this sick man was open to Him (*v.* 14), just as the life of the Samaritan woman (iv. 18). It is to be noticed that all the miracles recorded by St John, except the healing of the nobleman's son, were wrought spontaneously by Christ. But the question with which this work is prefaced is a peculiar feature.

Wilt thou] *i.e.* hast thou the will? desirest thou? The word is often ambiguous, as for example, v. 40, vi. 11, 67, vii. 17, viii. 44, ix. 27. The question was suggested by the circumstances of the man's case. It might seem that he acquiesced in his condition, and was unwilling to make any vigorous effort to gain relief. If it was so, the words were fitted to awaken attention, hope, effort, in one who had fallen into apathy. Comp. Acts iii. 4.

7. *The impotent man*] **The sick man** (ὁ ἀσθενῶν). The sufferer answers the thought which underlay the inquiry. The delay in his healing was due, as he explains, not to want of will but to want of means.

is troubled] The popular explanation of the phenomenon of an intermittent spring.

put] The original word (βάλλειν) is that which is commonly translated *cast*. In late Greek it is used very widely (*e.g.* xiii. 2, xviii. 11, xx. 25, 27), but it may express the necessary haste of the movement according to the gloss in *v.* 4.

8. The three features of the complete restoration are to be noticed (*rise*, *take up thy bed*, *walk*). The phrase occurs Mark ii. 9.

bed] The word (κράβαττος, Vulg. *grabbattus*), said to be of Macedonian origin, which is used here, occurs Mark ii. 4 ff. (note), vi. 55; Acts v. 15, ix. 33. It describes technically the bed of the poor—"a pallet."

The immediate sequel of the sign (9*b*—18).

In this section the various elements of the coming conflict are brought out distinctly; the significance of the cure as a work of power and judgment (*v.* 14), the accusations of the Jews (*vv.* 10, 16, 18), the self-vindication of Christ (*v.* 17).

9. *and on...the sabbath*] A new paragraph begins with these words: **Now on that day was a sabbath**, which prepares the way for the subsequent discourse. The form of the phrase is very remarkable (comp. ix. 14, xix. 31), and suggests the idea that the sabbath was a day of rest other than the weekly sabbath.

10. *The Jews*] See Introd. pp. ix, x.

unto him that was (**had been**) *cured*] The word and tense are contrasted with those found in *v.* 13.

It is the sabbath: **and** *it is not...to carry*] Rather, **to take up**, as in *vv.* 8, 9, 11, 12. The objectors would refer to such passages as Jer. xvii. 21 f. "If any one carries anything

11 He answered them, He that
made me whole, the same said unto
me, Take up thy bed, and walk.
12 Then asked they him, What
man is that which said unto thee,
Take up thy bed, and walk?
13 And he that was healed wist
not who it was: for Jesus had conveyed himself away, ‖a multitude
being in *that* place.
14 Afterward Jesus findeth him
in the temple, and said unto him,
Behold, thou art made whole: sin no
more, lest a worse thing come unto
thee.
15 The man departed, and told
the Jews that it was Jesus, which
had made him whole.
16 And therefore did the Jews
persecute Jesus, and sought to slay
him, because he had done these things
on the sabbath day.

from ulti- hat

---

from a public place to a private house on the sabbath...intentionally, he renders himself liable to the punishment of premature death (כרת) and stoning" ('Sabb.' 6 a, quoted by Wünsche).

11. *He answered them...*] **But he..** The authority of One who had wrought the miracle seemed to him to outweigh any legal enactment. He felt instinctively the presence of that which was greater than the sabbath.

the same] **even he**, with a marked emphasis on the pronoun (ἐκεῖνος). This usage is characteristic of St John, i. 18, 33, ix. 37, x. 1, xii. 48, xiv. 21, 26. Compare also Mark vii. 15, 20; Rom. xiv. 14; 2 Cor. x. 18.

12. *Then asked they...What man...which said...*] **They asked, Who is the** *man* **that** *said...* The introduction of *the man* marks the spirit of the inquiry, and suggests the contrast between the Divine Law and this (assumed) human teacher, who claimed to deal with it by his own power. Moreover, as the sufferer had spoken of his healing, these speak only of the technical offence, and pass by that work of power and mercy. Comp. *v.* 15.

Take up (omit *thy bed*) *and walk*] The words are given with great naturalness in an abrupt form.

13. *And he that...in that place*] **But** *he that...in* **the** *place.*

for Jesus had conveyed himself away] *for Jesus* **retired—withdrew**—silently and unperceived, from a place where He might be exposed to embarrassment; for this appears to be the force of the reference to the multitude, and not that the crowd made escape easier. The word (ἐκνεύειν, which occurs only here in New Testament) expresses literally, "to bend the head aside, to avoid a blow" (*declinavit a turba*, Vulg.). Comp. Judg. iv. 18, xviii. 26; 2 K. ii. 24, xxiii. 16; 3 Macc. iii. 22 (LXX.); Jos. 'Antt.' VII. 4. 2.

14. *Afterward*] **After these things.** Comp. *v.* 1, note.

findeth] The healing was incomplete till its spiritual lesson was brought out clearly. Though Christ had withdrawn from the multitude He sought (comp. i. 43, ix. 35) the object of His mercy; and so much at least the man had already learnt, that he repaired to the temple, as we must suppose, to offer thanks there for his restoration directly after his cure.

sin no more] The original (μηκέτι ἁμάρτανε, *noli peccare*, Vulg.) expresses rather *No longer continue to sin* (comp. 1 Joh. iii. 6, 9). How his sickness was connected with his sin must remain undefined; but the connexion is implied, yet in no such way as to lend colour to the belief in the direct connexion of all suffering with personal sin, which is corrected in ix. 3.

a worse thing] even than the sickness of thirty-eight years, by which the greater part of his life had been saddened.

15. *The man departed* (**went away**)...] It is difficult to understand the motive of the man in conveying this information to the Jews, since he knew the hostile spirit in which they regarded the cure. He was certainly not ungrateful, for he still speaks of Jesus as having cured him (*which had made him whole*, *v.* 11, and not *which had told him to take up his bed*, *v.* 12). He may have wished to leave the responsibility of his illegal act on the sabbath with One who had power to answer for it; or it may be simplest to suppose that he acted in obedience to the instructions of those whom, as a Jew, he felt bound to obey.

16. *And therefore* (διὰ τοῦτο, **for this cause**)...] This is the first open declaration of hostility to Christ (though the words *and sought to slay him*, which are wrongly added in this verse from *v.* 18, must be omitted); and it is based upon the alleged violation of the letter of the Law with regard to the sabbath, as in the other Gospels, Matt. xii. 2 ff. and parallels. The miracle just recorded called out the settled enmity of the Jews, but the phrase *because he did*, or rather *used to do*, *was in the habit of doing*, *these things* (acts of mercy which involved offences against the traditional interpretations of the Law) *on a sabbath*, shews that the feeling was not due to a solitary act, but to an obvious principle of action.

17 ¶ But Jesus answered them, My Father worketh hitherto, and I work.

18 Therefore the Jews sought the more to kill him, because he not only had broken the sabbath, but said also that God was his Father, making himself equal with God.

19 Then answered Jesus and said unto them, Verily, verily, I say unto you, The Son can do nothing of himself, but what he seeth the Father do:

---

17. The answer (see *v.* 19, note) of Christ contains in the briefest possible space the exposition of His office: *My Father* (ii. 16, xx. 17) *worketh hitherto* (ἕως ἄρτι, Vulg. *usque modo*, up to the present moment), **even until now**, *and I work*. That is to say, the rest of God after the creation, which the sabbath represents outwardly, and which I am come to realise, is not a state of inaction, but of activity, and man's true rest is not a rest *from* human earthly labour, but a rest *for* divine heavenly labour. Thus the merely negative, traditional, observance of the sabbath is placed in sharp contrast with the positive, final, fulfilment of spiritual service, for which it was a preparation. The works of Christ did not violate the Law, while they brought out the truth to which that tended. Cf. Matt. xii. 1 ff. and parallels. By the "work" of the Father we must understand at once the maintenance of the material creation and the redemption and restoration of all things, in which the Son co-operated with Him (Hebr. i. 3; Eph. i. 9 f.).

The form of the sentence is remarkable. Christ places His work as co-ordinate with that of the Father, and not as dependent on it. Comp. Mark ii. 27, 28 (*The Son of man is Lord also of the sabbath*).

The question of the action of God upon the Sabbath was much debated in the Jewish schools. "Why does not God," said a caviller, "keep the sabbath?" "May not a man," was the answer, "wander through his own house on the sabbath? The house of God is the whole realm above and the whole realm below" ('Shem. R.' xxx.). Comp. Philo, 'Leg. Alleg.' I. p. 46 M.

hitherto] **even until now.** The work of Christ which had excited the hostility of the Jews was, however little they could see it, really coincident with a working of God which knows no interruption.

18. The Jews rightly interpreted the words of the Lord. They saw that He claimed the power of abrogating the law of the Sabbath in virtue of His absolutely special relation to God: *He* **called God His own Father** (Rom. viii. 32)—His Father in a peculiar sense—*making Himself equal with God*, by placing His action on the same level with the action of God. Comp. x. 33. *For this reason the more they* (not only persecuted Him, *v.* 16, but) *sought to kill Him*. Comp. Matt. xii. 14, and parallels. Matt. xxvi. 65, note. Comp. viii. 59, x. 33; Mark ii. 7.

he...had broken] Literally, he *was loosing* (ἔλυε, Vulg. *solvebat*), *i.e.* he declared that the law of the sabbath was not binding. The word (λύω) expresses not the violation of the sanctity of the day in a special case, but the abrogation of the duty of observance. Comp. Matt. v. 19, xviii. 18. A prophet might absolve from the obligation of the law in a particular instance, but not generally.

The Nature and Prerogatives of the Son (19—29).

The first part of the comprehensive answer of the Lord to the Jews deals with His Nature and prerogatives (1) in relation to the Father (19—23), and (2) in relation to men (24—29).

The fact that the discourse was addressed to a small, trained, audience (see preliminary note) explains the close brevity of the reasoning.

vv. 19—23. The action and honour of the Son are coincident with the action and honour of the Father. It is through the action of the Son that men see the action of the Father, and it is by honouring the Son that they honour the Father.

The exposition of these thoughts is made in a series of statements bound together by "for" (γάρ) four times repeated.

The Son doeth nothing self-determined of Himself, which would be impossible (19*a*);

for His action is absolutely coincident in range with that of the Father (19*b*); and this can be;

for His Father shews Him His widening counsels, which extend to the exhibition of greater works than healing (20);

for it is the prerogative of the Son to give life (21), as is shewn to be the case;

for all judgment is given to Him, and men can see that He exerts this power (22).

Hence it follows that men should honour the Son even as they honour the Father (23).

19. *Then answered Jesus...*] *Jesus* **therefore** *answered....* He met their thoughts and their actions (comp. ii. 18, n.) by a justification of His own works and His divine claims as Messiah. This "answer" is not to be placed in immediate temporal connexion with what precedes.

Verily, verily] See i. 51, note. The teaching is "with authority" (Matt. vii. 28 f.).

The Son] iii. 35. The idea is simply that of the absolute relation of the Divine Persons, of

for what things soever he doeth, these also doeth the Son likewise.

20 For the Father loveth the Son, and sheweth him all things that himself doeth: and he will shew him greater works than these, that ye may marvel.

21 For as the Father raiseth up

---

the Son to the Father, and consequently this term is used (19—23), and not (as below *vv.* 30 ff.) "I"—the Christ whom you reject—or "the Son of God" (*v.* 25), or "Son of man" (*v.* 27), which emphasize the divine or human nature of the Lord relatively to man. At the same time the Son is regarded as "sent" (*vv.* 23 f.), and therefore as Incarnate. But this idea lies in the background here, where the immediate point is the justification of the statement in *v.* 17 from the essential relation of the Son to the Father. The argument is conducted by the Lord without a direct personal reference to Himself in such a way as to arrest the attention of the Jews, and not to drive them away at once. Perfect Sonship involves perfect identity of will and action with the Father. *The Son can do nothing of Himself*, self-determined without the Father, nothing, that is, **except He see the Father doing it** (*but what he seeth the Father do*). Separate action on His part is an impossibility, as being a contradiction of His unity with the Father (comp. v. 30 and xvi. 13). The limitation (**except He see...**) refers to *can do nothing*, and not to the last words (*of Himself*); and the coincidence of the action of the Father and of the Son is brought out by the exact turn of the phrase—*see the Father* **doing**, and not *do*.

can do nothing] The eternal law of right is (in human language) the definition of divine power. The words do not convey any limitation of the Son's working, but explain something as to its character. Comp. *v.* 30, iii. 27; Mark vi. 5; (Gen. xix. 22). For another aspect of this "cannot" see vii. 7, note.

of himself] *v.* 30, note; Num. xvi. 28 (LXX.). The truth lies in the very idea of Sonship.

for what things soever...] The negative statement is supplemented by a positive one ... *The Son can do nothing ... for* ... His action is not only coincident but coextensive with the action of the Father: *what things soever He doeth these also the* **Son doeth in like manner**, not in imitation, but in virtue of His sameness of nature.

20. *For the Father ...*] The action of the Son, as coincident and coextensive with that of the Father, depends upon the continuous revelation which the Father makes to Him in accordance with His eternal love: *for the Father loveth the Son;...* and this revelation, regarded under the limitations of human existence, is progressive, and signs of healing are only preparatory to *greater works; for as the Father ... quickeneth, even so the Son also quickeneth whom He* (unemphatic) *will.*

Thus we can see that there is a divine coherence, a divine meaning, in all nature and all history. The Son *sees* all, for the Father *shews* all to Him; and we also can see parts at least in Him. Comp. Matt. xi. 27.

loveth (the Son)] The word (φιλεῖν) marks personal affection based upon a special relation (xi. 3, 36; comp. Matt. x. 37), and not the general feeling of regard, esteem, consideration (ἀγαπᾷν) which comes from reflection and knowledge: the former feeling answers to nature, the latter to experience and judgment (iii. 35, x. 17), and so is specially appropriate to spiritual relations. This love expresses (so to speak) the moral side of the essential relation of the Father to the Son. And so it is through the Son that the personal love of God is extended to believers: xvi. 27; comp. Rev. iii. 19.

The sign of love is the perfect revelation of thought and feeling: xv. 15.

he will ... than these] The original order is more expressive: **greater works** (comp. xiv. 12) **than these will He shew** (comp. x. 32) **Him**; and He (so it is implied, *v.* 19) when He seeth them will do them in like manner, *that ye* (emphatic) *may marvel.* It cannot but appear strange at first sight that wonder is given as the object of Christ's works. The difficulty is removed by taking account of the pronoun: that *ye* who question my authority and are blind to my divine Sonship *may marvel.* Till Christ was recognised His works could at the most appear only to be prodigies: their effect would be astonishment, not belief. But wonder might give occasion for faith. Under this aspect "wonder" is presented in two remarkable traditional sayings of the Lord preserved by Clement of Alexandria ('Strom.' II. 9, 45): "He that wonders shall reign, and he that reigns shall rest:" "Wonder at that which is before you." This partial object of wonder, however, is contrasted with the general object in *v.* 23. Works—outward signs—may produce wonder, but judgment completed enforces honour. Comp. Plat. 'Theæt.' p. 155 D.

shew] x. 32. The divine works require the interpretation of sympathy. Such sympathy the Son has absolutely.

works] This is a characteristic term in St John (comp. Matt. xi. 2) in which Christ includes under the same category the manifold forms of His action. His "works" were fragments contributing to "the work" which

the dead, and quickeneth *them;* even so the Son quickeneth whom he will.
22 For the Father judgeth no man, but hath committed all judgment unto the Son:
23 That all *men* should honour the Son, even as they honour the Father. He that honoureth not the Son honoureth not the Father which hath sent him.

He came to finish (iv. 34, xvii. 4), and these He must needs work while it was day (ix. 4). Miracles from this point of view are regarded on the same level with the other works of Christ, though "miraculous" works may in a peculiar sense move to faith (v. 36, x. 25, 32, xiv. 10, 12, xv. 24). All works alike are designed to contribute to the redemption of the world (comp. ch. xvii. 21, note). See *v.* 36, n.

21. The progress in the dignity of the works of the Son follows from the extent of their sphere, *for as the Father raiseth the dead ... even so the Son* **also** ... The restoration of an impotent man is then but a beginning of that giving of life of which it was a sign. The vivifying power of the Father is described in its twofold physical aspect. He *raiseth up the dead and quickeneth:* that of the Son in reference to its moral law, *He quickeneth whom He will.* The "quickening" as it stands in the second clause is necessarily coextensive with the *raising the dead and quickening* in the first, which is not to be limited to any isolated "miraculous" acts, but extends to all communication of life, natural and spiritual. The main forms of "quickening" are distinguished afterwards, *vv.* 25, 28.

The definition *whom He will* marks (1) the efficacy of Christ's power, and (2) connects this communication of higher life with the counsels of infinite wisdom and love, and (3) shews its independence of outward descent (as from Abraham). There is no emphasis on the personal will of the Son (*whom He will*) as in *v.* 20 (which He *Himself* doeth).

The full significance of this claim of Christ to "quicken whom he will" is illustrated by the second of the 'Shemoneh Esreh,' the 'Eighteen [Benedictions],' of the Jewish Prayer Book. It is probable that this thanksgiving was used in substance in the apostolic age: "Thou, O Lord, art mighty for ever: Thou quickenest the dead: Thou art strong to save. Thou sustainest the living by Thy mercy: Thou quickenest the dead by Thy great compassion. Thou...makest good Thy faithfulness to them that sleep in the dust... Thou art faithful to quicken the dead. Blessed art Thou, O Lord, who quickenest the dead."

22. The fact that the Son possesses and exercises this quickening power is established by the fact that He has a still more awful prerogative. The quickening of men is contrasted with the judgment of men, which is the correlative of sin (iii. 17 ff.). And this judgment belongs to the Son (as *Son of man, v.* 27), *For* **not even doth the Father judge any man**, *but hath committed* (**given**) *all judgment* (or literally, *the judgment* which comes and will come, *wholly, in all its parts*, now in its first beginning and hereafter in its complete accomplishment) *unto the Son.*

the Father ... no man] The exact phrase of the original marks a climax: **not even doth the Father**—to whom this office might seem to pertain—**judge any man.**

committed] **given** (δέδωκεν), the word which is constantly used of the privileges and office of the Son: *v.* 36, iii. 35, vi. 37, 39, x. 29, xvii. 2, 4 ff., 22 ff. See *v.* 36, note.

23. The Son has received the prerogative of judgment, and it is through the exercise of this power that men come to perceive His true majesty. For it was committed to Him for this end, *that all* men *should honour* (not future, but present) *the Son even as they honour the Father* (x. 37, 38). Sooner or later, in loss or in sorrow, this must be. And there is also a converse form of the Truth. It is by honouring the Son that we can honour the Father; and *He that honoureth not the Son honoureth not the Father which sent Him* (comp. 1 John iv. 20; ch. xv. 24).

which hath sent him] **which sent Him.** These words mark the transition from the conception of *the Son* essentially to that of the Son revealed by the incarnation. The phrase *He that sent me* is peculiar to St John (comp. Rom. viii. 3). It is used only by the Lord absolutely of the Father, iv. 34, *vv.* 24, 30, vi. 38, 39, vii. 16, 28, 33, viii. 26, 29, ix. 4, xii. 44, 45, xiii. 20, xv. 21, xvi. 5. Elsewhere the full form, *the Father that sent me*, occurs, v. 37, vi. 44, viii. 16, 18, xii. 49, xiv. 24. Comp. i. 33 (He that sent me *to baptize*).

24—29. In these verses we pass from the consideration of the relation of the Son to the Father to that of the relation of Christ to men. The conception of the "greater works" of the Son, the quickening and the judgment of men, is defined more exactly in connexion with the Son as revealed by the Incarnation. At the same time, though the oblique form is generally preserved, the work and the mission of Christ are referred to directly (*my* word, Him that sent *me*, *v.* 24). In *v.* 24 the general ideas of all life and all judgment in connexion with the Son (21, 22) are restated: in *vv.* 25, 26, they are applied to the present order; in 28, 29, they are applied to the future order.

24 Verily, verily, I say unto you, He that heareth my word, and believeth on him that sent me, hath everlasting life, and shall not come into condemnation; but is passed from death unto life.

25 Verily, verily, I say unto you, The hour is coming, and now is, when the dead shall hear the voice of the Son of God: and they that hear shall live.

26 For as the Father hath life in himself; so hath he given to the Son to have life in himself;

27 And hath given him authority to execute judgment also, because he is the Son of man.

---

24. *Verily, verily*] *vv.* 19, 25. Comp. i. 51, note.

He that ... believeth on him ... everlasting life, and shall not come into condemnation ...] *He that heareth my word and* **believeth Him** *that sent me hath life* **eternal** and **cometh not into judgment**, *but is passed* **out of** *death* (*the* death that is truly death) **into** *life* (*the* life that is truly life). (Comp. 1 John iii. 14.) The two conditions of eternal life are (1) knowledge of the revelation made by the Son, and (2) belief in the truth of it, that is, belief in the word of the Father who speaks through the Son. Comp. xvii. 3. He who knows the Gospel and knows that the Gospel is true cannot but *have* life. Eternal life is not future but present, or rather it *is*, and so is above all time. Comp. iii. 18 f. For him who hath this life judgment is impossible. He has already gone beyond it. Comp. 1 John ii. 28, iv. 17.

believeth on him . .] **believeth him...** (πιστεύων τῷ π.). The difference between "believing a person or statement" (πιστεύειν τινί) and "believing on a person" (πιστεύειν εἰς τινά) is as clearly marked in Greek as in English, though it is destroyed here in A. V. and in viii. 31; Acts xvi. 34, xviii. 8; Tit. iii. 8; while it is preserved *vv.* 38, 46, viii. 45, 46; Rom. iv. 3; Acts xxvii. 25. The two phrases are contrasted in vi. 29, 30, viii. 30, 31; 1 John v. 10. To believe God or to believe the Lord is to acknowledge as true the message which comes from Him or the words which He speaks. It is assumed that the message does come from Him, and therefore to believe the message is to believe Him. So here Christ refers His word to the authority of the Father: compare *v.* 37.

shall not come] **cometh not.** The issues of action are regarded in their potential accomplishment in the present.

condemnation] **judgment.** Compare Introd. pp. xlviii ff.

from death unto ...] **out of** *death* **into ...** 1 John iii. 14. In his epistle St John speaks of "love to the brethren" as the personal proof of this transition. Such love flows from an acceptance in faith of Christ's word (1 John ii. 7, iii. 11). Death and life are, as it were, two spheres of existence, like darkness and light: 1 John v. 19, 20, ch. viii. 31, note.

25. The present manifestation of Christ's vivifying power in the spiritual resurrection (*is coming and now is*) is stated in contrast with the future manifestation in the general resurrection (*is coming*, *v.* 28). See iv. 23, 21. The hour was "coming," so far as the Christian dispensation truly began with the gift of Pentecost: but it "was" already while Christ openly taught among men.

the dead] the spiritually dead: this is the predominant idea, but at the same time we cannot exclude the outward signs of it as in the raising of Lazarus: comp. xi. 23 ff. For this use of the word see Matt. viii. 22; Luke xv. 24, 32; Rom. vi. 11; Eph. v. 14. It will be observed that the voice of power is attributed to the *Son of God.* Comp. xi. 4; contrast ix. 35.

they that hear] This phrase is not coextensive with *the dead.* The voice is addressed to the whole class: those who receive it (οἱ ἀκούσαντες) shall live. As yet the thought is of *life* only, and not of judgment, except so far as that is expressed in the want of life.

26. *as ... so ...*] The particles mark the *fact* of the gift and not the *degree* of it. Comp. *v.* 21; Matt. xiii. 40, &c.

so hath he given ...] **so gave He also...** The Son has not life only as given, but life *in Himself* as being a spring of life. "Nos non habemus vitam in nobis ipsis, sed in Deo nostro. Ille autem Pater vitam in semetipso habet; et talem genuit Filium qui haberet vitam in semetipso; non fieret vitæ particeps, sed ipse vita esset, cujus nos vitæ participes essemus" (August. 'Serm.' CXXVII. 9). The tense (*gave*) carries us back beyond time; and yet it has a further application to the incarnation, wherein the Son became also the Son of man (*v.* 27). The sovereignty of life is followed by the authority to judge, as in *vv.* 21, 22. Comp. vi. 57; Rev. i. 17.

27. *And hath given* (**gave**) *him ... judgment* (om. *also*) *because he is the Son of man* (**son of man** or **a son of man**)] The prerogative of judgment is connected with the true humanity of Christ (*Son of man*) and not with the fact that He is the representative of humanity (*the Son of man*). The Judge, even as the Advocate (Hebr. ii. 18), must share the nature of those who are brought before

28 Marvel not at this: for the hour is coming, in the which all that are in the graves shall hear his voice,

[c] Matt. 25. 46.

29 And shall come forth; [c]they that have done good, unto the resurrection of life; and they that have done evil, unto the resurrection of damnation.

30 I can of mine own self do nothing: as I hear, I judge: and my judgment is just; because I seek not

---

Him. The omission of the article concentrates attention upon the nature and not upon the personality of Christ. Comp. i. 1; Hebr. i. 1, 2 (ἐν τοῖς προφήταις...ἐν υἱῷ, in One who was a Son). The phrase (**son of man**) is found here only in the Gospel, but it occurs also Rev. i. 13, xiv. 14: *the Son of Man* occurs i. 51, iii. 13, 14, vi. 27, 53, 62, as often in the other Gospels. Comp. i. 51, additional note.

28. *Marvel not at this: for ...*] The partial spiritual quickening and judgment is consummated in a universal quickening and judgment. There is a marked contrast between the corresponding clauses of *vv.* 25, 28: *the dead* (*v.* 25), *all that are in the tombs* (*v.* 28): *cometh and now is* (*v.* 25), *cometh* (*v.* 28). Here the quickening is the inevitable result of the divine action (*all...shall hear*); before it followed from the concurrence of faith with the divine message (*they that hear shall live*).

Marvel not...] Comp. *v.* 20. Wonder is at most only a stage of transition. Each manifestation of Christ's power is a preparation for something greater.

29. It will be observed that there is a contrast between the one result of the present action of the Son, *shall live* (*v.* 25), and the complex result of His future action: *shall go forth ...*

they that have done (*that* **wrought**) *good...*] The "doing" of good is described by a word which sets it forth as issuing in a definite production (οἱ τὰ ἀγαθὰ ποιήσαντες), while in the second member the word is changed: *they that have done* (**did**) *evil* ... where the "doing" is regarded simply in the moral character of the action (οἱ τὰ φαῦλα πράξαντες). The same words (ποιεῖν, πράσσειν) are contrasted, ch. iii. 20, 21, note; Rom. i. 32, vii. 15, 19, xiii. 4. The distinction is well preserved in the Vulgate, *bona fecerunt... mala egerunt.*

For the contrast of *a resurrection of life* (2 Macc. vii. 14), and *a resurrection of judgment*, see *v.* 24. In one case the resurrection is accompanied by the full fruition of life, judgment being past: in the other resurrection issues in judgment.

of damnation] *of* **judgment** (κρίσεως). Comp. iii. 17 ff.

30. This verse forms a transition from the first section of the discourse to the second. At the same time it marks the passage from the indirect (*the Son*) to the personal (*I*) revelation of Christ. The truth of the divine Sonship, with which the discourse opened, is first repeated in a new form, *I* (ἐγώ) *can of mine own self do nothing;* and then the principle of Christ's judgment is laid down (*as I hear, I judge*), which is the ground of all true judgment.

I can...do nothing] Comp. *v.* 19, note.

of mine own self] Comp. vii. 17 f., 28, viii. 28, 42, (xii. 49, ἐξ ἐμ.), xiv. 10, (xi. 51), xv. 4, note, xvi. 13. The very idea of Sonship involves (in some sense) that of dependence. There is but one "fountain" of Deity. But under another aspect the Son "lays down His life of Himself" (x. 18).

as I hear, I judge] The judgment of the Son is based upon the perfect knowledge of the thoughts of the Father, as the action of the Son is based upon the perfect vision of His works. The "hearing" in this verse with regard to judgment corresponds to the "seeing" in *v.* 19 with regard to action.

because I seek...the will of the Father which hath sent me] *of* **Him that sent me** (iv. 34, vi. 38, 39). The two conditions of absolute justice are (1) negative: absence of all respect of self; and (2) positive: devotion to the will of the Father. In both these respects the just judgment of the Son is contrasted with the false judgment of the Jews, *vv.* 41—44.

The connexion between the obedience rendered by the Son, and the honour rendered to the Son (*v.* 23), must be noticed.

It will be observed that the "will" of Christ corresponds with His one unchanged personality (*I*, ἐγώ). Comp. Matt. xxvi. 39, and parallels. The thought of the verse is partially illustrated by a noble saying of R. Gamaliel: "Do His will as if it were thy will, that He may do thy will as if it were His will." But he continues: "Annul thy will before His will, that He may annul the will of others before thy will" ('Aboth,' II. 4).

The witness to the Son and the ground of unbelief (31—47).

This second main division of the discourse consists, like the first, of two parts. The witness to the Son is first laid open (31—40), and then the rejection of the witness in its cause and end (41—47).

31—40. Christ appeals to a witness separate from His own, and yet such that He has immediate knowledge of its truth. Such wit-

mine own will, but the will of the Father which hath sent me.

8. 31 [d]If I bear witness of myself, my witness is not true.

3. 32 ¶ [e]There is another that beareth witness of me; and I know that the witness which he witnesseth of me is true.

33 Ye sent unto John, and [f]he bare witness unto the truth. [f]chap. 1. 7.

34 But I receive not testimony from man: but these things I say, that ye might be saved.

35 He was a burning and a shining light: and ye were willing for a season to rejoice in his light.

---

ness is partly provisional and partly final. Of the former kind that of John the Baptist is the type (33—35). The latter lies in the witness of "works" leading up to the witness of the Father (36—40).

31. *If I* (emphatic) *bear witness of* (**concerning**)...] The stress lies on the pronoun, "If I alone and in fellowship with no other..." Comp. viii. 14.

is not true] The words anticipate an objection, and define the amount of truth which it contains. According to legal usage the testimony of a witness was not received in his own case. This principle the Jews might urge against Christ; and He acknowledges the deeper meaning which lay beneath it. If He asserted His claims self-prompted (*of Himself*) He would violate the absolute trust which the Son owed to the Father; though there was a sense in which He could bear witness of Himself (viii. 12 ff.) when the Father spoke through Him (viii. 18).

32. *There is another*] In due time and in due manner another bears witness. The whole scope of the statement decides that this other is "the Father" and not the Baptist. In the verses which follow the testimony of the Baptist is treated as provisional, and as being in a certain degree an accommodation. The testimony of the Father is that upon which the Son rests, *v.* 37, viii. 18.

that beareth witness] The action is present and continuous (ὁ μαρτυρῶν...μαρτυρεῖ).

I know...] In the certainty of this knowledge Christ could repose. Such witness could not but produce its true effect. The absolute knowledge spoken of here (οἶδα) is to be distinguished from the knowledge of experience (ἔγνωκα) in *v.* 42.

the witness which he witnesseth] This full form of expression, as distinguished from "his witness," emphasizes the idea of the continuity of the witness as a matter of actual experience.

33. *Ye* (emphatic) *sent...and he bare*...] *Ye* **have sent**...*and* **he hath borne**... The mission and the testimony are spoken of as abiding in their results. The prominent idea is not the historic fact (i. 32), but the permanent and final value of the witness (i. 34, iii. 26, v. 37, xix. 35).

The emphatic pronoun (*Ye* have sent...) marks a contrast between the standard of authority which the Jews set up and that which Christ admitted (*v.* 34). At the same time the reference to John follows naturally after the mysterious reference to "another" in whom some might think that they recognised him.

34. *But I receive not testimony from man*...] *But* though the witness of John was decisive according to your view, *I* (emphatic as distinguished from *you*) *receive not* **my witness** (τὴν μαρτυρίαν, the witness which characterizes the reality of my work and answers to it) *from* **a man** (even though he be a prophet), *but these things I say*—I appeal even to this imperfect witness, I urge every plea which may be expected to prevail with you—*that ye*—even ye—*might* (**may**) *be saved*.

35. *He was a burning and a shining light*...] *He was*—though now his work is ended by imprisonment or death—**the lamp that burneth and shineth** (*giveth light*)... The phrase may also be rendered, **the lamp that** is kindled **and shineth**, by the analogy of Matt. v. 15; but Luke xii. 35, Rev. iv. 5, viii. 10, are strongly against this interpretation. John the Baptist was the **lamp**, the derivative and not the self-luminous light (i. 8). Comp. Matt. vi. 22; 2 Pet. i. 19; but the word is used also of the Lamb, Rev. xxi. 23, where the glory of God, as the source of light, is placed in connexion with the Lamb, through whom (as the lamp of this vast temple) the light is conveyed in the city of God. The definite article (*the* lamp) simply marks the familiar piece of household furniture (comp. Mark iv. 21; Luke xi. 36). The epithets complete the image. The lamp is exhausted by shining; its illuminating power is temporary, and sensibly consumed. John the Baptist necessarily decreased (iii. 30). The title is eminently appropriate to the Baptist in his relation to Christ (*the Light*); but there is no evidence to shew that it was given to the herald of Messiah by tradition, though it was applied to several distinguished teachers. Compare Buxtorf, 'Lex.' s. v. בוצינא, p. 338. But while his glory lasted the Jews (*ye* emphatic) *were willing for a season* (*an hour*, 2 Cor. vii. 8; Gal. ii. 5; Philem. 15) *to rejoice* (ἀγαλλιασθῆναι) *in his light*. This exulting joy however shewed their real misunder-

36 ¶ But I have greater witness
than *that* of John: for the works
which the Father hath given me to
finish, the same works that I do, bear
witness of me, that the Father hath
sent me.
37 And the Father himself, which
hath sent me, [g]hath borne witness
of me. Ye have neither heard his
voice at any time, [h]nor seen his
shape.
38 And ye have not his word
abiding in you: for whom he hath
sent, him ye believe not.

[g] M... 17. 5...
[h] D... 12.

---

standing of his mission. They welcomed his power, but disregarded the solemn warning of his preaching of repentance. His stern presence became a mere spectacle. Comp. Luke vii. 24 ff.

36, 37 *a*. *But I have greater witness...*] More exactly: *But* **the witness which I** (emphatic) **have is greater** (more conclusive) *than that of John* (or *than John*), *for... the* **very** *works that I do bear witness of me ...and the Father which sent me*, **He** *hath borne witness*. The one witness was even then being given; the other was complete. The revelation made in Christ, and especially in His works of power, was a proof developed before the eyes of men. The historical revelation of the Old Testament consummated at the Baptism was already a finished whole, and recorded in the preparatory Scriptures of the old Covenant.

the works...given] "The works" of Messiah from the divine side were a complete whole (*hath given*); but they were gradually wrought out on earth (*that I should accomplish*, *v.* 34); and this accomplishment was the end proposed in the divine gift (*ἵνα*).

the works] This phrase is used, as generally in St John's Gospel (*v.* 20, n.), to describe the whole outward manifestation of Christ's activity, both those acts which we call supernatural and those which we call natural. All alike are wrought in fulfilment of one plan and by one power. The many "works" (vii. 3, ix. 3, x. 25, 32, 37 f., xiv. 10 ff., xv. 24) are parts of the one "work" (iv. 34, xvii. 4). The phrase occurs elsewhere in Matt. v. 16.

hath given (δέδωκεν)] The declaration of this relation of the Father to the Son (Incarnate) is characteristic of St John. The Father hath given all things in His hand (iii. 35, xiii. 3); He hath given Him all judgment (*vv.* 22, 27); He gave Him to have life in Himself (*v.* 26); He hath given Him a company of faithful servants (vi. 39; comp. vi. 65, xvii. 2, 6, 9, 12, 24, xviii. 9); He hath given Him commandment what to say (xii. 49) and to do (xiv. 31, xvii. 4; comp. xvii. 7 f.). He gave Him authority over all flesh (xvii. 2); He hath given Him His name (xvii. 11 f.) and glory (xvii. 24; comp. *v.* 22).

finish] **accomplish.** Comp. iv. 34, note.

that I do] The pronoun (ἐγώ) which is inserted in the common text must be omitted. It stands in x. 25, xiv. 12, and xiii. 7.

37. *the Father* (omit *himself*)...**He** (*ἐκεῖνος*) *hath borne witness...*] Side by side with the continuous witness of the Father (*v.* 32) there is a witness which is complete. This was given, in its outward form, in the prophetic teaching of the Old Testament closed by the work of the Baptist; and in its spiritual form, in the constitution of man whereby he recognises in Christ the fulfilment of the providential teaching of God. Comp. Introd. pp. xlv. ff.

37 *b*, 38. But still the double witness was unavailing. The words and visions of the Old Testament were fulfilled in Christ (i. 17). If He was rejected at His coming, they were inarticulate and unreal to the faithless. So too it was with the last witness at the Baptism (i. 32 ff.). Since therefore it is only through the Son that men can hear or see God (xiv. 9), the Jews by their disbelief of Christ failed to hear and see Him (*ye* is unemphatic); nor was His word, which answers from within to the revelation without, abiding in them (1 John ii. 14). This all follows from the words which are emphasized in the original by their position: *whom He sent, Him ye* (ὑμεῖς) *believe not*.

The passage is a summary of the mode and conditions of revelation. The teaching and the character of God can be discovered in nature and history, but His Word must be welcomed and kept in the soul in order that that which is without may be intelligible.

his voice...shape...] Comp. Luke iii. 22 (*voice, shape*), ix. 35. Comp. ch. xii. 28; Acts vii. 31, ix. 4, x. 13.

38. *his word*] Compare xvii. 6 ff.; 1 John i. 10, ii. 14, (Hebr. iv. 12). The word of God is a power within man, speaking to and through his conscience; not simply the sum of the earlier revelation under the old Covenant as an outward power; nor yet an independent illumination; but the whole teaching of Providence felt to be a divine message.

for (**because**)...] This is not alleged as the ground, but as the sign of what has been said. Comp. Luke vii. 47; 1 John iii. 14.

he hath sent] *he* **sent.** Comp. xx. 21, note.

39, 40. From the essential elements of revelation, external (*voice, shape*) and internal

39 ¶ Search the scriptures; for in them ye think ye have eternal life: and they are they which testify of me.
40 And ye will not come to me, that ye might have life.
41 I receive not honour from men.
42 But I know you, that ye have not the love of God in you.
43 I am come in my Father's name, and ye receive me not: if another

---

(*word*), the Lord passes to the record of Revelation in Scripture. This the Jews misused.

39. *Search the scriptures...*] **Ye search** *the Scriptures...* The original word may be either imperative (A.V.) or indicative. The indicative rendering is strongly recommended by the (1) immediate connexion, *ye search... and they...*; (2) the sense of *for in them ye think...*, which rather explains a practice than recommends a precept; (3) the general form of the passage: *ye have...ye have not...ye will not;* (4) the character of the Jews who reposed in the letter of the Old Testament instead of interpreting it by the help of the living Word. On the other side the position of the verb at the beginning of the sentence, and the omission of the pronoun, which occurs in the second clause, are in favour of the imperative rendering. But on the whole, the former view is the most probable. The insertion of the pronoun would weaken the stress which is laid on the idea of *searching*, and this is the central thought. The intense, misplaced diligence of search is contrasted with the futile result.

Search] ch. vii. 52; 1 Pet. i. 11. Comp. Rom. viii. 27; 1 Cor. ii. 10; Rev. ii. 23. The original word (ἐραυνᾶν) describes that minute, intense investigation of Scripture (דרש) which issued in the allegorical and mystical interpretations of the *Midrash*. A single example of the stress laid upon the written word will suffice: "Hillel used to say ...more Thorah (Law), more life (Prov. iii. 1 f.)... He who has gotten to himself words of Thorah, has gotten to himself the life of the world to come" ('Aboth,' II. 8. Compare 'Perek R. Meir' throughout; Taylor, 'Sayings of the Fathers,' pp. 113 ff.). The knowledge of God, it was thought, without repentance brought forgiveness of sins (Just. M. 'Dial.' § 141).

the scriptures] the book as distinguished from the living word (*v.* 38).

for (**because**)...*ye think*] because you for your part (ὑμεῖς), following your vain fancies, think falsely and superstitiously that in them —in their outward letter—ye have eternal life, without penetrating to their true, divine meaning. You repose where you should be moved to expectation. You set up your theory of Holy Scripture against the divine purpose of it.

and they...and ye will not...] The words mark a double failure. The scriptures witnessed of One whom the Jews rejected; they pointed to life which the Jews would not seek. There is a deep pathos in the simple co-ordination: *and...and...*

and they (ἐκεῖναι)...] those very scriptures which you idolize. Comp. i. 18, note.

which testify] still and always. Comp. *v.* 32. The teaching of the Old Testament is never exhausted. As we know more of Christ it reveals more to us concerning Him.

40. *And*] still, even with this testimony before you, the personal act of faith fails, *ye will not* (ye have no will to) *come unto me* (comp. Matt. xxiii. 37, ch. iii. 19) *that ye may have life*—"life" in its simplest form, the condition of all else (iii. 36, xx. 31), not qualified even as "eternal life" (*v.* 39).

ye will not] Man has that freedom of determination which makes him responsible. This truth is expressed in various forms in St John's Gospel (comp. vii. 17, viii. 44, vi. 67) side by side with the affirmation of the divine action through which the will is effective for good (vi. 44).

41—47. In this section Christ, starting from the fact of a want of will to believe in His hearers, unfolds the cause (41—44) and the end (45—47) of their rejection of Himself.

The ground of rejection (41—44) lies in a want of divine love in the Jews (*v.* 42), which is shewn by their inability to recognise Christ's self-sacrifice (*v.* 43), while they themselves pursued selfish ends (*v.* 44).

41. The connexion of thought with what precedes appears to lie in the anticipation of a natural objection. The condemnation which Christ pronounced might be referred to disappointed hope. It is, He replies, your spiritual life and not my own glory that I seek. I want nothing for myself, but I see a fatal defect in you. "Glory from men I receive not"—the order is emphatic, and contrasted with that in *v.* 34—"but I know you, that ye have not the love of God in you."

honour (**glory**) *from men*] The glory of Messiah lies in His perfect fellowship with the Father (comp. i. 14, ii. 11, xii. 41); and men shew their sympathy with Him by "the love of God." This the Jews had not, and their rejection of Christ was the sign of the fatal defect.

42. *I know*] by the knowledge of experience (ἔγνωκα). Comp. ii. 24, note.

the love of God] The phrase occurs elsewhere in the Gospels only in Luke xi. 42.

shall come in his own name, him ye will receive.

[i] chap. 12. 43 44 [i] How can ye believe, which receive honour one of another, and seek not the honour that *cometh* from God only?

45 Do not think that I will accuse you to the Father: there is *one* that accuseth you, *even* Moses, in whom ye trust.

46 For had ye believed Moses, ye would have believed me: [k] for he wrote of me. [k] Ge 15. Deu 15.

47 But if ye believe not his writings, how shall ye believe my words?

Comp. 1 John ii. 5, iii. 17, iv. 7, 9, v. 3; Rom. v. 5; 2 Cor. xiii. 14; 2 Thess. iii. 5; Jude 21. God is at once the Author and the Object of this love; and it is frequently difficult to determine whether the words express the quickening love of God towards man, or the responsive love of man towards God.

have...in you (ἐν ἑαυτοῖς)] Comp. *v.* 26, vi. 53; 1 John v. 10; Mark iv. 17.

43. The utter want of fellowship with God on the part of the Jews is exhibited in its contrasted results: *I* (emphatic) *am come* **in the name of my Father**, revealing God to you in this character, *and ye receive me not: if another shall come in his own name*, giving expression to his own thoughts, his own desires, which are in harmony with your own, *him ye will receive.*

in the name of my Father] ch. x. 25, that is, resting absolutely in Him who is my Father and whom I make known to you as such; not simply "as representing" or "by the authority of" my Father, though these ideas are included in that deeper and more comprehensive one. Comp. xiv. 13 f., xv. 16, xvi. 23 f., 26, xvii. 11, 12, xx. 31.

44. The Jews offered a complete contrast to Christ (*v.* 30); for they made the judgment of men their standard. Hence the cause of their faithlessness is summed up in the question which represents faith as an impossibility for them: *How can ye* (emphatic) *believe*, **seeing that ye receive glory** (the highest reward of action) *one of another* (comp. Matt. xxiii. 5); *and the* **glory** *that* cometh *from* **the only God** (not *from God only*) *ye seek not?* **The only God**, the one source of all glory, absolutely one in nature, stands in opposition to the "gods many" and to the many common dispensers of praise; to regard these in themselves is idolatry (comp. xii. 42, 43). The change of construction in the original is remarkable, from a causal participle (**seeing that ye receive**) to the finite verb (*ye seek not*). The first clause gives the sufficient reason of unbelief; the second an accompanying fact. Comp. i. 32.

45—47. The rejection of Christ carries condemnation with it. The accuser is found in the supposed advocate (*v.* 45); and unbelief in the vaunted belief (*v.* 47).

45. *Do not think...*] Though I lay bare the cause and nature of your unbelief, *do not think that I will accuse you to the Father* (not *my Father*); there is one *that accuseth you*, even *Moses* **on whom you have set your hope.** Disbelief in me is disbelief in him, in the record of the promises to the patriarchs (viii. 56), in the types of the deliverance from Egypt (iii. 14), in the symbolic institutions of the Law, in the promise of a prophet like to himself; *for* **it was of me** (the order is emphatic) *he wrote.* If ye were now at this very time his faithful disciples, you would be mine also. Christ was the essential subject of the Law as of the Prophets; and so of the permanent records of the earlier dispensation.

in whom ye trust] **on whom ye have set your hope** (εἰς ὃν ὑμεῖς ἠλπίκατε, Vulg. *in quo vos speratis*). Comp. 2 Cor. i. 10; 1 Tim. iv. 10, v. 5.

47. The converse of *v.* 46 also holds true. Disbelief in Moses involved disbelief in Christ. *If ye believe not his writings*, the testimony which he has given formally, solemnly, and which you profess to accept as authoritative, *how shall ye believe my words*, my sayings (iii. 34), which come to you without the recommendation of use and age? The essence of the disbelief which the Jews shewed to Moses lay in refusing to regard the Law as transitory. They failed to seize the principle of life by which it was inspired, and petrified the form. If they thus allowed their pride to interfere with their acceptance of the real teaching of Moses, they could much less admit the teaching of Christ. Outward zeal became spiritual rebellion.

writings] The original word (γράμματα) appears to mark the specific form rather than the general scope of the record (γραφαί). Comp. 2 Tim. iii. 15 f.

ADDITIONAL NOTES on CHAP. V. 1, 3.

The evidence for the identification of the unnamed feast in *v.* 1 is obscure and slight. The feast has in fact been identified with each of the three great Jewish festivals—the *Passover* (Irenæus, Eusebius, Lightfoot, Neander, Greswell, &c.), *Pentecost* (Cyril, Chrysostom,

Calvin, Bengel, &c.), and the feast of *Tabernacles* (Ewald, &c.). It has also been identified with the Day of *Atonement* (Caspari), the feast of *Dedication* (Petavius ?), and more commonly in recent times with the feast of *Purim* (Wieseler, Meyer, Godet, &c.).

The difficulty was felt at a very early time. The definite article (ἡ ἑορτή) was added as soon as the second century, and is found in a large number of copies, among which are ℵ, C, L, and the early Egyptian versions. It is however omitted by ABD, Origen, and a large number of later copies; and this combination of authorities is of far greater weight in such a case than the former. We may therefore safely conclude that the Evangelist speaks of "a feast," not of "the feast." If the definite article were authentic the reference would be to the Feast of Tabernacles, which was emphatically "the Feast of the Jews" (comp. Browne, 'Ordo Sæclorum,' p. 87), and not, as is commonly said, to the Passover. One MS., it may be added, inserts "of unleavened bread," and another "the Feast of Tabernacles."

The determination of the event, if it can be reached, has a decisive bearing both upon the chronology of St John's narrative, and upon the relation of St John's narrative to that of the Synoptists.

The fixed points between which the Feast lies are the Passover (ii. 23) and the Feeding of the Five Thousand; the latter event taking place, according to the universal testimony of MSS. and versions, "when the Passover was near at hand" (vi. 4).

The following details in St John bear more or less directly upon the date.

1. After leaving Jerusalem at the conclusion of the Passover (iii. 22), the Lord "tarried" in Judæa. This stay was sufficiently long to lead to results which attracted the attention of the Baptist's disciples (*l. c.*) and of the Pharisees (iv. 1).

2. On the other hand, the interval between the Passover and the Lord's return to Galilee was such that the memory of the events of that Feast was fresh in the minds of those who had been present at it (iv. 45); and from the mention of "the Feast" it is unlikely that any other great Feast had occurred since.

3. The ministry of the Baptist, who was at liberty after the Passover (iii. 26 ff.), is spoken of as already past at the unnamed Feast (v. 35).

4. To this it may be added that the language in which the Lord's action in regard to the Sabbath is spoken of, implies that His teaching on this was now familiar to the leaders of the people (v. 18, ἔλυε).

5. The phrase used in iv. 35 has special significance if the conversation took place either shortly after seedtime or shortly before harvest.

6. The circumstances of the conversation in ch. iv. suit better with summer than with early spring.

7. At the time when the healing took place the sick lay in the open air, under the shelter of the porches.

8. From vii. 21 ff. it appears that the Lord had not visited Jerusalem between this unnamed Feast and the Feast of Tabernacles, and that the incident of *v.* 1 ff. was fresh in the minds of the people at the later visit.

9. It is improbable that the Feast was one of those which St John elsewhere specifies by name (the *Passover*, ii. 13, vi. 4, xi. 55; the *Tabernacles*, vii. 2; the *Dedication*, x. 22).

A consideration of these data seems to leave the choice between *Pentecost*, *the Feast of Trumpets*, (*the Day of Atonement*) and *Purim*.

Purim (March) would fall in well with the succession of events; but the character of the discourse has no connexion with the thoughts of the Festival; and the Festival itself was not such as to give a natural occasion for such teaching.

Pentecost would suit well with the character of the discourse, but the interval between the Passover of ch. ii. and the Pentecost of the same year would scarcely leave sufficient time for the events implied in ch. iii., iv.; while to regard it as the Pentecost of the year after (McClellan) seems to make the interval too great.

It is scarcely likely that the *Day of Atonement* would be called simply "a festival," though Philo ('de septen.' § 23) speaks of it as "a festival of a fast" (νηστείας ἑορτή), but *the Feast of Trumpets* (the new moon of September), which occurs shortly before, satisfies all the conditions which are required. This "beginning of the year," "the day of memorial," was in every way a most significant day. It had, according to the contemporary interpretation of Philo, a double significance, national and universal: national in memory of the miraculous giving of the law with the sound of the trumpet; and universal as calling men to a spiritual warfare in which God gives peace (*l. c.* § 22). On this day, according to a very early Jewish tradition, God holds a judgment of men (Mishnah, 'Rosh Hashanah,' § II. and notes); as on this day He had created the world (Suren. on Mishnah, 'Rosh Hashanah,' § I, II. pp. 306, 313). Thus many of the main thoughts of the discourse, creation, judgment, law, find a remarkable illustration in the thoughts of the Festival, as is the case with the other Festival discourses in St John. These find expression in the ancient prayer attributed to Rav (second century), which is still used in the Synagogue service for the day: "This is the day of the beginning of Thy works, a memorial of the first day... And on the provinces is it decreed thereon, 'This one is for the sword;' and 'This for peace;' 'This one is for famine,' and 'This for plenty.'

And thereon are men (creatures) visited, that they be remembered for life and for death. Who is not visited on this day? for the remembrance of all that hath been formed cometh before Thee..." ('Additional Service for the New Year,' אתה זוכר). And again, shortly after (comp. *vv.* 37 f.): "Thou didst reveal Thyself in the cloud of Thy glory unto Thy holy people, to speak with them; from the heavens didst Thou make them to hear Thy voice, and Thou didst reveal Thyself to them in a dense bright cloud. Yea the whole world trembled at Thy presence, and the creatures of Thy making trembled because of Thee, when Thou, our King, didst reveal Thyself on Mount Sinai, to teach Thy people Thy Law and Thy commandments" (*id.* אתה נגלית).

NOTE ON THE READING IN *v.* 3 ff.

The various readings in *vv.* 3, 4 are very instructive. The last clause of *v.* 3 and the whole of *v.* 4 (ἐκδεχομένων...νοσήματι) is omitted by ℵBC*, *Memph.*, *Theb.*, *Syr. vt.*, and one Latin copy (*q*).

The last clause of *v.* 3 (ἐκδεχομένων...κίνησιν) is omitted by A*L; while it is contained in D, 1, 33, (*Latt.*), (*Syrr.*), and the great mass of later authorities.

The whole of *v.* 4 is omitted by D, 33, and by some Latin copies, and is marked as spurious in very many MSS.; while it is contained in AL, (*Latt.*), (*Syr.*), and the great mass of later authorities. The passage is not referred to by any writer except Tertullian (see below) earlier than Chrysostom, Didymus and Cyril of Alexandria.

Thus the whole passage is omitted by the oldest representatives of each great group of authorities. And, on the other hand, the whole passage is not contained in any authority, except Latin, which gives an ante-Nicene text. It is also to be noticed that the passage is inserted in the later texts of the *Memph.* and *Arm.*, which omit it, wholly or in part, in their earliest form.

The earliest addition to the original text was the conclusion of *v.* 3. This was a natural gloss suggested by *v.* 7, which is undisturbed.

The gloss in *v.* 4 probably embodied an early tradition; and Tertullian was acquainted with it ('de Bapt.' 5).

The glosses (though longer and more important) are like many which are found in ℵD, *Syr. vt.* and *Lat. vt.*, and the fact that they are not found in ℵ, *Syr. vt.*, and only partly in D, shews that they were for a time confined to North Africa.

It is obvious that there could be no motive for omitting the words, if they originally formed part of St John's text; nor could any hypothesis of arbitrary omission explain the partial omissions in the earliest authorities which omit; while all is intelligible if the words are regarded as two glosses. The most ancient evidence and internal probability perfectly agree.

CHAPTER VI.

1 *Christ feedeth five thousand men with five loaves and two fishes.* 15 *Thereupon the people would have made him king.* 16 *But withdrawing himself, he walked on the sea to his disciples:* 26 *reproveth the people flocking after him, and all the fleshly hearers of his word:* 32 *declareth himself to be the bread of life to believers.* 66 *Many disciples depart from him.* 68 *Peter confesseth him.* 70 *Judas is a devil.*

---

ii. CHRIST AND MEN (ch. vi.).

The record of a critical scene in Christ's work in Galilee follows the record of the critical scene at Jerusalem. At Jerusalem Christ revealed Himself as the Giver of life; here He reveals Himself as the Support and Guide of life. In the former case the central teaching was upon the relation of the Son to the Father; in this case it is on the relation of Christ to the believer.

This episode contains the whole essence of the Lord's Galilæan ministry. It places in a decisive contrast the true and false conceptions of the Messianic Kingship, the one universal and spiritual, the other local and material.

The record consists of three parts: *the signs* (*vv.* 1—21); *the discourses* (*vv.* 22—59); *the issue* (*vv.* 60—71).

The signs on the land and on the lake (1—21).

The two signs, *the Feeding of the Five Thousand* (1—15), and *the Walking on the Sea* (15—21), combine to shew Christ as the support of life and as the guide and strengthener of the toiling. Through His disciples He first satisfies the multitudes, and then He Himself, at first unseen and unrecognised, brings His labouring disciples to the haven of rest.

1—15. *The sign on the land, the feeding of the five thousand.*

The feeding of the five thousand is the only incident in the Lord's life, before His last visit to Jerusalem, which is recorded by all four Evangelists. The variations of detail in the four narratives are therefore of the deepest interest (Matt. xiv. 13—21; Mark vi. 30—44; Luke ix. 10—17; John vi. 1—15).

Generally it may be said that the Synoptic narratives are given in broad outline, as part of a prolonged ministry. St John's narrative is part of an isolated episode, but at the same time individual in detail. The actors in the former are the Lord and "the disciples," or the "twelve:" "the disciples say to Him."

AFTER these things Jesus went over the sea of Galilee, which is *the sea* of Tiberias.
2 And a great multitude followed him, because they saw his miracles which he did on them that were diseased.
3 And Jesus went up into a moun-

"He saith to them;" in the latter, the Lord, and Philip, and Andrew. As a natural consequence the conversation, of which St John has preserved characteristic fragments, is condensed into a simple form by the first three Evangelists; and, on the other hand, the circumstances which led up to the event are to be found only in the Synoptists, though we may detect traces of their influence in St John's record.

It follows that the two narratives are derived from two distinct sources; for it is not possible that the narrative of St John could have been derived from any one of the Synoptists, or from the common original from which they were finally derived.

The chronology of the event cannot be determined with absolute certainty. Some have supposed that the words τὸ πάσχα (*v.* 4) are a very early and erroneous gloss (1); and others again have suggested that chh. v. and vi. were transposed accidentally, perhaps at the time when chh. vi., xxi.—episodes of the Galilæan lake—were added on the last review of the Gospel (2).

Against (1) (Browne, 'Ordo Sæclorum,' pp. 84 ff.) it must be urged that all direct documentary evidence whatever supports the disputed words. The ground for suspecting them is derived indirectly from patristic citations, and it is by no means clear that there is not in the passages quoted a confusion between vi. 4 and vii. 2. Irenæus (II. 22, § 3) appears to interpret nigh (vi. 4, ἐγγύς) retrospectively. Comp. Mark vi. 39, note.

The transposition (2) (Norris, 'Journal of Philology,' 1871, pp. 107 ff.) would give a simple connexion of events, but in the absence of all external evidence it cannot be maintained.

Our knowledge of the details of the Lord's life is far too fragmentary to justify us in the endeavour to make a complete arrangement of those which have been recorded. The very abruptness of the transition in vi. 1 is characteristic of St John; comp. iii. 22, x. 22, xii. 1.

CHAP. VI. 1. *After these things*] See v. 1, note.

went] Rather, *departed*, **went away**, that is from the scene of His ministry at the time, which is left undetermined, and not from Jerusalem, as if this verse stood in immediate connexion with ch. v. The abruptness with which the narrative is introduced is most worthy of notice. All we read is that the departure "over the sea of Galilee" (*i.e.* to the east side of it) took place at some time after the visit to Jerusalem, which, as we have seen, probably took place at the feast of the New Year. The Passover also was near, if the present text in *v.* 4 is correct; but we learn nothing from St John as to the facts by which the incident was immediately preceded. This information must be sought from the other Gospels. And it is very significant that the Synoptists set the withdrawal of the Lord in connexion with two critical events. They all agree in stating that it followed upon tidings brought from without. St Matthew makes it consequent upon the account of the death of the Baptist brought by his disciples (xiv. 13). St Luke places it immediately after the return of the twelve from their mission, but without any definite combination of the two events (ix. 10). St Mark brings out more clearly that at least one object of the retirement was rest from exhausting labour (vi. 30, 31). These indications of a concurrence of motives exactly correspond to the fulness of life. And St Luke has preserved the link which combines them. "Herod," he says, "sought to see [Jesus]," troubled by the thought of a new John come to take the place of him whom he had murdered (ix. 9). The news of the death of the Baptist, of the designs of Herod, of the work of the twelve, coming at the same time, made a brief season of quiet retirement, and that outside the dominions of Herod, the natural counsel of wisdom and tenderness. St Luke alone gives the name of the place which was chosen for this object, "a city called Bethsaida" (ix. 10), that is the district of Bethsaida Julias in Gaulonitis, at the N.E. of the lake (Jos. 'Ant.' XVIII. 2. 1). This second city of the same name was probably present to the mind of St John when he spoke of "Bethsaida of *Galilee*" (xii. 21; but not i. 44) as the home of Philip. Perhaps we may add, that this withdrawal for calm devotion would be still more necessary, if it was intended to cover the period of the Passover, which the Lord could not celebrate at Jerusalem owing to the hostility shewn towards Him there not long before.

the sea of Tiberias] This is the name by which the lake was known to classical writers (Paus. v. 7, p. 391, λίμνη Τιβεριάς). The title occurs only here and in ch. xxi. 1 in the New Testament; and it will be noticed that in xxi. 1 no second name is given. The later incident was not contained in the common basis of the Synoptic accounts, and was not therefore connected with the Synoptic title of the lake. The name of Tiberias, the splendid but unholy capital

tain, and there he sat with his disciples.

[a] Lev. 23. 5. Deut. 16. 1. 4 [a] And the passover, a feast of the Jews, was nigh.

[b] Matt. 14. 14. 5 ¶ [b] When Jesus then lifted up *his* eyes, and saw a great company come unto him, he saith unto Philip, Whence shall we buy bread, that these may eat?

6 And this he said to prove him: for he himself knew what he would do.

7 Philip answered him, Two hundred pennyworth of bread is not suf-

---

which Herod the tetrarch had built for himself, is not mentioned in the New Testament except in these two places and in *v.* 23.

2. *followed*] not simply on this occasion but generally (ἠκολούθει). The verse describes most vividly the habitual work and environment and influence of Christ. The sense stands in contrast with that in Matt. xiv. 13; Luke ix. 11.

saw] **beheld** (ἐθεώρουν), *v.* 19. See ii. 23, note.

his miracles...] **the signs** *which he did...* This verb (ἐποίει, Vulg. *faciebat*), like those which precede, marks a continued ministry.

3. *into a mountain*] **into the mountain, and...** So *v.* 15. The use of the definite article implies an instinctive sense of the familiar landscape, the mountain range closing round the lake. This use is found also in the Synoptic narrative, Matt. v. 1, xiv. 23, xv. 29; Mark iii. 13, vi. 46; Luke vi. 12, ix. 28. St Matthew adds that it was "a desert spot" (xiv. 13).

sat] Literally, *was sitting*. The word has a life-like distinctness when taken in connexion with *v.* 5. Comp. Matt. xiii. 1, xv. 29.

4. *And* **(Now)** *the passover...was nigh*] *i.e.* "near at hand" (ii. 13, vii. 2, xi. 55), and not as Irenæus (?) and some moderns have taken it, "lately past." The notice of the feast is probably designed to give a clue to the understanding of the spiritual lessons of the miracle which are set forth in the discourse which followed (1 Cor. v. 7); and at the same time it serves to explain how trains of pilgrims on their way to Jerusalem may have been attracted to turn aside to the new Teacher, in addition to "the multitude" who were already attached to Him.

the feast of the Jews] *i.e.* "the well-known feast." The phrase when it stands alone signifies the Feast of Tabernacles, "the one great national feast." Compare vii. 2 (where the order is different), and v. 1, note.

5. *When Jesus then lifted up...and saw... come...he saith...*] **Jesus therefore having lifted up his eyes and seen that... cometh...saith.** Comp. iv. 35, (i. 38).

come (**cometh**)] Literally, *is coming*. Jesus and His disciples sailed across the lake (Matt. xiv. 13), but "the multitudes" observed their departure and reached Bethsaida on foot (Mark vi. 33). The point of time here is evidently the first arrival of the people. A day of teaching and healing must be intercalated before the miracle of feeding was wrought (Matt. xiv. 14; Mark vi. 34; Luke ix. 11). St John appears to have brought together into one scene, as we now regard it, the first words spoken to Philip on the approach of the crowd, and the words in which they were afterwards taken up by Andrew, when the disciples themselves at evening restated the difficulty (Matt. xiv. 15; Mark vi. 35; Luke ix. 12). If this view be true, so that the words addressed to Philip with his answer preceded the whole day's work, then the mention of "two hundred pennyworth of bread" made by the disciples in St Mark (vi. 37) gains great point, and so too the phrase "what He was about to do" (*v.* 6), which otherwise appears to be followed too quickly by its fulfilment. It appears also from *v.* 15 that the Lord came down from the mountain before the miracle was wrought.

Philip] i. 44 ff., xii. 21 f., xiv. 8 f.

Whence shall we...] The words are one expression of the feeling of tender compassion noticed by the Synoptists (Matt. xiv. 14; Mark vi. 34).

6. *to prove*] Literally, **trying** him, to see whether he could meet the difficulty. Comp. 2 Cor. xiii. 5; Rev. ii. 2. The word does not necessarily carry with it (as these passages shew) the secondary idea of temptation (comp. also Matt. xxii. 35; Mark xii. 15); but practically in the case of men such trial assumes for the most part this form, seeing that it leads to failure, either as designed by him who applies it (Matt. xvi. 1, xix. 3, xxii. 18, &c.), or consequent upon the weakness of him to whom it is applied (Hebr. xi. 17; 1 Cor. x. 13). Comp. Deut. xiii. 3.

for he himself knew...would **(was about to)** *do*] Throughout the Gospel the Evangelist speaks as one who had an intimate knowledge of the Lord's mind. He reveals both the thoughts which belong to His own internal, absolute knowledge (εἰδέναι, *vv.* 61, 64, xiii. 3, xviii. 4, xix. 28), and also those which answered to actual experience and insight (γινώσκειν, *v.* 15, iv. 1, v. 6, xvi. 19).

7. *Two hundred pennyworth*] *i.e.* between six and seven pounds worth. See Mark vi. 37. We cannot tell by what calculation this

ficient for them, that every one of
them may take a little.
8 One of his disciples, Andrew,
Simon Peter's brother, saith unto him,
9 There is a lad here, which hath
five barley loaves, and two small
fishes: but what are they among so
many?
10 And Jesus said, Make the men
sit down. Now there was much grass
in the place. So the men sat down,
in number about five thousand.
11 And Jesus took the loaves;
and when he had given thanks, he
distributed to the disciples, and the
disciples to them that were set down;
and likewise of the fishes as much as
they would.
12 When they were filled, he said
unto his disciples, Gather up the fragments that remain, that nothing be
lost.
13 Therefore they gathered *them*
together, and filled twelve baskets
with the fragments of the five barley loaves, which remained over and
above unto them that had eaten.
14 Then those men, when they
had seen the miracle that Jesus did,
said, This is of a truth that prophet
that should come into the world.
15 ¶ When Jesus therefore per-

---

exact sum was reached. The reference may be to some unrecorded fact.

every one of them] Omit *of them*.

8. *Andrew*] He appears elsewhere in connexion with Philip, i. 44, xii. 22.

9. *barley loaves*] *v.* 13. The detail is peculiar to St John. Comp. 2 K. iv. 42. Barley bread was the food of the poor. Wetstein (*ad loc.*) has collected a large number of passages to shew the small account in which it was held. See Judg. vii. 13 f.; Ezek. xiii. 19.

small fishes] Rather, **fishes**. It is worthy of remark that the original word (ὀψάρια) is found in the New Testament only in this passage and in ch. xxi. It may have been a familiar Galilæan word.

10. *And Jesus*] Omit *And*.

the men...the men] *the* **people** (τοὺς ἀνθρώπους)...*the men* (οἱ ἄνδρες)...*about five thousand*. The change of word in the latter case implies the remark added by St Matthew (xiv. 21) *beside women and children*.

much grass] See note on Mark vi. 39. The difference of the form in which the detail is introduced marks apparently the testimony of two eye-witnesses. This detail corresponds with the date, which is fixed (vi. 4) in the early spring.

11. *And Jesus...*] *Jesus* **therefore**, answering the obedience of faith.

when he had given thanks (*v.* 23)] By this act the Lord takes the place of the head of the family (comp. Luke xxiv. 30). The word itself is found elsewhere in St John only, xi. 41. This second passage suggests that the thanksgiving was rendered in acknowledgment of the revelation of the Father's will in accordance with which the miracle was wrought. In the parallels the word is *blessed* (yet comp. Matt. xv. 36; Mark viii. 6). The two words preserve the two aspects of the action in relation to the source and in relation to the mode of its accomplishment. Compare in this connexion Matt. xxvi. 26 f.; Mark xiv. 22 f.

he distributed to...them that...] The words *to the disciples...and the disciples* must be omitted. They are an obvious gloss introduced from St Matthew xiv. 19.

and likewise of] **likewise also of.**

12. *When they...said...*] **And** *when they...* **saith...**

fragments] *i.e.* **the pieces** broken for distribution (Ezek. xiii. 19). The command to collect these is preserved by St John only.

that remain] *that* **remain over**, and so in *v.* 13 (*which* **remained over**), where the same word is used.

13. *gathered...together*] **gathered...up.** The word is the same as in *v.* 12. The simple repetition gives character to the narrative.

twelve] The number implies that the work was given to the apostles, though they have not been specially mentioned. Comp. *v.* 70.

baskets] The stout wicker baskets (κοφίνους) as distinguished from the soft, flexible "frails" (σφυρίδες, Matt. xv. 37; Mark viii. 8). Juv. 'Sat.' III. 14, VI. 542.

14, 15. This incident is peculiar to St John, but St Luke has preserved a detail which illustrates it. He notices that Christ spoke to the multitudes "concerning the kingdom of God" (ix. 11); and it is natural to suppose that the excitement consequent upon the death of the Baptist, which in part led to the Lord's retirement, may have moved many to believe that He would place Himself at the head of a popular rising to avenge the murder.

14. *Then those men ... Jesus did ...*] **The people** (οἱ ἄνθρωποι) **therefore... he** *did...*

that prophet that should come...] **the** *prophet* **that cometh...** Comp. i. 21, 25, vii. 40. The phrase is peculiar to St John. Yet see Matt. xxi. 11, and Acts vii. 37.

ceived that they would come and take him by force, to make him a king, he departed again into a mountain himself alone.

c Matt. 14. 23. 16 [c] And when even was *now* come, his disciples went down unto the sea,

17 And entered into a ship, and went over the sea toward Capernaum. And it was now dark, and Jesus was not come to them.

18 And the sea arose by reason of a great wind that blew.

19 So when they had rowed about five and twenty or thirty furlongs, they see Jesus walking on the sea, and drawing nigh unto the ship: and they were afraid.

20 But he saith unto them, It is I; be not afraid.

21 Then they willingly received him into the ship: and immediately

---

15. *would* (**were about to**)...*take him by force* (ἁρπάζειν, Vulg. *ut raperent*)] Comp. Acts xxiii. 10; (Judg. xxi. 21, LXX.); Matt. xi. 12. The multitude wished to use Christ to fulfil their own ends even against His will. In this lies the foreshadowing of the sin of Judas, ch. xviii. 6.

make him a king] **make him king.**

departed] **withdrew** (ἀνεχώρησεν). Comp. Matt. ii. 12 ff., xiv. 13, xv. 21, &c.; Acts xxiii. 19.

again] It follows (*v.* 3) that He had descended towards the shore when the miracle took place.

himself alone] to pray, as is added in the parallel narratives (Matt. xiv. 23; Mark vi. 46). The dismissal of the apostles mentioned in Matt. xiv. 22; Mark vi. 45, is involved in these words (contrast *v.* 3). The apostles were first withdrawn from the influence of the multitude, and the mass of the people were then sent away; but some (*v.* 22) still lingered with vain hopes till the morning.

16—21. *The sign upon the lake.*

This incident is related also by St Matthew (xiv. 22 ff.) and by St Mark (vi. 45 ff.). The change in time, scene, persons, belongs to the significance of the sign.

16. Comp. Matt. xiv. 22 ff.; Mark vi. 45 ff.

when even was now come] The "second evening," from sunset till dark. Comp. Matt. xiv. 15, 23.

17. *into a ship*] The definite article is omitted in the true text, so that A. V. is correct.

went...toward] Literally, *set out on their way to...* Comp. iv. 30. This continuous toil is contrasted by the tense with the simple act which preceded it (κατέβησαν, ἤρχοντο).

was not **yet** *come...*] at the time when they finally started. It appears that some incidents are here omitted. Probably Jesus had directed the apostles to meet Him at some point on the eastern shore on their way to Capernaum.

18. The singular vividness of the description is to be noticed. Comp. Jonah i. 13 (LXX.).

19. *five and twenty...furlongs*] The lake is at its broadest about forty stades ("furlongs"), or six miles. Thus they were "in the middle" of the lake (Mark vi. 47), having for a time kept to the shore.

see] **behold.** The word marks the arrested, absorbed attention of the disciples. Comp. *v.* 2.

on the sea] The words might mean (as xxi. 1) "on the sea-shore," but the context and parallels determine the sense here. Comp. Job ix. 8 (LXX.).

were afraid] Comp. Matt. xiv. 26; Mark vi. 49; Luke xxiv. 37.

20. *It is I*] Comp. iv. 26, viii. 24, 28, 58, (ix. 9), xiii. 19, xviii. 5, 6, 8; Mark xiii. 6; Luke xxi. 8.

21. *willingly received*] Literally, *they were willing to take* (ἤθελον λαβεῖν, Vulg. *voluerunt accipere*). The imperfect in the original expresses a continuous state of feeling as distinguished from an isolated wish. It is commonly used of a desire which is not gratified (vii. 44, xvi. 19; Mark vi. 19, 48; Gal. iv. 20, &c.), but this secondary idea does not necessarily lie in the word. Here the force of the tense is adequately given by A. V., though in Mark vi. 48 the same word is used of the supposed purpose of the Lord to "pass by" the disciples, which was not fulfilled. Comp. Mark xii. 38; Luke xii. 46. Fear passed into joy. Compare Luke xxiv. 37 with John xx. 20.

at the land] The original phrase (ἐπὶ τῆς γῆς) may mean *in the direction of the land*, that is, "moving straight towards the land;" but it more probably means *on the land*, being used of the vessel run up on the beach. Comp. Ps. cvii. (cvi.) 30. The Synoptists notice that the opposing forces were removed (Matt. xiv. 32; Mark vi. 51, *the wind ceased*); St John that the desired end was gained. Both results followed at once from the presence of Christ welcomed.

went] The original word (ὑπῆγον) is somewhat remarkable. Comp. *v.* 67, vii. 33, note, xii. 11, xviii. 8. The idea of "withdrawing from," "leaving" something, seems to underlie it.

the ship was at the land whither they went.

22 ¶ The day following, when the people which stood on the other side of the sea saw that there was none other boat there, save that one whereinto his disciples were entered, and that Jesus went not with his disciples into the boat, but *that* his disciples were gone away alone;

23 (Howbeit there came other boats from Tiberias nigh unto the

---

It will be obvious that these two "signs" are introductory to the discourse which follows. Both correct limited views springing out of our material conceptions. Effects are produced at variance with our ideas of quantity and quality. That which is small becomes great. That which is heavy moves on the surface of the water. Contrary elements yield at a divine presence. Both "signs," in other words, prepare the way for new thoughts of Christ, of His sustaining, preserving, guiding power, and exclude deductions drawn from corporeal relations only. He can support men, though visible means fall short. He is with His disciples, though they do not recognise or see Him. And in both cases also the powers and action of men are needed. They receive and assimilate the food which is given; they take Christ into their boat before they reach their haven.

The remarks with which Augustine opens his explanation of the narrative are of permanent value. "Miracula quæ fecit Dominus noster Jesus Christus sunt quidem divina opera et ad intellegendum Deum de visibilibus admonent humanam mentem ... Nec tamen sufficit hæc intueri in miraculis Christi. Interrogemus ipsa miracula, quid nobis loquantur de Christo: habent enim si intellegantur linguam suam. Nam quia ipse Christus Verbum Dei est, etiam factum Verbi verbum nobis est" (August. 'in Johann. Tract.' XXIV. 1, 2).

The discourses at Capernaum (22—59).

The discourses which followed the feeding of the five thousand serve in part as an answer to the mistaken expectations of the multitude (*vv.* 14, 15), while they unfold those views of Christ's Person and work which became a decisive trial for the faith of the disciples who were already attached to Him. The short absence had been sufficient to remove the fear of immediate violence on the part of Herod; though it appears that the Lord withdrew not long afterwards to "the coasts of Tyre and Sidon" (Matt. xv. 21 ff.).

The discourses fall into three groups: *vv.* 26—40, *vv.* 41—51, *vv.* 52—58. Each group is introduced by some expression of feeling on the part of those to whom the words are addressed, a simple question (*v.* 25), a murmuring (*v.* 41), a contention among themselves (*v.* 52). The thoughts successively dealt with are distinct: (1) the search after life, (2) the relation of the Son to God and man, (3) the appropriation by the individual of the Incarnate Son; and it appears that the audience and place do not remain the same. There are evident breaks after *v.* 40, and *v.* 51. The "Jews" are introduced in *vv.* 41, 52, but not before. The last words were spoken "in synagogue" (*v.* 59), but it is scarcely conceivable that the conversation began there.

26—40. The first part of the discourses consists of answers to successive questions (*vv.* 25, 28, 30, 34). The conversation is natural and rapid; and deals in succession with the aim of religious effort (26, 27); the method (28, 29); the assurance (30—33); the fulfilment (34—40).

22—24. This long sentence is complicated and irregular in construction. The irregularity is due to the mention of two facts which are intercalated between the beginning and end of the sentence. The narrative would naturally have run: *The day following the multitude... when they saw* (*v.* 24) *that Jesus was not there...took shipping...*; but St John has inserted two explanatory clauses, the first to explain why they still lingered on the eastern shore in the hope of finding Jesus: *The day following*, **the multitude...saw** (εἶδον) *that there was...save one* (omit *whereinto his disciples were entered*) *and that Jesus...but that his disciples* **went** *away alone*; and the second to explain how they were themselves able to cross over: *howbeit there came boats from Tiberias...* As a consequence he begins the sentence again in *v.* 24, *When the multitude therefore saw...*, where the *saw* is not a simple resumption of the *saw* in *v.* 22, but the result of later observation.

22. *the people which stood*] *the* **multitude...**(and so in *v.* 24), some, that is, who still lingered when the rest were dismissed (Matt. xiv. 23), the more eager zealots, as it seems, who wished still to make Christ fulfil their designs. They were not more than could cross the lake in the boats which came over (*v.* 23).

23. *Howbeit there came other boats*] Omit *other* (reading ἀλλὰ ἦλθεν πλοῖα). These boats, perhaps, were driven by the "contrary wind" (Matt. xiv. 24) across the lake. Their coming probably explains the reference to the "disciples" in *v.* 24. At first the multitude

place where they did eat bread, after that the Lord had given thanks:)

24 When the people therefore saw that Jesus was not there, neither his disciples, they also took shipping, and came to Capernaum, seeking for Jesus.

25 And when they had found him on the other side of the sea, they said unto him, Rabbi, when camest thou hither?

26 Jesus answered them and said, Verily, verily, I say unto you, Ye seek me, not because ye saw the miracles, but because ye did eat of the loaves, and were filled.

27 [1]Labour not for the meat which perisheth, but for that meat which endureth unto everlasting life, which the Son of man shall give unto you: [d]for him hath God the Father sealed.

28 Then said they unto him, What shall we do, that we might work the works of God?

[1] Or, Wor

[d] Ma 17.

---

might have supposed that they had returned in one of them from some brief mission to the other side.

nigh unto the place] that is, to some unfrequented part of the shore, as driven by stress of weather.

the Lord] Comp. iv. 1, xi. 2, xxi. 7.

24. *they also*] *they* **themselves.** The force of the word is that they also did what they found the disciples had done.

25. *when camest...*] The idea suggested by *when*, as contrasted with the more natural *how*, is that of the separation from Christ; as if the people had pleaded, "We sought thee long and anxiously on the other side. Could it be that even then thou hadst left us?" If this turn is given to the words the connexion of the answer is obvious: "It is not me ye seek, but my gifts."

26. *not because ye saw the miracles...*] *not because* **ye saw signs**..., not because my works of healing and sustaining led you to look for other manifestations of spiritual glory. That one last miracle—a speaking sign—was to you a gross material satisfaction, and not a pledge, a parable of something higher. You failed to see in it the lesson which it was designed to teach, that I am waiting to relieve the hunger of the soul.

were filled] Literally, "were satisfied with food as animals with fodder" (ἐχορτάσθητε, Vulg. *saturati estis*, and so in *v.* 12). The original word is different from that used in *v.* 12. It is however used in connexion with the narrative in the other Gospels (Matt. xiv. 20, and parallels) without any disparaging sense; and it is not therefore possible to press the material idea which predominates in it (Luke xv. 16, xvi. 21). See Matt. v. 6; Luke vi. 21.

27. *Labour not for...*] **Work** *not for...* The verb stands emphatically at the head of the sentence. "Work, yea win by work, not..." Thus perhaps there is a contrast between "seeking" and "working." Comp. Isai. lv. 1 ff.

work...*give*] The contrast of these verbs is essential to the sense of the passage. The believer's work does not earn a recompense at the last, but secures a gift. Even common work may bring more than its natural result, "the meat which perisheth." And no work brings more than the possibility of blessings to be used. Comp. i. 12 f., note.

the meat which perisheth] that food (βρῶσις) which belongs to our material life; which supports life only by undergoing change; for material life is truly a process of death (comp. 1 Cor. vi. 13). It is possible too that there may be even at this point a reference to the manna: Exod. xvi. 20.

that (**the**) *meat which endureth* (**abideth**) *unto everlasting* (**eternal**) *life*] that food which suffers no change, but remains in the man as a principle of power issuing in eternal life. Comp. iv. 14.

the Son of man] This title suggests the thought which underlies the whole discourse. Christ is speaking of His relation to men in virtue of His perfect humanity. He, as the absolute representative of mankind, will give this food of the higher life—the life also being His gift, v. 25—*for Him* **the Father** (not *my Father*, *v.* 32), His Father and the Father of men, **sealed, even God** (ch. x. 36. See also v. 36 ff.).

shall give] as the issue of His work (*v.* 51); or perhaps as the crown of your work of faith in Him.

God the Father] **the Father...even God.** The addition of the divine name at the close of the sentence emphasizes the identification of God with "the Father" of "the Son of man." Comp. viii. 19.

sealed] solemnly set apart for the fulfilment of this charge and authenticated by intelligible signs. Comp. iii. 33, note.

28. *Then said they...What shall we do, that we might...*] *They said* **therefore**...*What* **must** *we do, that we* **may**... The questioners appear to admit in word the necessity of the higher aim of work, and inquire as to the method of reaching it; but the phrase *work the works of God* marks the external concep-

ohn 3. 29 Jesus answered and said unto
them, [e] This is the work of God,
that ye believe on him whom he hath
sent.

30 They said therefore unto him,
What sign shewest thou then, that
we may see, and believe thee? what
dost thou work?

31 [f] Our fathers did eat manna in [f] Exod. 16. 15.
the desert; as it is written, [g] He gave Numb. 11. 7.
them bread from heaven to eat. [g] Psal. 78 25.

32 Then Jesus said unto them,
Verily, verily, I say unto you, Moses
gave you not that bread from heaven;
but my Father giveth you the true
bread from heaven.

---

tion of the service of God to which they still clung. The *works of God*—works which He requires—are assumed to be the one condition of obtaining the spiritual food.

29. The Lord deals with the error and the truth in the question which was put to Him. In the one work which God requires of man and man owes to God, all fragmentary and partial works are included. It is a true work as answering to man's will, but it issues in that which is not a work. *This is the work of God, that ye believe on...* Comp. 1 John iii. 23 (*his commandment*).

that ye believe (ἵνα πιστεύητε)] The phrase marks not only the simple fact of believing (τὸ πιστεύειν), but the effort directed to and issuing in this belief. Comp. iv. 34, note. And again it expresses not the single decisive act (ἵνα πιστεύσητε, xiii. 19), but the continuous state of faith.

This simple formula contains the complete solution of the relation of faith and works. Faith is the life of works; works are the necessity of faith.

30. *They said therefore...*] as recognising the claim which Christ preferred, and seeking an authentication of it.

What sign shewest thou (emphatic) *then...*] Literally, *What then doest thou as a sign...* thou, with thy commands to us, peremptory as a second Moses? Christ had charged the questioners with misunderstanding His signs before (*v.* 26); they ask therefore for some clear attestation of His claims. And in this there is nothing inconsistent with the effect which the feeding of the multitude had produced on some. Great as that work was, their history taught them to look for greater. They ask, as in the Synoptists, for "a sign from heaven" (Matt. xvi. 1).

that we may see, and believe thee] In these words faith is reduced to simple belief in the truth of a message, and grounded upon the testimony of the senses. The "believing on Christ" (*v.* 29) is reduced to "believing Christ." Comp. viii. 30, 31, note.

what dost thou work?] The words take up the demand made on themselves. There is a work, they plead, for the teacher as well as for the hearer. The question expresses what was suggested by the emphatic pronoun (*thou*) just before. Words must be justified by works.

31. *did eat manna*] **the manna** [Ps. lxxvii. (lxxviii.) 24]. The miracle which Christ had wrought suggested the greater miracle of Moses, by which the people were sustained for forty years. There was a tradition ('Midrash Koheleth,' p. 73, quoted by Lightfoot and Wünsche) that "as the first Redeemer caused the manna to fall from heaven, even so should the second Redeemer (גואל אחרון) cause the manna to fall." For this sign then, or one like this, the people looked from Him whom they were ready to regard as Messiah. Compare Matt. xvi. 1; Mark viii. 11. The manna was a favourite subject with Jewish expositors. A single passage from Philo ('De profugis,' § 25, p. 566) may serve as an example of their interpretations: "[When the people] sought what it is which feeds the soul, for they did not, as Moses says, know what it was, they discovered by learning that it is the utterance (ῥῆμα) of God and the divine word (θεῖος λόγος) from which all forms of instruction and wisdom flow in a perennial stream. And this is the heavenly food which is indicated in the sacred records under the Person of the First Cause (τοῦ αἰτίου) saying, Behold I rain on you bread (ἄρτους) out of heaven (Exod. xvi. 4). For in very truth God distils from above the supernal wisdom on noble and contemplative minds; and they when they see and taste, in great joy, know what they experience, but do not know the Power which dispenses the gift. Wherefore they ask, What is this which is sweeter than honey and whiter than snow? But they shall be taught by the prophet that this is the bread which the Lord gave them to eat" (Exod. xvi. 15). Comp. Siegfried, 'Philo v. Alex.' s. 229.

from heaven] **out of** *heaven* (and so throughout), which came out of the heavenly treasures, and did not simply descend from a higher region.

32. *Then Jesus...*] *Jesus* **therefore...**

Moses gave...not that (**the**) *bread*] There is a double contrast. It was not Moses but God revealing Himself through Moses who gave the manna; and again the manna—the perishable bread—was not in the highest sense "bread from heaven," but rather the symbol of spiritual food.

gave you] The people are identified with their ancestors. If the reading "hath given" (δέδωκεν) be adopted, then the present realisa-

33 For the bread of God is he which cometh down from heaven, and giveth life unto the world.
34 Then said they unto him, Lord, evermore give us this bread.
35 And Jesus said unto them, I am the bread of life: he that cometh to me shall never hunger; and he that believeth on me shall never thirst.
36 But I said unto you, That ye also have seen me, and believe not.

---

tion of what Moses gave in a symbol is assumed.

but my Father giveth...] not in one miraculous act only, but now and at all times.

the true bread] that which fulfils absolutely, ideally, the highest conception of sustaining food (ἀληθινός). Comp. iv. 23, note. The exact form of the original is emphatic: *the bread out of heaven, the true* bread (τὸν ἀ. ἐκ τ. οὐ. τὸν ἀλ.).

33. *the bread of God*] the bread which God gives directly; not simply that which He gives by the hand of His servants. Comp. i. 29 (*the Lamb of God*), note.

he which cometh down...] **that which** *cometh down...* Christ does not identify Himself with "the bread" till the next answer; and the request of the Jews which follows shews that nothing more than the notion of heavenly bread was present to them (comp. *vv.* 41, 50). This new manna was distinguished from the old in that it was continuous in its descent and not for a time; and again it was not confined to one people, but was for the world.

cometh down] The phrase prepares the way for the interpretation which follows, *vv.* 38, 41.

unto the world] Without the Word, without Christ, the world can have no life. He makes the blessing, which was national, universal.

34. *Then said they...*] *They said* **therefore...** The Jews see in the words of Christ a mysterious promise which they cannot understand; but they interpret it according to their material hopes. *Lord, evermore*, not on one rare occasion but always, *give us this bread.* They acknowledge that the gift must be constant (1 Thess. v. 15, πάντοτε), though its effects are lasting.

35. *Jesus* (omit *and*) *said...*] The Jews asked for something from Christ: He offers them Himself. The great gift, if only it were rightly perceived, was already made.

I am the...] This form of expression is not found in the Synoptists. It occurs not unfrequently in St John's Gospel, and the figures with which it is connected furnish a complete study of the Lord's work. Compare *vv.* 41, 48, 51, viii. 12 (the Light of the world), x. 7, 9 (the Door), x. 11, 14 (the good Shepherd), xi. 25 (the Resurrection and the Life), xiv. 6 (the Way, the Truth, and the Life), xv. 1, 5 (the true Vine).

the bread of life] the food which supplies life: of which life is not a quality only (*v.* 51, *the living bread*), but (so to speak) an endowment which it is capable of communicating. Compare *the tree of life* (Gen. ii. 9, iii. 22, 24; Prov. iii. 18, xi. 30, xiii. 12, xv. 4; Rev. ii. 7, xxii. 2, &c.); *the water of life* (Rev. xxi. 6, xxii. 1, &c. Comp. Ps. xxxvi. (xxxv.) 9; Prov. x. 11, xiii. 14, xiv. 27, xvi. 22, fountain of life). The phrases "words (distinct utterances, sayings, ῥήματα) of life" (*v.* 68), and "the word (the whole revelation, λόγος) of life" (1 John i. 1) are nearly connected.

cometh...believeth] The first word presents faith in deed as active and outward; the second presents faith in thought as resting and inward. Each element is, it is true, implied in the other, but they can be contemplated apart. For *coming to me* see v. 40, *vv.* (37), 44 f., 65, vii. 37.

shall never hunger...shall never thirst] The double image, suggested it may be by the thought of the Passover, extends the conception of the heavenly food, and prepares the way for the double form under which it is finally described (*v.* 53). The gift of strength corresponds with the effort to reach to Christ; the gift of joy with the idea of repose in Christ.

shall never thirst] The exact form of expression in the original is remarkable and irregular (οὐ μὴ διψήσει πώποτε. Contrast iv. 14, οὐ μὴ διψήσει εἰς τὸν αἰῶνα). Perhaps it suggests the image of Christ present in all time and regarding the unfailing satisfaction of those who come to Him, as distinguished from a simple future.

36. *But...*] The gift was indeed made, but the presence of the gift was unavailing, for the condition required of those who should receive it was unfulfilled.

I said unto you...] The thought is contained in *v.* 26, and the reference may be to those words; but more probably the reference is to other words like them spoken at some earlier time.

That ye (omit *also*) *have seen me, and...*] The first conjunction (καί) emphasizes the fact: *that ye have* indeed *seen and...* Comp. ix. 37. The Lord returns to the words in *v.* 30 (*see, believe*), now that the question in *v.* 34 has been answered. He Himself was the sign which the Jews could not read. No other more convincing could be given.

37 All that the Father giveth me
shall come to me; and him that
cometh to me I will in no wise cast out.
38 For I came down from heaven,
not to do mine own will, but the will
of him that sent me.
39 And this is the Father's will
which hath sent me, that of all which
he hath given me I should lose nothing, but should raise it up again at
the last day.
40 And this is the will of him that
sent me, that every one which seeth
the Son, and believeth on him, may
have everlasting life: and I will raise
him up at the last day.

---

37. There is a pause in the discourse before this verse. The unbelief of the people was not a proof that the purpose of God had failed. Rather it gave occasion for declaring more fully how certainly the Son carried out the Father's will.

All that (**All that which**) *the Father... him that cometh...*] The first clause is a general and abstract statement (πᾶν ὅ); the second gives the concrete and individual realisation of it (τὸν ἐρχόμενον). Believers are first regarded as forming a whole complete in its several parts, a gift of the Father; and then each separate believer is regarded in his personal relation to the Son. In the first case stress is laid upon the successful issue of the coming, the arrival (ἥξει, *shall reach me*; comp. Rev. iii. 3, xv. 4, xviii. 8); in the second case on the process of the coming (τὸν ερχομενον, not τὸν ἐλθόντα) and the welcome.

The same contrast between the abstract conception and the concrete fulfilment of it is found in *vv.* 39 f. and xvii. 2. Compare also the use of the abstract form, 1 John v. 4 contrasted with v. 5, 18; and ch. iii. 6 contrasted with iii. 8.

giveth] Compare xvii. 2, 6, 9, 12, 24, xviii. 9.

I will in no wise...] The stern words to the Galilæans might have seemed to be a casting out, but the Lord shews that, on the contrary, they were not truly coming to Him.

cast out] Comp. xii. 31, ix. 34 f.

38. *For...*] *For* this is the Father's will, as is implied in the gift (*v.* 39), and *I am come down...*

I came down] **I am come down.** Comp. iii. 13; (Eph. iv. 9 f.?). With these exceptions the word is used of Christ's descent only in this discourse.

from heaven] In this verse the original preposition (according to the true reading) expresses the idea of leaving (ἀπό), in *v.* 42 (as iii. 13) of proceeding out of (ἐκ). In the one case the thought is that of sacrifice; in the other that of divinity.

not...mine own will] See v. 19 ff.

39. *this is the Father's will which hath...*] According to the true reading, *this is* **the will of him** *that...*

that of all..] The construction in the original is broken: "that *as for all that which he has given me I should not lose of it...*" Comp. vii. 38, (1 John ii. 24, 27), Luke xxi. 6.

hath given] The present used in *v.* 37 (*giveth*) is here changed into the past when the gift is looked at in relation to the will of the Father, and not to the waiting of the Son.

should lose nothing, but should raise it up] filled with a new life, transfigured and glorified. This is the issue of the communication of Christ to the Church. In this place the effect is represented as dependent on the Father's will; but when the words are repeated (*vv.* 40, 44, 54)—once in each great division of the discourses—the effect is referred to the will of the Son (*and I will raise him up*).

at the last day] The phrase is found only in St John, *vv.* 40, 44, 54, xi. 24, xii. 48. Comp. 1 John ii. 18. The plural occurs Acts ii. 17; James v. 3; 2 Tim. iii. 1.

40. *And...the will of him that sent me, that...*] **For**.. *the will* **of my Father,** *that...* The general fulfilment of the will of the Father passes into this further truth, that the contemplation of the Son and belief on Him brings with it eternal life.

seeth (**beholdeth**) *the Son*] Comp. xii. 45, xiv. 19, xvi. 10, 16, 19. The act of contemplation and faith is not momentary or past, but continuous.

have everlasting (**eternal**) *life*] not as future, but as present already as a divine power. Comp. *v.* 47, xvii. 3.

The possession of eternal life is followed by the crowning action of the Son: *and I*—I the Incarnate Son—*will raise him up.* Eternal life is consummated in the restoration to the believer of a transfigured manhood. So far from the doctrine of the Resurrection being, as has been asserted, inconsistent with St John's teaching on the present reality of eternal life, it would be rather true to say that this doctrine makes the necessity of the Resurrection obvious. He who feels that life *is* now, must feel that after death all that belongs to the essence of its present perfection must be restored, however much ennobled under new conditions of manifestation.

41—51. The second part of the discourses, which deals with the relation of Christ to God and to man, is directly connected both with the first and with the third part: with the

41 The Jews then murmured at him, because he said, I am the bread which came down from heaven.
h Matt. 13. 55. 42 And they said, hIs not this Jesus, the son of Joseph, whose father and mother we know? how is it then that he saith, I came down from heaven?
43 Jesus therefore answered and said unto them, Murmur not among yourselves.
44 No man can come to me, ex-

---

first by the reiteration of the office of the Son (*v.* 44), and with the third by the reference to Christ's "flesh" (*v.* 51). It touches on the greatest mysteries of Christ's life, the Incarnation and the Atonement (*vv.* 42, 51), and the greatest mysteries of man's life, the concurrence of the divine and human will, and the permanence of life (*vv.* 44, 45, 37 ff.). It is briefly an answer to the question, How can the spring and support of life be in Christ, who is truly man?

41. This verse seems to mark the presence of new persons and a new scene, as well as a new stage in the history. The verses 37—40 were probably addressed specially to the immediate circle of the disciples. Thus we can understand how the Jews dwelt on the words in which Christ identified Himself with the true spiritual food of the world, while they took no notice of the loftier prerogatives which followed from this truth, since the exposition of these was not directed to them.

The Jews then] *The Jews* **therefore**..., the representatives of the dominant religious party, full of the teaching of the schools.

murmured at (**concerning**) *him*] half in doubt (vii. 32, [12]) and half in dissatisfaction (*v.* 61; Luke v. 30). These murmurings probably found expression for some little time before they were answered. There is nothing to shew that they were first uttered in Christ's presence.

I am the bread which came down from heaven] The exact phrase does not occur in the previous record; but it is a fair combination of the three phrases in which the Lord had described Himself. *the bread of God is that which cometh down from heaven* (*v.* 33); *I am the bread of life* (*v.* 35); *I have come down from heaven* (*v.* 38).

42. *Is not this*...] There is perhaps a tinge of contemptuous surprise in the pronoun (οὗτος) as in *v.* 52, vii. 15, iii. 26, though it does not necessarily lie in the word, iv. 14, ix. 33, &c.

the son of Joseph] ch. i. 46. Comp. Luke iv. 22.

we know] The pronoun is emphatic: *whose father we*, directly in the way of our ordinary life, *know*... There was (so they argue from their point of view) no room for mistake upon the matter. The word *know* expresses simply acquaintance with the fact that Joseph was in popular esteem the father of Jesus (comp. vii. 27), and not personal acquaintance with him as still living.

how is it then that he saith] **how doth he now say**—*now*, at last, when for so long he has lived as one of ourselves?

I came down (**am come down**) *from heaven*] See *v.* 38, note.

43. *Jesus therefore answered*...] **Jesus answered**... The answer corresponds in some way with that given to Nicodemus (iii. 3). The false claim to knowledge, and the assertion of unsubstantial objections, are both met in the same manner. The Jews were unable to understand the divine descent of the Lord, which seemed irreconcileable with His actual circumstances. He replies that a spiritual influence is necessary before His true Nature can be discerned, and that such influence was promised by the prophets as one of the characteristic blessings of the Messianic age.

44. *No man can*...*draw him*] Compare v. 40, *ye will not come to me*. As in all similar cases this "coming to Christ" may be regarded from its human side, as dependent on man's will; or from its divine side, as dependent on the power of God. So St Bernard remarks in connexion with these words: "nemo quippe salvatur invitus" ('De grat. et lib. act.' XI.). Yet even the will itself comes from a divine nature, a divine gift (chh. i. 12 f., iii. 7 ff., viii. 47, vi. 65). The "drawing" of the Father is best illustrated by the "drawing" of the Son, xii. 32. The constraining principle is love stirred by self-sacrifice, a love which calls out, and does not destroy, man's freedom and issues in self-sacrifice. The mission of the Son by the Father (*which sent* [omit *hath*] *me*), the sovereign act of love (iii. 16), is thus brought into close connexion with the power exerted by the Father on men. Augustine (*ad loc.*) puts the thought most forcibly: "'Trahit sua quemque voluptas;' non trahit revelatus Christus a Patre? Quid enim fortius desiderat anima quam veritatem?" Comp. *v.* 68.

No man can come] This divine impossibility is the expression of a moral law. It is not anything arbitrary, but inherent in the very nature of things; it does not limit but it defines the nature of human power. Comp. v. 19 (note), 30 (of the Son), xii. 39, note.

come] Here and in *v.* 65 the "coming" (ἐλθεῖν) is regarded as complete, and not in progress as in *v.* 37, vii. 37 (ἐρχέσθω).

cept the Father which hath sent me draw him: and I will raise him up at the last day.

54. 45 [i] It is written in the prophets,
. 34. And they shall be all taught of God. Every man therefore that hath heard, and hath learned of the Father, cometh unto me.

46 Not that any man hath seen the Father, [k] save he which is of God, he hath seen the Father. [k] Matt. xi. 27

47 Verily, verily, I say unto you, He that believeth on me hath everlasting life.

48 I am that bread of life.

49 Your fathers did eat manna in the wilderness, and are dead.

50 This is the bread which com-

---

draw (ἑλκύσω)] Comp. Jer. xxxviii. (xxxi.) 3 (LXX.).

and I...] The Son takes up and completes what the Father has begun. The change in the position of the pronoun slightly modifies the force of this repeated clause. In *v.* 40 the believer and Christ are placed in remarkable juxta-position (ἀναστήσω αὐτὸν ἐγὼ, *him, I*); here the *I* stands first with a reference to the whole preceding clause (καὶ ἐγὼ ἀναστήσω αὐτόν).

45. The "drawing" of the Father is illustrated by a prophetic promise. And under this new image of "teaching" the power is seen in its twofold aspect; the divine and human elements are combined. The "hearing" brings out the external communication, the learning the internal understanding of it. "Videte quomodo trahit Pater: docendo delectat, non necessitatem imponendo" (Aug. *ad loc.*).

in the prophets] *i.e.* in the division of the Scriptures which is so called. Compare Acts xiii. 40, vii. 42 (*the book of the prophets*); ch. i. 45, note. The phrase is found substantially in Isai. liv. 13; and the central idea of it is the promise of direct divine teaching. Thus the emphasis lies on "taught of God" and not on "all." This teaching lies for us in the Person and Work of Christ interpreted by the Spirit.

taught of God (διδακτοὶ Θεοῦ, Vulg. *docibiles Dei*)] Comp. 1 Cor. ii. 13; 1 Thess. iv. 9 (θεοδίδακτοι). The phrase describes not only one divine communication, but a divine relationship. Believers are life-long pupils in the school of God (למודי ה״, Isaiah, *l.c.* Comp. Isai. viii. 16).

Every man therefore that hath heard, and hath learned of the Father...] **Every one that heareth from the Father and learneth** (ἀκούσας καὶ μαθὼν)... The fulfilment of the promise is followed by its proper consequence. The "hearing" and "learning" are presented as single events corresponding to a definite voice and revelation. The call is obeyed at once, though it may be fulfilled gradually; the fact of the revelation is grasped at once, though it may be apprehended in detail little by little.

from *the Father*] the message which comes *from the Father* (ἀκούσας παρὰ τ. π.). Compare i. 40, vii. 51, viii. 26, 40, xv. 15.

46. But though the revelation made by the Father is direct in one sense, yet it must not be understood to be immediate. "Hearing" and "learning" fall short of seeing The Father is seen only by the Son (i. 18. Comp. Matt. xi. 27, and parallels). He alone who is truly God can naturally see God. The voice of God came to men under the old Covenant, but in Christ the believer can now see the Father (xiv. 9) in part, and will hereafter see God as He is (1 John iii. 2).

he which is of (**from**, παρά)...] Comp. vii. 29, ix. 16, 33. The phrase implies not only mission (xvi. 27 f., *came forth from*), but also a present relation of close dependence.

he hath seen] when He was "with God" (i. 1) before He "became flesh." The words mark emphatically the unchanged personality of Christ before and after the Incarnation. The substitution *God* for *the Father* in some early texts (א*D) is a kind of gloss which is not unfrequent in the group.

47. At this point the discourse takes a fresh start. The objection of the Jews has been met, and the Lord goes on to develope the idea set forth in *vv.* 35, 36, taking up the last word: **He that believeth** (omit *on me*, the phrase stands absolutely) *hath* **eternal** *life.* The actual existence of true faith implies the right object of it. Comp. c. iii. 3, note.

hath] See *v.* 40, note.

48—51. There is a close parallelism and contrast between *vv.* 48—50 and 51. *The bread of life: the living bread—which cometh down...that...: which came down; if...may... not die: shall live for ever.* In the first case the result is given as part of the divine counsel (*that cometh down, that* [ἵνα]...); in the second as a simple historical consequence (*came down...if a man*...).

48. *that* (**the**, and so in *v.* 58) *bread of life*] See *v.* 35, note.

49. *Your fathers did eat manna* (**ate the manna**)...*and are dead* (**died**)] The words are quoted from the argument of the Jews, *v.* 31. The heavenly food under the old Dispensation could not avert death. This

eth down from heaven, that a man may eat thereof, and not die.

51 I am the living bread which came down from heaven: if any man eat of this bread, he shall live for ever: and the bread that I will give is my flesh, which I will give for the life of the world.

52 The Jews therefore strove among themselves, saying, How can this man give us *his* flesh to eat?

53 Then Jesus said unto them,

---

then was not *bread of life*, even in the sphere to which it belonged. Comp. iv. 13.

50. *This is the bread which cometh...that...*] **This** bread—the true manna—**is the bread which cometh**...*that*... It is best to take *this* [*bread*] as the subject (*v.* 48, *I am the bread of life*, further defined in *v.* 51), and *the bread which cometh down from heaven* as the predicate; compare *vv.* 33, 58. The interpretation which makes *this* the predicate (*the bread which cometh...is this*, that is, is of such a nature, *that*...) appears to destroy the connexion.

not die] Comp. viii. 51, note.

51. *I am the living bread*] able to communicate the life which I possess. He therefore who receives me receives a principle of life.

eat of this bread] Some ancient authorities read *eat of my bread*.

and the bread...] **yea** *and* (*and in fact*) *the bread* (καὶ...δὲ)... Comp. viii. 16 f., xv. 27; 1 John i. 3.

the bread...which I (ἐγώ) *will give*] The pronoun is emphatic, and brings out the contrast between Christ and Moses. At the same time a passage is made from the thought of Christ as the living bread (*I am*..) to the thought of the participation in Him (*I will give*...). This participation is spoken of as still future, since it followed in its fulness on the completed work of Christ. There is also a difference indicated here between that which Christ is and that which He offers. He is truly God and truly man (ἐγώ); He offers His "flesh," His perfect humanity, *for the life of the world*.

my flesh] "Flesh" describes human nature in its totality regarded from its earthly side. Comp. i. 14. See also i. 13, iii. 6, vi. 63, viii. 15, xvii. 2; 1 John ii. 16, iv. 2; 2 John 7; Rom. viii. 3; 1 Tim. iii. 16; Hebr. v. 7. The thought of death lies already in the word, but that thought is not as yet brought out, as afterwards by the addition of *blood*. Comp. Eph. ii. 14 ff.; Col. i. 22; 1 Pet. iii. 18.

The life of the world in the highest sense springs from the Incarnation and Resurrection of Christ. By His Incarnation and Resurrection the ruin and death which sin brought in are overcome. The thought here is of support and growth, and not of atonement (*I lay down my life for*... x. 11, 15, note). The close of the earthly life, the end of the life which is, in one aspect, of self for self, opens wider relations of life. Comp. xii. 24. At this point no more than the general truth is stated. It is not yet indicated how the "flesh" of Christ, the virtue of His humanity, will be communicated to and made effectual for mankind or men. That part of the subject is developed in the last division of the whole argument.

my flesh, which I will give for the life...] The true text gives simply *my flesh* **for** *the life*... For this shortened form compare 1 Cor. xi. 24. The omission of the clause *which I will give* turns the attention to the general action of Christ's gift rather than to the actual making of it. The special reference to the future Passion would distract the thought at this point, where it is concentrated upon the Incarnation and its consequences generally. See Additional Note.

52—59. This last section of the teaching on "the true bread from heaven" carries forward the conceptions given in *vv.* 41—51 to a new result. The question before was as to the Person of the Lord: "Is not this the son of Joseph?" The question now is as to the communication of that which He gives: "How can this man give us his flesh to eat?" How can one truly man impart to others his humanity, so that they may take it to themselves and assimilate it? The answer is in this case also not direct but by implication. The fact, and the necessity of the fact, dispense with the need for further inquiry. The life is a reality.

52. *The Jews* (*v.* 41, note)...*strove among themselves* (**one with another**, πρὸς ἀλλήλους, iv. 33, xvi. 17)] They did not all reject at once the teaching of Christ. There were divisions among them; and they discussed from opposite sides the problem raised by the last mysterious words which they had heard (comp. vii. 12, 40 ff., x. 19 ff.). It is important to notice how the Evangelist records the varying phases of contemporary feeling. "The Jews" were not yet all of one mind.

How can...] The old question (iii. 4, 9), which is again left without an explicit answer. The simple reassertion of the fact is opposed both in a negative (*v.* 53) and in a positive statement to the difficulty as to the manner.

to eat] The Jews transfer directly to "the flesh" what hitherto, as far as our record goes, has been said only of "the bread," now identified with it. There is no gross misunderstanding on their part, but a clear perception

Verily, verily, I say unto you, Except ye eat the flesh of the Son of man, and drink his blood, ye have no life in you.
54 Whoso eateth my flesh, and drinketh my blood, hath eternal life; and I will raise him up at the last day.
55 For my flesh is meat indeed, and my blood is drink indeed.
56 He that eateth my flesh, and drinketh my blood, dwelleth in me, and I in him.
57 As the living Father hath sent me, and I live by the Father: so he

---

of the claim involved in the Lord's words. Comp. iii. 4, iv. 15, viii. 33. See also Num. xi. 13.

53. The thought indicated in *v.* 51 is now developed in detail. The "flesh" is presented in its twofold aspect as "flesh" and "blood," and by this separation of its parts the idea of a violent death is presupposed. Further "the flesh" and "the blood" are described as "the flesh" and "the blood" "of the Son of man," by which title the representative character of Christ is marked in regard to that humanity which He imparts to the believer. And once again both elements are to be appropriated individually ("eat," "drink"). By the "flesh" in this narrower sense we must understand the virtue of Christ's humanity as living for us; by the "blood" the virtue of His humanity as subject to death. The believer must be made partaker in both. The Son of man lived for us and died for us, and communicates to us the effects of His life and death as perfect man. Without this communication of Christ men can have "no life in themselves." But Christ's gift of His flesh and His blood to a man becomes in the recipient a spring of life within. Comp iv. 14.

Then Jesus said...] *Jesus* **therefore** *said...* meeting the difficulty which was raised by an appeal to what is really a fact of experience.

eat...drink] To "eat" and to "drink" is to take to oneself by a voluntary act that which is without, and then to assimilate it and make it part of oneself. It is, as it were, faith regarded in its converse action. Faith throws the believer upon and into its object: this spiritual eating and drinking brings the object of faith into the believer.

drink his blood] The phrase is unique in the New Testament. To Jewish ears it could not but be full of startling mystery. The thought is that of the appropriation of "life sacrificed." St Bernard expresses part of it very well when he says ... hoc est si compatimini conregnabitis ('De Dil. Deo,' IV.). Compare 'in Psalm.' III. 3, "Quid autem est manducare eius carnem et bibere sanguinem nisi communicare passionibus eius et eam conversationem imitari quam habuit in carne?"

in you] Literally, *in* **yourselves**. Compare v. 26; Matt. xiii. 21. Without the Son men have no life; for in men themselves there is no spring of life. Even to the last their life is "in Christ" and not "in themselves."

54. *Whoso* (**He that**, as in *v.* 56) *eateth*] The verb used here (τρώγειν) expresses not only the simple fact of eating but the process as that which is dwelt upon with pleasure (Matt. xxiv. 38. Comp. ch. xiii. 18). So also the tense (ὁ τρώγων, contrast *v.* 45, ὁ ἀκούσας) marks an action which must be continuous and not completed once for all.

hath eternal life...] Compare *v.* 40, note.

55. *For my flesh...*] The possession and the highest manifestation of life follow necessarily from participation in Christ's "flesh" and "blood:" such is their power.

is meat indeed...] *My flesh is* **true** (ἀληθής, real) *meat...* It stands in the same relation to man's whole being, as food does to his physical being. It must first be taken, and then it must be assimilated.

56. The truth of *v.* 54 is traced to its necessary foundation. In virtue of Christ's impartment of His humanity to the believer, the believer may rightly be said to "abide in Christ" and Christ to "abide in the believer." The believer has therefore "eternal life," and in that, the certainty of a resurrection, a restoration in glory of the fulness of his present powers.

dwelleth] **abideth**, as the word is commonly rendered. So also xiv. 10, 17; 1 John iii. 17, 24, iv. 12, 13, 15, 16. The word is singularly frequent in St John (Gospel, Epistles), and the phrases "*abide in* [*Christ*]" and the like are peculiar to him (yet compare 1 Tim. ii. 15; 2 Tim. iii. 14).

in me, and I in him...] There is, so to speak, a double personality. The believer is quickened by Christ's presence, and he is himself incorporated in Christ. Compare xv. 4, xvii. 23; 1 John iii. 24, iv. 15 f. This twofold aspect of the divine connexion is illustrated by the two great images of the "body" and the "temple." "Manemus in illo cum sumus membra eius: manet autem ipse in nobis cum sumus templum eius" (Aug. 'in Joh.' XXVII. 6).

Some early authorities (D, &c.) add a remarkable gloss at the end of the verse: *even as the Father is in me and I in the Father. Verily, verily, I say unto you, unless ye receive* (λάβητε) *the body of the Son of man as the bread of life ye have not life in him.*

57. *As...so*] The same combination occurs xiii. 15; 1 John ii. 6, iv. 17.

the living Father] The title is unique. Compare the phrase *the living God*, Matt. xvi. 16; 2 Cor vi. 16; Hebr. vii. 25, &c.

that eateth me, even he shall live by me.

58 This is that bread which came down from heaven: not as your fathers did eat manna, and are dead: he that eateth of this bread shall live for ever.

59 These things said he in the synagogue, as he taught in Capernaum.

---

hath sent me (**sent** *me*)] The introduction of these words marks the fact that Christ speaks of His vital fellowship with the Father not as the Word only, but as the Son Incarnate, the Son of man. Comp. v. 23. And thus the acceptance of the divine mission by the Son, and His dependence in His humanity on the Father, are placed in some sense in correlation with the appropriation of the Incarnate Son (*he that eateth me*) by the Christian; so that the relation of the believer to Christ is prefigured in the relation of the Son to the Father. Compare x. 14, 15, note.

by (**because of**) *the Father...by* (**because of**) *me*] The preposition (διὰ τὸν πατέρα, Vulg. *propter patrem*) describes the ground or object (*for*, *on account of*), and not the instrument or agent (*by*, *through*, διὰ τοῦ π.). Complete devotion to the Father is the essence of the life of the Son; and so complete devotion to the Son is the life of the believer. It seems better to give this full sense to the word than to take it as equivalent to *by reason of;* that is, "I live because the Father lives."

the Father] not "my Father." Emphasis is laid upon the universal relationship. Comp. iv. 21, note.

he that eateth me] In this phrase we reach the climax of the revelation. The words *eat of the bread* (*vv.* 50, 51), *eat the flesh of the Son of man and drink His blood* (*v.* 53), rise at last to the thought of *eating Christ*. The appropriation of the food which Christ gives, of the humanity in which He lived and died, issues in the appropriation of Himself.

even he] **he also.** The insertion of the emphatic pronoun (κἀκεῖνος) immediately after the subject, which it repeats and emphasizes, is most remarkable. It appears to lay stress upon that relation of dependence which constitutes the parallel between the disciples and the Son. Compare xiv. 12.

shall live] not *liveth*. The fulness of the life was consequent upon the exaltation of Christ. Comp. xiv. 19.

58. These concluding words carry back the discourse to its commencement (*vv.* 33, 35). The fulfilment of the type of the manna in Christ, after it has been set forth in its complete form, is placed in direct connexion with the earlier event.

This is that (**the**) *bread which came...*] *This* bread, this heavenly food, which has been shewn to be Christ Himself, and His "flesh" (*v.* 51), *is the bread which came...* Contrast *v.* 50: *This is the bread which cometh....* Both aspects of Christ's work must be kept in mind. He came, and He comes.

not as your fathers did eat manna, and are dead] **not as the fathers did eat and died.** The construction is irregular. Naturally the sentence would have run: *This is the bread...heaven: he that eateth this bread...*, but the parenthetical clause expresses in a condensed form the contrast between the true and the typical manna. "The fact and the issue of the fact is *not as the fathers ate and died.*" Comp. 1 John iii. 12 (οὐ καθώς). The reference to the "death" of "the generation in the wilderness" would have a fuller meaning if the tradition were already current that this generation "had no part in the world to come" (quoted by Lightfoot on *v.* 39).

the *fathers*] This title, as distinguished from the common text *your fathers*, recognises the representative position which the early generation occupied.

the fathers...he that eateth...] There appears to be significance in the passage from the plural to the singular. Throughout the discourses the believer is dealt with as exercising personal faith and not only as one of a society. Compare *vv.* 35, 37, 40, 45, 47, 50, 51, 54, 56.

eateth of...] **eateth**, as in *vv.* 54, 56. The construction in *vv.* 26, 50, 51, is different (φαγεῖν ἐκ).

59. *in the synagogue*] This is the only notice of the kind in St John's Gospel, though the general custom is referred to, xviii. 20. The absence of the definite article in the original here and in xviii. 20, which leads to a form of expression (ἐν συναγωγῇ) not found elsewhere in the New Testament, seems to mark the character of the assemblage rather than the place itself: "when people were gathered for worship," "in time of solemn assembly" (comp. 1 Macc. xiv. 28). It is a fact of great interest that among the ruins which mark the probable site of Capernaum (Tell Hûm) are the remains of a handsome synagogue, of which Wilson says: "On turning over a large block [of stone] we found the pot of manna engraved on its face" (Warren's 'Recovery of Jerusalem,' pp. 344 ff.). This very symbol may have been before the eyes of those who heard the Lord's words. It may be added that the history of the manna (Exod. xvi. 4—36) is appointed to be read in the Synagogues at morning service.

as he taught] The phrase gives a marked emphasis to the words which have gone before.

60 Many therefore of his disciples, when they had heard *this*, said, This is an hard saying; who can hear it?
61 When Jesus knew in himself that his disciples murmured at it, he said unto them, Doth this offend you?
62 [l] *What* and if ye shall see the Son of man ascend up where he was before?
63 It is the spirit that quickeneth;

[l] chap. 3 13.

The crisis corresponds in character with that at Nazareth, Luke iv. 16 ff. Comp. Matt. xi. 23. Some early authorities add, what may be a true traditional gloss, "on a sabbath."

The Issue (60—71).

The discourses proved a trial to the faith of the disciples. The immediate effect was a "murmuring" among them which led to a clear affirmation of the divine conditions of discipleship (60—65). And this was followed by a separation between the faithful and the unfaithful, both visibly (66—69) and invisibly (70, 71).

60. *Many therefore*] not only of the misunderstanding multitude (28 ff.) and of the ill-disposed Jews (41 ff.), but *of the disciples* (*v.* 3) who had hitherto followed Him, *when they heard* (omit *had*) *this*, found the new teaching of life through death a burden too heavy to be borne.

hard saying] that is, difficult to receive, accept, appropriate. The idea is not that of obscurity. The discourse was offensive, and not unintelligible. It made claims on the complete submission, self-devotion, self-surrender of the disciples. It pointed significantly to death. The same word (σκληρός, Vulg. *durus*) occurs Jude 15, in a somewhat similar connexion. Compare Gen. xxi. 11, xlii. 7; 1 K. xii. 13 (LXX.).

saying] or rather, *speech, discourse* (λόγος, Vulg. *sermo*). The English representative of the original (*word*) is not sufficiently elastic to give its sense in all cases.

hear it] Listen to it (ἀκούειν αὐτοῦ) with patience, as ready to admit it. See vii. 40, x. 3, 16, 27, xii. 47, xviii. 37. The pronoun (αὐτοῦ) may be taken as personal: *who can hear him?* but this is an unlikely rendering.

61. *When Jesus knew in himself*] **But when Jesus...** See ii. 24, note.

murmured] Compare *v.* 41, note.

offend you] Compare xvi. 1, note.

62. *What and if ye shall see...*] **What then if ye should behold...** This incomplete question, which seems to leave open in some measure the alternatives of greater offence and possible victory, has been interpreted in two very different ways, by supplying in one case a negative answer: "Ye will not then be offended any more;" and in the other a positive: "Ye will then assuredly be still more offended." According to the first interpretation the "ascending up" is the Ascension as the final spiritualizing of the Lord's Person, whereby the offence of the language as to His flesh would be removed by the apprehension of the truth as to His spiritual humanity. In the second the "ascending up" is referred to the "elevation" on the Cross, and the offence caused by the reference to the death of Christ is regarded as increased by the death itself in its actual circumstances. Each of these two interpretations appears to contain elements of the full meaning. The whole context shews distinctly that the disciples were to be subjected to some severer trial. The turn of the sentence therefore must be: "If then ye see the Son of man ascending...ye will be, according to your present state, more grievously offended; for that trial you must still be disciplined." But, on the other hand, the Crucifixion alone could not be described as an "ascending up where Christ was before;" yet it was the first part of the Ascension, the absolute sacrifice of self which issued in the absolute triumph over the limitations of earthly existence. The Passion, the Resurrection, the Ascension, were steps in the progress of the "ascending up" through suffering, which is the great offence of the Gospel. The difficulty of accepting this completed fact is (though greater) of the same kind as the difficulty of accepting life only through the communicated humanity of the Incarnate Son.

the Son of man ascend up (**ascending**) *where he was before*] Compare viii. 58, xvii. 5, 24; Col. i. 17. No phrase could shew more clearly the unchanged personality of Christ. As "the Son of man" He speaks of His being in heaven before the Incarnation. "Filius Dei et filius hominis unus Christus... Filius Dei in terra suscepta carne, filius hominis in cælo in unitate personæ" (Aug. *ad loc.*).

63. *the spirit...the flesh...*] The same contrast occurs in iii. 6 (see note), 1 Pet. iii. 18. Just as in man the *spirit* is that part of his nature by which he holds fellowship with the unseen eternal order, and *the flesh* that part of it by which he holds fellowship with the seen temporal order, so the two words are applied to the working of Christ. Nothing can carry us beyond the limits of its own realm. The new life must come from that which belongs properly to the sphere in which it moves. Compare 1 Cor. xv. 45, (2 Cor. iii. 6). The truth is expressed in its most general form, and is not to be limited to the spiritual and

the flesh profiteth nothing: the words that I speak unto you, *they* are spirit, and *they* are life.

64 But there are some of you that believe not. For Jesus knew from the beginning who they were that believed not, and who should betray him.

65 And he said, Therefore said I unto you, that no man can come unto me, except it were given unto him of my Father.

66 ¶ From that *time* many of his disciples went back, and walked no more with him.

67 Then said Jesus unto the twelve, Will ye also go away?

68 Then Simon Peter answered

---

carnal apprehension of Christ's Person; or to the spiritual and external participation in the Holy Communion; or even to the spiritual and historical manifestation of Christ. Each of these partial thoughts has its place in the whole conception. Compare 2 Cor. v. 16.

the words] Here the definite utterances (ῥήματα, Vulg. *verba*, *v.* 68) and not the whole revelation (λόγος, Vulg. *sermo*, *v.* 60). The reference is to the clear unfolding of the complete relation of man and humanity to the Incarnate Saviour. Hence a marked emphasis is laid on the pronoun *I*: the words that *I* and no prophet, not even Moses (*v.* 32) before me; and on the tense: *the words that I* **have spoken** (λελάληκα, according to the true reading), and not generally *speak*, though in some sense all Christ's words are life-giving, as conveying something of this central truth.

For the exact sense of "the words" (τὰ ῥήματα) see iii. 34, viii. 47, xvii. 8.

are spirit, and they are life] that is, belong essentially to the region of eternal being, and so are capable of conveying that which they essentially are. Compare *v.* 68.

64. *But*] even so, in the closest circle of my disciples there are some to whom they convey no vivifying influence, because the human condition is unfulfilled: *there are* **of you** (ἐξ ὑμῶν) **some** *who believe not.* For the order compare *v.* 70 (*of you one*).

For Jesus knew] Compare ii. 24, note.

from the beginning] Compare xvi. 4, (xv. 27). From the first moment when the public work of Christ began (1 John ii. 7, 24, iii. 11; Luke i. 2). The phrase must always be relative to the point present to the mind of the writer or speaker; and here that seems to be fixed by *v.* 70.

who should (**who it was that should**) *betray him*] This first allusion to the sin of Judas evidently stands in a significant connexion with the first unveiling of the Lord's Passion. The word rendered *betray* (παραδιδόναι) means strictly *deliver up*, *to give into* the hands of another to deal with as he pleases (ch. xviii. 30, 35 f., xix. 16; Matt. v. 25, &c.). The title of "traitor" is only once applied to Judas in the New Testament: Luke vi. 16 (προδότης). In other words his act is regarded in relation to the Lord's Passion, and not to his sin.

65. *Therefore said I...*] **For this cause have I said...** The divine condition of discipleship was clearly stated, because the disciples would have to bear the trial of treachery revealed in their midst, which might seem to be inconsistent with Christ's claims, and with what they thought that they had found in Him. His choice even of Judas was not made without full knowledge (xiii. 18).

come unto me] Judas then, though "chosen out" (*v.* 70) and called, had not come to Christ (*v.* 37). He remained still in himself; and now at this crisis he can keep silence.

were given unto him of my Father] **have been** (or **be**) *given unto him of* **the Father.** Comp. iii. 27. There is a sense in which all life is the unfolding of the timeless divine will. The Father (not *my Father*) here is looked upon as the source (ἐκ) from whom all flows. Comp. x. 32; 1 Cor. vii. 7; (2 Cor. ii. 2). It must be noticed likewise how here the divine and human elements are placed in close juxtaposition, *given*, *come*. The mystery must be left with the assertion of both the concurrent parts, the will of God and the will of man.

66 ff. The "murmuring" issued in separation. This separation was partly open and partly secret. The same teaching which led some disciples to desert Christ, appears to have called out in Judas that deeper antagonism of spirit which was shewn at last in the betrayal.

66. *From that time*] **Upon this** (compare xix. 12), with the notion of dependence on what had now happened. The phrase is not simply temporal (ch. ix. 1; Luke x. 20; Acts ix. 33, xxiv. 10, xxvi. 4), nor simply causal (Rom. i. 4; Rev. xvi. 21, viii. 13).

went back (ἀπῆλθον εἰς τὰ ὀπίσω, Vulg. *abierunt retro*)] They not only left Christ, but gave up what they had gained with Him, and, so far as they could, reoccupied their old places, Phil. iii. 13.

walked no more with him] Compare vii. 1, xi. 54. The phrase gives a vivid portraiture of the Lord's life.

67. *Then said Jesus...*] *Jesus* **therefore** *said...* The test had been applied to the mass, and it was now necessarily applied to the innermost circle of disciples.

the twelve] These are spoken of as known, though they have not been mentioned before.

him, Lord, to whom shall we go? thou hast the words of eternal life.
16. 69 [m] And we believe and are sure that thou art that Christ, the Son of the living God.
70 Jesus answered them, Have not

The number is implied in *v.* 13. In the earlier part of the record (chh. i.—iv.) no such chosen company is noticed, a fact which is a slight sign of the distinctness with which the course of the work of Christ was impressed on the apostle's mind. He does not record the call of the twelve, yet it lies hidden and implied in his narrative. From another side the reference shews that St John assumes that his readers are familiar with the main facts of the history.

Will ye also...] The form of the question (μὴ θέλετε, Vulg. *numquid vultis?*) implies that such desertion is incredible and yet to be feared; but here the negation is virtually assumed. Compare vii. 47, 52, xviii. 17, 25.

go away...go (*v.* 68)...] Perhaps more exactly, **go** (ὑπάγειν, *v.* 21) ... **go away** (ἀπελθεῖν, *v.* 22)... The first word suggests the notion of the personal act in itself; the second that of separation. See vii. 33, note.

68. *Then Simon Peter* (omit *Then*)...] St Peter occupies the same representative place in St John's narrative as in the others. Comp. xiii. 6 ff., 24, 36, xviii. 10, xx. 2, xxi. 3. His reply is the strong confession that the apostles have found in Christ all that they could seek. The thought is of what Christ has, as they have known, and not of Himself: *thou* (unemphatic) *hast* in thy spiritual treasury ready to be brought forth according to our powers and necessities (Matt. xiii. 52) *the words*, or rather **words** *of eternal life*. This phrase may mean either (1) words—utterances (*v.* 63)—concerning eternal life; or (2) words bringing, issuing in, eternal life (1 John i. 1). The usage of St John is on the whole decidedly in favour of the second interpretation. Thus we find *the bread of life* (*vv.* 35, &c.), *the light of life* (viii. 12), *the water of life* (Rev. xxi. 6, xxii. 1, 17), *the tree of life* (Rev. ii. 7, xxii. 2, 14). St Peter does not speak of the completed Gospel ("the word"), but of specific sayings (ῥήματα, not τὰ ῥήματα) which had been felt to carry life with them. He had recognised the truth of what the Lord had said *v.* 63 (τὰ ῥήματα).

69. *And we*] The pronoun is emphatic; we who are nearest to Thee and have listened to Thee most devoutly.

believe and are sure] **have believed and know** (or rather, **have come to know**). The vital faith which grasps the new data of the higher life precedes the conscious intellectual appreciation of them. "Non cognovimus et credidimus...Credidimus enim ut cognosceremus; nam si prius cognoscere et deinde credere vellemus, nec cognoscere nec credere valeremus" (Aug. *ad loc.*). Comp. ch. x. 38; 2 Pet. i. 5.

In 1 John iv. 16 the words stand in the inverted order, but it will be noticed from the construction there that the words *have believed* qualify and explain, so to speak, *have come to know* (*know*), but do not go closely with *the love that God hath to us*, which depends directly on *know*.

that Christ, the Son of the living God] According to the true reading (see additional note), **the Holy One of God**. Mark i. 24; Luke iv. 34. The knowledge of the demoniacs reached to the essential nature of the Lord. Comp. Rev. iii. 7; 1 John ii. 20. See also ch. x. 36, and *v.* 27 of this chapter.

With this confession of St Peter that which is recorded in Matt. xvi. 16, which belongs to the same period but to different circumstances, must be compared. Here the confession points to the inward character in which the Apostles found the assurance of life; there the confession was of the public office and theocratic Person of the Lord. To suppose that the one confession is simply an imperfect representation of the other is to deny the fulness of the life which lies behind both. This confession must be compared with the confessions in ch. i. Here the confession is made after the disappointment of the popular hope, and reaches to the recognition of that absolute character of Christ which the demoniacs tried to reveal prematurely.

70. Even in those who still clung to Christ there was an element of unfaithfulness. Comp. xiii. 10 f.

Jesus answered...] The reply is to the confident affirmation of St Peter, who rested his profession of the abiding faithfulness of the apostles upon their perception of the Lord's nature. So far was this from leaving no ground for doubt that the Lord shews that even His own choice (*Did not I—even I—choose*) left room for a traitor among those whom He had chosen.

them] St Peter spoke for all, and the Lord still speaks to the twelve and not to their representative only.

Have not I chosen you twelve?] **Did not I choose you the twelve?** you the marked representatives of the new Israel, the patriarchs of a divine people. The reference is not to the number of the apostles, but to their special position (ὑμᾶς τοὺς δώδεκα: comp. xx. 24).

choose: xiii. 18, xv. 16 f. Compare Luke vi. 13; Acts i. 2, 24; 1 Cor. i. 27 f.: Eph. i. 4. On the choice of Judas see xiii. 18, note.

and one of you (**of you one**) *is a devil*]

I chosen you twelve, and one of you is a devil?

71 He spake of Judas Iscariot *the* *son* of Simon: for he it was that should betray him, being one of the twelve.

Even out of this chosen body (ἐξ ὑμῶν) one is faithless. There is a tragic pathos in the original order.

a devil] viii. 44, xiii. 2; 1 John iii. 8, 10; Rev. xii. 9, xx. 2. The fundamental idea seems to be that of turning good into evil (διαβάλλειν). The two great temptations are the characteristic works of "the devil." Hence Judas, by regarding Christ in the light of his own selfish views, and claiming to use His power for the accomplishment of that which he had proposed as Messiah's work, partook of that which is essential to the devil's nature. With this term applied to Judas we must compare that of *Satan* applied at no long interval to St Peter (Matt. xvi. 23). Judas wished to pervert the divine power which he saw to his own ends; St Peter strove to avert what he feared in erring zeal for his Lord.

71. *He spake...*] **Now** *he spake...*

Judas Iscariot the son of Simon] **Judas** the son **of Simon Iscariot.** The true reading here marks Iscariot as certainly a local name: *a man of Kerioth* (*Karioth*). The place is commonly identified with *Kerioth*, a town of Judah (Josh. xv. 25), according to the A. V., so that Judas alone was strictly a Judæan. But it appears that the rendering there is incorrect, and that Kerioth ought to be joined with Hezron (Kerioth-Hezron). May not the town be identified with the Kerioth (Καριώθ) of Moab mentioned in Jer. xlviii. 24?

he it was that should] *it was he* **that was about to** (ἔμελλεν παραδιδόναι)... Compare xii. 4; Luke xxii. 23. The phrase in *v.* 64 is different (ὁ παραδώσων).

being one of the twelve] The phrase (εἷς ἐκ τ. δ.) is slightly different from that in Matt. xxvi. 14, 47 and parallels (εἷς τ. δ.), and seems to mark the unity of the body to which the unfaithful member belonged. Compare xx. 24.

ADDITIONAL NOTES on CHAP. VI.

26—58. A brief summary of the argument of the three discourses furnishes the best clue to their general interpretation in view of the controversies which have attached to parts of them. Their central subject is Christ, truly man, the source and the support of life. They deal, as we have seen, with three questions in succession. How can man gain fellowship with God? How can one who is man be the source and support of life? How can the virtue of Christ's humanity be imparted to and appropriated by others? Or, putting the two last questions in their final form: Can the Incarnation be a fact? Can the Incarnate Son of God communicate Himself to men? They are, it is evident, questions of universal moment, which go to the very heart of faith; and according as they are answered bring separation or closer union at all times between Christ and His disciples.

1. The source of life.

Man's effort is combined and contrasted with God's gift (26, 27).

The divine work of man is faith in a Person (28, 29).

The attestation of the gift which He brings lies in the gift itself (30—33).

He is Himself the gift; and even through apparent failure He fulfils His work (34—38).

Belief in the Son is life now, and will be followed by resurrection (39, 40).

2. But how can One who is man thus unite earth and heaven?

The answer requires a spiritual preparation in the hearer (43, 44).

But in part it is answered in the promises of the Old Testament (45, 46).

In part too the believer must himself cooperate (47—50).

Christ gives what He is: the fulness of His humanity (51).

3. How again can men partake in the virtues of another's being?

The answer lies deep in the perception of the divine nature of the Son of man.

Man lives only by the participation in the virtues of His life and death (53—55).

This participation brings with it a personal union between the believer and Christ (56),

Which is the fulness of divine life (57, 58).

From first to last the gift to men on the part of God is set forth as Christ "the Son of man;" and the power by which man makes the gift his own is active "faith." The repetition of the title "the Son of man" three times in most significant connexions brings out very clearly the aspect of Christ's Person to which the teaching specially points (*vv.* 27, 53, 62). So also the stress laid on believing (πιστεύειν εἰς, *vv.* 29, 35, 40, 47) keeps in prominence the requirement from man. In the last section (52—58) "believing" is not mentioned, but the same effect is attributed to "eating the flesh and drinking the blood" of Christ as before to "believing" absolutely (*vv.* 47, 54, ἔχει ζωὴν αἰώνιον).

Here then the activity of faith is presented in its completest energy in connexion with the fullest description of the divine gift. The fundamental antithesis of the human and divine, which appears at the opening of the discourses, is thus distinctly expressed at the close.

It must not however be concluded that "eating the flesh of the Son of man and drinking His blood" is simply a metaphorical expression for "believing on Christ," or more specifically for "believing on Christ as having lived and died for men." It is quite unnatural to suppose that the earlier and plain words are involved in dark figures by the later phrases. On the contrary, these figures indicate the effective action and issue of faith, while they preserve and recognise the meeting together of the human and divine in the highest consummation of the destiny of man.

The progress which underlies the apparent monotony of the discourses is most conspicuously marked by the comparison of the corresponding phrases "believing on the Son of man," and "eating" the Son of man, and is indicated also in the recurrent forms of expression which seem at first sight to be identical. Thus *vv.* 33, 50, 58, which in their general structure and elements are closely connected, are yet found upon examination to be clearly distinguished:

v. 33. The bread of God is that which *cometh* down from heaven, and *giveth* (διδοὺς) *life to the world.*

v. 50. This (bread) [*v.* 48, I am the bread of life] is the bread which *cometh* down from heaven that *a man may eat of it* (ἐξ αὐτοῦ φάγῃ) *and not die.*

v. 58. This (bread) [*i.e.* I (*v.* 57)] is the bread which *came* down from heaven: *he that eateth* (τρώγων) *this bread shall live for ever.*

The general divine fact is stated first; next the divine purpose in connexion with man; and then last the historic fact as it is appropriated by individual men.

From what has been said it will be seen that the discourses spring naturally out of the position in which the Lord stood at a critical moment towards His disciples and the people, and are perfectly intelligible as an answer to the questionings among them conveyed in such a parabolic form (Matt. xiii. 34) as was suggested partly by the miracle of feeding, and partly by the memories of the passover. That which is outward is made the figure of the inward, and then, when the spiritual conception is fully developed, the outward imagery is again adopted in order to indicate fresh forms of the truth. The people had "eaten of the loaves" (*v.* 26); that which it was their highest blessing to do was to eat the Son of man (*v.* 57). This "eating" is essential for all, inasmuch as without it there is no life and no resurrection (*v.* 53). And further, this "eating" leads necessarily to life in the highest sense; it has no qualification (such as eating "worthily"); it is operative for good absolutely.

It follows that what is spoken of "eating φαγεῖν) of the bread which cometh down from heaven" (*v.* 51), "eating (φαγεῖν) the flesh of the Son of man" (*v.* 53), "eating (τρώγειν) His flesh, and drinking His blood" (*vv.* 54, 56), "eating (τρώγειν) Him" (*v.* 57), "eating (τρώγειν) the bread which came down from heaven" (*v.* 58)—the succession of phrases is most remarkable—cannot refer primarily to the Holy Communion; nor again can it be simply prophetic of that Sacrament. The teaching has a full and consistent meaning in connexion with the actual circumstances, and it treats essentially of spiritual realities with which no external act, as such, can be co-extensive. The well-known words of Augustine, *crede et manducasti*, "believe and thou *hast* eaten," give the sum of the thoughts in a luminous and pregnant sentence.

But, on the other hand, there can be no doubt that the truth which is presented in its absolute form in these discourses is presented in a specific act and in a concrete form in the Holy Communion; and yet further that the Holy Communion is the divinely appointed means whereby men may realise the truth. Nor can there be a difficulty to any one who acknowledges a divine fitness in the ordinances of the Church, an eternal correspondence in the parts of the one counsel of God, in believing that the Lord, while speaking intelligibly to those who heard Him at the time, gave by anticipation a commentary, so to speak, on the Sacrament which He afterwards instituted. But that which He deals with is not the outward rite, but the spiritual fact which underlies it. To attempt to transfer the words of the discourse with their consequences to the Sacrament is not only to involve the history in hopeless confusion but to introduce overwhelming difficulties into their interpretation, which can only be removed by the arbitrary and untenable interpolation of qualifying sentences.

In this connexion two points require careful consideration. The words used here of the Lord's humanity are "flesh" and "blood," and not as in every case where the Sacrament is spoken of in Scripture "body" and "blood." And again St John nowhere refers directly to the Sacraments of Baptism and Holy Communion as outward rites.

The second point need not cause any surprise. St John living in the centre of Christian society does not notice the institution of services which were parts of the settled experience of Church life. He presupposes them; and at the same time records the discourses in which the ideas clothed for us and brought near to us in the two Sacraments were set forth. He guards the Sacraments in this way from being regarded either as ends in themselves or as mere symbols. He enables us to see how they correspond with fundamental views of the relations of man to God; how they are included in one sense in the first teaching of the Gospel; how Christianity is essentially sacramental as Judaism is essentially typical; how, through the Incarnation, the relations between things outward and inward, things seen and unseen, are revealed to us as real and eternal, and not superficial and transitory.

The first point is evidently of critical importance for the understanding of the relation between the discourses and the Sacrament. The "flesh" is (so to speak) the constituent element of the human organization; the "body" is the organization itself. That which the believer must appropriate is, as we have seen, the virtue of Christ's humanity; through this, in the unity of His Person, Christ unites him to God. That which Christ presents to His Church in the institution of Holy Communion is His "Body." The term "flesh" marks that which must be assimilated, and suggests the due co-operation of the individual recipient for an effect which is absolute. The term "body" answers to the outward rite, which is primarily social (1 Cor. x. 16 f.). Or, to put the idea in a somewhat different light, the "flesh" expresses that which characterizes the essential limitation of that humanity which "the Word became," capable of an indefinite variety of manifestations, while the "body" is a specific manifestation. The one suggests the conception of the principle of human life; the other the unity of a particular form of human life. (The gloss in D on *v.* 56 shews how soon the distinction was neglected.)

Among early writers Augustine has expressed very clearly the relation of the discourse to the Sacrament, though he does not dwell on the difference of "flesh" and "body." "This food and drink," he writes, "Christ wishes to be understood as fellowship with His Body and members... The Sacrament of this thing, that is, of the unity of the Body and Blood of Christ, is prepared on the Lord's table (*in dominica mensa*) in some places daily, in other places at stated intervals, and is taken from the Lord's table, for some to life, for some to destruction (*ad exitium*); the thing itself however of which [that rite] is a sacrament, is for every man to life, to none to destruction, whoever partakes of it ('Tract. in Joh.' XXVI. 15)...This is therefore to eat that food (*escam*) and to drink that blood, to abide in Christ and to have Him abiding in oneself. And through this, he who does not abide in Christ and in whom Christ does not abide, doubtless does not eat His flesh (*procul dubio nec manducat carnem eius*, the addition *spiritualiter* is a false gloss). nor drink His blood, although he eats and drinks the Sacrament of so great a thing to his own judgment" (*Id.* § 18, *etiamsi tantæ rei sacramentum ad judicium sibi manducet et bibat* according to the MSS. The text as it is quoted in Art. XXIX. has been interpolated from the commentary of Bede).

NOTE ON READINGS IN CHAP. VI.

There are several readings of considerable interest in ch. vi. which require notice as illustrating the history of the text.

9. The common text reads *παιδάριον ἕν*. This is supported by A, the mass of later uncial and cursive MSS., some copies of *vt. Lat.*, *Vulg.*, the *Syriac* versions (except *Syr. vt.*), &c.

On the other hand, *ἕν* is omitted by ℵBDL and a fair number of later copies, including some very important cursives, the most important copies of *Lat. vt.*, *Syr. vt.*, Origen, Cyril Alex., Chrysostom, &c. (C is defective). Here it will be observed that the oldest representatives of each class of authorities omit the word in dispute, the oldest Greek MSS., the oldest forms of the oldest versions, and the oldest father who quotes the passage.

There can then be no doubt that *παιδάριον* alone should be read.

15. In this verse ℵ has one of those paraphrastic glosses which are characteristic of ℵD, *vt. Lat.* and *vt. Syr.* In place of *ἵνα ποιήσωσιν [αὐτὸν] βασιλέα*, which is read by all other authorities with one questionable exception, it reads *καὶ ἀναδεικνύναι βασιλέα*. This phrase is followed by *φεύγει* for *ἀνεχώρησεν*. This reading *φεύγει* is supported by other authorities of the same group, *vt. Lat.*, *Vulg.*, *Syr. vt.*; but such evidence only shews the wide extension of the gloss at a very early time.

Other examples of similar paraphrases in members of the same group occur in *v.* 17, *κατέλαβεν δὲ αὐτοὺς ἡ σκοτία* (for *καὶ σκοτία ἤδη ἐγεγόνει*) ℵD; 46, *ἑώρακεν τὸν θεόν* (for *ἑ. τὸν πατέρα*) ℵ*D *a b e*... 51, *ἐκ τοῦ ἐμοῦ ἄρτου* (for *ἐκ τούτου τοῦ ἄρτου*) ℵ *a e*... 57, *λαμβάνων* (for *τρώγων*) D.

51. The last clause of this verse is found in three forms:

(1)...*ὃν ἐγὼ δώσω ἡ σάρξ μου ἐστὶν ὑπὲρ τῆς τοῦ κόσμου ζωῆς*, BCDLT, *Latt.*, *Syr. vt.*, *Theb.*, (Orig.), &c.

(2)...*ὃν ἐγὼ δώσω ὑπὲρ τῆς τοῦ κόσμου ζωῆς ἡ σάρξ μου ἐστίν*, ℵ, (*m*).

(3)...*ὃν ἐγὼ δώσω ἡ σάρξ μου ἐστὶν ἣν ἐγὼ δώσω ὑπὲρ τῆς τοῦ κόσμου ζωῆς*. The mass of later MSS. (A is defective), *Syr. Pesh.* and *Hcl.*, *Memph.*, Clem. Al.

The insertion of the clause *ἣν ἐγὼ δώσω* in (3) is evidently an attempt to remove the harshness of the construction in (1), which is removed in (2) by a transposition. But the addition of such a clause as *ὑπὲρ τ. τ. κ. ζ.* to a sentence already grammatically complete in order to bring out a wider thought is completely in St John's style.

63. The common reading λαλῶ is supported by the great mass of later MSS., but by no early evidence whatever; all the oldest MSS., versions, and fathers reading λελάληκα, which at first sight seems to limit the statement unduly.

69. The words of St Peter's confession offer a most instructive example of the manner in which a (supposed) parallel influences a reading.

The words are given in different authorities in the following forms: *σὺ εἶ*

(1) *ὁ ἅγιος τοῦ θεοῦ* ℵBC*DL (A and T are defective).

(2) *ὁ χριστός, ὁ ἅγιος τοῦ θεοῦ*, *Memph.*, *Theb.*

(3) *ὁ υἱὸς τοῦ θεοῦ*, 17, *b*, *Syr. vt.*

(4) *ὁ χριστός, ὁ υἱὸς τοῦ θεοῦ*, *Latt.*

(5) *ὁ χριστός, ὁ υἱὸς τοῦ θεοῦ τοῦ ζῶντος*, the mass of MSS. and *Syr.* (except *Syr. vt.*).

The last form (5) is identical with that in Matt. xvi. 16, in which the authorities (practically) do not vary. It is then scarcely to be questioned that the language in St John has been brought into accord with St Matthew and not changed from it. The stages of the assimilation are preserved in (2), (3), (4). Two changes were made separately at a very early time, the addition of *ὁ χριστός* (Egyptian versions) and the substitution of *υἱός* for *ἅγιος*. These two changes were then combined, and this is the reading preserved in the mass of Latin copies. And finally the complete phrase of St Matthew was introduced by the addition of *τοῦ ζῶντος*.

71. The mass of later copies, with the Gothic and the later copies of the Vulgate, give the title Iscariot (*Ἰσκαριώτην*) to Judas, but the earlier MSS. (ℵ^c^BC with some others) and the best copies of the Vulgate connect it with Simon (*Ἰσκαριώτου*). In D and some early Latin copies the reading is simply *Σκαριώθ* (*carioth*), for which ℵ* and four other early authorities read (as D reads xii. 4, xiii. 2, 26, xiv. 22) *ἀπὸ καρυώτου*. In xii. 4, xiv. 22, the title undoubtedly belongs to Judas. Here and in xiii. 2, 26 it appears scarcely less certainly to belong to his father Simon. The natural conclusion is that it was a local name borne by father and son alike.

CHAPTER VII.

1 *Jesus reproveth the ambition and boldness of his kinsmen:* 10 *goeth up from Galilee to the feast of tabernacles:* 14 *teacheth in the temple.* 40 *Divers opinions of him among the people.* 45 *The Pharisees are angry that their officers took him not, and chide with Nicodemus for taking his part.*

II. THE GREAT CONTROVERSY (vii.—xii.).

The record of the great controversy at Jerusalem, during which faith and unbelief were fully revealed, falls into two parts. The first part (vii.—x.) contains the outline of the successive stages of the controversy itself; the second the decisive judgment (xi., xii.).

i. THE REVELATION OF FAITH AND UNBELIEF AT JERUSALEM (vii.—x.).

This central section of the whole Gospel contains events and discourses connected with two national festivals, *the Feast of Tabernacles* and *the Feast of Dedication*, which commemorated the first possession of Canaan and the great recovery of religious independence. Thus the festivals had a most marked meaning in regard to the life of the Jews, and this, as will be seen, influenced the form of the Lord's teaching.

There is a clear progress in the history. The discussions at the Feast of Tabernacles (vii., viii.) are characterized by waverings and questionings among the people. The discussions at the Feast of Dedication shew the separation already consummated (ix., x.).

(1) *The Feast of Tabernacles* (vii., viii.).

No section in the Gospel is more evidently a transcript from life than this. It reflects a complex and animated variety of characters and feelings. Jerusalem is seen crowded at the most popular feast with men widely differing in hope and position: some eager in expectation, some immovable in prejudice. There is nothing of the calm solemnity of the private discourse, or of the full exposition of doctrine before a dignified body, such as has been given before. All is direct, personal encounter. The "brethren" of the Lord (vii. 3 ff.), "the Jews" (vii. 1, 11, 13, 15, 35, viii. 22, 48, 52, 57), "the multitudes" (vii. 12 f.), "the multitude" (vii. 12, 20, 31 f., 40 f., 43, 49), "the people of Jerusalem" (vii. 25), "the Pharisees" (vii. 32, 47, viii. 13), "the chief-priests (*i.e.* the Sadducean hierarchy) and Pharisees" (vii. 32, 45, for the first time), Nicodemus (vii. 50), "the Jews who believed him" (viii. 31), appear in succession in the narrative, and all with clearly marked individuality. Impatient promptings to action (vii. 3 ff.), vague inquiries (vii. 11), debatings (vii. 12, 40 ff.), fear on this side and that (vii. 13, 30, 44), wonder (vii. 15, 46), perplexity (vii. 25 ff.), belief (vii. 31, viii. 30), open hostility (vii. 32), unfriendly criticism (vii. 23 ff., viii. 48 ff.), selfish belief in Christ's Messianic dignity (viii. 31 ff.), follow in rapid alternation. All is full of movement, of local

AFTER these things Jesus walked
in Galilee: for he would not
walk in Jewry, because the Jews
sought to kill him.
a Lev. 23. 34. 2 [a] Now the Jews' feast of tabernacles was at hand.
3 His brethren therefore said unto
him, Depart hence, and go into Judæa, that thy disciples also may see
the works that thou doest.
4 For *there is* no man *that* doeth
any thing in secret, and he himself
seeketh to be known openly. If
thou do these things, shew thyself to
the world.
5 For neither did his brethren believe in him.
6 Then Jesus said unto them, My
time is not yet come: but your time
is alway ready.

---

colour, of vivid traits of conflicting classes and tendencies.

The section is naturally divided into several distinct scenes. The circumstances of the visit (vii. 1—13). The discussions at "the midst of the feast" (14—36). The discussions on the last day (37—52). The after-teaching (viii. 12—20). The trial of true and false faith (21—59).

1. *The circumstances of the visit to the Feast of Tabernacles* (vii. 1—13).

CHAP. VII. **1—13.** In these verses there is a lively picture of the position which the Lord held at the time. Continued teaching in Judæa had become impossible (*v.* 1). His brethren impatiently pressed for some more decisive public manifestation of His power (*vv.* 3—9). The multitudes gathered at Jerusalem were divided between faith and distrust (*vv.* 11, 12). But the dominant party kept down all open discussion of His claims (*v.* 13). The description brings out distinctly various aspects of a work and a Person not yet fully revealed.

1. *After these things*] **And** *after these things*, that is, the whole crisis brought about by the miracle of feeding.

walked] ch. vi. 66, note.

would not walk in Jewry (**Judæa,** as *v.* 3)] The words imply a previous work in Judæa corresponding to that now accomplished in Galilee.

to kill him] See v. 18.

2. *the Jews' feast of tabernacles*] **the feast of the Jews, the feast of Tabernacles.** This feast was pre-eminent among the festivals "as the holiest and greatest" (Jos. 'Ant.' VIII. 4. 1). It fell on 15—22 Tisri (September, October), and thus there is an interval of six months after the events of ch. vi., of which the Evangelist records nothing. The record of some details of this period is given in Matt. xii.—xvii., xxi.

3. *His brethren*] See Lightfoot, Excursus II. on 'Galatians.' Perhaps we may conclude even from this notice, compared with Mark iii. 21, 31, that the brethren were elder brethren (*i.e.* sons of Joseph by a former marriage) who might from their age seek to direct the Lord.

therefore] since Jesus had not gone up to the last Passover.

thy disciples also may see (**behold**)...] not only those disciples who would be gathered from all parts to Jerusalem, but specially those who had been gained by earlier teaching in Judæa and Jerusalem, and who still remained there. From this notice it appears that miracles were wrought chiefly among strangers to arrest attention; and also that the Lord was accompanied only by a small group of followers in His Galilæan circuits.

4. *For there is no man that* (**no man**) *doeth any thing in secret*] as Christ did, for His works in Galilee and even beyond the borders of Galilee were practically withdrawn (such is the argument) from the observation of those who could best judge of their worth.

and he...seeketh (**and seeketh**) *to be known openly*] Literally, "to be in boldness" (ἐν παρρησίᾳ εἶναι, Vulg. *in palam esse*), to stand forth boldly as one urging his claims before the world without reserve or fear. Comp. Wisd. v. 1; Col. ii. 15. The words refer to the position claimed and not to the position gained ("to be publicly known"). The phrase however (בפרהסיא) is not unfrequent in Rabbinic writers in the sense of "in public" as opposed to "in secret," see Buxtorf, 'Lex.' *s. v.*

If thou do (**doest**)...] The words do not carry with them any definite denial of the fact (*v.* 3), but simply place the fact as the basis for the conclusion.

shew thyself] **manifest** *thyself*. The word (φανερόω) is characteristic of St John. Comp. xxi. 1, note, i. 31, ix. 3, xvii. 6.

to the world] viii. 26. Comp. xiv. 22.

5. *For neither* (**not even**) *did his brethren believe in him*] The phrase need not mean more than that they did not sacrifice to absolute trust in Him all the fancies and prejudices which they cherished as to Messiah's office. Thus their belief could not be a constant power (οὐκ ἐπίστευον) influencing their whole mode of thinking. They ventured to advise and urge when Faith would have been content to wait.

7 The world cannot hate you; but me it hateth, because I testify of it, that the works thereof are evil.

8 Go ye up unto this feast: I go
8. not up yet unto this feast; [b]for my
time is not yet full come.

9 When he had said these words unto them, he abode *still* in Galilee.

10 ¶ But when his brethren were gone up, then went he also up unto the feast, not openly, but as it were in secret.

11 Then the Jews sought him at the feast, and said, Where is he?

12 And there was much murmuring among the people concerning him: for some said, He is a good man: others said, Nay; but he deceiveth the people.

---

believe in him] Compare viii. 30, note.

6. *Then Jesus said...*] **Therefore Jesus saith...**

My time] the seasonable moment for the revelation of myself (ὁ καιρὸς ὁ ἐμός). The word ("season," καιρός) occurs in St John's Gospel only in this passage [v. 4 is a gloss]. As compared with "hour" (viii. 20, note) "season" appears to mark the fitness of time in regard to the course of human events, while "the hour" has reference to the divine plan.

your time (καιρός) *is alway ready*] Christ's brethren had no new thoughts to make known. What they had to say was in harmony with what others were feeling. Their *time was always ready*. They were in sympathy with the world; while Christ was in antagonism with the world. They risked nothing by joining in the festival pilgrimage; He kept back not only from the danger of open hostility, but also from the violence of mistaken zeal, lest some should "make Him a king" (vi. 15). The thought which underlies the verse corresponds with that in *v.* 17.

7. *cannot hate you*] This "cannot" answers to the law of moral correspondence. It is of frequent occurrence in St John's Gospel and in different relations. Thus it is used of the relation of "the Jews" to Christ (vii. 34, 36, viii. 21 f., 43 f., xii. 39), and of "the world" to the Paraclete (xiv. 17); and in another aspect of the relation of the believer to Christ, in his first approach (vi. 44, 65, iii. 3, 5), and in his later progress (xiii. 33, 36, xvi. 12); and yet again of the relation of the Son to the Father (v. 19, note). In each case the impossibility lies in the true nature of things, and is the other side of the divine "must" (xx. 9, note).

8. *Go ye up unto this feast* (**the** *feast*)] The pronoun is emphatic: Do ye, with your thoughts and hopes, go up (ὑμεῖς ἀνάβητε).

I go not up yet unto this feast] The sense may be "I go not up with the great train of worshippers." Nor indeed did Christ go to the feast as one who kept it. He appeared during the feast (*v.* 14), but then as a prophet suddenly in the temple. Perhaps however it is better to give a fuller force to the "going up" and to suppose that the thought of the next paschal journey, when "the time was fulfilled," already shapes the words. The true reading "not yet" (followed by A. V.) and also the exact phrase "this feast" give force to this interpretation. The Feast of Tabernacles was a festival of peculiar joy for work accomplished. At such a feast Christ had now no place.

is not yet full come] Literally, *is not yet* **fulfilled** (οὔπω πεπλήρωται). Comp. Luke xxi. 24; Acts vii. 23 (ἐπληροῦτο); Eph. i. 10; Gal. iv. 4.

9. *When he had said...*] **And having** *said...*

10. *But when...were gone up, then went he also up unto the feast*] *But when...were gone up* **to the feast**, *then went he also up.*

but as it were in secret] hidden as one solitary stranger and not the centre of an expectant band. Contrast the visit in ii. 13 (in power), v. 1 (as a pilgrim), and here, when Christ was withdrawn from the pilgrim-company, with the final visit in triumph, xii. 12 f.

11. *Then the Jews* (**The Jews therefore**) *sought him*] in the parties of Galilæan worshippers, asking of them *Where is he?* that famous teacher (ἐκεῖνος) whom we saw, and of whom we have since heard (ix. 12)? The question was asked half perhaps in ill-will and half in curiosity.

12. *murmuring*] Or perhaps here *muttering* (γογγυσμός, Vulg. *murmur*), as of men who did not dare to speak plainly and loudly what they felt. Comp. *v.* 32.

among the people] *among* **the multitudes**, that is, among the different groups of strangers who had come up to the festival, and such as consorted with them. This confluence and separation will explain the occurrence of the plural (ἐν τοῖς ὄχλοις) which is found here only in St John, as it occurs also once only in St Mark.

for some said] **some said.** The omission of the particle gives vividness to the description.

a good man] unselfish and true. Compare Mark x. 17.

deceiveth the people] **leadeth the multitude astray** (πλανᾷ, Vulg. *seducit*). Comp. *v.* 47. The thought is of practical and not of intellectual error.

13 Howbeit no man spake openly of him for fear of the Jews.

14 ¶ Now about the midst of the feast Jesus went up into the temple, and taught.

15 And the Jews marvelled, saying, How knoweth this man ‖letters, having never learned?

‖Or, *learning.*

16 Jesus answered them, and said, My doctrine is not mine, but his that sent me.

17 If any man will do his will, he shall know of the doctrine, whether it be of God, or *whether* I speak of myself.

18 He that speaketh of himself seeketh his own glory: but he that seeketh his glory that sent him, the

---

13. *no man*] whether he thought well or ill of Christ, *spake openly* (**boldly**) *of him for fear*—an all-pervading fear (διὰ τὸν φόβον)—*of the Jews*, the leaders of the "national" party, who had as yet not pronounced judgment openly though their inclination was plain.

openly] **boldly**. The original word (παρρησίᾳ) has a double sense. It may mean either without reserve or veil, giving free utterance to every thought plainly (x. 24, xi. 14, xvi. 25, 29, xviii. 20), or without fear (xi. 54). Here, and so probably in *v.* 26, it is used in the latter sense.

2. *The discussions at the midst of the Feast* (*vv.* 14—36).

14—36. The discussions at "the midst of the feast" lay open thoughts of three groups of men: "the Jews" (14—24), "some of the inhabitants of Jerusalem" (25—31), the envoys of "the chief priests and the Pharisees" (32—36). Each discussion constitutes a separate scene. "The multitude" is swayed to and fro by conflicting fears and hopes (20, 31 f.). In dealing with the successive questioners the Lord indicates the authority of His teaching, His connexion with the old dispensation, the brief space of the people's trial.

14—24. In the first scene in the temple Christ shews the source and the test of His teaching (16—18) as against the false interpretations of the Law (*v.* 19), which were against the spirit and history of the Law itself (20—24).

14. *the midst of the feast*] The feast properly lasted seven days, but to these an eighth day was added as "the last day" of the feast (*v.* 37), Lev. xxiii. 36; 2 Macc. x. 6.

into the temple, and taught] This is the first mention of the appearance of the Lord as a public teacher at Jerusalem. Compare vi. 59, vii. 28, viii. 20 (the case is different in x. 23), xviii. 20.

15. *And the Jews*] *The Jews* **therefore**, v. 10. Introd. p. ix.

marvelled] Matt. xxii. 22; Luke iv. 22.

knoweth...letters] Compare Acts xxvi. 24. The marvel was that Jesus shewed Himself familiar with the literary methods of the time, which were supposed to be confined to the scholars of the popular teachers.

having never learned] though He has never studied in one of the great schools (μὴ μεμαθηκώς). Christ was in the eyes of the Jews a merely self-taught enthusiast. They marvelled at His strange success, while they did not admit His irregular claims.

16. *Jesus answered*] *Jesus* **therefore** *answered*. The Lord's reply meets the difficulty of the questioners. His teaching was not self-originated (*My doctrine* (**teaching**) *is not mine*), but derived from a divine Master; infinitely greater than the popular Rabbis. And it had a twofold attestation—an inward criterion and an outward criterion; the first from its essential character, and the second from the character of Him who delivered it. He whose will was in harmony with the will of God could not but recognise the source of the teaching. And again, the absolute devotion of Christ to Him who sent Him was a sign of His truth.

17. *If any man will do* (θέλῃ τὸ θέλημα ποιεῖν, Vulg. *si quis voluerit voluntatem facere*)...] *i.e.* If it be any man's will to do His will. The force of the argument lies in the moral harmony of the man's purpose with the divine law so far as this law is known or felt. If there be no sympathy there can be no understanding. Religion is a matter of life and not of thought only. The principle is universal in its application. The *will of God* is not to be limited to the Old Testament revelation, or to the claims of Christ, but includes every manifestation of the purpose of God. A fine saying is attributed to "Rabban Gamaliel, the son of R. Jehudah ha-Nasi:" "Do His will as if it were thy will, that He may do thy will as if it were His will" ('Aboth,' II. 4).

speak of myself] Compare v. 30 note, xv. 4, note.

18. *his own glory*] Compare v. 30, 41 ff.

but he that seeketh...] The second part of the sentence is changed in form so as to take a positive shape, wrought out both in relation to thought absolutely (*is true*, ἀληθής, Vulg. *verax*) and action relating to others (*there is no unrighteousness in him*).

For the connexion of "falsehood" and "unrighteousness" see Rom. ii. 8; 1 Cor. xiii. 6; 2 Thess. ii. 12. Injustice is falsehood in deed.

same is true, and no unrighteousness
is in him.
. 24. 19 [c]Did not Moses give you the
law, and *yet* none of you keepeth the
. 5. law? [d]Why go ye about to kill me?
20 The people answered and said,
Thou hast a devil: who goeth about
to kill thee?
21 Jesus answered and said unto
them, I have done one work, and ye
all marvel.
22 [e]Moses therefore gave unto you [e] Lev. 12. 3.
circumcision; (not because it is of
Moses, [f]but of the fathers;) and ye [f] Gen. 17. 10.
on the sabbath day circumcise a man.
23 If a man on the sabbath day [1] Or, *without breaking the law of Moses.*
receive circumcision, [1]that the law
of Moses should not be broken; are

---

19. The principle laid down is applied to the condemnation of the Jews. They professed unbounded devotion to Moses, and yet they broke the Law because they were estranged from its spirit. Their ignorance of the Law had at last grown so great that they were prepared to murder Him who came to fulfil the Law.

Did not...the law, and yet none...the law?] **Did not...the law? and none...the law.** The question is an appeal to their own proud boast. Then follows their condemnation by the Lord.

Why go ye about (**seek ye**, and so *v.* 20) *to kill me?*] *v.* 1.

20. *The people*] **The multitude**, made up chiefly of pilgrims, and therefore unacquainted with the full designs of the hierarchy. Omit *and said.*

Thou hast a devil] Compare Matt. xi. 18; Luke vii. 33, where the same phrase is used of John the Baptist, as one who sternly and, in men's judgment, gloomily and morosely withdrew himself from the cheerfulness of social life. So here perhaps the words mean no more than "thou art possessed with strange and melancholy fancies; thou yieldest to idle fears." In a different context they assume a more sinister force, viii. 48 f., 52, x. 20. Yet even in these cases the sense does not go beyond that of irrationality.

21. *Jesus answered...*] The point of the answer lies in the indication of the ground of the hostility which ended in murderous designs. All alike—"the Jews" and "the multitude"—*marvelled* at that which should have been an intelligible illustration of the Law. This wonder contained the germ of open misunderstanding and opposition which, if followed to its legitimate development, could not but end in deadly enmity. If men failed to see the inner significance of the Law they must persecute Christ who came to interpret it and offer its fulfilment in the Gospel.

I have done (**did**) *one work*] ch. v. 1 ff. This special healing on the Sabbath is singled out of the many which Christ wrought (ii. 23, iv. 45) from its exceptional circumstances.

marvel] Yet even wonder may be a first step towards a truer apprehension of the divine lesson Compare v. 20.

22. *Moses therefore gave unto you...*] **For this cause Moses hath given you**, as an abiding ordinance... The cause referred to is the typical realisation of the lesson which underlies the restoration of the impotent man, as it is brought out in *v.* 23. The words *for this cause* certainly commence a new sentence, and do not close *v.* 21. In this respect the usage of St John is decisive, vi. 65, viii. 47.

not because (**that**) *it is...but...*] The words are parenthetical. The case was not simply a conflict of two Mosaic precepts. The law of circumcision was not in origin Mosaic; and thus in itself it carried men's thoughts back to the great ideas which the Mosaic Law was designed to embody. The Mosaic Law of the Sabbath was, on the other hand, new.

The connexion of *for this cause* with *not because* (*that*) appears to be against the usage of the language (vi. 46); 2 Cor. i. 24, iii. 5; Phil. iv. 17; 2 Thess. iii. 9: *I do not mean that...but...*; yet see xii. 6 (where ὅτι is repeated); and against the argument, for the point in question was not the origin of circumcision, though this furnished a subsidiary thought, but the fact of conflicting enactments in the Law which were adjusted in a particular manner.

on the (**a**) *sabbath*] if that happened to be the eighth day. The principle is distinctly recognised in the Mishna, 'Sabb.' XIX. 1. R. Akiva said: "Every work which can be done on the eve of the Sabbath does not set aside the Sabbath; but circumcision, which cannot be done on the eve of the Sabbath [if the eve be the seventh day], sets aside the Sabbath." Compare Lightfoot and Wetstein, *ad loc.*

23. *should not be broken*] by the violation of the commandment which enjoined circumcision on the eighth day. Comp. x. 35, v. 18, note.

are ye angry...because I have made (**I made**)...] The contrast is between the effect of circumcision which made (as it were) one member sound, and that of the miracle which made the whole paralysed man sound. If then the Law itself ratified the precedence of this act of partial healing over the ceremonial observance of the Sabbath, how much more lawful was the complete healing.

ye angry at me, because I have made a man every whit whole on the sabbath day?

[g] Deut. 1. 16.

24 [g] Judge not according to the appearance, but judge righteous judgment.

25 Then said some of them of Jerusalem, Is not this he, whom they seek to kill?

26 But, lo, he speaketh boldly, and they say nothing unto him. Do the rulers know indeed that this is the very Christ?

27 Howbeit we know this man whence he is: but when Christ cometh, no man knoweth whence he is.

28 Then cried Jesus in the temple as he taught, saying, Ye both know me, and ye know whence I

I have made...on the sabbath...] **I made... on a** *sabbath.*

a man every whit whole...] More exactly, *a whole man sound* (ὅλον ἄνθρωπον ὑγιῆ, Vulg. *totum hominem sanum*). *A whole man* regarded from the physical side, and not with the subordinate distinction of "soul and body." Comp. v. 14.

24. *Judge not according to the appearance*] superficially, by the external aspect, as the matter first presents itself (κατ' ὄψιν, Vulg. *secundum faciem*).

righteous judgment] Or rather, *the righteous judgment;* give the one true and complete decision of which the case admits. The truth is one.

25—31. In the second scene, which is still in the temple (*v.* 28), the Lord meets the popular objection which was urged against the belief that He was the Christ (*vv.* 25—27). He had perfect authority for His work, from Him whom the Jews "knew not" (*v.* 28 f.). So the people were divided by His words and works (*v.* 31).

25. *Then said some...Jerusalem...*] **Some therefore** *of them of Jerusalem said*, who were acquainted with the designs of the hierarchy, and yet not committed to them. Hence they are described by the local name (Ἱεροσολυμῖται, Vulg. (inexactly) *quidam ex Hierosolymis*), which occurs elsewhere in New Testament only in St Mark i. 5 (Vulg. *Hierosolymitæ*). The chain of sequence (**therefore**) is that the Lord had taken up the position of accuser when He was Himself accused.

26. *But* (**And**), *lo, he speaketh boldly*] Comp. *v.* 13.

Do the...know...the very Christ?] **Can it be that the rulers** *indeed know* (μήποτε ἔγνωσαν)...**the Christ?** Can it be that they have learnt, come to know ...? The words seem to mark some point of transition, as if a change might have passed over the Sanhedrin. Possibly (so the people argue) they have examined the matter, and found reason to decide in favour of Him whom they before opposed. Perhaps there is a reference to the examination in ch. v. 19 ff.

27. *Howbeit* (ἀλλά)...] The suspicion is at once set aside as impossible: *we know...no man knoweth.* The two words *know, knoweth* (οἴδαμεν, γινώσκει) offer a contrast between the knowledge which is full and abiding, and that which comes by progress and observation. Compare xiv. 7, ii. 24, note.

whence he is] *i.e.* we know His family and His home. Yet even so they thought of Nazareth and not of Bethlehem, David's city, *v.* 42. Compare Matt. xiii. 54 f. It seems to have been expected that Messiah would appear suddenly (perhaps from Dan. vii. 13, or from Isai. liii. 8), no one knew whence, while Christ had lived long among His countrymen in obscurity and yet known to them. According to a Jewish saying ('Sanhedr.' 97 a) "three things come wholly unexpected, Messiah, a god-send and a scorpion." According to another tradition, Messiah would not even know his own mission till he was anointed by Elijah. Just. M. 'Dial.' § 8, p. 226 B.

when Christ (**the Christ**) *cometh*] The exact expression (ὅταν ἔρχηται contrasted with ὅταν ἔλθῃ, *v.* 31) marks the actual moment when the coming is realised. The appearance is a surprise.

28. *Then cried Jesus...as he taught, saying*] **Jesus therefore**, as being acquainted with their partial knowledge and the conclusions which they drew from it, **cried aloud** (ἔκραξεν) *in the temple*, **teaching and saying.** The testimony is given publicly and with solemn emphasis. Comp. *v.* 37, xii. 44, i. 15. The original word (κράζω) occurs only in these places in the Gospel (xii. 13, xix. 12, are false readings).

The repetition of the words *in the temple* (comp. *v.* 14) seems to indicate a break between this scene and the last.

Ye both know me, and ye know (**and know**)...] The claim of the people of Jerusalem is drawn out at length (*me, and whence I am*), and its superficial truth is conceded. So far as mere outward experience goes, Christ answers, Ye do know me and my origin; but that is not all. *I am not come of myself*, self-commissioned, dependent on no other authority, *but He that sent me is true*, is one who completely satisfies the conception of a sender

am: and I am not come of myself, but he that sent me is true, whom ye know not.

29 But I know him: for I am from him, and he hath sent me.

30 Then they sought to take him: but no man laid hands on him, because his hour was not yet come.

31 And many of the people believed on him, and said, When Christ cometh, will he do more miracles than these which this *man* hath done?

32 ¶ The Pharisees heard that the people murmured such things concerning him; and the Pharisees and the chief priests sent officers to take him.

33 Then said Jesus unto them,

(ἀληθινός); it is on Him I rely, and from Him I draw my strength; and Him *ye* (emphatic) *know not*.

and I am not...] The facts which the people knew and the facts which they did not know are simply set side by side. Comp. *v.* 30, viii. 20, ix. 30; Mark xii. 12.

of myself] Compare v. 30, note.

is true] The word rendered *true* (ἀληθινός, compare iv. 23) retains its proper meaning. God is described as true not merely in so far as He gave a true message, but as one who really sent a messenger; a real Father, as it were, sending a real Son. The question was as to the authority of Christ.

ye know not] Comp. iv. 22. This fatal want of knowledge made their boast of knowledge vain. The words are a sad echo of the opening words. As they thought they knew Christ so they thought they knew God.

29. *I* (omit *But*)—as opposed to *you*—*know him, for* (**because**) *I am from him*] Now as always I rest upon Him, deriving my whole being from Him, *and he hath sent* (**sent**) *me*. The continuance of being and the historic mission are set side by side; and both are referred to God.

30. *Then they sought...*] *They sought* **therefore**—because of His claim to be sent from God—*to take him*. The subject is taken from "some of them of Jerusalem" (*v.* 25), those among them who are specially called "Jews." Compare *vv.* 32, 44, (viii. 20, 59), (x. 31), x. 39, xi. 57.

but no man...] **and** *no man...* Compare *v.* 28, note.

his hour] Compare xiii. 1, note.

31. *And many of the people...*] **But of the multitude**—in contrast with the leaders of Jerusalem—*many believed on him*, not only gave credence to what He said ("believed Him"), but surrendered themselves to His guidance. It does not appear that they yet definitely recognised Him as Messiah, because He had not yet openly asserted His claim to the title (x. 24), though they were prepared to do so.

When Christ cometh, will he...] **Will the Christ when He** *cometh...* The question (μή, Vulg. *num quid*) suggests the inference that Jesus must be the Christ, though the inference is not drawn.

this man hath done] *this man* **did**. They look back upon the "signs" which Christ had wrought as a whole, now seen dispassionately far off.

32—36. These verses describe the third scene in the controversy. The wishes of Christ's enemies (*v.* 30) soon found active expression. The Sanhedrin sent public officers to seize Him; and in their presence for the first time He announces His speedy and irrevocable departure from "the Jews" (*vv.* 33 f.), to their bewilderment (*vv.* 35 f.).

32. *The Pharisees*] Comp. iv. 1.

heard that the people murmured such things] *heard* **the multitude murmuring these** *things*, as being inwardly dissatisfied and irresolute.

the Pharisees and the chief priests] **the chief priests and Pharisees.** The combination occurs also in St Matthew: Matt. xxi. 45, xxvii. 62. The phrase probably describes the Sanhedrin under the form of its constituent classes. Comp. *v.* 45, note, xi. 47, 57, xviii. 3.

chief priests] The title appears to be given not only to those who had held the office of high-priest, like Annas (see ch. xviii. 13, note), and his son Eleazar, and Simon the son of Kamhit, and Ishmael the son of Phabi, who may all have been alive at the time, but also to members of the hierarchical families which were represented by these men, alike infamous in Jewish tradition. Comp. Derenbourg, 'Histoire de Palestine,' pp. 230 ff. Thus the title describes rather a political faction than a definite office. Comp. Acts iv. 6 (*as many as were of the kindred of the high priest*). See *v.* 45, xi. 47, 57, xii. 10, xviii. 3, (35), xix. 6, 15, 21.

Compare also Matt. xxvii. 1, note.

officers (ὑπηρέτας)] clothed with legal authority and obeying the instructions of the Council. Comp. *vv.* 45 f., xviii. 3, 12, 18, 22, xix. 6; Acts v. 22, 26.

33. *Then said Jesus unto them*] **Jesus therefore said.** The words have a wider application than to the officers.

Yet a little while am I with you, and *then* I go unto him that sent me.

[h chap. 13. 33.] 34 [h] Ye shall seek me, and shall not find *me:* and where I am, *thither* ye cannot come.

35 Then said the Jews among themselves, Whither will he go, that we shall not find him? will he go unto the dispersed among the [1] Gentiles, and teach the Gentiles?

[1 Or, Greeks.]

36 What *manner of* saying is this that he said, Ye shall seek me, and shall not find *me:* and where I am, *thither* ye cannot come?

---

a little while] It was about six months to the Last Passover.

with you] The "multitude," the "Jews," the "officers," are all grouped together in one body.

I go...] Three Greek words are thus translated in St John, and two of them in similar connexions. Each word expresses a distinct aspect of departure, and its special force must be taken into account in the interpretation of the passage in which it is found. The first word (ὑπάγω), which is used here, emphasizes the personal act of going in itself, as a withdrawal (viii. 14, 21 f., xiii. 3, 33, 36, xiv. 4 f., 28, xvi. 5, 10, 16 f.).

The second word (πόρεύομαι) marks the going as connected with a purpose, a mission, an end to be gained, a work to be done (*v.* 35, xiv. 3, 12, 28, xvi. 7, 28).

The third word (ἀπέρχομαι) expresses simple separation, the point left (vi. 68, xvi. 7, *go away*).

Their differences are very clearly seen in a comparison of xvi. 10 (ὑπάγω) with xiv. 28 (πορεύομαι), and the succession of words in xvi. 7—10 (πορευθῶ, ἀπέλθω, ὑπάγω).

unto him that sent me] During the discourses in this chapter the reference is to the authority of mission (*him that sent me*) and not of nature (*the Father*). The thought of *the Father* is added in ch. viii. 16, 18. These words themselves leave a riddle unsolved

34. *Ye shall seek me...*] not in penitence nor yet in anger, but simply in distress. You shall recall my words and works, and wish once again to see if it might be that in me there were deliverance. The thought is not of the Christ generally, but of the Lord Himself, whose power and love they had experienced. Comp. Luke xvii. 22. Contrast this ineffectual seeking with Matt. vii. 7.

and where I am...] The fact of failure is referred to the cause of failure. Christ is essentially there whither He goes. The stress in this place is laid upon the difference of character (*I am*) which involves separation, and not upon the simple historical separation. Comp. viii. 21, xiii. 33 (*I go*). The pronouns in the original are placed in emphatic juxtaposition (εἰμὶ ἐγὼ, ὑμεῖς...).

35. *Then said the Jews...*] *The Jews* **therefore** *said...* Those who claimed the monopoly of religious privileges are separated from the rest. Hence we have *among themselves* (xii. 19) and not *one to another*.

will he go] *will* **this man** *go*, this strange pretender (οὗτος). The pronoun here carries an accent of surprise and contempt. Comp. vi. 52.

that we shall not...] that we (ἡμεῖς) who stand in the closest connexion with all the people of God.

the dispersed among the Gentiles] **the dispersion among the Greeks** (ἡ διασπορὰ τῶν Ἑλλήνων, Vulg. *dispersio gentium*), the Jews, that is, who are scattered among the heathen Greek-speaking nations. The Jews who were still separated from their own land after the Return were called by two strikingly significant terms: the "Captivity" (גלות from גלה, *he made bare*, ἀποικία, μετοικεσία, αἰχμαλωσία), and the "Dispersion" (διασπορά), which has no distinct Hebrew correlative. The first marks their relation to their own land; the second their relation to the lands which they occupied. Their own land was stripped of them, and they were separated from their national privileges. On the other hand, they were so scattered among the nations as to become the seed of a future harvest. This thought is recognised in a striking comment on Hos. ii. 24, quoted by Wünsche: R. Eliezer said the Eternal has therefore scattered the Israelites among other nations that the heathen may attach themselves to them ('Pesach.' 87 b). *Diaspora* first occurs Deut. xxviii. 25. Comp. Isai. xlix. 6; Jer. xv. 7; 2 Macc. i. 27; 1 Pet. i. 1; James i. 1. For the genitive see 1 Pet. i. 1. This usage seems to be quite decisive against the interpretation "the dispersed Greeks."

and teach the Gentiles (**Greeks**)] make these isolated groups of Jews the starting-point (as the apostles actually did) of teaching among the Gentiles. This is the climax of irrationality. No true Messiah, no one seriously claiming the title, could (it is argued) entertain such a plan.

36. *What manner of saying is this...*] **What is this word**... In spite of all, Christ's words cannot be shaken off. They are not to be explained away. A vague sense remains that there is in them some unfathomed meaning.

23. 37 [i] In the last day, that great *day*
of the feast, Jesus stood and cried,
saying, If any man thirst, let him
come unto me, and drink.
. 18. 38 [k] He that believeth on me, as
the scripture hath said, out of his
belly shall flow rivers of living water.
39 ([l] But this spake he of the Spirit, [l] Isai. 44. 3. Joel 2. 28.
which they that believe on him should
receive: for the Holy Ghost was not

---

3. *The discussions on the last day of the Feast (vv. 37—52).*

The record of the circumstances of the last day of the Feast consists of a fragmentary utterance containing a most significant promise (37—39), together with its effect upon the multitude (40—44); and then more remotely upon the Sanhedrin (45—52).

37. *In the . . . the feast*] **Now on** *the last day*, **the** *great* day *of the feast*. The peculiar greatness of the eighth day lay in the fact that it was the close of the whole festival and kept as a Sabbath (Lev. xxiii. 36). It has been conjectured that it was observed in memory of the entrance into Canaan. At present it is treated as a separate Festival. Compare Lightfoot, *ad loc.*

stood] The original (εἱστήκει) is singularly vivid: *Jesus* **was standing**, watching, as it might be, the procession of the people from their booths to the temple, *and* then, moved by some occasion, **he** *cried*... Comp. i. 35, note, xviii. 5, note.

If any man thirst] The image appears to have been occasioned by the libations of water brought in a golden vessel from Siloam which were made at the time of the morning sacrifice on each of the seven days of the feast while Isai. xii. 3 was sung. It is uncertain whether the libations were made on the eighth day. If they were not made, the significant cessation of the striking rite on this one day of the feast would give a still more fitting occasion for the words.

unto me] The satisfaction lies in the access to Christ. Comp. vi. 35.

The pouring out of the water (like the use of the great lights, viii. 12), was a commemoration of one conspicuous detail of the life in the wilderness typified by the festival. The water brought from the rock supplied an image of future blessing to the prophets: Ezek. xlvii. 1, 12; Joel iii. 18. And that gift is definitely connected with the Lord by St Paul: 1 Cor. x. 4.

Christ therefore shews how the promise of that early miracle was completely fulfilled in Himself in a higher form. He who drank of that water thirsted again; but the water which He gave became a spring of water within. As in iv. 14 the thought passes at once from the satisfaction of personal wants to the satisfaction of the wants of others which follows on this.

Nothing can prove more clearly the intimate relation between the teaching recorded by St John and the Old Testament, than the manner in which Christ is shewn to transfer to Himself the figures of the Exodus (the brazen serpent, the manna, the water, the fiery pillar).

38. The connexion of the phrase *he that believeth on me*, either with the words which precede (*let him that believeth on me come to me and drink*), or with those which follow (*he that believeth on me as the Scripture hath said*, *i.e.* truly, in accordance with the divine word), is obviously against the spirit of the whole passage. The words are out of strict construction. Comp. vi. 39; (Rev. ii. 26, iii. 12, 21).

The sense of thirst—personal want—comes first; then with the satisfaction of this, the fulness of faith; and then, the refreshing energies of faith.

as the scripture hath said (**said**)] The reference is not to any one isolated passage, but to the general tenour of such passages as Isai. lviii. 11; Zech. xiv. 8, taken in connexion with the original image (Exod. xvii. 6; Num. xx. 11).

shall flow rivers] The reception of the blessing leads at once to the distribution of it in fuller measure. Compare the thought in iv. 14, vi. 57, v. 26. He who drinks of the Spiritual Rock becomes in turn himself a rock from within which the waters flow to slake the thirst of others.

There is a fine passage in Augustine's Commentary on this passage as to the character of Christ's gifts: 'in Joh. Tract.' XXXII. 9.

39. *But this spake he*] The inspired activity of the apostles did not commence till after Pentecost. Comp. Luke xxiv. 49.

they that believe on him should receive] *they that* **believed** *on him* **were about to** *receive* (*were to receive*)... The thought of the Evangelist goes back to the definite group of the first disciples (reading οἱ πιστεύσαντες not οἱ πιστεύοντες).

the Holy Ghost (**the Spirit**) *was not yet* given] The addition of the word *given* expresses the true form of the original, in which *Spirit* is without the article (οὔπω ἦν πνεῦμα). When the term occurs in this form, it marks an operation, or manifestation, or gift of the Spirit, and not the personal Spirit. Compare i. 33, xx. 22; Matt. i. 18, 20, iii. 11, xii. 28; Luke i. 15, 35, 41, 67, ii. 25, iv. 1.

because that] Comp. xvi. 7, note, xx. 17. The necessary limitations of Christ's historical presence with the disciples excluded that reali-

yet *given;* because that Jesus was not yet glorified.)

40 ¶ Many of the people therefore, when they heard this saying, said, Of a truth this is the Prophet.

41 Others said, This is the Christ. But some said, Shall Christ come out of Galilee?

m Matt. 2. 5. 42 [m]Hath not the scripture said, That Christ cometh of the seed of David, and out of the town of Bethlehem, where David was?

43 So there was a division among the people because of him.

44 And some of them would have taken him; but no man laid hands on him.

45 ¶ Then came the officers to the chief priests and Pharisees; and they said unto them, Why have ye not brought him?

46 The officers answered, Never man spake like this man.

47 Then answered them the Pharisees, Are ye also deceived?

---

sation of His abiding presence which followed on the Resurrection.

It is impossible not to contrast the mysteriousness of this utterance with the clear teaching of St John himself on the "unction" (χρίσμα) of believers (1 John ii. 20 ff.), which forms a commentary, gained by later experience, upon the words of the Lord.

glorified] This is the first distinct reference to the Lord's "glorification." The conception is characteristic of St John's Gospel (compare i. 14, ii. 11; Introd. p. xlvii.), and includes in one complex whole the Passion with the Triumph which followed. Thus St John regards Christ's death as a Victory (compare xii. 32 f. note, xi. 4, 40), following the words of the Lord who identified the hour of His death with the hour of His glorification (xii. 23 f.). In accordance with the same thought Christ spoke of Himself as already "glorified" when Judas had gone forth to his work (xiii. 31, note); and so He had already received His glory by the faith of His disciples before He suffered (xvii. 10, note). In another aspect His glory followed after His withdrawal from earth (xvii. 5, xvi. 14). By this use of the phrase the Evangelist brings out clearly the absolute divine unity of the work of Christ in His whole "manifestation" (1 John iii. 5, 8, i. 2), which he does not (as St Paul) regard in distinct stages as humiliation and exaltation.

40. *Many of the people therefore ... this saying*] **Some therefore of the multitude ... these words** (λόγους, Vulg. *sermones*, discourses), that is, as it appears, all the discourses at the festival, and not those on the last day only. Probably this judgment marks the general opinion.

said] The original verb in this verse and the next (ἔλεγον, Vulg. *dicebant*) describes vividly a repeated expression of opinion.

the Prophet] Comp. i. 21, (Deut. xviii. 15).

41. *Shall Christ come*] **Why, doth the Christ come** (μὴ γάρ)...

42. *That Christ*] *That* **the Christ.**

out of the town of Bethlehem, where ...] **From Bethlehem the village** *where*... Comp. Isai. xi. 1; Jer. xxiii. 5; Mic. v. 2. It seems strange that anyone should have argued from this passage that the writer of the Gospel was unacquainted with Christ's birth at Bethlehem. He simply relates the words of the multitude who were unacquainted with it (comp. Luke iv. 23); and there is a tragic irony in the fact that the condition which the objectors ignorantly assumed to be unsatisfied was actually satisfied.

43. *among the people*] **in the multitude.**

44. *some of them*] of the multitude. Part of "the common people" were now dissatisfied with Christ, and would have taken Him, as the people of Jerusalem (*v.* 30) and the Pharisees (*v.* 32) before.

45. *Then ... officers*] *The officers* **therefore** *came*, because they had found no opportunity for fulfilling their mission.

the chief priests and Pharisees] Regarded now as one body (πρὸς τοὺς ἀ. καὶ Φ.), the Sanhedrin, and not as the separate classes composing it, as in *v.* 32 (οἱ ἀ. καὶ οἱ Φ.). The day was a Sabbath and yet the council was gathered.

they said ... Why have ye not brought? **(Why did ye not bring?)**] The pronoun (ἐκεῖνοι) used in the first clause (*they said*) is that which generally marks the more remote subject (comp. Acts iii. 13). In the thought of the apostle these enemies of Christ fill up, as it were, the dark background of his narrative, ever present in the distance.

46. *Never man spake like this man*] *Never man* **so spake**, according to the true reading.

47. *Then ... the Pharisees*] *The Pharisees* **therefore** specially standing out from the whole body *answered them.* The hostility of opinion is stronger than that of office.

Are...deceived?] *Are ye also*—whose simple duty it is to execute our orders—**led astray** (*v.* 12)? Their fault was in action (*led astray*) rather than in thought (*deceived*).

48 Have any of the rulers or of the Pharisees believed on him?

49 But this people who knoweth not the law are cursed.

50 Nicodemus saith unto them,
p. 3. (ⁿhe that came to Jesus by night,
t. 17, being one of them,)
15. 51 ᵒDoth our law judge *any* man, before it hear him, and know what he doeth?

52 They answered and said unto him, Art thou also of Galilee? Search, and look: for out of Galilee ariseth no prophet.

53 And every man went unto his own house.

---

48. *of the rulers*] of the members of the Sanhedrin (cf. *v.* 26, iii. 1, xii. 42), whom you are bound to obey, or of the Pharisees whose opinions you are bound to accept. The original form is significant: **Hath any one** (μή τις) *of the rulers believed on him; or*, to take a wider range, *of the Pharisees?*

49. *this people*] *this* **multitude** of whom we hear, and by whose opinion you are influenced, *are cursed*. *As knowing not the law*, they were in the opinion of the wise "a people of the earth," such that he who gave them a morsel merited divine chastisement. A saying is given in 'Aboth' II. 6, "No brutish man is sinfearing, nor is one of the people of the earth pious." Compare Wetstein, *ad loc.* Men were divided into "people of the earth" and "fellows" (חברים), *i.e.* educated men.

50. *that came to Jesus by night*] *that came* **to him before**, according to the true reading.

being one of them] and therefore able to speak from a position of equality. So the question of *v.* 48 was answered.

51. *Doth our law...hear him*] Those who pleaded for the law really broke the law. Compare Deut. i. 16; Exod. xxiii. 1.

any man] **a man**; literally, "the man" (τὸν ἀ.) in each case which comes before them. Cf. ii. 25.

before it hear him] Literally, **except it first hear from himself**, *i.e.* "hear what he has to urge on his own side." The Law is personified. The true Judge is a living law.

52. *Art thou also of Galilee?*] and therefore moved by local feeling. At the same time by the choice of this term to characterize Christ's followers, the questioners contrast them contemptuously with the true Jews.

Search, and look: for...] **Search, and see that...** The particle (ὅτι) is ambiguous; but it seems on the whole better to give to it the sense "that" than "for."

ariseth (ἐγείρεται, not ἐγήγερται)] The reference appears to be not so much to the past as to the future. Galilee is not the true country of the prophets; we cannot look then for Messiah to come thence. The words have that semblance of general truth which makes them quite natural in this connexion, though Jonah, Hoshea, Nahum, and perhaps Elijah, Elisha and Amos were of Galilee. Thus it was said by R. Jehuda in the name of Rab that "the law was maintained by the dwellers in Judæa" ('Eruv.' 53, as quoted by Wünsche). Comp. Neubauer, 'La Geogr. du Talmud,' pp. 183 f.

The episode of the woman taken in adultery (vii. 53—viii. 11).

This account of a most characteristic incident in the Lord's life is certainly not a part of St John's narrative. The evidence against its genuineness, as an original piece of the Gospel, both external and internal, is overwhelming (see Additional Note); but on the other hand it is beyond doubt an authentic fragment of apostolic tradition. Probably its preservation was due to Papias. The incident seems to belong to the last visit to Jerusalem; and it is placed in this connexion in some MSS. of St Luke (after Luke xxi.).

The special importance of the narrative lies in the fact that it records the single case in which the Lord deals with a specific sinful act. And this He does (1) by referring the act to the inward spring of action, and (2) by declining to treat the legal penalty as that which corresponds to the real guilt. So there is opened to us a glimpse of a tribunal more searching, and yet more tender, than the tribunals of men.

53. *every man went*] More closely, **they went every man...but** *Jesus* (viii. 1)... Thus the contrast between the whole gathering in the temple (not the members of the Sanhedrin only) and Christ is made more complete.

ADDITIONAL NOTE on CHAP. VII. 39.

There is a singular and interesting variety of readings in the phrase which describes the gift of the Holy Spirit as yet future, though the sense is not materially affected by them.

(1) οὔπω γὰρ ἦν πνεῦμα, ℵT. The Egyptian Versions represent the same reading, though *Memph.* adds the article in its rendering.

(2) οὔπω γὰρ ἦν πνεῦμα ἅγιον, LX, Mass of authorities. (A is defective.)

(3) οὔπω γὰρ ἦν τὸ πνεῦμα ἅγιον ἐπ' αὐτοῖς, D, (*f*).

(4) οὔπω γὰρ ἦν πνεῦμα ἅγιον δεδομένον, B *e*.

All the readings have early authority. But while (1) explains the others, it is not easy to see how it could have been derived from them. The simple addition of ἅγιον in (2) was a natural assimilation with xx. 22; and the glosses (3) and (4) which appear to be of equal antiquity express the sense truly, which might easily appear to be obscure in the bare (and original) text. The ungrammatical form in D marks the process of corruption.

CHAPTER VIII.

1 *Christ delivereth the woman taken in adultery.* 12 *He preacheth himself the light of the world, and justifieth his doctrine:* 33 *answereth the Jews that boasted of Abraham,* 59 *and conveyeth himself from their cruelty.*

JESUS went unto the mount of Olives.

2 And early in the morning he came again into the temple, and all the people came unto him; and he sat down, and taught them.

3 And the scribes and Pharisees brought unto him a woman taken in adultery; and when they had set her in the midst,

4 They say unto him, Master, this woman was taken in adultery, in the very act.

5 [a] Now Moses in the law commanded us, that such should be stoned: but what sayest thou? [a] Lev. 20. 10.

6 This they said, tempting him, that they might have to accuse him.

CHAP. VIII. 1. *the mount of Olives*] The Mount of Olives is nowhere mentioned by name in St John's Gospel. It is mentioned several times in each of the other Gospels in connexion with the last scenes of the Life of the Lord.

2. *early in the morning* (ὄρθρου)] Compare Luke xxi. 38 (ὤρθριζεν).

he sat down] assumed the position of the authoritative teacher. Compare Matt. v. 1, xxiii. 2; Mark ix. 35.

3. *the scribes and* **the** *Pharisees*] This is a common title in the Synoptists for the body summarily described by St John as *the Jews*. Compare Luke v. 30, vi. 7, xi. 53, xv. 2. St John never names "the scribes."

brought (**bring**) *unto him*] We may suppose that the guilty woman had been brought first to them as a preparatory step to her trial.

4. *was taken*] **hath been** *taken*. The original (κατείληπται) brings the present reality of guilt vividly before the reader (Vulg. *modo deprehensa est*).

5. *Now Moses in the law . . . that such should be stoned* (**to stone such**)] Deut. xxii. 23 f. The punishment of stoning was specified in the case of a betrothed bride. The form of death in other cases was not laid down, and according to Talmudic tradition it was strangulation. It seems better therefore to suppose that this exact crime had been committed than to suppose any inaccuracy in the statement. It is said also that a priest's daughter was stoned if she committed adultery; but this was not a provision of the Law. Compare Lightfoot, *ad loc.*

but what] **what therefore...** Assuming this enactment as explicit, what conclusion canst thou draw for the guidance of our action in the present case? Thou claimest to speak with authority and to fulfil the Law: solve our difficulty now.

6. *This* (**And** (δέ) *this*) . . . *tempting him*] Compare Matt. xxii. 18. The dilemma corresponds to that in the question as to the tribute money. To affirm the binding validity of the Mosaic judgment would be to counsel action contrary to the Roman law. To set the Mosaic judgment aside would be to give up the claim to fulfil the Law. In either case there was material for accusation, practically fatal to the assumption of the Messiahship to which the Lord's teaching evidently pointed. He might be carried away into a premature declaration of His claims, and fall under the civil power; or he might disparage Moses, and lose the favour of the people. The "temptation" lay in the design to lead the Lord to one of these two answers.

wrote] Both here (κατέγραφεν), and in *v.* 8 (ἔγραφεν), the tense in the original presents the action as going on before the witnesses. It is quite vain to conjecture what was written, if indeed we are to understand anything more than the mere mechanical action of writing. The attitude represents one who follows out his own thoughts and is unwilling to give heed to those who question him. The very strangeness of the action marks the authenticity of the detail. The words added in italics in A. V. represent a gloss found in many MSS. (μὴ προσποιούμενος).

But Jesus stooped down, and with
his finger wrote on the ground, *as*
though he heard them not.
7 So when they continued asking
him, he lifted up himself, and said
t. 17. unto them, [b]He that is without sin
among you, let him first cast a stone
at her.
8 And again he stooped down, and
wrote on the ground.
9 And they which heard *it*, being
convicted by *their own* conscience,
went out one by one, beginning at
the eldest, *even* unto the last: and
Jesus was left alone, and the woman
standing in the midst.
10 When Jesus had lifted up himself, and saw none but the woman,
he said unto her, Woman, where are
those thine accusers? hath no man
condemned thee?
11 She said, No man, Lord. And
Jesus said unto her, Neither do I
condemn thee: go, and sin no more.
12 ¶ Then spake Jesus again un-
to them, saying, [c]I am the light of the [c]chap. 1. 5. & 9. 5.

---

7. *So when ...*] **But** *when...*

He that is without sin...] The colour of the word "sinless" is caught from the context. Though it would be unnatural to assume that all in the group of accusers were actually guilty of adultery, there is nothing unnatural in supposing that each could feel in himself the sinful inclination which had here issued in the sinful act. In this way the words of the Lord revealed to the men the depths of their own natures, and they shrank in that Presence from claiming the prerogative of innocence. At the same time the question as to the woman's offence was raised at once from a legal to a spiritual level. The judges were made to feel that freedom from outward guilt is no claim to sinlessness. And the offender in her turn was led to see that flagrant guilt does not bar hope. The Law as in a figure dealt with that which is visible; the Gospel penetrates to the inmost soul.

first] taking, as it were, the place of the witness; Deut. xvii. 7. For here the guiltless was required to take the place of a witness in a higher sense. There is nothing in the words which disparages legal punishment. These men were not the appointed instruments of the law.

8. *again he stooped down...and* **with his finger** *wrote...*] as unwilling to speak more.

9. *And they which heard...conscience, went out one by one*] *And* **they when they heard went out** *one by one*, as they felt the power of Christ's sentence. The interpolated clause (*being convicted by their own conscience*) is a true explanation of the sense.

beginning at the eldest ... (**the elders**)] whose sorrowful experience of life was the fullest. The word is not a title of office, but simply of age.

the woman standing (**being**) *in the midst*] She still remained bound as it were by her sin in the presence of Christ. "Two persons were left," Augustine says (*ad loc.*), "the unhappy woman and Compassion Incarnate" (*Relicti sunt duo, misera et misericordia*).

10. *When Jesus had...unto her*] **And Jesus lifting** *himself up said unto her*.

Woman ... thine accusers? hath ... thee?] *Woman*, **where are they? Did no one condemn thee?** The question marks the interval during which the Lord had waited for the effect of His words.

11. *She said ... And Jesus said unto her*] **And** *she said ... And Jesus* **said.**

Neither do I condemn thee] though I am truly sinless. The words are not words of forgiveness (Luke vii. 48), but simply of one who gives no sentence (comp. Luke xii. 14). The condemnation has reference to the outward punishment and not to the moral guilt: that is dealt with in the words which follow. "Ergo et Dominus damnavit, sed peccatum non hominem" (Aug. *ad loc.*).

go, and sin no more] **go thy way: from henceforth** *sin no more*. Comp. v. 14.

4. *The after teaching* (viii. 12—20).

The Lord had applied to Himself one of the typical miracles of the Exodus (vii. 37 ff.): in this section He seems to apply to Himself that of the fiery pillar. As "the light of the world" He is self-attested (*v.* 12 f.). But for the apprehension of His nature sympathy is needed (14, 15). At the same time even as the Lord's judgment was an expression of the divine will, so His witness included that of the Father (*vv.* 16—18), who could be recognised by those who truly knew Christ (*v.* 19).

12. *Then spake Jesus again...*] **Jesus therefore** *again spake...* The opinions about Jesus were divided. The rulers were blinded by their prejudices. Jesus **therefore** traces back doubt and unbelief to want of inner sympathy with Himself. At the same time (*again*, vii. 37) the second symbol of the festival was interpreted.

spake] This word compared with *cried* (vii. 37) suggests an occasion of less solemnity, probably after the Feast, but the time cannot be certainly determined.

world: he that followeth me shall not walk in darkness, but shall have the light of life.

13 The Pharisees therefore said unto him, Thou bearest record of thyself; thy record is not true.

14 Jesus answered and said unto them, [d]Though I bear record of myself, *yet* my record is true: for I know whence I came, and whither I go; but ye cannot tell whence I come, and whither I go.

[d] chap. 5. 31.

---

unto them] Not to the multitude of the pilgrims, but rather to the representatives of the Jewish party at Jerusalem (*the Pharisees*, *v.* 13; *the Jews*, *vv.* 22, 31). The words refer back to the subject of vii. 52. The "multitude" (vii. 20, 31, 32, 40, 43, 49), which figures throughout the last chapter, does not appear again till xi. 42.

I am the light of the world] In the court of the women, where this discourse was held (see *v.* 20), were great golden candelabra which were lighted on the first night of the Feast of Tabernacles, and perhaps on the other nights. The sight of these and the remembrance of the light which they had cast over the otherwise unbroken gloom of the city seems to have suggested the figure. But the lamps themselves were only images of the pillar of light which had guided the people in the wilderness, just as the libations (vii. 38) recalled the supply of water from the Rock. And it is to this finally that the words of the Lord refer. The idea of that light of the Exodus—transitory and partial—was now fulfilled in the living Light of the world. Compare Isai. xlii. 6, xlix. 6; Mal. iv. 2; Luke ii. 32. According to tradition "Light" was one of the names of Messiah. Compare Lightfoot and Wünsche, *ad loc.* The same title in all its fulness was given by the Lord to His disciples (Matt. v. 14); and St Paul (Phil. ii. 15) speaks of Christians as "luminaries" (φωστῆρες). God is "Light" absolutely (1 John i. 5).

light] Compare Introd. p. xlvii.

of the world] not of one nation only. This thought went beyond the popular hope. Buxtorf ('Lex.' s. v. נר) quotes a remarkable saying from Talm. Hieros. 'Sabb.' ch. 2, that "the first Adam was the light of the world."

that followeth] The thought of the pilgrimage still remains. The light is not for self-absorbed contemplation. It is given for action, movement, progress.

in darkness] *in* **the darkness.** The phrase does not simply describe an accompanying circumstance of the movement, but the sphere in which it takes place. "The darkness" is opposed to "the light" (compare i. 5, xii. 46; 1 John ii. 9, 11), and includes the conceptions of ignorance, limitation, death.

shall have] not only shall look upon, or regard from a distance, but receive so that it becomes his own, a part of his true self. Comp. iv. 14, vi. 57. The Pauline phrase "in Christ," or conversely "Christ in me," expresses the fundamental thought.

the light of life] the light which both springs from life and issues in life; of which life is the essential principle and the necessary result. Compare i. 4. Parallel phrases are *The bread of life* (vi. 35, note); *the water of life* (Rev. xxi. 6); *the tree of life*, Rev. xxii. 14; and perhaps *the crown of life*, James i. 12.

13. *Thou bearest record* (**witness**) *of* (**concerning**) *thyself*] This objection points to the very characteristic of Christ's Being. It must be as they say because Christ is the light. The reality, the character of light, is attested by its shining. If men deny that it does shine, then there is no more room for discussion.

thy record (**witness**) *is not true*] This is perhaps as much an independent assertion as a consequence from the fact that the witness to Christ was from Himself, and so formally imperfect. The Pharisees set their judgment against His assertion. He affirms a truth; they, as claiming equal right of knowledge, deny it. Lightfoot (*ad loc.*) gives some interesting examples of the application of the law of witness to a particular case ('Rosh Hashanah,' 1 ff.). "No man," it is said, "can give witness for himself" (Mishnah, 'Ketub.' II. 9).

14. *Though* (**Even if**) *I bear record* (**witness**) *of myself*, *my record* (**witness**) *is true...*] The reply meets the objection of the Pharisees. The witness of Christ to Himself was essentially complete, and they had not that equality of knowledge on which they presumed to rely. A strong emphasis is thrown upon the pronoun (*Even if I...*), to mark at once the peculiarity in the source and in the foundation of the witness. Compare v. 31. The "I" in the earlier passage marked the separate individuality; here it marks the fulness of the whole Person.

is true] in point of fact (ἀληθής), and not, as in xix. 35, in formal validity (ἀληθινή).

for (**because**) *I know...*] True witness even to a single fact in the spiritual life involves a knowledge of the past and of the future. In the past lie the manifold elements out of which the present grew; in the future lies the revelation of what the present implicitly contains. He can bear witness to himself who has such knowledge of his own being. This no man has, but the Son has it, and in virtue of it He can reveal the Father. Comp. xvi. 28.

15 Ye judge after the flesh; I
judge no man.
16 And yet if I judge, my judgment is true: for I am not alone,
but I and the Father that sent me.
t. 17. 17 [e]It is also written in your law,
18. that the testimony of two men is true.
18 I am one that bear witness of
myself, and the Father that sent me
beareth witness of me.
19 Then said they unto him,
Where is thy Father? Jesus answered,
Ye neither know me, nor my Father:
if ye had known me, ye should have
known my Father also.
20 These words spake Jesus in

---

ye cannot tell...] **ye know not...** To such knowledge the Pharisees could lay no claim. They could not even discern the immediate spiritual relationship of the Lord to the unseen order (*whence I come and* (**or**)...), and still less the mystery of the Incarnation (*whence I came...*) which underlay it.

15. The thought of "knowledge" passes into that of "judgment." The Pharisees had not the knowledge, nor could they in their present state gain the knowledge. They judged *after the flesh* (comp. 2 Cor. v. 16). They were content to form their conclusions on an imperfect, external, superficial examination. Without feeling any necessity for deeper or wider insight, they decided according to the appearance of things; and so by that part of our nature which deals with appearances. Christ, on the other hand, though He embraced in this knowledge all the circumstances, and aspects, and issues of life, *judged no man*. The time for this was not yet; nor was this His work (xii. 47).

The contrast in these words may be compared with that below in *v.* 23, (26?).

16. But this absence of judgment on Christ's part was not from any defect in the completeness of His knowledge. For He adds, *And yet* (**even**, vi. 51, note) *if I judge, my judgment is true...*

is true.. for (**because**)...] Not only *true* as answering to the special facts (ἀληθής, *v.* 14), but *true* as satisfying our perfect conception of what judgment ought to be (ἀληθινή, comp. iv. 23, note, and xix. 35), *because* it is not an isolated or personal judgment, but a judgment springing out of a conscious union with the Author of all Truth. A saying given in 'Pirke Aboth' (IV. 12) gives the characteristic thought which the Lord meets: "Judge not alone (יחידי), for none may judge alone save ONE."

17. *It is also written in your law, that the testimony...*] **And even in your law**—the Law which is your law—**it is written**...*that the* **witness**... The Pharisees had appealed to the Law; the Law then of which they claimed absolute possession (vii. 49) is shewn to decide against them (Deut. xix. 15). The phrase does not in any way disparage or set aside the Law as a divine revelation, but marks the Jewish claim (*v.* 56, *your father*).

It is...written] The exact form used here (γέγραπται) is found in St John of the old Scriptures only in this place (compare xx. 31). It is the common form of citation in other books. St John elsewhere uses the resolved form (γεγραμμένον ἐστίν), which is read here by *Cod. Sin.;* ii. 17, note, x. 34, (xv. 25).

of two men] The word "men" (δύο ἀνθρώπων) does not occur in the original text or in the LXX. It appears to be introduced here to indicate the superior force of the divine witness.

18. *I am one that bear witness ... beareth witness*] *I am* **he that beareth** *witness* (ὁ μαρτυρῶν)... The change in the form of the two clauses presents the difference of the mode in which the two witnesses give their testimony. He that gave the witness was one, but through Him the Father also spake and wrought: "*I am he that beareth witness; and*, at the same time, in and through me, *the Father beareth witness of me*, so that your objection loses its point." The witness of the Father from whom Christ came was given not merely in the miracles done but in the whole ministry of the Son.

19. *Then said they...*] **They said therefore...** The appeal to an absent, unseen, witness did not satisfy the Pharisees.

Where is thy Father?] The form of the question shews the spirit of the questioners. They do not say "Who is thy Father?" as if they were in uncertainty as to the reference, but "Where...?" implying that a reference to one whom they could not look upon and interrogate was of no avail for the purpose of the argument.

Ye neither know me, nor...] Rather, **Ye know neither me nor...** The question was futile. The mere fact that it was put shewed that the true answer to it could not be given or received. There must be knowledge of what we seek before we can profitably ask where to seek it.

With this question and answer the question of Philip and the answer given to it may be contrasted, xiv. 8 ff.

20. *These words spake Jesus* (**He**) *in the treasury*] The Treasury was in the Court of the women, the most public part of the temple (compare Mark xii. 41 ff.; Luke xxi. 1). The mention of the locality adds force to the

the treasury, as he taught in the temple: and no man laid hands on him; for his hour was not yet come.
21 Then said Jesus again unto them, I go my way, and ye shall seek me, and shall die in your sins: whither I go, ye cannot come.
22 Then said the Jews, Will he kill himself? because he saith, Whither I go, ye cannot come.

---

notice of the Lord's immunity from violence which follows. For the Sanhedrin held their sittings ordinarily in the chamber *Gazith*, which was situated between the Court of the women and the inner Court. So Jesus continued to teach within earshot of His enemies.

taught] Contrast Acts xxiv. 12.

and no man...] *and* yet *no man*... The strange contrast is expressed by the simple juxtaposition of the facts: *v.* 55, i. 10, iii. 19, 32, vi. 70, vii. 4, 30, ix. 30, xvi. 32, xx. 19.

laid hands on him] **took him**, as in vii. 30, 32, 44, &c.

his hour] Comp. ii. 4, vii. 30, xiii. 1, note.

5. *The trial of true and false faith* (21—59).

This section describes the spiritual crisis in the preaching to Israel. It consists of two parts. The first part (21—30) contains the distinct presentation of the one object of faith with the declaration of the consequences of unbelief (*v.* 24). This is closed by the notice of a large accession of disciples (*v.* 30). The second part (31—58) gives an analysis of the essential character and issues of selfish belief and false Judaism. This is closed by the first open assault upon the Lord with violence (*v.* 59).

21—30. The subject of these verses is that which had been already partly announced at the feast (vii. 33 ff.). Christ shews the momentous issues which hang upon His brief sojourn with the Jews (*v.* 21), who are essentially opposite to Him in character (*v.* 23), and therefore only to be delivered by transforming faith in Him (*v.* 24). At present a plainer revelation of Himself was impossible (*v.* 25 f.); but hereafter all would be made clear (*v.* 28). Meanwhile His work was His witness (*v.* 29). And this some were enabled to accept (*v.* 30).

21. *Then said Jesus again*...] **He therefore**—because while He was still able to speak freely (*v.* 20) there was yet time and opportunity for some at least to gain the knowledge which they lacked—*said again to them*, as He had said before, vii. 34, but now with a more distinct and tragic warning, *I go my way, and ye shall seek me, and shall die in your sins* (**sin**).

unto them] *v.* 12, note.

ye shall seek me] The emphasis lies (as in vii. 34) upon the word *seek*. There is no contrast here between "ye" and "me." The search was the search of despair under the pressure of overwhelming calamity; and the issue was not failure only but death, and death in sin, for the search under false motives, with false ends, was itself sin, an open, utter abandonment of the divine will.

your **sin**] The sin was one in its essence, though its fruits were manifold (*v.* 24). Hence the order here is, "in your sin shall ye die," while in *v.* 24 the emphasis is transposed ("ye shall die in your sins").

whither I (ἐγώ) *go, ye* (ὑμεῖς) *cannot come*] Compare vii. 34 (*where I am*...). Here the contrast of persons (*I*, *ye*) is distinctly marked, as containing the ground of the separation. When the same words are applied to the disciples (xiii. 33) the impossibility of following is shewn to be for a time only (xiii. 36).

22. *Then said the Jews*] *The Jews*, who were the speakers also in vii. 35, **therefore** *said*, in scornful contempt of such an assumption of superiority. The repetition of the imperfect (ἔλεγον, ἔλεγεν contrasted with εἶπεν, 21, 24, 28) marks the record as a compressed summary.

Will he (μήτι, iv. 29, note) *kill himself? because* (**that**)...] The bitterness of the mockery, like the sternness of the denunciation, is increased (vii. 35). The questioners assume that no way can be open to Jesus which is not equally open to them, unless it be the way to Gehenna opened by self-murder. Thither indeed they could not follow Him. By the Jews suicide was placed on the same level with murder, Joseph. 'B. J.' III. 8 (14). 5; and the darkest regions of the world below were supposed to be reserved for those who were guilty of the crime (ᾅδης δέχεται τὰς ψυχὰς σκοτιώτερος, Jos. *l. c.*).

23. The Lord meets the taunt of His opponents by developing that difference of nature in which lay at once the cause of their inability to follow Him, and the cause of their inability to understand Him. He and they belonged essentially to different regions; the spring of their life, the sphere of their thoughts, were separated from the spring and the sphere of His by an infinite chasm. The difference was equally great whether it was regarded in its final source or in its present manifestation. The circumstances of earthly life give scope for the embodiment of two characters absolutely opposed. For earthly life lies between and in connexion with two orders, and it includes in itself two orders. It may be swayed by higher or lower influences; it may be fashioned on a fleeting or on an eternal type. And between these there can be no fellowship.

23 And he said unto them, Ye are from beneath; I am from above: ye are of this world; I am not of this world.

24 I said therefore unto you, that ye shall die in your sins: for if ye believe not that I am *he*, ye shall die in your sins.

25 Then said they unto him, Who art thou? And Jesus saith unto them, Even *the same* that I said unto you from the beginning.

26 I have many things to say and to judge of you: but he that sent me is true; and I speak to the world those things which I have heard of him.

There can be in the way of nature no passage from the one to the other.

Ye are from beneath] Your whole being in its deepest principles is drawn from the powers of the lower, sensual, realm (ἐκ τῶν κάτω, Vulg. *de deorsum*); you are "flesh of flesh" (iii. 6). Comp. James iii. 15 ff. For the phrase "to be of" (εἶναι ἐκ) see *v.* 47, xviii. 37.

I am from above] drawing every inspiration, every feeling, every judgment from heaven (ἐκ τῶν ἄνω, Vulg. *de supernis*. Comp. Col. iii. 1 f.).

ye are of this world] true children of the fleeting order which you can see.

I am not of this world] but the bringer in of a new and spiritual order, to which entrance can be gained only by a new birth.

24. *I said therefore*] because this fatal chasm separates you from my true home and from the region of life, that *ye shall die*—here the emphasis is changed and lies upon the end "death," and not upon the state "sin"—*in your sins*, which in their varied form reveal the presence of the one fatal source (*v.* 21). *For* there is but one mode of escape from death, one means of obtaining life, one "way" of approaching the Father by which earth and heaven are united, even fellowship by Faith with Him who *is*, and who has become man, and *if ye believe not* (**unless ye believe**) *that I am, ye shall die in your sins.*

that I am] not simply "*that I am* the Messiah," such as your imagination has drawn for you; but far more than this, *that I am*, that in me is the spring of life and light and strength; that I present to you the invisible majesty of God; that I unite in virtue of my essential Being the seen and the unseen, the finite and the infinite.

The phrase "I am" (ἐγώ εἰμι) occurs three times in this chapter (*vv.* 24, 28, 58; comp. xiii. 19), and on each occasion, as it seems, with this pregnant meaning. Compare Deut. xxxii. 39; Isai. xliii. 10.

Elsewhere, in cases where the predicate is directly suggested by the context, this predicate simply is to be supplied: ch. ix. 9, xviii. 5, 6, 8. Comp. vi. 20; Matt. xiv. 27; Mark vi. 50, xiv. 62; Luke xxii. 70. And so it is used of the Messiah: Mark xiii. 6; Luke xxi. 8. Cf. Acts xiii. 25.

25. *Then said they...*] **They said therefore...**

Who art thou?] The question corresponds with the general translation "I am." The wish of the questioners is evidently to draw from the Lord an open declaration that He is "the Christ," that is the Deliverer such as they conceived of him.

And Jesus saith...] **Jesus saith...**

Even the same...*the beginning*] Among the many interpretations of this most difficult phrase two appear to have chief claim to consideration:

(1) *Altogether, essentially, I am that which I even speak to you.* That is to say, My Person is my teaching. The words of Christ are the revelation of the Word Incarnate; and

(2) *How is it that I even speak to you at all?* How is it that I so much as speak with you? That is to say, The question which you ask cannot be answered. The very fact that it is proposed makes it clear, as it has been clear before, that it is vain for me to seek to lead you by my words to a better knowledge of myself.

Of these two the second interpretation, which was in the main that of the Greek fathers, seems to fall in best with the general sense of the dialogue. See Additional Note.

26. We must suppose a pause after the last words, if they are taken interrogatively, and then the sad train of thought is continued. The Jews, even if they had misunderstood the revelation which Christ had given of Himself, and were unworthy of any further manifestation of His Person—and indeed in virtue of this their grievous fault—furnished many subjects for teaching and judgment. In them unbelief was embodied. So the sentence follows: *I have many things to say and to judge of* (**concerning**) *you.* The utterance of these judgments will widen the chasm between us. *But* they must be spoken at all cost; they are part of my divine charge; *he that sent me is true;* in His message there is no superfluity and no defect, and the **things which I heard from Him**, when I came on earth to do His will, **these speak I unto the world.**

but he...] It seems best to find the opposition (as above) in the anticipated failure of these further revelations. Others find it in a contrast between these personal judgments

27 They understood not that he spake to them of the Father.

28 Then said Jesus unto them, When ye have lifted up the Son of man, then shall ye know that I am *he*, and *that* I do nothing of myself; but as my Father hath taught me, I speak these things.

29 And he that sent me is with me: the Father hath not left me alone; for I do always those things that please him.

30 As he spake these words, many believed on him.

31 Then said Jesus to those Jews which believed on him, If ye con-

---

and the Father's commission; as if the sense were: "but these self-chosen subjects must be set aside; He that..." In this case however the force of the affirmation of the "truth" of the Father appears to be lost. The general scope of the words seems to be that the divine message must be delivered whatever its immediate effect may be.

speak to] The construction is very remarkable (λαλῶ εἰς τὸν κ.). It is not simply "address to the world," but "speak *into*, so that the words may reach as far as, spread through, the world." Christ stands, as it were, outside the world, mediating between two worlds. Comp. 1 Thess. ii. 9 (εἰς ὑμᾶς), iv. 8; Hebr. ii. 3.

I have heard] **I heard.** Comp. *v.* 28, note, xv. 15, note.

27. *They understood* (**perceived**) *not*...] preoccupied as they were with thoughts of an earthly deliverer, and perhaps with doubts as to the possibility that Jesus might have come to them from some one such as they looked for, who awaited the favourable time for his appearance.

28. *Then said Jesus unto them*] **Jesus therefore said**... because He read their imaginations and knew why they were offended by His Person and teaching, *When ye have lifted up the Son of man* by the Cross to His throne of glory, *then shall ye know*—**perceive** at last—*that I am, and that I do nothing of myself;* perceive, that is, that my being alike and my action are raised above all that is limited, and in absolute union with God.

lifted up] Compare xii. 32, note.

shall ye know] Compare Ezek. vii. 4, xi. 12, xii. 20.

that I do] It is not unlikely that the verb begins a new sentence, and does not depend on the "that" of the previous clause: "you shall then perceive my true Nature. Yes, and in fact my whole work answers to a divine guidance."

of myself] Compare v. 30, note, xv. 4, note.

do...speak these things] The present teaching was part of the appointed work of Christ. The last phrase is not general, as if it were equivalent to "so I speak," but is used with a specific reference to the revelations which the Lord was even now making.

my Father hath taught] **the Father taught.** The mission of the Son is regarded as the point when He received all that was required for His work. The teaching is so far looked upon as compressed into one supratemporal act, and gradually realised under the conditions of human life.

Compare the use of *I heard* (ἤκουσα, iii. 32, viii. 26, 40, xv. 15). On the other hand *I hear* is used in regard to special acts (v. 30).

29. The whole being of the Son was in absolute harmony with the being of the Father, and the Father was personally present with the Son. In one sense there was a separation at the Incarnation: in another sense there remained perfect unbroken fellowship. There was a "sending" and yet a "remaining together." He that "sent" was still with Him that "was sent." The pregnancy of the phrase must be observed.

the Father ... alone] **He**, even He that sent me (so the words run, omitting *the Father*), at that crisis **left me not** *alone*—the new relation was superadded to and did not destroy the old relation—and men themselves can see the signs of this abiding communion, *for* (**because**) *I*—I (ἐγώ), in the complete Person on which you look—*do always*—not fitfully, uncertainly, partially—*the things that please Him.*

for] The word seems to be used here as in Luke vii. 47, to indicate the sign of the truth of the statement made, and not to give the ground of the fact stated. The perfect coincidence of the will of the Son with the will of the Father is presented as the effect, and not as the reason of the Father's Presence. And yet here as always the two thoughts run into one another.

those things that please him] The service is positive, active, energetic, and not only a negative obedience, an abstention from evil. Comp. 1 John iii. 22; Exod. xv. 26; Isai. xxxviii. 3; Wisd. ix. 18.

30. *believed on him*] in the fullest sense: cast themselves upon Him, putting aside their own imaginations and hopes, and waiting till He should shew Himself more clearly. This energy of faith in a person (πιστεύειν εἰς, "to believe in any one") is to be carefully distinguished from the simple acceptance of a person's statements as true (πιστεύειν τινί, "to

tinue in my word, *then* are ye my disciples indeed;

32 And ye shall know the truth, and the truth shall make you free.

---

believe any one"), which is noticed in the next verse. The phrase is characteristic of St John's Gospel (ii. 11, iii. 16, 18, 36, iv. 39, vi. 29, 35, 40, 47, vii. 5, 31, 38 f., 48, ix. 35 f., x. 42, xi. 25 f., 45, 48, xii. 11, 36 f., 42, 44, 46, xiv. 1, 12, xvi. 9, xvii. 20). It occurs once only in the Synoptic Gospels (Matt. xviii. 6 ‖ Mark ix. 42), and there most significantly of the faith of "little ones." The common phrase (πιστεύειν τινί) occurs *vv.* 45 f., (ii. 22), iv. 21, (50), v. 24, 38, 46 f., xiv. 11. With this phrase "to believe in a person" must be compared the more definite phrase "to believe in his name," that is, to believe in him as characterized by the specific title implied (i. 12, ii. 23, iii. 18).

31—59. This conversation lays open the essential differences between the men who would have given permanence to the Old Dispensation and Christ who fulfilled it. The historical and the spiritual, the external and the moral, the temporal and the eternal, are placed side by side. The contrast is made more complete because Abraham and not Moses is taken as the representative of Judaism.

The successive pleas of the Jews give in a natural order the objections which they took to Christ's claims. "We are Abraham's seed:...how sayest thou, Ye shall be made free?" (*v.* 33). "Abraham is our father" (*v.* 39). "We were not born of fornication: we have one Father, even God" (*v.* 41). "Thou art a Samaritan, and hast a devil" (*v.* 48). "Art thou greater than our father Abraham, who died?" (*v.* 53). "Hast thou seen Abraham?" (*v.* 57). The first three press the claims of inheritance, of kinsmanship, of religious privilege: the last three contain decisive judgments on Christ's character, on His authority, on His implied divine nature.

With the help of the clue thus given it is more easy to follow the course of the argument. At the outset Christ promises freedom to those who honestly follow out an imperfect faith (31 f.). "But we are free" is the answer (*v.* 33). Not spiritually (*vv.* 33—36); nor does descent carry with it religious likeness (*vv.* 37—42). Inability to hear Christ betrays and springs from a close affinity with the powers of evil (*vv.* 43—47). Such a judgment is sober and true (*vv.* 48—50). The word which Christ brings is life-giving (*vv.* 51—53); and He Himself was before Abraham (*vv.* 54—58).

31. Among the body of new converts were some *Jews*—men, that is, characterized as retaining the mistaken views of the nation —**who believed Him**, who acknowledged His claims to Messiahship as true, who were convinced by what He said, but who still interpreted His promise and words by their own prepossessions (comp. vi. 15). They **believed Him** and did not *believe* **in** *Him.* The addition of the word "Jews" and the change in the construction of the verb distinguish sharply this group from the general company in *v.* 30; and the exact form of the original makes the contrast more obvious (οἱ πεπιστευκότες αὐτῷ Ἰουδαῖοι, not οἱ Ἰουδαῖοι οἱ πεπιστευκότες αὐτῷ).

Then said Jesus...] **Jesus therefore** *said* ...*which* **had believed Him.** See *v.* 30, note.

If ye...disciples indeed] *If ye*—even ye with your inveterate prejudices and most imperfect faith—**abide** *in my word ye* **are truly my disciples.** The emphasis lies on the pronoun (*ye*) and not, as we are inclined to place it, on the verb (*abide*). The sentence is a gracious recognition of the first rude beginning of faith. Even this, if it were cherished with absolute devotion, might become the foundation of better things. It included the possibility of a true discipleship, out of which knowledge and freedom should grow; for there is a discipleship of those who for the time are in ignorance and in bondage.

continue (**abide**) *in my word*] The *word*, the revelation of Christ, is at once the element in which the Christian lives, and the spring of his life. He abides in the word, and the word abides in him (v. 38; 1 John ii. 14, i. 10). Just so, in the language of St Paul, the believer lives in Christ and Christ in the believer (Gal. ii. 20). The phrase which is used here and in *vv.* 37, 43 (ὁ λόγος ὁ ἐμός) expresses the word which is truly characteristic of Christ and not simply that which He utters. Comp. xv. 9 note. His word is the word of God, xvii. 6, 14, 17.

32. *ye shall know the truth*] Comp. i. 17, v. 33. This Truth is no mere abstract speculation. It is living and personal. Comp. *v.* 36, and xiv. 6.

the truth shall make you free] The freedom of the individual is perfect conformity to the absolute—to that which *is.* Intellectually, this conformity is knowledge of the Truth: morally, obedience to the divine Law. This principle is that which Socrates (for example) felt after when he spoke of vice as ignorance; and the Stoics when they maintained that "the wise man alone is free." The Jews also had a saying, "Thou wilt find no freeman but him who is occupied in learning of the Law," and hence they substituted mystically *cheruth* (freedom) for *charuth* (graven) in Exod. xxxii. 16 ('Perek R. Meir,' 2. See

33 ¶ They answered him, We be Abraham's seed, and were never in bondage to any man: how sayest thou, Ye shall be made free?

34 Jesus answered them, Verily, verily, I say unto you, [f] Whosoever committeth sin is the servant of sin.

[f] Rom. 6. 20. 2 Pet. 2. 19.

35 And the servant abideth not in the house for ever: *but* the Son abideth ever.

36 If the Son therefore shall make you free, ye shall be free indeed.

37 I know that ye are Abraham's seed; but ye seek to kill me, because my word hath no place in you.

Taylor, *ad loc.*). These different thoughts are summed up in the noble paradox *Deo servire est libertas*.

33. *They answered...*] *i.e. the Jews who believed Him* who have just been characterized.

We be Abraham's seed] to whom the sovereignty of the world has been assured by an eternal and inalienable right. Comp. Matt. iii. 9; Luke iii. 8.

and were never (**have never yet been**) *in bondage to any man*] The episodes of Egyptian, Babylonian, Syrian and Roman conquests were treated as mere transitory accidents, not touching the real life of the people, who had never accepted the dominion of their conquerors or coalesced with them.

how ... free?] *How sayest thou*—thou, a solitary if a great teacher, against the voice of the national consciousness—*ye shall be made*—become—*free?*

34. The answer to the national boast of the Jews lies in the affirmation of the true principle of freedom (*Verily, verily*. Comp. *vv.* 51, 58).

Whosoever (**Every one that**) *committeth sin*] "To commit sin" (ποιεῖν τὴν ἁμαρτίαν) is not simply to commit single, isolated, acts of sin, but to live a life of sin (1 John iii. 4, 8). The exact contrast is *doing the Truth* (iii. 21; 1 John i. 6) on one side and *doing righteousness* on the other (1 John ii. 29, iii. 7). Sin as a whole—complete failure, missing of the mark, in thought and deed—is set over against Truth and Righteousness.

the servant] "the slave," "the bond-servant" (δοῦλος). The same image occurs in St Paul (Rom. vi. 17, 20).

35. The transition from the thought of bondage to sin to that of freedom through the Son is compressed. Bondage to sin is the general type of a false relationship to God. He who is essentially a bondman cannot be a son of God. Whatever may be his outward connexion with God it can last only for a time. Permanent union with God must rest upon an abiding and essential foundation. Even the history of Abraham shewed this: Ishmael was cast out; the promises centred in Isaac. Thus there is a two-fold change in thought, (1) from bondage to sin to the idea of bondage, and (2) from the idea of sonship (contrasted with the idea of bondage) to the Son. Comp. Gal. iv. 22 ff.; Rom. vi. 16 ff.

the house] Comp. xiv. 2; Hebr. iii. 6 (οἶκος).

but *the Son...ever*] **the Son** *abideth* **for ever.**

36. This general principle, illustrated in the origin of the Jewish people by the parable of Isaac and Ishmael, has one absolute fulfilment. The Son, the true Son, is one. Through Him alone—in Him, in fellowship with Him—can lasting freedom be gained, seeing that He alone is free, and abideth unchangeable for ever.

If the Son therefore] The Son and not the Father is represented as giving freedom, in so far as He communicates to others that which is His own.

free indeed] The word translated *indeed* (ὄντως) occurs here only in St John. It appears to express reality in essence from within, as distinguished from reality as seen and known (ἀληθῶς *v.* 31, i. 48, iv. 42, vi. 14, vii. 40). The conception of freedom which is given in this whole passage presents the principle which St Paul applied to the special case of external ordinances.

37. The conception of freedom having been thus illustrated, the Lord goes back to the claim of the Jews, and admits it in its historical sense.

I know that ye are Abraham's seed; but...] Outwardly ye are sons; but in fact you seek to destroy the true Son. Your conceptions of the Father's will and purpose are so fatally wrong that they place you—however little the final issue may be apparent now—in deadly hostility to me. You believe me, but you would make me fulfil your thoughts. When you find that this cannot be, you too will see the murderous spirit revealed in you.

The ground of the hostility of the Jews was the fact that the revelation of Christ (*my word*) made no way, no progress in them. It had in some sense found an entrance, but it made no successful progress in their hearts.

hath no place] **maketh no way in you, hath not free course in you** (οὐ χωρεῖ, Vulg. *non capit*). The sense given in A.V.

38 I speak that which I have seen with my Father: and ye do that which ye have seen with your father.

39 They answered and said unto him, Abraham is our father. Jesus saith unto them, If ye were Abraham's children, ye would do the works of Abraham.

40 But now ye seek to kill me, a man that hath told you the truth, which I have heard of God: this did not Abraham.

41 Ye do the deeds of your father.

---

is not supported by ancient authority; and the idea required is not that of "abiding," but of growth and movement. Comp. Wisd. vii. 23, 24.

38. And yet the word of Christ justly claimed acceptance, for it was derived from immediate knowledge of God. **The things** *which I* (ἐγώ)—I myself directly, in my own Person—*have seen with (in the presence of) the Father I speak.* Compare iii. 11, 32.

I have seen] The perfect revelation through the Son rests upon perfect and direct knowledge. He speaks to men in virtue of His immediate and open vision of God, which no man could bear (i. 18). The appeal to this Vision of God is peculiar to St John. Comp. iii. 32, vi. 46 (the Father); and though man naturally is unable to attain to the sight of God (v. 37; 1 John iv. 20), yet in Christ the believer does see Him now (xiv. 7, 9. Comp. iii. 11; 1 John iii. 6; 3 John 11), and shall see Him more completely (1 John iii. 2. Comp. Matt. v. 8; 1 Cor. xiii. 12).

and ye do that which ye have seen with your father] Or, according to the more probable reading, **the things which ye heard from...** The verb in the original (ποιεῖτε) is ambiguous. It may be imperative *do ye*, or indicative *ye do*. If it be taken as an imperative the sense will be: **and do ye therefore the things which ye heard from the Father:** fulfil in very deed the message which you have received from God, and in which you make your boast. If it be taken as an indicative "the father" must receive opposite interpretations in the two clauses (*my Father*, even God, and *your father*, even the devil: τοῦ πατρός is to be read in both places). The sense will then be: **and ye therefore**, tragically consistent, **do the things which ye heard from your father**, the devil, whose spiritual offspring ye are. This thought has not yet been distinctly expressed, and in *v.* 41 *your father* is distinctly written (τοῦ πατρὸς ὑμῶν, not τοῦ πατρός), but on the other hand *v.* 39 may be supposed to imply a special reference.

39. If "do" be taken imperatively in *v.* 38 the connexion is: "Do not speak to us of some general relationship of the Father, and raise a doubt as to our obedience: *our father* — the one head of our whole race and of none other—*is Abraham*, whom we obey beyond question." If it be taken indicatively then the answer is: "What is this covert reproach as to our obedience to our father? There can be no doubt as to whom we obey. *Our father is Abraham.*" The thought is somewhat different from that in the words *we are Abraham's seed.* This phrase *we are Abraham's seed* suggests the notion of rightful inheritance; *Abraham is our father* that of a personal relationship.

If ye were ... ye would do ... Abraham] There is great variety of reading in the Greek texts in this passage. The most probable reading gives the sense: *If ye* **are children** *of Abraham*, **do** (ποιεῖτε) **the works** *of Abraham.* Or perhaps it may be rendered: *If ye* **are children** *of Abraham*, **ye do the works** *of Abraham*, a supposition which is obviously false. The emphasis is laid upon the community of nature (*children*), and not upon the inheritance of privilege (*sons*).

For the use of *children* see i. 12, xi. 52; 1 John iii. 1, 2, 10, v. 2; and for *sons*, xii. 36 (of light); xvii. 12 (of destruction). Compare also Rom. ix. 8, and viii. 15—17 taken in connexion with Gal. iv. 6 f.

40. *But now...*] As things really are.

a man] The word *man* (ἄνθρωπον) stands in contrast with *of God*, and so brings out the element of condescension in the Lord's teaching which exposed Him to the hostility of the Jews; and at the same time it suggests the idea of human sympathy, which He might claim from them (*a man*), as opposed to the murderous spirit of the power of evil. The title is nowhere else used by the Lord of Himself. Compare Rom. v. 15; 1 Tim. ii. 5; Acts ii. 22, xvii. 31 (ἀνήρ).

the truth, which I have heard (**which I heard**)] Compare *v.* 28 note.

this did not Abraham] who faithfully obeyed each word of God, and paid honour to those who spoke in His name, as to Melchizedek and the angels (Gen. xiv., xviii.). In the traditions of the East, Abraham, "the Friend," is still spoken of as "full of loving-kindness."

41. *Ye do the deeds*] *Ye* **are doing** *the* **works** (as *v.* 38). The condemnation stands in a solemn isolation, and carries the thought back to *v.* 38: *Do ye*...nay, *ye do*...

Then said they to him, We be not
born of fornication; we have one Father, *even* God.
42 Jesus said unto them, If God
were your Father, ye would love me:
for I proceeded forth and came from
God; neither came I of myself, but
he sent me.
43 Why do ye not understand my
speech? *even* because ye cannot hear
my word.
44 [g] Ye are of *your* father the devil, [g] 1 Jo[hn] 8.

Then said they...] **They said...** The line of thought seems to be this. You admit, the Jews argue, that we are historically descended from Abraham (*v.* 37), but you deny that we are spiritually like Abraham (*v.* 39). You speak of another father whose spiritual seed we are. But we appeal to facts. Just as we are literally Abraham's true seed, so are we spiritually. *We*, with a proud emphasis, *we be* (**were**) *not born of fornication.* We do not owe our position to idolatrous desertion of Jehovah. We are the offspring of the union of God with His chosen people. Our spiritual descent is as pure as our historical descent.

42. The answer to the boast lies in the natural conditions of all kinsmanship. The true children of God in virtue of their nature can always recognise Him however He shews Himself. The Jews by their misunderstanding destroyed the claim which they set up. Cf. 1 John v. 1.

for I ... sent me] The Person and the Work of the Lord were both evidences of His Sonship. This He shews by placing His mission first in relation to His divine nature, and then in relation to its historic aspect. In the first clause the two points, the actual mission (**I came forth**, ἐξῆλθον), and the present fulfilment of the mission (**I am come**, ἥκω), are contemplated in their distinctness. In the second (**have I come**, ἐλήλυθα), they are brought together, so that the mission is regarded in its fulfilment.

proceeded forth and came...] **came** *forth from* (*i.e. out of*) *God and* **am come...** The first phrase (ἐκ τοῦ θεοῦ ἐξῆλθον, Vulg. *ex deo processi*) is most remarkable, and occurs only in one other place, xvi. 28, where the preposition has been variously disturbed, some copies reading *from the side of* (παρά), and others *away from* (ἀπό), but here there is no variation. The words can only be interpreted of the true divinity of the Son, of which the Father is the source and fountain. The connexion described is internal and essential, and not that of presence or external fellowship. In this respect the phrase must be distinguished from "came forth from" (ἐξελθεῖν ἀπό) used of the separation involved in the Incarnation under one aspect (xiii. 3, xvi. 30); and also from "came forth from the side of" (ἐξελθεῖν παρά), which emphasizes the personal fellowship of the Father and the Son (xvi. 27, xvii. 8). These differences of thought are clearly seen in xvi. 27, 28, 30. Augustine expresses the idea very well: "Ab illo processit ut Deus, ut æqualis, ut Filius unicus, ut Verbum Patris; et venit ad nos quia Verbum caro factum est ut habitaret in nobis. Adventus ejus, humanitas ejus: mansio ejus, divinitas ejus: divinitas ejus quo vivus, humanitas ejus qua vivus."

and came] *and* **I am come** (ἥκω). Comp. 1 John v. 20. In this word the stress is laid wholly on the present.

neither came I...] **for neither have I come** (ἐλήλυθα)... Comp. iii. 2, 19, v. 43, vii. 28, xii. 46, xvi. 28, xviii. 37. Here the present is connected with the past act on which it rests. The deeper meaning of the first clause explains the form of the second. My Being is inherently divine in its derivation; and so it is also in its manifestation to the world, *for neither—not even*—on this mission of infinite love *have I come of myself...* This act of supreme sacrifice is in absolute dependence on the Father's will. That which causes offence to you is done in obedience to Him.

of myself] Comp. v. 30, note.

43. If the Jews had been true children of God they would have recognised His Son. But yet more than this. They failed not only in instinctive feeling towards Christ, but also in intellectual apprehension of His teaching. They had no love for Him, and therefore they had no understanding of His Gospel. They could not perceive the meaning or the source of His *speech*, in which little by little He familiarly set forth His work (comp. iv. 42), because they could not grasp the purport of His Word, the one revelation of the Incarnate Son in which all else was included.

ye cannot] inasmuch as the wilful service of another power hinders you (*v.* 44). The fatal obstacle was one of their own making. Comp. vii. 7, note.

For the form of the sentence see *vv.* 46, 47.

44. *Ye*] There is a strong emphasis on the pronoun in answer to the *we*, *v.* 41, *Ye* so-called children of Abraham, children of God, *are of your father*, true children of your true father, *the devil, and the lusts* (desires) *of your father* **it is your will to** *do* (θέλετε ποιεῖν); you deliberately choose as your own the feelings, passions, ends, which belong to him. You are, so to speak, his voluntary organs; what he desires, that you carry out. A strange translation, which the original (ἐκ τοῦ πατρὸς τοῦ διαβ.) admits, and which has

and the lusts of your father ye will do. He was a murderer from the beginning, and abode not in the truth, because there is no truth in him. When he speaketh a lie, he speaketh of his own: for he is a liar, and the father of it.

45 And because I tell *you* the truth,
ye believe me not.
46 Which of you convinceth me
of sin? And if I say the truth, why
do ye not believe me?
47 [h]He that is of God hear- [h] 1 John 4
eth God's words: ye therefore hear 6.

---

been put forward by a few recent critics, found some support in early times, and is adopted by Macarius Magnes without remark (II. c. 21): "ye are of the father of the devil;" as if the Jews and the devil were alike the offspring of another spiritual progenitor. According to this view the Jews are said to be murderers and liars like the devil, who followed the pattern of his (and their) father. But the interpretation finds no support elsewhere in Scripture.

are of] draw your being from, and so reproduce in your character. Comp. iii. 31, viii. 23, 47, xv. 19, xvii. 14, 16, xviii. 36, 37; 1 John ii. 16, iii. 8, 10, 12, iv. 1 ff., v. 19.

the devil] xiii. 2; 1 John iii. 8, 10; Rev. xii. 9.

He was a murderer from the beginning] When creation was complete he brought death upon the race of men by his falsehood (Rom. v. 12). For even before he had fallen through want of truth. *He* **stood** *not in the truth* (ἐν τῇ ἀλ.)—the divine Sum of all truth—*because there is no truth* (οὐκ ἔστιν ἀλ.)—no fragmentary truth which has affinity with the Truth—*in him.*

The reference appears to be to the Fall and not to the death of Abel (1 John iii. 12). The death of Abel was only one manifestation of the ruin wrought by selfishness (see 1 John iii 8 ff.). Comp. Wisd. ii. 24.

and abode not...] *and* **stood** *not...* See Additional Note.

When he speaketh a lie...] **Whenever** *he* (the devil) *speaketh a lie* (τὸ ψεῦδος, the falsehood as opposed to the Truth as a whole, comp. *v.* 38), *he speaketh of his own;* his utterances are purely selfish, he draws them simply from within himself (contrast *v.* 42; 2 Cor. iii. 5), *for* (**because**) *he is a liar, and the father of it.*

of it] The original (αὐτοῦ) may be masculine, *of him, i.e.* the liar; or neuter, *of it, i.e.* the lie. Comp. Orig. 'in Joh. T.' VI. 3, ὁ πατὴρ αὐτῆς (the truth).

It is however most probable that this very difficult sentence should be translated quite differently: **Whenever** a man **speaketh a lie, he speaketh of his own, for his father also is a liar.** A man, that is, by lying reveals his parentage and acts conformably with it. The omission of the subject with the verb is certainly harsh (ὅταν λαλῇ), but scarcely more so than the other renderings of the pronoun (αὐτοῦ).

45. *And because...*] **But** *because...* If I had spoken falsehood, such is the argument, you would have recognised that which is kindred to yourselves, **but...** The final opposition between Christ and the devil lies in the opposition of Truth to Falsehood. And this opposition repeats itself in the children of the two spiritual heads. There must be that which is akin to Truth in us, if we are to believe Truth. If our souls are given up to a lie we cannot believe the truth addressed to us. The contrast between *I* and *ye* is made as sharp as possible. "But as for me, because I tell you...(ἐγὼ δὲ ὅτι)."

46. Falsehood in action is sin. Falsehood within must shew itself. From words then the appeal is made to acts. *Which of you convinceth* (**convicteth**) *me of sin?* Who, that is, arraigneth me on a just charge of sin? The word *sin* (ἁμαρτία) is not to be taken for *error* or *falsehood*, but for "sin" generally, according to the uniform usage of the New Testament, and here probably, from the connexion, as measured by the Law. The words suggest but they do not prove the sinlessness of Christ. The appeal is to a human standard, yet such an appeal on such an occasion carries far more with it.

convinceth] **convicteth.** Compare xvi. 8, note.

And if I say the truth...] **If I say truth,** that which is true: truth, and not the Truth, the part and not the whole revelation. The absence of sin includes necessarily the absence of falsehood. Hence the Lord takes it as proved that His words are true.

47. We must suppose a pause after 46a, and again after 46b. Then follows the final sentence. The true child of God alone can hear the words (τὰ ῥήματα), each separate message, of God. For this reason, because the power of hearing (*v.* 43) depended on inward affinity, the Jews could not hear, because they were not of God. Comp. xviii. 37, vii. 17, xii. 48 f., xiv. 23, note; 1 John iv. 6.

He that is of God] the true child of God, who draws his life and support from Him. Comp. (i. 13), iii. 31, viii. 23, xv. 19, xvii. 14, xviii. 36, 37; 1 John ii. 16, iii. 10, (12), iv. 1 ff., v. 19.

ye therefore...because...] **for this cause ye** *...because.* This combination in St John com-

them not, because ye are not of God.

48 Then answered the Jews, and said unto him, Say we not well that thou art a Samaritan, and hast a devil?

49 Jesus answered, I have not a devil; but I honour my Father, and ye do dishonour me.

50 And I seek not mine own glory: there is one that seeketh and judgeth.

51 Verily, verily, I say unto you,

---

monly refers back to a former principle, which is exemplified at the time in the immediate circumstances. Comp. v. 16, 18, x. 17, xii. 18, 39; 1 John iii. 1.

ye are not of God] The whole scope of the argument proves that this state does not exclude true moral responsibility. Comp. 1 John iii. 7 ff.

48. *Then answered the Jews...*] **The Jews** *answered...* The key-word (*the Jews*) is introduced again in this new phase of the argument.

Say we not well...?] The form of expression shews that the reproach was a current one; so that a glimpse is here offered of the common judgment on Christ. He was in the eye of "the Jews" a Samaritan, a bitter foe of their nationality, and withal a breaker of the Law, and a frantic enthusiast, who was not master of his own thoughts and words. Thus the Jews turned back upon Christ both the charges which He had brought against them, that they were not legitimate children of Abraham, and that they were of the devil as their spiritual father. The pronoun is emphatic (οὐ κ. λ. ἡμεῖς): "Are not we at last right...?"

thou art a Samaritan] There is bitter irony in the original words, from the position of the pronoun at the end of the clause, which it is difficult to reproduce. "Thou that boastest great things of a kingdom and a fulfilment of the Law, after all art but a Samaritan."

hast a devil (**demon**)] Comp. vii. 20, x. 20 f.

49. The contrast is between the persons *I* and *you*. "*I* (ἐγώ), even in these bold mysterious utterances which move your wonder, *have not a* **demon**, *but* speak only words of soberness, which I must speak that I may thereby fulfil my mission. By so doing *I honour my Father*, and am no Samaritan; *and ye* are unable to see the Father in the Son, and therefore *ye* (ὑμεῖς) *do dishonour me*."

The Lord leaves unnoticed the first epithet of reproach (*thou art a Samaritan*). He would not recognise the meaning which they attached to a difference of race.

50. *And...*] **But** when I speak of dishonour it is not that I shrink from it: *I seek not mine own glory*; that quest is not my part, but belongs to another; and *there is one that seeketh and judgeth*—that seeketh and in the very act of seeking judgeth. For he who has failed in giving to me what is due is thereby condemned; and the will of the Father is that all men should honour the Son even as they honour the Father (v. 23).

there is] v. 45, *v.* 54.

that...judgeth] The phrase is superficially opposed to v. 22. But the thought here is of the divine law which is self-executing in the very nature of things.

seeketh] Philo, in a paraphrase of Gen. xlii. 22, *his blood is required* (LXX. ἐκζητεῖται), writes: "He that requireth (ὁ ζητῶν, *he that seeketh*) is not man but God, or the Word, or the divine Law" ('de Jos.' 29, II. p. 66).

51. *Verily, verily*] These words (as always) introduce a new turn of thought. The claims of the Jews based upon their historical descent and their spiritual sonship have been met and set aside; and the Lord now returns to the declaration of *vv.* 31 f., but with this difference, that what was then regarded in relation to *state* is now regarded in relation to *action*. For "abiding in the word" we have "keeping the word," and for "freedom" we have "victory over death."

keep my saying] *keep my* **word**, "doctrinam credendo, promissa sperando, facienda obediendo," Bengel. The original term for "keep" (τηρεῖν) is characteristic of St John. It expresses rather the idea of intent watching than of safe guarding (φυλάσσειν). The opposite to "keeping (τηρεῖν) the word" in this form would be to disregard it; the opposite to "keeping (φυλάσσειν) the word" in the other form would be to let it slip. "Keeping the word" of Christ is also to be distinguished from "keeping His commandments" (1 John ii. 3, 5); the former marks the observance of the whole revelation in its organic completeness, and the latter the observance of definite precepts.

see death] The exact phrase (θεωρεῖν θάνατον) is not found elsewhere in New Testament. Comp. iii. 36 (ὄψ. ζωήν); Luke ii. 26; Hebr. xi. 5 (μὴ ἰδεῖν θαν.); Acts ii. 27, 31, xiii. 35 ff. (εἶδε διαφθοράν); Rev. xviii. 7 (πένθος ἰδεῖν).

The "sight" described here is that of long, steady, exhaustive vision, whereby we become slowly acquainted with the nature of the object to which it is directed. The words must be compared with Gen. ii. 17. There is that in the believer which never dies, even though he seems to die; and conversely, Adam

If a man keep my saying, he shall
never see death.
52 Then said the Jews unto him,
Now we know that thou hast a
devil. Abraham is dead, and the prophets; and thou sayest, If a man
keep my saying, he shall never taste
of death.
53 Art thou greater than our father Abraham, which is dead? and
the prophets are dead: whom makest
thou thyself?
54 Jesus answered, If I honour
myself, my honour is nothing: it is
my Father that honoureth me; of
whom ye say, that he is your
God:
55 Yet ye have not known him;
but I know him: and if I should say,
I know him not, I shall be a liar like

---

died at the moment of his disobedience, though he seemed still to live. Comp. xi. 26, vi. 50.

death] Just as "life" in St John is present, or rather eternal (xvii. 3), so "death" is not an event but a state, that selfish isolation which is the negation of life. Comp. xi. 25 f., vi. 50, v. 24; 1 John iii. 14.

52. *Then said the Jews...*] **The Jews** *said...* The name is repeated here as in *v.* 48 at the beginning of the answer to the new self-revelation.

we know] The direct statement, made in apparent good faith, and yet (as the hearers thought) obviously and flagrantly false, could only be explained on the supposition of evil possession.

Abraham...death] God had spoken to Abraham and to the prophets, and they had kept His word and yet died, who then was this with a word more powerful? For the objection is intensified by the fact that the Lord did not simply claim life for Himself, but, what was far more, claimed to communicate eternal life.

is dead] **died.** The argument rests upon the simple historic fact.

taste of death] The inaccuracy of quotation is significant. The believer, even as Christ (Hebr. ii. 9), does "taste of death," though he does not "see" it in the full sense of *v.* 51.

The phrase (comp. Matt. xvi. 28 and parallels) is not found in the Old Testament, but is common in Rabbinic writers (see Buxtorf, 'Lex.' s. v. טעם), and seems to come from the image of the "cup" of suffering: ch. xviii. 11; Rev. xviii. 6, xiv. 10. xvi. 19; Matt. xx. 22 f. parallels, xxvi. 39 parallels. The "cup of death" is an Arabian image. Comp. Gesen. 'Thes.' s. v. כוס.

53. *Art thou*] the Galilean, the Nazarene. Comp. iv. 12.

which is dead?.. are dead] More exactly, **seeing that he** (ὅστις) **died,** *and the prophets* **died.** For the use of the relative see Col. iii. 5; Phil. iv. 3; Eph. iii. 13; Hebr. x. 35; 1 John i. 2.

whom makest thou thyself?] Comp. v. 18, x. 33, xix. 7, 12; 1 John i. 10.

54 f. The Lord prefaces His answer as to the relative dignity of Abraham and Himself by a revelation of the principle in obedience to which the answer is given. It does not come from any personal striving after glory, but in obedience to the will of the Father which the Son knows absolutely and obeys. The Son "makes Himself" to be nothing: He is, and He declares Himself to be that which the Father, so to speak, makes Him.

If I honour myself, my honour...] *If I,* I in obedience to my own impulse, **glorify** *myself, my* **glory...** Comp. v. 31.

it is my Father that honoureth me] **there is my Father that glorifieth me.** I glorify not myself, nor need I to do it; there is one that glorifieth me... The construction is exactly parallel with *v.* 50.

your God] as claiming an exclusive connexion with Him.

55. *Yet ye have not known him*] **And,** while you make this claim (comp. *v.* 20, note), **ye have not come to know him** (οὐκ ἐγνώκατε) by the teaching of the Law and of the Prophets, and now of the Son Himself, *but I know* (οἶδα) *Him,* essentially; and if I should dissemble my knowledge, if I should withhold the message which I have to give, *if I should say I know Him not, I shall be* **like unto you, a liar.**

I know him] Comp. vii. 29. For the difference between progressive and absolute knowledge see iii. 10 f. The special ignorance of these Jews stands in contrast with the knowledge which was characteristic of the nation: iv. 22.

a liar] for to hide the truth is no less falsehood than to spread error. Compare 1 John ii. 4, 22, iv. 20, v. 10.

but...] even in this crisis of separation, when my words will be misunderstood and so widen the breach between us (cf. *v.* 26), I proclaim the knowledge which I have and fulfil my mission by keeping His word.

and keep his saying **(word)**] The relation of the Son to the Father is attested by the same active devotion as the relation of the believer to Christ (*v.* 51). Comp. xv. 10.

56. This then is the answer. There is no such comparison as you dream of between Abraham and me. *Abraham your father,* the

unto you: but I know him, and keep his saying.

56 Your father Abraham rejoiced to see my day: and he saw *it*, and was glad.

57 Then said the Jews unto him, Thou art not yet fifty years old, and hast thou seen Abraham?

58 Jesus said unto them, Verily, verily, I say unto you, Before Abraham was, I am.

59 Then took they up stones to cast at him: but Jesus hid himself, and went out of the temple, going through the midst of them, and so passed by.

---

father whom you delight to name (*v.* 53) and in whom you trust (*v.* 39), *rejoiced* with the joy of exultation in his eager desire, in his confident hope, *to see my day*, *and he saw it and was glad.* I am He for whom he looked as the fulfilment of all that was promised to him; and you, who profess to be his children, pretend that I do him dishonour in claiming power which he could not have.

rejoiced (ἠγαλλιάσατο, **exulted**) *to see*] The peculiar construction (ἵνα ἴδῃ, Vulg. *ut videret*) may be explained by considering that the joy of Abraham lay in the effort to see that which was foreshadowed. It lay not in the fact *that* he saw, nor was it *in order to* see; but partial vision moved him with the confident desire to gain a fuller sight. Winer's translation ('Gramm.' § XCIV. 8, c) "that he should see" obscures this sense.

my day] That is probably the historic manifestation of the Christ (comp. Luke xvii. 22) without any special reference to any particular point in it as the Passion. It may be however that the historic work of Christ is regarded in its consummation in the day which is spoken of emphatically as "that day," "the day of the Son of man" (Luke xvii. 30), "the day of Christ" (Phil. i. 6, 10, ii. 16).

he saw it] The reference cannot be to any present vision in Paradise (comp. Hebr. xi. 13). The tense of the original is decisive against this view. All conjecture must be uncertain, but there is nothing unnatural in the supposition that the faith shewn in the offering up of Isaac may have been followed by some deeper, if transient, insight into the full meaning of the promises then renewed. Such faith was in itself, in one sense, a vision of the day of Messiah.

According to the Jewish tradition ('Bereshith R.' 44 Wünsche) Abraham saw the whole history of his descendants in the mysterious vision recorded in Gen. xv. 8 ff. Thus he is said to have "rejoiced with the joy of the Law."

57. *Then said the Jews...*] **The Jews therefore** *said...*, still persisting in the literal interpretation of the words.

fifty years old] This age was the crisis of completed manhood (Num. iv. 3). There was an early tradition that Christ was between forty and fifty years old at the time of the Passion (Iren. 'Adv. Hær.' II. 22. 5 f.). This opinion was said to be derived from St John. However strange it may appear, some such a view is not inconsistent with the only fixed historic dates which we have with regard to the Lord's life, the date of His birth, His Baptism, and the banishment of Pilate.

hast thou seen...] The language of the Lord is again (*v.* 52) misquoted; and on this occasion the misquotation completely misrepresents the thought.

58. There can be no doubt as to the meaning of the final answer which follows as a natural climax to what had been said before. Abraham died: Christ was the Giver of life. Abraham was the father of the Jews: Christ was the centre of Abraham's hope. Abraham came into being as a man: Christ is essentially as God. And this closing revelation is prefaced by the solemn words which fix attention upon its substance. *Verily, verily, I say unto you, Before Abraham was*—was born, came to be—*I am* (πρὶν 'Α. γενέσθαι ἐγώ εἰμι, Vulg. *antequam fieret Abraham ego sum*).

I am] The phrase marks a timeless existence. In this connexion "I was" would have expressed simple priority. Thus there is in the phrase the contrast between the created and the uncreated, and the temporal and the eternal. At the same time the ground of the assurance in *v.* 51 is made known. The believer lives because Christ lives, and lives with an absolute life (comp. xiv. 19).

59. *Then took they up...*] *They took up* **therefore**..., as understanding rightly the claim which was advanced in the last words. If the sentence had been a simple affirmation of the claim to Messiahship, it would have been welcomed. Comp. x. 24. But it was the affirmation of a new interpretation of Messiah's nature and work. Comp. x. 30 f.

going through...passed by] This clause must be omitted in accordance with a combination of the best authorities.

ADDITIONAL NOTES on CHAP. VII. 53—VIII. 11 and CHAP. VIII. 25, 44.

VII. 53—VIII. 11.

External and internal evidence combine to shew beyond all reasonable doubt that this remarkable narrative is not a genuine portion of the Gospel of St John.

A. EXTERNAL EVIDENCE.

The external evidence against its genuineness may be briefly summed up:

1. It is omitted by all the oldest Greek MSS. with one exception, and by a considerable number of those later MSS. which generally give a very ancient text: ℵ[A]B[C]LTXΔ, 33, 131, 157, *2pe*, &c. [A and C are defective, but it is certain that they did not contain the passage from an estimate of the contents of the missing pages; L (eighth cent.) and Δ (ninth cent.) indicate a knowledge of the existence of the narrative, which was evidently not found in their archetypes, by leaving a small gap.]

2. The passage is marked by asterisks or obeli in many MSS. which contain it. Euthymius Zigabenus [more correctly, Zygadenus, †1118], the earliest Greek commentator who writes upon it, observes that it is not found in "the accurate copies" or is obelized in them, and that therefore it is not to be accounted genuine.

3. It is inserted in other places:
(*a*) At the end of the Gospel by 1 and about ten other MSS.
(*b*) After vii. 36 by 225.
(*c*) After Luke xxi. by 69 and three other MSS.

4. It is omitted by important Latin copies *af*, &c., by the Egyptian versions, by the Old Syriac (the Berlin fragment), by the Gothic version, and by the best MSS. of the Peshito and of the Armenian versions.

5. It was certainly not read as a part of the Gospel by Tertullian, Origen, Theodore of Mopsuestia, Chrysostom, Cyril of Alexandria; nor is there any evidence that it was known by Cyprian or Hilary.

6. The earliest Greek text (that in D) differs very considerably from the common text; and the variations in the section generally are far more considerable than in portions of the authentic text of St John.

In other words, it is omitted by the oldest representatives of every kind of evidence (MSS., versions, fathers); and the critical character of the text is such as to distinguish it from the rest of the book with which it is connected.

On the other hand,

1. It is found in D and in the mass of the later uncial and cursive manuscripts.

Jerome mentions that it was found in his time "in many Greek and Latin MSS. in the Gospel according to John" ('adv. Pelag.' II. 17). And Augustine suggests that the passage was removed from the [Latin] text by "some who were of slight faith, or rather hostile to the true faith," to avoid scandal ('De Conj. Adult.' II. 7). Several scholia which notice its omission remark that it was found in "ancient" or "most ancient" copies.

2. It is found in most Latin copies, *bc*, &c., Vulg.; in the Jerusalem Syriac; in the Æthiopic, and in some later versions.

3. It was read as part of the Gospel by Augustine, Ambrose, and many later Latin Fathers; and it is quoted in the Apostolical Constitutions (II. 24).

4. It is found in the Calendar of Lessons in K (ninth cent.); and it has been read in the Greek Church, partially but not universally, at the Festivals of several saints from a date earlier than the eighth century. It was also read in the service at Rome in the time of Gregory the Great.

On this evidence several observations offer themselves.

1. The text of D is conspicuous for additions similar in character to this narrative, though less in extent (*e.g.* Luke vi. 5); and some of these (*e.g.* Matt. xx. 28) obtained a wide currency, though they cannot be considered to be a part of the authentic evangelic text.

2. The statement of Jerome is, of course, beyond question; but even he implies that the majority of copies was on the other side; and it is clear from other similar statements that he did not speak on critical questions after a very large examination of authorities. The general assertions of late MSS. as to "the ancient copies" are neutralised by opposite assertions in other MSS.

3. The early Latin copies are just those which admitted interpolations most freely (*e.g.* Matt. xx. 28); and it is easily intelligible that if Jerome found any Greek authority for the narrative he would not remove the history from the text. The fact therefore that he left it in the Latin text (he did not insert it) proves no more than that he did not feel bound to expunge it.

The Jerusalem Syriac is a lectionary, and though it abounds in very ancient readings, the MS. is not earlier than the eleventh century.

4. The date of the present text of the Apostolic Constitutions is too uncertain to admit of the conclusion being drawn that the narrative was found by the writer in the Greek text of St John in the third century. He may have quoted the narrative (*e.g.*) from St Luke or from tradition. It is however not improbable that the narrative may have found a place in some Greek texts of the Gospel in the third century, though there is no direct evidence of the fact.

5. The evidence of the liturgical use of the

passage does not carry its existence as a part of the Gospel beyond the date given by direct documentary evidence.

6. Augustine's assertion as to the removal of the passage from the text of St John, on prudential grounds, which has been maintained by the modern scholars who defend the genuineness of the passage, is wholly at variance with the cardinal facts of the history of the text of the New Testament. Wilful corruptions of the apostolic writings, however recklessly they were imputed in controversy, are happily in fact all but unknown. Changes, and even such a change as the insertion of this passage, can be accounted for without recourse to the assumption of dishonesty.

Thus the only natural explanation of the unquestioned facts is that the narrative was current in the third century in a Greek but not in a Latin text, though over a narrow range; that towards the end of the fourth century it was introduced in various places, but particularly where it now stands, and was thence taken into the Latin texts; that from the sixth century onwards it was found more and more frequently in the Constantinopolitan texts and all but universally in the Latin texts, and in the course of time was partially introduced into other versions.

B. Internal Evidence.

The internal evidence leads forcibly to the same conclusion.

1. The language of the narrative is different from that of St John both in vocabulary and in structure.

Thus St John nowhere uses the terms *τὸ ὄρος τῶν ἐλαιῶν, οἱ γραμματεῖς, κατακρίνω*, which are found in all the Synoptists; nor again, *πᾶς ὁ λαός*, which is common in St Luke, while *λαός* occurs in St John only in a special sense in xi. 50, xviii. 14; nor *ὄρθρου* (St Luke), but *πρωΐ* or *πρωΐας*; nor *καθίσας ἐδίδασκεν*; nor *πορεύεσθαι* in the simple sense of "to go" without the subsidiary notion of a purpose (even in iv. 50).

In structure the continuous connexion of the sentences by *δέ* (*vv.* 2, 3, 6, 7, 9, 10, 11) is wholly without example in St John's narrative. Contrast (for example) xx. 1—9 (*οὖν*, *vv.* 2, 3, 6, 8; *δέ*, *vv.* 1, 4), or iv. 1—26 (*οὖν*, 1, 5, 6, 9; *δέ*, 4, 6. Most of the clauses are unconnected).

2. The general "tone" of the narrative is alien from St John, and akin to the tone of the common Synoptic basis.

But it may be asked how the narrative came to be inserted where we find it? The answer can, I believe, be given with tolerable certainty. A narrative very similar to this was preserved by Papias, and was found also in the Gospel according to the Hebrews (Euseb. 'H. E.' III. 40). The object of Papias was to collect traditions illustrative of "the oracles of the Lord." It is then a most natural conjecture (Lightfoot, 'Contemporary Review,' Oct. 1875, p. 847) that this incident was given by Papias in illustration of ch. viii. 15; and so was inserted in the text, on which it had been originally a marginal note, in the nearest convenient place. Comp. Ewald, 'Joh. Schr.' I. p. 271.

The incident appears to belong to the last visit to Jerusalem, so that the position which it occupies in St Luke is perhaps historically correct.

25. *Even the same...the beginning*] The numerous interpretations of this most obscure sentence fall into two main classes, according as it is taken affirmatively (1), or interrogatively (2).

(1) The affirmative interpretations again are twofold. In some *τὴν ἀρχήν* is taken adverbially, and in others as parallel with the relative *ὅτι* (*ὅ τι*).

According to the latter interpretation the sense is: "I am the Beginning (Rev. xxi. 6), that which I am even saying to you." This appears to be the sense of the early Latin translation: *Initium quod et loquor uobis*. But even if *τὴν ἀρχήν* could be attracted to *ὅτι* in this way at the beginning of the sentence, the use of *λαλῶ* and not *λέγω* appears to be fatal to such an interpretation, for it evidently refers to the conversation, the general teaching, of Christ, and not to any specific declaration.

It may be here noticed that Augustine's interpretation, which is based upon the later Latin text, *Principium, quia et loquor uobis*, is obviously inconsistent with the Greek. "Believe me to be the Beginning, because I am even speaking with you, because, that is, I have become humble for your sake..." This interpretation however was followed by many Latin fathers who were ignorant of Greek.

If *τὴν ἀρχήν* be taken adverbially, it may have the sense of "altogether, essentially," or "to begin with, first of all," or (perhaps) "all along."

Thus the following interpretations have been given:

(*a*) "Altogether, essentially I am what I even speak to you. My Person *is* my teaching." The words of Christ are, to express the idea otherwise, the revelation of the Word Incarnate.

(*β*) "To begin with, first of all, I am even that which I am saying, that is, the Light of the world, the source of life."

(*γ*) "Even that which I am speaking and have spoken to you, all along, from the first, that I am. My words from the beginning have made known my Person."

Of these interpretations (*a*) seems to be open to the least objection on the score of the Greek, and to give the best sense. In (*β*) *λέγω* and not *λαλῶ* would be required; and the sense given to *τὴν ἀρχήν* in (*γ*) is very questionable, while A.V. which gives a true sense to τὴν ἀρχὴν would require ἐλάλησα.

(2) On the whole it is probably best to treat the sentence as interrogative; or (which gives the same sense) as a sad exclamation which is half interrogative. This is the sense which is given to the words by the Greek fathers.

"How is it that I even speak to you at all?" "Why do I even so much as speak with you?" Or, "To think that, can it be that, I even speak with you."

The interrogative sense of ὅτι is illustrated by Mark ix. 28, (ii. 7), ix. 11. And for the order see Matt. xv. 16.

The interrogative rendering: "Do you ask that which all along I am even saying to you?" leaves τὴν ἀρχὴν without any real force.

(3) Others have connected τὴν ἀρχὴν with the next clause, "To begin with...I have many things to say...concerning you." But no adequate sense can be given in this case to the intervening words.

44. The reading of the best MSS. (ℵB*DLX, &c.), ΟΥΚΕϹΤΗΚΕΝ, that is οὐκ ἕστηκεν, which has been disregarded by editors, and arbitrarily altered into οὐχ ἕστηκεν (Tischendorf prints οὐκ ἕστηκεν), is undoubtedly correct. Comp. Rev. xii. 4. The verb is the imperfect of στήκω (ch. i. 26; Rom. xiv. 4; 1 Thess. iii. 8; 1 Cor. xvi. 13). The Vulgate, which regularly renders ἕστηκα *sto* (Matt. xii. 47, xx. 6; Acts i. 11, xxvi. 6, &c.), here translates rightly *in veritate non stetit*. The context requires a past tense, and the strong form of the verb ("stand firm:" comp. i. 26, στήκει) is perfectly appropriate to the place.

CHAPTER IX.

1 *The man that was born blind restored to sight.* 8 *He is brought to the Pharisees.* 13 *They are offended at it, and excommunicate him:* 35 *but he is received of Jesus, and confesseth him.* 39 *Who they are whom Christ enlighteneth.*

AND as *Jesus* passed by, he saw a man which was blind from *his* birth.

2 And his disciples asked him, saying, Master, who did sin, this man, or his parents, that he was born blind?

---

(2) *The Feast of Dedication* (ix., x.).

The true reading in x. 22 (**Then** *was the Feast of Dedication*) determines that ch. ix. and x. 1—21 is connected with the Feast of Dedication, and not, as is commonly supposed, with the Feast of Tabernacles. The latter connexion has found support from the false gloss added to viii. 59, which appears to have been suggested by the "passing by" in ix. 1. As it is ch. ix. begins abruptly like ch. vi. The contents of ix. 1—x. 21 have a close affinity with x. 22—39. The thought throughout is of the formation of the new congregation, the new spiritual Temple.

The section falls into three main divisions: the sign, with the judgments which were passed upon it (ix. 1—12, 13—34); the beginning and characteristics of the new society (ix. 35—41, x. 1—21); Christ's final testimony as to Himself (x. 22—39).

The Sign (1—12).

The narrative of the healing is marked by the same kind of vivid details as we have noticed before. The occasion of the miracle, the peculiarity of the mode of cure, the reference to Siloam, are without direct parallels, and yet in perfect harmony with other narratives. The variety of opinion among the people and the mention of "the man called Jesus" belong to the experience of an immediate witness.

CHAP. IX. **1.** *as Jesus passed by*] perhaps in the neighbourhood of the temple where the man was waiting for the alms of worshippers (Acts iii. 2). The word (παράγων), which is rarely used (Matt. ix. 9; Mark ii. 14; Matt. ix. 27, xx. 30; Mark xv. 21), directs notice to the attendant circumstances. The narrative has been generally connected with the events of the preceding chapter owing to the false reading in viii. 59. It stands really as an independent record.

he saw] Something in the man's condition seems to have arrested the attention of the Lord. The word is significant. Naturally we should have expected "the disciples saw and asked."

blind from his birth] The miracles recorded in St John's Gospel stand out each as a type of its class. Hence stress is laid upon this special fact.

2. The thoughts of the controversy recorded in ch. viii. seem to have passed away. At once "a great calm" has come. The Lord stands in the centre of His disciples, and not of an angry crowd. Yet the question of the disciples moves in the same spiritual region as the speculations on inherited religious privileges and divine Sonship. Such a question is perhaps the simplest and commonest form of inquiry into our relation to those who have gone before us.

Master] **Rabbi.** Comp. i. 38, 49, iii. 2, iv. 31, vi. 25, xi. 8. The use of the Aramaic term is characteristic of St John, though it is found Matt. xxvi. 25, 49; Mark ix. 5, xi. 21, xiv. 45.

who did sin...that he was...] *that* **he**

3 Jesus answered, Neither hath
this man sinned, nor his parents: but
that the works of God should be
made manifest in him.
4 I must work the works of him
that sent me, while it is day: the
night cometh, when no man can
work.
5 As long as I am in the world, [a] I [a] ch
am the light of the world.

---

should be... by the just sequence of punishment on guilt. It is assumed that the particular suffering was retributive. The only doubt is as to the person whose sin was so punished; whether it was the man himself either before birth or in some former state of existence, or the man's parents. The latter alternative was familiar to the Jews (Exod. xx. 5; Hebr. vii. 10); and there are traces of a belief in the pre-existence of souls, at least in later Judaism (Wisd. viii. 20).

Perhaps it is most natural to suppose that the question, which in itself belongs to a Jewish mode of thought, was asked without any distinct apprehension of the alternatives involved in it. Lightfoot (*ad loc.*) has a curious collection of Rabbinical passages illustrating different forms of opinion on this subject.

born blind] From the disciples' acquaintance with this fact it may be supposed that the history of the man was popularly known.

3. The Lord's answer deals only with the special case (comp. Luke xiii. 1 ff., and for the general idea towards which it is directed, Acts xxviii. 4); and that only so far as it is an occasion for action and not a subject for speculation. We are not concerned primarily with the causes which have determined the condition or circumstances of men, with the origin of evil in any of its forms, but with the remedying of that which is amiss and remediable. It is true always, in one way or other, that for us evil is an opportunity for the manifestation of the works of God. But evil never ceases to be evil; and it may be noticed that at the proper occasion the Lord indicates the connexion between sin and suffering: v. 14, Matt. ix. 2.

Neither hath...sinned, nor...] *Neither* **did... sin**, *nor*...so as to bring down on him, that is, this particular retribution.

but that...in him] *but* he was born blind *that the works of God*, the works of redemptive love which He has sent me to accomplish, *may be made manifest in him*. Comp. v. 36. The works themselves are real even though we cannot see them: they need (from this side) manifestation only. For the emphatic *but* compare xv. 25, note. Underneath what we can see and conclude there lies a truer cause of that which perplexes us most.

in him] The man is not treated as an instrument merely, but as a living representative of the mercy of God. His suffering is the occasion and not the appointed preparation for the miracle, though when we regard things from the divine side we are constrained to see them in their dependence on the will of God.

4. *I must ... sent me*] According to the more probable reading: **we** *must work the works of Him that sent me*. So the Lord associates His disciples with Himself as before in iii. 11. The truth is general and holds good of the Master and of the servants. They are sent for the manifestation of the works of God. But the obligation of the servant's charge comes from the Master's mission. The works are no longer regarded as "the works of God" generally, but "the works of Him that sent" the Son.

while it is day] while the appointed time for working still remains: Ps. civ. (ciii.) 23. "Day" and "night" are taken in their most general sense as the seasons for labour and rest in regard to the special end in view. After the Passion there was no longer the opportunity for the performance of the works characteristic of the historic Life of Christ. Then in one sense "night" came, and in a yet fuller sense a new day dawned for new works, to be followed by another night, another close. It is not to be supposed that the "night" here describes an abiding and complete rest of Christ: it presents rest only from the works which belong to the corresponding "day."

The image partially finds place in the 'Sayings of the Jewish Fathers:' "R. Tarphon (Tryphon) said, The day is short, and the task is great, and the workmen are sluggish, and the reward is much, and the Master of the house is urgent" ('Pirke Aboth,' II. 19).

the night cometh] **night cometh**... The order is significant. The emphasis is laid upon the certain and momentary advance of that which ends all successful efforts in the present order: *there cometh* swiftly and inevitably *night*, *when no man* (**one**) *can work*. The necessary cessation of labour is expressed in its completest form.

5. *As long as* (Vulg. *quamdiu*)... *world*] **Whensoever** *I am in the world* (ὅταν...ὦ)... The indefinite form of the statement suggests the thought of the manifold revelations of the Word. "Whensoever" and not only during that revelation which was then in the course of being fulfilled, but also in the time of the Patriarchs, and of the Law, and of the Prophets, and through the later ages of the Church, Christ is *the light of the world*. This

6 When he had thus spoken, he
spat on the ground, and made clay
the of the spittle, and he ‖ anointed the
son
s of eyes of the blind man with the clay,
ud
7 And said unto him, Go, wash
in the pool of Siloam, (which is by
interpretation, Sent.) He went his
way therefore, and washed, and came
seeing.
8 ¶ The neighbours therefore, and

---

universality of application is further brought out by the omission of the personal pronoun in both clauses of the sentence. The stress is thrown upon the character of the manifestation of the Son, and not as in the former place where the phrase occurs (viii. 12) upon the Person of the Son.

the light of the world] The omission of the definite article (φῶς τ. κ., as compared with viii. 12, τὸ φῶς τ. κ.) is not without significance; Christ is "light to the world" as well as "the one light of the world." The character is unchangeable, but the display of the character varies with the occasion. In this case it is shewn in personal illumination. Bodily sight is taken as the representation of the fulness of human vision (*vv.* 39 ff.).

6. *he spat on the ground...*] Comp. Mark vii. 33, viii. 23. We must suppose that the attention of the blind man was by this time fully roused, perhaps by the conversation just recorded, or by some words addressed to him.

The application of spittle to the eyes, which was considered very salutary (comp. Tac. 'Hist.' IV. 81), was expressly forbidden by Jewish tradition, on the Sabbath. See Wetstein or Lightfoot, *ad loc.* The kneading of the clay further aggravated the offence.

he anointed...the clay] *He anointed* **his eyes** *with the clay.* At first Christ may seem to work against the end for which His help is sought. Here He sealed, so to speak, the eyes which He designed to open. It is impossible to determine why the Lord chose this method of working the cure. In the end the mode proved all-important.

7. *wash*] *i.e.* thine eyes (νίψαι), Matt. vi. 17; ch. xiii. 6, note.

in (εἰς) *the pool*] *i.e.* go to the pool and wash thine eyes there.

Siloam, which is by interpretation (**which is interpreted**), *Sent*] The idea which underlies this note of the Evangelist appears to be that in vii. 37 f. The stream which issued from the heart of the rock was an image of Christ. In the passage of Isaiah (viii. 6) "the waters of Siloah that go softly" are taken as the type of the divine kingdom of David resting on Mount Zion, in contrast with "the waters of the river [Euphrates], strong and mighty, even the king of Assyria and all his glory," the symbol of earthly power. (Comp. Delitzsch, *l. c.*) So therefore here Christ works through "the pool," the "Sent," sent, as it were, directly from God, that He may lead the disciples once again to connect Him and His working with the promises of the prophets. Thus, in some sense, God Himself, whose law Christ was accused of breaking, was seen to cooperate with Him in the miracle. At the same time the charge tried the faith of the blind man.

Siloam] The name of the pool properly indicates a discharge of waters (ἀποστολή) "sent," in this case, from a subterranean channel. For the form see Ewald, 'Gramm.' § 156, 2, a. The pool, which still retains its old name, *Birket Silwan*, is one of the few undisputed sites at Jerusalem. It lies at the mouth of the Tyropœon Valley, south of the temple, "at the foot of Mount Moriah," in Jerome's words. "The two pools of Siloam were probably made for the irrigation of the gardens below, and seem always to have been a favourite place for washing purposes; besides the surface drainage they received a supply of water from the Fountain of the Virgin by means of a subterranean channel. The upper pool is small" [an oblong reservoir cut in the rock, about fifty feet long, sixteen feet broad, and eighteen feet deep], "and at the south-west corner has a rude flight of steps leading to the bottom; but the whole is fast going to ruin, and the accumulation of rubbish around is very great; a little below this a dam of solid masonry has been built across the valley, forming the end of the lower and larger pool, now nearly filled up with rich soil and covered with a luxuriant growth of fig trees" (Wilson, 'Notes on the Ordnance Survey of Jerusalem,' p. 79). See Ritter, 'Palestine,' IV. 148 ff (Eng. Tr.), and 'Dict. of Bible,' *s. v.*, for notices of the site in earlier writers.

Sent] The interpretation of the name connects the pool with Christ (xvii. 3, &c.), and not with the man. See above.

He went his way] He **went away**.

came] to his own home, as it appears from the context (*the neighbours*).

8. *The neighbours therefore...*] No mark of time is given. This scene may belong to the following day, as *v.* 13 ff. certainly do (*v.* 14).

they which...was blind] *they* **which saw**—used habitually to see, behold as a conspicuous object (οἱ θεωροῦντες)—**him before** *that* (or *because*) *he was* **a beggar**. The particle is capable of both meanings (*that*, *because*). In other passages (iv. 19, xii. 19) St John uses the phrase certainly for "see...that...;" here however "because" suits the context better: because he was a beggar in a public spot, they were familiar with his appearance.

they which before had seen him that
he was blind, said, Is not this he that
sat and begged?
9 Some said, This is he: others
said, He is like him: *but* he said, I
am *he*.
10 Therefore said they unto him,
How were thine eyes opened?
11 He answered and said, A man
that is called Jesus made clay, and
anointed mine eyes, and said unto
me, Go to the pool of Siloam, and
wash: and I went and washed, and I
received sight.
12 Then said they unto him, Where
is he? He said, I know not.
13 ¶ They brought to the Pharisees him that aforetime was blind.
14 And it was the sabbath day
when Jesus made the clay, and opened his eyes.
15 Then again the Pharisees also
asked him how he had received his
sight. He said unto them, He put
clay upon mine eyes, and I washed,
and do see.
16 Therefore said some of the
Pharisees, This man is not of God,

The circumstantiality of the narrative which follows seems to shew that the man himself related the events to the evangelist.

9. *Some said...others said, He...*] **Others** *said...others* **said No, but** *he...* Two classes of people apparently are mentioned different from the first group.

he said] The pronoun here and in *vv.* 11, 12, 28, 36 is remarkable (ἐκεῖνος). It presents the man as the chief figure in a scene viewed from without. "He, that signal object of the Lord's love...." (comp. ii. 21, v. 11, (x. 6), (xiii. 30), xix. 21), and not "He himself," in contrast with the opinions of others.

10. *How...*] *How* **then....** It is to be observed that all the stress is laid upon the *manner* and not upon the *fact*. Comp. *vv.* 15, 19, 26.

11. *He...and said*] **He answered.**

A man (**The man**, Vulg. *Ille homo*) *that is called Jesus*] Not "that is called the Christ." He had learnt the personal name of the Lord, but says nothing of His claims to Messiahship. The form of the sentence, however, points to the general attention which was directed to the Lord. It is "the man" not "a man;" the man of whom report speaks often.

Go to...of Siloam] *Go* **to Siloam.**

and I went...] **so** *I went.*

I received sight] Strictly, *I recovered my sight* (ἀνέβλεψα) (Matt. xi. 5; Mark x. 51 f.; Luke xviii. 41 ff.), for sight by nature belongs to a man even though he has been born blind. This sense appears to us better than: "I looked up" (Mark xvi. 4).

12. *Then said they* (**And** *they said*)...*Where is he* (ἐκεῖνος)] that strange, unwelcome teacher, of whom we hear so much. Comp. vii. 11, *v.* 10 note.

He said] *He* **saith.**

The judgments on the sign (13—34).

The examination of the man who was healed offers a typical example of the growth of faith and unbelief. On the one side the Pharisees, who take their stand on a legal preconception, grow more determined and violent: 16 (*debate, division*); 24 (*judgment*); 34 (*disgraceful expulsion*). On the other side the man gains courage and clearness in his answers: 17 (*He is a prophet. Opinion*); 30 ff. (*acceptance of discipleship*); and finally he openly confesses Christ, *v.* 38.

The characters thus live and move, and shew marked traits of individuality. There is nothing vague, nothing conventional, in the narrative. The record includes three scenes: the first examination of the man (13—17); the examination of his parents (18—23); the final examination and expulsion of the man (24—34).

13. *They brought* (**bring**) *to the Pharisees*] as the recognised judges in religious questions. There were in Jerusalem two smaller courts, or Synagogue Councils, and the man was probably taken to one of these. In the later sections of the narrative, *vv.* 18 ff., the general title *the Jews* is used.

14. *it was the sabbath day when...*] The original phrase, according to the oldest text, is remarkable. It reads literally, "It was a sabbath on the day on which," *i.e.* **the day was a Sabbath whereon** (ἦν σαββ. ἐν ᾗ ἡμέρᾳ). Comp. v. 9.

made the clay] The words mark the feature in the miracle which technically gave offence. Comp. v. 12.

15. *Then again...*] *Again* **therefore** *the Pharisees also*...as not content with the report of others (*vv.* 10, 11).

how he had received...] *how* **he received...** The answer is more curt than before (*v.* 11); and there is already something of impatience in the tone of it, which breaks out afterwards, *v.* 27. The making of the clay and the command to go to Siloam are passed over.

16. *Therefore said...*] because to the legalist no other conclusion seemed to be possible.

because he keepeth not the sabbath day. Others said, How can a man that is a sinner do such miracles? And there was a division among them.

17 They say unto the blind man again, What sayest thou of him, that he hath opened thine eyes? He said, He is a prophet.

18 But the Jews did not believe concerning him, that he had been blind, and received his sight, until they called the parents of him that had received his sight.

19 And they asked them, saying, Is this your son, who ye say was born blind? how then doth he now see?

20 His parents answered them and said, We know that this is our son, and that he was born blind:

21 But by what means he now seeth, we know not; or who hath opened his eyes, we know not: he is of age; ask him: he shall speak for himself.

22 These *words* spake his parents, because they feared the Jews: for the Jews had agreed already, that if any man did confess that he was Christ, he should be put out of the synagogue.

23 Therefore said his parents, He is of age; ask him.

24 Then again called they the man that was blind, and said unto him,

---

Others (**But** *others*) *said, How can...a sinner*] It is presupposed therefore that Christ had valid authority for the apparent violation of the Sabbath.

a division] as before "in the multitude" (vii. 43) and afterwards "in the Jews" (x. 19). One party, it will be noticed, laid stress upon the fact, the others upon a preconceived opinion by which they judged of the fact.

17. *They say*...**therefore**...*again*...] as hoping to elicit some fresh details.

What...eyes?] *What* **dost thou** (σύ) **say** —we appeal to your own judgment and to the impression made upon you—What **dost thou say** *of him*, **seeing that he opened** *thine eyes?* For the construction, see ii. 18.

He said (**And** *he said*), *He is a prophet*] Comp. iv. 19, (vi. 14), iii. 2.

18—23. The examination of the parents of the man follows the examination of the man himself. They shrink with singular naturalness from incurring the displeasure of the dominant party.

18. *But the Jews*...] *The Jews* **therefore**...seeing that they could not reconcile a real miracle with disregard to the Sabbath. They probably suspected some collusion on the part of the man.

The Jews represent the incredulous section of *the Pharisees* (*v.* 16). Comp. *v.* 22.

of him...sight] The original is unusual: "of the man himself that had..."

19. *And they asked*]... **And asked**...The words are closely connected with the preceding clause.

who ye say was...] **of whom** *ye* (ὑμεῖς) *say*, from whom we may expect certain information, **that he was**...

20. *His...them and said*] *His parents* **therefore answered** *and said*, because they were unwilling to incur any responsibility.

21. *But by what means*...] *But* **how**... as in *vv.* 10, 15, 19, 26.

we know not...we (ἡμεῖς) *know not*] The emphatic insertion of the pronoun in the second case gives a new turn to the phrase: "*we* directly, of our own experience, *know not*, as you appeal to us, **who opened** *his eyes*."

he is of age...himself] **ask him**, not us: **he is of age**, and therefore his answer will be valid, and he will not be slow to give it: *he* **will** *speak for himself*.

22. *These words spake*...] **These things said**...

had agreed...that...] had formed a compact among themselves (συνετέθειντο, Vulg. *conspiraverant*) to secure this end, *that*... Comp. Acts xxiii. 20. The idea is not that they had determined on a punishment, but that they had determined on an aim.

that he was Christ] The question had already been publicly debated, vii. 26 ff.; though the Lord had not so revealed Himself in Jerusalem (x. 24) as He had done in Samaria (iv. 26).

put out of the synagogue] xii. 42, xvi. 2. This excommunication appears to have been exclusion from all religious fellowship (comp. Matt. xviii. 17) from "the congregation of Israel." In later times there were different degrees of excommunication, the Curse (חרם), and the Isolation (שמתא). Comp. Buxtorf, 'Lex.' s. v. נדוי. Lightfoot and Wünsche, *ad loc.*

23. *Therefore*...] **For this cause**... (διὰ τοῦτο), seeing that the hostility of the Jews was now passing into action.

24—34. In the second examination the

Give God the praise: we know that this man is a sinner.

25 He answered and said, Whether he be a sinner *or no*, I know not: one thing I know, that, whereas I was blind, now I see.

26 Then said they to him again, What did he to thee? how opened he thine eyes?

27 He answered them, I have told you already, and ye did not hear: wherefore would ye hear *it* again? will ye also be his disciples?

28 Then they reviled him, and said, Thou art his disciple; but we are Moses' disciples.

29 We know that God spake unto Moses: *as for* this *fellow*, we know not from whence he is.

30 The man answered and said unto them, Why herein is a marvellous thing, that ye know not from whence he is, and *yet* he hath opened mine eyes.

31 Now we know that God heareth not sinners: but if any man be a

---

conflict is brought to a decisive issue. The man chooses the Saviour whom he had experienced before the Moses of the schools.

24. *Then again...the man...*] **So they called the man a second time**: we must suppose that he was dismissed after the confession in *v.* 17. As they could no longer question the fact, they seek to put a new construction upon it.

Give God the praise] **Give glory to God.** The phrase (δὸς δόξαν τῷ θεῷ) is a solemn charge to declare the whole truth. Compare Josh. vii. 19; 1 Esdr. ix. 8; (1 S. vi. 5). The man by his former declaration (*v.* 17) had really (so they imply) done dishonour to God. He was now required to confess his error: to recognise in the authoritative voice of "the Jews" his own condemnation, and to admit the truth of it. At the same time under this thought of the rendering of glory to God by the confession of error, lies the further idea that the cure was due directly to God, and that to Him, and not to "the man called Jesus," was gratitude to be rendered. This, however, is not the primary sense of the phrase, though it is natural so to interpret A. V.

we know...] *We*, the guardians of the national honour, the interpreters of the divine will, *we know* (ἡμεῖς οἴδαμεν)... The claim is to absolute knowledge, and no reasons are alleged for the conclusion.

a sinner] by the violation of the Sabbath (*v.* 16).

25. *He answered and said*] **He therefore answered.**

Whether...I know not] The order in the original is remarkable: *If he is a sinner*, as you assert, that *I know not.* The first clause is an echo of the words of the Pharisees, and the man simply states that his knowledge furnishes no confirmation of it. Comp. Luke xxii. 67; Acts iv. 19, xix. 2. In 1 John iv. 1 and elsewhere the order is different.

26. *Then said they...again*] **They said therefore to him.**

What did he...? how...?] The questions suggest that they were yet willing to believe, if the facts were not decisive against belief.

27. *I have told you...*] **I told** *you.*

will ye also...] **would** *ye also* (μὴ καὶ ὑμεῖς θέλετε)...the words go back to the *we, v.* 24: *ye* who make the proud claims of which we have all heard, *ye* as well as I a poor mendicant, *would ye*...Have you a real desire, if only you can yield to it, to *become his disciples?* The *would* points the idea suggested by the fresh interrogation.

28. *Then* (**And**) *they reviled him*] by questioning his loyalty to the law, and treating him as an apostate. Comp. Acts xxiii. 4.

his disciples] Literally, **that man's disciple.** Comp. *vv.* 12, 37. Christ is looked upon as separated from them by a great chasm.

29. *We know*] The claim to knowledge is repeated (*v.* 24) with a bitter emphasis. "Moses" and "this man" stand at the head of the two clauses to make the contrast sharper.

spake] *hath spoken* familiarly, face to face (λελάληκεν), and the words abide still.

as for (**but** *as for*)...*whence he is*] that is, with what commission, by whose authority, he comes. Comp. Matt. xxi. 25. The converse objection is urged, vii. 27. Pilate at last asks the question, xix. 9; and the Lord claims for Himself alone the knowledge of the answer, viii. 14.

30. *Why herein is a marvellous thing* (**the marvellous thing,** τὸ θαυμαστόν)] Comp. iv. 37. The particle brings out an affirmation drawn from the previous words. "That being so as you say, then assuredly..."

that ye (ὑμεῖς)] from whom we look for guidance...

and yet (καί) *he hath opened* (**he opened**)...] For the *and*, see viii. 20 note.

31. *Now we know*] **We know**, not you alone, nor I, but all men alike. The simple verb (οἴδαμεν) is contrasted with the strong personal affirmation in *vv.* 24, 29 (ἡμεῖς οἴδ.).

if any man be a worshipper of God, and doeth (*be* **devout** or **religious** *and* **do**)...]

worshipper of God, and doeth his will,
him he heareth.
32 Since the world began was it
not heard that any man opened the
eyes of one that was born blind.
33 If this man were not of God,
he could do nothing.
34 They answered and said unto
him, Thou wast altogether born in
sins, and dost thou teach us? And
mmu- they ‖ cast him out.
ed
35 Jesus heard that they had cast
him out; and when he had found him,
he said unto him, Dost thou believe
on the Son of God?
36 He answered and said, Who is
he, Lord, that I might believe on
him?
37 And Jesus said unto him, Thou
hast both seen him, and it is he that
talketh with thee.
38 And he said, Lord, I believe.
And he worshipped him.
39 ¶ And Jesus said, For judg-

The word (θεοσεβής) occurs here only in New Testament (comp. 1 Tim. ii. 10). The two phrases mark the fulfilment of duty to God and man.

32. *Since the world began*] The exact phrase (ἐκ τοῦ αἰῶνος) does not occur elsewhere in New Testament. Comp. Luke i. 70; Acts iii. 21, xv. 18 (ἀπ' αἰῶνος); Col. i. 26 (ἀπὸ τῶν αἰ.).

34. The order is very significant: "In sins wast thou born altogether." So the Jews at once interpret and apply the question of the disciples, *v.* 2. Blindness was but a sign of deeper and more prevailing infirmity.

teach us] The emphasis lies on "teach." "Dost thou, marked out as a sinner, assume the prerogative of instruction...."

cast him out] from the place of their meeting, with contempt and contumely, as unworthy of further consideration. Comp. Mark i. 43, note. The word does not describe the sentence of excommunication, which such a body was not competent to pronounce.

The beginning of the new Society (35—41).

The ejection of the blind man who had been healed from the council of the Pharisees furnished the occasion for the beginning of a new Society distinct from the dominant Judaism. For the first time the Lord offers Himself as the object of faith, and that in His universal character in relation to humanity, as "the Son of man." He had before called men to follow Him: He had revealed Himself, and accepted the spontaneous homage of believers: but now He proposes a test of fellowship. The universal Society is based on the confession of a new truth. The blind who acknowledge their blindness are enlightened: the seeing who are satisfied with their sight (*we know*) are proved to be blind.

35. *Jesus heard*] The man himself may well have spoken of his treatment.

when he had found (**having found**) *him, he said unto him*] Omit *unto him*. Comp. i. 43, v. 14. The "work of God" was not yet completed. *Modo lavat faciem cordis* in Augustine's words.

Dost thou believe on the Son of God (**man**)?] The emphasis of the pronoun is remarkable, and may be contrasted with *v.* 34. *Dost thou*, the outcast, thou that hast received outward sight, thou that hast borne a courageous testimony, *believe on* **the Son of Man**—cast thyself with complete trust on Him who gathers up in Himself, who bears and who transfigures all that belongs to man? The thought of "the Son of man" stands in true contrast with the selfish isolation of "the Jews." The new Society, seen here in its beginning, rests upon this foundation, wide as humanity itself. See Additional Note

36. *Who is he*...] **And** *who is he*... The conjunction marks the eager, urgent, wondering question. The thought which it meets seems to be beyond hope. Comp. Mark x. 26; Luke x. 29.

that I might (**may**)...] He asks that faith may find its object. His trust in Jesus is absolute.

37. *And Jesus said* (**Jesus saith**)... *Thou hast both seen him*—with the eyes which God hath even now opened—*and he that talketh with thee* **is he** (ἐκεῖνος). The natural form of the sentence would have been "Thou hast both seen Him and heard Him;" but the power of the immediate position gives shape to the latter clause. "He that talketh with thee familiarly, as man with man, is He, that sublime Person, who seems to stand far off from thought and experience."

38. Confession in word and deed follows at once on the revelation. In St John "worship" (προσκυνεῖν) is never used of the worship of mere respect (iv. 20 ff., xii. 20).

Lord, I believe] **I believe, Lord.** The order is significant.

39. *And Jesus said*] not directly to any one nor to any group of those about Him, but as interpreting the scene before Him. The separation between the old and the new was now consummated, when the rejected of

ment I am come into this world, that they which see not might see; and that they which see might be made blind.

40 And *some* of the Pharisees which were with him heard these words, and said unto him, Are we blind also?

41 Jesus said unto them, If ye were blind, ye should have no sin: but now ye say, We see; therefore your sin remaineth.

"the Jews" sank prostrate at the feet of the Son of man.

For judgment I (ἐγώ) *am come* (**I came**)...] not to execute judgment (κρίσις), but that judgment (κρίμα) might issue from His Presence. The Son was not sent to judge (iii. 17), but judgment followed from His advent in the manifestation of faith and unbelief (iii. 18 f.). The emphatic pronoun carries back the reference to the "Son of man."

this world] the world as made known to us in its present state, full of conflict and sin, and so distinguished from *the world* which includes all created being. The phrase occurs viii. 23, xi. 9, xii. 25, 31, xiii. 1, xvi. 11, xviii. 36; 1 John iv. 17.

that they...might...might...] *that they*...**may ...may...**

they which see not] The true commentary on these verses is Luke x. 21 ‖ Matt. xi. 25, and Matt. xii. 31, 32. The phrase must be taken literally to describe those who have no intellectual knowledge, no clear perception of the divine will and the divine law; the simple, the little children. These by apprehending the revelation of the Son of man grasp the fulness of the Gospel, and see. Those on the other hand who had knowledge of the Old Covenant, who were so far "wise and understanding," and rested in what they knew, by this very wisdom became incapable of further progress and unable to retain what they had.

be made (**become**) *blind*] By wilfully confining their vision men lose the very power of seeing. There is a contrast between "those that see not" (οἱ μὴ βλέποντες), and "those who are blind" (τυφλοί). The former have the power of sight though it is unused: the latter have not the power.

40. *And* (omit) *some of the Pharisees* (**Those of the Pharisees**) *which were with him...*] who still followed under the guise of discipleship (Matt. xii. 2 f., 38; Luke vi. 2; Mark xvi. 10, &c.), but clung to their own views of Messiah's work (viii. 31 ff.).

these words] **these things.**

Are we blind also?] *Are we* **also blind?** we who have acknowledged Thy claims in advance—we who in virtue of our insight (iii. 2) have come to know Thee while others are in doubt (x. 24)? Can it be that we who saw then have now lost the power of sight? The question (like the claim of Nicodemus, iii. 2, *we know*) is inspired by the pride of class. The answer lays open the responsibility of privilege. Better—such is the force of it—is the lack of knowledge, than knowledge real and misused. The claim of the Pharisees to sight is conceded so far as to leave them without excuse, when they failed to profit by it.

41. *ye should* (**would**) *have* (**have had**) *no sin*] Comp. xv. 22, 24, xix. 11; 1 John i. 8. Sin is regarded as something cleaving to the man himself, which has become (so to speak) part of him, and for which he is responsible.

but now ye say, We see] There seems to be a pathetic pause after these words. Then at last follows the sentence: "You plead the reality of your knowledge, and the plea, in this sense, is just. You are witnesses against yourselves. Then is there no further illumination. *Your sin abideth* (omit *therefore*)."

There is a remarkable saying assigned to R. Abuhu which expresses the thought of this verse. A Sadducee asked him, When cometh the Messiah? "Go first," was the answer, "and make dark this people." "What sayest thou? That is a reproach to me." "I appeal" answered the Rabbi "to Isai. lx. 2." ('Sanhedrin,' 99a, quoted by Wünsche on John iii. 19.)

ADDITIONAL NOTE on CHAP. IX. 35.

The ancient authorities are divided as to the reading of the title under which the Lord offers Himself as the object of faith. τὸν υἱὸν τοῦ ἀνθρώπου (*the Son of man*) is read by ℵBD, the Thebaic version, by copies of the Æthiopic, and by some texts of Chrysostom.

On the other hand, τὸν υἱὸν τοῦ θεοῦ (*the Son of God*) is read by ALX 1, 33, and apparently all other MSS. (C is defective), by the Latin and Syriac and Memphitic versions, by Tertullian, Cyril of Alexandria, &c.

Both readings were evidently very widely spread at the beginning of the third century; and though undoubtedly such a combination of MSS. as ℵBD is shewn by a wide induction to be practically irresistible, the case is one in which it is important to take internal evidence into account.

The titles "the Son of man" and "the Son of God" do not occur very frequently in St John, and each about the same number of times. Nor does there appear to have been any general tendency to substitute one for the other, or to introduce either one or the other. In v. 19, D and a few kindred authorities read "the Son of man" for "the Son." It is of much more importance that elsewhere in confessions the title used is uniformly "the Son of God" (i. 34, 50, xi. 27: comp. xx. 31); and partly for this reason the introduction of the Synoptic confession of St Peter in vi. 69 became natural and easy. At first sight indeed the demand for belief in "the Son of man" is difficult to understand. It seems certain that there could have been no inclination on the part of scribes to substitute this unusual phrase for the common one; and the evidence is too varied to admit of the supposition that "Son of man" was accidentally substituted for "Son of God." On the other hand, the converse change from "Son of man" to "Son of God" was very obvious, whether the change was made mechanically or as the correction of a supposed blunder.

All the probabilities of change are in favour of "the Son of man" as the original reading. A closer examination of the context shews that this title is required to bring out the full meaning of the scene. The man had been expelled with contumely by the religious leaders of his people. He had in the popular sense broken with Judaism. He was therefore invited to accept an object of faith larger than that which was offered by the current conceptions of Messiah, "the Son of God." It was not necessary that he should have any very distinct understanding of the full meaning of the phrase "the Son of man" (xii. 23, 34); but at least it must have suggested to him one who being Man was the hope of man. This is the elementary form of the confession of the Incarnation on which the universal Church rests.

An examination of the other passages (i. 51, iii. 13 f., vi. 27, 53, viii. 28, xii. 23, xiii. 31) in which the title occurs shews clearly that it is in each case (as here) an essential part of the teaching which they convey.

CHAPTER X.

1 *Christ is the door, and the good shepherd.* 19 *Divers opinions of him.* 24 *He proveth by his works that he is Christ the Son of God:* 39 *escapeth the Jews,* 40 *and went again beyond Jordan, where many believed on him.*

VERILY, verily, I say unto you, He that entereth not by the door into the sheepfold, but climbeth up some other way, the same is a thief and a robber.

2 But he that entereth in by

The nature of the new Society (x. 1—21).

The reception of the outcast of the Synagogue gave occasion for an exposition under familiar figures of the nature of the new Society. At first this is given generally. The relation of the Shepherd to the Fold and to the Sheep suggests the character of the work which Christ had to do in respect of the organization of the divine Church, and to the completeness of His power to claim His own true followers (1—6). Afterwards the images are applied directly. Christ shews how He fulfils the offices indicated by "the Door" (7—10), and by "the Shepherd" (11—16). He is "the Good Shepherd" in regard of His devotion (11—13) and of His sympathy (14—16). His work too rests on perfect fellowship with the Father (17, 18). Once again His words divide His hearers (19—21).

CHAP. X. 1—6. The point of connexion lies in the thought of the Pharisees as the shepherds of God's Fold in contrast with the shepherds who may perhaps have been seen gathering their flocks for the night's shelter on the hills, though the thought of the allegory is that of the morning's work. On one side were self-will and selfishness; on the other loyal obedience and devotion. Comp. Ezek. xxxiv. 2 ff.; Jer. xxiii. 1 ff.; Zech. xi. 3 ff.

The allegory is given at first in its complex form. All the elements stand together undistinguished. Afterwards the two chief facts are considered separately, the fold and the flock. In relation to the Fold Christ is the Door; in relation to the Flock He is the Good Shepherd. But for the present this personal application lies in the background. The teaching is general. Even in Old Testament times the "Word" was the Door. Augustine ('in Joh.' XLV. 9) says well: *tempora variata sunt non fides.*

1. *Verily, verily...*] The old thought is taken up upon a fresh stage: there is continuance at once and progress (*v.* 7).

the sheepfold] More exactly, *the fold of the sheep* (Vulg. *ovile ovium*). The two ideas of the fold and the flock are presented distinctly. Comp. *v.* 7, *the door of the sheep.*

climbeth up (over the fence) *some other way*] not coming from the pastures or from the shepherd's home (ἀλλαχόθεν), and thinking of himself only, he makes his own road and overleaps the barriers which are set.

is a thief...] *is a thief* who seeks to avoid detection, and *a robber*, who uses open force to secure his ends. For "robber" (λῃστής) see xviii. 40; Matt. xxvi. 55, and parallel; Luke x. 30; and for "thief" (κλέπτης), xii. 6; 1 Thess. v. 2 ff.

the door is the shepherd of the sheep.

3 To him the porter openeth; and the sheep hear his voice: and he calleth his own sheep by name, and leadeth them out.

4 And when he putteth forth his own sheep, he goeth before them, and the sheep follow him: for they know his voice.

5 And a stranger will they not follow, but will flee from him: for they know not the voice of strangers.

6 This parable spake Jesus unto them: but they understood not what things they were which he spake unto them.

7 Then said Jesus unto them again, Verily, verily, I say unto you, I am the door of the sheep.

---

2. *is the* (a) *shepherd of the sheep*] one, it may be, of many, but his true nature is shewn by his act. The absence of the article fixes attention on the character as distinct from the person.

Several flocks were often gathered into one fold for protection during the night. In the morning each shepherd passed into the fold to bring out his own flock; and he entered by the same door as they. Hence the emphatic repetition of "sheep" (*vv.* 2, 7). As several flocks were gathered in one fold, the sheep of the One Shepherd might be in several folds (*v.* 16).

3. *the porter* (Vulg. *ostiarius*)] the guardian to whose care the fold in each case is committed. Comp. Mark xiii. 34. Thus the interpretation will vary according to the special sense attached to the "sheep" and the "shepherd." The figure is not to be explained exclusively of the Holy Spirit or of the Father, or of Moses, or of John the Baptist, but of the Spirit acting through His appointed ministers in each case.

openeth] when the shepherd returns to seek out his sheep and lead them to pasture.

the sheep] all that are gathered within the fold, listen to his voice, as a shepherd's voice, even though they are not peculiarly *his own sheep*. But the shepherd of each flock *calleth his own sheep by name and leadeth them out*. First comes the personal recognition, and then follows the fulfilment of the specific office.

calleth...by name] Comp. Isai. xliii. 1, xlv. 3, xlix. 1 (cf. lxii. 2); Rev. iii. 5. The phrase "to be known" by God corresponds with this image: 1 Cor. viii. 3, xiii. 12; Gal. iv. 9. Each "sheep" has its own name. The word rendered *calleth* (φωνεῖ) is that which expresses personal address rather than general or authoritative invitation (καλεῖ).

4. *And when he putteth forth*] **When he hath put forth.** In part an idea of separation underlies the parable. There is a sense in which the true shepherd not only "leads forth," but also "puts forth his own sheep" with a loving constraint, as well as that in which the false shepherds "put forth" (ix. 34). With regard to the old fold of Israel the time for this separation was at hand.

his own sheep...] **all** *his own*... according to the true reading. So *when* the shepherd **hath put forth all his own**, *he* places himself at their head and *goeth before them*.

5. *And a stranger...*] **But** *a stranger* (ἀλλοτρίῳ)... Compare, for the application of the thoughts, 1 John iii. 6, 9, v. 18 (τηρεῖ αὐτόν).

strangers] as a class contrasted with the sons of God. Comp. Matt. xvii. 25 f.; (Hebr. xi. 34). These are not however the same as the "thieves and robbers."

6. *parable*] The original word (παροιμία, Vulg. *proverbium*) is elsewhere translated *proverb*, ch. xvi. 25, 29; (2 Pet. ii. 22). It occurs in Symmachus' translation of Ezek. xii. 22 f., xvi. 44, for משל (LXX. παραβολή). Comp. Ecclus. xlvii. 17. It suggests the notion of a mysterious saying full of compressed thought, rather than that of a simple comparison.

unto them] that is, the Pharisees of ix. 40.

but they understood not...] The men whose legal self-complacency has been already noted (ἐκεῖνοι), failed to perceive the true meaning of the allegory; the spiritual conceptions of the fold, the door, the sheep, the shepherd, were all strange to them (comp. *v.* 20).

7—10. After drawing the general picture of the true relation of the Teacher to the Society and the outward organization, the Lord interprets it in relation to Himself under two main aspects. He is "the Door of the sheep" (7—10), and also "the Good Shepherd" (11—16). The first application determines that He is the one means of entrance to the Church at all times. "Through Him" men enter, and "through Him" they find access to the full treasures of life.

7. *Then said Jesus...*] *Jesus* **therefore**... in order to bring out the chief points of teaching in the allegory, *said to them again*, probably after an interval (viii. 12, 21). There is at least a pause in thought.

Verily, verily...] The teaching is again advanced another stage. That which has been up to this time general is now set forth in its special and most complete fulfilment. The universal law of the divine revelation is presented in its absolute expression. For *he that*

8 All that ever came before me are thieves and robbers: but the sheep did not hear them.
9 I am the door: by me if any man enter in, he shall be saved, and shall go in and out, and find pasture.
10 The thief cometh not, but for to steal, and to kill, and to destroy:

---

entereth (*v.* 2) we read *I am* (*vv.* 7, 11). This being so, Christ reveals Himself under two distinct aspects. He is "the Door" in regard of the society (the Fold) to which He gives admission; He is "the Good Shepherd" in regard of the individual care with which He leads each member of His flock. The thoughts of Ezek. xxxiv. are everywhere present.

the door of the sheep] not the door of the fold. Even under this aspect the thought is connected with the life and not simply with the organization.

of the sheep] by which sheep alike and shepherd enter, and not simply the door *to the sheep*. The phrase includes the thought of *v.* 1 and of *v.* 9. Even the shepherds—except the One Shepherd—are sheep also.

8. *All that ever came...are*] Omit *ever*, which obscures the sense. The second verb fixes the application of the words to the immediate crisis of national expectation. The interpretation of the whole phrase lies in the word *came*, in which we may see the full significance of the title, *he that should come*, as in *v.* 10. Thus the term includes essentially the notions of false Messiahs and self-commissioned teachers.

The omission of *before me* in an important group of early authorities (ℵ*, *Theb.*, *Lat. vt.*, *Syrr.*, &c.; Vulg. *quotquot venerunt*) points to this interpretation, while it obscures it. They who "came" (comp. 1 John v. 6), who pretended to satisfy the national expectation inspired by the prophets, or to mould the national expectations after the Pharisaic type, who offered in any way that which was to be accepted as the end of the earlier dispensation, who made themselves "doors" of approach to God (Matt. xxiii. 14), were essentially and continued to be inspired by selfishness, whether their designs were manifested by craft or by violence, and whether they were directed to gain or to dominion. They were *thieves and robbers*. With them John the Baptist may be contrasted. He claimed only to prepare the way for one "coming" (i. 30).

before me...] of time. Christ came when "all things were ready," in the fulness of time; and therefore whoever anticipated by however little the moment of the divine revelation so far violated its harmony with life. The other interpretations, "instead of," "passing by," "apart from," "before my commission to them," do violence to the words, and express only fragments of the true idea.

did not hear them] Such as *were waiting for the consolation of Israel* found no satisfaction in the works or designs or promises of those who sought to substitute another hope for that which the true Christ realised. There was no "Gospel for the poor" (Luke vi. 20, vii. 22; Matt. xi. 5) till the Son of man came.

9. *the door*] The thought is now concentrated upon the office (*the door*), and not upon the relation (*the door of the sheep*).

by me] The emphatic order brings out the unique personal relation in which the Lord stands to the believer, even in regard to the society.

any man] The words are used quite generally, and not of the shepherds only. The one entrance once made (*if any one enter*) is followed by the assurance and the enjoyment of freedom (*he shall be saved* ...). These words evidently describe the blessings of all Christians, and not of teachers only.

he shall be saved, and shall go in and **go** *out, and* **shall** *find pasture*] The fulness of the Christian life is exhibited in its three elements—safety, liberty, support. Admission to the fold brings with it first security (*he shall be saved*). But this security is not gained by isolation. The believer *goes in and goes out* without endangering his position (Num. xxvii. 17; Deut. xxxi. 2); he exercises the sum of all his powers, claiming his share in the inheritance of the world, secure in his home. And while he does so *he finds pasture*. He is able to convert to the divinest uses all the fruits of the earth. But in all this he retains his life "in Christ," and he approaches all else "through Christ," who brings not only redemption but the satisfaction of man's true wants. Comp. vii. 37.

10. *The thief*...] Christ presents Himself in His relation to others (*through me if*...). His rivals stand by themselves. And here the meaner word (*thief* not *robber*) is chosen to shew the true nature of that which appears to be less hateful when it is seen in its more violent forms.

to destroy] Whoever sets up a selfish ideal, and falls short of the completeness of self-sacrifice, abridges the resources of men. He not only *steals* to satisfy his own ends, but in doing thus he necessarily *kills* and *destroys*. In the pursuit of his object he wastes life and he wastes the sustenance of life, even if he does not propose to himself such an end. This is a universal truth (*cometh*, not *came*); and contrasted with it is the single unparalleled fact **I came** (not *I am come*) *that* **men may** *have*

I am come that they might have life, and that they might have *it* more abundantly.

a Isai. 40. 11. Ezek. 34. 23.

11 [a]I am the good shepherd: the good shepherd giveth his life for the sheep.

12 But he that is an hireling, and not the shepherd, whose own the sheep are not, seeth the wolf coming, and leaveth the sheep, and fleeth: and the wolf catcheth them, and scattereth the sheep.

---

life and may have **abundance**. These two aims are contrasted with *kill* and *destroy:* the contrast to "steal" lies in the very fact of Christ's coming. And thus the work of Christ is presented in its two issues, which correspond with the two fatal issues of the selfish prophet: the gift of life, and the gift of abundance. Life in itself is not all. There must be also that which shall maintain, and strengthen, and extend the action of life; and this also Christ assures. His sheep "find pasture."

might have it (life)...*abundantly*] Rather, **may have abundance** (περισσὸν ἔχωσιν). The repetition of *have* (ἔχωσιν) points to this parallelism. The idea that the phrase points to something more than life, as the kingdom of heaven, or the participation in the Holy Spirit, expresses only part of the meaning, which is indicated in i. 16.

11—16. The last verse furnishes the transition from the social to the personal relation, from the *door* to the *shepherd.* Two points are specially brought out in the character of "the good shepherd," His perfect self-sacrifice (11—13), and His perfect knowledge (14, 15), which extends beyond the range of man's vision (16). The whole portraiture of "the Good Shepherd" is a commentary on Isai. liii. See Taylor, 'The Gospel in the Law,' pp. 107 ff.

11. *I am the good shepherd*] The exact form of the expression, *I am the shepherd, the good* (shepherd), carries back the thought to others who partially and imperfectly discharge the office which Christ discharges completely. The epithet itself is remarkable (ὁ π. ὁ καλός). It recalls the phrases "the true bread" (vi. 32), and "the true vine" (xv. 1), but it is somewhat different. Christ is not only the true shepherd (ὁ π. ὁ ἀληθινός), who fulfils the idea of the shepherd, but He is the good shepherd who fulfils the idea in its attractive loveliness. The epithet implies the correspondence between the nobility of the conception and the beauty of the realisation. The "good" is not only good inwardly (ἀγαθός), but good as perceived (καλός). In the fulfilment of His work "the Good Shepherd" claims the admiration of all that is generous in man.

the good shepherd] The character of the Good Shepherd is first described in itself; and then (14 ff.) the relation of Christ as the Good Shepherd to the flock. The first picture however is in itself general, and it is wrong to seek any direct application of the images of the "hireling" and of "the wolf," as contrasted with one another, to the Jews of the time. Both indeed find their counterparts at all times.

giveth his life] **layeth down** *his life* (as in *vv.* 15, 17, &c.). The A.V. comes from Vulg., which reads here *dat animam.* The phrase is peculiar to St John (in the New Testament), *vv.* 15, 17, xiii. 37, 38, xv. 13; 1 John iii. 16, and is not found elsewhere. The image has been explained from the custom of laying down the price for which anything is obtained (comp. Matt. xx. 28), as here the good of the sheep. The usage of St John (xiii. 4) rather suggests the idea of putting off and laying aside as a robe. The phrase "to lay down life" must be compared with the language in vi. 51, which expresses another aspect of the truth. It is possible that there may be a reference to Isai. liii. 10 (תשים נפשו).

for (ὑπέρ, *in behalf of*) *the sheep*] It is not said expressly for his sheep (*vv.* 3, 4, 26). The thought here is simply that of the intrinsic relation of shepherd and flock.

12. *But* (omit) *he that is an hireling, and not the* (a) *shepherd*...] As the good shepherd regards his duty, and is bound by nature to the sheep, so his rival is described as a hireling who does his work for his reward, and so is not connected essentially with the flock. The idea of "own" here is not that of individual possession (1 Pet. v. 2 f.), but of peculiar relationship (*v.* 3).

seeth] **beholdeth**. The whole soul of the hireling is concentrated (comp. vi. 19) for the time upon the approaching peril, and then his choice is made. Augustine (*ad loc.*) says tersely *fuga animi timor est.*

the wolf] The flock has its natural enemies; and when it passes, as it must, into the world, it is open to their attacks.

catcheth...the sheep] **seizeth** *them and scattereth* **the flock**. Some fall victims to the attack, and all lose their unity. Individuals perish: the society is broken up. The word to be supplied after *scattereth* is not "the sheep," which is wrongly inserted in many authorities, but "the flock."

catcheth] **seizeth** (or *snatcheth*). The word (ἁρπάζει) describes the suddenness as well as the violence of the assault. Comp. *v.* 28 f., Matt. xiii. 19; Acts xxiii. 10.

13 The hireling fleeth, because he is an hireling, and careth not for the sheep.

14 I am the good shepherd, and know my *sheep*, and am known of mine.

15 As the Father knoweth me, even so know I the Father: and I lay down my life for the sheep.

16 And other sheep I have, which are not of this fold: them also I must bring, and they shall hear my voice; [b]and there shall be one fold, *and* one shepherd. [b] Ezek 37. 22.

---

13. *The hireling fleeth*] This clause must be omitted on the authority of ℵ(A*)BDL 1, 33 *e*, *Memph.*, *Theb.*, &c. The abruptness of the true reading places in close contrast the fate of the false shepherd and of the sheep. The double issue of cowardice and suffering comes from the fact that he who should have been a guardian thinks of himself and not of his charge. According to the Jewish tradition (Lightfoot, *ad loc.*), the shepherd for hire was responsible for damage done by wild beasts to his flock.

careth not for...] Contrast 1 Pet. v. 7.

14—16. The Lord applies directly to Himself and to His flock the ideal of the Good Shepherd.

14, 15. *I am...and know...and am known of mine. As the Father...me, even so . . .*] *I am . . . and* **I** *know . . . and* **mine know me, even as the Father knoweth me and I know the Father**, according to the most ancient authorities.

The relation of Christ to His people corresponds with that of the Son to the Father. Comp. vi. 57, xiv. 20, xv. 10, xvii. 21. The words are not simply a comparison, but the one relation is (so to speak) a measure of the other. Christ first took our nature that we might afterwards receive His. Such mutual knowledge as is described involves sympathy, love, community of nature: 1 John iv. 7 f.; Gal. iv. 9; 1 Cor. viii. 3; ch. xvii. 3, 25.

15. Completeness of knowledge is consummated in completeness of sacrifice. Perfect sympathy calls out the perfect remedy. Christ does actually what the Good Shepherd is prepared to do. This thought leads to the prospect of the removal of the barriers between race and race by the death of Christ (Eph. ii. 13 ff.: comp. Hebr. xiii. 20). But in this discourse, as elsewhere, the law of the divine revelation is observed, "to the Jew first and afterwards to the Gentile."

16. By the anticipation of the Cross (xii. 32) the spiritual horizon is extended. The flock of Christ is not confined to those enclosed in the Jewish fold, whether in Palestine or elsewhere. Even before His death, while the wall of partition is still standing, He "has" other sheep, who even if they know Him not are truly His (comp. xi. 52). The words are the historical affirmation of the truth, i. 4, 9. For the general thought compare Matt. viii. 11 f.; Luke xiii. 28 f.

other sheep] In the case of the Gentiles there was no outward unity. They did not form a "fold" as the Jews, whose work was realised through an outward organization. They were "scattered abroad" (xi. 52); but still they were Christ's "sheep" in fact, and not only potentially.

them also I must bring] in obedience to the divine Law. Comp. xx. 9, note.

bring] Rather, **lead.** The idea is that of openly assuming the guidance of the sheep, and not that of gathering them into one body (συναγαγεῖν, xi. 52), or of conducting them to one place (προσαγαγεῖν). The tense points to the one act whereby the Shepherd took up His rightful position. This could only be by His death, which re-unites man with God and therefore man (as man) with man (xii. 32).

shall hear] Acts xxviii. 28. Such obedience is the sign that we are Christ's (*vv.* 4, 27).

there shall be one fold] **they shall become**—they shall present the accomplishment of the ancient prophecy—*one* **flock**, *one shepherd* (Ezek. xxxiv. 23). That which "is" in the eternal counsel and truth of things "becomes" in human history, and this stage by stage, and not by one complete transformation.

The translation "fold" for "flock" (*ovile* for *grex*) has been most disastrous in idea and in influence. See Additional Note. The change in the original from "fold" (αὐλή), to "flock" (ποίμνη), is most striking, and reveals a new thought as to the future relations of Jew and Gentile. Elsewhere stress is laid upon their corporate union (Rom. xi. 17 ff.), and upon the admission of the Gentiles to the Holy City (Isai. ii. 3); but here the bond of fellowship is shewn to lie in the common relation to One Lord. The visible connexion of God with Israel was a type and pledge of this original and universal connexion. The unity of the Church does not spring out of the extension of the old kingdom, but is the spiritual antitype of that earthly figure. Nothing is said of one "fold" under the new dispensation.

It may be added that the obliteration of this essential distinction between the "fold" and the "flock" in many of the later Western versions of this passage indicates, as it appears.

17 Therefore doth my Father love me, [c] because I lay down my life, that I might take it again.

[c] Isai. 53. 7, 8.

18 No man taketh it from me, but I lay it down of myself. I have power to lay it down, and I have power to take it again. [d] This commandment have I received of my Father.

[d] Acts 2. 24.

19 ¶ There was a division therefore again among the Jews for these sayings.

20 And many of them said, He hath a devil, and is mad; why hear ye him?

21 Others said, These are not the words of him that hath a devil. Can a devil open the eyes of the blind?

---

a tendency of Roman Christianity, and has served in no small degree to confirm and extend the false claims of the Roman see. See Additional Note.

The fulfilment of the promise began with the establishment of one church of Jew and Gentile (Eph. ii. 13 ff.) and goes forward until the consummation of all things (Rom. xi. 36).

17. *Therefore*] **For this reason** (διὰ τοῦτο) — namely, that the Good Shepherd freely offers Himself for His flock, to bring all into a true unity—*doth* **the Father** *love me.* The perfect love of the Son calls out (if we dare so speak) the love of the Father, just as man's love calls out the active love of Christ.

The reason thus gathered from the former verses is summed up in the sentence which follows: *because I*—the pronoun is emphatic, I, in the exercise of my personal will—*lay down my life* with this clear end in view, *that I* **may** (not *might*) *take it again.* The "that" (ἵνα) marks a definite purpose, and not merely a result or a condition. The sacrifice is not a casting away of a blessing of God, but is itself made in order to give the blessing fuller reality, and this end is here distinctly set forth. Christ died in order to rise to a completer life and to raise men with Him. This purpose evoked the love of the Father. Comp. xii. 32; Phil. ii. 9; Hebr. ii. 10, xii. 2.

18. *No man taketh it...*] The aoristic reading (ἦρεν), which is probably true, *no one took it from me.* opens a glimpse into the eternal counsel independent of time, into "being" as distinguished from "becoming." Comp. Rev. iv. 11 (ἦσαν καὶ ἐκτίσθησαν); i. 4. The work of Christ, the Incarnate Son, was, so to speak, already accomplished when He came. And this work was imposed by no constraining power at first (*took*) but was to its last issue fulfilled by the free-will of Christ Himself, in harmony with the will of the Father (v. 30, vii. 28, viii. 28, 42, xiv. 10). Here only does Christ claim to do anything "of Himself" (ἀπ' ἐμαυτοῦ). Compare a like contrast in v. 31, viii. 14, 18.

taketh it] "taketh it away" (αἴρει, Vulg. *tollit*), Matt. xiii. 12, xxv. 28 f.

I have power...] *I have* **right**. not simple ability, but just authority (ἐξουσία) to do so. The emphasis which is laid on the personal act of sacrifice is traced back to its ground in these words. The two parts of the one act of Redemption are set side by side (*I have right to lay down, I have right to ... take again*).

I have power (**right**) *to lay it down*] In the case of Christ even death itself was voluntary. His will to the last absolutely coincided with the Father's will, so that He could do what no man can do.

I have power (**right**) *to take it* (λαβεῖν) *again*] The words contain implicitly the mystery of the divine-human Person of the Lord, gathered up in His divine Personality. In virtue of this undying Personality (v. 26), He had power to revivify all that was dissolved by death, "taking" in this sense that which was given by the Father. Comp. ii. 19. Christ in His divine nature works with the Father. Thus the "right" of the Son to "take" life again completely harmonizes with the fact that the Resurrection is elsewhere referred to the Father, though the Son is the Resurrection.

This commandment] which is one and complete—to lay down life and to take it again—is the source of eternal life: xii. 49 f., xiv. 31. Thus the action of the Son is finally led back to His Father (*My Father*, and not simply *the Father*) in the sense of the phrase *of myself I do nothing.*

19. *There was* (**arose**) *a division* (omit *therefore*) *again among the Jews*] as vii. 43 (in the multitude), ix. 16 (in the Pharisees).

these sayings] *these* **words** (λόγους, Vulg. *sermones*), these discourses: not only the last parables, but all the discourses of this visit.

20. *He hath a devil* (**demon**)] Cf. vii. 20, viii. 48 ff.

why hear ye him?] This was said apparently by those who feared the effect which the teaching of Christ had.

21. *These are not the words...*] *the* **sayings** (ῥήματα, Vulg. *verba*) — the specific utterances which arrested their attention, and not the general teaching—of one **possessed with a demon** (δαιμονιζομένου). The teaching itself refutes the charge of madness: the act indicates the co-operation of a power greater than and different from that of a demon (*Can a* **demon** *open ...?*).

22 ¶ And it was at Jerusalem the
c. [e]feast of the dedication, and it was
winter.
23 And Jesus walked in the temple in Solomon's porch.
24 Then came the Jews round
about him, and said unto him, How
long dost thou ‖ make us to doubt? ‖ Or, *hold us in suspense?*
If thou be the Christ, tell us plainly.
25 Jesus answered them, I told

Christ's final public testimony to Himself before His passion (x. 22—38).

In this section the testimony of the Lord to Himself reaches its climax. In answer to a direct question put to Him in the temple at a season suggestive of great hope (22—24), He directs His interrogators to His teaching and His works (25), while He points out the ground of their unbelief (26). At the same time He claims for Himself a flock separate from the corrupt theocracy, for which He has provided the fulness of life through His absolute fellowship with the Father (27—30). This claim, which is practically an answer to the original question, leads to an outburst of violence (31). Christ again appeals to His works (32); and, in answer to the charge of blasphemy (33), shews that the Old Testament pointed to that fellowship of God and man which He at length presented (34—36). Finally, once again He appeals to His works. By accepting these as real and studying them, He shews that men may rise to a true view of His Nature (37, 38).

The argument evidently falls in completely with the occasion. While it reveals to careful inquiry the essential basis of St John's own teaching, it is wholly free from his peculiar language, and even superficially (35, 36) at variance with it.

22. *And it was at Jerusalem the feast of the dedication*] **At that time** *the feast of the dedication* **was held** (ἐγένετο) *at Jerusalem.* See Additional Note. The special mention of the time appears to be made in order to connect the subject of the Lord's teaching with the hopes associated with the last national deliverance. The Hymn which is at present used in Jewish Synagogues at the Festival records the successive deliverances of Israel, and contains a prayer for yet another. Christ in fact perfectly accomplished what the Maccabees wrought in a figure, and dedicated a new and abiding temple: ii. 18 ff.; (Hebr. x. 20). For the history of the Festival, which was kept about the middle of December (Kisleu 25, and seven following days), see 1 Macc. iv. 36 ff.; Jos. 'Ant.' XII. 7. 7 (XII. 11). It was known as "the Feast of lights," and the title chosen by the Lord in ix. 5 may refer to their custom of kindling the lights, no less than to the ceremonies of the Feast of Tabernacles.

it was winter (omit *and*)] The note is added, not simply as a mark of time, but as an explanation of the fact that the Lord chose a sheltered spot for His teaching.

23, 24. The vividness and particularity of the description (**was walking**, *surrounded*, *began to say*, the *porch of Solomon* [comp. viii. 20]) are to be noticed.

walked] **was walking.** The verb marks the circumstances of the special conversation.

Solomon's porch] Acts iii. 11, v. 12. "The eastern cloister," Jos. 'Ant.' XX. 8. 6. Probably the vast substructions now remaining may belong to it.

24. *Then came the Jews . . .*] **The Jews therefore** *came . . .*, because the place was a public resort, and offered an opportunity for a decisive interview.

round about] Acts xiv. 20. Probably they were resolved to bar escape.

dost thou make us to doubt?] **hold our minds in suspense.** The original word (αἴρεις) is used for "raising" the mind with various emotions as the case may be, here in doubt between hope and fear.

If thou be (**art**) *the Christ...*] The emphasis lies on the pronoun. *If thou*, far as thou art from our ideal and from our wishes, *if thou art* (εἰ σὺ εἶ) *the Christ, tell us....* The words seem to betray an unsatisfied longing which seeks rest, if it can be gained, even from this strange teacher. The notion that the question is asked with a deliberate evil intention is unsuited to the occasion. It was repeated with terrible emphasis afterwards, Luke xxii. 67.

tell us plainly] without reserve and without fear, vii. 13, note, xi. 14. As if they wished to add, "and we on our part will not be wanting to carry out your purpose and our own."

25. The answer is a test of faith. The Lord was the Christ of the Old Testament, and yet not the Christ of the Pharisaic hope. The questioners therefore are thrown back upon their own spiritual discernment. The words and the works of Christ reveal Him.

I told you] not indeed directly, as the woman of Samaria (iv. 26); that open declaration came only when hope was past and it could foster no false expectations (Matt. xxvi. 64, note); but yet Christ's words were such that faith could not have misunderstood their meaning. And even if His teaching had remained a riddle, His works might still have furnished the interpretation of it. Comp. xiv. 11.

you, and ye believed not: the works that I do in my Father's name, they bear witness of me.

26 But ye believe not, because ye are not of my sheep, as I said unto you.

27 My sheep hear my voice, and I know them, and they follow me:

28 And I give unto them eternal life; and they shall never perish, neither shall any *man* pluck them out of my hand.

---

ye believed not] *ye* **believe** *not*. The question is of their present state.

which *I do*] The emphatic pronoun (*which I*—I, the very person whom you see and despise—*do*) at once refers back to the *thou* of the Jews' question, and forward to the relation of the Son to the Father.

in my Father's name] as revealing, that is, the special connexion in which I stand to Him, and in virtue of that connexion. Comp. v. 43.

they] **these**. For the emphatic repetition of the subject, see vi. 46, vii. 18, xv. 5.

26. *But*] the fault lies not in the lack of witness. It is the power to apprehend it which is wanting. *You* on your part *believe not*, *because...*

not of my sheep...] The phrase calls back the teaching of the earlier part of the chapter: *vv.* 14 ff. The exact form of expression "the sheep that are mine" (τὰ πρόβατα τὰ ἐμά) is characteristic of St John. Comp. xv. 9, note.

as I said unto you] These words are to be omitted in accordance with ℵBL, &c., *Memph.*, *Theb.*, *Vulg.*, &c.

27—30. The connexion of this paragraph with that which precedes is not very obvious. It seems to lie in the affirmation of the existence of a society of believers though Israel was unfaithful. "You hear not; you fail to recognise your Messiah; but still there are those who welcome the blessings which I bring, and acknowledge in me a wider office and a higher Being."

27, 28. These verses admit of three distinct arrangements, either into three divisions of one, two, and three clauses respectively; or into three divisions of two clauses; or into two divisions of three clauses (as A.V.). According to the first arrangement the general truth is stated at the outset, and afterwards developed on its two sides:

My sheep hear my voice,
And I know them,
and they follow me:
And I give unto them eternal life;
and they shall never perish,
and no one shall snatch them out of my hand.

In this arrangement the thought is first of the sheep and then of the shepherd.

According to the second arrangement the sheep stand in each case first:

My sheep hear my voice,
and I know them;
And they follow me,
and I give unto them eternal life;
And they shall never perish,
and no one shall snatch them out of my hand.

So the knowledge (sympathy, love) of Christ answers to obedience; life to progress; victory to salvation.

However the symmetry of the thought is arranged the ground of all is the same, the unity in essence, and power, and will, of the Father and of the Son.

27. *hear...follow*] Both verbs are plural here as contrasted with the singular *vv.* 3, 4 (*hear*, *follow*). In one case the idea of the flock prevails, and in the other that of the separate sheep. The plural occurs: 4, *know;* 5, *follow*, *fly*, *know;* 8, *heard;* (14, *know*); 16, *hear*, *become;* 28, *perish*. The singular, *v.* 4 (ἀκολουθεῖ); *v.* 12, *are* (ἔστιν); 16, *are* (ἔστιν).

I know them] *v.* 14.

they follow] *v.* 4. Life is progress towards fuller knowledge, and not rest.

28. *I give*] Not simply "I will give." The offer is present and continuously appropriated.

they shall...hand] They are safe from inward dissolution and from outward violence.

neither shall any man pluck them] **and no one shall snatch them**, as a fact distinguished from *can snatch*, *v.* 29.

out of my hand] Comp. Wisd. iii. 1; Isai. xlix. 2, li. 16.

27, 28. The doctrine of "final perseverance" has been found in this passage. But we must carefully distinguish between the certainty of God's promises and His infinite power on the one hand, and the weakness and variableness of man's will on the other. If man falls at any stage in his spiritual life, it is not from want of divine grace, nor from the overwhelming power of adversaries, but from his neglect to use that which he may or may not use. We cannot be protected against ourselves in spite of ourselves. He who ceases to hear and to follow is thereby shewn to be no true believer, 1 John ii. 19. The difficulty in this case is only one form of the difficulty involved in the relation of an infinite to a finite being. The sense of the divine protection is at any moment sufficient to inspire confidence.

29 My Father, which gave *them*
me, is greater than all; and no *man*
is able to pluck *them* out of my Father's hand.
30 I and *my* Father are one.
31 Then the Jews took up stones
again to stone him.
32 Jesus answered them, Many
good works have I shewed you from
my Father; for which of those works
do ye stone me?
33 The Jews answered him, saying, For a good work we stone thee
not; but for blasphemy; and because
that thou, being a man, makest thyself God.

---

but not to render effort unnecessary. Comp. vi. 37, 39, 40, 44 f. St Paul combines the two thoughts, Phil. ii. 12 f.

29. *My Father...all*] The reading of the original text in this place is doubtful. See Additional Note. According to the most probable reading the translation is, **that which the Father hath given me** *is greater than all:* the faithful regarded in their unity, as a complete body, are stronger than every opposing power. This is their essential character, *and no one is able...* Comp. 1 John v. 4.

and no man ... my Father's (**the** *Father's*) *hand*] The thought, which is concrete in *v.* 28, is here traced back to its most absolute form as resting on the essential power of God in His relation of universal Fatherhood. The variations in expression all point in the same direction. Here it is said simply *snatch*, and not *snatch them; can snatch*, and not *shall snatch; the Father*, and not *my Father*.

30. *I and my Father are one*] *I and* **the Father** *are one*. Every word in this pregnant clause is full of meaning. It is *I*, not *the Son; the Father*, not *my Father;* one essence (ἕν, Vulg. *unum*), not one person (εἷς, Gal. iii. 28, *unus*); *are*, not *am*. The revelation is of the nature of Christ in the fulness of His double nature, of the incarnate Son in the fulness of His manifested being, and that in relation to *the Father*, to God as He is Father at once of the Son and of men. The Incarnation was the proof of the complete unity of the Father and the Son. Through that was shewn the true connexion of God and man. And so it is that the union of believers together is made dependent on the union of the Father and the Son (xvii. 22, according to the true reading).

It seems clear that the unity here spoken of cannot fall short of unity of essence. The thought springs from the equality of power (*my hand, the Father's hand*); but infinite power is an essential attribute of God; and it is impossible to suppose that two beings distinct in essence could be equal in power. Comp. Rev. xx. 6, xxii. 3.

The phrase was very commonly quoted in controversy from the time of Tertullian. The following passages will repay study: Tertull. 'adv. Prax.' 22; Hippol. 'c. Noet.' 7; Ambr. 'de Spir. S.' I. 111, 116; August. 'Coll. c. Max.' § 14.

31. *Then the Jews took up...*] *The Jews took up*, lifted up or bore. The word (ἐβάστασαν, d *bajulaverunt*, but Vulg. *sustulerunt*) describes that which is borne as a heavy weight rather than that which is seized, Gal. vi. 2, 5, 17. The stones probably were brought from a distance by the most eager assailants (contrast viii. 59, ἦραν). The works which were going on at the temple would supply them.

again] viii. 59.

32. *answered*] their accusation in action. Comp. ii. 18, note. Here the Lord did not withdraw Himself at once (viii. 59), but further unfolded the revelation which He had given, and held their judgment in suspense by His word.

good works] good in the sense of morally beautiful (καλά), so that they claimed directly the instinctive admiration of men.

shewed] A divine work is a revelation to be studied. It is emphatically "a sign" (ii. 18). Something is left for the witness to bring to the interpretation of the fact (v. 20).

from my (**the**) *Father*] proceeding from Him as their source (ἐκ τοῦ π.) and connected with Him as the stream with the spring. Comp. vi. 65, vii. 17, viii. 42, 47, xvi. 28. See also v. 36, xv. 24. Under this aspect it is important to observe that the Lord speaks not of *my Father* but of *the Father;* the relationship to which He appeals is with men and not with the Son only.

for which] The interrogation marks quality (διὰ ποῖον) and not simple definition (διὰ τί), Matt. xxi. 23; Acts iv. 7.

do ye stone me?] The pronoun (ἐμέ) is emphatic; *do ye stone me*, who truly reveal the Father in act. The irony of the speech becomes the expression of stern indignation. The miracles of Christ had in fact called out the bitterest hostility of the Jews.

33. *The Jews answered him* (omit, with the most ancient MSS., *saying*)...] The second clause defines and intensifies the charge in the first. It was not, they reply, simple blasphemy, derogation from the honour due to God, but the assumption by man of the divine prerogatives, which called for their action. Comp. xix. 7.

^f Psal. 82. 6.

34 Jesus answered them, ^f Is it not written in your law, I said, Ye are gods?

35 If he called them gods, unto whom the word of God came, and the scripture cannot be broken;

36 Say ye of him, whom the Father hath sanctified, and sent into the world, Thou blasphemest; because I said, I am the Son of God?

37 If I do not the works of my Father, believe me not.

---

34. *Jesus answered...*] The accusation of the Jews was grounded upon a false conception of the unity of God drawn from the Old Testament. This, they argued, was violated if Jesus, truly man, claimed to be One with God. The Lord therefore shews in His answer that even in the Old Testament there was a preparation for that union of God and man which He came to complete.

in your law] in the code to which you appeal, viii. 17. For the extension of the title "law" to the other Scriptures, see xii. 34, xv. 25; (Rom. iii. 19; 1 Cor. xiv. 21). The same usage is found in Rabbinic writers. Comp. Wünsche, *ad loc.*

The reference in Ps. lxxxii. 6 is to judges who indeed violated the laws of their august office, yet even so their office was no less divine.

35. The case is taken as an extreme one. *If* the Scripture *called them unto whom the word of God came:* if the direct divine call to a sacred office carried with it such a communication of the divine power as justified the attribution of the title: *do ye* (ὑμεῖς) *say*, ye who plead the strictest adherence to the law as your justification, *of him whom* . . .

he called] The subject is not defined in the original (εἰ...εἶπε). It may be taken from the preceding "I said;" or "the Scripture" may be supplied from the second clause.

the word of God] This phrase, which is used of the divine communication under the old covenant, cannot be without reference to the Word before the Incarnation, through whom God held converse with His people and made His will known. Comp. Luke xi. 49; Matt. xxiii. 34.

the scripture cannot be broken] The particular sentence (ἡ γραφή) which has been quoted. This appears to be always the force of the singular in St John. See ii. 22, note, xvii. 12, xx. 9, note.

broken] The word (λυθῆναι, Vulg. *solvi*) is peculiar and characteristic of St John: ii. 19, v. 18, note, vii. 23; 1 John iii. 8 (comp. Eph. ii. 14).

It must be noticed that St John records the permanent significance of the Old Testament no less than the Synoptists: xiii. 18, xvii. 12, xix. 24, 28, 36, compared with Matt. v. 18, &c.

36. In contrast with those who derived their title from the temporary mission of the Word stands that One *Whom the Father* Himself directly **sanctified**, set apart for His work, *and then sent into the world.* The two moments in the mission of the Son are thus distinguished in their complete complementary fulness. The translation ... *to Whom the Word of God came* (*and the Scripture cannot be broken*), *Whom* (*i.e. the Word of God*) *the Father ... sent...* is wholly alien from the style of St John. Yet see Cyril Alex. *ad loc.*

hath sanctified] **sanctified** (consecrated). Comp. xvii. 17, 19. This fact belongs to the eternal order. The term (ἡγίασεν, Vulg. *sanctificavit*) expresses the divine destination of the Lord for His work. This destination carries with it the further thought of the perfect endowment of the Incarnate Son. His divine Person, if it is allowable so to speak, included an essential capacity for the Incarnation, so that a term peculiarly appropriate to the human nature can be properly used of the unchangeable Person. The various manifestations of the Spirit to Christ after His Advent were results of this eternal consecration. Comp. vi. 27; Acts iv. 27, 30. The word is used of the divine consecration of prophets (Jer. i. 5; Ecclus. xlix. 7), of Moses (Ecclus. xlv. 4), of the chosen people (2 Macc. i. 25 f.; 3 Macc. vi. 3). Comp. vi. 69; 1 John ii. 20.

the Son of God?] **Son of God.** The absence of the article (see xix. 7) fixes attention on the character and not on the person. As the position of Christ was higher than that of the theocratic judges, so the title which He here assumes is lower (*Son of God*, *Gods*). But how, it may be asked, does this argument justify the phrase used in *v.* 30? The phrases *ye are Gods*, *Son of God*, *I and the Father are one*, do not appear to be homogeneous. The answer appears to be this:

1. Such a phrase as that in Ps. lxxxii. 6 really includes in a most significant shape the thought which underlies the whole of the Old Testament, that of a covenant between God and man, which through the reality of a personal relationship assumes the possibility of a vital union. Judaism was not a system of limited monotheism, but a theism always tending to theanthropism, to a real union of God and man. It was therefore enough to shew in answer to the accusation of the Jews that there lay already in the Law the germ of the truth which Christ announced, the union of God and man.

2. And again the words *I and the Father are one*, exclude the confusion of the divine Persons and so suggest the thought of a Son

38 But if I do, though ye believe not me, believe the works: that ye may know, and believe, that the Father *is* in me, and I in him.

39 Therefore they sought again to take him: but he escaped out of their hand,

40 And went away again beyond Jordan into the place where John at first baptized; and there he abode.

41 And many resorted unto him, and said, John did no miracle: but all things that John spake of this man were true.

42 And many believed on him there.

---

of the same essence with the Father. In this sense the title "Son of God" does completely answer to the former revelation.

It will be observed that though the title (ὁ λόγος) "the Word" is almost suggested by the current of thought, yet St John keeps his own phraseology apart from the record of the Lord's words.

37, 38. Once again (*v.* 32) the Lord appeals to His works. The inborn power of recognising the divine in deed is the starting-point: the end is the recognition of the absolute intercommunion of the Incarnate Son (*I*) and the Father.

believe me not] do not accept my statements as true. The question here is of the acceptance of a testimony and not of faith in a Person (*believe in me*). Comp. v. 24 (note), 46, vi. 30, viii. 31, 45 f., xiv. 11; 1 John iii. 23, v. 10; Acts xvi. 34, xviii. 8, xxvii. 25; Rom. iv. 3.

believe the works] accept as real the signs which testify of me, *v.* 25. To "believe the works" is the first step towards "believing for the works' sake" (xiv. 11).

The belief in the testimony of the works is the foundation of the general knowledge and the growing perception in all its manifold revelations of the inner fellowship of the Father and the Son (*that the Father is in me and I in* **the Father**). This fellowship itself is first realised in works and then in absolute Being. The fellowship of "being" between the Father and the Son must be compared with the fellowship of "abiding" of the believer and God described in 1 John iv. 16, a passage which has evidently been modified by this.

that ye may know, and believe...] *That ye may know and* **may understand**...perceive once for all, and then go on advancing in ever fuller perception (ἵνα γνῶτε καὶ γινώσκητε)... Comp. xvii. 21, 23; Phil. i. 9.

39. *Therefore they sought again*] *They sought again*... vii. 30, 32, 44.

to take] **to seize**. Their immediate violence (*v.* 31) was so far checked.

he escaped (**went forth**) *out of their hand*] The phrase (ἐξῆλθεν ἐκ) occurs only here. It marks the power of Christ's personal majesty as contrasted with the impotence of His adversaries. Their "hand" is contrasted in some sense with "His hand" (*v.* 28), and His "going forth" with their inability to carry away any from His Father's protection.

40—42. The testimony of works and the testimony of the Baptist, which now found no acceptance in Judæa, were welcomed beyond Jordan.

40. *And went away again...*] *And* **he** *went away again*... The clause commences a new section. The reference is probably to some recent and unrecorded visit. The events of i. 28 are too remote.

This sojourn in Peræa is noticed in the Synoptists, Matt. xix. 1; Mark x. 1; (Luke xviii. 15).

at first baptized] **was at first baptizing**, as recorded in i. 28, in contrast with iii. 23. So the narrative of the Lord's ministry closes on the spot where it began. The Evangelist naturally marks the scene where he had himself met Christ.

there he abode] outside Judæa. The emphasis lies upon the place.

41. *many resorted unto him, and said...*] The acceptance of Christ beyond the limits of Judæa serves to complete the picture of the incredulity of the Jews.

The verse contains a double opposition of the Baptist and Christ, as is indicated by the repetition of John's name. The first contrast lies in the fact that John wrought no sign, while Christ was working many (Matt. xix. 1); and the second in the fact that John was not indeed "he that should come," but a true herald. The second clause presupposes the acceptance of Jesus as the Messiah on the testimony of the signs which were seen.

John did no miracle] The notice shews how little inclination there was to invest popular teachers with miraculous powers. The new Elijah might have seemed above all men likely to shew signs.

42. *believed on him*] with the devotion of self-surrender, and did not simply (as *vv.* 37, 38) accept His statements.

there] with a pointed reference to *v.* 40; *there*, if not in Jerusalem.

ADDITIONAL NOTES on Chap. x. 16, 22, 29.

16. The two words αὐλή (*fold*) and ποίμνη (*flock*) are given in this passage without any variation in the Greek text; and the two words are distinguished in the Syriac (Peshito, Harclean, Hierosol.) and Egyptian versions.

The earliest Latin note upon the passage which I have observed is by Jerome (In Ezek. xlvi. 22): "Alias oves habeo quæ non sunt ex hoc *atrio;* et illas oportet me adducere, et vocem meam audient, et fiet unum *atrium* et unus pastor. Hoc enim Græcum αὐλή significat, quod Latina simplicitas in *ovile* transtulit." This observation is interesting for several reasons. It shews how perfunctory Jerome's criticism of the Latin text was. He distinctly prefers *atrium* to *ovile* as the rendering of αὐλή, and yet he did not introduce it into his revision. And again he implies that αὐλή stands in the Greek text in both places, which at least shews that he did not verify his reference.

Elsewhere, it may be added (In Isai. lx. 22), Jerome reads "unus *grex* et unus pastor," giving *grex* also as the rendering of αὐλή in the former clause.

The old Latin texts (*a*, *b*, *c*, *e*) read *ovile*, *grex;* the Latin of D reads *atrium*, *grex*, according to Jerome's suggestion; many mixed texts (*f*, *ff*², *cod. aur.*, but none of Bentley's MSS.) read *ovile*, *grex;* in the Latin of Δ, ποίμνη is represented by the strange alternatives *ovile* v. *pastorale*. Cyprian gives *ovile*, *grex*.

The reading in Augustine varies. In treating of the passage he reads *ovile*, *ovile*, without comment. Elsewhere (*e.g.* 'Serm.' 138. 5) he reads *ovile*, *grex*.

The standard text of the Vulgate (*Cod. Amiat.* &c.), gives *ovile*, *ovile*, and this reading became practically universal among Latin mediæval writers. Even Erasmus left the rendering unchanged; and so also did Beza until 1582. The phrase *unum ovile*, *unus pastor*, had evidently become sacred by use.

Luther truly rendered the Greek (*aus diesem Stalle*, *Eine Herde*), and so also did Tyndale and Coverdale (*fold*, *flock*). Wiclif, however, following the Vulgate, had already made "one fold" familiar in English; and this rendering was introduced into Cromwell's Bible, 1539, and retained its place down to 1611.

It would perhaps be impossible for any correction now to do away with the effects which a translation undeniably false has produced on popular ecclesiastical ideas.

22. The reading in this verse is of critical importance in regard to the connexion of the preceding discourses.

The early authorities are divided:

(1) ἐγένετο τότε is found in BL 33, and in the Thebaic and Armenian versions.

(2) ἐγένετο δέ in ℵADX, and the mass of MSS., in some old Latin copies, and in the Syriac versions.

(3) A small group of cursive mss., including some of importance (1, 225, 2pc, &c.), and the best copies of the Old Latin (*a*, *b*) have no connecting particle.

(4) The Memphitic version and one Latin copy at least (*gat*) represent both τότε and δέ.

There are also other slight variations in the renderings in versions.

These phenomena may be accounted for by supposing either that originally there was no connecting particle, or that it was one which caused difficulty.

The evidence in support of the first supposition, though considerable, appears to be inadequate; and τότε would be an unlikely particle to insert.

On the other hand, if τότε stood in the text originally it would create superficial difficulty from the apparent confusion of the feasts; and again it is an unusual word in St John, and not often found in this position, though in fact its unusual position is significant (Matt. xxiv. 21, xxvii. 16, "at that time, while these discussions as to the old church and the new were going on").

If δέ had been the true reading, it is not easy to see why it should have been changed. The origin of the τότε from the repetition of the last syllable of ἐγένετο is very unlikely. And, though δέ has no obvious difficulty, it is hard to suppose that St John would have indicated in such a way a fresh journey to Jerusalem (xiii. 1 is not a parallel), and the statement, "Now the Feast of Dedication took place (ἐγένετο) at Jerusalem," is on this supposition, as it seems, singularly without force.

On the whole therefore it is best to adopt the reading τότε, which has strong external and internal authority, and which brings the conversation in x. 1—18 into connexion with its sequel, *v.* 25 ff., and with a characteristic epoch.

29. In this verse the relative (*which*) and the comparative (*greater*) are masculine in some of the most important authorities and neuter in others; and there is a cross division in these differences. Thus, (1) B*, *Latt.*, *Memph.* read, ὅ, μεῖζον; (2) ℵL, ὅ, μείζων; (3) AB²X, ὅς, μεῖζον; (4) D, ὁ δεδωκώς, μείζων; (5) the mass of authorities, ὅς, μείζων.

The reading (2) is impossible. The readings (4) and (5) are evidently corrections: if either had been original, it would not have been disturbed. The choice lies between (1) and (3). Of these (1) has the most ancient authority, and is the most difficult and at the same time the most in accordance with the style of St John (vi. 39, xvii. 2). This reading has therefore been adopted in the notes.

If the masculine relative be adopted (ὅς) the sense is quite simple: *My Father which gave them to me is greater* (personally, μείζων, or rather, *a greater power*, μεῖζον: comp. Matt. xii. 6) *than all; and* (as a consequence) *no one is able*...

Hilary ('de Trin.' 7. 22; II. 12) takes the phrase in a wholly different sense as referring to the derivation of the Son's divine nature from the Father (Datio paterna sumptæ nativitatis professio est, et quod unum sunt, proprietas ex nativitate naturæ est: II. 12). Ambrose ('De Spir. Sancto,' III. 116: Dedit pater per generationem non per adoptionem) and Augustine (*ad loc.* Quid dedit Filio Pater majus omnibus? Ut ipse illi esset unigenitus Filius) take the same view. But the usage of St John (vi. 39, *all that which the Father hath given me*: comp. *v.* 37, xvii. 2, *all that which thou hast given Him*) seems distinctly to point to the society of the faithful as the Father's gift; and this interpretation brings the clause into parallelism with those which have gone before.

CHAPTER XI.

1 Christ raiseth Lazarus, four days buried. 45 Many Jews believe. 47 The high priests and Pharisees gather a council against Christ. 49 Caiaphas prophesieth. 54 Jesus hid himself. 55 At the passover they inquire after him, and lay wait for him.

---

ii. THE DECISIVE JUDGMENT (xi., xii.).

This last section of the record of the Lord's public ministry, represented by His great controversy at Jerusalem, consists of two parts. The first part contains the narrative of the final sign with its immediate consequences (xi.); the second part gives three typical scenes which mark the close of the work, together with a summary judgment upon its results (xii.).

1. *The final sign and its immediate issues* (xi.).

The narrative of the raising of Lazarus is unique in its completeness. The essential circumstances of the fact in regard to persons, manner, results, are given with perfect distinctness. The history is more complete than that in ch. ix. because the persons stand in closer connexion with the Lord than the blind man, and the event itself had in many ways a ruling influence on the end of His ministry.

Four scenes are to be distinguished: (1) The prelude to the miracle (1—16); (2) The scene at Bethany (17—32); (3) The miracle (33—44); (4) The immediate issues of the miracle (45—57).

In studying the history, several points must be kept in view.

1. The sign itself is the last of a series, which has evidently been formed (xx. 30 f.) with a view to the complete and harmonious exhibition of the Lord's work. The seven miracles of the ministry, which St John relates, form a significant whole (ii. 1 ff., iv. 46 ff., v. 1 ff., vi. 5 ff., 15 ff., ix. 1 ff., xi.). And in this respect it is of interest to notice that the first and last are wrought in the circle of family life, and among believers to the strengthening of faith (ii. 11, xi. 15); and both are declared to be manifestations of "glory" (ii. 11, xi. 4, 40). So the natural relations of men become the occasions of the revelation of higher truth.

2. The circumstances of the miracle ought to be minutely compared with those of the corresponding miracles recorded by the Synoptists (Mark v. 22 ff. and parallels; Luke vii. 11 ff.). The omission of the raising of Lazarus by the Synoptists is no more remarkable in principle than the omission of these raisings by St John. In each case the selection of facts was determined by the purpose of the record. The miracles wrought at Jerusalem were not included in the cycle of apostolic preaching which formed the basis of the Synoptic Gospels.

3. Numerous minute touches mark the fulness of personal knowledge, or the impression of an eye-witness: *e.g.* the relation of the family to Jesus (*v.* 5); the delay of two days (6); the exact position of Bethany (18); the presence of Jews (19); the secret message (28); the title "the Master" (*id.*); the pause of Jesus (30); the following of the Jews (31), and their weeping (33); the prostration of Mary (32); the successive phases of the Lord's emotion (33, 35, 38); the appearance of Lazarus (44).

4. Not less remarkable than this definiteness of detail are the silences, the omissions, in the narrative; *e.g.* as to the return of the messenger (*v.* 4); the message to Mary (27 f.); the welcome of the restored brother (44). Under this head too may be classed the unexpected turns of expression: *e.g.* "unto Judæa" (*v.* 7). *vv.* 11 f., *v.* 37.

5. That however which is most impressive in the narrative, as a history, is its dramatic vividness; and this in different respects. There is a clear individuality in the persons. Thomas stands out characteristically from the apostles. Martha and Mary, alike in their convictions, are distinguished in the manner of shewing them. Then again there is a living revelation of character in the course of the narrative; Martha reflects the influence of the Lord's words. The Jews are tried and separated. And above all the Lord is seen throughout. absolutely one in His supreme freedom, perfectly human and perfectly divine, so that it is felt that there is no want of harmony between His tears and His life-giving command.

NOW a certain *man* was sick,
named Lazarus, of Bethany,
the town of Mary and her sister
Martha.
a Matt. 26. 7. 2 ([a]It was *that* Mary which anointed the Lord with ointment, and
wiped his feet with her hair, whose
brother Lazarus was sick.)
3 Therefore his sisters sent unto
him, saying, Lord, behold, he whom
thou lovest is sick.
4 When Jesus heard *that*, he said,

---

6. With regard to the fact itself it is important to remark that, while it was a sign of the resurrection, the Evangelist makes it clear throughout that this raising to a corruptible life is essentially distinct from the Lord's rising again to a glorified life.

7. Apart from the antecedent assumption that a miracle is impossible, and that the record of a miracle must therefore be explained away, it is not easy to see any ground for questioning the literal exactness of the history. No explanation of the origin of the narrative on the supposition that it is unhistorical, has even a show of plausibility. Those who deny the fact are sooner or later brought to maintain either that the scene was an imposture, or that the record is a fiction. Both of these hypotheses involve a moral miracle.

8. No overwhelming influence is assigned to the miracle by the Evangelist. It is a "sign," a revelation of the divine glory, to those who believe, or who have sympathy with the truth. But others, apparently, without questioning the reality of the fact, simply find in it a call to more energetic opposition. The work arrests attention; and then it becomes a touchstone of character. In this respect it completely answers to the function assigned to miracles in the New Testament.

9. This last consideration helps to explain the omission of the miracle from the Synoptic narratives. For us the incident, as an external fact, has naturally a relative importance far greater than it had for the Evangelists. For them, as for the Jews, it was one of "many signs" (xi. 47), and not essentially distinguished from them. The entry into Jerusalem was the decisive event in which the issue of all Christ's earlier works was summed up. This therefore the Synoptists record. For St John, however, the raising of Lazarus was, as the other miracles, a spiritual revelation. It fell in then with his plan, as far as we can discern it, to relate it at length, while it did not fall in with the common plan of the Synoptic Gospels, which excluded all working at Jerusalem till the triumphal entry.

(1) *The prelude to the miracle* (1—16).

The record of the miracle is prefaced by an account of the external and moral circumstances under which it was wrought. The message as to the sickness of Lazarus was brought to the Lord in His retirement at Peræa. He declared what the end would be in mysterious terms, and still remained where He was (1—6). Then followed the announcement of His intention to return to Judæa, which served to shew the feeling of His disciples, alike in their weakness and in their devotion (7—16). Throughout the Lord speaks with the authority of certain knowledge (*vv.* 4, 15).

CHAP. XI. 1—6. The message to Peræa from Bethany.

1. *Now...was...*] The particle (δέ) marks the interruption to the retirement beyond Jordan (x. 40).

Lazarus] The name is a shortened form of Eleazar. It occurs again in Luke xvi. 20; Jos., 'B. J.' v. 13. 7, and in Rabbinic writers (לעזר), see Lightfoot, *ad loc.* All the attempts to identify Lazarus with the person in the parable or with the rich young man are quite baseless. It may also be added that the identification of Mary with Mary Magdalene is a mere conjecture supported by no direct evidence, and opposed to the general tenour of the Gospels.

of Bethany...the town...] The contrast of prepositions in the original text, *of* (ἀπό, Vulg. *a*) *Bethany*, sprung **from** (ἐκ, Vulg. *de*) *the town* (**village**, and so *v.* 30) *of...*, describes the actual residence, and the true home of Lazarus. The "village" may have been Bethany, or it may have been some other village (a certain village, Luke x. 38).

Mary...Martha] Mary is apparently put forward as the person best known from the event mentioned in *v.* 2 and related in ch. xii., though Martha seems to have been the elder sister (*vv.* 5, 19; Luke x. 38 f.). "This name of Martha is very frequent in the Talmudic authors" (Lightfoot, *ad loc.*).

2. *It was that Mary...*] The original is ambiguous. It may be either *But* (δέ) *Mary was she that...whose...*; or, as A. V., *But it was* (the) *Mary which...whose...* The verse obviously presupposes (as *v.* 1) a general knowledge of the Evangelic history.

the Lord] iv. 1, note.

3. *Therefore his sisters...*] **The sisters therefore**, feeling sure of His love in their sorrow.

behold] It was enough to state the fact; they offer no plea. "Sufficit ut noveris: non enim amas et deseris" (Augustine, *ad loc.*). The interjection is characteristic of St John. Comp. xvi. 29, note.

This sickness is not unto death, but
for the glory of God, that the Son of
God might be glorified thereby.
5 Now Jesus loved Martha, and
her sister, and Lazarus.
6 When he had heard therefore
that he was sick, he abode two days
still in the same place where he was.
7 Then after that saith he to *his*
disciples, Let us go into Judæa again.
8 *His* disciples say unto him, Master, the Jews of late sought to stone
thee; and goest thou thither again?
9 Jesus answered, Are there not
twelve hours in the day? If any man
walk in the day, he stumbleth not,

---

he whom thou lovest] with the natural affection of personal attachment (ὃν φιλεῖς, Vulg. *quem amas*). So they point the relation. The Evangelist uses a different word in *v.* 5 (ἠγάπα, Vulg. *diligebat*). For the distinction between the two words, see v. 20, note, xxi. 15, 17, notes.

4. *When Jesus...he said*] **But** *when Jesus heard* **it** *he said*. The words are for all. They are not a simple answer to the messengers, nor yet a simple lesson for the disciples. They contain an answer, and they kindle faith. And the messenger seems to have returned reassured by them, while they were also designed to suggest hope to the sisters when all hope was over (*v.* 40).

This sickness...thereby] *This sickness is not unto death* as its issue and end, *but for*—to serve and to advance—*the glory of God*, **in order that** *the Son of God* **may** *be glorified thereby*. The general object (*the glory of God*) is made specific in the particular end. The actual occurrence of death was in no way against this statement. It rather helped to realise the deeper fulness of the revelation.

for the glory] In every other place in St John (even i. 30; 3 John 7) the preposition used here (ὑπέρ, Vulg. *pro*) marks the notion of "sacrifice in behalf of;" and this idea lies under the narrative here. There was some mysterious sense in which the sick man suffered in behalf of God's glory, and was not merely a passive instrument. Thus the sickness is regarded in a triple relation: "unto" in respect of the actual result; "in behalf of" in respect of the suffering borne; "in order that" in respect of the divine purpose.

For the thought comp. ix. 3, x. 38.

the glory of God] the revelation of God in His victorious majesty: *v.* 40, xii. 41; Acts vii. 55 (δ. θ.); Rom. i. 23, (iii. 23, v. 2), (vi. 4).

might (**may**) *be glorified*] The phrase contains a clear allusion to the glory of the Lord won through the Passion. The raising of Lazarus by revealing Christ's power and character brought the hostility of His enemies to a crisis (*vv.* 47 ff.), and led to His final "glorifying:" xii. 23, xiii. 31.

5. *Now Jesus loved...*] The words are a preparation for *v.* 6. The Evangelist describes the Lord's affection for this family as that of moral choice (ἠγάπα: see *v.* 3, note). The passing notice of that which must have been the result of long and intimate intercourse is a striking illustration of the fragmentariness of the Evangelic records. Lazarus is not mentioned in Luke x. 38 ff.

6. *When he had heard therefore...*] **When therefore he heard...** The delay and the return were alike consequences of the same divine affection and of the same divine knowledge. Because the Lord loved the family He went at the exact moment when His visit would be most fruitful, and not just when He was invited.

he abode...Then after that] *he abode* **for the time...***then after* **this** (τότε μέν...ἔπειτα... Vulg. *tunc quidem...deinde post hoc...*).

two days] The journey would occupy about a day. Thus Lazarus died at the time when the message came (*vv.* 17, 39). Christ therefore did not wait for the death, but knew of the death. Meanwhile He finished the work which He had to do before going back to Judæa. The supposition that the interval was left in order that the Lord might raise the dead and not heal the sick, and so shew greater power and win greater glory, is alien equally from the spirit and from the letter of the narrative, *v.* 15.

7—16. The decision to visit Bethany.

7. *Let us go into Judæa again*] It is to be noticed that the words are not *let us go to Bethany*. The thought is of the hostile land of unbelief in contrast with Peræa (x. 40).

8. *Master*] **Rabbi**, ix. 2, note.

the Jews...again?] **Even now** (νῦν) *the Jews* **were seeking...***and* **art thou going** *thither again?* The English idiom hardly admits the vividness of the original.

9. The answer is exactly complementary to that in ix. 4. It is here laid down that there is an appointed measure of working time given, and consequently that as long as that lasts work can be done. On the other hand (ix. 4) there is only a limited time, and the work must be finished within it.

There is no warrant for applying the ideas of "night" and "stumbling" to any special aspects of the Lord's work, as in the case of men, xii. 35. The answer is, as a whole, a

because he seeth the light of this world.

10 But if a man walk in the night, he stumbleth, because there is no light in him.

11 These things said he: and after that he saith unto them, Our friend Lazarus sleepeth; but I go, that I may awake him out of sleep.

12 Then said his disciples, Lord, if he sleep, he shall do well.

13 Howbeit Jesus spake of his death: but they thought that he had spoken of taking of rest in sleep.

14 Then said Jesus unto them plainly, Lazarus is dead.

15 And I am glad for your sakes that I was not there, to the intent

---

parable of human action. All action is subject to corresponding conditions. Man does not carry within him all that he requires. In order to move in the world he must be illuminated by the light of the world. This law held true even of Christ's work on earth. It could be done, and at the same time it could only be done, while the "day" yet continued. A similar idea is expressed in Luke xiii. 32 f.

The journey to Bethany was not yet begun, so that the image was probably suggested by the early dawn.

10. *there is...him*] **the light is not** *in him:* the light which he needs for the fulfilment of his work.

11. *These things said he: and after that...*] *These things* **spake** *he, and after* **this**...

Our friend...sleepeth] More exactly: **Lazarus, our friend, is fallen asleep** (κεκοίμηται). Even so he still is "our friend" in that world of spirit. Comp. xv. 14 f.; Luke xii. 4. The Lord joins His disciples with Himself in one bond of friendship (*our* friend).

is fallen asleep] Acts vii. 60, xiii. 36; Matt. xxvii. 52; 1 Thess. iv. 13 ff., &c. The image is common in Rabbinic writings.

12. *Then said...sleep...*] **The disciples therefore** *said* **to him...if he is fallen asleep...** The misunderstanding followed from a false view of the promise in *v.* 4. The "sleep" seemed to the disciples to be the crisis of recovery, as, for example, in fever, due to the intervention of the Lord. And if this was so, the perilous journey was no longer necessary; still less could it be well to break the rest which had at last been given.

he shall do well] *he shall* **be saved** (Vulg. *salvus erit*). It is important to notice how the word "save" reaches through the whole of man's nature to every part of it. We cannot draw the line between what we are tempted to call the higher and the lower. The whole narrative is a revelation of life and death, *vv.* 25 f.

Comp. Matt. ix. 21 ff.; (Mark v. 28; Luke viii. 48); Mark vi. 56, x. 52; (Luke xviii. 42); Luke vii. 50, viii. 36, (viii. 50), xvii. 19; James v. 15.

13. *Howbeit Jesus spake...had spoken...*] **Now** *Jesus* **had spoken...spake...** The solemn word misunderstood is contrasted with the immediate interpretation of it (ὅτι... λέγει).

14. *Then said Jesus...*] *Then* **therefore** *Jesus said...* because the disciples had failed to catch the meaning of the words with which He had tried their spiritual discernment. It is clearly implied that the knowledge was supernatural. "Quid lateret eum qui creaverat?" (Aug.).

plainly] without reserve and without metaphor. See vii. 13, note, x. 24, xvi. 25, 29.

Lazarus is dead] Or strictly, *Lazarus died.* The thought is carried back to the critical moment on which the disciples rested in hope. It is interesting to contrast the phrase used before (*v.* 11), *is fallen asleep*, which describes the continuous state with that used here, *died*, which marks the single point of change.

15. *I am glad...believe*] *I am glad for your sakes, to the intent ye may believe, that I was not there.* The words *to the intent ye may believe* are brought into the closest connexion with *for your sakes*, so as to explain the strange saying. Christ is glad not for the death of Lazarus, but for the circumstances and issues of the death. It will be observed that the Lord speaks of His own actions, as if they were in some sense not self-determined.

I was not there] as if death would have been impossible in the presence of Christ.

believe] The word is used absolutely. Comp. i. 7, 50, iv. 41, 42, 48, 53, v. 44, vi. 36, 64, xi. 40, xii. 39, xiv. 29, xix. 35, xx. 29, 31 (iii. 12, 18, x. 25, xvi. 31, xx. 8, are somewhat different). The disciples did already believe in one sense (ii. 11, vi. 69). But each new trial offers scope for the growth of faith. So that which is potential becomes real. Faith can neither be stationary nor complete. "He who *is* a Christian is no Christian" (Luther).

nevertheless...] **but** (ἀλλά), not to dwell on present sorrow or joy to come. The word breaks abruptly the connecting thought. *Habet Dominus horas suas et moras.*

go unto him] not *thither*, but *unto him: unto him*, and not to the sisters who were mourning for him. Even as Christ spoke of Lazarus as still "a friend" (*v.* 11), so here He speaks of the body "sleeping" in the tomb as the man himself. He fixes the thoughts

ye may believe; nevertheless let us
go unto him.
16 Then said Thomas, which is
called Didymus, unto his fellowdis-
ciples, Let us also go, that we may
die with him.
17 Then when Jesus came, he
found that he had *lain* in the grave
four days already.
18 Now Bethany was nigh unto
Jerusalem, ‖ about fifteen furlongs off: ‖ That is, *about two miles.*
19 And many of the Jews came to
Martha and Mary, to comfort them
concerning their brother.
20 Then Martha, as soon as she
heard that Jesus was coming, went
and met him: but Mary sat *still* in
the house.

---

of the disciples upon a real present relationship of Lazarus to them and to Himself. That is now the ground of hope (xiv. 19: comp. Luke xx. 38; Matt. xxii. 32, note).

16. *Then said Thomas...*] *Thomas* **therefore** *said...* in answer to the invitation, as seeing that the resolution of the Master was fixed. There is no longer (*v.* 8) any objection.

which is called...] not as an additional name, but as the interpretation of Thomas (*Twin*). Comp. iv. 25, (xix. 17), i. 38. The same note is repeated xx. 24, xxi. 2. It is difficult to see why special prominence is given to this Greek equivalent of the Aramaic name. Perhaps Thomas may have been familiarly known in Asia Minor among the Gentile Christians as Didymus. The traditions as to his work in Parthia and India are late and uncertain.

Let us also] In *v.* 11 Christ had spoken of Himself alone; in *v.* 15 there is a general invitation. Thomas emphasizes the voluntariness of the act.

that we may die with him] *i.e.* Jesus, suggested by "we *also*." It seems strange that any one should have referred it to Lazarus.

that we may die] The words stand in sharp contrast with the Lord's words, *that ye may believe.* Thomas keeps strictly within the range of that which he knew. There was no doubt as to the hostility of the Jews (comp. Luke xxii. 33). He will not go one step beyond that which is plain and open. He will die for the love which he has, but he will not affect the faith which he has not.

The other passages in which St Thomas appears shew the same character, xiv. 5 (we know not whither...), xx. 25 ff.

(2) *The scene at Bethany* (17—32).

After giving a general view of the circumstances at Bethany (17—19), the Evangelist lays open the meaning of the miracle as a revelation to faith, in connexion with the hope and sorrow of Martha (20—27) and Mary (28—32). Martha's confession of faith is in words (*vv.* 22, 24, 27); Mary's is in simple self-surrender (*v.* 32); while both alike start from the expression of the same conviction (*vv.* 21, 32). It has been commonly observed, and with justice, that under very different circumstances the sisters shew the same differences of character as in Luke x. 38 ff. Martha is eager, impetuous, warm; Mary is more devoted and intense.

17—19. The position at Bethany.

17. *Then when...found*] **So Jesus,** *when he came, found..* The word "found" emphasizes the object of the Lord's journey. Comp. i. 43, ii. 14, v. 14, ix. 35.

18. *Bethany was...*] The whole scene in the apostle's mind is distinct both in place and time. He looks back on the spot (*nigh unto Jerusalem*) and the company (*the Jews had come*) as prepared by a divine fitness for the work to be wrought.

fifteen furlongs off] *i.e.* about two miles. The construction in the original is peculiar (ἀπὸ στ. δεκ...). Comp. xxi. 8; Rev. xiv. 20. The modern name of Bethany (see 'Dict. of Bible,' *s. v.*) (*El-Azarîyeh*) is derived from the miracle. See Wilson, 'Lands of the Bible,' I. 485.

19. *of the Jews*] *vv.* 31, 36, 45. This was the last trial. Natural human love gave them once more the opportunity of faith.

came...to comfort] **had come**...*to comfort.* During the seven days (שׁבעה) of solemn mourning it is still customary for friends to make visits of condolence. Comp. 1 S. xxxi. 14; 1 Chro. x. 12; Job ii. 13 ('Jewish Daily Prayers,' pp. xxx. f.). Lightfoot (*ad loc.*) gives many illustrations of the ancient usages.

20—27. The Lord and Martha.

20. *Then Martha...*] *Martha* **therefore...** (*vv.* 18, 19 are parenthetical). Martha appears to have been engaged in some household duty, and so first heard of the Lord's approach; Mary was still in her chamber, so that the tidings did not at once come to her (*v.* 29) Comp. Luke x. 38 ff.

that Jesus was coming] Literally, *that Jesus cometh.* He had been watched for while hope lasted, and the watch seems to have been still kept when hope was gone. The words appear to be the exact message brought to Martha: "Jesus is coming."

21 Then said Martha unto Jesus, Lord, if thou hadst been here, my brother had not died.

22 But I know, that even now, whatsoever thou wilt ask of God, God will give *it* thee.

23 Jesus saith unto her, Thy brother shall rise again.

24 Martha saith unto him, [b] I know [b] Lu[k]
that he shall rise again in the resur- 14. chap.
rection at the last day.

25 Jesus said unto her, I am the
resurrection, and the [c] life: he that [c] ch.
believeth in me, though he were dead,
yet shall he live:

26 And whosoever liveth and be-

---

21. *Then said Martha...Lord, if...*] **So** *Martha said...Lord, if...* The words are a simple expression of faith and love, without any admixture of complaint. Martha does not say, "if thou hadst come;" she does not even emphasize the pronoun. She thinks only of a necessary absence. See *v.* 32.

22. *But...now...*] **And** *now* (καὶ νῦν) *I know that...* even when death seems to have closed all. Faith reaches forth to that which it does not grasp. The words perhaps refer to the mysterious saying of the Lord (*v.* 4) which had been reported to her.

I know] *v.* 24. Contrast *I believe*, *v.* 27. The faith, if imperfect, is real.

The emphatic repetition of *God*, at the end of both clauses in the original, serves to bring out, as it were, the special relation in which Christ stood to God in Martha's thoughts. It is to be observed that Martha uses a word for the Lord's prayer (αἰτεῖν) which the Lord uses of others (xiv. 13 f., xv. 16, xvi. 23 f.), but never of Himself. Comp. xvi. 26, note.

23. *Thy brother shall rise again*] The whole history of the raising of Lazarus is a parable of Life through death (*vv.* 4, 11, 16), of life through what is called death, of death through what is called life (*v.* 50). Here then, at the beginning, the key-note is given. Whatever death may seem to be, there is a resurrection. Death is not the final conqueror. As yet the idea of "resurrection" is not defined. It is enough that the idea be recognised.

24. Martha acknowledges the doctrine of a resurrection, as an object of remote belief: as something of general but not of personal interest, and therefore powerless in the present bereavement: *I know that he shall rise again in the resurrection*, in that awful scene of universal awakening, *at the last day*, when all human interests cease.

the last day] vi. 39, note.

25. The reply of the Lord meets each implied difficulty. He does not set aside Martha's confession, as if her idea were faulty. He brings the belief which she held into connexion with man's nature as He had made and revealed it. The resurrection is not a doctrine but a fact: not future but present: not multitudinous, but belonging to the unbroken continuity of each separate life. The Resurrection is one manifestation of the Life: it is involved in the Life. It is a personal communication of the Lord Himself, and not a grace which He has to gain from another. Martha had spoken of a gift to be obtained from God and dispensed by Christ. Christ turns her thoughts to His own Person. He *is* that which men need. He does not procure the blessing for them. Compare iv. 15 ff., vi. 35 ff. *I am*—not I shall be hereafter—*I am*, even in this crisis of bereavement, in this immediate prospect of the Cross, *the Resurrection and the Life*. The word "Resurrection" comes first, because the teaching starts from death; but the special term is at once absorbed in the deeper word which includes it, Life (*shall live*, not *shall rise again*).

I am the resurrection...] Christ in the fulness of His Person does not simply work the Resurrection and give life: He is both. He does not say "I promise," or "I procure," or "I bring," but "I am." By taking humanity into Himself He has revealed the permanence of man's individuality and being. But this permanence can be found only in union with Him. Thus two main thoughts are laid down: Life (Resurrection) is present, and this Life is in a Person.

and the life] The context in which this revelation is given determines the sense in which it must be interpreted. Christ is the life of the individual believer, in Whom all that belongs to the completeness of personal being (*v.* 23, *thy brother*; *v.* 11, *our friend*) finds its permanence and consummation. The same statement is made again in the last discourses (xiv. 6 note), but in a different connexion, and with a different scope. Just as "the life" in combination with "the resurrection" fixes the thought upon the man, so "the life" in combination with "the way" and "the truth" fixes it upon the whole sum of existence (i. 4), to which every man contributes his "individual difference." Christ is the Life in both relations. He gives unity and stability to each man separately, and at the same time in virtue of this to the whole creation. St Paul expresses the same double truth when he speaks of the believer as "living in Christ" (Rom. vi. 11), and of "all things consisting in Him" (Col. i. 17).

26. The truth is presented in its two forms as suggested by Resurrection and Life. Some

lieveth in me shall never die. Believest thou this?

27 She saith unto him, Yea, Lord: I believe that thou art the Christ, the Son of God, which should come into the world.

28 And when she had so said, she went her way, and called Mary her sister secretly, saying, The Master is come, and calleth for thee.

29 As soon as she heard *that*, she arose quickly, and came unto him.

30 Now Jesus was not yet come into the town, but was in that place where Martha met him.

31 The Jews then which were with her in the house, and comforted her, when they saw Mary, that she rose up hastily and went out, followed

---

there were, like Lazarus, who had believed and died, some like Martha who yet lived and believed. Of the first it is said that the death of earth under which they had fallen is no real death: *He that believeth on me, though he were dead* (**even if he die**), *shall live*—shall live still, live on even through that change, and not resume life at some later time. And of the second that the life of heaven shall never be broken off: *Whosoever* (πᾶς) *liveth and believeth in me*, he that in that faith hath seized the true conception of life, *shall never die*. To him who is in Christ death is not what it seems to be. The insertion of the universal term in this clause gives amplitude to the promise.

The verse points to mysteries which have occupied the thoughts of Eastern and also of Western philosophers, as the famous verses of Euripides shew, "Who knoweth if to live be truly death, and death be reckoned life by those below?" ('Polyid.' Fragm. VII.: comp. 'Phryx.' Fragm. XIV.), and indicates a higher form of "corporate" life, such as St Paul expresses by the phrase "in Christ" (Gal. ii. 20; Col. iii. 4). Comp. xvii. 3, note.

Part of the thought is expressed in a saying in the Talmud: "What has man to do that he may live? Let him die. What has man to do that he may die? Let him live" ('Tamid,' 32 a). The last words of Edward the Confessor offer a closer parallel: "Weep not," he said, "I shall not die but live; and as I leave the land of the dying I trust to see the blessings of the Lord in the land of the living" (Richard of Cirencester, II. 292).

shall never die] According to the universal usage of St John this must be the sense of the original phrase (οὐ μὴ...εἰς τὸν αἰῶνα), and not "shall not die for ever." See iv. 14, viii. 51, 52, x. 28, xiii. 8.

Believest thou this?] *i.e. Is this thy belief?* (πιστεύεις τοῦτο;) not *Do you admit my statement?* (τούτῳ πιστεύεις;).

27. Martha accepts the revelation, and then falls back upon the confession of the faith which she had won. She does not say simply "I believe," repeating the form given; but "I—even I—the pronoun is emphatic—**have believed**"—"I have made this belief my own." And the belief which she expresses, though it falls short technically of Christ's declaration, being real as far as it goes, carries all else with it. He who holds firmly what he has gained will find afterwards that it contains far more than he has realised.

I have believed] Cf. iii. 18, vi. 69, xvi. 27, xx. 29; 1 John iv. 16, v. 10.

the Christ] of whom all the prophets spake.

the Son of God] who can restore the broken fellowship of man and His maker.

which should come (even **he that cometh**) *into the world*] for whom in both aspects men are ever looking. The title is peculiar. Comp. vi. 14; Matt. xi. 3; Luke vii. 19 f.

28—32. The Lord and Mary.

28. *had so said*] *had said* **this**: the confession in its many parts is yet one.

she went her way (**away**)] Her faith answering to the revelation left nothing more to be said. She had risen above private grief.

called...secretly, saying] **called, saying secretly.** In the three other places where the adverb occurs (Matt. i. 19, ii. 7; Acts xvi. 37) it precedes the word with which it is connected (λάθρᾳ εἰπ.). The message was given so that Mary might meet the Lord alone and that the ill-feeling of the Jews might not be called out.

The Master] used absolutely. Comp. xx. 16, xiii. 13 f.; Matt. xxvi. 18, and parallels. The title opens a glimpse into the private intercourse of the Lord and the disciples: so they spoke of Him.

calleth for (**calleth**) *thee*] The conversation with Martha is evidently not related fully. We cannot suppose (with Cyril of Alexandria) that Martha herself framed the message out of the general tenor of the Lord's words.

29. *As soon* (**And** *as soon*)...*arose* ... *and came* (**set forth**) *unto him*] The terms are singularly vivid. The momentary act (ἠγέρθη, contrast also ἀνέστη, *v.* 31) is contrasted with the continuous action which followed (ἤρχετο).

30. *but was* **still** *in that place...*] as though He would meet the sisters away from the crowd of mourners.

her, saying, She goeth unto the grave
to weep there.
32 Then when Mary was come
where Jesus was, and saw him, she
fell down at his feet, saying unto him,
Lord, if thou hadst been here, my
brother had not died.
33 When Jesus therefore saw her

---

31. *saying, She goeth* ...] **supposing** (δόξαντες) **that she was going...**

to weep (ἵνα κλαύσῃ, Vulg. *ut ploret*)] The verb describes the continuous, almost passionate, expression of sorrow. Comp. xvi. 20, xx. 11 ff. So it is used especially of wailing for the dead: Matt. ii. 18; Mark v. 38 f. &c., Luke vii. 13, viii. 52; Acts ix. 39. The word must be carefully distinguished from that used in *v.* 35.

The secrecy of Martha became of no avail, and so it came to pass that the work was wrought in the presence of a mixed body of spectators (Cyril).

32. *Then...was come ...feet* . . .] **Mary therefore, when she came** . . . *fell at his feet* with more demonstrative emotion than Martha (*v.* 21), as afterwards she is represented as "weeping," *v.* 33.

Lord, . . . died] The words are identical with those used by Martha save for the significant transposition of the pronoun (οὐκ ἄν μου ἀπ. ὁ ἀδ.), and represent without doubt what the sisters had said one to another: "If the Lord had been here . . . ."

(3) *The Miracle* (33—44).

The details of the working of the miracle bring out several features not so clearly seen elsewhere. The work is not a simple exertion of sovereign, impassive, power. It follows on a voluntary and deep apprehension of the sorrow in itself and in its source (*vv.* 33—38). At the same time the issue is absolutely known while the present pain is fully shared (39, 40). Such knowledge follows from the perfect sympathy between the Father and the Son. The Son's works are the open expression of the will of the Father which He has recognised (41, 42).

33—40. The Lord's grief. Faith on its trial.

33. No conversation and no answer follows the sister's address as before. This was the climax of natural grief which called for the act of power and not for the word of power only.

saw her (Mary) *weeping*] Martha seems to have calmly trusted to the promise of restoration which yet she could not understand (*v.* 39).

groaned in the spirit] The word rendered *groaned* (here and in *v.* 38, ἐνεβριμήσατο τῷ πνεύματι, Vulg. *fremuit* or *infremuit spiritu*), occurs in three other places in the New Testament (Matt. ix. 30; Mark i. 43, xiv. 5, where see notes).

In these places there is the notion of coercion springing out of displeasure. The feeling is called out by something seen in another which moves to anger rather than to sorrow. So here we may set aside those interpretations of the word which represent the emotion as grief only. For such a sense of the word there is no authority at all. So much is clear that the general notion of antagonism, or indignation, or anger, must be taken.

But further difficulty arises as to the construction. Is the verb absolute or not? Is the spirit the sphere, or the instrument, or the object of the emotion?

1. In the other passages of the New Testament the dative of the object is always added (and so also in Isai. xvii. 13, Symm.). If "the spirit" be the object here, what must we then understand by "the spirit" to which this vehement expression of feeling is directed? (α) Some have supposed that "the spirit" here is the seat of human feeling, which the Lord in respect of His divine nature checked in its intensity. But "the spirit" can hardly describe the passionate, sympathetic side of human nature; and this conception is inconsistent with the words "He troubled Himself" which follow. (β) Others again have taken "the spirit" to express, according to the common usage of the word, that part of the Lord's human nature whereby He was in immediate fellowship with His Father. And in this case two distinct views may be taken of the sense according as (1) the antagonism is with that which unduly shrinks from action, or (2) with that which unduly presses forward to action. If we follow the first idea the sense will be that the Lord "straitly charged," summoned up to vigorous conflict with death the spirit which might, humanly speaking, hang back from the terrible encounter which even through victory would bring His own death. If we follow the second the thought will be that the Lord checked the momentary impulse which arose within Him to exert His divine power at once, and first voluntarily brought Himself into complete sympathy with the sorrow which He came to relieve. According to the first of these two interpretations, "vehemently moved His spirit" would be parallel with "He troubled Himself:" according to the second, "He sternly checked His spirit" would be the complement of it. Both interpretations fall in with the general sense of the passage, but the second seems to be the most natural.

2. Against this view of the construction, which makes "the spirit" the object of the

weeping, and the Jews also weeping
which came with her, he groaned in
he the spirit, and †was troubled,
ed 34 And said, Where have ye laid
lf. him? They said unto him, Lord,
come and see.

35 Jesus wept.
36 Then said the Jews, Behold
how he loved him!
37 And some of them said, Could
not this man, [d]which opened the [d]chap. 9. 6
eyes of the blind, have caused that

---

verb, it may be urged that *in His Spirit* (τῷ πνεύματι) is used elsewhere in parallel passages to describe the sphere of feeling (Mark viii. 12; Luke x. 21; John xiii. 21). If then the verb be taken absolutely, which appears to be justified by the use below (ἐμβ. ἐν ἑαυτῷ), what is the implied object of the indignant antagonism? Various answers have been given. Some have supposed that the Lord felt indignation (*a*) with the Jews as hypocritical mourners at the scene, and soon to become traitors. But this seems to be inconsistent with the general tone of *vv.* 45 f.: and with the parallelism of the verse (*weeping*, *weeping*). Others (β) find the cause of indignation in the unbelief or misapprehension of the Jews and even of the sisters. But these faults have not been brought into prominence. The emotion is stirred by the sight of sorrow as sorrow, and not as unbelief or distrust or disappointment. Others again (γ) think that the Lord was indignant at the sight of the momentary triumph of evil, as death, or personally of Christ's adversary the devil, who had brought sin into the world, and death through sin, which was here shewn under circumstances of the deepest pathos. This interpretation accords well with the scope of the passage.

On the whole, therefore, the choice seems to lie between the senses 1 (β) (2), "He sternly checked His spirit;" and 2 (γ), "He groaned"—expressed, that is, indignant emotion—"in spirit." And the use of the word below (*v.* 38) leads to a decision in favour of the second of these renderings.

Whichever view however be taken, it must be remembered that the miracles of the Lord were not wrought by the simple word of power, but that in a mysterious way the element of sympathy entered into them. He took away the sufferings and diseases of men in some sense by taking them upon Himself, as is expressed in Matt. viii. 17. So it is said (Luke viii. 46) that He knew that power "had gone out from Him." Compare Hebr. v. 7. It has been suggested also that in this case the conflict was the heavier, seeing that Lazarus himself was called upon to undergo a life of suffering. The reader will recall Browning's interpretation of his after life in the 'Epistle of Karshish.'

in the spirit] St John distinctly recognises "the spirit" (πνεῦμα, xiii. 21, xix. 30) and "the soul" (ψυχή, x. 11 ff., xii. 27) as elements in the Lord's perfect humanity, like the other Evangelists (πνεῦμα, Matt. xxvii. 50; Mark ii. 8, viii. 12; Luke x. 21, xxiii. 46; ψυχή, Matt. xx. 28, xxvi. 38, and parallels).

was troubled] **troubled Himself.** It cannot be supposed that the peculiar turn of the phrase used here (ἐτάραξεν ἑαυτόν, Vulg. *turbavit se ipsum*), is equivalent to *was troubled* (ἐταράχθη, xiii. 21, Vulg. *turbatus est*). The force of it appears to be that the Lord took to Himself freely those feelings to which others are subject; and this feeling of horror and indignation He manifested outwardly. "Turbaris tu nolens: turbatus est Christus quia voluit" (Aug. *ad loc.* Compare his note on xiii. 21).

34. *Where . . . laid him?*] The question is remarkable as being the single place in the Gospel where the Lord speaks as seeking information. Yet see *v.* 17 (*found*).

They said (**say**) . . .] Apparently Martha and Mary, to whom we must suppose that the question was addressed.

come and see] The words are a strange echo of i. 46. (Rev. vi. 1, 5, 7.)

35. *wept*] The exact word (ἐδάκρυσεν, Vulg. *lacrimatus est*) occurs here only in the New Testament. It says just so much as that "tears fell from Him." Once it is recorded that Jesus "wept" with the sorrow of lamentation: Luke xix. 41 (ἔκλαυσεν). This weeping was for the death of a people, a church, and not of a friend. Here too the death of Lazarus is the type of the universal destiny of manhood. It must be noticed that St John notices incidentally many traits of the Lord's perfect manhood: thirst (iv. 7, xix. 28), fatigue (iv. 6), love (φιλεῖν, xx. 2); as in the other Gospels we find mention of hunger (Matt. iv. 2), joy (Luke x. 21), sorrow (Mark iii. 5; Matt. xxvi. 38), and anger (Mark iii. 5).

36. *Then said the Jews* . . .] **The Jews therefore said** . . . From *vv.* 45 f. it appears that some had joined the company who were not of Mary's friends.

how he loved (ἐφίλει Vulg. *amabat*) *him!*] Comp. xx. 2.

37. *And* (**But**) . . . *Could not* . . . *not have died* (**not die**)?] It is possible that the words are used in irony: as if the speakers would draw the conclusion that the former miracle must have been unreal, because no miracle was wrought when a deep personal feeling must have suggested it. Tears shewed love, and shewed it to be powerless. In

even this man should not have died?

38 Jesus therefore again groaning in himself cometh to the grave. It was a cave, and a stone lay upon it.

39 Jesus said, Take ye away the stone. Martha, the sister of him that was dead, saith unto him, Lord, by this time he stinketh: for he hath been *dead* four days.

40 Jesus saith unto her, Said I not unto thee, that, if thou wouldest believe, thou shouldest see the glory of God?

41 Then they took away the stone *from the place* where the dead was laid. And Jesus lifted up *his* eyes, and said, Father, I thank thee that thou hast heard me.

42 And I knew that thou hearest

---

favour of this view *v.* 46 (*But some of them* ...) may be quoted. But it is equally possible to regard the words as spoken in sincerity and ignorance. It can cause no difficulty that the tidings of the Galilæan raisings from the dead had not become current at Jerusalem (comp. Luke viii. 56).

of the blind] **of him that was blind** (τοῦ τ.). The phrase is a definite allusion to the miracle recorded in ch. ix.

38. *Jesus therefore*] as standing in the presence of this conflict of grief and doubt, and with a clear vision of the realities of death. His emotion at this point has less outward manifestation. If it be supposed that the last words were spoken in mockery, then we can see the occasion of the new struggle.

It was (**Now** *it was*) *a cave*...] The caves used as tombs were closed by stone doors, and in some cases by stones which could be rolled along a ledge to the opening into which they were fitted: Matt. xxviii. 2; Luke xxiv. 2; Mark xvi. 3, 4 (ἀνακεκύλισται). Thus the word rendered *lay upon it* does not necessarily describe a pit. The sense may be better given by **laid against it.**

39. *Jesus said* (**saith**), *Take ye away*] Comp. xx. 1, where the other Evangelists have *rolled away* or *rolled back*.

Martha ... saith ...] Mary having once expressed her last hope remains silent. Martha too had laid aside all present hope, at the Lord's bidding as she thought (*vv.* 23 ff.), and looked now for some future restoration, connected it may have been with the manifestation of Messiah's glory (*v.* 27).

the sister of him that was dead] The close relationship is mentioned in order to place in a clearer light the tender solicitude with which Martha shrinks from the disclosure of the ravages of death on one nearly bound to her.

for he hath been ...] It will be observed that the Evangelist gives no support to the exaggerated statements of later interpreters (*e.g.* Augustine, 'in Joh. Tract.' XLIX. 1, "resuscitavit fœtentem"). He simply records the natural words of the sister, who speaks of what she believes must be, and not of an ascertained fact.

dead *four days* (τεταρταῖος, Vulg. *quadriduanus*)] The full significance of the words appears from a passage of 'Bereshith R.' (p. 1143), quoted by Lightfoot: "It is a tradition of Ben Kaphra's: The very height of mourning is not till the third day. For three days the spirit wanders about the sepulchre, expecting if it may return into the body. But when it sees that the form or aspect of the face is changed [on the fourth day], then it hovers no more, but leaves the body to itself." "After three days," it is said elsewhere, "the countenance is changed."

40. The Lord directs Martha to the deeper meaning of His words. He does not simply say, *Thy brother shall rise again.* He answers the suggestion of corruption by the promise of "glory." The general description of the victory of faith (*v.* 26) contained necessarily a special promise. The fulfilment of that promise was a revelation of *the glory of God* (*v.* 4), for which Christ had from the first encouraged the sisters to look. In this way attention is called to the permanent lesson of the sign.

41—44. The Son's fellowship with the Father. He quickens by His word.

41. *Then* (**So**) *they took away the stone*] It was enough. No one gainsaid the Master's word. The remainder of the clause (*from the place* ... *laid*) must be omitted in accordance with most ancient authorities.

lifted up his *eyes*] xvii. 1.

Father] xii. 27 f.; xvii. 1, 24. 25; Matt. xi. 25; Luke xxiii. 34, 46.

I thank thee that thou hast heard (**heardest**) *me*] The prayer had been made before, and the answer to the prayer had been assured v. 4. It was now the occasion not for supplication but for thanksgiving. But this thanksgiving was not for any uncertain or unexpected gift (*v.* 22). It was rather a proclamation of fellowship with God. The sympathy in work (v. 19) and thought between the Father and the Son is always perfect and uninterrupted, and now it was revealed in action. Even in this sorrow the Son knew

me always: but because of the people which stand by I said *it*, that they may believe that thou hast sent me.

43 And when he thus had spoken, he cried with a loud voice, Lazarus, come forth.

44 And he that was dead came forth, bound hand and foot with graveclothes: and his face was bound about with a napkin. Jesus saith unto them, Loose him, and let him go.

45 Then many of the Jews which came to Mary, and had seen the things which Jesus did, believed on him.

46 But some of them went their ways to the Pharisees, and told them what things Jesus had done.

---

the end (*I* [ἐγὼ δέ] on my part, whatever may have been the misgivings of others, *knew that* ...); but that which He knew others denied, and by the open claim to the cooperation of God the Lord made a last solemn appeal to the belief of His adversaries.

This passage may help to an understanding of the true nature of prayer in the case of the Lord, as being the conscious realisation of the divine will, and not a petition for that which is contingent (comp. 1 John iii. 22). In the case of men prayer approximates to this more and more. It is not the setting up of the will of self, but the apprehension and taking to self of the divine will, which corresponds with the highest good of the individual. Comp. xv. 7, note.

42. At the close of *v.* 41 we must make a pause. The reflection which follows is spoken as a self-revelation to the disciples. It will be noticed also that the Lord uses the phrase "*because of the people* (**multitude**)," and not "*because of the Jews*," which would have been the natural phrase of the Evangelist, if this had been, as some have alleged, a free rendering of the Lord's words.

I said it] The thanksgiving for the prayer fulfilled was the proof of the divine mission of the Son. For by thanking God for a work not yet seen He gave a crucial test of His fellowship with God.

that they may believe] xvii. 21.

43. *cried*] xii. 13, xviii. 40, xix. 6, 12, 15.

with a loud voice] of intelligible command (φωνῇ). The contrast lies in the muttered incantations of sorcerers.

come forth (δεῦρο ἔξω, Vulg. *veni foras*)] Comp. xii. 17; Luke vii. 14, viii. 54. Death is treated as sleep (*v.* 11, v. 25, 28).

44. *And he* ...] **He**... The omission of the conjunction by the best ancient authorities increases the solemn emphasis of the statement.

It is unnecessary to speculate how Lazarus so bound came forth. The limbs may have been swathed separately, as was the Egyptian custom.

graveclothes] or, *bands* (κειρίαις, Vulg. *institis*); comp. xix. 40 (ὀθονίοις).

napkin] xx. 7. The trait marks an eyewitness.

Loose...*go* (ὑπάγειν)] The simple command, made necessary by the awe of the bystanders, corresponds with the Lord's action in the parallel records, Luke vii. 15 (*he gave him to his mother*); viii. 55 (*he commanded that something be given her to eat*). The narrative leaves the sequel untold.

(4) *The immediate results of the miracle* (45—57).

The miracle was a decisive test of faith and unbelief in those who witnessed it (45, 46). The Jews and the Lord prepare themselves for the end. The Council, acting now under the influence of the Sadducæan hierarchy, decide on the death of Christ (47—53); and Christ withdraws from "the Jews" and waits "with His disciples" in retirement for the feast time, while men anxiously look for His appearance (54—57). Comp. note on Luke ix. 51.

45 f. Men judge of the sign according to their nature.

45. *Then* ... *which came* ... *had seen* ...] *Many* **therefore** *of the Jews*, **even they that came** ... *and* **beheld**. "The Jews," as a general term here (comp. *v.* 37), seems to include others in addition to the friends of Mary. Curiosity may readily have led some to join the company on their way to the grave.

to Mary] The phrase is different from that in *v.* 19 (*to Martha and Mary*), in order to refer exactly to the circumstances of *v.* 31.

the things which Jesus did] **that** *which* **He** *did*. The singular, which has the best ancient authority, as compared with *the things which* (*v.* 46), marks the concentration of thought upon the crowning work.

46. *some of them*] of "the Jews," that is, and not as A.V. seems to express, of "the Jews who had come to Mary."

went their ways (**away**) *to the Pharisees*] Comp. v. 15, ix. 13. It is not possible to determine their motive. It may have been simple perplexity. There is no trace of malevolence (unless it be found in *v.* 37), while there is, on the other hand, no trace of

47 ¶ Then gathered the chief priests
and the Pharisees a council, and said,
What do we? for this man doeth
many miracles.
48 If we let him thus alone, all
men will believe on him: and the
Romans shall come and take away
both our place and nation.

49 And one of them, *named* Caiaphas, being the high priest that same
year, said unto them, Ye know nothing at all,
50 [e] Nor consider that it is expe- [e] cha 14.
dient for us, that one man should die
for the people, and that the whole
nation perish not.

---

faith. Want of sympathy made the messengers the occasion of the final catastrophe. Comp. v. 15.

47—53. The decision of the Sanhedrin.

47. *Then ... chief priests*] *The chief priests* **therefore**, inasmuch as it was evident that this last work could not but create a popular crisis at the coming feast.

The "chief priests"—the hierarchical Sadducæan party—take the lead. Comp. vii. 32 (true reading). So it is throughout: xi. 57, xii. 10, xviii. 3, 35, xix. 6, 15, 21. In the whole record after this chapter the Pharisees are mentioned only twice (xii. 19, 42), and then in a very different aspect.

The same fact appears also in the Synoptic narratives. The only mention of "the Pharisees" in the history of the Passion is Matt. xxvii. 62 (*the chief priests and Pharisees, i.e.* the Sanhedrin), while "the chief priests" take the place of the deadly enemies of Christ (Matt. xxvi. 3, 14, &c.).

So also in the Acts the Pharisees never stand out as the leading enemies of the Christian. On the contrary, in the two scenes where they appear they are represented as inclined to favour them: v. 34, xxiii. 6 ff. The priests and the Sadducees—who belonged to the same party—take up the opposition: iv. 1, v. 17, xxii. 30, xxiii. 14, xxv. 2. Saul, himself a Pharisee, was their emissary (ix. 21, xxvi. 10).

a council] that is, "a meeting of the Council." The word (*συνέδριον*, Vulg. *concilium*) occurs here only without the article (Matt. x. 17 is different).

What do we?] Not simply "What must we do?" (Acts iv. 16, *τί ποιήσομεν;*) as if there were room for quiet deliberation; but, What are we doing? What course are we taking? (*τί ποιοῦμεν;* Vulg. *Quid facimus?*) The crisis for action is present and urgent. There is no question of considering Christ's claims, even when His works are acknowledged. The matter is regarded only as it affects themselves.

this man] said contemptuously: ch. ix. 16.

48. *If we let...*] It is assumed that the multitude will place their own interpretation upon the miracles, and set Jesus at their head, and that He will lend Himself to their zeal. This being so, they argue that the Romans will interfere with their power because they are unable to suppress seditious risings.

take away] as something which was their possession. They look at the hypothetical catastrophe from its personal side as affecting themselves. The two finite verbs (*ἐλεύσονται καὶ ἄρουσιν*), instead of the participle and finite verb, give distinction to each element in the picture. Comp. xv. 16.

both our place and **our** *nation*] the visible seat of the theocracy, the Temple and the City (comp. Acts vi. 13, xxi. 28; [Matt. xxiv. 15]), and our civil organization.

49. *And* (**But**) *one of them*, named *Caiaphas...*] Comp. xviii. 13, note; Matt. xxvi. 3, note; Acts v. 17.

being ... year] *being* **high-priest that year**. The phrase is added not as though the office were annual, but to bring out that at this last crisis of the fate of the Jews Caiaphas was the religious head of the nation. So he spoke as their mouthpiece. Nothing can be more natural than that in the recollection of St John the year of the death of Christ —the end and the beginning—should stand out conspicuously from all history as "the year of the Lord." That Caiaphas was high-priest "in that year" (*v.* 51, xviii. 13) gave its character to his pontificate. Comp. c. xx. 19 (note); Mark iv. 35 (*that day*).

Ye know nothing] Ye (*ὑμεῖς*), who dwell on these scruples and these fears, do not even know the simplest rule of statesmanship, that one must be sacrificed to many. The emphatic pronoun is bitterly contemptuous. The unscrupulous Sadducee (Acts v. 17) contrasts the timid irresolution of mere Pharisees with his own clear policy of death (comp. xii. 19). They could not even see their own interest; they were dreaming of some kind of restraint when they might make use of a convenient victim. This thought brings out the force of the clause which follows: "*nor consider* (*λογίζεσθε*) *that it is expedient for* **you**" (not *for us*).

50. *the people...the...nation...*] The former title (*λαός*) marks the divine relationship: the latter (*ἔθνος*) the civil organization. Comp. Acts xxvi. 17, 23; 1 Pet. ii. 9 f.; (Luke ii. 10).

The word "nation" is applied to the Jews. Luke vii. 5, xxiii. 2, (John xviii. 35); Acts x. 22, xxiv. 2, 10, 17, xxvi. 4, xxviii. 19;

51 And this spake he not of himself: but being high priest that year, he prophesied that Jesus should die for that nation;

52 And not for that nation only, but that also he should gather together in one the children of God that were scattered abroad.

53 Then from that day forth they took counsel together for to put him to death.

54 Jesus therefore walked no more openly among the Jews; but went thence unto a country near to the wilderness, into a city called Ephraim, and there continued with his disciples.

55 ¶ And the Jews' passover was nigh at hand: and many went out of the country up to Jerusalem before the passover, to purify themselves.

56 Then sought they for Jesus, and spake among themselves, as they stood in the temple, What think ye, that he will not come to the feast?

---

and so constantly in the LXX., *e.g.* Exod. xxxiii. 1. This use is wholly distinct from that of the plural, "the nations" (τὰ ἔθνη).

51. *And ... spake ... that nation*] **Now this he said ... the** *nation.* The high-priest represented the divine headship of the Jews, and it was through him that an inspired decision was given on questions of doubt: Num. xxvii. 21. The true priest is, as Philo says, a prophet ('De Creat. Princ.' 8, II. p. 367). Here, in virtue of his office, Caiaphas so utters his own thoughts as to pronounce a sentence of God unconsciously. By a mysterious irony he interpreted the results of the death of Christ truly, though in a way directly opposite to that which he apprehended. Something of the irony which reaches its climax here is found in other parts of the Gospel: vii. 41, 42, xix. 21.

52. *that nation*] **the** *nation.* St John does not repeat the word "people." The Jews at this crisis had ceased to be "a people." They were a "nation" only, as one of the nations of the world. The elements of the true "people" were scattered throughout the world, as Jews, and Jews of the Dispersion, and Gentiles.

gather together **into** *one*] Not as locally united, but as partaking in a common life and relationship through and to Him. Comp. x. 16, xvii. 23. "The Christian at Rome feels the Indian to be one of his members, and Christ the Head of all" (Chrysostom).

the children of God...] These "scattered children of God" were truly "children of God," though they had not as yet received the full knowledge of their Father. Comp. x. 16. The title is not given by anticipation, but by a revelation of the true essence of things. They were the constituents of the new "people" (xii. 32; 1 John ii. 2), even as they witnessed to the original filial relation of man as man to God. The term *scattered abroad* (Vulg. *filios dei qui erant dispersi*) marks a broken unity and not only wide dispersion (Matt. xxvi. 31; Acts v. 37). Such is the state of mankind in relation to its divine original.

53. *Then from...took counsel together*] **So** *from...took counsel.* That which had been a desire before (v. 18), now became a settled plan. St John marks the growth of the hostility step by step: v. 16 ff., (vii. 1), vii. 32. 45 ff., viii. 59, ix. 22, x. 39.

54—57. A space of retirement and suspense.

54. *Jesus therefore ...*] withdrawing Himself from unnecessary perils.

walked] vii. 1.

openly] Comp. vii. 4.

went (**departed**) ... *unto a* (**the**) *country*] That is, the country as opposed to the parts about Jerusalem, as in the next verse.

Ephraim] Apparently the place mentioned with Beth-el in 2 Chro. xiii. 19 (Ophrah). In this case "the wilderness" is the wild country N.E. of Jerusalem.

continued ... disciples] **he abode** (ἔμεινεν) *with* **the** *disciples.*

55. *And* (**Now**) *the Jews' passover*] ii. 13 (otherwise in vi. 4). The contrast between the Jewish passover and "the Christian passover" is distinctly before the mind of the Evangelist (1 Cor. v. 7).

to purify themselves] Acts xxi. 24 ff.; ch. xviii. 28. For the passover absolute ritual purity was required by the general though not by a specific law of Moses: Lev. vii. 21. Comp. Num. ix. 10; 2 Chro. xxx. 17 ff. "Every man," saith R. Isaac, "is bound to purify himself for the feast" ('Rosh Hashanah' XVI. 2. Lightfoot). The phrase was transferred to a spiritual use, 1 John iii. 3.

56. *Then ... Jesus*] *They sought for Jesus* **therefore** ... as remembering the events of the last Feast, x. 22 ff. Comp. vii. 11 ff.

spake among themselves] *spake* **one with another** ... The phrase (ἔλεγον πρὸς ἀλλ.) seems to describe the many knots of questioners gathered from time to time.

as they stood in the temple] the scene of Christ's teaching.

What think ye? think ye *that* ...?] The words appear to be spoken in mere curiosity, without love or hatred.

57 Now both the chief priests and the Pharisees had given a commandment, that, if any man knew where he were, he should shew *it*, that they might take him.

CHAPTER XII.

1 Jesus excuseth Mary anointing his feet. 9 The people flock to see Lazarus. 10 The high priests consult to kill him. 12 Christ rideth into Jerusalem. 20 Greeks desire to see Jesus. 23 He foretelleth his death. 37 The Jews are generally blinded: 42 yet many chief rulers believe, but do not confess him: 44 therefore Jesus calleth earnestly for confession of faith.

THEN Jesus six days before the passover came to Bethany, where Lazarus was which had been dead, whom he raised from the dead.

2 There they made him a supper; and Martha served: but Lazarus was one of them that sat at the table with him.

3 Then took Mary a pound of

---

57. *Now* (omit *both*) *the chief priests...*] This was known, and hence came the anxious questionings of the people.

given a commandment] *given* **commands**. The plural seems to be on the whole the most probable reading. In either case the phrase implies that particular instructions had been given, and not only a general direction.

2. *The close of Christ's public ministry* (xii.).

St John's narrative differs from that of the Synoptists as to the close of the Lord's ministry, as it differs throughout, but in a converse manner. Hitherto he has recorded a controversy at Jerusalem which they omit. At the last visit they record a controversy which he omits. The omission follows from the structure of his gospel. He has already traced the conflict with Judaism in its essential features, and he has therefore no need to dwell on the final discussions which made clear to all what he has shewn in its successive stages. Hence he closes his record of the public ministry with three typical scenes in which the relation of the Lord to the disciples, to the multitude, and to the larger world outside is imaged, with a dark background of unbelief (xii. 1—36); and then he gives two summary judgments on the whole issue of Christ's work (37—50).

(1) *The feast at Bethany* (1—11).

This narrative must be compared with the Synoptic parallels (Matt. xxvi. 6 ff.; Mark xiv. 3 ff.), and contrasted with Luke vii. 36 ff. The event is transposed without any definite mark of time in the Synoptic narrative, in order to bring it into close connexion with the treachery of Judas which was called out by it. See notes on the passages referred to. In the incident recorded by St Luke the central fact is the washing of the Lord's feet "with tears." The sinner and the friend were equal in their devotion, yet widely separated in the manner in which they shewed it.

CHAP. XII. **1.** *Then Jesus...*] *Jesus* **therefore**... or, **So** *Jesus*... Such being the time (xi. 55) and the general circumstances (xi. 56 f.). The idea is suggested that "the hour" was now come (viii. 20).

six days before...] That is, apparently, on the 8th Nisan. See Matt. xxi. 1, note. If, as has been shewn to be the case (Matt. xxvi. additional note), the Crucifixion took place on the 14th Nisan, and if, which seems to be less certain, that day was a Friday, the date given by St John falls on the Sabbath. It must then be supposed that the feast took place in the evening after the close of the Sabbath. If the Passion fell on Thursday, for which strong reasons can be adduced ('Introd. to Gospels,' pp. 344 ff.), the arrival at Bethany took place on Friday. In this case the Sabbath was kept a day of rest, and followed by the feast. On either supposition the entrance into Jerusalem was made on the Sunday, the next (natural) day.

St John appears to mark the period as the new *Hexaemeron*, a solemn period of "six days," the time of the new Creation. His Gospel begins and closes with a sacred week (comp. i. 29, 35, 43, ii. 1).

came to Bethany] having joined the Paschal gathering from Galilee through Peræa near Jericho: Luke xviii. 35 and parallels. This pause at Bethany is not mentioned in the Synoptists; but there is nothing surprising in the omission. St Matthew and St Mark mention that during the days which followed the Lord "went out to Bethany" at night. (Matt. xxi. 17; Mark xi. 11. Comp. Luke xxi. 37.)

where Lazarus...the dead] We must read with the best ancient authorities, *where Lazarus was whom* **Jesus** *raised from the dead*. There is a solemn emphasis in the repetition of the Lord's name.

2. *There ... supper*] *They* (probably the people of the village) *made him* **therefore** ... *supper there*. The feast was a grateful recognition of the work done among them (*therefore*). The mention of Lazarus as one of those present hardly falls in with the idea that he and his sisters were the hosts. From Matt. xxvi. 6, Mark xiv. 4, it appears that the feast was held in the house of "Simon the leper."

ointment of spikenard, very costly, and anointed the feet of Jesus, and wiped his feet with her hair: and the house was filled with the odour of the ointment.

4 Then saith one of his disciples, Judas Iscariot, Simon's *son*, which should betray him,

5 Why was not this ointment sold for three hundred pence, and given to the poor?

6 This he said, not that he cared for the poor; but because he was a thief, and [a] had the bag, and bare what was put therein. [a] chap 13 29.

7 Then said Jesus, Let her alone:

2, 3. Martha and Mary at this common feast still fulfil their characteristic parts.

3. *Then took Mary...*] *Mary therefore took*...feeling by a divine intuition the full significance of the festival. The act of anointing was symbolic of consecration to a divine work. This Mary felt to be imminent. The name is not mentioned in the Synoptic narrative.

a pound (λίτραν, Vulg. *litram*)] xix. 39, note. St Matthew and St Mark say simply, "a flask" (ἀλάβαστρον). The word (λίτρα) was current among Jewish writers. Comp. Buxtorf, s. v. ליטרא.

of spikenard] The original phrase which occurs here and in St Mark (νάρδου πιστικῆς, Vulg. *nardi pistici* here and *nardi spicati* in St Mark) is of uncertain meaning. See note on Mark xiv. 3. In later Greek the epithet (πιστικός) is used in the sense of "trustworthy," and it may mean here "genuine," "pure;" or it may mean "liquid" (πίνω). Perhaps it is best to suppose that it is a local technical term.

the feet...his feet...] The repetition is significant, and so is the order of the original in the second clause: *with her hair his feet.* The Synoptists mention only the "pouring on the head." This was an ordinary mark of honour: Ps. xxiii. 5.

the house...ointment] The detail is peculiar to St John, and is one of those minute points which belong only to a personal impression at the time. The keen sense of the fragrance belongs to experience and not to imagination.

4. *Then ... Judas Iscariot*] **But** *Judas Iscariot, one of his disciples ... saith ...* Omit, with the best ancient authorities, *Simon's son.* These words are practically undisturbed in the three other places where they occur: vi. 71, xiii. 2, 26.

which should betray him] The purpose is represented as already present if hitherto undefined. Now it took shape. Judas expressed what others felt (*the disciples*, Matt. xxvi. 8; *some*, Mark xiv. 4). With him the thought answered to an evil spirit: with them it was a passing suggestion. It is natural that St John should assign to the one that which truly belonged to him only.

The parts of Mary and Judas in respect to the death of Christ are brought into sharp contrast. Mary in her devotion unconsciously provides for the honour of the dead. Judas in his selfishness unconsciously brings about the death itself.

5. *three hundred pence*] The same sum is mentioned in Mark xiv. 5. (So also *Let her alone*, *v.* 7.) Comp. Plin. 'H. N.' XII. 54 (25).

and given] *i.e.* the price of it.

the poor] The omission of the definite article in the original gives emphasis to the character as distinguished from the class. Comp. Matt. xi. 5; Luke xviii. 22.

The poor were not forgotten, as may be gathered from xiii. 29. And Christ Himself was the true image of the poor, as the poor hereafter were to be of Him.

6. *This he said...*] **Now** *this he said...*

and had the bag, and bare...] *and* **having** *the bag* **took** *what ...* The word "took" (ἐβάσταζεν, Vulg. *portabat* and *exportabat*) can from the context gain the sense *took away:* ch. xx. 15; and so it appears to be used here. If the simple meaning, *bare*, be adopted the force of the addition will be: "He was a thief, and from his position he could indulge his avarice at the expense of the disciples."

the bag] The box, or chest (γλωσσόκομον, Vulg. *loculos*). The word was adopted in Rabbinic. See Buxtorf, s. v. גלוסקמא.

The question has been asked why the office, which was itself a temptation, was assigned to Judas? The answer, so far as an answer can be given, seems to lie in the nature of things. Temptation commonly comes to us through that for which we are naturally fitted. Judas had gifts of management, we may suppose, and so also the trial which comes through that habit of mind. The work gave him the opportunity of self-conquest.

7. *Let her alone...*] The general sense of the answer is clear. This offering was but the beginning of the work indicated by it, and yet in itself most significant. The anointing to the sacred office was an anointing for the tomb. Judas found fault with an unfruitful expenditure. The words of the Lord shew that there is that which is unfruitful directly, and yet in accordance with our instincts. No one grudges the gifts of affection to the dead; and this natural sacrifice of love, acknowledged by all, Mary had made, though she knew not the full import of the act. The anointing

against the day of my burying hath she kept this.

8 For the poor always ye have with you; but me ye have not always.

9 Much people of the Jews therefore knew that he was there: and they came not for Jesus' sake only, but that they might see Lazarus also, whom he had raised from the dead.

10 ¶ But the chief priests consulted that they might put Lazarus also to death;

11 Because that by reason of him many of the Jews went away, and believed on Jesus.

12 ¶ [b] On the next day much peo- [b] M 8.
ple that were come to the feast, when they heard that Jesus was coming to Jerusalem,

---

was in truth the first stage in an embalming. Death would give the opportunity of completing what was begun; and that was rightly done which would find its fulfilment in the preparation for the burial.

The words as given in the Synoptists (Matt. xxvi. 12; Mark xiv. 8) dwell on the present import of the deed. St John recognises this, but points also to some further fulfilment which should follow.

against the day...she kept this] The reading which is supported by preponderant authority gives this sense: **Suffer her to keep it for the day of my preparation for burial** (Vulg. *ut in die sepulturæ meæ servet illud*). The interpretation of these words is difficult. If, as appears at first sight from the Synoptic parallels, the ointment was poured out, in what sense could it be said to be kept? Two explanations have been proposed: "Let her alone: she hath done all this, she hath preserved her treasure unsold, that she might keep it for my preparation for burial." And again: "Suffer her to keep it—this was her purpose, and let it not be disturbed—for my preparation for burial." Both explanations seem to fall in with the context. The latter perhaps with its apparent paradox is to be preferred, and the idiom by which a speaker throws himself into the past, and regards what is done as still a purpose, is common to all languages. It may, however, be questioned whether the Synoptists describe the consumption of the whole of the large amount of ointment mentioned by St John (κατέχεεν, Matt. xxvi. 7; Mark xiv. 3). Part may have been used for this preliminary, unconscious, embalming, and part reserved.

of my burying] **of my preparation for burial** (ἐνταφιασμοῦ). This preparation, the Lord implies, was now begun, though it was completed afterwards (xix. 40). Mary had done her part.

8. *always ye have*] Comp. Deut. xv. 11.

me ye have not always] For the other side of this truth see Matt. xxviii. 20, (xxv. 40). The juxtaposition by Christ of Himself and the poor is a revelation of His claims.

It is remarkable that the promise of the future record of the act of love (Matt. xxvi. 13; Mark xiv. 9) is omitted by the one evangelist who gives the name of the woman who shewed this devotion to her Master.

9. *Much...Jews*] **The common people** (ὁ ὄχλος πολύς, according to the most probable reading, in which the two words ὁ. π. form a compound noun, as in *v.* 12) *therefore of the Jews*... as contrasted here with their leaders (*v.* 10).

of the Jews] The original is not a simple genitive. A preposition is used (ἐκ, Vulg. *ex*) to mark the class *out of which* the multitude was formed. Comp. vi. 60, xvi. 17, iii. 1, vii. 48.

therefore] The report of the feast was naturally noised abroad.

knew] *i.e.* came to know: **learnt**.

came] perhaps on the evening of the Sabbath, when the feast took place.

not for Jesus' sake (διὰ τ. 'Ι.)...*but that* (ἀλλ' ἵνα)... The Evangelist gives the general and the specific purpose.

10. *the chief priests*] Here, as before, they are prepared for decisive measures. The sacrifice of the "one man" (xi. 50) soon involved the sacrifice of more.

11. *went away*] withdrew from their company (ὑπῆγον, Vulg. *abibant*).

(2) *The triumphal entry into Jerusalem* (14—19).

In this incident again St John's narrative is parallel to that of the Synoptists, but more exact in details. The Synoptists say nothing of the rest at Bethany; and it appears at first sight as if they placed the triumphal entry on the same day as the journey from Jericho (Matt. xx. 29 ff. and parallels). And yet in each case there is the sign of a break: Matt. xxi. 1; Luke xix. 29. And the return to Bethany noticed by St Mark (xi. 11) suggests at least that village for the starting point. The same passage of St Mark shews that the expulsion of the traders took place on the next day. So that it may be reasonably conjectured that the entry did not take place till the afternoon, when the Lord had time only to regard the whole state of things without doing any special work.

12. *the next day*] The day after the feast, according to the natural reckoning, *i.e.* on

13 Took branches of palm trees, and went forth to meet him, and cried, Hosanna: Blessed *is* the King of Israel that cometh in the name of the Lord.

14 And Jesus, when he had found a young ass, sat thereon; as it is written,

9. 9. 15 [c]Fear not, daughter of Sion: behold, thy King cometh, sitting on an ass's colt.

16 These things understood not his disciples at the first: but when Jesus was glorified, then remembered they that these things were written of him, and *that* they had done these things unto him.

17 The people therefore that was with him when he called Lazarus out of his grave, and raised him from the dead, bare record.

18 For this cause the people also met him, for that they heard that he had done this miracle.

19 The Pharisees therefore said among themselves, Perceive ye how

---

the morning of Sunday the 10th Nisan, in which the lamb was set apart, if the Crucifixion is placed on Thursday, Nisan 14.

much people (**the common people**) *that were come...*] contrasted again with the common people of the Jews. These were Galileans.

when they heard] from those who returned from Bethany. The whole narrative must be compared with Matt. xxi. 1 ff.; Mark xi. 1 ff.; Luke xix. 29 ff. in order to gain a sense of the tumultuous excitement of the scene. At last Christ yielded on the eve of the Passion to the enthusiasm of the people: vi. 15.

13. *branches of palm trees*] **the** *branches* (τὰ βαΐα) *of* **the** *palm-trees* which grew by the wayside. Compare 1 Macc. xiii. 51, the triumphal entry of Simon into Jerusalem. In Matt. xxi. 8; Mark xi. 8, the language is more general: "branches (κλάδους)" or "litter (στιβάδας) from the trees."

Hosanna] Ps. cxviii. (cxvii.) 25 (LXX. σῶσον δή). This Psalm appears to have been written as the dedication Psalm of the Second Temple; or, according to others, at the laying of its foundation-stone. In either case the significance of the reference is obvious. It has also been supposed that this Psalm was written for the Feast of Tabernacles after the Return (Ezra iii. 1 ff.). See note *ad loc.* If this were so the use of the palm-branches would gain a new force. The Psalm at present occupies a conspicuous place in the Jewish service for the New Moon.

The words *Blessed...Lord* in the Psalm are spoken by the Priest and Levites as a welcome to the worshippers at the temple.

Blessed...Lord] According to the true order: **Blessed is He that cometh in the name of the Lord, even the King of Israel.** The divine mission and the national work are set side by side, as in i. 49.

14. *when he had found*] St John is silent as to the method of "finding" detailed by the Synoptists.

a young ass] Comp. Mark xi. 2; Luke xix. 30 (πῶλον); Matt. xxi. 2 (ὄνον...καὶ πῶλον).

15. *Fear not...*] Zech. ix. 9. The action is a distinct symbol of humility. The Lord was separated indeed from the crowd, but yet in the humblest way. The stress must be laid not on the literal coincidence, but upon the fulfilment of the idea which the sign conveyed.

16. *These things ...*] the circumstances of the entry, the riding on the ass. The threefold repetition of the words is to be noticed.

understood not] Comp. ii. 22, vii. 39; (Luke xxiv. 25 f.). This entry was not apprehended in its true bearing till the Ascension had shewn the spiritual nature of the Lord's sovereignty.

glorified] *v.* 23 note.

they had done] The Evangelist assumes as known the part which the disciples had taken, though he has not himself spoken of it.

17. *The people* (**multitude**) *therefore that was with him when he...bare record* (**witness**)] To "bear witness" is used absolutely as in xix. 35. The phrase seems to imply more than simple attestation, and to carry with it some interpretation of the fact.

therefore] as stirred by the spiritual excitement of this great crisis.

when he called...and raised...] The parts of the miracle are distinguished just as they would be in the impressions of a spectator, and the speciality brings the scene forward as it was now described by those who had seen it.

18. *For this cause the people* (**multitude**) *...for that...*] Comp. v. 16 note; x. 17.

19. *The Pharisees therefore said...*] In a kind of irresolute despair. Their own plans had failed; and only the unscrupulous designs of "the chief priests" remained. "Signs" (*v.* 18) are a "trial," a "temptation" in the significant language of Deuteronomy (מסה, Deut. iv. 34, vii. 19, xxix. 3).

among themselves] as one body, and no longer part of a mixed assembly.

Perceive ye...] **Ye behold** (θεωρεῖτε, Vulg. *videtis*)... The words are a natural example of the way in which men blame the leaders who

ye prevail nothing? behold, the world is gone after him.

20 ¶ And there were certain Greeks among them that came up to worship at the feast:

21 The same came therefore to Philip, which was of Bethsaida of Galilee, and desired him, saying, Sir, we would see Jesus.

22 Philip cometh and telleth Andrew: and again Andrew and Philip tell Jesus.

23 ¶ And Jesus answered them, saying, The hour is come, that the Son of man should be glorified.

24 Verily, verily, I say unto you, Except a corn of wheat fall into the ground and die, it abideth alone:

---

carry out their own counsels. Some have strangely supposed that the words were spoken by the secret friends of the Lord. The verb may be imperative (as A. V.), but the indicative appears to be more likely.

behold (lo), *the world...*] The confession of the Samaritans (iv. 42) is fulfilled by this confession at Jerusalem. Wetstein gives Talmudic examples of the use of the phrase.

is gone **away**] So "they lost what they looked upon as their own" (Cyril).

(3) *The petition of the Greeks. The heavenly voice. The last warning* (20—36 a).

This section contains the only incident which St John has recorded from the eventful days between the entry into Jerusalem and the evening of the Last Supper. The time at which it occurred is not given distinctly, but from *v.* 36 it appears to have happened at the close of the conflict. It forms indeed the conclusion of the history. New characters appear on the scene, and the method and extent of the Lord's future sovereignty are plainly foreshewn (*v.* 32).

The narrative consists of three parts: the request (20—22); the answer, and the voice from heaven (23—33); the last warning (34—36 *a*).

20—22. These Greeks at the close of the Lord's Life bring the Gentile world into fellowship with Him as the Magi had done at the beginning. The tradition (Euseb. 'H. E.' I. 13) of the mission of Abgarus of Edessa has probably some reference to their request. The locality of the scene is not fixed. It may reasonably be placed in the outer court of the temple (*v.* 29).

20. *And* (**Now**)...*certain Greeks* (Ἕλληνες)] apparently proselytes of the gate; not Greek-speaking Jews (Ἑλληνισταί), nor yet simply heathen, seeing that they "came up" to the feast, though the whole burnt-offerings of Gentiles were accepted. See Lightfoot *ad loc.* Comp. ch. vii. 35; Acts xvii. 4, (viii. 27, x. 1).

that came up] *that* **went** *up* (ἀναβαινόντων). The Evangelist places himself outside the Holy City (ii. 13, v. 1, xi. 55).

21. *to Philip*] Philip's Greek name may indicate a foreign connexion. There was a considerable Greek population in Decapolis; and the mention of Philip's place of abode suggests some local reason for applying to him.

Sir] The glory of the Master gives honour to the disciple.

we would see Jesus] They use the human name and not the name of the office: *the Christ*. With them we may suppose that the Messianic hope passed into the larger hope of the "Saviour of the world" (iv. 42), so far as it assumed any definiteness.

see] Come into the presence of and then lay our thoughts before him.

22. *telleth Andrew*] He is unwilling without further counsel to grant or to refuse the strange request to bring Gentiles to the Lord. Comp. Matt. xv. 24.

Andrew] Andrew and Philip appear in connexion again i. 44, vi. 7, 8. Comp. Mark iii. 18.

and again...Jesus] **Andrew cometh** and *Philip*; **and they tell** *Jesus*. Andrew takes the first place. Comp. i. 41 ff. The change from the singular to the plural seems to mark the manner in which they gain courage together to bear the request to their Master.

23—36 a. The answer involves far more than the mere admission of the Greeks to the Lord's Presence. The extension of the Gospel to the world rests on the Death of Christ, on His rejection by His own people. This is on all sides a mystery, partly intelligible by what we see (23—26), yet, like a divine voice, only intelligible to those who receive it with sympathy (27—33), while the time of trial is short (34—36 *a*).

23. *Jesus answered* (**answereth**) *them*] the disciples. Probably the Greeks came with the disciples. The Lord then in their hearing, and in the hearing of the multitude, unfolded the deepest significance of their request in relation to the consummation of His own work. It is not easy to suppose either that the interview with the Greeks preceded *v.* 23, or that the interview was refused, or that it followed after this scene. On the other hand St John has preserved just so much of what was said in reply to their request as gives the permanent interpretation of the incident, and no more.

The hour is come] The inquiry of the Greeks heralded the proclamation of the Gospel to

but if it die, it bringeth forth much fruit.

x. 10. 25 [d]He that loveth his life shall lose it; and he that hateth his life in this world shall keep it unto life eternal.

26 If any man serve me, let him follow me; and where I am, there shall also my servant be: if any man serve me, him will *my* Father honour.

27 Now is my soul troubled; and what shall I say? Father, save me

---

the Gentiles. For this the Passion and the Resurrection were the necessary conditions. Comp. x. 15 ff.

The hour] xiii. 1, note.

that the Son of man...] The sentence stands in contrast with xi. 4. There the central idea is that of the Son as the representative of the Father in power: here that of the Son as the representative of humanity.

that (ἵνα)...*should be...*] This issue was part of the divine counsel. Comp. xiii. 1, xvi. 2 note, 32.

be glorified] The glory of the Son of man lay in the bringing to Himself of all men (*v.* 32) by the Cross, and rising through death above death (comp. *v.* 32, note). In this victory over death by death there is the complete antithesis to the Greek view of life, in which death was hidden. Comp. *v.* 16, vii. 39, xiii. 31 note, xvii. 1 note, ii. 11.

24—27. The fact which has been announced in *v.* 23 (*that...be glorified*) is illustrated in three successive stages. It is shewn that fuller life comes through death, glory through sacrifice, first by an example from nature (*v.* 24), then in the experience of discipleship (*v.* 25 f.), and lastly in relation to the Lord's Own work: He came that He might lay down His life in order to take it again (*v.* 27. Comp. x. 17).

24. *Verily, verily...*] The law of higher life through death is shewn in the simplest analogy. Every nobler form of being presupposes the loss of that which precedes.

a corn of wheat] **the** *corn...*, that element which has in it the principle of the new growth. Comp. 1 Cor. xv. 36 f.

fall into the ground] separated, that is, from all in which it had lived before. The same act is on one side a sowing and on the other a falling.

it abideth **by itself** *alone* (αὐτὸς μόνος)] In this sense isolation is truly death. Comp. vi. 51, note.

25. The general truth of *v.* 24 is presented in its final antithesis in relation to human life. Sacrifice, self-surrender, death, is the condition of the highest life: selfishness is the destruction of life. The language is closely parallel to words recorded by the Synoptists: Matt. x. 38 f.; Luke xvii. 33.

loveth...hateth his life] The original word (ψυχή) rendered "life" here and "soul" in *v.* 27 is comprehensive, and describes that which in each case expresses the fulness of man's continuous being. He who seeks to gather round himself that which is perishable, so far perishes with it: he who divests himself of all that is of this world only, so far prepares himself for the higher life.

shall lose it] **loseth** *it*, or perhaps, **destroyeth** *it* (ἀπολλύει). The selfish man works his own destruction. Comp. Matt. x. 39, xvi. 25; Luke ix. 24.

hateth] Luke xiv. 26, note.

in this world] so far as it is bound up with that which is outward and transitory. "This world" is opposed to the kingdom of Christ.

26. The truth expressed in *vv.* 24, 25 is applied specially to the claims of discipleship. Service is progressive (comp. xxi. 19 ff.), and the effort of "following" does not fail of its issue. Even now the disciple is with his Master (Col. iii. 3; comp. xiv. 3, xvii. 24). The "me" is in each case emphatic; and the repetition of the pronouns in the original is remarkable (ἐμοί, ἐμοί, ἐγώ, ὁ ἐμός).

follow] Comp. xxi. 19 ff., xiii. 33, 36. "Ubi bene erit sine illo? aut quando esse male poterit cum illo?" (Aug. *ad loc.*)

if any man...my (**the**) *Father honour*] There is a significant change of order in this clause. The emphasis lies on *any one*, Jew or Greek, and not on *me* as before. He who honours is not described as "my Father," but as "the Father," the Father of the Son and of the believer. Comp. Additional Note on iv. 21.

27. That which is true of the believer is true also of Christ. He gains His glory through suffering (Phil. ii. 9); and so He turns now from the general law to its personal application to Himself.

It will be noticed that in the life of the Lord we constantly find transitions from joy to sorrow (comp. Luke xix. 38 ff., 41 ff.); and conversely (Matt. xi. 20 ff., 25 ff.).

my soul (ψυχή)] in which was gathered up the fulness of present human life (*v.* 25, note). Comp. x. 11 ff.; Matt. xx. 28, xxvi. 38; Mark x. 45, xiv. 34; Acts ii. 27. With this "the spirit" is contrasted xi. 33, note. The "soul" (ψυχή, Vulg. *anima*) is the seat of the human affections: the "spirit" (πνεῦμα, Vulg. *spiritus*) is the seat of the religious affections, by which man holds converse with God.

is...troubled] The shock has come already, but the effects continue (τετάρακται, Vulg. *turbata est*; comp. xi. 33, note). The presence and the petition of the Greeks foreshadowed the judgment on the ancient people, and brought forward the means by which it would be accomplished. The prospect of this cata-

from this hour: but for this cause came I unto this hour.

28 Father, glorify thy name. Then came there a voice from heaven, *saying*, I have both glorified *it*, and will glorify *it* again.

29 The people therefore, that stood by, and heard *it*, said that it thundered: others said, An angel spake to him.

30 Jesus answered and said, This voice came not because of me, but for your sakes.

---

strophe was perhaps the crisis of the Lord's present conflict.

what shall I (*what* **must** *I*) *say?*] The conflict, as at the Temptation, is a real one. The thought of a possible deliverance is present though not admitted.

Father...hour] These words have been interpreted in two very different modes. Some have taken them as part of the interrogation: "Shall I say, save me from this hour?" and others have taken them as a real prayer. Against the former interpretation it may be urged that it does not fall in with the parallel clause which follows: *Father, glorify Thy name;* nor with the intensity of the passage; nor yet with the kindred passages in the Synoptists (Matt. xxvi. 39 and parallels).

If then the words be taken as a prayer for deliverance it is important to notice the exact form in which it is expressed. The petition is for deliverance *out of* (σῶσον ἐκ, Vulg. *salvifica me ex hora hac*) and not for deliverance *from* (ἀπό) the crisis of trial. So that the sense appears to be "bring me safely out of the conflict" (Hebr. v. 7), and not simply "keep me from entering into it." Thus the words are the true answer to the preceding question. "In whatever way it may be Thy will to try me, save me out of the deep of affliction." There is complete trust even in the depth of sorrow. Comp. Matt. *l. c.*

If this sense be adopted the adversative particle which follows (*but...*) has the meaning: "Nay, this I need not say: the end is known." The petition might seem to imply uncertainty, but here there was none. If, on the other hand, the words are taken as a prayer for deliverance *from* the conflict, or interrogatively, the *but* is a simple corrective: "Nay, this I cannot say, for I came to sustain it."

for this cause] Christ came that He might enter into the last conflict with sin and death, and being saved out of it win a triumph over death by dying. If the failure of Israel was a chief element in the Lord's sorrow, this was a step towards the universal work which He came to accomplish (Rom. xi. 11). Some have supposed that the words are anticipatory of the prayer which follows: "I came that Thy name might be glorified." This thought, however, is more naturally included in the former interpretation. The name of the Father was glorified by the Son's absolute self-sacrifice.

28. *Father, glorify thy name*] Reveal to men, and here to Greeks as the representatives of the heathen world, in all its majesty the fulness of this Thy title shewn in the Son. How this should be is not expressed, but the reference is clearly to the thought of *v.* 32. The voice is the assurance and not the actual fulfilment.

Then came there...] **Then came therefore...** The expression of the prayer carried with it the appropriate pledge of fulfilment.

a voice from (**out of**) *heaven*] The utterance was real and objective, that is, it was not a mere thunder-clap interpreted in this sense; yet, like all spiritual things, this voice required preparedness in the organ to which it was addressed. Thus in the *Bath Kol* the divine message was not the physical sound in itself but the offspring of it Wünsche on Mark i. 11 quotes an interesting tradition of a divine voice which witnessed to the worth of Hillel.

I have both glorified...] Or, more closely, *I* **both glorified** *it*, that is, My name as Father, in past time, *and will glorify it.* The reference is to historic facts in the life of Christ, as, for example, to the signs which He wrought as signs of the Father (comp. v. 23, xi. 40); or perhaps more especially to the great crises in His ministry, the Baptism (Matt. iii. 17) and the Transfiguration (Matt. xvii. 5), in which His Sonship, and so the Father's character, was revealed.

will glorify it again] This glorification was not a mere repetition but a corresponding manifestation of the Father's glory. The glorification during the limited, earthly ministry to Israel was followed by a glorification answering to the proclamation of the universal Gospel to the world.

29. *The people* (**multitude**)...*that stood by*] iii. 29; Matt. xxvi. 73. They were probably in the outer court of the temple.

and heard] Omit *it.* The object is left purposely undefined. For the mass the voice was mere sound. The apprehension of a divine voice depends upon man's capacity for hearing. This is seen specially in the narrative of St Paul's conversion: Acts ix. 7, xxii. 9, xxvi. 13 f. Comp. Acts ii. 6, 12 f.

that it **had** *thundered...An angel spake* (**hath spoken**) *to him*] These last felt that the utterance was articulate though they could not hear the words.

30. *Jesus answered*] the questionings which were rising in the hearts of the people and of the disciples, while yet He meets them only by pointing to the significance of the voice for those who received it.

This voice...sakes] *This voice* **hath not come for my sake**, *but for your sakes.* Comp.

31 Now is the judgment of this world: now shall the prince of this world be cast out.
32 And I, if I be lifted up from the earth, will draw all *men* unto me.
33 This he said, signifying what death he should die.
34 The people answered him, [e] We have heard out of the law that Christ abideth for ever: and how sayest

[e] Psal. 110. 4.

---

xi. 42. It came to test their faith and to strengthen it; and at the same time to make clear the importance of the crisis revealed by the Gentile request. The order of the original text is emphatic: "It is not for my sake this voice hath come..."

31. *Now is the judgment of this world*] Or rather, *a judgment*, one of many if a most solemn one. The Passion was the judgment of the world (Luke ii. 34 f.), which shewed both men's thoughts towards Christ, and the true position of the world towards God.

this world] Jew and Gentile are alike included in the sentence; but probably the thought is most clearly expressed in the condemnation of the Greek idolatry of beauty and pleasure.

Now...now] The balanced form of the sentence answers to solemn emotion.

the prince of this world] Comp. xiv. 30, xvi. 11; (Eph. ii. 2, vi. 12; 2 Cor. iv. 4). The title is common in Jewish writers (שר העולם). According to a remarkable tradition quoted by Lightfoot (*ad loc.*) God gave the whole world except Israel into the power of the angel of death (comp. Hebr. ii. 14). Under this image "the prince of the world" stands in absolute contrast to the "author of life" (Acts iii. 15). It should however be added that the angel of death was in no way connected with Satan.

shall...be cast out] from the region of his present sway. Comp. 1 John v. 19; (Luke x. 18).

32. *And I...unto me*] The opposition to the *prince of this world* is made as sharp as possible (κἀγὼ ἂν ὑ.). The phrase by which the Lord indicates His death (*be lifted up*, iii. 14, viii. 28; comp. Acts ii. 33, v. 31) is characteristic of the view under which St John represents the Passion. He does not ever, like St Paul (*e.g.* Phil. ii. 8, 9), separate it as a crisis of humiliation from the glory which followed. The "lifting up" includes death and the victory over death. In this aspect the crisis of the Passion itself is regarded as a glorification (xiii. 31); and St John sees the Lord's triumph in this rather than in the Return. Comp. 1 John v. 4—6.

from the earth] The original phrase (ἐκ τῆς γῆς) expresses not only "above the earth," but "out of the earth," as taken from the sphere of earthly action. Thus there appears to be a reference to the Resurrection, and not only to the Crucifixion. At the same time it is clear from iii. 14 f. that it is by the elevation on the Cross that Christ is offered as the Saviour to the vision of believers.

will draw] vi. 44; (Hos. xi. 4, Heb.). The Son "draws" by the Spirit which He sends, xvi. 7. And there is need of this loving violence, for men are "held back by the enemy."

all men] The phrase must not be limited in any way. It cannot mean merely "Gentiles as well as Jews," or "the elect," or "all who believe." We must receive it as it stands: Rom. v. 18, (viii. 32); 2 Cor. v. 15; (Eph. i. 10); 1 Tim. ii. 6; Hebr. ii. 9; 1 John ii. 2. The remarkable reading "all things" (πάντα, Vulg. *omnia*) points to a still wider application of Redemption (Col i. 20), though Augustine explains it of "creaturæ integritatem, id est, spiritum et animam et corpus" (*ad loc.*).

unto me] *unto* **myself**. Emphatically as the one centre of the Church, in whom all find their completeness.

33. *This...what death...*] **But** *this...signifying* **by** *what* (ποίῳ) *death...*, not as if this were the primary end of the words, but the nature of Christ's atoning death was indicated in the form of the reference to it. Cp. xviii. 32, xxi. 19.

34. *The people answered...*] **The multitude therefore** *answered...*, when they found the claims to the prerogatives of Messiahship put forth by one who called himself the Son of man (*v.* 23), and spoke of his removal from the people whom he should save. The difficulty was twofold: firstly, that the Lord assumed a universal and not a special title ("Son of man" and not "Son of David"), and also that this sovereignty was not to be exercised on earth.

out of the law] out of the book of the Covenant, the Old Testament generally. Comp. x. 34, note.

that Christ...] *that* **the** *Christ...* The belief that *the Christ abideth for ever* was probably based on Isai. ix. 7; Ps. cx. 4, lxxxix. 4 f.; Ezek. xxxvii. 25. Comp. Luke i. 32 f.

how sayest thou (σύ)...] in opposition to the Law, or, at least, in language which we cannot reconcile with it.

The Son of man...] The title is not recorded by St John as having been used here in this connexion by the Lord, but the teaching in *v.* 32 naturally led to it (*v.* 23). Such a quotation from unrecorded words is a significant illustration of the compression of the narrative. The Evangelist gives the critical elements of the discourse only. The complete phrase occurs iii. 14.

thou, The Son of man must be lifted up? who is this Son of man?

35 Then Jesus said unto them, Yet a little while is the light with you. Walk while ye have the light, lest darkness come upon you: for he that walketh in darkness knoweth not whither he goeth.

36 While ye have light, believe in the light, that ye may be the children of light. These things spake Jesus, and departed, and did hide himself from them.

37 ¶ But though he had done so many miracles before them, yet they believed not on him:

38 That the saying of Esaias the prophet might be fulfilled, which he

---

must...] Comp. xx. 9 note.

be lifted up] Comp. iii. 14 note.

who is...] The question clearly shews that the title "the Son of man" was not necessarily identified with "the Christ." Comp. Additional Note on ch. i. § 6, p. 34.

35. *Then Jesus said*...] *Jesus* **therefore** *said*... meeting their difficulties by charging them to use the opportunities which they still had for fuller knowledge. There was yet time, though the time was short. The words are not described as an "answer" (*v.* 30), but as an independent utterance.

a little while] The words correspond with the plea "abideth for ever." Comp. vii. 33, xiii. 33, xiv. 19, xvi. 16 ff.

with you] **among** *you*; in your midst. Comp. i. 14; (Acts ii. 29).

Walk] Progress was both possible and a necessary duty while the light shone, and as the light shone.

lest...come upon you] **that** *darkness* **overtake you not**, as it will do if you do not advance to a fuller knowledge of myself and my work before the coming time of trial. Then all movement will be perilous. You will wander in a wilderness without "the pillar of fire." Comp. Jer. xiii. 16.

overtake (καταλάβῃ, Vulg. *comprehendant*)] The same word is used i. 5, vi. 17 var. lect.; 1 Thess. v. 4.

for he that...in darkness...] **and** *he that... in* **the** *darkness*... The clause is added as the most general form of the natural completion of the former sentence: "and ye may not know whither ye go."

36. *While ye have* **the** *light*] There was need of progress and there was also need of faith, which should support hereafter. There is a change of order in the repeated clause: *Walk as ye have the light*, and *as ye have the light believe on the light*.

that ye...of light] *that ye may* **become sons of light**, and so have light in yourselves. Comp. Luke xvi. 8; 1 Thess. v. 5; (Eph. v. 8, *children*). This glorious transformation is the last issue of faith. Thus the last recorded words of Christ to the world are an exhortation and a promise. Comp. xvi. 33.

(4) *The judgment of the Evangelist* (36 b—43).

In this section the Evangelist speaks in his own person and connects the apparent failure of the Lord's work with the prophetic teaching of Isaiah. In form the passage resembles xx. 30 f., xxi. 23—25; and, in a less degree, iii. 16—21, 31—36.

These things...and did hide himself (**was hidden**, ἐκρύβη, Vulg. *abscondit se*)] viii. 59. The hiding was not His work but the work of His adversaries, as being the result of their want of faith.

37. *so many*] This seems to be the meaning of the word (τοσαῦτα), and not *so great*. Comp. vi. 9, xxi. 11. Of these many works (comp. ii. 23, iv. 45, vii. 31, xi. 47, xx. 30) St John has recorded only seven as types.

before them] There was no excuse for ignorance, Acts xxvi. 26.

they believed not on him] with self-devoted, trustful, patient faith in life; though many did believe with the concealed adhesion of conviction, *v.* 42.

38. *That the saying* (**word**)...] Such a fulfilment was a part of the design of God, and so necessary; inasmuch as the prophetic word described the actual relation of the divine message to those who heard it. This relation, which was already present to the divine Vision and had been fulfilled in the type, must needs be realised in the antitype; so that the complaint uttered by Isaiah against his own contemporaries might have been uttered even more truly by Christ.

The prophecy itself (Isai. liii. 1) sets forth the two sides of the divine testimony, the message as to the servant of God which appealed to the inward perception of truth; and the signs of the power of God which appealed outwardly to those who looked upon them. In both respects the testimony failed to find acceptance. The message was not believed; the signs were not interpreted. There is an interesting examination of the use of Isai. liii. in the New Testament in Taylor's 'Gospel in the Law,' ch. v.

who hath believed...hath...been revealed?] More exactly as a retrospect of failure: **who believed...was...revealed?**

our report?] If the words are spoken by the prophet, according to the common interpretation, then *our report* may mean either "the message which came from us, which we delivered," or "the message which came to

53. spake, [f] Lord, who hath believed our
o. report? and to whom hath the arm of
the Lord been revealed?

39 Therefore they could not believe, because that Esaias said again,

13. 40 [g] He hath blinded their eyes, and
hardened their heart; that they should not see with *their* eyes, nor understand with *their* heart, and be converted, and I should heal them.

41 These things said Esaias, when he saw his glory, and spake of him.

42 ¶ Nevertheless among the chief rulers also many believed on him;

---

us, which we received." The former interpretation is the more natural. Comp. Matt. iv. 24, xiv. 1, xxiv. 6.

the arm of the Lord] Luke i. 51; Acts xiii. 17.

39. *Therefore...*] **For this cause**, namely, that in the order of Providence the Gospel must be met by general unbelief, *they could not believe*... The fact which has been already noted (*they did not believe*) is now traced back to its ultimate origin which lay in the divine action. They did not believe, and they could not believe, **for** *that* **Isaiah** *said again: He* (that is God) *hath*... The want of belief was involved in the necessary truth of the prophetic word. This fulfilment again involved in the incredulous an inability to believe consequent upon the actual working of God according to His fixed laws. Comp. Rom. x. 16. And yet, further, this working of God, as we look at it in the order of succession, was consequent upon man's prior unbelief. The Jews were already in an unnatural and diseased state when the prophet was sent to them. Then came the punishment whereby those who would not give glory to God by willing faith were made to subserve to His glory. The revelation of Christ, like the preaching of Isaiah, was the very power by which the existing form of unbelief was carried to its full development.

Esaias said] The quotation differs alike from Heb. and LXX. St John transfers to God what is represented by Isaiah as the mission of the prophet (Isai. vi. 10); while the healing on the other hand is ascribed to Christ. Comp. Matt. xiii. 14 f.; Acts xxviii. 26 f.

Augustine's discussion of this passage is full of interest, though he examines it from a single and limited point of view: "hoc propheta prædixit quia Deus hoc futurum esse præscivit...malam quippe eorum voluntatem prævidit Deus."

40. *He hath blinded...and hardened...*] The change of tense in the original is remarkable: *He hath blinded...and he hardened* (ἐπώρωσεν)... The verb translated "hardened" describes the formation of a "callus" (πῶρος) in a part of the body, as the eyes (Job xvii. 7). Comp. Mark vi. 52, viii. 17; Rom. xi. 7; 2 Cor. iii. 14.

understand] **perceive** (νοήσωσιν). The word in Mark iv. 12 is different (συνιῶσιν).

With regard to the general scope of the passage it may be observed that: 1. As a fact disregard of impulses and motives to right-doing makes it more and more hard to obey them. 2. We may regard this law as acting mechanically; or we may see in it, in relation to man, the action of a divine power. 3. The latter supposition introduces no new difficulty; but on the other hand places this stern law in connexion with a wider scheme of action, which makes hope possible.

In this connexion it is important to observe that a divine "cannot" answers to the divine "must" (xx. 9, note). This "cannot" expresses a moral and not an external or arbitrary impossibility. Thus it defines while it does not limit the action of the Son (v. 19, 30; comp. Mark vi. 5); and so fixes the conditions of discipleship (iii. 5, vi. 44, 65, vii. 34—36, viii. 21 f.), of understanding (iii. 3, viii. 43 f.; xiv. 17), of faith (as here; comp. v. 44), of fruitfulness (xv. 4 f.), of progress (xvi. 12).

41. *when...glory*] According to the reading of the most ancient authorities: **because** *he saw his* (Christ's) *glory*... The prophecy was not only given at the time of the celestial vision but in consequence of it. The sight of the divine glory made clear the vast chasm between God and the people who bore His name.

he saw his glory, and spake of him (Christ)] The Targum renders the original words of Isaiah, *I saw the Lord*, by *I saw the Lord's glory*. St John states the truth to which this expression points, and identifies the divine Person seen by Isaiah with Christ. Thus what Isaiah saw was the glory of the Word, and of Him he spoke. His message, that is, was not merely addressed to his contemporaries only, but reached to the time of the fuller manifestation to the world of that glory which he himself saw in a vision. It is uncertain whether the last clause (*spake of him*) depends on the *because* or not; but the position of the *of him* in the original points to this connexion.

42. *Nevertheless among* (**even of**) *the... rulers* (the members of the Sanhedrin: iii. 1, vii. 26, 48) *many believed on him*] This complete intellectual faith (so to speak) is really the climax of unbelief. The conviction found no expression in life.

believed on him] It is remarkable that St

but because of the Pharisees they did
not confess *him*, lest they should be
put out of the synagogue:

[h] chap. 5. 44
43 [h]For they loved the praise
of men more than the praise of
God.

44 ¶ Jesus cried and said, He that
believeth on me, believeth not on me,
but on him that sent me.

45 And he that seeth me seeth
him that sent me.

46 [i]I am come a light into the [i] cha[p.] 19.
world, that whosoever believeth on
me should not abide in darkness.

John uses of this belief the phrase which marks the completeness of belief (ἐπιστ. εἰς). The belief only lacked confession, but this defect was fatal. Comp. ii. 23, where also a belief complete in itself is practically imperfect.

because of the Pharisees] Comp. vii. 13, ix. 22 (*the Jews*).

did not confess] *did not* **make confession.** The verb is used absolutely. Comp. Rom. x. 9, 10. The imperfect tense (ὡμολόγουν, Vulg. *confitebantur*) marks the continued shrinking from the act of faith.

lest they should (**that they should not**) *be put out of the synagogue*] ix. 22.

43. *the praise* (**glory**) *of men...praise* (**glory**) *of God*] Comp. v. 44. The words suggest a contrast with that vision of the divine glory in which God shewed what He had prepared for men (*v.* 41). Comp. Rom. iii. 23.

(5) *The judgment of the Lord* (44—50).

This final judgment appears to contain a summary of the Lord's teaching gathered up in the view of this crisis, and not to be a new utterance. It falls into three parts: the position of the believer (44—46), and of the unbeliever (47—49), and the fruit of the message (50). The Lord first speaks of His Person (44—46), and then of His words (47—50).

44. But *Jesus cried...*] The witness of the Lord is set over against the witness of the prophet and the unbelief of the people. It expresses as completely as possible His absolute self-sacrifice as contrasted with the selfishness of His enemies. He is lost (so to speak) in Him that sent Him. He judges no man. His teaching is simply the expression of His Father's command.

cried (ἔκραξε, Vulg. *clamabat*)] vii. 28, 37. The testimony was so given as to claim and arrest attention; and it was given once and for all (contrast Luke xviii. 39).

believeth not on me, but...] He looks beneath the surface and acknowledges a divine presence realised in and through me. As yet it was impossible for men to know how faith could repose in the Son Himself.

on him that sent me] not simply on "the Father" as representing a general connexion, but on Him who is the source of the special revelation of Christ.

45. *he that seeth* (**beholdeth**) *me seeth* (**beholdeth**)...] In this case the negative clause is not found. So far as the believer beheld Christ, he beheld Him from whom Christ came. Belief passed through the veil: vision apprehended outwardly God in His relation to men. Comp. Matt. x. 40. For the sense of "behold" see xvi. 16.

The form of the sentence differs in each particular from xiv. 9: *beholdeth* occupies the place of *hath seen; Him that sent me* of *the Father*. The thought here is of the intent, patient, progressive contemplation of Christ leading to the fuller knowledge of Him from whom He came; thus the thought is of the one decisive moment, of which the results were permanent.

The title "Father" emphasizes the idea of the natural, essential relation to the Son and to men: the phrase "He that sent me" brings out the idea of the special mission, as involving a peculiar charge and corresponding authority. Comp. iv. 34, v. 24, 30, vi. 38, vii. 16, (18), 28, 33, viii. 26, 29, ix. 4, xiii. 20, xv. 21, xvi. 5 (peculiar to St John, and used only by the Lord). The two ideas are combined, v. 23, 37, vi. 44, viii. 16, 18, xii. 49, xiv. 24; and distinguished, vi. 39, 40.

46. *I am come a light* (or as *light*) *into...*] This was the office of Christ, to make all things clear. His Person when seen in its fulness illuminates the mysteries of life. There is darkness over the world, and without Him it must remain. Faith in Him brings purer vision. Comp. *v.* 36. See also iii. 19, viii. 12, ix. 5, (i. 4).

There is a significant contrast between *I am come* (ἐλήλυθα) and *I came* (ἦλθον), *v.* 47. The one marks the abiding result; and the other the particular purpose. For the use of the former (ἐλήλυθα) see v. 43, vii. 28, viii. 42 (and ἦλθον), xvi. 28, xviii. 37, (iii. 19); and for the use of the latter (ἦλθον), viii. 14, ix. 39, x. 10, xii. 27, 47, (xv. 22).

should (**may**) *not abide in* **the** *darkness*] as being the normal state of men without Christ. The exact phrase occurs only here, yet see 1 John ii. 9, 11 (*is in the darkness*); and viii. 12, xii. 35; 1 John ii. 11 (*walk in the darkness*). Comp. 1 John iii. 14, *abide in death*; and the opposite 1 John ii. 10, *abide in the light*.

47. Christ now passes from the thought of His Person to that of His words: from

p. 3. 47 [k]And if any man hear my words, and believe not, I judge him not: for I came not to judge the world, but to save the world.

48 He that rejecteth me, and receiveth not my words, hath one that
k 16. judgeth him: [l]the word that I have spoken, the same shall judge him in the last day.

49 For I have not spoken of myself; but the Father which sent me, he gave me a commandment, what I should say, and what I should speak.

50 And I know that his commandment is life everlasting: whatsoever I speak therefore, even as the Father said unto me, so I speak.

---

me to *my sayings*. Faith is essentially personal. Unbelief stops short at the outward manifestations of the Person: it deals with the teaching.

Two cases appear to be regarded, the first that of the respectful hearer, who listens and does not; the second, that of the man who refuses to listen at all. From this it appears that the reading "believe" is foreign to the scope of *v.* 47.

hear my words (**sayings**, ῥημάτων)] not with true understanding of their full import (viii. 47), but yet with attention, x. 3, 16, 27, &c.).

and believe not] According to the true reading, **and keep** (φυλάξῃ, Matt. xix. 20; Luke xi. 28) **them not.**

I (emphatic) *judge him not*] There is no personal element in the accomplishment of the final issue. Christ came for judgment (ix. 39) and yet not to judge (comp. iii. 17, viii. 15). The judgment followed naturally (so to speak) from His manifestation. The Law (in the fullest sense) is the one accuser (v. 45). Men simply remain where they are (iii. 36) if they do not come to Christ. Their sentence lies in the nature of things. In this case the hearers were self-condemned.

48. *He that rejecteth* (ὁ ἀθετῶν, Vulg. *qui spernit*) *me...my words* (**sayings**)...] Luke x. 16.

hath one that judgeth him] The word may be refused, but it cannot be banished. It still clings to the hearer as his judge. Its work is even now begun as it shall hereafter be fully revealed.

the word that I have spoken (*I* **spake**)...] The "sayings" are all bound up in one great message (λόγος), delivered and felt in its entirety. For the unbelieving Jews it was now ended (*spake* is contrasted with *speak*, *v.* 50). Comp. xvii. 6, 8.

the word...the same (**that**) *shall judge him*...] The resumptive, isolating pronoun (ἐκεῖνος) places in emphatic prominence the teaching which is regarded as past and separated from those to whom it was addressed. It stands, as it were, in the distance, as a witness and an accuser. Comp. i. 18, v. 11 and note.

in the last day] ch. vi. 39, 40, 44, 54, xi. 24. The phrase is peculiar to St John's Gospel. Comp. 1 Cor. xv. 52 (*the last trumpet*); 1 John ii. 18 (*the last hour*).

49. *For...spoken*...] **Because I spoke not**... The essential inherent power of judgment lies in the word, since there is in it no admixture of a limited human personality. It is wholly divine.

of myself] The phrase (ἐξ ἐμαυτοῦ, Vulg. *ex me*) is peculiar and unique. It describes (so to speak) the source out of which a stream flows continuously, and not simply the point of origin from which movement started (ἀπ' ἐμ. v. 30, vii. 17, 28, viii. 28, 42, (x. 18), xiv. 10).

he gave me a commandment] **himself hath given me commandment.** The pronoun (as in *v.* 48) emphasizes the reference; and the tense of the verb (δέδωκεν) marks the continuance of the action of the command.

what I should say (εἴπω, Vulg. *dicam*), *and what I should speak* (λαλήσω, Vulg. *loquar*)] That is, as to the substantial contents and the varying manner of my message.

50. *And I know* (οἶδα)...] The word may find acceptance or rejection, but this remains sure. The commandment of the Father, His will manifested in my commission, is eternal life. The Father's commandment not only is directed towards life, to quicken or to support it. It is life. Truth realised is that by which we live. The commandment of God is the expression of absolute Truth. Comp. vi. 63, 68, xvii. 17.

Life eternal *is* and not simply *shall be*. Comp. iii. 36, v. 24, (39), vi. 54, xvii. 3 note. 1 John v. 12, 13.

whatsoever (**the things which**) *I speak therefore*...] The certainty of this assurance furnishes the one rule of Christ's teaching. He in the fulness of His divine-human Person (ἐγώ) speaks in complete agreement with the Father's injunctions, who is His Father and our Father. In part His message was fully given (*vv.* 48 f.): in part it was still to be given to the inner circle of His disciples.

THE SELF-REVELATION OF CHRIST TO THE WORLD has now been completed. In the remainder of the Gospel St John records

CHAPTER XIII.

1 *Jesus washeth the disciples' feet: exhorteth them to humility and charity.* 18 *He foretelleth, and discovereth to John by a token, that Judas should betray him:* 31 *commandeth them to love one another,* 36 *and forewarneth Peter of his denial.*

THE SELF-REVELATION OF CHRIST TO THE DISCIPLES.

This division of the Gospel, like the former, falls into two parts, THE LAST MINISTRY OF LOVE (xiii.—xvii.), and THE VICTORY THROUGH DEATH (xviii.—xx.); with an EPILOGUE (xxi.).

XIII.—XVII. THE LORD'S LAST MINISTRY OF LOVE.

This division of the Gospel, which is entirely peculiar to St John, with the exception of the revelation of treachery among the twelve, falls into three sections:

I. THE LAST ACTS OF LOVE AND JUDGMENT (xiii. 1—30).

II. THE LAST DISCOURSES (xiii. 31—xvi. 33).

III. THE PRAYER OF CONSECRATION (xvii.).

I. THE LAST ACTS OF LOVE AND JUDGMENT (xiii. 1—30).

St John's account of events at the Last Supper contains two scenes. The first is the manifestation in act of the Master's self-sacrificing love (1—20): the second is the separation of the selfish disciple (21—30).

The incidents are parallel with sections of the Synoptic Gospels; but there are very few points of actual correspondence in detail between the narratives of the Synoptists and of St John. The discussion recorded by St Luke (xxii. 24 ff.) has a close connexion of thought with the lesson of the feet-washing. And the words announcing the betrayal are identical in St Matthew (xxvi. 21; comp. Mark xiv. 18) and St John (xiii. 21). All the Evangelists record the surprise with which this announcement was received (Matt. xxvi. 22; Mark xiv. 19; Luke xxii. 23; John xiii. 22); and St Matthew notes that Judas was designated as the traitor (xxvi. 25). But the details which St John has preserved as to the manner of the designation are peculiar to him.

The omission of the record of the Institution of the Lord's Supper belongs to the plan of the Gospel. It is impossible on any theory to suppose that the author was unacquainted with the facts. But it is difficult to determine at what point in the narrative of St John the Institution is to be placed. It is scarcely necessary to refer to the opinion of those who have supposed (Lightfoot, &c.) that the supper described in John xiii. was held at Bethany (Matt. xxvi. 6 ff.), and that the journey to Jerusalem follows xiv. 31; so that the Institution took place on the following day. This view appears to be directly opposed to xiii. 38: to the significant parallel with Luke xxii. 24 ff.: and to the general unity of the discourses in xiii.—xvii.

But if it be assumed that the meal described in ch. xiii. is identical with that described in the Synoptists, as including the Institution of the Lord's Supper, where can the Institution be intercalated? was it before or after the departure of Judas (xiii. 30)?

The evidence on this point is extremely slender. In the narratives of St Matthew and St Mark there is nothing which tends to decide the question in one way or the other. The prophecy of the betrayal and the Institution are introduced by the same general words (*as they were eating*, Matt. xxvi. 26; Mark xiv. 22), and though the former stands first there is nothing to shew that the order is chronological. It is also to be noticed that in these Evangelists there is no separation of the blessing of the Bread and of the Cup. In the narrative of St Luke the arrangement is different. A cup is first given for distribution (xxii. 17). Then follows the giving of Bread, with the words of Institution (*v.* 19). Then, according to the present text, the giving of the Cup, with the words of Institution introduced by the clause *in like manner also the cup after supper* (*v.* 20); and in close connexion with this is given the prophecy of the betrayal. There is indeed good reason for thinking that the second reference to the Cup is a very early addition to the original text of St Luke taken from 1 Cor. xi. 25; and as it stands it may be treated parenthetically. In any case, however, St Luke distinctly places the prophecy of the betrayal after the distribution of the Sacramental Bread; and, like St Paul, he places this distribution during the supper, and the distribution of the Sacramental Cup after the supper. The other Synoptic narratives are perfectly consistent with this view. Judas then, if we adopt this interpretation of the narrative, was present at the distribution of the Sacramental Bread, and not present at the distribution of the Sacramental Cup. In other words, the distribution of the Bread must be placed before *v.* 30 in St John's narrative, and the distribution of the Cup after.

If now we look for a break in xiii. 1—30, it may be found between 16 and 17, or between 19 and 20; but hardly between 22 and 23. It is, however, more in accordance with St Luke's narrative to place the distribution of the Bread before *v.* 2. The distribution of the Cup may be placed after 30, or 33; but it seems on the whole best to place it after 32. The teaching of that Sacramental Act forms a bond between the thoughts of 32 and 33.

NOW [a] before the feast of the passover, when Jesus knew that his hour was come that he should depart out of this world unto the Father, having loved his own which were in the world, he loved them unto the end.

2 And supper being ended, the

---

1. *The self-sacrifice of love* (1—20).

The central idea of this record corresponds with one aspect of the Institution of the Eucharist, that of self-sacrifice. The incident evidently belongs to the same spiritual circumstances. The form of the narrative is marked by extreme minuteness and vividness of detail (*vv.* 4 ff.), and by directness of recollection (*v.* 11). The portraiture of St Peter is instinct with life: he acts and is acted upon.

The narrative consists of two parts, the action itself (2—11), and the commentary upon the action (12—20). The latter approaches very closely in form to the teaching preserved by the Synoptists (*e.g. vv.* 16 f.). The former is a parable in action (comp. Matt. xviii. 2 ff.).

CHAP. XIII. **1—4.** These verses are differently punctuated. Some suppose that the construction is broken, and that the principal verb is *rises* in *v.* 4, the *knowing* in *v.* 3 resuming the *knowing* of *v.* 1. It seems better, however (as A. V.), to take *v.* 1 as complete in itself, as it is grammatically complete, and to regard *v.* 2 as a fresh beginning. On this view *v.* 1 is an introduction to the whole cycle of teaching which follows (xiii.—xvii.), while *vv.* 2, 3 are the introduction to the special incident of the feet-washing, the symbolic manifestation of love.

Now before the feast...] The disjunctive particle (δέ, Vulg. *autem*) perhaps suggests a contrast with the temporary retirement noticed in xii. 36. Though Jesus had thus withdrawn Himself, yet before the crisis of His Passion He fully prepared His disciples for the issue.

before the feast] It is impossible to take these words either with *knowing* or with *having loved*. The clause can only go properly with the principal verb *loved*. The note of time consequently serves to mark the date of the manifold exhibition of love, of the acts and discourses which follow immediately afterwards. All these took place "before the feast," that is, on the evening (the commencement) of Nisan 14th; and in these last scenes before the Passover at which the Jewish type found its perfect fulfilment, the love of the Lord was revealed in its highest form.

when Jesus knew] **Jesus knowing**, that is, since He knew. This knowledge, which is spoken of as absolute (εἰδώς), prompted the crowning display of love. The thought is brought into prominence by the repetition of the word *world*. In the world the disciples were to find their trial, and to find it when their Master had passed out of the world. Hence came the necessity for such encouragements as follow: *e.g.* xvi. 33.

In His knowledge of the disciples' suffering the Lord forgot His own suffering, though foreknowledge intensifies sorrow.

his hour] Just as St John points out the moral conditions of the Lord's life in a divine "cannot" (see xii. 40 note), and a divine "must" (xx. 9 note), he also marks the divine sequence in its events. The crises of His several manifestations are absolutely fixed in time (ii. 4; comp. xi. 9 f., ix. 4). In each case this "hour" is appointed with a view to the issue to which it leads (xii. 23, ἵνα δοξασθῇ, and so here ἵνα μεταβῇ). Compare iv. 21, 23, v. 25, 28; 1 John ii. 18; Rev. xiv. 7, 15; John vii. 6, 8 (καιρός); Eph. i. 10 (τὸ πλήρωμα τῶν καιρῶν); Gal. iv. 4 (τὸ πλήρωμα τοῦ χρόνου). Till the hour comes Christ's enemies are powerless (vii. 30, viii. 20). When it has come He recognises its advent (xii. 27, xvii. 1).

that he should depart...] The purpose, as part of the divine counsel, is marked emphatically (ἵνα). Comp. xii. 23, xvi. 2 note.

depart] The exact word (μεταβῇ, Vulg. *transeat*) is only used here in this connexion. It marks the transference from one sphere to another: comp. v. 24; 1 John iii. 14. Death for Christ, and in Him for the Christian, is not an interruption of being but a change of the mode of being, a "going to the Father," to His Father and ours.

this world...the world] The demonstrative (ὁ κόσμος οὗτος, *this world*) seems to lay stress upon the present aspect of the world as transitory and unsatisfying. The phrase occurs viii. 23, ix. 39, (xi. 9), xii. 25, 31, xvi. 11, xviii. 36; 1 John iv. 17 (and in St Paul).

unto the Father] as describing the religious and moral relationship, and not simply the idea of power (*to God*).

his own] Acts iv. 23, xxiv. 23; 1 Tim. v. 8. Compare xvii. 6 ff. Contrast i. 11.

unto the end] **to the uttermost.** The original phrase (εἰς τέλος, Vulg. *in finem*) has two common meanings, (1) *at last*, and (2) *utterly*, *completely*. The first sense appears to be most natural in Luke xviii. 5, and the second in 1 Thess. ii. 16. It occurs very frequently in the LXX., and most often in connexion with words of destruction (*utterly*), or abandonment (*for ever*): Ps. xii. 1, (ix. 18, al. εἰς τὸν αἰῶνα), &c. It occurs, however, in other connexions, Ps. xv. 11, lxxiii. 3, xlviii. 8; and constantly in later Greek writers, *e.g.* 2 Clem. 19; Luc. 'Somn.' 9.

devil having now put into the heart of Judas Iscariot, Simon's *son*, to betray him;

3 Jesus knowing that the Father had given all things into his hands, and that he was come from God, and went to God;

4 He riseth from supper, and laid aside his garments; and took a towel, and girded himself.

5 After that he poureth water into a bason, and began to wash the disciples' feet, and to wipe *them* with the towel wherewith he was girded.

6 Then cometh he to Simon Pe-

There appears to be no authority for taking it here in the sense of *to the end of His earthly presence* (yet see Matt. x. 22, xxiv. 13 f.), and such a translation does not suit the connexion with *before the feast*. If, however, we take the words as expressing *loved them with a perfect love*, then the thought comes out clearly, "As Christ loved His disciples, and had before shewed His love, so now at this crisis, before the day of His Passion, He carried His love to the highest point, **He loved them to the uttermost.**"

2. *And supper being ended...*] *And*—as one special manifestation of this love—**during a supper** (δείπνου γινομένου)...

the devil ... him] Literally, according to the most ancient text, **the devil having already put it into his** (*Judas'*) **heart that Judas Iscariot the son of Simon shall betray him.** The transference of the subject from the former to the latter clause is not unnatural (*...into the heart of Judas... that he should...*); and it seems to be impossible to accept the rendering "the devil having conceived in his heart that..."

The separation of "Iscariot" from Judas in the original text, "Judas the son of Simon, Iscariot," clearly marks the title as local. Comp. vi. 71, where it is an epithet of Simon.

3. *Jesus* (omit) *knowing*] That is, as before, "since He knew." The knowledge that He was possessed of this divine authority was the ground of His act of service; just as in *v.* 1 the knowledge of His coming departure was the ground of His crowning display of love.

the Father] Not "His Father." The Son of man (*Jesus*) is now the conqueror.

had given...] Our idiom will not bear in the oblique the original tense *gave* (found in the oldest authorities), which, however, marks the true idea of the commission once given eternally. A similar remark applies to the verbs below, which are literally **came forth** and **goeth.**

all things] The sense of absolute sovereignty is the more impressive here in the prospect of apparent defeat. Even through treachery and death lay the way to the Resurrection.

into his hands] to deal with as He pleased, even when He was given "into the hands" of men: Matt. xvii. 22, xxvi. 45.

The original order is most emphatic: "and that it was from God He came forth, and unto God He is going." The title of power and glory is used in this clause, as that of affinity (*the Father*) in the former.

was come] *was* **come forth** on His mission to the world at the Incarnation. The preposition used here (ἀπό) marks a separation and not the source. Contrast viii. 42, note.

4. *He riseth from* **the** *supper, and laid* (**layeth**) *aside...*] There is nothing to indicate the occasion of the action. The phrase implies that the supper was already begun, so this feet-washing cannot have answered to that before the meal. We may assume that it was a parable in action exhibited in order to illustrate some thought of the coming kingdom which had just found expression. Comp. Luke xxii. 24 ff.; (Matt. xviii. 1 ff.). For this reason each step in the act of service is noted with the particularity of an eye-witness: the rising from among the group (ἐγ. ἐκ), the laying aside the upper robes (ἱμάτια), the taking the towel, the girding, the pouring out of the water, the washing, the wiping. When Christ serves, He serves perfectly.

and **he** *took...girded himself*] The form of expression emphasizes the preparation by Himself. Comp. Luke xii. 37, xvii. 8, and ch. xxi. 18, with Acts xii. 8. "Quid mirum si præcinxit se linteo qui formam servi accipiens habitu inventus est ut homo?" (Aug. *ad loc.*)

5. *After that...*] **Then** (εἶτα), xix. 27, xx. 27.

poureth] The original word (βάλλει, Vulg *mittit*), which is peculiar, is rendered in the same connexion elsewhere *putteth;* Matt. ix. 17 and parallels.

into a (**the**) *bason*] which stood ready for this accustomed use. Comp. 2 K. iii. 11.

began to wash] The actual scene is broken up into its parts, just as all the details of preparation had been separately noticed. Comp. Gen. xviii. 4, xix. 2, xxiv. 32, xliii. 24; Judg. xix. 21; 1 Tim. v. 10. Rabbinic commentators dwelt on the significance of Ezek. xvi. 9. "Among men," they said, "the slave washes his master; but with God it is not so." Comp. Lightfoot and Wetstein, *ad loc.*

6. *Then* (**So**) *cometh he...*] as He passed round, or rather as He began to pass round, the circle of the disciples. There is nothing to support the old notion that the action began

ter: and Peter saith unto him, Lord,
dost thou wash my feet?
7 Jesus answered and said unto
him, What I do thou knowest not
now; but thou shalt know hereafter.
8 Peter saith unto him, Thou
shalt never wash my feet. Jesus answered him, If I wash thee not, thou
hast no part with me.
9 Simon Peter saith unto him,
Lord, not my feet only, but also *my*
hands and *my* head.
10 Jesus saith to him, He that is
washed needeth not save to wash *his*

---

with Judas. It is more natural to suppose that the Lord began with St Peter. In that case his refusal to accept the service is more intelligible than it would be if others had already accepted it.

and Peter saith (**he saith**) *unto him*] The abruptness of the clause suits the vivid narrative.

dost thou...] The position of the pronouns in the original (σύ μου ν. τ. π., Vulg. *tu mihi l. p., thou my feet*) brings out the sharp contrast of the persons. The thought of the kind of service is subordinated to the fact of service rendered by the Master to the servant.

7. *What I do*] The chasm between the thoughts of the Lord and of the disciple is marked by the emphatic pronouns (ὃ ἐγὼ π. σὺ οὐκ οἶ.).

The meaning of the act could not be understood till the Lord was glorified. The interpretation depended on a full view of His Person and His work. Knowledge as absolute and complete (οὐκ οἶδας) is contrasted with the knowledge which is gained by slow experience (γνώσῃ "thou shalt learn" or "understand"). Comp. iii. 10, 11, note.

hereafter] Literally, *after these things:* iii. 22, v. 1, 14 (*afterward*), vi. 1, vii. 1, xix. 38, xxi. 1. In these places reference is made to a group of incidents, and not to one single scene. We must then understand here by "these things" all the circumstances of the Passion which was now begun. Even the interpretation given in *vv.* 12 ff. was only partially intelligible, until Christ's sacrifice of Himself was completed. Perfect knowledge began with the day of Pentecost.

8. St Peter takes up the thought of "hereafter." Nothing, he would argue, can ever alter my position in regard to my Lord. This is fixed eternally. *Thou shalt not wash my feet while the world lasts* (οὐ μὴ...εἰς τὸν αἰῶνα). He assumed that he could foresee all; hence his reverence takes the form of self-will, just as in the corresponding incident in Matt. xvi. 22, where also his self-willed reverence for Christ, as He interpreted His office, brings down a stern reproof.

If I wash thee not...] Christ meets the confidence of the Apostle with a declaration of the necessary separation which must ensue from the want of absolute submission. "Unless I render thee this service, unless, that is, thou receivest that which I offer, even when thou canst not understand my purpose, thou hast no part with me." The first condition of discipleship is self-surrender.

It appears to be foreign to the context to introduce any direct reference to the washing in Christ's blood (see *vv.* 13 ff.). Though, as Cyril says, we may see some such thought suggested by the words.

wash thee] not *thy feet*. Christ Himself chooses the manner in which He accomplishes the work which is effectual for the whole and not for a part.

thou hast no part...] thou hast no share in my kingdom, as a faithful soldier in the conquests of his captain. Comp. Matt. xxiv. 51; Deut. xii. 12, xiv. 27; Ps. l. 18.

9. St Peter, with characteristic impulsiveness, still answers in the same spirit as before. Just as he had wished to define what the Lord should not do, so now he wishes to define the manner in which that should be done which he admitted to be necessary. He would extend in detail to every part the action which Christ designed to fulfil in one way according to His Own will.

10. The reply of the Lord introduces a new idea. From the thought of the act of service as such, we are led to the thought of the symbolic meaning of the special act as a process of cleansing. The "washing" of a part of the body, feet, or hands, or head, is contrasted with the "bathing" of the whole. The "washing" in itself does not mark an essential change, but is referred to the total change already wrought. *He that is* **bathed** (ὁ λελουμένος) *needeth not save to wash* (νίψασθαι) *his feet.*

Some important authorities omit *save* and *his feet*. If this reading be adopted the emphasis will lie on *needeth not*. The after-cleansing may be an act of divine love, but it is not to be required at man's will. The form of the verb in some degree suggests this turn of meaning. It is not "to be washed," corresponding with the former phrase, but "to wash himself," or "to wash his own feet" (Matt. xv. 2; Mark vii. 3). But it is more probable that the omission was occasioned by the difficulty of reconciling the phrase with "clean every whit."

If however the common reading be retained, the sense will be that the limited cleansing, as now symbolized, is all that is needed. He who is bathed needs, so to speak, only to

feet, but is clean every whit: and ye
are clean, but not all.
11 For he knew who should betray him; therefore said he, Ye are
not all clean.
12 So after he had washed their
feet, and had taken his garments,
and was set down again, he said
unto them, Know ye what I have
done to you?
13 Ye call me Master and Lord:
and ye say well; for *so* I am.
14 If I then, *your* Lord and Master, have washed your feet; ye also
ought to wash one another's feet.
15 For I have given you an ex-

---

remove the stains contracted in the walk of life; just as the guest, after the bath, needs only to have the dust washed from his feet when he reaches the house of his host.

is clean every whit] The partial and superficial defilements, of hands, or head; or feet, do not alter the general character. The man, as a whole, the man as man, is clean.

and ye are clean, but not all] The thought of the partial defilement of the person passes into the thought of the partial defilement of the society. The apostles as a body were clean. The presence of one traitor, the stain-spot to be removed, did not alter the character of the company any more than the partial soiling of the feet alters the essential cleanness of the man.

Taken in this connexion the passage throws light on the doctrine of the holiness of the visible Church. And this the more because it seems impossible not to see in the word *bathed*, as contrasted with *washed*, a foreshadowing of the idea of Christian Baptism (Hebr. x. 22; comp. Eph. v. 26; Titus iii. 5). There is however no evidence to shew that the apostles themselves were baptized unless with John's baptism. The "bathing" in their case consisted in direct intercourse and union with Christ. For them this one special act of service was but an accessory to the continuous love of that companionship. (Comp. xv. 3.)

11. *he knew who should betray him*] More strictly, *him that was betraying him*. The act of treason was already in process. Contrast vi. 64 (fut.), vi. 71, xii. 4. The rendering "betray" adds something to the force of the original word. The exact word "traitor" (προδότης) is applied to Judas only in Luke vi. 16. Elsewhere the word used of him is some part of the verb "to deliver up" (παραδιδόναι), and not of the word "to betray" (προδιδόναι).

therefore said he...] The addition is quite natural if the writer's vivid recollection of the scene carries him back to the time when the words arrested the attention before they were fully intelligible. Otherwise it is difficult to account for the obvious explanation. No one who had always been familiar with the whole history would have added them.

12. *Know ye...*] Do you apprehend, perceive, understand the meaning of (γινώσκετε...;)...? See *v.* 7. The word in *v.* 17 is different (οἴδατε).

13. *Master* (*i.e.* Teacher) *and Lord*] According to the common titles *Rabbi* and *Mar*, corresponding to which the followers were "disciples" or "servants" (*v.* 16).

14. *If I then*, your *Lord* (**the Lord**) *and* **the** *Master...*] If I, the one who am by confession supreme, **washed** (ἔνιψα) even now your feet...

ye also ought...] The obligation is of a debt incurred (ὀφείλετε): Matt. xxiii. 16, 18. Comp. ch. xix. 7; 1 John ii. 6, iii. 16, iv. 11; Luke xvii. 10; Rom. xv. 1, &c. The interpretation given is thus that of the duty of mutual subjection and service, and specially with a view to mutual purifying. Comp. 1 Pet. v. 5.

15. *I have given you* (**I gave**) *you an example...*] Three different words are rendered "example" in New Testament. That which is used here (ὑπόδειγμα) is applied to separate, isolated subjects (comp. Hebr. iv. 11, viii. 5, ix. 23; James v. 10; 2 Pet. ii. 6) Contrast 1 Cor. x. 6, 11 (τύπος); Jude 7 (δεῖγμα).

It will be observed that the example of Christ is always offered in connexion with some form of self-sacrifice.

that...to you] Literally, *that as I did to you, ye also do.* The parallel is between "I" and "ye," and hence the words "to one another" are not added.

The custom of "feet-washing" has been continued in various forms in the Church. See Bingham, XII. 4, § 10. By a decree (Can. 3) of the xviith Council of Toledo (694) it was made obligatory on the Thursday in Holy Week "throughout the Churches of Spain and Gaul" (pedes unusquisque pontificum seu sacerdotum, secundum hoc sacrosanctum exemplum, suorum lavare studeat subditorum). In 1530 Wolsey washed, wiped and kissed the feet of 59 poor men at Peterborough (Cavendish, 'Life,' I. p. 242). The practice was continued by English sovereigns till the reign of James II.; and as late as 1731 the Lord High Almoner washed the feet of the recipients of the royal gifts at Whitehall on "Maundy Thursday." The present custom of "the feet-washing" in St Peter's is well known. The practice was retained by the Mennonites; and also by the United Brethren,

ample, that ye should do as I have
done to you.
t. 10. 16 [b] Verily, verily, I say unto you,
15. The servant is not greater than his
lord; neither he that is sent greater
than he that sent him.
17 If ye know these things, happy
are ye if ye do them.
18 ¶ I speak not of you all: I
know whom I have chosen: but that
. 41. the scripture may be fulfilled, [c] He
that eateth bread with me hath lifted
up his heel against me.
19 ‖ Now I tell you before it come, ‖ Or, *From henceforth.*
that, when it is come to pass, ye may
believe that I am *he*.
20 [d] Verily, verily, I say unto you, [d] Matt. 10. 40.
He that receiveth whomsoever I send
receiveth me; and he that receiveth
me receiveth him that sent me.
21 [e] When Jesus had thus said, [e] Matt. 26. 21.
he was troubled in spirit, and tes-

---

among whom it has now fallen into disuse. There is an interesting account of Lanfranc's rule at Bec in Church's 'Anselm,' pp. 49 ff. The ancient English usage is illustrated by Chambers, 'Divine Worship in England,' p. xxvi. The Roman Service is given by Daniel, 'Cod. Lit.' I. 412.

16. *Verily, verily...*] The words, as usual, preface the new lesson.

The servant (**A servant**) *is not...*] Comp. Matt. x. 24; (Luke vi. 40).

he that is sent] **one** *that is sent* (ἀπόστολος) —an apostle.

17. *If ye know* (οἴδατε) *these things...*] the lessons conveyed by the feet-washing. The "knowledge" here is that which a man has and not that which he acquires.

happy are ye...] The original word is that used in the "beatitudes" (μακάριοι, Vulg. *beati*). Knowledge is a blessing as the help to action. There is a Jewish saying: "If a man knows the Law but does not do thereafter, it had been better for him that he had not come into the world" ('Shemoth R.' quoted by Wünsche).

18. *I speak not of you all*] The treachery of Judas was as yet manifest only to Christ; but to Him all was clear and open. For Judas knowledge would not issue in the happiness of doing.

I know whom I have chosen (**I chose**)] and so I know that even of these twelve chosen one is false (vi. 70). The choice here spoken of is the historical choice to the apostolate. The thought of "election to salvation" is quite foreign to the context. Hence the stress lies on *I* (ἐγώ) *know*. There was no surprise to Christ in the faithlessness of Judas, though there was to others. See Additional Note.

but that...] *but* my choice was so made *that*... or more generally, *but* this has so come to pass *that*...(xix. 36). There is a necessary correspondence between the fortunes of the servants of God at all times. It was necessary that Christ should fulfil in His own experience what David (or perhaps Jeremiah) had felt of the falseness of friends.

The words may also be taken: "but, that the scripture may be fulfilled, he that..." This construction however seems to be less natural and obscures the contrast.

He that...me] The Greek in St John closely renders the Hebrew. See Introd. p. xiv.

He that eateth bread with me...] According to the better reading, **my bread**. The phrase means simply, my friend bound to me by the closest and most sacred ties.

hath lifted up (**lifted up**)...] The notion is that of brute violence, and not of the cunning of the wrestler.

19. *Now...*] **From henceforth** (ἀπ' ἄρτι, Vulg. *a modo*, Matt. xxvi. 64, note). Hitherto the Lord had borne His sorrow in secret. Now it was necessary to anticipate the bitterness of disappointment. The crisis was reached from which silence henceforward was impossible. Comp. Matt. xxvi. 64; ch. xiv. 7.

before it come **to pass**, *that...*] that is, in order that what might have seemed to be a fatal miscarriage, should be shewn to have been within the range of the Master's foresight. Thus the disciples would be enabled to trust in Him absolutely. His knowledge was not only of the main fact but of the details.

believe that I am he] Comp. viii. 24, note.

20. *Verily, verily...*] The verse appears to contain the converse truth to *v.* 16, arising however directly out of *v.* 19. The knowledge of the Master's greatness furnishes the measure of the envoy's greatness. If the treachery of one shook the confidence of the others, the assurance of what their office truly was served to restore it. Comp. Matt. x. 40; and especially Luke xxii. 24—30.

2. *The separation of the selfish apostle* (21—30).

The act of complete sacrifice was followed by an act of righteous judgment. Service rests on love. Apostacy is the fruit of self-seeking. To the last Judas appears to take to himself honour without misgiving (*v.* 26). The details (*vv.* 22, 24, 25) continue to reflect the vivid impressions of an eye-witness.

21. *was troubled in spirit*] Compare xi.

tified, and said, Verily, verily, I say
unto you, that one of you shall betray me.
22 Then the disciples looked one on
another, doubting of whom he spake.
23 Now there was leaning on Jesus' bosom one of his disciples, whom
Jesus loved.
24 Simon Peter therefore beckoned
to him, that he should ask who it
should be of whom he spake.
25 He then lying on Jesus' breast
saith unto him, Lord, who is it?
26 Jesus answered, He it is, to
whom I shall give a ‖ sop, when I ‖ Or, *morsel.*
have dipped *it*. And when he had

33, xii. 27, which are however both different. The emotion belongs to the highest region (τῷ πνεύματι), as it is called out by the prospect of a spiritual catastrophe. This agony is peculiar to St John. "Pereant argumenta philosophorum," Augustine exclaims, "qui negant in sapientem cadere perturbationes animorum."

testified] Comp. iv. 44. The revelation is here made with solemn assurance, where the clear statement follows the general warnings in *vv.* 10, 11. At the same time the effect upon the disciples is different. They seek now for some explanation of the words.

22. *Then* (omit) *the disciples looked* (ἔβλεπον, Vulg. *aspiciebant*) *one on another*] The words give a vivid reminiscence of the actual scene. The first effect of the Lord's words was silent amazement and perplexity.

doubting] "Their consciousness of innocence," as has been well said, "was less trustworthy than the declaration of Christ." The same word (ἀπορεῖσθαι) occurs Luke xxiv. 4; Acts xxv. 20; 2 Cor. iv. 8; Gal. iv. 20, and expresses rather bewilderment than simple doubt. The parallel in Luke xxii. 23 shews that the rendering "about whom" and not "about what" is right.

23. *Now there ... bosom*] **There was at table reclining on Jesus' bosom.** At this time, and for some time before and after, the Jews appear to have adopted the Western mode of reclining at meals. Lightfoot (*ad loc.*) quotes Talmudic glosses which shew that the guests lay resting on their left arms, stretched obliquely, so that the back of the head of one guest lay in the bosom of the dress of the guest above him. If three reclined together the centre was the place of honour, the second place that above (to the left), the third that below (to the right). If the chief person wished to talk with the second it was necessary for him to raise himself and turn round, for his head was turned away as he reclined. St Peter then, sitting in the second place, was not in a favourable position for hearing any whisper from the Lord, which would fall naturally on the ears of St John. This very incident therefore, in which it has been supposed that St John claims precedence over St Peter, shews on the contrary that he sets himself second to him.

whom Jesus loved] xix. 26, xxi. 7, 20 (ἠγάπα, Vulg. *diligebat*). The word in xx. 2 is different, and marks a different relationship (see note there). The title is first used here, and is naturally suggested by the recollection of this special incident. It marks an acknowledgment of love and not an exclusive enjoyment of love. Comp. xiii. 1, 34, xv. 12, xi. 5.

24. *beckoned*] **beckoneth** (Acts xxiv. 10), as the eyes of the disciples were turned in surprise from one to another.

that he should...spake] According to the true reading: **and saith to him, Tell us who it is of whom He speaketh.** St Peter thought that the Lord had already revealed to St John in an undertone the name of the false apostle.

25. *He then...breast*] **He leaning back as he was** *on Jesus' breast.* The phrase marks the recollection of an eye-witness. The sudden movement (ἀναπεσὼν ἐπί) is contrasted with the position (ἀνακείμενος ἐν) at the table (οὕτως, **as he was**, iv. 6); the "bosom" (ἐν τῷ κόλπῳ), the full fold of the robe, with the "breast" (ἐπὶ τὸ στῆθος), the actual body. Before this change of posture the disciple was so placed as to hear a whisper from the Lord, but not so as to address Him easily. The act rather than the place at table was preserved in tradition, xxi. 20. Polycr. ap. Euseb. 'H. E.' v. 24; Iren. III. 1; Euseb. 'H. E.' v. 8. Hence the title "the disciple that leant on Christ's breast" (ὁ ἐπιστήθιος). Comp. Routh, 'Rell. Sacr.' I. 42.

26. *Jesus answered*] **Jesus therefore answereth...** The question was not now to be put aside, but it was answered only for those who put it.

to whom...dipped it] **for whom I shall dip** (cf. Ruth ii. 14) **the sop and give it him.** The emphatic pronoun marks the significance of the action. It is an Eastern custom at present for the host to give a small ball of meat to the guest whom he wishes to honour. The reference here may be to this custom. By this act, which is not mentioned in the other Gospels, Christ answered the question of St John, Matt. xxvi. 25. Comp. Matt. xxvi. 23; Mark xiv. 20.

And...of Simon] **So having dipped the sop he taketh it and giveth it to Judas** *the son* **of Simon Iscariot.**

dipped the sop, he gave *it* to Judas Iscariot, *the son* of Simon.

27 And after the sop Satan entered into him. Then said Jesus unto him, That thou doest, do quickly.

28 Now no man at the table knew for what intent he spake this unto him.

29 For some *of them* thought, because Judas had the bag, that Jesus had said unto him, Buy *those things* that we have need of against the feast; or, that he should give something to the poor.

30 He then having received the sop went immediately out: and it was night.

---

27. **then** *Satan entered into him*] Comp. Luke xxii. 3. In that passage is the beginning (comp. *v.* 2), in this, the consummation of the design. Judas in his self-will appears to have interpreted the mark of honour so as to confirm him in his purpose. So St John emphasizes the moment: *after the sop then* (τότε)... at that moment the conflict was decided. It is to be noticed that the pronoun here and in *v.* 30 (ἐκεῖνος) isolates Judas and sets him as it were outside the company. Satan is mentioned here only in the Gospel. "Enter" of evil spirits occurs Matt. xii. 45; Mark v. 12 f.; Luke viii. 30 ff., xi. 26. Comp. Rev. xi. 11.

Then said Jesus...] **Jesus therefore saith...** knowing the final resolve of Judas.

That thou doest, do quickly] The work was in essence already begun. Therefore the Lord now removes the traitor from His presence. The command is not to do the deed as if that were any longer uncertain, but to do in a particular way what is actually being done. Repentance is no longer possible; and Christ welcomes the issue for Himself. These words were spoken openly; those in 24—6 secretly.

28. *Now no man...*] not even St John, who did not connect this injunction with the announcement which he had just received.

29. *For some...*] They were so far from a suspicion of the true import of the words that they interpreted them in different ways.

the bag] Comp. xii. 6.

had said (**said**)...*Buy...against* (**for**, εἰς) *the feast*] The words shew that the meal cannot have been the passover. Moreover if it had been, Judas would not have left while the meal was as yet unfinished.

to the poor] xii. 5 ff.; Gal. ii. 10.

30. *He then* (**So he**) *having received...*] Rather, *having taken* (λαβών). The word marks that Judas on his part appropriated the gift, which, from the repeated mention, was evidently significant. Comp. xx. 22, vii. 39, i. 12, v. 43, &c.

and it was night] The words cannot but mark the contrast of the light within with the outer darkness into which Judas "went forth." Comp. Rev. xxi. 25, xxii. 5; 1 Thess. v. 5; (ch. ix. 4, xi. 10). See also Luke xxii. 53. "*Erat autem nox:* et ipse qui exivit erat nox" (Aug. *ad loc.*).

II. THE LAST DISCOURSES (xiii. 31—xvi.).

The last discourses of the Lord are divided into two portions by the change of place at the close of ch. xiv. Thus we have

i. THE DISCOURSES IN THE UPPER ROOM (xiii. 31—xiv. 31).

ii. THE DISCOURSES ON THE WAY (xv., xvi.).

These two groups of revelations, while they have much in common, are distinguished both by their external form and by a pervading difference of scope. The first group consists in a great degree of answers to individual apostles. St Peter (xiii. 36), St Thomas (xiv. 5), St Philip (xiv. 8), and St Jude (xiv. 22), propose questions to which the Lord replies. In the second group the case is far different. After the little company had left the room a solemn awe seems to have fallen upon the eleven (comp. Mark x. 32). They no longer dared to ask what they desired to know (xvi. 17); and when they spoke it was as a body, with an imperfect confession of grateful faith (xvi. 29 f.). This outward difference between the two groups corresponds with an inward difference. In the first group the thought of separation, and of union in separation, predominates. In the second group the main thought is of the results of realised union, and of conflict carried on to victory. This progress in the development of the central idea of the discourses influences the treatment of the subjects which are common to the two sections. This will appear clearly when the parallel teaching on the "new commandment" of love (xiii. 34, xiv. 15, 21, 23 f. Comp. xv. 9 ff., 17), on the world (xiv. 22 ff. Comp. xv. 18 ff.; xvi. 1 ff.), on the Paraclete (xiv. 16 f., 25 f.; comp. xv. 26, xvi. 8 ff.), and on Christ's coming (xiv. 3, 18, 28; comp. xvi. 16, 22), is examined in detail.

These last discourses in St John bear the same relation to the fourth Gospel as the last eschatological discourses to the Synoptic Gospels (Matt. xxiv.; Mark xiii.; Luke xxi.). The two lines of thought which they repre-

31 ¶ Therefore, when he was gone out, Jesus said, Now is the Son of man glorified, and God is glorified in him.

32 If God be glorified in him, God shall also glorify him in himself, and shall straightway glorify him.

33 Little children, yet a little while

---

sent are complementary, and answer to the circumstances by which they were called out. Speaking in full view of the city and the temple the Lord naturally dwelt on the revolutions which should come in the organization of nations and the outward consummation of His kingdom. Speaking in the Upper Room and on the way to Gethsemane to the eleven, now separated from the betrayer, He dwelt rather on the inward consummation of His work and on the spiritual revolution which was to be accomplished. In the last case the situation no less than the teaching was unique. See Introduction, pp. lxiii. ff.

i. THE DISCOURSES IN THE UPPER ROOM (xiii. 31—xiv. 31).

This first group of discourses may be arranged naturally in four sections.

1. *Separation: its necessity and issue* (xiii. 31—38).
2. *Christ and the Father* (xiv. 1—11).
3. *Christ and the disciples* (xiv. 12—21).
4. *The law and the progress of Revelation* (xiv. 22—31).

1. *Separation: its necessity and issue* (xiii. 31—38).

This first section of the Lord's final revelation of Himself and of His work contains in germ the main thoughts which are afterwards unfolded. He declares (*vv.* 31—35) His victory (*vv.* 31, 32), His departure (*v.* 33), the characteristic of His Society (*vv.* 34, 35); and then, by the example of St Peter, He lays open the need of long and painful discipline for the disciples, in order that they may realise at last fellowship with Him (*vv.* 36—38). The central idea is that of separation, its nature, its necessity, its consequences; so that the whole current of the discourses flows directly from the historical position with which they are connected.

In this section, as afterwards, the absence of connecting particles is a characteristic feature of the narrative.

31. *Therefore, when* (**When therefore**) ...*Jesus said* (**saith**)] The departure of Judas marked the crisis of the Lord's victory. By this the company was finally "cleansed" (*v.* 10): and not only was the element of evil expelled, but it was used for the fulfilment of its appropriate part.

gone out] The departure was the free act of Judas. Contrast ix. 34 (ἐξέβαλον).

Now is...] This "now," with which the Lord turns to the faithful eleven, expresses at once the feeling of deliverance from the traitor's presence and His free acceptance of the issues of the traitor's work. Judas was the representative of that spirit of wilful self-seeking which was the exact opposite of the spirit of Christ. By his removal therefore the conflict with evil which Christ had sustained in His human nature (*the Son of Man*) was essentially decided. As very Man and the representative of humanity He had finally overcome. At the moment when Judas went out, charged to execute his purpose, the Passion, as the supreme act of self-sacrifice, was virtually accomplished.

the Son of man] This title, as has been already implied, is the key to the interpretation of the passage. The words are spoken of the relation of "the Son of man" to "God," and not of that of "the Son" to "the Father."

glorified] Perfect self-sacrifice even to death, issuing in the overthrow of death, is the truest "glory" (comp. xii. 23 f., x. 17 f.; comp. vii. 39, xii. 16, xvii. 5). Even the disciple in his degree "glorifies God" by his death (xxi. 19). Hence the attainment of glory by *the Son of Man* is rightly spoken of as past (**was** *glorified*, ἐδοξάσθη, Vulg. *clarificatus est*, not simply *is glorified*) in relation to the spiritual order, though it was yet future in its historical realisation. The thought throughout these last discourses is of the decisive act by which the Passion had been embraced. The redemptive work of Christ essentially was completed (xvii. 4, &c.).

and God is (**was**) *glorified in him*] The divine counsel (if we may so speak) was justified in Christ as man. Comp. xiv. 13, xvii. 4.

32. *If God ... in him*] This clause is omitted by the most ancient authorities, and mars the symmetry of the structure of *vv.* 31, 32, which is seen to be most remarkable by a literal rendering:

Now was glorified the Son of Man,
And God was glorified in Him:
And God shall glorify Him in Himself,
And straightway shall He glorify Him.

God shall also ... and shall straightway ...] **And** *God shall*...*and straightway* **shall He**... The "glory" realised in absolute sacrifice must necessarily be regarded under two aspects, subjectively and objectively. The inward victory carried with it the outward triumph. Even as God was glorified in the Son of Man, as man, when He took to Himself willingly the death which the traitor was preparing, so also it followed that God would

I am with you. Ye shall seek me: *f*and as I said unto the Jews, Whither I go, ye cannot come; so now I say to you.

f ch. 7. 34.

34 *g*A new commandment I give unto you, That ye love one another; as I have loved you, that ye also love one another.

g Lev. 19. 18. chap. 15. 17. 1 John 4. 21.

---

glorify the Son of Man in His own divine Being, by taking up His glorified humanity to fellowship with Himself (Acts vii. 55). This second clause is the complement of the first, *was glorified...shall glorify*, not separable from it in the divine counsel, though distinguished in man's apprehension. The glory of Christ is one, whether it is seen in the Betrayal, or in the Cross, or in the Resurrection, or in the Ascension. Each fact contemplated in its true character includes all. Comp. Phil. ii. 9.

in himself] The preposition (ἐν ἑαυτῷ) marks unity of being, and not simply unity of position (παρὰ σοί, xvii. 5). The "in him" here corresponds with "forth from Him" (ἐξ αὐτοῦ) in ch. xvi. 28.

straightway] The sufferings and the glories (1 Pet. i. 11) henceforth followed one another in unbroken succession. Comp. xii. 23.

33. Christ's revelation of the nature of the crisis as affecting Himself, is followed by a revelation of it as affecting His disciples. The realisation of His heavenly glory involved His withdrawal from earth. The time therefore was come in which it was necessary for Him to announce His departure to those who were nearest to Him, as He had done before with another purpose to the Jews. In this His friends and His enemies were alike, that they could not, being what they were, follow Him.

Little children] The exact word (τεκνία, Vulg. *filioli*) occurs here only in the Gospels (xxi. 5, παιδία); but in 1 John it is found six (or seven) times: in Gal. iv. 19 the reading is doubtful. The word (like τέκνον, i. 12, note) emphasizes the idea of kinsmanship; and the diminutive conveys an expression at once of deep affection and also of solicitude for those who as yet are immature. By using it here the Lord marks the loving spirit of the communication which He makes, and assures those whom He leaves of His tender sympathy with them in their bereavement. At the same time He indicates that they stand to Him in a relation corresponding to that in which He stands to the Father: comp. x. 14, xiv. 20, xvii. 21, 23.

yet a little while] *i.e.* it is but for a little while that I am with you: the moment of separation is at hand. Comp. vii. 33.

Ye shall seek me] in the coming times of trial after the Passion, and after the Resurrection, and after the Ascension, and even to the consummation of the age, in the manifold loneliness of toil. Comp. Luke xvii. 22. It must be noticed that the second clause, which was addressed to the Jews, "and ye shall not find me" (vii. 34), is not added here. The search of the disciples, if in sorrow, would not be finally in vain. The words recorded in Luke xxii. 35, 36 point to a similar contrast between the position of the disciples with the Lord and their position without Him. Augustine's epigrammatic comment is most worthy of notice: "Quæramus inveniendum; quæramus inventum. Ut inveniendus quæratur, occultus est; ut inventus quæratur, immensus est... Satiat quærentem in quantum capit, et invenientem capaciorem facit..."

as I said] viii. 21. Comp. vii. 34.

the Jews] iv. 22, xviii. 20, 36 note.

so now] Of the two particles which are rendered "now," one (νῦν) marks a point of time absolutely; and the other (ἄρτι, Vulg. *modo*), which is used here, marks a point of time relatively to past and to future, and thus includes the notion of development or progress. Comp. ix. 19, 25 (ἄρτι), 21 (νῦν), and see also xiii. 7, xvi. 12, 31; Rev. xii. 10 (ἄρτι).

The exact force of the "now" here therefore is that, in the due advance of the divine plan, the time was come for the disciples to learn that they must be left behind by their Master.

34, 35. The announcement of the coming separation leads to the indication of its purpose. The season of bereavement was to be a season of spiritual growth. To this end Christ gave a commandment fitted to lead His disciples to appropriate the lessons of His life, and so, by realising their true character, to follow and to find Him. In giving this commandment He speaks both as a Master and as a Father (*v.* 33, *little children*) who gives instructions to the various members of his household on the point of his departure.

34. *A new commandment...That ye love one another*] The last clause is commonly taken to convey the substance or scope of the commandment. In this case the "newness" of the commandment (which was old in the letter, Lev. xix. 18; Luke x. 27) must be sought in the newness of the motive and of the scope, inasmuch as the example of the self-sacrifice of Christ, begun in the Incarnation and consummated at His death, revealed to men new obligations and new powers. Comp. 1 John ii. 7 f. A man's "neighbour" was at last seen to be simply his fellow man (Luke x. 36), while this universal love was based upon a special love realised in the Christian society (ἀλλήλους). Thus Christ was recognised first

35 By this shall all *men* know that ye are my disciples, if ye have love one to another.

36 ¶ Simon Peter said unto him, Lord, whither goest thou? Jesus answered him, Whither I go, thou canst

---

as the life of the Church, and then as the life of humanity. In this way the full conception of His Person was gradually called out, as the sense of "brotherhood" was fulfilled in Him, and love became active as an inward power and not as a duty imposed, as self-sacrifice resting on universal and not on relative claims. Nothing in the context suggests that the intensity of the commandment was increased, as if men were now to love their neighbours more than themselves.

It has however been conjectured that the "new commandment" is the ordinance of the Holy Communion which was instituted to the end that Christians "might love one another," by recalling in that the crowning act of Christ's love. If this be so, the words, *that ye love one another*, give the purpose and not the substance of the commandment. It is however difficult to suppose that such an Institution would be spoken of as a "commandment" (ἐντολή, 1 John ii. 7, iii. 22 ff.); but even if this definite reference be not accepted, it seems best to preserve the force of the final particle (ἵνα ἀγαπᾶτε) as marking the scope and not simply the form of the new commandment.

The force of "the new commandment" is illustrated by the well-known answer of Hillel: "That which is hateful to thee thou shalt not do to thy neighbour (comrade, לחברך). This is the whole Law: the rest is only commentary" (Buxtorf, 'Lex.' s. v. סני). The positive and the absolute takes the place of the negative and the relative.

"*Mandatum novum do vobis, ut vos invicem diligatis:* non sicut se diligunt qui corrumpunt, nec sicut se diligunt homines quoniam homines sunt; sed sicut se diligunt quoniam dii sunt et filii Altissimi omnes, ut sint Filio eius unico fratres..." (Aug. *ad loc.*).

A...commandment] This one commandment includes the sum of the old Law. Comp. Rom. xiii. 10. It is universal in its scope, and universal also in its application. It belongs to common life. The transition from the plural to the singular in 1 John ii. 3, 7 is to be noticed.

even *as I have loved you*] This clause also is ambiguous. It may express either the character or the ground of the love of Christians. In the former case it is supposed that this clause is transposed and placed in the front for emphasis: "that ye also may love one another even as I have loved you," that is, with absolute devotion. Such a transposition however is foreign from St John's manner, and in this interpretation, *ye also* loses its force. Thus it seems better to take the clause as parallel with *a new commandment give I unto you.* The commandment is thus enforced by the example: "I enjoin the precept (or I appoint the ordinance), even as up to this last moment I loved you, in order that you also, inspired by me, may imitate my love, one towards another." Comp. 1 John iii. 16.

I have loved you] The exact form (ἠγάπησα, **I loved**) implies that Christ's work is now ideally finished. Comp. xv. 9, 12, xvii. 4.

35. *By* (ἐν) *this*] By the manifestation of love in the Christian society (ἐν ἀλλήλοις, Mark ix. 50; Rom. xv. 5), and not characteristically by works of power, the Master would be seen to be still present with the disciples. Comp. 1 John iii. 10.

The well-known anecdote of St John's extreme old age preserved by Jerome ('ad Galat.' vi. 10) is a striking comment on the commandment. It is related that the disciples of the apostle, wearied by his constant repetition of the words "Little children, love one another," which was all he said when he was often carried into their assembly, asked him why he always said this. "Because," he replied, "it is the Lord's commandment; and if it only be fulfilled it is enough."

all men] The spectacle of love was a witness to the world (comp. xiv. 31, xvii. 21), and so it was treated by the early apologists; as, for example, in the famous passage of Tertullian: "The heathen are wont to exclaim with wonder, See how these Christians love one another! for they hate one another; and how they are ready to die for one another! for they are more ready to kill one another..." ('Apol.' 39). This idea of the witness of Christian love is made prominent by the fact that the Lord says "all men shall perceive (γνώσονται) that ye are," and not simply "ye shall be." At a later time Chrysostom drew a remarkable picture of the divisions of Christians as hindering the conversion of the heathen ('Hom. in Joh.' 71 fin.).

my disciples] The original form of expression (ἐμοὶ μαθηταί) is peculiar and emphatic. Comp. xv. 8, iv. 34. This, it is implied, was the loftiest title to which they aspired.

36—38. The view of the position of the Lord—of His victory, His departure, the perpetuation of His work—is completed by a view of the position of the disciples as seen in their representative, of their doubts, their future attainment, their present weakness.

36. *said* (**saith**)...*whither goest thou?*] St Peter feels rightly that the fact of the Lord's departure (*v.* 33) is the central point of all that He has just said. In the prospect of this separation he cannot rest satisfied with

not follow me now; but thou shalt follow me afterwards.

37 Peter said unto him, Lord, why cannot I follow thee now? I will
26. [h]lay down my life for thy sake.

38 Jesus answered him, Wilt thou lay down thy life for my sake? Verily, verily, I say unto thee, The cock shall not crow, till thou hast denied me thrice.

---

the implied promise of support and of the realisation by the disciples of the character of their absent Master. If Christ were indeed "the King of Israel" (comp. xii. 15), where could His kingdom be established if not at Jerusalem (comp. vii. 35)? How could the King leave those who had followed Him till He had claimed and received His throne? The Latin rendering of the words (*Domine quo vadis?*) recalls the beautiful legend of St Peter's martyrdom (*Acta Pauli*, Hilgfd., 'N. T. extra Can.' IV. 72). For the incompleteness of St Peter's question see xvi. 5. His thoughts were fixed upon the material and not upon the spiritual departure and following.

answered him] Omit *him*. The question itself is not directly answered, but rather the thought which St Peter cherished as he made it. "Let me only know whither Thou goest," he seems to say, "and I will go with Thee." So the reply of the Lord checks and yet encourages the apostle. It is enough for him to know that he shall follow his Master, though not now. It was impossible for him to follow Christ at once, because he was as yet unfitted. The work which he had to accomplish would itself prepare him for this, and the question is mainly one of "going" and "following." The idea of time is subordinate here, while it is otherwise in *v.* 37. Comp. Matt. xx. 23. Comp. Aug. 'Tr.' 66, "Noli extolli præsumendo, non potes modo: noli dejici desperando, sequeris postea."

If the original words are compared with the parallel words in viii. 21 (and supr. *v.* 33) it will be observed that the sharp opposition of persons (*I, ye*) is not preserved here. In checking the disciple the Lord simply points out the impossibility of an immediate following, and does not insist on a contrast of character which makes the impossibility.

37. *Peter said* (**saith**)...*Lord, why cannot I follow thee* **even** *now* (ἄρτι, Vulg. *modo*)?] St Peter assumes that the way is one of peril, but he thinks that he has estimated the utmost cost; and even at the moment he claims to be ready.

lay down my life] See x. 11, note. The apostle confidently believes that he can lay down his life for Christ before Christ has laid down His life for him. At a later time he learnt that it was by Christ's Passion his own martyrdom became possible, xxi. 18, 19 (*Follow me*).

38. *Jesus answered him, Wilt thou* ...] **Jesus answereth**, *Wilt thou*... The exact repetition of St Peter's words gives a singular pathos to the reply. It is as if the Lord accepted their essential truth, and looked forward to their fulfilment across the long years of discipline and trial: "Wilt thou? yea, I know thou wilt; yet in a way how different from that of which thou art now thinking." Comp. Luke xxii. 31 ff. In St Matthew (xxvi. 33) and St Mark (xiv. 29) the prophecy of St Peter's denial is placed on the way to Gethsemane in connexion with the prophecy of the general desertion of the apostles. This latter warning may well have given occasion to a second expression of St Peter's individual zeal. Comp. xvi. 32. But in the narrative of St John, St Peter does not appear again till xviii. 10.

ADDITIONAL NOTE on CHAP. XIII. 18.

There are two groups of explanations of the choice of Judas. The first group regard the choice from the side of the divine counsel; the second from the side of the human call.

1. It is said that he was chosen in obedience to God's will in order that he might betray Christ; or, to represent the same conception from another point of view, in order that the redemption might be accomplished through his act.

2. It is said again by some that Christ in making His choice of Judas did not read the inmost depths and issues of his character; and by others that seeing all distinctly even to the end He kept him near to Himself as one trusted equally with the others of the twelve.

Both these forms of explanation involve partial solutions of infinite problems.

The question raised by the first group leads us at once to the final mystery of divine Providence. This, as far as we can represent it to ourselves, deals with general results and not with individual wills.

The question raised by the second group leads us at once to the final mystery of the union of perfect divinity and perfect humanity in the One Person of the Lord. And here the records of the Gospel lead us to believe that the Lord had perfect human knowledge realised in a human way, and therefore limited in some sense, and separable in consciousness from His perfect divine omniscience. He knew the thoughts of men absolutely in their manifold possibilities, and yet, as man, not in their actual future manifestations.

These two final mysteries are not created by the fact that Judas was chosen by Christ among the twelve. They really underlie all religious life, and indeed all finite life. For finite being includes the possibility of sin, and the possibility of fellowship between the Creator and the creature.

Thus we may be content to have this concrete mystery as an example—the most terrible example—of the issues of the two fundamental mysteries of human existence.

CHAPTER XIV.

1 *Christ comforteth his disciples with the hope of heaven:* 6 *professeth himself the way, the truth, and the life, and one with the Father:* 13 *assureth their prayers in his name to be effectual:* 15 *requesteth love and obedience,* 16 *promiseth the Holy Ghost the Comforter,* 27 *and leaveth his peace with them.*

LET not your heart be troubled: ye believe in God, believe also in me.

2 In my Father's house are many

2. *Christ and the Father* (xiv. 1—11).

This section corresponds closely in form to that which has gone before. The Lord first states the goal and the purpose of His departure (*vv.* 1—4); and then meets the two crucial difficulties which are expressed by St Thomas (*vv.* 5—7) and by St Philip (8—11), as to the reality of man's knowledge of the divine end of life.

CHAP. XIV. 1—4. The succession of thought implied in these verses is singularly impressive. The ground idea is that of departure, already stated: this departure is to the Father's abode, with a view to preparing a place for, and then coming again to, those who know the direction of the journey.

1. *Let not your heart*—the seat of feeling and faith (Rom. x. 10)—*be troubled*] Comp. *v.* 27. There had been already much to cause alarm on this evening: ch. xiii. 21 f., 33, 36; and, in particular, the last warning (xiii. 38) might well shake the confidence of the disciples. It is easy therefore to imagine the sad silence which followed that utterance, broken at last by these words, which for the first time open heaven to faith.

troubled] *v.* 27, xii. 27, xiii. 21.

ye believe in God, believe also in me] The original words are ambiguous and can be interpreted (as indeed they have been interpreted) in four ways, according as the verbs are taken severally as in the indicative or imperative mood:

1. *Ye believe in God*, and if this be true, as assuredly it is, *ye believe also in me.*

2. *Ye believe in God, believe also in me.* (Vulgate, A.V.)

3. *Believe in God, and* (as a natural consequence) *ye believe in me.*

4. *Believe in God* and believe in me.

The double imperative (4) suits the context best. The changed order of the object (Believe in God and in me believe) marks the development of the idea. "Believe in God, and vet more than this, let your faith find in *Me* one on whom it can rest." In Christ belief in God gained a present reality. The simultaneous injunction of faith in God and in Christ under the same conditions implies the divinity of Christ (πιστεύετε εἰς). The belief is "in Christ," and not in any propositions about Christ.

in God] The successive divine titles used in the opening verses are significant: *God, my Father* (*v.* 2), *the Father* (*v.* 6).

2. *In my Father's house*] the spiritual and eternal antitype of the transitory temple (ii. 16) in which I have the right of a son (comp. viii. 36). Even as the earthly temple included in its court many chambers (1 K. vi. 5, 6, 10; Ezek. xli. 6), so it is to be conceived of the heavenly, as far as earthly figures can symbolize that which is spiritual. The Homeric description of Priam's palace ('Il.' VI. 242 ff.) may help to give distinctness to the image. But it is impossible to define further what is thus shadowed out. Heaven is where God is seen as our Father. We dare not add any local limitation, even in thought, to this final conception. And so the vision of God sums up all that we can conceive of the future being of the redeemed.

many mansions] There is room enough for all there: though you may find no shelter among men (xvi. 1, 2), you shall find it amply with my Father. It does not appear that there is in this place any idea of the variety of the resting-places, as indicating different limitations of future happiness. Such an idea would be foreign to the context, though it is suggested by other passages of Scripture, and was current in the Church from the time of Tertullian.

mansions] The rendering comes from the Vulgate *mansiones*, which were resting-places, and especially the "stations" on a great road where travellers found refreshment. This appears to be the true meaning of the Greek word here; so that the contrasted notions of repose and progress are combined in this vision of the future. The word (μονή) occurs in N.T. only here and in *v.* 23.

mansions: if *it were* not *so*, I would
have told you. I go to prepare a
place for you.
3 And if I go and prepare a place
for you, I will come again, and receive you unto myself; that where I
am, *there* ye may be also.
4 And whither I go ye know, and
the way ye know.
5 Thomas saith unto him, Lord,

---

if it were not so, I would have told you, **for** *I go...*] Christ reminds His disciples that as He has told them tidings of sorrow so He would not have withheld anything from them. But as it is, His departure in fact carries with it the promise of their reception. Otherwise it would only avail partially. This connexion seems better than to regard the words *if it were not so...you* as a mere parenthesis, and to refer the "for," which must be inserted in accordance with the best authorities, to the "many mansions." The interrogative construction, "if it were not so, would I have told you that I go to prepare a place for you?" is far less probable: there is indeed no difficulty in supposing that a reference is made to words not directly recorded (cf. xii. 26, &c., vi. 36), but the question would be singularly abrupt. Still less likely is the rendering "if it were not so, I would have told you that I am going to prepare a place for you." For Christ was in fact going to prepare a place: *v.* 3.

to prepare a place] Comp. Num. x. 33. Christ by His Death and Resurrection opened heaven, and by the elevation of His humanity thus made ready a place for men. Comp. Hebr. vi. 20 (πρόδρομος).

3. *And if...*] This departure is itself the condition of the return: separation, the cessation of the present circumstances of fellowship, was the first step towards complete union.

I will come again, and receive...] **I come** *again and* **I will take...**] The idea of Christ's Presence (παρουσία) is distinctly implied here as in xxi. 22 f. (comp. 1 John ii. 28). This idea is less prominent in St John's Gospel and Epistles than in the other writings of the New Testament, because they belong to the period after the first great coming of Christ at the overthrow of the Theocracy by the destruction of Jerusalem.

But though the words refer to the last "coming" of Christ, the promise must not be limited to that one "coming" which is the consummation of all "comings." Nor again must it be confined to the "coming" to the Church on the day of Pentecost, or to the "coming" to the individual either at conversion or at death, though these "comings" are included in the thought. Christ is in fact from the moment of His Resurrection ever coming to the world and to the Church, and to men as the Risen Lord (comp. i. 9).

This thought is expressed by the use of the present *I come* as distinguished from the future *I will come*, as of one isolated future act. The "coming" is regarded in its continual present, or, perhaps it may be said, eternal reality. Comp. *vv.* 18, 28, (xvii. 11, 13), (xxi. 22 f.). On the other hand, see, for the definite historical fulfilment, xiv. 23.

Side by side with this constant coming, realised through the action of the Holy Spirit in the life of the Church (*v.* 26), is placed the personal, historical, reception of each believer (*I will take you to myself*) fulfilled through death.

unto myself] the centre and spring of your joy and glory. Christ will not fail His disciples, though they may fail (xiii. 38).

Augustine rightly observes that these phrases of "going" and "coming" are not to be interpreted of local transference: "Si bene intelligo, nec unde vadis nec unde venis, recedis: vadis latendo, venis apparendo."

The double correspondence in the language of the two clauses, *go—come; prepare a place—take you to myself*, gives distinctness to the two aspects of Christ's work.

that where I am...] Presence with Christ, as involving the vision of His glory (xvii. 24), carries with it participation in His Nature. Comp. 1 John iii. 2. See also vii. 34, 36, viii. 21 f., xii. 26.

4. *whither I go ye know, and the way ye know*] According to the true reading, *whither* **I go ye know the way.** However indistinct might be the conception which the disciples had of the goal to which the Lord was going, they could at least see the direction in which He went. His life, as they looked upon it, made this clear. Hence the pronoun is emphatic here—"whither I—I as ye know me—am going," while it does not occur in the earlier clauses of *v.* 3 or in St Thomas' repetition of the words *v.* 5; nor is the following "ye" emphatic.

5—11. The revelation which the Lord had given of the purpose of His approaching separation creates questioning among the disciples. How can they have any true conception of the "way" of which He spoke? How can they have any true knowledge of the Father? The first question is proposed by St Thomas (5—7); and the second by St Philip (8—11).

5. *Thomas saith*] xi. 16, note.

and how can we know the way?] The true text gives a short sentence: **how know we** *the way?* This question of St Thomas expresses a natural difficulty as to the Lord's

we know not whither thou goest; and how can we know the way?

6 Jesus saith unto him, I am the way, the truth, and the life: no man cometh unto the Father, but by me.

7 If ye had known me, ye should have known my Father also: and from henceforth ye know him, and have seen him.

8 Philip saith unto him, Lord, shew us the Father, and it sufficeth us.

---

statement. For us generally a clear apprehension of the end is the condition of knowing the way. But in spiritual things faith is content to move forward step by step. There is a happiness in "not seeing," xx. 29. The "way" is itself the revelation, and for man the only possible revelation, of the end.

6 f. The answer of the Lord is more comprehensive than the question of St Thomas. The question is answered by the first clause: "I am the way;" but such a statement itself requires interpretation, and this is given in the clauses which follow. To know Christ is to know all, to know both the goal and the way. He is in the fullest sense the way, and the guide, and the strength of men; and beside Him there is none other.

6. *I am* ...] not simply "I reveal," or "I "open," or "I make, as a prophet or a lawgiver." Christ is all Himself. The pronoun is emphatic, and at once turns the thoughts of the apostles from a method to a Person.

The beautiful paraphrase of the verse by Thomas a Kempis may be quoted in his own words: "Ego sum via, veritas et vita. Sine via non itur, sine veritate non cognoscitur, sine vita non vivitur. Ego sum via quam sequi debes: veritas cui credere debes: vita quam sperare debes." ('De imit.' III. 56.)

the way] by which the two worlds are united, so that men may pass from one to the other. Comp. Heb. ix. 8, x. 20; Eph. ii. 18. Hence, perhaps, the Christian faith is spoken of as "the way:" Acts ix. 2, xix. 9, 23, xxii. 4, xxiv. 22. The use of the corresponding word in the Chinese mystical system of Lao-tse is of interest. "In the mysticism of Lao the term [Tao, 'the way,' 'the chief way'] is applied to the supreme cause, the way or passage through which everything enters into life, and at the same time to the way of the highest perfection" (Tiele, 'Hist. of Rel.' p. 37).

the truth] in which is summed up all that is eternal and absolute in the changing phenomena of finite being. Comp. viii. 32, i. 14, 17; 1 John v. 6 in connexion with ch. xiv. 26; Eph. iv. 21. For St John's conception of Truth see Introduction, pp. xliv. f. See also Jer. x. 10 (Hebr.) and Maimonides, 'Yad Hach.' I. 1.

the life] by which the entire sum of being fulfils one continuous purpose, answering to the divine will (comp. i. 3, 4), no less than that by which each individual being is enabled to satisfy its own law of progress and to minister to the whole of which it is a part. Comp. xi. 25; Col. iii. 4.

It is most instructive to notice the two connexions in which Christ reveals Himself to be "the Life." Comp. xi. 25, note.

no man cometh unto the Father ...] Here for the first time the end of "the way," even the Father, is distinctly told.

but by (**through**) *me*] It is only through Christ that we can, though in God (Acts xvii. 28), apprehend God as the Father, and so approach the Father. The preposition probably marks the agent (comp. i. 3, 10, 17; 1 John iv. 9); but it is possible that Christ may represent Himself as the "door" (x. 1, 9). It does not follow that every one who is guided by Christ is directly conscious of His guidance.

7. *If ye had known me*—come to know (ἐγνώκειτε) me in the successive revelations of myself which I have made—*ye should have known*—have enjoyed a certain and assured knowledge of (ᾔδειτε) *my Father also*] "The Father" of *v.* 6 is now regarded under His special relation to Christ. The disciples, it is implied, would have had no need to ask about Christ's goal and theirs, if they had really known Him. The change of verb (ἐγνώκειτε, ᾔδειτε) and the change of order (εἰ ἐγνώκ. με, τὸν π. μ. ἂν ᾔδ.) are both significant. Comp. viii. 19.

from henceforth (omit *and*)—from this crisis in my self-revelation—*ye know him, and have seen him*] The announcement which Christ had made had placed the Nature of the Father in a clear light. The disciples could no longer doubt as to His character or purpose. In this sense they had "seen the Father," though God is indeed invisible (i. 18). They had looked upon Him as He is made known in His fatherly relation, and not as He is in Himself. From that time forward the knowledge and the vision became part of their spiritual being. Comp. 1 John ii. 13.

8. St Thomas remains silent. The same faith, we may suppose, which afterwards enabled him to give expression to the great confession, xx. 28, now kept him pondering on the meaning of Christ's words. St Philip, on the other hand, takes hold on the last word and seeks to obtain vision in a more unquestionable form. He wishes to gain bodily sight in place of the sight of the soul.

Philip] i. 46 (47); vi. 7, xii. 21 ff.

9 Jesus saith unto him, Have I been so long time with you, and yet hast thou not known me, Philip? he that hath seen me hath seen the Father; and how sayest thou *then*, Shew us the Father?

10 Believest thou not that I am in the Father, and the Father in me? the words that I speak unto you I speak not of myself: but the Father that dwelleth in me, he doeth the works.

11 Believe me that I *am* in the Father, and the Father in me: or else believe me for the very works' sake.

---

shew us] As the revelation was once made to Moses (Exod. xxxiii. 17 ff.), and as it has been promised in the prophets (Isai. xl. 5). The new dispensation naturally seemed to call for a new manifestation of the divine glory. The request at the same time implies the belief that Christ could satisfy it. Comp. Matt. xi. 27.

it sufficeth us] We shall be contented then even to be left alone; we shall ask and we shall need no more.

9. *Have I been...with you...*] The thought is primarily of the self-revelation of Christ, and not of the power of observation in the disciples (Have ye been...with me...).

...and yet hast thou not known...] **and dost thou not know me?** hast thou not come to know me (ἔγνωκας)? The life of Christ was the true manifestation of the Father, whose will and nature could be discerned in the acts and words of His Son. A theophany—an apparition of God's glory—could only go a little way in shewing His holiness and justice and love.

known me] The Lord does not say here "the Father;" He points out first the way to the end.

Philip] There is an evident pathos in this direct personal appeal. The only partial parallels in St John are in xx. 16 (*Mary*); xxi. 15 (*Simon son of John*); the insertion of *Thomas* in xx. 29 is a false reading. See also Luke xxii. 31, x. 41; Matt. xvi. 17, xvii. 25; Mark xiv. 37.

he that hath seen me hath seen the Father] hath seen not God in His absolute being (i. 18), but God revealed in this relation. Comp. xii. 45, xv. 24; Col. i. 15; Heb. i. 3. Comp. i. 18, note.

The words give for all time a definiteness to the object of religious faith; and it is impossible to mistake the claim which they express.

and (omit) *how sayest thou* (emphatic)] thou, who from the first didst obey my command (i. 43, 44), and recognise in me the fulfilment of the promises of God (i. 45), and appeal to sight as the proof of my claims (i. 46).

10. *Believest thou not...*] It was a question of belief, for the Lord had expressed the truth plainly at an earlier time, x. 38.

I am in the Father, and the Father in me] In x. 38, the order is different, inasmuch as the notion of divine power is there made the starting-point. The teaching of Christ shewed how He was in closest communion with the Father; His works shewed how the Father wrought in Him.

the words] the special utterances (τὰ ῥήματα), the parts of the one great message, xv. 7, xvii. 8. Comp. iii. 34, v. 47, vi. 63, 68, viii. 30, 47, x. 21, xii. 47 f.

speak (**say**)...*speak*] The former verb notes the substance (λέγω) and the latter the form of the teaching (λαλῶ). Comp. xii. 49 f., xvi. 18; Matt. xiii. 3, xiv. 27, xxiii. 1, xxviii. 18; Mark v. 36, vi. 50; Luke xxiv. 6; Rom. iii. 19, &c.

of myself] Comp. v. 19, note.

but the Father...] My teaching is not self-originated, but on the contrary my whole Life is the manifestation of the Father's will.

the Father that dwelleth in me, he doeth the works] According to the true reading, *the Father* **abiding in me doeth His works,** carrieth out actively His purpose in many ways, and my teaching is part of this purpose. "The works" were the elements of "the work" (iv. 34, xvii. 4, v. 36, ix. 4), and they are said to be wrought by the Son (x. 37) as by the Father. Comp. v. 19 f., notes.

The words and the works of Christ are pointed out as the two proofs of His union with the Father, the former appealing to the spiritual consciousness, the latter to the intellect. The former were a revelation of character, the latter primarily of power; and naturally the former have the precedence. Comp. xv. 24, note.

11. *Believe...*] The verb is here plural, πιστεύετε contrasted with πιστεύεις, *v.* 10). Philip had expressed the thoughts of his fellow-disciples, and now the Lord addresses all. *Believe me that*...accept my own statement as final.

or else] if my Person, my life, my words, do not command faith, then follow the way of reason, and from the divinity of my works deduce the divinity of my nature (cf. v. 36). Comp. x. 37 f., iii. 2.

3. *Christ and the disciples* (12—21).

In the last sub-section (8—11) the thoughts of the disciples were concentrated on the objective manifestation of God without them:

12 Verily, verily, I say unto you,
He that believeth on me, the works
that I do shall he do also; and greater
works than these shall he do; because
I go unto my Father.

13 [a] And whatsoever ye shall ask in [a] Ma[tt.]
my name, that will I do, that the [7.]
Father may be glorified in the Son.

14 If ye shall ask any thing in my
name, I will do *it*.

---

they are now turned to the subjective manifestation of God within them. Three aspects of this progressive revelation are brought out in succession. The disciples continue Christ's work in virtue of their relation to Him (12—14). He still carries out His work and provides for them "another Advocate" (15—17). He comes to them Himself (18—21).

A comparison of xiii. 33 ff., xiv. 1 ff., xiv. 12 ff., will shew a striking progress in the unfolding of the vision of Christ's departure.

12—14. Christ's departure enables the disciples to do through His intercession greater works than He had done, in order that the Father may be glorified in the Son.

12. *Verily, verily...*] Christ had appealed to His works as a secondary ground of belief. He now shews that the true believer will himself do the same works. Such works flow from the Son and from those in fellowship with Him; but the life and the nature lie deeper.

believeth on me] as the result of *believing me* (*v.* 11).

shall he do also...] The emphatic pronoun fixes attention upon the person already characterized Comp. vi. 57, and *vv.* 21, 26; xii. 48, ix. 37; v. 39, i. 18, 33.

greater works than these (which I do in my earthly ministry) *shall he do*] "greater" that is, as including the wider spiritual effects of their preaching which followed after Pentecost (Acts ii. 41). "Evangelizantibus discipulis...gentes etiam crediderunt; hæc sunt sine dubitatione majora" (Aug. *ad loc.*). There is no reference to miracles of a more extraordinary kind (*e.g.* Acts xix. 12), as if there were a possibility of this material comparison (yet comp. Matt. xxi. 21 f.). Nor can "greater" be regarded as equivalent to "more."

These "greater works" are also works of Christ, being done by those who "believe on Him."

because...] The elevation of Christ in His humanity to the right hand of God carries with it the pledge of the greater works promised. The idea is not that the disciples will henceforward work because Christ will be absent; but that His going increases their power (xvi. 7; comp. Eph. iv. 8 ff.; Phil. iv. 13). The emphatic pronoun (*I*) does not give a contrast with "ye," but brings out the fulness of Christ's personality.

my Father] **the Father** according to the true reading. The title gives the ground of fellowship.

13. *And whatsoever...*] This clause may be either a continuation of the former clause and dependent on "because;" or a new and independent clause carrying forward the thought one stage further. The second alternative appears to be preferable. The union of Christ, perfect man, with the Father gives the assurance of the greater works; and yet more, Christ for the glory of the Father will fulfil the prayer of the disciples.

ask (of God) *in my name*] The phrase *in my name* occurs here first. Compare *in the name of my Father*, v. 43, x. 25, (xii. 13), xvii. 6, 11, 12, 26, and the words of the Evangelist, i. 12, ii. 23, iii. 18, xx. 21.

Now at last the Lord has revealed His Person to the disciples, and they are enabled to apprehend His relation to themselves and to the Father. Thus the phrase occurs throughout this section of the Gospel. xiv. 26, "the Holy Spirit, whom the Father will send in my name;" xv. 16, "that whatsoever ye shall ask (αἰτῆτε, αἰτήσητε) the Father in my name, He may give you;" xvi. 23, "if ye shall ask (αἰτήσητε) anything of the Father, He will give it you in my name;" xvi. 24, "hitherto have ye asked (ᾐτήσατε) nothing in my name;" xvi. 26, "in that day ye shall ask (αἰτήσεσθε) in my name." Comp. xv. 21.

The meaning of the phrase is "as being one with me even as I am revealed to you." Its two correlatives are *in me* (vi. 56, xiv. 20, xv. 4 ff., xvi. 33; comp. 1 John v. 20); and the Pauline *in Christ*. It occurs elsewhere in the New Testament in Mark ix. 38, xvi. 17; Luke x. 17; Acts ii. 38, iii. 6, iv. 10. The phrase *in the name* (ἐν τῷ ὀνόματι) must be distinguished from the cognate phrases *into the name*, *on the name* (εἰς τὸ ὄνομα, ἐπὶ τῷ ὀνόματι, and τῷ ὀνόματι), which are also found.

Augustine remarks that the prayer in Christ's name must be consistent with Christ's character, and that He fulfils it as Saviour, and therefore just so far as it conduces to salvation.

that (**this**) *will I do*] There is exact conformity between the disciples' prayer and Christ's will. He promises Himself to do what they ask, and not only that they shall receive their petition.

that the Father...] that God may be openly revealed in majesty as Father in the Son, for he who obtains his prayer through Christ, who claims to act in the Father's name (v. 43), necessarily gains a more living and grateful sense of the Father's power and love. The

15 ¶ If ye love me, keep my commandments.
16 And I will pray the Father, and he shall give you another Comforter, that he may abide with you for ever;
17 *Even* the Spirit of truth; whom the world cannot receive, because it

---

condition—the furtherance of the Father's glory—furnishes the true limitation of prayer. Comp. xiii. 31 ("*the Son of man* ... and *God* ...").

14. *If ye shall ask any thing in my name...*] The most ancient authorities add *me: if ye shall ask* **me** *anything*... This reading gives a fresh and important thought. Prayer is to be made not only *in the name of Christ*, as pleading His office in union with Him; but also *to Christ*.

I will do it] Or perhaps **this** (or *that*) *will I do* (τοῦτο ποιήσω). The reading is uncertain; but on the whole it seems best to regard the personal pronoun as emphatic here (ἐγὼ ποιήσω), so that it marks as elsewhere the action of Christ in the fulness of His double nature.

15—17. Christ after His departure continues His work for His disciples, and provides for them an abiding Advocate. But the efficiency of His action for them depends upon their fellowship with Him through loving obedience.

15. *If ye love me...*] The thought of love follows that of faith (*v.* 12). Faith issues in works of power: love in works of devotion. The subject of the love of the disciples for Christ (comp. viii. 42) is peculiar to this and the following section (15—31).

keep] According to the true reading, **ye will keep**. Obedience is the necessary consequence of love. The imperative reading gives a false turn to the thought. Love carries with it practical devotion, and this calls out the intercession of the Lord; or, in other words, love for Christ finds practical expression in love for the brethren, which is His commandment (xiii. 34). Comp. xv. 10, xiv. 21, 23; (1 John v. 3).

my commandments] The commandments that are mine, characteristic of me (τὰς ἐντολὰς τὰς ἐμάς, comp. xv. 9 note, xv. 12: in *v.* 21, xv. 10, τὰς ἐντολάς μου). The phrase in this connexion is nothing short of a claim to divine authority.

It may be added that this conception of "keeping God's commandments given through Christ" is characteristic of St John's writings: xv. 10; 1 John ii. 3 f., iii. 24, v. 2 f.; 2 John 6; Rev. xii. 17. Compare with this wider meaning Matt. xix. 17; 1 Tim. vi. 14.

16. *And I will pray* (**ask**)...] I on my part, when the due time has come. Active love on the part of Christ corresponds to active love on the part of the disciples. The mission of the Paraclete is from the Father who sent His Son (iii. 17). In this lies the perfect assurance of love; so that there is a correspondence between "I will do" (*v.* 13) and "I will ask and he shall give." Comp. xvi. 7. On *ask* (ἐρωτᾶν) see xvi. 26 note.

the Father] In this common title lies the pledge that the prayer will be granted.

shall give] Not *send* simply (*v.* 26), but (as it were) assign to you as your own. Comp. iii. 16; 1 John iii. 1, 24, iv. 13; Matt. x. 20.

another Comforter (**Advocate**)] See Note at the end of the Chapter. The phrase appears to mark distinctly the Personality of the Paraclete, and His true Divinity. He is "another," yet such that in His coming Christ too may be said to come (*v.* 18).

abide with you] **be** *with you*, according to the true text. Three different prepositions are used to describe the relation of the Holy Spirit to believers. He is "with (μετά) them." He "abideth by (παρά) them." He is "in (ἐν) them." The first marks the relation of fellowship: comp. xiv. 9, xv. 27. The second that of a personal presence: comp. viii. 38, xiv. 23, 25, xvii. 5. The third that of individual indwelling: comp. xiv. 10 f.

for ever] Christ's historical Presence was only for a time. His spiritual Presence was "for all the days until the consummation of the age" (Matt. xxviii. 20). This Presence was fulfilled through the Spirit.

17. *the Spirit of truth*] the Spirit by whom the Truth finds expression and is brought to man's spirit (xv. 26, xvi. 13; 1 John iv. 6 [opposed to "the spirit of error"]. Comp. 1 John v. 6). Comp. 1 Cor. ii. 12 ff. The Truth is that which the Spirit interprets and enforces. The gen. after "Spirit" describes in some cases (1) its characteristic, and in other cases, (2) its source. In the first sense we read Eph. i. 13; Hebr. x. 29. Comp. Eph. i. 17; Luke xiii. 11; Rom. i. 4, viii. 15, xi. 8; 1 Cor. iv. 21; 2 Tim. i. 7. On the other hand we have 1 Cor. vi. 11; Rom. viii. 11; 1 Cor. ii. 11 f.

the world] Comp. Additional Note on i. 10.

cannot receive] because sympathy is a necessary condition for reception. The soul can apprehend that only for which it has affinity (1 Cor. ii. 14). They who stand apart from Christ have neither the spiritual eye to discern the Paraclete, nor the spiritual power to acknowledge Him. Immediate vision is the one test which the world admits. The world **beholdeth** (comp. ii. 23, note, xvi. 16) *him*

seeth him not, neither knoweth him: but ye know him; for he dwelleth with you, and shall be in you.

18 I will not leave you ‖ comfortless: I will come to you.

‖ Or, *orphans.*

19 Yet a little while, and the world seeth me no more; but ye see me: because I live, ye shall live also.

20 At that day ye shall know that

---

not, neither knoweth (comp. ii. 25, note) *him.* This inability to receive the Spirit is emphasized by the fact that "His own people" received not the Word (i. 11). Even of the disciples it is not said that they "see" the Paraclete.

because...for (**because**)...] It is to be noticed that the order of thought in the two clauses is reversed. With the world want of vision prevented possession. With the disciples the personal presence of the Paraclete brought knowledge, and with that knowledge the power of more complete reception. Comp. Matt. xxv. 29.

but (omit) *ye know him*] On the other hand, the disciples had so far realised their fellowship with Christ, that of them it could be said, even as they looked with uncertainty to the future, "ye know (γινώσκετε) Him," with a knowledge inchoate indeed, yet real. For in Christ the Spirit was truly present already, if not in His characteristic manifestation; just as Christ is present now with His Church in the Spirit. In this sense it could be said of the Spirit, even before Pentecost, *He abideth* **by** *you and* **is** *in you*, according to a reading which has strong support. For the time the Spirit was in Christ; afterwards Christ has been for us in the Spirit. And His Presence is twofold, in the Society and in the individual; He "abideth beside" us in the Church; and He "is" in each believer. The common reading "shall be in you" has considerable support, and the two forms in the original (ἔσται, ἐστί) are liable to confusion, but the present tense appears to be less like a correction. Comp. 2 John 2.

18—21. A third topic of consolation on Christ's departure lies in the fact that He will Himself come to the disciples, and make His Person clearer to them than before.

18. *I will not leave* (x. 12, xvi. 32, viii. 29) *you comfortless*] Orphans (Lam. v. 3), bereft of your natural and loving guardian (ὀρφανούς, Vulg. *orfanos*). Christ presents Himself to the disciples as a Father of "children" (xiii. 33), no less than as a brother (xx. 17; comp. Hebr. ii. 11 f.). "Ipse circa nos paternum affectum quodammodo demonstrat" (Aug. *ad loc.*). The very word which describes their sorrow confirms their sonship.

I will come] **I come**, ever and at all times I am coming. The positive promise is not for the future only, but abiding. Comp. *vv.* 3, 28, xxi. 22 f. The fulfilment of the promise began at the Resurrection, when Christ's humanity was glorified; and the promise was potentially completed at Pentecost. The life of the Church is the realisation of the Pentecostal coming of the Lord, which is to be crowned by His coming to Judgment. No one specific application of the phrase exhausts its meaning. Comp. *v.* 3, note.

19. *Yet a little while*] That is, to the close of Christ's earthly natural life (comp. vii. 33, xii. 35, μ. χρ.; xiii. 33, xvi. 16 ff., μικρ.). So long, in some sense, the world continued to "see" (**behold**) Christ even if they did not "know" Him, through the conditions of His transitory manifestation. The disciples, on the other hand, in virtue of the principle of spiritual life within them, did not wholly lose the power of "seeing" (**beholding**) Christ by His death. They "beheld Him," so far as they were still able to receive His revelations of Himself; they "did not behold Him" (xvi. 16), so far as they had not yet gained the lasting vision of His divine glory. The words exclude the error of those who suppose that Christ will "come" under the same conditions of earthly existence as those to which He submitted at His first coming.

because I live...also] The ground of the power of vision in the disciples, which the world lacked, lay in their fellowship with Christ, and in the capacity for the higher life involved in that fellowship. The fulness of their life, as of their sight, dated from Pentecost (*shall live*). Thus this first clause contains by implication the reason of the disciples' continuous sight of their Lord, while it gives also the promise of their more complete connexion with Him when He was raised from death. The open sight of God is the fulness of life, 1 John iii. 1 ff. Compare v. 26, vi. 57; and, in another aspect, 1 Cor. xv. 21 f.

If the words are taken (as the original allows) wholly or in part as a direct explanation of the former statement (*ye behold me, because I live and ye shall live*, or *ye behold me because I live, and ye shall live*) the sense is much feebler; and the construction is not in St John's manner. Comp. xiii. 14, xiv. 3, xv. 20.

20. *At that day*] of realised life (comp. xvi. 23, 26) you shall come to know by the teaching of the Spirit, what is for the time (*v.* 10) a matter of faith only, my union with Him who is not only "the Father," but "my Father," and then, in that knowledge, realise the fulness of your fellowship with me. "The

I *am* in my Father, and ye in me, and I in you.

21 He that hath my commandments, and keepeth them, he it is that loveth me: and he that loveth me shall be loved of my Father, and I will love him, and will manifest myself to him.

22 Judas saith unto him, not Iscariot, Lord, how is it that thou wilt manifest thyself unto us, and not unto the world?

23 Jesus answered and said unto him, If a man love me, he will keep my words: and my Father will love him, and we will come unto

---

day" corresponds to "the coming," but generally it marks each victorious crisis of the new apprehension of the Risen Christ.

I am in my Father] The converse truth (*my Father in me*, *vv.* 10 f., xvii. 21) is not brought forward here, because the thought is predominantly that of the consummation of life in the divine order, and not that of the divine working in the present order.

ye in me, and I in you] The union is regarded first in its spiritual completeness, and then in its historical completeness (comp. xvii. 21, 23, (26); 1 John iii. 24, iv. 13, 15, 16).

21. *He that hath...and keepeth...*] The first verb (*hath*) marks the actual possession, as of something which is clearly and firmly apprehended (v. 38); the second (*keepeth*), the personal fulfilment.

The verse is in part the converse of *v.* 15. There active obedience is seen to be the consequence of love. Here active obedience is the sign of the presence of love. Comp. xv. 10.

The variation of construction (*shall be loved by*, *I will love*) in the second clause is to be noticed (see *v.* 23). The passive form (*shall be loved by*) seems to bring out the idea of the conscious experience of love by the object of it. The believer loves and feels in himself the action of the Father through Christ (*my Father*).

will manifest myself] The exact force of the word (ἐμφανίζω) is that of presentation in a clear, conspicuous form (comp. Matt. xxvii. 53; Hebr. ix. 24; [Acts x. 40; Rom. x. 20]; Exod. xxxiii. 13, 18). It conveys therefore more than the idea of the disclosing of a hidden presence (ἀποκαλύπτω) or the manifesting of an undiscovered one (φανερόω). The action of the Spirit effectuates in the believer this higher manifestation of Christ, which more than supplies the place of His Presence under the conditions of earthly life. At the same time the revelation is Christ's own work: "I will manifest myself," and not "I shall be manifested" (comp. *v.* 18, note).

4. *The law and the progress of Revelation* (22—31).

The description which has been given (12—21) of the future relation of Christ to His disciples leads to a more general view of the nature of Revelation. This falls into three parts. First the condition of Revelation is laid down in answer to the question of St Jude (22—24); then the mode of Revelation is defined (25—27); and lastly the work of Christ for His people, fulfilled in heaven and on earth, is recapitulated (28—31).

22—24. On the side of man love and obedience are pre-requisites for the reception of divine communications. These Christ calls out, and to reject His teaching is to reject the teaching of God.

22. *Judas, not Iscariot*] Luke vi. 16; Acts i. 13. Comp. Matt. x. 3; Mark iii. 18. The distinguishing clause seems at once to mark that Judas Iscariot was the more conspicuous of the two bearing the name, and also to express the instinctive shrinking of the Evangelist from even the momentary identification of the speaker with the betrayer, though he had distinctly marked the departure of Iscariot (xiii. 30). If, as appears likely, St John's narrative took shape in oral teaching addressed to a circle of disciples, the addition may have met a look of surprise from the hearers.

Lord, how is it that...] *Lord*, **what hath come to pass** *that*... The question implies that some change must have come over the plans of the Lord. It is assumed that as Messiah He would naturally have revealed Himself publicly: something then must have happened, so Judas argues, by which the sphere of Christ's manifestation was limited. The thought is rather of a manifestation of glory than of a manifestation of judgment.

unto us] The emphatic position of the pronoun ("that it is to us thou wilt...") gives it the force of "to us, the apostles, only."

the world] which was the object of God's love (iii. 16) and Messiah's inheritance (Ps. ii. 8). An apostle now raises in another form the question which was raised by the Lord's brethren before: vii. 4.

23. *Jesus answered...*] The answer lies in the necessary conditions of revelation which the words describe. The power of receiving a divine Revelation depends upon active obedience, which rests upon personal love. Love to Christ brings the love of His Father (*my Father* and not simply *the Father*) to the disciple. And this is followed by the realisa-

him, and make our abode with him.

24 He that loveth me not keepeth not my sayings: and the word which ye hear is not mine, but the Father's which sent me.

25 These things have I spoken unto you, being *yet* present with you.

26 But the Comforter, *which is* the Holy Ghost, whom the Father will send in my name, he shall teach

---

tion and continuance of that fellowship through which God is revealed to man. Love, obedience, and knowledge are correlative. Compare *v.* 15, note.

my words] *my* **word**, the Gospel message in its total unity, and not as broken up into separate commands (*v.* 15), or separate parts (*v.* 24).

we will come...] This use of the plural (*we*) implies necessarily the claim to true divinity on the part of Christ; compare x. 30 (note), and contrast xx. 17 (note). For the idea compare Rev. iii. 20.

abode] The original word (μονή, Vulg. *mansio*), even in the changed connexion, carries the thought back to *v.* 2 (μοναί, *mansions*). The two aspects of the truth are necessary. Comp. 1 John iv. 15, ii. 24. The Christian abides with God, and God abides with the Christian.

with him (*vv.* 17, 25)] and not here *in him*. The idea is that of the recognition of the divine without (so to speak) and not of the consciousness of the divine within. The Christian sees God by him (παρ' αὐτῷ); he welcomes and finds a dwelling-place for God, and does not only feel Him in him. Compare for the general idea Lev. xxvi. 11 ff.

24. The love of the disciples fitted them, imperfect as they were, to receive Christ's revelation of Himself. The want of love in the world made revelation impossible for the world. This impossibility is indicated and traced to its final ground in the last clause, which corresponds in relation though not in form to the last clause of *v.* 23. Disobedience to Christ is in fact disobedience to God under the aspect of Love. To reject His word is to reject the Father's word. For such then as loved not Christ there could be no divine manifestation in the sense here implied. Comp. vii. 16.

keepeth not my sayings] *my* **words** (λόγους), the constituent parts of the one "word." The use of the plural here may perhaps mark the perception of the unity of the revelation of the Lord as characteristic of believers and impossible for unbelievers.

which ye hear] The clause is unemphatic, and appears simply to describe the divine message in its fulness as actually addressed to the apostles.

25—27. The earthly teaching of Christ was dependent on the circumstances under which it was given. His temporary "abiding with the disciples" was but an image of the future abiding (*v.* 23). So far (*these things*) He had been able to speak while those who heard could at least partly understand Him. There could not but be something which seemed incomplete, and something which seemed obscure to the hearers. But this teaching, now brought to its close, was to be completed and laid open by the teaching of the Spirit, which should be universal (*all things* as contrasted with *these things*). And meanwhile Christ gave His peace as an endowment for the time of waiting.

25. *These things...*] all that had been spoken on this evening in contrast with the further teaching (*all things*) of the Paraclete.

being yet present...] **while yet abiding...** The word used (μένων, Vulg. *manens*) keeps up the connexion between the transitory fellowship of Christ with the disciples on earth and His spiritual fellowship with them hereafter (μονὴν ποιησόμεθα, *v.* 23).

26. *the Comforter* (**Advocate**), *which is* (**even**) *the Holy Ghost* (**Spirit**), *whom the Father will send in my name*] As compared with Christ the Paraclete fulfils a double office: He teaches and He recalls Christ's teachings. His work indeed is to teach by bringing home to men the whole of Christ's teaching. The revelation of Christ in His Person and work was absolute and complete, but without the gradual illumination of the Spirit it is partly unintelligible and partly unobserved. Comp. xvi. 13; 1 John ii. 20, 27.

As Christ came "in His Father's name" (v. 43, x. 25), so the Spirit is sent "in His name." The purpose of Christ's mission was to reveal God as His Father, and through this to make known His relation to men, and to humanity, and to the world. The purpose of the Mission of the Holy Spirit is to reveal Christ, to make clear to the consciousness of the Church the full significance of the Incarnation. Christ's "name," all, that is, which can be defined as to His nature and His work, is the sphere in which the Spirit acts; and so little by little through the long life of the Church the meaning of the primitive confession "Jesus is Lord" (Rom. x. 9; 1 Cor. xii. 3) is made more fully known.

The sense of the promise is completely

you all things, and bring all things to
your remembrance, whatsoever I have
said unto you.
27 Peace I leave with you, my
peace I give unto you: not as the
world giveth, give I unto you. Let
not your heart be troubled, neither let
it be afraid.
28 Ye have heard how I said unto
you, I go away, and come *again* unto
you. If ye loved me, ye would rejoice, because I said, I go unto the

---

destroyed if "in my name" is interpreted as meaning nothing more than "as my representative" or "at my intercession."

the Holy Ghost] The full emphatic title (τὸ Πνεῦμα τὸ ἅγιον) occurs here only in the Gospel. The moral character of the Spirit as fashioning the life of the Church is added to the teaching power of the Spirit (*vv.* 16, 17), as the Revealer of the Truth. The title occurs in the words of the Lord in the Synoptic Gospels: Matt. xii. 32; Mark iii. 29; Luke xii. 10 (τὸ ἁ. πν.), 12 (τὸ ἁ. πν.); Mark xiii. 11; Matt. xxviii. 19 (τὸ ἁ. πν.).

he shall...] The emphatic masculine pronoun (ἐκεῖνος) brings out the personality of the Advocate, while at the same time it gathers up in the personality the various attributes which have been before indicated (i. 18, note).

teach...bring to remembrance...] The former office appears to find its fulfilment in the interpretation of the true character of Christ, of what He was, and what He did: the latter, in opening the minds of the disciples to the right understanding of Christ's words: comp. ii. 22. So the Gospel could be written. The "you" does not limit the teaching of the Spirit to the apostles, who were the representatives of the Church (*vv.* 16, 17), though the promise was potentially accomplished for them (xvi. 12 f.).

all things...whatsoever I have said] *all things* ... **that I said.** The time of teaching is now regarded as past. Comp. xvii. 6, &c. The position of the personal pronoun at the end of the sentence (according to the most probable reading: εἶπον ὑμῖν ἐγώ) is very significant.

27. *Peace*] The word is here a solemn farewell, just as in xx. 21 it is a solemn greeting. To "give peace" (נתן שלום) was a customary phrase of salutation (Buxtorf, 'Lex.' 2425). The Lord takes the common words and transforms them. "God gave to Phinehas," Philo writes in reference to Num. xxv. 12, "the greatest blessing, even peace, a blessing which no man is able to afford" ('De vit. Mos.' I. § 55, ii. 129).

I leave] The thought of separation is mingled with the thought of blessing. Even in departing the Lord leaves peace behind as His bequest. He will not disturb that peace which the disciples had found in Him and in part appropriated. On the contrary, He defines and confirms it and offers it to them as their own. "*Peace*, even *my peace*, *I give unto you*," that peace of which I am the absolute Lord and source (comp. xv. 9, note), not regarded on its outward side as the blessedness of the Messianic kingdom, but as the realised confidence of faith and fellowship with God. Comp. ch. xvi. 33; Col. iii. 15; Phil. iv. 7. So the Lord speaks in the immediate prospect of Death, by which peace was finally secured, Col. i. 20; Rom. v. 1.

I give] as an absolute possession, which now becomes your own. Comp. 1 John iii. 1.

not as the world giveth...] The primary thought is of the manner of the gift, which passes into that of the character of the gift. The gifts of the world are so made as to give the greatest pleasure at first (comp. ii. 10) The gifts of Christ grow in power and fulness of blessing. Thus in the consciousness of the beginnings of this divine gift of peace the disciples were encouraged to overcome inward misgivings and to face outward dangers. "Let not your heart be troubled, neither let it be fearful." The opening words of the chapter are repeated with a new force.

let it be afraid] **be fearful** (δειλιάτω). Comp. 2 Tim. i. 7; Matt. viii. 26; Mark iv. 40; Rev. xxi. 8 (where the "fearful," the "cowards," stand at the head of those devoted to the second death).

28—31. The last verse (*v.* 27) stands closely related to both of the sub-sections between which it stands. The peace of Christ attends the Church during the period of gradual revelation, and it flows from Christ's work accomplished in heaven as on earth. This latter thought is brought out in these verses under both aspects. The departure of Christ, the great mystery of His revelation, led to the more effectual fulfilment of His work in virtue of His perfected fellowship with the Father (28, 29); and the mode of His departure, through death, the penalty of sin, was a proof of obedience and love fitted to move the world (30, 31).

28. *Ye have heard*] **Ye heard.** The addition of the word seems to mark the effect of the announcement on the disciples. The revelation was made and carefully noted.

I said unto you] *vv.* 2—4.

and come again] *and* **I come.** The insertion of "again" narrows the application of the promise. See *v.* 18, note.

If ye loved me] if your minds had not been concentrated on yourselves: if you had

Father: for my Father is greater than I.

29 And now I have told you before it come to pass, that, when it is come to pass, ye might believe.

30 Hereafter I will not talk much with you: for the prince of this world cometh, and hath nothing in me.

31 But that the world may know that I love the Father; and as the Father gave me commandment, even so I do. Arise, let us go hence.

---

thought only of me and of the fulfilment of my work—

ye would rejoice] **have rejoiced**. The prospect of trouble is contrasted with the feeling of joy. But the joy is spoken of as the momentary feeling on realising the announcement (ἐχάρητε) and not as a continuous state. Sorrow there must be at separation, but it can be brightened by the knowledge of the cause.

because I said, I go] The words *I said* must be omitted in accordance with the best authorities. Attention is fixed on the fact itself, and not on the statement of the fact.

for my Father (**because the Father**) *is greater than I*] and therefore when my union with Him is made complete by my elevation I shall be able to carry out my work for all the children of the one Father more effectually. The ground of the disciples' joy, as based upon their love for Christ, must be sought primarily in the fact of His exaltation; but this carries with it the thought of the consequent more complete fulfilment of His purposes. The return of the Son to the Father was a good for Him, and this alone would have been a sufficient cause for the disciples' rejoicing. But His exaltation was also essentially related to the accomplishment of His mission. Thus the prospect of blessing to the disciples is necessarily included in that of Christ's going to the Father, though it is not put forward as the cause of their joy.

greater than I] It appears to be unquestionable that the Lord here speaks in the fulness of His indivisible Personality. The "I" is the same as in viii. 58, x. 30. The superior greatness of the Father must therefore be interpreted in regard to the absolute relations of the Father and the Son without violation of the one equal Godhead. The fact that there was an essential fitness, if we may so speak of mysteries which transcend human language, in the Incarnation of the Son, enables us in some measure to apprehend this distinction of greatness, and also how the return of the Son to the Father, after the fulfilment of His mission, would be a source of joy to those who loved Him. See Note at the end of the Chapter.

29. *And now*] at this crisis (xii. 31), when your faith is about to be put to the test.

I have told you] of my departure, and yet more of what is implied in it, *before it come to pass*. The mode of separation, not yet realised, would prove the greatest trial to the apostles' faith. But the results which followed such a Death would afterwards enable them to trust for ever. Comp. xiii. 19.

that ye might (**may**) *believe*] The absolute use of the word includes all the special manifestations of faith. Other references to the ground of assurance to be found in the Lord's predictions occur, xiii. 19, xvi. 4. Comp. i. 7, 51, iv. 42, 53, vi. 64.

30. *Hereafter I will not talk...*] Literally, **I will no more talk...**

the prince of this (**the**) *world*] xii. 31, note.

cometh] even now is coming in the persons of those whom he inspires. All other enemies are, as it were, the instruments of the one great enemy. The Lord, it will be observed, speaks of the chief and not of the subordinate spirits, and contemplates his action through men. Comp. Eph. vi. 10 ff.

and hath nothing in me] More exactly, *and* **in me he hath nothing**—nothing which falls under his power. There was in Christ nothing which the devil could claim as belonging to his sovereignty. In others he finds that which is his own, and enforces death as his due; but Christ offered Himself voluntarily. He was not of the world. "Sic ostendit non creaturarum sed peccatorum principem diabolum" (Aug. *ad loc.*).

Thus the words indirectly and by implication affirm the sinlessness of Christ, and His freedom from the power of death.

The two facts which shew the nature of Christ's Passion are first coordinated, and then His free action is contrasted with them: the prince...cometh *and* he hath...*but* that...

The Jews had a tradition that when the angel of death came before David he could not hurt him because he was occupied unceasingly with lofty thoughts (Wünsche, *ad loc.*).

31. The construction of this verse is somewhat uncertain. The first part may be dependent on the last clause: *arise, let us go hence...that the world...and that as...even so I do* (Matt. ix. 6); but this arrangement is too artificial, and foreign to St John's style. If then the last clause is separated from what precedes, there still remain two possible interpretations. The first clause may be dependent on "so I do:" *i.e.* I go to meet death *that the world...and even as...commandment*. But this arrangement is open to the same objection as the former one, and separates unnaturally the *even as...so...* It remains therefore to

take the opening phrase *but that* as elliptical (comp. ix. 3, xiii. 18, xv. 25; 1 John ii. 19): *but* I surrender myself to suffering and death —that cometh to pass which will come to pass —*that the world...* The force of the contrast is obvious: *but* though the prince of the world has no claim upon me, I freely offer myself to the uttermost powers of evil, to death the last punishment of sin, that in me the world itself may see the greater power of love, and so learn (if God will) that the kingdom of Satan is overthrown.

the world] Comp. xvii. 21, 23.

and as...] It is uncertain whether this clause depends on "know" or not. The sense is the same in both cases: obedience flows from love and manifests it. Comp. Hebr. v. 8; 1 John v. 3.

Arise, let us go hence] The coincidence of the phrase with Matt. xxvi. 46 is interesting. The words are such as would naturally be repeated under like circumstances. We must suppose that after these words were spoken the Lord, with the eleven, at once left the house and went on the way which finally led to Gethsemane; and consequently that the discourses which follow, xv.—xvii., were spoken after He had gone from the upper room and before He crossed the Kidron (xviii. 1).

The other supposition, that the Lord after rising still lingered in the room, as full of the thoughts of the coming events, appears to be wholly against the obvious interpretation of the narrative, and to disregard the clear distinction in character between the earlier and later discourses. On the other hand, the words in xviii. 1, *went forth...over the brook Kidron*, cause no difficulty, for this "going forth" is evidently in regard to the sacred city and not to the house; nor is there anything in the abruptness of the narrative unlike St John's method. Further, it may be said that if the command had not been acted upon some notice of the delay would have been given.

ADDITIONAL NOTES on CHAP. XIV. 16, 28.

16. The word παράκλητος, translated *Comforter* in this passage, is found in the New Testament only in the writings of St John. It occurs four times in the Gospel (xiv. 16, 26, xv. 26, xvi. 7), and is in these places uniformly translated *Comforter;* and once in his first Epistle (ii. 1), where it is translated *advocate*. There is no marginal rendering in any place.

This double rendering dates from Wiclif. Both the Wicliffite versions give *Comforter* throughout the Gospel and *advocate* in the Epistle. Tyndale has the same renderings; and the two words have been preserved in the later English Bibles (the Great Bible, the Bishops' Bible, Geneva, King James's) with the exception of the Rhemish, which gives *Paraclete* in the Gospel and *advocate* in the Epistle.

This variation, which is found also in Luther (*Tröster*, Gosp., *Fürsprecher*, Ep.), is unquestionably due to the influence of the Latin Vulgate, which has *Paracletus* (*Paraclĭtus*) in the Gospel and *advocatus* in the Epistle.

The early Latin copies are divided, and not always consistent, in the Gospel. In xv. 26 and xvi. 7, *Pal.*, and in xiv. 16, *Pal. Verc. Colb.*, give the rendering *advocatus*. In the other cases *Pal. Verc. Ver. Colb. Corb.* give *paracletus* (*paraclitus*). This division indicates the existence of the two renderings from the earliest times, so that it is not possible to say that one is a correction of the other. In the Epistle the rendering is (I believe) uniformly *advocatus*.

Nearly all the other early versions, the Syriac, Memphitic, Arabic, and Æthiopic, keep the original word *Paracletus;* and it is likely, both from this fact and from the use of the word in Rabbinic writers, that it found early and wide currency in the East. The Thebaic gives different renderings in the Gospel and in the Epistle (Lightfoot, 'Revision of New Testament,' p. 55, note).

Among the Latin Fathers in quotations from the Gospel, Tertullian generally adopts the rendering *advocatus*, though he uses also *paracletus*, and gives an independent rendering *exorator* ('de Pudic.' 19). *Advocatus* is also predominant in Novatian, Hilary, and Lucifer. Ambrose and Jerome on the other hand usually give *Paracletus*. *Consolator* occurs as a rendering in Hilary, Jerome, and Orosius. In the Epistle *advocatus* is found with little variation, though Ambrose, Victor, and Vigilius read in some places *Paracletus*.

The English rendering "Comforter" appears to have been formed directly from the verb "to comfort," *i.e.* to strengthen (comp. Wiclif, Eph. vi. 10, *be ye comforted*, ἐνδυναμοῦσθε, *confortamini*), an adaptation of *confortare*. The noun *confortator* does not appear to be found; nor is there, as far as I can learn, any corresponding French word.

Passing now from the history of the word in the translations of the New Testament, which finally leaves us with the choice between the retention of the original term *paracletus* and the rendering *advocatus*, we go on to consider the meaning of the word independently. This ought to be decisively determined by the form of the word and common usage, unless there be anything in the context which imperatively requires some other sense.

(*a*) The form of the word is unquestionably passive. It can properly mean only "one called to the side of another," and that with the secondary notion of counselling or supporting or aiding him. On these points the cognate forms (κλητός, ἀνάκλητος, ἀπόκλητος, ἔγκλητος, ἐπίκλητος, σύγκλητος, &c.) and the use of the verb (παρακαλεῖν) are decisive. No example of a like form with an active (middle) sense can be brought forward.

(β) The classical use of the word is equally clear. The word is used technically for the "advocates" of a party in a cause, and specially for advocates for the defence. So Demosthenes speaks of the entreaties and personal influence of advocates (αἱ τῶν παρακλήτων δεήσεις καὶ σπουδαί, 'De Falsa Leg.' p. 341. Comp. 'De Cor.' p. 275).

(γ) The word is not found in the LXX.; but in Job xvi. 2 παράκλητοι occurs in Aquila and Theodotion, for the LXX. παρακλήτορες (Symm. παρηγοροῦντες) as a rendering of the Hebrew מנחמים. There is however no reason to suppose that the two words are identical in meaning; and it is likely that the associations which had gathered round παράκλητος in the second century led to the substitution of a common for a rare word.

Philo uses the word several times and in characteristic senses as *advocate* or *intercessor*. "We must find," he writes, "a more powerful advocate by whom (the emperor) Gaius will be brought to a favourable disposition towards us (δεῖ παράκλητον...εὑρεῖν...ὑφ' οὗ Γάϊος ἐξευμενισθήσεται); and that advocate is the city of Alexandria ... and it will use its advocacy (παρακλητεύσει)..." ('Leg. in Flacc.' 968 B. Comp. p. 967 B).

And in another place, speaking of the function of the High Priest, he says, "It was necessary that he who has been consecrated to the Father of the Universe should employ as advocate (intercessor) one most perfect in virtue, even the Son, both to obtain forgiveness of sins and a supply of most bountiful blessings" (παρακλήτῳ χρῆσθαι τελειοτάτῳ τὴν ἀρετὴν υἱῷ πρός τε ἀμνηστίαν ἁμαρτημάτων καὶ χορηγίαν ἀφθονεστάτων ἀγαθῶν) ('de Vit. Mos.' III. § 14, ii. p. 155 C. Compare 'de Opif. Mundi,' p. 4 f.).

(δ) The word is not unfrequent in the Rabbinical writers. Buxtorf (s. v. פרקליט) gives several interesting examples of its use. "He who fulfils one precept gains for himself one advocate (παράκλητος); he who commits one transgression gains for himself one accuser" (κατήγορος. Comp. Rev. xii. 10). "In the heavenly judgment a man's advocates (παράκλητοι) are repentance and good works." "All the righteousness (comp. Matt. vi. 1) and mercy which an Israelite doeth in this world are great peace and great advocates between him and his Father in heaven." "An advocate is a good intercessor before a magistrate or king."

(ε) There are instances of the occurrence of the word in early Christian writers. Barnabas ('Ep.' xx.) speaks of those who are "advocates of the wealthy (πλουσίων παράκλητοι) and unjust judges of the poor." And in the Letter of the Churches of Vienne and Lyons, Vettius Epagathus, who had voluntarily pleaded the cause of his fellow Christians, is spoken of as "the advocate of the Christians who had the Advocate in himself, even the Spirit" (Euseb. 'H. E.' v. 1). "Who will be our advocate (παράκλητος) [at the last day]," we read in the Second Epistle of Clement, "if we be not found with works holy and just?" (II. Clem. 6).

(ζ) Thus the independent usage of the term is perfectly clear and in strict accordance with the form of the word. But on the other hand, the Greek Fathers in interpreting the passages of the New Testament commonly give the word an active sense, as if it were "the consoler," "the encourager," "the comforter" (ὁ παρακαλῶν). This sense is given to the word as early as Origen, if Ruffinus can be trusted. "Paraclete," he says, "in the Greek has the two meanings 'intercessor' and 'consoler' (deprecatorem et consolatorem) ... Paraclete when used of the Holy Spirit is generally understood as 'consoler'" ('De Princ.' II. 7. 4). The word is certainly so interpreted by Cyril of Jerusalem ('Cat.' XVI. 20, παράκλητος...διὰ τὸ παρακαλεῖν), Gregory of Nyssa ('adv. Eunom.' II. vol. ii. p. 532, Migne, τὸ ἔργον ποιῶν παρακλήτου... παρακαλῶν), and most later Greek Fathers (see Suicer, *s. v.*). This adaptation of the sense of παρακαλεῖν is in all probability no more than a not unnatural isolation of one function of the advocate, just indeed as "advocate" itself is regarded as the "pleader," and not as the person himself "called in." In this way the interpretation conveys a partial truth, but by an inaccurate method. The advocate does "console" and "comfort" when he is called to help. But this secondary application of the term cannot be used to confirm an original meaning which is at fatal variance with the form of the word, and also against undoubted use elsewhere. It may also be added that παρακαλεῖν is not found in the writings of St John, though it is common in the other parts of the New Testament.

The contexts in which the word occurs in the New Testament lead to the same conclusion as the form, and the independent usage of the word. In 1 John ii. 1, the sense *advocate* alone suits the argument, though the Greek Fathers explain the term as applied to the Lord in the same way as in the Gospel. In the Gospel again the sense of advocate, counsel, one who pleads, convinces, convicts, in a great controversy, who strengthens on the one hand and defends on the other, meeting formidable attacks, is alone adequate.

Christ as the Advocate pleads the believer's cause with the Father against the accuser

Satan (1 John ii. 1. Compare Rom. viii. 26, and also Rev. xii. 10; Zech. iii. 1). The Holy Spirit as the Advocate pleads the believer's cause against the world, John xvi. 8 ff. (comp. Iren. III. 17. 3); and also Christ's cause with the believer, John xiv. 26, xv. 26, xvi. 14.

28. The superior greatness of the Father, which is affirmed by Christ in the words *The Father is greater than I*, has been explained mainly in two ways.

1. Some have thought that they have reference to the essential Personality of the Son, and correspond to the absolute idea of the relation of Father to Son, in which the Father has, in Pearson's language, "something of eminence," "some kind of priority." According to this view the eminence of the Father lies in the fact that the Son has the divine Essence by communication.

2. Others again have supposed that the words have reference to the position of the Son at the time when they were spoken. On this supposition the eminence of the Father lies in His relation to the Son as Incarnate and not yet glorified.

Both views are perfectly consistent with the belief in the unity of the divine Nature, and therefore with the belief in the equality of the Godhead of the Son with the Godhead of the Father. And it will probably appear that the one view really implies the other; and that, as far as human thought can penetrate such a mystery, it is reasonable to "ground the congruity of the mission" of the Son upon the immanent pre-eminence of the Father.

Under any circumstances the opinions of early representative writers upon the passage offer a most instructive subject of study.

The earliest use of the passage is of disputed meaning. IRENÆUS († c. 202) in discussing Mark xiii. 32, says, "If any one inquire the reason wherefore the Father, communicating to the Son in all things, hath been declared by the Son to know alone the hour and the day, one could not find at present any [reason] more suitable or more becoming, or more free from danger, than this (for the Lord is the only true (*verax*) Master), [that it is] in order that we may learn through Him that the Father is over all things. *For the Father*, he says, *is greater than I*. And so the Father is announced by our Lord to have the pre-eminence in regard to knowledge, for this purpose, that we also......should leave perfect knowledge and such questions to God" ('adv. Hær.' II. 28. 8). It has been urged that the application of the thought to men shews that the reference is to the Incarnate Son in His humanity; and on the other hand, the general context of the passage and the teaching of Irenæus in other places (*e.g.* I. 7. 4) has been pressed to prove that he is speaking of the Son as Son.

Clement of Alexandria does not, as far as I know, refer to the passage. The interpretation of his successor ORIGEN († 253) is free from all ambiguity, though it needs to be guarded carefully. "I admit," he says, "that there may be some......who maintain that the Saviour is the most High God over all (ὁ μέγιστος ἐπὶ πᾶσι θεός), but we do not certainly hold such a view, who believe Him when He said Himself: *The Father who sent me is greater than I*" ('c. Cels.' VIII. 14); and again: "Clearly we assert......that the Son is not mightier than the Father, but inferior (οὐκ ἰσχυρότερον ἀλλ' ὑποδεέστερον). And this we say as we believe Him when He said, *The Father who sent me is greater than I*" (*id.* c. 15. Comp. 'In Joh. T.' VI. 23; VIII. 25).

The language of TERTULLIAN († c. 220), like that of Origen, is open to misconstruction, but it leaves no doubt as to the sense in which he understood the words. "The Father," he says, "is the whole substance (*tota substantia*), the Son is an outflow and portion of the whole (*derivatio* (c. 14) *totius et portio*), as He Himself declares: *because the Father is greater than I*... The very fact that the terms Father and Son are used shews a difference between them; for assuredly all things will be that which they are called, and will be called that which they will be; and the different terms cannot be ever interchanged" ('c. Prax.' 9).

NOVATIAN (c. 250) is scarcely less bold in his mode of expression: "It is necessary that [the Father] have priority (*prior sit*) as Father, since He who knows no origin must needs have precedence over (*antecedat*) Him who has an origin. At the same time [the Son] must be less, since He knows that He is in Him as having an origin because He is born" ('De Trin.' I. 31. The words *quodammodo, aliquo pacto*, found in the common texts are mere glosses).

The words do not appear to be noticed by Cyprian, though he quotes those which immediately precede. At the beginning of the Arian controversy they naturally came into prominence; and the language of ALEXANDER of Alexandria, in his letter to Alexander of Constantinople (c. 322), which is one of the fundamental documents of the Nicene controversy, bears witness to the sense in which they were generally accepted: "We must guard," he writes, "for the Unbegotten Father His proper dignity (οἰκεῖον ἀξίωμα), affirming that He has no author of His Being (μηδένα τοῦ εἶναι αὐτῷ τὸν αἴτιον λέγοντας); and we must assign the fitting honour to the Son, according to Him the generation from the Father without beginning (τὴν ἄναρχον παρὰ τοῦ πατρὸς γέννησιν)...holding that the being unbegotten is the sole property (ἰδίωμα) of the Father, seeing that the Saviour Himself said *My Father is greater than I*" ('Ep. Alex.' ap. Theod. 'H. E.' I. 4, p. 19).

ATHANASIUS does not dwell upon the words, but he also gives the same general sense to them: "Hence it is that the Son Himself hath not said *My Father is better* (κρείττων) *than I*, that no one should conceive Him to be foreign to His nature, but *greater*, not in size (μεγέθει) nor in time, but because of His generation from the Father Himself. Moreover in saying *He is greater* He again shews the proper character [the true divinity] of His essence (τὴν τῆς οὐσίας ἰδιότητα, *i.e.* as τῆς τοῦ πατρὸς οὐσίας ἴδιος)" ('Orat. c. Ar.' I. 58).

In another writing which is doubtfully attributed to him the word "greater" is explained in reference to the Incarnation (ἐπειδὴ ἄνθρωπος γέγονε, 'De Incarn. et c. Arian.' c. 4. Compare the spurious 'Sermo de Fide,' §§ 14, 34).

The COUNCIL OF SARDICA (A. D. 344?) adopts the same interpretation of the passage as universally admitted: "We confess that God is One; we confess that the Godhead of the Father and of the Son is One; nor does any one ever deny that the Father is greater than the Son, [greater] not because He is of another essence (οὐ δι' ἄλλην ὑπόστασιν), or for any other difference, but because the very name of Father is greater than that of Son" (Theod. 'H. E.' II. 8, p. 82).

BASIL († 379) refers to the passage several times, and definitely adopts the early interpretation, though he also connects the words with the Incarnation. "Since the Son's origin (ἀρχή) is from (ἀπό) the Father, in this respect the Father is greater, as cause and origin (ὡς αἴτιος καὶ ἀρχή). Wherefore also the Lord said thus, *My Father is greater than I*, clearly inasmuch as He is Father (καθὸ πατήρ). Yea, what else does the word Father signify unless the being cause and origin of that which is begotten of Him?" ('c. Eunom.' I. 25. Comp. 'c. Eunom.' I. 20). This idea he expresses elsewhere more fully: "The Son is second in order (τάξει) to the Father, because He is from (ἀπό) Him, and [second] in dignity (ἀξιώματι), because the Father is the 'origin' and cause of His Being" ('c. Eunom.' III. 1).

But at the same time he very distinctly maintains that superior "greatness" is in no way indicative of difference of essence, and indeed argues that the comparison in such a case implies co-essentiality ('Ep.' VIII. 5); and "there is also," he adds, "another thought included in the phrase. For what marvel is it if He confessed the Father to be greater than Himself, being the Word and having become flesh, when He was seen to be less than angels in glory and [less] than men in appearance (εἶδος)?" (*l. c.*).

GREGORY OF NAZIANZUS († 390) holds the same language as his early friend Basil. "Superior greatness (τὸ μεῖζον)," he says, "depends on cause (ἐστὶ τῆς αἰτίας), equality on nature" ('Orat.' 30, § 7. Comp. 'Orat.' 40, § 43, οὐ κατὰ φύσιν τὸ μεῖζον τὴν αἰτίαν δέ. οὐδὲν γὰρ τῶν ὁμοουσίων τῇ οὐσίᾳ μεῖζον ἢ ἔλαττον). And he sets aside the interpretation of the phrase which refers it solely to the humanity of Christ as inadequate: "To say that [the Father] is greater than [the Son] conceived as man (τοῦ κατὰ τὸν ἄνθρωπον νοουμένου) is certainly true, but no great thing to say. For what marvel is it if God is greater than man?" ('Orat.' 30, § 7).

HILARY († 368) maintains the same view in the West: "The Father is greater than the Son, and clearly greater (*plane major*), to whom He gives to be as great as He is Himself, and imparts the image of His own birthlessness (*innascibilitas*) by the mystery of birth, whom He begets of Himself after His own likeness (*ex se in suam formam generat*)..." ('De Trin.' IX. 54).

And again: "Who will not confess that the Father hath pre-eminence (*potiorem*), as ingenerate compared with generate (*ingenitum a genito*), Father with Son, the Sender with the Sent, He who wills with Him who obeys? and He Himself will be our witness: *The Father is greater than I*" ('De Trin.' III. 12. Comp. XI. 12; 'De Syn. c. Ar.' 64).

MARIUS VICTORINUS (c. 365) gives a remarkable expression to this opinion: "If the Son is the whole from the whole, and light from light, and if the Father has given to the Son all that He has...[the Son] is equal to the Father, but the Father is greater, because He has given to Him all things, and is the cause of the Son's being, and being in that particular way (*causa est ipse filio ut sit, ut isto modo sit. Ad hoc autem major quod actio inactuosa*)......Therefore [the Son] is equal [to the Father] and unequal" ('adv. Arian.' I. 13).

PHÆBADIUS (c. 350) combines both views: "*The Father is greater than I*; rightly greater because He alone is a cause without cause (*solus hic auctor sine auctore est*...), rightly greater because He did not Himself descend into the Virgin..." ('c. Ar.' c. 13).

EPIPHANIUS († 403) is, as usual, vague and unsatisfactory. "The Son," he says, "says this, honouring the Father as became Him, having been honoured more greatly by the Father. For it was necessary (ἔδει) indeed that the true (γνήσιον) Son should honour His own Father, to shew His true nature (γνησιότητα)......In so far as the Father is Father, and He is a true Son, He honours His own Father..." ('Ancor.' 17. Comp. 'Hor.' LXIX. 53. 17; LXII. 4. 7).

The thought of Epiphanius is more clearly expressed by the *Pseudo-Cæsarius*: "The Father is not greater than the Son in extent, or mass, or time, or season, or worth (ἀξίᾳ), or strength, or godhead, or greatness, or appearance; for none of these things have place in the divine Trinity. But inasmuch as the Father is Father, so the Son honours the Father with true filial respect (γνησιότητι τιμᾷ)" ('Dial.' I.; 'Resp.' XVIII.).

Towards the close of the fourth century the opinion began to gain currency that the superior greatness of the Father was referred to the human life of the Son. This was perhaps a natural consequence of the later developments of the Nicene Christology.

AMPHILOCHIUS (c. 380) is first of the Greek fathers, as far as I have observed, who distinctly refers the words to the Lord's human nature (without hesitation). "If you wish to know," he writes, as if the Lord Himself were speaking, "how my Father is greater than I, I spake from the flesh and not from the Person of the Godhead (ἐκ τῆς σαρκὸς εἶπον καὶ οὐκ ἐκ προσώπου θεότητος)" ('Exc.' XII.; Galland. VI. 502; ap. Theodoret. 'Dial.' I. Comp. 'Dial.' II. p. 151; 'Dial.' III. p. 248).

CHRYSOSTOM († 407) in his Commentary gives the early interpretation: "If any one," he writes, "say that the Father is greater in so far as He is the cause (αἴτιος) of the Son, we will not gainsay this. But this however does not make the Son to be of a different essence (ἑτέρας οὐσίας)" ('Hom.' LXX. *ad loc.*). Elsewhere ('Hom.' VIII. 'in Hebr.' § 2) he appears to admit the reference to the humanity of Christ. The passage which is commonly quoted as giving this view: "It is no marvel if [the Son] is less than the Father owing to the mystery of the Incarnation (διὰ τὴν οἰκονομίαν)," is from a spurious writing ('Hom. de Christo pasch.' III. p. 814).

CYRIL OF ALEXANDRIA († 444) discusses the passage at considerable length ('Thes.' XI.), and offers different views. He allows that the words can be rightly understood of the absolute relation of the Father to the Son as "the origin of His coeternal offspring" (ὡς ἀρχὴ τοῦ συναϊδίου γεννήματος). "While the Son," he writes, "is equal to the Father on the ground of essence (ἴσος κατὰ τὸν τῆς οὐσίας λόγον ὑπάρχων) and like in all things, He says that the Father is greater as being without beginning (ὡς ἄναρχον), having beginning Himself in respect of source only (κατὰ μόνον τὸ ἐξ οὗ, and not, that is, of time also. Greg. Naz. 'Orat.' 20, § 7), even while He has this subsistence (ὕπαρξιν) coincident with Him (the Father)" ('Thes.' *l. c.*).

In his commentary, on the other hand, he lays down peremptorily the other interpretation: "The Father was greater, as the Son was still a slave and in our condition (ἐν τοῖς καθ' ἡμᾶς)... We affirm that the Son was made less than the Father in so far as He has become man, that however He was restored to being on equality (εἶναι ἐν ἴσῳ) with Him that begat Him (τῷ φύσαντι) after His leaving the earth (μετὰ τὴν ἐντεῦθεν ἀποδημίαν)..." (*ad loc.*).

In the Latin Church this opinion found general acceptance. AMBROSE († 397) writes: "[Christ] says in the nature of man that about which [our adversaries] are wont to assail us wrongfully (*calumniari*) [arguing] that it is said: *The Father is greater than I*... He is less in the nature of man, and do you wonder if speaking from the character of man (*ex persona hominis*) He said that the Father was greater...?" ('De Fide,' II. 8. Comp. V. 18).

AUGUSTINE († 430) commonly refers the superior greatness of the Father to the Incarnate Son; but he acknowledges that it can be understood of the Son as Son: The words are written "partly on account of the Incarnation (*administratio suscepti hominis*) ... partly because the Son owes to the Father that He is; as He even owes to the Father that He is equal (*æqualis aut par*) to the Father, while the Father owes to no one whatever He is" ('de Fid. et Symb.' c. IX. (1. 8). Comp. 'c. Maxim.' I. 15; II. 25; III. 14; 'c. Serm. Ar.' 5; 'Coll. c. Max.' 14; 'De Trin.' I. 14, 22).

In later times the interpretation by which the words are referred to the humanity of Christ became almost universal in the West (*e.g.* Leo, A.D. 449, 'Ep. ad Flavian.' XXVIII. 4); Fulgentius (c. 533, 'Epist.' VIII. 16); Alcuin (c. 802, 'de Trin.' III. 7). Comp. Thom. Aqu. 'Summa,' III. 20. 1).

In the East, JOHN OF DAMASCUS († 754) carefully reproduced the teaching of the earlier Greek fathers: "If we say that the Father is the origin of the Son and greater, we do not indicate that He is before the Son (προτερεύειν) in time or nature, nor in any other point, except as being the cause (κατὰ τὸ αἴτιον); that is that the Son was begotten of the Father, and not the Father of the Son, and that the Father is the cause of the Son naturally (αἴτιος φυσικῶς), as we say that the fire does not come from the light, but rather the light from the fire. When therefore we hear that the Father is the origin of and greater than the Son, we must understand it in regard of the cause (τῷ αἰτίῳ νοήσωμεν)" ('De Fide,' I. 8).

The summary of opinions given by PHOTIUS († c. 891) may complete this review of ancient interpretations. "Our fathers," he writes, "have variously understood the phrase of the Gospel, *My Father is greater than I*, without injury to the truth. Some say that [the Father] is called greater as being the cause, which presents not difference of substance, but rather identity (οὐκ οὐσίας παραλλαγὴν ταὐτότητα δὲ μᾶλλον καὶ συμφυΐαν). ... Others have taken the word as referring to the human nature (κατὰ τὸ ἀνθρώπινον)....Some have conceded that the term greater is used in respect of the Word, but not absolutely and in regard of essence, but in respect of the Incarnation,... since He who remits nothing of His own excellence is greater than He who has descended to the lowest sufferings. ... One might reasonably understand that the phrase was used with regard to the understanding of the disciples, for they still were imperfectly acquainted with God and their Master, and supposed that the Father was far greater (comp. Isid. Pelus. 'Ep.' 334).... And perhaps there is nothing to prevent us from supposing that the term is used in condescension, fashioned in a humble form to meet the weakness of the hearers ..." ('Epist.' I. 47, al. 176, al. 'Quæst.' 95).

If we turn from these comments to the text of St John, it will be seen that (1) The Lord speaks throughout the Gospel with an unchanged and unchangeable Personality. The "I" (ἐγώ) is the same in viii. 58, x. 30, xiv. 28. (2) We must believe that there was a certain fitness in the Incarnation of the Son. (3) This fitness could not have been an accident, but must have belonged, if we may so speak, to His true Personal Nature. (4) So far then as it was fit that the Son should be Incarnate and suffer, and not the Father, it is possible for us to understand that the Father is greater than the Son as Son, in Person but not in Essence. Among English writers it is sufficient to refer to Bull; and to Pearson, 'On the Creed,' Art. 1, whose notes, as always, contain a treasure of patristic learning.

CHAPTER XV.

1 The consolation and mutual love between Christ and his members, under the parable of the vine. 18 A comfort in the hatred and persecution of the world. 26 The office of the Holy Ghost, and of the apostles.

I AM the true vine, and my Father is the husbandman.

ii. THE DISCOURSES ON THE WAY (xv., xvi.).

This second group of discourses falls into the following sections:

1. *The living union* (xv. 1—10).
2. *The issues of union: the disciples and Christ* (xv. 11—16).
3. *The issues of union: the disciples and the world* (xv. 17—27).
4. *The world and the Paraclete* (xvi. 1—11).
5. *The Paraclete and the disciples* (xvi. 12—15).
6. *Sorrow turned to joy* (xvi. 16—24).
7. *After failure victory* (xvi. 25—33).

1. *The living union* (xv. 1—10).

This first section, like the corresponding section in the first group, contains the thought which is pursued in detail in the following sections, the thought of corporate, living, fruitful union between believers and Christ, which is developed afterwards in its manifold issues of joy and sorrow. The succession of ideas appears to be this. The life in union is begun but not perfected (*vv.* 1, 2); and the vital relation must be "freely" maintained (*vv.* 3, 4) in view of the consequences which follow from its preservation and loss (*vv.* 5, 6). Such being the circumstances of union, the blessings of union (*vv.* 7, 8) and the absolute type of union (*vv.* 9, 10) are set forth more fully.

CHAP. XV. 1, 2. The first two verses present the elements of symbolic teaching without any direct interpretation, the vine, the branches, the husbandman, the dressing. The whole usage of the Lord leads to the belief that the image of the vine was suggested by some external object. Those who think that the discourses were spoken in the chamber suppose that the symbol was supplied by a vine growing on the walls of the house and hanging over the window; or by "the fruit of the vine" (Matt. xxvi. 29).

If the discourses were spoken on the way to the Mount of Olives, the vineyards on the hill sides, or, more specially, the fires of the vine-prunings by Kidron, may have furnished the image. If however the discourses and the High Priestly prayer (ch. xvii.) were spoken in the court of the temple (xvii. 1, note), then it is most natural to believe that the Lord interpreted the real significance of the golden vine upon the gates, which was at once the glory and the type of Israel (Jos. 'Antt.' XV. 11. 3; 'B. J.' V. 5. 4).

1. *I am the true vine*] The exact form of the phrase marks first the identification of Christ with the image, and then the absolute fulfilment of the image in Him, Christ: *I am the vine; the true vine* (comp. i. 9, vi. 32, ἀληθινός, x. 11). Christ in His Person brings to complete fulfilment these vital relations of the parts to the whole —of unity and multiplicity—of growth and identity, which are shadowed forth in the vine. But yet more than this, the vine was the symbol of the ancient Church (Hos. x. 1; Isai. v. 1 ff.; Jer. ii. 21; Ezek. xv. 2 ff., xix. 10 ff.; Ps. lxxx. 8 ff.; comp. Matt. xxi. 33; Luke xiii. 6; [Rev. xiv. 18 ff.]). Compare Lightfoot and Wünsche, *ad loc.* Thus two currents of thought are united by the Lord when He speaks of Himself as "the true, the ideal, vine." Israel failed to satisfy the spiritual truths symbolized in the natural vine; the natural vine only imperfectly realises

15. 2 [a] Every branch in me that beareth not fruit he taketh away: and every *branch* that beareth fruit, he purgeth it, that it may bring forth more fruit.

13. 3 [b] Now ye are clean through the word which I have spoken unto you.

4 Abide in me, and I in you. As the branch cannot bear fruit of itself, except it abide in the vine; no more can ye, except ye abide in me.

---

the idea which it expresses. In both respects Christ is "the ideal vine," as contrasted with these defective embodiments.

the husbandman] The "husbandman" here stands apart from the vine, because Christ brings forward His relation with believers in virtue of His true manhood. In this relation He stands even as they do to the Father (Hebr. v. 8), and (in some mysterious sense) He, in His Body, is still under the Father's discipline (comp. Col. i. 24). In the Synoptic parable the word is applied to the leaders of the people; Matt. xxi. 33, and parallels. Compare also Luke xiii. 7.

2. The construction in the original, "Every branch, if it bear not...every branch that beareth...," is slightly irregular. The words would have been naturally, "Every branch in me He tends carefully: if any bear no fruit He removes it; if any bear fruit He prunes it." But the indefinite hypothetical form (*πᾶν κλῆμα μὴ φέρον*) is changed in the second clause for the definite and positive (*πᾶν τὸ καρπὸν φέρον*).

Every branch] Believers are identified with Christ. We cannot conceive of a vine without branches. Yet the life is independent of any particular manifestation of it. A similar mystery lies in the image of the body (Eph. v. 30; Col. ii. 19).

In the old dispensation union with Israel was the condition of life; in the new, union with Christ.

in me] Even the unfruitful branches are true branches. They also are "*in Christ*," though they draw their life from Him only to bear leaves (Matt. xxi. 19). It is the work of the Great Husbandman to remove them. Comp. Matt. xiii. 28 f., 47 ff. How a man can be "in Christ," and yet afterwards separate himself from Him, is a mystery neither greater nor less than that involved in the fall of a creature created innocent.

taketh **it** *away*] It is not perhaps necessary to attempt to determine the mode of this removal. Death breaks the connexion between the unfaithful Christian and Christ (see Matt. *l. c.*).

he purgeth (**cleanseth**) *it*] The word **cleanseth** (*καθαίρει*), which is used of lustrations, appears to be chosen with a view to its spiritual application. Everything is removed from the branch which tends to divert the vital power from the production of fruit.

bring forth (**bear**) *more fruit*] Increased fruitfulness is the end of discipline, and to this all care is directed. The vine especially needs pruning. Every one who has seen a vineyard of choice vines knows how closely they are cut.

3, 4. The relation which has been generally indicated in *vv.* 1, 2 is now applied to the disciples. Christ's work is accomplished for them; but they must themselves appropriate it (*abide in me*); their will must cooperate with His will.

3. *Now ye are...*] **Already** *ye* (*ὑμεῖς*) *are...* The spiritual work represented by this "cleansing" was potentially completed for the apostles, the representatives of His Church. It remained that it should be realised by them (comp. Col. iii. 3, 5). They had been purified by the divine discipline (comp. xiii. 10). They were clean (*καθαροί*) "**because of** *the word*." The word, the whole revelation to which Christ had given expression, was the spring and source, and not only the instrument, of their purity (*διὰ τὸν λ.*, and not *διὰ τοῦ λ.*; comp. vi. 57). See viii. 31 f., v. 34; Eph. v. 26 (*ῥῆμα*); James i. 18.

clean] It is possible that the word may contain an allusion to Lev. xix. 23. For three years the fruit of "trees planted for food" was counted unclean (*ἀπερικάθαρτος*, LXX.).

4. But the permanence of the purity to which they had attained depended upon the permanence of their fellowship. The disciple must set his life in Christ, and let Christ live in him. The form of the sentence is necessarily obscure; but the second clause is not to be taken as a future: "Abide in me, and I will abide in you." Both parts are imperative in conception: "Do ye abide in me, and admit me to abide in you, let me abide in you." "Effect, by God's help, this perfect mutual fellowship, your abiding in me, my abiding in you." Both thoughts are essential to the completeness of the union. Comp. xiv. 10, 20. In one sense the union itself, even the abiding of Christ, is made to depend upon the will of the believer. The other side of the truth is given in *v.* 16.

of itself] not simply "in itself," but "from itself," as the source of its own vital energy. Comp. v. 19, vii. 18, xi. 51, xvi. 13. The form is peculiar to St John (2 Cor. x. 7 is a false reading). Comp. v. 30, note.

except it abide] The phrase is compressed. The limitation applies to the principal thought

5 I am the vine, ye *are* the branches: He that abideth in me, and I in him, the same bringeth forth much fruit: for ‖without me ye can do nothing.

‖ Or, *severed from me.*

6 If a man abide not in me, he is cast forth as a branch, and is withered; and men gather them, and cast *them* into the fire, and they are burned.

7 If ye abide in me, and my words abide in you, ye shall ask what ye will, and it shall be done unto you.

8 Herein is my Father glorified,

(*bear fruit*), and not to the defining addition (*of itself*), to which it is parallel. Comp. v. 19; Gal. ii. 16. The branch cannot bear fruit of itself: it cannot bear fruit except it abide in the vine.

no more can ye] Literally, **so neither** *can ye* bear fruit of yourselves, or bear fruit at all, except in vital fellowship with me.

5, 6. The consequences of union and of loss of union with Christ are set out in the sharpest contrast.

5. The repetition of the "theme" (*v.* 1) leads to the addition of the clause *ye are the branches*, which sums up definitely what has been implied in the former verses.

He that...the same (οὗτος "he, and none other, it is that") *bringeth forth* (**beareth**) *much fruit*] The thought is of the productiveness of the Christian life. The vine-wood is worthless. For fruitfulness there is need of "abiding," continuance, patient waiting, on the part of those already "in Christ."

for (**because**) *without* (**apart from**) *me...*] The force of the argument lies in the fact that, as the fruitfulness of the branch does not depend upon itself but upon Christ in whom it lives, He will fulfil His part while the vital connexion is maintained. In other words, he in whom Christ lives must be abundantly fruitful, for it is His life alone which brings forth fruit.

apart from *me*] not simply without my help, but separated from me. Comp. Eph. ii. 12; ch. i. 3.

do nothing] accomplish nothing, bring out no permanent result. The thought is directly of Christian action, which can only be wrought in Christ. At the same time the words have a wider application. Nothing that really "is" can be done without the Word, whose activity must not be limited when He has not limited it: x. 16, i. 9.

6. *he is cast forth*] This happens simultaneously with the cessation of the vital union with Christ (ἐβλήθη). It is not a future consequence, as at the last judgment, but an inevitable accompaniment of the separation. The use of the adverb "outside" (ἐβλήθη ἔξω not ἐξεβλήθη) suggests a new aspect of the union with Christ, the idea of a vineyard in addition to that of a vine.

a (**the**) *branch*] the unfruitful branch by which he is represented.

withered] inasmuch as it receives the living sap no longer.

men (**they**) *gather them*] The indefiniteness of the subject corresponds with the mysteriousness of the act symbolized. "They gather them (the branches and their antitypes) to whom the office belongs." Comp. Luke xii. 20. The description is directly that of the fate of the severed branches (αὐτά), out of which the application immediately follows. "Ligna vitis...præcisa (Ezek. xv. 5) nullis agricolarum usibus prosunt, nullis fabrilibus operibus deputantur. Unum de duobus palmiti congruit aut vitis aut ignis..." (Aug. *ad loc.*).

the fire] The image is of the fires kindled to consume the dressings of the vineyards. Comp. Matt. xiii. 41 f. The Lord leaves the image, just as it is, to work its proper effect.

7, 8. In these two verses the blessings of union are shewn in prayer fulfilled and fruit borne.

7. *If ye abide in me, and my words* (**sayings**) *abide in you......*] The second clause is changed in form (not "and I in you," as *v.* 4), because the thought now is of the communion of prayer. The *words* (ῥήματα), the definite sayings, here specified, go to make up "the word" (ὁ λόγος, *v.* 3). Comp. viii. 43, 47, 51, xii. 47, 48, xvii. 6, 8, 14.

ye shall ask what ye will] According to the true reading, **ask whatsoever ye will.** The petitions of the true disciples are echoes (so to speak) of Christ's words. As He has spoken so they speak. Their prayer is only some fragment of His teaching transformed into a supplication, and so it will necessarily be heard. It is important to notice how the promise of the absolute fulfilment of prayer is connected with the personal fellowship of the believer with Christ, both in the Synoptists, and in St John. Comp. Matt. xviii. 19, 20, and below *v.* 16. In the original "*whatsoever ye will*" stands first, to mark the freedom of the believer's choice, or (in other words) the coincidence of his will with the will of Christ. Comp. 1 John iii. 22.

it shall be done] More literally, "it shall come to pass (γενήσεται, Vulg. *fiet*) for you." The result is not due to any external or arbitrary exertion of power, but to the action of a law of life.

8. *Herein*] *In this*, that is, in the necessary

that ye bear much fruit; so shall ye be my disciples.

9 As the Father hath loved me, so have I loved you: continue ye in my love.

10 If ye keep my commandments, ye shall abide in my love; even as I have kept my Father's commandments, and abide in his love.

11 These things have I spoken

---

consequence of your abiding in me, which carries with it the certain fulfilment of your prayers, inasmuch as they correspond with the divine will. The pronoun looks back, while at the same time the thought already indicated is developed in the words which follow. The end which God regards in answering prayer is *that ye may bear much fruit* (ἵνα φέρητε). Comp. iv. 34, note.

is glorified] The tense (as in *v.* 6) marks the absolute coincidence of the extension of the Father's glory with the realisation of the believer's effectual union with Christ. In the fruitfulness of the vine lies the joy and glory of the "husbandman" (*v.* 1).

bear much fruit] The words point to the future activity of the apostles as founders of the Church through which the Risen Christ acts. Comp. *v.* 16.

and *so shall ye be* (**become**) *my disciples*] Or, according to another reading, **and ye shall become...** Something is always wanting to the completeness of discipleship. A Christian never "is," but always "is becoming" a Christian. And it is by his fruitfulness that he vindicates his claim to the name.

9, 10. The sphere and the condition of union are revealed in the absolute type of union, the relation of the Son to the Father.

9. This verse admits of two renderings. The last clause may be the conclusion to the two former: **Even as** *the Father* **loved** *me* **and I loved** *you*, **abide** *in my love*. Or it may be independent: **Even as** *the Father* **loved** *me* **I also loved** *you*. *Abide in my love*. Both constructions are in harmony with St John's style. (Comp. vi. 57, xiv. 12.) The latter perhaps brings out most distinctly the mysterious truth that the relation of the Father to the Son corresponds with that of the Son to believers (comp. vi. 57, x. 14, 15), which is further applied in *v.* 10. The use of the aorist (*loved*) in both cases may perhaps carry the relation out of time, and make it absolute in the divine idea. Comp. xvii. 14. But it is simpler to regard the tense as chosen with regard to a work now looked upon as completed, according to the usage which is not unfrequent in these discourses. Comp. xiii. 31.

continue (**abide**) *ye in my love*] The love of Christ is, as it were, the atmosphere in which the disciple lives. It is not something realised at a momentary crisis, but enjoyed continuously. And this enjoyment depends, on the human side, upon the will of man. It can be made the subject of a command.

my love] The exact form of the phrase, which is found here only (ἡ ἀγάπη ἡ ἐμή), as distinguished from that used in the next verse (ἡ ἀγάπη μου), emphasizes the character of the love, as Christ's: *the love that is mine*, the love that answers to my nature and my work. Thus the meaning of the words cannot be limited to the idea of Christ's love for men, or to that of man's love for Christ: they describe the absolute love which is manifested in these two ways, the love which perfectly corresponds with Christ's Being. There are many corresponding phrases in the Gospel, "*the joy that is mine*" (ἡ χαρὰ ἡ ἐμή, *v.* 11, iii. 29, xvii. 13); "*the judgment that is mine*" (ἡ κρίσις ἡ ἐμή, v. 30, viii. 16); "*the commandments that are mine*" (xiv. 15); "*peace that is mine*" (εἰρήνη ἡ ἐμή, xiv. 27). Comp. v. 30, vi. 38, vii. 6, 8, viii. 31, 37, 43, 51, 56, x. 26, 27, xii. 26, xv. 12, xvii. 24, xviii. 36.

10. The promise here is the exact converse of that in xiv. 15. Obedience and love are perfectly correlative. Love assures obedience; obedience assures love. The love of the disciples for Christ carries with it the purpose and the power of obedience; the spirit of obedience is more than the sign of love (xiii. 35); it secures to the disciples the enjoyment of Christ's love. The love of Christ as it is realised unites and includes inseparably man's love for Christ, and Christ's love for man.

even as I (ἐγώ) *have kept my* (**the**) *Father's ...*] The Filial relation of the Son to "the Father" (not "His Father") is set forth as the type of that of the disciple for his Master (comp. viii. 29). Though the terms in which this relation is described belong properly to the life of the Incarnate Son, yet the emphatic pronoun shews that the statement is true of the eternal being of the Son in His unchanged personality. Comp. i. 1.

in his love] The pronoun stands emphatically first, so that there is a complete parallel between the corresponding clauses (τοῦ πατρὸς τὰς ἐντολάς, αὐτοῦ ἐν τῇ ἀγάπῃ). The perfect love of complete devotion to God is the highest conceivable good.

2. *The issues of union: the disciples and Christ* (xv. 11—16).

The Revelation which has been made in the first section is applied in the sections which follow. The end of it is shewn to be twofold, to create joy in sacrifice (xv. 11—27),

unto you, that my joy might remain
in you, and *that* your joy might
be full.
c chap. 13. 34. 1 Thess. 4. 9. 1 John 3. 11.
12 [c] This is my commandment,
That ye love one another, as I have
loved you.
13 Greater love hath no man than
this, that a man lay down his life for
his friends.
14 Ye are my friends, if ye do
whatsoever I command you.
15 Henceforth I call you not ser-

---

and to preserve faith unshaken (xvi.). The first object is gained by shewing the issues of union for the believer in relation to Christ (*vv.* 11—16), and to the world (*vv.* 17—27). True joy, Christ's joy, springs out of the self-sacrifice of love (*vv.* 12, 13). The connexion of believers with Christ is one of love (*vv.* 14, 15); and it is stable because it rests on His choice (*v.* 16).

11. The love of Christ was the love of absolute self-sacrifice. Such self-sacrifice is the fulness of joy. Thus by enjoining continuance in His love Christ prepares His hearers to suffer for love's sake. *These things have I spoken unto you that my joy might remain* (**may be**) *in you:* that you may know and share the blessedness which belongs to my work, the exemplar of your own; *and* that so *your joy might be full* (**may be fulfilled**).

my joy] Literally, "the joy that is mine," characteristic of me (see *v.* 9, note): the joy of complete self-surrender in love to love. Other interpretations of the phrase, "the joy which I inspire," or "your joy in me," fall far short of the meaning required by the context. The rendering "that my joy may find its foundation and support in you," is even more alien from the sense of the passage.

your joy] There appears to be a marked contrast between "the joy that is Christ's," and "the joy of the disciples." The one is absolute (**may be** *in*), the other is progressive (**may be fulfilled**). The latter may perhaps be rightly taken to include all the elements of true human joy. This natural joy, in itself incomplete and transitory, had been ennobled by the self-surrender of the disciples to Christ; and the completion of their joy in the indirect sense was to be found in the consummation of the union thus commenced. That consummation however was to be accomplished through suffering.

12, 13. The connexion of *v.* 12 with *v.* 11 lies in the thought of joy springing out of self-sacrifice, of which Christ gives the absolute pattern. The many "commandments" (*v.* 10) are gathered up in the one "new commandment" (xiii. 34), the commandment which was emphatically Christ's, of which the end and purport was that Christians should love one another after the pattern of their Master, who gave up His life for them. He is the model (*v.* 13), the source (*vv.* 14, 15), and the support of love (*v.* 16).

12. *my commandment*] Literally, "the commandment that is mine," that answers to my nature and my mission (*v.* 9, note). Comp. 1 John iii. 16.

That ye love] The exact phrase of the original (ἵνα ἀγαπᾶτε) emphasizes the purpose as distinguished from the simple substance of the command.

as I have loved] More closely, **even as I loved.** See *v.* 9.

13. The love of Christ for men was the supreme ideal of love. *Greater love than this*, which I have shewn and still shew, *no one hath* or could have; a love so framed in its divine law and last issue, *that one should lay down his life for his friends.* Comp. 1 John iii. 16.

The implied end of Christ's love—death for another—is regarded as the final aim of human self-devotion. *This* points backward to *I have loved you;* and *that one lay down* does not seem to be a simple explanation of *this*, but rather a declaration of the spirit and purpose of love. Comp. iv. 34, *v.* 8, xvii. 3; 1 John iv. 17; 3 John 4

lay down] Comp. x. 11, note.

for his friends] Love is contemplated here from the side of him who feels it, so that the objects of it are spoken of as "friends," that is, "loved by him." In Rom. v. 8 the sacrifice of Christ is regarded from the opposite side, from the side of those for whom it was offered, and men are described as being in themselves sinners.

14. *Ye* (ὑμεῖς) *are...*] Christ returns from the general case (*any one*) to Himself, and shews what is required on man's side to complete the conception of that relationship which He has established with His disciples.

friends] The true believer receives the title which is characteristic of Abraham, "the father of the faithful," "the friend of God" (Isai. xli. 8; James ii. 23). The title occurs Luke xii. 4 in connexion with the prospect of suffering. The true disciples had been in Christ's sight all along what He now solemnly entitles them.

whatsoever] **the things which**, but probably the true reading is **that which**, so that the emphasis is still laid upon the unity of Christ's command (*v.* 12).

15. The relation of the believer to Christ, out of which springs his relation to his fellow-believer, is essentially one not of service but of love.

vants; for the servant knoweth not what his lord doeth: but I have called you friends; for all things that I have heard of my Father I have made known unto you.

16 Ye have not chosen me, but I have chosen you, and [d] ordained you, that ye should go and bring forth fruit, and *that* your fruit should remain: that whatsoever ye shall ask

[a] Matt. 28. 19.

Henceforth I call you not] **No longer do I call you**, as in the time when Christ had not fully revealed Himself. The relation of God to His people under the Law had been that of Master to servant. Comp. Matt. x. 24 f., and the imagery of the parables: Matt. xiii. 27 f., xviii. 23 ff., xxii. 4 ff., xxiv. 45 ff.; Mark xiii. 34; Luke xii. 37 ff., xiv. 17 ff., xvii. 10, xix. 13 ff. See also xiii. 16, xii. 26 (διάκονος).

servants] The disciples however still claimed the title for themselves. The less was included in the greater. Comp. *v.* 20.

for (**because**)...] Comp. viii. 34 ff.

knoweth not (with the knowledge of intuitive certainty) *what his lord doeth* (**is doing**)] At the very moment of action there is no sympathy between the lord and the slave, by which the mind of one is known to the other. The slave is an instrument (ἔμψυχον ὄργανον) and not a person. Comp. Rom. vii. 15.

his lord] The order of the original (αὐτοῦ ὁ κύριος) emphasizes the contrast of persons.

The order is changed in the second clause: *but* **you I have called** *friends*. The emphasis is laid on the personal character of the eleven. The title also is one finally conferred (εἴρηκα, *I have called*), and not simply used as the occasion arises (λέγω, *I call*).

for (**because**)] The perfect revelation of the Father's will involves the relation of friendship. To know God is to love Him. To receive the knowledge of Him is to experience His love. The Son therefore called those to whom He revealed the Father "friends" in act before He called them so in word.

The revelation both in communication (ἐγνώρισα, **I made known**) and in reception (ἤκουσα, **I heard**, comp. viii. 28, note) is here presented as complete. This is one side of the truth. But the complete revelation given in the Lord's Presence needed a fuller unfolding (xvi. 12). He had not yet died and risen. It was the work of the Spirit to interpret afterwards little by little what He had revealed in word and life implicitly once for all (xiv. 26, ἐν τῷ ὀνόματί μου, xvii. 26, τὸ ὄνομά σου).

16. The Lord having set forth the aim of Christian joy through self-devotion, resting on a personal relation to Himself, shews how it is within reach of attainment. The stability of the connexion of "friendship" between the Lord and His disciples is assured by the fact that its origin lies with the Lord and not with man. This manifestation of love, like the divine love itself (1 John iv. 10), was not called out by anything in man. It was of divine grace, and therefore essentially sure. **Ye did not choose me**, or more exactly, *It was not ye that chose me as your master*, as scholars ordinarily choose their master—the pronoun stands emphatically first—*but* **I chose you** *as my friends*. The choice may be either generally to discipleship, or specially to the apostolate. The use of the word in vi. 70 and xiii. 18 (comp. Acts i. 2), no less than the context, in which the eleven are regarded as representatives of the Lord in relation to His Church, favours the second interpretation. The power of the office of the apostles lay for them in the fact that it was not self-chosen.

I have chosen] **I chose.** The reference is to the historic fact of the calling, Luke vi. 13; Acts i. 2. Comp. ch. vi. 70.

and ordained (**appointed**, **sent**, ἔθηκα, Vulg. *posui*) *you*] The word simply describes the assignment of a special post, which here carries with it further duties (*that ye may*...). Comp. Hebr. i. 2; Rom. iv. 17; 2 Tim. i. 11.

that ye (ὑμεῖς) on your part, in virtue of your peculiar knowledge and gifts, *should go*...] The repetition of the pronoun (ὑμᾶς, ἵνα ὑμεῖς) brings out the distinctive responsibility of the apostles. At the same time the verb (*go*, ὑπάγητε) marks their separation from their Master (Matt. xx. 4, 7, &c.), while they went into the world as heralds of the gospel (Mark xvi. 15; Luke x. 3). Three points are noticed in their activity. They take up an independent place; they are effective; the effect which they work is lasting. In all this lies the promise of the foundation and perpetuity of the Church. Moreover even in apparent separation the strength of the disciple comes from union with his Lord, and thus for a moment the imagery of *vv.* 2 ff. is resumed (**bear** *fruit*, *fruit* **abide**).

that whatsoever] This clause is in one aspect subordinate to the former; and in another coordinate with it. The consummation of faith grows out of fruitful obedience; and on the other hand fruitful obedience coincides with the fulfilment of prayer.

The direct personal application of *vv.* 15, 16, to the apostles is emphatically marked by the ninefold repetition of the pronoun (*ye*, *you*). At the same time the words are to be extended in due measure to all disciples whom the eleven represented.

whatsoever ye shall ask of the Father] The conditions of prayer already laid down (*v.* 7) are here presented in another light. In the

of the Father in my name, he may give it you.

17 These things I command you, that ye love one another.

18 If the world hate you, ye know that it hated me before *it hated* you.

19 If ye were of the world, the world would love his own: but be-

---

former passage prayer was regarded as the echo of Christ's own words. Here it is regarded as flowing from the new connexion (*ask the Father*) realised in the revelation of the Son (*in my name*). Comp. xvi. 26 f. And there is another detail to be observed, by which the promise in this passage is further distinguished from that in xiv. 13, 14. There it is said of the fulfilment of prayer, *I will do it;* and here, *that He may give it you.* In the former place stress is laid upon the action of Christ; in this upon the privilege of the believer. The work is wrought by Christ, but through the believer. He receives that which enables him to accomplish his Lord's will. Comp. xvi. 23.

in my name] See xiv. 13, note. This clause marks the proper object of prayer as spiritual and eternal, and not transitory. Comp. 1 John v. 14, 15. "Hoc petimus in nomine Salvatoris quod pertinet ad rationem salutis" (Aug. *in loc.*).

3. *The issues of union: the disciples and the world* (xv. 17—27).

The love of Christians for Christ and for one another, which is the end of Christ's commandment, involves hatred on the part of the world (*vv.* 17, 18), which springs from an essential opposition of nature, and finally from ignorance of the Father (*vv.* 19—21). But none the less such hatred is inexcusable, for Christ fulfilling His mission both in word and work left no plea for those who rejected Him (*vv.* 22—25); and the conflict which He had begun the disciples are commissioned to continue with the help of the Paraclete (*vv.* 26, 27).

17—21. The disciples' work, as a work of love, corresponds not only in character but also in issue with that of their Master; it is met by hatred which marks an opposition of natures between believers and the world, and so witnesses in fact to the true fellowship of Christians with Christ, and to their knowledge of God. Comp. 1 John iii. 1. At first sight the hatred of the world for that which is essentially good and beautiful could not but be a strange trial to believers (comp. 1 Peter iv. 12 ff.). Christ meets the temptation beforehand by tracing the hatred to its origin. The lesson was soon applied: Acts v. 41.

17. This verse must be taken as the introduction of a new line of thought, and not, according to the modern texts, as the summing up in conclusion of what has gone before. On this point the usage in St John is conclusive against the received arrangement. Comp. xiv. 25, xv. 11, xvi. 1, 25, 33. The love of Christ for Christians is the antidote to and the occasion of the world's hatred, which is directed against the virtues rather than against the failings of Christians. Christ first establishes the foundation of this love, and then lays open the antagonism which believers must support.

These things I command] The commands are involved in the teaching which has developed the original injunction, *abide in me* (*v.* 4). The scope of all was to create mutual love (ἵνα ἀγαπᾶτε ἀλλήλους, *that ye* may *love...*).

18. *If the world hate* (hateth, μισεῖ) *you*] This is assumed to be the actual fact. Compare vii. 7. The verb which follows (γινώσκετε) may be either indicative, "ye know," or imperative, "know ye" (Vulg. *scitote*). In favour of the latter rendering the imperative in *v.* 20 (*remember*) can be quoted; and at the same time it is more natural to suppose that the attention of the disciples is now definitely called to a truth which they had but just learnt to recognise, than that reference should be made to a knowledge which at any rate they had been very slow to gain. Comp. 1 John iv. 2. Now that the issue was at hand the past could at length be more certainly interpreted than at an earlier time; and yet more, the immediate experience of the disciples interpreted the history of their Master.

hated (hath hated, μεμίσηκεν)] The conception is of a persistent, abiding feeling, and not of any isolated manifestation of feeling. The "Jews" are treated as part of the "world."

hated me before it hated you] The original phrase is very remarkable (ἐμὲ πρῶτον ὑμῶν, Vulg. *priorem vobis*), *me first of you*, *first in regard of you.* Comp. i. 15. The force of it appears to lie in the stress laid upon the essential union of those which follow with the source. The later life is drawn from the original life. It is not only that Christ was "before" the disciples as separate from them; He was also their Head.

19. The hatred of the world to the disciples could not but follow necessarily from the choice of Christ, by which they were drawn out of the world to Him. This hatred, therefore, became to them a memorial of their great hopes. Comp. Matt. v. 14 f.; Rom. viii. 17; 1 Pet. iv. 12 f.

If ye were of the world, the world would

cause ye are not of the world, but I
have chosen you out of the world,
therefore the world hateth you.
20 Remember the word that I
t. 10. said unto you, [e] The servant is not
13. greater than his lord. If they have
persecuted me, they will also persecute you; if they have kept my saying, they will keep yours also.
21 But all these things will they
do unto you for my name's sake,
because they know not him that
sent me.
22 If I had not come and spoken

---

love] The love (ἐφίλει) is that of nature, and not of moral choice (ἀγαπᾶτε, *v.* 17).

his (**its**) *own...you*] The love of the world is marked as selfish. It is directed to that which specially belongs to itself: to a quality and not to a person (τὸ ἴδιον, Vulg. *quod suum erat*). The fivefold repetition of "the world" brings out vividly the antagonist of Christ.

I have chosen] **I chose.** See *v.* 16, note.

20. *the word*] The reference appears to be not to xiii. 16, but to some earlier occasion on which the words were used, with an application like the present one, Matt. x. 24.

If they have persecuted (**they persecuted**) ...*if they have kept* (**they kept**)...] The subject is left indefinite, being naturally supplied from "the world," and the alternatives are simply stated. The disciples could look back and discern what they had to expect: some courageous followers, some faithful hearers, out of misunderstanding, or careless, or hostile multitudes.

kept (ἐτήρησαν)...] *my word*; "observed," "obeyed," and not (as it has been taken) watched with a malicious purpose. Comp. viii. 51 ff., xiv. 23, xvii. 6; 1 John ii. 5; Rev. iii. 8, 10, xxii. 7, 9. The phrase is peculiar to St John.

21. *But...*] The Lord, with an abrupt transition, anticipates the judgment and deals with it. Persecution and rejection were inevitable; but they were not really to be feared. The disciples could bear them, because they sprang from ignorance of God, and so indirectly witnessed that the disciples knew Him.

all these things] all that is included in the activity of antagonism.

do unto you] The original phrase, according to the true text, is very remarkable (ποιήσουσιν εἰς ὑμᾶς). The disciples were to be not only in fact the victims of the world's hatred, but the object which the world deliberately sought to overpower.

for my name's sake] Comp. Acts v. 41 (*for the name*); 1 Pet. iv. 14. The hostility of the Jews to the disciples was called out by the fact that these proclaimed Christ as being what He had revealed Himself to be, the Christ, the Son of the living God. This was His "name;" and it became the ground of accusation, because the Jews knew not God, that God whom they professed to honour, from whom Christ came. To emphasize this idea God is spoken of simply as "He that sent me," and not as "God," or "the Father," or "the Father that sent me." Comp. iv. 34, v. 24, 30, vi. 38, 39, vii. 16, 18, 28, 33, viii. 26, 29, ix. 4, xii. 44 f., xiii. 20, xvi. 5. See also xvi. 3, note.

because] The true knowledge of God carries with it the knowledge of Christ (viii. 42 (comp. 1 John v. 1); and conversely the knowledge of Christ is the knowledge of God (xii. 44). Comp. Luke xxiii. 34.

22—25. The Lord, having shewn the fact and the ground of the hatred which His disciples would experience, shews also that the hatred is without excuse and yet inevitable. To this end He marks the double testimony which He had Himself offered to His Person and to His office, the testimony of teaching (*vv.* 22, 23), and the testimony of works (24). He had made the Father known. The parallelism between the two declarations is remarkable:

If I had not come and spoken to them, they had not had sin:
But now they have no excuse for their sin.
He that hateth me hateth my Father also.
If I had not done among them the works which none other did, they had not had sin:
But now they have both seen and hated both me and my Father.

The same two forms of witness are appealed to in the same order in xiv. 10, 11. Compare also Matt. xiii. 16 f.; Luke x. 23 f.

22. *come*] The word appears to be used in its technical sense: "If I had not claimed the true functions of Messiah, and spoken in that capacity, and wrought "the works of the Christ," they might then have treated me as a mere man and rejected me without sin." Comp. ix. 41. The Jews had the power and the opportunity of discerning Christ's real nature, so that they were inexcusable. Compare Deut. xviii. 18, 19, where the responsibility of discernment is laid upon the people.

had sin] Compare ix. 41, note. The phrase is peculiar to St John (*v.* 24, xix. 11; 1 John i. 8). Compare the corresponding phrase "bear sin" (LXX. λαμβάνειν ἁμαρτίαν), Num. ix. 13, xiv. 34, xviii. 22, &c. In 1 John i. 8, the phrase is contrasted with "we have not sinned" (οὐχ ἡμαρτήκαμεν). Both

unto them, they had not had sin: but
now they have no [1] cloke for their sin. *Or, excuse.*
23 He that hateth me hateth my
Father also.
24 If I had not done among them
the works which none other man did,
they had not had sin: but now have
they both seen and hated both me and
my Father.

25 But *this cometh to pass*, that
the word might be fulfilled that is
written in their law, [f] They hated me [f] Psal. 19.
without a cause.
26 [g] But when the Comforter is [g] Luk. 49 chap. 26.
come, whom I will send unto you
from the Father, *even* the Spirit of
truth, which proceedeth from the Father, he shall testify of me:

---

mark the abiding effects of sin. But in the latter the act is the central point, and in the former the responsibility for the act.

but now] as it is, they have incurred sin and *have*... The words mark a sharp contrast. Compare Luke xix. 42, ch. viii. 40, ix. 41, xvi. 5, xvii. 13, xviii. 36; 1 Cor. vii. 14, xii. 20, &c.; and in St Paul in the form νυνὶ δέ, Rom. iii. 21, vi. 22, &c.

cloke] **excuse** (πρόφασιν περί, Vulg. *excusationem de*). Compare Ps. cxl. 4 (LXX.).

for (περί) *their sin*] in the matter of, concerning their sin. They have nothing which they can even plead in their own defence as in times of ignorance (1 Pet. i. 14; Acts xvii. 30; Rom. iii. 25).

23. *He that hateth me hateth*...] It is assumed that "the Jews" hate Christ; and so the necessary consequences of this feeling are laid open. Hatred of the Son as Son carries with it hatred of the Father, in which character He had revealed God. Here in connexion with teaching (*v.* 22) the inward disposition of hatred only is touched upon, and that in a general form (*he that hateth*). In *v.* 24 the feeling is marked in its historic form (*have seen and have hated*). For the combination *me*...*my Father* see 1 John ii. 23, v. 10.

24. For those who could not enter into the witness of words Christ added the subordinate witness of works (xiv. 10 ff., note). The works are characterized (*which none other did:* comp. Matt. ix. 33); the words are undefined (*come and spoken*). The works of Christ might be compared with other works; His words had an absolute power (vii. 46. Comp. Matt. vii. 29). Augustine (*in loc.*) has an interesting comparison of other miracles with the miracles of Christ.

both seen] so far as the works revealed outwardly the majesty and will of God, and of Christ, as the representative of God. Comp xiv. 9. Contrast v. 23.

25. *But* this cometh to pass *that*...*might* (**may**)...] Comp. i. 8, *but* he came *that*..., ix. 3, *but* this hath come to pass *that*..., xi. 4, xiii. 18, xiv. 31; 1 John ii. 19; Mark xiv. 49. However startling it might be that the Jews should reject Him whom they professed to reverence, by doing so they fulfilled the Scripture. Comp. Acts xiii. 27. It could not but be that the divine type, foreshadowed in the history of king and prophet, should be completely realised. Comp. xii. 38 f.

in their law] The Lord separates His society from the unfaithful synagogue (*their* law). The very books which the Jews claimed to follow condemned them. For the extension of the term "Law" to the Psalms see x. 34, note. The phrase occurs in Ps. xxxv. (xxxiv.) 19, and in Ps. lxix. (lxviii.) 4.

without a cause] "gratuitously" (δωρεάν, Vulg. *gratis*). Compare 1 S. xix. 5, xxv. 31; 1 K. ii. 31; Ps. xxxv. (xxxiv.) 7 [LXX.]. The hostility of the Jews to Christ, who was absolutely holy and loving, could have no justification. It was pure hatred without ground.

26, 27. There is a pause after *v.* 25. The Lord had dwelt on the hatred with which He had been met. Yet that was not to prevail. The hostility of the world is therefore contrasted with the power by which it should be overcome. In *vv.* 26, 27 the thought is of the vindication of the Lord; in ch. xvi. this passes into the thought of the support of the disciples.

26. *But* (omit) *when the Comforter* (**Advocate**) *is come*] Comp. xiv. 16, note.

I (ἐγώ) *will send*] Comp. xvi. 7. The use of this phrase, involving the claim to divine power at this crisis of rejection, is made most significant by the emphatic pronoun.

from the Father] The preposition (παρά) which is used in both clauses expresses properly position ("from the side of"), and not source (ἐξ, "out of"). The remarkable use in Luke vi. 19 is explained by Luke viii. 44.

the Spirit of truth] xiv. 17, xvi. 13; 1 John iv. 6. Christianity is itself "the Truth." It was the office of the Spirit to interpret and enforce it. The genitive describes the substance of that with which the Spirit dealt, and not a mere characteristic of the Spirit, that His witness is true.

proceedeth] The original term (ἐκπορεύεται, Vulg. *procedit*) may in itself either describe proceeding from a source, or proceeding on a mission. In the former sense the preposition

27 And ye also shall bear witness, because ye have been with me from the beginning.

CHAPTER XVI.

1 Christ comforteth his disciples against tribulation by the promise of the Holy Ghost, and by his resurrection and ascension: 23 assureth their prayers made in his name to be acceptable to his Father. 33 Peace in Christ, and in the world affliction.

THESE things have I spoken unto you, that ye should not be offended.

---

out of (ἐκ, *e*) would naturally be required to define the source (Rev. i. 16, &c.); on the other hand the preposition *from* (*from the side of*, παρά, *a*) is that which is habitually used with the verb *to come forth* of the mission of the Son, *e.g.* xvi. 27, xvii. 8. The use of the latter preposition (παρά) in this place seems therefore to shew decisively that the reference here is to the temporal mission of the Holy Spirit, and not to the eternal Procession. In accordance with this usage the phrase in the Creeds is uniformly "which proceedeth out of" (τὸ πν. τὸ ἅγιον τὸ ἐκ τοῦ πατρὸς ἐκπορευόμενον); and it is most worthy of notice that the Greek fathers who apply this passage to the eternal Procession instinctively substitute "out of" (ἐκ) for "from" (παρά) in their application of it: *e.g.* Theodore of Mopsuestia ('Cat.' *in loco*). At the same time the use of the present (*proceedeth*) in contrast with the future (*I will send*), brings out the truth that the mission of the Spirit consequent on the exaltation of the Son was the consummation of His earlier working in the world. In this respect the revelation of the mission of the Spirit to men (*which proceedeth, I will send*) corresponds to the revelation of the eternal relations of the Spirit (*from the Father, through the Son*).

from the Father] not *from My Father*. The mission is connected with the essential relation of God to man.

he (ἐκεῖνος)...*testify* (**bear witness**)...] Comp. xiv. 26, note.

The witness of the Spirit was not only given through the disciples (Matt. x. 19, 20), but is also given more widely in the continuous interpretation of the life of Christ by the experience of men.

27. *ye also shall bear witness*] The verb (μαρτυρεῖτε) may be indicative (*and* **ye also bear witness**), or imperative (*and do ye also bear witness*). The imperative seems at first sight to fall in better with the general tenour of the passage (*vv.* 18, 20); but on the other hand 3 John 12, which is evidently moulded on this passage, favours the indicative; and yet more, in these two verses Christ is speaking of the witness which should maintain His cause against the world and not enjoining duties. On the whole, therefore, the imperative is less appropriate. The present tense is used of the witness of the disciples, inasmuch as their witness was already begun in some sense, in contrast with that of the Spirit, which was consequent upon Christ's exaltation.

have been with...] **are** *with me*... The relation was present and unbroken. Comp. Luke xv. 31.

from the beginning] Comp. 1 John ii. 7, 24, iii. 11; and cc. vi. 64, xvi. 4 (ἐξ ἀρχῆς). The "beginning" is necessarily relative to the subject (comp. Matt. xix. 4, 8; Acts xxvi. 4; ch. viii. 44). Here it expresses the commencement of Messiah's public work (Acts i. 22; Luke i. 2).

For the two-fold witness see Acts v. 32. On the one side there is the historical witness to the facts, and on the other the internal testimony of personal experience.

4. *The world and the Paraclete* (xvi. 1—11).

In this section the manifestation of the hatred of the world is followed out to its last issues (1—4 *a*), in the prospect of that crisis of separation, which is the condition of the mission of the Paraclete (4 *b*—7), who finally tries and convicts the world (8—11). The antagonistic forces of the world and the Paraclete are portrayed in the most energetic opposition. The warning is answered by the promise.

CHAP. XVI. **1 ff.** In the last section the hatred of the world was exhibited in its general character as inevitable and inexcusable, in contrast to the witness to Christ; it is now shewn in its intense activity as the expression of a false religious zeal.

1. *These things*] The reference appears to be to the whole revelation of the vital union of the believer with Christ, of the self-sacrifice of Christians, of their power of devotion, of their suffering as sharers with Christ, of their witness coincident with the witness of the Spirit; and not only to the last section (xv. 17—27). Compare xv. 11.

not be offended (σκανδαλισθῆτε)] Comp. vi. 61. The image of stumbling over some obstacle in the way (σκάνδαλον, "offence," 1 John ii. 10), which is common in the first two Gospels (*e.g.* Matt. xiii. 21) and is found more rarely in St Luke, occurs in this form only in these two places in the Gospel of St John. It is expressed otherwise in xi. 9 f. (comp. Rom. ix. 32). The offence lay in the opposition on the part of the world to that which the disciples were taught to regard as rightly claiming the allegiance of all

2 They shall put you out of the synagogues: yea, the time cometh, that whosoever killeth you will think that he doeth God service.
3 And these things will they do unto you, because they have not known the Father, nor me.
4 But these things have I told you, that when the time shall come, ye may remember that I told you of

---

men, and especially in the opposition of Israel to that which was the true fulfilment of their national hopes. No trial could be greater to Jewish apostles than the fatal unbelief of their countrymen. Comp. Rom. x.

2. *out of the synagogues* (or rather **synagogue**)] *i.e.* excommunciate you. Comp. ix. 22, xii. 42.

yea (ἀλλά, Vulg. *sed*)] The exclusion from religious fellowship might seem the climax of religious hostility, but there was something more formidable still. The contrast is between what the disciples could perhaps anticipate, and the real extremity of hatred. *They shall put you out of the synagogue;* this, indeed, however grievous, you may be prepared to bear; *but* far more than this; *The* **hour** *cometh* that their full malignity may be shewn, when putting you to death will seem to be the performance of a religious duty.

the time (**hour**) *cometh, that*...] The issue is represented in relation to the whole divine purpose which it fulfilled (Luke ii. 35). This uttermost manifestation of the violence of unbelief was part of the counsel of God. He provided for such an end (ἔρχεται ἵνα). Comp. *v.* 32, xii. 23, xiii. 1.

whosoever...] **every one who**... This will be the universal spirit, not only among Jews, who will be the first adversaries of the Church, but among Gentiles, who will accuse you of impious crimes (Tac. 'Ann.' XV. 44; Suet. 'Nero,' 16).

doeth God service] **offereth service unto God** (d, *hostiam offerre Deo*, Vulg. *obsequium præstare Deo*). The phrase expresses the rendering of a religious service (λατρεία, Rom. ix. 4; Hebr. ix. 1, 6), and more particularly the rendering of a sacrifice as service (προσφέρειν, Hebr. v. 1 ff., viii. 3 f., ix. 7 ff. &c.). The slaughter of Christians, as guilty of blasphemy (Acts vii. 57 f., vi. 13), would necessarily be regarded by zealots as an act of devotion pleasing to God, and not merely as a good work. The Midrash on Num. xxv. 13 ([*Phinehas*] *made an atonement*) may serve as a commentary. "Was this said because he offered an offering (*Korban*)? No; but to teach them that every one that sheds the blood of the wicked is as he that offereth an offering" ('Midrash R.' *ad loc.*).

3. *do unto you*] Omit *unto you.* The action itself, without regard to the particular objects of it, is the central thought.

because they have not known...] *because they* **knew not**... This fatal error was the consequence of a failure to know God. The evil act followed upon the blinded thought. The Jews in their crisis of trial "did not recognise" (οὐκ ἔγνωσαν) the Father and Christ. Their sin is not placed in the want of knowledge in itself (οὐκ οἴδασι, xv. 21, viii. 19, vii. 28), but in the fact that when the opportunity of learning was given to them they did not gain the knowledge which was within their reach (comp. xvii. 25, i. 10).

In this connexion the change from "Him that sent me" (xv. 21) to "the Father" (not "my Father") is significant. "The Father" marks an absolute and universal relation of God to man which Christ came to reveal; "Him that sent me" marks the connexion of Christ with the Old Covenant.

4. *But these things have I told you*] *But* **these things have I spoken** *unto you.* The strong adversative (ἀλλά) is difficult to explain. The reference has been supposed to be to the words immediately preceding; as though it were implied that careful reflection might have shewn the disciples after Christ's death what must be their position. This being so, their Master might have left them to the teaching of experience, but for their sake He forewarned them. It is however perhaps more simple to take the *but* as abruptly breaking the development of thought; "but, not to dwell on the details of the future..."

these things] See *v.* 1, note.

when the time] *when* **their hour**, the appointed time for their accomplishment.

ye may...of them] *ye may* **remember them how that I** (ἐγώ) **told you.** Comp. xiii. 19. The pronoun *I* is emphatic. Christ Himself had foreseen what caused His disciples' perplexity. As knowing this they could be patient.

4 b ff. The revelation which has been given answers to a crisis of transition. The departure of Christ is the condition of the coming of the Paraclete. Separation and suffering are the preparation for victory.

And (**But**, δέ) *these things I said not unto you* (**told you not**) *at* (**from**) *the beginning*] The exact phrase (ἐξ ἀρχῆς) occurs in the New Testament only here and in ch. vi. 64. The preposition suggests the notion of that which flows "out of" a source in a continuous stream, rather than of that which first began from a certain point. Comp. Isai. xl. 21, xli. 26, xliii. 9 (LXX.); Ecclus. xxxix. 32.

them. And these things I said not unto you at the beginning, because I was with you.

5 But now I go my way to him that sent me; and none of you asketh me, Whither goest thou?

6 But because I have said these things unto you, sorrow hath filled your heart.

7 Nevertheless I tell you the truth; It is expedient for you that I go away: for if I go not away, the Comforter will not come unto you; but if I depart, I will send him unto you.

8 And when he is come, he will [1] reprove the world of sin, and of righteousness, and of judgment:

[1] Or, *convince*.

If this difference be regarded, the relation of this statement to the warnings of future trials given at earlier times as recorded by the Synoptists (Matt. v. 10, x. 16 ff.; Luke vi. 22 f.) becomes intelligible. The future fate of the disciples had not been unfolded little by little in unbroken order as a necessary consequence of their relation to Christ. Here and there it had been indicated before, but now it was shewn in its essential relation to their faith. But *these things* must not be limited to the prediction of sufferings only. Christ had spoken also of the new relation of the disciples to Himself through the Paraclete. This fresh revelation was part of the vision of the future now first unfolded.

because I was with you] Comp. Matt. ix. 15.

5. *But now I go my way to* (**go unto**)...] Hitherto Christ had Himself borne the storm of hostility, and shielded the disciples: now He was to leave them, and the wrath of His enemies would be diverted upon them, though they would have another Advocate. The clause is to be closely connected with that which follows: "I go my way and yet none of you..."

to him that sent me] My mission, in other words, is completed.

and none of you...] Christ was going; so much the disciples realised. But their thoughts were bent upon their own immediate loss, and no one asked how this departure affected Him; so completely had their own sorrow absorbed them. Thus they missed the abiding significance of His departure for themselves. The isolated questions of St Peter and St Thomas (xiii. 36, xiv. 5) are not inconsistent with these words. Those questions were not asked with a view to the Lord's glory; and much had been said since which might have moved the disciples to a persistency of inquiry.

6. *because I have said* (**spoken**) *these things*] Comp. *vv.* 1, 4. The prospect of misunderstanding and suffering and separation to be faced shut out all thoughts of consolation and strength.

7. *Nevertheless...*] **But** though you are silent, unable to look onward to the later issues of immediate separation, *I* (ἐγώ), I, on my part, fulfil to the last my ministry of love —*I tell you the truth, it is expedient for you that I* (ἐγώ) *go away*. The disciples were deceived by the superficial appearance of things. To remove their error Christ tells them *the truth*, revealing, laying bare, the reality which was hidden from eyes dimmed by sorrow.

It is expedient] Comp. xi. 50, xviii. 14. From opposite sides ("it is expedient for *us*," xi. 50; but here "it is expedient for *you*") the divine and human judgments coincide. Comp. vii. 39 note.

The personal pronoun in the first case (*that I go*) is emphatic. Attention is fixed upon the Person of the Lord as He was known, in order to prepare the hearers for the thought of "another Advocate" (xiv. 16).

for if I go not away] Here the emphasis is changed. The stress is laid upon the thought of departure. To bring out this idea still more clearly, that which is first spoken of as a "departure" with the predominant notion of separation (ἐὰν μὴ ἀπέλθω) is afterwards spoken of as a "journey," with the predominant notion of an end to be gained (ἐὰν πορευθῶ). In *v.* 10 the idea is that of a "withdrawal" (ὑπάγω). Comp. vii. 33, note.

the Comforter (**Advocate**) *will not come... I will send him...*] The absence of the pronoun before the verb here (πέμψω, I *will send;* compare ἐγὼ πέμψω, xv. 26, *I* will send) gives predominance to the thought of the Mission of the Spirit as a fact. Comp. Luke xxiv. 49; Acts i. 4. The departure of Christ was in itself a necessary condition for the coming of the Spirit to men. The withdrawal of His limited bodily Presence necessarily prepared the way for the recognition of a universal Presence. Comp. vii. 39. And again the presence of Christ with the Father, the consummation of His union with the Father as God and Man, was the preliminary to the Mission of the Spirit. He sent the Spirit in virtue of His ascended Manhood.

And yet again the mission and the reception of the Spirit alike required a completed atonement of Man and God (Hebr. ix. 26 ff.), and the glorifying of perfect humanity in Christ.

8 ff. The promise of the Paraclete is followed by the description of His victory. The synagogue has become the world; and the world finds its conqueror.

8. *And when he is come, he...*] *And* **he** (*ἐκεῖνος*) **when he is come...** The whole action

9 Of sin, because they believe not on me;

of the Spirit during the history of the Church is gathered up under three heads. The categories of *sin, righteousness and judgment*, include all that is essential in the determination of the religious state of man, and to these the work of the Paraclete is referred. His office is to **convict** (ἐλέγχειν, Vulg. *arguere*) the world—humanity separated from God, though not past hope—**concerning** (περί, "in the matter of") *sin and righteousness and judgment*.

The idea of "conviction" is complex. It involves the conceptions of authoritative examination, of unquestionable proof, of decisive judgment, of punitive power. Whatever the final issue may be, he who "convicts" another places the truth of the case in dispute in a clear light before him, so that it must be seen and acknowledged as truth. He who then rejects the conclusion which this exposition involves, rejects it with his eyes open and at his peril. Truth seen as truth carries with it condemnation to all who refuse to welcome it. The different aspects of this "conviction" are brought out in the usage of the word in the N.T. There is first the thorough testing of the real nature of the facts (ch. iii. 20; Eph. v. 13); and then the application of the truth thus ascertained to the particular person affected (James ii. 9; Jude 15, (22), 1 Cor. xiv. 24; 2 Tim. iv. 2; comp. Matt. xviii. 15; John viii. 9); and that in chastisement (1 Tim. v. 20; Titus i. 9, ii. 15; comp. Eph. v. 11); or with a distinct view to the restoration of him who is in the wrong (Rev. iii. 19; Hebr. xii. 5; Titus i. 13).

The effect of the conviction of the world by the Spirit is left undecided so far as the world is concerned; but for the Apostles themselves the pleading of the Advocate was a sovereign vindication of their cause. In the great trial they were shewn to have the right, whether their testimony was received or rejected. The typical history recorded in the Book of the Acts illustrates the decisive twofold action of the divine testimony (2 Cor. ii. 16); for the presentation of the Truth in its power must always bring life or death, but it may bring either; and in this respect the experience of the Apostles on the Day of Pentecost (Acts ii. 13, 41) has been the experience of the Church in all ages. The divine reproof is not simply a final sentence of condemnation; it is also at the same time a call to repentance, which may or may not be heard. The Gospel of St John itself, as has been well pointed out (Köstlin, 'Lehrbegriff,' 205) is a monument of the Spirit's conviction of the world concerning sin (iii. 19—21, v. 28 f., 38—47, viii. 21 ff., 34—47, ix. 41, xiv. 27, xv. 18—24); righteousness (v. 30, vii. 18, 24, viii. 28. 46, 50, 54, xii. 32, xiv. 31, xviii. 37); and judgment (xii. 31, xiv. 30, xvii. 15).

sin...righteousness...judgment] The three conceptions, sin, righteousness, and judgment, are given first in their most abstract and general form. These are the cardinal elements in the determination of man's spiritual state. In these his past and present and future are severally summed up. Then when the mind has seized the broad divisions of the spiritual analysis the central fact in regard to each is stated, from which the process of testing, of revelation, of condemnation, proceeds. In each case the world was in danger of a fatal error, and this error is laid open in view of the decisive criterion to which it is brought.

The three subjects are placed in a natural and significant order. The position of man is determined first; he is shewn to have fallen. And then the position of the two spiritual powers which strive for the mastery over him is made known; Christ has risen to the throne of glory; the prince of the world has been judged. The subjects may also be regarded from another point of sight. When the conviction concerning sin is complete, there remains for man the choice of two alternatives; on the one side there is a righteousness to be obtained from without; and on the other, a judgment to be borne.

So far it may be said that in the thought of "sin" man is the central subject, as himself sinful; in the thought of "righteousness," Christ, as alone righteous; in the thought of "judgment," the devil, as already judged.

Yet once again the three words, sin, righteousness, judgment, gain an additional fulness of meaning when taken in connexion with the actual circumstances under which they were spoken. The "world," acting through its representatives, had charged Christ as "a sinner" (John ix. 24). Its leaders "trusted that they were righteous" (Luke xviii. 9), and they were just on the point of giving sentence against "the prince of life" (Acts iii. 15) as a malefactor (John xviii. 30). At this point the threefold error (Acts iii. 17), which the Spirit was to reveal and reprove, had brought at last its fatal fruit.

of...of...] The Spirit will convict the world "concerning, in the matter of (περί) sin, of righteousness, of judgment." He will not simply convict the world as sinful, as without righteousness, as under judgment, but He will shew beyond contradiction that it is wanting in the knowledge of what sin, righteousness, and judgment really are; and therefore in need of a complete change (μετάνοια).

9 ff. *because...because...because*] Three distinct facts answering to the spiritual character-

10 Of righteousness, because I go to my Father, and ye see me no more;

11 Of judgment, because the prince of this world is judged.

---

istics of the world, of Christ, and of the prince of the world, are stated, which severally form the basis of the action of the Spirit. The conjunction is not to be taken simply as explanatory ("in so far as"), but as directly causal; "because this and this and this is beyond question, the innermost secrets of man's spiritual nature can be and are discovered." Comp. Luke ii. 34, 35.

9. *Of sin, because they believe not on me*] The want of belief in Christ when He is made known, lies at the root of all sin, and reveals its nature. Sin is essentially the selfishness which sets itself up apart from, and so against God. It is not defined by any limited rules, but expresses a general spirit. Christ is thus the touchstone of character. To believe in Him, is to adopt the principle of self-surrender to God. Not to believe in Him, is to cleave to legal views of duty and service which involve a complete misunderstanding of the essence of sin. The Spirit therefore, working through the written and spoken word, starts from the fact of unbelief in the Son of Man, and through that lays open what sin is. In this way the condition of man standing alone is revealed, and he is left without excuse. Comp. viii. 21, ix. 41.

10. *Of righteousness, because I go...*] The Person of Christ, offered as the object of man's faith, serves as a test of the true appreciation of sin. The historical work of Christ, completed at His Ascension, serves as a test of the true appreciation of righteousness. The Life and Death and Resurrection of the Son of God placed righteousness in a new light. By these the majesty of law and the power of obedience and the reality of a divine fellowship, stronger than death, were made known once for all. For a time the Lord had shewn in an outward form the perfect fulfilment of the Law, and the absolute conformity of a human life to the divine ideal. He had shewn also how sin carries with it consequences which must be borne; and how they had been borne in such a way that they were potentially abolished. In that life, closed by the return to the Father, there was a complete exhibition of righteousness in relation to God and man. The Son had received a work to do, and having accomplished it He returned not simply to heaven but to the Father who sent Him, in token of its absolute fulfilment. This revelation once given was final. *Because* nothing could be added to it (*I go to the Father*); because after that Christ was withdrawn from human eyes He had passed into a new sphere (*ye see me no more*), there was fixed for all time that by which men's estimate of righteousness might be tried. On the other hand, till Christ had been raised to glory "righteousness" had not been vindicated. The condemnation of Christ by the representatives of Israel shewed in the extremest form how men had failed to apprehend the nature of righteousness. The Spirit, therefore, starting from the fact of Christ's life, His suffering, and His glory, regarded as a whole, lays open the divine aspects of human action as concentrated in the Son of Man. In this way the possibilities of life are revealed in fellowship with Him who has raised humanity to heaven.

righteousness] The word occurs only in this passage in St John's Gospel. In his first Epistle it is found in the phrase "do righteousness" (ii. 29, iii. 7, 10; comp. Rev. xxii. 11, [xix. 11]). "Righteousness" is evidently considered in its widest sense. Each limited thought of righteousness, as of God's righteousness in the rejection of the Jews, or of man's righteousness as a believer, or even of Christ's righteousness, otherwise than as the fulfilment of the absolute idea in relation both to God and man, is foreign to the scope of the passage. The world is examined, convicted, convinced, as to its false theories of righteousness. In Christ was the one absolute type of righteousness; from him a sinful man must obtain righteousness. Just as sin is revealed by the Spirit to be something far different from the breaking of certain specific injunctions, so righteousness is revealed to be something far different from the outward fulfilment of ceremonial or moral observances. Comp. Matt. v. 20, vi. 33; Rom. iii. 21 f., x. 3.

I go to **the Father** (not *my Father*), *and ye see* (**behold**) *me no more*] The idea of the first clause is that of a completed work (viii. 14, xiii. 3); that of the second a changed mode of existence. There is no contrast in the second clause between the disciples and others; in the original the pronoun is not expressed, and the emphasis lies upon the verb, "ye **behold** me" (θεωρεῖτε). Comp. *vv.* 16 ff. The new mode of existence is indicated as absolute (*ye behold*), and not merely relative to the world (they shall behold).

11. *Of judgment, because the prince* (**ruler**) *of this world is* (**hath been**) *judged*] The world hitherto had passed sentence on success and failure according to its own standard. At length this standard had been overthrown. He in whom the spirit of the world was concentrated had been judged at the very moment and in the very act by which he appeared to common eyes to have triumphed. The Lord therefore looks forward to the consummation

12 I have yet many things to say unto you, but ye cannot bear them now.

13 Howbeit when he, the Spirit of truth, is come, he will guide you into all truth: for he shall not speak of himself; but whatsoever he shall hear, *that* shall he speak: and he will shew you things to come.

14 He shall glorify me: for he

---

of His own Passion as the final sentence in which men could read the issues of life and death. And the Spirit starting from this lays open the last results of human action in the sight of the Supreme Judge. In this way the final victory of right is revealed in the realisation of that which has been indeed already done.

judgment] Comp. Introd. iii. 18 f.

hath been *judged*] The victory was already won: xiii. 31. Comp. xii. 31.

the prince (**ruler**) *of this world*] Ch. xii. 31, xiv. 30.

5. *The Paraclete and the disciples* (xvi. 12—15).

The office of the Paraclete is not confined to the conviction of the world. He carries forward the work which Christ had begun for the disciples, and guides them into all the Truth (*vv.* 12, 13). By this He glorifies Christ (*v.* 14), to whom all things belong (*v.* 15).

This section distinctly marks the position of the apostles with regard to revelation as unique; and so also by implication the office of the apostolic writings as a record of their teaching. The same trust which leads us to believe that the apostles were guided into the Truth, leads us also to believe that by the providential leading of the Spirit they were so guided as to present it in such a way that it might remain in a permanent form.

12. *I have yet...*] The principles had been fully laid down (xv. 15); yet there was still need of a divine commentary to apply these to individual life, and to the formation of a universal Church. In especial the meaning of the Passion had to be unfolded, for though the Passion was potentially included in the Incarnation, neither the one nor the other could be grasped by the disciples till the Son of man was outwardly glorified.

bear] The original word (βαστάζειν, Vulg. *portare*, all. *bajulare*) implies that such teaching as that of the Cross would have been a crushing burden. Comp. ch. xix. 17; Luke xi. 46, xiv. 27, Gal. vi. 2, 5; Acts xv. 10. The Resurrection brought the strength which enabled believers to support it.

now] at this point in your spiritual growth (ἄρτι). The word stands emphatically at the end. Compare xiii. 33, note.

13. *when he...*] The whole verse describes an essentially personal action. The Spirit continues under new conditions that which Christ began.

the Spirit of truth...into all truth (**the truth**)] He who gives expression to the Truth (see xiv. 17) guides men into its fulness. He leads them not (vaguely) "into all truth," but "into all the Truth" (εἰς τὴν ἀλήθειαν πᾶσαν), into the complete understanding of and sympathy with that absolute Truth, which is Christ Himself. The order of the original is remarkable; the truth in all its parts (τὴν ἀλ. πᾶσαν, according to the true reading). Comp. v. 22; Matt. ix. 35; Acts xvi. 26; Rom. xii. 4.

Comp. Ps. xxv. (xxiv.) 5; Rev. vii. 17; (Acts viii. 31).

guide] Christ is "the way" by which men are led to "the truth." By Him we go to Him. The Spirit "guides" men who follow His leading; He does not "tell" His message without effort on their part. He also guides them "into the Truth," which is the domain upon which they enter, and not something to be gazed upon from afar.

Philo, commenting upon Ex. xvi. 23, has a corresponding phrase: "The mind [of Moses] would not have gone thus straight to the mark unless there had been a divine Spirit which guided it (τὸ ποδηγετοῦν) to the truth" ('De Vit. Mos.' III. 36, II. p. 176).

for he shall not...] The test of His true guidance lies in the fact that His teaching is the perfect expression of the one will of God: it is not "of Himself" (see xv. 4, note). That which is affirmed of the Son is affirmed also of the Spirit. Comp. ch. viii. 26, 40, xv. 15. But it may be observed that the message of the Son is on each occasion spoken of as definite (*I heard*, ἤκουσα), while the message of the Spirit is continuous or extended (*whatsoever he shall hear*, or *heareth*, ὅσα ἀκούσει, or ἀκούει, or ὅσα ἂν ἀκούσῃ). The message of Christ given in His historical, human life, was in itself complete at once. The interpretation of that message by the Spirit goes forward to the end of time.

whatsoever...] The message of the Spirit is continuous, and it is also complete. Nothing is kept back which is made known to Him in the order of the divine wisdom.

shall hear] The verb is left absolute. The fact which is declared is that the teaching of the Spirit comes finally from the one source of Truth. The words that follow shew that no distinction is made in this respect between that which is of the Father and that which is of Christ.

shall receive of mine, and shall shew *it* unto you.
15 All things that the Father hath are mine: therefore said I, that he shall take of mine, and shall shew *it* unto you.
16 A little while, and ye shall not see me: and again, a little while, and

---

and he...] A special part of the whole teaching is marked out with reference to the work of the apostles. They lived in a crisis of transition. For them the Spirit had a corresponding gift: *He will declare unto you the things that are coming.*

shew] Rather, **declare**. Comp. iv. 25; 1 John i. 5; 1 Pet. i. 12. The triple repetition of the phrase "he will declare to you" (ἀναγγελεῖ ὑμῖν) at the end of the three verses 13, 14, 15, gives a solemn emphasis to it.

things to come] **the things that are to come**, not simply some things to come, but the whole system of the world to be; or still more exactly "the things that are coming" (τὰ ἐρχόμενα, Vulg. *quæ ventura sunt*), "that future which even now is prepared, and in the very process of fulfilment." The phrase, which occurs here only in the N. T., corresponds with "he that cometh" (Luke vii. 19 f., &c.), and "the age that cometh" (Luke xviii. 30). The reference is, no doubt, mainly to the constitution of the Christian Church, as representing hereafter the divine order in place of the Jewish economy.

14. *He*—that divine Person to whom we are now looking afar off (ἐκεῖνος)—*shall glorify me*] The work of the Spirit in relation to the Son is presented as parallel with that of the Son in relation to the Father. Comp. xiv. 26, xvii. 4. He "glorifies" the Son, that is, makes Him known in His full majesty by gradual revelation, taking now this fragment and now that from the whole sum of Truth. For the manifestation of the Truth is indeed the glorification of Christ. The pronoun (ἐμέ) is placed emphatically before the verb. It was Christ, and none other, who was the subject of the Spirit's teaching.

for (**because**) *he shall...*] To make Christ better known is assumed to be the same as spreading His glory.

shall receive] *shall* **take** (as in *v.* 15). The original verb may be rendered either "receive" or "take." It suggests (as distinguished from δέχεσθαι) the notion of activity and effort on the part of the recipient; and in this connexion "take" brings out well the personal action of the Spirit. Comp. xx. 22, note.

of mine] All that is Christ's is at first contemplated in its unity (τὸ ἐμόν), and then in its manifold parts (*all things*).

15. *All things...mine*] Comp. xvii. 10.

therefore said I...] The message of the Spirit was a message of absolute divine Truth; that Truth which belonged to the Father belonged also to the Son; therefore Christ could say that the Spirit would take of that which was His in order to fulfil His works.

shall take] According to the true reading, **taketh**. The work is even now begun (λαμβάνει), and not wholly future (*shall take*, λήμψεται, *v.* 14).

6. *Sorrow turned to joy* (xvi. 16—24).

The prospect of the fulfilment of the work of the Paraclete for the world and for the disciples is followed by a revelation of the condition in which the disciples themselves will be. They are to stand in a new relation to Christ (16—18). A time of bitter sorrow is to be followed by joy (19, 20), by joy springing (so to speak) naturally out of the sorrow (21, 22); and this joy is to be carried to its complete fulfilment (23, 24).

In this and the following section the disciples again, though in a body and at first indirectly, appear as speakers. The form of the first part of the discourses is partly resumed at the close, though under new conditions.

16. *ye shall not see me...ye shall see me*] **ye behold me no more**...*ye shall see me.* The last clause, *because I go unto the Father*, must be omitted in accordance with a very strong combination of authorities. The words have evidently been introduced from *v.* 17; and they do not occur in the Lord's repetition of the sentence, *v.* 19. This verse offers a superficial contradiction to xiv. 19, which may perhaps have arrested the attention of the disciples. Comp. *v.* 12, viii. 14. In xiv. 19 the thought is of the contrast between the world and the disciples; here the thought is of the contrast between two stages in the spiritual history of the disciples themselves. As contrasted with the world the disciples never lost the vision of Christ. Their life was unbroken even as His life, and so also their direct relation to Him. But on the other hand, the form of their vision was altered. The vision of wondering contemplation, in which they observed little by little the outward manifestation of the Lord (θεωρία), was changed and transfigured into sight (ὄψις), in which they seized at once intuitively all that Christ was. As long as His earthly presence was the object on which their eyes were fixed, their view was necessarily imperfect. His glorified presence shewed Him in His true nature.

ye shall see me] The fulfilment of this promise must not be limited to any one special

ye shall see me, because I go to the Father.

17 Then said *some* of his disciples among themselves, What is this that he saith unto us, A little while, and ye shall not see me: and again, a little while, and ye shall see me: and, Because I go to the Father?

18 They said therefore, What is this that he saith, A little while? we cannot tell what he saith.

19 Now Jesus knew that they were desirous to ask him, and said unto them, Do ye inquire among yourselves of that I said, A little while, and ye shall not see me: and again, a little while, and ye shall see me?

20 Verily, verily, I say unto you, That ye shall weep and lament, but the world shall rejoice: and ye shall be sorrowful, but your sorrow shall be turned into joy.

21 A woman when she is in tra-

---

event, as the Resurrection, or Pentecost, or the Return. The beginning of the new vision was at the Resurrection; the potential fulfilment of it was at Pentecost, when the spiritual Presence of the Lord was completed by the gift of the Holy Spirit. This Presence slowly realised will be crowned by the Return. After each manifestation there is a corresponding return to the Father.

17. *Then said some of his disciples...*] *Some of his disciples* **therefore** *said...* The particularity of the expression, as compared with *v.* 29, iv. 33, seems to mark a distinct impression on the mind of the Evangelist as to the actual scene. He, we may suppose, was himself silent.

among themselves] Rather, **one to another** (πρὸς ἀλλήλους), iv. 33, and so xix. 24. The phrases in *v.* 19 (μετ' ἀλλήλων), and again in xii. 19 (πρὸς ἑαυτούς), are different.

What is this...] The difficulty of the disciples was twofold, (1) as to the fact itself which was announced, and (2) as to the reason which they felt to be alleged in explanation of it. It is best to keep the rendering *because*, for the conjunction (ὅτι) which introduces the second clause. It may however serve simply to introduce the words quoted: *and I go to the Father*. But *v.* 10 seems to shew that it was not only the departure which was perplexing, but also the consequences connected with it; and it is from this verse that the words are quoted, since they are not found in the true text of *v.* 16.

ye shall not see me] **ye behold me not.**

18. *What is this that he saith, A little while?*] **What is this little while whereof he speaketh?** What are these strange intervals, marked by separation and change, which break the tenour of our intercourse?

we cannot tell] **we know not.**

he saith] The original marks the difference between the purport of the saying (ὃ λέγει μικρόν, Vulg. *quod dicit modicum*), and the form in which the saying was conveyed (ὃ λαλεῖ, Vulg. *quid loquitur*). Comp. viii. 43, xii. 49.

19. *Now* (omit) *Jesus knew* (**perceived,** ἔγνω)] The word used probably indicates an outward occasion for the Lord's words, though indeed He read the heart. The anxious looks and whisperings of the disciples would alone be sufficient to reveal their wish. Compare v. 6, vi. 15 (γνούς); and on the other hand, vi. 6 (ᾔδει), xiii. 1, 3, xviii. 4 (εἰδώς). Comp. ii. 24, note.

of that I said] **concerning this, that** (ὅτι) **I said.**

ye shall not see me] **ye behold me not.**

20 ff. The Lord in His answer takes for granted that which He had already made known, and reveals the character of the double interval (20—22), and the new relation to the Father realised for the disciples by His departure (23, 24).

20. *ye shall...*] The order in this first clause is very remarkable (κλαύσετε καὶ θρηνήσετε ὑμεῖς). Attention is at once fixed on the sadness of the immediate future for the disciples. It is as if the Lord had said to them: "Sorrow and lamentation there shall be. Do not marvel at this. And they shall be your lot. Meanwhile the world shall rejoice. Yes: this shall be the issue of that first 'little while.' *Ye* (omit *and*) *shall be sorrowful; but your sorrow*, in that you think that you have lost me, *shall be turned into joy*. This shall be the issue of the second 'little while.'"

ye shall weep and lament] The words mark the open expression of intense sorrow. Such lamentation was the natural accompaniment of Christ's death. Comp. Luke xxiii. 27 f., ch. xx. 11.

the world shall rejoice] as having been freed from one who was a dangerous innovator as well as a condemner of its ways.

and (omit) *ye* (ὑμεῖς) *shall be sorrowful*] The inward feeling is now substituted for the outward expression of grief. The first sharp utterance of lamentation was to be followed by a more permanent sorrow. The words, which had an immediate fulfilment in the experience of the Apostles before the Resurrection, and again before Pentecost, have also a wider application. The attitude of sorrow

vail hath sorrow, because her hour is come: but as soon as she is delivered of the child, she remembereth no more the anguish, for joy that a man is born into the world.

22 And ye now therefore have sorrow: but I will see you again, and your heart shall rejoice, and your joy no man taketh from you.

23 And in that day ye shall ask me nothing. [a] Verily, verily, I say unto you, Whatsoever ye shall ask

[a] Matt. 7. 7.

---

marks in one aspect the state of the Church until the Return. Comp. *v.* 16, note.

turned into (ἐγένετο εἰς)] Comp. Matt. xxi. 42; Luke xiii. 19; Acts iv. 11, v. 36; 1 Pet. ii. 7; Rom. xi. 9; 1 Cor. xv. 45; Rev. viii. 11, xvi. 19. The sorrow itself is transformed.

21. *A woman*] The exact form of expression (ἡ γυνή) marks not simply a single case, but the universal law. The illustration is not taken from any one woman, but from woman as such.

for joy] *for* **the joy**, the special joy which answered to her pangs.

a man] a being endowed with all the gifts of humanity (ἄνθρωπος, Vulg. *homo*). The potential fulness of the completed life is regarded as present to the mother's mind.

born into the world] The complex phrase marks not only the fact but the sphere of the new life. The man is introduced to a place in the great order in which he has a part to play. Comp. viii. 26.

The image of a new birth is constantly applied to the institution of Messiah's kingdom. Comp. Matt. xxiv. 8; Mark xiii. 8 (ὠδῖνες); Rom. viii. 22 (συνωδίνει). And it is applied more generally to the passage to joy through sorrow: Isai. lxvi. 6 ff.; Hos. xiii. 13. St Paul uses the same image to describe the relation of an apostle to his converts, Gal. iv. 19.

22. *And ye* (ὑμεῖς) *now therefore*...] Or, *Ye also therefore now*.... The application of the image (*therefore*) clearly indicates that something more is intended by it than the mere passage of the disciples through suffering to joy. The proper idea of birth-throes is not that of the transition from suffering to joy, but of suffering as the necessary condition and preparation for joy. Under this aspect the disciples in some sense occupied the position of the mother. It was their office, as the representatives of the Church, to realise the Christ of the Resurrection and present Him to the world (comp. Rev. xii. 2 ff.). The time of transition from their present state to that future state was necessarily a period of anguish, and that time was even now come (*now ye have*). But the image is not exhausted by this application. It appears also to have a reference to Christ Himself. For Him death was as the travail-pain issuing in a new life (Acts ii. 24). His passage through the grave was as the new birth of humanity brought about through the extremity of sorrow.

have sorrow] The phrase is not identical with *be sorrowful*, but expresses the full realisation of sorrow. See iii. 15, note.

I will see you again] The implied reference to Christ as Himself rising through the Passion to His glory seems to have led to the use of the first person here, as contrasted with the second person which was used before (*vv.* 16, 19, *ye shall see me*). The highest blessing lies not in the thought that God is the object of our regard, but that we are objects of God's regard. Comp. Gal. iv. 9; 1 Cor. viii. 3; (ch. x. 14, 15).

and your joy...taketh (perhaps *shall take*)...] The sorrow of the disciples (*v.* 20) underwent a sudden transformation. Their joy was stable. The turn of the sentence implies that they would have enemies, but that their enemies would not prevail.

23. *in that day*] when the new relation is realised, and you enjoy the fulness of my glorified presence (xiv. 20). "That day" begins with Pentecost and is consummated at the Return. The Lord now brings before the disciples the consequences of this "going to the Father" (*v.* 17), perfect knowledge, the perfect fulfilment of prayer, perfect joy.

ye shall ask me (ἐμὲ οὐκ ἐρωτήσετε) *nothing*] **ye shall ask me no question.** All will then be clear. The mysteries which now perplex you will have been illuminated. You will not need to seek my guidance when you enjoy that of the Spirit. The verb (ἐρωτήσετε) appears to answer directly to the same word used before in *v.* 19 (ἐρωτᾶν), and so to be used in the same sense. The phrase may however be rendered (as A. V.) *ye shall ask me nothing*, in the sense "ye shall make no request of me." But the context appears to favour the other interpretation. Thus the change in the position of the disciples as suggested in this clause when compared with the next is twofold. Their relation to Christ (the pronoun *me* stands in a position of emphasis) is to be fulfilled in the recognition of a relation to the Father. The questioning of ignorance is to be replaced by the definite prayer which claims absolute accomplishment as being in conformity with the will of God. Comp. xv. 16 n.

Verily, verily...] According to uniform usage this formula introduces a new thought. The preceding clause must therefore, as it seems, be taken rather with what has gone before than with these words.

the Father in my name, he will give *it* you.

24 Hitherto have ye asked nothing in my name: ask, and ye shall receive, that your joy may be full.

25 These things have I spoken unto you in [1] proverbs: but the time cometh, when I shall no more speak unto you in [1] proverbs, but I shall shew you plainly of the Father.

26 At that day ye shall ask in my name: and I say not unto you, that I will pray the Father for you:

27 For the Father himself loveth

[1] Or, *parables.*

Whatsoever ye shall ask (αἰτήσητε)...*in my name, he*...] Rather, according to the true reading: **if ye shall ask anything of...he shall give it you in my name.**

the Father] The return of Christ to the Father restored in its completeness the connexion of man with God, which had been broken.

give it you in my name] Not only is the prayer offered in Christ's name (*v.* 24, xv. 16), but the answer is given in His name. Every divine gift represents in part the working of that Spirit who is sent in His name (xiv. 26).

24. *Hitherto*] As yet Christ Himself was not fully revealed. His name in its complete significance was not made known; nor had the disciples at present the power to enter into its meaning.

ask] The end is assumed to be already reached. The command implies a continuous prayer (αἰτεῖτε, Matt. vii. 7), and not a single petition (Mark vi. 22, αἴτησον).

may be full (**fulfilled**)] The phrase implies not only the fact (ἵνα...πληρωθῇ, xv. 11), but the abiding state which follows (ἵνα... ᾖ πεπληρωμενη, comp. xvii. 13; 1 John i. 4; 2 John 12). This fulness of joy is the divine end of Christ's work according to the Father's will.

7. *After failure, victory* (xvi. 25—33).

This section forms a kind of epilogue to the discourses. The Lord gathers up in a brief summary His present and future relations to the disciples (25—27), and the character of His mission (28). This is followed by a confession of faith on the part of the disciples (29, 30); to which the Lord replies with a warning, and with a triumphant assurance (31—33).

25—27. The teaching of *vv.* 23 f. is unfolded more fully in these verses. There will be hereafter no need of questioning, because the revelation will be plain (23 *a*, 25): the fulfilment of prayer in Christ's name will be absolute, because of the relation established between believers and the Father (23 *b*, f., 26 f.).

25. *These things...in proverbs*] All that had been said since they had left the Upper Room. Of these revelations part had been veiled in figures (the Vine, the Woman in travail), and part was for the time only half intelligible. A deeper meaning lay beneath the words, which could not yet be made plain. It seems to be unnatural to limit the reference to the answer to the question in *v.* 17. The description applies in fact to all the earthly teaching of the Lord. The necessity which veiled His teaching to the multitudes (Matt. xiii. 11 ff.) influenced, in other ways, His teaching to the disciples. He spoke as they could bear, and under figures of human limitation.

proverbs] Comp. x. 6, note.

but the time cometh] **the hour** *cometh.* Omit *but*. Comp. iv. 21, note. From the day of Pentecost, Christ, speaking through the Holy Spirit, has declared plainly the relation of the Father to men (*vv.* 13 ff., xiv. 26).

shew you] **tell** *you*, or **declare unto you**, *vv.* 13 ff.; 1 John i. 2 f. The original word according to the true text (ἀπαγγελῶ) marks the origin rather than the destination (ἀναγγελῶ) of the message.

plainly] without reserve, or concealment. Here the objective sense of the original term (παρρησίᾳ, Vulg. *palam*) prevails. See vii. 13, note.

26. *At that day*...] *v.* 23, note. The fulness of knowledge leads to the fulness of prayer. The clearer revelation of the Father issues in the bolder petitions "in the Son's name;" and this revelation is given by the Paraclete after Pentecost.

I say not...that I (ἐγώ)] Your confidence will then rest upon a direct connexion with God. I speak not therefore of my own intercession in support of your requests. This intercession however is still necessary (1 John ii. 1 f.) so far as the disciples realise imperfectly their position as sons.

pray (**ask**) *the Father for you*] not directly "in behalf of you," but "about you" (περὶ ὑμῶν), as inquiring what was the Father's will, and so laying the case before Him. Comp. Luke iv. 38; ch. xvii. 9, 20. This use of *ask* (ἐρωτᾶν) in connexion with prayer addressed to God is peculiar to St John. It expresses a request made on the basis of fellowship and is used in the Gospel only of the petitions of the Lord (contrast αἰτεῖν, xi. 22, note). This peculiarity of sense explains the use of the word in 1 John v. 16, where the circumstances exclude the idea of prayer for a brother in fellowship with the common Father.

you, because ye have loved me, and
have believed that I came out from
God.
28 I came forth from the Father,
and am come into the world: again, I
leave the world, and go to the Father.
29 His disciples said unto him, Lo,
now speakest thou plainly, and speakest no ‖ proverb.
30 Now are we sure that thou
knowest all things, and needest not
that any man should ask thee: by
this we believe that thou camest forth
from God.

‖ Or, *parable*

---

27. *the Father himself*, without any pleading on my part, *loveth you* with the love which springs from a natural relationship (φιλεῖ), for the disciples are also sons (Rom. viii. 15). Comp. v. 20; Rev. iii. 19. This assurance carries out yet further the promise in xiv. 21, 23 (ἀγαπᾷν).

ye have loved me (πεφιλήκατε)] The word is used here only in the Gospels of the affection of the disciples for their Lord (yet see xxi. 15 ff., note), and the juxtaposition of the pronouns (ὑμεῖς ἐμὲ πεφ.) gives force to the personal relationship. Comp. Matt. x. 37. The word is used also 1 Cor. xvi. 22. The love of the disciples is to be regarded no less as the sign than as the cause of the Father's love (xiv. 21, 23). His love made their love possible, and then again responded to it (1 John iv. 10; "donum Dei est diligere Deum," Aug. *ad loc.*). Their love is regarded both in its origin, and in its continuance (*have loved*, πεφιλήκατε): His love, in its present operation (*loveth*, φιλεῖ).

came out from God] According to the true reading, **came forth from the Father.** The preposition used here (παρά) denotes the leaving a position (as it were) by the Father's side (comp. xv. 26); that used in the next verse (ἐκ) an issuing forth from the Father as the spring of deity. The twofold requirement of true discipleship is laid down to be: (1) personal devotion, (2) belief in the personal (ἐγώ) mission of Christ from heaven (xvii. 8). The recognition of the Son depends on a right sense of His relation to the Father. The common reading (*from God*) obscures this thought.

28. *I came forth from...*] *I came* **out** *from....* No phrase could express more completely unity of essence than the true original of these words (ἐξῆλθον ἐκ). Comp. viii. 42, note. Thus the Lord, while He recognises the faith of the disciples, lays before them a revelation of deeper mysteries. The verse is indeed a brief summary of the whole historic work of Christ: clause answers to clause: the Mission, the Nativity; the Passion, the Ascension.

again] This revelation is complementary to the other. Comp. 1 John ii. 8.

leave the world] Comp. iv. 3, note.

go to the Father] That which was before (*vv.* 10, 17) described as a withdrawal (ὑπάγω), is now again described as a journey for a purpose (πορεύομαι). Comp. xiv. 12, 28.

29 f. The Lord had interpreted the disciples' thoughts, and they openly confess their gratitude and faith, as satisfied with what they can grasp already.

29. *said unto him*] **say.**

Lo, now...Now **we know...**] The revelation seemed to the disciples to have outrun the promise. Their Master had spoken of some future time in which He would give a clear declaration of the Father. They answer, *Now thou speakest plainly;* and we need not wait in darkness any longer. *Now we know* that which makes silent patience easy.

Lo] The sharp interjection is characteristic of St John's narrative. It occurs more often in his Gospel than in all the other books of the N. T. together. Comp. iii. 26, v. 14, xi. 36, xii. 19, xix. 4, 5, 14, &c.

plainly] "In plainness" (ἐν παρρησίᾳ); the slight change of form from *v.* 25 (παρρησίᾳ) marks a difference between the sphere of the revelation and the simple manner; ch. vii. 4; Eph. vi. 19; Col. ii. 15.

30. *Now are we sure*] *Now* **we know.** The discernment of their thought (*v.* 19) seemed to the disciples a sure pledge that all was open before Christ. A human helper needs to have the thoughts of those whom he has to help interpreted to him. In such a case the question is the natural prelude to assistance. So the disciples had hitherto stood towards Christ; but now they had gained a fresh confidence. It was enough for the believer to feel the want. The Lord would satisfy it as was best, without requiring to hear it from him.

by this] Literally "in this" (ἐν τούτῳ). The proof is rather vital (so to speak) than instrumental. Comp. 1 John ii. 3, 5, iii. 16, 19, 24, iv. 9, 10, 13, 17, v. 2. Conscious of the Lord's knowledge of their hearts, they found in this the assurance of His divine mission (ἀπὸ θεοῦ). The "that" (ὅτι) is to be connected with "believe," and gives the object of faith. St John's usage generally is against the connexion of the particle with "in this" in the sense of "because;" ch. xiii. 35; 1 John ii. 3, 5, iii. 19, 24, v. 2. In 1 John iv. 13 the two constructions occur together.

camest forth from God] This common confession of faith shews how little even yet

31 Jesus answered them, Do ye
now believe?
32 [b]Behold, the hour cometh, yea,
is now come, that ye shall be scattered, every man to ‖his own, and
shall leave me alone: and yet I am
not alone, because the Father is
with me.
33 These things I have spoken
unto you, that in me ye might have
peace. In the world ye shall have
tribulation: but be of good cheer; I
have overcome the world.

[b] Matt. 26. 31.

‖ Or, *his own home.*

CHAPTER XVII.

1 *Christ prayeth to his Father to glorify him,* 6 *to preserve his apostles,* 11 *in unity,* 17 *and truth,* 20 *to glorify them, and all other believers with him in heaven.*

---

the disciples had apprehended the nature of Christ. As a body they had not advanced as far as the Baptist.

31 ff. The answer of the Lord recognises the faith of the disciples, and indicates its incompleteness. The last trial had not yet come outwardly; but even this was already surmounted. In the victory of the Master the essential peace of the disciple was included.

31. *Do ye now believe?*] The words are half question, half exclamation (xx. 29). The power and the permanence of their faith are brought into doubt, and not its reality. The *now* (ἄρτι) marks more than a mere point of time (νῦν, *vv.* 29, 30). It suggests a particular state, a crisis; *v.* 12, xiii. 7, 33; Rev. xii. 10.

32. *yea, is now* (omit *now*) *come*] This clause, as contrasted with "and now is" (iv. 23), presents rather the fulfilment of condition than the beginning of a period.

that ye shall be scattered...and shall leave...] *that ye* **may be scattered**...*and* **leave**... Comp. *v.* 2 note. Even this was part of the divine counsel.

be scattered] Comp. ch. x. 12; Zech. xi. 16, xiii. 7; (Matt. xxvi. 31; 1 Macc. vi. 54).

to his own] *i.e.* "to his own home" (xix. 27; Luke xviii. 28, true reading), or (more generally) "to his own pursuits." The bond which had held them together in a society was to be broken; Matt. xxvi. 56.

and yet] For the use of the conjunction see viii. 20. It is natural to imagine a pause after which this clause is solemnly added.

is with me] both now and always. This truth must be set side by side with the mysterious reference to a moment of leaving in Matt. xxvii. 46 (ἐγκατέλιπες). See note on that passage.

33. *These things...*] All that has been spoken since the departure of Judas: the words to the faithful.

in me ye might (**may**) *have...In the world...*] The believer lives two lives in two different spheres, the eternal life *in Christ*, the temporal life *in the world*. There is distrust, division, isolation for a time, but Christ becomes again the centre of a vital union.

ye shall have] **ye have.** Even then their conflict had begun.

be of good cheer] The word (θαρσεῖτε) is found here only in St John. Comp. Matt. ix. 2, 22, xiv. 27; Mark x. 49.

I (ἐγώ) *have overcome the world*] The pronoun stands out with stronger emphasis from the absence of the pronoun of the second person in the parallel clause. Thus in His last recorded words of teaching before the Passion, the Lord claims the glory of a conqueror. Comp. 1 John v. 4 (ἡ νικήσασα). The Christian's victory is in virtue of that which Christ has already won for all time. The image of the "victory" of believers recurs constantly in 1 John and Rev. Elsewhere it is found only in Rom. viii. 37, xii. 21.

XVII. THE PRAYER OF CONSECRATION

1. This chapter stands alone in the Gospels. It contains what may be most properly called "the Lord's Prayer," the Prayer which He Himself used as distinguished from that which He taught to His disciples. On other occasions we read that the Lord "prayed" (Matt. xiv. 23 and parallels, xix. 13; Mark i. 35; Luke iii. 21, v. 16, ix. 18, 28 f., xi. 1), but here the complete outline of what He said is preserved. In this respect it is noticeable that the other Evangelists have recorded words used shortly afterwards at Gethsemane (Matt. xxvi. 36 ff. and parallels). The nearest parallel to the Prayer is the Thanksgiving in Matt. xi. 25 ff. St John, it may be added, never speaks in his narrative of the Lord as "praying," as the other Evangelists do, but on one occasion he gives words of thanksgiving which imply a previous prayer, xi. 41 f., and on another occasion he gives a brief prayer: xii. 27, note.

2. It is evident from *v.* 1 that the prayer was spoken aloud (comp. Matt. xi. 25 ff.). While it was a communing of the Son with the Father, it was at the same time a most solemn lesson by the Master for the disciples (*v.* 13). At the supreme crisis of the Lord's work they were allowed to listen to the interpretation of its course and issue, and to learn the nature of the office which they had themselves to fulfil. The words are a revelation of what He did and willed for men, and a type of that fellowship with the Father in which all is accomplished. Teaching is crowned by prayer. Such words, however little understood at the time, were likely to be treasured up, and to grow luminous by the divine teaching of later experience.

3. There is no direct evidence to shew where the Prayer was uttered. It is most natural to suppose that it followed directly after the close of the address to the disciples (xvi. 33); and in that case that it followed without change of place. The discourses again in cc. xv., xvi. allow no break, and, though they may have been spoken on the way, it seems more likely that xiv. 31 marks the departure to some fresh spot in which chapters xv.—xvii. were spoken. St John's usage admits such a change of scene without explicit notice; and the second group of discourses forms a distinct whole, which at least suggests corresponding external conditions.

It is scarcely possible that chapters xv., xvi. could have been spoken in the streets of the city. It is inconceivable that ch. xvii. should have been spoken anywhere except under circumstances suited to its unapproachable solemnity. The character of the descent to the Kidron, and of the ground on the western side, does not afford a suitable locality. The upper chamber was certainly left after xiv. 31. One spot alone, as it seems, combines all that is required to satisfy the import of these last words, the Temple Courts. It may be true that there is nothing in the narrative which points immediately to a visit there; but much in what is recorded gains fresh significance if regarded in connexion with the seat of the old worship. The central object was the great Golden Vine (comp. Fergusson, 'The Temples of the Jews,' pp. 151 ff.), from which the Lord derived the figure of His own vital relation to His people. Everything which spoke of a divine Presence gave force to the promise of a new Advocate. The warning of persecution and rejection found a commentary in the scenes with which the temple had been associated in the last few days. Nowhere, as it seems, could the outlines of the future spiritual Church be more fitly drawn than in the sanctuary of the old Church. Nowhere, it is clear, could our High Priest more fitly offer His work and Himself and believers to the Father, than in the one place in which God had chosen to set His Name.

It may indeed have been not unusual for Paschal pilgrims to visit the temple during the night. At least it is recorded that at the Passover "it was the custom of the priests to open the gates of the temple at midnight" (ἐκ μέσης νυκτός) (Jos. 'Antt.' XVIII. 2. 2). Such a visit, therefore, as has been supposed, is in no way improbable.

4. This prayer of consecration is the complement to the Agony. There is no inconsistency between the two parts of the one final conflict. Viewed from the divine side, in its essential elements, the victory was won (xiii. 31). Viewed from the human side, in its actual realisation, the victory was yet future (xiv. 30). All human experience bears witness in common life to the naturalness of abrupt transitions from joy to sadness in the contemplation of a supreme trial. The absolute insight and foresight of Christ makes such an alternation even more intelligible. He could see, as man cannot do, both the completeness of His triumph and the suffering through which it was to be gained. Something of the same kind is seen in the conflict of deep emotion joined with words of perfect confidence at the grave of Lazarus (xi. 11, 23, 33, 35, 38, 40 ff.); and again on the occasion of the visit of the Greeks (xii. 23, 27 f., 30 ff.).

5. The general scope of the prayer, which is at once a prayer and a profession and a revelation, is the consummation of the glory of God through Christ, the Word Incarnate, from stage to stage, issuing in a perfect unity (*vv.* 21 ff.). The Son offers Himself as a perfect offering, that so His disciples may be offered afterwards, and through them, at the last, the world may be won. In the perfected work of the Saviour lies the consecration of humanity. The Son declares the accomplishment of the Father's work, and this being accomplished expresses His own will (*v.* 24).

6. The chapter falls into three main sections:

I. THE SON AND THE FATHER (1—5);

II. THE SON AND HIS IMMEDIATE DISCIPLES (6—19);

III. THE SON AND THE CHURCH (20—26).

The subordinate divisions will be seen in the following analysis:

I. THE SON AND THE FATHER (1—5).

(*The past as the basis for the future.*)

Prayer for fresh glory as the condition of the Father's glory (1).
Such was Christ's work on earth in its
aim (2),
method (3).
This had been accomplished (4).
Christ therefore claims to resume His glory (5).

II. THE SON AND HIS IMMEDIATE DISCIPLES (6—19).

(*The Revelation of the Father by the Son.*)

1. The revelation given and accepted (6—8).
2. The disciples watched over though left (9—11).
3. The past work and the future aim (12, 13).
4. The conflict and the strength (14, 15).
5. The issue (16—19).

THESE words spake Jesus, and
lifted up his eyes to heaven,
and said, Father, the hour is come;
glorify thy Son, that thy Son also
may glorify thee:

2 [a] As thou hast given him power [a M 18.]
over all flesh, that he should give
eternal life to as many as thou hast
given him.

III. THE SON AND THE CHURCH (20—26).

(*The Revelation of the Son to the Church and to the world.*)

1. The unity of the Church the conviction of the world.
   By the faith of believers to come (20, 21).
   By the glory of the disciples (22, 23).
2. The progress of revelation.
   By the contemplation of the glory of the Son (24).
   By the revelation through the Son of the Father's name (25, 26).

I. THE SON AND THE FATHER (1—5).

1—5. The completion of the work given by the Father to the Son is the ground for His glorifying by the Father. The work of the Son was to give eternal life to men. This life is the knowledge of God. The glory of the Son, resting upon His perfected work, issues therefore in the glory of the Father; for to know God is to give Him honour.

CHAP. XVII. **1.** *These words*] **These things** (ταῦτα). The reference is to that which precedes. The Lord completed His words of warning and hope and love with the final assurance of victory, and then He turned from earth to heaven, from the disciples to the Father, from teaching to prayer.

lifted up...and said...] St John does not separate the two actions: **lifting up...he said...** The trait marks at once the new region to which the thoughts of the Lord are turned, and the sense of perfect fellowship with the spiritual world. Comp. ch. xi. 41; Luke xviii. 13; Acts vii. 55.

The attitude forms a natural contrast to Luke xxii. 41, and parallels.

Father] *vv.* 5, 11, 24, ch. xi. 41, xii. 27 f. Matt. xi. 25; (Luke x. 21); Luke xxii. 42, xxiii. 34, 46. Comp. Luke xi. 2. The form of the petition includes the ground on which it rests, the absolute relation of the Father to the Son. The prayer is not regarded as directly personal (*glorify me;* contrast xi. 41); nor is it in a universal type (*O God, glorify;* see Luke xviii. 11, 13, and also Mark xv. 34). If the prayer was (as is likely) spoken in Aramæan, we cannot but recall Mark xiv. 36; Rom. viii. 15; Gal. iv. 6 (Ἀββά).

the hour] Comp. vii. 30, viii. 20, xii. 23, xiii. 1, note. All the circumstances of redemption proceeded (*is come*, comp. ii. 4) according to a divine law. In the accomplishment of this there is no delay and no haste.

glorify thy Son, that thy (**the**) *Son...may* (omit *also*)...] The "glorifying" of the Son is the fuller manifestation of His true nature. This manifestation, given in the fact of His victory over death, established by the Resurrection and Ascension, is set forth as having for its end the fuller manifestation of the Father. It is through the Son that men know and see the Father, ch. xiv. 7 ff.; and the one end of all work and of all partial ends is the glory of the Father. The "glorifying" of the Son must not be limited to His support in the Passion, nor to His wider acknowledgment, though the revelation of His Being includes the thoughts which were suggested by these partial interpretations. Comp. xii. 23, note. The true commentary on the words is Phil. ii. 9 ff.

It must be observed that the prayer is expressed in an impersonal form. It is based upon essential relations (*thy Son*, *the Son*, not *me*, *I*). In this respect it corresponds to the promise in Ps. ii. 8. Comp. viii. 50.

2. *As thou hast given him power...*] **Even as thou gavest him authority...** The complete elevation of the Incarnate Son to His divine glory was necessarily presupposed in His mission. He received a legitimate authority (ἐξουσία) over humanity as its true Head, and this could only be exercised in its fulness after the Ascension. At the same time the exaltation of the Son as Saviour carried with it the glorification of the Father, as the spring of the eternal life which Christ sent through the Spirit from heaven.

thou gavest...] The original charge once given (ἔδωκας) is treated as the ground and measure of the prayer for its fulfilment. Nothing is said or implied as to the sovereignty of the Son over other created beings (*e.g.* angels). His office is regarded primarily in relation to man fallen.

authority] Comp. ch. v. 27; Matt. vii. 29, ix. 6, xxviii. 18. For the genitive (π. σαρκός) see Matt. x. 1; Mark vi. 7.

all flesh] The phrase is the rendering of a Hebrew phrase (כל בשר) which describes mankind in their weakness and transitoriness, as contrasted with the majesty of God, Gen. vi. 12; Ps. lxv. 2, cxlv. 21; Isai. xl. 5 f., xlix. 26, lxvi. 16, 23 f.; Joel ii. 28; Ezek. xx. 48, xxi. 5; Jer. xii. 12, xxv. 31; Job xii. 10, xxxiv. 15; and from that side of their nature in which they are akin to, and represent, the lower world, Gen. vi. 19, vii. 15 f., 21, viii. 17, ix. 11, 15 ff.; Ps. cxxxvi. 25; Jer. xxxii. 27, xlv. 5.

Comp. Matt. xxiv. 22; Luke iii. 6; Acts

3 And this is life eternal, that they might know thee the only true God, and Jesus Christ, whom thou hast sent.

---

ii. 17; 1 Pet. i. 24; Rom. iii. 20; 1 Cor. i. 29; Gal. ii. 16.

From this point of sight the whole clause brings out forcibly the scope of the Incarnation, as designed to bring a higher life to that which in itself was incapable of regaining fellowship with God. Comp. Iren. 'Adv. hær.' V. 16. 2.

At the same time the universality of the Gospel is laid open. Not all Israel only (Luke ii. 10, *all the people*, Matt. xv. 24), but all humanity are the subjects of Messiah (Matt. xxviii. 19).

give...to as many as thou hast...] The original form of expression is remarkable: **that all that** (πᾶν ὅ) **thou hast given him to them he should give.** The Christian body is first presented in its unity as a whole, and then in its individual members. Comp. *v.* 24, vi. 37.

The contrast implied in *all flesh* and *all that has been given*, marks a mystery of the divine working which we cannot understand. The sovereignty is universal, the present blessing is partial. Comp. iii. 16.

3. *And this is life eternal* (**the life eternal**)] The definition is not of the sphere (*in this*), but of the essence of eternal life (comp. xii. 50). The subject is taken from the former clause: *The life eternal*—the life eternal, of which Christ had just now (as ever) spoken (ἡ αἰώνιος ζωή)—*is this, that...* Eternal life lies not so much in the possession of a completed knowledge as in the striving after a growing knowledge. The *that* (ἵνα) expresses an aim, an end, and not only a fact. Comp. iv. 34, vi. 29. So too the tense of the verb (γινώσκωσι) marks continuance, progress, and not a perfect and past apprehension gained once for all. Comp. *v.* 23, x. 38; 1 John v. 20; ch. xiv. 31 (ἵνα γνῷ), xix. 4; 1 John iv. 7, 8 (γινώσκει, ἔγνω).

The construction which occurs here (αὕτη ἐστὶν ἡ αἰ. ζ. ἵνα...) is characteristic of St John, ch. xv. 12; 1 John iii. 11, 23, v. 3; 2 John 6. The force of the article (ἡ αἰ. ζ.) appears in the only other passages of the New Testament where it is found: Acts xiii. 46; 1 Tim. vi. 12 (1 John v. 20 is a false reading). Comp. 1 John i. 2, ii. 25 (ἡ ζ. ἡ αἰ.).

The knowledge which is life, the knowledge which from the fact that it is vital is always advancing (γινώσκωσι, see above), is twofold; a knowledge of God in His sole, supreme Majesty, and a knowledge of the revelation which He has made in its final consummation in the mission of Christ. To regard the phrase *the only true God* as embracing here both *thee* and *him whom thou didst send*, a construction adopted by Cæsarius (Cramer, 'Cat.' *ad loc.*) and by many Latin fathers from Augustine downwards, or to regard the juxtaposition of *thee, the only true God*, and *him whom thou didst send*, as in any way impairing the true divinity of Christ, by contrast with the Father, is totally to misunderstand the passage. It is really so framed as to meet the two cardinal errors as to religious truth which arise in all times, the error which finds expression in various forms of polytheism, and the error which treats that which is preparatory in revelation as final. On the one side men make for themselves objects of worship, many and imperfect. On the other side they fail to recognise Christ when He comes. The primary reference is, no doubt, to the respective trials of Gentile and Jew, but these include in themselves the typical trials of all ages.

Cyril of Alexandria (*ad loc.*) justly remarks that the knowledge of God as the Father really involves a knowledge of the Son as God. The true (ἀληθινός) God is the Father who is made known in and by the Son (1 John v. 20). And the revelation of God as Father, which is the Personal revelation of God as love in Himself, involves at the same time the knowledge of the Holy Spirit. The epigram which expresses the teaching of St Augustine, "ubi amor ibi Trinitas," has its fulfilment in this conception. Comp. Aug. 'De Trin.' VIII. 14, IX. 8.

The verse finds an instructive comment in the double command, ch. xiv. 1.

this is ...] Life—eternal life—is characteristically spoken of by St John as truly present: iii. 36, v. 24, vi. 47, 54; 1 John v. 12; and the possession of this life may become a matter of absolute knowledge: 1 John v. 13. At the same time this life is regarded as future in its realisation: iv. 14, 36, vi. 27, xii. 25. The two thoughts are united in vi. 40, see note.

might know] **may** *know*. In such a connexion "knowledge" expresses the apprehension of the truth by the whole nature of man. It is not an acquaintance with facts as external, nor an intellectual conviction of their reality, but an appropriation of them (so to speak) as an influencing power into the very being of him who "knows" them. "Knowledge" is thus faith perfected; and in turn it passes at last into sight (1 John iii. 2; comp. 1 Cor. xiii. 9 ff.). It is remarkable that the noun (γνῶσις, ἐπίγνωσις) is not found in the writings of St John; the verb on the contrary (γινώσκω) is relatively more frequent in these than in any other section of the New Testament. As in the corresponding case of "faith" (see ii. 23, note) St John dwells on the active exercise of the power, and not on the abstract idea.

4 I have glorified thee on the
earth: I have finished the work which
thou gavest me to do.
5 And now, O Father, glorify
thou me with thine own self with
the glory which I had with thee before the world was.
6 I have manifested thy name un-

---

the only true God] On the word "true" (ἀληθινός) see iv. 23, note. There are many to whom the name of God has been applied (1 Cor. viii. 4 ff.), but One only fulfils the conception which man can dimly form of the absolute majesty of God. Comp. Rom. xvi. 27; 1 Tim. vi. 15 f.

Jesus Christ, whom thou hast sent] **Him whom thou didst send, even Jesus Christ.** The emphasis is laid on the single historic fact of Christ's mission (*didst send*, ἀπέστειλας), and not on the continuity of its effects (*hast sent*, ἀπέσταλκας, v. 36, xx. 21, note).

even *Jesus Christ*] The occurrence of these words creates great difficulty. The difficulty is materially lessened if *Christ* is regarded as a predicate: "*that they know...Jesus* as *Christ.*" The general structure of the sentence however is unfavourable to this view. The complex name "Jesus Christ" appears to answer exactly to the corresponding clause, "the only true God." These two clauses are thus most naturally taken to define the persons indicated before, "Thee" and "Him whom Thou didst send." If we accept this construction we have then to consider whether the definitions are to be treated as literally parts of the prayer, or as words used by the Evangelist in his record of the prayer, as best fitted in this connexion to convey the full meaning of the original language. In favour of the latter view it may be urged (1) that the use of the name "Jesus Christ" by the Lord Himself at this time is in the highest degree unlikely, while the compound title, expressing as it did at a later time the combination of the ideas of true humanity and of divine office, may reasonably be supposed to give the exact sense of the Lord's thought; (2) that the phrase "the only true God" recalls the phrase of St John "the true God" (1 John v. 20), and is not like any other phrase used by the Lord; (3) that the clauses, while perfectly natural as explanations, are most strange if they are taken as substantial parts of the actual prayer. It is no derogation from the truthfulness of the record that St John has thus given parenthetically and in conventional language (so to speak) the substance of what the Lord said probably at greater length.

4, 5. *I have glorified* (**I glorified**)...*And now...glorify...*] The prayer of *v.* 1 is repeated from the opposite point of view. Here the glorifying of Christ is treated as a consequence of work done, and there as a preparation for work still remaining to be done. There is also this further difference in expression, that in *v.* 1 the form is indirect (*thy Son*), while here it is direct (*I, me*). The reason of this appears to be that in *v.* 1 the central idea is that of the general relation of Son and Father, while here the attention is fixed on what Christ had done as man. The eternal glory of the Son is to be resumed by the Incarnate Son.

The parallelism between *v.* 4 and *v.* 5 is very close: *I glorified thee upon earth: Do Thou glorify me with Thine own self* (*i.e.* in heaven). And in each case the personal relation is made emphatic by the juxtaposition of the pronouns (*I, Thee, v.* 4; *Me, Thou, v.* 5).

4. I glorified...] The historical mission of Christ is now regarded as ended; the earthly work is accomplished. By a life of absolute obedience and love Christ had revealed—and therefore glorified—the Father.

I have finished] According to the true reading, **having finished (perfected,** τελειώσας). The participle defines the mode in which the glory of God was secured: there is but one action. For the use of the word "perfect" (Vulg. *consummavi*) comp. iv. 34, note.

work...gavest (**hast given**)] Comp. v. 36. Here the work is contemplated in its unity, as accomplished, and there in its manifold parts, as still to be done. Christ's work is not self-chosen, but wrought out in perfect obedience.

5. *now*] when the hour has come, and the last sacrifice of humiliation is over.

with thine own self...with thee] The sense of the preposition in this construction (παρὰ σεαυτῷ, παρὰ σοί) in St John is always local (and not ethical), either literally (i. 40, iv. 40, xiv. 25, xix. 25; Rev. ii. 13) or figuratively, as expressing a direct spiritual connexion (viii. 38, xiv. 17, 23). The sense therefore here, in both cases, is "in fellowship with thee." The rendering "in thy sight," which is supported by the usage of other writers of the New Testament (Luke ii. 52; 2 Thess. i. 6; 1 Pet. ii. 4, &c.), is excluded alike by St John's usage and by the context.

Thus the verse presents a contrast between the state of the Incarnate Son and of the Eternal Word. The Person is one (*glorify me...which I had...*), but by the assumption of manhood the Son for a time emptied Himself of that which He afterwards received again.

which I had] in actual possession and not as the object of the divine thought. Comp i. 1. The "glory" here spoken of is not the predestined glory of Christ's humanity, but

to the men which thou gavest me
out of the world: thine they were,
and thou gavest them me; and they
have kept thy word.
7 Now they have known that all
things whatsoever thou hast given me
are of thee.
8 For I have given unto them
the words which thou gavest me;
and they have received *them*, [b] and [b] chap. 16. 27.

---

the glory of His divinity which He resumed on His Ascension.

before the world was] Comp. *v.* 24 note. The glory of the Eternal Word spoken of here is distinguished from the glory of Christ, the Incarnate Word, spoken of in *v.* 22, though the two correspond to one another. The one is supra-temporal (ἔδωκας. *v.* 24); the other is a present possession (δέδωκας, *v.* 22).

For St Paul's statement of the fulfilment of these words see Phil. ii. 9 ff.

II. THE SON AND THE DISCIPLES (6—19).

6 ff. The fulfilment by Christ of His work among men contained the promise of the wider work which should be accomplished for and through them on His exaltation. Thus the current of His prayer passes naturally into a new channel. As He had prayed for Himself, He prays for His disciples. The petition *glorify me* is represented in new relations by *keep them* (*v.* 11), and *sanctify them* (*v.* 17). The glory of Christ, and of the Father in Christ, was to be realised by the continuance and completion of that which He had begun in men.

6. The prayer for the disciples is based upon a threefold declaration of what they were in relation to Christ (*I manifested thy name to the men...*), in relation to the Father (*thine they were...*), and in themselves (*they have kept thy word*). Each statement is a plea in favour of the petitions which follow. Together they form a portraiture of true discipleship.

I have manifested] **I manifested.** The phrase is exactly parallel with "I glorified" in *v.* 4. Christ made known perfectly the name of God as Father in His life. Even to the Jew this conception of the relation of God to man was new. The revelation however was not made to all, but to those who by sympathy were fitted to receive it.

unto the men (τοῖς ἀνθρώποις)] The full form of the phrase (as contrasted with "to those whom...") seems to mark a certain correspondence between the revelation and the recipients of it. As men the disciples were enabled to receive the teaching of the Son of man (comp. i. 4).

gavest] Comp. *vv.* 2, 24, vi. 37, x. 29, xviii. 9. It is only by the influence of the Father that men can come to Christ, vi. 44, 65. Yet the critical act admits of being described from many sides. The Father is said to "draw" men (vi. 44), and Christ also draws them (xii. 32). Christ "chooses" men (vi. 70, xv. 16); and men freely obey His call.

thine] not only as creatures of God, or as representatives by birth of Israel, the chosen people, but as answering to the true character of Israel (i. 47).

thy word] The revelation of Christ as a whole (ὁ λόγος, Vulg. *sermo*) is spoken of as the Father's word (comp. vii. 16, xii. 48, 49). All was included implicitly in the word by which the disciples were bidden to seek Christ (vi. 45). As they "heard" this at first, so they continued to hear it. On *keep* (τηρεῖν) see viii. 51, note.

7, 8. These verses unfold the growth of discipleship which is summarised in the preceding clause (*they have kept thy word*). The disciples who followed Christ in obedience to the Father had come to know by actual experience the nature and the source of His mission. They trusted Him, and then they found out little by little in whom they had trusted.

7. *Now they have known*] *Now they* **know** (ἔγνωκαν), now they have learnt through the teaching of discipleship. The English present seems to express best, both here and in *v.* 8, the actual result of past experience. Comp. v. 42, vi. 69, viii. 52, 55, xiv. 9; 1 John ii. 4.

all things whatsoever thou hast given] It might have seemed simpler to say "all that I have," but by such a mode of expression the thought of the special charge committed to the Son would have been lost. And yet further, the reference is to all the elements of the Lord's Life and Work—His words and acts—which are severally attributed to the Father's love (v. 19, 30, viii. 28, xii. 49 f., xiv. 10), and now regarded in their abiding consequence (*are*, not *were*).

8. The fuller insight which the disciples gained into the being of Christ came through the gradual manifestations which He "gave" and they "received."

the words...] That teaching which was before (*v.* 6) regarded in its unity, is now regarded in its component elements (τὰ ῥήματα). That which was organically one, was made known in many parts according to the Father's will (*the words which thou gavest me*).

The contrast between "the word" (λόγος), the complete message, and "the saying" (ῥῆμα), the detached utterance, is frequently important in St John, and yet difficult to express without a paraphrase. Comp. v. 38

have known surely that I came out from thee, and they have believed that thou didst send me.

9 I pray for them: I pray not for the world, but for them which thou hast given me; for they are thine.

10 And all mine are thine, and thine are mine; and I am glorified in them.

11 And now I am no more in the world, but these are in the world, and I come to thee. Holy Father,

---

(*word*), 47 (*sayings*), vi. 60 (*word*), 63 (*sayings*), 68 (*sayings*), viii. 43 (*word*), 47 (*sayings*), 51 (*word*), xii. 47 (*sayings*), 48 (*word*), xv. 3 (*word*), 7 (*sayings*). The plural of "word" occurs x. 19, xiv. 24; "saying" does not occur in St John in the singular, though it is frequent in other parts of the New Testament.

they have received...and have known...and they have believed...] **they received...and know...and believed...** The issues of the reception of the successive relations of Christ are gathered under the two heads of knowledge and faith (comp. vi. 69, note), and both alike are directed to the recognition of Christ and His mission. The disciples in their converse with their Master perceived, and perceived truly, on such evidence as to exclude all doubt, that the source of His life was divine This was a matter on which they could themselves judge. So far the voice of conscience was authoritative as to the character of Christ. But beyond this they believed that Christ was directly sent by God to fulfil a special office. This was no longer within the province of knowledge; it was a conclusion of faith. Yet here again in due course "faith" is transformed into knowledge, *v.* 25.

9 ff. The Lord has set forth the character and the position of the disciples, what they had received and made their own; He now looks forward to their future. They are watched over though left (9—11).

9. *I pray for them*] The pronouns are emphatic: "I on my part, in answer to their devotion; I, thy Son, for those who have been faithful to Thee." The emphatic "I" occurs throughout the prayer; see specially *vv.* 4, 12, 14, 19. On the word for "pray" (ἐρωτῶ, "ask") see xvi. 26, note.

The exclusion of "the world" from Christ's prayer is no limitation of the extent of His love (comp. *v.* 21, note), but a necessary result of the immediate circumstances of the prayer. His work is fulfilled in ever-increasing circles of influence. At present He is interceding for those who have been prepared beforehand to continue His work; and in their behalf He pleads a request of which the fulfilment is guaranteed (so to speak) by a threefold claim. The disciples for whom intercession is made were indeed the Father's (*they are thine:* comp. *v.* 6), and therefore He could not but regard His own children. And further, in respect of their relation to Christ, so far as they had been attached to Him this also was a relation to the Father equally (*all things that are mine are thine*). And thirdly, this relation had issued in Christ's glory, and therefore in the glory of the Father, so that by the fulfilment of their part hitherto they called out fresh gifts of divine love (*I have been glorified in them*).

10. *all mine are thine...*] **all things that are mine are thine...** This general statement, which is expressed in the most comprehensive form, and does not include only persons, prepares the way for the next. Service rendered to Christ is rendered to the Father (xiii. 20), so that those who were from the first God's children had become nearer to His love by their faith in the Son of God. The second clause (*and* **the things that are thine** *are mine*) is not required by the argument, but serves to emphasize the assertion of the perfect communion of the Son and the Father. The words are not to be regarded as parenthetical, but as part of the exposition of the argument, which is made by parallel sentences.

I am (**I have been**) *glorified*] To "glorify" God (or Christ) is to make Him known or to acknowledge Him as being what He is (xii. 28, note). Here then Christ bears witness to the faith of the disciples who had been enabled to recognise and to confess Him even in His state of self-humiliation (vi. 69). This glory gained in the persons of the disciples is not looked upon as past (ἐδοξάσθην, xiii. 31), but as abiding (δεδόξασμαι, 1 Pet. i. 8; 2 Cor. iii. 10).

in them] Faithful disciples are the living monuments in which Christ's glory is seen. So also a church is the "glory" of its founder, 1 Thess. ii. 20.

11. The declaration of the grounds on which the prayer is urged is followed by the statement of the circumstances which make the prayer necessary. These are simply coordinated (*and...and...and*); and the bare enumeration of the facts is left without comment. Christ leaves the world, the disciples remain in the world; Master and scholars must then be separated, so that the old connexion will be broken. Christ goes to the Father; He enters therefore upon a new sphere of His mediatorial work, in which His mode of action will be changed.

And now I...but these...] **And I...and they...** See above.

keep through thine own name those whom thou hast given me, that they may be one, as we *are*.

12 While I was with them in the world, I kept them in thy name: those that thou gavest me I have kept, and none of them is lost, but the son of perdition; [c] that the scripture might be fulfilled. [c] Psal. 109. 8.

13 And now come I to thee; and

I come to thee] The return of Christ to the Father involves more than a local separation from His people. It has a spiritual correspondence with His "coming" into the world (viii. 14, xiii. 3), by which the idea of separation (*I am no more in the world*...) passes into that of a new union. It typified a new relation towards the disciples. For a time they would be unable to "see" Him (xvi. 10, 16 ff.), or to "follow" Him (xiii. 33, 36 f.: comp. vii. 33 ff., viii. 21 ff.). Yet this change was designed to contribute to their good (xvi. 7), and was to be followed by a fresh "coming" to them (xiv. 3 ff., 18, 23, 28, xxi. 22 f.).

Holy Father...] The substance of the prayer here at length finds expression when the pleas in support of it, and the occasion which calls it out, have been set forth. The unique phrase of address (*Holy Father*, comp. Rev. vi. 10; 1 John ii. 20; *v.* 25, *righteous Father*) suggests the main thought. The disciples hitherto had been kept apart from the corruption of the world by the present influence of Christ. The revelation of holiness which He had made had a power at once to separate and to unite. He asks that God, regarded under the separate aspects of purity and tenderness, may carry forward to its final issue (*that they may be one even as we are*) that training which He had Himself commenced, and that too in the same way (*keep in thy name*, comp. *v.* 12). The "name" of the Father, the knowledge of God as Father, is regarded as an ideal region of security in which the disciples were preserved. It is the ground of their safety and not of Christ's power.

keep through thine own name those whom thou hast given me] According to the text which is supported by overwhelming authority, the rendering must be: *keep* **them in thy name which thou hast given me**. The phrase is very remarkable, and has no exact parallel except in *v.* 12. Perhaps the same thought is found in Phil. ii. 9 f.; and it is illustrated by the imagery of the Apocalypse. Thus in Rev. ii. 17, a promise is made to the victorious Christian: *I will give him a white stone, and on the stone a new name written, which no man knoweth saving he that receiveth it;* and again it is said of "the Word of God:" *he had a name written that no man knew but he himself* (xix. 12); and again of the saints in glory, *they shall see his face, and his name shall be on their foreheads* (xxii. 4). These passages suggest the idea that the "giving of the Father's name" to Christ expresses the fulness of His commission as the Incarnate Word to reveal God. He came in His Father's name (v. 43), and to make that name known (comp. *vv.* 4 ff.). He spoke what He had heard (viii. 26, 40, xv. 15). And all spiritual truth is gathered up in "the name" of God, the perfect expression (for men) of what God is, which "name" the Father gave to the Son to declare when He took man's nature upon Him. Comp. Exod. xxiii. 21.

one, **even** *as we are*] The unity is not only of will and love but of nature, perfectly realised in absolute harmony *in Christ*. As the divine Unity consists with a variety of Persons, so too the final unity of men does not exclude but perfectly harmonizes the separate being of each in the whole.

as we are] The use of the plural pronoun in such a connection is a distinct assertion of sameness of essence. The "we" which unites the Father and Christ affirms that their nature is one. Comp. x. 28, 29.

12 f. The Lord looks back upon the work which He had wrought for the disciples (*v.* 12), now that He is passing into the new order (*v.* 13). The place which He had occupied (*I* [ἐγώ] *kept*) must hereafter be filled otherwise.

12. *While...with them* (omit *in the world*) *I kept...kept*] *While...with them I kept*—**guarded**. The tenses of the original verb (ἐτήρουν, ἐφύλαξα, Vulg. *servabam*, *custodivi*) mark respectively the continuous action of watching and its completed issue. The difference between the verbs themselves appears to be that "kept" (τηρεῖν) expresses the careful regard and observance of that which is looked at as without (*e.g.* Matt. xxvii. 36), while "guarded" (φυλάσσειν) describes the protection of something held as it were within a line of defence from external assaults.

in thy name: those that thou gavest me I have kept...] *in thy name* **that thou hast given me; and I guarded** them... as in *v.* 11.

but...] The excepting phrase (εἰ μή) does not necessarily imply that Judas is reckoned among those whom the Lord "guarded." The exception may refer simply to the statement "not one perished." Comp. Matt. xii. 4; Luke iv. 26, 27; Gal. i. 19, ii. 16; Rev. xxi. 27. Contrast xviii. 9.

the son of perdition] He whose character was defined by this terrible mark, 2 Thess. ii. 3; (2 S. xii. 5). Comp. xii. 36, note. The solemn repetition of cognate words in the ori-

these things I speak in the world,
that they might have my joy fulfilled
in themselves.
14 I have given them thy word;
and the world hath hated them, because they are not of the world, even
as I am not of the world.
15 I pray not that thou shouldest
take them out of the world, but
that thou shouldest keep them from
the evil.
16 They are not of the world,
even as I am not of the world.
17 Sanctify them through thy
truth: thy word is truth.
18 As thou hast sent me into the

---

ginal cannot be preserved ("not one perished but the son of perishing").

that the scripture...] Judas was lost, but even the fall of Judas found a place in the whole scheme of divine Providence, comp. xii. 38, note. The reference is to Ps. xli. 9 (ch. xiii. 18), rather than to Ps. cix. 8 (Acts i. 20).

13. *And now come I*...] **But now I come...** The old relation was on the point of being broken.

Christ was, so to speak, already on His way to the Father, but at the same time He had not yet left the world. His prayer therefore was offered while He was still on the scene of human conflict, that the disciples, conscious of His intercession, might be able when alone to realise in themselves (comp. xiv. 23) that joy, characteristic of Him (comp. xv. 11, note), which they had hitherto found in His presence.

these things I speak ... that they might (**may**)...] The prayer was uttered aloud that the disciples might draw strength from the words which they heard.

14, 15. The joy of Christ must be won through conflict. The disciples are strong by the Word of God and by the Lord's intercession, but the world naturally hates them.

14. *I* (ἐγώ) *have given*...] The revelation which the Lord had made is now regarded in its completeness (τὸν λόγον as compared with τὰ ῥήματα, *v.* 8), and in connexion with Himself (ἐγὼ δ.): *I* in the fulness of my presence *have given*... The disciples were furnished with their power, and the crisis which decided their future was over. When they came before the world *the world hath hated* (**hated**) *them*, shewed at once and decisively its position of antagonism to the Gospel. The single act (**hated**, ἐμίσησεν) is contrasted with the permanent endowment (δέδωκα). On the other hand, see xv. 18, 24 (μεμίσηκεν). These two facts, *I have given*... *and the world hated*..., form the conditions which determine the nature of the apostolic work.

thy word] Comp. *vv.* 6, note, 17, v. 38, viii. 31 f.

they are not of...] Comp. *v.* 16, viii. 23, note.

15. It might have seemed best that the Lord should remove His disciples from a scene of inevitable conflict. But for them, as for Himself (xii. 27), the conflict was the condition of victory. His prayer therefore was for their protection, and not for their withdrawal either by isolation or by removal.

from the evil] **out of the evil one.** The parallel words in 1 John v. 18, 19, seem to shew conclusively that the original phrase (ἐκ τοῦ πονηροῦ, Vulg. *ex malo*), which is of doubtful gender, is here masculine (*the evil one*). Just as Christ is Himself the medium or sphere in which the believer lives and moves (ἐν χριστῷ), so the prince of the world, the evil one, is the medium or sphere in which they live and move who are given up to him (ἐν τῷ πονηρῷ). The relation of man to good and evil is a personal relation; and the Lord prays that His disciples may be kept out of the range of the pervading influence of His enemy. He does not pray only that they may be delivered from the outward assault of the evil one (2 Thess. iii. 3, φυλάσσειν ἀπὸ τοῦ πονηροῦ), but that they may be preserved from resting within his domain. St John especially dwells on this personal character of the evil with which man has to contend, 1 John ii. 13, 14 (νενικήκατε τὸν πονηρόν); iii. 12 (ἐκ τοῦ πονηροῦ ἦν); v. 18 (ὁ πονηρός); v. 19 (ἐν τῷ πονηρῷ κεῖται). Comp. xii. 31, xiv. 30, xvi. 11. [Comp. ἐκ for ἐκ χειρός in LXX.: Job vi. 23; Ps. cxl. (cxxxix.). 1.]

16—19. The issue of the disciples' conflict is not only victory but complete consecration. The truth for which they are hated and by which they are strong (*v.* 14) is the power by which they are transformed.

16. The last clause of *v.* 14 is repeated as the ground of a new petition. Protection is to be followed by hallowing. The possibility of this complete consecration, no less than the certain prospect of hostility, lies in the affinity of the disciples to their Lord (*they are not... even as I am not*...). A transposition gives emphasis to the idea of "the world," which comes at the beginning and end of the verse (*of the world they are not...I am not of the world*).

17. *Sanctify*] *i.e.* **Consecrate,** *hallow.* Comp. x. 36, note.

The prayer is that the consecration which is represented by admission into the Christian society may be completely realised in fact;

world, even so have I also sent them
into the world.
19 And for their sakes I sanctify
truly fied. myself, that they also might be ‖ sanctified through the truth.

20 Neither pray I for these alone,
but for them also which shall believe
on me through their word;
21 That they all may be one; as
thou, Father, *art* in me, and I in

---

that every power and faculty, offered once for all, may in due course be effectually rendered to God (Rom. xii. 1). It is not enough for the Christian to be "kept" (*vv.* 11, 15); he must also advance.

through thy truth] **in the truth.** The "truth," the sum of the Christian revelation, "the word of God," at once embodied in Christ and spoken by Him, is (as it were) the element into which the believer is introduced, and by which he is changed. The "truth" is not only a power within him by which he is moved; it is an atmosphere in which he lives. The end of the Truth is not wisdom, which is partial, but holiness, which is universal.

thy word] The exact form of the original (ὁ λόγος ὁ σός), "the word that is thine," emphasizes the fact that Christ's teaching was "not His own, but His that sent Him" (vii. 16). And this teaching must not be limited to His spoken Word or to the written Word, but extended to every utterance of God in nature and history through the WORD.

The word of God is not only "true," but "truth," and has a transforming virtue. Comp. viii. 31. The phrase occurs in one of the Jewish prayers for the new year in a different connexion: "Purify our hearts to serve Thee in truth. Thou, O God, art Truth (Jerem. x. 10), and Thy word is Truth and standeth for ever."

18, 19. The sanctifying of the apostles is connected with two thoughts, firstly with that of their own work, and secondly with that of Christ's work for them. They needed the "sanctifying" which He Himself received (x. 36) in order that they might fulfil their office; and He made that sanctifying possible for them.

18. *As* (**Even** *as*) *thou hast sent* (**didst send**) *me...so have I also sent* (**did I also send**) *them...*] Comp. xx. 21 (πέμπω). The Lord appears to look upon the first mission of the apostles (Matt. x. 5; Mark vi. 7; Luke ix. 2) as including their whole future work. Comp. iv. 38. After His departure they continue His work. Comp. 1 John ii. 20.

19. *I sanctify* (**consecrate**) *myself...might* (**may**) *be sanctified* (**consecrated**)] The work of the Lord is here presented under the aspect of absolute self-sacrifice. He shewed through His life how all that is human may be brought wholly into the service of God; and this He did by true personal determination, as perfectly man. The sacrifice of life (Hebr. x. 6 f.) was now to be consummated in death, whereby the last offering of self was made. The fruits of His victory are communicated to His disciples. By union with Him they also are "themselves sanctified in truth," through the Spirit whose mission followed on His completed work, and who enables each believer to appropriate what Christ has gained (xvi. 14). Christ does for Himself (ἐγὼ ἁγιάζω ἐμαυτόν) that which is done for the disciples (ἵνα ὦσιν ἡγιασμένοι).

through the truth] **in truth** (ἐν ἀληθείᾳ), truly, really, and not merely in name or externally (comp. iv. 23, note). The absence of the article distinguishes this phrase from that in *v.* 17 (*in the truth*). Comp. 2 John 1; 3 John 1; Col. i. 6; Matt. xxii. 16.

III. THE SON AND THE CHURCH (20—26).

The prayer of the Lord is now extended from the Eleven to the Church, and through them to the world. There is to be a progress both in the breadth of unity, and in the apprehension of revelation. The unity of believers is the conviction of the world (20—23); and believers advance in knowledge of the Son and of the Father (24—26). Christ Himself prays for all in all time.

20—23. The unity of the first disciples (*v.* 11) is replaced by a larger unity (*vv.* 21, 23), which is regarded as influencing the world to faith (*v.* 21) and knowledge (*v.* 23).

20. *for them also which shall believe* (**which believe**)] The final issue is gathered up in a present. The Church of the future is regarded as actually in existence (*which believe* [τῶν πιστευόντων] and not *which shall believe* [τῶν πιστευσόντων, Vulg. *qui credituri sunt*]). The immediate success of the apostles carried with it that success which should be. Their "word" is the appointed means for the calling out of faith (Rom. x. 14 f.). This "word" is the "word" which they had received from Christ (*v.* 14), the interpretation as well as the assertion of the facts of Christ's life. In the arrangement of the original, *through their word* is closely connected with *believe*, so as to form a compound idea, which is followed by *in me*.

21. *That they all...that they also . that the world...*] The great end is regarded in its growing extension. The simple and absolute idea of unity comes first (*that all*...who now and hereafter believe); this is then definitely extended to the later generations of believers (*that they also*), and finally the effect on the world comes within the scope of the

thee, that they also may be one in us: that the world may believe that thou hast sent me.

22 And the glory which thou gavest me I have given them; that they may be one, even as we are one:

---

prayer. And the unity of believers is itself presented in a threefold form, as a unity of all, a unity similar to that of the Father and the Son, and a unity realised in the Father and the Son.

be one] Comp. x. 30, *vv.* 11, 22; (1 Cor. iii. 8).

as (**even as**)...] The idea of the divine unity, which has been given generally before (*v.* 11, and *v.* 22), is set out in detail in its correlative manifestation. Comp. x. 38, xiv. 10, 11, 20. There is, so to speak, an interchange of the energy of the divine Life (*Thou in me, and I in Thee*), which finds a counterpart in the harmonious relations of the members of the Church. The true unity of believers, like the Unity of Persons in the Holy Trinity with which it is compared, is offered as something far more than a mere moral unity of purpose, feeling, affection; it is, in some mysterious mode which we cannot distinctly apprehend, a vital unity (Rom. xii. 5; Eph. iv. 4). In this sense it is the symbol of a higher type of life, in which each constituent being is a conscious element in the being of a vast whole. In "the life," and in "the life" only, each individual life is able to attain to its perfection. Such a conception, however imperfectly it may be grasped, meets many of the difficulties which beset the conception of an abiding continuance of our present individual separation.

may be...in us] Omit *one*. The omission of "one" emphasizes the thought of their unity. They who are "in God and Christ" necessarily find unity in that fellowship. God is the essential centre of unity.

in us] Not simply *in Me* or *in Thee*. Elsewhere the relation is definitely connected with the Son, vi. 56, xv. 4, 5; (1 John iii. 24). It is through the Son that men are united with the Father (*v.* 23, *I in them*); and so they are said "to be in God and God in them" (1 John iv. 13, 16, ὁ θεός).

It will be observed that the prayer for unity is offered up when the Lord is looking towards the widest extension of the faith; and the full significance of the prayer is made plainer if we bear in mind the religious differences (*e.g.* Jew and Gentile) of the apostolic age, and the struggles through which the Catholic Church strove towards its ultimate victory.

that the world...] Two results in regard to the world are set forth by Christ. The first, *that it may believe that thou hast sent* (**didst send**) *me*, and the second, *that it may know that thou hast sent* (**didst send**) *me, and hast loved* (**didst love**) *them as thou hast loved* (**lovedst**) *me* (*v.* 23). The first has been already given as the mark of the disciples (*v.* 8, *faith*), and (in part) the second (*v.* 25, *knowledge*) has the same value. So also in xi. 42, the words used by the Lord at the raising of Lazarus are said to have been spoken *for the sake of the multitude, that they may believe that thou didst send me*. Such faith then as is here contemplated is at least the beginning of a true faith, and not a mere unwilling acknowledgment of the fact. In this connexion it must further be noticed that the verbs in *vv.* 21, 23 are both present (πιστεύῃ, γινώσκῃ) as contrasted with the aorists in *vv.* 8, 25. Thus it appears that the end which is proposed as the last reward of earthly work is that described in general terms in 1 Cor. xv. 28; Phil. ii. 10, 11. This end, as here regarded, is to be brought about by the spectacle of the unity of the disciples (comp. xiii. 35); and the same thought is expressed more fully in *v.* 23. The unity of disciples, therefore, while it springs out of a direct relation to Christ, must have some external expression that it may affect those without the Church.

the world] A comparison of Rom. xi. 25 ff. with this passage seems to indicate that the Lord looks forward to the time when "Israel" shall have become included in "the world," and at last prove the instrument of its conversion.

that thou (σύ)...] that Thou, the God of Israel, the God of the Covenant, and none other... Comp. *vv.* 8, 18, 23, 25, xi. 42.

22. The mention of the office of future believers, to evoke faith in the world, leads to the mention of their endowment. In the former verse the Lord prayed for the disciples; He now declares what He has Himself done for them (ἐγὼ δέδωκα). Hence the emphatic personal pronoun stands in the front of the sentence (κἀγώ...). He communicated to them the glory which He had Himself received. The gift of this glory (like the prayer in *v.* 21) has regard to a threefold consequence: *that they may be one...that they may be perfected in one...that the world may know...*

the glory which thou gavest (**hast given**)...] Comp. *vv.* 5, 24. This glory comes from the perfect apprehension of the Father as fulfilling His work of love (comp. *v.* 3). Viewed from another point of sight it is the revelation of the divine in man realised in and through Christ. So to know God as He accomplishes His will is to find all things transfigured; and as the Son of Man in His own Person experienced and shewed the Father's purpose, so He enabled His disciples to appropriate the

23 I in them, and thou in me, that they may be made perfect in one; and that the world may know that thou hast sent me, and hast loved them, as thou hast loved me.

24 [d] Father, I will that they also, whom thou hast given me, be with me where I am; that they may behold my glory, which thou hast given me: for thou lovedst

[d] chap 12 26.

---

truth which He made clear. Comp. xiii. 31, note. Such divine glory leads to the unity of all being. The fulness of this glory is to be made known hereafter in the Lord's presence; but meanwhile it is partially presented in the different manifestations of Christ's action in believers through the power and beauty and truth of the Christian life. But the idea of "the glory" cannot be limited to any one of these.

them] the members of the universal Church.

23. *I in them*...] This clause, standing in apposition to that which precedes, explains the nature of the double unity of believers in themselves and with God. Christ in the body of believers is the ground of their unity; and the Father is in Him. The unity of believers is therefore like that of the divine Persons and with Them. The two members of the clause suggest the full parallel: *I in them* and they in me: I in Thee *and Thou in me*.

that they] The possession of the divine "glory"—the absolute harmony of life—furnishes the sure foundation for spiritual unity.

made perfect (**perfected**) *in one*] brought (εἰς) to a final unity in which they attain their completeness (τετελειωμένοι εἰς ἕν, Vulg. *consummati in unum*). For *perfected* see Phil. iii. 12; Hebr. ii. 10, v. 9, vii. 28, ix. 9, x. 1, 14, xi. 40, xii. 23; 1 John ii. 5, iv. 12, 17, 18. That which is completed at once on the divine side has to be gradually realised by man. So the essential unity is personally apprehended, and issues in the perfection of each believer as he fulfils his proper part.

and (omit) *that the world may know ... hast sent* (**didst send**)...] not at once (γνῷ), but by slow degrees (γινώσκῃ). See *v.* 21, note. This knowledge (like the "belief" above) cannot be taken in any other general sense than that which is found in the other verses of the chapter (*v.* 8, &c.). It is the knowledge of grateful recognition and not of forced conviction.

hast loved (**lovedst**) *them, as*...(**lovedst**) *me*] The spiritual effect wrought in Christians, the visible manifestation of a power of love among them (comp. xiii. 35), is declared to be a sufficient proof of the divine mission of Him from whom it comes, and of the continuance in them of the divine working. This working is not however such as might have been anticipated. The life of believers shews the same contrasts of joy and apparent failure as the life of Christ. But those contrasts are no disparagement of the perfectness of the love of God towards them.

24—26. While believers overcome the world by their unity, they are themselves also to advance in the fulness of knowledge. This progress belongs in part to a higher order of being (*v.* 24); but it rests essentially on the knowledge of Christ as the interpreter of the Father (*v.* 25); and therefore is realised on earth as Christ makes Himself better known (*v.* 26).

24. The prospect of the completion of the work of believers leads directly to the thought of their bliss. In portraying this the Lord places side by side Him to whom, and the united body for whom, He speaks (πατήρ, ὃ δέδωκάς μοι). He no longer "prays," but gives expression to His "will." *I will that*... For the use of the word (θέλω) by Christ, see ch. xxi. 22, 23; Matt. viii. 3, xxiii. 37, xxvi. 39 and parallels, xv. 32, (xx. 14); Luke xii. 49.

It is further interesting to contrast this expression of Christ's own will in behalf of His disciples with His submission to His Father's will in His prayer for Himself, Mark xiv. 36.

they...whom...] **that which**... All believers regarded as one whole. See *v.* 2, note. The original runs literally: *Father, as for that which Thou hast given me, I will that...they also*...

The will of Christ for His people includes two things, first that they may be where He is (xii. 26, xiv. 3), and so attain in the end to the sphere for the time unattainable by them (xiii. 36. Comp. vii. 34); and secondly, as dependent on this, that they may behold His glory. Each of these two issues contains an element not contained in the corresponding gifts already described. Presence with Christ, as involving personal fellowship with Him in the sphere of His glorified being, is more than a union effected by His presence with the Church. And the contemplation of His glory, in its whole extent, by those lifted beyond the limits of time, is more than the possession of that glory according to the measure of present human powers.

where I am...may behold] as sharing in the Lord's kingdom, 2 Tim. ii. 12. The scene of this vision is not defined. Under one aspect it may be placed at the Lord's "Presence." But no one special application exhausts the meaning of the words. Comp. 1 John iii. 2; 2 Cor. iii. 18.

my glory, which thou hast given ...] The

me before the foundation of the world.

25 O righteous Father, the world hath not known thee: but I have known thee, and these have known that thou hast sent me.

26 And I have declared unto them thy name, and will declare *it:* that the love wherewith thou hast loved me may be in them, and I in them.

---

full expression (literally, *the glory that is mine, which...* See xv. 9, note) as compared with *the glory which...*(*v.* 22) is to be noticed. "The glory" is here regarded as belonging and answering to the very nature of the Son. Yet it is not simply the glory of the Word (*v.* 5), but the glory of the Incarnate Son (Phil. ii. 9). The "glory" of the Word, apart from the Incarnation, is not said in the language of the New Testament to be "given" to Him, though the Father is the "one fountain of Godhead." The "glory" here spoken of is the glory of a restored and consummated harmony of God and man, which is made the final object of the contemplation of believers, even as it is already potentially given to them (*v.* 22).

for...] **because...** The love of the Father for the Son belongs to the eternal order. This love when outwardly realised is seen as glory in the object of it. And since the Father's love continued unchanged towards the Incarnate Son, this love necessarily involved the fulfilment of His glory as the Redeemer and Perfecter of humanity. To be allowed to "behold" such glory is to be admitted to the contemplation of an inexhaustible object.

before the foundation...] Comp. Eph. i. 4; 1 Pet. i. 20. The corresponding phrase "since the foundation of the world" (ἀπὸ κ. κ.) is not unfrequent: Rev. (πρὸ καταβολῆς κόσμου; Vulg. *ante constitutionem mundi*) xiii. 8, xvii. 8; Hebr. iv. 3, &c.

The words distinctly imply the personal pre-existence of Christ. The thought of an eternal love active in the depths of divine Being presents, perhaps, as much as we can faintly apprehend of the doctrine of the essential Trinity.

25, 26. In these concluding verses the justification (if we may so speak) of the whole prayer is gathered up in a simple enumeration of the facts of the world's ignorance, Christ's knowledge, and the disciples' faith; and the substance of it in the twofold end, that the love of the Father for the Son, and the Son Himself, may be in the disciples, who henceforward represent Him.

25. *righteous Father*] The epithet (comp. *v.* 11, *Holy Father*) emphasizes the nature of the plea. It is to the righteousness of the Father that the Son appeals, and He had fitted them in part and would still more completely fit them to bear the vision of the divine beauty. Those for whom He speaks had in part proved their faith.

the world hath not known thee (**knew Thee not**)*: but I have known* (**knew**) *thee, and these have known* (**knew**)...] In the original a conjunction (καί) stands before "the world" which cannot easily be translated. It serves to co-ordinate the two main clauses, which bring out the contrast between the world and the disciples. The force of it is as if we were to say: "Two facts are equally true; it is true that the world knew Thee not; it is true that these knew that Thou didst send me." The first shewed that in the way of "nature" men had failed; the second that the Son had found partial welcome in the way of "grace" (comp. 1 Cor. i. 21).

but I have known (**knew**) *thee*] This clause comes parenthetically to prepare for the next. Even if the world failed to read the lesson which was offered to it, there was yet another channel by which the knowledge could be conveyed. The Son, as the eternal Word, had the knowledge, and He came to men, and as man realised the knowledge in human life, and found some at least who admitted His mission. Thus in virtue of the Incarnation that was at last gained by His disciples, which the world had not gained, even the true knowledge of the Father.

have known] **knew.** That which before (*v.* 8) had been described as a matter of faith, is now presented in its final acceptance as a matter of knowledge.

26. The revelation of the Father's name by Christ followed on the personal acknowledgment of His mission. This revelation, complete in one sense (*I made known*; comp. xv. 15), is none the less continuous (*I will make known*). It cannot be finished while the world lasts. The end of it is that the Father may regard the disciples in response to their growing faith even as He regarded the Son, and that they may feel His love (*that the love wherewith thou* **lovedst** *... in them;* comp. Rom. v. 5). The possibility of such a consummation lies in the fact of the Presence of the Son Himself in them (*I in them*).

I have declared...will declare it] **I made known...and will make it known,** henceforward by the Holy Spirit, whom Christ sent, xv. 26.

I in them] The last word of the Lord's prayer corresponds with the last word of His discourses: *I have overcome the world* (xvi. 33). He is Himself the source of victory and life.

CHAPTER XVIII.

1 *Judas betrayeth Jesus.* 6 *The officers fall to the ground.* 10 *Peter smiteth off Malchus' ear.* 12 *Jesus is taken, and led unto Annas and Caiaphas.* 15 *Peter's denial.* 19 *Jesus examined before Caiaphas.* 28 *His arraignment before Pilate.* 36 *His kingdom.* 40 *The Jews ask Barabbas to be let loose.*

XVIII.—XX. THE VICTORY THROUGH DEATH.

This last main division of the Gospel falls naturally into four principal sections:

I. The betrayal (xviii. 1—11).
II. The double trial (xviii. 12—xix. 16).
III. The end (xix. 17—42).
IV. The new life (xx.).

The last three sections, as will appear afterwards, require further subdivision.

1. In comparing the narrative of St John with the parallel narratives of the Synoptists, it must be observed generally that here, as everywhere, St John fixes the attention of the reader upon the ideas which the several events bring out and illustrate. The Passio and Resurrection are for him revelations of the Person of Christ. The objective fact is a "sign" of something which lies deeper. It is a superficial and inadequate treatment of his narrative to regard it as a historical supplement of the other narratives, or of the current oral narrative on which they were based. It does (it is true) become in part such a supplement, because it is a portrayal of the main spiritual aspects of the facts illustrated from the fulness of immediate knowledge, but the record is independent and complete in itself. It is a whole, and, like the rest of the Gospel, an interpretation of the inner meaning of the history which it contains.

Thus in the history of the Passion three thoughts among others rise into clear prominence:

(1) *The voluntariness of Christ's sufferings.*

xviii. 4.	xviii. 36.
— 8.	xix. 28.
— 11.	— 30.

(2) *The fulfilment of a divine plan in Christ's sufferings:*

xviii. 4.	xix. 11.
— 9.	— 24.
— 11.	— 28.

Comp. Luke xxii. 53.

(3) *The majesty which shines through Christ's sufferings:*

xviii. 6.	xix. 11.
— 20 ff.	— 26 f.
— 37.	— 36 f.

The narrative in this sense becomes a commentary on earlier words which pointed to the end,

(1) x. 17, 18. (2) xiii. 1. (3) xiii. 31.

2. In several places the full meaning of St John's narrative is first obtained by the help of words or incidents preserved by the Synoptists. His narrative assumes facts found in them:

e.g.	xviii. 11.	xviii. 40.
	— 33.	xix. 41.

3. The main incidents recorded by more than one of the other evangelists which are omitted by St John are:

The agony (Matt., Mark, Luke).
The traitor's kiss (Matt., Mark, Luke).
The desertion by all (Matt., Mark). Comp. John xvi. 32.
The examination before the Sanhedrin at night; the false witness; the adjuration; the great Confession (Matt., Mark).
The mockery as prophet (Matt., Mark, Luke).
The council at daybreak (Matt., Mark, Luke)
The mockery after condemnation (Matt., Mark)
The impressment of Simon (Matt., Mark, Luke)
The reproaches of spectators (Matt., Mark, Luke) *and of the robbers* (Matt., Mark, [Luke]).
The darkness (Matt., Mark, Luke).
The cry from Ps. xxii. (Matt., Mark).
The rending of the veil (Matt., Mark).
The confession of the centurion (Matt., Mark, Luke).

Other incidents omitted by St John are recorded by single Evangelists:

ST MATTHEW.

Power over the hosts of heaven.
Pilate's wife's message.
Pilate's hand-washing.
The self-condemnation of the Jews.
The earthquake.

ST MARK.

The flight of the young man.
Pilate's question as to the death of Christ.

ST LUKE.

The examination before Herod.
The lamentation of the women.
Three "words" from the cross (xxiii. 34, 43, 46).
The repentance of one of the robbers.

4. The main incidents peculiar to St John are:

The words of power at the arrest (xviii. 4—9).
The examination before Annas (xviii. 13—24).
The first conference of the Jews with Pilate, and Pilate's private examination (xviii. 28—37, xix. 9—11). Comp. Matt. xxvii. 11; Mark xv. 2; Luke xxiii. 3.
The first mockery, and the Ecce Homo (xix. 2—5).
Pilate's maintenance of his words (xix. 21, 22).

WHEN Jesus had spoken these words, [a] he went forth with his disciples over the brook Cedron, where was a garden, into the which he entered, and his disciples.
2 And Judas also, which betrayed

[a] Matt. 26. 36.

The last charge (xix. 25—27).
The thirst. "It is finished" (xix. 28—30).
The piercing the side (xix. 31—37).
The ministry of Nicodemus (xix. 39).

5. In the narrative of incidents recorded elsewhere St John constantly adds details, often minute and yet most significant; *e.g.*

xviii. 1.	xviii. 15.	xix. 17.
— 2.	— 16.	— 19.
— 10.	— 26.	— 23.
— 11.	— 28.	— 41.
— 12.	xix. 14.	

See the notes.

6. In the midst of great differences of detail the Synoptists and St John offer many impressive resemblances as to the spirit and character of the proceedings; *e.g.*

(1) The activity of the "High Priests" (*i.e.* the Sadducæan hierarchy) as distinguished from the Pharisees.

(2) The course of the accusation: civil charge: religious charge: personal influence.

(3) The silence of the Lord in His public accusations, with the significant exception, Matt. xxvi. 64.

(4) The tone of mockery.

(5) The character of Pilate; haughty, contemptuous, vacillating, selfish.

7. The succession of the main events recorded by the four Evangelists appears to have been as follows:

Approximate time.	
1 *a.m.*	*The agony.*
"	*The betrayal.*
"	*The conveyance to the high-priest's house, probably adjoining "the Booths of Hanan."*
2 *a.m.*	*The preliminary examination before Annas in the presence of Caiaphas.*
3 *a.m.*	*The examination before Caiaphas and the Sanhedrin at an irregular meeting at "the Booths."*
5 *a.m.*	*The formal sentence of the Sanhedrin in their own proper place of meeting,* Gazith *or* Beth Midrash (Luke xxii. 66); Matt. xxvii. 1 (πρωΐας γενομένης: comp. Mark xv. 1; Luke xxii. 66, ὡς ἐγένετο ἡμέρα). *The first examination before Pilate, at the palace.*
5.30 *a.m.*	*The examination before Herod.*
"	*The scourging and first mockery by the soldiers at the palace.*
6.30 *a.m.*	*The sentence of Pilate* (John xix. 14, ὥρα ἦν ὡς ἕκτη).
7 *a.m.*	*The second mockery by the soldiers of the condemned "King."*
9 *a.m.*	*The crucifixion, and rejection of the stupefying draught* (Mark xv. 25, ἦν ὥρα τρίτη).
12 *noon.*	*The last charge.*
12—3 *p.m.*	*The darkness* (Matt. xxvii. 45; Mark xv. 33; Luke xxiii. 44, ἦν ὡσεὶ ὥρα ἕκτη...ἕως ὥρας ἐννάτης).
3 *p.m.*	*The end.*

I. THE BETRAYAL. Jesus and the disciples; Judas and the adversaries (1—11).

The substance of this section is peculiar to St John, though it presents many points of contact with the Synoptic narratives. The conflict which the other Evangelists record is here presupposed and regarded in its issues. The victory follows the battle. The Lord acts freely and with sovereign and protecting power towards His enemies and His disciples at the moment when He is given over for death.

CHAP. XVIII. 1. *When Jesus had spoken...*] ch. xvii. 1.

he went forth] from the limits of the city (comp. 1 K. ii. 37), probably in the direction of the present St Stephen's Gate, by the same route as on other days when He went to the Mount of Olives (Luke xxi. 37, xxii. 39; Mark xi. 19; Matt. xxi. 17); but now Jerusalem was left. The Lord returned only to die there. In the parallel passages the same word (ἐξῆλθεν) is used, according to the context, of the departure from the upper room (Luke xxii. 39; Matt. xxvi. 30; Mark xiv. 26).

the brook Cedron (**Kidron**)] See Additional Note. This detail is peculiar to St John. The parallel narratives have simply "went to the Mount of Olives." The exact description is probably introduced with a significant reference to the history of the flight of David from Absalom and Ahithophel (2 S. xv. 23; comp. ch. xiii. 18). The "brook" (χείμαρρος, compare Neh. ii. 15; 1 Macc. xii. 37), *i.e.* winter torrent or ravine (נַחַל), Kidron, separating the Mount of Olives from the Temple-mount, is noticed several times in the Old Testament: 1 K. ii. 37, xv. 13; 2 K. xxiii. 4 ff.; 2 Chro. xxix. 16; Jer. xxxi. 40, and these passages mark the associations which would be called up by the mention of the name. For a description of the ravine and the "Wady" see 'Dictionary of the Bible,' *s. v.*

a garden] on the Mount of Olives (Luke xxii. 39). The name of the "small farm" (χωρίον) to which it belonged, Gethsemane, is given by St Matthew and St Mark (Matt. xxvi. 36, note; Mark xiv. 32). Josephus

him, knew the place: for Jesus ofttimes resorted thither with his disciples.

3 [b] Judas then, having received a band *of men* and officers from the chief priests and Pharisees, cometh

[b] Matt. 26. 47.

---

mentions that "gardens" (παράδεισοι) were numerous in the suburbs of Jerusalem ('B. J.' VI. 1. 1. Comp. ch. xix. 41). There is nothing in the context to indicate the exact position of the garden. The traditional site, which may be the true one, dates from the time of Constantine, when "the faithful were eager to offer their prayers there" (Euseb. 'Onom.' *s. v.*).

Commentators from Cyril downwards have drawn a parallel and contrast between the histories of the Fall and the Victory connected with the two "gardens," Eden and Gethsemane. But there is no indication in the Gospel that such a thought was in the mind of the Evangelist. Yet see Mark i. 13.

entered] The garden would naturally be enclosed by a fence which secured the privacy of the retreat. Some time passed (Matt. xxvi. 40) between the entry into the garden and the arrival of Judas. In this interval the Agony took place, of which St John says nothing, though he implies a knowledge of the event in *v.* 11. It is evident from xii. 27 that that incident is not alien from his narrative.

and his disciples] **himself** *and his disciples.* Judas was finally excluded from the divine company: xiii. 30.

2. *Judas also......knew the place*] The withdrawal of the Lord from the city was not now (x. 40) for the purpose of escaping from the assaults of His enemies. The place to which He retired was well known. Judas, no less than the other apostles, was acquainted with the spot. Thus the words meet by anticipation the scoff of Celsus that the Lord "was taken while trying to hide Himself and to escape in the most disgraceful way" (Orig. 'c. Cels.' II. 9), as Origen justly argues (*id.* c. 10).

which betrayed] The original (as in *v.* 5, ὁ παραδιδούς) marks the process of betrayal as going on, and not the single past act (ὁ παραδούς, Matt. xxvii. 3). Comp. xiii. 11. Judas was already engaged in the execution of his plan.

ofttimes] Comp. Luke xxii. 39, (xxi. 37). The word can scarcely be limited to the present visit to Jerusalem. It is reasonable to suppose that the owner was an open or secret disciple of Christ. Comp. Matt. xxvi. 18.

resorted] The exact force of the original is rather, "Jesus and (with) His disciples assembled (συνήχθη) there." The idea appears to be that of a place of gathering, where the Lord's followers met Him for instruction, and not simply of a restingplace during the night. But it is possible that the spot was used for this latter purpose also during the present visit (Luke xxi. 37, ηὐλίζετο), and that Judas expected to find all sleeping at the time of his arrival. But the Lord's nights were now, as at the other crises of His life, times of prayer (Luke vi. 12, ix. 28; comp. Luke v. 16).

3—8. A difficulty arises as to the reconciliation of the incidents described in this passage with the narrative of the betrayal in the Synoptists. In the Synoptists the arrest follows close upon the kiss of Judas, which St John does not mention (Matt. xxvi. 50; Mark xiv. 45 f., yet see Luke xxii. 48 ff.). It is very difficult to believe that the kiss either preceded *v.* 4, or came after *v.* 8. Perhaps it is simplest to suppose that the unexpected appearance of the Lord outside the enclosure discomposed the plan of Judas, who had expected to find the whole party resting within the garden, and that for the moment he failed to give the appointed sign, and remained awestricken in the crowd (*v.* 5). This being so, the event of *v.* 6 followed, and afterwards Judas, taking courage, came up to Christ (Matt. xxvi. 49 f.; Mark xiv. 45), who then repelled him (Luke xxii. 48) and again addressed the hesitating multitude.

Others suppose, with somewhat less probability, as it seems (but see Matt. xxvi. 49, note), that the kiss of Judas immediately preceded the first question, *Whom seek ye?* and that, touched by his Master's reproof (Luke xxii. 48), he fell back into the crowd. Either view presents an intelligible whole; but the phrase in *v.* 5 (*was standing*) is more appropriate to the attitude of one who hesitates to do that which he has purposed to do, than of one who has been already repulsed.

It may be added that, though St John does not mention the "sign" of Judas, yet he implies that he had undertaken to do more than guide the band to the place where Christ might be found, by noticing that he was with them after they had reached the spot (*v.* 5).

3. *Judas then* (**therefore**)...] using his knowledge for the furtherance of his design.

a band of men *and officers from* ...] **the** *band of* **soldiers** *and officers from*... The force is clearly divided in the original into two main parts: (1) the band of soldiers, and (2) the "officers" (police) despatched by "the chief priests and Pharisees" (the Sanhedrin). The soldiers were part of the well-known body of Roman soldiers stationed as a garrison in Antonia (comp. Matt. xxvii. 27; Mark xv. 16; Acts xxi. 31 f.; and also Jos. 'Ant.' XX. 4. 3; 'B. J.' V. 5. 8). The original word (σπεῖρα) is used by Polybius

thither with lanterns and torches and weapons.
4 Jesus therefore, knowing all things that should come upon him, went forth, and said unto them, Whom seek ye?
5 They answered him, Jesus of Nazareth. Jesus saith unto them, I

---

as the representative of the Latin *manipulus* (not *cohors:* see Polyb. XI. 23, with Schweighäuser's note), consisting of about 200 men, the third part of a cohort. Whether the word is taken here in this technical sense (*v.* 12, note), or (as is more likely) in the larger sense of "cohort," which it appears to bear in the New Testament, it will naturally be understood that only a detachment of the whole body was present with their commander (*v.* 12).

The "officers" (ὑπηρέται) who came with "the band" were members of the temple-police, who were under the orders of the Sanhedrin. Comp. vii. 32, 45 ff.; Acts v. 22, 26.

In the Synoptists the whole company is described in general terms (Matt. xxvi. 47; Mark xiv. 43; Luke xxii. 47; comp. xxii. 52), and the soldiers are not distinctly mentioned. But it is difficult to suppose that the priests would have ventured on such an arrest as that of Christ without communicating with the Roman governor, or that Pilate would have found any difficulty in granting them a detachment of men for the purpose, especially at the feast-time. Moreover, Pilate's early appearance (*v.* 28) at the court, no less than the dream of his wife (Matt. xxvii. 19, *that just man*), implies some knowledge of the coming charge. Perhaps too it is not fanciful to see a reference to the soldiers in the turn of the phrase "twelve *legions* of angels" (Matt. xxvi. 53).

The special mention of the soldiers and of the watch fixes attention on the combination of Gentile and Jew in this first stage of the Passion as afterwards.

the chief priests and Pharisees] *and* **the** *Pharisees*. Comp. xi. 47, note.

with lanterns and torches] Although the party had the light of the Paschal full moon, they prepared themselves also against the possibility of concealment on the part of Him whom they sought. The other Evangelists do not notice the lights. The detail belongs to a vivid impression of the scene received by an eye-witness. The temple-watch, to whom the "officers" belonged, made their rounds with torches ('Middoth' I. 2, quoted by Lightfoot on Rev. xvi. 15; and in a most interesting note on Luke xxii. 4), and were, for the most part, not regularly armed (Jos. 'B. J.' IV. 4. 6).

4. *Jesus therefore*...] There was, so to speak, a divine necessity which ruled the Lord's movements. By Him all was foreseen: and He who had before withdrawn Himself (viii. 59, xii. 36, v. 13, vi. 15), now that "His hour was come" anticipated the search for which His enemies had made provision, and went forth from the enclosure of the garden (opposed to *entered*, *v.* 1) to meet them (not simply from the innermost part of the garden or from the circle of the disciples: *v.* 26 proves nothing against this view). The clause corresponds with the words in St Matthew (xxvi. 46) and St Mark (xiv. 42), "Rise, let us be going," which are followed by, "Behold he is at hand that betrayeth me."

that should come...] More exactly, **all the things that were coming** (πάντα τὰ ἐρχόμενα). The Passion has already begun. Comp. xiii. 1, note. It must further be noticed that the Passion is spoken of in relation to the divine order (*the things that were coming*), and not as sufferings to be borne, or evil prepared by enemies. Comp. *v.* 11.

went (or *came*) *forth, and said*] ... *and* **saith**. According to the true reading the two acts are marked separately. Christ left the place in which He might have sought concealment; and then He addressed those who sought to take Him.

Whom seek ye?] The question (as in *v.* 8) is designed to shield the disciples, and at the same time to bring clearly before the mind of the assailants the purpose for which they had come, and who He was whom they sought. The words fall in completely with the circumstances. The Lord was not recognised in the uncertain light. The company who had come to apprehend Him naturally supposed that He would not Himself advance to meet them, but that the questioner must be some friend. The idea of early commentators, that they were miraculously blinded, finds no support in the narrative.

5. *Jesus of Nazareth*] The tinge of contempt (comp. Matt. ii. 23), which appears to lie in the title here, as borrowed from popular usage, is given better by the literal rendering, *Jesus* **the Nazarene** ('Ι. τὸν Ναζωραῖον, as distinguished from 'Ι. τὸν ἀπὸ Ναζαρέτ, i. 45). Comp. xix. 19; Matt. xxvi. 71; Mark xiv. 67. The title is characteristic of the first stage of the preaching of the Gospel, when the reproach was turned into glory: Acts ii. 22, iii. 6, iv. 10, vi. 14, (xxii. 8, xxvi. 9). It was also used by disciples at an earlier date: Mark x. 47, xvi. 6; Luke xviii. 37, xxiv. 19 Comp. Mark i. 24; Luke iv. 34.

Jesus (**He**) *saith* ... *I am he*] The same words (ἐγώ εἰμι) were used on several memorable occasions, (iv. 26), vi. 20, viii. 24, 28, 58, and on this evening, xiii. 19. For Judas at

am *he.* And Judas also, which betrayed him, stood with them.

6 As soon then as he had said unto them, I am *he*, they went backward, and fell to the ground.

7 Then asked he them again, Whom seek ye? And they said, Jesus of Nazareth.

8 Jesus answered, I have told you that I am *he:* if therefore ye seek me, let these go their way:

9 That the saying might be fulfilled, which he spake, [c] Of them which thou gavest me have I lost none.

[c] chap. 17 12.

10 Then Simon Peter having a

---

least they must have been significant, though, as they stand in the context, they simply reveal the Person sought, and not His nature. But the self-revelation of Christ tries to the uttermost and answers the thoughts which men have of Him.

And Judas ... stood ...] ... **was standing.** The one figure is singled out, as it were, and regarded as he stands. Comp. i. 35, note. There is nothing in the text to support the view that Judas was paralysed and unable to recognise Jesus.

6. *As soon then as he had said*...(or, *When therefore ... ὡς οὖν*)] Omit the *had*. The incident which follows is made to depend upon the Lord's words. It is vain to inquire whether the withdrawal and prostration of the band of men was due to "natural" or "supernatural" causes. On any view it was due to the effect which the presence of the Lord, in His serene majesty, had upon those who had come to take Him. Various circumstances may have contributed to the result. It may have been that Judas had led his company to expect some display of power. It may have been that he himself hoped for a decisive manifestation of Messiah in sovereignty now that the crisis had come. But the prostration seems to shew, at any rate, that the Lord purposed to declare openly to the disciples (comp. Matt. xxvi. 53), that it was of His own free choice that He gave Himself up. And this is the effect which the narrative is calculated to produce upon a reader. The Lord's assailants were overawed by Him in some way, and they fulfilled their commission only by His consent. Comp. vii. 46.

went backward, and fell ...] The whole action represents the effects of fear, awe, veneration, self-humiliation (Job i. 20), not of external force. Comp. Rev. i. 17. The exaggeration which describes the men as "falling backwards" is utterly alien from the solemn majesty of the scene.

7. *Then asked he them again*] **Again therefore** *he asked them*. This literal rendering of the original brings out the connexion more clearly than A. V. Those who had come to arrest the Lord hung back, and therefore He Himself again roused them to their work. The spirit of the Lord's words, thus addressed to the whole company, corresponds with that of the words addressed to Judas "*Is it this* for which thou art come?" (Matt. xxvi. 50, note).

Jesus of Nazareth] Even after Christ had made Himself known, His enemies only repeat the name which they had been taught, as if waiting for some further guidance.

8. *I have told you ... let these go*] **I told** *you*... In the interval which had passed since the Lord came out from the garden alone (*v.* 4), His disciples had gathered round Him (let *these* go), and for them He still intercedes. Their deliverance helped to place His own Passion in a clearer light. It was fitting that He should suffer alone, though afterwards others suffered for His sake. His death, in itself essentially unique, was separated outwardly from the death of His disciples. They were enabled to die because He had died first. Comp. Isai. lxiii. 3.

9. *That the saying* (*word*) ... *which thou gavest me have I lost*...] ...*which thou* **hast given** *me* **I lost.** The Evangelist sees in the care with which the Lord provided for the outward safety of His disciples, a fulfilment of His words, xvii. 12, which were spoken of the past, and which had also a wider spiritual application. But, at the same time, those words spoken in absolute knowledge looked to the end, and therefore included all the events of the Passion (comp. xvii. 4, note); and, further, the deliverance of the disciples from outward peril included the deliverance from a temptation which they would not at present (as appears from the history of St Peter) have been able to support. This special act of watchful protection was therefore one fulfilment, but neither the only nor the chief fulfilment, of what the Lord had said of His effective guardianship of those given to Him. The significant difference in the form of the words, as spoken and as referred to (*I lost not one*, as distinguished from *not one perished*), is to be noticed.

10. *Then Simon Peter* ...] *Simon Peter* **therefore**... foreseeing what was now about to happen (comp. xiii. 37). The Jews among the company seem to have been foremost in the arrest. The incident is described by all the Evangelists, but St John alone mentions the names of St Peter and Malchus. It is easy to see why these were not likely to be particu-

sword drew it, and smote the high priest's servant, and cut off his right ear. The servant's name was Malchus.

11 Then said Jesus unto Peter, Put up thy sword into the sheath: the cup which my Father hath given me, shall I not drink it?

12 Then the band and the captain and officers of the Jews took Jesus, and bound him,

13 And led him away to Annas

---

larised in the original oral Gospel, while both were alive and at Jerusalem (see Matt. xxvi. 51; Mark xiv. 47, and notes). In St Matthew and St Mark the incident appears to be placed after "the multitude" had "laid their hands on Jesus and taken" (ἐκράτησαν) Him (Matt. xxvi. 50; Mark xiv. 46); and St Luke implies the same (xxii. 51). St John, on the other hand, appears to place the "binding" afterwards. If it be so, the two accounts are easily reconcileable. It was perfectly natural that the Lord should be first seized by some of the more eager of the crowd, and then afterwards bound by the Roman guard (*v.* 12). St Peter's act fell in the brief space of confusion between these two events.

sword] It was forbidden to carry weapons on a feast-day.

the high priest's servant] or rather, **the servant** (δοῦλος) **of the high-priest.** The definite article (τὸν τοῦ ἀρχ. δ.) is preserved in all the Gospels. It is impossible to tell what position he held, or why the Evangelist records his name, which was not an uncommon one. The servant's prominent action evidently marked him out for St Peter's attack. And further it is difficult not to feel that the healing of the wound, recorded only by St Luke (xxii. 51), helps to explain the apostle's escape from arrest.

11. *Then said Jesus ... thy sword*] *Jesus* **therefore** *said* ... **the** *sword.* The words are given more at length in St Matthew, xxvi. 52 ff. The tone of the two records is identical, and the reference to the Scriptures, preserved only by St Matthew, serves to illustrate one side of the phrase "which my Father hath given me."

the cup ...] This clause is peculiar to St John. The same image occurs in the Synoptists, Matt. xx. 22 f. (note); Mark x. 38 f.; and in connexion with this scene, Matt. xxvi. 39 ff.; Mark xiv. 36; Luke xxii. 42. It seems impossible not to feel that the words include the answer to the prayer at the Agony, not recorded by St John (Matt. xxvi. 39, "O my Father...let this cup pass away"...), for now, after the prayer, that "cup" is spoken of as "the cup which my Father hath given me." The cup was not taken away, but given, and the Lord now shews that He had received it willingly. The image is found in several remarkable passages of the Old Testament: Ezek. xxiii. 31 ff.; Ps. lxxv. 8, &c.

II. The Double Trial (xviii. 12—xix. 16).

(i.) The ecclesiastical trial (xviii. 12—27).
(ii.) The civil trial (xviii. 28—xix. 16).

i. The ecclesiastical trial. Master and disciples. Jesus and the high-priest, Peter and the servants, xviii. 12—27.

The record of the examination before Annas is peculiar to the narrative of St John. The Evangelist appears to have been present at the inquiry (*vv.* 15, 19). See Additional Note.

12. *Then the band ... and officers* ...] *The band* **therefore** (or, **So** *the band*)... *and* **the** *officers*... Seeing that there was no longer any resistance. The enumeration—*the band, the captain, the officers*—is emphatic and impressive. All combined to take the willing prisoner. In particular it will be observed that the action of the Roman guard is now noticed. They probably secured the Lord and delivered Him to the priest's servants "bound" (comp. *v.* 24). The "bonds" are not mentioned in the Synoptists till afterwards (Matt. xxvii. 2, note; Mark xv. 1); yet such a precaution is implied in their narrative. It was the policy of the priestly party to represent Christ as a dangerous enemy to public order; and perhaps they really feared a rescue by the "people" (Matt. xxvi. 5). Early Christian writers laid stress upon the "binding" as marking the parallel with Isaac (Gen. xxii. 9; Melito, ap. Routh, 'Rell. Sacr.' I. 123 f.).

The title of the "captain" in the original (χιλίαρχος) favours the view that "the band" was a "cohort," and not a smaller body ("maniple"): comp. Acts xxi. 31. The word "chiliarch" was used as the equivalent of "tribune," the proper title of the commander of a "cohort;" and the other places in which a "band" (σπεῖρα) is spoken of in the New Testament suggest the same conclusion: Acts x. 1, xxvii. 1. The rendering of σπεῖρα in the Latin versions is uniformly *cohort*. The words "band" and "captain" may however be both used in a general and not in a technical sense for a detachment of soldiers and the officer in command of it. (Comp. Rev. vi. 15, xix. 18, and Suidas *s. v.* σπεῖρα.)

13. *led him* (om. *away*) *to Annas first*] Annas (or Hanan, Ananias, Ananus) is one of the most remarkable figures in the Jewish history of the time. His unexampled fortune was celebrated in that he himself and his five

l An- nt t l un- i- the , 4. p. 11.

first; for he was father in law to Caiaphas, which was the high priest that same year.‖

14 [d] Now Caiaphas was he, which gave counsel to the Jews, that it was expedient that one man should die for the people.

15 ¶ [e] And Simon Peter followed Jesus, and *so did* another disciple: that disciple was known unto the high priest, and went in with Jesus into the palace of the high priest.

16 But Peter stood at the door without. Then went out that other

[e] Matt. 26 58.

---

sons held the high-priesthood in succession. He was high-priest himself from A.D. 7—14 (Jos. 'Ant.' XVIII. 2. 1 f.); then, after a short time his son Eleazar held the office for a year; and after a year's interval, his son-in-law Joseph Caiaphas succeeded and held the office till A.D. 35—6 (Jos. *l. c.*). Another son of Annas succeeded Caiaphas, and three other sons afterwards held the office, the last of whom, who bore his father's name, put to death James the brother of the Lord (Jos. 'Ant.' XX. 8. 1). This mere record reveals the skilful intriguer who exercised through members of his family the headship of his party (comp. Luke iii. 2; Acts iv. 6). In the Talmud ('Pesach.' 57 a, quoted by Derenbourg, p. 232 n.) we find a curse on "the family of Hanan and their serpent-hissings" (comp. Matt. iii. 7). The relationship of Caiaphas to Annas is not mentioned by any writer except St John, and yet this relationship alone explains how Caiaphas was able to retain his office by the side of Annas and his sons.

The narrative of St John lends no support to the conjecture (which, however, may be true) that Annas held some high office at the time, as the presidency of the Sanhedrin, which gave him a constitutional right to take the lead in the inquiry. The reason given for the proceeding—his family connexion with Caiaphas—lays open alike the character of the man and the character of the trial. See Additional Note.

first] This word conveys a tacit correction of the popular misunderstanding of the Synoptic narratives. The Lord was examined before Caiaphas (*v.* 24), but there was also a prior examination.

which was the high priest that same year] See ch. xi. 49, note. Comp. Taylor, 'Sayings of the Jewish Fathers,' I. 19, note, III. 26, note (בו ביום).

14. *Now Caiaphas was he* ...] Ch. xi. 50. The clause appears to be added to shew presumptively what would be the selfish policy of a man who had chosen such a son. Annas exercised his power through those who were like him.

15. *followed*] The imperfect (ἠκολούθει) paints the action in progress. For the fact comp. Matt. xxvi. 58 and parallels. After the panic, in which all the disciples fled (Matt. xxvi. 56), some again took courage (Matt. xxvi. 58).

another disciple] not *the other* (ὁ ἄλλος). The reader cannot fail to identify the disciple with St John. Comp. xx. 2.

known (γνωστός. Comp. Luke ii. 44, xxiii. 49)] No tradition (so far as it appears) has preserved the nature of the connexion; nor is it possible to draw any satisfactory conclusion from the fact that both St John (Polycr. ap. Euseb. 'H. E.' V. 24) and St James the Just, "the brother of the Lord" (Epiph. 'Hær.' LXXVIII. 14), are said to have worn the πέταλον or plate attached to the high-priest's mitre.

unto the high priest] It is very difficult to decide who is here spoken of under the title. Annas is called the high-priest in Acts iv. 6, while Caiaphas is named at the same time without any title; and so Josephus ('Antt.' XVIII. 5. 3; comp. XVIII. 3 (2). 2) speaks of "Jonathan the son of Ananus (Annas) the high-priest" after the removal of Caiaphas. In Luke iii. 2, Annas and Caiaphas bear the title together. It is therefore at least possible that Annas may be referred to. On the other hand, Caiaphas has just been described as "the high-priest" (*v.* 13), and is so called again in *v.* 24, where Annas also is mentioned. These facts make it difficult to suppose that the title is abruptly used, without any explanation, to describe Annas.

the palace (**court**, see Matt. xxvi. 58; Mark xiv. 54 and notes) *of the high priest*] *i.e.* of Caiaphas. It is quite reasonable to suppose that Annas still retained a lodging, in what appears to have been an official residence. In this case there is no discrepancy between St John and the Synoptists as to the scene of St Peter's denials (the residence of Caiaphas). Nor indeed would there be any difficulty in supposing that Annas presided at an examination in the house of Caiaphas, though he did not live there. St Luke (xxii. 54) says that the Lord was led "into the house of the high priest," without mentioning any name. By this form of expression the Evangelist perhaps wished to indicate that He was not brought at once officially before Caiaphas, though He was taken to his palace. The language of St Matthew suggests the same idea (Matt. xxvi. 57, "to Caiaphas ... where ...").

The idea that a change of scene from the house of Annas to the house of Caiaphas is

disciple, which was known unto the high priest, and spake unto her that kept the door, and brought in Peter.

17 Then saith the damsel that kept the door unto Peter, Art not thou also *one* of this man's disciples? He saith, I am not.

18 And the servants and officers stood there, who had made a fire of coals; for it was cold: and they warmed themselves: and Peter stood with them, and warmed himself.

19 ¶ The high priest then asked Jesus of his disciples, and of his doctrine.

20 Jesus answered him, I spake openly to the world; I ever taught in the synagogue, and in the temple,

---

marked in this verse is most unnatural. The narrative of the whole section (*vv.* 13—27) implies an identity of scene.

16. *Peter stood*]...**was standing**. Comp. *v.* 5, note.

her that kept the door] Comp. Acts xii. 13.

17. *Then saith the damsel...*] **The maid therefore...** The acquaintance of St Peter with St John suggested the question. St John meanwhile (it must be supposed) had pressed on into the audience-chamber, so that St Peter was alone. St John, who remained closest to the Lord, was unmolested: St Peter, who mingled with the indifferent crowd, fell.

Art not thou also (**Art thou...**)...] as well as thy friend (John). The form of the question expresses surprise, and suggests a negative answer. See vi. 67, vii. 47, ix. 40. The contemptuous turn of the sentence, "one of the disciples of this man," corresponds with the same feeling. As the suggestion was made St Peter yielded to it. His answer both here and in *v.* 25 simply reflects the temper of his questioners.

18. *And the servants and officers stood there, who had made...*] **Now** *the servants and* **the** *officers*, **having made...were standing...** The Roman soldiers had now gone back, and the private servants of the high-priest (δοῦλοι), and the officers—the temple-police (ὑπηρέται)—alone remained.

a fire of coals] A charcoal fire. There was no bright flame, but a glow of light sufficient to shew the features of any one turned towards it, Luke xxii. 56 (πρὸς τὸ φῶς).

for it was cold] As a general rule, the nights in Palestine about Easter-time are said to be warm throughout. The cold on this occasion appears to be spoken of as unusual.

and Peter stood with them, and warmed himself] *and Peter* **also was with them, standing and warming himself**. Comp. *v.* 25. The two main ideas are kept distinct. Peter had joined the company of the indifferent spectators; he was engaged in a trivial act. Such outward indifference often veils the deepest emotion.

19. *The high priest then* (**therefore**)...] *i.e.* probably Caiaphas. See *v.* 15, note. The narrative is connected with *v.* 14. The Master is now contrasted with the disciple. It is probable that a better acquaintance with the history of the time would remove the difficulty which arises from Caiaphas taking the lead in the examination before Annas. Yet it is easy to imagine that arrangements may have been made for a private examination in the chamber of Annas, at which Caiaphas was himself present, and in which he took part. At the close of this unofficial proceeding, Annas, the real leader in the whole action, sent Jesus to Caiaphas for a formal trial.

of his disciples...of his doctrine (**teaching**)] This preliminary examination was directed to the obtaining (if possible) of materials for the formal accusation which was to follow. With this view, it was natural to inquire into the class, the character, the number of the Lord's disciples, and into the general substance of His teaching.

20. The Lord leaves unnoticed the question as to His disciples (comp. *v.* 8), and fixes the attention of the questioner upon Himself alone. Hence an emphatic pronoun stands at the head of each clause. *I* (ἐγώ), whatever others may have done with whom you wish to compare me, *I* **have spoken** *openly* ... *I* (ἐγώ) *ever taught* ... So the Lord presents His teaching first as a completed whole (*I have spoken*, xvi. 33), and then in its historic presentation (*I ever taught*). The form of the sentence at the same time suggests a contrast between the openness of His conduct and the treachery which His enemies had employed.

openly] Without reserve. Comp. vii. 13, note.

to the world] Comp. viii. 26. The teaching of the Lord was not addressed to any select group of followers, even if it was veiled in parables which required spiritual sympathy for their interpretation, Matt. xiii. 10 ff.

ever (*always*)] The word does not of course mean that the Lord's teaching was confined to these public places, but that at all times He used opportunities of speaking in them.

in the synagogue ...] Or rather, **in synagogue**, "when people were gathered in solemn assembly" (ἐν συναγωγῇ, as distinguished from ἐν ταῖς συναγωγαῖς, Matt. ix. 35, &c.). Comp. vi. 59, note.

whither the Jews always resort; and
in secret have I said nothing.
21 Why askest thou me? ask them
which heard me, what I have said unto
them: behold, they know what I said.
22 And when he had thus spoken,
one of the officers which stood by
, with struck Jesus [1] with the palm of his
d. hand, saying, Answerest thou the high
priest so?
23 Jesus answered him, If I have
spoken evil, bear witness of the evil:
but if well, why smitest thou me?

24 [f] Now Annas had sent him [f] Matt. 26
bound unto Caiaphas the high priest. 57.
25 And Simon Peter stood and
warmed himself. [g] They said there- [g] Matt. 26.
fore unto him, Art not thou also *one* 69.
of his disciples? He denied *it*, and
said, I am not.
26 One of the servants of the high
priest, being *his* kinsman whose ear
Peter cut off, saith, Did not I see
thee in the garden with him?
27 Peter then denied again: and
immediately the cock crew.

---

the Jews always resort] According to the true reading, **all the Jews resort (come together)**, and not a mere party or clique. The combination "always," "all" (πάντοτε, πάντες), is singularly emphatic. Christ was from first to last a universal teacher, and not the founder of a sect. In manner, time, place, audience, He sought absolute publicity.

in secret have I said] *in secret* **I spake.** The words simply exclude the purpose of concealment. What the disciples heard in the ear they were charged to proclaim on the housetops (Matt. x. 27)

21. *Why askest* ...] The accusers are bound to establish their charge independently.

which heard me, what I have said...they know ...] *which* **have heard** *me, what* **I spake...these** *know*... The tense (ἀκηκοότας, not ἀκούσαντας) and the pronoun (οὗτοι) seem both to point directly to persons actually present or close at hand, who were able to speak with full knowledge if they pleased. Thus the Lord claims that the examination may proceed in due order by the calling of witnesses; and, according to the rule, the witnesses for the defence were called first ('Sanh.' f. 32. 1; f. 40. 1, quoted by Lightfoot, 'Hor. Hebr.,' on *v.* 15).

22. *with...his hand*] Or, "with a rod." This latter sense suits perhaps better with the word used for "smiting" (δέρεις), though the sense given in the text appears to be more appropriate to the circumstances. Comp. xix. 3; Acts xxiii. 2 ff. This insult is to be distinguished from the corresponding acts mentioned, Matt. xxvi. 67; Luke xxii. 63, 64.

23. *If I have spoken* (rather, **spake**) *evil* ...] The Lord addresses the servant as one who had heard Him, and as such He challenges him to bear just evidence as to His words, and not to use mere violence. The reference (as it appears) is not to the words just uttered (*v.* 21), but to the teaching of the Lord which was called in question (*v.* 20, *I spake*; *v.* 21, *what I spake*; *v.* 23, *if I spake*). The old commentators saw in the calm rebuke a true interpretation of the precept, Matt. v. 39.

24. *Now Annas had sent him*...] *Annas* **therefore sent** *him*... The words cannot be rendered otherwise. See Additional Note. The private interrogation at which Caiaphas had assisted led to no decisive result. Annas therefore sent Jesus to the high-priest officially, but as one already stamped with a sign of condemnation (ἀπέστειλεν, despatched; comp. note on xx. 21). During the inquiry the Lord would naturally be set free. This explains the notice that He was (again) "bound" before going to Caiaphas.

25. *And Simon Peter stood and warmed himself*] *Simon Peter* **was standing and warming** *himself.* Comp. *v.* 18.

They said therefore ...] Since St Peter was evidently a stranger among them, attention was necessarily turned again to him, when the Lord was again brought into the court at the close of the private examination before Caiaphas, and so occasion was given for the second questioning. During this passage it would be easy for the Lord to turn and "look on Peter" (Luke xxii. 61), when He had already gone by near him.

Art not thou also ...] **Art thou**... The form of question is the same as that in *v.* 17. Something no doubt in St Peter's manner, as the Lord was led by, betrayed his love. Whereupon followed the words of surprise: *Can it be that thou also art one of His disciples?*

26. *being his kinsman* (*a kinsman* **of him**) ...] A detail which marks an exact knowledge of the household (*v.* 15).

in the garden] as one of His chosen disciples, who were gathered behind the Lord when He stood outside at the entrance facing the crowd (*v.* 4).

27. *Peter then* (**therefore**) ...] He was already committed to the denial. St John, like St Luke, omits all the aggravations of St Peter's denials (Matt. xxvi. 70, 72, 74; Mark xiv. 71).

[h] Matt. 27. 2. ‖ Or, *Pilate's house.* [i] Acts 10. 28.

28 ¶ [h] Then led they Jesus from Caiaphas unto ‖ the hall of judgment: and it was early; [i] and they themselves went not into the judgment hall, lest they should be defiled; but that they might eat the passover.

---

the cock crew] The indefinite form of the phrase (**a cock** *crew*) is far more expressive than A. V., which rather describes the time than the incident. The silence of the Evangelist, as to the repentance of St Peter, is illustrated by xxi. 15 ff., where the fact is presupposed. The episode of Peter's fall is given as the fulfilment of the Lord's word (xiii. 38), who knew to the last detail what he had to bear.

ii. The civil trial. The divine King and the Roman governor. The divine King and the apostate people. xviii. 28—xix. 16.

The detailed account of the private examinations before Pilate (xviii. 33—37, xix. 8—11) is peculiar to St John (comp. Matt. xxvii. 11 ff. and parallels; 1 Tim. vi. 13). St John probably went within the palace. He would not be deterred by the scruple of the Jews (*v.* 28) under such circumstances, and there does not appear to have been any other obstacle to entrance. The apostle who had followed the Lord to the presence of the high-priest would not shrink from following Him to the presence of the governor.

It will be noticed that St John's narrative explains the language of Pilate to the Jews and to the Lord, which is abrupt and unprepared in the Synoptic narratives.

The narrative falls into several distinct sections corresponding to scenes without and within the Prætorium.

1. Without the Prætorium. The Jews claim the execution of their sentence (xviii. 28—32).

2. Within the Prætorium. "The good confession." Christ a King (33—37).

3. Without the Prætorium. First declaration of innocence. Barabbas (38—40).

4. Within the Prætorium. Scourging: mockery (xix. 1—3).

5. Without the Prætorium. Second and third declarations of innocence. "Ecce homo," "Son of God" (4—7).

6. Within the Prætorium. The source of authority, and from this the measure of guilt (8—11).

7. Without the Prætorium. Conviction overpowered: the King abjured: the last sentence (12—16).

1. *vv.* 28—32. *Without the Prætorium: Pilate and the Jews: the claim and the refusal.*

28. *Then led they Jesus*] *They* **lead** *Jesus* **therefore...** Comp. Matt. xxvii. 1 f. The examination before Caiaphas (Matt. xxvi. 59 ff. and parallels) is implied, and also its necessary issue. The sentence was determined, but the Sanhedrin had no power to carry it out. The subject (*they*) is not exactly defined. The principal actors ("the chief priests and Pharisees," "the Jews") are everywhere present to the mind of the Evangelist. Comp. xix. 4.

hall of judgment] *the* **palace.** The official residence (head-quarters) of the Roman governor (πραιτώριον). This was the technical sense of *prætorium* in the provinces (comp. Acts xxiii. 35). At Rome the usage of the word was different (comp. Lightfoot, 'Philippians,' pp. 97 ff.). The building occupied by Pilate is commonly supposed to have been the palace built by Herod on the western hill of Jerusalem. This was certainly occupied at a later time by the Roman governors (Philo, 'Leg. ad Cai.' 1034), but there is not any direct evidence, as far as appears, that it was occupied by Pilate, and on the whole it seems to be more probable (comp. xix. 13) that Pilate occupied quarters in Antonia, according to the traditional view. See the Additional Note on Matt. xxvii. 2.

it was early] Comp. Matt. xxvii. 1 parallels. The term (πρωΐ) is used technically for the fourth watch, 3—6 a.m. (Mark xiii. 35). A condemnation to death at night was technically illegal (Matt. *l. c.* note). An early meeting of the Sanhedrin appears to have been held to confirm the decision already made, and so to satisfy the form of law, which however was broken by the infliction and execution of the sentence on the day of trial. A Roman court could be held at any time after sunrise. On this occasion it was probably held as early as possible. Pilate, as we may suppose, had been prepared for the charge when application was made for the detachment of soldiers.

they themselves] In contrast with the Lord, who was now probably committed again to the soldiers, and taken within the Prætorium (*v.* 33).

lest they should be...; but that they might...] **that they might not** *be*... **but might...**

be defiled] by entering a house from which all leaven had not been scrupulously removed. The prætorium was placed under the protection of tutelary deities (θεοὶ οἱ τοῦ ἡγεμονικοῦ πραιτωρίου, 'Journal of Philology,' 1876, pp. 126 ff.; comp. Tac. 'Hist.' III. 10), but such a dedication is out of the question at Jerusalem. Pilate had learnt by bitter experience with what fierceness the Jews resented every semblance of a violation of their religious feelings (Jos. 'Bel. Jud.' II. 9. 2. Comp. Philo, 'Leg. ad Cai.' § 38).

eat the passover] See note on Matt. xxvi.

29 Pilate then went out unto them, and said, What accusation bring ye against this man?

30 They answered and said unto him, If he were not a malefactor, we would not have delivered him up unto thee.

31 Then said Pilate unto them, Take ye him, and judge him according to your law. The Jews therefore said unto him, It is not lawful for us to put any man to death:

32 [k] That the saying of Jesus might be fulfilled, which he spake, signifying what death he should die. [k] Matt. 20. 19.

33 [l] Then Pilate entered into the judgment hall again, and called Jesus, and said unto him, Art thou the King of the Jews? [l] Matt. 27 11.

---

29. *Pilate then* (**therefore**)...*said* (**saith**)] Pilate is introduced quite abruptly, without any title or explanation, as one perfectly well known. Comp. Mark xv. 1; Luke xxiii. 1. In St Matthew he is commonly spoken of as "the governor" (Matt. xxvii. 2, note), a title not found in St John. The scrupulousness of Pilate needs some explanation (contrast Acts xxii. 24). The explanation is probably supplied by St Matthew (Matt. xxvii. 19) in the message of Pilate's wife, which at least indicates that the accusation of Jesus had made an impression upon her, and so probably in Pilate's household. There is a slight trace in the narrative of St Matthew (ch. xxvii. 19, note) of the informal manner in which the trial was in part conducted.

went out] The best authorities add "without" (ἔξω). St John appears to emphasize the fact that Pilate "went forth without" his own prætorium, as if it were symbolic of the whole proceeding.

What accusation] The words do not necessarily imply that Pilate was ignorant of the character of the charge (see *v.* 3). Pilate requires that the charge should be made formally.

30 f. The Jews were evidently unprepared for the governor's hesitation in such a case; and attempted to claim the fulfilment of their sentence without rendering account of the grounds on which it rested. Pilate met this affectation of independence by bidding them carry out their purpose to the end by their own authority: *Pilate* **therefore** *said, Take him* **yourselves** (ὑμεῖς). On this they are forced to confess that nothing less than death will satisfy them, and this punishment they cannot inflict.

malefactor] Literally, *doing evil* (κακὸν ποιῶν), actively engaged in evil. The word in St Luke, xxiii. 32, is different (κακοῦργος).

31. *Take ye him*...] *Take him* **yourselves**... The words have a tinge of irony (*yourselves*, *your* law); and Pilate implicitly reminds the Jews of the limits within which their power of "judgment" was confined.

The Jews said (om. *therefore*) ...] Pilate's words left them no alternative. They could not escape from revealing their purpose; and probably they now brought forward against Christ the charge of treason (Luke xxiii. 2) in order to move Pilate the more easily (*v.* 34).

It is not lawful ...] See Additional Note.

32. *the saying* (**word**) *of Jesus*...*signifying what death* (*by* **what manner of** *death*) ...] Ch. xii. 32 f. Comp. Matt. xx. 19. Crucifixion was not a Jewish punishment. The clause must not be interpreted to convey the idea that the Jews wished a particular form of death to be inflicted, but that the circumstances of the case led to this issue.

2. *vv.* 33—37. *Within the Prætorium: Pilate and Christ: the good confession and the light question.*

33. *Then Pilate* ...] *Pilate* **therefore**... The urgency of the Jews constrained him to make further inquiry.

called Jesus] The Lord was already inside the court (*v.* 28); but Pilate summoned Him to his immediate presence (ἐφώνησεν, comp. ix. 18, 24).

Art thou the King of the Jews?] The words may mean either "Art thou he who has just now become notorious under this title?" or, "Dost thou claim the title, as it is said?" The title itself would be likely to arrest Pilate's attention, whether he had heard it spoken of before in connexion with the entry into Jerusalem or only now from the Jews. And further, he would rightly conclude that the title, when thus put forward, would be fitted to call out any fanaticism which there might be in a political enthusiast. The full form which the accusation assumed is given in St Luke (xxiii. 2). See xix. 12. In each of the four Gospels the first words of Pilate to Jesus are the same: "Art thou the King of the Jews?" (Matt. xxvii. 11; Mark xv. 2; Luke xxiii. 3). The form of the sentence (σὺ εἶ ...;) suggests a feeling of surprise in the questioner: "Art thou, poor, and bound, and wearied, the King of whom men have spoken?" Comp. iv. 12.

King of the Jews] *v.* 39, xix. 3, 19, 21. Compare Matt. ii. 2, xxvii. 11, 29, 37; Mark xv. 2, 9, 12, 18, 26; Luke xxiii. 3, 37, 38. The theocratic title *the King of Israel* (i. 49, note) stands in marked contrast with this civil title.

34 Jesus answered him, Sayest thou
this thing of thyself, or did others tell
it thee of me?
35 Pilate answered, Am I a Jew?
Thine own nation and the chief
priests have delivered thee unto me:
what hast thou done?
36 Jesus answered, My kingdom
is not of this world: if my kingdom
were of this world, then would my
servants fight, that I should not be
delivered to the Jews: but now is
my kingdom not from hence.
37 Pilate therefore said unto him,
Art thou a king then? Jesus answered, Thou sayest that I am a

---

34. *Jesus answered* (om. *him*)] The short clauses are impressive: "Jesus answered"—"Pilate answered"—"Jesus answered."

34 f. *Sayest thou ... tell it thee of me* (or **tell thee** *of me*)] The Lord's question is suited to lead Pilate to reflect on the nature of the charge which he had to judge. In this sense it is an appeal to his conscience. If he admits the alleged assumption of the title to be a crime, he must ask himself whether the title has any meaning for him? whether he desires to learn what further it may signify? or whether he has simply adopted a vague accusation, an ambiguous phrase, at random? Pilate's reply affirms his utter indifference to matters which only concerned (as he assumes) a despised people. "Am I a Jew?" Is it then possible for me to care for these things? Yet in the words which follow he implies that there is something strange in the case. The Jews were ready for the most part to favour any asserter of their national liberty. Now they had brought one called their King to be put to death. "Thine own nation" (τὸ ἔθνος τὸ σόν), and no Roman informer, "and the chief priests, the natural leaders of the people, **delivered** (om. *have*) *thee unto me: what hast thou done?* or, more exactly, *what* **didst thou do**," that is, to turn those who would naturally favour such as thee into relentless enemies?

36. Without directly replying to Pilate, the Lord indicates the real ground of the antagonism of the people and of the rulers to Himself, and at the same time explains how He is a King: "His kingdom was not of this world" (κόσμος). He would not make any concessions to the false patriotism of zealots (vi. 15), and yet He did claim a sovereignty, a sovereignty of which the spring and source was not of earth but of heaven. In both respects He was opposed to those who professed from different sides to represent the nation ("the Jews"). But as a spiritual King He was open to no accusation of hostility to the empire. His willing surrender was a sufficient proof that he had never contemplated violence.

My kingdom ... my kingdom ... my servants (ὑπηρέται, *officers*, *vv.* 3, 12, &c.)] The possessive pronoun is in each case emphasized: "the kingdom, the servants (*i.e.* disciples and apostles), who truly answer to me, to my nature and my will." Comp. xv. 11, note, xii. 26. There is an obvious reference to the Jewish conceptions of a kingdom and to the Jewish "officers." The use of the word ὑπηρέτης (here only of Christians in the Gospels, comp. 1 Cor. iv. 1; Acts xiii. 5) corresponds with the royal dignity which Christ assumes.

is not of this world ... hence] does not derive its origin or its support from earthly forces. Comp. viii. 23, xv. 19, xvii. 14, 16; 1 John ii. 16, iv. 5. At the same time Christ's kingdom is "in the world," even as His disciples are (xvii. 11). This verse serves as a comment on Matt. ii. 1 ff., and brings out the full force of St Matthew's characteristic term "the kingdom of heaven." The solemnity of the rhythmical balance of the sentence in the original cannot but be felt: "My kingdom ... not of this world ... if of this world ... my kingdom." The substitution of "hence" for "of this world" in the last clause appears to define the idea of the world by an immediate reference to the representatives of it close at hand.

fight] The original (ἠγωνίζοντο) describes a continuous effort, and not merely one definite conflict: "they would now be striving" (Luke xiii. 24; 1 Cor. ix. 25; 1 Tim. vi. 12; 2 Tim. iv. 7), and not "they would have fought" at the moment of my arrest.

the Jews] The title occurs in the record of the Lord's words, iv. 22, xiii. 33, and above, *v.* 20 (comp. xi. 8). The colour of the word in these places is slightly different from that which it bears in the Evangelist's narrative. The simple idea of nationality prevails over that of religious antagonism.

but now] As the case really stands, ix. 41, xv. 22, 24.

37. *Art thou a king then?*] The particle (οὐκοῦν), which occurs here only in the New Testament, gives a tinge of irony to the words, which are half interrogative in form and half an exclamation: "So then, after all, thou art a king?" This scornful tone is further accentuated by the personal pronoun at the end of the sentence: "thou, a helpless prisoner." Comp. *v.* 33, i. 21, iv. 19, viii. 48.

Thou sayest...] The Lord neither definitely accepts nor rejects the title. He leaves the claim

king. To this end was I born, and for this cause came I into the world, that I should bear witness unto the truth. Every one that is of the truth heareth my voice.

38 Pilate saith unto him, What

---

as Pilate had put it forward. Pilate had quoted the words of others, and the Lord had made clear in what general sense they must be interpreted. He now signifies further the foundation and character of His sovereignty, and the right which He has to the allegiance of men.

that I am ...] The translation *Thou sayest* (*i.e.* rightly), *because I am ...* seems to be both unnatural as a rendering of the original phrase, and alien from the context.

To this end (εἰς τοῦτο) ... *that* (ἵνα, in order that)] The first words (*To this end*) affirm generally the fact of the sovereignty which Christ exercised: He was born for the very purpose that He should reign; and the last (*that I may*) the special application of it: His reign was directed to the execution of a divine purpose. Comp. Acts ix. 21; Rom. xiv. 9; 2 Cor. ii. 9; 1 Pet. iii. 9, iv. 6; 1 John iii. 8.

was I born...for this cause came I...] **have I been born...to this end am I come** *into the world* ... The two phrases appear to correspond in part with the two in ch. xvi. 28, "I came out from the Father, and am come into the world." The first marks the entrance upon a new form of being, the second defines the sphere of the Lord's mission (comp. ix. 39, note). Or again, the first marks the beginning of the earthly life, the second the preexistence with the Father. But as addressed to Pilate the words declared only the human birth (comp. Luke i. 35, τὸ γεννώμενον), though a deeper meaning lies beneath them. The emphatic pronoun at the head of the sentence (ἐγὼ εἰς τοῦτο ...), and the repeated clause *to this end*, fix attention upon the Speaker and His office. Christ not only affirms the fact of His kingship, but also bases the fact upon the essential law of His being. He places His own Person (ἐγώ) in contrast with all other men, whether they disbelieve (as Pilate) or believe. And He describes His coming as permanent in its effects (ἐλήλυθα) and not simply as a past historic fact (ἦλθον).

bear witness unto the truth...] Truth, absolute reality, is the realm of Christ. He marks out its boundaries; and every one who has a vital connexion with the Truth recognises His sway. He does not only "bear witness concerning the truth" (μαρτυρεῖν περί, i. 7, 8, &c.), but "bears witness to, maintains, the truth" (μαρτυρεῖν τινί, iii. 26), as John had done in his place, v. 33. Comp. Acts x. 43, xv. 8, &c.; 3 John 12.

that is of the truth] who draws from the truth the inspiration of his life (comp. 1 John ii. 21, iii. 19). The phrase is parallel to "that is of God" (viii. 47, note). Comp. also *v.* 36, iii. 31, viii. 23, xv. 19, xvii. 14; 1 John ii. 16, iii. 8 ff., and in a wider sense x. 16; Col. iv. 11. All who thus depend on that which is Christ's are His proper subjects. For the whole answer comp. 1 Tim. vi. 13. It is of great interest to compare this "confession" before Pilate with the corresponding "confession" before the high-priest, Matt. xxvi. 64. The one addressed to Jews is framed in the language of prophecy, the other addressed to a Roman appeals to the universal testimony of conscience. The one speaks of a future manifestation of glory, the other speaks of a present manifestation of truth. The one looks forward to the Return, the other looks backward to the Incarnation. It is obvious how completely they answer severally to the circumstances of the two occasions.

the truth] Compare Introd. p. xliv. Lightfoot on ch. vi. 27 quotes two remarkable passages which illustrate one idea of the word: "When the great synagogue had been weeping, praying, and fasting, for a long time, a little roll fell from the firmament to them in which was written Truth. R. Chaniach saith, Hence learn that Truth is the seal of God." ('Sanh. Bab.' f. 64. 1.) And again: "What is the seal of the holy blessed God? R. Bibai, in the name of R. Reuben, saith 'Truth' (אמת). But what is Truth? R. Bon saith, The living God and King eternal. Resh Lachish saith, א is the first letter of the alphabet, מ the middle, and ת the last: that is, I the Lord am the first ... and beside me there is no God ... and I am with the last" ('Sanh. Hieros.' f. 18).

The Lord's confession includes the fulfilment of the double hope. He is the King of the people of God, and the universal Saviour. Comp. iv. 25 ff., ix. 35 ff.

38. *What is truth?*] The question of Pilate does not deal with absolute Truth—the Truth as one—of which the Lord had spoken (ἡ ἀλήθεια), but simply with truth in any particular case (ἀλήθεια). There is nothing of real reverence or seriousness in his words, still less of awe. He does not shape, even in passing thought, a subject for earnest inquiry, but half sadly, half cynically, implies that even in ordinary matters truth is unattainable. It was so evidently to his mind in the matter before him; but so much at least was plain to his Roman clearness of vision, that the prisoner accused by His countrymen was no political intriguer. He therefore impatiently breaks off the examination which had (as he fancied) shewn him enough to decide the case,

is truth? And when he had said this, he went out again unto the Jews, and saith unto them, I find in him no fault *at all.*

[m] Matt 27. 15.
39 [m] But ye have a custom, that I should release unto you one at the passover: will ye therefore that I release unto you the King of the Jews?

40 [n] Then cried they all again, saying, Not this man, but Barabbas. Now Barabbas was a robber. [n] Acts 14.

---

that he may obtain the release of Jesus if possible. Corn. a Lapide gives an interesting series of answers to the question, "What is truth?" from classical and patristic writers. Though they have no direct connexion with Pilate's thought they will repay study.

The sending to Herod (Luke xxiii. 6 ff.) must be placed between *vv.* 37, 39.

3. *vv.* 38—40. *Without the Prætorium. The judgment of Pilate and the judgment of the Jews. The sentence, the offer, the demand, Jesus and Barabbas.*

38 ff. *And when* ...] The incident that follows is a complete revelation of a weak worldly character. Pilate addressed himself, as it seems, not to the leading accusers of Jesus (*the high-priests and Pharisees*), but to the crowd which had now gathered round them. He trusted that an expression of popular feeling would enable him to follow his own judgment without incurring any unpopularity. He saw that Jesus was evidently the victim of a party (Matt. xxvii. 18), and perhaps of a small party. Moreover the festival allowed him to effect his purpose without absolutely setting aside the sentence of the Sanhedrin. He suggests therefore that Jesus should be released according to the custom of the Passover. From the narrative of St Mark it appears that the demand for the fulfilment of this act of grace was first made by "the multitude" who had come up to the governor's house (ἀναβάς, Mark xv. 8), and it is not unlikely that some at least of the people hoped in this way (like Pilate) to deliver Jesus. The name of a notorious criminal was coupled with that of Jesus (Matt. xxvii. 17), that the wish of the people might be expressed more decisively. When the choice was put to them there was for a time a division of feeling, or hesitation (Mark xv. 11, note). At length the high-priests prevailed (comp. ch. xix. 6), and Pilate was then overpowered by the popular cry, from which he had expected to obtain convenient support. He had no firmness to support him when his scheme had failed; and at last, by a strange irony, he was forced to release a man guilty of the very form of crime which the chief priests had tried to fasten upon Christ.

I find in him no fault at all] *I find no* **charge** (or **crime**) *in him.* The pronoun is emphatic here and xix. 6 (not in xix. 4), and contains an implied contrast between the partizanship of the priests and the calm judgment of the Roman governor.

39. *at the passover*] The custom is made more general in St Matthew (xxvii. 15) and St Mark (xv. 6), "at feast time" (κατὰ ἑορτήν). Nothing is known of the origin of the custom, nor is it (as far as appears) noticed anywhere except in the Gospels. Comp. Matt. xxvii. 15, note.

the King of the Jews] The title is probably used, as afterwards (xix. 15), to throw contempt on the pretensions of the Jewish leaders.

40. *Then cried they all again* ...] *They* **cried out therefore** *again* with the loud cry which will make itself heard (ἐκραύγασαν). Comp. xi. 43, xii. 13, xix. 6, 12, 15. The people, in spite of their late enthusiasm, were driven by their selfish hopes to prefer one who had at least defied the Roman power to their divine King.

again] The word is a singular mark of the brevity of St John's narrative, which assumes much as known. The previous demands of the people have not been noticed by him.

a robber] One of those outlaws who not unfrequently (Acts xxi. 38) covered their violence with a cloke of patriotism (comp. Luke xxiii. 19; Mark xv. 7; Matt. xxvii. 16, note). There is an impressive pathos in the brief clause. Comp. xiii. 30.

ADDITIONAL NOTES on CHAP. XVIII.

12—24. It is interesting to compare the narratives of the Lord's trial preserved by the Evangelists with the rules laid down in Jewish tradition for the conduct of such cases. It may be impossible to determine the antiquity of the contents of the Mishna, but the following brief summary of the contents of the Tract 'Sanhedrin,' so far as they bear upon the subject, will shew in what respects the proceedings as to the Lord agreed with and differed from what was received as law at a very early date.

Capital offences were tried by an assembly of twenty-three (ch. 1 § 4): a false prophet could be tried only by the great Sanhedrin, or assembly of seventy-one (ch. 1 § 5).

The witnesses were strictly and separately examined in all cases, and the agreement of two was held to be valid (ch. 3 § 6; ch. 5 §§ 1 ff.).

In capital cases the witnesses were specially charged as to the momentous consequences of their testimony, and cautioned as to the peril of destroying life (ch. 4 § 5), and they were to say nothing by conjecture or hearsay.

The judges sat in a semicircle, the president being in the middle, so that all might be face to face (ch. 4 § 3).

In capital cases everything was so arranged as to give the accused the benefit of the doubt, and with this view the votes for acquittal were taken first (ch. 4 § 1).

In civil cases the trial might be continued and decided by night; and a decision either way might be given on the day of trial. In capital cases the trial could take place only by day; and while an acquittal might be pronounced on the day of trial, a sentence of condemnation could not be given till the next day. Hence such cases could not be tried on the eve of a Sabbath or of a Feast (ch. 4 § 1: comp. ch. 5 § 5).

Even on the way to execution opportunity was given to the condemned, four or five times, if need were, to bring forward fresh pleas (ch. 6 § 1); and at the last he was urged to confession, that he might not be lost hereafter (ch. 6 § 2). A crier preceded the condemned, saying, "A. B. the son of A. B. goes forth to be stoned for such and such an offence: the witnesses are C. and D. If any one can prove his innocence, let him come forward and give his reasons" (ch. 6 § 1).

In cases of blasphemy the witnesses were rigorously examined as to the exact language used by the accused. If their evidence was definite the judges stood and rent their garments (ch. 7 § 5).

The blasphemer was to be stoned (ch. 7 § 4). After stoning he was to be hung upon a gibbet (ch. 6 § 4), and taken down before night (*id.*) and buried in a common grave provided for the purpose (ch. 6 § 5).

13. Derenbourg ('Essai sur l'Histoire et la Géographie de la Palestine,' Paris, 1867) has called attention (pp. 466 ff.) to a remarkable passage of the Talmud ('Jer. Taanith,' IV 8), which mentions that "on the Mount of Olives there were two *cedars*, under one of which were four booths (shops, חנויות) for the sale of objects legally pure. In one of these, pigeons enough were sold for the sacrifices of all Israel." He conjectures that these booths were [part of] "the famous booths of the sons of Hanan (Annas)," to which the Sanhedrin retired when it left the chamber "Gazith" (see Add. Note on *v.* 31). The identification seems to be very plausible, notwithstanding Keim's peremptory contradiction (III. 352, note). Yet see the note on Matt. xxvii. 1. But whether "the booths" were on the Mount of Olives or adjoining the temple, the place was the seat of the dominant faction of Annas, the centre of their hierarchical tyranny. The night meeting of members of the Sanhedrin favourable to their policy would therefore naturally be held there. The regular meeting in the morning of the whole body (Matt. xxvii. 1) was, on the other hand (as it appears), held in the old place of assembly, "Gazith" (Matt. xxvii. 5, *ῥίψας ἐν τῷ ναῷ*). The language of St Luke points clearly to the difference of place of the two examinations (xxii. 66, *ἀπήγαγον εἰς τὸ συνέδριον αὐτῶν*, as contrasted with xxii. 54, *εἰς τὸν οἶκον τοῦ ἀρχιερέως*). Perhaps it will be felt that the record gains in solemnity if the Mount of Olives was the one scene of all the events of the night. Even the mention of Kidron by the secondary and popular name of the "ravine of the cedars" may contain an allusion to a scandal felt as a grievous burden at the time when the priests gained wealth from the sale of victims by the "two cedars." "The booths of the sons of Hanan," tradition adds, "were destroyed three years before the destruction of the temple" (Derenbourg, p. 468).

17, 18, 25—27. The differences in detail, which occur in the records of the threefold denial of the Lord by St Peter, offer a singularly instructive subject for study. The fact is one of the very few related at length by the four Evangelists, and it offers a crucial test for determining, in some aspects, the character of the narratives of the Gospels.

It must be premised:—

1. That each Evangelist records the prediction of a threefold denial:—

Matt. xxvi. 34 ("before the cock crow thou shalt deny me thrice").

Mark xiv. 30 ("before the cock crow twice thou shalt deny me thrice").

Luke xxii. 34 ("the cock shall not crow this day until thou hast thrice denied that thou knowest me").

John xiii. 38 ("the cock shall not crow till thou hast denied me thrice").

In St Matthew and St Mark the prediction occurs after the mention of the departure from the upper room; in St Luke and St John, during the account of the Supper. The particles of connexion in the first two Gospels ("then" [St Matthew], "and" [St Mark]) do not require, though they suggest, chronological sequence. There is no difficulty in supposing either that the record of the words has been transposed by St Matthew and St Mark, or that the prediction was repeated. Such repetitions belong naturally to a crisis of concentrated excitement.

2. That each Evangelist records three acts of denial:—

Matt. xxvi. 70, 72, 74.
Mark xiv. 68, 70, 71.
Luke xxii. 57, 58, 60.
John xviii. 17, 25, 27.

The first three Evangelists specially notice the fulfilment of the prediction: Matt. xxvi. 75; Mark xiv. 72; Luke xxii. 61. St John does not, though he obviously recalls the words spoken: xviii. 27, compared with xiii. 38.

It may be added that the narratives of St Matthew and St Mark represent in the main one original. The narratives of St Luke and St John are independent of one another and of the other two.

Under these circumstances the question arises (1) Whether the four Evangelists relate the same three acts of denial; and then (2) if so, whether the differences in detail admit of being reconciled.

It will be most convenient to examine in succession the four narratives of the first, second, and third denials, noticing the significant points in each.

(Table A.) Here there is an agreement (*a*) as to the place of the incident, the court of the high priest's palace, "outside" and "beneath" the room in which the Lord was being examined, and more particularly by "the fire" which had been lighted there. St John mentions the "standing by the fire" after the fact of the denial, but evidently in connexion with it.

(*b*) As to the chief actor, "a maid" (παιδίσκη), further described by St Mark as "a maid of the high priest," and defined by St John as "the maid that kept the door." There is not the least indication that the "maid" of St Matthew and St Mark could not be the portress.

(*c*) As to the fact of a direct address to St Peter, and of a reply by him to the speaker. And, further, there is a substantial agreement as to what was said.

On the other hand, the Synoptists speak of St Peter as "sitting," St John as "standing," and the words recorded are different. But there is no difference as to time. The incident mentioned by St Matthew and St Mark may have occurred at any time after entrance into the court (Matt. xxvi. 58; Mark xiv. 54).

(Table B.) Here the records are much more complicated: (*a*) Two places are mentioned, the "fore-court" (St Mark), with which the "porch" of St Matthew is to be connected, and the fire in the court which was the scene of the former denial.

(*b*) Many persons take part in the accusation of St Peter: "the same maid" as before (St Mark), "another maid" (St Matthew), "another man" (St Luke), are specified, and St John says, generally, "they said," *i.e.* the bystanders.

But it will be noticed that St Luke alone singles out one man who addresses St Peter, and to whom personally St Peter replies. The

TABLE A.

Matt. xxvi. 69, 70.	Mark xiv. 66—68 a.	Luke xxii. 55—57.	John xviii. 16—18.
Peter was sitting without in the court, and a damsel came unto him, saying,	As Peter was beneath in the court, there cometh one of the maids of the high priest; and when she saw Peter warming himself, she looked upon him and said,	Peter was sitting in the midst of them [in the court], and a certain maid, seeing him as he sat in the light *of the fire*, and earnestly looking upon him, said,	[John] spake unto her that kept the door, and brought in Peter. The maid therefore that kept the door saith to Peter,
Thou also wast with Jesus of Galilee	Thou also wast with Jesus of Nazareth.	This man also was with him.	Art thou also one of this man's disciples?
But he denied before them all, saying,	But he denied (ἠρνήσατο), saying,	But he denied (ἠρνήσατο), saying,	He saith,
I know not what thou sayest.	I know not, neither understand I what thou sayest.	Woman, I know him not.	I am not.
			Now the servants ... were standing, having made a fire of coals ... and Peter was with them, standing and warming himself.

TABLE B.

Matt. xxvi. 71, 72.	Mark xiv. 68 b—70.	Luke xxii. 58.	John xviii. 25.
And when he was gone out into the porch (πυλών), another maid (ἄλλη) saw him,	And he went out into the porch (τὸ προαύλιον, the fore-court), and a cock crew. And the maid (ἡ παιδίσκη) saw him again,	And after a little while (μετὰ βραχύ) another man (ἕτερος) saw him,	Peter was standing and warming himself.
And saith unto them that were there (τοῖς ἐκεῖ),	And began to say to them that stood by.	And said,	They said therefore to him,
This man also was with Jesus of Nazareth.	This is one of them.	Thou also art one of them.	Art thou also one of his disciples?
And again he denied (ἠρνήσατο) with an oath,	And he denied (ἠρνεῖτο) again.	But Peter said,	He denied (ἠρνήσατο), and said.
I do not know the man.		Man, I am not.	I am not.

TABLE C.

Matt. xxvi. 73, 74.	Mark xiv. 70, 71.	Luke xxii. 59, 60.	John xviii. 26, 27.
And after a while (μετὰ μικρόν), they that stood *there* came and said to Peter,	And after a while again they that stood by said (ἔλεγον) to Peter,	And about the space of one hour after, another confidently affirmed, saying,	One of the servants, being his kinsman whose ear Peter cut off, saith,
Surely thou also art one of them, for thy speech bewrayeth thee.	Surely thou art one of them, for thou art a Galilæan.	Of a truth this man also was with them, for he is a Galilæan.	Did not I see thee in the garden with them?
Then began he to curse and to swear, *saying*,	But he began to curse and to swear, *saying*,	And Peter said,	Peter therefore denied again ...
I do not know the man.	I do not know this man of whom ye speak.	Man, I know not what thou sayest.	

words of accusation recorded by St Matthew and St Mark are not addressed to St Peter at all, but spoken among the groups of servants, and St Mark implies a repeated denial (ἠρνεῖτο). The words recorded by St John express apparently what was said by several. So also the denials recorded by St Matthew, St Mark, and St John, are not given as addressed to any particular person, as in the former case. They simply record the fact of denial.

(Table C.) Here again the narratives are complicated. There is no mention of place; but some time, "about an hour" (St Luke), has elapsed since the last denial. In St Matthew and St Mark the charge is addressed to St Peter by many ("they that stood by"). In St Luke the question and answer are both personal; in St John the question is direct, but no specific answer is recorded.

The charges in this case are all supported by some personal identification of St Peter.

If now we endeavour to realise the scene it will, I think, be clear that there were three crises, three acts of denial. The first was an isolated incident, and the others in part arose out of it. The portress made no remark when St John brought in his friend. It was not likely that she should do so. But afterwards, noticing him by the fire-light, she spoke directly to him. The slight differences in detail admit of easy explanation. St Peter's restlessness is evident throughout the scene.

After St Peter had made his denial and then withdrawn, the subject was not forgotten. The portress, when she saw him again, after some interval, on being called to the door, spoke of him to others. One and another accused him. Probably at the time he made no answer, but went away, and ventured to return to the fire. Here again a definite accusation was made and a denial followed; but the imperfect in St Mark seems to indicate that the denial was in some way repeated. The third incident is similar. Conversation had been going on. St Peter had joined in it. His dialect shewed his origin. One of the servants recognised him. Thereupon many brought the charge against him, and St Peter met his assailants at once with words fragmentarily preserved in the different narratives.

Briefly then, let the scene be realised, with all the excitement of the night trial and the universal gathering of servants and officers, and the separate details given by the different Evangelists will be found completely in harmony with the belief that there were three "denials," that is three acts of denial, of which the several writers have taken such features as seemed to be most significant for their purpose. Thus in the narrative of St John there is an evident climax in the succession of questioners: the portress, the bystanders generally, a man who claims direct knowledge.

19—24. The true reading in *v.* 24 (Annas *therefore* sent him..., ἀπέστειλεν οὖν...) involves the consequence that the examination noticed in *vv.* 19—23 is not any part of the official examination before Caiaphas and the Sanhedrin (Matt. xxvi. 57, 59—68; Mark xiv. 53, 55—65), but previous to it. The same sense is given by the simple aorist without the conjunction (*Annas sent him* ...), though less sharply. The character of the examination itself leads to the same result. The examination in St John is evidently informal and private (comp. Matt. xxvi. 57, note). The Lord Himself is questioned, but there is no mention of witnesses (Matt. xxvi. 60 ff.), no adjuration, no sentence, no sign of any legal process. If *v.* 21 implies that others were present besides the retinue of the high-priest, they took no part in the proceedings (contrast Matt. xxvi. 66 ff.). On the other hand, if Annas was really the soul of the Sadducæan faction, nothing would be more natural than that he should provide for a preliminary interrogation which might decide the course to be taken in the Sanhedrin. There might still be opposition there. As it was, the accusers were in fact driven to seek evidence from the Lord's hearers, and to confess that it was inadequate for their purpose. Thus baffled, they called forth, under the most solemn circumstances, His great confession as Messiah. It may be added that some time necessarily elapsed between the arrest of the Lord and His appearance before the formal session of the Sanhedrin. This interval gave opportunity for the private examination. The details of the various examinations, which St John has preserved, all bear upon the universal aspect of Christ's work, its openness, self-justification, truthfulness, dependence upon the divine will. It will further be noticed that as St John alone gives the private examination before Annas, so also he alone gives the private examination before Pilate. He was probably present at both.

31. The words "It is not lawful for us to put any man to death" have been interpreted to mean that the Jews could not inflict a capital sentence at this particular time (the Passover), or in the particular manner which they desired (crucifixion). But there is nothing in the context to justify such a limitation of the sense. The whole action of Pilate (comp. xix. 10) shews that the question of life and death was legally in his hands alone; and the words must be taken as a simple and direct statement that the Jews could not put to death without the governor's authority. That this was so appears from the terms which describe the procurator's power (Jos. 'Antt.' XVIII. I. I; compare also 'Antt.' XVI. 2. 4, and XVI. 6). There is also a remarkable tradition preserved in different forms in the Talmud, that the Sanhedrin left their proper place of assembly, Gazith, and sat in Chanjuth (forty years before the destruction of the temple). Now it was forbidden to condemn to death except in Gazith (see 'Avoda Zara,' ed. Edzard, pp. 61 ff. and notes).

The passages quoted from the New Testament (John viii. 3, 59, vii. 26; Acts v. 33, vii. 57 f., xxi. 27 ff.; [Acts xii. 4]) to prove that the Jews could put to death, only shew that the Roman governors were not unwilling to tolerate exceptional acts of violence. Compare also Jos. 'B. J.' VI. 2. 4, and 'Antt.' XX. 9. 1, where it appears that the execution of James the Just in the interval between the departure of one governor and the arrival of his successor was treated as a grave usurpation of power.

The question is discussed thoroughly and conclusively by Langen, in a paper in the 'Theol. Quartal-Schrift,' 1862, III. pp. 411 ff. Compare also the same writer's 'Die letzten Lebenst.' § 256.

NOTE ON THE READINGS IN *vv.* 1, 15, 24.

1. The reading of this verse offers points of singular interest. The great majority both of ancient and later authorities give χ. τῶν Κέδρων (ℵ^c BCLX, &c., most cursives, and Origen, Cyril Al., and Chrysostom) (1). Two representatives of a very ancient text (ℵ*D) give τοῦ Κεδροῦ (2). Some few copies, which generally represent a later text (AS, &c.), give τοῦ Κεδρών (3). The second and third readings may be grouped together, for both represent the Hebrew name *Kidron*, though in different forms (Κεδρόν or Κεδρός—κέδρος, *cedar*, is feminine—and Κεδρών). The first, on the other hand, substitutes for the Hebrew name a significant Greek name (*of the cedars*) which is found also in the LXX. (2 S. xv. 23; 1 K. xv. 13). No one of the versions directly supports (1), but the Memphitic reads *of the cedar tree*, while the *cedri* of some old Latin copies is uncertain. The Thebaic and the Æthiopic give *Kedros* (masc.) (2). The Vulgate, Gothic, and Armenian, give *Kedron* (3).

At first sight it seems obvious to suggest that an original reading, τοῦ Κεδρών, gave rise to two corrections on the part of ignorant scribes, who altered either the article (τῶν Κέδρων) or the noun (τοῦ Κεδροῦ), in what they supposed to be a false concord.

But the division of the authorities is most unfavourable to this view. It seems incredible that no one of the most ancient Greek texts should have preserved the true reading. On the other hand, the name Kidron was well known, and an alteration from τῶν Κέδρων to τοῦ Κεδρών would appear as plausible to a scribe as to many modern scholars.

It must be added that the use of the name χ. τῶν Κέδρων in the LXX. (1 K. xv. 13, and as a various reading in 2 S. xv. 23; 1 K. iii. 37; 2 K. xxiii. 6, 12), supplies fair evidence that it was current; and the fact that the article is not added to the similar forms, Κισσῶν (Κισῶν) and Ἀρνῶν, proves conclusively that the name was not an accidental corruption. In Josephus the name is always declined (κεδρών, -ῶνος).

Such a paronomasia as is involved in the change from *Kidron* to "of the *cedars*" is perfectly natural; and the fact that cedars were found on the Mount of Olives at the time (see Note on *v.* 13) gives additional likelihood to the change. It is indeed possible that the name of the Wady and of the Torrent (קִדְרוֹן = the Black) was originally derived from the "dark" trees, and not from the "dark" water.

15. The best authorities (ℵ*AB[D]) omit the article (ἄλλος, not ὁ ἄλλος), which is not expressed in A. V.

24. An overwhelming preponderance of evidence (BC*LX 1, 33, &c.) requires the insertion of *therefore* (οὖν). This reading, which presents considerable difficulty at first sight, was variously corrected: first by substituting *now* (δέ) for *therefore* (ℵ 69, &c.), and then by omitting the conjunction altogether (A and most later MSS.); and a few authorities insert the whole clause, *Annas* ... *Caiaphas*, in *v.* 13, with *therefore* or *now*.

CHAPTER XIX.

1 *Christ is scourged, crowned with thorns, and beaten.* 4 *Pilate is desirous to release him, but being overcome with the outrage of the Jews, he delivered him to be crucified.* 23 *They cast lots for his garments.* 26 *He commendeth his mother to John.* 28 *He dieth.* 31 *His side is pierced.* 38 *He is buried by Joseph and Nicodemus.*

4. xix. 1—3. *Within the Prætorium. The governor's punishment. The soldiers' mockery.*

CHAP. XIX. 1—3. The narrative of St John leaves no doubt that the "scourging" (ἐμαστίγωσεν) was inflicted by Pilate as a punishment likely to satisfy the Jews. They had only just used the ominous word "crucify" (Luke xxiii 21), though they pointed to it from the first (xviii. 31). The governor therefore thought that as he had humoured them by the release of Barabbas they might be contented with the ignominy inflicted on the alleged pretender to royalty without insisting on His death. This is distinctly brought out in Luke xxiii. 22 ("I will therefore chastise him [παιδεύσω], and let

[a] Matt. 27. 26.

THEN [a] Pilate therefore took Jesus, and scourged *him*.

2 And the soldiers platted a crown of thorns, and put *it* on his head, and they put on him a purple robe,

3 And said, Hail, King of the Jews! and they smote him with their hands.

4 Pilate therefore went forth again, and saith unto them, Behold, I bring

---

him go"). It is not however to be supposed that when Christ was condemned to be crucified the scourging was repeated. The passing references (φραγελλώσας) in St Matthew (xxvii. 26) and St Mark (xv. 15)—St Luke is silent,—though they would convey the impression that the scourging immediately preceded the crucifixion, according to the common, but not universal, custom, do not necessarily bear that meaning. There is therefore no real discrepancy between the accounts of the Synoptists and of St John. The accounts of the mockery by the soldiers are to be explained otherwise. From the narrative of St John it is evident that the Lord was insulted by the emblems of mock royalty before His condemnation. From the narrative of St Matthew it is no less evident that mockery of the same kind took place after His condemnation (Matt. xxvii. 31, *and when ... they took off ... and led ...*). St Mark is less definite as to the time, and St Luke is silent altogether about the incident. In addition to this difference as to the time, there are also some minor differences in the details of the two narratives. St Matthew and St Mark both mention emphatically "the gathering of the whole band" (Matt. xxvii. 27; Mark xv. 16); both mention the insulting homage; St Matthew mentions and St Mark implies the reed-sceptre; the outrages described in St Matthew and St Mark are greater and more varied. In a word, the scene described by St Matthew and St Mark represents a more deliberate and systematic mockery than that described by St John. It is not perhaps difficult to imagine the whole course of the mockery. The conduct of Herod (Luke xxiii. 11) probably suggested the idea of it. Pilate found it fall in with his own design to release Jesus as being too insignificant for serious treatment. The design failed. The crown and the robe were therefore removed; for it is not conceivable that any prisoner could be brought so disguised before a judge for sentence. But after the sentence was given, the men who had already entered into the spirit of the travesty made use of their opportunity to carry out the contemptuous exhibition more completely; and "the soldiers of the governor" invited "the whole band" (Matt. xxvii. 27) to join them in their fierce sport. There does not appear to be anything artificial in this interpretation of the recorded facts or inconsistent with the character of the actors. St John (as in other places) gives that which explains the origin of the proceeding.

1. *Then Pilate therefore ...*] Pilate's last appeal to the Jews (xviii. 39) had failed, and he now endeavours to save the life of Christ by inflicting such a punishment as might move His enemies to pity. This was his punishment (*Pilate took ... and scourged ...* contrasted with *v.* 6, *Take ye ... and crucify ...*). Scourging was itself part of a capital sentence, but in this case it was inflicted arbitrarily by Pilate without any formal judgment.

For an account of the punishment see Matt. xxvii. 26, note. St Matthew (xxvii. 26) and St Mark (xv. 15) refer to the scourging simply as having taken place before the Lord was given over for execution. St Luke (xxiii. 22) records Pilate's offer to inflict the punishment without saying more. St John brings the two notices into union.

Recent investigations at Jerusalem have disclosed what may have been the scene of the punishment. In a subterranean chamber, discovered by Captain Warren, on what Mr Fergusson holds to be the site of Antonia—Pilate's Prætorium—"stands a truncated column, no part of the construction, for the chamber is vaulted above the pillar, but just such a pillar as criminals would be tied to to be scourged." The chamber "cannot be later than the time of Herod" (Fergusson, 'The Temples of the Jews,' p. 176; comp. p. 242).

2. *a crown of thorns*] Comp. Matt. xxvii. 29, note. The thought is rather of the victor's wreath (as Tiberius' wreath of laurel, which was seen upon his arms: Suet. 'Tib.' c. 17) than of the royal diadem.

a purple robe] Comp. Matt. xxvii. 28, note; Mark xv. 17; and also 1 Macc. viii. 14, x. 20, 62, xi. 58, xiv. 43 f. Reference has naturally been made to Rev. xix. 13 (Isai. lxiii. 1 ff.). This blood-stained robe was the true dress of a kingly conqueror.

3. *And said*] According to the best authorities, *And* **they came unto Him and** *said*. This vivid detail does not occur in the narratives of the parallel incident. The imperfect (ἤρχοντο, Vulg. *veniebant*) gives the picture of the separate formal acts of homage rendered by the soldiers in succession.

Hail, King of the Jews] The words are evidently a mocking echo of what they had heard. Like Pilate, they ridicule the people no less than the Lord.

smote him ...] Some old versions add "on the face." This is probably the true idea. The savage blow took the place of the kiss of homage. Comp. xviii. 22.

him forth to you, that ye may know
that I find no fault in him.
5 Then came Jesus forth, wearing
the crown of thorns, and the purple
robe. And *Pilate* saith unto them,
Behold the man!
6 When the chief priests therefore and officers saw him, they cried
out, saying, Crucify *him*, crucify *him*.
Pilate saith unto them, Take ye
him, and crucify *him*: for I find no
fault in him.
7 The Jews answered him, We
have a law, and by our law he ought

---

5. *vv.* 4—7. *Without the Prætorium. Pilate: "Behold, the man." The Jews: "He made himself the Son of God."*

4. *Pilate therefore* ...] **And** *Pilate* .... According to the most probable reading the action is not so much a consequence (*therefore*) as a part of what has gone before, *v.* 1 (*Pilate therefore ... and the soldiers ... and Pilate* ...).

again] xviii. 38. Pilate had returned within the Prætorium to order the scourging.

unto them] The chief actors (xviii. 38) remain constantly present to the mind of the Evangelist, though the episode *vv.* 1—3 has interrupted the narrative.

I bring him ... that ye may know ... no fault (**charge,** *i.e.* **crime**)...] If the charge had seemed reasonable the governor would naturally have let the law take its course. That he had not done so, but brought the accused out again, was a clear proof that he held the charge against Him to be groundless. Yet with strange inconsistency he had treated Him as partly guilty in order to conciliate unrighteous accusers. But to scourge a prisoner whom he pronounced innocent seemed nothing in his eyes if he could by such means gain his end. His words therefore are an appeal at once to the sense of humanity and to the sense of justice in Christ's accusers. See also Acts xxii. 24.

forth] Up to this time Christ had been within the Prætorium, xviii. 28.

5. *Then came Jesus* ...] *Jesus* **therefore** *came* ... In obedience to the governor's will Christ follows His judge into the presence of the people. He knows all, and so knowing endures all in absolute submission.

wearing ...] Each emphatic detail is repeated (the crown *of thorns*, the *purple* robe). This array of mockery is presented as the natural dress of Christ (*φορῶν*. Comp. Matt. xi. 8; James ii. 3; Rom. xiii. 4). So He was through life the suffering King, the true Soldier.

And he (Pilate) *saith unto them*] Though the name of the Lord has intervened, Pilate is the chief actor now in the apostle's mind. Comp. *v.* 4 (*them*). Roman and Jew stand face to face before Christ; and Pilate now, as Caiaphas before (xi. 49 f.), is an unconscious prophet.

Behold, the man!] Contrast *v.* 14 "Behold, your King!" These words of half-contemptuous pity were designed to change the fierceness of the spectators into compassion. Fear alike and envy, Pilate argues, must disappear at the sight of one enduring with absolute patience such humiliation. "Behold" is an interjection and not a verb: "See, here is before you *the man*." What lies behind that phrase is unspoken and unthought. It is however natural for us to compare the Lord's prophecy as to Himself with the High Priest's appeal (Matt. xxvi. 63 ff., "*tell us whether thou be... the Son of God*"... "*Thou hast said: nevertheless I say unto you: From henceforth* (ἀπ' ἄρτι) *ye shall see the Son of man*"...).

6. *the chief priests ... and officers* (**the** *officers*) ...] The chief priests and their subordinates at once, *when they saw him*, anticipated any possible outburst of pity. They "saw" not an object of compassion, but only Him whom they had already doomed. *Therefore* they give the signal and the command to others. With "loud cries" (*ἐκραύγασαν*) they demand death, and the death of the vilest malefactor. For the first time the name of the cross is openly used. The sharp, short sentence, **Crucify, crucify**, exactly reproduces the feelings of the moment, and expresses the answer to Pilate's half measures. The thought is wholly of the punishment. (Contrast Mark xv. 13 f., "Crucify him.") Death, the death of a slave, nothing short of this, is the purpose of the accusers. All the Evangelists agree in representing the special demand for crucifixion as being made towards the end of the trial, after the offer to release a prisoner according to the custom of the feast (Matt. xxvii. 22, Mark xv. 13, Luke xxiii. 21).

Take ye him ... no fault ...] *Take him* **yourselves**...*no* **charge (crime)**... Pilate met the peremptory demand of the priests as before (ch. xviii. 31, *Take Him yourselves and ... judge* ...) by ironically referring the whole case to their own action. He will not, so he seems to say, simply ratify their decisions. They ask for crucifixion: well, let them crucify—a thing impossible—if his voice is not to be heard.

7. The Jews take up Pilate's challenge and Pilate's judgment in an unexpected manner. He had said *Take him yourselves* (λαβ. αὐ. ὑμεῖς). They answer, If you appeal to us, we have a power which we have not yet

to die, because he made himself the Son of God.

8 ¶ When Pilate therefore heard that saying, he was the more afraid;

9 And went again into the judgment hall, and saith unto Jesus, Whence art thou? But Jesus gave him no answer.

10 Then saith Pilate unto him, Speakest thou not unto me? knowest thou not that I have power to crucify thee, and have power to release thee?

11 Jesus answered, Thou couldest have no power *at all* against me, except it were given thee from above:

---

invoked. *We have a law* (ἡμεῖς ν. ἔ.) to which you are bound to give effect, whatever you may think of it, *and* **according to the law** (τὸν νόμον) *he ought to die.* The emphatic "we" answers at once to the emphatic "ye" and to the emphatic "I" of the governor.

by our law] Rather (omitting ἡμῶν), **according to the law.** Levit. xxiv. 16. Comp. Matt. xxvi. 63, 65 and notes.

made himself] cc. v. 18, x. 33, viii. 53 n. The form of expression emphasizes the heinousness of the charge. The claim was asserted in action and not only in word. Comp. *v.* 12, "maketh himself a king."

the Son of God] The absence of the article (υἱὸν θεοῦ) fixes attention upon the general character of the nature claimed (**Son of God**) as distinguished from the special personality (comp. i. 1, note). A Roman would have no distinct idea of One to whom alone the title "Son of God" truly belongs.

6. *vv.* 8—11. *Within the Prætorium. The origin of Christ untold: the origin of authority revealed.*

8. Pilate had already recognised something mysterious in the Person and charge before him (see xviii. 29, note). The fact that Christ was said to have claimed a divine origin naturally deepened the strange fear which His presence inspired: Pilate not only *was afraid*, but he *was more afraid*. Could he have ignominiously scourged one who was in some sense sent by the national divinity? A Roman at this time, when Eastern religions were making themselves felt throughout the empire, would be able to attach a real if vague meaning to the title "Son of God;" and superstition goes with unbelief. Compare Matt. xxvii. 54, where we have an obvious echo of the same words.

that saying] Rather, **this** *saying* or *word* (λόγος): *i.e.* the general charge now brought against Christ, and not the exact title itself (ῥῆμα).

9. *And went ... judgment hall ...*] *And* **he** *went* ... **palace (prætorium).** The clause marks a new scene.

Whence art thou?] The question is put in a general form. Pilate looks to the answer for the relief or the confirmation of his misgivings. This indecision of the questioner, who indirectly asks from the Lord a revelation of Himself (comp. viii. 25, x. 24), explains the silence with which he was met. That silence was fitted to lead Pilate to reflect on what he had already heard (ch. xviii. 36); and a direct answer would have been either misleading or unintelligible. Moreover, the claim of justice, which was now in question, was not in any way affected by the circumstances of the Lord's descent. Compare the parallel incident Matt. xxvii. 13 f. See also Isai. liii. 7.

10. *Then saith Pilate* (*Pilate* **therefore** *saith*) ... *Speakest thou not unto me?*] The pronoun stands with emphasis at the head of the sentence (ἐμοὶ οὐ λ.;): silence before others might have been intelligible, but Pilate was supreme. His sentence was the final voice not of a party but of the law and the government: *I have power*—rightful authority (ἐξουσία) ...

to crucify ... to release] Better, *to* **release** ... *to* **crucify** ... The alternatives are presented with the most impressive distinctness. The order in the best authorities places the motive of hope before that of fear, which seems in itself to be more natural.

11. *Jesus answered* **him**, *Thou couldest* (**wouldest**) *have ...*] The claim of Pilate to the absolute possession of right to act as he pleases leads the Lord to speak again. There was truth and error in the claim. The two required to be distinguished in order that the real relation of the civil and the theocratic powers to the death of Christ might be laid open. In the order of the world Pilate had the authority which he claimed to have. It had been given to him to exercise authority. As the representative of the Emperor his judgment was legally decisive (Rom. xiii. 1). But still his right to exercise authority was derived, not inherent. Human government is only valid as the expression of the divine will. He therefore who exercises it is responsible, whatever he may suppose, to a higher power. So far however as any immediate result was concerned Pilate acted within the scope of the "authority which it had been given to him to exercise." "**For this reason**" the High-Priest, representing the theocracy, was more guilty. Pilate was guilty in using wrongfully his civil power. The High-Priest was doubly guilty, both in using wrongfully a higher (spiritual) power

therefore he that delivered me unto
thee hath the greater sin.
12 And from thenceforth Pilate
sought to release him: but the Jews
cried out, saying, If thou let this man
go, thou art not Cæsar's friend: whosoever maketh himself a king speaketh against Cæsar.
13 ¶ When Pilate therefore heard
that saying, he brought Jesus forth,

---

and in transgressing his legitimate rules of action. He had failed to fulfil his duty and he had violated its rules. It was the privilege of his office to recognise the Messiah, and to preserve the true spiritual independence of the people. By appealing to a heathen power to execute an unjust (xi. 49 f.) sentence on Christ, he had sinned against God by unfaithfulness, as well as by unrighteousness.

given thee] It does not appear that there is (as is commonly supposed) any reference to the fact that Pilate was an unconscious instrument of the divine will. In this respect the Chief Priests were in the same position; and there was nothing in the fulfilment of the counsel of God to modify the guilt of one or the other (comp. Acts ii. 23).

That which "was given," it must be noticed, is not the authority itself, but the possession and exercise of it (ἦν δεδομένον not ἦν δεδομένη).

from above] *i.e.* from God. Comp. Rom. xiii. 1 f. The words correct Pilate's assertion of independence. The notion that the clause refers to the reference of the case from "a higher tribunal" (the Sanhedrin) to the Roman Court is wholly unnatural, though it has the confident support of Coleridge. In speaking of the source of Pilate's authority it has been rightly felt that the Lord indicates the source of His own being (*whence* ...?). He spoke of that which He knew and as One who knew (ch. iii. 11).

therefore] **for this reason**, because power is a divine trust.

he that delivered me unto thee] Caiaphas, the personal representative of "the Jews" (xviii. 30—35; comp. Matt. xxvii. 2 note). The responsibility for the act is concentrated in him. There can be no reference to Judas in the surrender to Pilate (*to thee*).

hath ... sin] xv. 22, note.

7. *vv.* 12—16. *Without the Prætorium. The double sentence on the Accused and the accusers. The Christ rejected: the Emperor chosen.*

12. *And from thenceforth...If thou let this man go...*] **Upon this** (omit *and*)...*If thou* **release** *this man... Upon this, i.e.* "in consequence of this answer" (comp. vi. 66, note), and not simply "after this." The calm majesty of the Lord's words confirmed Pilate's fears. He now actively "sought" himself to release Jesus: before he had endeavoured to lead the Jews to suggest his release.

the Jews] The national title stands out in contrast with the plea which they urge. Pilate had refused to carry out a sentence based upon Jewish opinion. The official chiefs of the theocracy convert themselves therefore into jealous guardians of the rights of the empire, and accuse Pilate of negligence. The simple acceptance of the title of "king" is, they argue, a declaration of antagonism to the one emperor. The change in the tactics of the priests is remarkable. Under ordinary circumstances a Roman governor would not have scrupled to give effect to a sentence based on a national religious law. Perhaps the accusers felt that their proceedings had been irregular, and in the face of opposition judged it better to press a political rather than a religious offence. Compare Matt. xxvii. 1 note.

cried out] According to the most probable reading (ἐκραύγασαν) the thought found expression in one loud simultaneous cry, as distinguished from the repeated cries of a multitude (ἐκραύγαζον xii. 13). See *vv.* 6, 15, xviii. 40. On each occasion St John notices the loud, decisive utterance, though this may have found echoes. Compare Mark xv. 14 (ἔκραξαν) with Matt. xxvii. 23 (ἔκραζον).

Cæsar's friend] The phrase was a title of honour frequently given to provincial governors (see Wetstein *ad loc.*, Jos. 'Antt.' XIV. 10. 2; Luke ii. 1, note); but here it is probably used in a general and not in a technical sense: "a loyal supporter of the emperor."

whosoever (literally, **every one that**) *maketh ... speaketh against ...*] *i.e.* controverts the emperor's authority, and so virtually sets himself against him in rebellion. Comp. Rom. x. 21 (Isai. lxv. 2).

It will be observed how completely the successive charges of the Jews noticed by St John correspond with the natural progress of the examination. They first bring a general accusation of "evil doing." Pilate refuses to accept their judgment. They then press the title "King of the Jews" (implied in xviii. 33) as seditious. Pilate dismisses the charge (xviii. 39). They next bring forward a religious offence against their own law. This increases Pilate's unwillingness to act (xix. 12). So lastly, letting drop the formal accusations, civil and ecclesiastical, they appeal to Pilate's own fears. In this way they obtained their end by personal motives (Acts xiii. 28, ᾐτήσαντο. Comp. Luke xxiii. 24).

13. *When Pilate therefore ... that saying* (**these words**) ...] The new plea left Pilate to choose between yielding to an indefinite sense of reverence and right, and escaping the

and sat down in the judgment seat in a place that is called the Pavement, but in the Hebrew, Gabbatha.

14 And it was the preparation of the passover, and about the sixth hour: and he saith unto the Jews, Behold your King!

15 But they cried out, Away with *him*, away with *him*, crucify him. Pilate saith unto them, Shall I crucify

---

danger of a plausible accusation at Rome, before such a man as Tiberius (Tac. 'Ann.' III. 38). If a late date be assigned to the Crucifixion, Pilate's fear at that time would have been greater, for the suspicions of Tiberius became more cruel after the fall of Sejanus, Pilate's patron (A.D. 31, Suet.'Tib.'61). It was natural therefore that his fear of the emperor overcame his fear of Christ. His misrule gave him good cause for alarm, and he could easily persuade himself that there would be real peril in neglecting the information which was laid before him. A popular outbreak might follow, even against the will of the Leader whom he believed to be innocent of violent designs. His decision therefore was taken without any further discussion.

these words] the imputation on his loyalty, the suggestion of rebellion.

brought ... forth (**without**)] After the *Ecce homo* the Lord had been taken within the Prætorium (*v.* 9). The formal sentence was given in the open court. The judgment-seat (tribunal) was placed upon a conspicuous spot, which was called in Hebrew (Aramaic) *Gabbatha*, and in Greek Lithostroton, "a pavement." The courts of the temple were paved (2 Chro. vii. 3, Jos. 'B. J.' VI. I. 8), and it is not unlikely that there was a paved platform at the head of the steps leading from the temple to Antonia (Acts xxi. 40), where Pilate's tribunal could be conveniently placed (see however note on Matt. xxvii. 2). There can be no reference under the Hebrew name, to such a portable mosaic floor as Julius Cæsar carried about with him for his judgment-seat (Suet. 'Cæs.' 46).

sat down in the judgment seat] It has been suggested that the verb (ἐκάθισεν) is transitive (I Cor. vi. 4; Eph. i. 20), and that the sense is, "Pilate placed Him (Christ) on a seat," completing in this way the scene of the "Ecce Homo," by shewing the King on His throne. At first sight the interpretation is attractive, but the action does not seem to fall in with the position of a Roman governor, and the usage of the phrase elsewhere (Acts xii. 21, xxv. 6, 17) appears to be decisive against it. St John, it may be added, never uses the verb transitively.

The absence of the article before "judgment seat," in the original (ἐπὶ βήματος, according to the true reading), probably indicates that this was an improvised and not a regular tribunal. Contrast Acts xii. 21, xxv. 6, 17. In Matt. xxvii. 19 the verb is different. Comp. Jos. 'B. J.' II. 14. 8 f

in the Hebrew] **in Hebrew**, *i.e.* the vernacular dialect. *vv.* 17, 20, v. 2, xx. 16; Rev. ix. 11, xvi. 16. The adverb is found only in these places. Comp. Acts xxi. 40, xxii. 2, xxvi. 14.

Gabbatha] There can be little doubt that this represents *Gab Baitha* (גב ביתא), "the ridge (back) of the House," *i.e.* the temple. Comp. Talm. Jerus. 'San.' f. 18 d, quoted by Wünsche.

14. *the preparation of the passover*] The day before—the "Eve" of—the Passover. See note on Matt. xxvii.

and about (**it was** *about*) *the sixth hour*] *i.e.* about 6 *a.m.* See Additional Note.

The marking of the day and hour fixes attention on the crisis of the history.

Behold, your King!] The words are spoken with bitterness. The people had refused to regard the appeal to their humanity (*v.* 5); and Pilate now implies that the wounded and mocked Prisoner is alone fit to represent them (*saith to the Jews*). At the same time, too, he may intend to remind them of the welcome which Christ had received at His entry into Jerusalem. This was the end of that enthusiasm. The priests had overawed the people.

"Behold" is here, as in *v.* 5, an interjection: "See, here is the king, of whom you spoke, and who befits you!"

15. *But they ...*] *They* **therefore.** The pronoun (ἐκεῖνοι) isolates the adversaries of the Lord, and sets them in this last scene apart from and over against Him. With one loud universal cry (ἐκραύγασαν) they disclaim all connexion with the King whom Pilate assigned to them: "Away, away with him."

Pilate, however, still presses his reproaches: *Shall* (*Must*) *I crucify your King?* The emphasis lies on the last words. From the beginning to the end the thought of kingship runs through the whole examination before Pilate.

The chief priests] There is singular force in the exact definition of the speakers here. They are not simply described as "the Jews" (xviii. 31, xix. 7), nor yet as "the chief priests and the officers" (xix. 6). The official organs of the theocracy themselves proclaim that they have abandoned the faith by which the nation had lived. The sentence "We have no king but Cæsar" (the foreign emperor) is the legitimate end of their policy, the formal abdication of the Messianic hope. The kingdom of God, in the confession of its rulers, has

your King? The chief priests answered, We have no king but Cæsar.
27. 16 [b] Then delivered he him therefore unto them to be crucified. And they took Jesus, and led *him* away.
17 And he bearing his cross went forth into a place called *the place* of a skull, which is called in the Hebrew Golgotha:
18 Where they crucified him, and two other with him, on either side one, and Jesus in the midst.

---

become the kingdom of the world. In the place of the Christ they have found the emperor. They first rejected Jesus as the Christ, and then, driven by the irony of circumstances, they rejected the Christ altogether.

16. *Then* **therefore** *he delivered* ...] There was now no longer room for delay. The end was reached. The last word had been spoken. So the zealots for the Roman empire were empowered to work their will. But Pilate pronounced no sentence himself. He simply let the chief priests have their way (comp. Matt. xxvii. 26; Mark xv. 15; Luke xxiii. 25). He had conceded a little against justice in false policy (*v.* 1), and he was driven to concede all against his will. From St Matthew it appears that he typically abjured the responsibility for the act, while the Jews took Christ's blood upon themselves (Matt. xxvii. 24, 25). So they became the real executioners, and carried out the foreign law (*he delivered Him* **up** *to them*). Yet even so their dependence was also indicated: the last clause runs not *that they should crucify* (*v.* 6), but *that he should be crucified.*

In this last issue it will be noticed that the Jews and Pilate were self-condemned of a double treason: the Jews of treason to their true king, on the plea of religion, and Pilate of treason to his office on the plea of loyalty.

III. THE END (xix. 17—42).

The record of the last scene of the Passion contains very much that is peculiar to St John: the challenging of the title (20—22), the last bequest (25—27), two words (28—30), the piercing of the side (31—37), the ministry of Nicodemus (39 f.). For a time at least St John was an eye-witness (*vv.* 26, 35).

The narrative falls into the following sections:—

1. *The Crucifixion* (17—22).
2. *The two groups of bystanders* (23—27).
3. *The fulfilment* (28—30).
4. *The two requests* (31—42).

Generally it will be observed that St John dwells on the fulfilment of the Old Covenant, on prophecies and types (*vv.* 24, 28, 36, 37), and on the Majesty of the Lord in suffering. In all the will of God and the will of Christ is seen to be accomplished.

In especial St John seems to insist on details (*v.* 29) which tended to identify the Lord with the Paschal Lamb, both as offered and as consumed.

1. *vv.* 17—22. *The Crucifixion. The two and the King. The title challenged and confirmed.*

16 b. *They* **therefore** *took* **(received)** *Jesus, and he*...] Pilate "delivered up" and the "chief priests" "received Jesus." The word (παρέλαβον) may serve to recall the phrase at the beginning of the Gospel: *His own received* (παρέλαβον) *Him not* (i. 11). The Jews received Christ from the hands of the Roman governor for death: they did not receive Him from the teaching of their own prophets for life. They "received" Him and "crucified" Him (*v.* 18), though the Roman soldiers were their instruments (*v.* 23; Matt. xxvii. 27). The act was theirs, even while they carried it out "by the hand of lawless men (*i.e.* Gentiles)" (Acts ii. 23; comp. iii. 15).

17. *bearing his cross*] Or, according to the better reading, *bearing* **the cross for himself.** From the Synoptists (Matt. xxvii. 32; Mark xv. 21; Luke xxiii. 26) it appears that on the way Simon of Cyrene (see Mark *l. c.* note) was taken either to carry or to assist in carrying the cross. This the Lord at first bore **for Himself**; and the remarkable language of St Mark (xv. 22, φέρουσιν, see note) lends countenance to the belief that He sank beneath the burden. Comp. Matt. xxvii. 31 f. notes.

Many writers from the time of Melito (Routh, 'Rell. Sacrr.' I. 122) have seen in the history of Isaac (Gen. xxii. 6) a type of this incident. Comp. xviii. 12, note.

went forth] Comp. Hebr. xiii. 12 f. This "going forth" (xviii. 1) from the city answers to the "coming in" (ch. xii. 12): the "Via dolorosa" to the line of triumph.

Golgotha] See Matt. xxvii. 33, note.

18. *they crucified*] *i.e.* the Jews, not indeed directly but acting through the Roman soldiers (*v.* 23), to whom the charge of the execution was committed. For the nature of the punishment, see Matt. xxvii. 35, note.

two other] described as "robbers" (λῃσταί, comp. ch. xviii. 40) by St Matthew (xxvii. 38, see note) and St Mark (xv. 27), and as "malefactors" (κακοῦργοι, comp. xviii. 30) by St Luke (xxiii. 32). It may have been of design that these criminals were put to death with the Lord, in order to place His

19 ¶ And Pilate wrote a title, and put *it* on the cross. And the writing was, JESUS OF NAZARETH THE KING OF THE JEWS.

20 This title then read many of the Jews: for the place where Jesus was crucified was nigh to the city: and it was written in Hebrew, *and* Greek, *and* Latin.

21 Then said the chief priests of the Jews to Pilate, Write not, The King of the Jews; but that he said, I am King of the Jews.

22 Pilate answered, What I have written I have written.

---

alleged offence of treason on a level with theirs. Comp. ch. xviii. 40, note.

in the midst] as holding the position of pre-eminence in that scene of uttermost shame. Even in suffering Christ appears as a King. St John by the addition of this clause emphasizes the thought which the other Evangelists leave to be deduced (Matt. xxvii. 38; Mark xv. 27; Luke xxiii. 33).

19. *And Pilate...title* **also**, *and...*] It was not unusual to attach to the cross the name and offence of the sufferer (see Matt. xxvii. 37, note). This St John calls by the technical Roman term "titulus" (τίτλος).

And the writing was] *And* **there was written.** It appears likely that St John has preserved exactly one of the forms of the "title" (the Greek). The other Evangelists speak of "the inscription of his accusation" (ἡ ἐπιγραφὴ τῆς αἰτίας αὐτοῦ, Mark xv. 26), "his accusation" (ἡ αἰτία αὐτοῦ, Matt. xxvii. 37), and "an inscription" (ἐπιγραφή, Luke xxiii. 38).

The facts that Pilate himself drew up the inscription and caused it to be placed (*wrote ...and placed it*) on the cross are mentioned only by St John. The act appears to have been an afterthought (ἔγραψεν δὲ καὶ τ.); or the form of expression may perhaps imply that the placing of the Lord "in the midst" was due to Pilate's direction. The form of the sentence, which throws the emphasis on "title" and not on "Pilate," is in favour of this view. In either case the Roman governor found expression to the last for the bitterness which had been called out in him by the opposition of the Jews (*vv.* 14, 15). The incidents which have been related before explain perfectly why the title was written, and how the heathen governor completed the unwilling testimony of the Jewish priest (xi. 49 f.).

20. *in Hebrew*, and *Greek*, and *Latin*] Rather, according to the best authorities, *in Hebrew*, and **in Latin**, and **in Greek**. This detail also is peculiar to St John, for the corresponding clause in Luke xxiii. 38 is an interpolation. Such multilingual inscriptions were not uncommon in the Roman provinces. The correspondence between the different texts (it may be added) was in all probability not so much verbal as substantial.

The order of the languages, according to the true reading, answers to the position which they would naturally occupy: the national dialect, the official dialect, the common dialect. These three languages gathered up the results of the religious, the social, the intellectual, preparation for Christ, and in each witness was given to His office.

21. *Then said the chief priests...*] *The chief priests ... said* **therefore** ... The place was public, and the inscription was so written as to be intelligible (perhaps) to all the visitors at the Feast. "The chief priests of the Jews" were consequently anxious to make it clear that they and all whom they represented were not compromised by the condemnation of "the King." Pilate's shaft went home. Perhaps we may see in the difference of form between the title assigned by Pilate, "The King of the Jews" (ὁ βασιλεὺς τ. 'I.), and that suggested by the priests as claimed by Jesus, "King of the Jews" (βασιλεὺς τ. 'I.), an instinctive unwillingness on their part to connect in any way the Messianic dignity—"*the* Kingship"—with Him whom they had condemned. They wished to make Him a mere ordinary usurper (comp. *v.* 12). Or it may have been that they would not acknowledge even by implication that such a title was possible, keeping, as pure secularists, to their former assertion, "We have no king but Cæsar."

the chief priests of the Jews] This unique title appears to be used here to emphasize the contrast between the faithless priests and the true King; and also to indicate that this priesthood had given way to another. Comp. ii. 6, 13, notes.

22. When there was no longer personal danger Pilate held to his purpose. The trait corresponds perfectly with his character, and the form of the answer is characteristically Roman, though it is found also in Rabbinic writings.

The account which Philo gives of the character of Pilate ('Leg. ad Caium,' § 38), "self-willed at once and implacable" (μετὰ τοῦ αὐθάδους ἀμείλικτος), illustrates St John's description. When the people besought him to remove the shields, which he had set up in Herod's palace in honour of the emperor, he was unwilling alike to undo what he had done and to gratify any popular wish. At the

27. 23 ¶ [c] Then the soldiers, when
they had crucified Jesus, took his
garments, and made four parts, to
every soldier a part; and also *his*
coat: now the coat was without seam,
‖ woven from the top throughout.
it. 24 They said therefore among
themselves, Let us not rend it, but
cast lots for it, whose it shall be:
that the scripture might be fulfilled,
which saith, [d] They parted my rai- [d] Psal. 22. 18.
ment among them, and for my ves-
ture they did cast lots. These things
therefore the soldiers did.
25 ¶ Now there stood by the cross
of Jesus his mother, and his mother's

---

same time he was greatly alarmed lest the Jews should expose to Tiberius his various acts of "corruption, outrage, robbery, insult, contumely; his indiscriminate and continuous murders; his unceasing and most vexatious cruelty."

2. *vv.* 23—27. *The bystanders. Departure seen from two points of view: (a) The soldiers: unfeeling selfishness. The last despoiling* (23, 24). *(b) The friends: waiting love. The last bequest* (25—27).

23. *Then the soldiers...]* *The soldiers* **therefore...** as carrying out in the customary manner the sentence which they had to execute (*v.* 18). St John describes in minute detail what the other Evangelists state summarily (Matt. xxvii. 35; Mark xv. 24; Luke xxiii. 34), and explains what they say of "casting lots." See Matt. xxvii. 35, note.

his garments...also **the coat**] The large, loose, outer dress with girdle, &c. (τὰ ἱμάτια), and the close-fitting inner tunic or vest (χιτών). The former could be conveniently divided, but not the latter.

four parts] Comp. Acts xii. 4 (quaternion of soldiers).

without seam] Such was the tunic of the high-priest, Jos. 'Antt.' III. 6. 4.

Chrysostom, who may write from personal knowledge, thinks that the detail is added to shew "the poorness of the Lord's garments, and that in dress, as in all other things, He followed a simple fashion."

24. *They said therefore among themselves* (**one to another**, xvi. 17)] It is easy to imagine how St John (*v.* 26) watched earnestly each act, and listened as the soldiers talked over their work.

that the scripture ...] Omit *which saith.* The central thought in the original context (Ps. xxii. 18) is that the enemies of the Lord's Anointed treated Him as already dead, and so disposed of His raiment. Part was torn asunder, part was to be worn by another. St John marks how this double appropriation of Christ's dress was brought about; and he appears to have had in mind the contrast which exists in the original between the over-clothing (בגדים) and the body-dress (לבוש), though this is obscured in the LXX. translation which he quotes. Comp. Hofmann, 'Weiss. u. Erf.' II. 144 ff.

This reference to the psalm, it may be noticed, has been inserted from this place in Matt. xxvii. 35. See note there.

my raiment] *my* **garments**. The same word is used as in *v.* 23 (ἱμάτια).

25 ff. There were others at the Cross besides the soldiers. The two groups are placed in significant contrast ("the soldiers on the one hand [οἱ μὲν οὖν στ.]" ... "on the other there were standing [εἱστήκεισαν δέ]" ...). At the very moment when His executioners fulfil the last part of their office, Christ in calm sovereignty works for others. The soldiers at their will dispose of His raiment, but He Himself, even from the Cross, determines the relationships of life.

25. *Now there stood...*] More exactly, *But there were standing* (εἱστήκεισαν, not simply *stood.* See xviii. 5, note). This group seems to have formed the more courageous part of "the many beholding from afar," mentioned by St Matthew (xxvii. 55 f., see notes), who therefore notices the three by name, though he does not record that they approached the Cross.

The text leaves room for doubt as to the number of the women mentioned. According to one interpretation, the name "Mary the wife of Clopas" is added as explanatory of the preceding phrase, "His mother's sister," so that three women only are specified: according to another interpretation, two pairs of women are distinguished, the first two not named but signified only, "His mother and His mother's sister;" and the second two plainly named, "Mary the wife of Clopas and Mary Magdalene." The former interpretation would involve the most unlikely supposition that two sisters bore the same name. The parallelism of the second interpretation is like St John's style, and is supported by other considerations. St Mark (xv. 40) mentions among those present "Mary Magdalene, and Mary the mother of James the less and of Joses, and Salome" (comp. Matt. xxvii. 56). There is no doubt as to the identity of "Mary the wife of Clopas" and "Mary the mother of James the less." It seems natural therefore to suppose that when two groups of three stand out clearly in the same connexion, in which

||Or, *Clopas.*

sister, Mary the *wife* of ||Cleophas,
and Mary Magdalene.
26 When Jesus therefore saw his
mother, and the disciple standing
by, whom he loved, he saith unto
his mother, Woman, behold thy son!
27 Then saith he to the disciple,
Behold thy mother! And from that
hour that disciple took her unto his
own *home*.
28 ¶ After this, Jesus knowing
that all things were now accomplish-

---

two persons are the same, that the third is also the same; and so that "the sister of the Lord's mother" is "Salome," "the mother of the sons of Zebedee." This near connexion of St John with the mother of the Lord helps to explain the incident which follows, as well as the general relation in which St John stood to the Lord. The omission of the name of Salome, on this supposition, falls in with St John's usage as to his brother and to himself. It may be added that the Peshito (Syriac) version distinctly adopts this view by inserting *and* before "Mary the *wife* of Clopas."

Mary the wife *of Cleophas* (**Clopas**)] This seems to be the true meaning of the elliptical phrase (M. ἡ τοῦ Κλωπᾶ). "Clopas" must then be regarded as identical with "Alphæus" (Matt. x. 3). It is commonly supposed that both forms represent the Aramaic חלפי. The form "Cleophas" (A. V.) comes from late Latin MSS. and has no Greek authority.

There is no direct ground for identifying Clopas (Κλωπᾶς) with Cleopas (Κλεόπας), mentioned in Luke xxiv. 18, and none therefore for supposing that this Mary was either his "mother" or his "wife" or his "daughter."

It will be noticed that Mary Magdalene is introduced abruptly, as well known, without any explanation.

26. *When Jesus therefore ...*] All who were present at the scene acted according to their true natures: priests (*v.* 21), soldiers (*vv.* 23, 24), Jews (*v.* 31); and so Christ fulfilled the last office of filial piety. The soldiers treated Him as already dead (*v.* 24, note), and He still exercised His royal power over the souls of men.

whom he loved] See ch. xiii. 23, note. The clause is at once an explanation of what follows, and a word of thanksgiving; of humility, not of pride.

Woman] Comp. ii. 4, note. Special earthly relationships are now at an end. For Christ the title of parentage ("Mother") is exchanged for the common title of respect (γύναι). If, as appears most likely, the "brethren" of Christ were sons of Joseph by a former marriage, and St John was the son of the sister of the Lord's mother, the difficulty which has been felt as to the charge which he received in preference to the brethren, who appear among the first believers (Acts i. 14), wholly disappears. St John was nearest to the Virgin by ties of blood. Comp. *v.* 25, note.

27. *Behold, thy mother!*] Here no title of address is used. To St John the Lord stood in the same relation as before. The absence of a vocative in this clause (Hebr. ii. 11) fixes attention on the meaning of that which was used before.

The four exclamations in this chapter, the two of Pilate, *Behold, the man!* (*v.* 5), *Behold, your King!* (*v.* 14), and these two of the Lord, *Behold, thy son! Behold, thy mother!* form a remarkable picture of what Christ is and what He reveals men to be. The word "Behold" is in each case an interjection.

And from that hour] The words are to be understood literally, but it does not follow that St John's "home" was at Jerusalem (but see note on Mark i. 20). He at once accepted and fulfilled the duties of his new sonship. The crisis of Christ's Passion ("His hour," comp. xiii. 1) closed finally His individual relation, as man, to His earthly mother. The simple connexion of the word and the deed (*and*, not *therefore*) is full of meaning. The act was not so much a consequence drawn from that which the Lord had said as something felt to be included in it. Perhaps St John conveyed the mother of the Lord at once to his own lodging, and himself returned.

unto his own home] Comp. xvi. 32, note. St John probably had some substance, Mark i. 20, note.

Nothing is known with reasonable certainty of the later life of the mother of the Lord. Epiphanius was evidently unacquainted with any accepted tradition upon the subject ('Hær.' LXXVIII. 11). He leaves it in doubt whether she accompanied St John to Asia Minor or not. But in the course of time surmises were converted into facts; and Nicaphorus Callisti († c. 1350, 'Hist. Eccles.' II. 3) relates that she lived with St John at Jerusalem for eleven years after the death of the Lord, and died there in her 59th year. The site of the "Tomb of the Virgin," just to the north of the garden of Gethsemane, is not mentioned by any traveller of the first six centuries, and the later tradition that the church there was built by Helena is certainly false. See Quaresmius, II. 240 ff.; Williams, 'Holy City,' II. 434 ff. From a passage in a Synodical Letter of the Council of Ephesus (A.D. 431, 'Conc.' III. 573, Labbe) it appears that, according to another tradition, the mother of the Lord accompanied St John to Ephesus and was buried there.

69. ed, *that the scripture might be fulfilled, saith, I thirst.
29 Now there was set a vessel full
of vinegar: and they filled a spunge
with vinegar, and put *it* upon hyssop,
and put *it* to his mouth.
30 When Jesus therefore had received the vinegar, he said, It is

---

3. *vv.* 28—30. *The work accomplished: the willing death.*

28. *After this*] The phrase is not indefinite, as "after these things," see ch. v. 1. The ministry of Christ to others was ended. Then notice is taken of His own suffering. But all thought is concentrated upon the Lord Himself, upon His words and His actions; and it may be for this reason that St John omits all mention of the three hours' darkness (Matt. xxvii. 45; Mark xv. 33).

knowing] Comp. ch. xiii. 1.

were now accomplished] **are now finished.** The A. V. loses the striking parallel between this clause "are now finished" (ἤδη τετέλεσται) and what follows, "It is finished" (τετέλεσται).

that the scripture might be fulfilled] This clause can be connected either with the words which precede ("were now accomplished that the ...") or with the words which follow ("...accomplished, that the scripture might be fulfilled, saith ..."). The stress which the Evangelist lays upon the fulfilment of prophetic words in each detail of Christ's sufferings appears to shew that the latter interpretation is correct. The "thirst," the keen expression of bodily exhaustion, was specified as part of the agony of the Servant of God (Ps. lxix. 21), and this Messiah endured to the uttermost. The incident loses its full significance unless it be regarded as one element in the foreshadowed course of the Passion. Nor is there any difficulty in the phrase "are now finished" as preceding it. The "thirst" was already felt, and the feeling included the confession of it. The fulfilment of the Scripture (it need scarcely be added) was not the object which the Lord had in view in uttering the word, but there was a necessary correspondence between His acts and the divine foreshadowing of them.

be fulfilled] *be* **accomplished, perfected.** The word used (τελειωθῇ, Vulg. *consummaretur*, for which some copies substitute the usual word πληρωθῇ) is very remarkable. It appears to mark not the isolated fulfilling of a particular trait in the scriptural picture, but the perfect completion of the whole prophetic image. This utterance of physical suffering was the last thing required that Messiah might be "made perfect" (Hebr. ii. 10, v. 7 ff.), and so the ideal of prophecy "made perfect" in Him. Or, to express the same thought otherwise, that "work" which Christ came to "make perfect" (ch. iv. 34, xvii. 4) was written in Scripture, and by the realisation of the work the Scripture was "perfected." Thus under different aspects of this word and of that which it implies, prophecy, and the earthly work of Christ, and Christ Himself, were "made perfect."

29. The act on this occasion (contrast Luke xxiii. 36) appears to have been a natural act of compassion, and not at all of mockery. The emphasis is laid upon the physical suffering of the Lord, and not upon the manner in which it was met.

Now (omit) *there was ... vessel ... vinegar*] It seems to be certain from Luke xxiii. 36 that the "vinegar" was thin sour wine, the ordinary drink of the soldiers. This may have been brought by them for their own use during the long watch. The mention of the "vessel set" is peculiar to St John.

and they filled ... and put it ...] **having therefore placed a sponge full of the vinegar upon hyssop they put it ...** St John's narrative leaves the persons undetermined. "They" may refer to the soldiers whose action has been described above, or "the Jews," who are in his mind the real agents throughout (*v.* 16). The account in St Matthew (xxvii. 48, see note) and St Mark (xv. 36), with equal vagueness, refers the action to "one of them that stood by," but since St Luke (xxiii. 36) speaks of "the soldiers" as having offered "vinegar" to the Lord at an earlier stage of His Passion, there can be little doubt that one of these, touched with awe by what had intervened, now brought in compassion the draught which had been offered in mockery before.

hyssop] In St Matthew and St Mark "a reed" is mentioned, which is probably to be distinguished from the hyssop; though the "hyssop" has been frequently identified with the caper-plant, which has stems three or four feet long. Comp. Matt. xxvii. 48, note, and the 'Dictionary of the Bible,' *s. v.*

30. *received*] The Lord, it will be noticed, asked for and received this slight refreshment, which restored natural forces, while He refused the stupefying potion which was before offered to Him. See Matt. xxvii. 34, note. He gave up life while in full possession of the powers of life.

It is finished] Comp. *v.* 28. The earthly life had been carried to its issue. Every essential point in the prophetic portraiture of Messiah had been realized (Acts xiii. 29). The last suffering for sin had been endured. The "end" of all had been gained. Nothing was left undone or unborne. The absence of a definite subject forces the reader to call up

finished: and he bowed his head, and gave up the ghost.

31 The Jews therefore, because it was the preparation, that the bodies should not remain upon the cross on the sabbath day, (for that sabbath day was an high day,) besought Pilate that their legs might be broken, and *that* they might be taken away.

32 Then came the soldiers, and

---

each work which was now brought to an end. Comp. Luke xviii. 31, xxii. 37, and the phrase of St Paul, 2 Tim. iv. 7. See Matt. xxvii. 50, note.

gave up the ghost (**His spirit**)] The death itself is described as a voluntary act (Tertull. 'Apol.' ch. 21, p. 58, "Suffixus spiritum cum verbo sponte dimisit prævento carnificis officio"). Among later writers who dwell on this idea, Augustine (*in loc.*) may be specially quoted: "Quis ita dormit quando voluerit, sicut Jesus mortuus est quando voluit? Quis ita vestem ponit quando voluerit, sicut se carne exuit quando vult? Quis ita cum voluerit abit, quomodo ille cum voluit obiit? Quanta speranda vel timenda potestas est judicantis, si apparuit tanta morientis?" In this sense the words stand in close relation with the phrase of St Paul, *He gave up Himself* (παρέδωκεν ἑαυτόν, Eph. v. 2, 25; Gal. ii. 20). Comp. 1 Pet. ii. 23, and, under another aspect, Acts vii. 59. St Luke (xxiii. 46) gives the words which the Lord used (παρατίθεμαι, Ps. xxxi. 5). Such a willing surrender of life was an exact fulfilment of what the Lord had said of Himself, ch. x. 17 f. Under these circumstances it may not be fitting to speculate on the physical cause of the Lord's death, but it has been argued that the symptoms agree with a rupture of the heart, such as might be produced by intense mental agony (Stroud, 'The physical cause of the Death of Christ,' 1847, 1871; see note on *v.* 34). In connexion with St John's language here it may be noticed that in the Apocalypse he seems to avoid the word "died" in speaking of the Lord: i. 18, ii. 8 (γενέσθαι νεκρός); yet see c. xii. 33, xi. 51. The phrases in the parallel accounts are different, Matt. xxvii. 50 (ἀφῆκεν τὸ πνεῦμα); and Mark xv. 37; Luke xxiii. 46 (ἐξέπνευσεν).

The "seven words from the Cross," which are preserved some by one Evangelist and some by another, form a whole which requires to be studied by itself. One is given by St Matthew and St Mark only. Three are peculiar to St Luke, and three to St John. The following list presents the order in which they appear to have been uttered.

(*a*) Before the darkness.

1. *Father, forgive them; for they know not what they do* (ποιοῦσιν), Luke xxiii. 34.
2. *Verily I say, To day shalt thou be with me in paradise* (Luke xxiii. 43).
3. *Woman, behold, thy son! ... Behold, thy mother!* (John xix. 26 f.).

(*β*) During the darkness: towards the close.

4. *My God, my God, why didst thou forsake me?* (Matt. xxvii. 46; Mark xv. 34).

(*γ*) At the close of the darkness.

5. *I thirst* (John xix. 28).
6. *It is finished* (John xix. 30).
7. *Father, into thy hands I commend my spirit* (Luke xxiii. 46).

The last word of the Lord which St John records is a voice of triumph. Comp. xvi. 33.

4. *vv.* 31—42. *The two requests: shame turned to honour.*

(a) *The request of the Jews. The sign of life in the crucified Lord* (*vv.* 31—37).

31—37. The main thought of this section is that of the Life of the Lord in Death. The sign of life is called out by wanton insult: the unconscious agency of enemies effects the fulfilment of the divine purpose.

The incidents are peculiar to St John. Yet see the early addition to St Matt. xxvii. 49, "But another took a spear and pierced His side, and there came out water and blood."

31. *The Jews therefore* ...] The connexion is not with that which immediately precedes, for the Jews did not yet know of Christ's death. But the narrative goes back to follow out the conduct of the chief actors in the tragedy (*vv.* 7, 20); they had wrought their will, and now they were eager to satisfy the letter of the Law: Deut. xxi. 22 f. Jos. 'B. J.' IV. 5. 2. Comp. xviii. 28.

Under any circumstances the dead bodies ought to have been removed before night; but this obligation became more urgent on the day of the Crucifixion, since that day preceded a great Festival, "the first day of unleavened bread" (Exod. xii. 16; Lev. xxiii. 7), which, according to the common view, coincided on this occasion with the weekly Sabbath (see Matt. xxvi., note), so that the day was "a great day" in itself, and by the concurrence of two "Sabbaths."

besought] Rather, **asked** (ἠρώτησαν), as for that which they might reasonably expect to be granted.

legs ... broken] This terrible punishment (σκελοκοπία, *crurifragium*) was inflicted (like crucifixion) upon slaves (Sen. 'De ira,' III. 32) and others who had incurred the anger of irresponsible masters (Suet. 'Aug.' 67; 'Tib.' 44; Sen. 'De ira,' III. 18; comp. Euseb. 'H. E.' v.

brake the legs of the first, and of the
other which was crucified with him.
33 But when they came to Jesus,
and saw that he was dead already,
they brake not his legs:
34 But one of the soldiers with
a spear pierced his side, and forthwith
came there out blood and water.
35 And he that saw *it* bare record, and his record is true: and he

---

21). It was no part of the punishment of crucifixion itself, but was inflicted in this case, and perhaps generally in Jewish crucifixions (Lact. IV. 26), in order to hasten death. Compare Lipsius, 'De cruce,' II. 14. The punishment was abolished, together with crucifixion, by the first Christian emperor Constantine (Lipsius, III. 14).

32. *Then...the soldiers*] *The soldiers* **therefore**,—to whom the carrying out of the execution had been committed—*came* from their place of guard to fulfil these new instructions.

the first ... the other ...] starting perhaps from the two sides at which they had been stationed.

34. The wantonness of the soldiers' violence was in part checked (*they brake not his legs*), *but one* of them, in order, no doubt, to learn the certainty of the Lord's death, *pierced His side.* The word which describes the wound (ἔνυξεν) is used both of a light touch (Ecclus. xxii. 19) and of a deep gash (Jos. 'B. J.' III. 7. 35). Here there is no doubt that the latter is described, both from the weapon used (λόγχῃ, Vulg. *lancea*, the long lance of a horseman) and from the object of the blow. The word is quite distinct from that used in *v.* 37 (ἐξεκέντησαν, *pierced through*, or *deeply:* 1 Chro. x. 4). The reading of the Latin Vulgate, *opened* (*aperuit*), comes from a false reading of the Greek (ἤνοιξεν for ἔνυξεν).

blood and water] It has been argued (with the greatest plausibility and authority by Dr Stroud, 'The physical cause of the Death of Christ,' ed. 2, 1871) that this is a natural phenomenon. The immediate cause of death was (it is said) a rupture of the heart, which was followed by a large effusion of blood into the pericardium. This blood, it is supposed, rapidly separated into its more solid and liquid parts (*crassamentum* and *serum*), which flowed forth in a mingled stream, when the pericardium was pierced by the spear from below. But it appears that both this and the other naturalistic explanations of the sign are not only inadequate but also inconsistent with the real facts. There is not sufficient evidence to shew that such a flow of blood and water as is described would occur under the circumstances supposed, and the separation of the blood into its constituent parts is a process of corruption, and we cannot but believe that even from the moment of death the Body of the Lord underwent the beginnings of that change which issued in the Resurrection. The issuing of the blood and water from His side must therefore be regarded as a sign of life in death. It shewed both His true humanity and (in some mysterious sense) the permanence of His human life. Though dead, dead in regard to our mortal life, the Lord yet lived; and as He hung upon the cross He was shewn openly to be the source of a double cleansing and vivifying power, which followed from His death and life.

The Sign by which this revelation was made becomes intelligible from the use of the terms "blood" and "water" elsewhere in the writings of St John. 1. "Blood" is the symbol of the natural life (comp. i. 13); and so especially of life as sacrificed; and Christ by dying provided for the communication of the virtue of His human life: vi. 53—56, xii. 24 ff. Comp. Rev. i. 5, v. 9, vii. 14. 2. "Water" is the symbol of the spiritual life (see iv. 14, iii. 5, and vii. 38; [Zech. xiv. 8]); and Christ by dying provided for the outpouring of the Spirit: xvi. 7. Comp. Rev. xxi. 6, xxii. 1, 17, [vii. 17]. The cleansing from sin and the quickening by the Spirit are both consequent on Christ's death.

Thus we are brought by this sign of "blood and water" to the ideas which underlie the two Sacraments and which are brought home to faith in and through them; and the teaching of the third and sixth chapters is placed at once in connexion with the Passion. It is through the death of Christ, and His new Life by Death, that the life of the Spirit and the support of the whole complex fulness of human life is assured to men. The symbols of the Old Covenant (Hebr. ix. 19) found their fulfilment in the New.

Comp. 1 John v. 6 ff. Lightfoot quotes a remarkable tradition from 'Shemoth R.' 122 a, based on the interpretation of Ps. lxxviii. 20 (ויזובו מים), that "Moses struck the rock twice, and first it gushed out blood and then water."

For a summary of the patristic interpretations of the passage see Additional Note.

35. See Introduction, pp. xxv. ff.

He that **hath seen** (ὁ ἑωρακώς) **hath borne witness** (μεμαρτύρηκεν, not ἐμαρτύρησεν), and his **witness** is true: and he knoweth that he saith **things that are true** that **ye also may** believe.

his **witness** *is true* (ἀληθινή)] *i.e.* it answers to the full conception of adequate testimony. Comp. viii. 16, 14 and notes.

ye] *ye* **also**, even as the apostle himself,

knoweth that he saith true, that ye
might believe.
36 For these things were done,
f Exod. 12. 46. Numb. 9. 12. Psal. 34. 20. *f* that the scripture should be fulfilled,
A bone of him shall not be broken.
37 And again another scripture
g Zech. 12. 10. saith, *g* They shall look on him whom
they pierced.
38 ¶ *h* And after this Joseph of *h* Matt. 27. 57.
Arimathæa, being a disciple of Jesus,
but secretly for fear of the Jews, besought Pilate that he might take
away the body of Jesus: and Pilate
gave *him* leave. He came therefore,
and took the body of Jesus.
39 And there came also Nico-

---

who had had the privilege of witnessing these signs of the truth of the Gospel.

believe] On this absolute use of the word see i. 7.

36. *For these things were done* (rather, **came to pass**) ...] The stress is laid upon the correspondence of the two facts with the details of type and prophecy. It was wonderful, as the events fell out, that the legs of Christ were not broken: it was further wonderful, when He had escaped this indignity, that His side was pierced. The first fact pointed the student of Scripture to the fulfilment in Jesus of the symbolism of the Law: the second to the fulfilment in Him of the promises as to the representative of Jehovah. For the two passages quoted are not to be regarded only as isolated quotations, but also as indicating the two great lines of preparatory teaching to which they severally belong.

the scripture] *i.e.* the passage of scripture. See ii. 22, note.

A bone ...] Exod. xii. 46; (Num. ix 12). Comp. 1 Cor. v. 7. The ordinance extended to the burnt-offerings (Lev. i. 6, *into his pieces*). That which was offered to God might not be arbitrarily mutilated. It was fitting that it should be brought to Him in its full strength. And conversely God preserves "the righteous" (Acts iii. 14, &c.), so that "not one of his bones is broken" (Ps. xxxiv. 20), even in his uttermost distress. The spiritual correspondence of the fact with the phrase in the Psalm should not be overlooked.

37. *They shall look* ...] Zech. xii. 10. See note. Comp. Introduction, p. xiv. "The Jews" are the subject of the whole sentence. The Crucifixion was their act (*v.* 16); and in unbelief and in belief they represent the world. It is important to notice that the prophetic vision is referred to Christ under a twofold aspect. As presented by the prophet himself, it is the vision of a Saviour late recognised by a penitent people (comp. ch. xii. 32). As applied in the Apocalypse, it is primarily the vision of one slain returning to Judgment (Rev. i. 7). Perhaps these two aspects of Christ's death are reconciled in that final Truth which lies at present beyond our sight.

pierced] *v.* 34, note.

(b) *The request of Joseph of Arimathæa. The quickening of love in disciples* (*vv.* 38—42).

38—42. Just as the last section deals with the unconscious ministry of enemies, this deals with the devoted ministry of friends. The Death of the Lord evoked in disciples that courage which had been latent during His lifetime (*secretly*, *v.* 38, *by night at the first*, *v.* 39). From this point of sight it is natural that the ministry of the women should be passed over (Matt. xxvii. 61; Mark xv. 47; Luke xxiii. 55 f.): their continued service revealed no sudden growth of love or self-sacrifice.

All the Evangelists record the request of Joseph. St John alone notices the offering and the presence of Nicodemus (*vv* 39 f.).

38. *after this*] More exactly, *after* **these things** (μετὰ ταῦτα): the phrase marks an indefinite, general, sequence and not a direct sequence (μετὰ τοῦτο, *v.* 28). Comp. vi. 1, note. The form of expression is of importance here because it shews that the Evangelist does not (as has been supposed) place the request of Joseph after the incident related in *vv.* 32 ff., but simply after the issue of the crucifixion: comp. Mark xv. 44 f.

Joseph of Arimathæa] Matt. xxvii. 57 ff. (*a rich man*); Mark xv. 43 f. (*an honourable councillor*, *i.e.* a member of the Sanhedrin); Luke xxiii. 50 f. (*a good man and just* ...). See notes on these passages.

for fear of the Jews] xii. 42, vii. 13. St Mark adds most significantly, with a clear reference to this fact: *Joseph ... went in boldly unto Pilate* ... literally, **having dared** (τολμήσας), having ventured on an act foreign to his natural temper (Mark xv. 43, note).

besought] *v.* 31, note.

take away] The permission given to Joseph is in complete harmony with the instructions given to the soldiers (*v.* 31 f., *that they might be taken away*). Joseph would be able to prefer his request after the death of the Lord (Mark xv. 44), and before the bodies were removed in the ordinary course. Thus he "took down" the Lord's Body (Mark xv. 46; Luke xxiii. 53), either assisting in or directing the act.

gave him leave] This was in accordance with Roman law except in extreme cases. See the passage quoted by Wetstein on Matt.

demus, which at the first came to Jesus by night, and brought a mixture of myrrh and aloes, about an hundred pound *weight*.

40 Then took they the body of Jesus, and wound it in linen clothes with the spices, as the manner of the Jews is to bury.

41 Now in the place where he was crucified there was a garden; and in the garden a new sepulchre, wherein was never man yet laid.

42 There laid they Jesus therefore because of the Jews' preparation *day*; for the sepulchre was nigh at hand.

---

xxvii. 58. An avaricious governor was able to sell the privilege of burial (Cic. 'Verr.' V. 45), yet Pilate did not do this (Mark xv. 45, ἐδωρήσατο): see note *in loc.* and contrast Matt. xxviii. 14. Compare also the burial of the bodies of John the Baptist (Matt. xiv. 12) and St Stephen (Acts viii. 2) by their friends.

the body of Jesus] According to the best authorities, **his** *body*.

39. *And there came also ...*] The order of the words, corresponding to that in the former clause, seems to suggest the thought that the act of Joseph gave Nicodemus courage to join him.

which...came to Jesus (*to* **him**)] iii. 1 ff., vii. 50. The addition of the words "by night" here (not in vii. 50 according to the true reading) is designed apparently to contrast this open act of reverence to Christ, done before the day had closed, with the secrecy of his first visit. The use of the phrase "at the first" probably implies at the same time that Nicodemus had come to Christ on other occasions; though it may indicate only the beginning of the Lord's ministry (comp. ch. x. 40).

and brought (**bringing**) *a mixture* (or, according to a probable reading, **a roll**) *of myrrh and aloes*] Comp. Ps. xlv. 8, "All thy garments are myrrh and aloes..." The compound was made of the gum of the myrrh tree (comp. Matt. ii. 11; 'Dict. of Bible,' *s. v.*) and a powder of the fragrant aloe wood.

The amount of the preparation ("about a hundred pound weight," that is, a hundred Roman pounds of nearly twelve ounces) has caused some needless difficulty. The intention of Nicodemus was, without doubt, to cover the Body completely with the mass of aromatics (comp. 2 Chro. xvi. 14): for this purpose the quantity was not excessive as a costly gift of devotion.

40. *Then took they ...*] *They took* **therefore** ... as uniting in the pious service.

wound (**bound**) *it in linen clothes* (**cloths**)] The exact word used (ὀθόνια) is found also in Luke xxiv. 12, a verse which appears to have been a very early addition to St Luke's Gospel. The diminutive form which is used in Greek medical writings for bandages, seems to distinguish these "swathes" in which the Body was bound from "the linen cloth" (σινδών) mentioned by the other Evangelists, in which it was "wrapped" (ἐνε-ύλιξεν as contrasted with ἔδησαν).

the manner of the Jews] as contrasted with that (*e.g.*) of the Egyptians, who removed parts of the body before embalming (Herod. II. 86 ff.). The phrase may, however, only mark the Jewish custom of embalming as contrasted with burning: comp. Tac. 'Hist.' V. 3.

to bury] Or more exactly, *to prepare for burial.* Comp. ch. xii. 7; Matt. xxvi. 12; Mark xiv. 8. The same word (ἐνταφιάζειν) is used in the LXX. for the "embalming" of Jacob (Gen. l. 2 f.). The process indicated is the simple wrapping of the dead body in swathes of linen cloth covered with thick layers of the aromatic preparation.

41. *a garden*] Comp. xviii. 1. The scene of the betrayal and the scene of the triumphant rest answer one to the other. The detail is peculiar to St John.

Josephus relates of Uzziah ('Ant.' IX. 10. 4, κήποις), and of Manasseh ('Ant.' X. 3. 2, παραδείσοις), that they were buried in their "gardens."

a new sepulchre] St Matthew adds that it belonged to Joseph (xxvii. 60, see note), and all the Synoptists notice that it was cut in the rock. The fact that "no one had ever yet been laid in it" (comp. Luke xxiii. 53) is emphasized (as it appears) to shew that the Lord was not brought into contact with corruption.

42. *There ... because ...*] The embalmment could not (according to their views) be deferred, and for this ample provision was made. But it is implied that the sepulchre in which the Lord was laid was not chosen as His final resting-place.

laid they] From another point of view it is said most naturally (Acts xiii. 29) of "the Jews and their rulers" generally, that "they placed" Christ in the tomb. It was the act of both, on the one side from the aspect of devotion and on the other from the aspect of hatred.

Jesus] Comp. xi. 11, note.

the Jews' preparation day] Comp. ii. 13, xi. 55, "the passover of the Jews;" xix. 21, "the chief priests of the Jews." This use of the term "preparation" is unfavourable to the view that it is used simply for the day of the week (Friday).

ADDITIONAL NOTES on Chap. xix.

Note on St John's reckoning of Hours.

St John mentions a definite hour of the day on four occasions:

(1) i. 39, *about the tenth hour.*
(2) iv. 6, *about the sixth hour.*
(3) iv. 52, *at the seventh hour.*
(4) xix. 14, *about the sixth hour.*

He also records this saying of the Lord, "Are there not twelve hours in the day?" (xi. 9).

The question therefore arises whether the incidents of which the time is given furnish any clue to the mode of reckoning: whether, that is, the hours were reckoned from 6 *p.m.* to 6 *a.m.* and from 6 *a.m.* to 6 *p.m.* according to the common ancient mode followed by the Jews, or from midnight to noon, and from noon to midnight, according to the modern Western mode.

The different passages will first be examined separately, in order that it may be seen how far the context helps to determine the answer.

(1) i. 39. After the mention of the hour, it is said that the disciples abode with Jesus "that day" (τὴν ἡμέραν ἐκείνην). It appears likely also that Jesus left the Baptist early in the day (i. 35 ff.). It is then scarcely conceivable that it was 4 *p.m.* (4 *a.m.* is out of the question) before He reached the place "where He abode;" and even less conceivable that the short space of the day then remaining should be called "that day," which, in fact, appears to have been full of incident. On the other hand, 10 *a.m.* suits both conditions. It is an hour by which a wayfarer would seek to have ended his journey; and it would leave practically "a day" for intercourse.

(2) iv. 6. In this case the hour marks a pause on a journey: the visit of the disciples to a town to purchase provisions; a coming of a woman to the well to draw water. It can scarcely be questioned that these three things fall in better with 6 *p.m.* than with noon. It is most unlikely that a woman would come from a distance at midday to the well, and on the other hand, evening was the usual time: Gen. xxiv. 11. It is more natural that the purchases would be made when the day's travel was over. Sychar too was at about the usual distance of a day's journey from within the borders of Judæa, and arrangements would probably be made to spend the night outside the city, which was afterwards entered by special invitation (iv. 30, 40). If the incident fell in summer (v. 1, Additional Note) there would be ample time for the conversation and the return to the city.

(3) iv. 52. The uncertainty of the site of Cana causes a little difficulty in determining the time required for the journey from Capernaum to Cana. This may however be fairly reckoned at about four or five hours. (Comp. Jos. 'Vit.' c. 17: a night journey from Cana to Tiberias.) It is then possible that the father may have planned that his journey to and from Cana should be included in one natural day, and that he did not meet his servants till after 6 *p.m.*, when they would perhaps speak of 1 *p.m.* as "yesterday, about the seventh hour" (comp. Luke xxiii. 54); though such a usage of "yesterday" appears to be distinctly at variance with St John's own usage of "day:" xx. 19 (comp. Luke xxiv. 29, 33) Still it is more likely that the words of Jesus were spoken to the nobleman at Cana in the evening at seven o'clock, when it was already too late for him to return home that night, and that he returned to Capernaum on the next morning, when his servants met him on the way. In this case, of course, the sense, and not the phrase of the servants is given.

(4) xix. 14. In this place it is admitted that the date of noon cannot be brought into harmony with the dates of St Mark (xv. 25). But if we suppose that the time approximately described was about 6.30 *a.m.* it is not difficult to fit in all the events of the trial: see p. 288.

So far then the examination of the passages themselves is decidedly favourable to the supposition that the modern Western reckoning of the hours is followed by St John. The mention of "twelve hours in the day" has no bearing on the decision one way or other; for we commonly use the same phrase though we reckon from midnight to noon.

It must however be admitted that this mode of reckoning hours was unusual in ancient times. The Romans (Mart. IV. 8) and Greeks, no less than the Jews, reckoned their *hours* from sunrise. But the Romans reckoned their civil *days* from midnight (Aul. Gell. III. 2; comp. Matt. xxvii. 19, "this day,") and not from sunrise, or from sunset (as the Jews). And there are also traces of reckoning the hours from midnight in Asia Minor. Polycarp is said ('Mart. Pol.' c. 21) to have been martyred at Smyrna "at the eighth hour." This, from the circumstances, must have been 8 *a.m.* Pionius again is said to have been martyred (at Smyrna also) at "the tenth hour," which can hardly have been 4 *p.m.*, since such exhibitions usually took place before noon. These two passages furnish a sufficient presumption that St John, in using what is the modern reckoning, followed a practice of the province in which he was living and for which he was writing.

The subject has been discussed at length by Dr Townson, 'Discourses,' pp. 215—250; and again, quite lately, with great exactness, by Mr McClellan, 'New Testament,' I. pp. 737 ff.

Note on "The Acts of Pilate."

The part which Pilate occupies in the history of the Passion attracted the attention of

Christian writers at an early time. He came to be regarded by many as the representative of the better instincts of heathendom overpowered by the relentless malice of the Jews. A large and popular literature grew up, consisting of "Acts," "Letters" and legends of the death of Pilate. Of these writings, the "Acts," which form the first part of what is known as "the Gospel of Nicodemus," are the most important and the most ancient. The "Acts" were in circulation in the middle of the second century; and the texts still preserved have, as it appears beyond all doubt, been formed, by successive revisions and interpolations, from that original. In its present shape the narrative may probably be referred to a Greek text of the 4th century. Much of it is unquestionably earlier. But even when regarded only as a late and apocryphal commentary on the records of the Gospels, it has great interest. The narrative is found in Greek and Latin copies; and a Coptic fragment also remains as old as the 5th century. All the MSS. give substantially the same outline, though the variations in detail and language are very considerable.

The narrative opens with the formal complaint of a body of Jews, headed by "Annas and Caiaphas," and including "Gamaliel" and "Alexander" (Acts iv. 6), addressed to Pilate. They accuse Jesus of saying that He is "Son of God and King," of wishing to abrogate the law, and of violating the sabbath by cures, wrought by evil arts (γόης ἐστί), and pray that He may be brought before him. Pilate orders an officer to summon Him. The officer, who had been present at the triumphal entry, spreads a robe before Him to walk on; and when Jesus enters the court, the standards bend before Him in the hands of their bearers. The same act of adoration is afterwards repeated when the Jews depute twelve of the strongest of their number to hold the standards. Pilate, in amazement, is about to rise, when the message of his wife (a proselyte, Procula) is brought to him. "See," said the Jews, "He is, as we told you, an enchanter." On this, Pilate asks Jesus, "What do these witness against Thee? Sayest Thou nothing?" Jesus answered, "If they had not had authority (ἐξουσία), they would have spoken nothing: each one has authority over his own mouth to speak good and bad: they themselves shall see to it." "What shall we see?" is the rejoinder. "We have seen that Thou wast born of fornication: that Thy Birth brought the slaughter of the infants at Bethlehem: that Thy father and Thy mother fled in fear to Egypt." On this, certain of the Jews attest that the mother of the Lord was duly wedded to Joseph. Then follows St John xviii. 29—37, transcribed almost verbally; but Pilate's last question is not left unanswered: "Truth," Jesus saith to him, "is from heaven." Pilate saith: "Is there not truth on earth?" Jesus saith to Pilate: "Seest thou? How are they that speak the truth judged by those that have the authority upon earth?" The Jews then press the charge of blasphemy. "What shall I do to Thee?" Pilate asks of Jesus. "As it was given thee," is the answer. "How given?" Jesus saith to him: "Moses and the prophets prophesied of my Death and Resurrection." On this, when Pilate charges the Jews to inflict the punishment which is due, they answer, "We wish Him to be crucified." This demand leads to the most remarkable addition to the Gospel narrative. A number of the disciples, Nicodemus, the paralytic of Bethesda, a blind man, a leper, the woman who had the issue of blood (Veronica), and others, plead for the Saviour who had healed them.

Pilate therefore again seeks to set Christ free, but is finally met by the cry, "We acknowledge Cæsar for our king, not Jesus. The Magi brought gifts to Him as a king, but Herod sought to kill Him." "Is this He," he then asks, "whom Herod sought?" And when he hears that He is, he washes his hands, places the guilt upon the accusers, and gives his sentence: "Thy nation hath proved Thee to be king, I therefore pronounce that Thou be scourged and then crucified in the garden where Thou wast taken; and that two malefactors, Dysmas and Gestas, be crucified with Thee."

It is needless to pursue the narrative further, or to dwell upon the strange contrast which it offers to the Gospels. The thought of Pilate as the executor of the divine will which runs through it finds its most remarkable expression in an account of his execution by the order of "the Emperor." After he had ended a prayer to the Lord for pardon, a voice came from heaven, saying, "All the generations and the families of the Gentiles shall bless thee, because under thee (ἐπὶ σοῦ) were fulfilled all these things that were spoken by the prophets about me; and thou too hast to appear as my witness at my second coming, when I shall judge the twelve tribes of Israel and those that confessed not to my name" ('Parad. Pil.' § 10).

The texts of the different copies of the "Acts" and other writings are given most completely by Tischendorf in his 'Evangelia Apocrypha,' 203 ff. Thilo has given an elaborate commentary on the *Evangelium Nicodemi* in his 'Codex Apocryphus N. T.' I. 490 ff., and his 'Prolegomena,' § 8 pp. cxviii. ff., give a very full literary history of the book. Tischendorf has published a slight essay on the relation of the Acts to the Gospels ('Pilati circa Christum judicio'...1855), and the date and composition of the book have been discussed by Lipsius (1871) after other German scholars. "The Gospel of Nicodemus" was translated into Anglo-Saxon; and it was repeatedly printed in English in the sixteenth century.

ON THE PATRISTIC INTERPRETATION OF XIX. 34.

The patristic interpretation of ch. xix. 34 offers an instructive example of the method and characteristics of ancient commentators. It will therefore be worth while to quote at some length without further discussion the views of the Greek and Latin fathers upon the passage. The reader will judge how far there is any general consent between the different writers or any clear independence of judgment in dealing with the original text.

I. GREEK FATHERS:

The earliest writer[1] who distinctly refers to the passage is CLAUDIUS APOLLINARIS (c. 170 A.D.).

Apollinaris speaks of the Lord as Him "who had His holy side pierced (ἐκκεντηθεὶς, John xix. 37), who poured forth from His side the two elements that again purify (τὰ δύο πάλιν καθάρσια), water and blood (the order is changed), word and spirit..." (Routh, 'Rell.' I. 161). The introduction of the word "again" appears to connect the water and the blood with the use of water and blood under the old Covenant. As to the deeper meaning of the sign, Apollinaris, according to the most probable view, interprets it of the word of the gospel (λόγος), and of the sanctification of the spirit (πνεῦμα), that is of the historic and of the inward testimony. There may be also a further but obscure reference to the human and divine natures of the Lord.

ORIGEN in two places dwells upon the phenomenon as a divine sign. "In the case of all other dead bodies," he writes, "the blood is coagulated, and pure water does not flow from them. But in the case of Jesus the marvel in His dead body was that even in the dead body there was blood and water poured forth from His sides" ('c. Cels.' II. c. 36; cf. c. 69.).

"How great," he writes again, "was His mercy that for our salvation He not only was made Flesh, but descended even to the dead, and in death itself has the marks of the living. For water and blood came forth from His side" ('Comm. in Thess.' IV. 15, quoted by Jerome 'Ep. ad Minerv. et Alex.' § 10, if indeed the quotation from Origen extends so far. In a fragment of his commentary on the Galatians [V. 268 ed. Lommatzsch] he treats the sign as a proof of the reality of the Lord's body).

[1] A passage quoted by Clement from a Valentinian writer ('Excc. ex Theod.' § 61) must be excepted, in which the issuing of the blood and water is interpreted of the expulsion of the passions from the Body of the Lord. Irenæus alludes to the "mixed cup" (V. 2. 3; [IV. 33. 2]), but without any reference to St John. In another early writing, the 'Letter of the Churches of Vienne and Lyons' (Euseb. 'H. E.' V. 1), the effusion of water appears to be connected with ch. vii. 38.

EUSEBIUS OF CÆSARÆA ('Dem. Ev.' X. 8, p. 504) treats the passage as a fulfilment of Ps. xxii. 14, "I am poured out like water," without dwelling further upon it.

CYRIL OF JERUSALEM applies the twofold issue to the two baptisms of blood and water ('Cat.' III. 10): "The Saviour redeeming the world through the cross, being pierced in His side, brought forth (ἐξήγαγεν) blood and water, in order that some in seasons of peace may be baptized in water, others in seasons of persecution may be baptized in their own blood (ἐν οἰκείοις αἵμασιν, the blood of their death)."

CHRYSOSTOM ('Hom.' LXXXV. *in loc.*) interprets the fact of the two sacraments: "Not without a purpose (ἁπλῶς) or by chance did those springs come forth, but because the Church consisteth of these two together (ἐξ ἀμφοτέρων τούτων συνέστηκε). And those that are initiated know it, being regenerate by water (ἀναγεννώμενοι) and nourished (τρεφόμενοι) by the Blood and Flesh. Hence the Sacraments (τὰ μυστήρια) take their beginning; in order that when thou drawest near to the awful Cup thou mayest so approach, as drinking from the very Side."

CYRIL OF ALEXANDRIA (*ad loc.*) thinks that "God appointed the fact as an image and firstfruits, so to speak, of the Mystic Blessing (Εὐλογία; see Suicer, *s.v.*) and Holy Baptism. For Holy Baptism is really of Christ and from Christ; and the power of the Mystic Blessing springs (ἀνέφυ) for us out of the Holy Flesh."

The recently discovered work of MACARIUS MAGNES has an interesting note on the passage, though the text is unhappily corrupt: "One of the soldiers pierced the side... in order that when blood flowed and water in a gushing stream, by the blood they may be delivered who occupied the place of captivity, and by the water they may be washed who bear the stripes of sins. Certainly this hath been done not without a purpose, but of Providence, as though the divine forethought laid down that it should come to pass; for since [from the side came the origin of sin] it was necessary that from the side should flow the source of salvation: from the side came the sting (ἡ πληγή), from the side the spring (ἡ πηγή): from the side the malady, from the side the cure..." (I. 18).

The same thoughts occur in a homily 'On the Passion' (§ 25), falsely attributed to Athanasius (IV. 186 ff., ed. Migne), as also in Apollinarius, Euthymius, Theophylact, and Tertullian, quoted below; and more particularly in a quotation from Antiochus of Ptolemais in Cramer's 'Catena,' *ad loc.*

A very remarkable note of APOLLINARIUS [of Laodicea] is given in the 'Catena' of Corderius upon the passage: "The Lord offered a side for a side: the woman [Eve] was a side, and the evil which came from here is undone (λύεται) by the Lord's Passion. For from that side proceeded the counsel which brought ruin on man; but from the holy side water is poured forth and blood, through which the world is cleansed, as we get ourselves washed of our sins, since the elements which were separated in the Law come together in Him. For there were [under the Law] sprinklings of blood for purification (πρὸς κάθαρσιν), and baptisms by water for sanctification (πρὸς ἁγνισμόν). Since therefore all things were devised beforehand in regard to Christ, the Body of the Lord furnished both these to the world, sacred blood and holy water, even when it was already dead in human fashion; for He hath in Himself great power of life."

JOHN OF DAMASCUS ('De fide,' IV. 9) gives the same interpretation: Christ "caused to flow for us from His holy and undefiled side a fountain of remission: water for regeneration and washing (ἐπίκλυσις) of sin and corruption; blood as a drink to furnish life everlasting (πότον ζωῆς ἀϊδίου πρόξενον)."

EUTHYMIUS ZIGABENUS (*ad loc.*) gives both the interpretations, that of the two baptisms and of the two sacraments. The latter is given in the words of Chrysostom and may be an interpolation. The former has some details of interest. "The event (he writes) is supernatural, and clearly shews that He who was pierced was more than man. For blood will not proceed from a dead man, though one pierce the body ten thousand times. Further, the Saviour is pierced in the side by a spear because the side of Adam was pierced by sin, that is Eve, healing the wound of (Adam's) side by the wound of (His own) side. And He causes blood and water to issue, fashioning (καινουργῶν) two baptisms, that by blood (of martyrdom), and that by water (of regeneration), and by the stream of these He washes away the stream of sin."

THEOPHYLACT (*ad loc.*) gives the interpretation of Chrysostom, adding among other things the reference to Eve, and then connects the twofold issue with "the mixed chalice:" "Let the Armenians," he says, "be ashamed who do not mix water with the wine in the Mysteries. For they do not believe, as it seems, that water also was poured forth from the side, which is the more marvellous, but only blood; and hence they do away with the greater part of the marvel; I mean that the blood is a mark that the Crucified was man, but the water that He was more than man, that He was God." Compare Binterim, 'Denkwürdigkeiten,' IV. 2, p. 55, where an opposite interpretation is quoted; and Anselm, 'Ep.' CVII.

II. LATIN FATHERS:

TERTULLIAN regarded the twofold issue as typical of the two baptisms of water and of blood. "Martyrdom," he writes, "is another baptism...whence also water and blood, the elements of both washings (*utriusque lavacri paratura*), flowed from the wound in the Lord's side" ('De Pudic.' c. XXII. p. 435).

At the same time, while he fully developes this application, he appears also to indicate a reference to the Eucharist in the mention of "the blood." "We have also a second washing (*lavacrum*), itself a distinct one (*unum et ipsum*), namely, that of blood; of which the Lord says, 'I have a baptism to be baptized with' (Luke xii. 50), when He had been already baptized. For He had come 'through water and blood,' as John wrote (1 John v. 6), to be baptized by water, to be glorified by blood. Hence to make us 'called' by water, 'chosen' by blood, He sent forth these two baptisms from the wound of His pierced side; that so those who believed on His blood might be washed with water, and those who had washed with water might also drink His blood. His [baptism of blood] is the baptism which both stands in place of (*repræsentat*) the baptism of water (*lavacrum*) when it has not been received, and restores [its blessing] when it has been lost." ('De Bapt.' c. XVI. p. 203; comp. c. IX.)

In another place he compares the death of Christ with the sleep of Adam (Gen. ii. 21 ff.), for He so died "that from the wound inflicted on His side the Church, the true Mother of the living, might be shaped." ('De An.' c. XLIII. p. 304.)

There is not, as far as I am aware, any reference to the incident in the genuine works of CYPRIAN. But in the works appended to his writings the water and blood are explained of the two baptisms ('De Singul. Apostt.' p. 392 Rig.), and more generally of the cleansing power of Christ's Passion both initially and through the whole life. ('De Pass. Chr.' p. 339.)

NOVATIAN (c. 10) sees in the sign a proof of the reality of Christ's Body.

AMBROSE starts from the main idea of Origen, and then interprets the sign generally. "After death the blood in our bodies coagulates; but from that body still incorrupt though dead the life of all flowed. For water and blood came forth: the former to wash, the latter to redeem" ('in Luc.' X. § 135).

And again: "Why water? why blood? Water to cleanse: blood to redeem. Why from the side? Because whence came the guilt, thence came the grace. The guilt was through the woman: the grace was through the Lord Jesus Christ" ('De sacram.' V. 1).

JEROME follows Tertullian in referring the

sign to the "two Baptisms." (Ep. LXIX. (ad Oceanum) § 6): "The side of Christ is wounded by the spear, and the sacraments of baptism and martyrdom are poured forth together (*pariter*)."

RUFINUS ('Comm. in Symb.' § 23) also interprets the sign of the two baptisms with the addition of some new thoughts. "This," he writes, "has a mystical meaning, for Christ had said that out of his belly shall proceed living waters (vii. 38). But He caused blood to issue also (*produxit*), which the Jews prayed to come upon themselves and upon their children. Hence He caused water to issue to wash the believing, and blood to condemn the faithless. It may also be understood to represent the two-fold grace of baptism: the one which is given by the baptism of water, the other which is sought through martyrdom by the shedding of blood: for both have the name of baptism. Further, if the question is asked why it was from the side rather than from any other member that the Lord is said to have caused water and blood to issue, I think that the woman [Eve] is indicated in the side through the rib (Gen. ii. 21, 22). And so because the fountain of sin and death issued from the first woman, who was a rib of the first Adam, the fountain of redemption and life is made to issue from the rib of the second Adam."

AUGUSTINE interprets the issue of "the two Sacraments:" "The sleep of the man" (Adam), he writes, "was the death of Christ; for when He hung lifeless on the Cross, His side was pierced by the spear, and thence flowed forth blood and water, which we know to be the sacraments, by which the Church [the antitype of Eve] is built up ('de Civ.' XXII. c. 17).

And again (*ad loc.*): "The soldier did not smite or wound, but opened (*aperuit*, according to the false reading ἤνοιξεν) Christ's side, that in some sense the door of life should be laid open there, whence the Sacraments of the Church flowed, without which there is no entrance to the life which is true life. That blood was poured out for the remission of sins: that water tempers the cup of salvation (*salutare poculum*); this gives both the laver and the cup (*potus*)."

PRUDENTIUS, with a poet's license, represents the spear-wound as piercing through the breast of Christ from right to left, as C. a Lapide understands him. From one opening (the larger) flowed the blood, from the other, the water.

"O novum cæde stupenda vulneris miraculum!
Hinc cruoris fluxit unda, lympha parte ex altera:
Lympha nempe dat lavacrum, tum corona ex sanguine est."
('Cath.' IX. 85 ff. Compare Areval's note.)

"Ipse loci (sc. cæli) est dominus, laterum cui vulnere utroque,
Hinc cruor effusus fluxit et inde latex.
Ibitis hinc, ut quisque potest, per vulnera Christi,
Evectus gladiis alter, et alter aquis."
('Peristeph.' VIII. 15 ff.)

"Trajectus per utrumque latus laticem atque cruorem
Christus agit: sanguis victoria, lympha lavacrum est."
('Dittoch.' XLII.)

LEO applies the passage to illustrate the doctrine of Christ's Manhood and Deity (Ep. XXVIII. 'ad Flav.' § 5). "When the side of the Crucified was opened (*aperto*) by the soldier's spear, let [the impugner of the true doctrine of Christ's Person] understand whence flowed the blood and the water, that the Church of God might be refreshed (*rigaretur*) both by the laver and by the cup.... 'There are three that bear witness, the spirit and the water and the blood, and these three are one:' the spirit, that is, of sanctification, and the blood of redemption, and the water of baptism, which 'three' are 'one' and remain undivided, and nothing in them is separated from its connexion; for the Catholic Church lives and advances in this faith, that neither is the manhood in Christ Jesus believed without His true divinity, nor His divinity without His true humanity."

One later comment may be added. RUPERT OF DEUTZ ('Comm. in Joh.' XIII. pp. 365 f.) explains the sign of the whole virtue of the Lord's Passion transferred to men: "We are redeemed by blood: we are washed by water... The Lord was baptized in His own Passion, and when already dead by that issue enabled us to share in His saving death... Therefore not blood only, nor water only, flowed from the Saviour's side; because the divine order of our salvation requires both. For we were not redeemed for this that He should possess us such as we were before... In order then that there might be that by which we could be washed from our sins, water, which could only wash bodily impurities, was united to blood, which is the price of our redemption, and from that union obtained virtue and power to be worthy of cooperating with the Holy Spirit to wash away the invisible impurities of sins."

CHAPTER XX.

1 *Mary cometh to the sepulchre:* 3 *so do Peter and John, ignorant of the resurrection.* 11 *Jesus appeareth to Mary Magdalene,* 19 *and to his disciples.* 24 *The incredulity, and confession of Thomas.* 30 *The scripture is sufficient to salvation.*

IV. THE NEW LIFE. (c. xx.)

1. St John's record of the Resurrection corresponds with his record of the Passion. It is not simply a history, still less an exhaustive history, but a revelation of spiritual truth through outward facts. Writing in the centre of a Christian Church to those who were familiar with the historic groundwork of the Gospel, the Evangelist recounts from his own experience just those incidents which called out in the disciples the fulness of belief triumphant over personal sorrow, and common fear, and individual doubt. Each historical character is also typical: each detail has a permanent lesson. And as related to the whole plan of the Gospel St John's narrative of the Resurrection is the counterpart and complement to his narrative of the Passion. His history of the Passion is the history of the descent of selfishness to apostacy: his history of the Resurrection is the history of the elevation of love into absolute faith. It lays open a new Life in Christ, and a new life in men.

2. The incidents recorded by more than one of the other Evangelists which are omitted by St John are:

The angel's message to the two Marys and Salome (Matt., Mark).

The appearance to two disciples, not apostles (Luke, Mark).

The last charge and promise (Matt., Mark).

3. Other incidents omitted by St John are recorded by single Evangelists:

ST MATTHEW.

The earthquake: the descent of the angel who removes the stone: the panic of the guards.

The report of the guards, and the device of the high priests (xxviii. 1 ff.).

Words at the appearance on the Galilæan mount. (Comp. Mark xvi. 15 ff.)

ST MARK.

Reproaches of the disciples for unbelief (xvi. 14).

ST LUKE.

An appearance to St Peter (xxiv. 34; comp. 1 Cor. xv. 5).

The conversation on the way to Emmaus (xxiv. 13 ff.; comp. Mark xvi. 12 f.).

Words at the meeting with the eleven and others (xxiv. 36 ff.).

The appearance before the Ascension (xxiv. 44 ff.).

Compare also Acts i. 1—12, ii. 24—33, iii. 15, v. 30 ff., x. 40 ff., 1 Cor. xv. 5—8.

The enumeration of the appearances of the Lord "raised on the third day according to the Scriptures," which is given by St Paul in this last passage, is of the deepest interest. The introduction of the phrase "he was seen" (ὤφθη) in *vv.* 5, 6, 7, 8, breaks them up into four groups, separated (as it may be reasonably concluded) in time and place.

(1) *To Peter: to the "twelve"* (Jerusalem).

(2) *To above five hundred brethren at once* (Galilee).

(3) *To James: to "all the apostles"* (Jerusalem).

(4) *To St Paul himself.*

It will be observed that St Paul says nothing of the appearance to Mary Magdalene. He is silent indeed as to all the events directly connected with the sepulchre.

The use of the phrase *he was seen* (ὤφθη) in no way limits the appearance to a vision as distinguished from a real personal manifestation of the Risen Christ. (Acts vii. 26. Comp. Acts xiii. 31.)

4. The main incidents peculiar to St John are:

The gift of the power of absolution.

The appearance on the second Lord's day.

To these must be added the incidents of ch. xxi.

That however which is most characteristic of St John here, as elsewhere, is the clear revelation of individual traits by the course of the events; St Peter, St John, Mary Magdalene, St Thomas, stand out with a distinct personality in these two last chapters.

5. While there are very great differences in the details of the several Evangelic narratives, there are also remarkable points of agreement between them, both as to the general features of the history, and as to its circumstances.

All the Evangelists concur in the following main particulars:

No description is given of the act of Resurrection.

The manifestations were made only to believers. (Contrast the account in the apocryphal "Gospel of Nicodemus.")

The manifestations were made not only to separate persons, but to companies.

They were determined by the Lord's pleasure: He shewed Himself.

They were received with hesitation at first.

No mere report was accepted.

The Revelation issued in a conviction of the presence of the Living Lord with the disciples.

There is agreement also as to several characteristic circumstances:

The visit of women to the sepulchre in the early morning was the starting-point of hope.

a Matt. 28. 1. Mark 16. 1.

THE a first *day* of the week cometh Mary Magdalene early, when
it was yet dark, unto the sepulchre,
and seeth the stone taken away from
the sepulchre.
2 Then she runneth, and cometh

The removal of the stone first raised questionings.

The revelations of angels preceded the manifestation of the Lord Himself.

The Lord revealed Himself to Mary Magdalene first.

6. It is most difficult to construct with any certainty a consecutive view of the few unconnected incidents which have been preserved. The following table gives a provisional arrangement of the facts connected with the first Easter-Day.

Approximate time.	
Just before 6 *p.m. Saturday.*	*Mary Magdalene and Mary the* [*mother*] *of James go to view the sepulchre* (Matt. xxviii. 1).
After 6 *p.m. Saturday.*	*The purchase of spices by Mary Magdalene, Mary the* [*mother*] *of James and Salome* (Mark xvi. 1).
Very early on Sunday.	*The Resurrection, followed by the earthquake, the descent of the angel, the opening of the tomb* (Matt. xxviii. 2—4).
5 *a.m.*	*Mary Magdalene, Mary the* [*mother*] *of James and Salome, probably with others, start for the sepulchre in the twilight. Mary Magdalene goes before the others, and returns at once to Peter and John* (John xx. 1 ff.).
5.30 *a.m.*	*Her companions reach the sepulchre when the sun had risen* (Mark xvi. 2). *A vision of an angel. Message to the disciples* (Matt. xxviii. 5 ff.; Mark xvi. 5 ff.).
6 *a.m.*	*Another party, among whom is Joanna, come a little later, but still in the early morning* (Luke xxiv. 1 ff.). Comp. Mark xvi. 1 note. *A vision of "two young men." Words of comfort and instruction* (Luke xxiv. 4 ff.).
6.30 *a.m.*	*The visit of Peter and John* (John xx. 3—10). *A vision of two angels to Mary Magdalene* (John xx. 11—13). *About the same time the company of women carry their tidings to the apostles* (Luke xxiv. 10 f.).
7 *a.m.*	*The Lord reveals Himself to Mary Magdalene* (John xx. 14—18; Mark xvi. 9). *Not long after He reveals Himself, as it appears, to the company of women who are returning to the sepulchre. Charge to the brethren to go to Galilee* (Matt. xxviii. 9 f.).
4—6 *p.m.*	*The appearance to the two disciples on the way to Emmaus* (Luke xxiv. 13 ff.; Mark xvi. 12).
After 4 *p.m.*	*An appearance to St Peter* (Luke xxiv. 34; comp. 1 Cor. xv. 5).
8 *p.m.*	*The appearance to the eleven and others* (Luke xxiv. 36 ff.; Mark xvi. 14; John xx. 19 ff.).

The main difficulties are due to the extreme compression of St Matthew's narrative, in which there is no clear distinction of points of time. The incidents and the spectators are brought together in a general picture. (Comp. Matt. xxviii. 9, note.)

7. It will strike the careful student that there is a remarkable order in the types of faith in the Lord's Resurrection which St John notices successively. The "beloved disciple" "believes" in consequence of a triple sign, without any manifestation of the Lord Himself (xx. 8). Mary Magdalene believes, not through sight or even through sound, but through the personal voice of love (xx. 14—16). The "disciples" believe when they see the Lord's wounds (xx. 20). St Thomas believes when his own test is offered to him (xx. 27 f.). It seems impossible to regard these slowly widening victories of love without feeling the permanent significance of their common lesson. There is however a faith higher than all these which in various degrees depended on outward experience (xx. 29).

8. The main record of St John falls into four divisions:

(1) *The actual facts. The triple sign verified* (xx. 1—9).

(2) *The revelation to personal love. The Lord transfigures devotion* (*vv.* 10—18).

(3) *The revelation to fearful disciples. The Lord gives peace and authority to His society* (*vv.* 19—23).

(4) *The revelation to the anxious questioner. The Lord gives conviction by sight and blessing to faith* (*vv.* 24—29).

The central thought of the whole is the passage from sight to faith.

After the narrative of the Resurrection is completed there follows a brief notice of the scope of the Gospel (*vv.* 30 f.).

1. *The actual facts. The triple sign verified* (*vv.* 1—9).

This section falls into two parts. The evidence of Mary Magdalene (*vv.* 1 f.), the evidence of St Peter and St John (*vv.* 3—9). Mary attests the first sign, the opened sepulchre; St Peter and St John attest the two other signs, the empty sepulchre, and the

13. to Simon Peter, and to the [b]other
1. disciple, whom Jesus loved, and saith
unto them, They have taken away
the Lord out of the sepulchre, and we
know not where they have laid him.
3 Peter therefore went forth, and
that other disciple, and came to the
sepulchre.
4 So they ran both together: and
the other disciple did outrun Peter,
and came first to the sepulchre.
5 And he stooping down, *and look-*

---

carefully ordered grave-clothes. Comp. Matt. xxviii. 1 ff.; Mark xvi. 1 ff.; Luke xxiv. 10—12.

CHAP. XX. 1. *The first day of the week*] **But on the ....** Comp. Matt. xxviii. 1, note.

Mary Magdalene] Comp. xix. 25. St Luke alone of the Evangelists mentions her before the history of the Passion, Luke viii. 2.

when it was yet dark] Mary Magdalene appears to have reached the sepulchre before the other women of her company. Comp. Matt. xxviii. 1; Mark xvi. 2, and notes. St Luke combines the varied ministry and testimony of all the women in one notice, xxiii. 55 f., xxiv. 10.

the stone ... from the sepulchre] All the Evangelists mention the removal of "the stone," and St Mark notices this especially as the sight which first attracted the attention of the visitants to the sepulchre, Mark xvi. 4. The Synoptists speak of "rolling away" (ἀποκυλίειν) the stone (comp. Tristram, 'Land of Israel,' pp. 396 f., ed. 3). The phrase used by St John is very peculiar, "taken, lifted out of" (ἠρμένον ἐκ), as filling up the opening of the sepulchre.

2. *Then she runneth ...*] *She runneth* **therefore ....** Apparently Mary Magdalene made no further search. She hastily (if rightly) concluded that the sepulchre must be empty from what she saw at a distance. The stone would not have been removed unless with the object of taking away the body. It is clear that she had no vision of angels before she returned, and received no message, as those with whom she is associated by St Mark (xvi. 1) and St Matthew (xxviii. 1).

cometh to Simon Peter] In spite of his fall, which was by this time probably known, St Peter was still regarded as one of the natural leaders among the disciples, comp. Luke xxii. 32.

the other disciple, whom Jesus loved] The word here used for *loved* (ἐφίλει, Vulg. *amabat*) is different from that used in xiii. 23, xxi. 7, 20 (ἠγάπα, Vulg. *diligebat*), and marks a personal affection (comp. xi. 3). At the same time the difference of this phrase ("the other disciple whom ...") from the corresponding phrase ("that disciple whom ...," xxi. 7) leads to the conclusion that both disciples alike are described here as objects of the same feeling. Simon Peter was one marked by the personal affection of the Lord even as St John was "the other."

The repetition of the preposition ("to Simon Peter...," "to the other...") suggests some distinction in their place of lodging. The mother of the Lord, it cannot be forgotten, was with St John.

They have taken] The rapid boldness of the conclusion is characteristic of a woman's eager nature. The subject is indefinite: it may be "the Jews" (comp. xix. 4), or it may be "those who provided the temporary resting-place" (xix. 42, comp. *v.* 15).

the Lord] For her the dead body is still "the Lord." Comp. xix. 42. For the absolute use of the term see iv. 1, note.

we know not] By the plural Mary identifies herself with those who had started on the visit with her, though in fact she had not waited till they came to the tomb. Compare *v.* 13, "I know not," in connexion with "my Lord," spoken in her solitude to (apparent) strangers.

3. The form of the sentence is singularly expressive. Peter at once takes the lead ("went forth," aorist); **the** *other disciple* attaches himself, as it were, to his decisive guidance, then both are represented on their way, *and* **they went on their way toward** (not *and came to*) *the sepulchre*. Comp. Matt. xxviii. 1, note. Compare xii. 22 for the singular, and iv. 30 for the combination of aor. and imp. See also vi. 17. For the incident compare Luke xxiv. 12, note, 24.

4. *So they ran both together*] Literally, *But they began to run* (ἔτρεχον), *the two together.* Mary is naturally forgotten in the description. St John recalls that which was most vividly impressed upon him at the time.

did outrun] Literally, *ran on in front* (προέδραμεν) *more quickly than Peter*, as the younger man; starting on suddenly (so the tense seems to imply), perhaps when he came in sight of the sepulchre.

5. *stooping down, and looking in*] The original word (παρακύπτω), which is thus paraphrased, occurs in *v.* 11 and in the parallel passage, Luke xxiv. 12, and again in 1 Pet. i. 12; James i. 25. The idea which it conveys is that of looking intently with eager desire and effort (literally *bending beside*) at that which is partially concealed. Comp. Ecclus. xiv. 23, xxi. 23; Song of Sol. ii. 9.

saw] **seeth.** The simple sight here (βλέπει) is distinguished from the intent regard (θεωρεῖ) of St Peter when he entered the sepulchre; and in this connexion it is significant

ing in, saw the linen clothes lying;
yet went he not in.
6 Then cometh Simon Peter following him, and went into the sepulchre, and seeth the linen clothes
lie,
7 And the napkin, that was about
his head, not lying with the linen
clothes, but wrapped together in a
place by itself.
8 Then went in also that other
disciple, which came first to the sepulchre, and he saw, and believed.
9 For as yet they knew not the
scripture, that he must rise again
from the dead.

---

that St John does not see "the napkin," the small cloth, lying apart.

yet went he not in] A natural feeling of awe would arrest one of the character of St John. He had already seen enough to fill his soul with anxious thoughts.

6. *Then cometh Simon Peter*] *Simon Peter* **therefore also** *cometh*, while St John still lingers outside.

went into] at once without a look or a pause.

and seeth the linen clothes lie...] *and* **he beholdeth** *the linen* **cloths** (and *v.* 7) **lying.** The abrupt change of tense marks a break in the progress of the thought. The entrance is courageously made: then follows the experience. The word *beholdeth* (θεωρεῖ, see 12, 14) expresses the earnest intent gaze of the apostle as his eye passes from point to point.

7. *the napkin*] Comp. xi. 44.

about (**upon**) *his head*] The absence of the name is noticeable. The mind of the writer is filled with the thought of Christ. Compare *v.* 15.

wrapped together in a place by itself] Literally, *apart in one place*. There were no traces of haste. The deserted tomb bore the marks of perfect calm. The grave-clothes had been carefully removed, which would be a work of time and difficulty, and laid in two separate places. It was clear therefore that the body had not been stolen by enemies; it was scarcely less clear that it had not been taken away by friends.

8. *Then* (**Therefore**) *went in also that* (**the**) *other...*] He no longer shrank from entering the grave which had been now certainly found empty. *He went in ... and saw* (εἶδε) *and believed.* All is gathered in one sentence without break or change of form (contrast *v.* 6). He "saw" what St Peter had seen, the clear signs of the removal of the body of the Lord, and "believed."

The exact interpretation of the word "believed" is difficult. It is not likely that it means simply "believed that the body had been removed as Mary Magdalene reported." Such a conclusion was rather a matter of natural and immediate inference from what he saw. The use of the word absolutely rather points to the calm patient acceptance of a mystery as yet in part inexplicable with full confidence in the divine love. The threefold sign of the stone removed, the empty sepulchre, the grave-clothes leisurely arranged, indicated something still to be more fully shewn, and the apostle waited in trustful expectation for the interpretation. Perhaps the word may have even a fuller sense, and imply that St John believed in some way that the Lord was alive. There is thus a sharp contrast between "believed" and "knew" (comp. vi. 69, note). In such a case there ought to have been no scope for faith; the fact should have been one of knowledge. If the apostles had really entered into the meaning of the Scriptures they would have known that the Life, the Resurrection, of Christ was a divine necessity for which death was a condition. But St John, like the other disciples ("they knew not"), had failed to read the lesson of the Old Testament, even by the help of the Lord's teaching. Now he is in some sense separated from them (*he believed ... they knew not*).

9. *For as yet ...*] Comp. Luke xxiv. 21; Mark xvi. 14. The belief in the Resurrection was produced in spite of the most complete unreadiness on the part of the disciples to accept it. So far from being based on a previous interpretation of scripture, the fact itself first illuminated the sense of scripture. Comp. Luke xxiv. 25, 45. The chief priests knew of the Lord's words as to His rising again, and in their fear took measures to counteract them (Matt. xxvii. 63 ff., see note), while the disciples in their love failed to recall the same words for their consolation. This contrast is a revelation of character, and will be recognised as profoundly true, if account be taken of the different conceptions which unbelievers and disciples had of the Person and of the Death and of the Resurrection of Christ.

the scripture] The reference is probably to Ps. xvi. 10. Comp. Acts ii. 24 ff., xiii. 35. The Evangelist speaks of some express testimony (ἡ γραφή, comp. xvii. 12, note), and not of the general contents of scripture (κατὰ τὰς γραφάς, 1 Cor. xv. 3 f.).

must] This divine necessity (δεῖ) is shewn to run through the last unexpected events of the Lord's earthly life; Matt. xxvi. 54; Mark viii. 31; Luke ix. 22, xvii. 25, xxii. 37, xxiv. 7, 26, 44, (46); John iii. 14, xii. 34, note; Acts i. 16. See also ii. 4 (ὥρα), note.

10 Then the disciples went away again unto their own home.

11 ¶ But Mary stood without at the sepulchre weeping: and as she wept, she stooped down, *and looked* into the sepulchre,

12 And seeth two angels in white sitting, the one at the head, and the other at the feet, where the body of Jesus had lain.

13 And they say unto her, Woman, why weepest thou? She saith unto them, Because they have taken away my Lord, and I know not where they have laid him.

14 And when she had thus said, she turned herself back, and saw Jesus standing, and knew not that it was Jesus.

15 Jesus saith unto her, Woman, why weepest thou? whom seekest thou? She, supposing him to be the

---

2. *The revelation to personal love. The Lord transfigures devotion* (*vv.* 10—18).

The details of this section are peculiar to St John. The bare fact is mentioned, Mark xvi. 9. It is significant that the first manifestation of the Risen Lord was granted to the patient watching of love. In this sense, Prov. viii. 17 found fulfilment. The late tradition (Sedul. 'Carm. Pasch.' v. 361 ff.) which represents the Lord as appearing first to His mother rests on no authority.

10. *Then the disciples went away...*] *The disciples* **therefore...**, as feeling that nothing more could be learnt upon the spot.

The angels which had been seen by the women did not appear to the apostles. Such manifestations necessarily follow the laws of a spiritual economy. Comp. *v.* 12.

11. *But Mary*] whose return has not been noticed, remained when the apostles went away: "A stronger affection riveted to the spot one of a weaker nature" (Aug.). Yet she did not venture to enter the sepulchre, even after the apostles had done so. She **continued standing** (εἱστήκει) *at the sepulchre without*, i. 35, note.

and (**so**) *as she wept, she stooped down, and looked...*] just as St John had done: *v.* 5.

12. *And seeth...the one* (**one**) *at the head, and the other* (**one**) *at the feet*] like the cherubim on the mercy-seat, between which the "Lord of hosts dwelt," Exod. xxv. 22; 1 S. iv. 4; 2 S. vi. 2; Ps. lxxx. 1, xcix. 1.

seeth] **beholdeth.** Both here and in *v.* 14 the word (θεωρεῖ) suggests the idea of a silent contemplation for a time.

two angels] Comp. *v.* 10, note. This is the only place where angels are mentioned in the narrative of the Evangelist. Comp. i. 52, xii. 29 (v. 4 is an early interpolation).

in white] Matt. xxviii. 3; Mark xvi. 5; Acts i. 10. The same elliptical phrase is used Rev. iii. 4. Comp. Matt. xvii. 2, and parallels, Rev. iii. 5, 18, iv. 4, vi. 11, vii. 9, 13, xix. 14.

13. *they say unto her*] The pronoun (ἐκεῖνοι) which is inserted here, like the name which is inserted in *v.* 15, marks the pause during which Mary regarded those before her without speaking.

Mary repeats, with two significant variations, the words which she had addressed to the apostles (*v.* 2). It is easy to understand how they were repeated in her heart again and again as the sum of all her thoughts; but she now says *My Lord* (not *the Lord*), and *I know* (not *we know*); the relation and the loss are, in this case, regarded as personal, and not as general. The familiar boldness of the words, spoken without special excitement or alarm, shews how the whole soul of the speaker was absorbed in one object.

The extreme simplicity of the narrative, it may be added, reflects something of the solemn majesty of the scene. The sentences follow without any connecting particles till *v.* 19. (Comp. c. xv.)

14. *When* (omit *And*) *she had thus said, she turned...*] as unwilling to continue a conversation which promised no help. The vision of angels makes no impression upon her. We can imagine also that she became conscious of another Presence, as we often feel the approach of a visitor without distinctly seeing or hearing him. It may be too that the angels looking towards the Lord shewed some sign of His coming.

and saw...] and **beholdeth...** Comp. *vv.* 6, 12.

knew not] She was pre-occupied with her own reflections. We see that only which we have the inward power of seeing. Till Mary was placed in something of spiritual harmony with the Lord she could not recognise Him. Comp. Luke xxiv. 16; Matt. xxviii. 17; ch. xxi. 4.

15. The first words of the Lord, His first recorded words after the Resurrection, are a repetition of the angel's words, but with an important addition. He partly interprets the grief of the mourner by asking, *Whom seekest thou?* She has lost some one (not something; i. 38).

the gardener] and therefore a friend, Matt. xxvii. 60; ch. xix. 41 f. The conjecture

gardener, saith unto him, Sir, if thou have borne him hence, tell me where thou hast laid him, and I will take him away.

16 Jesus saith unto her, Mary. She turned herself, and saith unto him, Rabboni; which is to say, Master.

17 Jesus saith unto her, Touch me not; for I am not yet ascended

---

was natural, both from the place and from the time.

if thou (emphatic; "if thou and not our enemies,") *have* (**hast**) *borne Him...Him...Him*] Mary makes no answer to the inquiry. Her heart is so full of the Person to whom it referred that she assumes that He is known to her questioner: "palam omnibus esse credit, quod a suo corde nec ad momentum recedere potest" (Bern. 'In Cant.' VII. 8). The trait is one of those direct reflections of life which mark St John's Gospel.

and I...] Love makes her strength appear to be sufficient.

16. We must suppose a short pause, during which Mary resumes her former position, and receiving no answer, becomes lost in her grief again. While she is thus lost Jesus "calleth her by name," *Mary* (Μαριάμ); and in that direct personal address awakens the true self (Luke viii. 2; Mark xvi. 9). What the word of common interest (*woman*) could not do, the word of individual sympathy does at once (comp. ch. x. 3).

She turned] once again (as *v.* 14), but this time with a clear answer of reverent recognition, *and saith unto him*, **in Hebrew**, *Rabboni*, *Master* (Teacher). Yet the title, while it reveals her devotion, reveals also the imperfection of her faith (contrast *v.* 28).

in Hebrew] The words must be added to the text. The exact term in the original text (Ἑβραϊστί) is found only in St John's Gospel and in the Apocalypse. The notice of this detail for Greek readers seems to mark clearly what was the language of the most intimate intercourse of the Lord and His disciples. Comp. Acts xxii. 2, xxvi. 14.

Rabboni (**Rabbuni**)] The word occurs also in Mark x. 51. It is strictly "my Master," but, as in Rabbi, the pronominal affix ceased to have any very distinct force. Here only is the term "Master" applied to the Lord after the Resurrection. The exact term (רַבּוֹנִי, or רַבּוּנִי) is used as a title of respect in the Targums (Gen. xxiii. 15). The interpretation "Master" (διδάσκαλε), which is added by the Evangelist, fixes the meaning, and excludes the higher sense of "the divine Lord" (רבון עלמא), which has been sometimes given to it, as if it expressed a recognition of the Lord's higher Nature. The preservation of the form is one of those little touches which stamp the Evangelist as a Jew of Palestine (Delitzsch, 'Ztschr. f. luther. Theol.' 1878, s. 7). It is said that the form preserved in the original text (*Rabbuni*), which has been lost in the Vulgate and A. V. (*Rabboni*), is "Galilæan" (Böttcher, 'Lehrb.' § 64): if this be so, the trait is more significant.

17. *Touch me not; for I am...*] The words imply, what a few copies here state by an interpolated clause, that Mary started up and ran to Christ, perhaps to clasp His feet (comp. Matt. xxviii. 9), and the exact form (μή ἅπτου) implies further that she was already clinging to Him when He spoke. Thus she expressed in word and act the strength and the failure of her love, which the Lord disciplined and raised by His answer. The reason by which the Lord checked this expression of devotion can be differently apprehended. The "for" may refer (1) to the whole sentence which follows (*I am not...your God*), or (2) only to the first clause (*I am not...Father*). In the first case the imminent, though not realised, Ascension of the Lord would be regarded as forbidding the old forms of earthly intercourse. In the second case the Ascension would be presented as the beginning and condition of a new union. The latter seems to be unquestionably the true view, and falls in with the moral circumstances of the incident. Mary substituted a knowledge of the humanity of Christ for a knowledge of His whole Person: "Quod vides hoc solum me esse putas: noli me tangere" (Aug. 'In Joh.' XXVI. 3). She thought that she could now enjoy His restored Presence as she then apprehended it. She assumed that the return to the old life exhausted the extent of her Master's victory over death. Therefore in His reply Christ said: "Do not cling to me, as if in that which falls under the senses you can know me as I am; for there is yet something beyond the outward restoration to earth which must be realised, before that fellowship towards which you reach can be established as abiding. *I am not yet ascended to* **the Father**. When that last triumph is accomplished, then you will be able to enjoy the communion which is as yet impossible ('Sic tangitur ab iis a quibus bene tangitur, ascendens ad Patrem, manens cum Patre, æqualis Patri.' Aug. *l. c.*). Meanwhile, this is the reward of thy love, that thou shalt bear the message of the coming and more glorious change to those to whom thou didst bear the tidings of what seemed to be thy loss and theirs." Comp. Bern. 'Serm. in Cant.' XXVIII. 9 f. The spiritual temper of Mary will be seen to be the exact opposite of that of

to my Father: but go to my brethren, and say unto them, I ascend unto my Father, and your Father; and *to* my God, and your God.
18 Mary Magdalene came and told the disciples that she had seen the Lord, and *that* he had spoken these things unto her.
19 ¶ [c] Then the same day at evening, being the first *day* of the

[c] Mark 16. 14.

Thomas. She is satisfied with the earthly form which she recognises. Thomas, having thought that the restoration of the earthly life was impossible, rises from the recognition of the earthly form to the fullest acknowledgment of the divine: *v.* 28.

Touch] The idea appears to be that of "holding," in the desire to retain, and not of "touching" with a view to ascertain the corporeal reality of the Presence. Under other circumstances the Lord invited the disciples to "handle" His Person; Luke xxiv. 39, *v.* 27; comp. 1 John i. 1.

my Father] The most ancient authorities omit the pronoun, reading **the Father**. The general conception of Fatherhood is given first, and this is afterwards defined and distinguished.

but go to my brethren...] The new title (Matt. xxviii. 10) follows from the use of the words "the Father." Spiritual relationships now take the place of natural relationships. Comp. xix. 26, note; Matt. xii. 48 f. The title occurs very significantly in the record of the first action of the Christian society: Acts i. 15 (*in the midst of the* **brethren**).

I ascend...] Not "I shall ascend," but "I am ascending." In one sense the change symbolized by the visible Ascension was being wrought for the apostles during the forty days, as they gradually became familiarised with the phenomena of Christ's higher Life.

The message which Mary was charged to bear was one of promise as well as of fulfilment. Christ did not say "I have risen again," as though the disciples could as yet understand the meaning of the words, but "I ascend." The end was not to be grasped yet. The Resurrection was a beginning as well as a fulfilment.

unto my Father, and your Father] He who is *the Father* is Father of Christ and Father of men in different ways; of Christ by nature, of men by grace. And just as the Lord separated Himself from men while He affirmed His true Humanity by taking to Himself the title of "the Son of Man," so here, while He affirms the true divine sonship of believers, He separates their sonship from His own. Comp. Hebr. ii. 11; Rom. viii. 29.

my God, and your God] In His perfect humanity Christ speaks of the Father as His God: Matt. xxvii. 46. Comp. Rev. iii. 2, 12 (not ii. 7).

In the epistles of St Paul the compound title "the God and Father of our Lord Jesus Christ" is not unfrequent: Rom. xv. 6; 2 Cor. i. 3, xi. 31; Eph. i. 3. Comp. 1 Cor. xv. 24.

18. *came and told*] **cometh and telleth.** The exact form of expression is remarkable: "cometh telling" (ἔρχεται...ἀγγέλλουσα), and not "having come (or coming) telleth." The emphasis is thrown on Mary's immediate departure on her mission. For this purpose she was ready to leave the Lord at once. In the best authorities her words are partly direct and partly oblique: *She...telleth*, **I have seen** *the Lord; and* **how** *that he* **said** *these things unto her.*

3. *The revelation to fearful disciples. The Lord gives peace and authority to His society* (*vv.* 19—23).

The details of this section are peculiar to St John—the closed doors, the fear of the Jews, the absence of St Thomas, the mission, the promise; but the fact of the appearance to the assembled disciples on the evening of the first Easter day is recorded by St Luke, xxiv. 36, and St Mark, xvi. 14 (ἀνακειμένοις).

The clauses in St Luke which correspond most closely with St John (Luke xxiv. 36 *b*, 40) appear to have been very early [apostolic] additions to his original text.

19. *Then the same day at evening, being the first day...*] **When therefore it was evening on that day, the first day...** The form of expression is singularly full and emphatic.

When therefore...] The appearance to Mary Magdalene was (so to speak) necessarily supplemented by an appearance to the Church. The several revelations to individuals (Luke xxiv. 31, 34) prepared the way for this manifestation to the body; and gave occasion for the gathering of the disciples. It could not but be that the tidings, which must have been spread through the company of believers, should cause many to come together, and perhaps to the "upper room" where the Last Supper was held. Comp. Acts i. 13.

on that day] that memorable day, the birthday of Christian life. Comp. i. 39 (40), v. 9, xi. 53, (xiv. 20, xvi. 23, 26), xix. 27, 31, xxi. 3; Mark iv. 35. The phrase corresponds with *that year;* xi. 49, note.

evening] Comp. Luke xxiv. 29, 33, 36. The hour was evidently late, about 8 *p.m.* Time must be allowed for the return of the disciples from Emmaus, who were not likely

week, when the doors were shut where the disciples were assembled for fear of the Jews, came Jesus and stood in the midst, and saith unto them, Peace *be* unto you.

20 And when he had so said, he shewed unto them *his* hands and his side. Then were the disciples glad, when they saw the Lord.

21 Then said Jesus to them again, Peace *be* unto you: as *my* Father hath sent me, even so send I you.

22 And when he had said this, he breathed on *them*, and saith

---

to leave Jerusalem till after the evening prayer (Acts iii. 1).

when the doors were shut] Comp. *v.* 26. The clause can only have been added to mark the miraculousness of the Lord's appearance. He came not in any ordinary, natural way (comp. Luke xxiv. 31). It is vain to speculate as to the manner in which He came. All that is set before us is that He was not bound by the present conditions of material existence which we observe. The Evangelist, it must be added, simply states the facts. He does not, as some later commentators, represent the Lord as coming through the closed doors, or entering in any definite manner.

where the disciples were (omit *assembled*)] "the eleven and they that were with them" in the words of St Luke (xxiv. 33). Though St Thomas was absent, the apostles as a body ("the eleven") were assembled.

for fear of the Jews] Comp. vii. 13. This clause explains the careful closing of the room. Rumours of the Resurrection had been spread, and it was as yet uncertain what policy the popular leaders would adopt.

Peace be unto you] This was the ordinary salutation (comp. Luke x. 5), which is still in use, but here it was employed with a peculiar force. The disciples were troubled, alarmed, fearful (comp. Luke xxiv. 37), and the Risen Lord by His Presence announced confidence and victory. Compare Gen. xliii. 23 and ch. xiv. 27, the last words spoken (and perhaps spoken in the same room) before the Lord "went out" to His Passion.

20. *when he had so said* (**said this**), *he shewed unto them his hands and his side*] Literally, according to the most ancient text, **both** *His hands and His side unto them.* There is a solemn pathos in the full form of description. St Luke notices "His hands and His feet" (xxiv. 40). St John had specially recorded the piercing of the side, and hence he naturally recalled that wound.

Then were the disciples] **The disciples therefore were** *glad*... At first "they believed not for joy" (Luke xxiv. 41); but the joy of kindled hope became only fuller when it was changed into the joy of conviction; *when they saw* (ἰδόντες, comp. xvi. 16) *the Lord*, and knew beyond all doubt (20) that it was He Himself.

the Lord] *v.* 2.

21. *Then said Jesus* (**Jesus therefore said**) *to them again*...] The necessary preparation was now completed. When doubt was overcome the new work was announced. The first "Peace" was the restoration of personal confidence: the second "Peace" was the preparation for work. Both however are equally extended to all present.

as my Father (**the Father**) *hath sent me*...] The mission of Christ is here regarded not in the point of its historical fulfilment (*sent*), but in the permanence of its effects (*hath sent*). The form of the fulfilment of Christ's mission was now to be changed, but the mission itself was still continued and still effective. The apostles were commissioned to carry on Christ's work, and not to begin a new one. Their office was an application of His office according to the needs of men. See Additional Note.

22. *breathed on them*] Comp. Gen. ii. 7 (LXX.). The same image which was used to describe the communication of the natural life, is here used to express the communication of the new, spiritual, life of re-created humanity.

The "breath" (πνεῦμα) is an emblem of the Spirit, iii. 8; and by "breathing," as Augustine observes, the Lord shewed that the Spirit was not the Spirit of the Father only but also His own.

The act is described as one (ἐνεφύσησε) and not repeated. The gift was once for all, not to individuals but to the abiding body.

on them...unto them] There is nothing to limit the pronoun to "the ten." It appears from Luke xxiv. 33, that there was a general gathering of the believers in Jerusalem (*those with them:* in *v.* 24 "the twelve" are evidently distinguished from "the disciples"). There is a Jewish legend that when Moses laid his hand on Joshua, God said, "In this world only individuals possess the gift of prophecy, but in 'the world to come' (the Messianic age) all Israelites shall be seers: Joel iii. 1" ('Midrash Tanchuma,' 65 c, quoted by Wünsche).

Receive] Literally, *Take* (λάβετε). The choice of word seems to mark the personal action of man in this reception. He is not wholly passive even in relation to the divine gift. The same word is used of "life" (x. 17 f.) and "words" (xii. 48). The phrase recurs Acts viii. 15, 17, 19, (x. 47, ἔλ. τὸ π. τὸ ἅ.). xix. 2.

unto them, Receive ye the Holy Ghost:

att. 18. 23 [d]Whose soever sins ye remit, they are remitted unto them; *and* whose soever *sins* ye retain, they are retained.

---

the Holy Ghost] Or rather, in order to express the absence of the article, *a gift of the Holy Ghost* (comp. vii. 39), even the power of the new life proceeding from the Person of the Risen Christ. The presence of this new life of humanity in the disciples communicated to them by Christ was the necessary condition for the descent of the Holy Spirit on the day of Pentecost. The Spirit which the Lord imparted to them was His Spirit, or, as it may be expressed, the Holy Spirit as dwelling in Him. By this He first quickened them, and then sent, according to His promise, the Paraclete to be with them, and to supply all power for the exercise of their different functions. The relation of the Paschal to the Pentecostal gift is therefore the relation of quickening to endowing. The one answers to the power of the Resurrection, and the other to the power of the Ascension (Godet); the one to victory and the other to sovereignty. The characteristic effect of the Pentecostal gift was shewn in the exercise of supremacy potentially universal. The characteristic effect of the Paschal gift was shewn in the new faith by which the disciples were gathered into a living society (comp. Luke xxiv. 45). All those interpretations of the words which limit them to a particular gift, as of working miracles, or of knowledge, or the like, fall completely short of the meaning which points to an endowment not occasional but perpetual. To regard the words and act as a promise only and a symbol of the future gift is wholly arbitrary and unnatural.

23. The pronouns in this case are unemphatic. The main thought which the words convey is that of the reality of the power of absolution from sin granted to the Church, and not of the particular organization through which the power is administered. There is nothing in the context, as has been seen, to shew that the gift was confined to any particular group (as the apostles) among the whole company present. The commission therefore must be regarded properly as the commission of the Christian society and not as that of the Christian ministry. (Comp. Matt. v. 13, 14.) The great mystery of the world, absolutely insoluble by thought, is that of sin; the mission of Christ was to bring salvation from sin, and the work of His Church is to apply to all that which He has gained. Christ risen was Himself the sign of the completed overthrow of death, the end of sin, and the impartment of His Life necessarily carried with it the fruit of His conquest. Thus the promise is in one sense an interpretation of the gift. The gift of the Holy Spirit finds its application in the communication or withholding of the powers of the new Life.

The promise, as being made not to one but to the society, carries with it of necessity, though this is not distinctly expressed, the character of perpetuity; the society never dies (comp. *v.* 21). In this respect the promise differs essentially from that to St Peter (Matt. xvi. 18 f., see note), which was distinctly personal. And the scope of the promise differs from that formerly given to the society (Matt. xviii. 18 f., see note), which concerns the enactment of ordinances and not the administration of that which is purely spiritual. At the same time this promise carries that forward to a higher region. As that promise gave the power of laying down the terms of fellowship, so this gives a living and abiding power to declare the fact and the conditions of forgiveness. The conditions, as interpreted by the apostolic practice, no less than by the circumstances of the case, refer to character (comp. Luke xxiv. 47). The gift, and the refusal of the gift, are regarded in relation to classes and not in relation to individuals. The use of the plural appears in some degree to indicate this (ἄν τινων, αὐτοῖς); and still more the necessity of giving to "retain" an application corresponding to that of "remit." It is impossible to contemplate an absolute individual exercise of the power of "retaining;" so far it is contrary to the scope of the passage to seek in it a direct authority for the absolute individual exercise of the "remitting." At the same time the exercise of the power must be placed in the closest connexion with the faculty of spiritual discernment consequent upon the gift of the Holy Spirit. Comp. 1 John ii. 18 ff.

remit] This is the only place in St John's Gospel where the word occurs in this connexion. Comp. 1 John i. 9, ii. 12. The use is frequent in the Synoptists.

remitted...retained] The use of the perfect in these two words (ἀφέωνται, according to the most probable reading, and κεκράτηνται) expresses the absolute efficacy of the power. No interval separates the act from the issue. There is perfect harmony, perfect coincidence, between the divine voice through the society and the divine will.

retain] hold fast, so that they may not pass away from him to whom they attach. The word (κρατεῖν) is used several times in the Apocalypse of "holding fast doctrine" and the like (ii. 13 ff., 25, iii. 11).

24 ¶ But Thomas, one of the twelve, called Didymus, was not with them when Jesus came.

25 The other disciples therefore said unto him, We have seen the Lord. But he said unto them, Except I shall see in his hands the print of the nails, and put my finger into the print of the nails, and thrust my hand into his side, I will not believe.

26 ¶ And after eight days again his disciples were within, and Thomas with them: *then* came Jesus, the doors being shut, and stood in the midst, and said, Peace *be* unto you.

27 Then saith he to Thomas, Reach hither thy finger, and behold my hands; and reach hither thy hand, and thrust *it* into my side: and be not faithless, but believing.

---

4. *The revelation to the anxious questioner. The Lord gives conviction by sight and blessing to faith* (*vv.* 24—29).

This section is entirely peculiar to St John.

24. *Thomas*] Comp. xi. 16, note.

the twelve] Comp. vi. 67, note.

was not with them] The cause of the absence of St Thomas is not expressed or hinted at. It is easy to imagine that one of his temperament (see xi. 16) would prefer to wait in solitude for some light upon the mystery of the Passion.

25. *The other disciples therefore...*] The assurance of joy was of necessity conveyed to him who had not received it; and it was given in its completest form, *We have seen the Lord*, where the absence of a pronoun in the original throws the stress upon the verb.

The reply of St Thomas reveals how he had dwelt upon the terrible details of the Passion. The wounds of the Lord are for him still gaping, as he had seen them. He must be able to reconcile that reality of death with life before he can believe. Just as before (xi. 16) he sets the most extreme case before himself and will face that. It is further to be remarked that the Lord had offered the test of touch to the disciples on the former occasion (Luke xxiv. 39, 40). It is likely therefore that St Thomas shaped his words according to what they had told him (*v.* 20, *hands*, *side*). The correspondence is full of interest.

print...print] The reading *place* for *print* (τόπον for τύπον) in the second instance is nothing more than an early and natural mistake. The repetition of the same word is significant; and the A. V. has obliterated another example of the same use by substituting, here and in *v.* 27, *thrust thy hand* for **put** (βάλω) *thy hand* in the second clause.

I will not believe] The emphatic denial (οὐ μὴ πιστεύσω, comp. vi. 37) corresponds with the temper which hopes at once and fears intensely. "Thou fool (Raca)," is a Jewish saying, "if thou hadst not seen thou wouldest not have believed: thou art a mocker" ('Baba Bathra,' 75 a, quoted by Wünsche).

26. *after eight days...*] During this interval, as far as appears, the disciples were left to ponder over and take into their hearts the facts of Easter Day. No fresh manifestations seem to have been made to them. At length therefore they were free, as the Festival and the Sabbath were over, to go to Galilee. Yet it was natural for them to look for some fresh token of hope on the first weekly return of the day of the Resurrection. Nothing is said of the time of their gathering. It may have been in the evening (*i.e.* the beginning of the Jewish day), when they were preparing for their departure from Jerusalem on the morrow. However this may have been Thomas, in spite of his unsatisfied misgivings, had not left their company. He shewed faith in act if not in thought. On the other hand the ten had not excluded him, though unconvinced, from their society.

again ... within ...] The words imply that the gathering was held in the same place and under the same circumstances as before. Yet it is perhaps not without meaning that the words "for fear of the Jews" (*v.* 19) are not repeated. The power of the new life had freed them from this, though their doors were closed. The phrase "his disciples" (*v.* 19 "the disciples"), when the Lord's name has not preceded, will be noticed. Comp. xix. 4, note.

then came Jesus] The original unconnected phrase is far more solemn: **Jesus cometh.**

27. *Then saith he ...*] By recalling St Thomas' own words the Lord shews that He was present at the very time when St Thomas was questioning His Resurrection.

behold] **see** (ἴδε, *v.* 25). One look was enough.

be not ...] Rather, "become not." Belief and unbelief both grow. St Thomas "was" not, but he "was on the way to be," faithless. And yet further the tense of the verb (μὴ γίνου) marks the process as continually going on. The transformation is regarded as present and not as a future result.

The exact correspondence of the two words "faithless," "believing," in the original (ἄπιστος, πιστός) cannot be adequately rendered in English: "unbelieving" ... "believing," and "faithless" ... "faithful," both fall short of the idea.

28 And Thomas answered and said
unto him, My Lord and my God.
29 Jesus saith unto him, Thomas,
because thou hast seen me, thou hast
believed: blessed *are* they that have
not seen, and *yet* have believed.
p. 21. 30 ¶ [e] And many other signs truly
did Jesus in the presence of his disciples, which are not written in this
book:
31 But these are written, that ye
might believe that Jesus is the Christ,
the Son of God; and that believing
ye might have life through his name.

---

28. Everything combines to shew that St Thomas did not employ the test which he had himself proposed (*e.g. hast seen*, not *hast felt*). The presence of the Lord enabled him to feel at once that what he had unconsciously desired was something more than could be assured to him by mere sensible testing. He recognised the Lord, but that was not all. So far the criterion which he imagined might have brought conviction. But he knew also that his Lord was more than man. Having set before himself distinctly the extent of his hope he was better able than others to perceive how the revelation of the Lord went beyond it. In his example it is seen that faith is not measured by sight, while it is the interpretation of actual phenomena.

And (omit) *Thomas... My Lord and my God*] The words are beyond question addressed to Christ (*saith unto him*), and cannot but be understood as a confession of belief as to His Person (comp. 'Syn. Œc.' v. Can. 12, *De tribus capitulis*) expressed in the form of an impassioned address. The discipline of self-questioning, followed by the revelation of tender compassion and divine knowledge, enabled St Thomas to rise to the loftiest view of the Lord given in the Gospels. His sublime, instantaneous confession, won from doubt, closes historically the progress of faith which St John traces. At first (ch. i. 1) the Evangelist declared his own faith: at the end he shews that this faith was gained in the actual intercourse of the disciples with Christ. The record of this confession therefore forms the appropriate close to his narrative; and the words which follow shew that the Lord accepted the declaration of His Divinity as the true expression of faith. He never speaks of Himself directly as God (comp. v. 18), but the aim of His revelation was to lead men to see God in Him.

29. *Thomas, because ...*] Omit *Thomas*. There is a power and clearness in the confession which rests on thought and vision, but the Lord shews a happier triumph. The first clause of His reply is half interrogative, half exclamatory (comp. xvi. 31). Then follows the great promise for all ages, based on the experience of the first week of the proclamation of the good tidings: *Blessed are they that* **saw not** *and yet believed*, believed not simply from the word of others but from actual experience, which told them that Christ was risen, because He was indeed with them. Report, like sight, is the occasion, and not the final stay of faith. The change of tense in the participle (πεπίστευκας ... ἰδόντες) evidently marks the statement as realised already in the Christian society. There must have been many disciples who had only heard of the appearances on Easter Day, and of these some at least had believed. Their "happiness" (μακάριοι, comp. Matt. v. 3 ff.) lay in the fact that at once they were in sympathy with the facts of the unseen order.

This last and greatest of the Beatitudes is the peculiar heritage of the later Church. Comp. 1 Pet. i. 6 ff.

The close and purpose of the record (*vv.* 30, 31).

30. The particle of connexion in this verse is difficult to express (πολλὰ μὲν οὖν ... ταῦτα δὲ ...). The Evangelist seems to say, looking back upon the representative events which he had related, crowned by the events of the Resurrection: "*So then* (οὖν), as naturally might be expected by any reader who has followed the course of my narrative, *many other signs did Jesus ... but* out of the whole sum *these are written* ..." (For the construction see Mark xvi. 19 f.; Luke iii. 18 f.; Acts viii. 4 f., and often; the μέν answers to δε in *v.* 31, and the οὖν marks the transition.) The "signs" referred to cannot be limited to those of the Risen Christ, though these illuminated and interpreted the remainder. The clause "in the presence of His disciples," however, belongs primarily to these, inasmuch as they were confined to the experience of believers. The statement is of primary importance in connexion with the scope of the Gospel. It was not St John's purpose to write a "Life" of the Lord. His work was a Gospel and not a biography.

31. *that ye might...ye might have life through*] *that ye* **may**...*ye* **may** *have life* **in**... The object of the Gospel is described under its two main aspects, intellectual and moral. It was designed to produce a two-fold conviction, and through this the enjoyment of a life-giving faith: *these things are written* in order that readers *may believe*, *that Jesus*—perfect man—*is the Christ*, the fulfiller of the hopes and promises of Israel (comp. Matt. i. 16), and also *the Son of God* (comp. Luke iii. 23, 38), the fulfiller of the destiny of mankind: and then, in virtue of this belief, held as a present power, *may have life in His name*, that is, in fellowship with Him as revealed in the fulness of His double nature. This declaration of the purpose of the Gospel corresponds most closely with the Apostle's declaration of the purpose of his Epistle, 1 John i. 3, 4. In both cases a historic message is made the spring of the highest blessing of "life," of divine "fellowship."

have life] Comp. 1 John v. 13. The general relation between the Christology of the Gospel and of the first Epistle of St John is of the highest interest and significance. In the Gospel the Evangelist shews step by step that the historic Jesus was the Christ, the Son of God (opposed to mere "flesh"); in the Epistle he re-affirms that the Christ, the Son of God, was true man (opposed to mere "spirit:" 1 John iv. 2). The correspondences and differences are equally striking.

ADDITIONAL NOTE on CHAP. XX. 21.

In this verse the tenses of the verbs (ἀπέσταλκε [not ἀπέστειλε] and πέμπω) (I.), and the difference of the verbs themselves (ἀποστέλλω—πέμπω), require to be noticed (II.).

I. The mission of Christ is sometimes (1) contemplated in the one specific fact of the Incarnation (ἀπέστειλε *aor.*); sometimes (2) it is contemplated in its abiding issues (ἀπέσταλκε, *perf.*). A study of the passages in which the two forms are severally used will bring out their exact meaning.

1. In the following passages the aorist (ἀπέστειλε) is used; iii. 17, 34, viii. 42 (in combination with the perfect ἐλήλυθα), x. 36, xi. 42, xvii. 3, 8 (with ἐξῆλθον), 18 (with ἀπέστειλα of the disciples), 21, 23, 25. In these passages there is no variation of reading. In the following passages ἀπέστειλε is unquestionably the true reading, though the variant ἀπέσταλκε occurs in some early authorities: v. 38 (with πιστεύετε), vi. 29 (with ἵνα πιστεύητε), vi. 57 (with ζῶ), vii. 29 (with εἰμί); 1 John iv. 10.

In all these cases it will be found that the exact force of the teaching lies in the actual fact of Christ's mission.

2. The perfect (ἀπέσταλκε) is far more rare. It occurs without any variation in 1 John iv. 14 (with τεθεάμεθα and μαρτυροῦμεν). It is also unquestionably the true reading in v. 36, xx. 21; 1 John iv. 9, though the variant ἀπέστειλε is found in these passages.

The use of the perfect elsewhere is sufficiently frequent to shew that it preserves its proper sense, and describes a mission which continues in its present effects. Comp. ch. v. 33, Luke iv. 18; Acts vii. 35 (read ἀπέσταλκεν σὺν χειρί), ix. 17, x. 20, xv. 27, xvi. 36; 2 Cor. xii. 17 (in connexion with ἐπλεονέκτησα, συναπέστειλα).

The combined use of the aorist and perfect in 1 John iv. 9 ff. is singularly instructive.

II. The contrast between the verbs (ἀποστέλλω, πέμπω) in the two clauses is obviously significant. Both verbs are used of the mission of the Son, and of the mission of believers, but with distinct meanings. The former (ἀποστέλλω) corresponds with the idea of our own words "despatch" and "envoy," and conveys the accessory notions of a special commission, and so far of a delegated authority in the person sent. The simple verb πέμπω marks nothing more than the immediate relation of the sender to the sent.

The passages in which ἀποστέλλω is used by St John of the Mission of the Son have been already quoted.

It is used of the mission of the disciples: iv. 38, xvii. 18. Comp. Matt. x. 5, 16, xxi. 34, 36, xxiii. 37; Mark vi. 7; Luke ix. 2, xxii. 35.

The force of the word is illustrated by the other passages in which it is found: i. 6, 19, 24, iii. 28, v. 33, vii. 32, xi. 3. These passages help to bring out the meaning of the phrase in xviii. 24, by which it is implied that the Lord was "despatched" to Caiaphas as already bearing His condemnation, and stamped with the mark of Annas.

The usage of πέμπω in St John as applied to the Mission of the Son is distinguished grammatically from that of ἀποστέλλω. Ἀποστέλλω is always used in finite tenses, and πέμπω is always used in the participial form (*e.g.* ὁ πέμψας με, ὁ πατὴρ ὁ πέμψας), though ὁ ἀποστείλας is found elsewhere: Matt. x. 40; Mark ix. 37; Luke ix. 48, x. 16.

Πέμπω is used of disciples here and in ch. xiii. 20. It is also used of the Spirit, xiv. 26, xvi. 7.

The two words appear in close connexion, i. 19, 22, 24, iv. 34, 38 (a contrast to this passage), v. 36, 37, 38, vi. 29, 38, 44, 57, vii. 28, 29. In chapters xii.—xvi. πέμπω only is used; in ch. xvii. only ἀποστέλλω, and so also in Ep. 1.

The general result of the examination of these facts seems to be that in this charge the Lord presents His own Mission as the one abiding Mission of the Father; this He fulfils through His church. His disciples receive no new commission, but carry out His. Comp. Matt. xxviii. 20; Hebr. iii. 1. They are not (in this respect) His envoys, but in a secondary degree envoys of the Father. Comp. 2 Cor. v. 20; Col. i. 24. Their work too begins with the reception of the new life (*I am sending*, not *I will send* Compare *I ascend*).

CHAPTER XXI.

1 Christ appearing again to his disciples was known of them by the great draught of fishes. 12 He dineth with them: 15 earnestly commandeth Peter to feed his lambs and sheep: 18 foretelleth him of his death: 22 rebuketh his curiosity touching John. 25 The conclusion.

AFTER these things Jesus shewed
himself again to the disciples at
the sea of Tiberias; and on this wise
shewed he *himself*.
2 There were together Simon
Peter, and Thomas called Didymus,
and Nathanael of Cana in Galilee,

EPILOGUE, ch. xxi.

This chapter is evidently an appendix to the Gospel, which is completed by ch. xx. It is impossible to suppose that it was the original design of the Evangelist to add the incidents of ch. xxi. after ch. xx. 30 f., which verses form a solemn close to his record of the great history of the conflict of faith and unbelief in the life of Christ. And the general scope of the contents of this chapter is distinct from the development of the plan which is declared to be completed in ch. xx. The manifestation of the Lord which is given in detail in it is not designed to create faith in the fact of His Resurrection, but to illustrate His action in the Society; He guides and supports and assigns their parts to His disciples.

On the other hand it is equally clear that xxi. 1—23 was written by the author of the Gospel. The style and the general character of the language alike lead to this conclusion; and there is no evidence to shew that the Gospel was published before the appendix was added to it.

The occasion of the addition is probably to be found in the circulation of the saying of the Lord as to St John (xxi. 23). The clear exposition of this saying carried with it naturally a recital of the circumstances under which it was spoken.

The contents of the chapter are peculiar to St John.

The narrative falls into two main divisions:

I. The Lord and the body of disciples. Their work: His gift (xxi. 1—14).

II. The Lord and individual disciples. His determination of their work (xxi. 15—23).

The two last verses (24, 25) contain an identification of the writer of the Gospel, and a renewed testimony (comp. xx. 30) to the infinite multiplicity of Christ's works.

1. THE LORD AND THE BODY OF DISCIPLES (1—14). This section falls into two parts:

i. The work of the disciples first wrought of their own pleasure (1—3), and then in obedience to the Lord's directions (4—11).

ii. The Lord's gift of sustenance (12—14).

i. The Work of the Disciples (1—11).

CHAP. XXI. 1. *After these things*] Comp. v. 1, vi. 1. Such an indefinite mark of time is not unsuitable to the character of this narrative as an appendix to the original plan of the Gospel.

shewed himself] Rather, **manifested** *himself*. The same word (φανερόω) is used of the appearances of the Lord after the Resurrection in the conclusion of St Mark's Gospel, xvi. 12, 14. The active form, which occurs in this verse only (contrast *v.* 14), marks the appearance as depending on the Lord's will. He was so pleased to reveal Himself. Comp. ii. 11, vii. 4. This special manifestation of the Risen Christ is part of the whole "manifestation" through the Incarnation (ch. i. 31; 1 John i. 2, iii. 5, 8; comp. 1 Tim. iii. 16; 1 Pet. i. 20) which is consummated at the Return (1 John ii. 28, iii. 2; comp. Col. iii. 4; 1 Pet. v. 4).

again] The word does not exclude the idea of other intervening manifestations, but places the narrative which follows as parallel with the former narratives in being a manifestation to "the disciples" (xx. 19, 24 f.), that is, in all probability, the apostles, the disciples in the narrower sense, though "the twelve" were not all assembled on this occasion, but at most "seven" only. See note on *v.* 2.

at the sea of Tiberias] Comp. vi. 1. This name does not occur elsewhere in the Gospels. The return of the disciples to Galilee is indicated in Matt. xxviii. 7; Mark xvi. 7. Before the Ascension they came again to Jerusalem and continued there till after Pentecost (Acts i. 4). The words in Luke xxiv. 44 ff. appear to be a summary of teaching at different times during the forty days. It is important to observe that St John takes account of both groups of appearances of the Risen Lord. St Matthew only notices the appearance to "the eleven" in Galilee, and St Luke only appearances at Jerusalem.

and on this wise shewed he himself] More exactly, *and* **he manifested** himself **on this wise**. The repetition of a prominent word is characteristic of St John's style. The Evangelist states the fact first, and then, as it were after a pause, goes back to recall the details of it. Comp. xiii. 1 ff.

2. *There were together*] The enumeration which follows seems to shew that all present belonged to the same neighbourhood.

Thomas] In Acts i. 13, Thomas is joined with Philip, so that he may have been of Bethsaida (i. 44).

Nathanael] See i. 45. The addition "of Cana" throws light upon the connexion of

and the *sons* of Zebedee, and two other of his disciples.

3 Simon Peter saith unto them, I go a fishing. They say unto him, We also go with thee. They went forth, and entered into a ship immediately; and that night they caught nothing.

4 But when the morning was now come, Jesus stood on the shore: but the disciples knew not that it was Jesus.

5 Then Jesus saith unto them, ‖ Children, have ye any meat? They answered him, No. ‖ Or, *Sirs.*

6 And he said unto them, Cast the net on the right side of the ship, and ye shall find. They cast therefore, and now they were not able to draw it for the multitude of fishes.

7 Therefore that disciple whom Jesus loved saith unto Peter, It is the Lord. Now when Simon Peter

---

i. 45 ff. and ii. 1 ff., where the detail is not given.

the sons of Zebedee] Matt. xx. 20, xxvi. 37, xxvii. 56.

two other] The record of the first chapter suggests that these two may have been Andrew (i. 41) and Philip (i. 43 ff.). Yet it is more probable that these two were "disciples" in the wider sense, and that St John places himself and his brother last among the apostles. Under any circumstances the position of "the sons of Zebedee" in the enumeration is not that which any other writer than St John would have given to them.

3. *Simon Peter*] Even here St Peter takes the lead in action. The disciples seem to have continued their ordinary work, waiting calmly for the sign which should determine their future. Comp. Luke xxii. 36; 2 Thess. iii. 8; Acts xviii. 3.

We also go] Literally, **come.**

They went forth] from the house, probably at Capernaum or Bethsaida, in which they were now staying.

a ship (**the** *ship*)] Omit *immediately*. Comp. vi. 17 ff. In the first place where the word occurs (vi. 17) there is no article according to the true reading. Here "the ship" is mentioned as part of the ordinary equipment for the fisher's work. It may be naturally supposed that when St Peter "left all" (Luke v. 11) those who retained possession of his property respected his right when he reclaimed it. The word "immediately" must be omitted.

in *that night*] The emphatic pronoun (ἐν ἐκείνῃ τῇ ν.) perhaps implies that the want of success was unusual with them. The night was the most favourable time for fishing. Comp. Luke v. 5.

4. *when the morning was now come*] The true reading (γινομένης for γενομένης) gives the more vivid picture: *when* **the day was now breaking.** The exact time is significant for the interpretation of the incident.

stood...on...] Came, as the phrase implies (ἔστη εἰς), from some unknown quarter, and stood on *the* **beach** (αἰγιαλός). See Acts xxvii. 39 f., xxi. 5; Matt. xiii. 2, 48. Comp. xx. 19, 26. Interpreters at all times have pointed to the significant contrast in the positions of the Lord and the disciples, He on the firm ground, they on the restless waters.

but (rather **howbeit**)...*knew not*...] The clause is added as something strange (μέντοι, iv. 27, xii. 42). It is vain to give any simply natural explanation of the failure of the disciples to recognise Christ. After the Resurrection He was known as He pleased, and not necessarily at once (ch. xx. 14 ff.; Luke xxiv. 31). Yet it is easy to understand that the disciples were preoccupied with their work, as Mary Magdalene with her sorrow (xx. 14, an exact parallel), so that the vision of the divine was obscured.

5. *Then Jesus* (*Jesus* **therefore**)...] as desiring to bring them to a knowledge of Himself. The words might be taken as the question of one who wished to buy what they had.

Children] The original word (παιδία) marks the difference of age or position, and not the tie of relationship (τεκνία, ch. xiii. 33). Comp. 1 John ii. 13, 18 (παιδία) with 1 John ii. 1, 12 (true reading τεκνία), 28, iii. 7, 18, iv. 4, v. 21). Here it is probably no more than a familiar address. The form of the question in the original (μήτι) suggests a negative answer. See iv. 29.

meat] Probably something to eat with bread (προσφάγιον, which answers to the Attic ὄψον). This was commonly fish, so that the synonymous word (ὀψάριον) came to be used for fish (ch. vi. 9 f.).

6. *on the right side*] The definiteness of the command (contrast Luke v. 4) explains the readiness with which it was obeyed.

to draw it] up into the boat (ἑλκύσαι), as contrasted with the "dragging" (σύρειν) it after the boat. In the end it was "drawn" up to the land (*v.* 11). Wilson speaks of the fish in the lake as being seen "in dense masses" ('Recovery of Jerusalem,' p. 341).

7. *Therefore that disciple...*] He was able to read in a moment by a certain sympathy with Christ the meaning of the sign. In this

heard that it was the Lord, he girt *his* fisher's coat *unto him*, (for he was naked,) and did cast himself into the sea.

8 And the other disciples came in a little ship; (for they were not far from land, but as it were two hundred cubits,) dragging the net with fishes.

9 As soon then as they were come to land, they saw a fire of coals there, and fish laid thereon, and bread.

10 Jesus saith unto them, Bring of the fish which ye have now caught.

11 Simon Peter went up, and drew the net to land full of great fishes, an hundred and fifty and three: and for all there were so many, yet was not the net broken.

---

power of insight Christ's love to him was illustrated, so that the title becomes, as it were, a thanksgiving. See ch. xiii. 23.

Now when Simon Peter heard...] *Simon Peter* **therefore having** *heard...* The revelation came to him from without, and no longer from within (Matt. xvi. 17), but he at once acted upon it. He could not wait for the slow progress of the boat, but with swift resolve "cast himself into the sea" (contrast Matt. xiv. 28 ff.), having first "girt his coat (ἐπενδύτης, an upper garment. See LXX. 1 S. xviii. 4, "robe;" 2 S. xiii. 18; the word was adopted in later Hebrew for the "frock" of labourers) about him," with instinctive reverence for the presence of his Master. While engaged in his work he was "naked," that is, probably, stripped of all but his light under-garment (comp. 1 S. xix. 24; Isai. xx. 2; Amos ii. 16), though at present the word applies literally to Galilæan fishermen; but these poor men, who have no boats, occupy a different position from the apostles (Tristram, 'Land of Israel,' pp. 425 ff. ed. 3).

8. *in a little ship*] *in* **the boat** (τὸ πλοιάριον). The change of word may point to the use of some smaller vessel which was attached to the "ship," as the words are distinguished in vi. 22; or it may be a more exact description of the vessel.

for they...] The clause explains how they could easily do what is described, and soon gain the shore. The distance was about a hundred yards.

9. *As soon then as ... they saw ...*] **So when ...** *they* **see ...** They hasten to meet the Lord before they have secured their prize (*v.* 10). *The fire of coals*, *i.e.* of charcoal (ἀνθρακιά, xviii. 18), the *fish* (ὀψάριον), and the *bread* (loaf, ἄρτος), are spoken of in such a way as to suggest the thought that they were provided supernaturally. The Lord provides as He will, through human labour naturally, or otherwise.

fish...bread...] Rather, **a fish...a loaf...** Compare *v.* 13, *the fish...the loaf...* The thought of unity seems to be distinctly presented (1 Cor. x. 17).

10. The command was probably given in order to mark the gifts of the Lord as gifts to be used. Perhaps the use of ὀψάριον (fish as food) here as contrasted with ἰχθύς (fish generally) in the next verse emphasizes the idea.

11. *Simon Peter* **therefore** *went up*] Peter at once—again first in action—enters the vessel to which the net was fastened, and then draws it up after him on to the land.

an hundred and fifty and three] Jerome quotes an opinion that there were so many kinds of fish, and adds that one of each kind was taken to shew the universality of the work of the apostles ('In Ezech.' xlvii. 9). For other interpretations see Additional Note. The record of the exact number probably marks nothing more than the care with which the disciples reckoned their wonderful draught. The significant differences between the circumstances of the miraculous draught of fishes at the beginning of the Lord's ministry (Luke v. 1 ff.), and of this after the Resurrection, have frequently been noted. Augustine draws them out very well. The one miracle, he says, was the symbol of the Church at present, the other of the Church perfected; in the one we have good and bad, in the other good only; there Christ also is on the water, here He is on the land; there the draught is left in the boats, here it is landed on the beach; there the nets are let down as it might be, here in a special part; there the nets are rending, here they are not broken; there the boats are on the point of sinking with their load, here they are not laden; there the fish are not numbered, here the number is exactly given ('In Joh.' CXXII. 7). It seems impossible not to acknowledge that there is a spiritual meaning in these variations of the two narratives which consistently converge to distinct ends.

ii. The Lord's Gift (12—14).

The completion of the apostles' work, hallowed now by the offering of first-fruits, is followed by the bestowal of the Lord's blessing. As He had made their labour fruitful, so now He gives them of His Own. The absence of connecting particles in the true text of *vv.* 12 f. gives a peculiar solemnity to the description.

12 Jesus saith unto them, Come *and* dine. And none of the disciples durst ask him, Who art thou? knowing that it was the Lord.

13 Jesus then cometh, and taketh bread, and giveth them, and fish likewise.

14 This is now the third time that Jesus shewed himself to his disciples, after that he was risen from the dead.

15 ¶ So when they had dined, Jesus saith to Simon Peter, Simon, *son* of Jonas, lovest thou me more

---

12. *dine*] Rather, **breakfast** (ἀριστήσατε). The ἄριστον was the morning meal, as contrasted with the afternoon meal (δεῖπνον). Comp. Luke xiv. 12. In St Matthew xxii. 4 ff., the guests invited to "the breakfast" refuse the invitation and go away to their day's work.

The Lord seems to have been still standing at some little distance when He gave the invitation. The disciples held back in awe. They "knew that it was the Lord;" and still it is evident that He was in some way changed.

And none ... ask] Omit *And*. The original word for *ask* (ἐξετάσαι) describes precise and careful inquiry and examination, Matt. ii. 8, x. 11. There is a conviction of reality which (in a sense) precludes certain forms of investigation as unfitting.

13. *Jesus then* ...] Omit *then*. As the disciples hang back "Jesus cometh," and gives to them of "the bread" and "the fish" which He had Himself provided. The articles in the original (τὸν ἄρτον, τὸ ὀψάριον) point back to *v.* 9. Nothing is said either as to the use of the fish caught (*v.* 10) or of the Lord Himself sharing the meal. He appears only as the Giver of the food which He brings, and this fact probably explains the absence of the customary "blessings" or "thanksgiving" (vi. 11; Luke xxiv. 30).

14. *This is now* ...] 2 Pet. iii. 1. Comp. *v.* 1. The "third" time most probably refers to manifestations to "the disciples" in a body. St John himself relates three appearances before this, the first being to Mary Magdalene, xx. 11 ff. Perhaps the form of expression (*this is now* [ἤδη] ...) may be chosen with a view to distinguish this appearance, which was not preserved in the popular tradition, from the later appearances which were preserved in it. It is possible also that "the third time" may describe "groups" or "days" of appearances; the appearances on the first day being reckoned as one appearance; but the exact interpretation of the words seems to be more natural.

II. THE LORD AND INDIVIDUAL DISCIPLES (15—23).

This section also falls into two parts:

i. The work of St Peter: to act (15—19).

ii. The work of St John: to wait (20—23).

shewed himself] **was manifested.** See *v.* 1 n.

The contents are peculiar to St John.

i. The work of St Peter. The apostolic charge (15—17); the personal issue (18, 19).

15. *So when they had dined* (**breakfasted**)...] After the common meal the personal charge followed naturally.

saith to Simon Peter, Simon, son of Jonas (**John**, and so *vv.* 16, 17; see i. 42, note)] The contrast of the names is significant. The address of the Lord, thrice repeated, recalls the first words addressed to St Peter (i. 42), when he received the surname Cephas (Peter). At the same time it must be observed that the Lord never addresses St Peter by his new surname; nor does St Paul speak of him by the Greek form of it (Peter) according to the true text, but only as Cephas. On the other hand, the surname is commonly used either alone or with Simon in the narrative of the Gospels, and always in the Greek form. This varying usage, which exactly corresponds with the circumstances under which the title was substituted for the original name, is a striking indication of the exactness of the records, and specially of the exactness of the record of the Lord's words (Matt. xvi. 17, xvii. 25; Mark xiv. 37; Luke xxii. 31; comp. Acts x. 5 ff.).

son of Jonas (**John**)] The mention of St Peter's natural descent here (comp. i. 42; Matt. xvi. 17) appears to direct attention in the first place to the man in the fulness of his natural character, as distinguished from the apostle.

lovest thou me more than these?] *i.e.* more than these, thy fellow-disciples, love me. The reference is probably to St Peter's words (ch. xiii. 37; Matt. xxvi. 33), in which he had claimed for himself the possession of supreme devotion (comp. xv. 12 ff.). In the record of St Matthew (*l.c.*) this profession is placed in immediate connexion with the Lord's promise of an appearance in Galilee after His Resurrection, which gives peculiar force to the question. It is unnatural to suppose that "*these*" is neuter, and that the Lord refers to the instruments or fruits of the fisher's craft.

lovest (ἀγαπᾷς, Vulg. *diligis*)] It will be noticed that the foundation of the apostolic office is laid in love and not in belief. Love (ἀγάπη) in its true form includes Faith (comp. 1 Cor. xiii. 13).

Yea, Lord...] St Peter in his answer affirms his personal attachment to the Lord, appealing to the Lord's own knowledge; but his

than these? He saith unto him, Yea, Lord; thou knowest that I love thee. He saith unto him, Feed my lambs.
16 He saith to him again the second time, Simon, *son* of Jonas, lovest thou me? He saith unto him, Yea, Lord; thou knowest that I love thee. He saith unto him, Feed my sheep.
17 He saith unto him the third time, Simon, *son* of Jonas, lovest thou me? Peter was grieved because he said unto him the third time, Lovest thou me? And he said unto him, Lord, thou knowest all things; thou knowest that I love thee. Jesus saith unto him, Feed my sheep.
18 Verily, verily, I say unto thee,

---

profession differs in two important points from the question proposed. He does not assume any superiority over others (*more than these*): and he lays claim only to the feeling of natural love (φιλῶ σε, Vulg. *amo te*), of which he could be sure. He does not venture to say that he has attained to that higher love (ἀγαπᾶν) which was to be the spring of the Christian life (ch. xiii. 34, xiv. 15, 21, 28, &c.). Moreover now he says nothing of the future, nothing of the manifestation of his love (xiii. 37). Comp. Bernard, 'Serm. de div.' XXIX. fin.

thou (emphatic) *knowest*] Experience had taught St Peter to distrust his own judgment of himself. Even when the fact is one of immediate consciousness he rests his assertion on the Lord's direct insight.

Feed my lambs] In response to the sincere confession the Lord imposes a charge which shews that He accepts the apostle's answer. The privilege and the work of love are identical. The image is now changed. The fisher's work is followed by the shepherd's work. Those who are brought together and taken out of "the many waters" need to be fed and tended. This office of the shepherd with which St Peter is entrusted is regarded under three different aspects. The first portrayed here is the simplest and humblest. The little ones in Christ's flock need support, which they cannot obtain of themselves; this the apostle is charged to give them.

Feed] The original word (βόσκειν), which occurs again in *v.* 17, is found elsewhere in the New Testament only of swine (Matt. viii. 30, 33; Mark v. 11, 14; Luke viii. 32, 34, xv. 15). As distinguished from the word which follows (*v.* 16, ποιμαίνειν) it expresses the providing with food.

16. A short pause, as we must suppose, followed; and then the question was repeated **a second time**, but so that the thought of comparison is omitted: *Simon, son of* **John**, *lovest* (ἀγαπᾷς) *thou me?* St Peter's answer is identically the same as before. He still shrinks from taking to himself the loftier word. In reply the Lord lays upon him a new part of the shepherd's duty: **Tend**—be shepherd of—*my sheep*. The lambs require to be fed; the sheep require to be guided. The watchful care and rule to be exercised over the maturer Christians calls for greater skill and tenderness than the feeding of the young and simple.

Feed] **Tend** (ποίμαινε), Acts xx. 28; 1 Pet. v. 2; Matt. ii. 6. Comp. Rev. ii. 27, &c.; Jude 12. The Vulgate does not distinguish *feed* and *tend* (*pasce*, *pasce*).

17. *lovest thou* (φιλεῖς, Vulg. *amas*) *me*] When the Lord puts the question "the third time," He adopts the word which St Peter had used. Just as the idea of comparison was given up before, so now the idea of the loftiest love is given up. It is as if the Lord would test the truth of the feeling which St Peter claimed.

The three questions could not but recall the three denials; and the form of this last question could not but vividly bring back the thought of the failure of personal devotion at the moment of trial. So *Peter was grieved* not only that the question was put again, but that this *third time* the phrase was changed; that the question was not only put once again, but at the same time put so as to raise a doubt whether he could indeed rightly claim that modified love which he had professed. His "grief" lay in the deep sense that such a doubt might well be suggested by the past, even if it were at the time ungrounded. Men might reasonably distrust his profession of sincerity after his fall, but he appealed to the Lord (*Thou* (σύ) *knowest...*).

The answer of St Peter meets the points in the changed question. He leaves out the affirmation (*Yea, Lord*) of his former reply and throws himself wholly on the Lord, upon His absolute knowledge, and upon His special knowledge. *Lord, Thou knowest* (οἶδας) *all things*, and at this moment *Thou* **seest** (γινώσκεις) *that I love Thee*. The knowledge to which he appeals is not only that of divine intuition, but of immediate observation. Comp. ii. 25, note. The Vulgate again fails to distinguish the two words.

In reply the Lord completed His commission, *Feed* (βόσκε) *my sheep*. The mature no less than the young Christians require their appropriate sustenance. Provision must be made for their support as well as for their guidance. And this is the last and most difficult part of the pastor's office.

When thou wast young, thou girdedst thyself, and walkedst whither thou wouldest: but when thou shalt be old, thou shalt stretch forth thy hands, and another shall gird thee, and carry *thee* whither thou wouldest not.

19 This spake he, signifying by what death he should glorify God.

---

my lambs...my sheep...my sheep...] It will be noticed that the Lord retains His own right to those who are committed to the apostle's care. Comp. 1 Pet. v. 2 f. Augustine paraphrases admirably: "Si me diligis, non te pascere cogita, sed oves meas sicut meas pasce, non sicut tuas; gloriam meam in eis quære, non tuam, dominium meum non tuum..." ('In Joh.' CXXIII. 5).

18. The threefold apostolic charge resting on the assurance of personal love was given. The revelation of the personal issues of that love followed. There was a most true sense in which the bold declaration of the apostle (xiii. 37) was destined to find a literal fulfilment: *Verily, verily, I say to thee......*

Verily, verily] The Risen Christ uses once more His familiar formula.

When thou wast young (νεώτερος, Vulg. *junior*, lit. *younger*)] The earlier outward freedom of St Peter in his youth is contrasted with his final complete outward bondage. At the moment he stood between the two states. Perhaps the thought of a converse growth of spiritual freedom underlies the image.

when thou shalt be old] The martyrdom of St Peter is placed in the year A.D. 64, and he seems to have been already of middle age (Matt. viii. 14).

stretch forth thy hands] as helpless and seeking help.

gird thee] bind thee as a condemned criminal.

whither thou wouldest not] The way to a violent death must always be terrible, because unnatural; and that exactly in proportion as the violation of nature by such an end is realised. Comp. xii. 27.

19. *This spake he* (**Now this he spake**) *signifying* (comp. xii. 33, xviii. 32) *by what* (**what manner of**) *death...*] The crucifixion of St Peter at Rome is attested by Tertullian ('Scorp.' 15) and later writers. Origen further stated that he was crucified with his head downwards at his own request (Euseb. 'H. E.' III. 1). Though the language of the Lord has very commonly been adapted to the details of crucifixion, it does not appear that it points directly to anything more than martyrdom, when "another girded him," and he was taken "whither he would not." The "stretching forth the hands" can hardly be referred primarily to the position on the cross, since this detail is placed first.

he should glorify God] Literally, **he shall glorify**. The construction in xviii. 32 is different. The Evangelist throws himself back to the time when the death of St Peter was as yet future. As martyrdom was a "glorifying God," so conversely the martyr himself was said to be "glorified" by his death. Comp. vii. 39, xii. 23, and Suicer *s. v.* δοξάζειν.

Follow me] The end of martyrdom having now been shewn, the Lord repeated the command given before under different circumstances to others (i. 43; Matt. viii. 22, ix. 9, xix. 21), "Follow me." What had been impossible before the apostle's fall became possible for him now (xiii. 36 ff.).

The command itself, as given before and after the Resurrection, has necessarily different though analogous meanings. During the Lord's earthly life following Him implied the abandonment of previous occupations (Matt. ix. 9) and duties (Matt. viii. 22); attendance upon Him even when He entered on strange and mysterious paths; participation in disgrace and danger (Matt. x. 38). Now to "follow Christ" required further the perception of His course; the spiritual discernment by which His movements can still be discovered; and yet further the readiness to accept martyrdom as the end.

These different thoughts appear to have a place in the words *follow me*, but the command had also, as appears from the next verse (*following*), a literal meaning also, though it is impossible to decide for what purpose the Lord called St Peter away from the other disciples.

Augustine's comment on the promise of the glory of future martyrdom to the penitent and restored apostle is pregnant with thought: "Hunc invenit exitum ille negator et amator; præsumendo elatus, negando prostratus, flendo purgatus, confitendo probatus, patiendo coronatus; hunc invenit exitum ut pro ejus nomine perfecta dilectione moreretur, cum quo se moriturum perversa festinatione promiserat. Faciat ejus resurrectione firmatus, quod immature pollicebatur infirmus. Hoc enim oportebat ut prius Christus pro Petri salute, deinde Petrus pro Christi prædicatione moreretur. Præposterum fuit quod audere cœperat humana temeritas, cum istum disposuisset ordinem veritas. Animam suam se positurum pro Christo Petrus putabat, pro liberatore liberandus; cum Christus venisset animam suam positurus pro suis ovibus in quibus erat et Petrus; quod ecce jam factum est...Jam pretio pro te fuso, nunc est [Petre] ut sequaris emptorem, et sequaris omnino usque ad mortem crucis" ('In Joh.' CXXIII.

And when he had spoken this, he
saith unto him, Follow me.
20 Then Peter, turning about,
p. 13. seeth the disciple [a]whom Jesus loved
20. 2. following; which also leaned on his
breast at supper, and said, Lord,
which is he that betrayeth thee?
21 Peter seeing him saith to Jesus,
Lord, and what *shall* this man *do?*

22 Jesus saith unto him, If I will
that he tarry till I come, what *is that*
to thee? follow thou me.
23 Then went this saying abroad
among the brethren, that that disciple should not die: yet Jesus said
not unto him, He shall not die; but,
If I will that he tarry till I come,
what *is that* to thee?

---

4). It is impossible to translate adequately this epigrammatic African Latin.

ii. The work of St John.

20. *Peter* (omit *Then*), *turning about*] The command of the Lord appears to have been accompanied by some symbolic action. As St Peter literally obeyed the call thus expressed under a figure, and moved away from the group of the apostles, something attracted his attention, and he "turned about" to the direction indicated (ἐπιστραφείς, Mark v. 30). The whole picture is full of life.

the disciple...] Comp. xiii. 23, note.

which also leaned (**leaned back**)...**the** *supper*] The reference is to the special act of the apostle (ἀνέπεσεν), and not to the position which he occupied at the table (ἦν ἀνακείμενος, xiii. 23). The notice is added here to explain the close connexion of St John with St Peter, and the confidence with which St John ventured to follow even without a special invitation.

21. *Peter* **therefore...**] No question could be more natural. The fact that St John was following was itself an unspoken question as to the future, an asking of the Lord's will.

Lord, and...] The original is singularly brief and pregnant, "Lord, and this man, what?" (Κύριε, οὗτος δὲ τί; Vulg. *Domine, hic autem quid?*) What of him? What shall he suffer or do? what shall be his lot?

22. In the Lord's answer the emphasis is laid upon the pronouns "him" and "thou" (ἐὰν αὐτὸν θ...σύ μοι ἀκ.). The thought is of the individual offices of disciples. St Peter's fortune corresponded with his work, and so too St John's.

If I will (comp. xvii. 24, note) *that...*] The hypothetical form of the sentence veils the divine counsel. Experience has shewn what that was.

abide *till I come*] The exact force of the original is rather "while I am coming" (ἕως ἔρχομαι). The "coming" is not regarded as a definite point in future time, but rather as a fact which is in slow and continuous realisation. The prominent idea is of the interval to be passed over rather than of the end to be reached. Comp. ix. 4, xii. 35 f.; Mark vi. 45 (ἀπολύει); 1 Tim. iv. 13; Luke xix. 13 (ἐν ᾧ); Matt. v. 25. "Abiding" is the correlative to "following;" and according to the manifold significance of this word it expresses the calm waiting for further light, the patient resting in a fixed position, the continuance in life.

The "coming" of the Lord is no doubt primarily "the second coming" (παρουσία, 1 John ii. 28); but at the same time the idea of Christ's "coming" includes thoughts of His personal coming in death to each believer. And yet further the coming of Christ to the Society is not absolutely one. He "came" in the destruction of Jerusalem. Thus St John did tarry till the great "coming," nor is there anything fanciful in seeing an allusion to the course of the history of the Church under the image of the history of the apostles. The type of doctrine and character represented by St John is the last in the order of development. In this sense he abides still. Comp. xiv. 3, note; and Rev. ii. 5, 16, iii. 11, xvi. 15, xxii. 7, 12, 20.

what is that to thee?] The arrangement of the various parts in the whole body of the Church does not concern men. That rests with the divine will, and the divine will is unfolded in the course of life.

23. *Then went this saying...*] *This saying* (*word*) **therefore** *went* ... the words which the Lord had spoken. These were inexactly repeated, and taken to affirm "that that disciple dieth not." The tradition that St John was sleeping in his grave at Ephesus, and that the moving dust witnessed to the breathing of the saint beneath, survived for a long time. Augustine mentions it doubtfully "on the authority of grave men" ('In Joh.' CXXIV. 2).

among the brethren] This use of the phrase which is common in the book of the Acts (ix. 30, &c.) is found here only in the Gospels (comp. ch. xx. 17; Luke xxii. 32).

yet Jesus...] The manner in which the error is corrected seems to shew clearly that it had not been refuted by fact, or, in other words, that this Epilogue to the Gospel was written by St John. The apostle, still alive and looking to the uncertainty of the future, rests on the simple repetition of the precise language of the Lord. He does not claim to know all that He meant; he repeats what He

24 This is the disciple which testifieth of these things, and wrote these things: and we know that his testimony is true.

b chap. 20. 30.

25 [b] And there are also many other things which Jesus did, the which, if they should be written every one, I suppose that even the world itself could not contain the books that should be written. Amen.

---

said. The true interpretation of the words was for history.

It is obvious that St Peter and St John occupy in this narrative representative positions both as to their work and as to the issue of their work. The one is the minister of action whose service is consummated by the martyrdom of death: the other is the minister of thought and teaching whose service is perfected in the martyrdom of life. Augustine ('In Joh.' CXXIV. 3) has a very interesting comparison of the two charges, which is thus summed up: "Perfecta me sequatur actio, informata meæ passionis exemplo: inchoata vero contemplatio maneat donec venio, perficienda cum venero." See also the Preface to the Commentary of Rupert of Deutz.

CONCLUDING NOTES: *vv.* 24, 25.

These two verses appear to be separate notes attached to the Gospel before its publication. The form of *v.* 24, contrasted with that of xix. 35, shews conclusively that it is not the witness of the Evangelist. The words were probably added by the Ephesian elders, to whom the preceding narrative had been given both orally and in writing. See Introduction, p. xxxv. The change of person in *v.* 25 (*I suppose*, compared with *we know*) marks a change of authorship. It is quite possible that this verse may contain words of St John (comp. xx. 30), set here by those who had heard them.

24. *testifieth...testimony*] **beareth witness...witness.** The witness is spoken of as present, but the form of the phrase (ὁ μαρτυρῶν, contrast ὁ γράψας) does not in itself shew conclusively that the apostle was alive at the time when the note was written (comp. i. 15), though this is the most natural interpretation (comp. v. 32, 33).

these things] The phrase may be referred to the whole contents of the Gospel (xx. 31), or be limited to the narrative of ch. xxi.

we know] The plural (contrast xix. 35) taken in connexion with *this is the disciple* and *I suppose* (*v.* 25) seems to be undoubtedly a true plural, and not a usage like 1 John i. 1. Compare Col. iv. 3, where there is a corresponding change from the apostolic group (Col. i. 1) to St Paul himself.

true] true in fact (ἀληθής). The thought is not brought out here as in xix. 35, that it satisfies the ideal conditions of testimony (ἀληθινή). The words read like an echo of 3 John 12.

25. *I suppose*] The word (οἶμαι) is rare in the N.T. (comp. Phil. i. 17; James i. 7). From the form of the sentence (ἐὰν γράφηται... χωρήσειν) it appears that the recollection of the other deeds was still fresh, so that the record of them was possible.

could not contain] The bold expression answers to a deep truth. A complete account (*every one*) of the perfect human (*Jesus*) life of the Lord would be practically infinite.

Amen] is no part of the original text.

ADDITIONAL NOTES on CHAP. XXI.

11. The precise statement of the number has naturally attracted the attention of commentators from early times, and the interpretations which have been assigned to it do more than form a sample of ingenious combinations. They illustrate a method of viewing Scripture which, however different from our own, was at one time nearly universal. It will then be not without use and interest to notice one or two of the prominent explanations of the number which have been offered.

There is, as far as I have noted, no explanation of the number preserved in the great ante-Nicene fathers, Clement, Irenæus, and Origen, Tertullian and Cyprian. But Cyril of Alexandria (†444) and Augustine (†430) have probably preserved earlier interpretations in their own comments.

CYRIL of ALEXANDRIA (*in loc.*), followed by AMMONIUS the PRESBYTER (Cramer Cat.' *in loc.*), Euthymius (doubtfully) and Theophylact (*ad loc.*), regards the number as being significant in its three simple elements: 100 + 50 + 3. The 100, he says, represents the fulness of the Gentiles, for 100 (= 10 × 10) is "the fullest number," and as such it is used to describe the Lord's full flock (Matt. xviii. 12) and full fertility (Matt. xiii. 8). The 50 represents "the remnant of Israel according to election," which falls short of completeness $\left(50=\frac{100}{2}\right)$. The 3 indicates the Holy Trinity, to whose glory all alike are gathered.

AUGUSTINE ('in Joh. Tr.' CXXII.) adopts a more complicated interpretation. *Ten*, he says, is the number of the Law. But the Law without grace kills. To the number of the Law therefore we add *seven*, the number of the Spirit, in order to obtain the fulness of the divine revelation as a power of life. But, he then adds, the sum of the numbers from one to seventeen inclusive is one hundred and fifty-three (1 + 2 + 3 &c. + 17 = 153). So that the number 153 signifies all those who are included in the saving operation of divine grace, which makes reconciliation with the Law. Nor is this all. The *three* is the symbol of the Trinity; and the triple fifty brings out the idea of unity in the Spirit, who is revealed in a sevenfold operation (50 = 7 × 7 + 1).

GREGORY THE GREAT adopts in part the symbolism of Augustine, but employs it even more ingeniously. The Evangelist, he writes, would not have given the exact number unless he had deemed that it contained a mystery. All action under the Old Testament is ruled by the Decalogue; and under the New Testament by the *seven* gifts of the Spirit (Isai. xi. 2). Our action, therefore, under both aspects can be represented by 10 + 7. But it is by faith in the Holy Trinity that action is made effectual. We therefore multiply 17 by 3 and obtain the number 51, which expresses the idea of true rest, being unity added to the number of the year of jubilee. This symbol of rest (51) is again multiplied by three and we gain the result 153, the symbol of the elect citizens of the heavenly country, the final heirs of rest ('Hom.' XXIV. 4).

RUPERT of DEUTZ ('In Joh.' XIV.) regards the three numbers as representing the proportions of three different classes united in one faith. The "hundred" are the married, who are the most numerous, the "fifty" the widowed or continent who are less numerous, the "three," the least in number, are the virgins. "But," he adds, "there is much that has been profitably written on this 153 by learned divines, which the careful reader will easily find."

BRUNO ASTENSIS (xith—xiith cent.; the homilies were wrongly published under the name of Eusebius of Emesa) adopts a simpler view. "Three," he says, "has the same significance as 150 = 3 × 50. There are three parts of the world, Asia, Africa, Europe. Therefore 150 + 3 represents the sum of all the faithful throughout the world." (*In loc.* [Hom. LXXI.] Migne, 'Patrol.' CXLV. 599.)

It may be worth while to add, if such interpretations seem alien from our way of thinking, that Volkmar has recently surpassed them in extravagance. He gravely argues ('Mose Prophetie' 61 f.) that the number represents *Simeon Bar Jona Kepha*. To obtain this result he is obliged to leave out one letter in *Kepha*, and to give the Hebrew letters values inconsistent with ancient usage.

NOTE ON THE READINGS IN *vv.* 15 ff.

The readings in the three charges of the Lord are somewhat perplexed.

15. *Βόσκε τὰ ἀρνία μου.* So ℵABLX and almost all: Vulg. *agnos*. But C*D read *πρόβατα*, and old Lat. *oves*. In this case however the reading cannot be doubtful. The substitution of *πρόβατα* shews the tendency of scribes.

16. *Ποίμαινε τὰ προβάτιά μου.* So BC, "some old copies."

But ℵADX and nearly all others read *πρόβατα*. Old Lat. *oves*. Vulg. *agnos*.

The reading here may be fairly considered doubtful. The force of the diminutive is seen below.

17. *Βόσκε τὰ προβάτιά μου.* So ABC.

But ℵDX and nearly all others *πρόβατα*. Lat. *oves* (some *agnos*). Λ *ἀρνία*.

In this case there can be little doubt that *προβάτια* is the true reading. The diminutive, which is a form of tender endearment, goes naturally with *βόσκε*. In the second charge there is no special fitness in the diminutive, though the use of the diminutive throughout has an appropriateness to the circumstances.